T0235730

Lecture Notes in Computer Science   12302

Dang Van Hung · Oleg Sokolsky (Eds.)

Automated Technology for Verification and Analysis

18th International Symposium, ATVA 2020
Hanoi, Vietnam, October 19–23, 2020
Proceedings

 Springer

Editors
Dang Van Hung
Vietnam National University (VNU-UET)
Hanoi, Vietnam

Oleg Sokolsky
University of Pennsylvania
Philadelphia, PA, USA

ISSN 0302-9743 ISSN 1611-3349 (electronic)
Lecture Notes in Computer Science
ISBN 978-3-030-59151-9 ISBN 978-3-030-59152-6 (eBook)
https://doi.org/10.1007/978-3-030-59152-6

LNCS Sublibrary: SL2 – Programming and Software Engineering

This Springer imprint is published by the registered company Springer Nature Switzerland AG
The registered company address is: Gewerbestrasse 11, 6330 Cham, Switzerland

Preface

This volume contains the papers presented at the 18th International Symposium on Automated Technology for Verification and Analysis (ATVA 2020) held in Hanoi, Vietnam, during October 19–23, 2020.

The ATVA series of symposia is dedicated to promoting research in theoretical and practical aspects of automated analysis, verification, and synthesis by providing an international venue for the researchers to present new results. At the same time, they provide a forum for interaction between the regional and international research communities and industry in the field.

ATVA 2020 received 75 full paper submissions coauthored by researchers from 29 countries. Each submission was reviewed by at least three Program Committee (PC) members with the help from reviewers outside the PC. After 10 days of online discussions, the committee decided to accept 32 papers for presentation at the conference.

We would like to express our gratitude to all the researchers who submitted their work to the symposium. We are particularly thankful to all colleagues who served on the PC, as well as the external reviewers, whose hard work in the review process helped us prepare the conference program. The international diversity of the PC as well as external reviewers is noteworthy as well: PC members and external reviewers have affiliations with institutes in 20 countries.

Special thanks go to the three invited speakers – Tobias Nipkow, from TU Munich, Germany; Klaus Havelund, from CalTech and NASA JPL, USA; and David Dill, from Stanford University, USA. The papers of the two first invited talks are included in this volume.

A number of colleagues have worked very hard to make this conference a success. We wish to express our thanks to the Local Organizing Committee: Hung Pham Ngoc, Hieu Vo Dinh, and many student volunteers. We would also like to thank the University of Engineering and Technology of the Vietnam National University, Hanoi, Vietnam, the host of the conference, who provided various support and facilities for organizing the conference and its tutorials. Finally, we are thankful for the institutional and financial support from Vingroup Innovation Foundation (VINIF) and Toshiba Software Development in Vietnam (TSDV).

The conference program was prepared with the help of EasyChair. We thank Springer for continuing to publish the conference proceedings.

October 2020

Dang Van Hung
Oleg Sokolsky

Organization

General Chair

Son Bao Pham   Vietnanm National University (VNU), Hanoi, Vietnam

Program Committee Chairs

Dang Van Hung   UET-VNU, Vietnam
Oleg Sokolsky   University of Pennsylvania, USA

Steering Committee

E. Allen Emerson   The University of Texas at Austin, USA
Teruo Higashino   Osaka University, Japan
Oscar H Ibarra   University of California, Santa Barbara, USA
Insup Lee   University of Pennsylvania, USA
Doron A Peled   Bar-Ilan University, Israel
Farn Wang   National Taiwan University, Taiwan
Hsu-Chun Yen   National Taiwan University, Taiwan

Program Committee

Dang Van Hung   UET-VNU, Vietnam
Oleg Sokolsky   University of Pennsylvania, USA
Mohamed Faouzi Atig   Uppsala University, Sweden
Ondrej Lengal   Brno University of Technology, Czech Republic
Christel Baier   TU Dresden, Germany
Orna Kupferman   Hebrew University, Israel
Chih-Hong Cheng   Fortiss Research Institute of the Free State of Bavaria, Germany
Erika Abraham   RWTH Aachen University, Germany
Tachio Terauchi   Waseda University, Japan
Yu-Fang Chen   Academia Sinica, Taiwan
Zhilin Wu   Institute of Software, Chinese Academy of Sciences, China
Pham Ngoc Hung   UET-VNU, Vietnam
Borzoo Bonakdarpour   Iowa State University, USA
Truong Anh Hoang   UET-VNU, Vietnam
Alexandre Duret-Lutz   LRDE, EPITA, France
Ezio Bartocci   Technical University of Vienna, Austria
Javier Esparza   Technical University of Munich, Germany
Xuan Dong Li   Nanjing University, China

viii   Organization

Doron Peled	Bar-Ilan University, Israel
Do Van Tien	Budapest University of Technology and Economics, Hungary
Dimitar Guelev	Bulgarian Academy of Sciences, Bulgaria
Bernd Finkbeiner	Saarland University, Germany
Keijo Heljanko	University of Helsinki, Finland
Krishnendu Chatterjee	Institute of Science and Technology (IST), Austria
Sven Schewe	The University of Liverpool, UK
Franck Cassez	Macquarie University, Australia
Jun Sun	Singapore University of Technology and Design, Singapore
Lu Feng	University of Virginia, USA
Hakjoo Oh	Korea University, South Korea
Udi Boker	Interdisciplinary Center (IDC) Herzliya, Israel
Luca Bortolussi	University of Trieste, Italy
Michael Tautschnig	Queen Mary University of London, UK
Bow-Yaw Wang	Academia Sinica, Taiwan
Lijun Zhang	Institute of Software, Chinese Academy of Sciences, China
Quan Thanh Tho	Ho Chi Minh University of Technology, Vietnam
David Lo	SMU, Singapore
Swen Jacobs	CISPA Helmholtz Center for Information Security, Germany
Farn Wang	National Taiwan University, Taiwan
Meenakshi D'Souza	International Institute of Information Technology, India
Vo Dinh Hieu	VNU, Vietnam
Indranil Saha	Indian Institute of Technology Kanpur, India

Additional Reviewers

Andrea Turrini
Yong Li
Malte Schledjewski
Alexander Rabinovich
Lei Bu
Carbone
Tobias Meggendorfer
Salomon Sickert
Maximilian Weininger
Minxue Pan
Wenchao Yu
Meiyi Ma
Ennio Visconti
Meiyi Ma
Shibashis Guha

Etienne Renault
Fathiyeh Faghih
Luca Laurenti
Lukáš Holík
Catalin Dima
Vijay Ganesh
Yu Wang
Shuling Wang
Jingyi Wang
Roman Rabinovich
Ales Smrcka
Yun-Sheng Chang
Mouhammad Sakr
Mikhail Raskin
Linzhang Wang

Norine Coenen
Christoph Haase
Mouhammad Sakr
Adrien Pommellet
Niklas Metzger
Jianhua Zhao
Song Gao
Francesca Cairoli
Wei-Lun Tsai
Taolue Chen
Tony Sloane
Tzu-Chi Lin

Lei Bu
Tobias Meggendorfer
Andrea Turrini
Jesko Hecking-Harbusch
Yong Li
Vojtěch Havlena
Peter Habermehl
Philipp J. Meyer
Mikhail Raskin
Laurent Doyen
A. R. Balasubramanian
Hongfei Fu

Sponsoring Institutions

Vingroup Innovation Foundation (VINIF)
Toshiba Software Development in Vietnam (TSDV)

Contents

Logics

Techniques for Verification, Analysis and Testing

Model Checking and Decision Procedures

Invited Papers

First-Order Timed Runtime Verification Using BDDs

Klaus Havelund[1](✉) and Doron Peled[2](✉)

[1] Jet Propulsion Laboratory, California Institute of Technology, Pasadena, USA
klaus.havelund@jpl.nasa.gov
[2] Department of Computer Science, Bar Ilan University, Ramat Gan, Israel
doron.peled@gmail.com

Abstract. Runtime Verification (RV) expedites the analyses of execution traces for detecting system errors and for statistical and quality analysis. Having started modestly, with checking temporal properties that are based on propositional (yes/no) values, the current practice of RV often involves properties that are parameterized by the data observed in the input trace. The specifications are based on various formalisms, such as automata, temporal logics, rule systems and stream processing. Checking execution traces that are data intensive against a specification that requires strong dependencies between the data poses a non-trivial challenge; in particular if runtime verification has to be performed online, where many events that carry data appear within small time proximities. Towards achieving this goal, we recently suggested to represent relations over the observed data values as BDDs, where data elements are enumerated and then converted into bit vectors. We extend here the capabilities of BDD-based RV with the ability to express timing constraints, where the monitored events include clock values. We show how to efficiently operate on BDDs that represent both relations on (enumerations of) values and time dependencies. We demonstrate our algorithm with an efficient implementation and provide experimental results.

1 Introduction

Runtime verification provides techniques for monitoring system executions, online and offline, against a formal specification. The monitored system is instrumented to report to the monitor on the occurrence of relevant events that may also include related data values. The monitor observes the input events and keeps some internal *summary* of the prefix of the execution observed so far, which allows computing whether an evidence for a violation of the specification is already available. RV can complement the use of testing and verification techniques during the system development, e.g. by performing offline log file analysis. It can also be used online as part of protecting a system against an unwanted situation and averting it [26]. This is particularly important in

The research performed by the first author was carried out at Jet Propulsion Laboratory, California Institute of Technology, under a contract with the National Aeronautics and Space Administration. The research performed by the second author was partially funded by Israeli Science Foundation grant 1464/18: "Efficient Runtime Verification for Systems with Lots of Data and its Applications".

D. V. Hung and O. Sokolsky (Eds.): ATVA 2020, LNCS 12302, pp. 3–24, 2020.
https://doi.org/10.1007/978-3-030-59152-6_1

safety-critical systems such as aerospace systems, transportation systems, power plants, and medicine.

One main challenge in applying RV is to increase the scope of the properties that can be monitored. The goal is to provide algorithms for monitoring richer, and yet succinct specification formalisms while ensuring that the algorithms are efficient enough to catch up with the speed of information arrival; especially if we want to apply them online. We recently suggested to use BDDs [11, 12] to represent relations between data elements that appear during the execution. We extend this approach and present here a BDD-based algorithm for full first-order linear temporal logic with time constraints. Consider the following property (the syntax and semantics will be described later).

$$(close \rightarrow \mathbf{P}\,open) \tag{1}$$

It expresses that when *close* happens, *open* must have already happened (**P** stands for *previously*). To monitor this property, it is enough to remember if *open* was reported to the monitor so that it can be checked when *close* is reported. The classical algorithm [23] keeps two sets of Boolean variables, pre and now, in the summary, for the *previous* and the *current* value of each subformula, respectively. These variables are updated every time a new event is reported. For example, for the property $\mathbf{P}\,open$ (*open* has happened in the past), we keep pre($\mathbf{P}\,open$) and now($\mathbf{P}\,open$) and update now($\mathbf{P}\,open$) := now($open$) $\vee$ pre($\mathbf{P}\,open$), where now($open$) is *true* if *open* holds in the most recent event. An example of a first-order temporal specification is the following.

$$\forall f\,(close(f) \rightarrow \mathbf{P}\,open(f)) \tag{2}$$

It asserts that every file that is closed was opened before. Here, we need to keep in the summary a *set* of all the opened files so that we can compare them to the closing of files. In general, the summary in this case extends the one used for the propositional case by keeping for each subformula the set of assignments, essentially a relation between the values assigned to the free variables that satisfy it: pre for the prefix without the last event, and now for the current prefix. These sets can be updated using database operations between relations, corresponding to the Boolean operations in the propositional case.

An extension of the logic, in another dimension, allows the properties to refer to the progress of time. The reported events appear with some integer timing value. We do not assume that the system reports to the monitoring program in each time unit or that only a single event occurs within a time unit. We also leave open the unit of measurement for time values (seconds, minutes, etc.). An example of such a specification is

$$\forall f\,(closed(f) \rightarrow \mathbf{P}_{\leq 20}\,open(f)) \tag{3}$$

which asserts that every file f that is closed was opened not longer than 20 time units before.

An RV algorithm for first-order LTL was presented in [7], and implemented in the MonPoly tool, based on two alternative approaches: one allows unrestricted negation and the relations are represented as *regular sets* and, subsequently, automata [25]; another one with restricted negation in which relations are represented explicitly and are subjected to database operators (e.g., join). In [7], an RV algorithm for first-order temporal logic with time constraints was presented. In [19], an algorithm that performs RV on first-order logic using BDDs was suggested and a related tool was constructed. BDDs are directed acyclic graphs that can often achieve a very compact representation of Boolean functions. In this context, a BDD represents the relationship between values of free variables that satisfy a given subformula in the summary. In that work, instead of representing the data values themselves, enumerations of these values were used. This allows a relatively short representation of big data values and using BDDs over a relatively small number of bits. It helps obtaining a good compactness for the BDDs due to common patterns in adjacent enumerations. The algorithm for the first-order logic is simple and quite similar to the propositional algorithm. Using a special reserved value to represent all the values that were not seen before allows the algorithm to easily deal with unconstrained negation.

In this work, we build upon this latter BDD-based construction and extend it to include in the temporal logic also timing constraints. This includes adapting the RV algorithm to reflect the timing constraints and extending the BDD representation to represent timing information as well as data values. We do this while keeping the summary compact and easy to update using BDD operations. We show how to perform updates on relations over both (enumerations of) data values and timing values, including Boolean and simple arithmetical operations. This is quite a nontrivial use of BDDs, applied to the context of runtime verification. Albeit the mixed use of the BDD representation and the addition of timing constraints, we manage to keep the basic algorithm similar to the propositional one. We follow the theory with an implementation that extends that of [19] and present experimental results.

Related Work. RV over propositional logic with timing constraints appears in [10,33]. In [16], an RV algorithm for propositional LTL that returns optimal (minimal or maximal) values that make the specification correct with respect to the observed trace was presented. Other work on data-centric runtime verification include the systems based on trace slicing, where data values are mapped to copies of propositional automata [1,29,31], formula rewriting [5,17], and rule-based monitoring [4,6,18], tree-automata [3] and SMT solving [13]. Applying arithmetic operations to sets of values, represented using BDD appeared in [14].

2 Propositional Past LTL with Timing

RV is often restricted to monitoring executions against specification properties that contain only the *past* modalities [27], where it is implicitly assumed that the specification needs to hold for *all* the prefixes of the execution[1]. These properties correspond to temporal *safety properties* [2], where a failure can always be detected on a finite prefix as soon as it occurs [10]. Expressing safety properties in this form allows an efficient runtime verification algorithm that is only polynomial in the size of the specification [23]. The syntax of propositional past timed linear temporal logic is as follows:

$$\varphi ::= true \mid p \mid (\varphi \wedge \varphi) \mid \neg \varphi \mid (\varphi \mathcal{S} \varphi) \mid (\varphi \mathcal{S}_{\leq \delta} \varphi) \mid (\varphi \mathcal{Z}_{\leq \delta} \varphi) \mid (\varphi \mathcal{S}_{> \delta} \varphi) \mid \ominus \varphi$$

---

[1] This is equivalent to saying that the specification is of the form $\Box \varphi$, where φ contains only past modalities; we omit here the implied $\Box$, which is a *future modality*.

where p is a *proposition* from a finite set of propositions P, with S standing for *since*, and $\ominus$ standing for *previous-time*. The formula $(\varphi S \psi)$ has the standard interpretation that ψ must be true in the past and φ must be true since then. The formula $\ominus \varphi$ is true in the current state if φ is true in the previous state. The formula $(\varphi S_{\leq \delta} \psi)$ has the same meaning as $(\varphi S \psi)$, except that ψ must have occurred within δ time units. The formula $\varphi Z_{\leq \delta} \psi$ is similar to $\varphi S_{\leq \delta} \psi$, except that it requires ψ to be satisfied in the past; it is not sufficient if ψ is satisfied in the current state. Finally, $(\varphi S_{> \delta} \psi)$ has the same meaning as $(\varphi S \psi)$, except that ψ must have occurred more than δ time units ago. One can also write $(\varphi \lor \psi)$ instead of $\neg(\neg \varphi \land \neg \psi)$, $(\varphi \rightarrow \psi)$ instead of $(\neg \varphi \lor \psi)$, $\mathbf{P}\,\varphi$ (*previous* φ) instead of $(true\, S\, \varphi)$ and $\mathbf{H}\,\varphi$ (*history* φ) instead of $\neg \mathbf{P} \neg \varphi$. We also define $P_{\leq \delta} \varphi = (true S_{\leq \delta} \varphi)$, $\mathbf{P}_{> \delta} \varphi = (true S_{> \delta} \varphi)$, $\mathbf{H}_{\leq \delta} = \neg P_{\leq \delta} \neg \varphi$, $\mathbf{H}_{> \delta} = \neg \mathbf{P}_{> \delta} \neg \varphi$, $(\varphi \mathcal{R}_{\leq \delta} \psi) = \neg(\neg \varphi S_{\leq \delta} \neg \psi)$ and $(\varphi \mathcal{R}_{> \delta} \psi) = \neg(\neg \varphi S_{> \delta} \neg \psi)$.

LTL formulas are interpreted over executions $\xi = \langle P, L, \tau \rangle$, where

- P is a finite set of *propositions*,
- $L : \mathbb{N} \mapsto 2^P$, where $\mathbb{N}$ are the positive integers,
- $\tau : \mathbb{N} \mapsto \mathbb{N}$ is a monotonic function (representing clock values). We may, but do not have to, assume that $\tau(1) = 0$.

We will refer to $\xi(i) = \langle i, L(i), \tau(i) \rangle$ as the ith *event* in ξ, which satisfies the propositions $L(i)$ and occurs at time $\tau(i)$. The semantics is defined as follows:

- $\xi, i \models true$.
- $\xi, i \models p$ if $p \in L[i]$.
- $\xi, i \models \neg \varphi$ if not $\xi, i \models \varphi$.
- $\xi, i \models (\varphi \land \psi)$ if $\xi, i \models \varphi$ and $\xi, i \models \psi$.
- $\xi, i \models (\varphi S \psi)$ if for some $1 \leq j \leq i$, $\xi, j \models \psi$, and for all $j < k \leq i$ it holds that $\xi, k \models \varphi$.
- $\xi, i \models (\varphi S_{\leq \delta} \psi)$ if there exists some $1 \leq j \leq i$, such that $\tau(i) - \tau(j) \leq \delta$ and $\xi, j \models \psi$, and for all $j < k \leq i$ it holds that $\xi, k \models \varphi$.
- $\xi, i \models (\varphi Z_{\leq \delta} \psi)$ if there exists some $1 \leq j < i$, such that $\tau(i) - \tau(j) \leq \delta$ and $\xi, j \models \psi$, and for all $j < k \leq i$ it holds that $\xi, k \models \varphi$.
- $\xi, i \models (\varphi S_{> \delta} \psi)$ if there exists some $1 \leq j < i$, such that $\tau(i) - \tau(j) > \delta$ and $\xi, j \models \psi$, and for all $j < k \leq i$ it holds that $\xi, k \models \varphi$.
- $\xi, i \models \ominus \varphi$ if $i > 1$ and $\xi, i - 1 \models \varphi$.

We say that an execution ξ satisfies a property φ iff for every i, it holds that $\xi, i \models \varphi$. Note that this is *discrete time* semantics. We also do not require that every time instance must have a corresponding event. Thus, $(\varphi S \psi)$ means that φ has been holding for every reported event since ψ held.

3   Runtime Verification for Propositional Past LTL

3.1   Algorithm for Propositional Past LTL Without Time Constraints

The dynamic programming algorithm for propositional past LTL without timing constraints described in [23] is based on the observation that the semantics of the past time formulas $\ominus \varphi$ and $(\varphi S \psi)$ in the current step i is defined in terms of the semantics in the previous step $i-1$ of a subformula. The algorithm operates on a summary that includes two vectors (arrays) of Boolean values indexed by subformulas: pre for the previous observed prefix, which excludes the last seen event, and now for the current prefix, which includes the last seen event. The algorithm is as follows.

1. Initially, for each subformula φ of the specification η, $\text{now}(\varphi) := \textit{false}$.
2. Observe the next event[2] $\langle i, L(i), \tau(i) \rangle$ as input.
3. Let $\text{pre} := \text{now}$.
4. Make the following updates for each subformula. If φ is a subformula of ψ then $\text{now}(\varphi)$ is updated before $\text{now}(\psi)$.
   - $\text{now}(p) := (p \in L(i))$.
   - $\text{now}(\textit{true}) := \textit{true}$.
   - $\text{now}((\varphi \wedge \psi)) := \text{now}(\varphi) \wedge \text{now}(\psi)$.
   - $\text{now}(\neg \varphi) := \neg \text{now}(\varphi)$.
   - $\text{now}((\varphi S \psi)) := \text{now}(\psi) \vee (\text{now}(\varphi) \wedge \text{pre}((\varphi S \psi)))$.
   - $\text{now}(\ominus \varphi) := \text{pre}(\varphi)$.
5. if $\text{now}(\eta) = \textit{false}$ then report "error".
6. Goto step 2.

3.2 RV for Propositional Past LTL with Timing Constraints

We describe the additions to the algorithm in Sect. 3.1 for the subformulas that contain timing constraints, i.e., $(\varphi S_{\leq \delta} \psi)$, $(\varphi Z_{\leq \delta} \psi)$ and $(\varphi S_{> \delta} \psi)$. For each of these subformulas, we add to the summary two integer variables τpre and τnow, which represent timers that measure the time since a point that is relevant for calculating their truth value in the current state. These variables are initialized to -1 and their values will be updated based on the time difference $\Delta = \tau(i) - \tau(i-1)$ between the current event $\xi(i)$ and the previous one $\xi(i-1)$.

The Propositional Algorithm for $(\varphi S_{\leq \delta} \psi)$

This subformula asserts that at position i in the trace, there is some earlier (or current) position j, where $\tau(e_i) - \tau(e_j) \leq \delta$ and where $(\varphi S \psi)$ started to hold, until and including the current event. The summary needs to remember not only that ψ has happened and φ kept holding since, but also to update the time duration that has passed. There can be multiple such positions j where ψ held, but we only need to refer to the last (most recent) such position j, since it has the smallest value, hence also the time constraint will be the latest to expire.

The summary has the integer $\textit{time}$ variables $\tau\text{now}(\varphi S_{\leq \delta} \psi)$ and $\tau\text{pre}(\varphi S_{\leq \delta} \psi)$, which can have the values $[-1 \dots \delta]$. This value is the distance from the most recent point where $(\varphi S \psi)$ started to hold within an interval of δ time units. The values from $[0 \dots \delta]$ correspond to the case where $\text{pre}/\text{now}(\varphi S_{\leq \delta} \psi) = \textit{true}$ and -1 corresponds to the case where $\text{pre}/\text{now}(\varphi S_{\leq \delta} \psi) = \textit{false}$. The update rule for $\tau\text{now}(\varphi S_{\leq \delta} \psi)$ and $\text{now}(\varphi S_{\leq \delta} \psi)$ is as follows:

---

[2] We ignore at this point the clock value component $\tau(i)$.

if now(ψ) **then** τnow$(\varphi S_{\leq\delta}\psi) := 0$	[restart timer]
else if τpre$(\varphi S_{\leq\delta}\psi) \neq -1$ and now(φ) **then**	[$(\varphi S_{\leq\delta}\psi)$ continues to hold?]
if τpre$(\varphi S_{\leq\delta}\psi) + \Delta > \delta$ **then**	[distance too big?]
τnow$(\varphi S_{\leq\delta}\psi) := -1$	[$(\varphi S_{\leq\delta}\psi)$ does not hold]
else τnow$(\varphi S_{\leq\delta}\psi) := \tau$pre$(\varphi S_{\leq\delta}\psi) + \Delta$	[update distance]
else τnow$(\varphi S_{\leq\delta}\psi) := -1$;	[$(\varphi S_{\leq\delta}\psi)$ does not hold]
now$(\varphi S_{\leq\delta}\psi) := (\tau$now$(\varphi S_{\leq\delta}\psi) \neq -1)$	

The Propositional Algorithm for $(\varphi Z_{\leq\delta}\psi)$

This subformula is similar to $(\varphi S_{\leq\delta}\psi)$, but requires that ψ has happened in the past, *excluding* the current time, and not more than δ time units in the past; if ψ holds now, this is not sufficient for $(\varphi Z_{\leq\delta}\psi)$ to hold. This modality is required to express properties such as

$$\forall f \; open(f) \rightarrow \neg(true \; Z_{\leq 20} \; open(f))$$

which asserts that we have not witnessed two openings of the same file in proximity of 20 ticks or less. Note that the previous-time $\ominus$ operator does not help in expressing the above property, since $\ominus$ refers to the previous event, which is not guaranteed to have occurred exactly one clock tick earlier. The algorithm sets the timer to the distance from the last event, if φ holds now, and ψ held in the previous event. Then it updates the timer by adding Δ as long as φ continues to hold and we are within the time distance δ.

if now(φ) **then**	
if pre(ψ) and $\Delta \leq \delta$ **then** τnow$(\varphi Z_{\leq\delta}\psi) := \Delta$	[initiate timer]
else	
if τpre$(\varphi Z_{\leq\delta}\psi) \neq -1$ **and** τpre$(\varphi Z_{\leq\delta}\psi) + \Delta \leq \delta$ **then**	[distance still OK?]
τnow$(\varphi Z_{\leq\delta}\psi) := \tau$pre$(\varphi Z_{\leq\delta}\psi) + \Delta$	[update distance]
else τnow$(\varphi Z_{\leq\delta}\psi) := -1$	
else τnow$(\varphi Z_{\leq\delta}\psi) := -1$;	
now$(\varphi Z_{\leq\delta}\psi) := (\tau$now$(\varphi Z_{\leq\delta}\psi) \neq -1)$	

The Propositional Algorithm for $(\varphi S_{>\delta}\psi)$

We update τnow$(\varphi S_{>\delta}\psi)$, which is the current time distance to where $(\varphi S\psi)$ (the untimed version of the subformula) started to hold. We update it according to the *earliest* (i.e., furthest in the past) occurrence where this held, since this is the larger distance, hence the first to satisfy the timing constraint. If this occurrence becomes irrelevant (since φ does not hold in the current prefix) then later observed occurrences become irrelevant too. When this happens, we either zero the counter, in case that ψ currently holds, or otherwise set it to -1 to signal that $(\varphi S\psi)$ does not currently hold. We restrict the counter to $\delta + 1$; any value that is bigger than that will result in the same conclusion, and we want to keep that value small[3]. Now $\varphi S_{>\delta}\psi$ currently holds when the value of this counter is bigger than δ.

---

[3] In fact, when $\Delta > \delta$, we use $\delta + 1$ instead.

if $\mathrm{now}(\varphi) \wedge \mathrm{tpre}(\varphi \mathcal{S}_{>\delta} \psi) \geq 0$ **then**
$\quad \mathrm{tnow}(\varphi \mathcal{S}_{>\delta} \psi) := \min(\mathrm{tpre}(\varphi \mathcal{S}_{>\delta} \psi) + \Delta, \delta + 1)$
else if $\mathrm{now}(\psi)$ **then** $\mathrm{tnow}(\varphi \mathcal{S}_{>\delta} \psi) := 0$ [restart counter]
else $\mathrm{tnow}(\varphi \mathcal{S}_{>\delta} \psi) := -1$;   [$(\varphi \mathcal{S}_{>\delta} \psi)$ does not hold]
$\mathrm{now}(\varphi \mathcal{S}_{>\delta} \psi) := (\mathrm{tpre}(\varphi \mathcal{S}_{>\delta} \psi) > \delta)$

4 First-Order Past LTL

First-order past LTL allows quantification over the values of variables that appear as parameters in the specification. In the context of RV, these values can appear within the monitored events. For example, $close(f)$ indicating that f is being closed. We saw in the introduction Property (2), which asserts that a file cannot be closed unless it was opened before. A more refined specification requires that a file can be closed only if it was opened before, but also has not been closed since:

$$\forall f \, (close(f) \longrightarrow \ominus(\neg close(f) \mathcal{S} \, open(f))) \tag{4}$$

An *assignment* over a set of variables W maps each variable $x \in W$ to a value from its associated domain. For example $[x \rightarrow 5, y \rightarrow \text{“abc”}]$ is an assignment that maps x to 5 and y to "abc". A predicate consists of a predicate name and a variable or a constant of the same type[4]. E.g., if the predicate name p and the variable x are associated with the domain of strings, then $p(\text{“gaga”})$, $p(\text{“lady”})$ and $p(x)$ are predicates. The predicates G with constant parameters are called *ground predicates*. A model, i.e., an execution (or a trace), ξ is a pair $\langle L, \tau \rangle$, where

1. $L : \mathbb{N} \mapsto 2^G$, and
2. $\tau : \mathbb{N} \mapsto \mathbb{N}$ is a monotonic function representing integer clock values.

An *event* in ξ is a triple $\xi(i) = \langle i, L(i), \tau(i) \rangle$ for $i \geq 1$.

4.1 Syntax

As in the propositional case, we restrict ourselves to *safety* properties, hence introduce only the past modalities.

$$\varphi ::= true \mid p(a) \mid p(x) \mid (\varphi \wedge \varphi) \mid \neg \varphi \mid (\varphi \mathcal{S} \varphi) \mid (\varphi \mathcal{S}_{\leq \delta} \varphi) \mid (\varphi \mathcal{Z}_{\leq \delta} \varphi) \mid (\varphi \mathcal{S}_{>\delta} \varphi) \mid \ominus \varphi \mid \exists x \, \varphi$$

We can also define $\forall x \varphi$ as $\neg \exists \neg \varphi$, and all the additional operators defined for the propositional case in Sect. 2.

---

[4] For simplicity of the presentation, but without restricting the algorithms or the implementation, we present here only unary predicates.

4.2 Semantics

Let $free(\varphi)$ be the set of free, i.e., unquantified, variables of subformula φ. Let $\gamma[x \mapsto a]$ be an assignment that agrees with the assignment γ, except for the binding $x \mapsto a$. Then $\gamma, \xi, i \models \varphi$, where γ is an assignment that contains $free(\varphi)$, and $i \geq 1$, is defined as follows:

- $\gamma, \xi, i \models true$.
- $\gamma, \xi, i \models p(a)$ if $p(a) \in L(i)$.
- $\gamma[x \mapsto a], \xi, i \models p(x)$ if $p(a) \in L[i]$.
- $\gamma, \xi, i \models (\varphi \wedge \psi)$ if $\gamma, \xi, i \models \varphi$ and $\gamma, \xi, i \models \psi$.
- $\gamma, \xi, i \models \neg\varphi$ if not $\gamma, \xi, i \models \varphi$.
- $\gamma, \xi, i \models (\varphi S \psi)$ if there exists some $1 \leq j \leq i$, such that $\gamma, \xi, j \models \psi$ and and for all $j < k \leq i$ it holds that $\gamma, \xi, k \models \varphi$.
- $\gamma, \xi, i \models (\varphi S_{\leq \delta} \psi)$ if there exists some $1 \leq j \leq i$, such that $\tau(i) - \tau(j) \leq \delta$ and $\gamma, \xi, j \models \psi$, and for all $j < k \leq i$ it holds that $\gamma, \xi, k \models \varphi$.
- $\gamma, \xi, i \models (\varphi Z_{\leq \delta} \psi)$ if there exists some $1 \leq j < i$, such that $\tau(i) - \tau(j) \leq \delta$ and $\gamma, \xi, j \models \psi$, and for all $j < k \leq i$ it holds that $\gamma, \xi, k \models \varphi$.
- $\gamma, \xi, i \models (\varphi S_{> \delta} \psi)$ if there exists some $1 \leq j < i$, such that $\tau(i) - \tau(j) > \delta$ and $\gamma, \xi, j \models \psi$, and for all $j < k \leq i$ it holds that $\gamma, \xi, k \models \varphi$.
- $\gamma, \xi, i \models \ominus\varphi$ if $i > 1$ and $\gamma, \xi, i - 1 \models \varphi$.
- $\gamma, \xi, i \models \exists x\, \varphi$ if there exists $a \in domain(x)$ such that $\gamma[x \mapsto a], \xi, i \models \varphi$.

We write $\xi \models \varphi$ for a formula φ without free variables when $\varepsilon, \xi, i \models \varphi$ for each i, where ε is the empty assignment.

5   RV for First-Order Past LTL Using BDDs

We describe an algorithm for monitoring first-order past LTL properties with time constraints. The untimed version and an implementation of it was presented in [19].

5.1   RV for First-Order Past LTL Without Time Constraints Using BDDs

For the purpose of self containment, we first present the RV algorithm for the first-order past LTL without timing constraints, as presented in [19]. Then, in the next section we will show how to expand this into the logic with time constraints.

Using BDDs to Represent Relations

Our algorithm is based on representing relations between data elements (and, as we discuss later, timers, which are small integers) using Ordered Binary Decision Diagrams (OBDD, although we write simply BDD) [11]. A BDD is a compact representation for a Boolean valued function as a directed acyclic graph (DAG), see, e.g., Figs. 1 and 2.

A BDD is obtained from a tree that represents a Boolean formula with some Boolean variables $x_1 \ldots x_k$ by gluing together isomorphic subtrees. Each non-leaf node is labeled with one of the Boolean variables. A non-leaf node x_i is the source of two arrows leading to other nodes. A dotted-line arrow represents that x_i has the Boolean value *false* (i.e.,

0), while a thick-line arrow represents that it has the value *true* (i.e., 1). The nodes in the DAG have the same order along all paths from the root (hence the letter 'O' in OBDD). However, some of the nodes may be absent along some paths, when the result of the Boolean function does not depend on the value of the corresponding Boolean variable. Each path leads to a leaf node that is marked by either *true* or *false*, corresponding to the Boolean value returned by the function for the Boolean values on the path.

A Boolean function, and consequently a BDD, can represent a set of integer values as follows. Each integer value is, in turn, represented using a bit vector: a vector of bits $x_1 \ldots x_k$ represents the integer value $x_1 \times 1 + x_2 \times 2 + \ldots x_k \times 2^k$, where the bit value of x_i is 1 for *true* and 0 for *false* and where x_1 is the *least* significant bit, and x_k is the *most* significant. For example, the integer 6 can be represented as the bit vector 110 (the most significant bit appears to the left) using the bits $x_1 = 0$, $x_2 = 1$ and $x_3 = 1$. To represent a *set* of integers, the BDD returns *true* for any combination of bits that represent an integer in the set. For example, to represent the set $\{4,6\}$, we first convert 4 and 6 into the bit vectors 100 and 110, respectively. The Boolean function over x_1, x_2, x_3 is $(\neg x_1 \wedge x_3)$, which returns *true* exactly for these two bit vector combinations.

This can be extended to represent relations, or, equivalently, a set of tuples over integers. The Boolean variables are partitioned into n bitstrings $x_1 = x_1^1, \ldots, x_{k_1}^1$, $x_n = x_1^n, \ldots, x_{k_n}^n$, each representing an integer number, forming the bit string[5]:

$$x_1^1, \ldots, x_{k_1}^1, \ldots, x_1^n, \ldots, x_{k_n}^n.$$

Using BDDs over Enumerations of Values

The summary for the first-order RV algorithm without timing constraints consists of BDDs $pre(\varphi)$ and $now(\varphi)$ for all subformulas of the monitored property. In the propositional case, these summary elements have Boolean values. For the first-order case, each summary element for a subformula φ is conceptually a relation between values of the free variables in φ. However, instead of representing these values directly, according to their different domains (e.g., integers, strings), these relations are represented as BDDs over the *enumerations* of values, and not directly over the values themselves.

During RV, when a value (associated with a variable in the specification) appears for the first time in an observed event, we assign to it a new *enumeration*. Values can be assigned consecutive enumeration values; however, a refined algorithm can reuse enumerations that were used for values that can no longer affect the verdict of the RV process, see [21]. We use a hash table to point from the value to its enumeration so that in subsequent appearances of this value the same enumeration will be used. For example, if the runtime verifier sees the input events *open*(a), *open*(b), *open*(c), it may encode them as the bit vectors 000, 001 and 010, respectively.

The described results in several advantages:

1. It allows a shorter representation of very big values in the BDDs; the values are compacted into a smaller number of bits. Furthermore, if a big data value occurs multiple times, we avoid representing that big value multiple times in the BDDs.

---

[5] In the implementation the same number of bits are used for all variables: $k_1 = k_2 = \ldots = k_n$.

2. It contributes to the compactness of the BDDs because enumerations of values that are not far apart often share large bit patterns.
3. The first-order RV algorithm is simple and very similar to the propositional algorithm; the Boolean operators over summary elements: conjunction, disjunction and negation, are replaced by the same operators over BDDs. This also simplifies the implementation.
4. Given an efficient BDD package, the implementation can be very efficient. On can also migrate between BDD packages.
5. Full use of negation also follows easily.

Example 1 - BDDs without Time

As an example consider the following formula concerning the correctness of command execution. It states that for all commands m, if the command succeeds execution, then there must have been a dispatch of that command in the past with some priority p, and no failure since the dispatch:

$$\forall m(suc(m) \rightarrow \exists p(\neg fail(m) \, S \, dis(m,p)))\tag{5}$$

Let us apply this property to the first two events of the following trace, where each event includes a single ground predicate. It consists of the dispatch of two commands, sending of telemetry data and success of the two commands:

$$\langle dis(stop,1), dis(off,2), tel(speed,2), suc(stop), suc(off) \rangle\tag{6}$$

We shall now focus on the current assignments to the free variables m and p satisfying the subformula $\varphi = \neg fail(m) \, S \, dis(m,p)$, represented as a BDD. After the first event $dis(stop,1)$ this BDD corresponds to the assignment $[m \mapsto stop, p \mapsto 1]$. The algorithm (to be shown below) will for each variable enumerate the data observed in events, in this case[6], assume that $stop$ gets enumerated as 6 (binary 110) and 1 also gets enumerated as 6 (binary 110) (note that values for different variables get enumerated individually, and therefore can be mapped to the same enumerations). This mapping is recorded in the hash map for each variable from values to enumerations. Say we represent the enumeration for the value of each of the variables m and p using three bits: $m_1 m_2 m_3$ and $p_1 p_2 p_3$, with m_1 and p_1 being the least significant bits. The assignment $[m \mapsto stop, p \mapsto 1]$ will then be represented by a BDD which accepts the bit vector $m_1 m_2 m_3 p_1 p_2 p_3 = 011011$. This BDD is shown in Fig. 1a. The BDD has 6 nodes, named $0, \ldots, 5$. The nodes 0, 1 and 2 represent $m_1 m_2 m_3$, and the nodes 3, 4 and 5 represent $p_1 p_2 p_3$. Following the arrows from node 0 on the top to the leaf node 1 (*true*) at the bottom, we indeed see the binary pattern 011011 (dotted-line arrows = 0 and thick-line arrows = 1).

Consider now the second event $dis(off,2)$. Here off gets enumerated as 5 (binary 101), just as 2 gets enumerated as 5 (binary 101) - again, variables get enumerated individually. The BDD in Fig. 1b represents the set of assignments: $\{[m \mapsto stop, p \mapsto 1], [m \mapsto off, p \mapsto 2]\}$. The BDD is the union of the BDD in Fig. 1a and a BDD representing the path 101101.

---

[6] The example BDDs are generated by our tool.

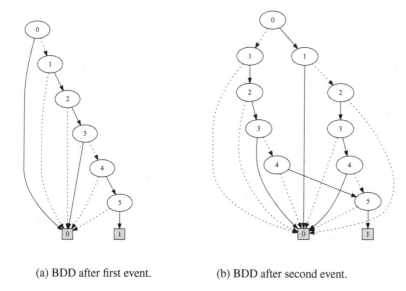

(a) BDD after first event.   (b) BDD after second event.

Fig. 1. The BDDs for the formula $(\neg fail(m) \; \mathcal{S} \; dis(m, p))$ after the first event and after the second event.

The BDD-based Algorithm for First-order Past LTL

We use a hash table to map values to their enumerations. When a ground predicate $p(a)$ occurs in the execution matching with $p(x)$ in the monitored property, the procedure **lookup**(x, a) is used to return the enumeration of a: it checks if a is already hashed. If not, i.e., this is a's first occurrence, then it will be hashed and assigned a new enumeration that will be returned by **lookup**. Otherwise, **lookup** returns the value hashed under a, which is the enumeration that a received before. A better compactness is achieved where each value is hashed separately for each variable x that matches it in the specification formula, hence **lookup**(x, a) is not necessarily the same as **lookup**(y, a).

We can use a counter for each variable x, counting the number of different values appearing so far for x. When a new value appears, this counter is incremented and the value is converted to a Boolean representation (a bit vector). Note, however, that any enumeration scheme is possible, as shown in Example 1 above.

The function **build**(x, A) returns a BDD that represents the set of assignments where x is mapped to (the enumeration of) v for $v \in A$. This BDD is independent of the values assigned to any variable other than x, i.e., they can have any value. For example, assume that we use three Boolean variables (bits) x_1, x_2 and x_3 for representing enumerations over x (with x_1 being the least significant bit), and assume that $A = \{a, b\}$, **lookup**$(x, a) = 001$, and **lookup**$(x, b) = 011$. Then **build**(x, A) is a BDD representation of the Boolean function $x_1 \wedge \neg x_3$.

Intersection and union of sets of assignments are translated simply to conjunction and disjunction of their BDD representation, respectively, and complementation becomes BDD negation. We will denote the Boolean BDD operators for conjunction, disjunction and negation as $\wedge$, $\vee$ and $\neg$ (confusion should be avoided with the corresponding operations applying on propositions). To implement the existential (universal, respectively) operators, we use the BDD existential (universal, respectively) operators over the Boolean variables that represent (the enumerations of) the values of x. Thus, if B_φ is the BDD representing the assignments satisfying φ in the current state of the monitor, then $\exists x_1, \ldots, x_k(B_\varphi)$ is the BDD that is obtained by applying the BDD existential quantification repeatedly on the BDD variables $x_1 \ldots, x_k$. Finally, $\mathrm{BDD}(\bot)$ and $\mathrm{BDD}(\top)$ are the BDDs that return uniformally *false* or *true*, respectively.

The dynamic programming algorithm, shown below, works similarly to the algorithm for the propositional case shown in Sect. 3. That is, it operates on two vectors (arrays) of values indexed by subformulas: pre for the state before the last event, and now for the current state after the last event. However, while in the propositional case the vectors contain Boolean values, in the first-order case they contain BDDs.

1. Initially, for each subformula φ of the specification η, $\mathrm{now}(\varphi) := \mathrm{BDD}(\bot)$.
2. Observe a new event (as a set of ground predicates) s as input.
3. Let pre := now.
4. Make the following updates for each subformula. If φ is a subformula of ψ then $\mathrm{now}(\varphi)$ is updated before $\mathrm{now}(\psi)$.
   - $\mathrm{now}(true) := \mathrm{BDD}(\top)$.
   - $\mathrm{now}(p(a)) := \text{if } p(a) \in s \text{ then } \mathrm{BDD}(\top) \text{ else } \mathrm{BDD}(\bot)$.
   - $\mathrm{now}(p(x)) := \mathbf{build}(x, A) \text{ where } A = \{a \mid p(a) \in s\}$.
   - $\mathrm{now}((\varphi \wedge \psi)) := \mathrm{now}(\varphi) \wedge \mathrm{now}(\psi)$.
   - $\mathrm{now}(\neg\varphi) := \neg\mathrm{now}(\varphi)$.
   - $\mathrm{now}((\varphi \, \mathcal{S} \, \psi)) := \mathrm{now}(\psi) \vee (\mathrm{now}(\varphi) \wedge \mathrm{pre}((\varphi \mathcal{S} \psi)))$.
   - $\mathrm{now}(\ominus \varphi) := \mathrm{pre}(\varphi)$.
   - $\mathrm{now}(\exists x \, \varphi) := \exists x_1, \ldots, x_k \, \mathrm{now}(\varphi)$.
5. if $\mathrm{now}(\eta) = \mathrm{BDD}(\bot)$ then report "error".
6. Goto step 2.

An important component of the algorithm is that, at any point during monitoring, enumerations that are not used in the pre and now BDDs represent all values that have *not* been seen so far in the input events. We specifically reserve one enumeration, with bit vector value of $11 \ldots 11$ (i.e., all ones), to represent all values not seen yet. This trick allows us to use a finite representation and quantify existentially and universally over *all* values in infinite domains while allowing unrestricted use of negation in the temporal specification.

5.2   The BDD-based Algorithm for First-Order Past LTL with Time Constraints

We describe now *changes* to the algorithm in Sect. 5.1 for handling the subformulas with the timing constraints $(\varphi \mathcal{S}_{\leq\delta}\psi)$, $(\varphi \mathcal{Z}_{\leq\delta}\psi)$ and $(\varphi \mathcal{S}_{>\delta}\psi)$.

BDDs Representing Relations Over Data and Time

Analogously to the propositional case, in the first-order case we need to add to the summary, for subformulas with timing constraints, in addition to the BDDs for $\mathrm{pre}(\varphi)$

and now(φ), also BDDs of the time $\tau pre(\varphi)$ and $\tau now(\varphi)$. These BDDs contain the relevant time that has passed that is needed in order to check the timing constraint.

Each assignment or tuple in such a BDD is over some number of data data variables $x^1 \ldots x^n$ and, in adddition, a timing variable t, forming the BDD bits:

$$x_1^1, \ldots, x_k^1, \ldots, x_1^n, \ldots, x_k^n, t_1, \ldots, t_m$$

These integer values are, either,

1. enumerations of data values, for each x^i, as explained above, or
2. the time t that has passed since the event that causes the tuple of data values to be included.

In order to keep the representation finite and small, $2\delta + 1$ is used as the limit on t. That is, after we update t, we compare it against δ. When t goes beyond δ we can store just $\delta + 1$ since we just need to know that it passed δ. During computation, when we observe a Δ that is bigger than δ, we cut it down to $\delta + 1$ for the same reason, before we add to t. Finally, since adding $\Delta = \delta + 1$ to a $t \leq \delta$ gives max $2\delta + 1$, then this is the biggest number we need to store in a BDD. Consequently, the number of bits needed to store time is $log_2(2\delta + 1)$.

Example 2 - BDDs with Time

We add a timing constraint to the formula (5) in Example 1, stating that when a command succeeds it must have been dispatched in the past within 3 time units:

$$\forall m(suc(m) \rightarrow \exists p(\neg fail(m) \ S_{\leq 3} \ dis(m, p))) \tag{7}$$

Let us apply this property to the first two events of the following trace, which is the trace (6) from Example 1, augmented with clock values following @-signs. We keep the time constraint and clock values small and consecutive, to keep the BDD small for presentation purposes:

$$\langle dis(stop, 1)@1, dis(off, 2)@2, tel(speed, 2)@3, suc(stop)@4, suc(off)@5 \rangle \tag{8}$$

The BDD for the subformula $\varphi = \neg fail(m) \ S_{\leq 3} \ dis(m, p)$ at the third event $tel(speed, 2)$, shown in Fig. 2, reflects that two (010 in binary) time units have passed since $dis(stop, 1)$ occurred, and one time unit (001 in binary) has passed since $dis(off, 2)$ has occurred. The BDD is effectively an augmentation of the BDD in Fig. 1b, with the additional three nodes 6, 7, and 8, representing respectively the bits t_1, t_2, and t_3 for the timer value, with t_1 (node 6) being the least significant bit.

BDD Update Operators on Relations Over Data and Time Constraints

When a new event occurs, depending on the type of the subformula with timing constraint, we need to update the timers in τnow that count the time that has passed since a tuple of values has entered. Subsequently, τpre will be updated when the next event will occur. The difference between the clock value of the current event and the clock value of the previous one is Δ, and the timer is incremented, as explained above, by

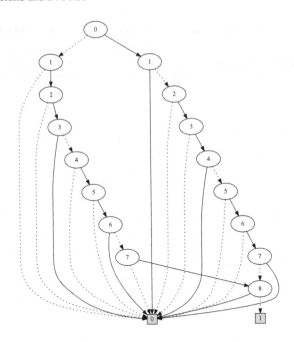

Fig. 2. The BDD for the formula $(\neg\textit{fail}(m)\ \mathcal{S}_{\leq 3}\ \textit{dis}(m,p))$ at the third event.

$min(\Delta,\delta+1)$. We also need to be able to check whether after adding Δ, the value of the time difference exceeds the time constraint δ.

Abstractly, given a relation R over data elements and time values, we need to construct two relations[7]:

- $R+\Delta = \{(x^1,\ldots,x^n,t+\Delta)|(x^1,\ldots,x^n,t)\in R\}$. This can be done by
    1. Constructing a relation $\mathcal{T} = \{(t,t')\,|\,t\geq 0 \wedge t' = t+\Delta\}$.
    2. Taking the *join* of R and $\mathcal{T}$. The join is basically the tuples that agree on the values of their common variables.
    3. Projecting out the (old) t values, and then renaming the (new) t' values as t.
- $R > \delta = \{(x^1,\ldots,x^n,t)\in R\,|\,t > \delta\}$. This can by done by
    1. Constructing $T_\delta = \{t\,|\,t > \delta\}$.
    2. Taking the join between R and T_δ.

We show now how to translate these set operators into BDDs. For $R+\Delta$, we construct a Boolean formula $addconst(t,t',\Delta)$ that expresses relation $\mathcal{T}$ between the Boolean variables of t and t'. For $R > \delta$, we construct a Boolean formula $gtconst(t,\delta)$ that corresponds to T_δ. These formulas are translated to BDDs. Then, taking the join of two BDDs is done by first completing the two BDDs to be over the same bits; since the BDDs are independent of the missing bits, this is trivial, keeping the same BDD structure. Then the intersection between these BDDs is obtained via the BDD conjunction ($\wedge$) operator.

---

[7] Recall that all values are restricted to $2\delta+1$ and if $\Delta > \delta$, then $\delta+1$ is used instead of Δ.

The Boolean formula *addconst*. The Boolean formula $addconst(t, t', \Delta)$ is satisfied by a pair of integer values t and t', represented as the bit vectors $t_1 \ldots t_m$ and $t'_1, \ldots, t'_m$, respectively, when $t' = t + \Delta$. The integer constant Δ is represented using the bit vector $\Delta_1 \ldots \Delta_m$. The formula uses the additional bits $r_1, \ldots, r_m$, where r_i is the carry-over from the ith bits, according to Binary addition. This allows presenting the formula in an intuitive way, following standard binary addition and in obtaining a formula that is linear in the number of bits. When translating the formula to a BDD, existential quantification is applied to remove the Boolean variables $r_1, \ldots, r_m$.

$addconst(t, t', \Delta) = \wedge_{1 \leq i \leq m} (t'_i \leftrightarrow (t_i \oplus \Delta_i \oplus r_i))$
where $r_1 = false$,
$\qquad$ **for** $1 \leq i < m$: $r_{i+1} = ((r_i \wedge (t_i \vee \Delta_i)) \vee (\neg r_i \wedge t_i \wedge \Delta_i))$

The formula *gtconst*. The formula $gtconst(t, \delta)$ is *true* when t is bigger than δ. Both t and δ are integers represented as bit vectors $t_1 \ldots t_m$ and $\delta_1 \ldots \delta_m$, respectively. This holds when there is an index $1 \leq i \leq m$ such that $t_i = 1$ (*true*) and $\delta_i = 0$ (*false*), and where for $m \geq j > i, t_j = \delta_j$. When translating the formula to a BDD, existential quantification is applied to the Boolean variables $r_0, \ldots, r_m$, which are used to propagate the check from the least to the most significant bit.

$gtconst(t, \delta) = r_m$
where $r_0 = false$,
$\qquad$ **for** $1 \leq i \leq m$: $r_i = ((t_i \wedge \neg \delta_i) \vee ((t_i \leftrightarrow \delta_i) \wedge r_{i-1}))$

We describe now the additions required in Step 4 of the algorithm presented in Sect. 5.1.

The First-order Algorithm for $(\varphi \, \mathcal{S}_{\leq \delta} \, \psi)$

The BDDs pre/now$(\varphi \mathcal{S}_{\leq \delta} \psi)$ generalize the Boolean summaries for the propositional past LTL, by representing enumerations of the values of the free variables that satisfy this subformula, e.g., with the bits $x_1^1, \ldots, x_k^n$. The BDDs τpre/τnow$(\varphi \mathcal{S}_{\leq \delta} \psi)$ relate the values of the free variables that satisfy this subformula with the timer values that keep the time elapsed since the point where the values of the free variables were observed.

Generalizing from the propositional case, we need to compare and update timing values *per each assignment* to the free variables of a subformula $(\varphi \mathcal{S}_{\leq \delta} \psi)$. An example is the assignments (tuples) $\{[x \mapsto me, y \mapsto 72, t \mapsto 6], [x \mapsto you, y \mapsto 62, t \mapsto 9]\}$ for the subformula $(\varphi \mathcal{S}_{\leq \delta} \psi)$, where t is assigned to the time units that has elapsed. We represent that using BDDs, where the values for x and y follow the previous conventions, with the bits $x_1 \ldots x_k$ and $y_1 \ldots y_k$ encoding the enumerations for the values for x and y, respectively, and the bits $t_1, \ldots, t_m$ that represent the time passed since their introduction.

We will also use the following BDD constructions: $rename(B, x, y)$ renames the bits $x_1 \ldots x_k$ in the BDD B as $y_1 \ldots y_k$ and $BDD0(x)$ is a BDD where all the x_i bits are a constant 0, representing the Boolean expression $\neg x_1 \wedge \ldots \wedge \neg x_k$.

The update of the BDD τnow$(\varphi \mathcal{S}_{\leq \delta} \psi)$ is similar to the updates of the *if* statements in the propositional case, applied to all the values of the free variables of this subformula and uses the BDD constructed from the formula *gtconst*. While in the propositional case we kept the values $[-1, 0, \ldots, \delta]$, with -1 representing *false*, here we need only keep the assignments for the free variables of the subformula that correspond to $[0 \ldots \delta]$. Tuples of variable values that do not satisfy the time constraint are simply not represented by the BDD. This simplifies the formalization.

$$\tau now(\varphi S_{\leq\delta}\psi) := (now(\psi) \wedge BDD0(t)) \bigvee (\neg now(\psi) \wedge now(\varphi) \wedge$$
$$rename(\exists t_1 \ldots t_m (addconst(t, t', \Delta) \wedge \neg gtconst(t', \delta) \wedge \tau pre(\varphi S_{\leq\delta}\psi)), t', t)) ;$$
$$now(\varphi S_{\leq\delta}\psi) := \exists t_1 \ldots t_m \tau now(\varphi S_{\leq\delta}\psi)$$

That is, either ψ holds now and we reset the timer t to 0, or ψ does not hold now but φ does, and the previous t value is determined by $\tau pre(\varphi S_{\leq\delta}\psi)$, to which we add Δ, giving t', which must not be greater than δ. Then t is removed by quantifying over it, and t' renamed to t (t' becomes the new t). The BDD for $now(\varphi S_{\leq\delta}\psi)$ is obtained from $\tau now(\varphi S_{\leq\delta}\psi)$ by projecting out the timer value.

Note that the Boolean operators $\wedge$ and $\vee$ on BDDs represent *join* and *cojoin*, respectively. This means that before the operator is applied, its two parameters are extended to have the same BDD variable bits (where the missing bits are assigned to all possible combinations).

The First-Order Algorithm for $(\varphi \, \mathcal{Z}_{\leq\delta} \, \psi)$

The update of the BDD $now(\varphi \mathcal{Z}_{\leq\delta}\psi)$ is, conceptually, similar case-wise to the updates of the *if* statements of the propositional case, applied to all the values of the free variables of this formula.

$$\tau now(\varphi \mathcal{Z}_{\leq\delta}\psi) :=$$
$$now(\varphi) \wedge$$
$$((pre(\psi) \wedge \Delta \leq \delta \wedge EQUAL(t, \Delta))$$
$$\vee$$
$$(\neg pre(\psi) \wedge$$
$$rename(\exists t_1 \ldots t_m (addconst(t, t', \Delta) \wedge \neg gtconst(t', \delta) \wedge \tau pre(\varphi \mathcal{Z}_{\leq\delta}\psi)), t', t)));$$
$$now(\varphi \mathcal{Z}_{\leq\delta}\psi) := \exists t_1 \ldots t_m \tau now(\varphi \mathcal{Z}_{\leq\delta}\psi)$$

Where $EQUAL(t, c) = \exists z_1 \ldots z_m (BDD0(z) \wedge addconst(z, t, c))$, expressing that t is equal to c by adding $z = 0$ to c to obtain t. The formula says that φ must hold now and one of two cases must hold. In the first case, ψ holds in the previous state, $\Delta \leq \delta$, and t is initialized to Δ. In the second case, ψ not hold in the previous state, and (using the same procedure as for the previous subformula) the previous t value is determined by $\tau pre(\varphi \mathcal{Z}_{\leq\delta}\psi)$, to which we add Δ, giving t', which must not be greater than δ. Then t is removed by quantifying over it, and t' renamed to t (t' becomes the new t). Note that $\Delta \leq \delta$ is a Boolean condition, and, depending on its value, can be translated into the BDD representing the constants *true* or *false*.

The First-Order Algorithm for $(\varphi S_{>\delta}\psi)$

Monitoring the subformula $(\varphi S_{>\delta}\psi)$ is, conceptually, similar case-wise to the propositional case.

$\tau now(\varphi S_{>\delta}\psi) :=$
 $(now(\psi) \wedge (\neg pre(\varphi S_{>\delta}\psi) \vee \neg now(\varphi)) \wedge BDD0(t)) \vee$
 $(now(\varphi) \wedge rename(previous, t', t))$
where $previous = \exists t_1 \ldots t_m \, (\tau pre(\varphi S_{>\delta}\psi) \wedge ((\neg gtconst(t,\delta) \wedge addconst(t,t',\Delta)) \vee$
 $(gtconst(t,\delta) \wedge EQUAL(t', \delta+1)));$
$now(\varphi S_{>\delta}\psi) := \exists t_1 \ldots t_m \, (\tau now(\varphi S_{>\delta}\psi) \wedge gtconst(t,\delta))$

When ψ currently holds and either $\varphi S_{>\delta}\psi$ did not hold in the previous state or φ does not hold now, we reset the timer t to 0. When φ holds we compute t' using the **where**-clause as follows and then rename it to t; t takes its value from $\tau pre(\varphi S_{>\delta}\psi)$, which is calculated based on the previous step. This means that $(\varphi S_{>\delta}\psi)$ held in the previous step. If t was then not greater than δ, we add Δ to t to obtain t'. Otherwise (t was already greater than δ), we set t' to $\delta+1$ to reduce the size of the time values we have to store.

6 Implementation and Evaluation

6.1 Implementation

The DEJAVU tool, previously presented in [19] for the untimed case, was extended to capture the extension of the first-order LTL logic with time. The DEJAVU tool assumes that each state contains one[8] ground predicate, called an *event*. The tool, programmed in Scala, reads a specification containing one or more properties, and generates a Scala program, which can be applied to a log file containing events[9] in CSV (Comma Separated Value) format. The generated monitor program produces a verdict (true or false) for each event in the log, although only failures are reported to the user. It uses the JavaBDD package [24] for generating and operating BDDs. As an example, consider the property (7) from Example 2. The generated monitor uses an enumeration of the subformulas of the original formula in order to evaluate the subformulas bottom up for each new event. Figure 3 (right) shows the decomposition of the formula into subformulas (an Abstract Syntax Tree - AST), indexed by numbers from 0 to 8, satisfying the invariant that if a formula φ_1 is a subformula of a formula φ_2 then φ_1's index is bigger than φ_2's index. The evaluation function of the generated monitor (~900 LOC in total), which is applied for each event, is shown in Fig. 3 (left). In each step the evaluate function re-computes the now array from highest to lowest index, and returns true (ok) iff now(0) is not BDD($\bot$).

6.2 Evaluation

We have performed an evaluation of DEJAVU by verifying variants of the properties shown in Fig. 4 on a set of traces of varying length and structure. Each property is verified with, and without, time constraints. The *command* property is the previously discussed property (7) in Example 2. The *access* property is similar to a property evaluated

---

[8] This restriction from the theory and algorithm presented above is made because our experience shows that this is by far the most common case.

[9] The tool can also be applied for online monitoring with some small adjustments.

```
def evaluate (): Boolean = {
  now(8) = build("dis")(V("m"),V("p"))
  now(7) = build("fail")(V("m"))
  now(6) = now(7).not()
  now(5) = (now(8).and(zeroTime)).or(
    now(6).and(pre(5))
    .and(DeltaBDD).and(deltaBDD)
    .and(addConst(t,tp,D,c))
    .and(gtConst(tp,d).not ())
    . exist (var_d). exist (var_D)
    . exist (var_c). exist (var_t)
    .replace(tp_to_t_map)
  )
  now(4) = now(5).exist(var_t)
  now(3) = now(4).exist(var_p)
  now(2) = build("suc")(V("m"))
  now(1) = now(2).not().or(now(3))
  now(0) = now(1).forAll (var_m)
  val error = now(0).isZero
  tmp = now; now = pre; pre = tmp
  ! error
}
```

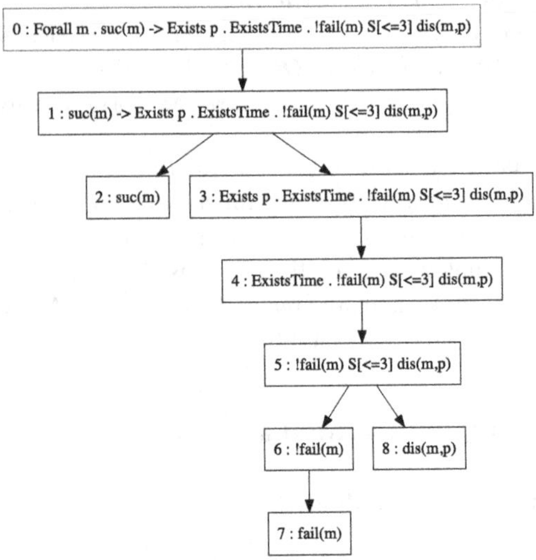

0 : Forall m . suc(m) -> Exists p . ExistsTime . !fail(m) S[<=3] dis(m,p)

1 : suc(m) -> Exists p . ExistsTime . !fail(m) S[<=3] dis(m,p)

2 : suc(m)

3 : Exists p . ExistsTime . !fail(m) S[<=3] dis(m,p)

4 : ExistsTime . !fail(m) S[<=3] dis(m,p)

5 : !fail(m) S[<=3] dis(m,p)

6 : !fail(m)   8 : dis(m,p)

7 : fail(m)

Fig. 3. Monitor (left) and AST (right) for the property.

in [19]. It states that if a file f is accessed by a user u, then the user should have logged in within 50 time units and not yet logged out, and the file should have been opened within 50 time units and not yet closed. The next properties concern operations of the Mars rover Curiosity [28]. The *boots* property concerns booting of instruments (passed as event parameters). A boot is initiated by a boot-start and terminated by a boot-end. The property states that for any instrument, we do not want to see a double boot (a boot followed by a boot), where the boots last longer than 20 s, and where the distance between the boots is less than 5 s. Finally, the *mobraces* and *armraces* properties follow the same pattern but for two different constants. The *mobraces* property states that during the execution of the command MOB_PRM (a dispatch of the command followed by the success of the command), which reports mobility parameters to ground; there should be no error in radio transmission of telemetry to ground. In addition the command must succeed in no more than 5 s. The *armraces* property states the same for the ARM_PRM command that transmits robotic arm parameters to ground. These two last properties in fact reflect a known (benign) race condition in the software of the Curiosity rover, caused when a thread servicing the radio is starved and generates the warning tr_err which indicates missing telemetry. This happens because the thread is preempted by higher priority threads that are processing one of two commands MOB_PRM and ARM_PRM.

Table 1 shows the results of the evaluation, performed on a Mac Pro laptop, running the Mac OS X 10.14.6 operating system, with a 2.9 GHz Intel Core i9 processor and 32 GB of memory. Each property is evaluated on one or more traces, numbered 1–

---

prop commands : **Forall** m . suc(m) → **Exists** p . ! fail (m) S[<=50] dis(m,p)

prop access : **Forall** u . **Forall** f .
    access(u,f) → ((! logout(u) S[<=50] login(u)) & (!close (f) S[<=50] open(f)))

prop boots: ! **Exists** i . (boot_e(i) & !P[<=20] boot_s(i) &
    @ (!boot_e(i) S (boot_s(i) & (!boot_e(i) S[<=5] (boot_e(i) &
    !P[<=20] boot_s(i) & @ (!boot_e(i) S boot_s(i)))))))

prop mobraces : suc("MOB_PRM") → (P[<=5] dis("MOB_PRM") &
    @ (!(suc("MOB_PRM") | **Exists** msg . tr_err(msg) S dis("MOB_PRM")))

prop armraces : suc("ARM_PRM") → (P[<=5] dis("ARM_PRM") &
    @ (!(suc("ARM_PRM") | **Exists** msg . tr_err(msg) S dis("ARM_PRM")))

Fig. 4. Evaluation properties.

15. Six of these traces are taken from [19] (traces nr. 1, 2, 3 and 7, 8, 9), and which are very data heavy, requiring lots of data to be stored by the monitor. The remaining traces require storing less information (and perhaps are more realistic). Traces 1–13 were generated for the experiment and are artificial, stress testing DEJAVU. Traces 14 and 15 are real logs of events reported by the Mars Curiosity rover, transmitted to JPL's ground operations (trace 14 is a prefix of the longer trace 15). For each trace is shown length in number of events, depth in terms of how many data values must be stored by the monitor, and whether it was verified without time constraints (no constr.) or with time constraints. A depth for the ACCESS property of e.g. 5,000 can mean that there at some point has been 5,000 users that have logged in and not yet logged out. Events in the logs 1–12 have consecutive clock values 1, 2, 3, ... Resulting trace analysis times are provided in minutes and seconds. In addition the factor of slowdown is shown for verifying with time constraints compared to verification without time constraints (execution time with constraints divided by execution time without constraints).

The interpretation of the results is as follows. By observing the factor numbers in the rightmost column, it is clear that there is a cost to monitoring timed properties compared to monitoring properties without time constraints. This holds for all traces. Furthermore, the larger the time constraints, the more calculations the monitor has to perform on bit strings representing time values. The performance of DEJAVU is acceptable for time constraints that require no more than 7 bits of storage. We observed, however, that going beyond 7 bits causes the monitor execution to become considerably slower. This corresponds to time constraints beyond 63.5 (note that for a time constraint of δ one needs $log_2(2\delta + 1)$ bits, see page page 13). The reason for this is not understood at the time of writing, and remains to be explored.

Table 1. Evaluation data. The factors (rightmost column) show how much slower verification of formulas with time constraints are compared to the untimed version of those formulas.

Property	Trace nr.	Trace length	Depth	Time constraint	Time	Factor
COMMANDS	1	11,004	8,000	no constr.	1.0 s	
				50	1.8 s	1.8
	2	110,004	80,000	no constr.	1.7 s	
				50	13.2 s	7.8
	3	1,100,004	800,000	no constr.	9.3 s	
				50	2 min 5.8 s	13.5
	4	10,050	25	no constr.	0.7 s	
				50	1.0 s	1.4
	5	100.050	25	no constr.	1.1 s	
				50	1.8	1.6
	6	1,000,050	25	no constr.	2.6 s	
				50	5.9 s	2.3
ACCESS	7	11,006	5000	no constr.	0.9 s	
				50	3.7 s	4.1
	8	110,006	50,000	no constr.	2.2 s	
				50	16.7 s	7.6
	9	1,100,006	500,000	no constr.	15.2 s	
				50	3 min 53.9 s	15.4
	10	10.100	25	no constr.	0.8 s	
				50	1.7 s	2.1
	11	100,100	25	no constr.	1.1s	
				50	8.4 s	7.6
	12	1,000,100	25	no constr.	2.6 s	
				50	1 min 15.9 s	29.2
BOOTS	13	10,012	low	no constr.	0.2 s	
				2	0.4 s	2.0
				20	0.8 s	4.0
				50	5.1 s	25.5
				60	7.2 s	36.0
MOB + ARM RACES	14	50,000	low	no constr.	0.3 s	
				10	0.7 s	2.3
				60	1.0 s	3.3
	15	96,795	low	no constr.	0.5 s	
				10	1.0 s	2.0
				60	1.6 s	3.2

7   Conclusions

We extended the theory and implementation of runtime verification for first-order past (i.e., safety) temporal logic from [19] to include timing constraints. The untimed algorithm was based on representing relations over data values using BDDs. The use of BDDs over enumerations of the data values as integers, and subsequently, bit vectors, allowed an efficient representation that was shown, through an implementation and experiments, to allow the monitoring of large execution traces.

This was extended here to allow timing constraints, as in $(\varphi \mathcal{S}_{\leq \delta} \varphi)$, $(\varphi \mathcal{Z}_{\leq \delta} \varphi)$ and $(\varphi \mathcal{S}_{>\delta} \varphi)$, with each event in the input trace including an integer clock value. The addition of timing constraints was done by extending the BDDs to represent relations over both enumeration of data and timer values. This required the use of nontrivial operations over BDDs that allow updating relations while performing arithmetic operations on the timer values. We extended the tool DEJAVU, and reported on some of the experimental results performed with time constraints.

References

1. Allan, C.: Adding trace matching with free variables to AspectJ. In: OOPSLA 2005, pp. 345–364. IEEE (2005)
2. Alpern, B., Schneider, F.B.: Recognizing Safety and Liveness. Distrib. Comput. **2**(3), 117–126 (1987). https://doi.org/10.1007/BF01782772
3. D'Angelo, B.: LOLA: Runtime monitoring of synchronous systems. In: TIME 2005, pp. 166–174 (2005)
4. Barringer, H., Goldberg, A., Havelund, K., Sen, K.: Rule-based runtime verification. In: Steffen, B., Levi, G. (eds.) VMCAI 2004. LNCS, vol. 2937, pp. 44–57. Springer, Heidelberg (2004). https://doi.org/10.1007/978-3-540-24622-0_5
5. Barringer, H., Havelund, K.: TRACECONTRACT: a Scala DSL for trace analysis. In: Butler, M., Schulte, W. (eds.) FM 2011. LNCS, vol. 6664, pp. 57–72. Springer, Heidelberg (2011). https://doi.org/10.1007/978-3-642-21437-0_7
6. Barringer, H., Rydeheard, D., Havelund, K.: Rule systems for run-time monitoring: from EAGLE to RULER. In: Sokolsky, O., Taşıran, S. (eds.) RV 2007. LNCS, vol. 4839, pp. 111–125. Springer, Heidelberg (2007). https://doi.org/10.1007/978-3-540-77395-5_10
7. Basin, D.A., Klaedtke, F., Müller, S., Zalinescu, E.: Monitoring metric first-order temporal properties. J. ACM **62**(2), 1–45 (2015)
8. Basin, D.A., Klaedtke, F., Zalinescu, E.: Algorithms for monitoring real-time properties. Acta Informatica **55**(4), 309–338 (2018)
9. Bauer, A., Leucker, M., Schallhart, C.: The good, the bad, and the ugly, but how ugly is ugly? In: Sokolsky, O., Taşıran, S. (eds.) RV 2007. LNCS, vol. 4839, pp. 126–138. Springer, Heidelberg (2007). https://doi.org/10.1007/978-3-540-77395-5_11
10. Bauer, A., Leucker, M., Schallhart, C.: Runtime verification for LTL and TLTL. ACM Trans. Softw. Eng. Methodol. **20**(4), 1–64 (2011)
11. Bryant, R.E.: Symbolic Boolean manipulation with ordered binary-decision diagrams. ACM Comput. Surv. **24**(3), 293–318 (1992)
12. Burch, J.R., Clarke, E.M., McMillan, K.L., Dill, D.L., Hwang, L.J.: Symbolic model checking: 10^{20} states and beyond. In: LICS 1990, pp. 428–439 (1990)
13. Decker, N., Leucker, M., Thoma, D.: Monitoring modulo theories. J. Softw. Tools Technol. Transfer **18**(2), 205–225 (2016)
14. Clarke, E.M., McMillan, K.L., Zhao, X., Fujita, M., Yang, J.C.Y.: Spectral transforms for large Boolean functions with applications to technology mapping. Formal Methods Syst. Des. **10**(2/3), 137–148 (1997)

15. Falcone, Y., Fernandez, J.-C., Mounier, L.: Runtime verification of safety-progress properties. In: Bensalem, S., Peled, D.A. (eds.) RV 2009. LNCS, vol. 5779, pp. 40–59. Springer, Heidelberg (2009). https://doi.org/10.1007/978-3-642-04694-0_4

16. Faymonville, P., Finkbeiner, B., Peled, D.: Monitoring parametric temporal logic. In: McMillan, K.L., Rival, X. (eds.) VMCAI 2014. LNCS, vol. 8318, pp. 357–375. Springer, Heidelberg (2014). https://doi.org/10.1007/978-3-642-54013-4_20

17. Hallé, S., Villemaire, R.: Runtime enforcement of web service message contracts with data. IEEE Trans. Serv. Comput. **5**(2), 192–206 (2012)

18. Havelund, K.: Rule-based runtime verification revisited. Int. J. Softw. Tools Technol. Transfer **17**(2), 143–170 (2014). https://doi.org/10.1007/s10009-014-0309-2

19. Havelund, K., Peled, D., Ulus, D.: First-order temporal logic monitoring with BDDs. In: FMCAD 2017, pp. 116–123. IEEE (2017)

20. Havelund, K., Peled, D.: Efficient Runtime Verification of First-Order Temporal Properties. In: Gallardo, M.M., Merino, P. (eds.) SPIN 2018. LNCS, vol. 10869, pp. 26–47. Springer, Cham (2018). https://doi.org/10.1007/978-3-319-94111-0_2

21. Havelund, K., Peled, D.: BDDs on the run. In: Margaria, T., Steffen, B. (eds.) ISoLA 2018. LNCS, vol. 11247, pp. 58–69. Springer, Cham (2018). https://doi.org/10.1007/978-3-030-03427-6_8

22. Havelund, K., Reger, G., Thoma, D., Zălinescu, E.: Monitoring events that carry data. In: Bartocci, E., Falcone, Y. (eds.) Lectures on Runtime Verification. LNCS, vol. 10457, pp. 61–102. Springer, Cham (2018). https://doi.org/10.1007/978-3-319-75632-5_3

23. Havelund, K., Roşu, G.: Synthesizing monitors for safety properties. In: Katoen, J.-P., Stevens, P. (eds.) TACAS 2002. LNCS, vol. 2280, pp. 342–356. Springer, Heidelberg (2002). https://doi.org/10.1007/3-540-46002-0_24

24. JavaBDD. http://javabdd.sourceforge.net

25. Henriksen, J.G.: Mona: monadic second-order logic in practice. In: Brinksma, E., Cleaveland, W.R., Larsen, K.G., Margaria, T., Steffen, B. (eds.) TACAS 1995. LNCS, vol. 1019, pp. 89–110. Springer, Heidelberg (1995). https://doi.org/10.1007/3-540-60630-0_5

26. Könighofer, B.: Shield synthesis. Form. Methods Syst. Des. **51**(2), 332–361 (2017)

27. Manna, Z., Pnueli, A.: Completing the temporal picture. Theor. Comput. Sci. **83**, 91–130 (1991)

28. Mars Science Laboratory (MSL) mission website: http://mars.jpl.nasa.gov/msl

29. Meredith, P.O.,Jin, D., Griffith, D., Chen, F., Rosu, G.: An overview of the MOP runtime verification framework. Int. J. Softw. Tools Technol. Transfer **14**(3), 249–289. Springer (2012). https://doi.org/10.1007/s10009-011-0198-6

30. Peled, D., Havelund, K.: Refining the safety–liveness classification of temporal properties according to monitorability. In: Margaria, T., Graf, S., Larsen, K.G. (eds.) Models, Mindsets, Meta: The What, the How, and the Why Not?. LNCS, vol. 11200, pp. 218–234. Springer, Cham (2019). https://doi.org/10.1007/978-3-030-22348-9_14

31. Reger, G., Cruz, H.C., Rydeheard, D.: MARQ: monitoring at Runtime with QEA. In: Baier, C., Tinelli, C. (eds.) TACAS 2015. LNCS, vol. 9035, pp. 596–610. Springer, Heidelberg (2015). https://doi.org/10.1007/978-3-662-46681-0_55

32. Roşu, G., Bensalem, S.: Allen linear (Interval) temporal logic – translation to LTL and monitor synthesis. In: Ball, T., Jones, R.B. (eds.) CAV 2006. LNCS, vol. 4144, pp. 263–277. Springer, Heidelberg (2006). https://doi.org/10.1007/11817963_25

33. Rozier, K.Y., Schumann, J.: R2U2: tool Overview. In: RV-CuBES, vol. 3, pp. 138–156 (2017)

Verified Textbook Algorithms
A Biased Survey

Tobias Nipkow$^{(\boxtimes)}$ (iD), Manuel Eberl (iD), and Maximilian P. L. Haslbeck (iD)

Technische Universität München, Munich, Germany

Abstract. This article surveys the state of the art of verifying standard textbook algorithms. We focus largely on the classic text by Cormen *et al.* Both correctness and running time complexity are considered.

1 Introduction

Correctness proofs of algorithms are one of the main motivations for computer-based theorem proving. This survey focuses on the verification (which for us always means machine-checked) of textbook algorithms. Their often tricky nature means that for the most part they are verified with interactive theorem provers (*ITPs*).

We explicitly cover running time analyses of algorithms, but for reasons of space only those analyses employing ITPs. The rich area of automatic resource analysis (e.g. the work by Jan Hoffmann *et al.* [103, 104]) is out of scope.

The following theorem provers appear in our survey and are listed here in alphabetic order: ACL2 [111], Agda [31], Coq [25], HOL4 [181], Isabelle/HOL [150, 151], KeY [7], KIV [63], Minlog [21], Mizar [17], Nqthm [34], PVS [157], Why3 [75] (which is primarily automatic). We always indicate which ITP was used in a particular verification, unless it was Isabelle/HOL (which we abbreviate to Isabelle from now on), which remains implicit. Some references to Isabelle formalizations lead into the *Archive of Formal Proofs* (*AFP*) [1], an online library of Isabelle proofs.

There are a number of algorithm verification frameworks built on top of individual theorem provers. We describe some of them in the next section. The rest of the article follows the structure and contents of the classic text by Cormen *et al.* [49] (hereafter abbreviated by *CLRS*) fairly closely while covering some related material, too. Material present in CLRS but absent from this survey usually means that we are not aware of a formalization in a theorem prover.

Because most theorem provers are built on a logic with some kind of functional programming language as a sublanguage, many verifications we cite pertain to a functional version of the algorithm in question. Therefore we only mention explicitly if a proof deals with an imperative algorithm.

It must be emphasized that this survey is biased by our perspective and covers recent work by the authors in more depth. Moreover it is inevitably incomplete. We encourage our readers to notify us of missing related work.

© Springer Nature Switzerland AG 2020
D. V. Hung and O. Sokolsky (Eds.): ATVA 2020, LNCS 12302, pp. 25–53, 2020.
https://doi.org/10.1007/978-3-030-59152-6_2

2   Programming and Verification Frameworks

In this section we will describe how the various systems that appear in our survey support program verification. The theorem provers ACL2, Agda, Coq, HOL, Isabelle, Minlog, Nqthm and PVS are based on logics that subsume a functional programming language. By default that is the language algorithms must be formulated in. ACL2 and Nqthm are special in two regards: their logic contains the programming language Lisp whereas the other theorem provers typically rely on some sort of compiler into functional languages like SML, OCaml, Haskell, Scala and even JavaScript; ACL2 also supports imperative features [35] directly.

KeY and KIV are primarily program verification systems but with inbuilt provers. They support modular verification and stepwise refinement. KeY focuses on the verification of Java programs, KIV on refinement and the automatic generation of executable programs in multiple target languages.

Why3 also falls into the program verification category. It has its own programming and specification language WhyML, which is mostly functional but with mutable record fields and arrays. Verification conditions are discharged by Why3 with the help of various automated and interactive theorem provers. WhyML can be translated into OCaml but can also be used as an intermediate language for the verification of C, Java, or Ada programs.

Mizar is the odd one out: it does not have any built-in notion of algorithm and its proofs about algorithms are at an abstract mathematical level.

There are various approaches for algorithm verification. Two important categories are the following:

Explicit Programming Language (Deep Embedding). One can define a programming language – functional or imperative – with a convenient set of constructs, give it a formal semantics, and then express an algorithm as a program in this language. Additionally, a cost model can be integrated into the semantics to enable formal reasoning about running time or other resource use. The actual analysis is then typically done with some sort of program logic (e.g. a Hoare-style calculus). When embedded in a theorem prover, this approach is often referred to as a *deep embedding*.

Directly in the Logic (No Embedding). As was mentioned before, many ITPs offer functionality to define algorithms directly in the logic of the system – usually functionally. This approach is more flexible since algorithms can use the full expressiveness of the system's logic and not only some fixed restricted set of language constructs. One possible drawback of this approach is that it can be difficult or even impossible to reason about notions such as running time explicitly. A possible workaround is to define an explicit cost function for the algorithm, but since there is no formal connection between that function and the algorithm, one must check by inspection that the cost function really does correspond to the incurred cost. Another disadvantage is that, as was said earlier, most logics do not have builtin support for imperative algorithms.

Hybrids between these two approaches also exist (such as *shallow embeddings*). And, of course, the different approaches can be combined to reap the advantages of all of them; e.g. one can show a correspondence between the running time of a deeply-embedded algorithm and a cost function specified as a recurrence directly in the logic, so that results obtained about the latter have a formal connection to the former.

Imperative Verification Frameworks. As examples of such combined approaches, both Coq and Isabelle provide frameworks for the verification of imperative algorithms that are used to verify textbook algorithms.

The CFML tool [41] allows extracting a *characteristic formula* – capturing the program behaviour, including effects and running time – from a Caml program and importing it into Coq as an axiom. The CFML library provides tactics and infrastructure for Separation Logic with time credits [42] that allow to verify both functional correctness and running time complexity.

Sakaguchi [176] presented a library in Coq that features a state-monad and extraction to OCaml with mutable arrays.

Imperative-HOL is a monadic framework with references and arrays by Bulwahn *et al.* [38] which allows code generation to ML and Haskell with references and mutable arrays. Lammich [118] presents a simplified fragment of LLVM, shallowly embedded into Isabelle, with a code generator to LLVM text. Both Imperative-HOL and Isabelle-LLVM come with a Separation Logic framework and powerful proof tools that allow reasoning about imperative programs. Zhan and Haslbeck [201] extend Imperative-HOL with time and employ Separation Logic with time credits.

Isabelle Refinement Framework. There are several techniques for verifying algorithms and data structures. Many verification frameworks start in a "bottom-up" manner from a concrete implementation and directly generate verification conditions which are then discharged automatically or interactively. Another technique is to model an algorithm purely functionally, prove its correctness abstractly and then prove that it is refined by an imperative implementation. For example, Lammich [122] and Zhan [200] employ this technique for the verification of algorithms in Imperative-HOL.

A third approach is best described as "top-down": an abstract program capturing the algorithmic idea is proved correct, refined stepwise to a more concrete algorithm and finally an executable algorithm is synthesized. The Isabelle Refinement Framework [127] constitutes the top layer of a tool chain in Isabelle that follows that approach. It allows specifying the result of programs in a nondeterminism monad and provides a calculus for stepwise refinement. A special case is data refinement, where abstract datatypes (e.g. sets) are replaced by concrete datatypes (e.g. lists). Many algorithms have been formalized in this framework and we will mention some of them in the main part of this paper. Lammich provides two backends to synthesize an executable program and produce a refinement proof from an abstract algorithm: The Autoref tool [114] yields a purely functional implementation by refining abstract datatypes with data structures from the Isabelle Collections Framework [121]. The Sepref tool [118,119] synthesizes efficient imperative implementations in Imperative-HOL and LLVM. Haslbeck and Lammich [95] extended the Isabelle Refinement Framework and Sepref to reason abstractly about the running time of programs and synthesize programs that preserve upper bounds through stepwise refinement down to Imperative-HOL with time [201].

2.1 Approaches for Randomized Algorithms

There are various approaches for reasoning about randomized algorithms in a formal way. Analogously to the non-randomized setting described in Sect. 2, there again exists an entire spectrum of different approaches:

- fully explicit/deeply-embedded approaches
- "no embedding" approaches that model randomized algorithms directly in the logic as functions returning a probability distribution
- shallow embeddings, e.g. with shallow deterministic operations but explicit random choice and explicit "while" loops. Examples are the approaches by Petcher and Morrisett [165] in Coq and by Kaminski et al. [110] on paper (which was formalized by Hölzl [105]).
- combined approaches that start with a program in a deeply-embedded probabilistic programming language and then relate it to a distribution specified directly in the logic, cf. e.g. Tassarotti and Harper [188].

Next, we will explore the different approaches that exist in an ITP setting to represent probability distributions. This is crucial in the "no embedding" approach, but even in the other cases it is useful to be able to give a formal semantics to the embedded programming language, prove soundness of a program logic, etc. The first work known to us on formalizing randomized algorithms is by Hurd [109] and represented randomized algorithms as deterministic algorithms taking an infinite sequence of random bits as an additional input. However, it seems that later work preferred another approach, which we will sketch in the following.

Generally, the idea is to have a type constructor M of probability distributions, i.e. $M(\alpha)$ is the type of probability distributions over elements of type α. This type constructor, together with two monadic operations $return : \alpha \to M(\alpha)$ and $bind : M(\alpha) \to (\alpha \to M(\beta)) \to M(\beta)$, forms the *Giry monad* [84], which in our opinion has emerged as the most powerful and natural representation for randomized programs in an ITP setting.

The exact definition and scope of $M(\alpha)$ varies. The following approaches are found in popular ITPs:

- For their formalization of quicksort in Coq, Van der Weegen and McKinna [193] represented distributions as trees whose leaves are deterministic results and whose nodes are uniformly random choices. While well-suited for their use case, this encoding is not ideal for more general distributions.

- Isabelle mostly uses *probability mass functions* (PMFs), i.e. functions $\alpha \rightarrow [0, 1]$ that assign a probability to each possible result (which only works for distributions with countable support). The same approach is also used by Tassarotti and Harper [187] in Coq.
- As an earlier variation of this, Audebaud and Paulin-Mohring [14] used the CPS-inspired encoding $(\alpha \rightarrow [0, 1]) \rightarrow [0, 1]$ of PMFs in Coq.
- Isabelle contains a very general measure theory library [106] in which distributions are functions $\text{Set}(\alpha) \rightarrow [0, 1]$ that assign a probability to every measurable set of results. This is the most expressive representation and allows for continuous distributions (such as Gaussians) as well. It can, however, be tedious to use due to the measurability side conditions that arise. PMFs are therefore preferred in applications in Isabelle whenever possible.

The main advantage of having probability distributions in the logic as first-class citizens is again expressiveness and flexibility. It is then even possible to prove that two algorithms with completely different structure have not just the same expected running time, but exactly the same distribution. For imperative randomized algorithms or fully formal cost analysis, one must however still combine this with an embedding, as done by Tassarotti and Harper [188].

One notable system that falls somewhat outside this classification is *Ellora* by Barthe *et al.* [19]. This is a program logic that is embedded into the EasyCrypt theorem prover [18], which is not a general-purpose ITP but still general enough to allow analysis of complex randomized algorithms.

This concludes the summary of the verification frameworks we consider. The rest of the paper is dedicated to our survey of verified textbook foundations and algorithms. We roughly follow the structure and contents of CLRS.

3   Mathematical Foundations

3.1   Basic Asymptotic Concepts

Landau symbols ("Big-O", "Big-Theta", etc.) are common in both mathematics and in the analysis of algorithms. The basic idea behind e.g. a statement such as $f(n) \in O(g(n))$ is that $f(n)$ is bounded by some multiple of $g(n)$, but different texts sometimes differ as to whether "bounded" means $f(n) \leq g(n)$ or $f(n) \leq |g(n)|$ or even $|f(n)| \leq |g(n)|$. Usually (but not always), the inequality need also only hold "for sufficiently large n". In algorithms contexts, f and g are usually functions from the naturals into the non-negative reals so that these differences rarely matter. In mathematics, on the other hand, the domain of f and g might be real or complex numbers, and the neighbourhood in which the inequality must hold is often not $n \rightarrow \infty$, but e.g. $n \rightarrow 0$ or a more complicated region. Finding a uniform formal definition that is sufficiently general for all contexts is therefore challenging.

To make matters worse, informal arguments involving Landau symbols often involve a considerable amount of hand-waving or omission of obvious steps: consider, for instance, the fact that

$$\exp\left(\frac{x+1}{\sqrt{x}+1}\right)x^a(\log x)^b \in O\bigl(e^x\bigr) \ . \tag{1}$$

This is intuitively obvious, since the first factor on the left-hand side is "roughly" equal to $e^{x/2}$. This is exponentially smaller than the e^x on the right-hand side and therefore eclipses the other, polynomial–logarithmic factors. Doing such arguments directly in a formally rigorous way is very tedious, and simplifying this process is a challenging engineering problem.

Another complication is the fact that pen-and-paper arguments, in a slight abuse of notation, often use $O(g(n))$ as if it were one single function. The intended meaning of this is "there exists some function in $O(g(n))$ for which this is true". For example, one writes $e^{\sqrt{n+1}} = e^{\sqrt{n}+O(1/\sqrt{n})}$, meaning "there exists some function $g(n) \in O(1/\sqrt{n})$ such that $e^{\sqrt{n+1}} = e^{\sqrt{n}+g(n)}$." This notation is very difficult to integrate into proof assistants directly.

Few ITPs have support for Landau-style asymptotics at all. In the following, we list the formalizations that we are aware of:

- Avigad *et al.* [15] defined "Big-O" for their formalization of the Prime Number Theorem, including the notation $f =_o g +_o O(h)$ for $f(x) = g(x) + O(h(x))$ that emulates the abovementioned abuse of notation at least for some simple cases. However, their definition of O is somewhat restrictive and no longer used for new developments.
- Eberl defined the five Landau symbols from CLRS and the notion of asymptotic equivalence ("$\sim$"). These are intended for general-purpose use. The neighbourhood in which the inequality must hold is $n \to \infty$ by default, but can be modified using filters [107], which allow for a great degree of flexibility. This development is now part of the Isabelle distribution. A brief discussion of it can be found in his article on the Akra–Bazzi theorem [59].
- Guéneau *et al.* [87] (Coq) define a "Big-O-like domination relation for running time analysis, also using filters for extra flexibility.
- Affeldt *et al.* [6] (Coq) define general-purpose Landau symbols. Through several tricks, they fully support the abovementioned "abuse of notation".

It seems that the filter-based definition of Landau symbols has emerged as the canonical one in an ITP context. For algorithm analysis, the filter in question is usually simply $n \to \infty$ so that this extra flexibility is not needed, but there are two notable exceptions:

- Multivariate "Big-O" notation is useful e.g. if an algorithm's running time depends on several parameters (e.g. the naïve multiplication of two numbers m and n, which takes $O(mn)$ time). This can be achieved with *product filters*.
- Suppose we have some algorithm that takes $O(\log n)$ time on sorted lists xs for large enough n, where $n = |xs|$ is the length of the list. This can be expressed naturally as $\text{time}(xs) \in O_F(\log |xs|)$ w.r.t. a suitable filter F. For instance, in Isabelle, this filter can be written as

$$\text{length } \textbf{going-to } \text{at\_top } \textbf{within } \{xs.\ \text{sorted } xs\} \ .$$

In addition to that, Coq and Isabelle provide mechanisms to facilitate asymptotic reasoning:

- Affeldt *et al.* [6] provide a proof method called "near" in Coq that imitates the informal pen-and-paper reasoning style where in asymptotic arguments, one can assume properties as long as one can later justify that they hold *eventually*. This can lead to a more natural flow of the argument.
- Motivated by the proof obligations arising from applications of the Master theorem, Eberl [59] implemented various *simplification procedures* in Isabelle that rewrite Landau-symbol statements into a simpler form. Concretely, there are procedures to
  - cancel common factors such as $f(x)g(x) \in O(f(x)h(x))$,
  - cancel dominated terms, e.g. rewriting $f(x) + g(x) \in O(h(x))$ to $f(x) \in O(h(x))$ when $g(x) \in o(f(x))$ and
  - simplify asymptotic statements involving iterated logarithms, e.g. rewriting $x^a(\log x)^b \in O(x^c(\log \log x)^d)$ to equations/inequalities of a, b, c, d.
- Lastly, Eberl [60] provides an Isabelle proof method to prove limits and Landau-symbol statements for a large class of real-valued functions. For instance, it can solve the asymptotic problem (1) mentioned earlier fully automatically.

3.2   The Master Theorem

CLRS present the Master theorem for divide-and-conquer recurrences and use it in the running time analysis of several divide-and-conquer algorithms. They also briefly mention another result known as the Akra–Bazzi theorem and cite the streamlined version due to Leighton [130]. This result generalizes the Master theorem in several ways:

- The different sub-problems being solved by recursive calls are not required to have the same size.
- The recursive terms are not required to be exactly $f(\lfloor n/b \rfloor)$ or $f(\lceil n/b \rceil)$ but can deviate from n/b by an arbitrary sub-linear amount.
- While the "balanced" case of the original Master theorem requires $f(n) \in \Theta(n^{\log_b a}(\log n)^k)$, the Akra–Bazzi theorem also works for a much larger class of functions.

The only formalized result related to this that we are aware of is Eberl's formalization of Leighton's version of the Akra–Bazzi theorem [59]. CLRS state that the Akra–Bazzi Theorem "can be somewhat difficult to use" – probably due to its rather technical side conditions and the presence of an integral in the result. However, Eberl's formalization provides several corollaries that combine the first and second advantage listed above while retaining the ease of application of the original Master theorem.

Eberl gives some applications to textbook recurrences (mergesort, Karatsuba multiplication, Strassen multiplication, median-of-medians selection). Zhan and

Haslbeck [201] also integrated Eberl's work into their work on verifying the asymptotic time complexity of imperative algorithms (namely imperative versions of mergesort, Karatsuba and median-of-medians). Rau and Nipkow [173] used Eberl's Master theorem to prove the $O(n \log n)$ running time of a closest-pair-of-points algorithm.

4   Sorting and Order Statistics

4.1   Sorting

Verification of textbook sorting algorithms was a popular pastime in the early theorem proving days (e.g. [32]) but is now more of historic interest. To show that the field has progressed, we highlight three verifications of industrial code.

The sorting algorithm TimSort (combining mergesort and insertion sort) is the default implementation for generic arrays and collections in the Java standard library. De Gouw et al. [86] first discovered a bug that can lead to an `ArrayIndexOutOfBoundsException` and suggested corrections. Then De Gouw et al. [85] verified termination and exception freedom (but not full functional correctness) of the actual corrected code using KeY.

Beckert et al. [20], again with KeY, verified functional correctness of the other implementation of sorting in the Java standard library, a dual pivot quicksort algorithm.

Lammich [120] verified a high-level assembly-language (LLVM) implementation of two sorting algorithms: introsort [140] (a combination of quicksort, heapsort and insertion sort) from the GNU C++ library (libstdc++) and pdqsort, an extension of introsort from the Boost C++ libraries. The verified implementations perform on par with the originals.

Additionally, we mention a classic meta result that is also presented in CLRS: Eberl [56] formally proved the $\Omega(n \log n)$ lower bound for the running time of comparison-based sorting algorithms in Isabelle.

4.2   Selection in Worst-Case Linear Time

Eberl [57] formalized a functional version of the deterministic linear-time selection algorithm from CLRS including a worst-case analysis for the sizes of the lists in the recursive calls. Zhan and Haslbeck [201] refined this to an imperative algorithm, including a proof that it indeed runs in linear time using Eberl's formalization of the Akra–Bazzi theorem (unlike the elementary proof in CLRS). However, the imperative algorithm they formalized differs from that in CLRS by some details. Most notably, the one in CLRS is in-place, whereas the one by Zhan and Haslbeck is not. Formalizing the in-place algorithm would require either a stronger separation logic framework or manual reasoning to prove that the recursive calls indeed work on distinct sub-arrays.

5   Data Structures

5.1   Elementary Data Structures

We focus again on two noteworthy verifications of actual code. Polikarpova *et al.* [167,168] verify EiffelBase2, a container library (with emphasis on linked lists, arrays and hashing) that was initially designed to replace EiffelBase, the standard container library of the Eiffel programming language [136]. A distinguishing feature is the high degree of automation of their Eiffel verifier called AutoProof [78]. The verification uncovered three bugs. Hiep *et al.* [100] (KeY) verified the implementation of a linked list in the Java Collection framework and found an integer overflow bug on 64-bit architectures.

5.2   Hash Tables

The abstract datatypes sets and maps can be efficiently implemented by hash tables. The Isabelle Collections Framework [121] provides a pure implementation of hash tables that can be realized by Haskell arrays during code generation. Lammich [116,122] also verified an imperative version with rehashing in Imperative-HOL. Filliâtre and Clochard [72] (Why3) verified hash tables with linear probing. Pottier [170] verified hash tables in CFML with a focus on iterators. Polikarpova *et al.* (see above) also verified hash tables. These references only verify functional correctness, not running times.

5.3   Binary Search Trees

Unbalanced binary search trees have been verified many times. Surprisingly, the functional correctness, including preservation of the BST invariant, almost always require a surprising amount of human input (in the form of proof steps or annotations). Of course this is even more the case for balanced search trees, even ignoring the balance proofs. Most verifications are based on some variant of the following definition of BSTs: the element in each node must lie in between the elements of the left subtree and the elements of the right subtree. Nipkow [146] specifies BSTs as trees whose inorder list of elements is sorted. With this specification, functional correctness proofs (but not preservation of balancedness) are fully automatic for AVL, red-black, splay and many other search trees.

5.4   AVL and Red-Black Trees

Just like sorting algorithms, search trees are popular case studies in verification because they can often be implemented concisely in a purely functional way. We merely cite some typical verifications of AVL [47,74,152,172] and red-black trees [12,41,52,74] in various theorem provers.

We will now consider a number of search trees not in CLRS.

5.5 Weight-Balanced Trees

Weight-balanced trees were invented by Nievergelt and Reingold [143,144] (who called them "trees of bounded balance"). They are balanced by size rather than height, where the size $|t|$ of a tree t is defined as the number of nodes in t. A tree is said to be α-balanced, $0 \leq \alpha \leq 1/2$, if for every non-empty subtree t with children l and r, $\alpha \leq \frac{|l|+1}{|t|+1} \leq 1-\alpha$. Equivalently we can require $\frac{\min(|l|,|r|)+1}{|t|+1} \leq \alpha$. Insertion and deletion may need to rebalance the tree by single and double rotations depending on certain numeric conditions. Blum and Mehlhorn [28] discovered a mistake in the numeric conditions for deletion, corrected it and gave a very detailed proof. Adams [5] used weight-balanced trees in an actual implementation (in ML) but defined balancedness somewhat differently from the original definition. Haskell's standard implementation of sets, Data.Set, is based on Adams's implementation. In 2010 it was noticed that deletion can break α-balancedness. Hirai and Yamamoto [102], unaware of the work by Blum and Mehlhorn, verified their own version of weight-balanced trees in Coq, which includes determining the valid ranges of certain numeric parameters. Nipkow and Dirix [149] provided a verified framework for checking validity of specific values for these numeric parameters.

5.6 Scapegoat Trees

These trees are due to Anderson [11], who called them *general balanced trees*, and Galperin and Rivest [81], who called them *scapegoat trees*. The central idea: don't rebalance every time, rebuild a subtree when the whole tree gets "too unbalanced", i.e. when the height is no longer logarithmic in the size, with a fixed multiplicative constant. Because rebuilding is expensive (in the worst case it can involve the whole tree) the worst case complexity of insertion and deletion is linear. But because earlier calls did not need to rebalance, the amortized complexity is logarithmic. The analysis by Anderson was verified by Nipkow [147].

5.7 Finger Trees

Finger trees were originally defined by reversing certain pointers in a search tree to accelerate operations in the vicinity of specific positions in the tree [88]. A functional version is due to Hinze and Paterson [101]. It can be used to implement a wide range of efficient data structures, e.g. sequences with access to both ends in amortized constant time and concatenation and splitting in logarithmic time, random access-sequences, search trees, priority queues and more. Functional correctness was verified by Sozeau [182] (Coq) and by Nordhoff et al. [155]. The amortized complexity of the deque operations was analysed by Danielsson [50] (Agda).

5.8 Splay Trees

Splay trees [179] are self-adjusting binary search trees where items that have been searched for are rotated to the root of the tree to adjust to dynamically changing access frequencies. Nipkow [145, 146] verified functional correctness and amortized logarithmic complexity.

5.9 Braun Trees

Braun trees are binary trees where for each node the size of the left child is the same or one larger than the size of the right child [108, 174]. They lend themselves to the implementation of extensible arrays and priority queues in a purely functional manner [162]. They were verified by Nipkow and Sewell [153] in great depth. McCarthy *et al.* [133] demonstrate their Coq library for running time analysis by proving the logarithmic running time of insertion into Braun trees.

6   Advanced Design and Analysis Techniques

6.1   Dynamic Programming

It is usually easy to write down and prove correct the recursive form of a dynamic programming problem, but it takes work to convert it into an efficient implementation by memoizing intermediate results. Wimmer *et al.* [196] automated this process: a recursive function is transformed into a monadic one that memoizes results, and a theorem stating the equivalence of the two functions is proved automatically. The results are stored in a so-called *state monad*. Two state monads were verified: a purely functional state monad based on search trees and the state monad of Imperative-HOL using arrays. The imperative monad yields implementations that have the same asymptotic complexity as the standard array-based algorithms. Wimmer *et al.* verify two further optimizations: bottom-up order of computation and an LRU cache for reduced memory consumption. As applications of their framework, they proved the following algorithms correct (in their recursive form) and translated them into their efficient array-based variants: Bellman-Ford, CYK (context-free parsing), minimum edit distance and optimal binary search trees. Wimmer [195] also treated Viterbi's algorithm in this manner.

Nipkow and Somogyi [154] verified the straightforward recursive cubic algorithm for optimal binary search trees and Knuth's quadratic improvement [113] (but using Yao's simpler proof [199]) and applied memoization.

6.2   Greedy Algorithms

One example of a greedy algorithm given in CLRS is Huffman's algorithm. It was verified by Théry [189] (Coq) and Blanchette [27]. For problems that exhibit a matroid structure, greedy algorithms yield optimal solutions. Keinholz [112] formalizes matroid theory. Haslbeck *et al.* [95, 96] verify the soundness and running time of an algorithm for finding a minimum-weight basis on a weighted matroid and use it to verify Kruskal's algorithm for minimum spanning trees.

7   Advanced Data Structures

7.1   B-Trees

We are aware of two verifications of imperative formulations of B-trees. Malecha *et al.* [131] used Ynot [141], an axiomatic extension to Coq that provides facilities for writing and reasoning about imperative, pointer-based code. The verification by Ernst *et al.* [64] is unusual in that it combines interactive proof in KIV with the automatic shape analysis tool TVLA [175].

7.2   Priority Queues

We start with some priority queue implementations not in CLRS. Priority queues based on Braun trees (see Sect. 5.9) were verified by Filliâtre [70] (Why3) and Nipkow and Sewell [153]. Two self-adjusting priority queues are the skew heap [180] and the pairing heap [77]. Nipkow and Brinkop [145,148] verified their functional correctness (also verified in Why3 [69,164]) and amortized logarithmic running times. Binomial heaps (covered in depth in the first edition of CLRS) were verified by Meis *et al.* [135] (together with skew binomial heaps [36]), Filliâtre [71] (Why3) and Appel [13] (Coq).

The above heaps are purely functional and do not provide a `decrease-key` operation. Lammich and Nipkow [124] designed and verified a simple, efficient and purely functional combination of a search tree and a priority queue, a "priority search tree". The salient feature of priority search trees is that they offer an operation for updating (not just decreasing) the priority associated with some key; its efficiency is the same as that of the update operation.

Lammich [117] verified an imperative array-based implementation of priority queues with `decrease-key`.

7.3   Union-Find

The union-find data structure for disjoint sets is a frequent case-study: it was formalized in Coq [48,176,192] and Isabelle [122]. Charguéraud, Pottier and Guéneau [42,43,87] were the first to verify the amortized time complexity $O(\alpha(n))$ in Coq using CFML. Their proof follows Alstrup *et al.* [10].

8   Graph Algorithms

8.1   Elementary Graph Algorithms

Graph-searching algorithms are so basic that we only mention a few notable ones. BFS for finding shortest paths in unweighted graphs was verified by participants of a verification competition [76] (in particular in KIV). Lammich and Sefidgar [125] verified BFS for the Edmonds–Karp algorithm. Lammich and Neumann [123] as well as Pottier [169] (Coq) verified DFS and used it for algorithms of different complexity, ranging from a simple cyclicity checker to strongly connected components algorithms. Wimmer and Lammich [198] verified an enhanced version of DFS with subsumption. Bobot [29] verified an algorithm for topological sorting by DFS in Why3.

Strongly Connected Components. There are several algorithms for finding strongly connected components (SCCs) in a directed graph. Tarjan's algorithm [186] was verified by Lammich and Neumann [123,142]. Chen *et al.* verified Tarjan's algorithm in Why3, Coq and Isabelle and compared the three formalizations [45,46]. Lammich [115] verified Gabow's algorithm [79] (which was used in a verified model checker [65]), and Pottier [169] (Coq) verified the SCC algorithm featured in CLRS, which is attributed to Kosaraju.

8.2   Minimum Spanning Trees

Prim's algorithm was first verified by Abrial *et al.* [4] in B [3] and on a more abstract level by Lee and Rudnicki [129] (Mizar). Guttmann [89,90] verified a formulation in relation algebra, while Nipkow and Lammich [124] verified a purely functional version.

Kruskal's algorithm was verified by Guttmann [91] using relation algebras. Functional correctness [97] and time complexity [95] of an imperative implementation of Kruskal's algorithm were verified by Haslbeck, Lammich and Biendarra.

8.3   Shortest Paths

The Bellman-Ford algorithm was verified as an instance of dynamic programming (see Sect. 6.1).

Dijkstra's Algorithm. Dijkstra's algorithm has been verified several times. The first verifications were conducted by Chen, Lee and Rudnicki [44,129] (Mizar) and by Moore and Zhang [138] (ACL2). While these formalizations prove the idea of the algorithm, they do not provide efficient implementations. Charguéraud [41] verifies an OCaml version of Dijkstra's algorithm parameterized over a priority queue data structure (without a verified implementation). A notable point is that his algorithm does not require a `decrease-key` operation.

Nordhoff and Lammich [156] use their verified finger trees (see Sect. 5.7) that support `decrease-key` to obtain a verified functional algorithm. Lammich later refined the functional algorithm down to an imperative implementation using arrays to implement the heap [117]. Zhan [200] also verified the imperative version using his auto2 tool. Finally, Lammich and Nipkow [124] used their red-black tree based priority queues that also support `decrease-key` to obtain a simple functional implementation.

The Floyd–Warshall Algorithm. Early verifications by Paulin-Mohring [161] (Coq), Berger *et al.* [22] (Minlog), and Berghofer [23] relied on program extraction from a constructive proof and only targeted the Warshall algorithm for computing the transitive closure of a relation. Filliâtre and Clochard [73] (Why3) verified an imperative implementation of the Warshall algorithm. Wimmer [194] verified the functional correctness of the Floyd–Warshall algorithm for the APSP problem including detection of negative cycles. The main complication is to prove that destructive updates can be used soundly. This and the detection of negative cycles are left as an exercise to the reader in CLRS. The resulting functional implementation (with destructive updates) was later refined to an imperative implementation by Wimmer and Lammich [197].

8.4   Maximum Network Flow

The first verification of the Ford–Fulkerson method, at an abstract level, was by Lee [128] (Mizar). Lammich and Sefidgar [125] verified the Ford–Fulkerson method and refined it down to an imperative implementation of the Edmonds–Karp algorithm. They proved that the latter requires $O(|V| \cdot |E|)$ iterations. On randomly generated networks, their code is competitive with a Java implementation by Sedgewick and Wayne [177]. In further work [126] they verified the generic push–relabel method of Goldberg and Tarjan and refined it to both the relabel-to-front and the FIFO push–relabel algorithm. They also performed a running time analysis and benchmarked their algorithms against C and C++ implementations.

Haslbeck and Lammich [95] provided a proper running time analysis of the Edmonds–Karp algorithm and proved the complexity $O(|V| \cdot |E| \cdot (|V| + |E|))$.

8.5   Matching

Edmonds' famous blossom algorithm [62] for finding maximum matchings in general graphs was verified by Abdulaziz [2].

Hamid and Castelberry [92] (Coq) verified the Gale–Shapley algorithm [80] for finding stable marriages.

9   Selected Topics

9.1   Matrix Operations

Palomo-Lozano et al. formalized Strassen's algorithm for matrix multiplication in ACL2 [158], but only for square matrices whose size is a power of two. Dénès et al. formalized a slightly more efficient variant of it known as Winograd's algorithm in Coq [51] for arbitrary matrices. Garillot et al. formalized the LUP decomposition algorithm from CLRS in Coq [83].

9.2   Linear Programming

The simplex algorithm was formalized by Allamigeon and Katz [9] (Coq) and by Spasić and Marić [132,183]. The latter was repurposed into an incremental algorithm that can emit unsatisfiable cores by Bottesch et al. [30]. Parsert and Kaliszyk [159] extended this to a full solver for linear programming.

9.3   Polynomials and FFT

The recursive Fast Fourier Transform was formalized in various systems. We are aware of the formalizations in ACL2 by Gamboa [82], in Coq by Capretta [39], in HOL4 by Akbarpour and Tahar [8] and in Isabelle by Ballarin [16].

9.4   Number-Theoretic Algorithms

Most of the basic number theory shown in CLRS (GCDs, modular arithmetic, Chinese remainder theorem) is available in the standard libraries of various systems and we will therefore not give individual references for this and focus entirely on the algorithms.

Hurd formalized the Miller–Rabin test [109] in HOL4. Stüwe and Eberl [185] formalized Miller–Rabin and some other related tests (Fermat[1] and Solovay–Strassen) in Isabelle. In all cases, what was shown is that a prime is always correctly classified as prime and that a composite is correctly classified with probability at least $\frac{1}{2}$. The running time analysis is not particularly interesting for these algorithms, and although they are randomized algorithms, the randomness is of a very simple nature and thus not very interesting either.

Beyond the primality-testing algorithms in CLRS, Chan [40] gave a HOL4 formalization of the correctness and polynomial running time of the AKS, which was the first deterministic primality test to be proved to run in polynomial time.

9.5   String Matching

The Knuth–Morris–Pratt algorithm was verified by Filliâtre in Coq and Why3 [67,68]. Hellauer and Lammich [99] verified a functional version of this algorithm and refined it to Imperative-HOL. Lammich [118] synthesized verified LLVM code. The Boyer–Moore string searching algorithm [33] was covered in the first edition of CLRS. Boyer and Moore [34] (Nqthm) and Moore and Martinez [137] (ACL2) verified different variants of this algorithm; Toibazarov [190] verified the preprocessing phase of the variant considered by Moore and Martinez. Besta and Stomp [26] (PVS) verified the preprocessing phase of the original algorithm.

9.6   Computational Geometry

Convex hull algorithms have been popular verification targets: Pichardie and Bertot [166] (Coq) verified an incremental and a package wrapping algorithm, Meikle and Fleuriot [134] verified Graham's scan and Brun *et al.* [37] (Coq) verified an incremental algorithm based on hypermaps. Dufourd and Bertot [24,53] (Coq) verified triangulation algorithms based on hypermaps.

Rau and Nipkow [173] verified the divide-and-conquer closest pair of points algorithm and obtained a competitive implementation.

---

[1] The Fermat test is called PSEUDOPRIME in CLRS.

9.7   Approximation and Online Algorithms

Stucke [184] (Coq and Isabelle) verified an approximation algorithm for vertex colouring in relation algebra. Eßmann *et al.* [66] verified three classic algorithms and one lesser-known one for vertex cover, independent set, load balancing and bin packing. Haslbeck and Nipkow [98] formalized online algorithms and verified several deterministic and randomized algorithms for the list update problem.

9.8   Randomized Algorithms

In addition to the randomized algorithms from CLRS, we will also list some from the classic textbook *Randomized Algorithms* by Motwani and Raghavan [139]. All work was done using PMFs unless stated otherwise (refer to Sect. 2.1 for a discussion of the various approaches).

The first work on a non-trivial randomized algorithm in an ITP was probably Hurd's [109] previously-mentioned formalization of the Miller–Rabin primality test in HOL (using an infinite stream of random bits to encode the randomness). The primality tests formalized by Stüwe and Eberl [185] are technically also randomized algorithms, but the probabilistic content is very small.

The expected running time of the coupon collector problem was treated by Kaminski *et al.* [110] using their Hoare-style calculus for the pGCL language (on paper). Hölzl [105] formalized their approach in Isabelle.

Barthe *et al.* analyzed several probabilistic textbook problems using a program logic called *Ellora* [19], which is embedded into the EasyCrypt system [18]:

- expected running time of the coupon collector problem
- tail bounds on the running time of Boolean hypercube routing
- probability of incorrectly classifying two different polynomials as equal in probabilistic polynomial equality checking

The correctness of CLRS's RANDOMIZE-IN-PLACE, also known as the Fisher–Yates shuffle, was verified by Eberl [54].

The correctness and expected running time of randomized quicksort was formalized by Van der Weegen and McKinna [193] (Coq) using their "decision tree" approach mentioned earlier and by Eberl [58,61]. Both additionally treated the case of average-case deterministic quicksort: Van der Weegen and McKinna proved that its expected running time is $O(n \log n)$, whereas Eberl additionally proved that it has exactly the same distribution as randomized quicksort.

Eberl [55,61] proved that random binary search trees (BSTs into which elements are inserted in random order) have logarithmic expected height and internal path length. He also proved that the distribution of the internal path length is precisely the same as that of the running time of randomized quicksort.

Haslbeck *et al.* [61,94] formalized randomized treaps [178] and proved that their distribution is precisely equal to that of random BSTs, regardless of which order the elements are inserted. The analysis is particularly noteworthy because it involves continuous distributions of trees, which require a non-trivial amount of measure theory.

Haslbeck and Eberl [93] also defined skip lists [171] and formally analyzed two of the most algorithmically interesting questions about them, namely the expected height and the expected path length to an element.

Tassarotti and Harper [187] developed a general cookbook-style method for proving tail bounds on probabilistic divide-and-conquer algorithms in Coq. They applied this method to the running time of randomized quicksort and the height of random BSTs. Later [188] they used a hybrid approach that combines a program logic for a deeply embedded imperative language with high-level reasoning in Coq to analyze skip lists (restricted to two levels for simplicity).

Acknowledgements. We thank Andrew Appel, Gilles Barthe, Arthur Charguéraud, Cyril Cohen, Gidon Ernst, Jean-Christophe Filliâtre, Walter Guttmann, Reiner Hähnle, Peter Lammich, J Moore, Joseph Tassarotti, Laurent Théry, René Thiemann and Simon Wimmer for their help in compiling this survey and Jasmin Blanchette for nitpicking. This research is supported by DFG Koselleck grant NI 491/16-1.

References

1. Archive of Formal Proofs. http://www.isa-afp.org
2. Abdulaziz, M., Mehlhorn, K., Nipkow, T.: Trustworthy graph algorithms (invited talk). In: Rossmanith, P., Heggernes, P., Katoen, J. (eds.) 44th International Symposium on Mathematical Foundations of Computer Science, MFCS 2019. LIPIcs, vol. 138, pp. 1:1–1:22. Schloss Dagstuhl - Leibniz-Zentrum für Informatik (2019). https://doi.org/10.4230/LIPIcs.MFCS.2019.1
3. Abrial, J.: The B-book - Assigning Programs to Meanings. Cambridge University Press (1996). https://doi.org/10.1017/CBO9780511624162
4. Abrial, J.-R., Cansell, D., Méry, D.: Formal derivation of spanning trees algorithms. In: Bert, D., Bowen, J.P., King, S., Waldén, M. (eds.) ZB 2003. LNCS, vol. 2651, pp. 457–476. Springer, Heidelberg (2003). https://doi.org/10.1007/3-540-44880-2_27
5. Adams, S.: Efficient sets - a balancing act. J. Funct. Program. **3**(4), 553–561 (1993). https://doi.org/10.1017/S0956796800000885
6. Affeldt, R., Cohen, C., Rouhling, D.: Formalization techniques for asymptotic reasoning in classical analysis. J. Form. Reasoning **11**(1), 43–76 (2018). https://doi.org/10.6092/issn.1972-5787/8124
7. Ahrendt, W., Beckert, B., Bubel, R., Hähnle, R., Schmitt, P.H., Ulbrich, M. (eds.): Deductive Software Verification - The KeY Book - From Theory to Practice, LNCS, vol. 10001. Springer, Cham (2016), https://doi.org/10.1007/978-3-319-49812-6
8. Akbarpour, B., Tahar, S.: A methodology for the formal verification of FFT algorithms in HOL. In: Hu, A.J., Martin, A.K. (eds.) FMCAD 2004. LNCS, vol. 3312, pp. 37–51. Springer, Heidelberg (2004). https://doi.org/10.1007/978-3-540-30494-4_4
9. Allamigeon, X., Katz, R.D.: A formalization of convex polyhedra based on the simplex method. In: Ayala-Rincón, M., Muñoz, C.A. (eds.) ITP 2017. LNCS, vol. 10499, pp. 28–45. Springer, Cham (2017). https://doi.org/10.1007/978-3-319-66107-0_3

10. Alstrup, S., Thorup, M., Gørtz, I.L., Rauhe, T., Zwick, U.: Union-find with constant time deletions. ACM Trans. Algorithms **11**(1), 6:1–6:28 (2014). https://doi.org/10.1145/2636922

11. Andersson, A.: Improving partial rebuilding by using simple balance criteria. In: Dehne, F., Sack, J.-R., Santoro, N. (eds.) WADS 1989. LNCS, vol. 382, pp. 393–402. Springer, Heidelberg (1989). https://doi.org/10.1007/3-540-51542-9_33

12. Appel, A.W.: Efficient verified red-black trees (2011). https://www.cs.princeton.edu/~appel/papers/redblack.pdf

13. Appel, A.W.: Verified Functional Algorithms, August 2018. https://softwarefoundations.cis.upenn.edu/vfa-current/index.html

14. Audebaud, P., Paulin-Mohring, C.: Proofs of randomized algorithms in Coq. Sci. Comput. Program. **74**(8), 568–589 (2009). https://doi.org/10.1016/j.scico.2007.09.002

15. Avigad, J., Donnelly, K., Gray, D., Raff, P.: A formally verified proof of the prime number theorem. ACM Trans. Comput. Logic **9**(1) (2007). https://doi.org/10.1145/1297658.1297660

16. Ballarin, C.: Fast Fourier Transform. Archive of Formal Proofs, October 2005. http://isa-afp.org/entries/FFT.html, Formal proof development

17. Bancerek, G., et al.: Mizar: state-of-the-art and beyond. In: Kerber, M., Carette, J., Kaliszyk, C., Rabe, F., Sorge, V. (eds.) CICM 2015. LNCS (LNAI), vol. 9150, pp. 261–279. Springer, Cham (2015). https://doi.org/10.1007/978-3-319-20615-8_17

18. Barthe, G., Dupressoir, F., Grégoire, B., Kunz, C., Schmidt, B., Strub, P.-Y.: EasyCrypt: a tutorial. In: Aldini, A., Lopez, J., Martinelli, F. (eds.) FOSAD 2012-2013. LNCS, vol. 8604, pp. 146–166. Springer, Cham (2014). https://doi.org/10.1007/978-3-319-10082-1_6

19. Barthe, G., Espitau, T., Gaboardi, M., Grégoire, B., Hsu, J., Strub, P.-Y.: An assertion-based program logic for probabilistic programs. In: Ahmed, A. (ed.) ESOP 2018. LNCS, vol. 10801, pp. 117–144. Springer, Cham (2018). https://doi.org/10.1007/978-3-319-89884-1_5

20. Beckert, B., Schiffl, J., Schmitt, P.H., Ulbrich, M.: Proving JDK's dual pivot quicksort correct. In: Paskevich and Wies [160], pp. 35–48, https://doi.org/10.1007/978-3-319-72308-2_3

21. Berger, U., Miyamoto, K., Schwichtenberg, H., Seisenberger, M.: Minlog - a tool for program extraction supporting algebras and coalgebras. In: Corradini, A., Klin, B., Cîrstea, C. (eds.) CALCO 2011. LNCS, vol. 6859, pp. 393–399. Springer, Heidelberg (2011). https://doi.org/10.1007/978-3-642-22944-2_29

22. Berger, U., Schwichtenberg, H., Seisenberger, M.: The Warshall algorithm and Dickson's lemma: two examples of realistic program extraction. J. Autom. Reasoning **26**(2), 205–221 (2001). https://doi.org/10.1023/A:1026748613865

23. Berghofer, S.: Program extraction in simply-typed higher order logic. In: Geuvers, H., Wiedijk, F. (eds.) TYPES 2002. LNCS, vol. 2646, pp. 21–38. Springer, Heidelberg (2003). https://doi.org/10.1007/3-540-39185-1_2

24. Bertot, Y.: Formal verification of a geometry algorithm: a quest for abstract views and symmetry in coq proofs. In: Fischer, B., Uustalu, T. (eds.) ICTAC 2018. LNCS, vol. 11187, pp. 3–10. Springer, Cham (2018). https://doi.org/10.1007/978-3-030-02508-3_1

25. Bertot, Y., Castéran, P.: Interactive Theorem Proving and Program Development - Coq'Art: The Calculus of Inductive Constructions. Texts in Theoretical Computer Science. An EATCS Series, Springer, Cham (2004). https://doi.org/10.1007/978-3-662-07964-5

26. Besta, M., Stomp, F.A.: A complete mechanization of correctness of a string-preprocessing algorithm. Formal Methods Syst. Des. **27**(1–2), 5–17 (2005). https://doi.org/10.1007/s10703-005-2243-0

27. Blanchette, J.C.: Proof pearl: Mechanizing the textbook proof of Huffman's algorithm. J. Autom. Reasoning **43**(1), 1–18 (2009). https://doi.org/10.1007/s10817-009-9116-y

28. Blum, N., Mehlhorn, K.: On the average number of rebalancing operations in weight-balanced trees. Theor. Comput. Sci. **11**, 303–320 (1980). https://doi.org/10.1016/0304-3975(80)90018-3

29. Bobot, F.: Topological sorting (2014). http://toccata.lri.fr/gallery/topological_sorting.en.html, formal proof development

30. Bottesch, R., Haslbeck, M.W., Thiemann, R.: Verifying an incremental theory solver for linear arithmetic in Isabelle/HOL. In: Herzig, A., Popescu, A. (eds.) FroCoS 2019. LNCS (LNAI), vol. 11715, pp. 223–239. Springer, Cham (2019). https://doi.org/10.1007/978-3-030-29007-8_13

31. Bove, A., Dybjer, P., Norell, U.: A brief overview of agda – a functional language with dependent types. In: Berghofer, S., Nipkow, T., Urban, C., Wenzel, M. (eds.) TPHOLs 2009. LNCS, vol. 5674, pp. 73–78. Springer, Heidelberg (2009). https://doi.org/10.1007/978-3-642-03359-9_6

32. Boyer, R.S., Moore, J S.: Proving theorems about LISP functions. In: Nilsson, N. (ed.) International Joint Conference on Artificial Intelligence. pp. 486–493. William Kaufmann (1973) http://ijcai.org/Proceedings/73/Papers/053.pdf

33. Boyer, R.S., Moore, J.S.: A fast string searching algorithm. Commun. ACM **20**(10), 762–772 (1977). https://doi.org/10.1145/359842.359859

34. Boyer, R.S., Moore, J.S.: A computational logic handbook, Perspectives in Computing, vol. 23. Academic Press, New York (1979)

35. Boyer, R.S., Strother Moore, J.: Single-threaded objects in ACL2. In: Krishnamurthi, S., Ramakrishnan, C.R. (eds.) PADL 2002. LNCS, vol. 2257, pp. 9–27. Springer, Heidelberg (2002). https://doi.org/10.1007/3-540-45587-6_3

36. Brodal, G.S., Okasaki, C.: Optimal purely functional priority queues. J. Funct. Program. **6**(6), 839–857 (1996). https://doi.org/10.1017/S095679680000201X

37. Brun, C., Dufourd, J., Magaud, N.: Designing and proving correct a convex hull algorithm with hypermaps in Coq. Comput. Geom. **45**(8), 436–457 (2012). https://doi.org/10.1016/j.comgeo.2010.06.006

38. Bulwahn, L., Krauss, A., Haftmann, F., Erkök, L., Matthews, J.: Imperative functional programming with Isabelle/HOL. In: Mohamed, O.A., Muñoz, C., Tahar, S. (eds.) TPHOLs 2008. LNCS, vol. 5170, pp. 134–149. Springer, Heidelberg (2008). https://doi.org/10.1007/978-3-540-71067-7_14

39. Capretta, V.: Certifying the fast Fourier transform with coq. In: Boulton, R.J., Jackson, P.B. (eds.) TPHOLs 2001. LNCS, vol. 2152, pp. 154–168. Springer, Heidelberg (2001). https://doi.org/10.1007/3-540-44755-5_12

40. Chan, H.L.J.: Primality testing is polynomial-time: a mechanised verification of the AKS algorithm. Ph.D. thesis, Australian National University (2019). https://openresearch-repository.anu.edu.au/bitstream/1885/177195/1/thesis.pdf

41. Charguéraud, A.: Program verification through characteristic formulae. In: Hudak, P., Weirich, S. (eds.) Proceeding of the 15th ACM SIGPLAN International Conference on Functional Programming. ICFP 2010, pp. 321–332. ACM (2010). https://doi.org/10.1145/1863543.1863590

42. Charguéraud, A., Pottier, F.: Machine-checked verification of the correctness and amortized complexity of an efficient union-find implementation. In: Urban, C., Zhang, X. (eds.) ITP 2015. LNCS, vol. 9236, pp. 137–153. Springer, Cham (2015). https://doi.org/10.1007/978-3-319-22102-1_9

43. Charguéraud, A., Pottier, F.: Verifying the correctness and amortized complexity of a union-find implementation in separation logic with time credits. J. Autom. Reasoning **62**(3), 331–365 (2019). https://doi.org/10.1007/s10817-017-9431-7

44. Chen, J.C.: Dijkstra's shortest path algorithm. Formalized Mathematics **11**(3), 237–247 (2003). http://fm.mizar.org/2003-11/pdf11-3/graphsp.pdf

45. Chen, R., Cohen, C., Lévy, J., Merz, S., Théry, L.: Formal proofs of Tarjan's strongly connected components algorithm in Why3, Coq and Isabelle. In: Harrison, J., O'Leary, J., Tolmach, A. (eds.) 10th International Conference on Interactive Theorem Proving, ITP 2019. LIPIcs, vol. 141, pp. 13:1–13:19. Schloss Dagstuhl - Leibniz-Zentrum für Informatik (2019). https://doi.org/10.4230/LIPIcs.ITP.2019.13

46. Chen, R., Lévy, J.: A semi-automatic proof of strong connectivity. In: Paskevich and Wies [160], pp. 49–65. https://doi.org/10.1007/978-3-319-72308-2_4

47. Clochard, M.: Automatically verified implementation of data structures based on AVL trees. In: Giannakopoulou, D., Kroening, D. (eds.) VSTTE 2014. LNCS, vol. 8471, pp. 167–180. Springer, Cham (2014). https://doi.org/10.1007/978-3-319-12154-3_11

48. Conchon, S., Filliâtre, J.: A persistent union-find data structure. In: Russo, C.V., Dreyer, D. (eds.) Workshop on ML, 2007. pp. 37–46. ACM (2007). https://doi.org/10.1145/1292535.1292541

49. Cormen, T.H., Leiserson, C.E., Rivest, R.L., Stein, C.: Introduction to Algorithms, 3rd Edition. MIT Press (2009). http://mitpress.mit.edu/books/introduction-algorithms

50. Danielsson, N.A.: Lightweight semiformal time complexity analysis for purely functional data structures. In: Necula, G.C., Wadler, P. (eds.) Proceedings of the 35th ACM SIGPLAN-SIGACT Symposium on Principles of Programming Languages, POPL 2008. pp. 133–144. ACM (2008). https://doi.org/10.1145/1328438.1328457

51. Dénès, M., Mörtberg, A., Siles, V.: A refinement-based approach to computational algebra in Coq. In: Beringer, L., Felty, A. (eds.) ITP 2012. LNCS, vol. 7406, pp. 83–98. Springer, Heidelberg (2012). https://doi.org/10.1007/978-3-642-32347-8_7

52. Dross, C., Moy, Y.: Auto-active proof of red-black trees in SPARK. In: Barrett, C., Davies, M., Kahsai, T. (eds.) NFM 2017. LNCS, vol. 10227, pp. 68–83. Springer, Cham (2017). https://doi.org/10.1007/978-3-319-57288-8_5

53. Dufourd, J.-F., Bertot, Y.: Formal study of plane Delaunay triangulation. In: Kaufmann, M., Paulson, L.C. (eds.) ITP 2010. LNCS, vol. 6172, pp. 211–226. Springer, Heidelberg (2010). https://doi.org/10.1007/978-3-642-14052-5_16

54. Eberl, M.: Fisher-yates shuffle. Archive of Formal Proofs, September 2016. http://isa-afp.org/entries/Fisher_Yates.html, Formal proof development

55. Eberl, M.: Expected shape of random binary search trees. Archive of Formal Proofs, April 2017. http://isa-afp.org/entries/Random_BSTs.html, Formal proof development

56. Eberl, M.: Lower bound on comparison-based sorting algorithms. Archive of Formal Proofs, March 2017. http://isa-afp.org/entries/Comparison_Sort_Lower_Bound.html, Formal proof development

57. Eberl, M.: The median-of-medians selection algorithm. Archive of Formal Proofs, December 2017. http://isa-afp.org/entries/Median_Of_Medians_Selection.html, Formal proof development

58. Eberl, M.: The number of comparisons in quicksort. Archive of Formal Proofs, March 2017. http://isa-afp.org/entries/Quick_Sort_Cost.html, Formal proof development

59. Eberl, M.: Proving divide and conquer complexities in Isabelle/HOL. J. Autom. Reasoning **58**(4), 483–508 (2017). https://doi.org/10.1007/s10817-016-9378-0

60. Eberl, M.: Verified real asymptotics in Isabelle/HOL. In: Proceedings of the International Symposium on Symbolic and Algebraic Computation. ISSAC 2019. ACM, New York (2019). https://doi.org/10.1145/3326229.3326240

61. Eberl, M., Haslbeck, M.W., Nipkow, T.: Verified analysis of random binary tree structures. In: J. Automated Reasoning (2020). https://doi.org/10.1007/s10817-020-09545-0

62. Edmonds, J.: Paths, trees, and flowers. Can. J. Math. **17**, 44–467 (1965). https://doi.org/10.4153/CJM-1965-045-4

63. Ernst, G., Pfähler, J., Schellhorn, G., Haneberg, D., Reif, W.: KIV: overview and verifythis competition. Int. J. Softw. Tools Technol. Transf. **17**(6), 677–694 (2015). https://doi.org/10.1007/s10009-014-0308-3

64. Ernst, G., Schellhorn, G., Reif, W.: Verification of B$^+$ trees by integration of shape analysis and interactive theorem proving. Software Syst. Model. **14**(1), 27–44 (2015). https://doi.org/10.1007/s10270-013-0320-1

65. Esparza, J., Lammich, P., Neumann, R., Nipkow, T., Schimpf, A., Smaus, J.-G.: A fully verified executable LTL model checker. In: Sharygina, N., Veith, H. (eds.) CAV 2013. LNCS, vol. 8044, pp. 463–478. Springer, Heidelberg (2013). https://doi.org/10.1007/978-3-642-39799-8_31

66. Eßmann, R., Nipkow, T., Robillard, S.: Verified approximation algorithms. In: Peltier and Sofronie-Stokkermans [163], pp. 291–306. https://doi.org/10.1007/978-3-030-51054-1_17

67. Filliâtre, J.C.: Knuth-Morris-Pratt string searching algorithm. http://toccata.lri.fr/gallery/kmp.en.html, formal proof development

68. Filliâtre, J.-C.: Proof of imperative programs in type theory. In: Altenkirch, T., Reus, B., Naraschewski, W. (eds.) TYPES 1998. LNCS, vol. 1657, pp. 78–92. Springer, Heidelberg (1999). https://doi.org/10.1007/3-540-48167-2_6

69. Filliâtre, J.C.: Skew heaps (2014). http://toccata.lri.fr/gallery/skew_heaps.en.html, formal proof development

70. Filliâtre, J.C.: Purely applicative heaps implemented with Braun trees (2015). http://toccata.lri.fr/gallery/braun_trees.en.html, formal proof development

71. Filliâtre, J.C.: Binomial heaps (2016). http://toccata.lri.fr/gallery/binomial_heap.en.html, formal proof development

72. Filliâtre, J.C., Clochard, M.: Hash tables with linear probing (2014). http://toccata.lri.fr/gallery/linear_probing.en.html, formal proof development

73. Filliâtre, J.C., Clochard, M.: Warshall algorithm (2014), http://toccata.lri.fr/gallery/warshall_algorithm.en.html, formal proof development

74. Filliâtre, J.-C., Letouzey, P.: Functors for proofs and programs. In: Schmidt, D. (ed.) ESOP 2004. LNCS, vol. 2986, pp. 370–384. Springer, Heidelberg (2004). https://doi.org/10.1007/978-3-540-24725-8_26

75. Filliâtre, J.-C., Paskevich, A.: Why3 — where programs meet provers. In: Felleisen, M., Gardner, P. (eds.) ESOP 2013. LNCS, vol. 7792, pp. 125–128. Springer, Heidelberg (2013). https://doi.org/10.1007/978-3-642-37036-6_8

76. Filliâtre, J., Paskevich, A., Stump, A.: The 2nd verified software competition: Experience report. In: Proceedings of the 1st International Workshop on Comparative Empirical Evaluation of Reasoning Systems, pp. 36–49 (2012). http://ceur-ws.org/Vol-873/papers/paper_6.pdf

77. Fredman, M.L., Sedgewick, R., Sleator, D.D., Tarjan, R.E.: The pairing heap: a new form of self-adjusting heap. Algorithmica 1(1), 111–129 (1986). https://doi.org/10.1007/BF01840439

78. Furia, C.A., Nordio, M., Polikarpova, N., Tschannen, J.: Autoproof: auto-active functional verification of object-oriented programs. Int. J. Softw. Tools Technol. Transf. 19(6), 697–716 (2017). https://doi.org/10.1007/s10009-016-0419-0

79. Gabow, H.N.: Path-based depth-first search for strong and biconnected components. Inf. Process. Lett. 74(3–4), 107–114 (2000). https://doi.org/10.1016/S0020-0190(00)00051-X

80. Gale, D., Shapley, L.S.: College admissions and the stability of marriage. Am. Math. Monthly 69(1), 9–15 (1962)

81. Galperin, I., Rivest, R.L.: Scapegoat trees. In: Ramachandran, V. (ed.) Proceedings of the Fourth Annual ACM/SIGACT-SIAM Symposium on Discrete Algorithms, pp. 165–174. ACM/SIAM (1993). http://dl.acm.org/citation.cfm?id=313559.313676

82. Gamboa, R.: The correctness of the fast Fourier transform: a structured proof in ACL2. Formal Methods Syst. Des. 20(1), 91–106 (2002)

83. Garillot, F., Gonthier, G., Mahboubi, A., Rideau, L.: Packaging mathematical structures. In: Berghofer, S., Nipkow, T., Urban, C., Wenzel, M. (eds.) TPHOLs 2009. LNCS, vol. 5674, pp. 327–342. Springer, Heidelberg (2009). https://doi.org/10.1007/978-3-642-03359-9_23

84. Giry, M.: A categorical approach to probability theory. In: Banaschewski, B. (ed.) Categorical Aspects of Topology and Analysis. LNM, vol. 915, pp. 68–85. Springer, Heidelberg (1982). https://doi.org/10.1007/BFb0092872

85. de Gouw, S., de Boer, F.S., Bubel, R., Hähnle, R., Rot, J., Steinhöfel, D.: Verifying OpenJDK's sort method for generic collections. J. Autom. Reasoning 62(1), 93–126 (2019). https://doi.org/10.1007/s10817-017-9426-4

86. de Gouw, S., Rot, J., de Boer, F.S., Bubel, R., Hähnle, R.: OpenJDK's Java.utils.Collection.sort() is broken: the good, the bad and the worst case. In: Kroening, D., Păsăreanu, C.S. (eds.) CAV 2015. LNCS, vol. 9206, pp. 273–289. Springer, Cham (2015). https://doi.org/10.1007/978-3-319-21690-4_16

87. Guéneau, A., Charguéraud, A., Pottier, F.: A fistful of dollars: formalizing asymptotic complexity claims via deductive program verification. In: Ahmed, A. (ed.) ESOP 2018. LNCS, vol. 10801, pp. 533–560. Springer, Cham (2018). https://doi.org/10.1007/978-3-319-89884-1_19

88. Guibas, L.J., McCreight, E.M., Plass, M.F., Roberts, J.R.: A new representation for linear lists. In: Hopcroft, J.E., Friedman, E.P., Harrison, M.A. (eds.) Proceedings of the 9th Annual ACM Symposium on Theory of Computing, pp. 49–60. ACM (1977). https://doi.org/10.1145/800105.803395

89. Guttmann, W.: Relation-algebraic verification of Prim's minimum spanning tree algorithm. In: Sampaio, A., Wang, F. (eds.) ICTAC 2016. LNCS, vol. 9965, pp. 51–68. Springer, Cham (2016). https://doi.org/10.1007/978-3-319-46750-4_4

90. Guttmann, W.: An algebraic framework for minimum spanning tree problems. Theor. Comput. Sci. 744, 37–55 (2018). https://doi.org/10.1016/j.tcs.2018.04.012

91. Guttmann, W.: Verifying minimum spanning tree algorithms with stone relation algebras. J. Log. Algebraic Methods Program **101**, 132–150 (2018). https://doi.org/10.1016/j.jlamp.2018.09.005

92. Hamid, N.A., Castleberry, C.: Formally certified stable marriages. In: Proceedings of the 48th Annual Southeast Regional Conference. ACM SE 2010. ACM (2010). https://doi.org/10.1145/1900008.1900056

93. Haslbeck, M.W., Eberl, M.: Skip lists. Archive of Formal Proofs, January 2020. http://isa-afp.org/entries/Skip_Lists.html, Formal proof development

94. Haslbeck, M.W., Eberl, M., Nipkow, T.: Treaps. Archive of Formal Proofs, February 2018. http://isa-afp.org/entries/Treaps.html, Formal proof development

95. Haslbeck, M.P.L., Lammich, P.: Refinement with time – refining the runtime of algorithms in Isabelle/HOL. In: Harrison, J., O'Leary, J., Tolmach, A. (eds.) Interactive Theorem Proving, ITP 2019. LIPIcs, vol. 141, pp. 20:1–20:18. Schloss Dagstuhl - Leibniz-Zentrum für Informatik (2019). https://doi.org/10.4230/LIPIcs.ITP.2019.20

96. Haslbeck, M.P.L., Lammich, P., Biendarra, J.: Kruskal's algorithm for minimum spanning forest. Archive of Formal Proofs, February 2019. http://isa-afp.org/entries/Kruskal.html, Formal proof development

97. Haslbeck, M.P.L., Lammich, P., Biendarra, J.: Kruskal's algorithm for minimum spanning forest. Arch. Formal Proofs 2019 (2019), https://www.isa-afp.org/entries/Kruskal.html

98. Haslbeck, M.P.L., Nipkow, T.: Verified analysis of list update algorithms. In: Lal, A., Akshay, S., Saurabh, S., Sen, S. (eds.) Foundations of Software Technology and Theoretical Computer Science, FSTTCS 2016. LIPIcs, vol. 65, pp. 49:1–49:15. Schloss Dagstuhl - Leibniz-Zentrum für Informatik (2016). https://doi.org/10.4230/LIPIcs.FSTTCS.2016.49, https://doi.org/10.4230/LIPIcs.FSTTCS.2016.49

99. Hellauer, F., Lammich, P.: The string search algorithm by knuth, morris and pratt. Archive of Formal Proofs, December 2017. http://isa-afp.org/entries/Knuth_Morris_Pratt.html, Formal proof development

100. Hiep, H.-D.A., Maathuis, O., Bian, J., de Boer, F.S., van Eekelen, M., de Gouw, S.: Verifying OpenJDK's LinkedList using KeY. TACAS 2020. LNCS, vol. 12079, pp. 217–234. Springer, Cham (2020). https://doi.org/10.1007/978-3-030-45237-7_13

101. Hinze, R., Paterson, R.: Finger trees: a simple general-purpose data structure. J. Funct. Program. **16**(2), 197–217 (2006). https://doi.org/10.1017/S0956796805005769

102. Hirai, Y., Yamamoto, K.: Balancing weight-balanced trees. J. Funct. Program. **21**(3), 287–307 (2011). https://doi.org/10.1017/S0956796811000104

103. Hoffmann, J.: Types with potential: polynomial resource bounds via automatic amortized analysis. Ph.D. thesis, Ludwig Maximilians University Munich (2011). http://edoc.ub.uni-muenchen.de/13955/

104. Hoffmann, J., Aehlig, K., Hofmann, M.: Multivariate amortized resource analysis. ACM Trans. Program. Lang. Syst. **34**(3), 14:1–14:62 (2012). https://doi.org/10.1145/2362389.2362393

105. Hölzl, J.: Formalising semantics for expected running time of probabilistic programs. In: Blanchette, J.C., Merz, S. (eds.) ITP 2016. LNCS, vol. 9807, pp. 475–482. Springer, Cham (2016). https://doi.org/10.1007/978-3-319-43144-4_30

106. Hölzl, J., Heller, A.: Three chapters of measure theory in Isabelle/HOL. In: van Eekelen, M., Geuvers, H., Schmaltz, J., Wiedijk, F. (eds.) ITP 2011. LNCS, vol. 6898, pp. 135–151. Springer, Heidelberg (2011). https://doi.org/10.1007/978-3-642-22863-6_12

107. Hölzl, J., Immler, F., Huffman, B.: Type classes and filters for mathematical analysis in Isabelle/HOL. In: Blazy, S., Paulin-Mohring, C., Pichardie, D. (eds.) ITP 2013. LNCS, vol. 7998, pp. 279–294. Springer, Heidelberg (2013). https://doi.org/10.1007/978-3-642-39634-2_21

108. Hoogerwoord, R.R.: A logarithmic implementation of flexible arrays. In: Bird, R.S., Morgan, C.C., Woodcock, J.C.P. (eds.) MPC 1992. LNCS, vol. 669, pp. 191–207. Springer, Heidelberg (1993). https://doi.org/10.1007/3-540-56625-2_14

109. Hurd, J.: Verification of the Miller-Rabin probabilistic primality test. J. Log. Algebraic Methods Program. **56**(1–2), 3–21 (2003). https://doi.org/10.1016/S1567-8326(02)00065-6

110. Kaminski, B.L., Katoen, J.-P., Matheja, C., Olmedo, F.: Weakest precondition reasoning for expected run–times of probabilistic programs. In: Thiemann, P. (ed.) ESOP 2016. LNCS, vol. 9632, pp. 364–389. Springer, Heidelberg (2016). https://doi.org/10.1007/978-3-662-49498-1_15

111. Kaufmann, M., Moore, J.S., Manolios, P.: Computer-Aided Reasoning: An Approach. Kluwer Academic Publishers, Norwell (2000)

112. Keinholz, J.: Matroids. Archive of Formal Proofs, November 2018. http://isa-afp.org/entries/Matroids.html, Formal proof development

113. Knuth, D.E.: Optimum binary search trees. Acta Inf. **1**, 14–25 (1971). https://doi.org/10.1007/BF00264289

114. Lammich, P.: Automatic data refinement. In: Blazy, S., Paulin-Mohring, C., Pichardie, D. (eds.) ITP 2013. LNCS, vol. 7998, pp. 84–99. Springer, Heidelberg (2013). https://doi.org/10.1007/978-3-642-39634-2_9

115. Lammich, P.: Verified efficient implementation of Gabow's strongly connected component algorithm. In: Klein, G., Gamboa, R. (eds.) ITP 2014. LNCS, vol. 8558, pp. 325–340. Springer, Cham (2014). https://doi.org/10.1007/978-3-319-08970-6_21

116. Lammich, P.: Refinement to Imperative/HOL. In: Urban and Zhang [191], pp. 253–269. https://doi.org/10.1007/978-3-319-22102-1_17

117. Lammich, P.: Refinement based verification of imperative data structures. In: Avigad, J., Chlipala, A. (eds.) Proceedings of the 5th ACM SIGPLAN Conference on Certified Programs and Proofs, pp. 27–36. ACM (2016). https://doi.org/10.1145/2854065.2854067

118. Lammich, P.: Generating verified LLVM from Isabelle/HOL. In: Harrison, J., O'Leary, J., Tolmach, A. (eds.) Interactive Theorem Proving, ITP 2019. LIPIcs, vol. 141, pp. 22:1–22:19. Schloss Dagstuhl - Leibniz-Zentrum für Informatik (2019). https://doi.org/10.4230/LIPIcs.ITP.2019.22

119. Lammich, P.: Refinement to imperative HOL. J. Autom. Reasoning **62**(4), 481–503 (2019). https://doi.org/10.1007/s10817-017-9437-1

120. Lammich, P.: Efficient verified implementation of Introsort and Pdqsort. In: Peltier, N., Sofronie-Stokkermans, V. (eds.) IJCAR 2020. LNCS (LNAI), vol. 12167, pp. 307–323. Springer, Cham (2020). https://doi.org/10.1007/978-3-030-51054-1_18

121. Lammich, P., Lochbihler, A.: The Isabelle collections framework. In: Kaufmann, M., Paulson, L.C. (eds.) ITP 2010. LNCS, vol. 6172, pp. 339–354. Springer, Heidelberg (2010). https://doi.org/10.1007/978-3-642-14052-5_24

122. Lammich, P., Meis, R.: A Separation Logic Framework for Imperative HOL. Archive of Formal Proofs, November 2012. http://isa-afp.org/entries/Separation_Logic_Imperative_HOL.html, Formal proof development

123. Lammich, P., Neumann, R.: A framework for verifying depth-first search algorithms. In: Leroy, X., Tiu, A. (eds.) Proceedings of the 2015 Conference on Certified Programs and Proofs. CPP 2015, pp. 137–146. ACM (2015). https://doi.org/10.1145/2676724.2693165

124. Lammich, P., Nipkow, T.: Proof pearl: purely functional, simple and efficient priority search trees and applications to Prim and Dijkstra. In: Harrison, J., O'Leary, J., Tolmach, A. (eds.) Interactive Theorem Proving, ITP 2019. LIPIcs, vol. 141, pp. 23:1–23:18. Schloss Dagstuhl - Leibniz-Zentrum für Informatik (2019). https://doi.org/10.4230/LIPIcs.ITP.2019.23

125. Lammich, P., Sefidgar, S.R.: Formalizing the Edmonds-Karp algorithm. In: Blanchette, J.C., Merz, S. (eds.) ITP 2016. LNCS, vol. 9807, pp. 219–234. Springer, Cham (2016). https://doi.org/10.1007/978-3-319-43144-4_14

126. Lammich, P., Sefidgar, S.R.: Formalizing network flow algorithms: a refinement approach in Isabelle/HOL. J. Autom. Reasoning **62**(2), 261–280 (2019). https://doi.org/10.1007/s10817-017-9442-4

127. Lammich, P., Tuerk, T.: Applying data refinement for monadic programs to Hopcroft's algorithm. In: Beringer, L., Felty, A. (eds.) ITP 2012. LNCS, vol. 7406, pp. 166–182. Springer, Heidelberg (2012). https://doi.org/10.1007/978-3-642-32347-8_12

128. Lee, G.: Correctnesss of Ford-Fulkerson's maximum flow algorithm. Formalized Math. **13**(2), 305–314 (2005). http://fm.mizar.org/2005-13/pdf13-2/glib_005.pdf

129. Lee, G., Rudnicki, P.: Correctness of Dijkstra's shortest path and Prim's minimum spanning tree algorithms. Formal. Math. **13**(2), 295–304 (2005). http://fm.mizar.org/2005-13/pdf13-2/glib_004.pdf

130. Leighton, T.: Notes on better master theorems for divide-and-conquer recurrences (MIT lecture notes) (1996), https://courses.csail.mit.edu/6.046/spring04/handouts/akrabazzi.pdf

131. Malecha, J.G., Morrisett, G., Shinnar, A., Wisnesky, R.: Toward a verified relational database management system. In: Hermenegildo, M.V., Palsberg, J. (eds.) Proceedings of the 37th ACM SIGPLAN-SIGACT Symposium on Principles of Programming Languages, POPL 2010, pp. 237–248. ACM (2010). https://doi.org/10.1145/1706299.1706329

132. Marić, F., Spasić, M., Thiemann, R.: An incremental simplex algorithm with unsatisfiable core generation. Archive of Formal Proofs, August 2018. http://isa-afp.org/entries/Simplex.html, Formal proof development

133. McCarthy, J., Fetscher, B., New, M., Feltey, D., Findler, R.B.: A coq library for internal verification of running-times. In: Kiselyov, O., King, A. (eds.) FLOPS 2016. LNCS, vol. 9613, pp. 144–162. Springer, Cham (2016). https://doi.org/10.1007/978-3-319-29604-3_10

134. Meikle, L.I., Fleuriot, J.D.: Mechanical theorem proving in computational geometry. In: Hong, H., Wang, D. (eds.) ADG 2004. LNCS (LNAI), vol. 3763, pp. 1–18. Springer, Heidelberg (2006). https://doi.org/10.1007/11615798_1

135. Meis, R., Nielsen, F., Lammich, P.: Binomial heaps and skew binomial heaps. Archive of Formal Proofs, October 2010. http://isa-afp.org/entries/Binomial-Heaps.html, Formal proof development

136. Meyer, B.: Eiffel: The Language. Prentice-Hall (1991). http://www.eiffel.com/doc/#etl

137. Moore, J S., Martinez, M.: A mechanically checked proof of the correctness of the Boyer-Moore fast string searching algorithm. In: Broy, M., Sitou, W., Hoare, T. (eds.) Engineering Methods and Tools for Software Safety and Security, pp. 267–284. IOS Press (2009)

138. Moore, J.S., Zhang, Q.: Proof pearl: Dijkstra's shortest path algorithm verified with ACL2. In: Hurd, J., Melham, T. (eds.) TPHOLs 2005. LNCS, vol. 3603, pp. 373–384. Springer, Heidelberg (2005). https://doi.org/10.1007/11541868_24

139. Motwani, R., Raghavan, P.: Randomized Algorithms. Cambridge University Press, Cambridge (1995)

140. Musser, D.R.: Introspective sorting and selection algorithms. Softw. Pract. Exp. **27**(8), 983–993 (1997). https://doi.org/10.1002/(SICI)1097--024X(199708)27: 8<983::AID-SPE117>3.0.CO;2-%23

141. Nanevski, A., Morrisett, G., Shinnar, A., Govereau, P., Birkedal, L.: Ynot: dependent types for imperative programs. In: Hook, J., Thiemann, P. (eds.) Proceeding of the 13th ACM SIGPLAN International Conference on Functional Programming, ICFP 2008. pp. 229–240. ACM (2008). https://doi.org/10.1145/1411204. 1411237

142. Neumann, R.: CAVA – A Verified Model Checker. Ph.D. thesis, Technische Universität München (2017). http://nbn-resolving.de/urn/resolver.pl?urn:nbn: de:bvb:91-diss-20170616-1342881-1-9

143. Nievergelt, J., Reingold, E.M.: Binary search trees of bounded balance. In: Fischer, P.C., Zeiger, H.P., Ullman, J.D., Rosenberg, A.L. (eds.) Proceedings of the 4th Annual ACM Symposium on Theory of Computing, pp. 137–142. ACM (1972). https://doi.org/10.1145/800152.804906

144. Nievergelt, J., Reingold, E.M.: Binary search trees of bounded balance. SIAM J. Comput. **2**(1), 33–43 (1973). https://doi.org/10.1137/0202005

145. Nipkow, T.: Amortized complexity verified. In: Urban and Zhang [191], pp. 310–324. https://doi.org/10.1007/978-3-319-22102-1_21

146. Nipkow, T.: Automatic functional correctness proofs for functional search trees. In: Blanchette, J.C., Merz, S. (eds.) ITP 2016. LNCS, vol. 9807, pp. 307–322. Springer, Cham (2016). https://doi.org/10.1007/978-3-319-43144-4_19

147. Nipkow, T.: Verified root-balanced trees. In: Chang, B.E. (ed.) Programming Languages and Systems, APLAS 2017. LNCS, vol. 10695, pp. 255–272. Springer (2017). https://doi.org/10.1007/978-3-319-71237-6_13

148. Nipkow, T., Brinkop, H.: Amortized complexity verified. J. Autom. Reasoning **62**(3), 367–391 (2019). https://doi.org/10.1007/s10817-018-9459-3

149. Nipkow, T., Dirix, S.: Weight-balanced trees. Archive of Formal Proofs, March 2018. http://isa-afp.org/entries/Weight_Balanced_Trees.html, Formal proof development

150. Nipkow, T., Klein, G.: Concrete Semantics - With Isabelle/HOL. Springer, Cham (2014). https://doi.org/10.1007/978-3-319-10542-0, http://www.concrete-semantics.org/

151. Nipkow, T., Paulson, L.C., Wenzel, M.: Isabelle/HOL. LNCS, vol. 2283. Springer, Heidelberg (2002). https://doi.org/10.1007/3-540-45949-9

152. Nipkow, T., Pusch, C.: AVL trees. Archive of Formal Proofs, March 2004. http://isa-afp.org/entries/AVL-Trees.html, Formal proof development

153. Nipkow, T., Sewell, T.: Proof pearl: Braun trees. In: Blanchette, J., Hritcu, C. (eds.) Proceedings of the 9th ACM SIGPLAN International Conference on Certified Programs and Proofs, CPP 2020, pp. 18–31. ACM (2020). https://doi.org/ 10.1145/3372885.3373834

154. Nipkow, T., Somogyi, D.: Optimal binary search trees. Archive of Formal Proofs, May 2018. http://isa-afp.org/entries/Optimal_BST.html, Formal proof development

155. Nordhoff, B., Körner, S., Lammich, P.: Finger trees. Archive of Formal Proofs, October 2010. http://isa-afp.org/entries/Finger-Trees.html, Formal proof development

156. Nordhoff, B., Lammich, P.: Dijkstra's shortest path algorithm. Archive of Formal Proofs, January 2012. http://isa-afp.org/entries/Dijkstra_Shortest_Path.html, Formal proof development

157. Owre, S., Shankar, N.: A brief overview of PVS. In: Mohamed, O.A., Muñoz, C., Tahar, S. (eds.) TPHOLs 2008. LNCS, vol. 5170, pp. 22–27. Springer, Heidelberg (2008). https://doi.org/10.1007/978-3-540-71067-7_5

158. Palomo-Lozano, F., Inmaculada Medina-Bulo, J.A.A.J.: Certification of matrix multiplication algorithms. In: Theorem Proving in Higher Order Logics, Supplemental Proceedings, TPHOLs 2001 (2001)

159. Parsert, J., Kaliszyk, C.: Linear programming. Archive of Formal Proofs, August 2019. http://isa-afp.org/entries/Linear_Programming.html, Formal proof development

160. Paskevich, A., Wies, T. (eds.): VSTTE 2017. LNCS, vol. 10712. Springer, Cham (2017). https://doi.org/10.1007/978-3-319-72308-2

161. Paulin-Mohring, C.: Extraction de programmes dans le Calcul des Constructions. (Program Extraction in the Calculus of Constructions). Ph.D. thesis, Paris Diderot University, France (1989). https://tel.archives-ouvertes.fr/tel-00431825

162. Paulson, L.C.: ML for the Working Programmer, 2nd edn. Cambridge University Press, Cambridge (1996)

163. Peltier, N., Sofronie-Stokkermans, V. (eds.): IJCAR 2020. LNCS (LNAI), vol. 12167. Springer, Cham (2020). https://doi.org/10.1007/978-3-030-51054-1

164. Pereira, M.: Pairing heaps (2016). http://toccata.lri.fr/gallery/pairing_heap.en.html, formal proof development

165. Petcher, A., Morrisett, G.: The foundational cryptography framework. In: Focardi, R., Myers, A. (eds.) POST 2015. LNCS, vol. 9036, pp. 53–72. Springer, Heidelberg (2015). https://doi.org/10.1007/978-3-662-46666-7_4

166. Pichardie, D., Bertot, Y.: Formalizing convex hull algorithms. In: Boulton, R.J., Jackson, P.B. (eds.) TPHOLs 2001. LNCS, vol. 2152, pp. 346–361. Springer, Heidelberg (2001). https://doi.org/10.1007/3-540-44755-5_24

167. Polikarpova, N., Tschannen, J., Furia, C.A.: A fully verified container library. In: Bjørner, N., de Boer, F. (eds.) FM 2015. LNCS, vol. 9109, pp. 414–434. Springer, Cham (2015). https://doi.org/10.1007/978-3-319-19249-9_26

168. Polikarpova, N., Tschannen, J., Furia, C.A.: A fully verified container library. Formal Asp. Comput. 30(5), 495–523 (2018). https://doi.org/10.1007/s00165-017-0435-1

169. Pottier, F.: Depth-first search and strong connectivity in Coq. In: Journées Francophones des Langages Applicatifs (JFLA), January 2015. http://gallium.inria.fr/~fpottier/publis/fpottier-dfs-scc.pdf

170. Pottier, F.: Verifying a hash table and its iterators in higher-order separation logic. In: ACM SIGPLAN Conference on Certified Programs and Proofs (CPP), pp. 3–16, January 2017. https://doi.org/10.1145/3018610.3018624, http://gallium.inria.fr/~fpottier/publis/fpottier-hashtable.pdf

171. Pugh, W.: Skip lists: a probabilistic alternative to balanced trees. Commun. ACM 33(6), 668–676 (1990). https://doi.org/10.1145/78973.78977

172. Ralston, R.: ACL2-certified AVL trees. In: Eighth International Workshop on the ACL2 Theorem Prover and Its Applications. ACL2 2009, pp. 71–74. ACM (2009). https://doi.org/10.1145/1637837.1637848

173. Rau, M., Nipkow, T.: Verification of closest pair of points algorithms. In: Peltier and Sofronie-Stokkermans [163], pp. 341–357. https://doi.org/10.1007/978-3-030-51054-1_20

174. Rem, M., Braun, W.: A logarithmic implementation of flexible arrays (1983). memorandum MR83/4. Eindhoven University of Technology

175. Sagiv, S., Reps, T.W., Wilhelm, R.: Parametric shape analysis via 3-valued logic. ACM Trans. Program. Lang. Syst. **24**(3), 217–298 (2002). https://doi.org/10.1145/514188.514190

176. Sakaguchi, K.: Program extraction for mutable arrays. In: Gallagher, J.P., Sulzmann, M. (eds.) FLOPS 2018. LNCS, vol. 10818, pp. 51–67. Springer, Cham (2018). https://doi.org/10.1007/978-3-319-90686-7_4

177. Sedgewick, R., Wayne, K.: Algorithms, 4th Edition. Addison-Wesley, Upper Saddle River (2011)

178. Seidel, R., Aragon, C.R.: Randomized search trees. Algorithmica **16**(4/5), 464–497 (1996). https://doi.org/10.1007/BF01940876

179. Sleator, D.D., Tarjan, R.E.: Self-adjusting binary search trees. J. ACM **32**(3), 652–686 (1985). https://doi.org/10.1145/3828.3835

180. Sleator, D.D., Tarjan, R.E.: Self-adjusting heaps. SIAM J. Comput. **15**(1), 52–69 (1986). https://doi.org/10.1137/0215004

181. Slind, K., Norrish, M.: A brief overview of HOL4. In: Mohamed, O.A., Muñoz, C., Tahar, S. (eds.) TPHOLs 2008. LNCS, vol. 5170, pp. 28–32. Springer, Heidelberg (2008). https://doi.org/10.1007/978-3-540-71067-7_6

182. Sozeau, M.: Program-ing finger trees in Coq. In: Hinze, R., Ramsey, N. (eds.) Proceedings of the 12th ACM SIGPLAN International Conference on Functional Programming. ICFP 2007, pp. 13–24. ACM (2007). https://doi.org/10.1145/1291220.1291156

183. Spasić, M., Marić, F.: Formalization of incremental simplex algorithm by stepwise refinement. In: Giannakopoulou, D., Méry, D. (eds.) FM 2012. LNCS, vol. 7436, pp. 434–449. Springer, Heidelberg (2012). https://doi.org/10.1007/978-3-642-32759-9_35

184. Stucke, I.: Reasoning about cardinalities of relations with applications supported by proof assistants. In: Höfner, P., Pous, D., Struth, G. (eds.) RAMICS 2017. LNCS, vol. 10226, pp. 290–306. Springer, Cham (2017). https://doi.org/10.1007/978-3-319-57418-9_18

185. Stüwe, D., Eberl, M.: Probabilistic primality testing. Archive of Formal Proofs, February 2019. http://isa-afp.org/entries/Probabilistic_Prime_Tests.html, Formal proof development

186. Tarjan, R.E.: Depth-first search and linear graph algorithms. SIAM J. Comput. **1**(2), 146–160 (1972). https://doi.org/10.1137/0201010

187. Tassarotti, J., Harper, R.: Verified tail bounds for randomized programs. In: Avigad, J., Mahboubi, A. (eds.) ITP 2018. LNCS, vol. 10895, pp. 560–578. Springer, Cham (2018). https://doi.org/10.1007/978-3-319-94821-8_33

188. Tassarotti, J., Harper, R.: A separation logic for concurrent randomized programs. Proc. ACM Program. Lang. **3**(POPL), 64:1–64:30 (2019). https://doi.org/10.1145/3290377

189. Théry, L.: Formalising Huffman's algorithm. Research report, Università degli Studi dell'Aquila (2004) https://hal.archives-ouvertes.fr/hal-02149909

190. Toibazarov, E.: An ACL2 proof of the correctness of the preprocessing for a variant of the Boyer-Moore fast string searching algorithm. Honors thesis, Computer Science Dept., University of Texas at Austin (2013). see www.cs.utexas.edu/users/moore/publications/toibazarov-thesis.pdf

191. Urban, C., Zhang, X. (eds.): ITP 2015. LNCS, vol. 9236. Springer, Cham (2015). https://doi.org/10.1007/978-3-319-22102-1

192. Vafeiadis, V.: Adjustable references. In: Blazy, S., Paulin-Mohring, C., Pichardie, D. (eds.) ITP 2013. LNCS, vol. 7998, pp. 328–337. Springer, Heidelberg (2013). https://doi.org/10.1007/978-3-642-39634-2_24

193. van der Weegen, E., McKinna, J.: A machine-checked proof of the average-case complexity of quicksort in Coq. In: Berardi, S., Damiani, F., de'Liguoro, U. (eds.) TYPES 2008. LNCS, vol. 5497, pp. 256–271. Springer, Heidelberg (2009). https://doi.org/10.1007/978-3-642-02444-3_16

194. Wimmer, S.: Formalized timed automata. In: Blanchette, J.C., Merz, S. (eds.) ITP 2016. LNCS, vol. 9807, pp. 425–440. Springer, Cham (2016). https://doi.org/10.1007/978-3-319-43144-4_26

195. Wimmer, S.: Hidden Markov models. Archive of Formal Proofs, May 2018. http://isa-afp.org/entries/Hidden_Markov_Models.html, Formal proof development

196. Wimmer, S., Hu, S., Nipkow, T.: Verified Memoization and dynamic programming. In: Avigad, J., Mahboubi, A. (eds.) ITP 2018. LNCS, vol. 10895, pp. 579–596. Springer, Cham (2018). https://doi.org/10.1007/978-3-319-94821-8_34

197. Wimmer, S., Lammich, P.: The Floyd-Warshall algorithm for shortest paths. Archive of Formal Proofs, May 2017. http://isa-afp.org/entries/Floyd_Warshall.html, Formal proof development

198. Wimmer, S., Lammich, P.: Verified model checking of timed automata. In: Beyer, D., Huisman, M. (eds.) TACAS 2018. LNCS, vol. 10805, pp. 61–78. Springer, Cham (2018). https://doi.org/10.1007/978-3-319-89960-2_4

199. Yao, F.F.: Efficient dynamic programming using quadrangle inequalities. In: Miller, R.E., Ginsburg, S., Burkhard, W.A., Lipton, R.J. (eds.) Proceedings of the 12th Annual ACM Symposium on Theory of Computing, pp. 429–435. ACM (1980). https://doi.org/10.1145/800141.804691

200. Zhan, B.: Efficient verification of imperative programs using Auto2. In: Beyer, D., Huisman, M. (eds.) TACAS 2018. LNCS, vol. 10805, pp. 23–40. Springer, Cham (2018). https://doi.org/10.1007/978-3-319-89960-2_2

201. Zhan, B., Haslbeck, M.P.L.: Verifying asymptotic time complexity of imperative programs in Isabelle. In: Galmiche, D., Schulz, S., Sebastiani, R. (eds.) IJCAR 2018. LNCS (LNAI), vol. 10900, pp. 532–548. Springer, Cham (2018). https://doi.org/10.1007/978-3-319-94205-6_35

Neural Networks and Machine Learning

Verifying Recurrent Neural Networks
Using Invariant Inference

Yuval Jacoby[1(✉)], Clark Barrett[2(✉)], and Guy Katz[1(✉)]

[1] The Hebrew University of Jerusalem, Jerusalem, Israel
{yuval.jacoby,g.katz}@mail.huji.ac.il
[2] Stanford University, Stanford, USA
clarkbarrett@stanford.edu

Abstract. Deep neural networks are revolutionizing the way complex systems are developed. However, these automatically-generated networks are opaque to humans, making it difficult to reason about them and guarantee their correctness. Here, we propose a novel approach for verifying properties of a widespread variant of neural networks, called *recurrent neural networks*. Recurrent neural networks play a key role in, e.g., speech recognition, and their verification is crucial for guaranteeing the reliability of many critical systems. Our approach is based on the inference of *invariants*, which allow us to reduce the complex problem of verifying recurrent networks into simpler, non-recurrent problems. Experiments with a proof-of-concept implementation of our approach demonstrate that it performs orders-of-magnitude better than the state of the art.

1 Introduction

The use of *recurrent neural networks* (*RNNs*) [13] is on the rise. RNNs are a particular kind of deep neural networks (DNNs), with the useful ability to store information from previous evaluations in constructs called *memory units*. This differentiates them from *feed-forward neural networks* (*FFNNs*), where each evaluation of the network is performed independently of past evaluations. The presence of memory units renders RNNs particularly suited for tasks that involve context, such as machine translation [7], health applications [25], speaker recognition [34], and many other tasks where the network's output might be affected by previously processed inputs.

Part of the success of RNNs (and of DNNs in general) is attributed to their very attractive generalization properties: after being trained on a finite set of examples, they generalize well to inputs they have not encountered before [13]. Unfortunately, it is known that RNNs may react in highly undesirable ways to certain inputs. For instance, it has been observed that many RNNs are vulnerable to *adversarial inputs* [6,32], where small, carefully-crafted perturbations are added to an input in order to fool the network into a classification error. This example, and others, highlight the need to *formally verify* the correctness of RNNs, so that they can reliably be deployed in safety-critical settings. However, while DNN verification has received significant attention in recent years

© Springer Nature Switzerland AG 2020
D. V. Hung and O. Sokolsky (Eds.): ATVA 2020, LNCS 12302, pp. 57–74, 2020.
https://doi.org/10.1007/978-3-030-59152-6_3

(e.g., [2,4,5,8,10,12,15,19,20,26,27,33,35,36]), almost all of these efforts have been focused on FFNNs, with very little work done on RNN verification.

To the best of our knowledge, the only existing general approach for RNN verification is via *unrolling* [1]: the RNN is duplicated and concatenated onto itself, creating an equivalent feed-forward network that operates on a sequence of k inputs simultaneously, as opposed to one at a time. The FFNN can then be verified using existing verification technology. The main limitation of this approach is that unrolling increases the network size by a factor of k (which, in real-world applications, can be in the hundreds [34]). Because the complexity of FFNN verification is known to be worst-case exponential in the size of the network [18], this reduction gives rise to FFNNs that are difficult to verify—and is hence applicable primarily to small RNNs with short input sequences.

Here, we propose a novel approach for RNN verification, which affords far greater scalability than unrolling. Our approach also reduces the RNN verification problem into FFNN verification, but does so in a way that is independent of the number of inputs that the RNN is to be evaluated on. Specifically, our approach consists of two main steps: (i) create an FFNN that *over-approximates* the RNN, but which is the same size as the RNN; and (ii) verify properties over this over-approximation using existing techniques for FFNN verification. Thus, our approach circumvents any duplication of the network or its inputs.

In order to perform step (i), we leverage the well-studied notion of *inductive invariants*: our FFNN encodes time-invariant properties of the RNN, which hold initially and continue to hold after the RNN is evaluated on each additional input. Automatic inference of meaningful inductive invariants has been studied extensively (e.g., [28,30,31]), and is known to be highly difficult [29]. We propose here an approach for generating invariants according to *predefined templates*. By instantiating these templates, we automatically generate a candidate invariant I, and then: (i) use our underlying FFNN verification engine to prove that I is indeed an invariant; and (ii) use I in creating the FFNN over-approximation of the RNN, in order to prove the desired property. If either of these steps fail, we refine I (either strengthening or weakening it, depending on the point of failure), and repeat the process. The process terminates when the property is proven correct, when a counter-example is found, or when a certain timeout value is exceeded.

We evaluate our approach using a proof-of-concept implementation, which uses the Marabou tool [20] as its FFNN verification back-end. When compared to the state of the art on a set of benchmarks from the domain of speaker recognition [34], our approach is orders-of-magnitude faster. Our implementation, together with our benchmarks and experiments, is available online [16].

The rest of this paper is organized as follows. In Sect. 2, we provide a brief background on DNNs and their verification. In Sect. 3, we describe our approach for verifying RNNs via reduction to FFNN verification, using invariants. We describe automated methods for RNN invariant inference in Sect. 4, followed by an evaluation of our approach in Sect. 5. We then discuss related work in Sect. 6, and conclude with Sect. 7.

2 Background

2.1 Feed-Forward Neural Networks and Their Verification

An FFNN N with n layers consists of an input layer, $n-2$ hidden layers, and an output layer. We use s_i to denote the *dimension* of layer i, which is the number of neurons in that layer. We use $v_{i,j}$ to refer to the j-th neuron in the i-th layer. Each hidden layer is associated with a weight matrix W_i and a bias vector b_i. The FFNN input vector is denoted as v_1, and the output vector of each hidden layer $1 < i < n$ is $v_i = f\left(W_i v_{i-1} + b_i\right)$, where f is some element-wise activation function (such as $\mathrm{ReLU}(x) = \max(0, x)$). The output layer is evaluated similarly, but without an activation function: $v_n = W_{n-1}v_{n-1} + b_n$. Given an input vector v_1, the network is evaluated by sequentially calculating v_i for $i = 2, 3, \ldots, n$, and returning v_n as the network's output.

A simple example appears in Fig. 1. This FFNN has a single input neuron $v_{1,1}$, a single output neuron $v_{3,1}$, and two hidden neurons $v_{2,1}$ and $v_{2,2}$. All bias values are assumed to be 0, and we use the common $\mathrm{ReLU}(x) = \max(0, x)$ function as our activation function. When the input neuron is assigned $v_{1,1} = 4$, the weighted sum and activation functions yield $v_{2,1} = \mathrm{ReLU}(4) = 4$ and $v_{2,2} = \mathrm{ReLU}(-4) = 0$. Finally, we obtain the output $v_{3,1} = 4$.

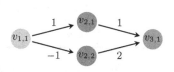

Fig. 1. A simple feed-forward neural network.

FFNN Verification. In FFNN verification we seek inputs that satisfy certain constraints, such that their corresponding outputs also satisfy certain constraints. Looking again at the network from Fig. 1, we might wish to know whether $v_{1,1} \leq 5$ always entails $v_{3,1} < 20$. Negating the output property, we can use a verification engine to check whether it is possible that $v_{1,1} \leq 5$ and $v_{3,1} \geq 20$. If this query is unsatisfiable (**UNSAT**), then the original property holds; otherwise, if the query is satisfiable (**SAT**), then the verification engine will provide us with a counter-example (e.g., $v_{1,1} = -10, v_{3,1} = 20$ in our case).

Formally, we define an FFNN verification query as a triple $\langle P, N, Q \rangle$, where N is an FFNN, P is a predicate over the input variables x, and Q is a predicate over the output variables y. Solving this query entails deciding whether there exists a specific input assignment x_0 such that $P(x_0) \wedge Q(N(x_0))$ holds (where $N(x_0)$ is the output of N for the input x_0). It has been shown that even for simple FFNNs and for predicates P and Q that are conjunctions of linear constraints, the verification problem is NP-complete [18]: in the worst-case, solving it requires a number of operations that is exponential in the number of neurons in N.

2.2 Recurrent Neural Networks

Recurrent Neural Networks (RNNs) are similar to FFNNs, but have an additional construct called a *memory unit*. Memory units allow a hidden neuron to *store* its assigned value for a specific evaluation of the network, and have that value become part of the neuron's weighted sum computation in the *next* evaluation. Thus, when evaluating the RNN in time step $t + 1$, e.g. when the RNN reads the $t + 1$'th word in a sentence, the results of the t previous evaluations can affect the current result.

A simple RNN appears in Fig. 2. There, node $\tilde{v}_{2,1}$ represents node $v_{2,1}$'s memory unit (we draw memory units as squares, and mark them using the tilde sign). When computing the weighted sum for node $v_{2,1}$, the value of $\tilde{v}_{2,1}$ is also added to the sum, according to its listed weight (1, in this case). We then update $\tilde{v}_{2,1}$ for the next round, using the vanilla RNN update rule: $\tilde{v}_{2,1} := v_{2,1}$. Memory units are initialized to 0 for the first evaluation, at time step $t = 1$.

Time Step	$v_{1,1}$	$v_{2,1}$	$\tilde{v}_{2,1}$	$v_{3,1}$
1	0.5	0.5	0	0.5
2	1.5	2	0.5	2
3	-1	1	2	1
4	-3	0	1	0

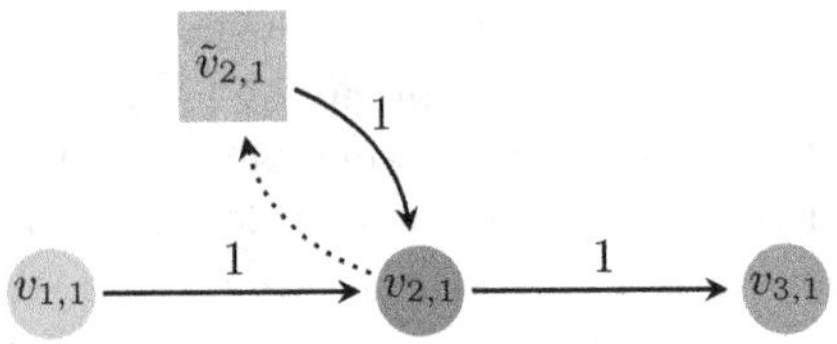

Fig. 2. An illustration of a toy RNN with the ReLU activation function. Each row of the table represents a single time step, and depicts the value of each neuron for that step. Using a t superscript to represent time step t, we observe that $v_{2,1}^t$ is computed as $\max(0, \tilde{v}_{2,1}^t + v_{1,1}^t)$, according to the ReLU function.

The FFNN definitions are extended to RNNs as follows. We use the t superscript to indicate the timestamp of the RNN's evaluation: e.g., $v_{3,2}^4$ indicates the value that node $v_{3,2}$ is assigned in the 4'th evaluation of the RNN. We associate each hidden layer of the RNN with a square matrix H_i of dimension s_i, which represents the weights on edges from memory units to neurons. Observe that each memory unit in layer i can contribute to the weighted sums of all neurons in layer i, and not just to the neuron whose values it stores. For time step $t > 0$, the evaluation of each hidden layer $1 < i < n$ is now computed by $v_i^t = f\left(W_i v_{i-1}^t + H_i \tilde{v}_i^t + b_i\right)$, and the output values are given by $v_n^t = W_n v_{n-1}^t + H_n v_n^{t-1} + b_n$. By convention, we initialize memory units to 0 (i.e. for every memory unit $\tilde{v}$, $\tilde{v}^1 = 0$). For simplicity, we assume that each hidden neuron in the network has a memory unit. This definition captures also "regular" neurons, by setting the appropriate entries of H to 0.

While we focus here on vanilla RNNs, our technique could be extended to, e.g., LSTMs or GRUs; we leave this for future work.

RNN Verification. We define an RNN verification query as a tuple $\langle P, N, Q, T_{\max} \rangle$, where P is an input property, Q is an output property, N is an RNN, and $T_{\max} \in \mathbb{N}$ is a bound on the time interval for which the property should hold. P and Q include linear constraints over the network's inputs and outputs, and may also use the notion of time.

As a running example, consider the network from Fig. 2, denoted by N, the input predicate $P = \bigwedge_{t=1}^{5}(-3 \leq v_{1,1}^{t} \leq 3)$, the output predicate $Q = \bigvee_{t=1}^{5}(v_{3,1}^{t} \geq 16)$, and the time bound $T_{\max} = 5$. This query searches for an evaluation of N with 5 time steps, in which all input values are in the range $[-3, 3]$, and such that at some time step the output value is at least 16. By the weights of N, it can be proved that $v_{3,1}^{t}$ is at most the sum of the ReLUs of inputs so far, $v_{3,1}^{t} \leq \sum_{i=1}^{t} \mathrm{ReLU}(v_{1,1}^{i}) \leq 3t$; and so $v_{3,1}^{t} \leq 15$ for all $1 \leq t \leq 5$, and the query is UNSAT.

2.3   Inductive Invariants

Inductive invariants [29] are a well-established way to reason about software with loops. Formally, let $\langle Q, q_0, T \rangle$ be a transition system, where Q is the set of states, $q_0 \in Q$ is an initial state, and $T \subseteq Q \times Q$ is a transition relation. An invariant I is a logical formula defined over the states of Q, with two properties: (i) I holds for the initial state, i.e. $I(q_0)$ holds; and (ii) I is closed under T, i.e. $(I(q) \wedge \langle q, q' \rangle \in T) \Rightarrow I(q')$. If it can be proved (in a given proof system) that formula I is an invariant, we say that I is an inductive invariant.

Invariants are particularly useful when attempting to verify that a given transition system satisfies a *safety property*. There, we are given a set of bad states B, and seek to prove that none of these states is reachable. We can do so by showing that $\{q \in Q \mid I(q)\} \cap B = \emptyset$. Unfortunately, automatically discovering invariants for which the above holds is typically an undecidable problem [29]. Thus, a common approach is to restrict the search space—i.e., to only search for invariants with a certain syntactic form.

3   Reducing RNN Verification to FFNN Verification

3.1   Unrolling

To date, the only available general approach for verifying RNNs [1] is to transform the RNN in question into a *completely equivalent*, feed-forward network, using *unrolling*. An example appears in Fig. 3. The idea is to leverage $T_{\max}$, which is an upper bound on the number of times that the RNN will be evaluated. The RNN is duplicated $T_{\max}$ times, once for each time step in question, and its memory units are removed. Finally, the nodes in the i'th copy are used to fill the role of memory units for the $i + 1$'th copy of the network.

While unrolling gives a sound reduction from RNN verification to FFNN verification, it unfortunately tends to produce very large networks. When verifying a property that involves t time steps, an RNN network with n memory units will be transformed into an FFNN with $(t - 1) \cdot n$ new nodes. Because the FFNN verification problem becomes exponentially more difficult as the network size increases [18], this renders the problem infeasible for large values of t. As scalability is a major limitation of existing FFNN verification technology, unrolling can currently only be applied to small networks that are evaluated for a small number of time steps.

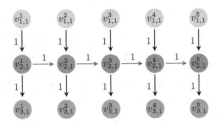

Fig. 3. Unrolling the network from Fig. 2, for $T_{max} = 5$ time steps. The edges in red fill the role of the memory units of the original RNN. The number of neurons in the unrolled network is 5 times the number of neurons in the original. (Color figure online)

3.2 Circumventing Unrolling

We propose a novel alternative to unrolling, which can reduce RNN verification to FFNN verification without the blowup in network size. The idea is to transform a verification query $\varphi = \langle P, N, Q, T_{max} \rangle$ over an RNN N into a different verification query $\hat{\varphi} = \langle \hat{P}, \hat{N}, \hat{Q} \rangle$ over an FFNN $\hat{N}$. $\hat{\varphi}$ is not equivalent to φ, but rather *over-approximates* it: it is constructed in a way that guarantees that if $\hat{\varphi}$ in UNSAT, then φ is also UNSAT. As is often the case, if $\hat{\varphi}$ is SAT, either the original property truly does not hold for N, or the over-approximation is too coarse and needs to be refined; we discuss this case later.

A key point in our approach is that $\hat{\varphi}$ is created in a way that captures the notion of time in the FFNN setting, and without increasing the network size. This is done by incorporating into $\hat{P}$ an *invariant* that puts bounds on the memory units as a function of the time step t. This invariant does not precisely compute the values of the memory units—instead, it bounds each of them in an interval. This inaccuracy is what makes $\hat{\varphi}$ an over-approximation of φ. More specifically, the construction is performed as follows:

1. $\hat{N}$ is constructed from N by adding a new input neuron, t, to represent time. In line with standard FFNN definitions, t is treated as a real number.
2. For every node v with memory unit $\tilde{v}$, in $\hat{N}$ we replace $\tilde{v}$ with a regular neuron, v^m, which is placed in the input layer. Neuron v^m will be connected to the network's original neurons with the original weights, just as $\tilde{v}$ was.[1]
3. We set $\hat{P} = P \wedge (1 \leq t \leq T_{max}) \wedge I$, where I is a formula that bounds the values of each new v^m node as a function of the time step t. The constraints in I constitute the invariant over the memory units' values.
4. The output property is unchanged: $\hat{Q} = Q$.

We name $\hat{\varphi}$ and $\hat{N}$ constructed in this way the *snapshot query* and the *snapshot network*, respectively, and denote $\hat{\varphi} = \mathcal{S}(\varphi)$ and $\hat{N} = \mathcal{S}(N)$. The intuition behind this construction is that query $\hat{\varphi}$ encodes a snapshot (an assignment of t)

---

[1] Note that we slightly abuse the definitions from Sect. 2, by allowing an input neuron to be connected to neurons in layers other than its preceding layer.

in which all constraints are satisfied. At this point in time, the v^m nodes represent the values stored in the memory units (whose assignments are bounded by the invariant I); and the input and output nodes represent the network's inputs and outputs at time t. Clearly, a satisfying assignment for $\hat{\varphi}$ does not necessarily indicate a counter-example for φ; e.g., because the values assigned to v^m might be impossible to obtain at time t in the original network. However, if $\hat{\varphi}$ is UNSAT then so is φ, because there does not exist a point in time in which the query might be satisfied. Note that the construction only increases the network size by 1 (the v^m neurons replace the memory units, and we add a single neuron t).

Time-Agnostic Properties. In the aforementioned construction of $\hat{\varphi}$, the original properties P and Q appear, either fully or as a conjunct, in the new properties $\hat{P}$ and $\hat{Q}$. It is not immediately clear that this is possible, as P and Q might also involve time. For example, if P is the formula $v_{1,2}^7 \geq 10$, it cannot be directly incorporated into $\hat{P}$, because $\hat{N}$ has no notion of time step 7.

For simplicity, we assume that P and Q are *time-agnostic*, i.e. are given in the following form: $P = \bigwedge_{t=1}^{T_{\max}} \psi_1$ and $Q = \bigvee_{t=1}^{T_{\max}} \psi_2$, where ψ_1 and ψ_2 contain linear constraints over the inputs and outputs of N, respectively, at time stamp t. This formulation can express queries in which the inputs are always in a certain interval, and a bound violation of the output nodes is sought. Our running example from Fig. 2 has this structure. When the properties are given in this form, we set $\hat{P} = \psi_1$ and $\hat{Q} = \psi_2$, with the t superscripts omitted for all neurons. This assumption can be relaxed significantly; see Sect. 8 of the appendix in the full version of the paper [17].

Example. We demonstrate our approach on the running example from Fig. 2. Recall that $P = \bigwedge_{t=1}^5 (-3 \leq v_{1,1}^t \leq 3)$, and $Q = \bigvee_{t=1}^5 (v_{3,1}^t \geq 16)$. First, we build the snapshot network $\hat{N}$ (Fig. 4) by replacing the memory unit $\tilde{v}_{2,1}$ with a regular neuron, $v_{2,1}^m$, which is connected to node $v_{2,1}$ with weight 1 (the same weight previously found on the edge from $\tilde{v}_{2,1}$ to $v_{2,1}$), and adding neuron t to represent time. Next, we set $\hat{P}$ to be the conjunction of (i) P, with its internal conjunc-

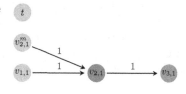

Fig. 4. The feed-forward snapshot network $\hat{N}$ for the RNN from Fig. 2.

tion and t superscripts omitted; (ii) the time constraint $1 \leq t \leq 5$; and (iii) the invariant that bounds the values of $v_{2,1}^m$ as a function of time: $v_{2,1}^m \leq 3(t-1)$. Our new verification query is thus:

$$\langle \underbrace{v_{1,1} \in [-3,3] \wedge t \in [1,5] \wedge (v_{2,1}^m \leq 3(t-1))}_{\hat{P}}, \hat{N}, \underbrace{v_{3,1} \geq 16}_{\hat{Q}} \rangle$$

This query is, of course, UNSAT, indicating that the original query is also UNSAT. Note that the new node t is added solely for the purpose of including it in constraints that appear in $\hat{P}$.

The requirement that I be an invariant over the memory units of N ensures that our approach is sound. Specifically, it guarantees that I allows any assignment for v^m that the original memory unit $\tilde{v}$ might be assigned. This is formulated in the following lemma (whose proof, by induction, is omitted):

Lemma 1. *Let $\varphi = \langle P, N, Q, T_{\max} \rangle$ be an RNN verification query, and let $\hat{\varphi} = \langle \hat{P}, \hat{N}, \hat{Q} \rangle$ be the snapshot query $\hat{\varphi} = \mathcal{S}(\varphi)$. Specifically, let $\hat{P} = P \wedge (1 \leq t \leq T_{\max}) \wedge I$, where I is an invariant that bounds the values of each v^m. If $\hat{\varphi}$ is UNSAT, then φ is also UNSAT.*

3.3 Constructing $\hat{\varphi}$: Verifying the Invariant

A key assumption in our reduction from RNN to FFNN verification was that we were supplied some invariant I, which bounds the values of the v^m neurons as a function of the time t. In this section we make our method more robust, by including a step that verifies that the supplied formula I is indeed an invariant. This step, too, is performed by creating an FFNN verification query, which can then be dispatched using the back-end FFNN verification engine. (We treat I simultaneously as a formula over the nodes of $\mathcal{S}(N)$ and those of N; the translation is performed by renaming every occurrence of v^m to $\tilde{v}^t$, or vice versa.)

First, we adjust the definitions of an inductive invariant (Sect. 2.3) to the RNN setting. The state space Q is comprised of states $q = \langle \mathcal{A}, t \rangle$, where $\mathcal{A}$ is the current assignment to the nodes of N (including the assignments of the memory units), and $t \in \mathbb{N}$ represents time step. For another state $q' = \langle \mathcal{A}', t' \rangle$, the transition relation $T(q, q')$ holds if and only if: (i) $t' = t + 1$; i.e., the time step has advanced by one; (ii) for each neuron v and its memory unit $\tilde{v}$ it holds that $\mathcal{A}'[\tilde{v}] = \mathcal{A}[v]$; i.e., the vanilla RNN update rule holds; and (iii) the assignment $\mathcal{A}'$ of all of the network's neurons constitutes a proper evaluation of the RNN according to Sect. 2; i.e., all weighted sums and activation functions are computed properly. A state q_0 is initial if $t = 1$, $\tilde{v} = 0$ for every memory unit, and the assignment of the network's neurons constitutes a proper evaluation of the RNN.

Next, let I be a formula over the memory units of N, and suppose we wish to verify that I is an invariant. Proving that I is in invariant amounts to proving that $I(q_0)$ holds for any initial state q_0, and that for every two states $q, q' \in Q$, $I(q) \wedge T(q, q') \rightarrow I(q')$. Checking whether $I(q_0)$ holds is trivial. The second check is more tricky; here, the key point is that because q and q' are consecutive states, the memory units of q' are simply the neurons of q. Thus, we can prove that I holds for q' by looking at the snapshot network, assuming that I holds initially, and proving that $I[v^m \mapsto v, t \mapsto t + 1]$, i.e. the invariant with each memory unit v^m renamed to its corresponding neuron v and the time step advanced by 1, also holds. The resulting verification query, which we term φ_I, can be verified using the underlying FFNN verification back-end.

We illustrate this process using the running example from Fig. 2. Let $I = v_{2,1}^m \leq 3(t-1)$. I holds at every initial state q_0; this is true because at time $t = 1$, $v_{2,1}^m = 0 \leq 3 \cdot 0$. Next, we assume that I holds for state $q = \langle \mathcal{A}, t \rangle$ and prove that it holds for $q = \langle \mathcal{A}', t+1 \rangle$. First, we create the snapshot FFNN $\hat{N}$, shown in Fig. 4. We then extend the original input property $P = \bigwedge_{t=1}^{5}(-3 \leq v_{1,1}^{t} \leq 3)$ into a property P' that also captures our assumption that the invariant holds at time t: $P' = (-3 \leq v_{1,1} \leq 3) \wedge (v_{2,1}^{m} \leq 3(t-1))$. Finally, we prepare an output property Q' that asserts that the invariant does not hold for $v_{2,1}$ at time $t+1$, by renaming $v_{2,1}^{m}$ to $v_{2,1}$ and incrementing t: $Q' = \neg(v_{2,1} \leq 3(t+1-1))$. When the FFNN verification engine answers that $\varphi_I = \langle P', \mathcal{S}(N), Q' \rangle$ is UNSAT, we conclude that I is indeed an invariant. In cases where the query turns out to be SAT, I is not an invariant, and needs to be refined.

Given a formula I, the steps described so far allow us to reduce RNN verification to FFNN verification, in a completely sound and automated way. Next we discuss how to automate the generation of I, as well.

4   Invariant Inference

4.1   Single Memory Units

In general, automatic invariant inference is undecidable [29]; thus, we employ here a heuristic approach, that uses *linear templates*. We first describe the approach on a simple case, in which the network has a single hidden node v with a memory unit, and then relax this limitation. Note that the running example depicted in Fig. 2 fits this case. Here, inferring an invariant according to a linear template means finding values α_l and α_u, such that $\alpha_l \cdot (t-1) \leq \tilde{v}^t \leq \alpha_u \cdot (t-1)$. The value of $\tilde{v}^t$ is thus bounded from below and from above as a function of time. In our template we use $(t-1)$, and not t, in order to account for the fact that $\tilde{v}^t$ contains the value that node v was assigned at time $t-1$. For simplicity, we focus only on finding the upper bound; the lower bound case is symmetrical. We have already seen such an upper bound for our running example, which was sufficiently strong for proving the desired property: $\tilde{v}_{2,1}^t \leq 3(t-1)$.

Once candidate α's are proposed, verifying that the invariant holds is performed using the techniques outlined in Sect. 3. There are two places where the process might fail: (i) the proposed invariant cannot be proved (φ_I is SAT), because a counter-example exists. This means that our invariant is *too strong*, i.e. the bound is too tight. In this case we can weaken the invariant by increasing α_u; or (ii) the proposed invariant holds, but the FFNN verification problem that it leads to, $\hat{\varphi}$, is SAT. In this case, the invariant is *too weak*: it does not imply the desired output property. We can strengthen the invariant by decreasing α_u.

This search problem leads us to binary search strategy, described in Algorithm 1. The search stops, i.e. an optimal invariant is found, when $ub - lb \leq \epsilon$ for a small constant ϵ. The algorithm fails if the optimal linear invariant is found, but is insufficient for proving the property in question; this can happen if φ is indeed SAT, or if a more sophisticated invariant is required.

Discussion: Linear Templates. Automated invariant inference has been studied extensively in program analysis (see Sect. 6). In particular, elaborate templates have been proposed, which are more expressive than the linear template

Algorithm 1. Automatic Single Memory Unit Verification$(P, N, Q, T_{\max})$

1: $lb \leftarrow -M, \; ub \leftarrow M$ ▷ M is a large constant
2: **while** $ub - lb \geq \epsilon$ **do**
3:     $\alpha_u \leftarrow \frac{ub+lb}{2}, \quad I \leftarrow v_{2,1}^m \leq \alpha_u \cdot (t-1)$
4:     **if** φ_I is UNSAT **then**
5:         Construct $\hat{\varphi}$ using invariant I
6:         **if** $\hat{\varphi}$ is UNSAT **then**
7:             **return** True
8:         $ub \leftarrow \alpha_u$ ▷ Invariant too weak
9:     **else**
10:        $lb \leftarrow \alpha_u$ ▷ Invariant too strong
11: **return** False

that we use. The approach we presented in Sect. 3 is general, and is compatible with many of these templates. Our main motivation for focusing on linear templates is that most FFNN verification tools readily support linear constraints, and can thus verify the φ_I queries that originate from linear invariants. As we demonstrate in Sect. 5, despite their limited expressiveness, linear invariants are already sufficient for solving many verification queries. Extending the technique to work with more expressive invariants is part of our ongoing work.

Multiple Memory Units in Separate Layers. Our approach can be extended to RNNs with multiple memory units, each in a separate layer, in an iterative fashion: an invariant is proved separately for each layer, by using the already-proved invariants of the previous layers. As before, we begin by constructing the snapshot network in which all memory units are replaced by regular neurons. Next, we work layer by layer and generate invariants that over-approximate each memory unit, by leveraging the invariants established for memory units in the previous layers. Eventually, all memory units are over-approximated using invariants, and we can attempt to prove the desired property by solving the snapshot query. An example and the general algorithm for this case appears in Sect. 9 of the appendix in the full version of the paper [17].

4.2 Layers with Multiple Memory Units

We now extend our approach to support the most general case: an RNN with layers that contain multiple memory units. We again apply an iterative, layer-by-layer approach. The main difficulty is in inferring invariants for a layer that has multiple memory units, as in Fig. 5: while each memory unit belongs to a single neuron, it affects the assignments of all other neurons in that layer. We propose to handle

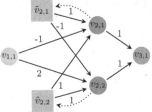

Fig. 5. An RNN where both memory units affect both neurons of the hidden layer: $v_{2,1}^t = \text{ReLU}(\tilde{v}_{2,1}^t + \tilde{v}_{2,2}^t - v_{1,1}^t)$; and $v_{2,2}^t = \text{ReLU}(-\tilde{v}_{2,1}^t + \tilde{v}_{2,2}^t + 2v_{1,1}^t)$.

this case using separate linear invariants for upper- and lower-bounding each of the memory units. However, while the invariants have the same linear form as in the single memory unit case, *proving* them requires taking the other invariants of the same layer into account. Consider the example in Fig. 5, and suppose we have α_l^1, α_u^1 and α_l^2, α_u^2 for which we wish to verify that

$$\alpha_l^1 \cdot (t-1) \leq \tilde{v}_{2,1}^t \leq \alpha_u^1 \cdot (t-1) \qquad\qquad \alpha_l^2 \cdot (t-1) \leq \tilde{v}_{2,2}^t \leq \alpha_u^2 \cdot (t-1) \quad (1)$$

In order to prove these bounds we need to dispatch an FFNN verification query that assumes Eq. 1 holds and uses it to prove the inductive step:

$$\tilde{v}_{2,1}^{t+1} = v_{2,1}^t = \mathrm{ReLU}(-\tilde{v}_{1,1}^t + \tilde{v}_{2,1}^t + \tilde{v}_{2,2}^t) \leq \alpha_u^1 \cdot (t+1-1) \qquad (2)$$

Similar steps must be performed for $\tilde{v}_{2,1}^{t+1}$'s lower bound, and also for $\tilde{v}_{2,2}^{t+1}$'s lower and upper bounds. The key point is that because Eq. 2 involves $\tilde{v}_{2,1}^t$ and $\tilde{v}_{2,2}^t$, multiple α terms from Eq. 1 may need to be used in proving it. This interdependency means that later changes to some α value might invalidate previously acceptable assignments for other α values. This adds a layer of complexity that did not exist in the cases that we had considered previously.

For example, consider the network in Fig. 5, with $P = \bigwedge_{t=1}^3 -3 \leq v_{1,1}^t \leq 3$, and $Q = \bigvee_{t=1}^3 v_{3,1}^t \geq 100$. Our goal is to find values for α_l^1, α_u^1 and α_l^2, α_u^2 that will satisfy Eq. 1. Let us consider $\alpha_l^1 = 0, \alpha_u^1 = 8, \alpha_l^2 = 0$ and $\alpha_u^2 = 0$. Using these values, the induction hypothesis (Eq. 1) and the bounds for $v_{1,1}$, we can indeed prove the upper bound for $\tilde{v}_{2,1}^{t+1}$:

$$\tilde{v}_{2,1}^{t+1} = v_{2,1}^t = \mathrm{ReLU}(-\tilde{v}_{1,1}^t + \tilde{v}_{2,1}^t + \tilde{v}_{2,2}^t) \leq \mathrm{ReLU}(3 + 8(t-1) + 0) \leq 8t$$

Unfortunately, the bounds $0 \leq \tilde{v}_{2,2}^t \leq 0$ are inadequate, because $\tilde{v}_{2,2}^t$ can take on positive values. We are thus required to adjust the α values, for example by increasing α_u^2 to 2. However, this change invalidates the upper bound for $\tilde{v}_{2,1}^{t+1}$, i.e. $\tilde{v}_{2,1}^{t+1} \leq 8t$, as that bound relied on the upper bound for $\tilde{v}_{2,2}^t$; Specifically, knowing only that $1 \leq t \leq 3, -3 \leq v_{1,1}^t \leq 3, 0 \leq \tilde{v}_{2,1}^t \leq 8(t-1)$ and $0 \leq \tilde{v}_{2,2}^t \leq 2(t-1)$, it is impossible to show that $\tilde{v}_{2,1}^{t+1} = v_{2,1}^t \leq 8t$.

The example above demonstrates the intricate dependencies between the α values, and the complexity that these dependencies add to the search process. Unlike in the single memory unit case, it is not immediately clear how to find an initial invariant that simultaneously holds for all memory units, or how to strengthen this invariant (e.g., which α constant to try and improve).

Finding an Initial Invariant. We propose to encode the problem of finding initial α values as a *mixed integer linear program* (MILP). The linear and piecewise-linear constraints that the α values must satisfy (e.g., Eq. 2) can be precisely encoded in MILP using standard big-M encoding [18]. There are two main advantages to using MILP here: (i) an MILP solver is guaranteed to return a valid invariant, or soundly report that no such invariant exists; and (ii) MILP instances include a *cost function* to be minimized, which can be used to optimize the invariant. For example, by setting the cost function to be $\sum \alpha_u - \sum \alpha_l$, the MILP solver will typically generate tight upper and lower bounds.

The main disadvantage to using MILP is that, in order to ensure that the invariants hold for all time steps $1 \leq t \leq T_{\max}$, we must encode all of these steps in the MILP query. For example, going back to Eq. 2, in order to guarantee that $v_{2,1}^{t+1} = \text{ReLU}(-v_{1,1}^t + v_{2,1}^t + v_{2,2}^t) \leq \alpha_u^1 \cdot t$, we would need to encode within our MILP instance the fact that $\bigwedge_{t=1}^{T_{\max}} \left(\text{ReLU}(-v_{1,1}^t + v_{2,1}^t + v_{2,2}^t) \leq \alpha_u^1 \cdot t \right)$. This might render the MILP instance difficult to solve for large values of $T_{\max}$. However, we stress that this approach is quite different from, and significantly easier than, unrolling the RNN. The main reason is that these MILP instances are each generated for a single layer (as opposed to the entire network in unrolling), which renders them much simpler. Indeed, in our experiments (Sect. 5), solving these MILP instances was never the bottleneck. Still, should this become a problem, we propose to encode only a subset of the values of $t \in \{1, \ldots, T_{\max}\}$, making the problem easier to solve; and should the α assignment fail to produce an invariant (this will be discovered when φ_I is verified), additional constraints could be added to guide the MILP solver towards a correct solution. We also describe an alternative approach, which does not require the use of an MILP solver, in Sect. 10 of the appendix in the full version of the paper [17].

Strengthening the Invariant. If we are unable to prove that $\hat{\varphi}$ is UNSAT for a given I, then the invariant needs to be strengthened. We propose to achieve this by invoking the MILP solver again, this time adding new linear constraints for each α, that will force the selection of tighter bounds. For example, if the current invariant is $\alpha_l = 3, \alpha_u = 7$, we add constraints specifying that $\alpha_l \geq 3 + \epsilon$ and $\alpha_u \leq 7 - \epsilon$ for some small positive ϵ—leading to stronger invariants.

5   Evaluation

Our proof-of-concept implementation of the approach, called *RnnVerify*, reads an RNN in TensorFlow format. The input and output properties, P and Q, and also $T_{\max}$, are supplied in a simple proprietary format, and the tool then automatically: (i) creates the FFNN snapshot network; (ii) infers a candidate invariant using the MILP heuristics from Sect. 4; (iii) formally verifies that I is an invariant; and (iv) uses I to show that $\hat{\varphi}$, and hence φ, are UNSAT. If $\hat{\varphi}$ is SAT, our module refines I and repeats the process for a predefined number of steps.

For our evaluation, we focused on neural networks for *speaker recognition*—a task for which RNNs are commonly used, because audio signals tend to have temporal properties and varying lengths. We applied our verification technique to prove *adversarial robustness* properties of these networks, as we describe next.

Adversarial Robustness. It has been shown that alarmingly many neural networks are susceptible to *adversarial inputs* [32]. These inputs are generated by slightly perturbing correctly-classified inputs, in a way that causes the misclassification of the perturbed inputs. Formally, given a network N that classifies inputs into labels $l_1, \ldots, l_k$, an input x_0, and a target label $l \neq N(x_0)$, an adversarial input is an input x such that $N(x) = l$ and $\|x - x_0\| \leq \delta$; i.e., input x is very close to x_0, but is misclassified as label l.

Adversarial robustness is a measure of how difficult it is to find an adversarial example—and specifically, what is the smallest δ for which such an example exists. Verification can be used to find adversarial inputs or rule out their existence for a given δ, and consequently can find the smallest δ for which an adversarial input exists [3].

Speaker Recognition. A speaker recognition system receives a voice sample and needs to identify the speaker from a set of candidates. RNNs are often applied in implementing such systems [34], rendering them vulnerable to adversarial inputs [23]. Because such vulnerabilities in these systems pose a security concern, it is important to verify that their underlying RNNs afford high adversarial robustness.

Benchmarks. We trained 6 speaker recognition RNNs, based on the VCTK dataset [37]. Our networks are of modest, varying sizes of approximately 220 neurons: they each contain an input layer of dimension 40, one or two hidden layers with $d \in \{2, 4, 8\}$ memory units, followed by 5 fully connected, memoryless layers with 32 nodes each, and an output layer with 20 nodes. The output nodes represent the possible speakers between which the RNNs were trained to distinguish. In addition, in order to enable a comparison to the state of the art [1], we trained another, smaller network, which consists of a single hidden layer. This was required to accommodate technical constraints in the implementation of [1]. All networks use ReLUs as their activation functions.

Next, we selected 25 random, fixed input points $X = \{x_1, \ldots, x_{25}\}$, that do not change over time; i.e. $x_i \in \mathbb{R}^{40}$ and $x_i^1 = x_i^2 = \ldots$ for each $x_i \in X$. Then, for each RNN N and input $x_i \in X$, and for each value $2 \leq T_{\max} \leq 20$, we computed the ground-truth label $l = N(x_i)$, which is the label that received the highest score at time step $T_{\max}$. We also computed the label that received the second-highest score, l_{sh}, at time step $T_{\max}$. Then, for every combination of N, $x_i \in X$, and value of $T_{\max}$, we created the query $\langle \bigwedge_{t=1}^{T_{\max}} (\|x'^t - x_i^t\|_{L_\infty} \leq 0.01), N, l_{sh} \geq l \rangle$. The allowed perturbation, at most 0.01 in L_∞ norm, was selected arbitrarily. The query is only SAT if there exists an input x' that is at distance at most 0.01 from x, but for which label l_{sh} is assigned a higher score than l at time step $T_{\max}$. This formulation resulted in a total of 2850 benchmark queries over our 6 networks.

Results. We began by comparing our technique to the state-of-the-art, unrolling-based RNSVerify tool [1], using the small network we had trained. Each dot in Fig. 6 represents a tool's average run time on the 25 input points, for a specific $T_{\max}$. Both methods returned UNSAT on all queries; however, the runtimes clearly demonstrate that our approach is far less sensitive to large $T_{\max}$ values. In a separate experiment, our tool was able to solve a verification query on the same network with $T_{\max} = 180$ in 2.5 s, whereas RNSVerify timed out after 24 h.

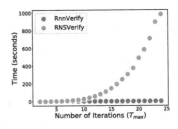

Fig. 6. Average running time (in seconds) of RnnVerify and RNSVerify, as a function of $T_{\max}$.

Next, we used RnnVerify on all 2850 benchmark queries on the 6 larger networks. The results appear in Sect. 11 of the appendix in the full version of the paper [17], and are summarized as follows: (i) RnnVerify terminated on all benchmarks, with a median runtime of 5.39 s and an average runtime of 48.67 s. The maximal solving time was 5701 s; (ii) 85% of RnnVerify's runtime was spent within the underlying FFNN verification engine, solving φ_I queries. This indicates that as the underlying FFNN verification technology improves, our approach will become significantly more scalable; (iii) for 1919 (67%) of the benchmarks, RnnVerify proved that the RNN was robust around the tested point. For the remaining 931 benchmarks, the results are inconclusive: we do not know whether the network is vulnerable, or whether more sophisticated invariants are needed to prove robustness. This demonstrates that for a majority of tested benchmarks, the linear template proved useful; and (iv) RnnVerify could generally prove fewer instances with larger values of $T_{\max}$. This is because the linear bounds afforded by our invariants become more loose as t increases, whereas the neuron's values typically do not increase significantly over time. This highlights the need for more expressive invariants.

6   Related Work

Due to the discovery of undesirable behaviors in many DNNs, multiple approaches have been proposed for verifying them. These include the use of SMT solving [15,18,20,24], LP and MILP solving [8,33], symbolic interval propagation [35], abstract interpretation [9,10], and many others (e.g., [2,11,14,21, 26,27]). Our technique focuses on RNN verification, but uses an FFNN verification engine as a back-end. Consequently, it could be integrated with many of the aforementioned tools, and will benefit from any improvement in scalability of FFNN verification technology.

Whereas FFNN verification has received a great deal of attention, only little research has been carried out on RNN verification. Akintunde et al. [1] were the first to propose such a technique, based on the notion of unrolling the network into an equivalent FFNN. Ko et al. [22] take a different approach, which aims at quantifying the robustness of an RNN to adversarial inputs—which can be regarded as an RNN verification technique tailored for a particular kind of properties. The scalability of both approaches is highly sensitive to the number of time steps, T_{max}, specified by the property at hand. In this regard, the main advantage of our approach is that it is far less sensitive to the number of time steps being considered. This affords great potential for scalability, especially for long sequences of inputs. A drawback of our approach is that it requires invariant inference, which is known to be challenging.

In a very recent paper, Zhang et al. [38] propose a verification scheme aimed at RNNs that perform cognitive tasks. This scheme includes computing polytope invariants for the neuron layers of an RNN, using abstract interpretation and fixed-point analysis. We consider this as additional evidence of the usefulness of invariant generation in the context of RNN verification.

Automated invariant inference is a key problem in program analysis. A few notable methods for doing so include abstract-interpretation (e.g., [30]); counterexample-guided approaches (e.g., [28]); and learning-based approaches (e.g., [31]). It will be interesting to apply these techniques within the context of our framework, in order to more quickly and effectively discover useful invariants.

7   Conclusion

Neural network verification is becoming increasingly important to industry, regulators, and society as a whole. Research to date has focused primarily on FFNNs. We propose a novel approach for the verification of recurrent neural networks—a kind of neural networks that is particularly useful for context-dependent tasks, such as NLP. The cornerstone of our approach is the reduction of RNN verification to FFNN verification through the use of inductive invariants. Using a proof-of-concept implementation, we demonstrated that our approach can tackle many benchmarks orders-of-magnitude more efficiently than the state of the art. These experiments indicate the great potential that our approach holds. In the future, we plan to experiment with more expressive invariants, and also to apply *compositional verification* techniques in order to break the RNN into multiple, smaller networks, for which invariants can more easily be inferred.

Acknowledgements. This work was partially supported by the Semiconductor Research Corporation, the Binational Science Foundation (2017662), the Israel Science Foundation (683/18), and the National Science Foundation (1814369).

References

1. Akintunde, M., Kevorchian, A., Lomuscio, A., Pirovano, E.: Verification of RNN-based neural agent-environment systems. In: Proceedings 33rd Conference on Artificial Intelligence (AAAI), pp. 6006–6013 (2019)

2. Bunel, R., Turkaslan, I., Torr, P., Kohli, P., Mudigonda, P.: A unified view of piecewise linear neural network verification. In: Proceedings of the 32nd Conference on Neural Information Processing Systems (NeurIPS), pp. 4795–4804 (2018)

3. Carlini, N., Katz, G., Barrett, C., Dill, D.: Provably Minimally-Distorted Adversarial Examples, 2017. Technical report. https://arxiv.org/abs/1709.10207

4. Cheng, C.-H., Nührenberg, G., Huang, C.-H., Ruess, H.: Verification of binarized neural networks via inter-neuron factoring. In: Proceeding of the 10th Working Conference on Verified Software: Theories, Tools, and Experiments (VSTTE), pp. 279–290 (2018)

5. Cheng, C.-H., Nührenberg, G., Ruess, H.: Maximum resilience of artificial neural networks. In: D'Souza, D., Narayan Kumar, K. (eds.) ATVA 2017. LNCS, vol. 10482, pp. 251–268. Springer, Cham (2017). https://doi.org/10.1007/978-3-319-68167-2_18

6. Cisse, M., Adi, Y., Neverova, N., Keshet, J.: Houdini: fooling deep structured visual and speech recognition models with adversarial examples. In: Proceedings of the 30th Advances in Neural Information Processing Systems (NIPS), pp. 6977–6987 (2017)

7. Devlin, J., Chang, M., Lee, K., Toutanova, K.: BERT: pre-training of deep bidirectional transformers for language understanding, 2018. Technical report. http://arxiv.org/abs/1810.04805

8. Ehlers, R.: Formal verification of piece-wise linear feed-forward neural networks. In: D'Souza, D., Narayan Kumar, K. (eds.) ATVA 2017. LNCS, vol. 10482, pp. 269–286. Springer, Cham (2017). https://doi.org/10.1007/978-3-319-68167-2_19

9. Elboher, Y.Y., Gottschlich, J., Katz, G.: An abstraction-based framework for neural network verification. In: Lahiri, S.K., Wang, C. (eds.) CAV 2020. LNCS, vol. 12224, pp. 43–65. Springer, Cham (2020). https://doi.org/10.1007/978-3-030-53288-8_3

10. Gehr, T., Mirman, M., Drachsler-Cohen, D., Tsankov, E., Chaudhuri, S., Vechev, M.: AI2: safety and robustness certification of neural networks with abstract interpretation. In: Proceedings of the 39th IEEE Symposium on Security and Privacy (S&P) (2018)

11. Gokulanathan, S., Feldsher, A., Malca, A., Barrett, C., Katz, G.: Simplifying neural networks using formal verification. In: Proceedings of the 12th NASA Formal Methods Symposium (NFM) (2020)

12. Goldberger, B., Adi, Y., Keshet, J., Katz, G.: Minimal modifications of deep neural networks using verification. In: Proceedings of the 23rd International Conference on Logic for Programming, Artificial Intelligence and Reasoning (LPAR), pp. 260–278 (2020)

13. Goodfellow, I., Bengio, Y., Courville, A.: Deep Learning. MIT Press, Cambridge (2016)

14. Gopinath, D., Katz, G., Păsăreanu, C., Barrett, C.: DeepSafe: a data-driven approach for assessing robustness of neural networks. In: Proceedings 16th International Symposium on on Automated Technology for Verification and Analysis (ATVA), pp. 3–19 (2018)

15. Huang, X., Kwiatkowska, M., Wang, S., Wu, M.: Safety verification of deep neural networks. In: Majumdar, R., Kunčak, V. (eds.) CAV 2017. LNCS, vol. 10426, pp. 3–29. Springer, Cham (2017). https://doi.org/10.1007/978-3-319-63387-9_1

16. Jacoby, Y., Barrett, C., Katz, G.: RnnVerify (2020). https://github.com/yuvaljacoby/RnnVerify

17. Jacoby, Y., Barrett, C., Katz, G.: Verifying recurrent neural networks using invariant inference (Full Version) (2020). Technical report. https://arxiv.org/abs/2004.02462

18. Katz, G., Barrett, C., Dill, D.L., Julian, K., Kochenderfer, M.J.: Reluplex: an efficient SMT solver for verifying deep neural networks. In: Majumdar, R., Kunčak, V. (eds.) CAV 2017. LNCS, vol. 10426, pp. 97–117. Springer, Cham (2017). https://doi.org/10.1007/978-3-319-63387-9_5

19. Katz, G., Barrett, C., Dill, D., Julian, K., Kochenderfer, M.: Towards proving the adversarial robustness of deep neural networks. In: Proceedings of the 1st Workshop on Formal Verification of Autonomous Vehicles, (FVAV), pp. 19–26 (2017)

20. Katz, G., et al.: The Marabou framework for verification and analysis of deep neural networks. In: Dillig, I., Tasiran, S. (eds.) CAV 2019. LNCS, vol. 11561, pp. 443–452. Springer, Cham (2019). https://doi.org/10.1007/978-3-030-25540-4_26

21. Kazak, Y., Barrett, C., Katz, G., Schapira, M.: Verifying Deep-RL-Driven systems. In: Proceedings of the 1st ACM SIGCOMM Workshop on Network Meets AI & ML (NetAI), pp. 83–89 (2019)

22. Ko, C., Lyu, Z., Weng, T., Daniel, L., Wong, N., Lin, D.: POPQORN: quantifying robustness of recurrent neural networks. In: Proceedings of the 36th IEEE International Conference on Machine Learning and Applications (ICML) (2019)

23. Kreuk, F., Adi, Y., Cisse, M., Keshet, J.: Fooling end-to-end speaker verification with adversarial examples. In: Proceedings of the IEEE International Conference on Acoustics, Speech and Signal Processing (ICASSP), pp. 1962–1966 (2018)

24. Kuper, L., Katz, G., Gottschlich, J., Julian, K., Barrett, C., Kochenderfer, M.: Toward scalable verification for safety-critical deep networks. Technical report (2018). https://arxiv.org/abs/1801.05950

25. Lipton, Z., Kale, D., Elkan, C., Wetzel, R.: Learning to diagnose with LSTM recurrent neural networks. In: Proceedings of the 4th International Conference on Learning Representations (ICLR) (2016)

26. Lomuscio, A., Maganti, L.: An approach to reachability analysis for feed-forward ReLU neural networks. Technical report (2017). http://arxiv.org/abs/1706.07351

27. Narodytska, N., Kasiviswanathan, S., Ryzhyk, L., Sagiv, M., Walsh, T.: Verifying Properties of Binarized Deep Neural Networks. Technical report (2017). http://arxiv.org/abs/1709.06662

28. Nguyen, T., Antonopoulos, T., Ruef, A., Hicks, M.:Counterexample-guided approach to finding numerical invariants. In: Proceedings of the 11th Joint Meeting on Foundations of Software Engineering (FSE), pp. 605–615 (2017)

29. Padon, O., Immerman, N., Shoham, S., Karbyshev, A., Sagiv, M.: Decidability of inferring inductive invariants. In: Proceedings of the 43th Symposium on Principles of Programming Languages (POPL), pp. 217–231 (2016)

30. Sharma, R., Dillig, I., Dillig, T., Aiken, A.: Simplifying loop invariant generation using splitter predicates. In: Gopalakrishnan, G., Qadeer, S. (eds.) CAV 2011. LNCS, vol. 6806, pp. 703–719. Springer, Heidelberg (2011). https://doi.org/10.1007/978-3-642-22110-1_57

31. Si, X., Dai, H., Raghothaman, M., Naik, M., Song, L.: Learning loop invariants for program verification. In: Proceedings of the 32nd Conference on Neural Information Processing Systems (NeurIPS), pp. 7762–7773 (2018)

32. Szegedy, C., et al.: Intriguing Properties of Neural Networks. Technical report (2013). http://arxiv.org/abs/1312.6199

33. Tjeng, V., Xiao, K., Tedrake, R.: Evaluating robustness of neural networks with mixed integer programming. In: Proceedings of the 7th International Conference on Learning Representations (ICLR) (2019)

34. Wan, L., Wang, Q., Papir, A., Lopez-Moreno, I.: Generalized end-to-end loss for speaker verification. Technical report (2017). http://arxiv.org/abs/1710.10467
35. Wang, S., Pei, K., Whitehouse, J., Yang, J., Jana, S.: Formal security analysis of neural networks using symbolic intervals. In: Proceedings of the 27th USENIX Security Symposium, pp. 1599–1614 (2018)
36. Wu, H., et al.: Parallelization techniques for verifying neural networks. Technical report (2020). https://arxiv.org/abs/2004.08440
37. Yamagishi, J., Veaux, C., MacDonald, K.: CSTR VCTK corpus: English multi-speaker corpus for CSTR voice cloning toolkit. University of Edinburgh (2019). https://doi.org/10.7488/ds/2645
38. Zhang, H., Shinn, M., Gupta, A., Gurfinkel, A., Le, N., Narodytska, N.: Verification of recurrent neural networks for cognitive tasks via reachability analysis. In: Proceedings of the 24th Conference of European Conference on Artificial Intelligence (ECAI) (2020)

NeuralExplorer: State Space Exploration of Closed Loop Control Systems Using Neural Networks

Manish Goyal$^{(\boxtimes)}$ and Parasara Sridhar Duggirala

Department of Computer Science, University of North Carolina at Chapel Hill,
Chapel Hill, USA
{manishg,psd}@cs.unc.edu

Abstract. In this paper, we propose a framework for performing state space exploration of closed loop control systems. Our approach involves approximating sensitivity and a newly introduced notion of inverse sensitivity by a neural network. We show how the approximation of sensitivity and inverse sensitivity can be used for computing estimates of the reachable set. We then outline algorithms for performing state space exploration by generating trajectories that reach a neighborhood. We demonstrate the effectiveness of our approach by applying it not only to standard linear and nonlinear dynamical systems, but also to nonlinear hybrid systems and also neural network based feedback control systems.

Keywords: State space exploration · Sensitivity · Inverse Sensitivity · Neural Networks · Testing · Approximation · Falsification

1 Introduction

Advances in hardware and software have made it easier to integrate sophisticated control algorithms in embedded devices. While such control algorithms might improve the performance of the system, they make the task of verification and validation very challenging. In a typical work flow, after deploying the control algorithm, the control designer generates a few test cases and checks if the specification is satisfied. Given that the state space is continuous and the dynamics are often nonlinear, finding the trajectory that violates the specification is similar to searching for a needle in a haystack. For example, consider a regulation application where the output of the control system is required to eventually converge to a set point s within the error threshold of δ. Therefore, the output should remain in the interval $[s - \delta, s + \delta]$ after a specified settling time. The control designer would first test the control algorithm by generating a test suite. If all of the executions in the test suite satisfy the specification, the control designer would like to generate test cases that are close to violating the specification. Given the nonlinearity of the dynamics, the control designer does not have a method to generate the next test input that results in a higher value of error than observed in the test suite.

In some instances, the designer can encode the property as a temporal logic formula and use off-the-shelf falsification tools for generating a trajectory that violates

© Springer Nature Switzerland AG 2020
D. V. Hung and O. Sokolsky (Eds.): ATVA 2020, LNCS 12302, pp. 75–91, 2020.
https://doi.org/10.1007/978-3-030-59152-6_4

the specification. Such an approach has a few drawbacks. First, falsification tools are geared towards finding a trajectory that violates the given specification, not necessarily to help the control designer in state space exploration. Second, if the specification (error threshold δ or the settling time) is changed, the results from the falsification analysis are no longer useful. Finally, the falsification tools require the specification to be provided in a temporal logic such as signal temporal logic or metric temporal logic. While such specification might be useful in the verification and deployment phase, they are a hindrance during the design and exploration phase. Currently there are no tools that aid control designer in performing systematic testing of closed loop control systems.

In this paper, we present *NeuralExplorer*, a technique for performing state space exploration of closed loop control systems using neural networks. NeuralExplorer can supplement the testing procedure by helping the designer generate test cases that reach a target or a neighborhood. The artifact that helps us in this endeavor is *sensitivity*. Informally, sensitivity of a closed loop system is the change in the trajectory of the system as a result of perturbing the initial condition. The backward time notion of sensitivity is called *inverse sensitivity*. Given a sample set of trajectories, we train a neural network to approximate the sensitivity and inverse sensitivity functions. These neural networks are then used to generate a trajectory (or trajectories) that reaches a destination (or a neighborhood around it).

Our framework has three primary advantages. First, since NeuralExplorer relies only on the sample test cases, it does not require a model of the system and can be applied to a black-box systems. Second, since sensitivity is a fundamental property of the closed loop system, approximating it using a neural network is generalizable to trajectories that are beyond the test cases generated by the control designer. Third, a control designer can develop intuition about the convergence and divergence of trajectories by querying the neural network. In evaluating our framework, we were not only able to perform state space exploration for standard linear and nonlinear dynamical systems, but also for nonlinear hybrid systems and neural network based feedback control systems. We believe that NeuralExplorer is useful for generating corner cases and supplements some of the existing testing and reachable set computation procedures.

2   Related Work

Reachability analysis is often employed for proving the safety specification of safety critical control system [4, 11]. Some of the recent works in this domain are SpaceEx [22], Flow* [9], CORA [3] and HyLAA [7]. These techniques use a symbolic representation for the reachable set of states. While these are useful for proving that the safety specification is satisfied, generating counterexamples using reachability analysis is still an area of research [24].

For generating trajectories that violate a given safety specification, falsification techniques are widely applied [15, 19]. In these techniques, the required specification is specified in a temporal logic such as Metric Temporal Logic (MTL) [31] or Signal Temporal Logic (STL) [32, 35]. Given a specification, falsification techniques generate several sample trajectories and use various heuristics [2, 12, 23, 38, 43, 48] for generating trajectories that violate the specification. Prominent tools in this domain include S-Taliro [5] and Breach [13].

Bridging falsification and reachability are simulation driven verification methods [14, 16, 20, 28]. These methods compute an upper bound on the sensitivity of the trajectories and compute an overapproximation of the reachable set using sample trajectories. While these techniques bridge the gap between falsification and verification, they suffer from curse of dimensionality. That is, the number of trajectories generated might increase exponentially with the dimensions. C2E2 [17], and DryVR [21] are some of the well known tools in this domain.

Given the rich history of application of neural networks in control [33, 36, 37] and the recent advances in software and hardware platforms, neural networks are now being deployed in various control tasks. As a result, many verification techniques are now being developed for neural network based control systems [18, 30, 44, 47]. Additionally, techniques for verification of neural networks deployed in other domains have been proposed [27, 45, 46].

In this paper, we use neural networks to approximate an underlying property of sensitivity and inverse sensitivity. We believe that this is a valid approach because recently, many neural network based frameworks for learning the dynamics or their properties have been proposed [8, 34, 39–42].

3   Preliminaries

We denote the elements of the state space as x to be elements in $\mathbb{R}^n$. Vectors are denoted as v. We denote the dynamics of the plant as

$$\dot{x} = f(x, u) \tag{1}$$

Where x is the state space of the system that evolves in $\mathbb{R}^n$ and u is the input space in $\mathbb{R}^m$.

Definition 1 (Unique Trajectory Feedback Functions). *A feedback function* $u = g(x)$ *is said to be unique trajectory feedback function if the closed loop system* $\dot{x} = f(x, g(x))$ *is guaranteed existence and uniqueness of the solution for the initial value problem for all initial points* $x_0 \in \mathbb{R}^n$.

Notice that for a feedback function to give a unique trajectory feedback, it need not be differentiable. From the sufficient conditions of ODE solutions, it is sufficient if $g(x)$ is continuous and is lipschitz.

Definition 2 (Trajectories of Closed Loop System). *Given a unique trajectory feedback function* $u = g(x)$, *a trajectory of closed loop system* $\dot{x} = f(x, g(x))$, *denoted as* $\xi_g(x_0, t)$ $(t \geq 0)$, *is the solution of the initial value problem of the differential equation* $\dot{x} = f(x, g(x))$ *with initial condition* x_0. *We often drop the feedback function* g *when it is clear from the context.*

We extend the notion of trajectory to include backward time trajectories as well. Given $t > 0$, *the backward time trajectory* $\xi_g(x_0, -t) = x$ *such that* $\xi_g(x, t) = x_0$. *We denote backward time trajectory as* $\xi^{-1}(x_0, t)$.

Given $x_0, x_1 \in \mathbb{R}^n$ and $t > 0$ such that $\xi(x_0, t) = x_1$, then $\xi^{-1}(x_1, t) = x_0$. It is trivial to observe that $\xi^{-1}(\xi(x_0, t), t) = x_0$.

Definition 3 (Sensitivity of Trajectories). *Given an initial state x_0, vector v, and time t, the sensitivity of the trajectories, denoted as $\Phi(x_0, v, t)$ is defined as.*

$$\Phi(x_0, v, t) = \xi(x_0 + v, t) - \xi(x_0, t).$$

Informally, sensitivity is the vector difference between the trajectories starting from x_0 and $x_0 + v$ after time t. We extend the definition of sensitivity to backward time trajectories as

$$\Phi^{-1}(x_0, v, t) = \xi^{-1}(x_0 + v, t) - \xi^{-1}(x_0, t).$$

We call $\Phi^{-1}(x_0, v, t)$ as inverse sensitivity function. Informally, inverse sensitivity function gives us the perturbation of the initial condition that is required to displace the trajectory passing through x_0 by v. Observe that $\xi(\xi^{-1}(x_0, t) + \Phi^{-1}(x_0, v, t), t) = x_0 + v$.

For general nonlinear differential equations, analytic representation of the trajectories of the ODEs need not exist. If the closed loop system is a smooth function, then the infinite series for the trajectories is given as

$$\xi(x_0, t) = x_0 + \mathcal{L}_f(x_0)t + \mathcal{L}_f^2(x_0)\frac{t^2}{2!} + \mathcal{L}_f^3(x_0)\frac{t^3}{3!} + \dots \tag{2}$$

Where $\mathcal{L}_f^i$ is the ith order Lie-derivative over the field $f(x, g(x))$ at the state x_0. Hence, one can write the sensitivity function as

$$\Phi(x_0, v, t) = v + (\mathcal{L}_f(x_0 + v) - \mathcal{L}_f(x_0))t + (\mathcal{L}_f^2(x_0 + v) - \mathcal{L}_f^2(x_0))\frac{t^2}{2!} + \dots \tag{3}$$

$\Phi^{-1}(x_0, v, t)$ is obtained by substituting $-f$ for f in Eq. 3. When the closed loop dynamics is linear, i.e., $\dot{x} = Ax$, it is easy to observe that $\Phi(x_0, v, t) = e^{At}v$, $\Phi^{-1}(x_0, v, t) = e^{-At}v$ where e^{At} (e^{-At}) is the matrix exponential of the matrix At ($-At$). Observe that for linear systems, the inverse sensitivity function is independent of the state x_0. For nonlinear dynamical systems, one can truncate the infinite series up to a specific order and obtain an approximation. However, for hybrid systems that have state based mode switches, or for feedback functions where the closed loop dynamics is not smooth or is discontinuous, such an infinite series expansion is hard to compute. The central idea in this paper is to approximate Φ and Φ^{-1} using a neural network and perform state space exploration using such neural networks.

4   Neural Network Approximations of Sensitivity and Inverse Sensitivity

Given a domain of operation $D \subseteq \mathbb{R}^n$, one can generate a finite set of trajectories for testing the system operation in D. Often, these trajectories are generated using numerical ODE solvers which return trajectories sampled at a regular time step. For approximating sensitivity and inverse sensitivity, we generate a finite number of time bounded trajectories where the step size, time bound, and the number of trajectories are specified by the user. The trajectories can be generated either according to a probability distribution specified by the user or from specific initial configurations provided by her.

Given a sampling of a trajectory at regular time interval with step size h, i.e., $\xi(x_0, 0), \xi(x_0, h), \xi(x_0, 2h), \ldots, \xi(x_0, kh)$, we make two observations. First, any prefix or suffix of this sequence is also a trajectory, albeit, of a shorter duration. Hence, from a given set of trajectories, one can generate more *virtual trajectories* that have shorter duration. Second, given two trajectories (real or virtual) starting from initial states x_1 and x_2, $(x_1 \neq x_2)$, We have the two following observations.

$$\Phi(x_1, x_2 - x_1, t) = \xi(x_2, t) - \xi(x_1, t) \tag{4}$$

$$\Phi^{-1}(\xi(x_1, t), \xi(x_2, t) - \xi(x_1, t), t) = x_2 - x_1. \tag{5}$$

Given an initial set of trajectories, we generate virtual trajectories and use Eqs. 4 and 5 for generating all tuples $\langle x_0, v, t, v_{sen} \rangle$ and $\langle x_0, v, t, v_{isen} \rangle$ such that $v_{sen} = \Phi(x_0, v, t)$ and $v_{isen} = \Phi^{-1}(x_0, v, t)$. This data is then used for training and evaluation of the neural network to approximate the sensitivity and inverse sensitivity functions. We denote these networks as NN_Φ and $NN_{\Phi^{-1}}$ respectively.

4.1   Evaluation on Standard Benchmarks

For approximating the sensitivity and inverse sensitivity functions, we pick a standard set of benchmarks consisting of nonlinear dynamical systems, hybrid systems, and control systems with neural network feedback functions. Most of the benchmarks are taken from standard hybrid systems benchmark suite [1,6,29]. The benchmarks Brussellator, Lotka, Jetengine, Buckling, Vanderpol, Lacoperon, Roesseler, Steam, Lorentz, and Coupled vanderpol are continuous nonlinear systems, where Lorentz and Roesseler are *chaotic* as well. SmoothHybrid Oscillator and HybridOscillator are nonlinear hybrid systems. The remaining benchmarks Mountain Car and Quadrotor are selected from [30], where the state feedback controller is given in the from of neural network.

For each benchmark, we generated a given number (typically 30 or 50) of trajectories, where the step size for ODE solvers and the time bound are provided by the user. We do not know how much data is required to obtain a required amount of accuracy. The trade offs between the amount of data required, training time, and accuracy of the approximation is a subject of future research. The data used for training the neural network is collected as described in previous subsection. We use 90% of the data for training and 10% for testing.

We used Python Multilayer Perceptron implemented in Keras [10] library with Tensorflow as the backend. The network has 8 layers with each layer having 512 neurons. The optimizer used is stochastic gradient descent. The network is trained using Levenberg-Marquardt backpropagation algorithm optimizing the mean absolute error loss function, and the Nguyen-Widrow initialization.

The activation function used to train the network is **relu** for all benchmarks except `Mountain car` for which **sigmoid** performs better because the NN controller is sigmoid-based. Note that the choice of hyper-parameters such as number of layers and neurons, the loss and activation functions is empirical, and is motivated by our prior work [25]. We evaluate the network performance using root mean square error (MSE) and mean relative error (MRE) metrics. The training and evaluation are performed on a system running Ubuntu 18.04 with a 2.20 GHz Intel Core i7-8750H CPU with 12 cores and 32 GB RAM. The network training time, MSE and MRE for learning inverse sensitivity function are given in Table 1. The reader is addressed to [26] for the training performance of the neural network tasked with learning sensitivity function.

Table 1. Learning inverse sensitivity function. Parameters and performance of neural network tasked with learning inverse sensitivity function. The set of benchmarks includes nonlinear dynamical, hybrid and neural network based feedback control systems. Time bound is number of steps for which the system simulation is computed.

Benchmark		Dims	Step size (sec)	Time bound	Training Time (min)	MSE	MRE
Continuous Nonlinear Dynamics	Brussellator	2	0.01	500	67.0	1.01	0.29
	Buckling	2	0.01	500	42.0	0.59	0.17
	Lotka	2	0.01	500	40.0	0.50	0.13
	Jetengine	2	0.01	300	34.0	1.002	0.26
	Vanderpol	2	0.01	500	45.50	0.23	0.23
	Lacoperon	2	0.2	500	110.0	1.8	0.46
	Roesseler	3	0.02	500	115.0	0.44	0.07
	Lorentz	3	0.01	500	67.0	0.48	0.08
	Steam	3	0.01	500	58.0	0.13	0.057
	C-Vanderpol	4	0.01	500	75.0	0.34	0.16
Hybrid/NN Systems	HybridOsc.	2	0.01	1000	77.0	0.31	0.077
	SmoothOsc.	2	0.01	1000	77.5	0.23	0.063
	Mountain Car	2	-	100	10.0	0.005	0.70
	Quadrotor	6	0.01	120	25.0	0.0011	0.16

Table 2. Evaluations. The results of reachTarget after iteration count 1 and 5. We compute average absolute distance d_a and relative distance d_r over 500 iterations of our algorithm for each benchmark. Additionally, a range of values is obtained for d_a and d_r by performing the evaluation on 10 different targets.

Benchmark	Dims	Iteration count = 1			Iteration count = 5		
		d_a	d_r	Time (ms)	d_a	d_r	Time (ms)
Brussellator	2	[0.19–1.87]	[0.23–0.74]	11.38	[0.003–0.22]	[0.01–0.12]	31.34
Buckling	2	[1.67–11.52]	[0.17–0.45]	13.61	[0.36- 2.09]	[0.06–0.31]	34.51
Lotka	2	[0.08–0.24]	[0.21–0.45]	12.38	[0.02–0.07]	[0.09–0.22]	34.28
Jetengine	2	[0.05 -0.20]	[0.19–0.28]	15.96	[0.0004–0.05]	[0.006–0.14]	38.26
Vanderpol	2	[0.29–0.58]	[0.16–0.66]	12.34	[0.03–0.18]	[0.04–0.16]	34.02
Lacoperon	2	[0.03–0.13]	[0.12–0.28]	17.18	[0.003–0.03]	[0.02–0.16]	37.34
Roesseler	3	[0.72–2.02]	[0.20–0.34]	16.08	[0.21–0.63]	[0.06–0.14]	38.26
Lorentz	3	[1.24–5.60]	[0.29–0.58]	24.72	[0.20–0.70]	[0.05–0.17]	60.18
Steam	3	[1.59–5.21]	[0.31–0.67]	8.68	[0.41–1.8]	[0.08–0.30]	69.80
C-Vanderpol	4	[0.87–1.72]	[0.34–0.60]	17.44	[0.20–0.40]	[0.07–0.18]	44.86
HybridOsc	2	[0.28–0.92]	[0.13–0.29]	16.70	[0.03–0.31]	[0.01–0.10]	45.82
SmoothOsc	2	[0.37–1.09]	[0.13- 0.23]	52.22	[0.04–0.42]	[0.02–0.18]	136.72
Mountain Car	2	[0.004–0.24]	[0.08–0.22]	138.90	[0.0002–0.005]	[0.03–0.12]	266.76
Quadrotor	6	[0.014–1.09]	[0.10–0.67]	284.96	[0.004–0.04]	[0.02–0.13]	668.78

5   Space Space Exploration Using Neural Network Approximation

In this section, we present various applications in the domain of state space exploration using the neural network approximation of sensitivity and inverse sensitivity. The goal of state space exploration is to search for trajectories that satisfy or violate a given specification. In this paper, we primarily concern ourselves with a safety specification, that is, whether a specific trajectory reaches a set of states labelled as *unsafe*. In order to search for such trajectories, we present four different algorithms that use neural networks that approximate sensitivity and inverse sensitivity. The main reason for providing a variety of such algorithms is to demonstrate the flexibility of the framework and the wide variety of ways in which it can be used. The reader is referred to [26] for additional experimental results of these techniques.

5.1   Reaching a Specified Destination Using Inverse Sensitivity Approximation

In the course of state space exploration, after testing the behavior of the system for a given set of test cases, the control designer might choose to explore the system behavior that reaches a destination or approaches the boundary condition for safe operation. Given a domain of operations D, we assume that the designer provides a desired target state z (with an error threshold of δ) that is reached by a trajectory at time t. Our goal is to generate a trajectory ξ such that $\xi(t)$ visits a state in the δ neighborhood of z.

Our approach for generating the target trajectory is as follows. First, we generate a random trajectory ξ from the initial state x, and compute the difference vector of target state z and $\xi(t)$ (i.e., $z - \xi(t)$). We now use the neural network approximation of the inverse sensitivity function and estimate the perturbation required in the initial set such that the trajectory after time t goes through z (i.e., $NN_{\Phi^{-1}}(\xi(t), z - \xi(t), t)$). Since the neural network can only approximate the inverse sensitivity function, the trajectory after the perturbation (i.e., $x + NN_{\Phi^{-1}}(\xi(t), z - \xi(t), t)$) need not visit δ neighborhood of the destination. However, we can repeat the procedure until a threshold on the number of iterations is reached or the δ threshold is satisfied. The pseudo code of this procedure, denoted as reachTarget, is given in Algorithm 1.1.

---

input : System simulator ξ, time bound T, trained neural network $NN_{\Phi^{-1}}$, time instance
$t \leq T$, destination state $z \in D$, iteration count I, initial set θ, and threshold δ

output: State $x \in \theta$, d_r, $d_a \triangleq \|\xi(x,t) - z\|_2$ such that $d_a \leq \delta$

1 $x \leftarrow x_{random} \in \theta; i \leftarrow 1;$
2 $x_0 \leftarrow \xi(x,t); d_a \leftarrow \|x_0 - z\|_2;$
3 $d_{init} \leftarrow d_a; d_r \leftarrow 1;$
4 **while** $(d_a > \delta)$ & $(i \leq I)$ **do**
5 $\quad v \leftarrow x_0 - z;$
6 $\quad v^{-1} \leftarrow NN_{\Phi^{-1}}(x_0, v, t);$
7 $\quad x \leftarrow x + v^{-1}; x_0 \leftarrow \xi(x,t);$
8 $\quad d_a \leftarrow \|x_0 - z\|_2; i \leftarrow i + 1;$
9 **end**
10 $d_r \leftarrow \dfrac{d_a}{d_{init}};$
11 **return** $(x, d_r, d_a);$

Algorithm 1.1: reachTarget. Finding an initial state from which the simulation goes within δ-neighborhood of destination z at time t. $\|\cdot\|_2$ is the $l2$-norm. The algorithm returns best candidate for the falsifying initial state, absolute distance d_a, and relative distance d_r wrt initial d_a.

In Algorithm 1.1, $\xi(x,.)$ is the simulation generated by ξ for the state x; x_0 is the simulation state at time t; $v^{-1} \triangleq \Phi^{-1}(x_0, v, t)$ is the inverse sensitivity function which is learned using neural network $NN_{\Phi^{-1}}$. The *absolute distance* d_a is the euclidean distance between simulation state at time t and the destination z. d_r is the *relative distance* with respect to the initial absolute distance d_{init}. Since v^{-1} is an estimate of the perturbation required in the initial set, a new anchor trajectory with initial state $x + v^{-1}$ is generated and the new distance d_a between $\xi(x,t)$ and z is computed. The **while** loop runs until either δ threshold is reached or iteration count I is exhausted.

Evaluation of reachTarget on Standard Benchmarks. We evaluate the performance of reachTarget algorithm by picking a random target state z in the domain of interest and let it generate a trajectory that goes through the neighborhood ($\delta = 0.01$ or 0.001) of the target at a specified time t. We use random target states in order to evaluate the performance of the search procedure in the entire domain and not bias it to a specific sub-space. Typically, reachTarget executes the loop in lines 4–9 for 10 times before reaching the target. In Table 2, we present the relative and absolute distance between the target and the state reached by the trajectory generated by reachTarget after one or five iterations of the loop. The demonstration of the procedure is shown in Fig. 1.

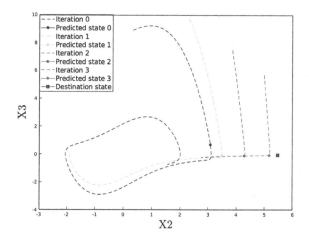

Fig. 1. Illustration of reachTarget. We highlight the result of executing reachTarget on Coupled Vanderpol. Iteration 0 is the trajectory from x_{random}. Subsequent 3 trajectories are labeled as Iteration 1, 2 and 3 respectively. As shown, with each iteration, the trajectory moves closer to the destination.

We now discuss a few variations of our algorithm and their evaluation approaches. *Uncertainty in time:* The control designer might not be interested in reaching the target at a precise time instance as long as it lies within a bounded interval of time. In such cases, one can iterate reachTarget for every step in this interval and generate a trajectory that approaches the target. Consider the designer is interested in finding the maximum distance (or, height) the car can go to on the left hill in Mountain Car. By providing an ordered list of target states and a time interval, she can obtain the maximum distance as well the time instance at which it achieves the maxima. If there is no state in the given initial set from which the car can go to a particular target, the approach, as a side effect, can also provide a suitable initial candidate that takes the car as close as possible to that target. Similarly, in Quadrotor, one can find an initial state from which the system can go to a particular location during a given time interval.

Generalization: Based on our Mountain Car experiment, we observed that, for the given initial set, the maximum distance the car can achieve on the left hill is approx. 1.17. However, even after expanding the initial set from $[-0.55, -0.45][0.0, 0.0]$ to $[-0.60, -0.40][0.0, 0.0]$, our approach finds the maximum achievable distance (1.3019) such that the car can still reach on the top of the right hill (shown in Fig. 2). This shows that our neural network is able to generalize the inverse sensitivity over trajectories that go beyond the test cases considered during the training process.

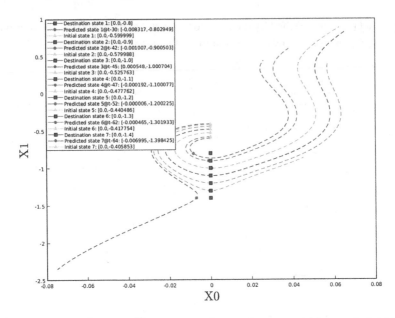

Fig. 2. Generalization Computing the maximum distance the car can achieve on the left hill after expanding the initial set.

Discussion: It can be observed from Table 2 that our technique is capable of achieving below 10% relative distance in almost all cases after 5 iterations. That is, the trajectory generated by reachTarget algorithm after 5 iterations is around 10% away from the target than the initial trajectory. This was the case even for chaotic systems, hybrid systems, and for control systems with neural network components. While training the neural network might be time taking process, the average time for generating new trajectories that approach the target is very fast (less than a second for all cases). The high relative distance in some cases might be due to high dimensionality or large distance to the target which may be reduced further with more iterations.

5.2 Falsification of Safety Specification

One of the widely used methods for performing state space exploration are falsification methods [38,43]. Here, the specification is provided in some temporal logic such as Signal or Metric Temporal Logic [31,35]. The falsifier then generates a set of test executions and computes the *robustness* of trajectory with respect to the specification. It then invokes heuristics such as stochastic global optimization for discovering a trajectory that violates the specification.

Given an unsafe set U, we provide a simple algorithm to falsify safety specifications. We generate a fixed number (m) of random states in the unsafe set U. Then, using the reachTarget sub-routine, generate trajectories that reach a vicinity of the randomly generated states in U. We terminate the procedure when we discover an execution that enters the unsafe set U. For Simulated annealing benchmark, we compare the number of trajectories generated by S-Taliro with the trajectories generated using inverse sensitivity in Fig. 3. S-Taliro takes 121 s with quadratic optimization and 11 s with analytical distance computation, NeuralExplorer obtains a falsifying trajectory in 2.5 s. Similar performance gain is observed in a few other benchmarks.

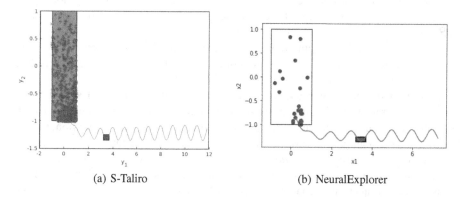

(a) S-Taliro   (b) NeuralExplorer

Fig. 3. Falsification in Simulated Annealing using S-Taliro and NeuralExplorer. The red box in each of the figures denotes the unsafe set and the other box denotes the initial set. Each of the points in the initial set represents a sample trajectory generated by the falsification engine. (Color figure online)

Falsification using approximation of inverse sensitivity enjoys a few advantages over other falsification methods. First, since our approach approximates the inverse sensitivity, and we use the reachTarget sub-routine; if the approximation is accurate to a certain degree, each subsequent trajectory generated would make progress towards the destination. Second, if the safety specification is changed slightly, the robustness of the trajectories with respect to new specification and the internal representation for the stochastic optimization solver has to be completely recomputed. However, since our trajectory generation does not rely on computing the robustness for previously generated samples, our algorithm is effective even when the safety specification is modified.

The third and crucial advantage of our approach lies when the falsification tool does not yield a counterexample. In those cases, the typical falsification tools cannot provide any geometric insight into the reason why the property is not satisfied. However, using an approximation of inverse sensitivity, the system designer can envision the required perturbation of the reachable set in order to move the trajectory in a specific direction. This geometric insight would be helpful in understanding why a specific trajectory does not go into the unsafe set.

Considering these advantages, the results demonstrated in Fig. 3 should not be surprising. We also would like to mention that these advantages come at the computational price of training the neural networks to approximating the inverse sensitivity. We observed that in some other examples, S-Taliro terminates with a falsification trajectory faster than our approach. The reasons for such cases and methods to improve falsification using NeuralExplorer are a topic of future work.

5.3 Density Based Search Methods for State Space Exploration

One of the most commonly used technique for performing state space exploration is generation of trajectories from a set of random points generated using an apriori distribution. Based on the proximity of these trajectories to the *unsafe* set, this probability distribution can further be refined to obtain trajectories that move closer to the unsafe set. However, one of the computational bottlenecks for this is the generation of trajectories. Since the numerical ODE solvers are sequential in nature, the refinement procedure for probability distribution is hard to accelerate.

For this purpose, one can use the neural network approximation of sensitivity to *predict* many trajectories in an embarassingly parallel way. Here, a specific set of initial states for the trajectories are generated using a pre-determined distribution. Only a few of the corresponding trajectories for the initial states are generated using numerical ODE solvers. These are called as *anchor trajectories*. The remainder of trajectories are not generated, but rather predicted using the neural network approximation of sensitivity and anchor trajectories. That is, $\xi(x_i, t) + \Phi_{NN}(x_i, x_j - x_i, t)$. Additionally, the designer has the freedom to choose only a subset of the initial states for only a specific time interval for prediction and refine the probability distribution for generating new states. This would also allow us to specifically focus on a time interval or a trajectory without generating the prefix of it. An example of predictive trajectory generation for performing *reachability analysis* on Vanderpol oscillator is provided in Fig. 4.

5.4 Density Based Search for Falsification

Similar to the inverse sensitivity based falsification, one can use the density based search space method for generating trajectories that reach a destination and violate a safety specification. The forward density based search procedure would work as follows. First, an anchor trajectory is generated and time instances of this trajectory that are closer to the unsafe set are identified. Then a set of new initial states are generated according to an apriori decided distribution. Instead of generating the trajectories from these initial states using ODE solvers, the *predicted trajectories* using the anchor trajectory and neural network approximation of sensitivity are generated specifically for the time intervals of interest. Then, the initial state with the predicted trajectory that is closest to the unsafe set is chosen and a new anchor trajectory from the selected initial state is generated. This process of generating anchor trajectory, new distribution of initial states is continued until you reach within the given threshold around the unsafe set. Demonstration of this procedure for Vanderpol system is shown in Fig. 5. Notice that this approach gives an underlying intuition about the geometric behavior of neighboring trajectories.

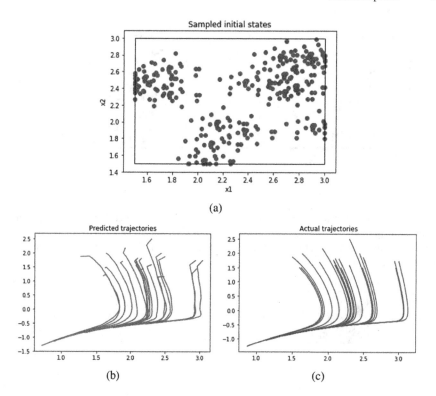

(a)

(b)

(c)

Fig. 4. State space exploration on Vanderpol. A cluster of points is sampled in the neighborhood of a reference state. Actual trajectories as well as predicted trajectories obtained by the neural network which approximates sensitivity function are shown. (Color figure online)

A similar method for density based estimation using inverse sensitivity approximation can also be devised. Instead of sampling the initial set, the density based method for inverse sensitivity generates random states around the unsafe set to be reached and then, using reachTarget, explores states in the initial set that reach these unsafe configurations at a particular time instance. In addition, it maintains the distance of each trajectory from the unsafe set. In this manner, one can classify states in the initial set based on their respective trajectories' distances to the unsafe set. This results into a density map that can provide some geometric insights about initial configurations. An example of such a density map generated is given in Fig. 6. In Fig 6(a), the trajectories starting from the states in the bottom left side of the initial set either go into the unsafe set or are much closer to it compared to the states in the upper right side. Also, observe how the density map changes by changing the unsafe specification in Fig. 6(b).

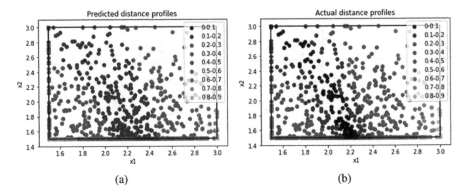

(a)   (b)

Fig. 5. Density based search for *falsification* **using sensitivity in** `Vanderpol`**.** The perturbation in the neighborhood of reference state are greedily chosen in an iterative manner so as to minimize the distance to unsafe state. The sampled states are classified based on their euclidean distance to the unsafe state.

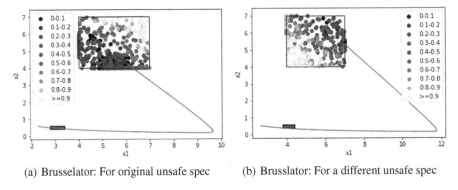

(a) Brusselator: For original unsafe spec   (b) Brusslator: For a different unsafe spec

Fig. 6. Density based search for *falsification* **using inverse sensitivity in** `Brusselator`**.** The initial states explored in the falsification process are colored according to their distance to the unsafe set. These color densities help in identifying regions in the initial set potentially useful for falsification. Notice the difference in the color densities as we select a difference unsafe spec.

6   Conclusion and Future Work

We presented NeuralExplorer framework for state space exploration of closed loop control systems using neural network. Our framework depends on computing neural network approximations of two key properties of a dynamical system called sensitivity and inverse sensitivity. We have demonstrated that for standard benchmarks, these functions can be learned with less than 20% relative error. We demonstrated that our method can not only be applied to standard nonlinear dynamical systems but also for control systems with neural network as feedback functions.

Using these approximations of sensitivity and inverse sensitivity, we presented new ways to performing state space exploration. We also highlighted the advantages of the falsification methods devised using the approximations. Additionally, we demonstrated that our techniques give a geometric insight into the behavior of the system and provide more intuitive information to the user, unlike earlier black box methods. We believe that these techniques can help the system designer in search of the desired executions.[1]

In future, we intend to extend this work to handle more generic systems such as feedback systems with environmental inputs. We believe such a black-box method for generating adversarial examples can be integrated into generative adversarial training for training neural networks for control applications.

Acknowlegements. This material is based upon work supported by the Air Force Office of Scientific Research under award number FA9550-19-1-0288 and National Science Foundation (NSF) under grant numbers CNS 1739936, 1935724. Any opinions, findings, and conclusions or recommendations expressed in this material are those of the author(s) and do not necessarily reflect the views of the United States Air Force or National Science Foundation.

References

1. Benchmarks of continuous and hybrid systems. https://ths.rwth-aachen.de/research/projects/hypro/benchmarks-of-continuous-and-hybrid-systems/
2. Abbas, H., Fainekos, G.: Linear hybrid system falsification through local search. In: Bultan, T., Hsiung, P.-A. (eds.) ATVA 2011. LNCS, vol. 6996, pp. 503–510. Springer, Heidelberg (2011). https://doi.org/10.1007/978-3-642-24372-1_39
3. Althoff, M.: An introduction to CORA 2015. In: Proceedings of the Workshop on Applied Verification for Continuous and Hybrid Systems (2015)
4. Alur, R., Dang, T., Ivančić, F.: Progress on reachability analysis of hybrid systems using predicate abstraction. In: Maler, O., Pnueli, A. (eds.) Hybrid Systems: Computation and Control (2003)
5. Annpureddy, Y., Liu, C., Fainekos, G., Sankaranarayanan, S.: S-TaLiRo: a tool for temporal logic falsification for hybrid systems. In: Abdulla, P.A., Leino, K.R.M. (eds.) TACAS 2011. LNCS, vol. 6605, pp. 254–257. Springer, Heidelberg (2011). https://doi.org/10.1007/978-3-642-19835-9_21
6. Bak, S., Beg, O.A., Bogomolov, S., Johnson, T.T., Nguyen, L.V., Schilling, C.: Hybrid automata: from verification to implementation. Int. J. Softw. Tools Technol. Transfer **21**(1), 87–104 (2017). https://doi.org/10.1007/s10009-017-0458-1
7. Bak, S., Duggirala, P.S.: Hylaa: a tool for computing simulation-equivalent reachability for linear systems. In: Proceedings of the 20th International Conference on Hybrid Systems: Computation and Control (2017)
8. Chen, R.T.Q., Rubanova, Y., Bettencourt, J., Duvenaud, D.: Neural ordinary differential equations (2018)
9. Chen, X., Ábrahám, E., Sankaranarayanan, S.: Flow*: an analyzer for non-linear hybrid systems. In: Sharygina, N., Veith, H. (eds.) Computer Aided Verification (2013)
10. Chollet, F., et al.: Keras. https://github.com/fchollet/keras (2015)
11. Dang, T., Maler, O.: Reachability analysis via face lifting. In: Henzinger, T.A., Sastry, S. (eds.) HSCC 1998. LNCS, vol. 1386, pp. 96–109. Springer, Heidelberg (1998). https://doi.org/10.1007/3-540-64358-3_34

---

[1] All the code and examples for the evaluations performed in this section are available at https://github.com/mag16154/NeuralExplorer.

12. Deshmukh, J.V., Fainekos, G.E., Kapinski, J., Sankaranarayanan, S., Zutshi, A., Jin, X.: Beyond single shooting: iterative approaches to falsification. In: American Control Conference, ACC (2015)

13. Donzé, A.: Breach, A toolbox for verification and parameter synthesis of hybrid systems. In: Computer Aided Verification, 22nd International Conference, CAV 2010. Proceedings (2010)

14. Donzé, A., Maler, O.: Systematic simulation using sensitivity analysis. In: Bemporad, A., Bicchi, A., Buttazzo, G. (eds.) HSCC 2007. LNCS, vol. 4416, pp. 174–189. Springer, Heidelberg (2007). https://doi.org/10.1007/978-3-540-71493-4_16

15. Donzé, A., Maler, O.: Robust satisfaction of temporal logic over real-valued signals. In: Formal Modeling and Analysis of Timed Systems - 8th International Conference, FORMATS 2010. Proceedings (2010)

16. Duggirala, P.S., Mitra, S., Viswanathan, M.: Verification of annotated models from executions. In: Proceedings of the Eleventh ACM International Conference on Embedded Software (2013)

17. Duggirala, P.S., Mitra, S., Viswanathan, M., Potok, M.: C2E2: a verification tool for stateflow models. In: Baier, C., Tinelli, C. (eds.) TACAS 2015. LNCS, vol. 9035, pp. 68–82. Springer, Heidelberg (2015). https://doi.org/10.1007/978-3-662-46681-0_5

18. Dutta, S., Chen, X., Jha, S., Sankaranarayanan, S., Tiwari, A.: Sherlock - a tool for verification of neural network feedback systems: demo abstract. In: HSCC (2019)

19. Fainekos, G.E., Pappas, G.J.: Robustness of temporal logic specifications for continuous-time signals. TCS (2009)

20. Fan, C., Mitra, S.: Bounded verification with on-the-fly discrepancy computation. In: International Symposium on Automated Technology for Verification and Analysis, pp. 446–463 (2015)

21. Fan, C., Qi, B., Mitra, S., Viswanathan, M.: DRYVR: data-driven verification and compositional reasoning for automotive systems. In: CAV (1) (2017)

22. Frehse, G.,et al.: SPACEEX: scalable verification of hybrid systems. In: Proceedings of the 23rd International Conference on Computer Aided Verification (CAV) (2011)

23. Ghosh, S., et al.: Diagnosis and repair for synthesis from signal temporal logic specifications. In: Proceedings of the 19th International Conference on Hybrid Systems: Computation and Control (2016)

24. Goyal, M., Duggirala, P.S.: On generating a variety of unsafe counterexamples for linear dynamical systems. In: ADHS (2018)

25. Goyal, M., Duggirala, P.S.: Learning robustness of nonlinear systems using neural networks (2019). https://sites.google.com/view/dars2019/home

26. Goyal, M., Duggirala, P.S.: Neuralexplorer: state space exploration of closed loop control systems using neural networks. CoRR, abs/2007.05685 (2020)

27. Huang, X., Kwiatkowska, M., Wang, S., Wu, M.: Safety verification of deep neural networks. In: CAV (1) (2017)

28. Huang, Z., Mitra, S.: Proofs from simulations and modular annotations. In: Proceedings of the 17th International Conference on Hybrid Systems: Computation and Control (2014)

29. Immler, F.: ARCH-COMP18 category report: continuous and hybrid systems with nonlinear dynamics. In: ARCH@ADHS (2018)

30. Ivanov, R., Weimer, J., Alur, R., Pappas, G.J., Lee, I.: verisig: verifying safety properties of hybrid systems with neural network controllers (2018)

31. Koymans, R.: Specifying real-time properties with metric temporal logic. Real-time systems (1990)

32. Kyriakis, P., Deshmukh, J.V., Bogdan, P.: Specification mining and robust design under uncertainty: a stochastic temporal logic approach. ACM Trans. Embed. Comput. Syst. (2019)

33. Lewis, F., Jagannathan, S., Yesildirak, A.: Neural Network Control of Robot Manipulators and Non-linear Systems. CRC Press, Austin (1998)
34. Long, Z., Lu, Y., Ma, X., Dong, B.: PDE-net: learning PDEs from data. In: Proceedings of the 35th International Conference on Machine Learning, pp. 3208–3216 (2018)
35. Maler, O., Nickovic, D., Pnueli, A.: Checking temporal properties of discrete, timed and continuous behaviors. In: Avron, A., Dershowitz, N., Rabinovich, A. (eds.) Pillars of Computer Science. LNCS, vol. 4800, pp. 475–505. Springer, Heidelberg (2008). https://doi.org/10.1007/978-3-540-78127-1_26
36. Miller, W., Werbos, P., Sutton, R.: Neural Networks for Control. A Bradford book, MIT Press (1995). https://books.google.com/books?id=prjMtIr_yT8C
37. Moore, K.L.: Iterative Learning Control for Deterministic Systems. Springer, London (2012). https://doi.org/10.1007/978-1-4471-1912-8
38. Nghiem, T., Sankaranarayanan, S., Fainekos, G., Ivancić, F., Gupta, A., Pappas, G.J.: Montecarlo techniques for falsification of temporal properties of non-linear hybrid systems. In: Proceedings of the 13th ACM International Conference on Hybrid Systems: Computation and Control (HSCC 2010) (2010)
39. Pan, S., Duraisamy, K.: Long-time predictive modeling of nonlinear dynamical systems using neural networks. Complexity (2018)
40. Pathak, J., Hunt, B., Girvan, M., Lu, Z., Ott, E.: Model-free prediction of large spatiotemporally chaotic systems from data: a reservoir computing approach. Phys. Rev. Lett. **120**(2), 024102 (2018)
41. Phan, D., Paoletti, N., Zhang, T., Grosu, R., Smolka, S.A., Stoller, S.D.: Neural state classification for hybrid systems. In: Proceedings of the Fifth International Workshop on Symbolic-Numeric Methods for Reasoning About CPS and IoT (2019)
42. Raissi, M., Perdikaris, P., Karniadakis, G.E.: Multistep neural networks for data-driven discovery of nonlinear dynamical systems (2018)
43. Sankaranarayanan, S., Fainekos, G.E.: Falsification of temporal properties of hybrid systems using the cross-entropy method. In: Hybrid Systems: Computation and Control (2012)
44. Sun, X., Khedr, H., Shoukry, Y.: Formal verification of neural network controlled autonomous systems. In: Proceedings of the 22nd ACM International Conference on Hybrid Systems: Computation and Control (2019)
45. Sun, Y., Huang, X., Kroening, D., Sharp, J., Hill, M., Ashmore, R.: Structural test coverage criteria for deep neural networks. ACM Trans. Embedded Comput. Syst. (2019)
46. Tjeng, V., Xiao, K.Y., Tedrake, R.: Evaluating robustness of neural networks with mixed integer programming. In: ICLR (Poster). OpenReview.net (2019)
47. Tran, H.D., Cai, F., Diego, M.L., Musau, P., Johnson, T.T., Koutsoukos, X.: Safety verification of cyber-physical systems with reinforcement learning control. ACM Trans. Embed. Comput. Syst. (2019)
48. Zutshi, A., Deshmukh, J.V., Sankaranarayanan, S., Kapinski, J.: Multiple shooting, cegar-based falsification for hybrid systems. In: Proceedings of the 14th International Conference on Embedded Software (2014)

DeepAbstract: Neural Network Abstraction for Accelerating Verification

Pranav Ashok[1], Vahid Hashemi[2], Jan Křetínský[1],
and Stefanie Mohr[1(✉)]

[1] Technical University of Munich, Munich, Germany
muehlbes@in.tum.de
[2] Audi AG, Ingolstadt, Germany

Abstract. While abstraction is a classic tool of verification to scale it up, it is not used very often for verifying neural networks. However, it can help with the still open task of scaling existing algorithms to state-of-the-art network architectures. We introduce an abstraction framework applicable to fully-connected feed-forward neural networks based on clustering of neurons that behave similarly on *some* inputs. For the particular case of ReLU, we additionally provide error bounds incurred by the abstraction. We show how the abstraction reduces the size of the network, while preserving its accuracy, and how verification results on the abstract network can be transferred back to the original network.

1 Introduction

Neural networks (NN) are successfully used to solve many hard problems reasonably well in practice. However, there is an increasing desire to use them also in safety-critical settings, such as perception in autonomous cars [Che+17a], where reliability has to be on a very high level and that level has to be guaranteed, preferably by a rigorous proof. This is a great challenge, in particular, since NN are naturally very susceptible to adversarial attacks, as many works have demonstrated in the recent years [Pap+16; AM18; Don+18; SVS19]. Consequently, various verification techniques for NN are being developed these days. Most verification techniques focus on proving robustness of the neural networks [CNR17; Ehl17; Hua+17; Kat+17; Geh+18; Sin+19b], i.e. for a classification task, when the input is perturbed by a small ε, the resulting output should be labeled the same as the output of the original input. Reliable analysis of robustness is computationally extremely expensive and verification tools struggle to scale when faced with real-world neural networks [Dvi+18].

This research was funded in part by TUM IGSSE Grant 10.06 *PARSEC*, the German Research Foundation (DFG) project 383882557 *Statistical Unbounded Verification* (KR 4890/2-1), the DFG research training group *CONVEY* (GRK 2428), and the project *Audi Verifiable AI*.

D. V. Hung and O. Sokolsky (Eds.): ATVA 2020, LNCS 12302, pp. 92–107, 2020.
https://doi.org/10.1007/978-3-030-59152-6_5

Abstraction. [CGL94; Cla+00] is one of the very classic techniques used in formal methods to obtain more understanding of a system as well as more efficient analysis. Disregarding details irrelevant to the checked property allows for constructing a smaller system with a similar behaviour. Although abstraction-based techniques are ubiquitous in verification, improving its scalability, such ideas have not been really applied to the verification of NN, except for a handful of works discussed later.

In this paper, we introduce an abstraction framework for NN. In contrast to syntactic similarities, such as having similar weights on the edges from the previous layer [ZYZ18], our aim is to provide a behavioural, semantic notion of similarity, such as those delivered by predicate abstraction, since such notions are more general and thus more powerful. Surprisingly, this direction has not been explored for NN. One of the reasons is that the neurons do not have an explicit structure like states of a program that are determined by valuations of given variables. What are actually the values determining neurons in the network?

Note that in many cases, such as recognition of traffic signs or numbers, there are finitely many (say k) interesting data points on which and on whose neighbourhood the network should work well. Intuitively, these are the key points that determine our focus, our scope of interest. Consequently, we propose the following equivalence on neurons. We evaluate the k inputs, yielding for each neuron a k-tuple of its activation values. This can be seen as a vector in $\mathbb{R}^k$. We stipulate that two neurons are similar if they have similar vectors, i.e, very close to each other. To determine reasonable equivalence classes over the vectors, we use the machine-learning technique of k-means clustering [HTF09]. While other techniques, e.g. principal component analysis [Bis06], might also be useful, simple clustering is computationally cheap and returns reasonable results. To summarize in other words, in the lack of structural information about the neurons, we use empirical behavioural information instead.

Applications. Once we have a way of determining similar neurons, we can merge each equivalence class into a single neuron and obtain a smaller, abstracted NN. There are several uses of such an NN. Firstly, since it is a smaller one, it may be preferred in practice since, generally, smaller networks are often more robust, smoother, and obviously less resource-demanding to run [Che+17b]. Note that there is a large body of work on obtaining smaller NN from larger ones, e.g. see [Che+17b; Den+20]. Secondly, and more interestingly in the safety-critical context, we can use the smaller abstract NN to obtain a guaranteed solution to the original problem (verifying robustness or even other properties) in two distinct ways:

1. The smaller NN could replace the original one and could be easier to verify, while doing the same job (more precisely, the results can be ε-different where we can compute an upper bound on ε from the abstraction).
2. We can analyze the abstract NN more easily as it is smaller and then transfer the results (proof of correctness or a counterexample) to the original one, provided the difference ε is small enough.

The latter corresponds to the classic abstraction-based verification scenario. For each of these points, we provide proof-of-concept experimental evidence of the method's potential.

Our contribution is thus the following:

- We propose to explore the framework of abstraction by clustering based on experimental data. For feed-forward NN with ReLU, we provide error bounds.
- We show that the abstraction is also usable for compression. The reduction rate grows with the size of the original network, while the abstracted NN is able to achieve almost the same accuracy as the original network.
- We demonstrate the verification potential of the approach: (i) In some cases where the large NN was not analyzable (within time-out), we verified the abstraction using existing tools; for other NN, we could reduce verification times from thousands to hundreds of seconds. (ii) We show how to transfer a proof of robustness by a verification tool DeepPoly [Sin+19a] on the abstract NN to a proof on the original network, whenever the clusters do not have too large radii.

Related Work. In contrast to compression techniques, our abstraction provides a mapping between original neurons and abstract neurons, which allows for transferring the claims of the abstract NN to the original one, and thus its verification.

The very recent work [YGK19] suggests an abstraction, which is based solely on the sign of the effect of increasing a value in a neuron. While we can demonstrate our technique on e.g. 784 dimension input (MNIST) and work with general networks, [YGK19] is demonstrated only on the Acas Xu [JKO18] networks which have 5 dimensional input; our approach handles thousands of nodes while the benchmark used in [YGK19] is of size 300. Besides, we support both classification and regression networks. Finally, our approach is not affected by the number of outputs, whereas the [YGK19] grows exponentially with respect to number of outputs.

[PA19] produces so called Interval Neural Networks containing intervals instead of single weights and performs abstraction by merging these intervals. However, they do not provide a heuristic for picking the intervals to merge, but pick randomly. Further, the results are demonstrated only on the low-dimensional Acas Xu networks.

Further, [SB15] computes a similarity measure between incoming weights and then starts merging the most similar ones. It also features an analysis of how many neurons to remove in order to not lose too much accuracy. However, it does not use clustering on the semantic values of the activations, but only on the syntactic values of the incoming weights, which is a very local and thus less powerful criterion. Similarly, [ZYZ18] clusters based on the incoming weights only and does not bound the error. [HMD16] clusters weights in contrast to our activation values) using the k-means clustering algorithm. However, the focus is on weight-sharing and reducing memory consumption, treating neither the abstraction mapping nor verification.

Finally, abstracting neural networks for verification purposes was first proposed by [PT10], transforming the networks into Boolean constraints.

2   Preliminaries

We consider simple feedforward neural networks, denoted by D, consisting of one input layer, one output layer and one or more hidden layers. The layers are numbered $1, 2, \ldots, L$ with 1 being the *input layer*, L being the *output layer* and $2, \ldots, L - 1$ being the *hidden layers*. Layer ℓ contains n_ℓ neurons. A neuron is a computation unit which takes an input $h \in \mathbb{R}$, applies an *activation function* $\phi : \mathbb{R} \to \mathbb{R}$ on it and gives as output $z = \phi(h)$. Common activation functions include tanh, sigmoid or ReLU [MHN13], however we choose to focus on ReLU for the sake of simplicity, where $\mathrm{ReLU}(x)$ is defined as $\max(0, x)$. Neurons of one layer are connected to neurons of the previous and/or next layers by means of weighted connections. Associated with every layer ℓ that is not an output layer is a *weight matrix* $W^{(\ell)} = (w_{i,j}^{(\ell)}) \in \mathbb{R}^{n_{\ell+1} \times n_\ell}$ where $w_{i,j}^{(\ell)}$ gives the weights of the connections to the ith neuron in layer $\ell+1$ from the jth neuron in layer ℓ. We use the notation $W_{i,*}^{(\ell)} = [w_{i,1}^{(\ell)}, \ldots, w_{i,n_\ell}^{(\ell)}]$ to denote the incoming weights of neuron i in layer $\ell + 1$ and $W_{*,j}^{(\ell)} = [w_{1,j}^{(\ell)}, \ldots, w_{n_{\ell+1},j}^{(\ell)}]^\intercal$ to denote the outgoing weights of neuron j in layer ℓ. Note that $W_{i,*}^{(\ell)}$ and $W_{*,j}^{(\ell)}$ correspond to the ith row and j^{th} column of $W^{(\ell)}$ respectively. The input and output of a neuron i in layer ℓ is denoted by $h_i^{(\ell)}$ and $z_i^{(\ell)}$ respectively. We call $\mathbf{h}^\ell = [h_1^{(\ell)}, \ldots, h_{n_\ell}^{(\ell)}]^\intercal$ the vector of *pre-activations* of layer ℓ and $\mathbf{z}^\ell = [z_1^{(\ell)}, \ldots, z_{n_\ell}^{(\ell)}]^\intercal$ the vector of *activations* of layer ℓ, where $z_i^{(\ell)} = \phi^{(\ell)}(h_i^{(\ell)})$. A vector $\mathbf{b}^{(\ell)} \in \mathbb{R}^{n_\ell}$ called *bias* is also associated with all hidden layers ℓ.

In a feedforward neural network, information flows strictly in one direction: from layer ℓ_m to layer ℓ_n where $\ell_m < \ell_n$. For an n_1-dimensional input $\boldsymbol{x} \in \mathcal{X}$ from some input space $\mathcal{X} \subseteq \mathbb{R}^{n_1}$, the output $\boldsymbol{y} \in \mathbb{R}^{n_L}$ of the neural network D, also written as $\boldsymbol{y} = D(\boldsymbol{x})$ is iteratively computed as follows:

$$\mathbf{h}^{(0)} = \boldsymbol{x}$$
$$\mathbf{h}^{(\ell+1)} = W^{(\ell)} \mathbf{z}^{(\ell)} + \mathbf{b}^{(\ell+1)} \tag{1}$$
$$\mathbf{z}^{(\ell+1)} = \phi(\mathbf{h}^{(\ell+1)}) \tag{2}$$
$$\boldsymbol{y} = \mathbf{z}^{(L)}$$

where $\phi(x)$ is the column vector obtained on applying ϕ component-wise to $\boldsymbol{x}$. We sometimes write $\mathbf{z}^{(\ell)}(\boldsymbol{x})$ to denote the output of layer ℓ when $\boldsymbol{x}$ is given as input to the network.

We define a *local robustness* query to be a tuple $Q = (D, \boldsymbol{x}, \boldsymbol{\delta})$ for some network D, input $\boldsymbol{x}$ and perturbation $\boldsymbol{\delta} \in \mathbb{R}^{|\boldsymbol{x}|}$ and call D to be robust with respect to Q if $\forall \boldsymbol{x}' \in [\boldsymbol{x} - \boldsymbol{\delta}, \boldsymbol{x} + \boldsymbol{\delta}] : D(\boldsymbol{x}') = D(\boldsymbol{x})$. In this paper, we only deal with local robustness.

3   Abstraction

In classic abstraction, states that are similar with respect to a property of interest are merged for analysis. In contrast, for NN, it is not immediately clear which neurons to merge and what similarity means. Indeed, neurons are not actually states/configurations of the system; as such, neurons, as opposed to states with values of variables, do not have inner structure. Consequently, identifying and dropping irrelevant information (part of the structure) becomes more challenging. We propose to merge neurons which compute a similar function *on some set* X *of inputs*, i.e., for each input $x \in X$ to the network, they compute ε-close values. We refer to this as I/O-similarity. Further, we choose to merge neurons only within the same layer to keep the analysis and implementation straightforward.

In Sect. 3.1, we show a straightforward way to merge neurons in a way that is sensible if they are I/O-similar. In Sect. 3.2, we give a heuristic for partitioning neurons into classes according to their I/O-similarity. While this abstraction idea is not limited to verification of robustness, it preserves the robustness of the original network particularly well, as seen in the experiments in Sect. 5.

3.1   Merging I/O-Similar Neurons

I/O-similar neurons can be merged easily without changing the behaviour of the NN too much. First, we explain the procedure on an example.

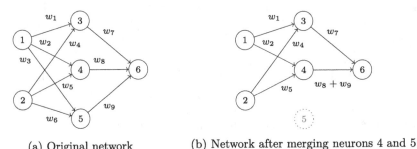

(a) Original network   (b) Network after merging neurons 4 and 5

Fig. 1. Before and after merge: neuron 4 is chosen as a representative of both 4 and 5. On merging, the incoming weights of neuron 5 are deleted and its outgoing weight is added to the outgoing weight of neuron 4.

Example 1. Consider the network shown in Fig. 1a. The network contains 2 input neurons and 4 ReLU neurons. For simplicity, we skip the bias term in this example network. Hence, the activations of the neurons in the middle layer are given as follows: $z_3 = ReLU(w_1z_1 + w_4z_2)$, $z_4 = ReLU(w_2z_1 + w_5z_2)$, $z_5 = ReLU(w_3z_1 + w_6z_2)$; and the output of neuron 6 is $z_6 = ReLU(w_7z_3 + w_8z_4 + w_9z_5)$. Suppose that for all inputs in the dataset, the activations of neurons 4 and 5 are 'very' close, denoted by $z_4 \approx z_5$. Then, $z_6 = ReLU(w_7z_3 + w_8z_4 + w_9z_5)$.

Algorithm 1. Abstract network D with given clustering K_L

1: **procedure** ABSTRACT(D, X, K_L)
2:     $\tilde{D} \leftarrow D$
3:     **for** $\ell \leftarrow 2, \ldots, L-1$ **do**
4:         $A \leftarrow \{\mathbf{a}_i^{(\ell)} \mid \mathbf{a}_i^{(\ell)} = [\tilde{z}_i^{(\ell)}(x_1), \ldots, \tilde{z}_i^{(\ell)}(x_N)]$ where $x_i \in X\}$
5:         $\mathcal{C} \leftarrow$ KMEANS($A, K_L(\ell)$)
6:         **for** $C \in \mathcal{C}$ **do**
7:             $\tilde{W}_{*,rep(C)}^{(\ell)} \leftarrow \sum_{i \in C} W_{*,i}^{(\ell)}$
8:         **delete** $C \setminus \{rep(C)\}$ from $\tilde{D}$
     return $\tilde{D}$

Since neurons 4 and 5 behave similarly, we abstract the network by merging the two neurons as shown in Fig. 1b. Here, neuron 4 is chosen as a representative of the "cluster" containing neurons 4 and 5, and the outgoing weight of the representative is set to the sum of outgoing weights of all the neurons in the cluster. Note that the incoming weights of the representative do not change. In the abstracted network, the activations of the neurons in the middle layer are now given by $\tilde{z}_3 = ReLU(w_1\tilde{z}_1 + w_4\tilde{z}_2) = z_3$ and $\tilde{z}_4 = ReLU(w_2\tilde{z}_1 + w_5\tilde{z}_2) = z_4$ with neuron 5 being removed. The output of neuron 6 is therefore $\tilde{z}_6 = ReLU(w_7\tilde{z}_3 + (w_8 + w_9)\tilde{z}_4) = ReLU(w_7z_3 + (w_8 + w_9)z_4) = ReLU(w_7z_3 + w_8z_4 + w_9z_4) \approx z_6$, which illustrates that merging preserves the behaviour of the network.

Formally, the process of merging two neurons p and q belonging to the same layer ℓ works as follows. We assume, without loss of generality, that p is retained as the representative. First, the abstract network $\tilde{D}$ is set to the original network D. Next, $\tilde{W}^{(\ell-1)}$ is set to $W^{(\ell-1)}$ with the qth row deleted. Further, we set the outgoing weights of the representative p to the sum of outgoing weights of p and q, $\tilde{W}_{*,p}^{(\ell)} = W_{*,p}^{(\ell)} + W_{*,q}^{(\ell)}$. This procedure is naturally extendable to merging multiple I/O-similar neurons. It can be applied repeatedly until all desired neurons are merged. For the interested reader, the correctness proof and further technical details are made available in [Ash+20, Appendix A.1].

Proposition 1 (Sanity Check). *If for neurons p and q, for all considered inputs $x \in X$ to the network D, $z_p = z_q$, then the network $\tilde{D}$ produced as described above, in which p and q are merged by removing q and letting p serve as their representative, and by setting $\tilde{W}_{*,p}^{(\ell)} = W_{*,p}^{(\ell)} + W_{*,q}^{(\ell)}$, will have the same output as D on all inputs $x \in X$. In other words, $\forall x \in X\ D(x) = \tilde{D}(x)$.*

3.2 Clustering-Based Abstraction

In the previous section, we saw that multiple I/O-similar neurons can be merged to obtain an abstract network behaving similar to the original network. However, the quality of the abstraction depends on the choice of neurons used in the merging. Moreover, it might be beneficial to have multiple groups of neurons that are merged separately. While multiple strategies can be used to identify

---

Algorithm 2. Algorithm to identify the clusters

1: **procedure** IDENTIFY-CLUSTERS(D, X, α)
2:      $\tilde{D} \leftarrow D$
3:      **for** $\ell \leftarrow 2, ..., L - 1$ **do**   ▷ Loops through the layers
4:          **if** $accuracy(\tilde{D}) > \alpha$ **then**
5:              $K_L(\ell) \leftarrow$ BINARYSEARCH$(\tilde{D}, \alpha, \ell)$ ▷ Finds optimal number of clusters
6:              $\tilde{D} \leftarrow$ ABSTRACT$(\tilde{D}, X, K_L)$
7:      **return** K_L

---

such groups, in this section, we illustrate this on one of them — the unsupervised learning approach of *k-means clustering* [Bis06], as a proof-of-concept.

Algorithm 1 describes how the approach works in general. It takes as input the original (trained) network D, an input set X and a function K_L, which for each layer gives the number of clusters to be identified in that layer. Each $x \in X$ is input into $\tilde{D}$ and for each neuron i in layer ℓ, an $|X|$-dimensional vector of observed activations $\mathbf{a}_i^{(\ell)} = [z_i^{(\ell)}(x_1), \ldots, z_i^{(\ell)}(x_{|X|})]$ is constructed. These vectors of activations, one for each neuron, are collected in the set A. We can now use the k-means algorithm on the set A to identify $K_L(\ell)$ clusters. Intuitively, k-means aims to split the set A into $K_L(\ell)$ clusters such that the pairwise squared deviations of points in the same cluster is minimized. Once a layer is clustered, the neurons of each cluster are merged and the neuron closest to the centroid of the respective cluster, denoted by $rep(C)$ in the pseudocode, is picked as the cluster representative. As described in Sect. 3.1, the outgoing connections of all the neurons in a cluster are added to the representative neuron of the cluster and all neurons except the representative are deleted.

While Algorithm 1 describes the clustering procedure, it is still a challenge to find the right K_L. In Algorithm 2, we present one heuristic to identify a good set of parameters for the clustering. It is based on the intuition that merging neurons closer to the output layer impacts the network accuracy the least, as the error due to merging is not multiplied and propagated through multiple layers. The overarching idea is to search for the best k-means parameter, $K_L(\ell)$, for each layer ℓ starting from the first hidden layer to the last hidden layer, while making sure that the merging with the said parameter (K_L) does not drop the accuracy of the network beyond a threshold α.

The algorithm takes a trained network D as input along with an input set X and a parameter α, the lower bound on the accuracy of the abstract network. The first hidden layer $(\ell = 2)$ is picked first and k-means clustering is attempted on it. The parameter $K_L(\ell)$ is discovered using the BINARYSEARCH procedure which searches for the lowest k such that the accuracy of the network abstracted with this parameter is the highest. We make a reasonable assumption here that a higher degree of clustering (i.e. a small k) leads to a higher drop in accuracy. Note that this might cause the BINARYSEARCH procedure to work on a monotone space and we might not exactly get the optimal. However, in our experiments, the binary search turned out to be a sufficiently good alternative to brute-force search. The algorithm ensures that merging the clusters as prescribed by K_L does not drop the accuracy of the abstracted network below α.[1] This process is now repeated on $\tilde{D}$ starting with the next hidden layer. Finally, K_L is returned, ready to be used with Algorithm 1.

Now we present two results which bound the error induced in the network due to abstraction. The first theorem applies to the case where we have clustered groups of I/O-similar neurons in each layer for the set X of network inputs.

Let for each neuron i, $\mathbf{a}_i = [z_i(x_1), \ldots, z_i(x_N)]$ where $x_j \in X$, and let $\tilde{D} = $ ABSTRACT(D, X, K_L) for some given K_L. Define $\boldsymbol{\epsilon}^{(\ell)}$, the maximal distance of a neuron from the respective cluster representative, as

$$\boldsymbol{\epsilon}^{(\ell)} = [\epsilon_1^{(\ell)}, \ldots, \epsilon_{n_\ell}^{(\ell)}]^\mathsf{T} \qquad \text{where} \qquad \epsilon_i^{(\ell)} = \|\mathbf{a}_i - \mathbf{a}_{r_{C_i}}\| \tag{3}$$

where $\|\cdot\|$ denotes the Euclidean norm operator, C_i denotes the cluster containing i and r_{C_i} denotes the representative of cluster C_i. Further, define the absolute error due to abstraction in layer ℓ as $\boldsymbol{err}^{(\ell)} = \tilde{\mathbf{z}}^{(\ell)} - \mathbf{z}^{(\ell)}$.

Theorem 1 (Clustering-induced error). *If the accumulated absolute error in the activations of layer ℓ is given by $\boldsymbol{err}^{(\ell)}$ and $\boldsymbol{\epsilon}^{(\ell+1)}$ denotes the the maximal distance of each neuron from their cluster representative (as defined in Eqn. 3) of layer $\ell + 1$, then the absolute error $\boldsymbol{err}^{(\ell+1)}$ for all inputs $\boldsymbol{x} \in X$ can be bounded by*

$$|\boldsymbol{err}^{(\ell+1)}| \leq |W^{(\ell)}\boldsymbol{err}^{(\ell)}| + \boldsymbol{\epsilon}^{(\ell+1)}$$

and hence, the absolute error in the network output is given by $\boldsymbol{err}^{(L)}$.

The second result considers the local robustness setting where we are interested in the output of the abstracted network when the input $\boldsymbol{x} \in X$ is perturbed by $\delta \in \mathbb{R}^{|\boldsymbol{x}|}$.

Theorem 2. *If the inputs $\boldsymbol{x} \in X$ to the abstract network $\tilde{D}$ are perturbed by $\delta \in \mathbb{R}^{|\boldsymbol{x}|}$, then the absolute error in the network output due to both abstraction and perturbation denoted by $\boldsymbol{err}_{total}$ is bounded for every $\boldsymbol{x} \in X$ and is given by*

$$|\boldsymbol{err}_{total}| \leq |\tilde{W}^{(L)} \ldots \tilde{W}^{(1)}\delta| + |\boldsymbol{err}^{(L)}|$$

where $\tilde{W}^{(\ell)}$ is the matrix of weights from layer ℓ to $\ell + 1$ in $\tilde{D}$, L is the number of layers in $\tilde{D}$ and $\boldsymbol{err}^{(L)}$ is the accumulated error due to abstraction as given by Theorem 1.

In other words, these theorems allow us to compute the absolute error produced due to the abstraction alone; or due to both (i) abstraction and (ii) perturbation of input. Theorem 2 gives us a direct (but naïve) procedure to perform local robustness verification by checking if there exists an output neuron i with a lower bound $(\tilde{D}_i(x) - (E_{total})_i)$ greater than the upper bound $(\tilde{D}_j(x) + (E_{total})_j)$ of all other output neurons j. The proofs of both theorems can be found in [Ash+20, Appendix A.2].

---

[1] Naturally, the parameter α has to be less than or equal to the accuracy of D.

4 Lifting Guarantees from Abstract NN to Original NN

In the previous section, we discussed how a large neural network could be abstracted and how the absolute error on the output could be calculated and even used for robustness verification. However, the error bounds presented in Theorem 2 might be too coarse to give any meaningful guarantees. In this section, we present a proof-of-concept approach for lifting verification results from the abstracted network to the original network. While in general the lifting depends on the verification algorithm, as a demonstrative example, we show how to perform the lifting when using the verification algorithm DeepPoly [Sin+19a] and also how it can be used in conjunction with our abstraction technique to give robustness guarantees on the original network.

We now give a quick summary of DeepPoly. Assume that we need to verify that the network D labels all inputs in the δ-neighborhood of a given input $x \in X$ to the same class; in other words, check if D is locally robust for the robustness query (D, x, δ). DeepPoly functions by propagating the interval $[x - \delta, x + \delta]$ through the network with the help of abstract interpretation, producing over-approximations (a lower and an upper bound) of activations of each neuron. The robustness query is then answered by checking if the lower bound of the neuron representing one of the labels is greater than the upper bounds of all other neurons. We refer the interested reader to [Sin+19a, Section 2] for an overview of DeepPoly. Note that the algorithm is sound but not complete.

If DeepPoly returns the bounds $\tilde{l}$ and $\tilde{u}$ for the abstract network $\tilde{D}$, the following theorem allows us to compute $[\hat{l}, \hat{u}]$ such that $[\hat{l}, \hat{u}] \supseteq [l, u]$, where $[l, u]$ would have been the bounds returned by DeepPoly on the original network D.

Theorem 3 (Lifting guarantees). *Consider the abstraction $\tilde{D}$ obtained by applying Algorithm 1 on a ReLU feedforward network D. Let $\tilde{l}^{(\ell)}$ and $\tilde{u}^{(\ell)}$ denote the lower bound and upper bound vectors returned by DeepPoly for the layer ℓ, and let $\tilde{W}_{+}^{(\ell)} = \max(0, \tilde{W}^{(\ell)})$ and $\tilde{W}_{-}^{(\ell)} = \min(\tilde{W}^{(\ell)}, 0)$ denote the +ve and -ve entries respectively of its ℓth layer weight matrix. Let $\epsilon^{(\ell)}$ denote the vector of maximal distances of neurons from their cluster representatives (as defined in Eq. 3), and let x be the input we are trying to verify for a perturbation $[-\delta, \delta]$. Then for all layers $\ell < L$, we can compute*

$$\hat{u}^{(\ell)} = \max \left(0, \begin{array}{l} \tilde{W}_{+}^{(\ell-1)}(\hat{u}^{(\ell-1)} + \epsilon^{(\ell-1)}) \\ + \tilde{W}_{-}^{(\ell-1)}(\hat{l}^{(\ell-1)} - \epsilon^{(\ell-1)}) \\ + \tilde{b}^{(\ell)} \end{array} \right) \qquad \hat{l}^{(\ell)} = \max \left(0, \begin{array}{l} \tilde{W}_{+}^{(\ell-1)}(\hat{l}^{(\ell-1)} - \epsilon^{(\ell-1)}) \\ + \tilde{W}_{-}^{(\ell-1)}(\hat{u}^{(\ell-1)} + \epsilon^{(\ell-1)}) \\ + \tilde{b}^{(\ell)} \end{array} \right)$$

where $\hat{u}^{(1)} = \tilde{u}^{(1)} = u^{(1)} = x + \delta$ and $\hat{l}^{(1)} = \tilde{l}^{(1)} = l^{(1)} = x - \delta$ such that

$$[\hat{l}, \hat{u}] \supseteq [l, u]$$

where $[l, u]$ is the bound computed by DeepPoly on the original network.

For output layer $\ell = L$, the application of the $\max(0, \cdot)$-function is omitted, the rest remains the same.

In other words, this theorem allows us to compute an over-approximation of the bounds computed by DeepPoly on the original network D by using only the abstract network, thereby allowing a local robustness proof to be lifted from the abstraction to the original network. Note that while this procedure is sound, it is not complete since the bounds computed by Theorem 3 might still be too coarse. An empirical discussion is presented in Sect. 5, an example of the proof lifting can be seen in [Ash+20, Appendix A.5], and the proof is given in [Ash+20, Appendix A.3].

5 Experiments

We now analyze the potential of our abstraction. In particular, in Sect. 5.1, we look at how much we can abstract while still guaranteeing a high test accuracy for the abstracted network. Moreover, we present verification results of abstracted network, suggesting a use case where it replaces the original network. In Sect. 5.2, we additionally consider lifting of the verification proof from the abstracted network to the original network.

We ran experiments with multiple neural network architectures on the popular MNIST dataset [LeC98]. We refer to our network architectures by the shorthand $L \times n$, for example "6×100", to denote a network with L fully-connected feedforward hidden layers with n neurons each, along with a separate input and output layers whose sizes depend on the dataset — 784 neurons in the input layer and 10 in the output layer in the case of MNIST. We implemented the abstraction technique described in Sect. 3.2 using the popular deep learning library TensorFlow [Aba+15] and the machine learning library Scikit-learn [Ped+11]. For the verification, we used the DeepPoly implementation available in the ERAN toolbox[2].

Remark on Acas Xu. We do not run experiments on the standard NN verification case study Acas Xu [JKO18]. The Acas Xu networks are very compact, containing only 6 layers with 50 neurons each. The training/test data for these networks are not easily available, which makes it difficult to run our data-dependent abstraction algorithm. Further, the network architecture cannot be scaled up to observe the benefits of abstraction, which, we conjecture, become evident only for large networks possibly containing redundancies. Moreover, the specifications that are commonly verified on Acas Xu are not easily encodable in DeepPoly.

5.1 Abstraction Results

First, we generated various NN architectures by scaling up the number of neurons per layer as well as the number of layers themselves and trained them on MNIST. We generated various NN architectures by scaling up the number of

---

[2] Available at github.com/eth-sri/ERAN.

neurons per layer as well as the number of layers themselves and trained them on MNIST. For doing so, we split the dataset into three parts: one for the training, one for validation and one for testing. The training is then performed on the training dataset by using common optimizers and loss functions. The training was stopped when the accuracy on the validation set did not increase anymore. The NN on MNIST were trained on 60000 samples from the whole dataset. Of these, 10% are split for validation, thus there are 54000 images for the training itself and 6000 images for validation. The optimizer used for the training process is ADAM, which is an extension to the stochastic gradient descent. To prevent getting stuck in local minima, it includes the first and second moments of the gradient. It is a common choice for the training of NN and performed reasonably well in this application. Its parameter are set to the default from TensorFlow, namely a learning rate of 0.001, $\beta_1 = 0.9$, $\beta_2 = 0.999$ and $\epsilon = 1e - 07$.

For MNIST, the most reasonable loss function is the sparse categorical crossentropy. The training process was stopped when the loss function on the validation data did not decrease anymore. Usually, the process would stop after at most 10 epochs. Then, we executed our clustering-based abstraction algorithm (Algorithm 1) on each trained network allowing for a drop in accuracy on a test dataset of at most 1%.

Size of the Abstraction. Table 1 gives some information about the quality of the abstraction - the extent to which we can abstract while sacrificing accuracy of at most 1%. We can see that increasing the width of a layer (number of neurons) while keeping the depth of the network fixed increases the number of neurons that can be merged, i.e. the reduction rate increases. We conjecture that there is a minimum number of neurons per layer that are needed to simulate the behavior of the original network. On the other hand, interestingly, if the depth of the network is increased while keeping the width fixed, the reduction rate seems to hover around 15–20%.

Figure 2 demonstrates the potential of the clustering-based abstraction procedure in compressing the network. Here, the abstraction is performed layer after layer from layer 1 to layer 6. We cluster as much as possible permitting the test accuracy of the network to drop by at most 1%. Unsurprisingly, we get more reduction in the later (closer to output) layers compared to the initial. We conjecture that this happens as the most necessary information is already processed and computed early on, and the later layers transmit low dimensional information. Interestingly, one may observe that in layers 4, 5 and 6, all network architectures ranging from 50 to 500 neurons/layer can be compressed to an almost equal size around 30 nodes/layer.

Verifying the Abstraction. As mentioned in the Sect. 1, we found that the abstraction, considered as a standalone network, is faster to verify than the original network. This opens up the possibility of verifying the abstraction and replacing the original network with it, in real-use scenarios. In Fig. 3, we show the time it takes to verify the abstract network using DeepPoly against the time

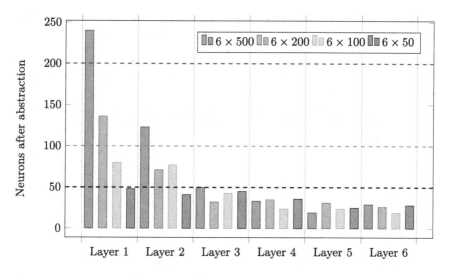

Fig. 2. Plot depicting the sizes of the abstract networks when initialized with 4 different architectures and after repetitively applying clustering-based abstraction on the layers until their accuracy on the test set is approximately 95%.

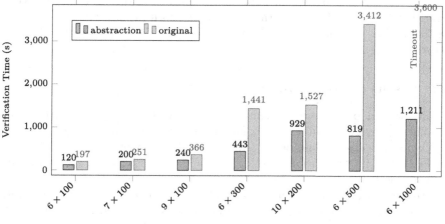

Fig. 3. Accelerated verification after abstracting compared to verification of the original. The abstracted NN are verified directly without performing proof lifting, as if they were to replace the original one in their application. The time taken for abstracting (not included in the verification time) is 14, 14, 20, 32, 37, 53, and 214 s respectively.

taken to verify the respective original network. Note that the reduction rate and accuracy drop of the corresponding networks can be found in Table 1 above.

Table 1. Reduction rate of abstracted neural networks with different architectures along with the drop in accuracy (measured on an independent test set). In the top half, the number of layers (depth) is varied and in the bottom half, the number of neurons per layer (width) is increased. This table shows that the clustering-based abstraction works better with wider networks. The networks were originally trained to reach an accuracy on the test set of around 96.3% to 98.2%.

Network Arch.	Accuracy Drop (%)	Reduction Rate (%)
3×100	0.40	15.5
4×100	0.41	15.5
5×100	0.21	21.2
6×100	0.10	13.3
6×50	0.10	5.7
6×100	0.10	13.3
6×200	0.10	30.2
6×300	0.20	39.9
6×1000	0.01	61.7

Clearly, there is a significant improvement in the run time of the verification algorithm; for the 6×1000 case, the verification algorithm timed out after 1 hour on the original network while it finished in less than 21 mins on the abstract network.

5.2   Results on Lifting Verification Proof

Finally, we ran experiments to demonstrate the working of the full verification pipeline — involving clustering to identify the neurons that can be merged, performing the abstraction (Sect. 3.2), running DeepPoly on the abstraction and finally lifting the verification proof to answer the verification query on original network (Sect. 4).

We were interested in two parameters: (i) the time taken to run the full pipeline; and (ii) the number of verification queries that could be satisfied (out of 200). We ran experiments on a 6×300 network that could be verified to be locally robust for 197/200 images in 48 minutes by DeepPoly. The results are shown in Table 2. In the best case, our preliminary implementation of the full pipeline was able to verify robustness for 195 images in 36 mins — 13 s for clustering and abstracting, 35 min for verification, and 5 s for proof lifting. In other words, a 14.7% reduction in network size produced a 25% reduction in verification time. When we pushed the abstraction further, e.g. last row of Table 2, to obtain a reduction of 19.4% in the network size, DeepPoly could still verify robustness of the abstracted network for 196 images in just 34 minutes (29% reduction). However, in this case, the proof could not be lifted to the original network as the over-approximations we obtained were too coarse.

Table 2. Results of abstraction, verification and proof lifting of a 6×300 NN on 200 images to verify. The first column gives the number of neurons removed in layers 3, 4, 5 and 6 respectively. The second column shows the reduction in the size of the abstracted network compared to the original. We also report the number of images for which the original network could be proved robust by lifting the verification proof.

Removed Neurons	Reduction Rate (%)	Images Verified	Verification Time (min)
15, 25, 100, 100	13.33	195	36
15, 50, 100, 100	14.72	195	36
25, 25, 100, 100	13.89	190	36
25, 50, 100, 100	15.28	190	36
25, 100, 100, 100	18.06	63	35
50, 100, 100, 100	19.44	0	34

This points to the interesting fact that the time taken in clustering and proof lifting are indeed not the bottlenecks in the pipeline. Moreover, a decrease in the width of the network indeed tends to reduce the verification time. This opens the possibility of spending additional computational time exploring more powerful heuristics (e.g. principal component analysis) in place of the naïve k-means clustering in order to find smaller abstractions. Moreover, a counterexample-guided abstraction refinement (CEGAR) approach can be employed to improve the proof lifting by tuning the abstraction where necessary.

6 Conclusion

We have presented an abstraction framework for feed-forward neural networks using ReLU activation units. Rather than just syntactic information, it reflects the semantics of the neurons, via our concept of I/O-similarity on experimental values. In contrast to compression-based frameworks, the abstraction mapping between the original neurons and the abstract neurons allows for transferring verification proofs (transferring counterexamples is trivial), allowing for abstraction-based verification of neural networks.

While we have demonstrated the potential of the new abstraction approach by a proof-of-concept implementation, its practical applicability relies on several next steps. Firstly, I/O-similarity with the Euclidean distance ignores even any linear dependencies of the I/O-vectors; I/O-similarity with e.g. principal component analysis thus might yield orders of magnitude smaller abstractions, scaling to more realistic networks. Secondly, due to the correspondence between the proofs, CEGAR could be employed: one can refine those neurons where the transferred constraints in the proof become too loose. Besides, it is also desirable to extend the framework to other architectures, such as convolutional neural networks.

References

[Aba+15] Abadi, M., et al.: TensorFlow: Large-Scale Machine Learning on Heterogeneous Systems. Software available from tensorflow.org. (2015). https://www.tensorflow.org/

[AM18] Akhtar, N., Mian, A.: Threat of adversarial attacks on deep learning in computer vision: a survey. In: IEEE Access, vol. 6, pp. 14410–14430 (2018)

[Ash+20] Ashok, P., et al.: DeepAbstract: neural network abstraction for accelerating verification. Technical report (2020). arXiv: 2006.13735 [cs.LO]

[Bis06] Christopher M Bishop. Pattern recognition and machine learning. springer, 2006

[CGL94] Clarke, E.M., Grumberg, O., Long, D.E.: Model checking and abstraction. ACM Trans. Program. Lang. Syst. **16**(5), 1512–1542 (1994)

[Che+17a] Chen, X., et al.: Multi-view 3d object detection network for autonomous driving. In: CVPR (2017)

[Che+17b] Yu, C., et al.: A Survey of Model Compression and Acceleration for Deep Neural Networks. In: CoRR abs/1710.09282 (2017)

[Cla+00] Clarke, E.M., et al.: Counterexample-guided abstraction refinement. In: CAV (2000)

[CNR17] Chih-Hong, C., Nührenberg, G., Ruess, H.: Maximum resilience of artificial neural networks. In: ATVA (2017)

[Den+20] Lei, D., et al.: Model compression and hardware acceleration for neural networks: a comprehensive survey. In: Proceedings of the IEEE **108**(4), 485–532 (2020)

[Don+18] Dong, Y., et al.: Boosting adversarial attacks with momentum. In: CVPR (2018)

[Dvi+18] Krishnamurthy, D., et al.: A dual approach to scalable verification of deep networks. In: UAI (2018)

[Ehl17] Rüdiger, E.: Formal verification of piece-wise linear feed- forward neural networks. In: ATVA (2017)

[Geh+18] Timon, G., et al.: Ai2: safety and robustness certification of neural networks with abstract interpretation. In: 2018 IEEE Symposium on Security and Privacy (SP) (2018)

[HMD16] Han, S., Mao, H., Dally, W.J.: Deep compression: compressing deep neural network with pruning, trained quantization and huffman coding. In: ICLR (2016)

[HTF09] Trevor Hastie, Robert Tibshirani, and Jerome Friedman. The elements of statistical learning: data mining, inference, and prediction. Springer Science & Business Media, 2009

[Hua+17] Huang, X., et al.: Safety verification of deep neural networks. In: CAV, no. 1 (2017)

[JKO18] Julian, K.D., Kochenderfer, M.J., Owen, M.P.: Deep Neural Network Compression for Aircraft Collision Avoidance Systems. In: CoRR abs/1810.04240 (2018)

[Kat+17] Guy, K., et al.: Reluplex: an efficient SMT solver for verifying deep neural networks. In: CAV, no. 1 (2017)

[LeC98] LeCun, Y.: The MNIST database of handwritten digits. http://yann.lecun.com/exdb/mnist/ (1998)

[MHN13] Maas, A.L., Hannun, A.Y., Ng, A.Y.: Rectifier nonlinearities improve neural network acoustic models. In: ICML (2013)

[PA19] Pavithra, P., Zahra, R.A.: Abstraction based output range analysis for neural networks. In: NeurIPS (2019)

[Pap+16] Papernot, N., et al.: The limitations of deep learning in adversarial settings. In: EuroS&P. IEEE (2016)

[Ped+11] Pedregosa, F., et al.: Scikit-learn: machine Learning in Python. J. Mach. Learn. Res. **12**, 2825–2830 (2011)

[PT10] Luca, P., Armando, T.: An abstraction-refinement approach to verification of artificial neural networks. In: CAV (2010)

[SB15] Suraj, S., Venkatesh Babu, R.: Data-free parameter pruning for deep neural networks. In: BMVC (2015)

[Sin+19a] Singh, G., et al.: An abstract domain for certifying neural networks. In: Proceedings ACM Program. Lang. vol. 3.POPL, 41:1–41:30 (2019)

[Sin+19b] Singh, G., et al.: Boosting robustness certification of neural networks. In: ICLR (Poster) (2019)

[SVS19] Su, J., Vasconcellos Vargas, D., Sakurai, K.: One pixel attack for fooling deep neural networks. IEEE Trans. Evol. Comput. **23**(5), 828–841 (2019)

[YGK19] Elboher, Y.Y., Gottschlich, J., Katz, G.: An abstraction-based framework for neural network verification. In: arXiv e-prints, arXiv:1910.14574 (2019)

[ZYZ18] Zhong, G., Yao, H., Zhou, H.: Merging neurons for structure compression of deep networks. In: ICPR (2018)

Faithful and Effective Reward Schemes for Model-Free Reinforcement Learning of Omega-Regular Objectives

Ernst Moritz Hahn[1], Mateo Perez[2(✉)], Sven Schewe[3], Fabio Somenzi[2], Ashutosh Trivedi[2], and Dominik Wojtczak[3]

[1] University of Twente, Enschede, The Netherlands
[2] University of Colorado Boulder, Boulder, USA
Mateo.Perez@colorado.edu
[3] University of Liverpool, Liverpool, UK

Abstract. Omega-regular properties—specified using linear time temporal logic or various forms of omega-automata—find increasing use in specifying the objectives of reinforcement learning (RL). The key problem that arises is that of faithful and effective translation of the objective into a scalar reward for model-free RL. A recent approach exploits Büchi automata with restricted nondeterminism to reduce the search for an optimal policy for an ω-regular property to that for a simple reachability objective. A possible drawback of this translation is that reachability rewards are sparse, being reaped only at the end of each episode. Another approach reduces the search for an optimal policy to an optimization problem with two interdependent discount parameters. While this approach provides denser rewards than the reduction to reachability, it is not easily mapped to off-the-shelf RL algorithms. We propose a reward scheme that reduces the search for an optimal policy to an optimization problem with a single discount parameter that produces dense rewards and is compatible with off-the-shelf RL algorithms. Finally, we report an experimental comparison of these and other reward schemes for model-free RL with omega-regular objectives.

1 Introduction

A significant challenge to widespread adoption of reinforcement learning (RL) is the faithful translation of designer's intent to the scalar reward signal required by RL algorithms [19]. Logic-based specifications help in two ways: by precisely capturing the intended objective, and by allowing its automatic translation to a reward function. Omega-regular objectives, such as those expressed in Linear Temporal Logic (LTL) [25] and by ω-automata [28], have recently been proposed to specify learning objectives for both model-based [10,20] and model-free RL.

Model-free RL algorithms do not construct a model of the environment; hence, they often scale better than model-based algorithms. However, applying model-free RL to ω-regular properties requires one to address separate concerns:

© Springer Nature Switzerland AG 2020
D. V. Hung and O. Sokolsky (Eds.): ATVA 2020, LNCS 12302, pp. 108–124, 2020.
https://doi.org/10.1007/978-3-030-59152-6_6

1. Finding the right automata representation to build product MDPs with ω-regular acceptance conditions on the fly [13].
2. Translating the acceptance condition into a reward assignment that is appropriate for RL, such as reachability or maximizing an overall reward earned.
3. Computing policies that maximize expected reward with a RL technique, like Q-learning, which normally applies discounting to the rewards.

In addressing these concerns, one strives to achieve an overall translation that is *faithful* (maximizing reward means maximizing probability of achieving the objective) and *effective* (RL quickly converges to optimal strategies). In this paper, we focus on the second step, and explore its interplay with the third step when using off-the-shelf RL tools and techniques.

The first approach to learning for ω-regular objectives used deterministic Rabin automata [30]. While the reduction used from Rabin automata to rewards does not have the required correctness properties [12]—there is still no direct translation from Rabin automata to rewards—this work opened the door to using reinforcement learning for temporal and ω-regular properties.

The problems with handling Rabin automata suggest that one should use automata with simpler acceptance mechanisms, like Büchi automata. However, Büchi automata require nondeterminism to recognize all ω-regular languages. Nondeterministic machines can use unbounded look-ahead to resolve nondeterministic choices. However, model checking and reinforcement learning (RL) for Markov Decision Process (MDPs [29]) have a game setting, which restricts the resolution of nondeterminism to be based on the past.

Being forced to resolve nondeterminism on the fly, an automaton may end up rejecting words it should accept, so that using it can lead to incorrect results. Due to this difficulty, initial solutions to game solving and probabilistic model checking have been based on deterministic automata—usually with Rabin or parity acceptance conditions. For two-player games, Henzinger and Piterman proposed the notion of *good-for-games (GFG)* automata [16]. These are nondeterministic automata that simulate [9,15,26] a deterministic automaton that recognizes the same language. The existence of a simulation strategy means that nondeterministic choices can be resolved without look-ahead.

On an MDP, however, the controller is not facing a strategic opponent who may take full advantage of the automaton's inability to resolve nondeterminism on the fly. Vardi was the first to note that probabilistic model checking is possible with Büchi automata only capable of restricted nondeterminism [37]. *Limit deterministic Büchi automata (LDBA)* [6,11,31] make no nondeterministic choice after seeing an accepting transition. They still recognize all ω-regular languages and are, under mild restrictions [31], *suitable* for probabilistic model checking.

The second generation of methods for reinforcement learning therefore used such limit-deterministic Büchi automata [3,12,14]. These papers differ significantly in how they translate the Büchi condition into rewards. The first approach [12] reduces to reachability: in a nutshell, it translates traversing an accepting transition to reaching a fresh target state with a low probability $1 - \zeta$, and to continuing to traverse the product MDP with high probability ζ. The second approach [3] assigns fixed rewards whenever passing an accepting transition, while using a complex discounting strategy: when passing an accepting transition, the reward is given and a discount factor of $\gamma_B \in]0,1[$ is applied to the remaining rewards, whereas when traversing a non-accepting transition no reward is given, and a different discount factor $\gamma \in]0,1[$ is applied. For the approach to be correct, it is required that γ_B be a function of γ with the property that, when γ goes to 1, $\frac{1-\gamma}{1-\gamma_B(\gamma)}$ goes to 0. The advantage of this method is that rewards appear earlier, but at the cost of having two parameters (that are not independent of each other), and an overhead in the calculation. The third approach [14] uses a constant discount factor $\gamma \in]0,1]$, which (while not technically correct [3,12]) usually works and provides good results in practice.

We use transformations on the reward structure from our reachability reduction in [12] to infer simple alternative total and discounted reward structures that favor the same strategies as the reachability reduction from [12] and therefore inherit the correctness from there. The total reward structure keeps the accepting sink, and simply provides a reward whenever an accepting transition is taken, regardless of whether or not the sink is reached. We show that this increases the expected payoff obtained from a strategy by a constant factor, thus preserving preferences between different strategies.

The discounted reward structure does not introduce the accepting sink, but works on the unadjusted product MDP. It uses a biased discount, where a discount is only made when an accepting transition is passed. This is closely related to [3], but keeps the vital separation of concerns that allows us to keep the proofs simple and the method easy to use and understand: We introduce a reduction that produces a faithful reward structure with a single variable ζ. Coupled to a learning technique that uses discounted rewards, our approach is equivalent to that of [3] (though it suggests that γ is really a function of γ_B, not the other way round), but with a clear separation of concerns: the smaller factor γ_B (which corresponds to $\zeta \cdot \gamma$ in this setting) is the ingredient that makes the reward structure faithful, the larger discount factor γ simply provides contraction.

A good reward scheme should promote fast learning by giving dense rewards with low variance. It should also be compatible with off-the-shelf RL algorithms, so that state-of-the-art algorithms may be used promptly and with little effort. The rewards produced by the scheme of [12] tend to be sparse because they are only possible at the end of an episode, when the target state is reached. On the other hand, the reachability-based rewards can be directly used with any off-the-shelf RL algorithm [17,32]. The total reward structure provides dense rewards and is straightforward to integrate with off-the-shelf RL algorithms. However, it is affected by the high variability of the return. Discounted rewards fix the problem with variability, but require the implementations of RL algorithms to accommodate state-dependent discounts.

While the reward transformations are ways to 'shape' rewards in the literal sense of arranging them in a way that they appear early, they are orthogonal to classic reward shaping techniques like adding potentials to MDP states [22,27].

As an orthogonal approach, it is a potentially helpful addition to all the reward schemes discussed above.

Reward machines [5,18] is a related notion of providing a formal structure to specify rewards. Reward machines are Mealy machines where the inputs are the observations of the MDP and the outputs are scalar rewards. The key difference of reward machines from ours is that reward machines interpret specification of finite traces (e.g. LTL on finite prefixes [8]). Moreover, they allow specification of arbitrary scalar rewards for various events, while in our work the reward is given strictly according to the formal specification.

This paper is organized as follows. After the preliminaries, we first introduce the novel total reward and then the new faithful total rewards based on biased discounts (Sects. 3.2 and 3.3) for good-for-MDP automata. In Sect. 4, we discuss how to use Q-learning for this faithful reward scheme. In Sect. 5, we evaluate the impact of the contributions of the paper on reinforcement learning algorithms. Section 6 presents conclusions.

2   Preliminaries

A *nondeterministic Büchi automaton* is a tuple $\mathcal{A} = \langle \Sigma, Q, q_0, \Delta, \Gamma \rangle$, where Σ is a finite *alphabet*, Q is a finite set of *states*, $q_0 \in Q$ is the *initial state*, $\Delta \subseteq Q \times \Sigma \times Q$ are transitions, and $\Gamma \subseteq Q \times \Sigma \times Q$ is the transition-based *acceptance condition*.

A *run* r of $\mathcal{A}$ on $w \in \Sigma^\omega$ is an ω-word $r_0, w_0, r_1, w_1, \ldots$ in $(Q \times \Sigma)^\omega$ such that $r_0 = q_0$ and, for $i > 0$, it is $(r_{i-1}, w_{i-1}, r_i) \in \Delta$. We write $\inf(r)$ for the set of transitions that appear infinitely often in the run r. A run r of $\mathcal{A}$ is *accepting* if $\inf(r) \cap \Gamma \neq \emptyset$.

The *language*, $L_{\mathcal{A}}$, of $\mathcal{A}$ (or, *recognized* by $\mathcal{A}$) is the subset of words in Σ^ω that have accepting runs in $\mathcal{A}$. A language is ω-*regular* if it is accepted by a Büchi automaton. An automaton $\mathcal{A} = \langle \Sigma, Q, Q_0, \Delta, \Gamma \rangle$ is *deterministic* if $(q, \sigma, q'), (q, \sigma, q'') \in \Delta$ implies $q' = q''$. $\mathcal{A}$ is *complete* if, for all $\sigma \in \Sigma$ and all $q \in Q$, there is a transition $(q, \sigma, q') \in \Delta$. A word in Σ^ω has exactly one run in a deterministic, complete automaton.

A *Markov decision process (MDP)* $\mathcal{M}$ is a tuple $\langle S, s_0, A, T, \Sigma, L \rangle$ where S is a finite set of states, s_0 is a designated initial state, A is a finite set of *actions*, $T : S \times A \to \mathcal{D}(S)$, where $\mathcal{D}(S)$ is the set of probability distributions over S, is the *probabilistic transition function*, Σ is an alphabet, and $L : S \times A \times S \to \Sigma$ is the *labeling function* of the set of transitions. For a state $s \in S$, $A(s)$ denotes the set of actions available in s. For states $s, s' \in S$ and $a \in A(s)$, we have that $T(s, a)(s')$ equals $\Pr(s'|s, a)$.

A *run* of $\mathcal{M}$ is an ω-word $s_0, a_1, \ldots \in S \times (A \times S)^\omega$ such that $\Pr(s_{i+1}|s_i, a_{i+1}) > 0$ for all $i \geq 0$. A finite run is a finite such sequence. For a *run* $r = s_0, a_1, s_1, \ldots$ we define the corresponding labeled run as $L(r) = L(s_0, a_1, s_1), L(s_1, a_2, s_2), \ldots \in \Sigma^\omega$. We write $Runs(\mathcal{M})$ $(FRuns(\mathcal{M}))$ for the set of runs (finite runs) of $\mathcal{M}$ and $Runs_s(\mathcal{M})$ $(FRuns_s(\mathcal{M}))$ for the set of runs (finite runs) of $\mathcal{M}$ starting from state s. When the MDP is clear from the context we drop the argument $\mathcal{M}$.

A strategy in $\mathcal{M}$ is a function $\mu : FRuns \to \mathcal{D}(A)$ such that for all finite runs r we have $supp(\mu(r)) \subseteq A(\mathsf{last}(r))$, where $supp(d)$ is the support of d and $\mathsf{last}(r)$ is the last state of r. Let $Runs^{\mu}_s(\mathcal{M})$ denote the subset of runs $Runs_s(\mathcal{M})$ that correspond to strategy μ and initial state s. Let $\Sigma_{\mathcal{M}}$ be the set of all strategies. A strategy μ is *pure* if $\mu(r)$ is a point distribution for all runs $r \in FRuns$ and we say that μ is *stationary* if $\mathsf{last}(r) = \mathsf{last}(r')$ implies $\mu(r) = \mu(r')$ for all runs $r, r' \in FRuns$. A strategy is *positional* if it is both pure and stationary.

The behavior of an MDP $\mathcal{M}$ under a strategy μ with starting state s is defined on a probability space $(Runs^{\mu}_s, \mathcal{F}^{\mu}_s, \mathrm{Pr}^{\mu}_s)$ over the set of infinite runs of μ from s. Given a random variable over the set of infinite runs $f : Runs \to \mathbb{R}$, we write $\mathbb{E}^{\mu}_s\{f\}$ for the expectation of f over the runs of $\mathcal{M}$ from state s that follow strategy μ. A *Markov chain* is an MDP whose set of actions is singleton. For any MDP $\mathcal{M}$ and stationary strategy μ, let $\mathcal{M}_{\mu}$ be the Markov chain resulting from choosing the actions in $\mathcal{M}$ according to μ.

Given an MDP $\mathcal{M}$ and an automaton $\mathcal{A} = \langle \Sigma, Q, q_0, \Delta, \Gamma \rangle$, we want to compute an optimal strategy satisfying the objective that the run of $\mathcal{M}$ is in the language of $\mathcal{A}$. We define the *semantic satisfaction* probability for $\mathcal{A}$ and a strategy μ from state s as:

$$\mathsf{PSem}^{\mathcal{M}}_{\mathcal{A}}(s, \mu) = \mathrm{Pr}^{\mu}_s\{r \in Runs^{\mu}_s : L(r) \in L_{\mathcal{A}}\} \text{ and}$$
$$\mathsf{PSem}^{\mathcal{M}}_{\mathcal{A}}(s) = \sup_{\mu} \left(\mathsf{PSem}^{\mathcal{M}}_{\mathcal{A}}(s, \mu) \right) .$$

A strategy μ_* is optimal for $\mathcal{A}$ if $\mathsf{PSem}^{\mathcal{M}}_{\mathcal{A}}(s, \mu_*) = \mathsf{PSem}^{\mathcal{M}}_{\mathcal{A}}(s)$.

When using automata for the analysis of MDPs, we need a syntactic variant of the acceptance condition. Given an MDP $\mathcal{M} = \langle S, s_0, A, T, \Sigma, L \rangle$ and an automaton $\mathcal{A} = \langle \Sigma, Q, q_0, \Delta, \Gamma \rangle$, the *product* $\mathcal{M} \times \mathcal{A} = \langle S \times Q, (s_0, q_0), A \times Q, T^{\times}, \Gamma^{\times} \rangle$ is an MDP augmented with an initial state (s_0, q_0) and accepting transitions $\Gamma^{\times}$. The function $T^{\times} : (S \times Q) \times (A \times Q) \to \mathcal{D}(S \times Q)$ is defined by

$$T^{\times}((s, q), (a, q'))((s', q')) = \begin{cases} T(s, a)(s') & \text{if } (q, L(s, a, s'), q') \in \Delta \\ 0 & \text{otherwise.} \end{cases}$$

Finally, $\Gamma^{\times} \subseteq (S \times Q) \times (A \times Q) \times (S \times Q)$ is defined by $((s, q), (a, q'), (s', q')) \in \Gamma^{\times}$ if, and only if, $(q, L(s, a, s'), q') \in \Gamma$ and $T(s, a)(s') > 0$. A strategy $\mu^{\times}$ on the product defines a strategy μ on the MDP with the same value, and vice versa. (For a stationary $\mu^{\times}$, μ may need memory.) We define the *syntactic satisfaction* probabilities as

$$\mathsf{PSat}^{\mathcal{M}}_{\mathcal{A}}((s, q), \mu^{\times}) = \mathrm{Pr}^{\mu}_s\{r \in Runs^{\mu^{\times}}_{(s,q)}(\mathcal{M} \times \mathcal{A}) : \inf(r) \cap \Gamma^{\times} \neq \emptyset\}$$
$$\mathsf{PSat}^{\mathcal{M}}_{\mathcal{A}}(s) = \sup_{\mu^{\times}} \left(\mathsf{PSat}^{\mathcal{M}}_{\mathcal{A}}((s, q_0), \mu^{\times}) \right) .$$

Note that $\mathsf{PSat}^{\mathcal{M}}_{\mathcal{A}}(s) = \mathsf{PSem}^{\mathcal{M}}_{\mathcal{A}}(s)$ holds for a deterministic $\mathcal{A}$. In general, $\mathsf{PSat}^{\mathcal{M}}_{\mathcal{A}}(s) \leq \mathsf{PSem}^{\mathcal{M}}_{\mathcal{A}}(s)$ holds, but equality is not guaranteed because the optimal resolution of nondeterministic choices may require access to future events.

An automaton $\mathcal{A}$ is *good for MDPs* (GFM), if $\mathsf{PSat}_{\mathcal{A}}^{\mathcal{M}}(s_0) = \mathsf{PSem}_{\mathcal{A}}^{\mathcal{M}}(s_0)$ holds for all MDPs $\mathcal{M}$ [13]. For an automaton to match $\mathsf{PSem}_{\mathcal{A}}^{\mathcal{M}}(s_0)$, its non-determinism is restricted not to rely heavily on the future; rather, it must be possible to resolve the nondeterminism on-the-fly. In this paper we only consider GFM automata, which have this ability.

For ω-regular objectives, optimal satisfaction probabilities and strategies can be computed using graph-theoretic techniques over the product structure. However, when the MDP transition structure is unknown, such techniques are not applicable. Model-free reinforcement learning overcomes this limitation.

3   Faithful Translation of Objectives to Rewards

The problem we address is the following:

> *Given MDP $\mathcal{M}$ with unknown transition structure and a GFM Büchi automaton $\mathcal{A}$ accepting an ω-regular objective φ, compute a strategy optimal for $\mathcal{A}$, that is, a strategy that maximizes the probability that $\mathcal{M}$ satisfies φ.*

Reinforcement learning (RL) provides a framework to compute optimal strategies from repeated interactions with an MDPs with unknown transition structure. It consists of maximizing the expectation of a scalar reward. Of the two main approaches to RL, *model-free* and *model-based*, the former, which is asymptotically space-efficient [33], has been shown to scale well [35].

Bridging the gap between ω-regular specifications and model-free RL requires a translation from specification to scalar reward such that a model-free RL algorithm maximizing scalar rewards produces a policy that maximizes the probability to satisfy the specification. We call this requirement *faithfulness*. Another key requirement on such a translation is *effectiveness*: the reward should be formulated to help mainstream RL algorithms (such as Q-learning [38]) to reliably and quickly learn such optimal policies. We next present three solutions to the faithfulness requirement. From the approach of [12] we derive two reward schemes that translate the maximization of satisfaction probability to total reward and discounted reward problems. In Sects. 4 and 5 we discuss their effectiveness.

3.1   Reachability Rewards

The reduction from [12] (see Fig. 1) was the first faithful translation of ω-regular objectives to scalar rewards for model-free RL. Maximizing the chance to realize an ω-regular objective given by an MDP Büchi automaton $\mathcal{A}$ for an MDP $\mathcal{M}$ is reduced to maximizing the chance to meet the reachability objective in the augmented MDP $\mathcal{R}^\zeta$ (for $\zeta \in]0,1[$) obtained from $\mathcal{M} \times \mathcal{A}$ by

- adding a new target state t (either as a sink with a self-loop or as a point where the computation stops; we choose here the latter view) and by
- making the target t a destination of each accepting transition τ of $\mathcal{M} \times \mathcal{A}$ with probability $1 - \zeta$ and multiplying the original probabilities of all other destinations of an accepting transition τ by ζ.

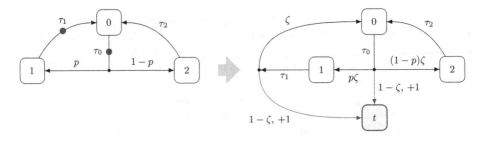

Fig. 1. Reachability reward scheme.

We define the probability to reach the sink t in $\mathcal{R}^\zeta$ as

$$\mathsf{PSat}_t^{\mathcal{R}^\zeta}((s,q),\mu) = \Pr{}_s^\mu\{r \in \mathit{Runs}_{(s,q)}^\mu(\mathcal{R}^\zeta) : r \text{ reaches } t\}$$

$$\mathsf{PSat}_t^{\mathcal{R}^\zeta}(s) = \sup_\mu \left(\mathsf{PSat}_t^{\mathcal{R}^\zeta}((s,q_0),\mu)\right) .$$

Theorem 1 ([12]). *The following holds:*

1. $\mathcal{R}^\zeta$ *(for $\zeta \in {]}0,1{[}$) and $\mathcal{M} \times \mathcal{A}$ have the same set of strategies.*
2. *For a positional strategy μ, the chance of reaching the target t in $\mathcal{R}_\mu^\zeta$ is 1 if, and only if, the chance of satisfying the Büchi objective in $(\mathcal{M} \times \mathcal{A})_\mu$ is 1:*
   $$\mathsf{PSat}_t^{\mathcal{R}^\zeta}((s_0,q_0),\mu) = 1 \iff \mathsf{PSat}_{\mathcal{A}}^{\mathcal{M}}((s_0,q_0),\mu) = 1.$$
3. *There is a $\zeta_0 \in {]}0,1{[}$ such that, for all $\zeta \in [\zeta_0, 1{[}$, an optimal reachability strategy μ for $\mathcal{R}^\zeta$ is an optimal strategy for the Büchi objective in $\mathcal{M} \times \mathcal{A}$:*
   $$\mathsf{PSat}_t^{\mathcal{R}^\zeta}((s_0,q_0),\mu) = \mathsf{PSat}_t^{\mathcal{R}^\zeta}(s_0) \Rightarrow \mathsf{PSat}_{\mathcal{A}}^{\mathcal{M}}((s_0,q_0),\mu) = \mathsf{PSat}_{\mathcal{A}}^{\mathcal{M}}(s_0).$$

3.2 Total and Dense Rewards

Theorem 1 proves the faithfulness of the translation to reachability of [12], which, however, has a drawback. For ζ close to 1, the rewards occur late: they are *sparse*. Addressing this concern leads to our second translation, which produces *denser* rewards and reduces the problem to the maximization of *total* reward.

   We build, for a GFM Büchi automaton $\mathcal{A}$ and an MDP $\mathcal{M}$, the augmented MDP $\mathcal{T}^\zeta$ (for $\zeta \in {]}0,1{[}$) obtained from $\mathcal{M} \times \mathcal{A}$ in the same way as $\mathcal{R}^\zeta$, i.e., by

- adding a new sink state t (as a sink where the computation stops) and
- by making the sink t a destination of each accepting transition τ of $\mathcal{M} \times \mathcal{A}$ with probability $1 - \zeta$ and by multiplying the original probabilities of all other destinations of an accepting transition τ by ζ.

Unlike $\mathcal{R}^\zeta$, MDP $\mathcal{T}^\zeta$ is equipped with a total reward (also known as undiscounted reward) objective, where taking an accepting (in $\mathcal{M} \times \mathcal{A}$) transition τ provides a reward of 1, regardless of whether it leads to the sink t.

Let $N(r)$ be the number of accepting transitions in a run r of $\mathcal{T}^\varsigma$. Then,

$$\mathsf{ETotal}^{\mathcal{T}^\varsigma}((s,q),\mu) = \mathbb{E}^\mu_{(s,q)}\{N(r) : r \in Runs^\mu_{(s,q)}(\mathcal{T}^\varsigma)\}$$
$$\mathsf{ETotal}^{\mathcal{T}^\varsigma}(s) = \sup_\mu \left(\mathsf{ETotal}^{\mathcal{T}^\varsigma}((s,q_0),\mu)\right) .$$

Note that the set of runs with $N(r) = \infty$ has probability 0 in $Runs^\mu_{(s,q)}(\mathcal{T}^\varsigma)$: they are the runs that infinitely often do not move to t on an accepting transition, where the chance that this happens at least n times is ς^n for all finite n.

Theorem 2. *The following holds:*

1. *MDP $\mathcal{T}^\varsigma$ (for $\varsigma \in\,]0,1[$), MDP $\mathcal{R}^\varsigma$ (for $\varsigma \in\,]0,1[$), and product MDP $\mathcal{M} \times \mathcal{A}$ have the same set of strategies.*
2. *For a positional strategy μ, the expected reward for $\mathcal{T}^\varsigma_\mu$ is r if, and only if, the chance of reaching the target t in $\mathcal{R}^\varsigma_\mu$ is $r/(1-\varsigma)$:*
   $\mathsf{PSat}^{\mathcal{R}^\varsigma}_t((s_0,q_0),\mu) = (1-\varsigma)\mathsf{ETotal}^{\mathcal{T}^\varsigma}((s_0,q_0),\mu)$.
3. *The expected reward for $\mathcal{T}^\varsigma_\mu$ is in $\left[0,(1-\varsigma)^{-1}\right]$.*
4. *The chance of satisfying the Büchi objective in $(\mathcal{M} \times \mathcal{A})_\mu$ is 1 if, and only if, the expected reward for $\mathcal{T}^\varsigma_\mu$ is $(1-\varsigma)^{-1}$.*
5. *There is a $\varsigma_0 \in\,]0,1[$ such that, for all $\varsigma \in [\varsigma_0,1[$, a strategy μ that maximizes the reward for $\mathcal{T}^\varsigma$ is an optimal strategy for the Büchi objective in $\mathcal{M} \times \mathcal{A}$.*

Proof. (1) Obvious, because all the states and their actions are the same apart from the sink state t for which the strategy can be left undefined.

(2) The sink state t can only be visited once along any run, so the expected number of times a run starting at (s_0, q_0) while using μ is going to visit t is the same as its probability of visiting t , i.e., $\mathsf{PSat}^{\mathcal{R}^\varsigma}_t((s_0,q_0),\mu)$. The only way t can be reached is by traversing an accepting transition and this always happens with the same probability $(1-\varsigma)$. So the expected number of visits to t is the expected number of times an accepting transition is used, i.e., $\mathsf{ETotal}^{\mathcal{T}^\varsigma}((s_0,q_0),\mu)$, multiplied by $(1-\varsigma)$.

(3) follows from (2), because $\mathsf{PSat}^{\mathcal{R}^\varsigma}_t((s_0,q_0),\mu)$ cannot be greater than 1.

(4) follows from (2) and Theorem 1 (2).

(5) follows from (2) and Theorem 1 (3).

$\square$

3.3 Discounted and Dense Rewards

The expected undiscounted reward for $\mathcal{T}^\varsigma_\mu$ can be viewed as the expected total sum of dynamically discounted rewards for $(\mathcal{M} \times \mathcal{A})_\mu$, by giving a reward of ς^i when passing through an accepting transition when i *accepting* transitions have been used before. We call these ς-*biased discounted rewards*.

Let $\mathcal{D} = \mathcal{M} \times \mathcal{A}$ and, for a run r with $N(r) = n$ accepting transitions, let the ζ-biased discounted reward be $\mathsf{Disct}_\zeta(r) = \sum_{i=0}^{n-1} \zeta^i = \frac{1-\zeta^n}{1-\zeta}$ if $n < \infty$ or $\mathsf{Disct}_\zeta(r) = \sum_{i=0}^{\infty} \zeta^i = \frac{1}{1-\zeta}$ if $n = \infty$. Let

$$\mathsf{EDisct}_\zeta^{\mathcal{D}}((s,q),\mu) = \mathbb{E}_{(s,q)}^\mu \{ \mathsf{Disct}_\zeta(r) : r \in Runs_{(s,q)}^\mu(\mathcal{D}) \}$$

$$\mathsf{EDisct}_\zeta^{\mathcal{D}}(s) = \sup_\mu \left(\mathsf{EDisct}_\zeta^{\mathcal{D}}((s,q_0),\mu) \right) .$$

Theorem 3. *For every positional strategy μ, the expected reward for $\mathcal{T}_\mu^\zeta$ is equal to the expected total ζ-biased discounted reward for $\mathcal{D}_\mu$, i.e., for every start state (s,q) we have:* $\mathsf{EDisct}_\zeta^{\mathcal{D}}((s,q),\mu) = \mathsf{ETotal}^{\mathcal{T}^\zeta}((s,q),\mu)$.

Proof. Note that for any start state (s,q) and $n \geq 0$:

$$\Pr{}_s^\mu \{ r \in Runs_{(s,q)}^\mu(\mathcal{T}^\zeta) : N(r) > n \} = \Pr{}_s^\mu \{ r \in Runs_{(s,q)}^\mu(\mathcal{D}) : N(r) > n \} \cdot \zeta^n .$$

This is because the only transition-wise difference between $\mathcal{T}^\zeta$ and $\mathcal{D}$ is that every time an accepting transition is passed through in $\mathcal{T}^\zeta$, the process stops at the sink node with probability $1 - \zeta$. Therefore, in order to use more than n accepting transitions in $\mathcal{T}^\zeta$, the non-stopping option has to be chosen n times in a row, each time with probability ζ.

For any random variable $X : \Omega \to \mathbb{N} \cup \{\infty\}$ we have $\mathbb{E}X = \sum_{n \geq 0} \Pr(X > n)$. Now from the definition of $\mathsf{EDisct}_\zeta^{\mathcal{D}}((s,q),\mu)$ and $\mathsf{ETotal}^{\mathcal{T}^\zeta}((s,q),\mu)$ we get:

$$\mathsf{EDisct}_\zeta^{\mathcal{D}}((s,q),\mu) = \sum_{n \geq 1} \Pr{}_{(s,q)}^\mu \{ r \in Runs_{(s,q)}^\mu(\mathcal{D}) : N(r) = n \} \cdot \sum_{0 \leq i < n} \zeta^i$$

$$+ \Pr{}_{(s,q)}^\mu \{ r \in Runs_{(s,q)}^\mu(\mathcal{D}) : N(r) = \infty \} \cdot \sum_{i \geq 0} \zeta^i$$

$$\overset{(*)}{=} \sum_{n \geq 0} \Pr{}_{(s,q)}^\mu \{ r \in Runs_{(s,q)}^\mu(\mathcal{D}) : N(r) > n \} \cdot \zeta^n$$

$$= \sum_{n \geq 0} \Pr{}_{(s,q)}^\mu \{ r \in Runs_{(s,q)}^\mu(\mathcal{T}^\zeta) : N(r) > n \}$$

$$= \mathsf{ETotal}^{\mathcal{T}^\zeta}((s,q),\mu) ,$$

where $(*)$ follows by expanding the products and joining up the terms that have a common factor of the form ζ^n. □

This improves over [3] because it provides a clearer separation of concerns: the only discount factor represents the *translation to reachability*. The use of Q-learning [35] introduces two other parameters, the discount factor γ and the learning rate α, with $\gamma, \alpha \in]0, 1[$. For fixed parameters, Q-learning works in the limit when the parameters are chosen in the right order—e.g., $\lim_{\gamma \uparrow 1} \lim_{\alpha \downarrow 0}$ of the expected value works, while $\lim_{\alpha \downarrow 0} \lim_{\gamma \uparrow 1}$ does not—and when experimenting with different learning approaches, it is useful to separate concerns, rather then mixing parameters from the learning mechanism with those required for faithfulness.

Thus, using only one discount parameter, ζ, instead of two (called γ and γ_B in [3]) parameters (that are not independent) to guarantee faithfulness provides a clean separation of concerns: Reinforcement learning will still use a discount for effectiveness, but the role of the two parameters is neatly separated. This formulation offers a simpler proof, and provides better intuition: discount whenever you have earned a reward. It also lends itself to implementation with convergent RL algorithms—as long as they support state-dependent discounts. The discount rate on accepting edges is multiplied by ζ instead of assigning a decaying reward of ζ^i. This does not change the optimal strategies and the expected reward from the initial state remains the same.

4   Q-Learning and Effectiveness

We next discuss the applicability of Q-learning to the faithful reward schemes presented in Sect. 3. Recourse to Blackwell optimality allows us to deal also with undiscounted rewards, even though a naive use of Q-learning may produce incorrect results in this case.

Q-learning [38] is a well-studied model-free RL approach to compute an optimal strategy for discounted rewards. Q-learning computes so-called Q-values for every state-action pair. Intuitively, once Q-learning has converged to the fixed point, $Q(s, a)$ is the optimal reward the agent can get while performing action a after starting at s. The Q-values can be initialized arbitrarily, but ideally they should be close to the actual values. Q-learning learns over a number of episodes, each consisting of a sequence of actions with bounded length. An episode can terminate early if a sink-state or another non-productive state is reached. Each episode starts at the designated initial state s_0. The Q-learning process moves from state to state of the MDP using one of its available actions and accumulates rewards along the way. Suppose that in the i-th step, the process has reached state s_i. It then either performs the currently (believed to be) optimal action $a_i = \max_a Q_i(s_{i+1}, a)$ (so-called *exploitation* option) or, with probability ϵ, picks uniformly at random one of the actions available at s_i (so-called *exploration* option). Either way, the Q-value is updated as follows:

$$Q_{i+1}(s_i, a_i) = (1 - \alpha_i)Q_i(s_i, a_i) + \alpha_i(r_i + \gamma \cdot \max_a Q_i(s_{i+1}, a)) \ ,$$

where $\alpha_i \in {]}0, 1{[}$ is the learning rate and $\gamma \in {]}0, 1]$ is the discount factor. Note the model-freeness: this update does not depend on the set of transitions nor their probabilities. For all other pairs s, a we have $Q_{i+1}(s, a) = Q_i(s, a)$, i.e., they are left unchanged. Watkins and Dayan showed the convergence of Q-learning [38].

Theorem 4 (Convergence). *For $\lambda < 1$, bounded rewards $|r_i| \leq B$ and learning rates $0 \leq \alpha_i < 1$ satisfying: $\sum_{i=0}^{\infty} \alpha_i = \infty$ and $\sum_{i=0}^{\infty} \alpha_i^2 < \infty$, we have that $Q_i(x, a) \to Q(s, a)$ as $i \to \infty$ for all $s, a \in S \times A$ almost surely.*

However, in the total reward setting that corresponds to Q-learning with discount factor $\gamma = 1$, Q-learning may not converge, or converge to incorrect values as shown below.

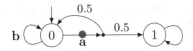

Example 1. Consider the MDP in Fig. 2 with reachability rewards (Sect. 3.1) and assume the following parameters: $\alpha = \zeta = 1/2, \epsilon > 0$, $\gamma = 1$. All Q-values are initialized to 0. It can be checked that after taking action **a** at state 0 and reaching the sink-state t (with

Fig. 2. Q-learning with total reward may converge to a wrong fixed point or not at all. The accepting transition is marked with a green dot. (Color figure online)

probability $1 - \zeta$, not depicted) would result in setting $Q(0, \mathbf{a}) = (1 - \alpha) \cdot 0 + \alpha \cdot 1 = 1/2$. Repeating this n times in a row (with probability $\geq (\epsilon/2)^n$) would lead to $Q(0, \mathbf{a}) = 1 - 1/2^n$. Taking then m times action **b** (again with positive probability), would result in setting $Q(0, \mathbf{b})$ to $(1 - 1/2^m)(1 - 1/2^n)$, which tends to 1 as n and m increase. Note that the value of $Q(0, \mathbf{b})$ can never decrease as its update rule is $Q(0, \mathbf{b}) = \max_a Q(0, a)$. Therefore, even if Q-learning converges, $\max_a Q(0, a)$ can be far away from the actual value of state 0, which is clearly smaller than $3/4$, as the dead-end node 2 with 0 reward is reached with probability $> \zeta/2 = 1/4$. The situation is even worse when we consider total and dense reward (Section 3.2). Following the same learning path (but never reaching the sink-state t) would result in $Q(0, \mathbf{b}) = n/2$ and $Q(0, \mathbf{a}) = (1 - 1/2^m)n/2$, and so $Q(0, a)$ will almost surely diverge to ∞ as the number of episodes increases.

To solve total-reward problems using Q-learning, we exploit the concept of Blackwell-optimal strategies. Given an MDP $\mathcal{M}$, we say that a strategy μ is Blackwell-optimal if there exists a $\lambda_0 \in]0,1[$ such that μ is λ-discount optimal for all $\lambda \in]\lambda_0, 1[$. Moreover, if $\mathcal{M}$ has n states and all transition probabilities are rational with numerator and denominator bounded from above by M, then λ_0 is bounded from above by $1 - ((n!)^2 2^{2n+3} M^{2n^2})^{-1}$ [1,17,24]. The following theorem enables the application of Q-learning for discounted reward problem for total-reward when total rewards are bounded.

Theorem 5 (Blackwell-Optimality [23]). *Let $\mathcal{M}$ be an MDP and $\rho : S \times A \to \mathbb{R}$ be a reward function such that for every strategy μ of $\mathcal{M}$ expected total reward is finite, then every Blackwell-optimal strategy is total-reward optimal.*

All of the reward schemes introduced in the previous section can be reduced to total reward objectives with bounded expected total reward and hence Q-learning can be applied with discount factor left as a hyperparameter.

5   Experiments

We carried out our experiments in the tool MUNGOJERRIE [12], which reads MDPs described in the PRISM language [21], and ω-regular automata written in the HOA format [2,7]. MUNGOJERRIE provides an interface for RL algorithms akin to that of [4] and supports probabilistic model checking.

We compared four reward schemes. Reachability reward (RR) is the scheme from [12]. Total reward (TR) is the scheme from Sect. 3.2. Discounted reward (DR) is the scheme from Sect. 3.3, which is equivalent to that of [3]. We will consider these methods the same in our analysis. Simple reward (SR) is a reward mechanism which provides +1 reward on accepting edges and 0 reward otherwise, similar to [30] restricted to Büchi objectives. Although this reward scheme is known not to be faithful [12], we compare it to see its practical value.

Table 1. Q-learning results. Times are in seconds.

Name	States	Aut	Prod	Prob	RR	TR	DR	SR
twoPairs	4	4	16	1	0.04	0.04	0.06	1.23
riskReward	4	2	8	1	0.05, 0.05	0.30	0.07, 0.07	0.97
deferred	41	1	41	1	0.11	0.04, 0.23	0.12	1.43
grid5x5	25	3	75	1	1.56	6.97, 7.34	0.46	20.69
trafficNtk	122	13	462	1	0.09, 0.09	0.73	0.13, 0.14	2.11
windy	123	2	240	1	3.34, 3.64	29.37, 35.18	1.14	18.64
windyKing	130	2	256	1	1.02	20.55, 20.69	1.30	36.77
windyStoch	130	2	260	1	42.94, 52.28	56.57	4.28	67.55
frozenSmall	16	3	48	0.823	0.29, 0.48	0.83, 1.08	0.38	8.74
frozenLarge	64	3	192	1	0.94	6.47, 8.98	2.08	25.34
othergrid6	36	25	352	1	1.06, 1.17	5.31, 12.77	1.70	44.58

For our RL algorithm, we selected Q-learning [38] due to its widespread use and convergence guarantees. As with any RL algorithm, the performance of Q-learning depends on the hyperparameter values. We ran a grid search on the RMACC Summit supercomputer [34] across hyperparameter combinations for all examples and methods. The examples are taken from [12]. In the grid search, we varied ζ (equivalently, γ_B), the exploration rate ϵ, the learning rate α, the episode number, the episode length, and whether the learning rate decayed. The variations made to these parameters were selected by hand. Statistics for each grid point are based on three runs. The grid search required 207,900 runs and took over 100 days of CPU time. All methods require a sufficiently high discount factor. We used the very high value of $\gamma = 0.99999$ for all runs. A value so close to 1 is prone to cause, in practice, many of the problems that may occur in the undiscounted case. However, we also experimented with lower discount factors, and they provided very similar results.

The selection of the "best" parameters from our grid search makes use of two criteria. Criterion 1 is based on reward maximization. Given a reward scheme, an automaton, and an MDP, there is a maximum reward achievable. In the spirit of the model-free application of these methods, we estimated these maxima based on the recorded initial value in the Q-table. This can be determined without knowledge of the structure of the MDP and without additional computation. We then removed all sets of parameters which produced average values that were not within 5% of the maximum. If Q-learning has converged, we know that the value of the initial state of the Q-table is the value of the optimal strategy. However, if Q-learning has overestimated these values, then this criterion will select parameters that are the most prone to overestimation. Criterion 2 is based on using full knowledge of the MDP and access to the model checker. We fixed the strategies produced after learning completed and used the model checker to compute the probability of satisfaction of the property under these strategies. We then removed all sets of parameters which produced average values that were not within 1% of the maximum probability of satisfaction of the property.

In Table 1, we report the fastest time of all parameter values that remain after applying Criterion 1. Of these, we mark with bold red face those that fail Criterion 2 and report the fastest time of all parameter values that remain after applying both criteria.

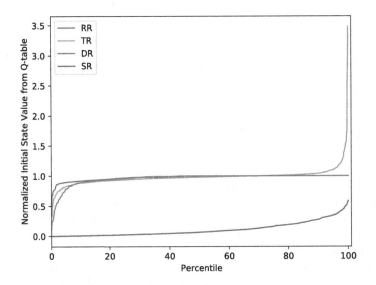

Fig. 3. Plot depicting inaccurate estimation of Q-values for TR and SR.

5.1　Inaccuracies in Estimation of Q-Values

In order to understand the performance of these reward schemes with Q-learning under our criteria, consider the example `riskReward`, which has two strategies: one leads to an accepting edge at every step with probability 0.9; the other leads to an accepting edge every other step with probability 1. This example shows that SR is not a faithful reward scheme [12] because the strategy that maximizes the probability of satisfaction does not maximize the SR reward. Since the strategy reported in Table 1 for SR is optimal for the satisfaction of the property, we know that Q-learning did not converge to a reward-maximizing strategy for the chosen values of the hyperparameters. From this, we can see that Criterion 1 may not rule out parameters that do not produce reward-maximizing strategies. We believe that this is because Criterion 1 selects based on Q-values, which may not be accurate estimates of the actual values obtained by optimal strategies.

In Fig. 3, for each method we plot the values of the initial state from the Q-table of all grid points in increasing order. Each value in the figure was normalized such that an optimal reward maximization strategy for that method has a value of 1. Note that TR and SR do not have their values saturate like RR and DR. When we apply Criterion 1 to TR and SR, we remove all parameters that do not produce Q-values close to the top of the peaks that can be seen in the figure. As this filters out most of the runs, this offers an explanation for the longer running times of these methods. For SR, the Q-values do not converge. This is likely due to the fact that with a very large discount factor, SR needs more training than the other methods to converge to larger Q-values. For TR, we overestimate the value by up to about 3.5 times. We believe that this is due to Q-learning's tendency to overestimate the value of the optimal strategy.

As we discussed in Sect. 4, these methods rely on the contraction provided by discounting to be correct, and we have seen in Example 1 that in the undiscounted case the Q-value can go to infinity even in the absence of a strategy that wins with positive probability. While the contraction provided by the discount factor counters this effect, for a discount factor as high as the one chosen in the experiments the contraction is relatively weak. An extremely small learning rate would be needed to contain this effect. Additionally, the high variance reward of TR exacerbates the positive bias present in the estimator implemented by Q-learning. Double Q-learning [36] is a technique that mitigates this overestimation by using an estimator which is negatively biased. We believe that utilizing such techniques warrants further investigation.

In summary, Table 1 suggests that RR and DR perform similarly. The lower reward variance of DR explains why Criterion 1 selects optimal strategies for the satisfaction of the property more often than with RR. SR takes longer than the other methods under our criteria. On the other hand, TR is not well suited for Q-learning. While its denser reward may help to guide the learner, the inaccuracy in the Q-value estimates from this method negates this benefit. However, we do not know if these issues extend to other RL algorithms or if other algorithms may take better advantage of the denser reward of TR.

6   Discussion and Future Work

The three concerns to be addressed when applying model-free RL to ω-regular properties are:

1. Finding the right automata representation.
2. Translating the acceptance condition into a faithful reward scheme.
3. Computing policies that maximize expected reward with an RL technique.

In [13], we addressed the first concern by introducing Good-for-MDP automata. This paper addresses the other two issues.

There have been two correct results for reinforcement learning of ω-regular properties on MDPs. We have shown how to change the older of the two reward schemes, [12], to allow for earlier rewards in Sect. 3.2, and to obtain a biased discount scheme quite directly from there in Sect. 3.3. This biased discount scheme is significantly simpler than the scheme suggested in [3], which uses two entangled discount factors. Moreover, we have shown that the reward scheme from [3] can be viewed as the result of using the simple biased discount scheme from Sect. 3.3 embedded in a standard discounted Q-learning. We have therefore connected the known reward structures and provided simple intuitive explanations—in the form of a separation of concerns—for the reward structure used in [3]. Besides offering a simpler proof and new insights, it opens up an avenue of future work to see if other RL techniques will benefit from ζ-biased discounted rewards without the common detour through discounting.

Acknowledgment. This work utilized resources from the University of Colorado Boulder Research Computing Group, which is supported by the National Science Foundation (awards ACI-1532235 and ACI-1532236), the University of Colorado Boulder, and Colorado State University. This work was supported by the Engineering and Physical Sciences Research Council through grant EP/P020909/1 and by the National Science Foundation through grant 2009022.

References

1. Andersson, D., Miltersen, P.B.: The complexity of solving stochastic games on graphs. In: Algorithms and Computation, pp. 112–121 (2009)
2. Babiak, T., et al.: The hanoi omega-automata format. In: Kroening, D., Păsăreanu, C.S. (eds.) CAV 2015. LNCS, vol. 9206, pp. 479–486. Springer, Cham (2015). https://doi.org/10.1007/978-3-319-21690-4_31
3. Bozkurt, A.K., Wang, Y., Zavlanos, M.M., Pajic, M.: Control synthesis from linear temporal logic specifications using model-free reinforcement learning. CoRR, abs/1909.07299 (2019)
4. Brockman, G., et al.: OpenAI Gym. CoRR, abs/1606.01540 (2016)
5. Camacho, A., Toro Icarte, R., Klassen, T.Q., Valenzano, R., McIlraith, S.A.: LTL and beyond: formal languages for reward function specification in reinforcement learning. In: Joint Conference on Artificial Intelligence, pp. 6065–6073 (2019)
6. Courcoubetis, C., Yannakakis, M.: The complexity of probabilistic verification. J. ACM **42**(4), 857–907 (1995)
7. cpphoafparser (2016). https://automata.tools/hoa/cpphoafparser. Accessed 05 Sept 2018
8. De Giacomo, G., Vardi, M.Y.: Linear temporal logic and linear dynamic logic on finite traces. In: IJCAI, pp. 854–860 (2013)
9. Etessami, K., Wilke, T., Schuller, R.A.: Fair simulation relations, parity games, and state space reduction for Büchi automata. SIAM J. Comput. **34**(5), 1159–1175 (2005)
10. Fu, J., Topcu, U.: Probably approximately correct MDP learning and control with temporal logic constraints. In: Robotics Science and Systems (2014)

11. Hahn, E.M., Li, G., Schewe, S., Turrini, A., Zhang, L.: Lazy probabilistic model checking without determinisation. In: Concurrency Theory, pp. 354–367 (2015)

12. Hahn, E.M., Perez, M., Schewe, S., Somenzi, F., Trivedi, A., Wojtczak, D.: Omega-regular objectives in model-free reinforcement learning. In: Vojnar, T., Zhang, L. (eds.) TACAS 2019. LNCS, vol. 11427, pp. 395–412. Springer, Cham (2019). https://doi.org/10.1007/978-3-030-17462-0_27

13. Hahn, E.M., Perez, M., Schewe, S., Somenzi, F., Trivedi, A., Wojtczak, D.: Good-for-MDPs automata for probabilistic analysis and reinforcement learning. In: Tools and Algorithms for the Construction and Analysis of Systems, pp. 306–323 (2020)

14. Hasanbeig, M., Kantaros, Y., Abate, A., Kroening, D., Pappas, G.J., Lee, I.: Reinforcement learning for temporal logic control synthesis with probabilistic satisfaction guarantees. In: Conference on Decision and Control, December 2019

15. Henzinger, T.A., Kupferman, O., Rajamani, S.K.: Fair simulation. In: Mazurkiewicz, A., Winkowski, J. (eds.) CONCUR 1997. LNCS, vol. 1243, pp. 273–287. Springer, Heidelberg (1997). https://doi.org/10.1007/3-540-63141-0_19

16. Henzinger, T.A., Piterman, N.: Solving games without determinization. In: Ésik, Z. (ed.) CSL 2006. LNCS, vol. 4207, pp. 395–410. Springer, Heidelberg (2006). https://doi.org/10.1007/11874683_26

17. Hordijk, A., Yushkevich, A.A.: Handbook of Markov Decision Processes Methods and Applications, pp. 231–267. Springer, New York (2002). https://doi.org/10.1007/978-1-4615-0805-2

18. Icarte, T.R., Klassen, T.Q., Valenzano, R.A., McIlraith, S.A.: Using reward machines for high-level task specification and decomposition in reinforcement learning. In: Conference on Machine Learning, pp. 2112–2121, July 2018

19. Irpan, A.: Deep reinforcement learning doesn't work yet. https://www.alexirpan.com/2018/02/14/rl-hard.html (2018)

20. Křetínský, J., Pérez, G.A., Raskin, J.-F.: Learning-based mean-payoff optimization in an unknown MDP under omega-regular constraints. In: CONCUR, vol. 118, LIPIcs, pp. 8:1–8:18 (2018)

21. Kwiatkowska, M., Norman, G., Parker, D.: PRISM 4.0: verification of probabilistic real-time systems. In: Gopalakrishnan, G., Qadeer, S. (eds.) CAV 2011. LNCS, vol. 6806, pp. 585–591. Springer, Heidelberg (2011). https://doi.org/10.1007/978-3-642-22110-1_47

22. Lavaei, A., Somenzi, F., Soudjani, S., Trivedi, A., Zamani, M.: Formal controller synthesis for unknown continuous-space MDPs via model-free reinforcement learning. In: International Conference on Cyber-Physical Systems, April 2020

23. Lewis, M.E.: Bias optimality. In: Feinberg, E.A., Shwartz, A. (eds.) Handbook of Markov Decision Processes, pp. 89–111. Springer, Boston (2002). https://doi.org/10.1007/978-1-4615-0805-2_3

24. Liggett, T.M., Lippman, S.A.: Short notes: stochastic games with perfect information and time average payoff. SIAM Rev. **11**(4), 604–607 (1969)

25. Manna, Z., Pnueli, A.: The Temporal Logic of Reactive and Concurrent Systems *Specification*. Springer (1991)

26. Milnerm, R.: An algebraic definition of simulation between programs. Int. Joint Conf. Artif. Intell. **23**, 481–489 (1971)

27. Ng, A.Y., Harada, D., Russell, S.J.: Policy invariance under reward transformations: theory and application to reward shaping. In: International Conference on Machine Learning, pp. 278–287 (1999)

28. Perrin, D., Pin, J.-É.: Infinite Words: Automata, Semigroups. Elsevier, Logic and Games (2004)

29. Puterman, M.L.: Markov Decision Processes: Discrete Stochastic Dynamic Programming. Wiley, New York (1994)
30. Sadigh, D., Kim, E., Coogan, S., Sastry, S.S., Seshia, S.A.: A learning based approach to control synthesis of Markov decision processes for linear temporal logic specifications. In: CDC, pp. 1091–1096, December 2014
31. Sickert, S., Esparza, J., Jaax, S., Křetínský, J.: Limit-deterministic Büchi automata for linear temporal logic. In: Chaudhuri, S., Farzan, A. (eds.) CAV 2016. LNCS, vol. 9780, pp. 312–332. Springer, Cham (2016). https://doi.org/10.1007/978-3-319-41540-6_17
32. Somenzi, F., Trivedi, A.: Reinforcement learning and formal requirements. In: Zamani, M., Zufferey, D. (eds.) NSV 2019. LNCS, vol. 11652, pp. 26–41. Springer, Cham (2019). https://doi.org/10.1007/978-3-030-28423-7_2
33. Strehl, A.L., Li, L., Wiewiora, E., Langford, J., Littman, M.L.: PAC model-free reinforcement learning. In: International Conference on Machine Learning, ICML, pp. 881–888 (2006)
34. RMACC Summit Supercomputer. https://rmacc.org/rmaccsummit
35. Sutton, R.S., Barto, A.G.: Reinforcement Learnging: An Introduction. MIT Press, 2nd edn (2018)
36. van Hasselt, H.: Double Q-learning. In: Advances in Neural Information Processing Systems, pp. 2613–2621 (2010
37. Vardi, M.Y.: Automatic verification of probabilistic concurrent finite state programs. In: Foundations of Computer Science, pp. 327–338 (1985)
38. Watkins, C.J.C.H., Dayan, P.: Q-learning. Mach. Learn. 8(3–4), 279–292 (1992)

Automata

Practical "Paritizing" of Emerson-Lei Automata

Florian Renkin[(⊠)], Alexandre Duret-Lutz, and Adrien Pommellet

LRDE, EPITA, Le Kremlin-Bicêtre, France
{frenkin,adl,adrien}@lrde.epita.fr

Abstract. We introduce a new algorithm that takes a *Transition-based Emerson-Lei Automaton* (TELA), that is, an ω-automaton whose acceptance condition is an arbitrary Boolean formula on sets of transitions to be seen infinitely or finitely often, and converts it into a *Transition-based Parity Automaton* (TPA). To reduce the size of the output TPA, the algorithm combines and optimizes two procedures based on a *latest appearance record* principle, and introduces a *partial degeneralization*. Our motivation is to use this algorithm to improve our LTL synthesis tool, where producing deterministic parity automata is an intermediate step.

1 Introduction

Let us consider the transformation of ω-automata with arbitrary Emerson-Lei acceptance into ω-automata with parity acceptance. Our inputs are *Transition-based Emerson-Lei Automata* (TELA), i.e., automata whose edges are labeled with integer marks like ⓿, ❶, ❷,... and whose acceptance condition is a positive Boolean formula over terms such as $\mathsf{Fin}(❶)$ or $\mathsf{Inf}(❷)$ that specifies which marks should be seen infinitely or finitely often in accepting runs. Our algorithm processes a TELA with any such acceptance condition, and outputs a TELA whose acceptance can be interpreted as a *parity max odd* (resp. *even*) condition, i.e., the largest mark seen infinitely often along a run has to be odd (resp. even). Figure 1 on page 9 and Fig. 3 on page 10 show an example of input and output.

While *non-deterministic Büchi automata* are the simplest ω-automata able to represent all ω-regular languages, deterministic Büchi automata are less expressive; as a consequence, applications that require determinism usually switch to more complex acceptance conditions like Rabin, Streett, or parity. Parity can be regarded as the simplest of the three, in the sense that any parity automaton can be converted into a Rabin or a Streett automaton without changing its transition structure. Parity acceptance is especially popular among game solvers, as parity games can be solved with memoryless strategies and arise in many problems.

Our motivation comes from one such problem: *reactive synthesis from LTL specifications*, i.e., building an I/O transducer whose input and output signals satisfy an LTL specification φ [4]. The high-level approach taken by our ltlsynt tool [20], or even by the SyntComp'19 winner Strix [18], is to transform the LTL

© Springer Nature Switzerland AG 2020
D. V. Hung and O. Sokolsky (Eds.): ATVA 2020, LNCS 12302, pp. 127–143, 2020.
https://doi.org/10.1007/978-3-030-59152-6_7

formula into a *deterministic transition-based parity automaton* (DTPA), interpret the DTPA as a parity game by splitting the alphabet on inputs and outputs, then solve the game and use any winning strategy to synthesize a transducer. Let us zoom on the first step: transforming an LTL formula into a DTPA.

One of the many methods to transform an LTL formula into a DTPA is to first convert the LTL formula into a non-deterministic Büchi automaton, and then determinize this automaton using some variant of Safra's construction to obtain a DTPA [22,23]. This is the current approach of ltlsynt [20]. However, since the introduction of the HOA format [2] allowing the representation of TELA, we have seen the development of several tools for converting LTL formulas into TELA: for instance delag [21], ltl2da and ltl2na (all three part of newer versions of Owl [13]), ltl3tela [19], or Spot's ltl2tgba -G (see Sect. 5), all trying to reduce the size of their output by using acceptance formulas more closely related to the input LTL formulas. An alternative way to transform an LTL formula into a DTPA is therefore to first transform the LTL formula into a deterministic TELA, and then "paritize" the result. This paper focuses on such a paritization procedure. Note that our construction preserves the deterministic nature of its input but also works on non-deterministic automata.

Our procedure adapts for TELA, optimizes, and combines a few existing transformation procedures. For instance there exists a procedure called SAR (*state appearance record*) [16,17] that converts a state-based Muller automaton into a state-based parity automaton, and a similar but more specialized procedure called IAR (*index appearance record*) [16,17] for transforming a Rabin or Streett automaton into a parity automaton. These two procedures are based on a *latest appearance record* (LAR), i.e., a structure that keeps track of the latest occurring state or the latest occurring unsatisfied Rabin/Streett pair (the term LAR is sometimes used to describe SAR [10]). We describe the adaptation of these two procedures in Sect. 3. In the context of a TELA, we introduce a simplified SAR called CAR (*color appearance record*) that only tracks colors, and the IAR algorithm has already been adapted by Křetínský et al. [15]. A third transformation, also described in Sect. 3, can be used as a preprocessing before the previous procedures: this is a *partial degeneralization*, i.e. an extension of the classical degeneralization procedure [1,11] that will replace any sub-formula of the form $\bigwedge_i \mathsf{Inf}(m_i)$ (resp. $\bigvee_i \mathsf{Fin}(m_i)$) by a single $\mathsf{Inf}(m_j)$ (resp. $\mathsf{Fin}(m_j)$) in the acceptance condition.

In Sect. 4 we present our "paritization" procedure that combines the above procedures with some additional optimizations. Essentially the automaton is processed one strongly-connected component (SCC) at a time, and for each SCC the acceptance condition is simplified before choosing the most appropriate transformation to parity.

This paritization procedure is implemented in Spot 2.9. In Sect. 5 we show how the combination of all the improvements outperforms the straightforward CAR algorithm in practice.

2   Transition-Based Emerson-Lei Automata

Emerson-Lei Automata were defined [8] and named [24] in the 80s, and provide a way to describe a Muller acceptance condition using a positive Boolean formula over sets of states that must be visited finitely or infinitely often. Below we define the transition-based version of those automata, as used in the *Hanoi Omega-Automata Format* [2]. Instead of working directly with sets of transitions, we label transitions by multiple colored marks, as can be seen in Figs. 1, 2 and 3.

Let $M = \{0, \ldots, n-1\}$ be a finite set of n contiguous integers called the set of *marks* or *colors*, from now on also written $M = \{\mathbf{0}, \mathbf{1}, \ldots\}$ in our examples. We define the set $\mathcal{C}(M)$ of *acceptance formulas* according to the following grammar, where m stands for any mark in M:

$$\alpha ::= \top \mid \bot \mid \mathsf{Inf}(m) \mid \mathsf{Fin}(m) \mid (\alpha \wedge \alpha) \mid (\alpha \vee \alpha)$$

Acceptance formulas are interpreted over subsets of M. For $N \subseteq M$ we define the satisfaction relation $N \models \alpha$ according to the following semantics:

$$N \models \top \quad N \models \mathsf{Inf}(m) \text{ iff } m \in N \quad N \models \alpha_1 \wedge \alpha_2 \text{ iff } N \models \alpha_1 \text{ and } N \models \alpha_2$$
$$N \not\models \bot \quad N \models \mathsf{Fin}(m) \text{ iff } m \notin N \quad N \models \alpha_1 \vee \alpha_2 \text{ iff } N \models \alpha_1 \text{ or } N \models \alpha_2$$

Intuitively, an Emerson-Lei automaton is an ω-automaton labeled by marks and whose acceptance condition is expressed as a positive Boolean formula on sets of marks that occur infinitely often or finitely often in a run. More formally:

Definition 1 (Transition-based Emerson-Lei Automata). *A* transition-based Emerson-Lei automaton *(TELA) is a tuple* $\mathcal{A} = (Q, M, \Sigma, \delta, q_0, \alpha)$ *where* Q *is a finite set of states,* M *is a finite set of marks,* Σ *is a finite input alphabet,* $\delta \subseteq Q \times \Sigma \times 2^M \times Q$ *is a finite set of transitions,* $q_0 \in Q$ *is an initial state, and* $\alpha \in \mathcal{C}(M)$ *is an acceptance formula.*

Given a transition $d = (q_1, \ell, A, q_2) \in \delta$, we write $d = q_1 \xrightarrow{\ell, A} q_2$. A *run* r of $\mathcal{A}$ is an infinite sequence of transitions $r = (s_i \xrightarrow{\ell_i, A_i} s'_i)_{i \geq 0}$ in δ^ω such that $s_0 = q_0$ and $\forall i \geq 0$, $s'_i = s_{i+1}$. Since Q is finite, for any run r, there exists a position $j_r \geq 0$ such that for each $i \geq j_r$, the transition $s_i \xrightarrow{\ell_i, A_i} s'_i$ occurs infinitely often in r. Let $\mathsf{Rep}(r) = \bigcup_{i \geq j_r} A_i$ be the set of colors **rep**eated infinitely often in r. A run r is *accepting* if $\mathsf{Rep}(r) \models \alpha$, and we then say that $\mathcal{A}$ *accepts* the word $(\ell_i)_{i \geq 0} \in \Sigma^\omega$. The *language* $\mathcal{L}(\mathcal{A})$ is the set of words accepted by $\mathcal{A}$. Two TELA are *equivalent* if they have the same language. By extension, the language of a state $q \in Q$ is the language of the automaton using q as initial state.

Example 1. In the automaton of Fig. 1, the run r that repeats infinitely the two transitions $\rightarrow\!\textcircled{0}\overset{\textbf{3}}{\underset{\textbf{2}\ \textbf{4}}{\rightleftarrows}}\textcircled{1}$ has $\mathsf{Rep}(r) = \{\textbf{2}, \textbf{3}, \textbf{4}\}$. Since $\mathsf{Rep}(r)$ satisfies the acceptance condition (written below the automaton) r is an accepting run.

A TELA's acceptance formula can be used to express many classical ω-automata acceptance conditions, as shown in Table 1. Note that colors may

Table 1. Shape of classical acceptance formulas. The variables $m, m_0, m_1, \ldots$ stand for any acceptance marks in $M = \{0, 1, \ldots\}$ to allow multiple occurrences.

Büchi	$\mathsf{Inf}(m)$
generalized Büchi	$\bigwedge_i \mathsf{Inf}(m_i)$
co-Büchi	$\mathsf{Fin}(m)$
generalized co-Büchi	$\bigvee_i \mathsf{Fin}(m_i)$
Rabin	$\bigvee_i \left(\mathsf{Fin}(m_{2i}) \wedge \mathsf{Inf}(m_{2i+1})\right)$
Rabin-like	$\bigvee_i \left(\mathsf{Fin}(m_{2i}) \wedge \mathsf{Inf}(m_{2i+1})\right) \vee \bigvee_j \mathsf{Inf}(m_j) \vee \bigvee_k \mathsf{Fin}(m_k)$
Streett	$\bigwedge_i \left(\mathsf{Inf}(m_{2i}) \vee \mathsf{Fin}(m_{2i+1})\right)$
Streett-like	$\bigwedge_i \left(\mathsf{Inf}(m_{2i}) \vee \mathsf{Fin}(m_{2i+1})\right) \wedge \bigwedge_j \mathsf{Inf}(m_j) \wedge \bigwedge_k \mathsf{Fin}(m_k)$
parity max even	$\mathsf{Inf}(2k) \vee (\mathsf{Fin}(2k-1) \wedge (\mathsf{Inf}(2k-2) \vee (\mathsf{Fin}(2k-3) \wedge \ldots)))$
parity max odd	$\mathsf{Inf}(2k+1) \vee (\mathsf{Fin}(2k) \wedge (\mathsf{Inf}(2k-1) \vee (\mathsf{Fin}(2k-2) \wedge \ldots)))$

appear more than once in most formulas; for instance $(\mathsf{Fin}(\mathbf{0}) \wedge \mathsf{Inf}(\mathbf{1})) \vee (\mathsf{Fin}(\mathbf{1}) \wedge \mathsf{Inf}(\mathbf{0}))$ is a Rabin acceptance formula.

The only unusual formulas of Table 1 are the *Rabin-like* and *Streett-like* conditions. A Rabin-like formula $\bigvee_i \left(\mathsf{Fin}(m_{2i}) \wedge \mathsf{Inf}(m_{2i+1})\right) \vee \bigvee_j \mathsf{Inf}(m_j) \vee \bigvee_k \mathsf{Fin}(m_k)$ can be converted into the Rabin formula $\bigvee_i \left(\mathsf{Fin}(m_{2i}) \wedge \mathsf{Inf}(m_{2i+1})\right) \vee \bigvee_j (\mathsf{Fin}(a) \wedge \mathsf{Inf}(m_j)) \vee \bigvee_k (\mathsf{Fin}(m_k) \wedge \mathsf{Inf}(b))$ by introducing two new marks a and b such that a occurs nowhere in the automaton and b occurs everywhere. Therefore, without loss of generality, we may describe algorithms over Rabin automata, but in practice we implement those over Rabin-like acceptance conditions.

When discussing Rabin acceptance, it is common to mention the number of *Rabin pairs*, i.e., the number of disjuncts in the formula; we use the same vocabulary for Rabin-like, even if some of the pairs only have one term. Dually, the number of pairs in a Streett-like formula is the number of conjuncts.

Remark 1. Formula $\mathsf{Fin}(\mathbf{0}) \wedge \mathsf{Inf}(\mathbf{1})$ can be seen as Rabin with one pair, or a Streett-like with two pairs. Similarly, a generalized Büchi is also Streett-like.

Remark 2. Any sub-formula of the form $\bigvee_i \mathsf{Inf}(m_i)$ (resp. $\bigwedge_i \mathsf{Fin}(m_i)$) can be replaced by a single $\mathsf{Inf}(a)$ (resp. $\mathsf{Fin}(a)$) by introducing a mark a on all transitions where any m_i occurred. Thus, any parity automaton can be rewritten as Rabin-like or Streett-like without adding or removing any transition: to produce a Rabin-like (resp. Streett-like) acceptance, rewrite the parity acceptance formula in disjunctive normal form (resp. CNF) and then replace each term of the form $\bigwedge_i \mathsf{Fin}(m_i)$ (resp. $\bigvee_i \mathsf{Inf}(m_i)$) by a single Fin (resp. Inf).

Definition 2 (Strongly Connected Component). *Let us consider a TELA $\mathcal{A} = (Q, M, \Sigma, \delta, q_0, \alpha)$. A strongly connected component (SCC) is a non-empty set of states $S \subseteq Q$ such that any ordered pair of distinct states of S can be connected by a sequence of transitions of δ. We note $\mathcal{A}_{|S} = (S, M, \Sigma, \delta', q'_0, \alpha)$ a sub-automaton induced by S, where $\delta' = \delta \cap (S \times \Sigma \times 2^M \times S)$, and $q'_0 \in S$ is an arbitrary state of S. An SCC S is said accepting if $\mathscr{L}(\mathcal{A}_{|S}) \neq \emptyset$.*

3   Specialized Transformations

We describe three algorithms that transform the acceptance condition of a TELA. The first two output an equivalent TELA with parity acceptance: CAR (Sect. 3.1) works for any input, while IAR (Sect. 3.2) is specialized for Rabin-like or Streett-like inputs. The third algorithm is a *partial degeneralization* (Sect. 3.3): it takes an automaton with any acceptance formula α, and produces an automaton where any generalized Büchi (resp. generalized co-Büchi) subformula of α have been replaced by a Büchi (resp. co-Büchi) formula. Optimizations common to these algorithms are listed in Sect. 3.4.

3.1   Color Appearance Record

Consider a set of marks $M = \{0, 1, \ldots, n-1\}$ and a TELA $\mathcal{A} = (Q, M, \Sigma, \delta, q_0, \alpha)$. Let $\Pi(M)$ be the set of *permutations* of M. We can represent a permutation $\sigma \in \Pi(M)$ by a table $\langle \sigma(0), \sigma(1), \ldots, \sigma(n-1) \rangle$.

The *Color Appearance Record* (CAR) algorithm pairs such permutations of colors with states of the input automaton in order to keep track of the history of colors visited in the corresponding run of $\mathcal{A}$, in the order they were last seen. Output states are therefore elements of $Q^{CAR} = Q \times \Pi(M)$.

We *update* histories with a function $\mathcal{U} : \Pi(M) \times M \to \Pi(M) \times 2^M$, such that $\mathcal{U}(\sigma, c) = (\langle c, \sigma(0), \sigma(1), \ldots, \sigma(i-1), \sigma(i+1), \ldots, \sigma(n-1)\rangle, \{\sigma(0), \sigma(1), \ldots, \sigma(i)\})$ where $i = \sigma^{-1}(c)$ is the position of color c in σ. In other words, $\mathcal{U}(\sigma, c)$ moves c to the front of σ by rotating the first $i+1$ elements: it returns the new permutation and the set of rotated elements. This update function can be generalized to a set of colors recursively as follows:

$$\widetilde{\mathcal{U}}(\sigma, \emptyset) = (\sigma, \emptyset)$$
$$\widetilde{\mathcal{U}}(\sigma, \{c\} \cup C) = (\rho, R \cup S) \text{ where } (\pi, R) = \widetilde{\mathcal{U}}(\sigma, C) \text{ and } (\rho, S) = \mathcal{U}(\pi, c)$$

That is to say, $\widetilde{\mathcal{U}}(\sigma, C)$ moves the colors in C to the front of σ and also returns set of colors corresponding to the updated prefix. The order in which colors in C are moved to the front of σ is unspecified and may affect the size of the output automaton (see Sect. 3.4).

Let $M' = \{0, \ldots, 2n+1\}$ be the output marks. We define the transition relation $\delta^{CAR} \subseteq Q^{CAR} \times \Sigma \times 2^{M'} \times Q^{CAR}$ as follows:

$$\delta^{CAR} = \left\{ (q, \sigma) \xrightarrow{x, \{c\}} (q', \pi) \,\middle|\, q \xrightarrow{x, C} q' \in \delta, \, (\pi, R) = \widetilde{\mathcal{U}}(\sigma, C), \, c = 2|R| + [R \not\models \alpha] \right\}$$

where $[R \not\models \alpha]$ is a shorthand for 0 if $R \models \alpha$ and for 1 if $R \not\models \alpha$.

Theorem 1. *For any TELA $\mathcal{A} = (Q, M, \Sigma, \delta, q_0, \alpha)$ over the marks $M = \{0, \ldots, n-1\}$, there exists an equivalent TELA $\mathcal{A}' = (Q^{CAR}, M', \Sigma, \delta^{CAR}, (q_0, \pi_0), \alpha')$ where α' is a parity max even formula over $2n + 1$ colors. The initial permutation can be any $\pi_0 \in \Pi(M)$.*

The proof is similar to that of the *state appearance record* algorithm [16], but we track colors instead of states. The intuition is that any cycle r' of $\mathcal{A}'$ corresponds to a cycle r of $\mathcal{A}$. If the union of the colors visited by r is R, then all the states in r' necessarily have all colors of R to the front of their history, there will be at least one transition t of r' for which the number of colors rotated by $\widetilde{\mathcal{U}}$ is $|R|$, and for all the other transitions this number will be lesser or equal. Therefore, the color $2|R| + [R \not\models \alpha]$ selected for this transition t will be the highest of $\mathsf{Rep}(r')$ and will cause r' to be accepting iff r is accepting.

Note that this construction may produce $|Q| \times n!$ states in the worst case.

Example 2. The CAR arrow at the top-right of Fig. 2 shows an application of CAR on a small example. Let us ignore the fact that there is no initial state in these "automata" and focus on how transitions of the output (above the arrow) are built from the transitions of the input (below). Assuming we want to build the successors of the output state $(1_1, \langle 0, 2, 1 \rangle)$, we look for all successors of input state 1_1. One option is $(1_1) \text{—②→} (0_1)$. We compute the history $\widetilde{\mathcal{U}}(\langle 0, 2, 1 \rangle, \{②\})$ of the destination state by moving ② to the front of the current history, yielding $\langle 2, 0, 1 \rangle$. The destination state is therefore $(0_1, \langle 2, 0, 1 \rangle)$. Two colors $R = \{❶, ②\}$ have been moved in the history by this transition, and since $R \models \alpha$ the transitions is labeled by color $2 \times |R| + 0 = ④$. Another successor is the loop $(1_1) \text{↺} ❶$. In this case, color ❶, already at the front of the history, is moved onto itself, so the output is a loop. Since $R = \{❶\} \not\models \alpha$, that loop is labeled by $2 \times |R| + 1 = ❸$.

3.2 Index Appearance Record

While CAR can be used to transform Rabin or Streett automata into parity automata, there exists an algorithm more suitable for these subclasses of TELA. Let $\mathcal{A} = (Q, M, \Sigma, \delta, q_0, \alpha)$ be a TELA with a Rabin acceptance condition $\alpha = \bigvee_{i \in \mathcal{I}} (\mathsf{Fin}(p_i) \wedge \mathsf{Inf}(r_i))$. We call (p_i, r_i) a *Rabin pair*, where p_i is the *prohibited* color, and r_i the *required* color.

We define the set of *index appearance records* as the set $\Pi(\mathcal{I})$ of permutations of Rabin pair indices. The output states $Q^{\mathrm{IAR}} = Q \times \Pi(\mathcal{I})$ are equipped with such a record to track the history of indices of the Rabin pairs (p_i, r_i) in the order the colors p_i were last seen.

We update those IAR using a function $\mathcal{U} : \Pi(\mathcal{I}) \times \mathcal{I} \to \Pi(\mathcal{I})$, such that $\mathcal{U}(\sigma, i) = \langle i, \sigma(0), \sigma(1), \ldots, \sigma(j-1), \sigma(j+1), \ldots, \sigma(|\mathcal{I}| - 1) \rangle$ where $j = \sigma^{-1}(i)$ is the position of the index i in σ. In other words, $\mathcal{U}(\sigma, i)$ moves i to the front of σ by rotating the first $j + 1$ elements. This update function can be generalized to a set of indices recursively with $\widetilde{\mathcal{U}}(\sigma, \emptyset) = \sigma$ and $\widetilde{\mathcal{U}}(\sigma, \{i\} \cup I) = \widetilde{\mathcal{U}}(\widetilde{\mathcal{U}}(\sigma, i), I)$.

When processing a transition labeled by colors $C \subseteq M$, we need to update the history for all indices $P(C) = \{i \in \mathcal{I} \mid p_i \in C\}$ of a prohibited color.

This construction builds an automaton with *parity max odd* acceptance over the color $M' = \{0, 1, \ldots, |\mathcal{I}| + 2\}$. The transitions $\delta^{\mathrm{IAR}} \subseteq Q^{\mathrm{IAR}} \times \Sigma \times 2^{M'} \times Q^{\mathrm{IAR}}$ of the output automaton can be defined as:

$$\delta^{\text{IAR}} = \left\{ (q,\sigma) \xrightarrow{x,\{c\}} (q',\pi) \;\middle|\; \begin{matrix} q \xrightarrow{x,C} q' \in \delta,\; \pi = \tilde{\mathcal{U}}(\sigma, P(C)),\; m = \mathcal{M}(\sigma,C), \\ c = 2m + 1 + [m \geq 0 \wedge p_{\sigma(m)} \in C] \end{matrix} \right\}$$

where $\mathcal{M}(\sigma,C) = \max(\{-\frac{1}{2}\} \cup \{i \in \{0,1,|\mathcal{I}|-1\} \mid p_{\sigma(i)} \in C \vee r_{\sigma(i)} \in C\})$ is the rightmost index of σ corresponding to a pair with a color in C, or $-\frac{1}{2}$ if no such index exists.

Theorem 2 ([15]). *For any TELA $\mathcal{A} = (Q,M,\Sigma,\delta,q_0,\alpha)$ over the marks $M = \{0,\ldots,n-1\}$ and such that α is a Rabin condition, there exists an equivalent TELA $\mathcal{A}' = (Q^{\text{IAR}}, M', \Sigma, \delta^{\text{IAR}}, (q_0,\pi_0), \alpha')$ where α' is a parity max odd acceptance formula over $2n+2$ colors. The initial permutation π_0 can be chosen arbitrarily. A dual construction transforms Streett into parity max even.*

For proof, we refer the reader to Löding [16] (for state-based acceptance) and to Křetínský et al. [15] (who adapted it to TELA).

For the intuition behind the definition of c in δ^{IAR}, imagine a transition $(q,\sigma) \xrightarrow{x,\{c\}} (q',\pi)$ on a cycle r' of $\mathcal{A}'$, and a matching transition $q \xrightarrow{x,C} q'$ from $\mathcal{A}$. Assume the corresponding cycle r of the input automaton visits all colors in $C' = \text{Rep}(r)$. Because they are on the cycle r', the IARs σ, π, and the others on that cycle have all their indices $P(C')$ to the left of the permutation. When we scan the IAR σ from the right to the left to find the maximal index $m = \mathcal{M}(\sigma,C)$ corresponding to a pair matching C, three situations can occur: (1) If $m \geq 0$ and $p_{\sigma(m)} \in C$, we know that we are in the left part, and that all Rabin pairs of indices $\sigma(0),\ldots,\sigma(m)$ are not satisfied on this cycle: the transition is labeled with $c = 2m+2$ to indicate so. (2) If $m \geq 0$ and $p_{\sigma(m)} \notin C$, it *may* be the case that m is in the right part of the IAR, meaning that the Rabin pair of index $\sigma(m)$ is satisfied. We label the transition with $c = 2m+1$ to indicate acceptance, but this might be canceled by a another transition emitting a higher even value if $p_{\sigma(i)}$ appears elsewhere on this cycle. (3) Finally $m = -\frac{1}{2}$ occurs when $C = \emptyset$, in this case the transition is labeled by $c = 0$ as no pair is satisfied.

This procedure generates an automaton with $|Q| \times |\mathcal{I}|!$ states in the worst case, but unless colors occur multiple times in α, we usually have $|\mathcal{I}| \leq n/2$, making IAR preferable to CAR.

Example 3. The arrow IAR in Fig. 2 shows an example of IAR at work on a Rabin automaton with two pairs. The output transition $\boxed{2\langle 01\rangle}\text{-④→}\boxed{2\langle 10\rangle}$, corresponds to a loop labeled by $C = \{\mathbf{0},\mathbf{2}\}$ in the input. Since $\mathbf{0}$ is prohibited in Rabin pair 1, index 1 has to move to the front of the history. Furthermore, the rightmost index of $\langle 01\rangle$ with a color in C is also $m = 1$ and corresponds to $p_1 = \mathbf{0} \in C$, this justifies that the output transition is labeled by $2m+1+1 = \mathbf{④}$.

3.3 Partial Degeneralization

We now define the partial degeneralization of a TELA A according to some subset D of its colors. Our intent is to modify A in such a way that we can replace any sub-formula of the form $\bigwedge_{d \in D} \mathsf{Inf}(d)$ in its acceptance condition α by a single $\mathsf{Inf}(e)$ for some new color e. Similarly, any sub-formula of the form $\bigvee_{d \in D} \mathsf{Fin}(d)$ will be replaced by $\mathsf{Fin}(e)$. We denote such a substitution of sub-formulas by $\alpha[\bigwedge_{d \in D} \mathsf{Inf}(d) \leftarrow \mathsf{Inf}(e)][\bigvee_{d \in D} \mathsf{Fin}(d) \leftarrow \mathsf{Fin}(e)]$.

The construction ensures that the runs of the output that see all colors of D infinitely often also see e infinitely often. To do that, we consider an ordering of $\{d_0, d_1, \ldots d_{|D|-1}\}$ of D, and equip each state of the output automaton by a *level* in $L = \{0, 1, \ldots |D| - 1\}$. We jump from level i to level $i + 1$ whenever we use a transition labeled by d_i; thus, we reach a level i only after having met the i first colors of D. We jump down to level 0 when a transition t leaving a state at level $|D| - 1$ is labeled by $d_{|D|-1}$; moreover, since any cycle going through t will have seen all colors in D, we can add the new color e to t.

An optimization, commonly done in degeneralization procedures [1,11], is that transition labeled by multiple consecutive colors of D may skip several levels. Let us define this *skipping* of levels more formally as a function $\mathcal{S} : L \times 2^M \to L \times 2^{\{e\}}$ that takes a level i and a set C of colors seen by some transition, and returns the new level j and a subset that is either $\emptyset$ or $\{e\}$ to indicate whether the new color should be added to the output transition.

$$\mathcal{S}(i, C) = \begin{cases} (j, \emptyset) & \text{if } j < |D| \\ (j - |D|, \{e\}) & \text{if } j \geq |D| \end{cases}, \text{ where}$$

$$j = \max\left(k \in \{i, i+1, \ldots, i+|D|\} \,\middle|\, \{d_i, d_{(i+1) \bmod |D|}, \ldots, d_{(k+|D|-1) \bmod |D|}\} \subseteq C\right).$$

Theorem 3. *Let $\mathcal{A} = (Q, M, \Sigma, \delta, q_0, \alpha)$ be a TELA, and let $C \subseteq M$ be a set of marks. Let $D = \{d_0, d_1, \ldots, d_{|C|-1}\}$ be some ordering of the colors of C, and let $L = \{0, 1, \ldots, |C|\}$ be a set of levels.*

$\mathcal{A}$ is equivalent to its partial degeneralization according to C, defined by automaton $\mathcal{A}' = (Q', M', \Sigma, \delta', (q_0, i_0), \alpha')$ where $Q' = Q \times L$, $M' = M \cup \{e\}$ for some new color $e \notin M$, $\alpha' = \alpha[\bigwedge_{d \in D} \mathsf{Inf}(d) \leftarrow \mathsf{Inf}(e)][\bigvee_{d \in D} \mathsf{Fin}(d) \leftarrow \mathsf{Fin}(e)]$, and $\delta' = \left\{ (q_1, i) \xrightarrow{\ell, C} (q_2, j) \,\middle|\, q_1 \xrightarrow{\ell, C \cap M} q_2 \in \delta, \mathcal{S}(i, C \cap M) = (j, C \setminus M) \right\}$. The initial level can be any $i_0 \in L$.

First, note that this procedure does not remove any color from the automaton. This is because even though subformulas of the form $\bigwedge_{d \in D} \mathsf{Inf}(d)$ are removed from α, other parts of α, preserved in α', may still use colors in D. Of course, colors that do not appear in α' may be removed from the automaton as a subsequent step, and this is done in our implementation.

Moreover, because the algorithm keeps all used colors, the construction is valid for any subset $D \subseteq M$, even one that does not correspond to a conjunction of Inf or disjunction of Fin in α. In such a case, the construction enlarges the automaton without changing its acceptance condition.

Finally, in the case where α is a generalized Büchi condition over the marks M, and $D = M$, then the resulting α' will be $\mathsf{Inf}(e)$, and removing all the now useless original colors will have the same effect as a classical degeneralization. In this sense, the degeneralization is a special case of the partial degeneralization.

Similarly, this procedure can also be seen as a generalization of the transformation of generalized-Rabin automata into Rabin automata [12].

Example 4. In Fig. 2, the arrow $\text{PD}_{\{1,3\}}$ denotes the application of a partial degeneralization according to the set $M = \{\text{❶}, \text{❸}\}$. This allows to rewrite acceptance's sub-formula $\text{Fin}(\text{❶}) \vee \text{Fin}(\text{❸})$ as $\text{Fin}(\text{❹})$ with a new color. Output states (q, i) are written as q_i for brevity. The ordering of colors is $d_0 = \text{❸}$, $d_1 = \text{❶}$.

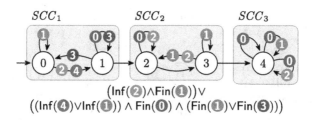

$$\big(\text{Inf}(\text{❷}) \wedge \text{Fin}(\text{❶})\big) \vee$$
$$\big(\,(\text{Inf}(\text{❹}) \vee \text{Inf}(\text{❶})) \wedge \text{Fin}(\text{⓿}) \wedge (\text{Fin}(\text{❶}) \vee \text{Fin}(\text{❸}))\big)$$

Fig. 1. Some arbitrary input TELA, to be paritized. For readability, letters are not displayed.

3.4   Optimizations

We now describe several optimizations for the aforementioned constructions.

Jump to Bottom: The choice of the initial permutation π_0 in the CAR, in the IAR, or of the initial level i_0 in the partial degeneralization is arbitrary. With a bad selection of those values, a cycle can be turned into a lasso. For instance, if we consider the input automaton $\rightarrow\!\!\text{(}x\text{)} \underset{\text{❶}}{\overset{\text{⓿}}{\rightleftarrows}} \text{(}y\text{)}$, applying CAR with $\pi_0 = \langle 0, 1 \rangle$ produces an automaton with the following structure: $\rightarrow\!\!\boxed{x\langle 01 \rangle} \!\rightarrow\! \boxed{y\langle 01 \rangle} \rightleftarrows \boxed{x\langle 10 \rangle}$, whereas $\pi_0 = \langle 1, 0 \rangle$ would yield $\rightarrow\!\!\boxed{x\langle 10 \rangle} \rightleftarrows \boxed{y\langle 01 \rangle}$.

Instead of guessing the correct initialization, we simply use the fact that two states (q, σ) and (q, π) recognize the same language: after the algorithm's execution, we redirect any transition leading to a state (q, σ) to the copy (q, π) that lies in the bottommost SCC (in some topological ordering of the SCCs). The initial state is changed similarly. The input and output automata should have then the same number of SCCs.

This optimization applies to CAR, IAR, partial degeneralization, or combinations of those. E.g., if partial degeneralization is used before CAR or IAR, leading to states of the form $((q, i), \sigma)$, the search for an equivalent state in the bottom SCC needs only consider q, and can simplify both constructions at once.

A similar simplification was initially proposed in the context of IAR for simplifying one SCC at a time [15]. Heuristics used in degeneralization algorithms to select initial level upon entering a new SCC [1] are then unnecessary.

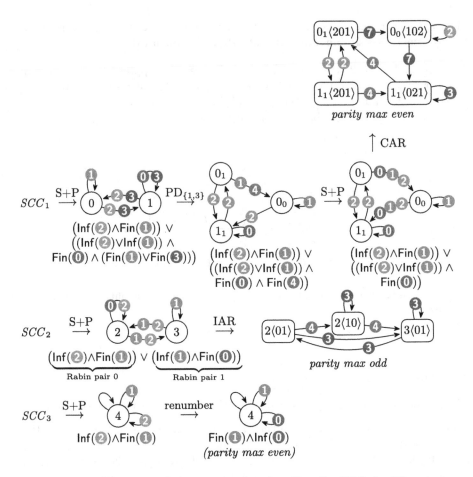

Fig. 2. Intermediate steps of the construction, handling the SCCs in different ways. These steps are explained at various places through Sects. 3 and 4.

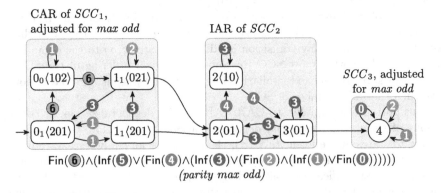

Fig. 3. Paritization of the automaton of Fig. 1, combining the transformed SCCs of Fig. 2 after adjustment to a common acceptance condition.

History Reuse: When processing an input transition labeled with multiple colors, the insertion order of those colors (resp. Rabin pair indices) in front of the history during an update of the CAR (resp. IAR) is arbitrary. Křetínský et al. [15] suggested to check previously built states for one with a compatible trail of the history, in order to avoid creating new states. While implementing this optimization, we noticed that sometimes we can find multiple compatible states: heuristically selecting the most recently created one (as opposed to the oldest one) produces fewer states on average in our benchmark. It seems to create tighter loops and larger "lasso prefixes" that can later be removed by the *jump to bottom* optimization. Such history reuse can also be done *a posteriori* once a candidate automaton has been built, to select better connections.

Heuristic Selection of Move Order: When an input transition is labeled with multiple colors, but no compatible destination state already exists to apply the previous optimization, we select the order in which colors are moved to the front of the history using a heuristic. Colors that are common to all incoming transitions of the destination states are moved last, so they end up at the beginning of the history. For instance in the CAR construction of Fig. 2, this is how the order ⟨102⟩ is chosen as destination history for transition (0_1)—❶⓿❷→(0_0): ❶ is common to all edges going to 0_0, so we want it at the front of the history.

SCC-aware Algorithms: These algorithms benefit from considering the SCCs of the original automaton. For CAR and IAR, the histories attached can be restricted to the colors present in the SCC [15]. The partial degeneralization needs not modify SCCs that do not contain all the colors C to degeneralize.

Heuristic Ordering of Colors to Degeneralize: Our implementation of the partial degeneralization tries to guess, for each SCC, an appropriate ordering of the color to degeneralize: this is done by maintaining the order as a list of equivalence classes of colors, and refining this order as new transitions are processed. For instance if we degeneralize for the colors $C = \{⓿,❶,❷,❸\}$, the initial order will be ⟨{⓿,❶,❷,❸}⟩ , then if the first transition we visit has colors {❶,❸} the new order will be refined to ⟨{❶,❸},{⓿,❷}⟩ and we jump to level 2 as we have now seen the first equivalence class of size 2.

Propagation of Colors: To favor the grouping of colors in the dynamic ordering of the partial degeneralization, and in the history reuse optimization of IAR and CAR, we propagate colors as much as possible in SCCs. Ignoring transitions that are self-loops or that do not have both extremities in the same SCC, colors common to all incoming transitions of a state can be copied to all outgoing transitions and vice-versa. E.g., (x)—⓿→(y)—⓿❶→(z)←❷ is seen as the equivalent (x)←⓿→(y)←⓿❶→(z)←❷ , showing that cycles with ❶ always have ⓿.

The next section goes one step further in SCC-awareness, by actually simplifying the acceptance condition for each SCC according to the colors present. The paritization strategy to apply (CAR, IAR, identity, ...) can then be chosen independently for each SCC.

4 Paritization with Multiple Strategies

We now describe our paritization algorithm taking as input a TELA $\mathcal{A}$:

(1) Enumerate the SCCs S_i of $\mathcal{A}$. For each S_i, perform the following operations:

(a) Consider the sub-automaton $\mathcal{A}_{|S_i}$.

(b) Simplify its acceptance condition by removing unused colors ($\mathsf{Fin}(i)$ becomes $\top$, and $\mathsf{Inf}(i)$ becomes $\bot$ for any color i unused in $\mathcal{A}_{|S_i}$), or dually, colors that appear everywhere. Colors that always appear together can be replaced by a single color, and disjunctions of Inf or conjunctions of Fin can be reduced as discussed in Remark 2.

(c) Propagate colors in the SCC (Sect. 3.4).

(d) If the simplified acceptance condition contains conjunctions of Inf or disjunctions of Fin, apply the partial degeneralization construction (maybe multiple times) for all those terms, and remove unused colors. Since this incurs a blowup of the state-space that is linear (maybe multiple times) in the number of colors removed, it generally helps the CAR construction which has a worst case factorial blowup in the number of colors. Also, after this step, the acceptance condition might match more specialized algorithms in the next step. Jump to step 1b as the acceptance changed.

(e) Transform the automaton $\mathcal{A}_{|S_i}$ into a *parity max* automaton R_i using the first applicable procedure from the following list:

– If $\mathscr{L}(\mathcal{A}_{|S_i})$ is empty [3], strip all colors and set the acceptance condition to $\bot$, which is a corner case for *parity max even* formula. (For *parity max* acceptances, transitions without color can be interpreted as having color -1.);

– Do nothing if the acceptance is already a *parity max* formula;

– If the acceptance has the shape $\mathsf{Inf}(m_0) \vee (\mathsf{Fin}(m_1) \wedge (\mathsf{Inf}(m_2) \vee ...))$ of a *parity max*, renumber the colors $m_0, m_1, \ldots$ in decreasing order to get a *parity max* formula;

– Adjust the condition to $\mathsf{Inf}(\mathbf{0})$ and the labeling of the transitions if this is a deterministic Rabin-like automaton that is Büchi-type (this requires a transition-based adaptation of an algorithm by Krishnan et al. [14]); note that $\mathsf{Inf}(\mathbf{0})$ is also a *parity max even* formula.

– Dually, adjust the condition to $\mathsf{Fin}(\mathbf{0})$ if this is a deterministic Streett-like automaton that is co-Büchi-type, since $\mathsf{Fin}(\mathbf{0})$ is also a *parity max odd* formula.

– If the automaton is Rabin-like or Streett-like, apply IAR to obtain a *parity max* automaton. When the acceptance formula can be interpreted as both Rabin-like or Streett-like we use the interpretation with the fewest number of pairs (cf. Remark 1).

– Otherwise, apply CAR to obtain a *parity max* automaton.

(2) Now that each automaton $\mathcal{A}_{|S_i}$ has been converted into an automaton R_i whose *parity* acceptance is either *max odd* or *max even*, adjust those acceptance conditions by incrementing or decrementing the colors of some R_i so that they can all use the same acceptance, and stitch all R_i together to form

the final automaton R. For any transition of $\mathcal{A}$ that goes from state q in SCC i to state q' in SCC j, R should have a transition for each copy of q in R_i and going to one copy of q' in R_j. Similarly, the initial state of R should be any copy of the initial state of $\mathcal{A}$.

(3) As a final cleanup, the number of colors of R can be reduced by computing the Rabin-index of the automaton [5].

Figures 1, 2 and 3 show this algorithm at work on a small example with three SCCs. Figure 3 shows the result of step 2. Executing step 3 would reduce the number of colors to 2 (or to 3 if uncolored transitions are disallowed).

We now comment the details of Fig. 2. The notation S+P refers to the Simplification of the acceptance condition (step 1b) and the Propagation of colors in the SCC (step 1c). On SCC_1, step 1b replaces ❹ by ❷, because these always occur together, and step 1c adds ❷ on the transition from 1 to 0. After partial degeneralization, the sub-formula $\mathsf{Fin}(⓪) \wedge \mathsf{Fin}(❹)$ can be fused into a single $\mathsf{Fin}(⓪)$ (see Remark 2) by simply replacing ❹ by ⓪ in the automaton, and after that the marks on the transitions before and after state 0_0 are propagated by step 1c. The resulting automaton is neither Rabin-like nor Streett-like, so it is transformed to parity using CAR; however the history of the states only have 3 colors to track instead of the original 5. In SCC_2, $\mathsf{Fin}(❸)$ and $\mathsf{Inf}(❹)$ can be replaced respectively by $\top$ and $\bot$ because ❸ and ❹ are not used. The acceptance condition is therefore reduced to the Rabin acceptance condition displayed, and IAR can be used instead of CAR. (Using CAR would build at least 4 states.) Finally SCC_3's acceptance conditions reduces to $\mathsf{Inf}(❷) \wedge \mathsf{Fin}(①)$. Renumbering the colors to $\mathsf{Fin}(①) \wedge \mathsf{Inf}(⓪)$ gives us a parity max odd acceptance.

To stitch all these results together, as in Fig. 3, we adjust all automata to use *parity max odd*: in SCC_1 this can be done for instance by decrementing all colors and in SCC_3 by incrementing them (handling any missing color as -1).

Our implementation uses an additional optimization that we call the *parity prefix detection*. If the acceptance formula has the shape $\mathsf{Inf}(m_0) \vee (\mathsf{Fin}(m_1) \wedge (\mathsf{Inf}(m_2) \vee (...\beta)))$, i.e., it starts like a *parity max* formula but does not have the right shape because of β, we can apply CAR or IAR using only β while preserving the color $m_0, m_1, m_2, \ldots$ of the parity prefix, and later renumber all colors so the formula becomes *parity max*. This limits the colors that CAR and IAR have to track, so it reduces the number of states in the worst case.

5   Experimental Evaluation

The simple CAR described in Sect. 3.1, without the optimizations of Sect. 3.4 was implemented in Spot 2.8 [7] as a function `to_parity()`. It can be used by Spot's `ltlsynt` tool with option `--algo=lar`; in that case the LTL specification φ passed to `ltlsynt` is converted to a deterministic TELA $\mathcal{A}_\varphi$ with arbitrary acceptance and then transformed into a parity automaton $\mathcal{P}_\varphi$ with `to_parity()` before the rest of the LTL synthesis procedure is performed.

The TELA $\mathcal{A}_\varphi$ built internally by `ltlsynt` can be obtained using Spot's `ltl2tgba -G -D` command: the construction is similar to the `delag` tool [21] and regards the original formula as a Boolean combination of LTL sub-formulas φ_i, translating each φ_i to a deterministic TELA $\mathcal{A}_{\varphi_i}$ (by combining classical LTL-to-generalized-Büchi translation [6] with specialized constructions for subclasses of LTL [9], or a Safra-based procedure [23]), and combining those results using synchronized products to obtain a TELA whose acceptance condition is the Boolean combination of the acceptance conditions of all the $\mathcal{A}_{\varphi_i}$.

In Spot 2.9, to_parity() was changed to implement Sect. 4 and the optimizations of Sect. 3.4. We are therefore in position to compare the improvements brought by those changes on the transformation of $\mathcal{A}_\varphi$ to $\mathcal{P}_\varphi$.[1]

We evaluate the improvements on two sets of automata:

syntcomp contains automata generated with ltl2tgba -G -D from LTL formulas from the sequential TLSF track of SyntComp'2017. Among those automata, we have removed those that already had a parity acceptance (usually Büchi acceptance). The remaining set contains 32 automata with a generalized-Büchi condition, and 84 with a condition that mixes Fin and Inf terms (only 1 of these can be considered Rabin-like or Streett-like). The average number of accepting SCCs is 1.9 (min. 1, med. 1, max. 4). The average number of states is 46 (min. 1, med. 13, max. 986).

randltl contains 273 automata built similarly, from random LTL formulas. Furthermore, we have ensured that no automaton has parity acceptance, and all of them use at least 5 colors (med. 5, avg. 5.2, max. 9). The average number of accepting SCCs is 1.7 (min. 1, med. 1, max. 5). The average number of states is 5.8 (min. 1, med. 4, max. 41). Only 13 of these automata have a Rabin-like or Streett-like acceptance condition.

The improvement of our new paritization based on multiple strategies over our old unoptimized CAR implementation is shown on Fig. 4.

Table 2 selectively disables some optimizations to evaluate their effect on the number of output states. Configuration "all − x" means that optimization x is disabled. *Rabin to Büchi* is the detection of Rabin-like (or Streett-like) automata that are Büchi (or co-Büchi) realizable at step 1e. *Parity prefix* is the optimization mentioned at the very end of Sect. 4. *Simplify acc*, *propagate colors*, and *partial degen* correspond respectively to steps 1b and 1c, and 1d. Partial degeneralization appears to be the most important optimization, because in addition to reducing the number of colors, it may help to use IAR or even simpler construction. The propagation of colors, which allows more flexibility in the selection of histories, is the second best optimization. *Hist. reuse* corresponds to the history reuse described in Sect. 3.4. *all − reuse latest* has history reuse enabled, but uses the oldest compatible state instead of the latest—hence our heuristic of using the latest compatible state. Finally *Unoptimized CAR* is a straightforward implementation of CAR given for comparison.

To assert the effect of the improved paritization on ltlsynt, we ran the entire SyntComp'17 benchmark (including formulas omitted before) with a timeout of 100 seconds, and counted the number of cases solved by different configurations

---

[1] To reproduce these results, see https://www.lrde.epita.fr/~frenkin/atva20/.

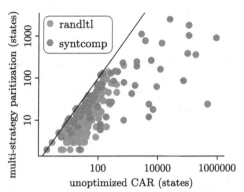

Fig. 4. Comparison of the new multi-strategy paritization (Sect. 4) against the unoptimized CAR (Sect. 3.1)

Table 2. Effect of disabling different optimizations on the arithmetic and geometric means of the number of states on both benchmarks

configuration	amean	gmean
all	48.71	14.43
all − Rabin to Büchi	48.72	14.45
all − parity prefix	48.97	14.54
all − simplify acc	49.32	15.07
all − hist. reuse	51.01	15.18
all − reuse latest	51.05	15.29
all − propagate colors	55.69	16.91
all − partial degen	2165.50	20.20
unoptimized CAR	5375.02	45.16

Table 3. Number of SyntComp'17 cases solved by `ltlsynt` under different configurations, with a timeout of 100 s. PAR-2 (penalized average runtime) sums the time of all successful instances, plus twice the timeout for unsuccessful ones.

option	approach to paritization	# solved	PAR-2
--algo=lar.old	LTL to determ. TELA, then CAR of Sect. 3.1	175	7262 s
--algo=sd	LTL to Büchi, then split input/output variables, then Safra-based determinization [20]	177	6879 s
--algo=ds	LTL to Büchi, then Safra-based determinization, then split input/output variables [20]	180	6671 s
--algo=lar	LTL to determ. TELA, then approach of Sect. 4	185	6296 s

of `ltlsynt`, as reported in Table 3. We can see that improving CAR with all the tricks of Sect. 4 allowed the `ltlsynt`'s LAR-based approach to perform better than `ltlsynt`'s Safra-based approaches.

6   Conclusion

We have presented a procedure that converts any TELA into a transition-based parity automaton. Our algorithm combines algorithms that are transition-based adaptations or generalizations of known procedures (e.g., CAR is a adaption of the classical SAR and partial degeneration extends the standard generalization technique), thus this paper can also be read as a partial survey of acceptance condition transformations presented under a unified framework.

The CAR construction, which is the general case for our paritization algorithm, produces smaller automata than the classical SAR, as it tracks colors instead of states, and uses transition-based acceptance. We further improved this construction by applying more specialized algorithms in each SCC (IAR [15], detection of Büchi-realizable SCCs [14], detection of empty SCCs [3], detection of parity) after simplifying their acceptance.

The proposed partial degeneralization procedure is used as a preprocessing step to reduce conjunctions of Inf or disjunction of Fin in the acceptance condition, and to reduce the number of colors that CAR and IAR have to track. Since partial degeneralization only causes a linear blowup in the number of colors removed, it generally helps the CAR construction whose worst case scenario incurs a factorial blowup in the number of colors. Furthermore, after partial degeneralization, the acceptance condition may match more specialized algorithms.

The implementation of the described paritization procedure is publicly available in Spot 2.9. While our motivation stems from one approach to produce deterministic parity automata used in Spot, this paritization also works with non-deterministic automata: it preserves the determinism of the input.

Acknowledgment. The unoptimized CAR definition of Sect. 3.1 was first implemented in Spot by Maximilien Colange.

References

1. Babiak, T., Badie, T., Duret-Lutz, A., Křetínský, M., Strejček, J.: Compositional approach to suspension and other improvements to LTL translation. In: Bartocci, E., Ramakrishnan, C.R. (eds.) SPIN 2013. LNCS, vol. 7976, pp. 81–98. Springer, Heidelberg (2013). https://doi.org/10.1007/978-3-642-39176-7_6

2. Babiak, T., et al.: The hanoi omega-automata format. In: Kroening, D., Păsăreanu, C.S. (eds.) CAV 2015. LNCS, vol. 9206, pp. 479–486. Springer, Cham (2015). https://doi.org/10.1007/978-3-319-21690-4_31

3. Baier, C., Blahoudek, F., Duret-Lutz, A., Klein, J., Müller, D., Strejček, J.: Generic emptiness check for fun and profit. In: Chen, Y.-F., Cheng, C.-H., Esparza, J. (eds.) ATVA 2019. LNCS, vol. 11781, pp. 445–461. Springer, Cham (2019). https://doi.org/10.1007/978-3-030-31784-3_26

4. Bloem, R., Chatterjee, K., Jobstmann, B.: Graph Games and reactive synthesis. Handbook of Model Checking, pp. 921–962. Springer, Cham (2018). https://doi.org/10.1007/978-3-319-10575-8_27

5. Carton, O., Maceiras, R.: Computing the Rabin index of a parity automaton. Informatique théorique et applications **33**(6), 495–505 (1999)

6. Duret-Lutz, A.: LTL translation improvements in Spot 1.0. Int. J. Critical Comput. Based Syst. **5**(1/2), 31–54 (2014)

7. Duret-Lutz, A., Lewkowicz, A., Fauchille, A., Michaud, T., Renault, É., Xu, L.: Spot 2.0 — A framework for LTL and ω-automata manipulation. In: Artho, C., Legay, A., Peled, D. (eds.) ATVA 2016. LNCS, vol. 9938, pp. 122–129. Springer, Cham (2016). https://doi.org/10.1007/978-3-319-46520-3_8

8. Emerson, E.A., Lei, C.-L.: Modalities for model checking: branching time logic strikes back. Sci. Comput. Program. **8**(3), 275–306 (1987)

9. Esparza, J., Křetínský, J., Sickert, S.: One theorem to rule them all: a unified translation of LTL into ω-automata. In: LICS 2018, pp. 384–393. ACM (2018)

10. Farwer, B.: ω-Automata, LNCS 2500, chap. 1, pp. 3–20. Springer, Heidelberg (2001)
11. Gastin, P., Oddoux, D.: Fast LTL to Büchi automata translation. In: CAV 2001, LNCS 2102, pp. 53–65. Springer, Cham (2001)
12. Křetínský, J., Esparza, J.: Deterministic automata for the (F,G)-Fragment of LTL. In: Madhusudan, P., Seshia, S.A. (eds.) CAV 2012. LNCS, vol. 7358, pp. 7–22. Springer, Heidelberg (2012). https://doi.org/10.1007/978-3-642-31424-7_7
13. Křetínský, J., Meggendorfer, T., Sickert, S.: Owl: a library for ω-words, automata, and LTL. In: Lahiri, S.K., Wang, C. (eds.) ATVA 2018. LNCS, vol. 11138, pp. 543–550. Springer, Cham (2018). https://doi.org/10.1007/978-3-030-01090-4_34
14. Krishnan, S.C., Puri, A., Brayton, R.K.: Deterministic ω-automata vis-a-vis deterministic Büchi automata. In: ISAAC 1994, LNCS 834, pp. 378–386. Springer, Cham (1994)
15. Křetínský, J., Meggendorfer, T., Waldmann, C., Weininger, M.: Index appearance record for transforming rabin automata into parity automata. In: Legay, A., Margaria, T. (eds.) TACAS 2017. LNCS, vol. 10205, pp. 443–460. Springer, Heidelberg (2017). https://doi.org/10.1007/978-3-662-54577-5_26
16. Löding, C.: Methods for the transformation of ω-automata: complexity and connection to second order logic. Diploma thesis, Institue of Computer Science and Applied Mathematics (1998)
17. Löding, C.: Optimal bounds for transformations of automata. In: Rangan, C.P., Raman, V., Ramanujam, R. (eds.) FSTTCS 1999. LNCS, vol. 1738, pp. 97–109. Springer, Heidelberg (1999). https://doi.org/10.1007/3-540-46691-6_8
18. Luttenberger, M., Meyer, P.J., Sickert, S.: Practical synthesis of reactive systems from LTL specifications via parity games. Acta Informatica, **57**, 3—36 (2020). Originally published on 21 November 2019
19. Major, J., Blahoudek, F., Strejcek, J., Sasaráková, M., Zboncáková, T.: `ltl3tela`: LTL to small deterministic or nondeterministic Emerson-Lei automata. In: ATVA 2019, LNCS 11781, pp. 357–365. Springer, Cham (2019)
20. Michaud, T., Colange, M.: Reactive synthesis from LTL specification with Spot. In: SYNT 2018 (2018). http://www.lrde.epita.fr/dload/papers/michaud.18.synt.pdf
21. Müller, D., Sickert, S.: LTL to deterministic Emerson-Lei automata. In: GandALF 2017, vol. 256 of EPTCS, pp. 180–194 (2017)
22. Piterman, N.: From nondeterministic büchi and streett automata to deterministic parity automata. Logical Methods Comput. Sci. **3**(3), 1057–1065 (2007)
23. Redziejowski, R.: An improved construction of deterministic omega-automaton using derivatives. Fundamenta Informaticae **119**(3–4), 393–406 (2012)
24. Safra, S., Vardi, M.Y.: On ω-automata and temporal logic. In: STOC 1989, pp. 127–137. ACM (1989)

Complexity of Verification and Synthesis of Threshold Automata

A. R. Balasubramanian$^{(\boxtimes)}$ ⓘ, Javier Esparza ⓘ, and Marijana Lazić ⓘ

Technische Universität München, Munich, Germany
bala.ayikudi@tum.de, {esparza,lazic}@in.tum.de

Abstract. Threshold automata are a formalism for modeling and analyzing fault-tolerant distributed algorithms, recently introduced by Konnov, Veith, and Widder, describing protocols executed by a fixed but arbitrary number of processes. We conduct the first systematic study of the complexity of verification and synthesis problems for threshold automata. We prove that the coverability, reachability, safety, and liveness problems are NP-complete, and that the bounded synthesis problem is Σ_p^2 complete. A key to our results is a novel characterization of the reachability relation of a threshold automaton as an existential Presburger formula. The characterization also leads to novel verification and synthesis algorithms. We report on an implementation, and provide experimental results.

Keywords: Threshold automata · Distributed algorithms · Parameterized verification

1 Introduction

Many concurrent and distributed systems consist of an arbitrary number of communicating processes. Parameterized verification investigates how to prove them correct for any number of processes [1].

Parameterized systems whose processes are indistinguishable and finite state are often called *replicated systems*. A global state of a replicated system is completely determined by the number of processes in each state. Models of replicated systems differ in the communication mechanism between processes. Vector Addition Systems (VAS) and their extensions [2,7,9,11] can model rendez-vous, multiway synchronization, global resets and broadcasts, and other mechanisms. The decidability and complexity of their verification problems is well understood [1,2,8,10,24].

Transition guards of VAS-based replicated systems are *local*: Whether a transition is enabled or not depends only on the current states of a *fixed* number of processes, independent of the total number of processes. Konnov *et al.*

This project has received funding from the European Research Council (ERC) under the European Union's Horizon 2020 research and innovation programme under grant agreement No. 787367 (PaVeS).

D. V. Hung and O. Sokolsky (Eds.): ATVA 2020, LNCS 12302, pp. 144–160, 2020.
https://doi.org/10.1007/978-3-030-59152-6_8

observed in [15] that local guards cannot model fault-tolerant distributed algorithms. Indeed, in such algorithms often a process can only make a step if it has received a message from a *majority* or some fraction of the processes. To remedy this, they introduced *threshold automata*, a model of replicated systems with shared-variable communication and *threshold guards*, in which the value of a global variable is compared to an affine combination of the total numbers of processes of different types. In a number of papers, Konnov *et al.* have developed and implemented verification algorithms for safety and liveness of threshold automata [14–18]. Further, Kukovec *et al.* have obtained decidability and undecidability results [19] for different variants of the model. However, contrary to the VAS case, the computational complexity of the main verification problems has not yet been studied.

We conduct the first systematic complexity analysis of threshold automata.[1] In the first part of the paper we show that the parameterized coverability and reachability problems are NP-complete. Parameterized coverability asks if some configuration reachable from some initial configuration puts at least one process in a given state, and parameterized reachability asks if it puts processes in *exactly* a given set of states, leaving all other states unpopulated. The NP upper bound is a consequence of our main result, showing that the reachability relation of threshold automata is expressible in existential Presburger arithmetic. In the second part of the paper we apply this expressibility result to prove that the model checking problem of *Fault-Tolerant Temporal Logic* (ELTL$_{FT}$) [18] is NP-complete, and that the problem of synthesizing the guards of a given automaton, studied in [21], is Σ_p^2 complete. The last part of the paper reports on an implementation of our novel approach to the parameterized (safety and liveness) verification problems. We show that it compares favorably to ByMC, the tool developed in [17].

2   Threshold Automata

We introduce threshold automata, illustrating the definitions on the example of Fig. 2, a model of the Byzantine agreement protocol of Fig. 1.

Environments. Threshold automata are defined relative to an *environment* $Env = (\Pi, RC, N)$, where Π is a set of *parameters* ranging over $\mathbb{N}_0$, $RC \subseteq \mathbb{N}_0^\Pi$ is a *resilience condition* expressible as an integer linear formula, and $N: RC \to \mathbb{N}_0$ is a linear function. Intuitively, a valuation of Π determines the number of processes of different kinds (e.g., faulty) executing the protocol, and RC describes the admissible combinations of parameter values. Finally, N associates to a each admissible combination, the number of copies of the automaton that are going to run in parallel, or, equivalently, the number of processes explicitly modeled. In a Byzantine setting, faulty processes behave arbitrarily, and so we do not model

---

[1] A full version of this paper containing additional details and proofs can be found at https://arxiv.org/abs/2007.06248.

```
1 var  myval_i ∈ {0,1}
2 var  accept_i ∈ {false, true} ← false
3
4 while  true  do  (in one atomic step)
5   if  myval_i = 1
6     and not  sent  ECHO  before
7   then send ECHO to  all
8
9   if  received  ECHO  from  at  least
10      t + 1  distinct  processes
11      and not  sent  ECHO  before
12   then send ECHO to  all
13
14   if  received  ECHO  from  at  least
15      n − t  distinct  processes
16   then  accept_i ← true
17 od
```

Fig. 1. Pseudocode of a reliable broadcast protocol from [26] for a correct process i, where n and t denote the number of processes, and an upper bound on the number of faulty processes. The protocol satisfies its specification (if $myval_i = 1$ for every correct process i, then eventually $accept_j = true$ for some correct process j) if $t < n/3$.

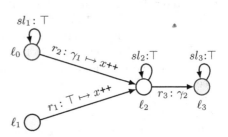

Fig. 2. Threshold automaton modeling the body of the loop in the protocol from Fig. 1. Symbols γ_1, γ_2 stand for the threshold guards $x \geq (t+1) - f$ and $x \geq (n-t) - f$, where n and t are as in Fig. 1, and f is the actual number of faulty processes. The shared variable x models the number of ECHO messages sent by correct processes. Processes with $myval_i = b$ (line 1) start in location ℓ_b (in green). Rules r_1 and r_2 model sending ECHO at lines 7 and 12. The self-loop rules $sl_1, \ldots, sl_3$ are stuttering steps. (Color figure online)

them explicitly; in this case, the system consists of one copy of the automaton for every correct process. In the crash fault model, processes behave correctly until they crash, they must be modeled explicitly, and the system has a copy of the automaton for each process, faulty or not.

Example 1. In the threshold automaton of Fig. 2, the parameters are n, f, and t, describing the number of processes, the number of faulty processes, and the maximum possible number of faulty processes, respectively. The resilience condition is the set of triples (i_n, i_f, i_t) such that $i_n/3 > i_t \geq i_f$; abusing language, we identify it with the constraint $n/3 > t \geq f$. The function N is given by $N(n, t, f) = n - f$, which is the number of correct processes.

Threshold Automata. A *threshold automaton* over an environment *Env* is a tuple TA $= (\mathcal{L}, \mathcal{I}, \Gamma, \mathcal{R})$, where $\mathcal{L}$ is a nonempty, finite set of *local states* (or *locations*), $\mathcal{I} \subseteq \mathcal{L}$ is a nonempty subset of *initial locations*, Γ is a set of *global variables* ranging over $\mathbb{N}_0$, and $\mathcal{R}$ is a set of *transition rules* (or just *rules*), formally described below.

A *transition rule* (or just a *rule*) is a tuple $r = (from, to, \varphi, \boldsymbol{u})$, where *from* and *to* are the *source* and *target* locations, $\varphi \colon \Pi \cup \Gamma \to \{true, false\}$ is a conjunction of *threshold guards*, and $\boldsymbol{u} \colon \Gamma \to \{0, 1\}$ is an *update*. We often let $r.from, r.to, r.\varphi, r.\boldsymbol{u}$ denote the components of r. Intuitively, r states that a process can move from *from* to *to* if the current values of Π and Γ satisfy φ, and when it moves it updates the current valuation $\boldsymbol{g}$ of Γ by performing the update $\boldsymbol{g} := \boldsymbol{g} + \boldsymbol{u}$. Since all components of $\boldsymbol{u}$ are nonnegative, the values of global variables never decrease. A *threshold guard* φ has one of the following two forms:

- $x \geq a_0 + a_1 \cdot p_1 + \ldots + a_{|\Pi|} \cdot p_{|\Pi|}$, called a *rise guard*, or
- $x < a_0 + a_1 \cdot p_1 + \ldots + a_{|\Pi|} \cdot p_{|\Pi|}$, called a *fall guard*,

where $x \in \Gamma$ is a shared variable, $p_1, \ldots, p_{|\Pi|} \in \Pi$ are the parameters, and $a_0, a_1, \ldots, a_{|\Pi|} \in \mathbb{Q}$ are rational coefficients. Since global variables are initialized to 0, and they never decrease, once a rise (fall) guard becomes true (false) it stays true (false). We call this property *monotonicity of guards*. We let Φ^{rise}, Φ^{fall}, and Φ denote the sets of rise guards, fall guards, and all guards of TA.

Example 2. The rule r_2 of Fig. 2 has ℓ_0 and ℓ_2 as source and target locations, $x \geq (t+1) - f$ as guard, and the number 1 as update (there is only one shared variable, which is increased by one).

Configurations and Transition Relation. A *configuration* of TA is a triple $\sigma = (\boldsymbol{\kappa}, \boldsymbol{g}, \boldsymbol{p})$ where $\boldsymbol{\kappa} \colon \mathcal{L} \to \mathbb{N}_0$ describes the number of processes at each location, and $\boldsymbol{g} \in \mathbb{N}_0^{|\Gamma|}$ and $\boldsymbol{p} \in RC$ are valuations of the global variables and the parameters. In particular, $\sum_{\ell \in \mathcal{L}} \boldsymbol{\kappa}(\ell) = N(\boldsymbol{p})$ always holds. A configuration is *initial* if $\boldsymbol{\kappa}(\ell) = 0$ for every $\ell \notin \mathcal{I}$, and $\boldsymbol{g} = \boldsymbol{0}$. We often let $\sigma.\boldsymbol{\kappa}, \sigma.\boldsymbol{g}, \sigma.\boldsymbol{p}$ denote the components of σ.

A configuration $\sigma = (\boldsymbol{\kappa}, \boldsymbol{g}, \boldsymbol{p})$ *enables* a rule $r = (from, to, \varphi, \boldsymbol{u})$ if $\boldsymbol{\kappa}(from) > 0$, and $(\boldsymbol{g}, \boldsymbol{p})$ satisfies the guard φ, i.e., substituting $\boldsymbol{g}(x)$ for x and $\boldsymbol{p}(p_i)$ for p_i in φ yields a true expression, denoted by $\sigma \models \varphi$. If σ enables r, then TA can *move* from σ to the configuration $r(\sigma) = (\boldsymbol{\kappa}', \boldsymbol{g}', \boldsymbol{p}')$ defined as follows: (i) $\boldsymbol{p}' = \boldsymbol{p}$, (ii) $\boldsymbol{g}' = \boldsymbol{g} + \boldsymbol{u}$, and (iii) $\boldsymbol{\kappa}' = \boldsymbol{\kappa} + \boldsymbol{v}_r$, where $\boldsymbol{v}_r(from) = -1$, $\boldsymbol{v}_r(to) = +1$, and $\boldsymbol{v}_r = 0$ otherwise. We let $\sigma \to r(\sigma)$ denote that TA can move from σ to $r(\sigma)$.

Schedules and Paths. A *schedule* is a (finite or infinite) sequence of rules. A schedule $\tau = r_1, \ldots, r_m$ is *applicable* to configuration σ_0 if there is a sequence of configurations $\sigma_1, \ldots, \sigma_m$ such that $\sigma_i = r_i(\sigma_{i-1})$ for $1 \leq i \leq m$, and we define $\tau(\sigma_0) := \sigma_m$. We let $\sigma \xrightarrow{*} \sigma'$ denote that $\tau(\sigma) = \sigma'$ for some schedule τ, and say that σ' is *reachable* from σ. Further we let $\tau \cdot \tau'$ denote the concatenation of two schedules τ and τ', and, given $\mu \geq 0$, let $\mu \cdot \tau$ the concatenation of τ with itself μ times.

A *path* or *run* is a finite or infinite sequence $\sigma_0, r_1, \sigma_1, \ldots, \sigma_{k-1}, r_k, \sigma_k, \ldots$ of alternating configurations and rules such that $\sigma_i = r_i(\sigma_{i-1})$ for every r_i in the sequence. If $\tau = r_1, \ldots, r_{|\tau|}$ is applicable to σ_0, then we let $\mathsf{path}(\sigma_0, \tau)$ denote the path $\sigma_0, r_1, \sigma_1, \ldots, r_{|\tau|}, \sigma_{|\tau|}$ with $\sigma_i = r_i(\sigma_{i-1})$, for $1 \leq i \leq |\tau|$. Similarly, if τ is an infinite schedule. Given a path $\mathsf{path}(\sigma, \tau)$, the set of all configurations in the path is denoted by $\mathsf{Cfgs}(\sigma, \tau)$.

3   Coverability and Parameterized Coverability

We say that configuration σ *covers* location ℓ if $\sigma.\kappa(\ell) > 0$. We consider the following two *coverability* questions in threshold automata:

Definition 1 ((Parameterized) coverability). *The* coverability problem *consists of deciding, given a threshold automaton* TA, *a location* ℓ *and an initial configuration* σ_0, *if some configuration reachable from* σ_0 *covers* ℓ. *The* parameterized coverability problem *consists of deciding, given* TA *and* ℓ, *if there is an initial configuration* σ_0 *and a configuration reachable from* σ_0 *that covers* ℓ.

Sometimes we also speak of the *non-parameterized coverability* problem, instead of the coverability problem, to avoid confusion. We show that both problems are NP-hard, even when the underlying threshold automaton is acyclic. In the next section, we show that the reachability and parameterized reachability problems (which subsume the corresponding coverability problems) are both in NP.

Theorem 1. *Parameterized coverability in threshold automata is NP-hard, even for acyclic threshold automata with only constant guards (i.e., guards of the form* $x \geq a_0$ *and* $x < a_0$*).*

Proof. (Sketch.) We prove NP-hardness of parameterized coverability by a reduction from 3-SAT. The reduction is as follows: (See Fig. 3 for an illustrative example). Let φ be a 3-CNF formula with variables $x_1, \ldots, x_n$. For every variable x_i we will have two shared variables y_i and $\bar{y}_i$. For every clause C_j, we will have a shared variable c_j. Intuitively, each process begins at some state ℓ_i and then moves to either $\top_i$ or $\bot_i$ by firing either $(\ell_i, \top_i, \bar{y}_i < 1, y_i\text{++})$ or $(\ell_i, \bot_i, y_i < 1, \bar{y}_i\text{++})$ respectively. Moving to $\top_i$ ($\bot_i$ resp.) means that the process has guessed the value of the variable x_i to be true (false resp). Once it has chosen a truth value, it then increments the variables corresponding to all the clauses which it satisfies and moves to a location ℓ_{mid}. If it happens that all the guesses were correct, a final rule gets unlocked and processes can move from ℓ_{mid} to ℓ_F. The key property we need to show is that if some process moves to $\top_i$ then no other process can move to $\bot_i$ (and vice versa). This is indeed the case because if a process moves to $\top_i$ from ℓ_i, it would have fired the rule $(\ell_i, \top_i, \bar{y}_i < 1, y_i\text{++})$ which increments the shared variable y_i, and so falsifies the guard of the corresponding rule $(\ell_i, \bot_i, y_i < 1, \bar{y}_i\text{++})$, and therefore no process can fire it. Similarly, if $(\ell_i, \bot_i, y_i < 1, \bar{y}_i\text{++})$ is fired, no process can fire $(\ell_i, \top_i, \bar{y}_i < 1, y_i\text{++})$.

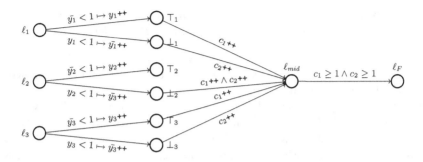

Fig. 3. Threshold automaton TA_φ corresponding to the formula $\varphi = (x_1 \vee \neg x_2 \vee x_3) \wedge (\neg x_1 \vee \neg x_2 \vee \neg x_3)$. Note that setting x_1 to true and x_2 and x_3 to false satisfies φ. Let σ_0 be the initial configuration obtained by having 1 process in each initial location ℓ_i, $1 \leq i \leq 3$, and 0 in every other location. From ℓ_1 we increment y_1 and from ℓ_2 and ℓ_3 we increment $\bar{y}_2$ and $\bar{y}_3$ respectively, thereby making the processes go to $\top_1, \bot_2, \bot_3$ respectively. From there we can move all the processes to ℓ_{mid}, at which point the last transition gets unlocked and we can cover ℓ_F.

A modification of the same construction proves

Theorem 2. *The coverability problem is NP-hard even for acyclic threshold automata with only constant rise guards (i.e., guards of the form $x \geq a_0$).*

Constant Rise Guards. Theorem 2 puts strong constraints to the class of TAs for which parameterized coverability can be polynomial, assuming P $\neq$ NP. We identify an interesting polynomial case.

Definition 2. *An environment $Env = (\Pi, RC, N)$ is* multiplicative *for a TA if for every $\mu \in \mathbb{N}_{>0}$ (i) for every valuation $\boldsymbol{p} \in RC$ we have $\mu \cdot \boldsymbol{p} \in RC$ and $N(\mu \cdot \boldsymbol{p}) = \mu \cdot N(\boldsymbol{p})$, and (ii) for every guard $\varphi := x \,\square\, a_0 + a_1 p_1 + a_2 p_2 + \ldots a_k p_k$ in TA (where $\square \in \{\geq, <\}$), if $(y, q_1, q_2, \ldots, q_k)$ is a (rational) solution to φ then $(\mu \cdot y, \mu \cdot q_1, \ldots, \mu \cdot q_k)$ is also a solution to φ.*

Multiplicativity is a very mild condition. To the best of our knowledge, all algorithms discussed in the literature, and all benchmarks of [18], have multiplicative environments. For example, in Fig. 2, if the resilience condition $t < n/3$ holds for a pair (n, t), then it also holds for $(\mu \cdot n, \mu \cdot t)$; similarly, the function $N(n, t, f) = n - f$ also satisfies $N(\mu \cdot n, \mu \cdot t, \mu \cdot f) = \mu \cdot n - \mu \cdot f = \mu \cdot N(n, t, f)$. Moreover, if $x \geq t + 1 - f$ holds in σ, then we also have $\mu \cdot x \geq \mu \cdot t + 1 - \mu \cdot f$ in $\mu \cdot \sigma$. Similarly for the other guard $x \geq n - t - f$.

This property allows us to reason about multiplied paths in large systems. Namely, condition (ii) from Definition 2 yields that if a rule is enabled in σ, it is also enabled in $\mu \cdot \sigma$. This plays a crucial role in Sect. 5 where we need the fact that a counterexample in a small system implies a counterexample in a large system.

Theorem 3. *Parameterized coverability of threshold automata over multiplicative environments with only constant rise guards is P-complete.*

Proof. (Sketch.) P-hardness is proved by giving a logspace-reduction from the Circuit Value problem ([20]) which is well known to be P-hard. In the following, we sketch the proof of inclusion in P.

Let $\mathsf{TA} = (\mathcal{L}, \mathcal{I}, \Gamma, \mathcal{R})$ be a threshold automaton over a multiplicative environment $Env = (\Pi, RC, N)$ such that the guard of each transition in $\mathcal{R}$ is a constant rise guard. We construct the set $\widehat{\mathcal{L}}$ of locations that can be reached by at least one process, and the set of transitions $\widehat{\mathcal{R}}$ that can occur, from at least one initial configuration. We initialize two variables $X_{\mathcal{L}}$ and $X_{\mathcal{R}}$ by $X_{\mathcal{L}} := \mathcal{I}$ and $X_{\mathcal{R}} := \emptyset$, and repeatedly update them until a fixed point is reached, as follows:

- If there exists a rule $r = (\ell, \ell', true, \boldsymbol{u}) \in \mathcal{R} \setminus X_{\mathcal{R}}$ such that $\ell \in X_{\mathcal{L}}$, then set $X_{\mathcal{L}} := X_{\mathcal{L}} \cup \{\ell'\}$ and $X_{\mathcal{R}} := X_{\mathcal{R}} \cup \{r\}$.
- If there exists a rule $r = (\ell, \ell', (\wedge_{1 \leq i \leq q}\, x_i \geq c_i), \boldsymbol{u}) \in \mathcal{R} \backslash X_{\mathcal{R}}$ such that $\ell \in X_{\mathcal{L}}$, and there exists rules $r_1, r_2, \ldots, r_q$ such that each $r_i = (\ell_i, \ell'_i, \varphi_i, \boldsymbol{u}_i) \in X_{\mathcal{R}}$ and $\boldsymbol{u}_i[x_i] > 0$, then set $X_{\mathcal{L}} := X_{\mathcal{L}} \cup \{\ell'\}$ and $X_{\mathcal{R}} := X_{\mathcal{R}} \cup \{r\}$.

In the full version of the paper, we prove that after termination $X_{\mathcal{L}} = \widehat{\mathcal{L}}$ holds. Intuitively, multiplicativity ensures that if a reachable configuration enables a rule, there are reachable configurations from which the rule can occur arbitrarily many times. This shows that any path of rules constructed by the algorithm is executable.

4   Reachability

We now consider reachability problems for threshold automata. Formally, we consider the following two versions of the reachability problem:

Definition 3 ((Parameterized) reachability). *The reachability problem consists of deciding, given a threshold automaton* TA, *two sets* $\mathcal{L}_{=0}, \mathcal{L}_{>0}$ *of locations, and an initial configuration* σ_0, *if some configuration* σ *reachable from* σ_0 *satisfies* $\sigma.\kappa(\ell) = 0$ *for every* $\ell \in \mathcal{L}_{=0}$ *and* $\sigma.\kappa(\ell) > 0$ *for every* $\ell \in \mathcal{L}_{>0}$. *The parameterized reachability problem consists of deciding, given* TA *and* $\mathcal{L}_{=0}, \mathcal{L}_{>0}$, *if there is an initial configuration* σ_0 *such that some* σ *reachable from* σ_0 *satisfies* $\sigma.\kappa(\ell) = 0$ *for every* $\ell \in \mathcal{L}_{=0}$ *and* $\sigma.\kappa(\ell) > 0$ *for every* $\ell \in \mathcal{L}_{>0}$.

Notice that the reachability problem clearly subsumes the coverability problem and hence, in the sequel, we will only be concerned with proving that both problems are in NP. This will be a consequence of our main result, showing that the reachability relation of threshold automata can be characterized as an existential formula of Presburger arithmetic. This result has several other consequences. In Sect. 5 we use it to give a new model checking algorithm for the fault-tolerant logic of [18]. In Sect. 7 we report on an implementation whose runtime compares favorably with previous tools.

Reachability Relation as an Existential Presburger Formula. Fix a threshold automaton $\mathsf{TA} = (\mathcal{L}, \mathcal{I}, \Gamma, \mathcal{R})$ over an environment Env. We construct an existential Presburger arithmetic formula ϕ_{reach} with $(2|\mathcal{L}| + 2|\Gamma| + 2|\Pi|)$ free variables such that $\phi_{reach}(\sigma, \sigma')$ is true iff σ' is reachable from σ.

Let the *context* of a configuration σ, denoted by $\omega(\sigma)$, be the set of all *rise* guards that evaluate to true and all *fall* guards that evaluate to false in σ. Given a schedule τ, we say that the path $\mathsf{path}(\sigma, \tau)$ is *steady* if all the configurations it visits have the same context. By the monotonicity of the guards of threshold automata, $\mathsf{path}(\sigma, \tau)$ is steady iff its endpoints have the same context, i.e., iff $\omega(\sigma) = \omega(\tau(\sigma))$. We have the following proposition:

Proposition 1. *Every path of a threshold automaton with k guards is the concatenation of at most $k + 1$ steady paths.*

Using this proposition, we first construct a formula ϕ_{steady} such that $\phi_{steady}(\sigma, \sigma')$ holds iff there is a *steady* path $\mathsf{path}(\sigma, \tau)$ such that $\tau(\sigma) = \sigma'$.

The Formula ϕ_{steady}. For every rule $r \in \mathcal{R}$, let x_r be a variable ranging over non-negative integers. Intuitively, the value of x_r will represent the number of times r is fired during the (supposed) path from σ to σ'. Let $X = \{x_r\}_{r \in \mathcal{R}}$. We construct ϕ_{steady} step by step, specifying necessary conditions for σ, σ' and X to satisfy the existence of the steady path, which in particular implies that σ' is reachable from σ.

Step 1. σ and σ' must have the same values of the parameters, which must satisfy the resilience condition, the same number of processes, and the same context:

$$\phi_{base}(\sigma, \sigma') \equiv \sigma.\boldsymbol{p} = \sigma'.\boldsymbol{p} \,\wedge\, RC(\sigma.\boldsymbol{p}) \,\wedge\, N(\sigma.\boldsymbol{p}) = N(\sigma'.\boldsymbol{p}) \,\wedge\, \omega(\sigma) = \omega(\sigma').$$

Step 2. For a location $\ell \in \mathcal{L}$, let $out_1^\ell, \ldots, out_{a_\ell}^\ell$ be all outgoing rules from ℓ and let $in_1^\ell, \ldots, in_{b_\ell}^\ell$ be all incoming rules to ℓ. The number of processes in ℓ after the execution of the path is the initial number, plus the incoming processes, minus the outgoing processes. Since x_r models the number of times the rule r is fired, we have

$$\phi_{\mathcal{L}}(\sigma, \sigma', X) \equiv \bigwedge_{\ell \in \mathcal{L}} \left(\sum_{i=1}^{a_\ell} x_{in_i^\ell} - \sum_{j=1}^{b_\ell} x_{out_j^\ell} = \sigma'.\kappa(\ell) - \sigma.\kappa(\ell) \right)$$

Step 3. Similarly, for the shared variables we must have:

$$\phi_{\Gamma}(\sigma, \sigma', X) \equiv \bigwedge_{z \in \Gamma} \left(\sum_{r \in \mathcal{R}} (x_r \cdot r.\boldsymbol{u}[z]) = \sigma'.\boldsymbol{g}[z] - \sigma.\boldsymbol{g}[z] \right)$$

Step 4. Since $\mathsf{path}(\sigma, \tau)$ must be steady, if a rule is fired along $\mathsf{path}(\sigma, \tau)$ then its guard must be true in σ and so

$$\phi_{\mathcal{R}}(\sigma, X) \equiv \bigwedge_{r \in \mathcal{R}} x_r > 0 \,\Rightarrow\, (\sigma \models r.\varphi)$$

Step 5. Finally, for every rule r that occurs in $\mathsf{path}(\sigma, \tau)$, the path must contain a "fireable" chain leading to r, i.e., a set of rules $S = \{r_1, \ldots, r_s\} \subseteq \mathcal{R}$ such that all rules of S are executed in $\mathsf{path}(\sigma, \tau)$, there is a process in σ at $r_1.from$, and the rules $r_1, \ldots, r_s$ form a chain leading from $r_1.from$ to $r.from$. We capture this by the constraint

$$\phi_{appl}(\sigma, X) \equiv \bigwedge_{r \in \mathcal{R}} \left(x_r > 0 \Rightarrow \bigvee_{S = \{r_1, r_2, \ldots, r_s\} \subseteq \mathcal{R}} \phi^r_{chain}(S, \sigma, X) \right)$$

where

$$\phi^r_{chain}(S, \sigma, X) \equiv \bigwedge_{r \in S} x_r > 0 \wedge \sigma.\kappa(r_1.from) > 0 \wedge \bigwedge_{1 < i \le s} r_{i-1}.to = r_i.from \wedge r_s = r$$

Combining the Steps. Define $\phi_{steady}(\sigma, \sigma')$ as follows:

$$\phi_{steady}(\sigma, \sigma') \equiv \phi_{base}(\sigma, \sigma') \wedge$$
$$\exists X \ge 0. \, \phi_{\mathcal{L}}(\sigma, \sigma', X) \wedge \phi_\Gamma(\sigma, \sigma', X) \wedge \phi_{\mathcal{R}}(\sigma, X) \wedge \phi_{appl}(\sigma, X) \, .$$

where $\exists X \ge 0$ abbreviates $\exists x_{r_1} \ge 0, \ldots, \exists x_{r_{|\mathcal{R}|}} \ge 0$. By our discussion, it is clear that if there is a steady path leading from σ to σ', then $\phi_{steady}(\sigma, \sigma')$ is satisfiable. The following theorem proves the converse.

Theorem 4. *Let* TA *be a threshold automaton and let* $\sigma, \sigma' \in \Sigma$ *be two configurations. Formula* $\phi_{steady}(\sigma, \sigma')$ *is satisfiable if and only if there is a steady schedule* τ *with* $\tau(\sigma) = \sigma'$.

Observe that, while ϕ_{steady} has exponential length in TA when constructed naïvely (because of the exponentially many disjunctions in ϕ_{appl}), its satisfiability is in NP. Indeed, we first non-deterministically guess one of the disjunctions for each conjunction of ϕ_{appl} and then check in nondeterministic polynomial time that the (polynomial sized) formula with only these disjuncts is satisfiable. This is possible because existential Presburger arithmetic is known to be in NP [13].

The Formula ϕ_{reach}. By Proposition 1, every path from σ to σ' in a threshold automaton with a set Φ of guards can be written in the form

$$\sigma = \sigma_0 \xrightarrow{*} \sigma'_0 \to \sigma_1 \xrightarrow{*} \sigma'_1 \to \sigma_2 \ldots \sigma_K \xrightarrow{*} \sigma'_K = \sigma'$$

where $K = |\Phi| + 1$, and $\sigma_i \xrightarrow{*} \sigma'_i$ is a steady path for each $0 \le i \le K$. It is easy to see from the definition of the transition relation between configurations that we can construct a polynomial sized existential Presburger formula ϕ_{step} such that $\phi_{step}(\sigma, \sigma')$ is true iff σ' can be reached from σ by firing at most one rule. Thus, we define $\phi_{reach}(\sigma, \sigma')$ to be

$$\exists \sigma_0, \sigma'_0, \ldots, \sigma_K, \sigma'_K \left(\sigma_0 = \sigma \wedge \sigma'_K = \sigma' \wedge \bigwedge_{0 \le i \le K} \phi_{steady}(\sigma_i, \sigma'_i) \wedge \bigwedge_{0 \le i \le K-1} \phi_{step}(\sigma'_i, \sigma_{i+1}) \right)$$

Theorem 5. *Given a threshold automaton* TA*, there is an existential Presburger formula* ϕ_{reach} *such that* $\phi_{reach}(\sigma, \sigma')$ *holds iff* $\sigma \xrightarrow{*} \sigma'$.

As deciding the truth of existential Presburger formulas is in NP, we obtain:

Corollary 1. *The reachability and parameterized reachability problems are in NP.*

Remark 1. In [14] an algorithm was given for parameterized reachability of threshold automata in which the updates of all rules contained in loops are equal to $\mathbf{0}$. Our algorithm does not need this restriction.

5   Safety and Liveness

We recall the definition of *Fault-Tolerant Temporal Logic* ($\mathsf{ELTL_{FT}}$), the fragment of LTL used in [18] to specify and verify properties of a large number of fault-tolerant algorithms. $\mathsf{ELTL_{FT}}$ has the following syntax, where $S \subseteq \mathcal{L}$ is a set of locations and $guard \in \Phi$ is a guard:

$$\psi ::= pf \mid \mathbf{G}\,\psi \mid \mathbf{F}\,\psi \mid \psi \wedge \psi \qquad cf ::= S = 0 \mid \neg(S = 0) \mid cf \wedge cf$$
$$pf ::= cf \mid gf \Rightarrow cf \qquad\qquad gf ::= guard \mid gf \wedge gf \mid gf \vee gf$$

An infinite path $\mathsf{path}(\sigma, \tau)$ starting at $\sigma = (\kappa, \mathbf{g}, \mathbf{p})$, satisfies $S = 0$ if $\kappa(\ell) = 0$ for every $\ell \in S$, and $guard$ if $(\mathbf{g}, \mathbf{p})$ satisfies $guard$. The rest of the semantics is standard. The negations of specifications of the benchmarks [3–6,12,22,23,25,26] can be expressed in $\mathsf{ELTL_{FT}}$, as we are interested in finding possible violations.

Example 3. One specification of the algorithm from Fig. 1 is that if $myval_i = 1$ for every correct process i, then eventually $accept_j = true$ for some correct process j. In the words of the automaton from Fig. 2, a violation of this property would mean that initially all correct processes are in location ℓ_1, but no correct process ever reaches location ℓ_3. In $\mathsf{ELTL_{FT}}$ we write this as

$$\{\ell_0, \ell_2, \ell_3\} = 0 \,\wedge\, \mathbf{G}\,(\{\ell_3\} = 0)\,.$$

This has to hold under the fairness constraint

$$\mathbf{G}\,\mathbf{F}\left(((x \geq t+1 \vee x \geq n-t) \Rightarrow \{\ell_0\}=0) \,\wedge\, \{\ell_1\}=0 \,\wedge\, (x \geq n-t \Rightarrow \{\ell_2\}=0) \right).$$

As we have self-loops at locations ℓ_0 and ℓ_2, a process could stay forever in one of these two states, even if it has collected enough messages, i.e., if $x \geq t+1$ or $x \geq n-t$. This is the behavior that we want to prevent with such a fairness constraint. Enough sent messages should force each process to progress, so the location eventually becomes empty. Similarly, as the rule leading from ℓ_1 has a trivial guard, we want to make sure that all processes starting in ℓ_1 eventually (send a message and) leave ℓ_1 empty, as required by the algorithm.

Fig. 4. The cut graph of a formula $\mathbf{F}\,(a \wedge \mathbf{F}\,b \wedge \mathbf{F}\,c \wedge \mathbf{G}\,d \wedge \mathbf{G}\,\mathbf{F}\,e)$ (left) and one lasso shape for a chosen topological ordering $a \leq \mathbf{F}\,b \leq \mathbf{F}\,c \leq loop_{st} \leq \mathbf{G}\,\mathbf{F}\,e \leq loop_{end}$ (right).

In this section we study the following problem:

Definition 4 (Parameterized safety and liveness). *Given a threshold automaton* TA *and a formula* φ *in* $\mathsf{ELTL}_{\mathsf{FT}}$, *check whether there is an initial configuration* σ_0 *and an infinite schedule* τ *applicable to* σ_0 *such that* $\mathsf{path}(\sigma_0, \tau) \models \varphi$.

Since parameterized coverability is NP-hard, it follows that parameterized safety and liveness is also NP-hard. We prove that for automata with *multiplicative environments* (see Definition 2) parameterized safety and liveness is in NP.

Theorem 6. *Parameterized safety and liveness of threshold automata with multiplicative environments is in NP.*

The proof, which can be found in the full version, is very technical, and we only give a rough sketch here. The proof relies on two notions introduced in [18]. First, it is shown in [18] that every $\mathsf{ELTL}_{\mathsf{FT}}$ formula is equivalent to a formula in *normal form* of shape $\phi_0 \wedge \mathbf{F}\,\phi_1 \wedge \cdots \wedge \mathbf{F}\,\phi_k \wedge \mathbf{G}\,\phi_{k+1}$, where ϕ_0 is a propositional formula and $\phi_1, \ldots, \phi_{k+1}$ are themselves in normal form. Further, formulas can be put in normal form in polynomial time. The second notion introduced in [18] is the *cut graph* $Gr(\varphi)$ of a formula in normal form. For our sketch it suffices to know that $Gr(\varphi)$ is a directed acyclic graph with two special nodes $loop_{st}$ and $loop_{end}$, and every other node is a subformula of φ in normal form (see Fig. 4).

For a formula $\varphi \equiv \phi_0 \wedge \mathbf{F}\,\phi_1 \wedge \ldots \wedge \mathbf{F}\,\phi_k \wedge \mathbf{G}\,\phi_{k+1}$, we will say that its *local proposition* is ϕ_0 and its *global proposition* is the local proposition of ϕ_{k+1}. It is shown in [18] that, given $\varphi = \phi_0 \wedge \mathbf{F}\,\phi_1 \wedge \cdots \wedge \mathbf{F}\,\phi_k \wedge \mathbf{G}\,\phi_{k+1}$, some infinite path satisfies φ iff there exists a topological ordering $v_0, v_1, \ldots, v_c = loop_{st}, v_{c+1}, \ldots, v_l = loop_{end}$ of the cut graph and a path $\sigma_0, \tau_0, \sigma_1, \ldots, \sigma_c, \tau_c, \ldots, \sigma_{l-1}, \tau_{l-1}, \sigma_l$ such that, roughly speaking, (among other technical conditions) every configuration σ_i satisfies the local proposition of v_i and every configuration in $\mathsf{Cfgs}(\sigma_i, \tau_i)$ satisfies the global proposition of every v_j where $j \leq i$.

Using multiplicativity and our main result that reachability is definable in existential Presburger arithmetic, we show that for every proposition p, we can construct an existential formula $\phi_p(\sigma, \sigma')$ such that: If there is a path between σ and σ', all of whose configurations satisfy p, then $\phi_p(\sigma, \sigma')$ is satisfiable. Further, if $\phi_p(\sigma, \sigma')$ is satisfiable, then there is a path between $2 \cdot \sigma$ and $2 \cdot \sigma'$ all of whose configurations satisfy p. (Here $2 \cdot \sigma = ((2 \cdot \sigma.\kappa), (2 \cdot \sigma.\mathbf{g}), (2 \cdot \sigma.\mathbf{p}))$.) Then, once we have fixed a topological ordering $V = v_0, \ldots, v_l$, (among other conditions), we check if there are configurations $\sigma_0, \ldots, \sigma_l$ such that for every i, σ_i satisfies the local proposition of v_i and for every $j \leq i$, $\phi_{p_j}(\sigma_i, \sigma_{i+1})$ is satisfiable where p_j is the global proposition of v_j. Using multiplicativity, we then show that this procedure is sufficient to check if the given specification φ is satisfied.

Our algorithm consists therefore of the following steps: (1) bring φ in normal form; (2) construct the cut graph $Gr(\varphi)$; (3) guess a topological ordering of the nodes of $Gr(\varphi)$; (4) for the guessed ordering, check in nondeterministic polynomial time if the required sequence $\sigma_0, \ldots, \sigma_l$ exists.

Remark 2. From an algorithm given in [18] one can infer that parameterized safety and liveness is in NP for threshold automata with multiplicative environments, where all cycles are simple, and rules in cycles have update $\mathbf{0}$. (The NP bound was not explicitly given in [18].) Our algorithm only requires multiplicativity.

6 Synthesis of Threshold Guards

We study the *bounded synthesis* problem for constructing parameterized threshold guards in threshold automata satisfying a given specification.

Sketch Threshold Automata. Let an *indeterminate* be a variable that can take values over rational numbers. We consider threshold automata whose guards can contain indeterminates. More precisely, a *sketch* threshold automaton is a tuple $\mathsf{TA} = (\mathcal{L}, \mathcal{I}, \Gamma, \mathcal{R})$, just as before, except for the following change. Recall that in a threshold automaton, a guard is an inequality of one of the following two forms:

$$x \geq a_0 + a_1 \cdot p_1 + \ldots + a_{|\Pi|} \cdot p_{|\Pi|} \quad \text{or} \quad x < a_0 + a_1 \cdot p_1 + \ldots + a_{|\Pi|} \cdot p_{|\Pi|}$$

where $a_0, a_1, \ldots, a_{|\Pi|}$ are rational numbers. In a sketch threshold automaton, some of the $a_0, a_1, \ldots, a_{|\Pi|}$ can be *indeterminates*. Moreover, indeterminates can be shared between two or more guards.

Given a sketch threshold automaton TA and an assignment μ to the indeterminates, we let $\mathsf{TA}[\mu]$ denote the threshold automaton obtained by substituting the indeterminates by their values in μ. We define the *bounded synthesis* problem:

> Given: An environment Env, a sketch threshold automaton TA with indeterminates $v_1, \ldots, v_m$, a formula φ of $\mathsf{ELTL_{FT}}$, and a polynomial p.
> Decide: Is there an assignment μ to $v_1, \ldots, v_m$ of size $O(p(|\mathsf{TA}| + |\varphi|))$ (i.e., the vector $(\mu(v_1), \ldots, \mu(v_m))$ of rational numbers can be encoded in binary using $O(p(|\mathsf{TA}| + |\varphi|))$ bits) such that $\mathsf{TA}[\mu]$ satisfies $\neg\varphi$ (i.e., such that for every initial configuration σ_0 in $\mathsf{TA}[\mu]$, every infinite run starting from σ_0 satisfies $\neg\varphi$)?

We say that an assignment μ to the indeterminates makes the environment multiplicative if the conditions of Definition 2 are satisfied after plugging in the assignment μ in the automaton. In the following, we will only be concerned with assignments which make the environment multiplicative.

Since we can guess an assignment in polynomial time, by Theorem 6 it follows

Theorem 7. *Bounded synthesis is in Σ_2^p.*

By a reduction from the Σ_2-SAT problem, we also provide a matching lower bound.

Theorem 8. *Bounded synthesis is Σ_2^p-complete.*

The *synthesis* problem is defined as the bounded synthesis problem, but lifting the constraint on the size of μ. While we do not know the exact complexity of the synthesis problem, we can show that, for a large and practically motivated class of threshold automata introduced in [21], the synthesis problem reduces to the bounded synthesis problem. We proceed to describe and motivate the class.

The parameter variables of fault-tolerant distributed algorithms usually consist of a variable n denoting the number of processes running the algorithm and various "failure" variables for the number of processes exhibiting different kinds of failures (for example, a variable t_1 might be used to specify the number of Byzantine failures, a variable t_2 for crash failures, etc.). The following three observations are made in [21]:

(1) The resilience condition of these algorithms is usually of the form $n > \sum_{i=1}^{k} \delta_i t_i$ where t_i are parameter variables and δ_i are natural numbers.
(2) Threshold guards typically serve one of two purposes: to check if at least a certain fraction of the processes sends a message (for example, $x > n/2$ ensures that a strict majority of processes has sent a message), or to bound the number of processes that crash.
(3) The coefficients of the guards are rational numbers with small denominators (typically at most 3).

By (2), the structure of the algorithm guarantees that the value of a variable x never goes beyond n, the number of processes. Therefore, given a threshold guard template $x \bowtie \boldsymbol{u} \cdot \boldsymbol{\pi} + v$, where $\boldsymbol{u}$ is a vector of indeterminates, $\boldsymbol{\pi}$ is a vector of parameter variables, v is an indeterminate, and $\bowtie$ is either $\geq$ or $<$, we are only interested in assignments μ of $\boldsymbol{u}$ and v which satisfy $0 \leq \mu(\boldsymbol{u}) \cdot \nu(\boldsymbol{\pi}) + \mu(v) \leq n$ for every valuation $\nu(\boldsymbol{\pi})$ of $\boldsymbol{\pi}$ respecting the resilience condition. Guards obtained by instantiating guard templates with such a valuation μ are called *sane guards* [21].

The following result is proved in [21]: Given a resilience condition $n > \sum_{i=1}^{k} \delta_i t_i$, and an upper bound D on the denominator of the entries of μ (see (1) and (3) above), the numerators of the entries of μ are necessarily of polynomial size in $k, \delta_1, \ldots, \delta_k$. Therefore, the synthesis problem for sane guards and bounded denominator, as introduced in [21], reduces to the bounded synthesis problem, and so it can be solved in Σ_2^p time. Moreover, the reduction used in Theorem 8 to prove Σ_2^p-hardness yields sketch threshold automata with sane guards, and so the the synthesis problem for sane guards and bounded denominator is also Σ_2^p-complete.

7   Experimental Evaluation

Following the techniques presented in this paper, we have verified a number of threshold-based fault-tolerant distributed algorithms.

Table 1. The experiments were run on a machine with Intel® Core™ i5-7200U CPU with 7.7 GiB memory. The time limit was set to be 5 h and the memory limit was set to be 7 GiB. TLE (MLE) means that the time limit (memory limit) exceeded for the particular benchmark.

Input	Case (if more than one)	Threshold automaton		Time, seconds	
		$|\mathcal{L}|$	$|\mathcal{R}|$	Our tool	ByMC
nbacg		24	64	11.84	10.29
nbacr		77	1031	490.79	1081.07
aba	Case 1	37	202	251.71	751.89
aba	Case 2	61	425	2856.63	TLE
cbc	Case 1	164	2064	MLE	MLE
cbc	Case 2	73	470	2521.12	36.57
cbc	Case 3	304	6928	MLE	MLE
cbc	Case 4	161	2105	MLE	MLE
cfls	Case 1	41	280	50.5	55.87
cfls	Case 2	41	280	55.88	281.69
cfls	Case 3	68	696	266.56	7939.07
cfls	hand-coded TA	9	26	7.17	2737.53
clcs	Case 1	101	1285	1428.51	TLE
clcs	Case 2	70	650	1709.4	11169.24
clcs	Case 3	101	1333	TLE	MLE
clcs	hand-coded TA	9	30	37.72	TLE
bosco	Case 1	28	152	58.11	89.64
bosco	Case 2	40	242	157.61	942.87
bosco	Case 3	32	188	59	104.03
bosco	hand-coded TA	8	20	20.95	510.32

Benchmarks. Consistent broadcast (**strb**) [26] is given in Fig. 1 and its threshold automaton is depicted in Fig. 2. The algorithm is correct if in any execution either all correct processes or none set accept to true; moreover, if all correct processes start with value 0 then none of them accept, and if all correct processes start with value 1 then they all accept. The algorithm is designed to tolerate Byzantine failures of less than one third of processes, that is, if $n > 3t$. Folklore Reliable Broadcast (**frb**) [5] that tolerates crash faults and Asynchronous Byzantine agreement (**aba**) [3] satisfy the same specifications as consistent broadcast, under the same resilience condition.

Non-blocking atomic commit (**nbacr**) [23] and (**nbacg**) [12] deal with faults using failure detectors. We model this by introducing a special location such that a process is in it if and only if it suspects that there is a failure of the system.

Condition-based consensus (**cbc**) [22] reaches consensus under the condition that the difference between the numbers of processes initialized with 0 and 1 differ by at least t, an upper bound on the number of faults. We also check algorithms that allow consensus to be achieved in one communication step, such as **cfcs** [6], **c1cs** [4], as well as Byzantine One Step Consensus **bosco** [25].

Evaluation. Table 1 summarizes our results and compares them with the results obtained using the ByMC tool [17]. Due to lack of space, we have omitted those experiments for which both ByMC and our tool took less than 10 s.

We implemented our algorithms in Python and used Z3 as a back-end SMT solver for solving the constraints over existential Presburger arithmetic. Our implementation takes as input a threshold automaton and a specification in ELTL$_{FT}$ and checks if a counterexample exists. We apply to the latest version of the benchmarks of [17]. Each benchmark yields two threshold automata, a hand-coded one and one obtained by a data abstraction of the algorithm written in Parametric Promela. For automata of the latter kind, due to data abstraction, we have to consider different cases for the same algorithm. We test each automaton against all specifications for that automaton.

Our tool outperforms ByMC in all automata with more than 30 states, with the exception of the second case of cbc. It performs worse in most small cases, however in these cases, both ByMC and our tool take less than 10 s. ByMC works by enumerating all so-called *schemas* of a threshold automaton, and solving a SMT problem for each of them; the number of schemas can grow exponentially in the number of guards. Our tool avoids the enumeration. Since the number of schemas for the second case of cbc is just 2, while the second case of aba and third case of cf1s have more than 3000, avoiding the enumeration seems to be key to our better performance.

References

1. Bloem, R., et al.: Decidability of Parameterized Verification. Synthesis Lectures on Distributed Computing Theory. Morgan & Claypool Publishers, San Rafael (2015)
2. Blondin, M., Haase, C., Mazowiecki, F.: Affine extensions of integer vector addition systems with states. In: CONCUR. LIPIcs, vol. 118, pp. 14:1–14:17. Schloss Dagstuhl - Leibniz-Zentrum fuer Informatik (2018)
3. Bracha, G., Toueg, S.: Asynchronous consensus and broadcast protocols. J. ACM **32**(4), 824–840 (1985)
4. Brasileiro, F., Greve, F., Mostefaoui, A., Raynal, M.: Consensus in one communication step. In: Malyshkin, V. (ed.) PaCT 2001. LNCS, vol. 2127, pp. 42–50. Springer, Heidelberg (2001). https://doi.org/10.1007/3-540-44743-1_4
5. Chandra, T.D., Toueg, S.: Unreliable failure detectors for reliable distributed systems. J. ACM **43**(2), 225–267 (1996)
6. Dobre, D., Suri, N.: One-step consensus with zero-degradation. In: DSN, pp. 137–146 (2006)
7. Dufourd, C., Finkel, A., Schnoebelen, P.: Reset nets between decidability and undecidability. In: Larsen, K.G., Skyum, S., Winskel, G. (eds.) ICALP 1998. LNCS, vol. 1443, pp. 103–115. Springer, Heidelberg (1998). https://doi.org/10.1007/BFb0055044
8. Esparza, J.: Decidability and complexity of Petri net problems—An introduction. In: Reisig, W., Rozenberg, G. (eds.) ACPN 1996. LNCS, vol. 1491, pp. 374–428. Springer, Heidelberg (1998). https://doi.org/10.1007/3-540-65306-6_20
9. Esparza, J., Finkel, A., Mayr, R.: On the verification of broadcast protocols. In: LICS, pp. 352–359. IEEE Computer Society (1999)
10. Esparza, J., Nielsen, M.: Decidability issues for petri nets - a survey. Bull. EATCS **52**, 244–262 (1994)
11. German, S.M., Sistla, A.P.: Reasoning about systems with many processes. J. ACM **39**(3), 675–735 (1992)
12. Guerraoui, R.: Non-blocking atomic commit in asynchronous distributed systems with failure detectors. Distrib. Comput. **15**(1), 17–25 (2002). https://doi.org/10.1007/s446-002-8027-4
13. Haase, C.: A survival guide to Presburger arithmetic. ACM SIGLOG News **5**(3), 67–82 (2018)
14. Konnov, I., Lazic, M., Veith, H., Widder, J.: Para^2: parameterized path reduction, acceleration, and SMT for reachability in threshold-guarded distributed algorithms. Formal Methods Syst. Des. **51**(2), 270–307 (2017)
15. Konnov, I., Veith, H., Widder, J.: On the completeness of bounded model checking for threshold-based distributed algorithms: reachability. In: Baldan, P., Gorla, D. (eds.) CONCUR 2014. LNCS, vol. 8704, pp. 125–140. Springer, Heidelberg (2014). https://doi.org/10.1007/978-3-662-44584-6_10
16. Konnov, I., Veith, H., Widder, J.: On the completeness of bounded model checking for threshold-based distributed algorithms: reachability. Inf. Comput. **252**, 95–109 (2017)
17. Konnov, I., Widder, J.: ByMC: Byzantine model checker. In: Margaria, T., Steffen, B. (eds.) ISoLA 2018. LNCS, vol. 11246, pp. 327–342. Springer, Cham (2018). https://doi.org/10.1007/978-3-030-03424-5_22
18. Konnov, I.V., Lazic, M., Veith, H., Widder, J.: A short counterexample property for safety and liveness verification of fault-tolerant distributed algorithms. In: POPL 2017, pp. 719–734 (2017)

19. Kukovec, J., Konnov, I., Widder, J.: Reachability in parameterized systems: all flavors of threshold automata. In: CONCUR, pp. 19:1–19:17 (2018)
20. Ladner, R.E.: The circuit value problem is log space complete for p. SIGACT News **7**(1), 18–20 (1975)
21. Lazić, M., Konnov, I., Widder, J., Bloem, R.: Synthesis of distributed algorithms with parameterized threshold guards. In: OPODIS. LIPIcs, vol. 95, pp. 32:1–32:20 (2017)
22. Mostéfaoui, A., Mourgaya, E., Parvédy, P.R., Raynal, M.: Evaluating the condition-based approach to solve consensus. In: DSN, pp. 541–550 (2003)
23. Raynal, M.: A case study of agreement problems in distributed systems: non-blocking atomic commitment. In: HASE, pp. 209–214 (1997)
24. Schmitz, S., Schnoebelen, P.: The power of well-structured systems. CoRR abs/1402.2908 (2014)
25. Song, Y.J., van Renesse, R.: Bosco: one-step Byzantine asynchronous consensus. In: Taubenfeld, G. (ed.) DISC 2008. LNCS, vol. 5218, pp. 438–450. Springer, Heidelberg (2008). https://doi.org/10.1007/978-3-540-87779-0_30
26. Srikanth, T., Toueg, S.: Simulating authenticated broadcasts to derive simple fault-tolerant algorithms. Distrib. Comput. **2**, 80–94 (1987). https://doi.org/10.1007/BF01667080

On (I/O)-Aware Good-For-Games Automata

Rachel Faran$^{(\boxtimes)}$ and Orna Kupferman$^{(\boxtimes)}$

School of Engineering and Computer Science, Hebrew University, Jerusalem, Israel
{rachelmi,orna}@cs.huji.ac.il

Abstract. Good-For-Games (GFG) automata are nondeterministic automata that can resolve their nondeterministic choices based on the past. The fact that the synthesis problem can be reduced to solving a game on top of a GFG automaton for the specification (that is, no determinization is needed) has made them the subject of extensive research in the last years. GFG automata are defined for general alphabets, whereas in the synthesis problem, the specification is over an alphabet $2^{I \cup O}$, for sets I and O of input and output signals, respectively. We introduce and study (I/O)-*aware GFG automata*, which distinguish between nondeterminism due to I and O: both should be resolved in a way that depends only on the past; but while nondeterminism in I is hostile, and all I-futures should be accepted, nondeterminism in O is cooperative, and a single O-future may be accepted. We show that (I/O)-aware GFG automata can be used for synthesis, study their properties, special cases and variants, and argue for their usefulness. In particular, (I/O)-aware GFG automata are unboundedly more succinct than deterministic and even GFG automata, using them circumvents determinization, and their study leads to new and interesting insights about hostile vs. collaborative nondeterminism, as well as the theoretical bound for realizing systems.

1 Introduction

Synthesis is the automated construction of systems from their specifications [6, 18]. The system should *realize* the specification, namely satisfy it against all possible environments. More formally, the specification is a language L of infinite words over an alphabet $2^{I \cup O}$, where I and O are sets of input and output signals, respectively, and the goal is to build a reactive system that outputs assignments to the signals in O upon receiving assignments to the signals in I, such that the generated sequence of assignments, which can be viewed as an infinite computation in $(2^{I \cup O})^{\omega}$, is in L [18]. The common approach for solving the synthesis problem is to define a two-player game on top of a deterministic automaton $\mathcal{D}$ for L. The positions of the game are the states of $\mathcal{D}$. In each round of the game, one player (the environment) provides an input assignment in 2^I, the second player (the system) responds with an output assignment in 2^O, and the game transits to the corresponding successor state. The goal of the system is to respond in a way so that the sequence of visited positions satisfies the

© Springer Nature Switzerland AG 2020
D. V. Hung and O. Sokolsky (Eds.): ATVA 2020, LNCS 12302, pp. 161–178, 2020.
https://doi.org/10.1007/978-3-030-59152-6_9

acceptance condition of $\mathcal{D}$. Thus, the generated computation is in L. The system has a winning strategy in the game iff the language L is (I/O)-realizable [9].

Now, if one replaces $\mathcal{D}$ by a nondeterministic automaton $\mathcal{A}$ for L, the system has to respond not only with an output, but also with a transition of $\mathcal{A}$ that should be taken. This is problematic, as this choice of a transition should accommodate all possible future choices of the environment. In particular, if different future choices of the environment induce computations that are all in the language of $\mathcal{A}$ yet require different nondeterministic choices, the system cannot win. Thus, it might be that L is realizable and still the system has no winning strategy in the game.

Some nondeterministic automata are, however, good for games. The study of such automata started in [13], by means of tree automata for derived languages. It then continued by means of *good for games* (GFG) word automata [11].[1] Intuitively, a nondeterministic automaton $\mathcal{A}$ is GFG if it is possible to resolve its nondeterminism in a manner that only depends on the past and still accepts all the words in the language. Formally, $\mathcal{A}$ over an alphabet Σ and state space Q is GFG if there is a *strategy* $g : \Sigma^* \rightarrow Q$, such that for every word $w = \sigma_1 \cdot \sigma_2 \cdots \in \Sigma^\omega$, the sequence $g(w) = g(\epsilon), g(\sigma_1), g(\sigma_1 \cdot \sigma_2), \ldots$ is a run of $\mathcal{A}$ on w, and whenever w is accepted by $\mathcal{A}$, the run $g(w)$ is accepting. Thus, the strategy g, which *witnesses* $\mathcal{A}$'s GFGness, maps each word $x \in \Sigma^*$ to the state that is visited after x is read. Obviously, there exist GFG automata: deterministic ones, or nondeterministic ones that are *determinizable by pruning* (DBP); that is, ones that just add transitions on top of a deterministic automaton.[2] In terms of expressive power, it is shown in [13,17] that GFG automata with an acceptance condition γ (e.g., Büchi) are as expressive as deterministic γ automata. In terms of succinctness, GFG automata on infinite words are more succinct (possibly even exponentially) than deterministic ones [4,12]. Further research studies decidability, typeness, complementation, construction, and minimization for GFG automata [1,3,5,12], as well as GFG automata for ω-pushdown languages [15]. Beyond its computational advantages, the use of GFG automata circumvents cumbersome determinization constructions that traditional synthesis algorithms involve [14,19].

Recall that in order to be GFG, an automaton needs a strategy $g : \Sigma^* \rightarrow Q$ that resolves nondeterminism in a way that depends only on the past. We argue that this is a too strong requirement for the synthesis problem. There, $\Sigma = 2^{I \cup O}$, and we suggest to distinguish between nondeterminism due to the 2^I component of each letter, which is hostile, and nondeterminism due to the 2^O component, which is cooperative. As a simple example, consider the nondeterministic Büchi (in fact, looping) automaton $\mathcal{A}_1$ over $2^{\{a,b\}}$ appearing in Fig. 1. The Boolean

---

[1] GFGness is also used in [7] in the framework of cost functions under the name "history-determinism".

[2] In fact, DBP automata were the only examples known for GFG automata when the latter were introduced in [11]. As explained there, however, even DBP automata are useful in practice, as their transition relation is simpler than the one of the embodied deterministic automaton and it can be defined symbolically.

assertions on the transitions describe the letters with which they can be taken. For example, the transition from q_0 to q_1 can be taken with the letters $\{a\}$ or $\{a, b\}$. Note that $\mathcal{A}_1$ is not GFG. Indeed, a strategy $g : (2^{\{a,b\}})^* \to Q$ neglects either the word $\{a\}^\omega$, in the case $g(\{a\}) = q_1$, or the word $\{a\} \cdot \{a, b\}^\omega$, in the case $g(\{a\}) = q_2$. Assume that a is an input signal and b is an output signal, and that we play the synthesis game on top of $\mathcal{A}_1$. Since the system controls the assignment to b, it wins the game: on input $\{a\}$, it can proceed to q_1, and keep assigning true to b, staying forever in q_1, or it can proceed to q_2 and keep assigning false to b, staying forever in q_2.

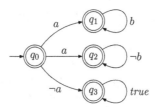

Fig. 1. The automaton $\mathcal{A}_1$ is not GFG, yet is $(\{a\}/\{b\})$-aware GFG.

We introduce and study (*I/O*)-*aware GFG automata*, which distinguish between nondeterminism due to I and O: both should be resolved in a way that depends on the past; but while nondeterminism in I is hostile, and the strategy witnessing the GFGness should address all possible "*I*-futures", nondeterminism in O is cooperative, and a single "*O*-future", which the strategy chooses, is sufficient. More formally, an automaton $\mathcal{A}$ over $2^{I \cup O}$ is (*I/O*)-aware GFG if for every word $w_I \in (2^I)^\omega$, if w_I is *hopeful*, namely it can be paired with a word $w_O \in (2^O)^\omega$ to a computation accepted by $\mathcal{A}$, then the pairing as well as the accepting run of $\mathcal{A}$ can be produced in an on-line manner, thus in a way that only depends on the past. For example, the automaton $\mathcal{A}_1$ from Fig. 1 is $(\{a\}/\{b\})$-aware GFG, as given the a-component of a letter, there is a strategy that pairs it with a b-component and a transition of $\mathcal{A}_1$ in a way that all the hopeful words in $(2^{\{a\}})^\omega$ are paired with a word in $(2^{\{b\}})^\omega$ and an accepting run on the obtained computation.

After introducing (*I/O*)-aware GFG automata, our first set of results concerns their applications and decidability. First, we show that nondeterminisitic (*I/O*)-aware GFG automata are *sound and complete for* (*I/O*)-*realizability*: the system has a winning strategy in a game played on them iff the specification is (*I/O*)-realizable. Note that using a nondeterministic automaton is always sound. The use of deterministic automata, then GFG automata, and now (*I/O*)-aware GFG automata, is required for the completeness. We conclude that the synthesis problem for (*I/O*)-aware GFG automata with acceptance condition γ can be solved in the same complexity as deciding games with γ winning conditions. Thus, it coincides with the complexity for deterministic automata. In particular, for (*I/O*)-aware nondeterministic Büchi automata, the synthesis problem can be solved in quadratic time. Then, we study the problem of deciding whether a given nondeterministic automaton is (I/O)-aware GFG. We show that the problem is reducible to the problem of deciding whether the projection of $\mathcal{A}$ on I is GFG, and following [3], conclude that it is polynomial for Büchi automata. We also extend the notion of DBP automata to the (I/O)-aware setting, and study the relation between DBP and (I/O)-aware DBP automata, as well as the relation between (I/O)-aware DBP and (I/O)-aware GFG automata.

It is tempting to believe that the more signals we identify as outputs, the "more (I/O)-aware GFG" the automaton is. Our second set of results has to do with the fact that the above intuition is wrong. Essentially, this follows from the fact that while nondeterminism in O is cooperative, a strategy that witnesses (I/O)-aware GFGness has to "cover" only hopeful input words, and the identification of signals as outputs may make some input words hopeful. In particular, while all deterministic automata are GFG, not all deterministic automata are (I/O)-aware GFG. In order to address this phenomenon, we introduce (I^+/O^-)-*aware GFG automata*: an automaton $\mathcal{A}$ is (I^+/O^-)-aware GFG if there is a partition $\langle I', O' \rangle$ of $I \cup O$ such that $I \subseteq I'$ and $\mathcal{A}$ is (I'/O')-aware GFG. Intuitively, since $I \subseteq I'$, then the system has less control in the $\langle I', O' \rangle$ partition, which we show to imply that (I^+/O^-)-aware GFG automata are sound and complete for (I/O)-realizablity. As discussed above, however, the connection between controlability and GFGness is not monotone. Consequently, while deciding (I/O)-aware GFGness for Büchi automata is polynomial, we show that deciding their (I^+/O^-)-aware GFGness requires a check of all possible partitions of $I \cup O$, and is NP-complete in $|I \cup O|$.

(I/O)-aware GFG automata significantly extend the type of automata that are sound and complete for (I/O)-realizability. A natural problem that follows is the generation of small (I^+/O^-)-aware GFG automata. Our third set of results concerns this challenge, and its tight relation to the problem of generating small realizing (I/O)-transducers. We describe two heuristics in this front. In the first, we introduce the notion of (I/O)-*coverage* between automata, which together with (I/O)-aware GFGness entails preservation of (I/O)-realizability. We then discuss generation of small (I/O)-covering automata, showing that (I/O)-aware GFG automata are unboundedly more succinct than deterministic and even GFG automata. Intuitively, while an automaton may need a large state space in order to recognize all computations, an (I/O)-aware GFG automaton that is used for synthesis may reject some of the computations, as long as it covers all hopeful input words. While (I/O)-covering GFG automata under-approximate the specification, our second heuristic is *counter-example guided inductive synthesis* (CEGIS), and it generates over-approximating GFG automata. Unlike earlier CEGIS efforts [2,20,21], our starting point is an LTL formula, and we iteratively refine GFG automata that over-approximate the specification and its complement. Our GFG automata are obtained by applying the subset construction on the nondeterministic automaton and adding nondeterministic transitions to states associated with strict subsets of the successor subset. Working with the subset construction is always sound and complete for safety automata. For Büchi automata, refinement steps are needed in cases richer information that is needed for keeping track of visits in accepting states. Working with GFG automata, we let the winning strategy use small subsets, in particular follow the nondeterministic automaton when possible.

2 Preliminaries

2.1 Automata

A *nondeterministic word automaton* over a finite alphabet Σ is $\mathcal{A} = \langle \Sigma, Q, q_0, \delta, \alpha \rangle$, where Q is a set of states, $q_0 \in Q$ is an initial state, $\delta : Q \times \Sigma \to 2^Q \setminus \{\emptyset\}$ is a total transition function, and α is an acceptance condition. We say that $\mathcal{A}$ is *deterministic* if for every $q \in Q$ and $\sigma \in \Sigma$, we have that $|\delta(q, \sigma)| = 1$. A *run* of $\mathcal{A}$ on an infinite word $\sigma_0, \sigma_1, \dots \in \Sigma^\omega$ is a sequence of states $r = q_0, q_1, \dots$, where for every position $i \geq 0$, we have that $q_{i+1} \in \delta(q_i, \sigma_i)$. We use $inf(r)$ to denote the set of states that r visits infinitely often. Thus, $inf(r) = \{q : q_i = q \text{ for infinitely many } i\text{-s}\}$.

We consider *parity* acceptance condition, where $\alpha : Q \to \{1, \dots, k\}$, and a run r is accepting iff $\min_{q \in inf(r)}(\alpha(q))$ is even. We also consider *Büchi* acceptance condition, where $\alpha \subseteq Q$, and a run is accepting iff it visits states in α infinitely often; that is, $\alpha \cap inf(r) \neq \emptyset$. Finally, we consider *looping* automata, which are a special case of Büchi automata in which all states except for one rejecting sink are in α (equivalently, $\alpha = Q$ and the transition function need not be total). The *language* of $\mathcal{A}$, denoted $L(\mathcal{A})$, is the set of all words $w \in \Sigma^\omega$ such that $\mathcal{A}$ has an accepting run on w.

We use three letter acronyms in $\{D,N\} \times \{P,B,L\} \times \{W\}$ to denote classes of word automata. The first letter indicates whether this is a deterministic or nondeterministic automaton, and the second indicates the acceptance condition. For example, NLW is a nondeterministic looping automaton.

We say that a nondeterministic automaton is *good for games* (GFG, for short) if its nondeterminism can be resolved based on the past [11]. Formally, a nondeterministic automaton $\mathcal{A} = \langle \Sigma, Q, q_0, \delta, \alpha \rangle$ is GFG if there exists a function $g : \Sigma^* \to Q$ such that the following hold: (1) $g(\epsilon) = q_0$, (2) The strategy g is compatible with δ; thus, for every $w \cdot \sigma \in \Sigma^* \times \Sigma$, we have that $g(w \cdot \sigma) \in \delta(g(w), \sigma)$, and (3) The strategy g "covers" all words in $L(\mathcal{A})$; thus for every word $w = \sigma_0 \cdot \sigma_1 \dots \in L(\mathcal{A})$, the run that g induces on w, namely $g(\epsilon), g(\sigma_0), g(\sigma_0 \cdot \sigma_1), \dots$, is accepting. We then say that g *witnesses* the GFG-ness of $\mathcal{A}$.

2.2 Games

A *game* is a tuple $G = \langle V_{\text{AND}}, V_{\text{OR}}, E, \alpha \rangle$, where V_{AND} and V_{OR} are disjoint sets of positions, owned by Player AND and Player OR, respectively. Let $V = V_{\text{AND}} \cup V_{\text{OR}}$. Then, $E \subseteq V \times V$ is an edge relation, and α is a winning condition, defining a subset of V^ω. A *play* is an infinite sequence of positions $v_0, v_1, \dots \in V^\omega$, such that for every index $i \geq 0$, we have that $\langle v_i, v_{i+1} \rangle \in E$. A play $\pi \in V^\omega$ is *winning* for Player OR if π satisfies α, and is winning for Player AND otherwise. We focus here on *Büchi* games, where $\alpha \subseteq V$ and π satisfies α if it visits the positions in α infinitely often.

Starting from some position $v_0 \in V$, the players generate a play in G as follows. In every round, if the current position is $v \in V_j$, for $j \in \{\text{AND}, \text{OR}\}$, then Player j chooses a successor v' of v, and the play proceeds to position v'. A *strategy* for a player $j \in \{\text{AND}, \text{OR}\}$ is a function $f_j : V^* \times V_j \to V$ such that for every $u \in V^*$ and $v \in V_j$, we have that $\langle v, f_j(u, v) \rangle \in E$. Thus, a strategy for Player j maps the history of the game so far, when it ends in a position v owned by Player j, to a successor of v. Two strategies $f_{\text{AND}}, f_{\text{OR}}$, and an initial position v_0 induce a play $\pi = v_0, v_1, v_2 \cdots \in V^\omega$, where for every $i \geq 0$, if $v_i \in V_j$, for $j \in \{\text{AND}, \text{OR}\}$, then $v_{i+1} = f_j((v_0, \ldots, v_{i-1}), v_i)$. We say that π is the *outcome* of $f_{\text{OR}}, f_{\text{AND}}$, and v_0, and denote $\pi = outcome(f_{\text{OR}}, f_{\text{AND}}, v_0)$.

We say that a position $v \in V$ is winning for Player OR if there exists a strategy f_{OR} such that for every strategy f_{AND}, we have that $outcome(f_{\text{OR}}, f_{\text{AND}}, v)$ is winning for Player OR. We then say that f_{OR} is a *winning strategy* of Player OR from v. We define similarly winning positions and strategies for Player AND.

It is known that Büchi games are *determined*. That is, every position in a Büchi game is winning for exactly one of the players. Solving a game is deciding which vertices are winning for every player. Büchi games can be solved in quadratic time [22].

2.3 Synthesis

Consider two finite sets I and O of input and output signals, respectively. For two words $w_I = i_0 \cdot i_1 \cdot i_2 \cdots \in (2^I)^\omega$ and $w_O = o_0 \cdot o_1 \cdot o_2 \cdots \in (2^O)^\omega$, we define $w_I \oplus w_O$ as the word in $(2^{I \cup O})^\omega$ obtained by merging w_I and w_O. Thus, $w_I \oplus w_O = (i_0 \cup o_0) \cdot (i_1 \cup o_1) \cdot (i_2 \cup o_2) \cdots$.

An (I/O)-*transducer* models a finite-state system that generates assignments to the output signals while interacting with an environment that generate assignments to the input signals. Formally, an (I/O)-transducer is $\mathcal{T} = \langle I, O, S, s_0, \rho, \tau \rangle$, where S is a set of states, $s_0 \in S$ is an initial state, $\rho : S \times 2^I \to S$ is a transition function, and $\tau : S \to 2^O$ is a labelling function on the states. Intuitively, $\mathcal{T}$ models the interaction of an environment that generates at each moment in time a letter in 2^I with a system that responds with letters in 2^O. Consider an input word $w_I = i_0 \cdot i_1 \cdots \in (2^I)^\omega$. The *run* of $\mathcal{T}$ on w_I is the sequence $s_0, s_1, s_2 \ldots$ such that for all $j \geq 0$, we have that $s_{j+1} = \rho(s_j, i_j)$. The *output* of $\mathcal{T}$ on w_I is then $w_O = o_1 \cdot o_2 \cdots \in (2^O)^\omega$, where $o_j = \tau(s_j)$ for all $j \geq 1$. Note that the first output assignment is that of s_1, thus $\tau(s_0)$ is ignored. This reflects the fact that the environment initiates the interaction. The *computation of* $\mathcal{T}$ on w_I, denoted $\mathcal{T}(w_I)$, is then $w_I \oplus w_O$. Thus, $\mathcal{T}(w_I) = i_0 \cup o_1, i_1 \cup o_2, \ldots \in (2^{I \cup O})^\omega$.

For an automaton $\mathcal{A}$ over $2^{I \cup O}$, we say that $\mathcal{T}$ (I/O)-*realizes* $\mathcal{A}$ if for every input word $w_I \in (2^I)^\omega$, the computation of $\mathcal{T}$ on w_I is in $L(\mathcal{A})$. If there exists an (I/O)-transducer $\mathcal{T}$ that (I/O)-realizes $\mathcal{A}$, then we say that $\mathcal{A}$ is (I/O)-

realizable. The *synthesis* problem is to decide, given an automaton $\mathcal{A}$, whether $\mathcal{A}$ is (I/O)-realizable, and if so, to return an (I/O)-transducer that realizes it.

Given an NBW $\mathcal{A} = \langle 2^{I \cup O}, Q, q_0, \delta, \alpha \rangle$ with a total δ, we define the *synthesis game* $G_{\text{SYN}}(\mathcal{A}, I, O)$ as follows. Intuitively, the game is played over Q, and starts at q_0. Let q be the position of the game at the beginning of some round. The round proceeds as follows: first, Player AND, who represents the environment, chooses a letter $i \in 2^I$. Then, Player OR, who represents the system, chooses a letter $o \in 2^O$ and a state q' such that $q' \in \delta(q, i \cup o)$, and the game proceeds to q'. Formally, we define $G_{\text{SYN}}(\mathcal{A}, I, O) = \langle V_{\text{AND}}, V_{\text{OR}}, E, \alpha \rangle$, where $V_{\text{AND}} = Q$, $V_{\text{OR}} = Q \times 2^I$, and $E = \{\langle q, \langle q, i \rangle \rangle : q \in V_{\text{AND}} \text{ and } i \in 2^I\} \cup \{\langle \langle q, i \rangle, q' \rangle : \text{ there is } o \in 2^O \text{ such that } q' \in \delta(q, i \cup o)\}$.

We say that an automaton $\mathcal{A}$ over alphabet $2^{I \cup O}$ is *sound and complete for (I/O)-realizability* when $\mathcal{A}$ is (I/O)-realizable iff q_0 is a winning state for Player OR in $G_{\text{SYN}}(\mathcal{A}, I, O)$. Note that all NBWs are sound for (I/O)-realizability, in the sense that if q_0 is a winning state for the system in $G_{\text{SYN}}(\mathcal{A}, I, O)$, then $\mathcal{A}$ is (I/O)-realizable. However, there are (I/O)-realizable NBWs for which q_0 is not winning for Player OR. The inherent difficulty in $\mathcal{A}$ being nondeterministic lies in the fact that each move of Player OR to a successor state in $\mathcal{A}$ should accommodate all possible future choices of Player AND. If different future choices of Player AND induce computations that are all in the language of $\mathcal{A}$ yet require different nondeterministic choices, then Player OR cannot win.

3 (I/O)-Aware Good-for-Games Automata

For an automaton $\mathcal{A}$ over $2^{I \cup O}$ and a word $w_I \in (2^I)^\omega$, we say that w_I is *hopeful in $\mathcal{A}$* if there exists a word $w_O \in (2^O)^\omega$ such that $w_I \oplus w_O \in L(\mathcal{A})$. Consider a nondeterministic automaton $\mathcal{A} = \langle 2^{I \cup O}, Q, q_0, \delta, \alpha \rangle$, and let $g : (2^I)^* \to 2^O \times Q$ be a function. We denote the first and second components of g by g_O and g_Q, respectively. That is, for a word $w_I \in (2^I)^*$, we have that $g(w_I) = \langle g_O(w_I), g_Q(w_I) \rangle$. We say that $\mathcal{A}$ is *(I/O)-aware GFG* if there exists a function $g : (2^I)^* \to 2^O \times Q$ such that the following hold.

1. $g(\epsilon) = \langle \emptyset, q_0 \rangle$,
2. The strategy g is compatible with δ. Thus for every $w_I \in (2^I)^*$ and $i \in 2^I$, we have that $g_Q(w_I \cdot i) \in \delta(g_Q(w_I), i \cup g_O(w_I))$, and
3. The strategy g "covers" all input words that are hopeful in $\mathcal{A}$. Thus for every w_I that is hopeful in $\mathcal{A}$, we have that $g_Q(w_I) = g_Q(\epsilon), g_Q(i_0), g_Q(i_0 \cdot i_1), \dots$ is an accepting run on $w_I \oplus (g_O(\epsilon) \cdot g_O(i_0) \cdot g_O(i_0 \cdot i_1) \cdots)$.

Example 1. Consider the nondeterministic Büchi (in fact, looping) automaton $\mathcal{A}_2$ over $2^{\{a,b,c\}}$ appearing in Fig. 2. Missing transitions lead to a rejecting sink.

Note that $\mathcal{A}_2$ is not GFG. Indeed, a strategy $g : (2^{\{a,b,c\}})^* \to Q$ neglects either the word $\{a, b\}^\omega$, in the case $g(\{a, b\}) = q_1$, or the word $\{a, b\} \cdot \{a, b, c\}^\omega$, in the case $g(\{a, b\}) = q_2$.

Assume that a and b are input signals and c is an output signal. Now, a function $g : (2^{\{a,b\}})^* \to 2^{\{c\}} \times Q$ such that $g(\epsilon) = \langle \emptyset, q_0 \rangle$, $g(\{a, b\}) = \langle \emptyset, q_2 \rangle$,

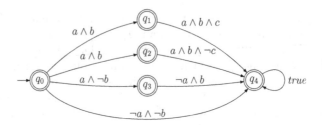

Fig. 2. The automaton $\mathcal{A}_2$ is not GFG, yet is $(\{a,b\}/\{c\})$-aware GFG.

$g(\{a\}) = \langle \emptyset, q_3 \rangle$ and $g(\emptyset \cdot (2^{\{a,b\}})^*) = g(\{a\} \cdot \{b\} \cdot (2^{\{a,b\}})^*) = g(\{a,b\} \cdot \{a,b\} \cdot (2^{\{a,b\}})^*) = \langle \emptyset, q_4 \rangle$, witnesses that $\mathcal{A}_2$ is $(\{a,b\}/\{c\})$-aware GFG. Intuitively, identifying c as an output enables $\mathcal{A}_2$ to accept only one of the words $\{a,b\}^\omega$ and $\{a,b\} \cdot \{a,b,c\}^\omega$. □

As demonstrated in Example 1, the distinction between the nondeterminism in I and O makes some automata good for games. Beyond being applicable to more specifications, the cooperative nature of the nondeterminism in O makes (I/O)-aware GFG automata unboundedly more succinct than GFG automata. Indeed, a GFG automaton may need a large state space in order to recognize all computations, whereas an (I/O)-aware GFG automaton only needs to cover all hopeful input words. Similarly, determinization, even in GFG automata, may be needed in order to accept in an on-line manner all computations, and is not needed if we only care to accept a subset of them. We get back to this point in Sect. 7.

Remark 1 [(I/O)-aware DBP automata]. Translating LTL formulas to non-deterministic automata, one typically uses the Büchi acceptance condition [23], which motivates our focus on NBWs. For safety properties, one ends up with NLWs – nondeterministic looping automata. As studied in [4,16], GFG NLWs are *determinizable by prunning* (DBP, for short); that is, their transition function embodies a deterministic transition function that recognizes the same language. Extending the study to the (I/O)-aware setting is possible: We say that an NBW $\mathcal{A}$ is (I/O)-*aware DBP* if it is possible to resolve the nondeterministic choices of $\mathcal{A}$ by choosing, for every state q and assignment $i \in 2^I$, a transition from q that agrees with i, in a way that covers all input sequences that are hopeful in $\mathcal{A}$. In the full version, we define (I/O)-aware DBP automata formally and show that all the known results about DBPness extend easily to the (I/O)-aware setting. In particular, while every (I/O)-aware DBP automaton is (I/O)-aware GFG, the reverse direction is valid only for (I/O)-aware GFG NLWs. □

4   Synthesis with (I/O)-Aware GFG Automata

In this section we show that, as has been the case with GFG automata, (I/O)-aware GFG automata are sound and complete for (I/O)-realizability. Also, in spite of their succinctness, the complexity of the synthesis problem for (I/O)-aware GFG automata coincides with that of deterministic automata, and the problem of deciding whether a given automaton is (I/O)-aware GFG is not more complex than the problem of deciding whether a given automaton is GFG.

Theorem 1. (I/O)-aware GFG automata are sound and complete for (I/O)-realizability.

Proof. Consider an (I/O)-aware GFG automaton $\mathcal{A} = \langle 2^{I \cup O}, Q, q_0, \delta, \alpha \rangle$. We show that q_0 is winning for Player OR (the system) in $G_{\mathrm{SYN}}(\mathcal{A}, I, O)$ iff $\mathcal{A}$ is (I/O)-realizable.

The first direction holds for general automata: if Player OR wins $G_{\mathrm{SYN}}(\mathcal{A}, I, O)$, then his winning strategy induces an (I/O)-transducer that (I/O)-realizes $\mathcal{A}$.

For the other direction, assume that $\mathcal{A}$ is a realizable (I/O)-aware GFG automaton. Let $g : (2^I)^* \to 2^O \times Q$ be a function that witnesses $\mathcal{A}$'s (I/O)-aware GFGness, and let $G_{\mathrm{SYN}}(\mathcal{A}, I, O) = \langle Q, Q \times 2^I, E, \alpha \rangle$ be the synthesis game. We describe a winning strategy for Player OR in $G_{\mathrm{SYN}}(\mathcal{A}, I, O)$. Consider a prefix of a play $q_0, \langle q_0, i_0 \rangle, q_1, \langle q_1, i_1 \rangle, \ldots, q_k, \langle q_k, i_k \rangle$. A winning strategy for Player OR is to move from $\langle q_k, i_k \rangle$ to $g_Q(i_0 \cdot i_1 \cdots i_k)$. By the second condition on (I/O)-aware GFGness, the function g is compatible with δ, and so the above move exists. In addition, since $\mathcal{A}$ is realizable, then all the words in $(2^I)^\omega$ are hopeful in $\mathcal{A}$. Then, by the third condition on (I/O)-aware GFGness, we have that the run that g_Q produces is accepting. Therefore, this strategy is indeed winning for Player OR. □

Example 2. Consider again the automaton $\mathcal{A}_2$ from Example 1. Let $I = \{a, b\}$ and $O = \{c\}$. It is easy to see that Player OR does not win the synthesis game on $\mathcal{A}_2$. Indeed, Player AND can win by starting with input $\{b\}$. Since $\mathcal{A}_2$ is $(\{a, b\}/\{c\})$-aware GFG, we can conclude that $\mathcal{A}_2$ is not $(\{a, b\}/\{c\})$-realizable.   □

The following corollary follows immediately from Theorem 1 and from the known complexity of deciding Büchi games [22].

Corollary 1. *The synthesis problem for (I/O)-aware automata with acceptance condition γ can be solved in the complexity of deciding games with winning condition γ. In particular, the synthesis problem for (I/O)-aware NBWs can be solved in quadratic time.*

We turn to study the complexity of deciding whether a given automaton is (I/O)-aware GFG. For an NBW $\mathcal{A} = \langle 2^X, Q, q_0, \delta, \alpha \rangle$ and a partition $\langle I, O \rangle$ of X, we define the *projection* of $\mathcal{A}$ on I as $\mathcal{A}_{|I} = \langle 2^I, Q, q_0, \delta', \alpha \rangle$, where for every two states $q_1, q_2 \in Q$ and letter $i \in 2^I$, we have that $q_2 \in \delta'(q_1, i)$ iff there exists $o \in 2^O$ such that $q_2 \in \delta(q_1, i \cup o)$. Thus, $\mathcal{A}_{|I}$ is obtained from $\mathcal{A}$ by hiding the 2^O-component in its transitions. Note that $\mathcal{A}_{|I}$ accepts all the words in $(2^I)^\omega$ that are hopeful in $\mathcal{A}$.

Lemma 1. *For every automaton $\mathcal{A}$ over 2^X and every partition $\langle I, O \rangle$ of X, we have that $\mathcal{A}$ is (I/O)-aware GFG iff $\mathcal{A}_{|I}$ is GFG.*

Lemma 1 implies the following. The result for NBWs also uses [3].

Corollary 2. *Consider an acceptance condition γ. The complexity of deciding (I/O)-aware GFGness for γ automata coincides with the complexity of deciding GFGness for γ automata. In particular, deciding (I/O)-aware GFGness for NBWs can be done in polynomial time.*

5   Non-monotonicity of (I/O)-Aware GFGness

For a set X of signals and two partitions $\langle I, O \rangle$ and $\langle I', O' \rangle$ of X to input and output signals, we say that $\langle I, O \rangle$ *has less control than* $\langle I', O' \rangle$ if $I' \subseteq I$ (equivalently, $O' \supseteq O$). That is, in $\langle I', O' \rangle$, the system assigns values to all the signals in O and possibly some more, which have been assigned by the environment in the partition $\langle I, O \rangle$.

Consider a specification NBW $\mathcal{A}$ over the alphabet 2^X. It is not hard to see that if $\langle I, O \rangle$ has less control than $\langle I', O' \rangle$ and $\mathcal{A}$ is (I/O)-realizable, then $\mathcal{A}$ is also (I'/O')-realizable. Indeed, an (I'/O')-transducer that realizes $\mathcal{A}$ can be obtained from an (I/O)-transducer that realizes $\mathcal{A}$ by moving the signals in $I \setminus I'$ from the transitions to the output function, and arbitrarily pruning nondeterminism. On the other hand, as we shall see below, the NBW $\mathcal{A}$ may be (I/O)-aware GFG and not (I'/O')-aware GFG, and vice-versa. We first study the two extreme partitions, namely the ones when the system has all or no control.

Lemma 2. *Every NBW over 2^X is $(\emptyset/X)$-aware GFG. Every NBW over 2^X is $(X/\emptyset)$-aware GFG iff it is GFG.*

We continue to the general case, showing that the identification of signals as input or output can both improve and harm (I/O)-aware GFGness. We start with an example.

Example 3. Consider again the NLW $\mathcal{A}_2$ from Example 1. As we have seen there, $\mathcal{A}_2$ is not GFG, yet is $(\{a, b\}/\{c\})$-aware GFG. Here, we claim that $\mathcal{A}_2$ is not $(\{a\}/\{b, c\})$-aware GFG. Thus, identifying b as an output signal harms (I/O)-aware GFGness. Indeed, a function that attempts to witness $(\{a\}/\{b, c\})$-aware GFGness is $g : (2^{\{a\}})^* \to 2^{\{b, c\}} \times Q$, and it neglects either the word $\{a\}^\omega$, in the case $g_Q(\{a\}) = q_3$, or the word $\{a\} \cdot \emptyset^\omega$, in the case $g_Q(\{a\}) \in \{q_1, q_2\}$. □

In Theorem 2 below we generalize Example 3 and show that the alternation between positive and negative effect of control on (I/O)-aware GFGness is unboundedly long. The proof can be found in the full version.

Theorem 2 [(I/O)**-aware GFGness is not monotone**]. *For every $k \geq 1$, we can define a DLW $\mathcal{A}^k$ over an alphabet $2^{\{x_1, x_2 \ldots, x_{2k}\}}$, such that for all $1 \leq j \leq k$, we have that $\mathcal{A}^k$ is not $(\{x_1, \ldots, x_{2j-1}\}/\{x_{2j}, \ldots, x_{2k}\})$-aware GFG and is $(\{x_1, \ldots, x_{2j}\}/\{x_{2j+1}, \ldots, x_{2k}\})$-aware GFG.*

When, however, the specification is (I/O)-realizable, then monotonicity holds for partitions that have less control than $\langle I, O \rangle$:

Theorem 3. *Consider an (I/O)-realizable NBW $\mathcal{A}$ and a partition $\langle I', O' \rangle$ that has less control than $\langle I, O \rangle$. If $\mathcal{A}$ is (I'/O')-aware GFG, then $\mathcal{A}$ is also (I/O)-aware GFG.*

Proof. Consider an (I/O)-realizable NBW $\mathcal{A} = \langle 2^{I \cup O}, Q, q_0, \delta, \alpha \rangle$, and let $\langle I', O' \rangle$ be a partition that has less control than $\langle I, O \rangle$. That is, $I \subseteq I'$. Assume that $\mathcal{A}$ is (I'/O')-aware GFG and let $g' : (2^{I'})^* \to 2^{O'} \times Q$ and $f : (2^I)^* \to 2^O$ be functions that witness $\mathcal{A}$'s (I'/O')-aware GFGness and (I/O)-realizability, respectively. We define a function $g : (2^I)^* \to 2^O \times Q$ that witnesses $\mathcal{A}$'s (I/O)-aware GFGness.

Essentially, we construct g as follows. Given a word $w_I \in (2^I)^*$, we first use f in order to extend w_I to a word over $2^{I'}$, and then apply g' on the extended word. Formally, for $w_I = i_0, i_1, \cdots \in (2^I)^*$, let $w_O = f(i_0), f(i_0 \cdot i_1), \cdots \in (2^O)^*$. That is, w_O is the word that f pairs with w_I. Let $C = O \setminus O'$ be the set of signals for which control is lost in the transition from the partition $\langle I, O \rangle$ to $\langle I', O' \rangle$. Let $u \in (2^C)^*$ be the projection of w_O on C. That is, $u = f(i_0) \cap C, f(i_0 \cdot i_1) \cap C, \cdots \in (2^C)^*$. Note that $C = I' \setminus I$. Thus, we can define $w_{I'} = w_I \oplus u \in (2^{I'})^*$, and we define $g(w_I) = \langle g'_O(w_{I'}) \cup c, g'_Q(w_{I'}) \rangle$, where c is the last letter of u.

Since $\mathcal{A}$ is (I'/O')-aware GFG, the function g' induces an accepting run of $\mathcal{A}$ on every word in $(2^{I'})^\omega$ that is hopeful in $\mathcal{A}$. This holds also for the word generated above, and so the function g witnesses $\mathcal{A}$'s (I/O)-aware GFGness. □

6 (I^+/O^-)-Aware Good-for-Games Automata

The non-monotonicity of the behavior of the signals discussed in Sect. 5 points to a bothering situation. In particular, an automaton may be GFG, in fact even deterministic, and hence be sound and complete for (I/O)-realizability, and still not be (I/O)-aware GFG. In this section we address this by defining (I^+/O^-)-aware GFG automata, which consider, given $\mathcal{A}$, all the partitions of $I \cup O$ with respect to which $\mathcal{A}$ is sound and complete for (I/O)-realizability.

For an NBW $\mathcal{A} = \langle 2^{I \cup O}, Q, q_0, \delta, \alpha \rangle$, we say that $\mathcal{A}$ is (I^+/O^-)-aware GFG if there exists a partition $\langle I', O' \rangle$ that has less control than $\langle I, O \rangle$, namely $I \subseteq I'$, such that $\mathcal{A}$ is (I'/O')-aware GFG. Note that every (I/O)-aware GFG automaton is (I^+/O^-)-aware GFG. In fact, by Lemma 2, every GFG automaton is (I^+/O^-)-aware GFG. However, as Lemma 2 implies, there are (I^+/O^-)-aware GFG automata that are not GFG or not (I/O)-aware GFG. We first argue that (I^+/O^-)-aware GFG automata are sound and complete for (I/O)-realizability.

Theorem 4. (I^+/O^-)-*aware GFG automata are sound and complete for (I/O)-realizability.*

Proof. Let $\mathcal{A} = \langle 2^{I \cup O}, Q, q_0, \delta, \alpha \rangle$ be an (I^+/O^-)-aware GFG automaton, and let $\langle I', O' \rangle$ be a partition that has less control than $\langle I, O \rangle$ and for which $\mathcal{A}$ is

(I'/O')-aware GFG. We show that Player OR wins $G_{\text{SYN}}(\mathcal{A}, I, O)$ iff $\mathcal{A}$ is (I/O)-realizable. The first direction holds for general NBWs. For the other direction, assume that $\mathcal{A}$ is (I/O)-realizable. Then, as $\langle I', O' \rangle$ has less control than $\langle I, O \rangle$, Theorem 3 implies that $\mathcal{A}$ is (I/O)-aware GFG. Therefore, by Theorem 1, Player OR wins $G_{\text{SYN}}(\mathcal{A}, I, O)$. □

Theorem 4 enables us to extend Corollary 1 to (I^+/O^-)-aware GFG automata:

Corollary 3. *The synthesis problem for (I^+/O^-)-aware automata with acceptance condition γ can be solved in the complexity of deciding games with winning condition γ. In particular, the synthesis problem for (I^+/O^-)-aware NBWs can be solved in quadratic time.*

We turn to study the complexity of deciding (I^+/O^-)-aware GFGness. As we shall see, the non-monotonicity suggests that one should check all possible partitions of $I \cup O$. Formally, we have the following. The NP-hardness proof relate the choice of a partition with a choice of a satisfying assignment to a 3CNF formula.

Theorem 5. *Consider an NBW $\mathcal{A} = \langle 2^{I \cup O}, Q, q_0, \delta, \alpha \rangle$. The problem of deciding whether $\mathcal{A}$ is (I^+/O^-)-aware GFG is polynomial in $|Q|$ and NP-complete in $|I \cup O|$.*

7 (I/O)-Awareness and Synthesis

A natural problem that follows from our results is the generation of small (I^+/O^-)-aware GFG automata. Thus, given an NBW $\mathcal{A}$, return a minimal (I^+/O^-)-aware GFG automaton equivalent to $\mathcal{A}$. In this section we argue that the equivalence requirement is too strong and can be relaxed to produce even smaller automata. We relate the problem of generating (I/O)-aware GFG automata with that of generating realizing (I/O)-transducers, and show how it sheds light on an important open problem, namely whether minimal realizing transducers for NBW specifications with n states need $2^{O(n \log n)}$ or only $2^{O(n)}$ states. We also suggest a heuristic algorithm that solves synthesis given a specification and its negation, possibly avoiding determinization and getting a transducer with less than $2^{O(n \log n)}$ states.

7.1   Minimal (I/O)-Transducers

We start with the definition of *covering* automata, which replaces the equivalence condition. For two automata $\mathcal{A}$ and $\mathcal{A}'$ over $2^{I \cup O}$, we say that $\mathcal{A}'$ (I/O)-*covers* $\mathcal{A}$ if $L(\mathcal{A}') \subseteq L(\mathcal{A})$ and $L(\mathcal{A}_{|I}) = L(\mathcal{A}'_{|I})$. Thus, every word in $(2^I)^\omega$ that is hopeful in $\mathcal{A}$ is hopeful also in $\mathcal{A}'$, and $\mathcal{A}'$ does not extend the language of $\mathcal{A}$.

[3] Moreover, $\mathcal{A}'$ (I^+/O^-)-*covers* $\mathcal{A}$ if there is a partition $\langle I', O' \rangle$ that has less control than $\langle I, O \rangle$ such that $L(\mathcal{A}') \subseteq L(\mathcal{A})$ and $L(\mathcal{A}_{|I'}) = L(\mathcal{A}'_{|I'})$. We then say that $\mathcal{A}'$ (I^+/O^-)-covers $\mathcal{A}$ with $\langle I', O' \rangle$. Note that if $\mathcal{A}'$ (I/O)-covers $\mathcal{A}$, then $\mathcal{A}'$ also (I^+/O^-)-covers $\mathcal{A}$ (with the partition $\langle I, O \rangle$), yet, as has been the case with (I^+/O^-)-awareness, allowing coverage with partitions with less control strictly strengthen the definition, and, as we show below, is still sound and complete for (I/O)-realizability.

Theorem 6. *Consider two automata $\mathcal{A}$ and $\mathcal{A}'$ over $2^{I \cup O}$. If $\mathcal{A}'$ (I^+/O^-)-covers $\mathcal{A}$ with $\langle I', O' \rangle$ and is (I'/O')-aware GFG, then $\mathcal{A}'$ is sound and complete for (I/O)-realizability of $\mathcal{A}$.*

Proof. We prove that Player OR wins $G_{\text{SYN}}(\mathcal{A}', I, O)$ iff $\mathcal{A}$ is (I/O)-realizable. The first direction is easy: if Player OR wins $G_{\text{SYN}}(\mathcal{A}', I, O)$, then $\mathcal{A}'$ is (I/O)-realizable. Since $L(\mathcal{A}') \subseteq L(\mathcal{A})$, then every transducer that (I/O)-realizes $\mathcal{A}'$ also (I/O)-realizes $\mathcal{A}$, thus $\mathcal{A}$ is (I/O)-realizable.

For the other direction, assume that $\mathcal{A}$ is (I/O)-realizable, and let $\mathcal{T}$ be a transducer that (I/O)-realizes $\mathcal{A}$. Consider a word $w_I \in (2^I)^\omega$. Let $w_{I'} = \mathcal{T}(w_I) \cap (2^{I'})^\omega$, that is, $w_{I'}$ is the projection on I' of the computation of $\mathcal{T}$ on w_I. Clearly, $w_{I'} \in L(\mathcal{A}_{|I'})$, and therefore, $w_{I'} \in L(\mathcal{A}'_{|I'})$. Let $g : (2^{I'})^* \to 2^{O'} \times Q$ be a function that witnesses that $\mathcal{A}'$ is (I'/O')-aware GFG. We describe a winning strategy for Player OR in $G_{\text{SYN}}(\mathcal{A}', I, O)$. Recall that in $G_{\text{SYN}}(\mathcal{A}', I, O)$, Player OR responds to a sequence of input letters over 2^I with an output letter in 2^O and an according transition. Essentially, Player OR uses $\mathcal{T}$ in order to extend a given sequence of input letters in $(2^I)^*$ to a sequence of letters in $(2^{I'})^*$, and then plays accordingly to g. Formally, we extend the notion of computations of $\mathcal{T}$ to finite words. Consider a prefix of a play $q_0, \langle q_0, i_0 \rangle, q_1, \langle q_1, i_1 \rangle, \ldots, q_k, \langle q_k, i_k \rangle$. A winning strategy for Player OR in $G_{\text{SYN}}(\mathcal{A}', I, O)$ is to move from $\langle q_k, i_k \rangle$ to $g_Q((2^{I'})^* \cap \mathcal{T}(w_I))$, where $w_I = i_0 \cdot i_1 \cdots i_k$. Recall that for all $w_I \in (2^I)^\omega$, we have that $w_{I'}$ is hopeful in $\mathcal{A}'$. Therefore, the above strategy is winning for Player OR. $\qquad \square$

Theorem 6 implies that one can solve synthesis for an automaton $\mathcal{A}$ by constructing an (I'/O')-aware GFG automaton $\mathcal{A}'$ that (I^+/O^-)-covers $\mathcal{A}$ with $\langle I', O' \rangle$, rather than an equivalent one, and solving $G_{\text{SYN}}(\mathcal{A}', I, O)$.

Remark 2. Note that for $\mathcal{A}'$ to (I^+/O^-)-cover $\mathcal{A}$ with $\langle I', O' \rangle$, the $L(\mathcal{A}_{|I}) = L(\mathcal{A}'_{|I})$ requirement is strengthened to $L(\mathcal{A}_{|I'}) = L(\mathcal{A}'_{|I'})$. This is crucial. That is, it may be the case that $\mathcal{A}$ is realizable, yet Player OR loses $G_{\text{SYN}}(\mathcal{A}', I, O)$ for an (I^+/O^-)-aware GFG automaton $\mathcal{A}'$ such that $L(\mathcal{A}_{|I}) = L(\mathcal{A}'_{|I})$ and $L(\mathcal{A}') \subseteq L(\mathcal{A})$. As an example, consider an automaton $\mathcal{A}$ over $2^{\{a,b,c\}}$ with $L(\mathcal{A}) = (2^{\{a,b,c\}})^\omega$, and the automaton $\mathcal{A}_2$ from Example 1. Let $I = \{a\}$ and

---

[3] Note that the definition is different than *open implication* in [10], where $\mathcal{A}'$ *open implies* $\mathcal{A}$ if every (I/O)-transducer that (I/O)-realizes $\mathcal{A}'$ also (I/O)-realizes $\mathcal{A}'$. For example, an empty $\mathcal{A}'$ open implies every unrealizable $\mathcal{A}$, yet need not (I/O)-cover it.

$O = \{b, c\}$. It is easy to see that all the words in $(2^{\{a\}})^\omega$ are hopeful in $\mathcal{A}_2$, and that $L(\mathcal{A}_2) \subseteq L(\mathcal{A})$. In addition, $\mathcal{A}$ is clearly realizable. Recall that $\mathcal{A}_2$ is $(\{a, b\}/\{c\})$-aware GFG, thus it is (I^+/O^-)-aware GFG. Yet, Player OR looses $G_{\mathrm{SYN}}(\mathcal{A}_2, I, O)$. Indeed, a winning strategy for Player AND is to start with input $\{a\}$, and then choose input $\emptyset$ if Player OR responds with output in which b is true, and choose input $\{a\}$ otherwise.   □

We turn to study the size of a minimal (I/O)-covering (I/O)-aware GFG NBW. Since unboundedly large parts of the specification automaton may not be needed for its realization, we have the following.

Lemma 3. *Consider an NBW $\mathcal{A}$. An (I/O)-aware GFG NBW that (I/O)-covers $\mathcal{A}$ may be unboundedly smaller than any GFG automaton equivalent to $\mathcal{A}$.*

Theorem 7. *Consider an (I/O)-realizable NBW $\mathcal{A}$. The size of a minimal (I/O)-aware GFG NBW that (I/O)-covers $\mathcal{A}$ coincides with the size of a minimal (I/O)-transducer that (I/O)-realizes $\mathcal{A}$.*

Proof. It is easy to see that if $\mathcal{A}$ is realizable, then an (I/O)-transducer that (I/O)-realizes $\mathcal{A}$ can be viewed as an (I/O)-aware GFG NLW that (I/O)-covers $\mathcal{A}$. Conversely, a winning strategy for the system on $G_{\mathrm{SYN}}(\mathcal{A}, I, O)$, for an (I/O)-aware GFG NBW $\mathcal{A}$, can be viewed as an (I/O)-transducer that (I/O)-realizes $\mathcal{A}$. Note that since our definition of (I/O)-transducers has the output assignments in the states, we actually need $2^{|O|}$ copies of each state. These copies, however, are not needed if one considers (I/O)-transducers with output assignments on the transitions.   □

We continue to the problem of generating small covering (I/O)-aware GFG NBWs. By Theorem 7, the latter coincides with the problem of generating small realizing transducers. The currently known upper bound for the size of a realizing transducer, starting with a specification NBW $\mathcal{A}$ with n states, is $2^{O(n \log n)}$, and is based on playing the synthesis game on a deterministic automaton equivalent to $\mathcal{A}$. Unlike the case of determinization, no matching lower bound is known. Below we relate the existence of such a lower bound with the existence of an NBW that is easy to complement yet hard to determinize.

Theorem 8. *Let $n \geq 1$. If there is an NBW $\mathcal{A}_n$ with n states such that (1) $\mathcal{A}_n$ is easy to complement: there is an NBW $\mathcal{A}'_n$ with $O(n)$ states such that $L(\mathcal{A}'_n) = \Sigma^\omega \setminus L(\mathcal{A}_n)$, yet (2) $\mathcal{A}_n$ is hard to determinize: a DBW equivalent to $\mathcal{A}_n$ needs at least $2^{O(n \log n)}$ states, then there is a realizable NBW $\mathcal{B}_n$ with $O(n)$ states such that the minimal realizing transducer for $\mathcal{B}_n$ needs at least $2^{O(n \log n)}$ states.*

Proof. Let Σ be the alphabet of $\mathcal{A}_n$. We define $\mathcal{B}_n$ over $\Sigma \times \{0, 1\}$ so that $L(\mathcal{B}_n)$ contains all words $w \oplus v$ such that $w \in L(\mathcal{A}_n)$ iff v has infinitely many 1's. Thus, the projection on Σ is in $L(\mathcal{A}_n)$ iff the projection on $\{0, 1\}$ has infinitely many 1's.

It is not hard to see that we can define $\mathcal{B}_n$ by an NBW with $O(n)$ states. Indeed, we can define $\mathcal{B}_n$ as the union of an NBW $\mathcal{B}_n^1$ for words $w \oplus v$ such that $w \in L(\mathcal{A}_n)$ and v has infinitely many 1's and an NBW $\mathcal{B}_n^2$ for words $w \oplus v$ such that $w \notin L(\mathcal{A}_n)$ and v has finitely many 1's. The NBW $\mathcal{B}_n^1$ is the product of $\mathcal{A}_n$, which has n states, with a 2-state DBW for "infinitely many 1's", so its size is $O(n)$. The NBW $\mathcal{B}_n^2$ is the product of an NBW that complements $\mathcal{A}_n$, and which, by Condition (1), has $O(n)$ states, with a 3-state NBW for "only finitely many 1's". So the size of $\mathcal{B}_n^2$ is also $O(n)$.

Now, if we view Σ as an input alphabet and view $\{0, 1\}$ as an output alphabet, then a $(\Sigma/\{0, 1\})$-transducer for $\mathcal{B}_n$ induces a DBW for $\mathcal{A}$ of the same size (note we refer here to Σ and $\{0, 1\}$ as input and output alphabets, rather than signals, but this is a technical issue, as we could have encoded them). To see this, consider a $(\Sigma/\{0, 1\})$-transducer $\mathcal{T}_n = \langle \Sigma, \{0, 1\}, S, s_0, \rho, \tau \rangle$ that realizes $\mathcal{B}_n$, and let $\mathcal{D}_n = \langle \Sigma, S, s_0, \rho, \alpha \rangle$ be a DBW with $\alpha = \{s : \tau(s) = 1\}$. We claim that $L(\mathcal{D}_n) = L(\mathcal{A}_n)$. Indeed, since $\mathcal{T}_n$ realizes $\mathcal{B}_n$, then for every input word $w \in \Sigma^\omega$, the computation of $\mathcal{T}_n$ on w has infinitely many 1's iff $w \in L(\mathcal{A}_n)$. Hence, the run of $\mathcal{D}_n$ on w visits α infinitely often iff $w \in L(\mathcal{A}_n)$. Hence, by Condition (2), the transducer $\mathcal{T}_n$ needs at least $2^{O(n \log n)}$ states. □

Remark 3. Theorem 8 refers to languages that are DBW-recognizable. It is easy to extend it to all ω-regular languages by considering DPWs. □

7.2 Using Over-Approximating GFG Automata

In Sect. 7.1, we suggest the use of GFG automata that under-approximate the specification. In this section we suggest a heuristic that starts with an LTL formula φ and is based on GFG automata that over-approximate NBWs for φ and $\neg\varphi$. The GFG automaton that over approximates an NBW $\mathcal{A}$ is obtained by applying the subset construction on $\mathcal{A}$ and adding nondeterministic transitions to states associated with strict subsets of the successor subset. By working with the over-approximations of both φ and $\neg\varphi$, we iteratively refine the subset construction, adding information that makes the state spaces closer to that of DPWs for φ and $\neg\varphi$. This continues until we get a transducer that realizes φ or $\neg\varphi$, typically much earlier than full determinization is performed. Our method follows the counter-example guided inductive synthesis (CEGIS) [2,20,21] approach, which iteratively computes candidate solutions to the synthesis problem, and refines them accordingly to counterexample traces. However, program executions in CEGIS are finite, while the reactive systems that we consider produce infinite interactions.

We now describe the heuristic in more detail. For an NBW $\mathcal{A} = \langle 2^{I \cup O}, Q, q_0, \delta, \alpha \rangle$, the *nondeterministic subset construction* of $\mathcal{A}$ is NSC($\mathcal{A}$) = $\langle 2^{I \cup O}, 2^Q, \{q_0\}, \delta', \alpha' \rangle$, where $S' \in \delta'(S, \sigma)$ iff $S' \subseteq \cup_{q \in S} \delta(q, \sigma)$, and $S \in \alpha'$ iff $S \cap \alpha \neq \emptyset$. That is, NSC($\mathcal{A}$) extends the subset construction of $\mathcal{A}$ by adding transitions, for every $S \in 2^Q$ and $\sigma \in 2^{I \cup O}$, to all the subsets of $\delta(S, \sigma)$. Note that α' contains all sets whose intersection with α is not empty, and so NSC($\mathcal{A}$)

over-approximates $\mathcal{A}$, thus $L(\mathcal{A}) \subseteq L(\text{NSC}(\mathcal{A}))$. In addition, $\text{NSC}(\mathcal{A})$ is DBP, and so it is GFG with respect to the deterministic subset construction of $\mathcal{A}$.

Given an LTL formula φ, let $\mathcal{A}_\varphi$ and $\mathcal{A}_{\neg\varphi}$ be NBWs for φ and $\neg\varphi$, respectively. By determinacy of games, $\mathcal{A}_\varphi$ is (I/O)-realizable iff $\mathcal{A}_{\neg\varphi}$ is not (O/I)-realizable.[4] We use $\tilde{\mathcal{A}}_\varphi$ and $\tilde{\mathcal{A}}_{\neg\varphi}$ to denote the over-approximations of $\mathcal{A}_\varphi$ and $\mathcal{A}_{\neg\varphi}$, respectively, generated during the algorithm. Initially, $\tilde{\mathcal{A}}_\varphi = \text{NSC}(\mathcal{A}_\varphi)$ and $\tilde{\mathcal{A}}_{\neg\varphi} = \text{NSC}(\mathcal{A}_{\neg\varphi})$. In every iteration, we solve both $G_{\text{SYN}}(\tilde{\mathcal{A}}_\varphi, I, O)$ and $G_{\text{SYN}}(\tilde{\mathcal{A}}_{\neg\varphi}, O, I)$. Since we work with over-approximations, the following three outcomes are possible.

1. Player AND wins $G_{\text{SYN}}(\tilde{\mathcal{A}}_{\neg\varphi}, O, I)$. Then, we conclude that φ is realizable, the winning strategy for Player AND induces a transducer that realizes φ, and we are done.
2. Player AND wins $G_{\text{SYN}}(\tilde{\mathcal{A}}_\varphi, I, O)$. Then, we conclude that φ is not realizable, and we are done.
3. Player OR wins in both games. Note this is possible only due to the over-approximation. We model-check the single computation w that is the outcome of the interaction of the winning strategies of Player OR in the games. If $w \models \varphi$, we conclude that $\tilde{\mathcal{A}}_\varphi$ needs to be refined. At this point we may also model check the transducer induced by the winning strategy of Player OR in $G_{\text{SYN}}(\tilde{\mathcal{A}}_{\neg\varphi}, O, I)$, and conclude that φ is not realizable if the transducer satisfies $\neg\varphi$. Dually, if $w \not\models \varphi$, we conclude that $\tilde{\mathcal{A}}_{\neg\varphi}$ needs to be refined, and we may model check the transducer induced by the winning strategy of Player OR in $G_{\text{SYN}}(\tilde{\mathcal{A}}_\varphi, I, O)$, and conclude it realizes φ. If model checking fails, or if we decide to skip it, we refine (possibly both $\mathcal{A}_\varphi$ and $\mathcal{A}_{\neg\varphi}$, one according to w and one with respect to the counterexample obtained from the model checking) and continue to the next iteration.

It is left to describe the refinement. Essentially, the refinement of $\tilde{\mathcal{A}}_\varphi$ (and similarly for $\tilde{\mathcal{A}}_{\neg\varphi}$) with respect to a counterexample word w excludes w from $\tilde{\mathcal{A}}_\varphi$, and is done in a way that eventually results in a GFG automaton for $\mathcal{A}_\varphi$, unless the procedure halts in an earlier iteration. The refinement may use any on-the-fly determinization construction whose state space consists of information on top of the subset construction (e.g., Safra trees [19] or reduced trees [8]). Let $\mathcal{D}_\varphi$ be a DPW for $\mathcal{A}_\varphi$, and let r be the run of $\mathcal{D}_\varphi$ on w. By the way we defined and have refined $\tilde{\mathcal{A}}_\varphi$ so far, the states in r can be mapped to the states of $\tilde{\mathcal{A}}_\varphi$. For example, in the first iteration, where the states of $\tilde{\mathcal{A}}_\varphi$ are subsets of states in $\mathcal{A}_\varphi$, we use the fact that each state in $\mathcal{D}_\varphi$ is associated with such a subset. We use this mapping in order to refine states of $\tilde{\mathcal{A}}_\varphi$ that are mapped to by different states along r, and update the acceptance condition of $\tilde{\mathcal{A}}_\varphi$ accordingly. See the full version for an example.

---

[4] A more precise definition of the dual setting adds to the realizability notation the parameter of "who moves first". Then, $\mathcal{A}_\varphi$ is (I/O)-realizable with the environment moving first iff $\mathcal{A}_{\neg\varphi}$ is not (O/I)-realizable with the system (that is, the player that generates signals in O) moving first. Adding this parameter is easy, yet makes the writing more cumbersome, so we give it up.

As with other counterexample-guided refinement methodologies, several heuristics concerning the choice of a counterexample are possible. Here, we also suggest heuristics for the choice of winning strategy in both $G_{\mathrm{SYN}}(\tilde{\mathcal{A}}_\varphi, I, O)$ and $G_{\mathrm{SYN}}(\tilde{\mathcal{A}}_{\neg\varphi}, O, I)$. This is where the GFGness of the nondeterministic subset construction plays a role. We say that a winning strategy for a player is *minimalistic* if for every state associated with a subset $S \subseteq 2^Q$ that she chooses, every state that is associated with a subset $S' \subset S$ is losing for her. By choosing minimalistic strategies, we avoid determinization associated with large sets, whenever possible. In fact, when $\mathcal{A}_\varphi$ is (I/O)-aware GFG, a winning strategy may coincide with the GFG strategy. In addition, in the case Player OR wins both of the games, we can consider several winning strategies, and either refine or check the induced transducer with respect to each one of them.

In the worst case, the algorithm halts when either $\tilde{\mathcal{A}}_\varphi$ or $\tilde{\mathcal{A}}_{\neg\varphi}$ is a DPW for φ or $\neg\varphi$, respectively. Thus, their size bounds the number of iterations. In each iteration, we solve two parity games, check whether a single computation satisfies φ, and optionally model-check a transducer – all these are done in less than exponential time, and so the overall time complexity is doubly exponential in $|\varphi|$, meeting the lower bound for LTL synthesis.

References

1. Abu Radi, B., Kupferman, O.: Minimizing GFG transition-based automata. In: Proceedings of 46th ICALP. LIPIcs, vol. 132 (2019)
2. Alur, R., et al.: Syntax-Guided Synthesis. IEEE (2013)
3. Bagnol, M., Kuperberg, D.: Büchi good-for-games automata are efficiently recognizable. In: Proceedings of the 38th FSTTCS. LIPIcs, vol. 132 (2018)
4. Boker, U., Kuperberg, D., Kupferman, O., Skrzypczak, M.: Nondeterminism in the presence of a diverse or unknown future. In: Fomin, F.V., Freivalds, R., Kwiatkowska, M., Peleg, D. (eds.) ICALP 2013. LNCS, vol. 7966, pp. 89–100. Springer, Heidelberg (2013). https://doi.org/10.1007/978-3-642-39212-2_11
5. Boker, U., Kupferman, O., Skrzypczak, M.: How deterministic are Good-for-Games automata? In: Proceedings of the 37th FSTTCS. LIPIcs, vol. 93 (2017)
6. Church, A.: Logic, arithmetics, and automata. In: Proceedings of International Congress of Mathematicians (1963)
7. Colcombet, T.: The theory of stabilisation monoids and regular cost functions. In: Albers, S., Marchetti-Spaccamela, A., Matias, Y., Nikoletseas, S., Thomas, W. (eds.) ICALP 2009. LNCS, vol. 5556, pp. 139–150. Springer, Heidelberg (2009). https://doi.org/10.1007/978-3-642-02930-1_12
8. Fisman, D., Lustig, Y.: A modular approach for Büchi determinization. In: Proceedings of the 26th CONCUR (2015)
9. Grädel, E., Thomas, W., Wilke, T.: Automata, Logics, and Infinite Games: A Guide to Current Research. LNCS, vol. 2500. Springer, Heidelberg (2002). https://doi.org/10.1007/3-540-36387-4
10. Greimel, K., Bloem, R., Jobstmann, B., Vardi, M.: Open implication. In: Aceto, L., Damgård, I., Goldberg, L.A., Halldórsson, M.M., Ingólfsdóttir, A., Walukiewicz, I. (eds.) ICALP 2008. LNCS, vol. 5126, pp. 361–372. Springer, Heidelberg (2008). https://doi.org/10.1007/978-3-540-70583-3_30

11. Henzinger, T.A., Piterman, N.: Solving games without determinization. In: Ésik, Z. (ed.) CSL 2006. LNCS, vol. 4207, pp. 395–410. Springer, Heidelberg (2006). https://doi.org/10.1007/11874683_26

12. Kuperberg, D., Skrzypczak, M.: On determinisation of good-for-games automata. In: Halldórsson, M.M., Iwama, K., Kobayashi, N., Speckmann, B. (eds.) ICALP 2015. LNCS, vol. 9135, pp. 299–310. Springer, Heidelberg (2015). https://doi.org/10.1007/978-3-662-47666-6_24

13. Kupferman, O., Safra, S., Vardi, M.Y.: Relating word and tree automata. Ann. Pure Appl. Logic 138(1–3), 126–146 (2006)

14. Kupferman, O., Vardi, M.Y.: Safraless decision procedures. In: Proceedings of the 46th FOCS (2005)

15. Lehtinen, K., Zimmermann, M.: Good-for-games ω-pushdown automata. In: Proceedings of the 35th LICS (2020)

16. Morgenstern, G.: Expressiveness results at the bottom of the ω-regular hierarchy. M.Sc. thesis, The Hebrew University (2003)

17. Niwiński, D., Walukiewicz, I.: Relating hierarchies of word and tree automata. In: Morvan, M., Meinel, C., Krob, D. (eds.) STACS 1998. LNCS, vol. 1373, pp. 320–331. Springer, Heidelberg (1998). https://doi.org/10.1007/BFb0028571

18. Pnueli, A., Rosner, R.: On the synthesis of a reactive module. In: Proceedings of the 16th POPL (1989)

19. Safra, S.: On the complexity of ω-automata. In: Proceedings of the 29th FOCS (1988)

20. Solar-Lezama, A.: Program synthesis by sketching. Ph.D. thesis, UC Berkeley (2008)

21. Solar-Lezama, A., Tancau, L., Bodik, R., Seshia, S.A., Saraswat, V.: Combinatorial sketching for finite programs. In: Proceedings of the 12th ASPLOS (2006)

22. Vardi, M.Y., Wolper, P.: Automata-theoretic techniques for modal logics of programs. J. Comput. Syst. Sci. 32(2), 182–221 (1986)

23. Vardi, M.Y., Wolper, P.: Reasoning about infinite computations. I&C 115(1), 1–37 (1994)

Urgent Partial Order Reduction for Extended Timed Automata

Kim G. Larsen, Marius Mikučionis, Marco Muñiz[✉], and Jiří Srba

Department of Computer Science, Aalborg University, Aalborg, Denmark
{kgl,marius,muniz,srba}@cs.aau.dk

Abstract. We propose a partial order reduction method for reachability analysis of networks of timed automata interacting via synchronous channel communication and via shared variables. Our method is based on (classical) symbolic delay transition systems and exploits the urgent behavior of a system, where time does not introduce dependencies among actions. In the presence of urgent behavior in the network, we apply partial order reduction techniques for discrete systems based on stubborn sets. We first describe the framework in the general setting of symbolic delay time transition systems and then instantiate it to the case of timed automata. We implement our approach in the model checker UPPAAL and observe a substantial reduction in the reachable state space for case studies that exhibit frequent urgent behaviour and only a moderate slowdown on models with limited occurence of urgency.

1 Introduction

Partial order reduction techniques [4] based on persistent sets [14], ample sets [22] or stubborn sets [17,27] have proved beneficial for the state space exploration of systems that exhibit high degree of concurrency. As many actions in such systems can be (in a syntax-driven manner) considered as independent, these techniques will explore only a subset of the possible interleavings of independent actions while preserving the property of the system we are interested in.

The techniques of partial order reductions for untimed system have only recently been extended to *timed* systems with indication of success. For more than two decades timed systems have resisted several partial order reduction attempts, largely caused by the fact that time introduces additional dependencies between actions that will normally be considered as independent. In [15] the authors show a potential for stubborn reductions for networks of timed automata, however using only approximate abstraction approach. A new idea of exploiting urgency in timed systems in order to facilitate efficient partial order reduction appeared in [8] in the context of timed-arc Petri nets with discrete time.

We take the idea of urgency-based [23] partial order reduction one step further and extend the method towards the case of networks of extended timed automata in the UPPAAL style, including handshake and broadcast communication primitives, communication over shared variables as well as a C-like imperative programming language allowing for complex computation over discrete

© Springer Nature Switzerland AG 2020
D. V. Hung and O. Sokolsky (Eds.): ATVA 2020, LNCS 12302, pp. 179–195, 2020.
https://doi.org/10.1007/978-3-030-59152-6_10

structured variables. Our main contribution is a partial order reduction method for urgent behavior based on the classical (zone-based) symbolic semantics for networks of timed automata and its efficient implementation in the industrial strength real-time verification tool UPPAAL. An additional challenge is to develop static analysis for the rich modeling language of UPPAAL and combine it with symbolic model checking techniques in a sound way. On a number of experiments we show the applicability of the proposed method w.r.t. state-space and time reduction.

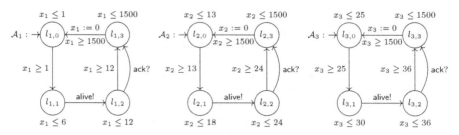

(a) Three sensors of the simplified fire alarm system

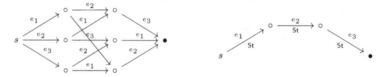

(b) Fragment of the full and reduced transition systems for the system in Figure 1a

Fig. 1. Simplified fire alarm system

Fire Alarm System Example. To illustrate the effect of our urgency-based partial order reduction technique, we consider a simplified version of an industrial fire alarm system [11]. The system uses a communication protocol based on the Time Division Multiple Access (TDMA) paradigm, and has over 100 sensors each of them assigned a unique time slot for sending and receiving messages. Figure 1a shows a down-scaled and simplified version of the system with three sensors, each modeled as a timed automaton. Each sensor has its own clock x_i, with the corresponding TDMA slot modeled by guards in ($x_i \geq 1500$) and invariants ($x_i \leq 1500$). At the end of the TDMA cycle i.e. when $x_i = 1500$ every sensor resets its clock and goes back to its initial location. Figure 1b left shows the fragment of the reachable transition system starting at the configuration $s = ((l_{1,3}, l_{2,3}, l_{3,3}), x_1 = x_2 = x_3 = 1500)$ where time progress is disabled due to the invariants $x_i \leq 1500$. The transitions are induced by the edges $e_i = \langle l_{i,3}, \tau, x_i \geq 1500, x_i = 0, l_{i,0} \rangle$. States of the form ∘ denote the so-called zero time states where time cannot progress, whereas the filled state • denotes a situation where time can delay. Figure 1b right shows the corresponding reduced transition system that contains only one interleaving sequence that allows us to reach the state where time can delay again.

Related Work. The most related work in [8] presents an urgent partial order reduction method for *discrete* time systems based on stubborn set construction [17,27]. The method is instantiated to timed-arc Petri nets and compared to our case, it does not consider discrete data structures nor any communication primitives. In our work we focus on *continuous* time systems modeled as networks of timed automata, requiring us to use symbolic transition system as the underlying semantic model. The idea of applying partial order reduction for independent events that happen at the same time also appeared in [9] however this methods is not as efficient as ours because it is static (precomputed before the state space exploration). In our approach we apply a dynamic reduction that on-the-fly identifies independent actions even in the presence of communication between the components, possibly sharing some resources.

Partial order reduction techniques applied to timed automata [2] include the early works [7,10,19] based on the notion of local and global clocks or the concept of covering as generalized dependencies. However, there is not provided any experimental evaluation of the proposed techniques. There exist also techniques based on event zones [18,21] and on merging zones from different interleaved executions [25]. These are exact techniques comparable to approximate convex-hull abstraction which is by now superseded by the exact LU-abstraction [5]. More recently, over-approximative methods based on abstracted zone graphs were also studied in [15]. The main difference is that our approach is an exact method that is applicable directly to the state-of-the-art techniques implemented in UPPAAL.

Finally, *quasi-equal clocks* [16] are clocks for which in all computations their values are equal or if one clock gets reset then a reset must urgently eventually occur also for the other clocks, assuming that resets occur periodically. Reductions using quasi-equal clocks yield exponential savings and have been used to verify a number of industrial systems. However, this approach is based on syntactic transformations and requires a method for detecting quasi-equal clocks [20]. Our approach fully automatizes reductions based on quasi-equal clocks and further generalizes to scenarios where clock resets have irregular reset periods.

2   Partial Order Reduction for Symbolic Delays

We describe the general idea of our partial order reduction technique in terms of symbolic delay transition systems. Intuitively a symbolic delay corresponds to time elapsing in the zone graph for timed automata or flow in the region graph of a hybrid system. Let A be a set of actions and δ a symbolic delay with $A \cap \{\delta\} = \emptyset$.

Definition 1 (Symbolic Delay Transition System). *A symbolic delay transition system is a tuple* $(S, s_0, \rightarrow)$ *where* S *is a set of states,* $s_0 \in S$ *is the initial state, and* $\rightarrow \subseteq S \times (A \cup \{\delta\}) \times S$ *is the transition relation.*

If $(s, \alpha, s') \in \rightarrow$ we write $s \xrightarrow{\alpha} s'$. In this paper we consider only deterministic systems: a transition system is *deterministic* if $s \xrightarrow{\alpha} s'$ and $s \xrightarrow{\alpha} s''$ implies $s' = s''$. For the rest of this section, let us assume a fixed symbolic delay transition system $(S, s_0, \rightarrow)$ and a set of goal states $G \subseteq S$.

A state $s \in S$ is *zero time* if it can not delay, denoted by $\mathsf{zt}(s)$ and defined by $\mathsf{zt}(s)$ iff $\forall s' \in S, \alpha \in A \cup \{\delta\}.\ s \xrightarrow{\alpha} s' \implies \alpha \in A$. A *reduction* is a function $\mathsf{St} : S \rightarrow 2^A$. A reduced transition relation is a relation $\underset{\mathsf{St}}{\rightarrow} \subseteq \rightarrow$ such that $s \underset{\mathsf{St}}{\xrightarrow{\alpha}} s'$ iff $s \xrightarrow{\alpha} s'$ and $\alpha \in \mathsf{St}(s) \cup \{\delta\}$. For a given state $s \in S$ we define $\overline{\mathsf{St}(s)} \overset{\text{def}}{=} A \setminus \mathsf{St}(s)$ to be the set of all actions not in $\mathsf{St}(s)$. Given a sequence of labels $w = \alpha_1 \alpha_2 \alpha_3 \ldots \alpha_n \in (A \cup \{\delta\})^*$ we write $s \xrightarrow{w} s'$ iff $s \xrightarrow{\alpha_1} \ldots \xrightarrow{\alpha_n} s'$. If a sequence w of length n is such that $s \xrightarrow{w} s'$ we also write $s \rightarrow^n s'$. The set of *enabled actions* at state $s \in S$ is $\mathsf{En}(s) \overset{\text{def}}{=} \{a \in A \mid \exists s' \in S.\ s \xrightarrow{a} s'\}$.

The *reachability problem*, given a symbolic delay transition system $(S, s_0, \rightarrow)$ and a set of goal states G, is to decide whether there is $s' \in G$ such that $s_0 \rightarrow^* s'$.

Definition 2 (Reachability Preserving Reduction). *A reduction* St *is reachability preserving if it satisfies the following conditions:*

$(\mathcal{Z})\ \forall s \in S.\ \neg\mathsf{zt}(s) \implies \mathsf{En}(s) \subseteq \mathsf{St}(s)$

$(\mathcal{D})\ \forall s, s' \in S.\ \forall w \in \overline{\mathsf{St}(s)}^*.\ \mathsf{zt}(s) \wedge s \xrightarrow{w} s' \implies \mathsf{zt}(s')$

$(\mathcal{R})\ \forall s, s' \in S.\ \forall w \in \overline{\mathsf{St}(s)}^*.\ \mathsf{zt}(s) \wedge s \xrightarrow{w} s' \wedge s \notin G \implies s' \notin G$

$(\mathcal{W})\ \forall s, s' \in S.\ \forall w \in \overline{\mathsf{St}(s)}^*.\ \forall a \in \mathsf{St}(s).\ \mathsf{zt}(s) \wedge s \xrightarrow{wa} s' \implies s \xrightarrow{aw} s'$

If a delay is possible at state s Condition $\mathcal{Z}$ will ensure that there is no reduction. Condition $\mathcal{D}$ ensures that states which can delay are preserved. Condition $\mathcal{R}$ ensures that goal states are preserved and finally Condition $\mathcal{W}$ corresponds to the classical stubborn set requirement that stubborn actions can be commuted to the beginning of the execution. The following theorem was proved in [8] for the case of timed transitions systems.

Theorem 1 (Reachability Preservation). *Let* St *be a reachability preserving reduction. Let* $s \in S$ *and* $s \rightarrow^n s'$ *for some* $s' \in G$ *then* $s \underset{\mathsf{St}}{\rightarrow}^m s''$ *for some* $s'' \in G$ *where* $m \leq n$.

3   Extended Timed Automata (XTA)

We apply our method to the theory of timed automata [2]. Our formal model is *extended timed automata* and it is an abstract representation of modeling formalism used in the tool UPPAAL [6].

Clocks and Discrete Variables. Let X be a set of *clocks*. A *clock valuation* is a function $\mu : X \rightarrow \mathbb{R}_{\geq 0}$. We use $\mathcal{V}(X)$ to denote the sets of all valuations for clocks in X. Let V be a set of *discrete variables*. The function D assigns to each variable $v \in V$ a finite domain $D(v)$. A *variable valuation* is a function $\nu : V \rightarrow \bigcup_{v \in V} D(v)$ that maps variables to values such that $\nu(v) \in D(v)$. We use $\mathcal{V}(V)$ to denote the set of all variable valuations. We let μ_0 resp. ν_0 to denote the valuation that maps every clock resp. variable to the value 0.

Expressions. We use expr to denote an expression over V. We assume that expressions are well typed and for expression expr we use $D(\text{expr})$ to denote its domain. Given a variable valuation ν and an expression expr, we use $\text{expr}^\nu \in D(\text{expr})$ to denote the value of expr under ν. We use $V(\text{expr}) \in 2^V$ to denote the set of variables in expr such that for all $v \in V(\text{expr})$ and for all $\nu, \nu' \in \mathcal{V}(V)$ if $\nu(v) = \nu'(v)$ then $\text{expr}^\nu = \text{expr}^{\nu'}$.

Constraints. The set $B(X)$ is the set of *clock constraints* generated by the grammar $\phi ::= x \bowtie \text{expr} \mid \phi_1 \wedge \phi_2$, where $x \in X$, $D(\text{expr})$ is the domain of all natural numbers $\mathbb{N}$ and $\bowtie \in \{<, \leq, \geq, >\}$. The set $B(V)$ is a set of *Boolean variable constraints* over V. The set $B(X, V)$ of constraints comprises $B(X)$, $B(V)$, and conjunctions over clock and variable constraints. Given a constraint $\phi \in B(X, V)$, we use $X(\phi)$ to denote the set of clocks in ϕ, and $V(\phi)$ to denote the set of variables in ϕ. We define the evaluation of a constraint $\phi \in B(X, V)$ as ϕ^ν where expressions in ϕ are evaluated under ν.

Updates. A *clock update* is of the form $x := \text{expr}$ where $x \in X$, and $D(\text{expr}) = \mathbb{N}$. A *variable update* is of the form $v := \text{expr}$ where $v \in V$ and $D(v) = D(\text{expr})$. The set $U(X, V)$ of *updates* contains all finite, possibly empty sequences of clock and variable updates. Given clock valuation $\mu \in \mathcal{V}(X)$, variable valuation $\nu \in \mathcal{V}(V)$, and update $r \in U(X, V)$, we use r^ν to denote the update resulting after evaluating all expressions in r under ν, we use $X(r)$ to denote the set of clocks in r, and $V(r)$ to denote the set of variables in r. We let $[\![r^\nu]\!] : \mathcal{V}(X) \cup \mathcal{V}(V) \to \mathcal{V}(X) \cup \mathcal{V}(V)$ be a map from valuations to valuations. We use $\mu[r^\nu]$ to denote the updated clock valuation $[\![r^\nu]\!](\mu)$. Analogously, for variable valuation ν', we use $\nu'[r^\nu]$ to denote the updated variable valuation $[\![r^\nu]\!](\nu')$.

Channels. Given a set C of *channels*, the set $H(C)$ of synchronizations over channels is generated by the grammar $h ::= c[\text{expr}]! \mid c[\text{expr}]? \mid \tau$, where $c \in C$, $D(\text{expr}) = \mathbb{N}$, and τ represents an internal action. Given a variable valuation ν, for synchronization h of the form $c[\text{expr}]!$ we use h^ν to denote $c[\text{expr}^\nu]!$, and similar for synchronizations of the form $c[\text{expr}]?$.

Definition 3 (Extended Timed Automata XTA). *A extended timed automaton $\mathcal{A}$ is a tuple $(L, L^u, L^c, l_0, X, V, H(C), E, I)$ where: L is a set of locations, $L^u \subseteq L$ denotes the set of urgent locations in L, $L^c \subseteq L$ denotes the set of committed locations in L and $L_u \cap L_c = \emptyset$, $l_0 \in L$ is the initial location, X is a nonempty the set of clocks, V is the set of variables, $H(C)$ is a set of channels expressions for set of channels C, $E \subseteq L \times H(C) \times B(X) \times B(V) \times U(X, V) \times L$ is a set of edges between locations with a channel expressions, a clock guard, a variable guard, an update set, and $I : L \to B(X)$ assigns clock invariants to locations.*

Definition 4 (Network of XTA). *A network $\mathcal{N}$ of XTA consists of a finite sequence $\mathcal{A}_1, \ldots, \mathcal{A}_n$ of XTA, where $\mathcal{A}_i = (L_i, L_i^u, L_i^c, l_i^0, X_i, V_i, H(C)_i, E_i, I_i)$ for $1 \leq i \leq n$. Locations are pairwise disjoint i.e. $L_i \cap L_j = \emptyset$ for $1 \leq i, j \leq n$*

and $i \neq j$. The set of locations is $L = \cup_{i=1}^{n} L_i$, analogously for urgent L^u and committed L^c locations. The set of clocks is $X = \cup_{i=1}^{n} X_i$ and the set of variables is $V = \cup_{i=1}^{n} V_i$. The set of channel expressions is $H(C) = \cup_{i=1}^{n} H(C)_i$. The set of edges is $E = \cup_{i=1}^{n} E_i$. A location vector is a vector $\boldsymbol{l} = (l_1, \ldots, l_n)$, and $\boldsymbol{l}_0 = (l_1^0, \ldots, l_n^0)$ is the initial location vector. The invariant function over location vectors is $I(\boldsymbol{l}) = \bigwedge_i I_i(l_i)$.

We write $\boldsymbol{l}[l_i'/l_i]$ to denote the vector where the i-th element l_i of $\boldsymbol{l}$ is replaced by l_i'. We write $\boldsymbol{l}^i$ to denote the i-th element of $\boldsymbol{l}$.

Zones. We assume the canonical satisfaction relation "$\models$" between valuations and constraints in $B(X)$ and $B(V)$. The set $B^+(X)$ of *extended clock constraints* is generated by the grammar $\phi ::= x \bowtie c \mid \phi_1 \wedge \phi_2 \mid x - y \bowtie c$, where $x, y \in X$, $c \in \mathbb{N}$ and $\bowtie \in \{<, \leq, \geq, >\}$. A *zone* $\llbracket Z \rrbracket$ is a set of clock valuations described by an extended clock constraint $Z \in B^+(X)$ where $\llbracket Z \rrbracket \stackrel{\text{def}}{=} \{\mu \in \mathcal{V}(X) \mid \mu \models Z\}$. When it is clear from the context, we use Z and $\llbracket Z \rrbracket$ interchangeably. We define $Z^\uparrow \stackrel{\text{def}}{=} \{\mu + d \mid \mu \in Z, d \in \mathbb{R}_{\geq 0}\}$, where for $d \in \mathbb{R}_{\geq 0}$, $\mu + d$ maps each clock $x \in X$ to the value $\mu(x) + d$. For zone Z and update r we define $Z[r] \stackrel{\text{def}}{=} \{\mu[r] \mid \mu \in Z\}$.

For timed automata we consider the set of actions $A = 2^E$ that corresponds to the discrete transitions induced by the edges E, and δ is the delay action induced by non-zero delay transitions. We can now define the symbolic semantics of networks of timed automata in terms of a zone graph (see e.g. [1]).

Definition 5 (Semantics of a Network of XTA). *Let $\mathcal{N} = \mathcal{A}_1, \ldots, \mathcal{A}_n$ be a network of TA. Its semantics is defined as a symbolic delay transition system (zone graph) $(S, s_0, \rightarrow)$, where $S \subseteq (L_i \times \cdots \times L_n) \times B^+(X) \times \mathcal{V}(V)$ is the set of states comprising a location vector, a zone, and a variable valuation, $s_0 = (\boldsymbol{l}_0, \{\mu_0\}, \nu_0)$ is the initial state, and $\rightarrow \subseteq S \times (A \cup \{\delta\}) \times S$ is the transition relation defined by:*

- *delay transition, $(\boldsymbol{l}, Z, \nu) \xrightarrow{\delta} (\boldsymbol{l}, Z^\uparrow \wedge I(\boldsymbol{l})^\nu, \nu)$ if $\boldsymbol{l}^i \notin L_i^u \cup L_i^c$ for $1 \leq i \leq n$, and $\exists \mu \in Z, d \in \mathbb{R}_{\geq 0}. d > 0 \wedge \mu + d \models I(\boldsymbol{l})^\nu$,*

- *internal transition, $(\boldsymbol{l}, Z, \nu) \xrightarrow{\{e_i\}} (\boldsymbol{l}[l_i'/l_i], Z', \nu')$ if $e_i = (l_i, \tau, \phi, \psi, r, l_i') \in E_i$ s.t. $Z' = (Z \wedge I(\boldsymbol{l})^\nu \wedge \phi^\nu)[r^\nu] \wedge I(\boldsymbol{l}[l_i'/l_i])^{\nu'}$, where $Z' \neq \emptyset$, $\nu' = \nu[r^\nu]$, $\nu \models \psi^\nu$, and if $\boldsymbol{l}^k \in L_k^c$ for some $1 \leq k \leq n$ then $l_i \in L_i^c$,*

- *handshake transition, $(\boldsymbol{l}, Z, \nu) \xrightarrow{\{e_i, e_j\}} (\boldsymbol{l}[l_j'/l_j, l_i'/l_i], Z', \nu')$ if there exists $e_i = (l_i, h_i!, \phi_i, \psi_i, r_i, l_i') \in E_i$ and $e_j = (l_j, h_j?, \phi_j, \psi_j, r_j, l_j') \in E_j$ s.t. $h_i^\nu = h_j^\nu$, and $Z' = (Z \wedge I(\boldsymbol{l})^\nu \wedge \phi_i^\nu \wedge \phi_j^\nu)[r_i^\nu][r_j^\nu] \wedge I(\boldsymbol{l}[l_j'/l_j, l_i'/l_i])^{\nu'}$, where $Z' \neq \emptyset$, $\nu \models (\psi_i^\nu \wedge \psi_j^\nu)$, $\nu' = \nu[r_i^\nu][r_j^\nu]$, and if $\boldsymbol{l}^k \in L_k^c$ for some $1 \leq k \leq n$ then $l_i \in L_i^c$ or $l_j \in L_j^c$.*

In the following, we are given a network of TA $\mathcal{N} = \mathcal{A}_1, \ldots, \mathcal{A}_n$ with locations L, clocks X, variables V, and induced symbolic transition system $(S, s_0, \rightarrow)$.

Definition 6 (Properties). *A formula is given by the grammar $\phi ::= \text{deadlock} \mid l \mid x \bowtie c \mid \psi_v \mid \phi_1 \wedge \phi_2$, where $l \in L$, $x \in X$, $\bowtie \in \{<, \leq, \geq, >\}$,*

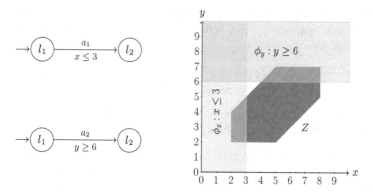

Fig. 2. Two components with actions a_1 and a_2. Actions are enabled at zone Z. Note that executing a_1 will disable a_2 and vice versa.

$c \in \mathbb{N}$, and ψ_v is a Boolean constraint for $v \in V$. Let $(l, Z, \nu) \in S$ be a state. The satisfaction of a formula is inductively defined as follows:

$$
\begin{aligned}
(l, Z, \nu) &\models \text{deadlock} && \text{iff } \exists \mu \in Z, \forall d \in \mathbb{R}_{\geq 0}.\mathsf{En}((l, \{\mu + d\}, \nu)) = \emptyset \\
(l, Z, \nu) &\models l && \text{iff } l^i = l \text{ for some } i \text{ with } 1 \leq i \leq n \\
(l, Z, \nu) &\models x \bowtie c && \text{iff } \exists \mu \in Z. \ \mu \models x \bowtie c \\
(l, Z, \nu) &\models \psi_v && \text{iff } \nu \models \psi_v \\
(l, Z, \nu) &\models \phi \wedge \psi && \text{iff } (l, Z, \nu) \models \phi \text{ and } (l, Z, \nu) \models \psi
\end{aligned}
$$

A network satisfies ϕ iff its initial state can reach a state that satisfies ϕ.

4 Reachability Preserving Reduction for XTA

In this section we provide syntactic based sound approximations for all the elements required by our technique. In Subsect. 4.1 we give a semantic definition for independence of actions, then we describe a syntactic independence relation. In Subsect. 4.2 we identify the relevant actions which need to be included in the stubborn set to preserve states which can delay. Finally, in Subsect. 4.3 we describe the stubborn sets for preserving goal states. For the rest of this section we are given a network $\mathcal{N} = \mathcal{A}_1, \ldots, \mathcal{A}_n$, with edges E and components $\mathcal{A}_i = (L_i, L_i^u, L_i^c, l_{i_0}, X_i, V_i, H(C)_i, E_i, I_i)$, the corresponding transition system $(S, s_0, \rightarrow)$ with actions $A = 2^E$, and state $s = (l, Z, \nu)$.

4.1 Independence for Actions

The notion of *independence of actions* plays a key role in partial order reduction. Intuitively two actions are independent if they can not disable each other and they commute.

Definition 7 (Independence of Actions). *An* independence *relation for state* $s \in S$ *is a symmetric, anti-reflexive relation* $\leftrightsquigarrow_s \subseteq A \times A$ *satisfying the following conditions for each* $(a_1, a_2) \in \leftrightsquigarrow_s$:

1. $\forall s' \in S.\ s \xrightarrow{a_1} s' \wedge a_2 \in \mathsf{En}(s) \implies a_2 \in \mathsf{En}(s')$
2. $a_1 \in \mathsf{En}(s) \wedge a_2 \in \mathsf{En}(s) \implies \exists s' \in S.\ s \xrightarrow{a_1 a_2} s' \wedge s \xrightarrow{a_2 a_1} s'$

If $(a_1, a_2) \in \leftrightsquigarrow_s$ *they are* independent *at* s *denoted by* $a_1 \leftrightsquigarrow_s a_2$. *Otherwise they are* dependent *at* s *denoted by* $a_1 \rightsquigarrow_s a_2$.

In what follows we will provide a syntactic independence relation on actions. Toward this goal, first we define operations on actions and we define a syntactic independence relation on operations.

Additional Notation. For a given edge $e = (l, h, \phi, \psi, r, l') \in E$ we use $src(e)$, $dst(e)$ to denote the source location l and the destination location l' of edge e. Given actions $a, a' \in A$, for action a we define its *preset* as $\mathsf{Pre}(a) \overset{\text{def}}{=} \{src(e) \in L \mid e \in a\}$, and its *poset* as $\mathsf{Post}(a) \overset{\text{def}}{=} \{dst(e) \in L \mid e \in a\}$. We use $\mathsf{Active}(a) \overset{\text{def}}{=} \{\mathcal{A}_i \mid \mathcal{A}_i \text{ is in } \mathcal{N} \text{ and } \exists l \in \mathsf{Pre}(a).\ l \in L_i\}$ to denote the active components for a. We use $\mathsf{Parallel}(a, a') \overset{\text{def}}{=} \mathsf{Active}(a) \cap \mathsf{Active}(a') = \emptyset$ to denote that actions a and a' correspond to different components. For convenience we define *Operations for Actions in TA*. The set of all operations is the set containing all constraints and resets i.e. Op is the power set of $B(X, V) \cup U(X, V)$. The set of *operations* for action $a \in A$ is given by, $\mathsf{Op}(a) \overset{\text{def}}{=} \mathsf{Guard}(a) \cup \mathsf{Update}(a)$. Where the set of guards is $\mathsf{Guard}(a) \overset{\text{def}}{=} \bigcup \{\phi \wedge \psi \wedge I(l) \wedge I(l') \mid (l, h, \phi, \psi, r, l') \in a\}$, and the set of updates is $\mathsf{Update}(a) \overset{\text{def}}{=} \bigcup \{r \mid (l, h, \phi, \psi, r, l') \in a\}$. Given an operation $\mathsf{op} \in \mathsf{Op}$, the set of variables which op increments is given by $\mathsf{Inc}(\mathsf{op}) = \{v \in V(\mathsf{op}) | \exists r \in \mathsf{op} \text{ and } r \text{ includes } v := v + 1 \text{ with } D(v) = \mathbb{N}\}$. Analogously the set $\mathsf{Dec}(\mathsf{op})$ contains the variables which op decrements $\mathsf{Dec}(\mathsf{op}) = \{v \in V(\mathsf{op}) | \exists r \in \mathsf{op} \text{ and } r \text{ includes } v := v - 1 \text{ with } D(v) = \mathbb{N}\}$. The clocks and variables the operation writes is given by $\mathsf{Write}(\mathsf{op}) \overset{\text{def}}{=} \bigcup_{r \in \mathsf{op}'} \{xv \mid r \in U(X, V) \text{ and } xv := \mathsf{expr} \text{ is in } r\}$, where op' is obtained from op by removing increment and decrement updates, formally $\mathsf{op}' = \mathsf{op} \setminus \{xv := \mathsf{expr} \in \mathsf{op} \mid \mathsf{expr} \text{ is of the form } xv + 1 \text{ or } xv - 1\}$ The set $\mathsf{Readleq}(\mathsf{op}) = \{xv \in X \cup V \mid xv \leq \mathsf{expr} \in \mathsf{op} \text{ or } xv < \mathsf{expr} \in \mathsf{op}\}$ is the set containing clock and variables which appear in less and equal comparisons. Analogously the set $\mathsf{Readgeq}(\mathsf{op})$ contains clock and variables which appear in greater and equal comparisons in op. The clocks and variables the operation reads is given by $\mathsf{Read}(\mathsf{op}) \overset{\text{def}}{=} X(\mathsf{op}') \cup V(\mathsf{op}')$ where op' is obtained from op by removing less (greater) and equal comparisons, formally $\mathsf{op}' = \mathsf{op} \setminus \{xv \bowtie \mathsf{expr} \in \mathsf{op} \mid \bowtie \in \{<, >, \geq\}\}$. Note that given a zone, a clock constraint can modify (write to) other clocks. Finally $\Gamma_x(Z) \overset{\text{def}}{=} \{\mu(x) \mid \mu \in Z\}$ is the set of real values for clock x in zone Z.

Definition 8 (Independence of Operations). *Given operations* $\mathsf{op}_1, \mathsf{op}_2 \in \mathsf{Op}$ *and state* s, *operation* op_1 *is independent of operation* op_2 *at* s *denoted by*

$\mathsf{op}_1 \not\rightsquigarrow_s^\sharp \mathsf{op}_2$ *iff the following hold:*
(1) $\mathsf{Read}(\mathsf{op}_1) \cap (\mathsf{Write}(\mathsf{op}_2) \cup \mathsf{Inc}(\mathsf{op}_2) \cup \mathsf{Dec}(\mathsf{op}_2)) = \emptyset$
(2) $\mathsf{Readleq}(\mathsf{op}_1) \cap (\mathsf{Write}(\mathsf{op}_2) \cup \mathsf{Inc}(\mathsf{op}_2)) = \emptyset$
(3) $\mathsf{Readgeq}(\mathsf{op}_1) \cap (\mathsf{Write}(\mathsf{op}_2) \cup \mathsf{Dec}(\mathsf{op}_2)) = \emptyset$
(4) $\mathsf{Write}(\mathsf{op}_1) \cap (\mathsf{Write}(\mathsf{op}_2) \cup \mathsf{Inc}(\mathsf{op}_2) \cup \mathsf{Dec}(\mathsf{op}_2)) = \emptyset$
(5) $\mathsf{Inc}(\mathsf{op}_1) \cap (\mathsf{Write}(\mathsf{op}_2) \cup \mathsf{Dec}(\mathsf{op}_2)) = \emptyset$
(6) $\mathsf{Dec}(\mathsf{op}_1) \cap (\mathsf{Write}(\mathsf{op}_2) \cup \mathsf{Inc}(\mathsf{op}_2)) = \emptyset$
(7) $\{x \mid x \in X(\mathsf{op}_1) \cup X(\mathsf{op}_2) \text{ and } |\Gamma_x(Z)| \neq 1 \text{ and } \mathsf{op}_1, \mathsf{op}_2 \in B(X, V)\} = \emptyset$
If $\mathsf{op}_1 \not\rightsquigarrow_s^\sharp \mathsf{op}_2$ *and* $\mathsf{op}_2 \not\rightsquigarrow_s^\sharp \mathsf{op}_1$ *the we write* $\mathsf{op}_1 \not\leftrightsquigarrow_s^\sharp \mathsf{op}_2$ *and say that* op_1 *and* op_2 *are independent at s. We write* $\mathsf{op}_1 \leftrightsquigarrow_s^\sharp \mathsf{op}_2$ *iff* op_1 *and* op_2 *are dependent.*

Intuitively two operations are independent if they read and write in different variables, note that increments and decrements are treated specially. Additionally for timed automata we need to consider that applying a guard affects a number of clocks. As an example consider Fig. 2, we have that $Z \cap \phi_x \neq \emptyset$ and $Z \cap \phi_y \neq \emptyset$. However, if we apply ϕ_x we have that $(Z \cap \phi_x) \cap \phi_y = \emptyset$ this will cause the corresponding actions to disable each other. Condition (7) is not satisfied for clocks x or y in zone Z. Therefore we have $\phi_x \leftrightsquigarrow_s^\sharp \phi_y$. Note that Condition (7) is rather strong, since only zones which are lines or points will satisfy it (which is often the case in urgent states), relaxing this condition is subject of future work. Given two independent operations, we can conclude with a number of rules which are useful for showing that two actions do not disable each other and commute in extended timed automata.

Lemma 1. *Given state* $s = (l, Z, \nu)$*, constraints* $\phi, \phi' \in B(X)$*, update* $r \in U(X)$*, and variable valuations* $\nu, \nu_1 \in \mathcal{V}(V)$*. The following hold:*
(1) *if* $\phi \not\rightsquigarrow_s^\sharp r$ *then* $[\![(Z \wedge \phi^\nu)[r^\nu]]\!] = [\![Z[r^\nu] \wedge \phi^\nu]\!]$
(2) *if* $[\![(Z \wedge \phi^\nu)[r^\nu] \wedge \phi^\nu]\!] \neq \emptyset$ *then* $[\![(Z \wedge \phi^\nu)[r^\nu] \wedge \phi^\nu]\!] = [\![(Z \wedge \phi^\nu)[r^\nu]]\!]$
(3) *if* $\phi \not\rightsquigarrow_s^\sharp \phi'$ *and* $\mu \in [\![Z \wedge (\phi')^\nu]\!]$ *and* $[\![Z \wedge \phi^{\nu_1}]\!] \neq \emptyset$ *then* $\mu \in [\![(Z \wedge (\phi')^{\nu_1})]\!]$
(4) *if* $\forall x \in X(\phi).|\Gamma_x(Z)| = 1$ *and* $[\![Z \wedge \phi^\nu]\!] \neq \emptyset$ *and* $[\![Z \wedge \phi^{\nu_1}]\!] \neq \emptyset$ *then*
$[\![Z \wedge \phi^\nu]\!] = [\![Z \wedge \phi^{\nu_1}]\!]$

Lemma 1 (1) states that if a reset is independent of a constraint then the reset does not affect the constraint. Lemma 1 (2) does not require independent operations, in our proofs it is used to remove redundant application of invariants from components which are not involved in transitions. Lemma 1 (3) implicitly uses Condition (7) from Definition 8 to show that a valuation satisfying a guard is preserved after applying another guard. Lemma 1 (4) states that if a guard ϕ has been updated (via increment or decrement which in our case always produce a "bigger" constraint), then because of the shape of the zone the intersections will produce the same set.

Definition 9 (Syntactic Independence of Actions). *Given a state* $s = (l, Z, \nu)$ *with* $l = (l_1, \ldots, l_n)$ *and two actions* $a_1, a_2 \in A_s^\sharp$*. Actions* a_1 *and* a_2 *are syntactically independent at state s denoted by* $a_1 \not\leftrightsquigarrow_s^\sharp a_2$ *if and only if the*

following conditions hold:
(Ind1) $\mathsf{Pre}(a_1) \cap \mathsf{Pre}(a_2) = \emptyset$
(Ind2) $\exists l \in F(a_1). l \in L^c \iff \exists l \in F(a_2). l \in L^c$ for $F \in \{\mathsf{Pre}, \mathsf{Post}\}$.
(Ind3) $\forall op_1 \in \mathsf{Op}(a_1), op_2 \in \mathsf{Op}(a_2). op_1 \leadsto\!\!\!\!/\,_s^\sharp op_2$
(Ind4) $\forall i \in \{1,2\}, op \in \mathsf{Op}(a_i), j \in \{1, \ldots, n\}. l^j \notin \mathsf{Pre}(a_i) \implies op \leadsto\!\!\!\!/\,_s^\sharp I(l^j)$

Condition (Ind1) ensures that the source locations for the actions are disjoint. Condition (Ind2) takes into account the semantics of committed locations and prevents actions from disabling each other. Condition (Ind3) ensures that all the operations on the actions are independent. Finally Condition (Ind4) ensures that the operations in actions a_i for $i \in \{1,2\}$ do not modify the invariant of other components which could disable action a_{3-i}. When these syntactic conditions are satisfied we have the following theorem.

Theorem 2. *Given a zero time state* $s \in S$ *and two actions* $a_1, a_2 \in A_s^\sharp$. *If* $a_1 \leadsto\!\!\!\!/\,_s^\sharp a_2$ *then* $a_1 \leadsto\!\!\!\!/\,_s a_2$.

Our analysis uses the current state $s = (l, Z, \nu)$ to conclude if two actions are independent at s. In particular we use the zone Z in Definition 8 Condition (7) to detect clock constraint dependencies. Due to this condition we can make assumptions about the shape of the zone Z which allow us to conclude that if the actions were syntactically independent at s then so they are in states reachable via independent actions.

Corollary 1. *Given state* s, *action* $a \in A_s^\sharp$, *and* $A' = \{a' \in A_s^\sharp \mid a \leadsto_s^\sharp a'\}$. *Then* $\forall s' \in S.a' \in (A_s^\sharp \setminus A'), w \in (A_s^\sharp \setminus A')^*. \mathsf{zt}(s) \wedge s \xrightarrow{w} s' \xrightarrow{a'} s'' \implies a \leadsto\!\!\!\!/\,_{s'}^\sharp a'$.

4.2 Preserving Non-zero Time States

In order to satisfy Condition $\mathcal{D}$ from Definition 2, which ensures that the reduction preserves states that can delay, we need to include particular actions to the stubborn set. In XTA time can not elapse at an urgent (committed) location or if invariant is stopping time.

Definition 10 (Time Enabling Action). *An action* $a \in A$ *is a time enabling action at zero time state* $s = (l, Z, \nu)$ *if executing a may cause time to elapse. Formally* $\mathsf{tea}^\sharp(a, s)$ *iff* $(\exists l \in \mathsf{Pre}(a). l \in L^u \cup L^c) \bigvee (\forall \mu \in Z, d \in \mathbb{R}_{\geq 0}. \mu + d \models I(l) \implies d = 0)$.

Consider again Fig. 1a and the zero time state $s = ((l_{1,3}, l_{2,3}, l_{3,3}), x_1 = x_2 = x_3 = 1500)$ and actions $a_i = \{(l_{i,3}, \tau, x_i \geq 1500, x_i = 0, l_{i,0})\}$. The actions are time enabling actions i.e. $\mathsf{tea}^\sharp(a_i, s)$ for $i \in \{1, 2, 3\}$. Note that as long as a time enabling action is enabled, time can not elapse. Thus executing independent actions can not cause time to progress.

Lemma 2. *Let* $s \in S$, $a \in \mathsf{En}(s)$ *with* $\mathsf{tea}^\sharp(a, s)$ *and* $Delay_s^\sharp \overset{def}{=} \{a\} \cup \{a' \in A_s^\sharp \mid a \leadsto_s^\sharp a'\}$. *Then* $\forall s' \in S, w \in (A_s^\sharp \setminus Delay_s^\sharp)^*. s \xrightarrow{w} s' \wedge \mathsf{zt}(s) \implies \mathsf{zt}(s')$.

4.3 Preserving Goal States

In order to satisfy Condition $\mathcal{R}$ from Definition 2, which ensures that the reduction preserves goal states, we need to include actions whose execution is necessary to reach a goal state.

Definition 11 (Interesting Actions for Properties). *For formula φ and state s such that $s \not\models \varphi$. The set $\varphi_s^\sharp \subseteq A_s^\sharp$ is defined recursively based on the structure of φ as given by the following table:*

Formula φ	$\varphi_s^\sharp$
l	$\{a \in A_s^\sharp \mid l \in \mathsf{Post}(a)\}$
deadlock	$pick\ a \in \mathsf{En}(s)\ then\ \{a\} \cup$ $\{a' \in A_s^\sharp \mid (\mathsf{Pre}(a) \cap \mathsf{Pre}(a') \neq \emptyset) \vee (\mathsf{Parallel}(a, a') \wedge a \leftrightsquigarrow_s^\sharp a'\}$
$x \bowtie c$	$\{a \in A_s^\sharp \mid \exists op \in \mathsf{Update}(a).\ x \bowtie c \leftrightsquigarrow_s^\sharp op\}$
$\varphi_v\ for\ v \in V$	$\{a \in A_s^\sharp \mid \exists op \in \mathsf{Op}(a).\ \varphi_v \leftrightsquigarrow_s^\sharp op\}$
$\varphi_1 \wedge \varphi_2$	$(\varphi_i)_s^\sharp\ for\ some\ i \in \{1, 2\}\ where\ s \not\models \varphi_i$

Lemma 3. *Given a state s, a formula φ, and the set $\varphi_s^\sharp$. Then $\forall s' \in S, w \in (A_s^\sharp \setminus \varphi_s^\sharp)^*.\ s \xrightarrow{w} s' \wedge \mathsf{zt}(s) \wedge s \not\models \varphi \implies s' \not\models \varphi.$*

5 Computing Stubborn Sets in UPPAAL

We shall first provide a high level algorithm to compute a reachability preserving reduction for networks of timed automata and then discuss details related to the implementation of our technique in the model checker UPPAAL.

5.1 Algorithm

Assume a given network of XTA and reachability formula φ. During the reachability analysis, we repeatedly use Algorithm 1 at every generated state s to compute a reduction $\mathsf{St}^\sharp$ that satisfies the conditions from Definition 2. At Line 1, we output $\mathsf{En}(s)$ should the state s be non-zero time state, thus satisfying Condition $\mathcal{Z}$. Line 3 includes all actions that are relevant for the preservation of the reachability of states that can delay or belong to the goal states. Together with Lemma 2 and Lemma 3 this ensures that Condition $\mathcal{D}$ and Condition $\mathcal{R}$ are satisfied. Finally, the while loop starting at Line 5 ensures Condition $\mathcal{W}$. The while loop considers an action $a \in \mathsf{St}_s^\sharp$, if this action is not enabled then it will include all necessary actions which can enable it. This is done by adding actions which modify the location vector at Line 11, or by adding actions which modify the guards in a at Line 14. In the case where action a is enabled then the for loop at Line 16 includes all actions that are not independent with a.

Additionally, note that the set $A_s^\sharp$ is finite and in each iteration the size of $\mathsf{St}_s^\sharp$ can only increase because the only operation applied to $\mathsf{St}_s^\sharp$ is union. In the worst case we have $\mathsf{St}_s^\sharp = A_s^\sharp$ and hence the algorithm terminates.

Theorem 3 (Total Correctness). *Let $\mathcal{N}$ be a network of XTA and φ a formula. Algorithm 1 terminates and $\mathsf{St}^\sharp$ is a reachability preserving reduction where $\mathsf{St}^\sharp(s)$ is the output of Algorithm 1 for every state $s \in S$.*

Algorithm 1. Computing conditional stubborn sets

Input Network $\mathcal{A}_1, \ldots, \mathcal{A}_n$, state $s = (l, Z, \nu)$, and formula φ.
Output Conditional stubborn set $\mathsf{St}_s^\sharp$

1: **if** $\neg\mathsf{zt}(s)$ **then return** $\mathsf{En}(s)$;
2: compute $A_s^\sharp$ and $\varphi_s^\sharp$;
3: **if** $\forall a \in \varphi_s^\sharp.\ \neg\mathsf{tea}^\sharp(a, s)$ **then** pick $a \in \mathsf{En}(s)$ with $\mathsf{tea}^\sharp(a, s)$; $\varphi^\sharp := \varphi^\sharp \cup \{a\}$;
4: $W := \varphi_s^\sharp$; $R := A_s^\sharp$; $\mathsf{St}_s^\sharp := W$
5: **while** $W \neq \emptyset$ and $\mathsf{En}(s) \cap \mathsf{St}_s^\sharp \neq \mathsf{En}(s)$ **do**
6:     Pick $a \in W$; $W := W \setminus \{a\}$; $\mathsf{St}_s^\sharp := \mathsf{St}_s^\sharp \cup \{a\}$; $R := R \setminus \{a\}$;
7:     **if** $a \notin \mathsf{En}(s)$ **then**
8:         **for all** $e \in a$ **do**
9:             **if** $src(e)$ is not in l **then**
10:                 **for all** $a' \in R$ **do**
11:                     **if** $src(e) \in \mathsf{Post}(a')$ **then** $W := W \cup \{a'\}$;
12:                 **if** exists $g \in \mathsf{Guard}(\{e\})$ such that $s \not\models g$ **then**
13:                     **for all** $a' \in R$ **do**
14:                         **if** $\exists r \in \mathsf{Update}(a').\ g \leadsto_s^\sharp r$ **then** $W := W \cup \{a'\}$;
15:     **if** $a \in \mathsf{En}(s)$ **then**
16:         **for all** $a' \in R$ **do**
17:             **if** $(\mathsf{Pre}(a) \cap \mathsf{Pre}(a') \neq \emptyset) \vee (\mathsf{Parallel}(a, a') \wedge a \leadsto_s^\sharp a')$ **then**
18:                 $W := W \cup \{a'\}$;
19: **return** $\mathsf{St}_s^\sharp$;

5.2 Implementation Details

Algorithm 1 is inserted as a state successor filter after the state successors are computed. This filter passes through only the states that are the result of stubborn actions. To improve the efficiency, the stubborn set is computed only when the origin state is urgent and has more than one successor, otherwise the filter just forwards all successors without any reduction. In the following we describe a number of optimizations that we included in our implementation.

Reachable Actions. In previous sections we have defined $A = 2^E$, as the set of actions. This set is unnecessary large and unpractical. The set of *reachable actions* from s can be semantically defined as $A_s \stackrel{\text{def}}{=} \{a \in A \mid \exists s', s'' \in S, w \in A^*.\ s \xrightarrow{w} s' \xrightarrow{a} s''\}$. Our goal is to compute the smallest set $A_s^\sharp$ such that $A_s \subseteq A_s^\sharp \subseteq A$. Computing a small set has the advantage that potentially less dependencies are introduced, additionally it will reduce the computation time of stubborn sets. We implemented a static analysis in order to compute the set $A_s^\sharp$. Our analysis exploits the fact that time can not elapse at a state s, and thus actions that require a delay to become enabled need not be included in $A_s^\sharp$. For the performance sake, the approximation $A_s^\sharp$ is computed in two steps. The first step is prior to state exploration and is only executed once. In this step for each edge we compute the set of edges it can reach without doing a delay operation. The starting edge is assumed to be enabled and thus we start with all possible clock assignments in conjunction with the source invariant. If clocks are compared against constants, we add the constraints. Otherwise, if integer variables appear on the guards, we relax (loose) all the information on the affected clock. The second step is executed at every urgent state and it is done by using precomputed data structures from the previous step that collect for every enabled edge the set of edges it can reach and then composes them into actions.

Broadcast Channels. Many UPPAAL models use broadcast channels, however the set of possible broadcast synchronizations is exponentially large in terms of the number of potential receivers (in contrast to linear complexity of handshake synchronizations) and hence untenable for larger networks. Instead of computing all possible synchronizations, we compute one super-action for each broadcast sending edge, combining all potential receiving edges from other processes—this serves as a safe over-approximation. Such combined treatment avoids exponential blowup of broadcast actions at the cost of overly-conservative dependency checks, which considers a super-set of associated variables instead of precise sets involving a particular subset of receiving edges. In addition to broadcast synchronizations, the static analysis also supports arrays and C-like structures by expanding them into individual variables. Array indices, references and functions calls are over-approximated by using the ranges from variable types.

Precomputed Data Structures. To make our implementation fast, we precompute a number of data structures required by our technique. Examples include, edges leading to locations, some property base sets, reachable edges from locations. In particular, in order to compute the dependence between actions, the associated variable sets are also precomputed in advance for each action. These variable sets are then used to construct a dependency matrix over all reachable actions, thus making the action dependency check a constant-time lookup during verification.

6   Experiments

Table 1 shows the results of our POR implementation applied on a number of industrial case studies[1]. The experiments were run on a cluster with AMD EPYC 7551 processor with the timeout of 10 h (and 15GB of RAM) for all models except for SecureRideSharing where the timeout was 48 h (and 200 GB of RAM). The model instances are suffixed with a number indicating the increasing amount of parallel components (sensors and the like).

FireAlarm is a simplified version of IndustFireAlarm [11] for the communication protocol of a wireless sensor network from German Company SeCa GmbH as described in Sect. 1. The AGless300 corresponds to a requirement from EN-54 standard that a sensor failure is reported in less than 300 s. A stricter property AGless100 is added to evaluate the performance when a property does not hold.

---

[1] Reproducibility package https://github.com/DEIS-Tools/upor.

Table 1. Experimental results. Satisfiability results agree for all queries. Queries with * were not satisfied. The reduction is the ratio of performance without POR and with POR. OOM indicates out of memory.

Model	Query	Without POR		With POR		Reduction ratio	
		States	Time s	States	Time s	States	Time
FireAlarm4	AGnotdeadlock	27	<0.01	22	<0.01	1.23	–
FireAlarm20	AGnotdeadlock	1048635	148.41	270	0.01	3883.83	14841
FireAlarm100	AGnotdeadlock	–	OOM	5350	5.18	–	–
IndustFireAlarm13	AGless100*	931496	97.57	24296	2.81	38.34	34.72
IndustFireAlarm15	AGless100*	3684136	571.75	27672	3.84	133.14	148.89
IndustFireAlarm17	AGless100*	14694312	2884.18	31496	5.09	466.55	566.64
IndustFireAlarm19	AGless100*	58734632	15878.47	35768	7.20	1642.1	2205.34
IndustFireAlarm30	AGless100*	–	OOM	67272	27.92	–	–
IndustFireAlarm100	AGless100*	–	OOM	585272	2753.54	–	–
IndustFireAlarm13	AGless300	3731370	439.50	102570	12.73	36.38	34.52
IndustFireAlarm15	AGless300	14742718	2570.36	116862	17.69	126.15	145.30
IndustFireAlarm17	AGless300	58784210	12833.69	132946	23.15	442.17	554.37
IndustFireAlarm19	AGless300	–	OOM	150822	32.83	–	–
IndustFireAlarm30	AGless300	–	OOM	281172	128.08	–	–
IndustFireAlarm100	AGless300	–	OOM	2380752	12715.08	–	–
IndustFireAlarm13	AGnotdeadlock	3731320	388.63	63618	4.96	58.65	78.35
IndustFireAlarm15	AGnotdeadlock	14742668	2215.16	65654	5.68	224.55	389.99
IndustFireAlarm17	AGnotdeadlock	58784160	11202.80	67818	6.47	866.79	1731.50
IndustFireAlarm19	AGnotdeadlock	–	OOM	70110	8.00	–	–
IndustFireAlarm30	AGnotdeadlock	–	OOM	85004	17.85	–	–
IndustFireAlarm100	AGnotdeadlock	–	OOM	270504	530.46	–	–
SecureRideSharing6	AGlessMaxFail	200141	2.23	200141	5.60	1	0.40
SecureRideSharing7	AGlessMaxFail	7223770	95.60	7223770	252.61	1	0.38
SecureRideSharing8	AGlessMaxFail*	85622469	1467.49	85622469	3691.46	1	0.40
SecureRideSharing9	AGlessMaxFail*	1961298623	43548.8	1961298623	106223.46	1	0.41
SecureRideSharing6	AGnotdeadlock	200141	3.05	184973	6.3	1.08	0.48
SecureRideSharing7	AGnotdeadlock	7223770	122.29	2428033	93.21	2.98	1.31
SecureRideSharing8	AGnotdeadlock	97539581	2058.40	39387328	1845.46	2.48	1.12
SecureRideSharing9	AGnotdeadlock	–	OOM	944892374	55481.09	–	–
TTAC4	AGnotdeadlock	12213203	308.40	11414483	379.51	1.07	0.81
TTAC5	AGnotdeadlock	217259289	6724.25	204152089	8679.56	1.06	0.77
TTPA6	AGnotdeadlock	668421	27.30	668421	55.82	1	0.49
TTPA7	AGnotdeadlock	3329080	166.34	3329080	337.06	1	0.49
TTPA8	AGnotdeadlock	18073077	1096.79	18073077	2229.04	1	0.49
FB14	AGnotdeadlock	98310	138.22	98310	139.5	1	0.99
FB15	AGnotdeadlock	196614	698.54	196614	702.61	1	0.99
FB16	AGnotdeadlock	393222	2794.58	393222	2788.83	1	1

Results show exponentially increasing savings in both number of states and computation time.

The SecureRideSharing models a fault-tolerant, duplicate-sensitive aggregation protocol for wireless sensor networks [3,12]. This case study did not show reductions until special treatment for broadcast synchronizations and variable increments was implemented. The AGnotdeadlock property shows substantial reductions, and one instance times out when POR is not used, however for the

AGlessMaxFail query the state space is not reducible and the verification time is more than doubled due to variables reverenced in the query.

The TTAC models a Timed Triggered Architecture protocol [13] used in drive-by-wire vehicles. The TTPA models a Time-Triggered Protocol for SAE class A sensor/actuator networks [26]. The model FB models the Field Buss scheduling protocol [24]. These case studies were selected as they do not allow for any state space reduction, thus allowing us to observe the time-overhead of our method. This overhead varies from almost no overhead for the FB models to twice as slow for the TTPA models.

7   Conclusion

We presented an application of partial order reduction based on stubborn sets to the model of network of timed automata in the UPPAAL style, including a detailed analysis of both clock and discrete variable dependencies among the different components. The method allows us to reduce the state space in the situations where a sequence of mutually independent actions is performed while the network is in an urgent configuration where time cannot elapse (caused by the fact that at least one component is in urgent/committed location or there is a clock invariant imposing the urgency). Our method is implemented in the tool UPPAAL and the experiments confirm that for the models with enough independent concurrent behavior in urgent situations, we can achieve exponential speedup in the reachability analysis. For models with limited urgent behavior, the overhead of our method is still acceptable (with the worst-case ratio of about 0.4 slowdown). These results are highly encouraging, yet further optimizations can be achieved by a more detailed static analysis of independent actions, one of the directions for future research.

Acknowledgments. We thank Christian Herrera and Sergio Feo Arenis for providing the models we use in our experimental section.

References

1. Aceto, L., Ingolfsdottir, A., Larsen, K., Srba, J.: Reactive Systems: Modelling, Specification and Verification, p. 195. Cambridge University Press, Cambridge (2007)
2. Alur, R., Dill, D.L.: A theory of timed automata. Theor. Comput. Sci. **126**(2), 183–235 (1994)
3. Feo-Arenis, S., Westphal, B.: Formal verification of a parameterized data aggregation protocol. In: Brat, G., Rungta, N., Venet, A. (eds.) NFM 2013. LNCS, vol. 7871, pp. 428–434. Springer, Heidelberg (2013). https://doi.org/10.1007/978-3-642-38088-4_29
4. Baier, C., Katoen, J.-P.: Principles of Model Checking. The MIT Press, Cambridge (2008)
5. Behrmann, G., Bouyer, P., Larsen, K.G., Pelánek, R.: Lower and upper bounds in zone-based abstractions of timed automata. Int. J. Softw. Tools Technol. Transf. **8**(3), 204–215 (2006). https://doi.org/10.1007/s10009-005-0190-0

6. Behrmann, G., David, A., Larsen, K.G.: A tutorial on UPPAAL. In: Bernardo, M., Corradini, F. (eds.) SFM-RT 2004. LNCS, vol. 3185, pp. 200–236. Springer, Heidelberg (2004). https://doi.org/10.1007/978-3-540-30080-9_7

7. Bengtsson, J., Jonsson, B., Lilius, J., Yi, W.: Partial order reductions for timed systems. In: Sangiorgi, D., de Simone, R. (eds.) CONCUR 1998. LNCS, vol. 1466, pp. 485–500. Springer, Heidelberg (1998). https://doi.org/10.1007/BFb0055643

8. Bønneland, F.M., Jensen, P.G., Larsen, K.G., Muñiz, M., Srba, J.: Start pruning when time gets urgent: partial order reduction for timed systems. In: Chockler, H., Weissenbacher, G. (eds.) CAV 2018. LNCS, vol. 10981, pp. 527–546. Springer, Cham (2018). https://doi.org/10.1007/978-3-319-96145-3_28

9. Bozga, M., Graf, S., Ober, I., Ober, I., Sifakis, J.: The IF toolset. In: Bernardo, M., Corradini, F. (eds.) SFM-RT 2004. LNCS, vol. 3185, pp. 237–267. Springer, Heidelberg (2004). https://doi.org/10.1007/978-3-540-30080-9_8

10. Dams, D., Gerth, R., Knaack, B., Kuiper, R.: Partial-order reduction techniques for real-time model checking. Formal Aspects Comput. **10**(5–6), 469–482 (1998). https://doi.org/10.1007/s001650050028

11. Feo-Arenis, S., Westphal, B., Dietsch, D., Muñiz, M., Andisha, A.S.: The wireless fire alarm system: ensuring conformance to industrial standards through formal verification. In: Jones, C., Pihlajasaari, P., Sun, J. (eds.) FM 2014. LNCS, vol. 8442, pp. 658–672. Springer, Cham (2014). https://doi.org/10.1007/978-3-319-06410-9_44

12. Gobriel, S., Mosse, D., Brustoloni, J., Melhem, R.: Ridesharing: fault tolerant aggregation in sensor networks using corrective actions. In: The 3rd Annual IEEE SECON, vol. 2, pp. 595–604, October 2006

13. Godary, K.: Validation temporelle de réseaux embarqués critiques et fiables pour l automobile. Ph.D. thesis, Ins. National des Sc. Appliquées de Lyon, France (2004)

14. Godefroid, P. (ed.): Partial-Order Methods for the Verification of Concurrent Systems. LNCS, vol. 1032. Springer, Heidelberg (1996). https://doi.org/10.1007/3-540-60761-7

15. Hansen, H., Lin, S.-W., Liu, Y., Nguyen, T.K., Sun, J.: Diamonds are a girl's best friend: partial order reduction for timed automata with abstractions. In: Biere, A., Bloem, R. (eds.) CAV 2014. LNCS, vol. 8559, pp. 391–406. Springer, Cham (2014). https://doi.org/10.1007/978-3-319-08867-9_26

16. Herrera, C., Westphal, B., Feo-Arenis, S., Muñiz, M., Podelski, A.: Reducing quasi-equal clocks in networks of timed automata. In: Jurdziński, M., Ničković, D. (eds.) FORMATS 2012. LNCS, vol. 7595, pp. 155–170. Springer, Heidelberg (2012). https://doi.org/10.1007/978-3-642-33365-1_12

17. Kristensen, L.M., Schmidt, K., Valmari, A.: Question-guided stubborn set methods for state properties. FM Syst. Des. **29**(3), 215–251 (2006). https://doi.org/10.1007/s10703-006-0006-1

18. Lugiez, D., Niebert, P., Zennou, S.: A partial order semantics approach to the clock explosion problem of timed automata. Theor. Comput. Sci. **345**(1), 27–59 (2005)

19. Minea, M.: Partial order reduction for model checking of timed automata. In: Baeten, J.C.M., Mauw, S. (eds.) CONCUR 1999. LNCS, vol. 1664, pp. 431–446. Springer, Heidelberg (1999). https://doi.org/10.1007/3-540-48320-9_30

20. Muñiz, M., Westphal, B., Podelski, A.: Detecting quasi-equal clocks in timed automata. In: Braberman, V., Fribourg, L. (eds.) FORMATS 2013. LNCS, vol. 8053, pp. 198–212. Springer, Heidelberg (2013). https://doi.org/10.1007/978-3-642-40229-6_14

21. Niebert, P., Qu, H.: Adding invariants to event zone automata. In: Asarin, E., Bouyer, P. (eds.) FORMATS 2006. LNCS, vol. 4202, pp. 290–305. Springer, Heidelberg (2006). https://doi.org/10.1007/11867340_21

22. Peled, D.: All from one, one for all: on model checking using representatives. In: Courcoubetis, C. (ed.) CAV 1993. LNCS, vol. 697, pp. 409–423. Springer, Heidelberg (1993). https://doi.org/10.1007/3-540-56922-7_34

23. Perin, M., Faure, J.: Coupling timed plant and controller models with urgent transitions without introducing deadlocks. In: 17th International Conference on Emerging Technologies & Factory Automation, ETFA 2012, pp. 1–9. IEEE (2012)

24. Petalidis, N.: Verification of a fieldbus scheduling protocol using timed automata. Comput. Inform. **28**, 655–672 (2009)

25. Salah, R.B., Bozga, M., Maler, O.: On interleaving in timed automata. In: Baier, C., Hermanns, H. (eds.) CONCUR 2006. LNCS, vol. 4137, pp. 465–476. Springer, Heidelberg (2006). https://doi.org/10.1007/11817949_31

26. Steiner, W., Elmenreich, W.: Automatic recovery of the TTP/A sensor/actuator network. In: WISES (2003)

27. Valmari, A., Hansen, H.: Stubborn set intuition explained. In: Koutny, M., Kleijn, J., Penczek, W. (eds.) Transactions on Petri Nets and Other Models of Concurrency XII. LNCS, vol. 10470, pp. 140–165. Springer, Heidelberg (2017). https://doi.org/10.1007/978-3-662-55862-1_7

Eliminating Message Counters
in Threshold Automata

Ilina Stoilkovska[1,2], Igor Konnov[1], Josef Widder[1(✉)], and Florian Zuleger[2]

[1] Informal Systems, Vienna, Austria
{igor,josef}@informal.systems
[2] TU Wien, Vienna, Austria
{stoilkov,zuleger}@forsyte.at

Abstract. Threshold automata were introduced to give a formal semantics to distributed algorithms in a way that supports automated verification. While transitions in threshold automata are guarded by conditions over the number of globally sent messages, conditions in the pseudocode descriptions of distributed algorithms are usually formulated over the number of locally received messages. In this work, we provide an automated method to close the gap between these two representations. We propose threshold automata with guards over the number of received messages and present abstractions into guards over the number of sent messages, by eliminating the receive message counters. Our approach allows us for the first time to fully automatically verify models of distributed algorithms that are in one-to-one correspondence with their pseudocode. We prove that our method is sound, and present a criterion for completeness w.r.t. LTL$_{-X}$ properties (satisfied by all our benchmarks).

1 Introduction

In distributed algorithms, the actions that a process takes locally depend on the messages it has received from the other processes in the system. To enable an action, a process checks if a quorum has been obtained (e.g., majority, two-thirds, etc.) by counting the received messages. Statements such as *"wait until $n - t$ ECHO messages are received"* or *"if more than $n/2$ messages with the same value are received"*, where n is the number of processes and t is the upper bound on the number of faults, are commonly found in the pseudocode of various algorithms.

The root cause that an action becomes enabled is not that enough messages are *received* (which is information local to a process), but that enough processes have *sent* messages (which is information global to the system). This leads to redundancy when producing a formal model: the information about whether an action is enabled is present in the global state of the system, as well as in the

---

Partially supported by: Austrian Science Fund (FWF) via NFN RiSE (S11403, S11405) and doctoral college LogiCS W1255; Interchain Foundation, Switzerland.

D. V. Hung and O. Sokolsky (Eds.): ATVA 2020, LNCS 12302, pp. 196–212, 2020.
https://doi.org/10.1007/978-3-030-59152-6_11

local state of the processes. As [11] shows, this redundancy may lead to spurious counterexamples when applying abstraction-based model checking, which prevents abstraction-based techniques from scaling beyond small examples.

Threshold automata [13] were introduced to model and verify asynchronous fault-tolerant distributed algorithms. They are effective for verification, as they eliminate this redundancy by only allowing expressions over the global variables (i.e., the variables that count the number of sent messages). That is, it suffices to translate the check whether a quorum has been obtained to a check whether enough messages have been sent. For many algorithms, this translation can easily be done manually, as was the case in [12] (and [20], for synchronous algorithms).

However, different classes of algorithms, such as, e.g., Ben-Or's randomized consensus algorithm [2], have more complex guards, where conditions over receive variables can occur in negated form. To model such algorithms in the threshold automata framework, one needs to translate negated conditions over receive variables to positive conditions over the global variables. Owing to implicit assumptions about the values of the receive and global variables, imposed by the asynchronous computation and faulty environment, eliminating the receive variables by hand becomes increasingly tedious and error-prone.

In this paper, we propose an automated method that translates guard expressions over the local receive variables into guard expressions over the global variables. We explicitly encode the relationship between the receive and global variables using a so-called *environment assumption*. The input is a threshold automaton, whose rules contain conditions over the receive variables, and an environment assumption. The output is a threshold automaton where the receive variables are eliminated. We make the following contributions:

1. We introduce a new variant of threshold automata that allows guards over receive variables, and thus is a formalization which captures the constructs that appear in the pseudocode found in the literature.
2. To eliminate the receive variables, we use quantifier elimination for Presburger arithmetic [9,16,17]. This results in quantifier-free guard expressions over the shared variables, and constitutes a valid input to ByMC [14].
3. We show that this method is sound, i.e., that the resulting system is an over-approximation of the original system. For completeness, we present classes of threshold automata for which eliminating receive message counters preserves linear temporal properties without the next operator ($\mathsf{LTL_{-X}}$).
4. In our experiments, we specified several fault-tolerant distributed algorithms with guards over receive variables. We implemented our technique in a prototype, and used it to obtain guards over global variables. When comparing the automatically generated automata to the manually constructed ones, we found flaws, such as missing or redundant rules, or incorrect guards in the manual benchmarks (which were done by some of the authors of this paper).
5. We verified the correctness of the resulting threshold automata using ByMC.

In this way, we establish a fully automated pipeline, that for a given algorithm: starts from a formal model that captures its pseudocode, produces a formal model suitable for verification, and automatically verifies its correctness.

```
1    bool   v := input_value({0, 1});
2    int   rnd := 1;
3    while   (true)      do
4    send   (R,rnd,v)      to  all;
5    wait for    n - t messages (R,rnd,        *);
6    if   received more than (n + t) / 2
7        messages (R,rnd,w)           then
8    send   (P,rnd,w,D)      to  all;
9    else send    (P,rnd,?)      to  all;
10   wait for    n - t messages (P,rnd,        *);
11   if   received at least t + 1
12       message (P,rnd,w,D)            then  {
13   v := w;
14   if   received more than (n + t) / 2
15       messages (P,rnd,w,D)            then
16   decide w;
17   }
18   else    v := random({0, 1});
19   rnd := rnd + 1;
20   od
```

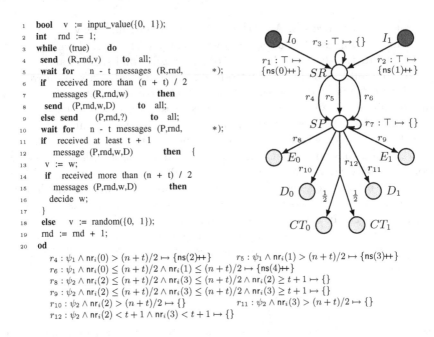

$r_4 : \psi_1 \wedge \mathsf{nr}_i(0) > (n+t)/2 \mapsto \{\mathsf{ns}(2)\mathord{+}\mathord{+}\}$ $r_5 : \psi_1 \wedge \mathsf{nr}_i(1) > (n+t)/2 \mapsto \{\mathsf{ns}(3)\mathord{+}\mathord{+}\}$

$r_6 : \psi_1 \wedge \mathsf{nr}_i(0) \leq (n+t)/2 \wedge \mathsf{nr}_i(1) \leq (n+t)/2 \mapsto \{\mathsf{ns}(4)\mathord{+}\mathord{+}\}$

$r_8 : \psi_2 \wedge \mathsf{nr}_i(2) \leq (n+t)/2 \wedge \mathsf{nr}_i(3) \leq (n+t)/2 \wedge \mathsf{nr}_i(2) \geq t+1 \mapsto \{\}$

$r_9 : \psi_2 \wedge \mathsf{nr}_i(2) \leq (n+t)/2 \wedge \mathsf{nr}_i(3) \leq (n+t)/2 \wedge \mathsf{nr}_i(3) \geq t+1 \mapsto \{\}$

$r_{10} : \psi_2 \wedge \mathsf{nr}_i(2) > (n+t)/2 \mapsto \{\}$ $r_{11} : \psi_2 \wedge \mathsf{nr}_i(3) > (n+t)/2 \mapsto \{\}$

$r_{12} : \psi_2 \wedge \mathsf{nr}_i(2) < t+1 \wedge \mathsf{nr}_i(3) < t+1 \mapsto \{\}$

Fig. 1. The pseudocode of the probabilistic Byzantine consensus protocol by Ben-Or [2], with $n > 5t$, and its TA where $\psi_1 \equiv \mathsf{nr}_i(0) + \mathsf{nr}_i(1) \geq n - t$ and $\psi_2 \equiv \mathsf{nr}_i(2) + \mathsf{nr}_i(3) + \mathsf{nr}_i(4) \geq n - t$. We use the notation $r : \varphi \mapsto \{\mathsf{ns}(m)\mathord{+}\mathord{+} \mid m \in M\}$, where φ is the rule guard, and $\{\mathsf{ns}(m)\mathord{+}\mathord{+} \mid m \in M\}$ is the set of increments of send variables.

2 Overview on Our Approach

We discuss our approach using the example in Fig. 1. It shows the pseudocode of the probabilistic consensus algorithm by Ben-Or [2], which describes the behavior of one process. A system consists of n processes, f of which are faulty; there is an upper bound $t \geq f$ on the number of faults. We comment on some typical peculiarities of the pseudocode in Fig. 1: v in line 4 is a program variable, w in line 7 is an (implicitly) existentially quantified variable whose scope ranges from line 6 to line 8 (similarly in lines 11–13 and lines 14–16). Besides, the tuple notation of messages hides the different types of its components: In line 8, the quadruple (P, rnd, w, D) is sent, where P and D are message tags (from a finite domain), while rnd is an algorithm variable (integer), and w is the mentioned existentially quantified variable. In the other branch, in line 9 the triple $(P, rnd, ?)$ is sent, that is, the "w, D" pair is replaced by the single tag '?'. We highlight these constructs to emphasize the difficulty of understanding the algorithm descriptions given in pseudocode, as well as the need for formal models. Irrespective of this formalization challenge, this algorithm and many other fault-tolerant distributed algorithms typically contain the following constructs:

- setting the values of local variables, e.g., line 13,
- sending a message of type m, for $m \in M$, e.g., line 4,
- waiting until enough messages of some type have been received, e.g., line 5.

Threshold Automata. In this paper, we present a method for obtaining a formal model of a fault-tolerant distributed algorithm starting from its pseudocode. In Sect. 3, we generalize *threshold automata (TA)* [13], and propose the extension as a formalism to faithfully encode fault-tolerant distributed algorithms. The TA specifies the behavior of one process; a parallel composition of multiple copies of a TA specifies the behavior of a distributed system in a faulty environment.

The TA shown on the right in Fig. 1 models one iteration of the while-loop starting in line 3. It resembles a control flow graph, where:

- the *locations* of the TA encode the values of the local variables and the value of the program counter. For example, I_0 encodes that a process sets v to 0 in line 1, while E_0 encodes the same assignment in line 13.
- sending a message $m \in M$ is captured by incrementing the send variable $\mathsf{ns}(m)$. For example, a process with initial value 0 sends $(R, rnd, 0)$ in line 4. We say that the message $(R, rnd, 0)$ is of type 0, and model the sending by a process moving from I_0 to SR, and incrementing the variable $\mathsf{ns}(0)$.
- waiting until enough messages are received is modeled by keeping processes in a so-called *wait location*, defined in Sect. 4. For example, once a process sends a message in line 4, it moves to line 5, where it waits for $n - t$ messages that can be either $(R, rnd, 0)$ or $(R, rnd, 1)$. In the TA, the wait location SR encodes that the process has sent a message of type either 0 or 1, and that it now waits to receive at least $n - t$ messages of type 0 or 1.

Eliminating Receive Variables. In Sect. 4, we introduce two types of TA: rcvTA, which have local transitions guarded by expressions over *local* receive variables $\mathsf{nr}_i(m)$, and sndTA, where the guards are over *global* send variables $\mathsf{ns}(m)$, for $m \in M$. We use rcvTA to encode the behavior of a single process, and sndTA for verification purposes. The approaches in [12,13] encoded distributed algorithms using sndTA, and defined techniques for verifying safety and liveness properties of systems of sndTA. Thus, to apply these techniques to systems of rcvTA, our goal is to automatically generate sndTA, given a rcvTA.

In Sect. 5, we propose an abstraction from rcvTA to sndTA, which translates guards over $\mathsf{nr}_i(m)$ to guards over $\mathsf{ns}(m)$, for $m \in M$, based on *quantifier elimination*. The translation incorporates the relationship between the send and receive variables in asynchronous faulty environments, encoded using an *environment assumption* Env. The environment assumption depends on the fault model; e.g., for Byzantine faults, Env has constraints of the kind: $\mathsf{nr}_i(m) \leq \mathsf{ns}(m) + f$, that is, a process can receive up to f messages more than the ones sent by correct processes, where f is the number of faulty processes. Given a guard φ over the receive variables, to obtain a guard $\hat{\varphi}$ over the send variables, we apply quantifier elimination to the formula $\varphi' \equiv \exists \mathsf{nr}_i(0) \dots \exists \mathsf{nr}_i(|M| - 1) \, (\varphi \wedge \mathsf{Env})$. This produces a quantifier-free formula $\hat{\varphi}$ over the send variables, equivalent to φ'.

We implemented a prototype tool that automatically generates guards over the send variables. We used Z3 [10] to automate the quantifier elimination step. We encoded several algorithms from the literature using rcvTA, translated them to sndTA using our prototype tool, and used ByMC [14] to verify their correctness, which we report on in Sect. 8. For instance, for the guard $\varphi_6 \equiv nr_i(0) + nr_i(1) \geq n - t \wedge nr_i(0) \leq (n + t)/2 \wedge nr_i(1) \leq (n + t)/2$, of rule r_6 in Fig. 1, our prototype tool applies quantifier elimination to the formula $\exists nr_i(0) \ldots \exists nr_i(4) \ (\varphi_6 \wedge \mathsf{Env})$ and outputs the guard $\widehat{\varphi_6} \equiv ns(0) + ns(1) + f \geq n - t \wedge ns(0) + f \geq (n - 3t)/2 \wedge ns(1) + f \geq (n - 3t)/2 \wedge \widehat{\mathsf{Env}}$, where $\widehat{\mathsf{Env}}$ is what remains of Env after eliminating $nr_i(0), \ldots, nr_i(4)$.

Soundness and Criteria for Completeness. In Sect. 6, we show that a system of n copies of a generated sndTA is an *overapproximation* of a system of n copies of the original rcvTA, i.e., we show that the translation is sound. This allows us to check the properties of a system of n copies of rcvTA by checking the properties of the system of n copies of sndTA. In general, the translation is not complete. We characterize a class of TA, for which we show that the overapproximation is *precise* w.r.t. LTL$_{-X}$ properties. We call these TA *common*, as they capture common assumptions made by algorithm designers. A TA is common if a process either: (1) does not wait for messages of the same type in different wait locations, or (2) in a given wait location, it waits for *more* messages of the same type than in any of its predecessor wait locations. We propose a formalization of these two assumptions, which allows us to classify the TA of all our benchmarks as common. In Sect. 7, we present a construction which given an infinite trace of the system of n copies of sndTA, builds an infinite *stutter-equivalent* trace of the system of n copies of a common rcvTA.

3   Threshold Automata

Let M denote the set of types of messages that can be sent and received by the processes. A process i, for $1 \leq i \leq n$, has three kinds of variables:

- *local* variables, x_i, visible only to process i, that store values local to process i, such as, e.g., an initial value or a decision value;
- *receive* variables $nr_i(m)$, visible only to process i, that accumulate the number of messages of types $m \in M$ that were received by process i;
- *send* variables, $ns(m)$, shared by all processes, that accumulate the number of messages of types $m \in M$ that were sent by the processes.

A *threshold automaton* TA is a tuple $(\mathcal{L}, \mathcal{I}, \mathcal{R}, \Gamma, \Delta, \Pi, RC, \mathsf{Env})$ whose components are defined below.

Locations $\mathcal{L}$, $\mathcal{I}$. The *locations* $\ell \in \mathcal{L}$ encode the current value of the process local variables x_i, together with information about the program counter. The *initial locations* in $\mathcal{I} \subseteq \mathcal{L}$ encode the initial values of the process local variables.

Variables Γ, Δ. The set Γ of *shared variables* contains send variables $ns(m)$, for $m \in M$, ranging over $\mathbb{N}$. The set Δ of *receive variables* contains receive variables

$\mathrm{nr}_i(m)$, for $m \in M$, ranging over $\mathbb{N}$. Initially, the variables in Γ and Δ are set to 0. As they are used to count messages, their value cannot decrease.

Parameters Π, Resilience Condition RC. We assume that the set Π of *parameters* contains at least the parameter n, which denotes the total number of processes. The *resilience condition RC* is a linear integer arithmetic expression over the parameters from Π. Let $\boldsymbol{\pi}$ be the $|\Pi|$-dimensional *parameter vector*, and let $\mathbf{p} \in \mathbb{N}^{|\Pi|}$ be its valuation. If $\mathbf{p}$ satisfies the resilience condition *RC*, we call it an *admissible valuation* of $\boldsymbol{\pi}$, and define the set $\mathbf{P}_{RC} = \{\mathbf{p} \in \mathbb{N}^{|\Pi|} \mid \mathbf{p} \models RC\}$ of admissible valuations of $\boldsymbol{\pi}$. The mapping $N : \mathbf{P}_{RC} \to \mathbb{N}$ maps $\mathbf{p} \in \mathbf{P}_{RC}$ to the number $N(\mathbf{p})$ of processes that participate in the algorithm. For each process i, we assume $1 \le i \le N(\mathbf{p})$.

For example, the algorithm in Fig. 1 has three parameters: $n, t, f \in \Pi$. The resilience condition is $n > 5t \wedge t \ge f$. An admissible valuation $\mathbf{p} \in \mathbf{P}_{RC}$ is $\langle 6, 1, 1 \rangle$, as $\mathbf{p}[n] > 5\mathbf{p}[t] \wedge \mathbf{p}[t] \ge \mathbf{p}[f]$.

Rules $\mathcal{R}$. The set $\mathcal{R}$ of *rules* defines how processes move from one location to another. A *rule* $r \in \mathcal{R}$ is a tuple $(\textit{from}, \textit{to}, \varphi, \mathbf{u})$, where $\textit{from}, \textit{to} \in \mathcal{L}$ are locations, φ is a *guard*, and $\mathbf{u}$ is a $|\Gamma|$-dimensional *update vector* of values from the set $\{0, 1\}$. The guard φ is used to check whether the rule can be executed, and will be defined below. The update vector $\mathbf{u}$ captures the increment of the shared variables.

For example, in Fig. 1, executing the rule $r_1 = (I_0, SR, \top, \mathbf{u})$ moves a process i from location I_0 to location SR, by incrementing the value of $\mathrm{ns}(0)$. That is, $r_1.\mathbf{u}[\mathrm{ns}(0)] = 1$, and for every other shared variable $g \in \Gamma$, with $g \ne \mathrm{ns}(0)$, we have $r_1.\mathbf{u}[g] = 0$. Observe that the guard of r_1 is $r_1.\varphi = \top$, which means that r_1 can be executed whenever process i is in location I_0.

Propositions. Let $\boldsymbol{\gamma}$ denote the $|\Gamma|$-dimensional *shared variables vector*, and $\boldsymbol{\delta}$ the $|\Delta|$-dimensional *receive variables vector*. To express guards and temporal properties, we consider the following propositions:

- ℓ-*propositions*, $\mathrm{p}(\ell)$, for $\ell \in \mathcal{L}$, (which will be used in Sect. 6),
- r-*propositions*, $\mathbf{a} \cdot \boldsymbol{\delta} \ge \mathbf{b} \cdot \boldsymbol{\pi} + c$, such that $\mathbf{a} \in \mathbb{Z}^{|\Delta|}, \mathbf{b} \in \mathbb{Z}^{|\Pi|}, c \in \mathbb{Z}$,
- s-*propositions*, $\mathbf{a} \cdot \boldsymbol{\gamma} \ge \mathbf{b} \cdot \boldsymbol{\pi} + c$, such that $\mathbf{a} \in \mathbb{Z}^{|\Gamma|}, \mathbf{b} \in \mathbb{Z}^{|\Pi|}, c \in \mathbb{Z}$.

Guards. A *guard* φ is a Boolean combination of r-propositions and s-propositions. We denote by $\mathsf{Vars}_\Delta(\varphi) = \{\mathrm{nr}_i(m) \in \Delta \mid \mathrm{nr}_i(m) \text{ occurs in } \varphi\}$ the set of receive variables that occur in the guard φ. A guard φ is evaluated over tuples $(\mathbf{d}, \mathbf{g}, \mathbf{p})$, where $\mathbf{d} \in \mathbb{N}^{|\Delta|}, \mathbf{g} \in \mathbb{N}^{|\Gamma|}, \mathbf{p} \in \mathbf{P}_{RC}$ are valuations of the vectors $\boldsymbol{\delta}$ of receive variables, $\boldsymbol{\gamma}$ of shared variables, and $\boldsymbol{\pi}$ of parameters. We define the semantics of r-propositions and s-propositions, the semantics of the Boolean connectives is standard. An r-proposition holds in $(\mathbf{d}, \mathbf{g}, \mathbf{p})$, i.e., $(\mathbf{d}, \mathbf{g}, \mathbf{p}) \models \mathbf{a} \cdot \boldsymbol{\delta} \ge \mathbf{b} \cdot \boldsymbol{\pi} + c$ iff $(\mathbf{d}, \mathbf{p}) \models \mathbf{a} \cdot \boldsymbol{\delta} \ge \mathbf{b} \cdot \boldsymbol{\pi} + c$ iff $\mathbf{a} \cdot \mathbf{d} \ge \mathbf{b} \cdot \mathbf{p} + c$. Similarly for s-propositions, we have $(\mathbf{d}, \mathbf{g}, \mathbf{p}) \models \mathbf{a} \cdot \boldsymbol{\gamma} \ge \mathbf{b} \cdot \boldsymbol{\pi} + c$ iff $(\mathbf{g}, \mathbf{p}) \models \mathbf{a} \cdot \boldsymbol{\gamma} \ge \mathbf{b} \cdot \boldsymbol{\pi} + c$ iff $\mathbf{a} \cdot \mathbf{g} \ge \mathbf{b} \cdot \mathbf{p} + c$.

The guard $r_4.\varphi$ of rule r_4 in the TA in Fig. 1 is a conjunction of two r-propositions, as $\mathsf{nr}_i(0) > (n + t)/2$ is equivalent to $2\mathsf{nr}_i(0) \geq n + t + 1$. We have $\mathsf{Vars}_\Delta(r_4.\varphi) = \{\mathsf{nr}_i(0), \mathsf{nr}_i(1)\}$ and $\mathsf{Vars}_\Gamma(r_4.\varphi) = \emptyset$.

Environment Assumption Env. The environment assumption Env is a conjunction of linear integer arithmetic constraints on the values of the receive, shared variables, and parameters. It is used to faithfully model the assumptions imposed by the fault model and the message communication. For example, for Byzantine faults, we have the environment assumption

$$\mathsf{Env} \equiv \bigwedge_{r \in \mathcal{R}} \mathsf{Env}(r.\varphi), \text{ for } \mathsf{Env}(r.\varphi) \equiv \bigwedge_{M' \subseteq M(r.\varphi)} \sum_{m \in M'} \mathsf{nr}_i(m) \leq \sum_{m \in M'} \mathsf{ns}(m) + f$$

where $M(r.\varphi)$ are the message types of the receive variables that occur in the guard $r.\varphi$, i.e., $m \in M(r.\varphi)$ iff $\mathsf{nr}_i(m) \in \mathsf{Vars}_\Delta(r.\varphi)$. The constraint $\mathsf{Env}(r.\varphi)$ states that the number of received messages of types in $M' \subseteq M(r.\varphi)$, is bounded by the number of sent messages of types in M' and the number f of faults.

4   Modeling Distributed Algorithms with **TA**

The definition of TA we presented in Sect. 3 is very general. To faithfully model the sending and receiving of messages in fault-tolerant distributed algorithms, we introduce *elementary* TA, by imposing several restrictions on the locations and the guards on the rules.

We first define wait locations. A location $\ell \in \mathcal{L}$ is a *wait location* iff (W1) there exists exactly one $r \in \mathcal{R}$ with $r = (\ell, \ell, \top, \mathbf{0})$, and (W2) there exists at least one $r \in \mathcal{R}$ with $r = (\ell, \ell', \varphi, \mathbf{u})$, with $\ell \neq \ell'$, where $r.\varphi \neq \top$. A process in a wait location $\ell \in \mathcal{L}$ uses the self-loop rule (W1) to stay in ℓ while it awaits to receive enough messages, until some guard of a (W2) is satisfied. The process uses the rules (W2) to move to a new location once the number of messages passes some threshold. The self-loop rule is unguarded and updates no shared variables, that is, its guard is $\top$ and its update vector is $\mathbf{0}$. The outgoing rules that are not self-loops are guarded and can contain updates of shared variables.

In Fig. 1, SR is a wait location, as it has a self-loop rule $r_3 = (SR, SR, \top, \mathbf{0})$ as well as three guarded outgoing rules, $r_4, r_5,$ and r_6, that are not self-loops.

Definition 1. *A threshold automaton* $\mathsf{TA} = (\mathcal{L}, \mathcal{I}, \mathcal{R}, \Gamma, \Delta, \Pi, RC, \mathsf{Env})$ *is elementary iff r.from is a wait location for every* $r \in \mathcal{R}$*, with* $r.\varphi \neq \top$*.*

We now define the two kinds of elementary TA: *receive* and *send* TA. To do so, we introduce a *receive guard*, as a Boolean combination of r-propositions and s-propositions, and a *shared guard*, as a Boolean combination of s-propositions.

Definition 2 (Receive TA). *The elementary* TA $(\mathcal{L}, \mathcal{I}, \mathcal{R}_\Delta, \Gamma, \Delta, \Pi, RC, \mathsf{Env}_\Delta)$ *is a receive* TA *(denoted by* rcvTA*) if $r.\varphi$ is a receive guard, for* $r \in \mathcal{R}_\Delta$*.*

Definition 3 (Send TA). *The elementary* TA $(\mathcal{L}, \mathcal{I}, \mathcal{R}_\Gamma, \Gamma, \Delta, \Pi, RC, \mathsf{Env}_\Gamma)$ *is a send* TA *(denoted by* sndTA*) if $\Delta = \emptyset$, and $r.\varphi$ is a shared guard, for* $r \in \mathcal{R}_\Gamma$*. We omit Δ from the signature, and define* sndTA $= (\mathcal{L}, \mathcal{I}, \mathcal{R}_\Gamma, \Gamma, \Pi, RC, \mathsf{Env}_\Gamma)$*.*

For example, the TA in Fig. 1 is a rcvTA. In the remainder of this section, we define the semantics of the parallel composition of $N(\mathbf{p})$ copies of receive and send TA as an asynchronous transition system and counter system, respectively.

4.1 Asynchronous Transition System ATS(p)

Definition 4 (ATS(p)). *Given a rcvTA and* $\mathbf{p} \in \mathbf{P}_{RC}$, *the triple* $\mathsf{ATS}(\mathbf{p}) = \langle S(\mathbf{p}), S_0(\mathbf{p}), T(\mathbf{p}) \rangle$ *is an asynchronous transition system, where* $S(\mathbf{p}), S_0(\mathbf{p})$, *are the set of* states *and* initial states, *and* $T(\mathbf{p})$ *is the* transition relation.

A *state* $s \in S(\mathbf{p})$ is a tuple $s = \langle \boldsymbol{\ell}, \mathbf{g}, \mathbf{nr}_1, \dots, \mathbf{nr}_{N(\mathbf{p})}, \mathbf{p} \rangle$, where $\boldsymbol{\ell} \in \mathcal{L}^{N(\mathbf{p})}$ is a vector of *locations*, such that $\boldsymbol{\ell}[i] \in \mathcal{L}$, for $1 \leq i \leq N(\mathbf{p})$, is the current location of the process i, the vector $\mathbf{g} \in \mathbb{N}^{|\Gamma|}$ is a valuation of the shared variables vector $\boldsymbol{\gamma}$, and the vector $\mathbf{nr}_i \in \mathbb{N}^{|M|}$, is a valuation of the receive variables vector $\boldsymbol{\delta}$ for process i. Each state $s \in S(\mathbf{p})$ satisfies the constraints imposed by the environment assumption Env_{Δ}. A state s_0 is *initial*, i.e., $s_0 \in S_0(\mathbf{p}) \subseteq S(\mathbf{p})$, if $\boldsymbol{\ell} \in \mathcal{I}^{N(\mathbf{p})}$, and $\mathbf{g}, \mathbf{nr}_1, \dots, \mathbf{nr}_{N(\mathbf{p})}$ are initialized to $\mathbf{0}$.

A *receive guard* $r.\varphi$, for $r \in \mathcal{R}_{\Delta}$, is evaluated over tuples (s, i), where $s \in S(\mathbf{p})$ and $1 \leq i \leq N(\mathbf{p})$. We define $(s, i) \models r.\varphi$ iff $(s.\mathbf{nr}_i, s.\mathbf{g}, s.\mathbf{p}) \models r.\varphi$.

Given two states, $s, s' \in S(\mathbf{p})$, we say that $(s, s') \in T(\mathbf{p})$, if there exists a process i, for $1 \leq i \leq N(\mathbf{p})$, and a rule $r \in \mathcal{R}_{\Delta}$ such that: (T1) $s.\boldsymbol{\ell}[i] = r.\textit{from}$ and $(s, i) \models r.\varphi$, (T2) $s'.\mathbf{g} = s.\mathbf{g} + r.\mathbf{u}$, (T3) $s'.\boldsymbol{\ell}[i] = r.\textit{to}$, (T4) $s.\mathbf{nr}_i[m] \leq s'.\mathbf{nr}_i[m]$, for $m \in M$, and (T5) for all j such that $1 \leq j \leq N(\mathbf{p})$ and $j \neq i$, we have $s'.\boldsymbol{\ell}[j] = s.\boldsymbol{\ell}[j]$ and $s'.\mathbf{nr}_j[m] = s.\mathbf{nr}_j[m]$, for $m \in M$. A rule $r \in \mathcal{R}_{\Delta}$ is *enabled* in a state $s \in S(\mathbf{p})$ if there exists a process i with $1 \leq i \leq N(\mathbf{p})$ such that (T1) holds. A state $s' \in S(\mathbf{p})$ is the *result* of applying r to s if there exists a process i, with $1 \leq i \leq N(\mathbf{p})$, such that r is enabled in s and if s' satisfies (T2) to (T5).

A *path* in $\mathsf{ATS}(\mathbf{p})$ is the finite sequence $\{s_i\}_{i=0}^{k}$ of states, such that $(s_i, s_{i+1}) \in T(\mathbf{p})$, for $0 \leq i < k$. A path $\{s_i\}_{i=0}^{k}$ is an *execution* if $s_0 \in S_0(\mathbf{p})$.

4.2 Counter System CS(p)

Definition 5 (CS(p) [13]). *Given a sndTA and* $\mathbf{p} \in \mathbf{P}_{RC}$, *the triple* $\mathsf{CS}(\mathbf{p}) = \langle \Sigma(\mathbf{p}), I(\mathbf{p}), R(\mathbf{p}) \rangle$ *is a counter system, where* $\Sigma(\mathbf{p}), I(\mathbf{p})$ *are the sets of config- urations and* initial configurations, *and* $R(\mathbf{p})$ *is the* transition relation.

A *configuration* $\sigma \in \Sigma(\mathbf{p})$ is the triple $\sigma = \langle \boldsymbol{\kappa}, \mathbf{g}, \mathbf{p} \rangle$, where the vector $\boldsymbol{\kappa} \in \mathbb{N}^{|\mathcal{L}|}$ is a vector of *counters*, s.t. $\sigma.\boldsymbol{\kappa}[\ell]$, for $\ell \in \mathcal{L}$, counts how many processes are in location ℓ, and the vector $\mathbf{g} \in \mathbb{N}^{|\Gamma|}$ is the valuation of the shared variables vector $\boldsymbol{\gamma}$. Every configuration $\sigma \in \Sigma(\mathbf{p})$ satisfies the constraint $\sum_{\ell \in \mathcal{L}} \sigma.\boldsymbol{\kappa}[\ell] = N(\mathbf{p})$ and the environment assumption Env_{Γ}. A configuration σ_0 is *initial*, i.e., $\sigma_0 \in I(\mathbf{p}) \subseteq \Sigma(\mathbf{p})$, if $\sigma_0.\boldsymbol{\kappa}[\ell] = 0$, for $\ell \in \mathcal{L} \setminus \mathcal{I}$, and $\sigma_0.\mathbf{g} = \mathbf{0}$.

A *shared guard* $r.\varphi$, for $r \in \mathcal{R}_{\Gamma}$, is evaluated over $\sigma \in \Sigma(\mathbf{p})$ as follows. As $r.\varphi$ is a Boolean combination of *s*-propositions, we have $\sigma \models r.\varphi$ iff $(\sigma.\mathbf{g}, \sigma.\mathbf{p}) \models r.\varphi$.

Given $\sigma, \sigma' \in \Sigma(\mathbf{p})$, we say that $(\sigma, \sigma') \in R(\mathbf{p})$ if there exists a rule $r \in \mathcal{R}_{\Gamma}$ such that: (R1) $\sigma.\boldsymbol{\kappa}[r.\textit{from}] \geq 1$ and $\sigma \models r.\varphi$, (R2) $\sigma'.\mathbf{g} = \sigma.\mathbf{g} + r.\mathbf{u}$,

(R3) $\sigma'.\kappa[r.from] = \sigma.\kappa[r.from] - 1$ and $\sigma'.\kappa[r.to] = \sigma.\kappa[r.to] + 1$, and (R4) for all $\ell \in \mathcal{L} \setminus \{r.from, r.to\}$, we have $\sigma'.\kappa[\ell] = \sigma.\kappa[\ell]$. The rule $r \in \mathcal{R}_\Gamma$ is *enabled* in $\sigma \in \Sigma(\mathbf{p})$ if it satisfies condition (R1). We call $\sigma' \in \Sigma(\mathbf{p})$ the *result* of applying r to σ, if r is enabled in σ and σ' satisfies the conditions (R2) to (R4).

The *path* and *execution* in $\mathsf{CS}(\mathbf{p})$ are defined analogously as for $\mathsf{ATS}(\mathbf{p})$.

5   Abstracting rcvTA to sndTA

We perform the abstraction from rcvTA to sndTA in two steps. First, we add the environment assumption Env_Δ as a conjunct to every receive guard occurring on the rules of the rcvTA. Second, we eliminate the receive variables to obtain the shared guards and environment assumption Env_Γ of sndTA.

Let $\mathsf{rcvTA} = (\mathcal{L}, \mathcal{I}, \mathcal{R}_\Delta, \Gamma, \Delta, \Pi, RC, \mathsf{Env}_\Delta)$ be a receive TA and let $\mathsf{rcvTA}' = (\mathcal{L}, \mathcal{I}, \mathcal{R}'_\Delta, \Gamma, \Delta, \Pi, RC, \mathsf{Env}_\Delta)$ be the receive TA obtained by adding the environment assumption Env_Δ as a conjunct to every receive guard $r.\varphi$, for $r \in \mathcal{R}_\Delta$.

Definition 6. *Given a rule $r \in \mathcal{R}_\Delta$, its corresponding rule in rcvTA' is the rule $r' \in \mathcal{R}'_\Delta$, such that $r'.from = r.from$, $r'.to = r.to$, $r'.\mathbf{u} = r.\mathbf{u}$, and*

$$r'.\varphi = \mathsf{addEnv}_\Delta(r.\varphi) \,, \text{ where } \mathsf{addEnv}_\Delta(r.\varphi) = \begin{cases} \top & \text{if } r.\varphi = \top \\ r.\varphi \wedge \mathsf{Env}_\Delta & \text{otherwise} \end{cases}$$

Proposition 1. *For every rule $r \in \mathcal{R}_\Delta$, state $s \in S(\mathbf{p})$, and process i, for $1 \le i \le N(\mathbf{p})$, we have $(s, i) \models r.\varphi$ iff $(s, i) \models \mathsf{addEnv}_\Delta(r.\varphi)$.*

Proposition 1 follows from Definitions 4 and 6. As a result of it, composing $N(\mathbf{p})$ copies of rcvTA and $N(\mathbf{p})$ copies of rcvTA' results in the same $\mathsf{ATS}(\mathbf{p})$.

Given the $\mathsf{rcvTA}' = (\mathcal{L}, \mathcal{I}, \mathcal{R}'_\Delta, \Gamma, \Delta, \Pi, RC, \mathsf{Env}_\Delta)$, obtained from rcvTA by Definition 6, we now construct a $\mathsf{sndTA} = (\mathcal{L}, \mathcal{I}, \mathcal{R}_\Gamma, \Gamma, \Pi, RC, \mathsf{Env}_\Gamma)$ whose locations, shared variables, and parameters are the same as in rcvTA and rcvTA', and whose rules $\mathcal{R}_\Gamma$ and the environment assumption Env_Γ are defined as follows.

Definition 7. *Given a rule $r' \in \mathcal{R}'_\Delta$, its corresponding rule in sndTA is the rule $\hat{r} \in \mathcal{R}_\Gamma$, such that $\hat{r}.from = r'.from$, $\hat{r}.to = r'.to$, $\hat{r}.\mathbf{u} = r'.\mathbf{u}$, and*

$$\hat{r}.\varphi = \mathsf{eliminate}_\Delta(r'.\varphi), \text{ with } \mathsf{eliminate}_\Delta(r'.\varphi) = \begin{cases} \top & \text{if } r'.\varphi = \top \\ \mathsf{QE}(\exists \boldsymbol{\delta}\ r'.\varphi) & \text{otherwise} \end{cases}$$

where $\boldsymbol{\delta}$ is the $|\Delta|$-dimensional vector of receive variables, and QE is a quantifier elimination procedure for linear integer arithmetic.

The environment assumption Env_Γ of sndTA is the formula $\mathsf{eliminate}_\Delta(\mathsf{Env}_\Delta)$.

To obtain the shared guards of a sndTA, we apply quantifier elimination to eliminate the existentially quantified variables from the formula $\exists \boldsymbol{\delta}\ r.\varphi \wedge \mathsf{Env}_\Delta$, where $r.\varphi$ is a receive guard. The result is a quantifier-free formula over the shared variables, which is logically equivalent to $\exists \boldsymbol{\delta}\ r.\varphi \wedge \mathsf{Env}_\Delta$. We obtain the environment assumption Env_Γ of a sndTA in a similar way. The following proposition is a consequence of Definition 7 and quantifier elimination.

Proposition 2. *For every rule $r' \in \mathcal{R}'_\Delta$ and state $s \in S(\mathbf{p})$, if there exists a process i, with $1 \leq i \leq N(\mathbf{p})$, such that $(s, i) \models r'.\varphi$, then $s \models \mathsf{eliminate}_\Delta(r'.\varphi)$.*

The converse of the above proposition does not hold in general, i.e., if $r.\varphi$ is a receive guard, $s \models \mathsf{eliminate}_\Delta(r'.\varphi)$ does not imply $(s, i) \models r.\varphi$, for some $1 \leq i \leq N(\mathbf{p})$. However, by quantifier elimination, $s \models \mathsf{eliminate}_\Delta(r'.\varphi)$ implies $s \models \exists \boldsymbol{\delta} \; r'.\varphi$.

6   Soundness

The construction of sndTA defined in Sect. 5 is sound. Given a rcvTA and its corresponding sndTA, we show that there exists a simulation relation between the system $\mathsf{ATS}(\mathbf{p}) = \langle S(\mathbf{p}), S_0(\mathbf{p}), T(\mathbf{p}) \rangle$, induced by rcvTA, and the counter system $\mathsf{CS}(\mathbf{p}) = \langle \Sigma(\mathbf{p}), I(\mathbf{p}), R(\mathbf{p}) \rangle$, induced by sndTA. From this, we conclude that every ACTL^* formula over a set AP of atomic propositions that holds in $\mathsf{CS}(\mathbf{p})$ also holds in $\mathsf{ATS}(\mathbf{p})$. In this paper, the set AP of *atomic propositions* contains ℓ-propositions and s-propositions (cf. Sect. 3).

Evaluating AP. We define two labeling functions: $\lambda_{S(\mathbf{p})}$ and $\lambda_{\Sigma(\mathbf{p})}$. The function $\lambda_{S(\mathbf{p})} : S(\mathbf{p}) \to 2^{\mathrm{AP}}$ assigns to a state $s \in S(\mathbf{p})$ the set of atomic propositions from AP that hold in s. The function $\lambda_{\Sigma(\mathbf{p})} : \Sigma(\mathbf{p}) \to 2^{\mathrm{AP}}$ is defined analogously. We define the semantics of ℓ-propositions: $\mathrm{p}(\ell)$ holds in $s \in S(\mathbf{p})$, i.e., $s \models \mathrm{p}(\ell)$, iff there exists a process i, with $1 \leq i \leq N(\mathbf{p})$, such that $s.\boldsymbol{\ell}[i] = \ell$. The ℓ-proposition $\mathrm{p}(\ell)$ holds in $\sigma \in \Sigma(\mathbf{p})$, that is, $\sigma \models \mathrm{p}(\ell)$ iff $\sigma.\boldsymbol{\kappa}[\ell] \geq 1$.

Simulation. A binary relation $R \subseteq S(\mathbf{p}) \times \Sigma(\mathbf{p})$ is a *simulation relation* [1] if:

1. for every $s_0 \in S_0(\mathbf{p})$, there exists $\sigma_0 \in I(\mathbf{p})$ such that $(s_0, \sigma_0) \in R$,
2. for every $(s, \sigma) \in R$ it holds that:
   (a) $\lambda_{S(\mathbf{p})}(s) = \lambda_{\Sigma(\mathbf{p})}(\sigma)$,
   (b) for every state $s' \in S(\mathbf{p})$ such that $(s, s') \in T(\mathbf{p})$, there exists a configuration $\sigma' \in \Sigma(\mathbf{p})$ such that $(\sigma, \sigma') \in R(\mathbf{p})$ and $(s', \sigma') \in R$.

We introduce an *abstraction mapping* from the set $S(\mathbf{p})$ of states of $\mathsf{ATS}(\mathbf{p})$ to the set $\Sigma(\mathbf{p})$ of configurations of $\mathsf{CS}(\mathbf{p})$.

Definition 8. *The* abstraction mapping $\alpha_{\mathbf{p}} : S(\mathbf{p}) \to \Sigma(\mathbf{p})$ *maps* $s \in S(\mathbf{p})$ *to* $\sigma \in \Sigma(\mathbf{p})$, *s.t.* $\sigma.\boldsymbol{\kappa}[\ell] = |\{i \mid s.\boldsymbol{\ell}[i] = \ell\}|$, *for* $\ell \in \mathcal{L}$, $\sigma.\mathbf{g} = s.\mathbf{g}$, *and* $\sigma.\mathbf{p} = s.\mathbf{p}$.

The main result of this section is stated in the theorem below. It follows from: (i) a state s in $\mathsf{ATS}(\mathbf{p})$ and its abstraction $\sigma = \alpha_{\mathbf{p}}(s)$ in $\mathsf{CS}(\mathbf{p})$ satisfy the same atomic propositions, a consequence of the semantics of atomic propositions, and (ii) if a rule $r \in \mathcal{R}_\Delta$ is enabled in s, then the rule $r \in \mathcal{R}_\Gamma$, obtained by Definitions 6 and 7, is enabled in σ, a consequence of Propositions 1 and 2.

Theorem 1. *The binary relation* $R = \{(s, \sigma) \mid s \in S(\mathbf{p}), \sigma \in \Sigma(\mathbf{p}), \sigma = \alpha_{\mathbf{p}}(s)\}$ *is a simulation relation.*

7   Sufficient Condition for Completeness

We introduce the class of *common* rcvTA, that formalizes assumptions often implicitly assumed by distributed algorithms designers. In a common rcvTA, for every two wait locations ℓ and ℓ', where ℓ' is reachable from ℓ, either: (1) a process waits for messages of different types in ℓ and ℓ', or (2) a process waits for more messages of the same type in ℓ' than in ℓ. Below, we give one possible formalization of common rcvTA, which allows us to establish stutter-trace inclusion [1] between the counter system $CS(\mathbf{p})$ and the system $ATS(\mathbf{p})$.

Theorem 2. *Let rcvTA be common, and sndTA its corresponding send TA. For every execution of $CS(\mathbf{p})$ induced by sndTA, there exists a stutter-equivalent execution of $ATS(\mathbf{p})$ induced by the common rcvTA.*

From Theorem 2, every LTL_{-X} formula satisfied in $ATS(\mathbf{p})$ is also satisfied in $CS(\mathbf{p})$. As LTL_{-X} is a fragment of $ACTL^*$, a consequence of Theorems 1 and 2 is:

Corollary 1. *Let rcvTA be common, and sndTA its corresponding send TA. Let ϕ be an LTL_{-X} formula over the set AP of atomic propositions. For a given $\mathbf{p} \in \mathbf{P}_{RC}$, we have $ATS(\mathbf{p}) \models \phi$ iff $CS(\mathbf{p}) \models \phi$.*

We define the properties of common rcvTA, that allow us to show Theorem 2.

Definition 9. *A guard φ is monotonic iff for every $\mathbf{d}, \mathbf{d}' \in \mathbb{N}^{|\Delta|}$, $\mathbf{g}, \mathbf{g}' \in \mathbb{N}^{|\Gamma|}$, $\mathbf{p} \in \mathbf{P}_{RC}$, $(\mathbf{d}, \mathbf{g}, \mathbf{p}) \models \varphi$, $\mathbf{d}[m] \leq \mathbf{d}'[m]$, for $m \in M$, and $\mathbf{g}[g] \leq \mathbf{g}'[g]$, for $g \in \Gamma$, implies $(\mathbf{d}', \mathbf{g}', \mathbf{p}) \models \varphi$.*

The monotonicity of the guards captures constraints imposed by the message communication and distributed computation. It states that a monotonic guard changes its truth value at most once as the processes update the values of the receive and shared variables.

Definition 10. *Let $P_\Delta = \{D_1, \ldots, D_k\}$ be a partition over the set Δ of receive variables. An environment assumption Env_Δ is:*

- *P_Δ-independent iff Env_Δ is of the form $Env_\Delta = \bigwedge_{D \in P_\Delta} \psi_D$, where ψ_D is a subformula of Env_Δ, such that $Vars_\Delta(\psi_D) = D$.*
- *D-closed under joins, for $D \in P_\Delta$, iff for every $\mathbf{d}, \mathbf{d}' \in \mathbb{N}^{|\Delta|}$, $\mathbf{g} \in \mathbb{N}^{|\Gamma|}$, and $\mathbf{p} \in \mathbf{P}_{RC}$, such that $\mathbf{d}[m] = \mathbf{d}'[m]$, for $nr_i(m) \in \Delta \setminus D$, we have $(\mathbf{d}, \mathbf{g}, \mathbf{p}) \models Env_\Delta$ and $(\mathbf{d}', \mathbf{g}, \mathbf{p}) \models Env_\Delta$ implies $(\max\{\mathbf{d}, \mathbf{d}'\}, \mathbf{g}, \mathbf{p}) \models Env_\Delta$.*

The constraints of a P_Δ-independent environment assumption Env_Δ are expressions over disjoint sets of variables. Under P_Δ-independence, for an environment assumption Env_Δ which is D-closed under joins, for $D \in P_\Delta$, there exists a maximal valuation of the variables in D such that Env_Δ is satisfied.

For Byzantine faults, Env_Δ is D-closed under joins for some $D \in P_\Delta$ iff $|D| = 1$. To show a counterexample for $|D| > 1$, consider some $D = \{nr_i(0), nr_i(1)\}$ of size 2. Let φ be the receive guard $\varphi = nr_i(0) + nr_i(1) \geq n - t$. Then, Env_Δ

has the following three conjuncts: (i) $\mathsf{nr}_i(0) \leq \mathsf{ns}(0) + f$, (ii) $\mathsf{nr}_i(1) \leq \mathsf{ns}(1) + f$, and (iii) $\mathsf{nr}_i(0) + \mathsf{nr}_i(1) \leq \mathsf{ns}(0) + \mathsf{ns}(1) + f$. Consider $f = \mathsf{ns}(0) = \mathsf{ns}(1) = 1$, $\mathsf{nr}_i(0) = 2$, $\mathsf{nr}_i(1) = 1$, and $\mathsf{nr}_i(0) = 1$, $\mathsf{nr}_i(1) = 2$. Taking the maximum of these two valuations violates the constraint (iii). We remark that for crash faults, Env_Δ is always D-closed under joins for all $D \in P_\Delta$.

The rule r is a *predecessor* of rule r', for $r, r' \in \mathcal{R}_\Delta$, iff $r.\varphi \neq \top$, $r'.\varphi \neq \top$, and $r'.from$ is reachable from $r.from$ by a path that starts with r.

Definition 11. *A* $rcvTA = (\mathcal{L}, \mathcal{I}, \mathcal{R}_\Delta, \Gamma, \Delta, \Pi, RC, \mathsf{Env}_\Delta)$ *is* common *iff*

- *there exists a partition* P_Δ, *where* $\mathsf{Vars}_\Delta(r.\varphi) \in P_\Delta$, *for* $r \in \mathcal{R}_\Delta$,
- Env_Δ *is* P_Δ-*independent*
- *for every two rules* $r, r' \in \mathcal{R}_\Delta$, *such that* r *is a predecessor of* r' *either*
    1. $\mathsf{Vars}_\Delta(r.\varphi) \cap \mathsf{Vars}_\Delta(r'.\varphi) = \emptyset$, *or*
    2. Env_Δ *is* $\mathsf{Vars}_\Delta(r'.\varphi)$-*closed under joins and the guard* $r'.\varphi$ *is monotonic*.

The rcvTA of all our benchmarks are common. They are either: Byzantine, with non-overlapping variables on the guards outgoing of wait locations or with partition elements of size 1; or crash-faulty. Consider Fig. 1. We have $P_\Delta = \{\mathsf{Vars}_\Delta(r_{SR}.\varphi), \mathsf{Vars}_\Delta(r_{SP}.\varphi)\}$, where $\mathsf{Vars}_\Delta(r_{SR}.\varphi) = \{\mathsf{nr}_i(0), \mathsf{nr}_i(1)\}$, and $\mathsf{Vars}_\Delta(r_{SP}.\varphi) = \{\mathsf{nr}_i(2), \mathsf{nr}_i(3), \mathsf{nr}_i(4)\}$. For Byzantine faults and the partition P_Δ, we have Env_Δ is P_Δ-independent. For $r_{SP} \in \{r_8, \ldots, r_{12}\}$ and its predecessors $r_{SR} \in \{r_4, \ldots, r_6\}$ SR, we have $\mathsf{Vars}_\Delta(r_{SP}) \cap \mathsf{Vars}_\Delta(r_{SR}) = \emptyset$.

Stutter-Equivalent Executions. Let rcvTA be common, and let sndTA be its corresponding send TA. Given an infinite execution $exec_{\mathsf{CS}} = \{\sigma_j\}_{j\in\mathbb{N}}$ in $\mathsf{CS}(\mathbf{p})$, induced by sndTA, we construct an infinite execution $exec_{\mathsf{ATS}} = \{s_i\}_{i\in\mathbb{N}}$ in $\mathsf{ATS}(\mathbf{p})$, induced by the common rcvTA, which is stutter-equivalent to $exec_{\mathsf{CS}}$ as follows:

1. constructing the initial state s_0 of $exec_{\mathsf{ATS}}$, and
2. for every transition (σ, σ') in $exec_{\mathsf{CS}}$, extending the execution $exec_{\mathsf{ATS}}$ either by a single transition or by a path consisting of two transitions.

The construction satisfies the following invariants: (I1) given $\sigma \in \Sigma(\mathbf{p})$, which is the origin of the transition (σ, σ') in step 2, and the state $s \in S(\mathbf{p})$ at the tail of $exec_{\mathsf{ATS}}$ before executing step 2, it holds that $\sigma = \alpha_{\mathbf{p}}(s)$, and (I2) for every process i, with $1 \leq i \leq N(\mathbf{p})$, and $s \in S(\mathbf{p})$ at the tail of $exec_{\mathsf{ATS}}$, it holds that $s.\mathbf{nr}_i[m] = 0$, for $m \in M$, such that $\mathsf{nr}_i(m)$ occurs on guards of rules that process i has not applied before reaching $s.\ell[i]$.

Constructing the Initial State. Let $\sigma_0 \in I(\mathbf{p})$ be the initial configuration of $exec_{\mathsf{CS}}$. We construct a state $s_0 \in S(\mathbf{p})$ such that $\sigma_0 = \alpha_{\mathbf{p}}(s_0)$, where $s_0.\mathbf{nr}_i[m] = 0$, for $m \in M$ and $1 \leq i \leq N(\mathbf{p})$.

Proposition 3. *Given* $\sigma_0 \in I(\mathbf{p})$, *the state* $s_0 \in S(\mathbf{p})$, *such that* $\sigma_0 = \alpha_{\mathbf{p}}(s_0)$ *and* $s_0.\mathbf{nr}_i[m] = 0$, *for* $m \in M$ *and* $1 \leq i \leq N(\mathbf{p})$, *is an initial state in* $\mathsf{ATS}(\mathbf{p})$.

Extending the Execution exec$_\text{ATS}$. The construction of *exec*$_\text{ATS}$ proceeds iteratively: given a transition (σ, σ') in *exec*$_\text{CS}$, the execution *exec*$_\text{ATS}$ is extended by a single transition or a path consisting of two transitions. Let $r \in \mathcal{R}_\Delta$ denote the rule in rcvTA, which was used to construct the rule $r \in \mathcal{R}_\Gamma$, that was applied in the transition (σ, σ'). Let s be the state at the tail of *exec*$_\text{ATS}$. By the invariant of the construction, $\alpha_\mathbf{p}(s) = \sigma$. There are two cases:

1. r is enabled in s – *exec*$_\text{ATS}$ is extended by a single transition (s, s'),
2. r is not enabled in s – *exec*$_\text{ATS}$ is extended by two transitions: (s, s'), (s', s'').

When r is enabled in s, the construction picks such a process i, and applies the rule r to the state s, such that the receive variables of process i are not updated. The result is the state s', such that: (A1) $s'.\ell[i] = r.to$ and $s'.\mathbf{g} = s.\mathbf{g} + r.\mathbf{u}$, (A2) $s'.\mathbf{nr}_i[m] = s.\mathbf{nr}_i[m]$, for $m \in M$, that is, the process i does update its receive variables, (A3) for all j such that $1 \leq j \leq N(\mathbf{p})$, and $i \neq j$, we have $s'.\ell[j] = s.\ell[j]$ and $s'.\mathbf{nr}_j[m] = s.\mathbf{nr}_j[m]$, for $m \in M$.

Proposition 4. *Suppose r is enabled in s. Let $s' \in S(\mathbf{p})$ be obtained by applying* (A1)–(A3). *Then, $(s, s') \in T(\mathbf{p})$ is a transition in* ATS(**p**).

In the case when r is not enabled in s, there is no process i, with $1 \leq i \leq N(\mathbf{p})$ and $s.\ell[i] = r.from$, such that $(s, i) \models r.\varphi$. This can happen if $r.\varphi$ is a receive guard, i.e., $\ell = r.from$ is a wait location. By $\sigma.\kappa[\ell] \geq 1$ and the invariant (I1), there exists a process i in the wait location ℓ. The construction extends *exec*$_\text{ATS}$ with: one transition in which the receive variables of process i are updated to values $\mathbf{nr} \in \mathbb{N}^{|\Delta|}$, such that $r.\varphi$ becomes enabled, and a second transition in which process i applies the rule r, without updating its receive variables.

By quantifier elimination and Definition 11, we can find values $\mathbf{nr}$ that satisfy $r.\varphi$, where only the values of variables in $\text{Vars}_\Delta(r.\varphi)$ get updated, i.e., where $\mathbf{nr}[m] = s.\mathbf{nr}_i[m]$ for $\text{nr}_i(m) \in \Delta \setminus \text{Vars}_\Delta(r.\varphi)$. For the values $\mathbf{nr}[m]$, for $\text{nr}_i(m) \in \text{Vars}_\Delta(r.\varphi)$, we take the maximum of $s.\mathbf{nr}_i[m]$ and the values for $\text{nr}_i(m)$ in some arbitrary valuation that satisfies $r.\varphi$. Thus, process i can apply the self-loop rule $r' = (\ell, \ell, \top, \mathbf{0})$ to update its receive variables to $\mathbf{nr}$. The result is a state s', such that: (B1) $s'.\ell[i] = s.\ell[i]$ and $s'.\mathbf{g} = s.\mathbf{g}$, (B2) $s'.\mathbf{nr}_i[m] = \mathbf{nr}[m]$, for $m \in M$, (B3) for all j such that $1 \leq j \leq N(\mathbf{p})$, and $i \neq j$, we have $s'.\ell[j] = s.\ell[j]$ and $s'.\mathbf{nr}_j[m] = s.\mathbf{nr}_j[m]$, for $m \in M$. The rule r is enabled in s', as $s'.\ell[i] = \ell$ and $(s', i) \models r.\varphi$, and is applied to s', using (A1)–(A3), resulting in the state s''.

Proposition 5. *Suppose r is not enabled in s. Let $s' \in S(\mathbf{p})$ be obtained by applying* (B1)–(B2). *Then, $(s, s') \in T(\mathbf{p})$ is a transition in* ATS(**p**).

We sketch how to prove Proposition 5 using the assumptions from Definition 11. If there exists a predecessor r_p of the rule r, such that $\text{Vars}_\Delta(r_p.\varphi)$ and $\text{Vars}_\Delta(r.\varphi)$ overlap, the monotonicity of $r.\varphi$ ensures that $(\mathbf{nr}, s.\mathbf{g}, s.\mathbf{p}) \models r.\varphi$, which implies $(s', i) \models r.\varphi$. Using P_Δ-independence and $\text{Vars}_\Delta(r.\varphi)$-closure under joins of Env_Δ we can reason only about the variables from $\text{Vars}_\Delta(r.\varphi)$ to show that $(\mathbf{nr}, s.\mathbf{g}, s.\mathbf{p}) \models \text{Env}_\Delta$, from which $s' \models \text{Env}_\Delta$ follows. Otherwise, i.e., if $\text{Vars}_\Delta(r_p.\varphi)$ and $\text{Vars}_\Delta(r.\varphi)$ do not overlap, $(s', i) \models r.\varphi$ and $s' \models \text{Env}_\Delta$ follow from the P_Δ-independence of Env_Δ and the invariant (I2).

Table 1. The algorithms we encoded as rcvTA and the model checking results. The columns stand for: QE – the time to produce a sndTA for a given rcvTA as input; $|\Phi|$ – the number of properties checked with ByMC; sndTA $\models \phi$ and TA $\models \phi$ – the time ByMC took to verify all the properties of the automatically generated sndTA and the manually encoded TA, respectively; $\Rightarrow$ – if all, some, or none of the sndTA guards imply the manual TA guards; +**L**, **F** – guard implications after adding lemmas or fixes.

Algorithm	Reference	Faults	QE	$|\Phi|$	sndTA $\models \phi$	TA $\models \phi$	$\Rightarrow$	+**L, F**
ABA	[7, Fig. 3]	Byzantine	0.43 s	3	0.94 s	0.8 s	all	–
Ben-Or-Byz	[2, Prot. B]	Byzantine	1.04 s	4	36.4 s	0.64 s	some	all
Ben-Or-clean	[2, Prot. A]	clean crash	0.78 s	4	2 m 8 s	1.03 s	some	all
Ben-Or-crash	[2, Prot. A]	crash	1.31 s	4	4 × M.O	23 h, 2 × M.O	some	all
Bosco	[18, Alg. 1]	Byzantine	2.01 s	5	30 h 5 m	9 m 14 s	some	some
CC-clean	[15, Fig. 1]	clean crash	0.65 s	3	0.95 s	0.67 s	all	–
CC-crash	[15, Fig. 1]	crash	0.33 s	3	1 h 59 m	40.8 s	all	–
FRB	[8, Fig. 4]	crash	0.14 s	3	3.66 s	0.97 s	none	all
RS-Bosco	[18, Alg. 2]	Byzantine	9.51 s	5	–	–	some	some
STRB	[19, Fig. 2]	Byzantine	0.31 s	3	0.97 s	0.75 s	all	–

Stutter-equivalence. For a given common rcvTA and its corresponding sndTA, the construction produces an infinite execution $exec_{\text{ATS}}$ in $\text{ATS}(\mathbf{p})$, given an infinite execution $exec_{\text{CS}}$ in $\text{CS}(\mathbf{p})$. Propositions 3, 4 and 5 ensure that $exec_{\text{ATS}}$ is an execution in $\text{ATS}(\mathbf{p})$. The invariants (I1) and (I2) are preserved during the construction. When r is enabled in s, it is easy to check that $\alpha_{\mathbf{p}}(s') = \sigma'$, where s' is obtained by (A1)–(A3), and no receive variables are updated. When r is not enabled in s, we have $\alpha_{\mathbf{p}}(s') = \sigma$, and $\alpha_{\mathbf{p}}(s'') = \sigma'$ where s' is obtained by (B1)–(B2), and s'' by (A1)–(A3). Here, only the receive variables of process i occurring on the rule r applied in s' are updated. Stutter-equivalence follows from (I1) and because s and σ satisfy the same atomic propositions.

8 Experimental Evaluation

In our experimental evaluation, we: (1) encoded several distributed algorithms from the literature as rcvTA, (2) implemented the method from Sect. 5 in a prototype tool that produces the corresponding sndTA, (3) compared the output to the existing manual encodings from the benchmark repository [3], and (4) verified the properties of the sndTA using the tool ByMC [14].

Encoding rcvTA. To encode distributed algorithms as rcvTA, we extended the TA format defined by ByMC with declarations of receive variables and environment constraints. For each of our benchmarks (Table 1), there already exists a manually produced TA. For some crash-tolerant benchmarks, we also encoded a "clean crash" variant, where the crashed processes do not send messages.

Applying Quantifier Elimination. We implemented a script that parses the input rcvTA, and creates a sndTA according to the abstraction from Sect. 5, whose rules have shared guards, obtained by applying Z3 [10] tactics for quantifier elimination [5,6], to formulas of the form $\exists \delta \ r.\varphi \wedge Env_\Delta$, where $r.\varphi$ is a receive guard. For all our benchmarks, the sndTA is generated within seconds (cf. Table 1).

Analyzing the sndTA. We used Z3 to check whether the guards for the automatically generated sndTA imply the guards of the manually encoded TA from the benchmark repository [3]. With this check we are able to either verify that the earlier, manually encoded, TA faithfully model the benchmark algorithms, or detect discrepancies, which we investigated further. Due to our completeness result (Section 7), our technique produces the strongest possible guards. Hence, we expected implication for all the benchmarks we considered. This is indeed the case for ABA, CC-*, and STRB. To our surprise, the implication did not hold for all the guards of the other benchmarks.

For Ben-Or-crash and FRB, we found flaws in the manual encodings. These algorithms tolerate crash faults, where the number of messages sent by faulty processes is stored in shared variables $ns_f(m)$, and the environment assumption has constraints of the form $nr_i(m) \leq ns(m) + ns_f(m)$. We identified that the variables $ns_f(m)$ did not occur in the manual guards, that is, it was assumed that $nr_i(m) \leq ns(m)$. We fixed the manual guards by adding the variables $ns_f(m)$. This made the benchmark Ben-Or-crash harder to check than previously reported in [4]: For the corrected TA, ByMC checked two properties in a day and ran out of memory for the other two (and for all four properties when checking the sndTA). By adding $ns_f(m)$ to the manual guards of FRB we verified that the automatically generated guards are indeed stronger.

For all the Ben-Or-* benchmarks, we had to add lemmas to the environment assumption Env_Δ in order to verify that the automatically generated guards imply the manual guards. The key finding is that these lemmas were implicitly used in the manual encoding of the benchmarks in [4]. For instance, to get guards for $r_8, \ldots, r_{12}$ in Fig. 1 that imply the manual guards, we added the lemma $ns(2) = 0 \vee ns(3) = 0$ to Env_Δ. To ensure soundness, it suffices to check (with Z3) that the rules which increment $ns(2)$ or $ns(3)$ cannot both be enabled.

For the most complicated benchmarks, Bosco and RS-Bosco, we could not find the right lemmas which ensure that all automatically generated guards imply all manual guards. Further, after inspecting the manual guards for several hours, we were not able to establish if the manual guards which are not implied are indeed wrong. Still, we successfully verified the properties of sndTA for Bosco with ByMC. Checking the manual TA for RS-Bosco requires running ByMC on an MPI cluster, to which we currently have no access. Hence, we could not verify RS-Bosco.

Model Checking with ByMC. We verified the properties of eight out of ten sndTA that our script produced. We ran ByMC with both the automatically generated sndTA and the already existing manual TA as input (the results are in Table 1). The timeout for ByMC was set to 24 h for each property that we checked. The experiments were run on a machine with 2,8 GHz Quad-Core Intel Core i7 and 16 GB. We used Z3 v4.8.7 and ByMC v2.4.2.

Quantifier elimination for $\exists \delta\; r.\varphi \wedge \mathsf{Env}_\Delta$ in Presburger arithmetic may produce a quantifier-free formula which contains divisibility constraints; that are not supported by ByMC. We encountered divisibility constraints in the automatically generated guards for the benchmarks Bosco and RS-Bosco. To apply ByMC, we extend our analysis by a phase that generates different versions of the rcvTA according to the different evaluations of the divisibility constraints. For example, if the divisibility constraint $n\%2 = 0$ occurs on a guard, we create two versions of the rcvTA: one where n is odd, and one where n is even. Based on these two rcvTA, our script produces two sndTA, which we check with ByMC.

9 Conclusions

Our automated method helped in finding glitches in the existing encoding of several benchmarks, which confirms our motivation of automatically constructing threshold automata. In addition to the glitches discussed in Sect. 8, we found the following problems in manual encodings: redundant rules (whose guards always evaluate to false), swapped guards (on rules r, r', where the guard of r should be $r'.\varphi$, and vice versa), and missing rules (that were omitted). This indicates that there is a real benefit of producing guards automatically.

However, our experimental results show that ByMC performs worse on the sndTA than on the manual TA. Since the automatically generated guards have more s-propositions than the manual guards, the search space that ByMC explores is larger than for the manual TA. In this paper, we focus on soundness and completeness of the translation rather than on efficiency. We suggest that a simplification step which eliminates redundant s-propositions will lead to a performance comparable to manual encodings, and we leave that for future work.

References

1. Baier, C., Katoen, J.P.: Principles of Model Checking. MITP (2008)
2. Ben-Or, M.: Another advantage of free choice (extended abstract): completely asynchronous agreement protocols. In: PODC (1983)
3. https://github.com/konnov/fault-tolerant-benchmarks
4. Bertrand, N., Konnov, I., Lazić, M., Widder, J.: Verification of randomized consensus algorithms under round-rigid adversaries. In: CONCUR (2019)
5. Bjørner, N.: Linear quantifier elimination as an abstract decision procedure. In: IJCAR (2010)
6. Bjørner, N., Janota, M.: Playing with quantified satisfaction. In: LPAR (2015)
7. Bracha, G., Toueg, S.: Asynchronous consensus and broadcast protocols. J. ACM **32**(4), 824–840 (1985)
8. Chandra, T.D., Toueg, S.: Unreliable failure detectors for reliable distributed systems. J. ACM **43**(2), 225–267 (1996)

9. Cooper, D.C.: Theorem proving in arithmetic without multiplication. Mach. Intell. **7**(91–99), 300 (1972)
10. De Moura, L., Bjørner, N.: Z3: an efficient SMT solver. In: TACAS (2008)
11. John, A., Konnov, I., Schmid, U., Veith, H., Widder, J.: Parameterized model checking of fault-tolerant distributed algorithms by abstraction. In: FMCAD (2013)
12. Konnov, I., Lazić, M., Veith, H., Widder, J.: A short counterexample property for safety and liveness verification of fault-tolerant distributed algorithms. In: POPL (2017)
13. Konnov, I., Veith, H., Widder, J.: On the completeness of bounded model checking for threshold-based distributed algorithms: reachability. Inf. Comput. **252**, 95–109 (2017)
14. Konnov, I., Widder, J.: ByMC: byzantine model checker. In: ISOLA (2018)
15. Mostéfaoui, A., Mourgaya, E., Parvédy, P.R., Raynal, M.: Evaluating the condition-based approach to solve consensus. In: DSN (2003)
16. Presburger, M.: Über die Vollständigkeit eines gewissen Systems der Arithmetik ganzer Zahlen, in welchem die Addition als einzige Operation hervortritt. Comptes Rendus du I congres de Mathématiciens des Pays Slaves (1929)
17. Pugh, W.: A practical algorithm for exact array dependence analysis. Commun. ACM **35**(8), 102–114 (1992)
18. Song, Y.J., van Renesse, R.: Bosco: one-step byzantine asynchronous consensus. In: DISC (2008)
19. Srikanth, T., Toueg, S.: Simulating authenticated broadcasts to derive simple fault-tolerant algorithms. Distrib. Comput. **2**, 80–94 (1987)
20. Stoilkovska, I., Konnov, I., Widder, J., Zuleger, F.: Verifying safety of synchronous fault-tolerant algorithms by bounded model checking. In: TACAS (2019)

Logics

Context-Aware Temporal Logic
for Probabilistic Systems

Mahmoud Elfar[✉] [ID], Yu Wang[ID], and Miroslav Pajic[ID]

Duke University, Durham, NC 27708, USA
{mahmoud.elfar,yu.wang94,miroslav.pajic}@duke.edu,
http://cpsl.pratt.duke.edu

Abstract. In this paper, we introduce the context-aware probabilistic
temporal logic (CAPTL) that provides an intuitive way to formalize system requirements by a set of PCTL objectives with a context-based priority structure. We formally present the syntax and semantics of CAPTL
and propose a synthesis algorithm for CAPTL requirements. We also
implement the algorithm based on the PRISM-games model checker.
Finally, we demonstrate the usage of CAPTL on two case studies: a
robotic task planning problem, and synthesizing error-resilient scheduler
for micro-electrode-dot-array digital microfluidic biochips.

Keywords: Markov-decision process · Temporal logic · Model
checking · Probabilistic systems · Synthesis

1 Introduction

The correct-by-design paradigm in Cyber-Physical Systems (CPS) has been a
central concept during the design phase of various system components. This
paradigm requires the abstraction of both the system behavior and the design
requirements [22,23]. Typically, the system behavior is modeled as a discrete
Kripke structure, with nondeterministic transitions representing various actions
or choices that need to be resolved. In systems where probabilistic behavior is
prevalent, formalisms such as Markov decision processes (MDPs) are best suited.
The applications of correct-by-design synthesis paradigm span CPS fields such as
robot path and behavior planning [6,18], smart power grids [24], safety-critical
medical devices [15], and autonomous vehicles [25].

Temporal logic (TL) can be utilized to formalize CPS design requirements.
For example, Linear Temporal Logic (LTL) [2] is used to capture safety and
reachability requirements over Boolean predicates defined over the state space.
Similarly, computation tree logic (CTL) [2] allows for expressing requirements
over all computations branching from a given state. Probabilistic computation
tree logic (PCTL) can be viewed as a probabilistic variation of CTL to reason
about the satisfaction probabilities of temporal requirements.

The choice of which TL to use is both a science and an art. Nevertheless,
fundamental factors include expressiveness (i.e., whether the design requirements

© Springer Nature Switzerland AG 2020
D. V. Hung and O. Sokolsky (Eds.): ATVA 2020, LNCS 12302, pp. 215–232, 2020.
https://doi.org/10.1007/978-3-030-59152-6_12

of interest can be expressed by the logic), and the existence of model checkers that can verify the system model against the design requirement, synthesize winning strategies, or generate counterexamples. Although prevalent TLs can be inherently expressive, two notions are oftentimes overlooked, namely, how easy it is to correctly formalize the design requirements, and whether existing model checkers are optimized for such requirements. The more complex it becomes to formalize a given requirement, the more likely it is that human error is introduced in the process.

In particular, we focus in this paper on requirements that are naturally specified as a set of various objectives with an underlying priority structure. For instance, the objective of an embedded controller might be focused on achieving a primary task. However, whenever the chances of achieving such task fall below a certain threshold, the controller shall proceed with a fail-safe procedure. Such requirement, while being easy to state and understand, can prove challenging when formalized for two reasons. First, multiple objectives might be involved with a priority structure, i.e., one objective takes priority over another. Second, the context upon which the objectives are switched is of probabilistic nature, i.e., it requires the ability to prioritize objectives based on probabilistic invariants.

To this end, in this work we consider the problem of modeling and synthesis of CPS modeled as MDPs, with context-based probabilistic requirements, where a context is defined over probabilistic conditions. We tackle this problem by introducing the context-aware probabilistic temporal logic (CAPTL). CAPTL provides intuitive means to formalize design requirements as a set of objectives with a priority structure. For example, a requirement can be defined in terms of primary and secondary objectives, where switching from the former to the latter is based upon a probabilistic condition (i.e., a context). The ability to define context as probabilistic conditions sets CAPTL apart from similar TLs.

In addition to providing the syntax and semantics of CAPTL for MDPs, we investigate the problem of synthesizing winning strategies based on CAPTL requirements. Next, we demonstrate how the synthesis problem can be reduced to a set of PCTL-based synthesis sub-problems. Moreover, for deterministic CAPTL requirements with persistence objectives, we propose an optimized synthesis algorithm. Finally, we implement the algorithm on top of PRISM-games [19], and we show experimental results for two case studies where we synthesize a robotic task planner, and an error-resilient scheduler for microfluidic biochips.

The rest of this section discusses related work. Preliminaries and a motivating example are provided in Sect. 2. In Sect. 3 we introduce the syntax and semantics of CAPTL. The CAPTL-based synthesis problem is introduced in Sect. 4, where we first explore how a CAPTL requirement can be approached using PCTL, followed by our proposed synthesis algorithm. For evaluation, we consider two case studies in Sect. 5. Finally, we conclude the paper in Sect. 6. Full proofs can be found in the extended version of this paper [9].

Related Work. The problem of multi-objective model checking and synthesis has been studied in literature, spanning both MDPs and stochastic games, for various properties, including reachability, safety, probabilistic queries, and reward-based requirements [11,13,14]. Our work improves upon the multi-objective synthesis paradigm by enabling priorities over the multiple objectives as we will show in Sect. 2. One prevalent workaround is to define multiple reward structures, where states are assigned tuples of real numbers depicting how favorable they are with respect to multiple criteria. The synthesis problem is then reduced to an optimization problem over either a normalized version of the rewards (i.e., assigning weights), or one reward with logical constraints on the others [1,7]. Results are typically presented as Pareto curves, depicting feasible points in the reward space [14]. Our work differs in two aspects. First, we use probabilities as means to define priorities rather than reward structures. Second, the mechanics needed to define context-based priorities are an integral part of CAPTL.

Perhaps the closest notion to our context-based prioritization scheme are probabilistic invariant sets (PIS) [17]. Both CAPTL and PIS involve the identification of state-space subsets that maintain a probability measure within specific bounds. While prevalent in the field of probabilistic programs [3], PIS was not considered in the field of CPS synthesis, despite the fact that (non-probabilistic) invariant sets are used in controller design [4]. The problem of merging strategies for MDPs that correspond to different objectives has been investigated [5,27]. Our approach, however, is primarily focused on formalizing the notion of context-based priorities within the specification logic itself rather than altering the original model. While one can argue that PCTL alone can be used to define priorities by utilizing nested probabilistic operators, the nesting is typically limited to qualitative operators [20]. In contrast, CAPTL relaxes such limitation by allowing quantitative operators as well. Moreover, CAPTL-based synthesis provides an insight into which objective is being pursued at a given state.

2   Problem Setting

Preliminaries. For a measurable event E, we denote its probability by $\Pr(E)$. The powerset of A is denoted by $\mathcal{P}(A)$. We use $\mathbb{R}$, $\mathbb{N}$ and $\mathbb{B}$ for the set of reals, naturals and Booleans, respectively. For a sequence or a vector π, we write $\pi[i]$, $i \in \mathbb{N}$, to denote the i-th element of π.

We formally model the system as an MDP. MDPs feature both probabilistic and nondeterministic transitions, capturing both uncertain behaviors and nondeterministic choices in the modeled system, respectively. We adopt the following definition for a system model as an MDP [2].

Definition 1 (System Model). *A system model is an MDP $\mathcal{M} = (S, Act, \mathbf{P}, s_0, AP, L)$ where S is a finite set of states; Act is a finite set of actions; $\mathbf{P} : S \times Act \times S \rightarrow [0,1]$ is a transition probability function s.t. $\sum_{s' \in S} \mathbf{P}(s, a, s') \in \{0,1\}$ for $a \in Act$; s_0 is an initial state; AP is a set of atomic propositions; and $L : S \rightarrow \mathcal{P}(AP)$ is a labeling function.*

Given a system $\mathcal{M}$, a *path* is a sequence of states $\pi = s_0 s_1 \ldots$, such that $\mathbf{P}(s_i, a_i, s_{i+1}) > 0$ where $a_i \in Act(s_i)$ for all $i \geq 0$. The trace of π is defined as $trace(\pi) = L(s_0)L(s_1) \cdots$. We use $FPath_{\mathcal{M},s}$ ($IPath_{\mathcal{M},s}$) to denote the set of all finite (infinite) paths of $\mathcal{M}$ starting from $s \in S$. We use $Paths_{\mathcal{M},s}$ to denote the set of all finite and infinite paths starting from $s \in S$. If $\mathbf{P}(s, a, s') = p$ and $p > 0$, we write $s \xrightarrow{a,p} s'$ to denote that, with probability p, taking action a in state s will yield to state s'. We define the *cardinality* of $\mathcal{M}$ as $|\mathcal{M}| = |S| + |\mathbf{P}|$, where $|\mathbf{P}|$ is the number of non-zero entries in $\mathbf{P}$.

A *strategy* (also known as a policy or a scheduler) defines the behavior upon which nondeterministic transitions in $\mathcal{M}$ are resolved. A *memoryless* strategy uses only the current state to determine what action to take, while a *memory-based* strategy uses previous states as well. We focus in this work on pure memoryless strategies, which are shown to suffice for PCTL reachability properties [2].

Definition 2 (Strategy). *A (pure memoryless) strategy of $\mathcal{M} = (S, Act, \mathbf{P}, s_0, AP, L)$ is a function $\sigma : S \to Act$ that maps states to actions.*

By composing $\mathcal{M}$ and σ, nondeterministic choices in $\mathcal{M}$ are resolved, reducing the model to a *discrete-time Markov chain* (DTMC), denoted by $\mathcal{M}^\sigma$. We use $\mathrm{Pr}^\sigma_{\mathcal{M},s}$ to denote the probability measure defined over the set of infinite paths $IPath^\sigma_{\mathcal{M},s}$. The function $Reach(\mathcal{M}, s, \sigma)$ denotes the set of reachable states in $\mathcal{M}$ starting from $s \in S$ under strategy σ, while $Reach(\mathcal{M}, s)$ denotes the set of all reachable states from s under any strategy.

We use *probabilistic computation tree logic* (PCTL) to formalize system objectives as temporal properties with probabilistic bounds, following the grammar

$$\Phi ::= \top \mid a \mid \neg\Phi \mid \Phi \wedge \Phi \mid \mathbb{P}_J[\varphi], \quad \varphi ::= \mathsf{X}\Phi \mid \Phi\mathsf{U}\Phi \mid \Phi\mathsf{U}^{\leq k}\Phi,$$

where $J \subseteq [0,1]$, and X and U denote the *next* and *until* temporal modalities, respectively. Other derived modalities include $\Diamond$ (*eventually*), $\Box$ (*always*), and W (*weak until*). Given a system $\mathcal{M}$ and a strategy σ, the PCTL satisfaction semantics over $s \in S$ and $\pi \in Paths^\sigma_{\mathcal{M},s}$ is defined as follows [2,12]:

$$
\begin{aligned}
s, \sigma &\models a & &\Leftrightarrow a \in L(s) \\
s, \sigma &\models \neg\Phi & &\Leftrightarrow s \not\models \Phi \\
s, \sigma &\models \Phi_1 \wedge \Phi_2 & &\Leftrightarrow s \models \Phi_1 \wedge s \models \Phi_2 \\
s, \sigma &\models \mathbb{P}_J[\varphi] & &\Leftrightarrow \mathrm{Pr}\{\pi \mid \pi \models \varphi\} \in J \\
\pi, \sigma &\models \mathsf{X}\Phi & &\Leftrightarrow \pi[1] \models \Phi \\
\pi, \sigma &\models \Phi_1 \mathsf{U} \Phi_2 & &\Leftrightarrow \exists j \geq 0. \left(\pi[j] \models \Phi_2 \wedge (\forall 0 \leq k < j. \pi[k] \models \Phi_1)\right) \\
\pi, \sigma &\models \Phi_1 \mathsf{U}^{\leq n} \Phi_2 & &\Leftrightarrow \exists 0 \leq j \leq n. \left(\pi[j] \models \Phi_2 \wedge (\forall 0 \leq k < j. \pi[k] \models \Phi_1)\right)
\end{aligned}
$$

PCTL can be extended with *quantitative queries* of the form $\mathbb{P}_{\min}[\varphi]$ ($\mathbb{P}_{\max}[\Phi]$) to compute the minimum (maximum) probability of achieving φ [12,26], i.e.,

$$\mathbb{P}_{\min}[\varphi] = \inf_{\sigma \in \Sigma} \mathrm{Pr}^\sigma_{\mathcal{M},s}\left(\{\pi \mid \pi \models \varphi\}\right), \quad \mathbb{P}_{\max}[\varphi] = \sup_{\sigma \in \Sigma} \mathrm{Pr}^\sigma_{\mathcal{M},s}\left(\{\pi \mid \pi \models \varphi\}\right).$$

We will denote such queries as $\mathbb{P}_{\mathrm{opt}}$ (read: optimal), where $\mathrm{opt} \in \{\max, \min\}$.

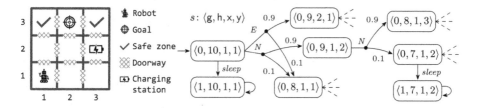

Fig. 1. A motivating example of a robot (left) and part of its model (right).

Motivating Example. Consider the simple grid-world shown in Fig. 1(left). The robot can move between rooms through doorways where obstacles can be probabilistically encountered (e.g., closed doors), requiring the robot to consume more power. The robot state is captured as a tuple s : (g, h, x, y), where $g \in \{on, sleep, error\}$ is the robot's status, $h \in \{0, 1, \ldots, 10\}$ is the robot's battery level, and x and y are its current coordinates. As shown in Fig. 1(right), the system can be modeled as $\mathcal{M} = (S, Act, \mathbf{P}, s_0, AP, L)$, where $Act = \{N, S, E, W, sleep, error\}$, and $s_0 = (0, 10, 1, 1)$. Suppose that the main objective for the robot is to reach the goal with a charge $h > 3$ (objective A). However, if the probability of achieving objective A is less than 0.8, the robot should prioritize reaching the charging station and switch to *sleep* mode (objective B). Moreover, if the probability of achieving objective B falls below 0.7, the robot should stop and switch to *err* mode, preferably in one of the safe zones (objective C).

Now let us examine how such requirements can be formalized. Let $\varphi_A = \Diamond(goal \wedge (h > 3) \wedge on)$, $\varphi_B = \Diamond(chrg \wedge (h > 3) \wedge on)$, and $\varphi_C = \Diamond(error)$. One can use PCTL to capture each objective separately as the reachability queries $\Phi_A = \mathbb{P}_{\max}[\varphi_A]$, $\Phi_B = \mathbb{P}_{\max}[\varphi_B]$, and $\Phi_C = \mathbb{P}_{\max}[\varphi_C]$. A multi-objective query $\Phi_1 = \Phi_A \vee \Phi_B \vee \Phi_C$ does not capture the underlying priority structure in the original requirements. In fact, an optimal strategy for Φ_1 always chooses the actions that reflect the objective with the highest probability of success, resulting in a strategy where the robot simply signals an error from the very initial state. Similarly, the use of $\Phi_2 = \mathbb{P}_{\max}[\varphi_A W \varphi_B]$ does not provide means to specify the context upon which switching from φ_A to φ_B occurs. Attempts featuring multi-objective queries with nested operators, such as $\Phi_3 = \mathbb{P}_{\max}[\varphi_A \wedge \mathbb{P}_{\max \geq 0.8}[\varphi_A]] \vee \mathbb{P}_{\max}[\varphi_B \wedge \mathbb{P}_{\max < 0.8}[\varphi_A]]$, have several drawbacks. First, correctly formalizing the requirement is typically cumbersome and hard to troubleshoot. Second, to the best of our knowledge, nested queries in the form of $\mathbb{P}_{opt \in J}$ are not supported by model checkers. Third, the semantics of the formalized requirement is potentially different from the original one. For instance, Φ_3 allows the system to pursue φ_A even after switching to φ_B if the probability of achieving φ_A rises again above 0.8—a behavior that was not called for in the original requirement.

Consequently, in this paper we focus on two problems: the formalization of PCTL objectives with an underlying context-based priority structure, and the

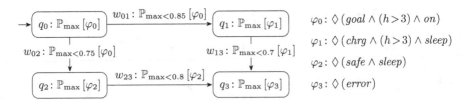

Fig. 2. The CAPTL requirement for the running example.

synthesis of strategies for such objectives. The first problem is addressed by introducing CAPTL in Sect. 3, while the second is addressed in Sect. 4. We will use this motivating example as a running one throughout the rest of this paper.

3   Context-Aware Temporal Logic

CAPTL Syntax. CAPTL features two pertinent notions, namely, objectives and contexts. Let $\mathcal{M}$ be our system model, and let $\varXi$ be the set of all possible PCTL path formulas defined for $\mathcal{M}$. In CAPTL, we define an *objective* q as a conjunctive optimization query $q = \bigwedge_{i=1}^{m} \mathbb{P}_{\mathrm{opt}}[\varphi_i]$, $\varphi_i \in \varXi$, $m > 0$. When $m > 1$, q resembles a multi-objective optimization query in the conjunctive form. Otherwise, in the simplest form where $m = 1$, q is a single-objective query.

A *context* $w_{\langle q, q' \rangle}$ marks a state where switching from objective q to objective q' is required. Formally, we define a context w over $\varXi$ as a set of satisfaction queries in the disjunctive normal form $w = \bigvee_{j=1}^{n} \bigwedge_{i=1}^{m} \mathbb{P}_{\mathrm{opt} \in J_{ij}}[\varphi_{i,j}]$, $\varphi_{ij} \in \varXi$, $J \subseteq [0,1]$. Intuitively, in a state where $w_{\langle q, q' \rangle}$ is satisfied, the system switches from q to q'. Notice that the context definition utilizes the operator $\mathbb{P}_{\mathrm{opt} \in J_{ij}}$ with an interval, i.e., a context is evaluated at a given state as a boolean value in $\mathbb{B}$. In contrast, the objective definition utilizes the operator $\mathbb{P}_{\mathrm{opt}}$ without intervals, i.e., a quantitative optimization query that can return a numerical value in $[0,1]$.

A *CAPTL requirement* defines a set of objectives to be satisfied, in addition to a set of contexts, representing the probabilistic conditions upon which objectives are prioritized. Formally, we define the syntax of a CAPTL requirement as follows.

Definition 3 (CAPTL Requirement). *Given a set of PCTL path formulas $\varXi$, a CAPTL requirement is a tuple $\mathcal{A} = (Q, W, \varXi, \hookrightarrow, q_0)$ where*

- *$Q \subset \{ \bigwedge_{i=1}^{m} \mathbb{P}_{\mathrm{opt}}[\varphi_i] \mid \varphi_i \in \varXi \}$ is a finite nonempty set of objectives over $\varXi$,*
- *$W \subset \left\{ \bigvee_{j=1}^{n} \bigwedge_{i=1}^{m} \mathbb{P}_{\mathrm{opt} \in J_{ij}}[\varphi_{i,j}] \mid \varphi_{ij} \in \varXi, J_{ij} \subseteq [0,1] \right\}$ is a set of contexts,*
- *$\hookrightarrow \subseteq Q \times W \times Q$ is a conditional transition relation, and*
- *$q_0 \in Q$ is an initial objective.*

In a CAPTL requirement $\mathcal{A}$, each state $q \in Q$ represents an objective, i.e., an optimization query to be satisfied. The conditional transition relation $\hookrightarrow$ defines how objectives are allowed to change. For instance, if $q \xrightarrow{w} q'$, a shorthand for $(q, w, q') \in \hookrightarrow$, then the objectives are switched from q to q' if w is satisfied.

Notice that contexts are used as labels for the conditional transition relation. In the rest of this paper, we will overload the notation and use $W : Q \rightarrow \mathcal{P}(W)$ to denote the set of contexts emerging from a given objective. We will also use $Q(q, w) = q'$ to denote that objective q has a context w that leads to q'.

Example 1. For the running example, Fig. 2 shows an example of a CAPTL requirement $\mathcal{A}$ where $Q = \{q_0, q_1, q_2, q_3\}$, $W = \{w_{01}, w_{02}, w_{13}, w_{23}\}$, and $\hookrightarrow = \{\langle q_0, w_{01}, q_1 \rangle, \langle q_0, w_{02}, q_2 \rangle, \langle q_1, w_{13}, q_3 \rangle, \langle q_0, w_{23}, q_3 \rangle\}$. The requirement starts by prioritizing $q_0 = \mathbb{P}_{\max}[\varphi_0]$. If $\mathbb{P}_{\max}[\varphi_0] \in [0.75, 0.85)$, the context w_{01} becomes true, and by executing $q_0 \xrightarrow{w_{01}} q_1$, $q_1 = \mathbb{P}_{\max}[\varphi_1]$ is prioritized. Similarly, if $\mathbb{P}_{\max}[\varphi_0] \in [0, 0.75)$, w_{02} becomes true, executing $q_0 \xrightarrow{w_{02}} q_2$ where $q_2 = \mathbb{P}_{\max}[\varphi_2]$ is prioritized. Notice that objectives can have a single context, e.g., $W(q_1) = \{w_{13}\}$; multiple contexts, e.g., $W(q_0) = \{w_{01}, w_{02}\}$; or none, e.g., $W(q_3) = \varnothing$.

CAPTL Semantics for MDPs. We progressively define CAPTL semantics for MDPs by first defining the satisfaction semantics for objectives and contexts. Let $q = \mathbb{P}_{\max}[\varphi]$ be the objective at state s, and let Σ be the set of all strategies for $\mathcal{M}$. We say that $s, \sigma^* \models q$ if $\sigma^* \in \Sigma$ such that

$$\mathrm{Pr}_{\mathcal{M}}^{\sigma^*, s} = \sup_{\sigma \in \Sigma} \mathrm{Pr}_{\mathcal{M}, s}^{\sigma} \left(\{\pi \in Paths_{\mathcal{M}, s}^{\sigma} \mid \pi \models \varphi\} \right). \tag{1}$$

In that case, we call σ^* a *local strategy*, i.e., an optimal strategy w.r.t. $\langle q, s \rangle$.

Definition 4 (Local Strategy). *Let* $q_i = \mathbb{P}_{\mathrm{opt}}[\varphi_i]$ *be an objective. A* local *(optimal) strategy for* $\langle q_i, s_i \rangle$ *is a strategy* $\sigma_{\langle q_i, s_i \rangle} \in \Sigma$ *such that*

$$\mathrm{Pr}_{\mathcal{M}, s_i}^{\sigma_{\langle q_i, s_i \rangle}} = \mathop{\mathrm{opt}}_{\sigma \in \Sigma} \mathrm{Pr}_{\mathcal{M}, s_i}^{\sigma} \left(\{\pi \in Paths_{\mathcal{M}, s_i}^{\sigma} \mid \pi \models \varphi_i\} \right)$$

Next, let $(q, w, q') \in \hookrightarrow$, where $w = \mathbb{P}_{\leq c}[\varphi]$. Let $s_k \in Reach(\mathcal{M}, s, \sigma^*)$, where σ^* is the local strategy for $\langle q, s \rangle$. We say that $s_k \models w$ if

$$\sup_{\sigma \in \Sigma} \mathrm{Pr}_{\mathcal{M}, s_k}^{\sigma} \left(\{\pi \in Paths_{\mathcal{M}, s_k}^{\sigma} \mid \pi \models \varphi\} \right) \leq c. \tag{2}$$

Note that contrary to (1), the set of paths $\{\pi\}$ in (2) is *not* limited to those induced by the local strategy σ^*. Moreover, if $\exists \pi = s \ldots s_i \ldots s_k \in FPath_{\mathcal{M}, s}^{\sigma}$ s.t. $s_i \models w$, and $s_i \not\models w$ for all $i < k$, then s_k is called a *switching state*, i.e., the first state on a path π to satisfy w, triggering a switch from q to q'.

Definition 5 (Switching Set). *Let* $q = \mathbb{P}_{\mathrm{opt}}[\varphi]$ *and* $\sigma^* \in \Sigma$ *such that* $s_0, \sigma^* \models q$. *The corresponding* switching set $S_q \subseteq Reach(\mathcal{M}, s_0, \sigma^*)$ *is defined as*

$$S_q = \left\{ s_k \mid \exists \pi = s_0 \ldots s_i \ldots s_k \in FPath_{\mathcal{M}, s_0}^{\sigma^*} \text{ s.t. } s_i \not\models \bigvee_{w \in W(q)} w, \forall i < k; s_k \models \bigvee_{w \in W(q)} w \right\}.$$

We use $S_q^{q'}$ *to denote the set of switching states from* q *to* q'.

An objective is *active* in a state s if it is being pursued at that state.

Definition 6 (Active Objective). *Let* $\mathcal{A} = (Q, W, \Xi, \hookrightarrow, q_0)$ *and* $\mathcal{M} = (S, Act, \mathbf{P}, s_0, AP, L)$. *An* activation function $g : S \to \mathcal{P}(Q)$ *is defined inductively as: (i)* $g(s_0) \ni q_0$; *and (ii)* $g(s) \ni q'$ *if* $g(s) \ni q$ *and* $s \in S_q^{q'}$. *We say objective* $q \in Q$ *is* active at state $s \in S$ *if* $g(s) \ni q$.

As captured in Definition 4, local strategies are tied to their respective objectives. Consequently, a local strategy is switched whenever an objective is switched as well, and the new local strategy substitutes its predecessor. We call the set of local strategies a *strategy profile*, and the resulting behavior a *protocol*.

Definition 7 (Protocol). *Let* $\mathcal{A} = (Q, W, \Xi, \hookrightarrow, q_0)$ *and* $\mathcal{M} = (S, Act, \mathbf{P}, s_0, AP, L)$. *Given a strategy profile* $\sigma = \{\sigma_{\langle q,s \rangle} \dots\}$, *the induced* (optimal) *protocol is a (partial) function* $\Pi : Q \times S \nrightarrow Act \cup \mathcal{P}(W)$ *such that*

- $\Pi(q, s) = \sigma_{\langle q,s \rangle}(s) \in Act$ *iff* $q \in g(s)$ *and* $s \notin S_q$; *and*
- $\Pi(q, s) \ni w_{\langle q,q' \rangle}$, *where* $w_{\langle q,q' \rangle} \in W$, *iff* $q \in g(s)$ *and* $s \in S_q^{q'}$.

Given $\langle q, s \rangle$, a protocol assigns either an optimal action based on the local strategy associated with q, or a context to switch the active objective itself. We will use $\mathfrak{P}$ to denote the set of all possible protocols.

Definition 8 (System-Protocol Composition). *Let* $\mathcal{M} = (S, Act, \mathbf{P}, s_0, AP, L)$ *and* $\Pi : Q \times S \nrightarrow Act \cup \mathcal{P}(W)$ *be a compatible protocol. Their composition is defined as* $\mathcal{M}^{\Pi} = \left(\hat{Q}, Act \cup W, \hat{\mathbf{P}}, \hat{s}_0, \hat{L} \right)$ *where* $\hat{Q} \subseteq Q \times S$, $\hat{s}_0 = \langle q_0, s_0 \rangle$, *and*

$$\hat{\mathbf{P}}(\langle q, s \rangle, a, \langle q', s' \rangle) = \begin{cases} \mathbf{P}(s, a, s') & \text{if } \Pi(q, s) = a, \ q' = q, \\ 1 & \text{if } \Pi(q, s) = w, \ s' = s, \ q' = Q(q, w), \\ 0 & \text{otherwise.} \end{cases}$$

We now define the CAPTL satisfaction semantics as follows.

Definition 9 (CAPTL Satisfaction Semantics). *Let* $\mathcal{A} = (Q, W, \Xi, \hookrightarrow, q_0)$, $\mathcal{M} = (S, Act, \mathbf{P}, s_0, AP, L)$, *and* $\Pi : Q \times S \nrightarrow Act \cup \mathcal{P}(W)$. *The* CAPTL *satisfaction semantics is defined inductively as follows:*

$$\mathcal{M}, \Pi \models q \Leftrightarrow \Pr_{\mathcal{M}^{\Pi}}(\{\pi \in Paths_{\mathcal{M}^{\Pi}} \mid last(\pi) = \langle q, s' \rangle, s' \models q\}) \geqslant 1,$$
$$\mathcal{M}, \Pi \models_c \mathcal{A} \Leftrightarrow \Pr_{\mathcal{M}^{\Pi}}(\{\pi \in Paths_{\mathcal{M}^{\Pi}} \mid last(\pi) = \langle q, s' \rangle, s' \models q, q \in Q\}) = c,$$
$$\mathcal{M}, \Pi \models \mathcal{A} \Leftrightarrow \mathcal{M}, \Pi \models_{\geqslant 1} \mathcal{A}.$$

CAPTL semantics dictate that $\mathcal{M}$ and Π satisfy $\mathcal{A}$ if every path $\pi \in Paths_{\mathcal{M}^{\Pi}}$ ends with a state $s \in S$ where $q \ni g(s)$ and $s \models q$, i.e., the system reaches some state s where some objective q is both active and satisfied.

CAPTL Fragments. A CAPTL requirement is *nondeterministic* if for some $q \in Q$, $\exists w_i, w_j \in W(q)$ such that $S_q^{q_i} \cap S_q^{q_j} \neq \varnothing$. That is, at least one objective has two or more contexts that can be active at the same state. If that is not the case, then the CAPTL requirement is *deterministic*. We now identify a fragment of deterministic CAPTL requirements where the following two conditions are met. First, every $q \in Q$ is a quantitative PCTL persistence objective. Second, every $w \in W(q)$ is a qualitative PCTL persistence objective over the same persistence set as in q. This is formally captured in the following definition.

Definition 10 (Persistence CAPTL). *A CAPTL requirement $\mathcal{A} = (Q, W, \Xi, \hookrightarrow, q_0)$ is persistent if (i) every $q \in Q$ is of the form $q = \mathbb{P}_{\max}[\Diamond \Box B]$ for some $B \subseteq S$ and (ii) if $W(q) \neq \varnothing$ then for any $w_{\langle q, q_j \rangle} \in W(q)$, it holds that $w_{\langle q, q_j \rangle} = \mathbb{P}_{\max \in J_j}[\Diamond \Box B]$ where (J_j) are disjoint intervals satisfying $\cup_j J_j = [0, c)$ for some $0 < c \leq 1$.*

A persistence CAPTL (P-CAPTL) requirement allows for defining persistence objectives, where each objective maximizes the probability of (i.e., prioritizes) reaching a corresponding persistence set. Contexts in this case can be understood as lower bounds of their respective objectives. That is, an objective is pursued as long as, at any transient state, the probability of achieving such objective does not drop below a certain threshold. The requirement also ensures that at most one context is satisfied at any state, eliminating any nondeterminism in $\mathcal{A}$.

Example 2. Continuing Example 1, Fig. 3 shows the persistence CAPTL requirement for the robot. Notice that all objectives are in the form $\mathbb{P}_{\max}[\Diamond \Box B]$. Also, the intervals $[0.75, 0.85)$ and $[0, 0.75)$ of w_{01} and w_{02}, respectively, are disjoint, hence at most one context in $W(q_0) = \{w_{01}, w_{02}\}$ can be satisfied at any state.

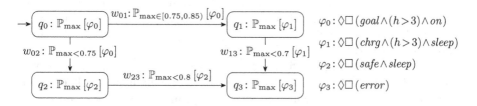

Fig. 3. The persistence CAPTL requirement for the running example.

4   CAPTL-Based Synthesis

In this section we first define the synthesis problem for CAPTL requirements. Next, we examine a general procedure for deterministic CAPTL where the synthesis problem is reduced to solving a set of PCTL-based strategy synthesis problems. Finally, we utilize the underlying structure of persistence properties to propose a synthesis procedure optimized for P-CAPTL requirements.

In the rest of this section, let $\mathcal{M} = (S, Act, \mathbf{P}, s_0, AP, L)$ and $\mathcal{A} = (Q, W, \Xi, \hookrightarrow, q_0)$. We assume that a probabilistic model checker is given (e.g., PRISM-games [19] or UPPAAL STRATEGO [8]) that can accept an MDP-based model $\mathcal{M}$ and a PCTL formula Φ as inputs, and provides the following functions:

- REACH :: $(\mathcal{M}, s) \mapsto R \subseteq S$ returns the set of reachable states $R = Reach(\mathcal{M}, s)$.
- VERIFY :: $(\mathcal{M}, s, \Phi) \mapsto b \in \mathbb{B}$ returns the Boolean value $\top$ if $\mathcal{M}, s \models \Phi$, and returns $\bot$ otherwise.
- SYNTH :: $(\mathcal{M}, s, \Phi) \mapsto (\sigma, c)$ returns a policy $\sigma \in \Sigma$ s.t. $\Pr(\mathcal{M}_s^\sigma \models \Phi) = c$ for some $c \in [0, 1]$.

We also assume that the model checker functions terminate in finite time and return correct answers. We now define the CAPTL synthesis problem as follows.

Definition 11 (CAPTL Synthesis Problem). *Given* $\mathcal{M} = (S, Act, \mathbf{P}, s_0, AP, L)$ *and* $\mathcal{A} = (Q, W, \Xi, \hookrightarrow, q_0)$, *the CAPTL synthesis problem seeks to find a protocol* $\Pi : Q \times S \nrightarrow Act \cup W$ *such that* $\mathcal{M}, \Pi \models \mathcal{A}$.

PCTL-Based Approach. The synthesis problem can be reduced to solving a set of PCTL-based synthesis queries as demonstrated in Algorithm 1. Starting with $\langle q_0, s_0 \rangle$, the algorithm verifies whether any context $w \in W(q_0)$ is satisfied, and if true, adds w to the protocol and switches to the next objective. If no context is satisfied, the algorithm synthesizes a local strategy and adds the corresponding optimal action to the protocol.

Proposition 1. *Algorithm 1 terminates; and returns* Π, c *iff* $\mathcal{M}, \Pi \models_c \mathcal{A}$.

Synthesis for P-CAPTL. We now propose a synthesis algorithm optimized for persistence CAPTL. To this end, we show that for a given persistence objective, synthesizing a local strategy in the initial state suffices. In a manner similar to switching states (see Definition 5), we devise a partition of reachable states for every objective. We will use those concepts to define a system-CAPTL composition and show that it is bisimilar to $\mathcal{M}^\Pi$.

Let $R = Reach(\mathcal{M}, s_0)$. We first note that given $\mathcal{M}$ and $q = \mathbb{P}_{opt}[\Diamond\Box B]$, existing model checking and synthesis algorithms typically compute a least fixed point (LFP) vector $\mathbf{x}_q \in [0, 1]^{|R|}$, where $\mathbf{x}_q[s]$ is the optimal probability of satisfying $\Diamond\Box B$ at state $s \in R$ (e.g., see [2,16]). That is, when SYNTH $(\mathcal{M}, s_0, q)$ is called, $\mathbf{x}_q$ is computed, but only $c = \mathbf{x}_q[s_0]$ is returned (i.e., the value at the initial state). We exploit this fact by implementing a function REACHP :: $(\mathcal{M}, s, q) \mapsto \mathbf{x}_q$ that returns the LFP vector $\mathbf{x}_q$ associated with q.

Lemma 1 (Local Strategy Dominance). *Let* $\mathcal{M} = (S, Act, \mathbf{P}, s_0, AP, L)$ *and* $q = \mathbb{P}_{max}[\Diamond\Box B]$. *For all* $s \in Reach(\mathcal{M}, s_0)$, $\sigma_{\langle q, s \rangle} = \sigma_{\langle q, s_0 \rangle}|_{Reach(\mathcal{M}, s)}$.

Lemma 1 signifies that a local strategy for q in the initial state (i.e., $\sigma_{\langle q, s_0 \rangle}$) subsumes all local strategies for the same probabilistic reachability objective in every $s \in R$. Next, for every $q \in Q$, let us define the following partition of R:

Algorithm 1: PCTL-Based Synthesis

Input: $\mathcal{M} = (S, Act, \mathbf{P}, s_0, AP, L)$, $\mathcal{A} = (Q, W, \Xi, \hookrightarrow, q_0)$
Result: Π, c such that $\mathcal{M}, \Pi \models_c \mathcal{A}$

1 **foreach** $q \in Q$ **do** $\hat{S}_q \leftarrow \varnothing$, $\bar{S}_q \leftarrow \varnothing$
2 $\Pi \leftarrow \varnothing$, $\hat{S}_{q_0} \leftarrow \{s_0\}$, $q \leftarrow q_0$, $\mathbf{C} \leftarrow \mathbf{0}_{Q \times S} \in [0,1]^{Q \times S}$, $repeat \leftarrow \top$
3 **while** $\hat{S}_q \neq \varnothing$ **do**
4 $\quad$ Let $s \in \hat{S}_q$, $\hat{S}_q \leftarrow \hat{S}_q \setminus \{s\}$, $\bar{S}_q \leftarrow \bar{S}_q \cup \{s\}$
5 $\quad$ **while** $repeat$ **do** $repeat \leftarrow \bot$
6 $\quad\quad$ **foreach** $w \in W(q)$ **do**
7 $\quad\quad\quad$ **if** VERIFY$(\mathcal{M}, s, w) = \top$ **then**
8 $\quad\quad\quad\quad$ $\Pi \leftarrow \Pi \cup \{(s, q, w)\}$, $q \leftarrow Q(q, w)$, $repeat \leftarrow \top$, **break**
9 $\quad$ $(\sigma, \mathbf{C}(q, s)) \leftarrow$ SYNTH$(\mathcal{M}; s, q)$, $\Pi \leftarrow \Pi \cup \{(s, q, \sigma(s))\}$
10 $\quad$ $\hat{S}_q \leftarrow \hat{S}_q \cup (Post(\mathcal{M}, s, \sigma(s)) \setminus \bar{S}_q)$
11 $c \leftarrow$ VERIFY$\left(\mathcal{M}^\Pi, \langle q_0, s_0 \rangle, \mathbb{P}\left[\Diamond \bigvee_{q \in Q}(\langle q, s \rangle \wedge \mathbf{C}(q, s) = 1)\right]\right)$

- $R_q^q = \{s \in R \mid \forall w = \mathbb{P}_{\max \in J}[\Diamond \Box B] \in W(q), \mathbf{x}_q[s] \notin J\}$, i.e., the states in R where, if q is active, keep pursuing q.
- $R_q^{q'} = \{s \in R \mid \exists w = \mathbb{P}_{\max \in J}[\Diamond \Box B] \in W(q), \mathbf{x}_q[s] \in J, Q(q, w) = q'\}$, i.e., the states in R where, if q is active, switch to q'.

Lemma 2 (Partitioning). *Let* $\mathcal{M} = (S, Act, \mathbf{P}, s_0, AP, L)$, $\mathcal{A} = (Q, W, \Xi, \hookrightarrow, q_0)$, *and* $R = Reach(\mathcal{M}, s_0)$. *For every* $q \in Q$, $\bigcup_{q' \in Q} R_q^{q'} = R$; *and* $R_q^{q'} \cap R_q^{q''} = \varnothing$ *for every* $q' \neq q''$.

Proof Sketch. From Definition 10, the intervals $(J_w)_{w \in W(q)}$ are disjoint; hence $(R_q^{q'})_{q' \neq q}$ are disjoint as well, and that $R_q^q = R / \left(\bigcup_{q' \neq q} R_q^{q'} \right)$. $\quad\square$

Example 3. Returning to the P-CAPTL requirement specified in the running example (see Fig. 3), Fig. 4 depicts the partitioning of the state-space based on q_0, q_1, q_2 and q_3. Notice that for any $q \in Q$, the sets $(R_q^{q'})_{q' \in Q}$ are pairwise disjoint, where $\bigcup_{q' \in Q} R_q^{q'} = Reach(\mathcal{M}, s_0)$. For example, $R_{q_0}^{q_0}$, $R_{q_0}^{q_1}$ and $R_{q_0}^{q_2}$ do not intersect, and their union spans $R = Reach(\mathcal{M}, s_0)$. In this case, $R_{q_0}^{q_3} = \varnothing$ since there is no direct context emerging from q_0 to q_3.

Definition 12 (System-CAPTL Composition). *Let* $\mathcal{M} = (S, Act, \mathbf{P}, s_0, AP, L)$, $\mathcal{A} = (Q, W, \Xi, \hookrightarrow, q_0)$, *and* $\sigma = \{\sigma_{\langle q, s_0 \rangle} \mid q \in Q\}$. *Their composition is defined as the automaton* $\mathcal{M}_{\mathcal{A}}^\sigma = (V, \overline{Act}, \mathbf{P}_v, \rightarrow', v_0, AP, \bar{L})$ *where* $V \subseteq S \times Q \times \Gamma$, *and* $\Gamma = \{①, ②\}$; $\overline{Act} = Act \cup W \cup \{\tau\}$, *where* τ *is a stutter action*; $v_0 = \langle s_0, q_0, ② \rangle$; $\bar{L} : V \rightarrow \mathcal{P}(AP)$ *such that* $\bar{L}(\langle s, q, \gamma \rangle) = L(s)$; *and the transition relation* $\rightarrow'$ *is defined using the following compositional rules:*

$$[R1] \frac{s \xrightarrow{a, p} s' \wedge \sigma_{\langle q, s_0 \rangle}(s) = a}{\langle s, q, ① \rangle \xrightarrow{a, p}{}' \langle s', q, ② \rangle} \quad [R2] \frac{s \in R_q^q}{\langle s, q, ② \rangle \xrightarrow{\tau}{}' \langle s, q, ① \rangle} \quad [R3] \frac{s \in R_q^{q'}}{\langle s, q, ② \rangle \xrightarrow{w_{\langle q, q' \rangle}}{}' \langle s, q', ② \rangle}.$$

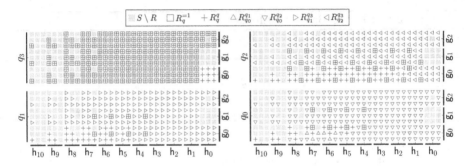

Fig. 4. Partitioning the state-space of the running example using q_0, q_1, q_2, and q_3. For example, $\langle q_1, g_0, h_5, 2, 1 \rangle = \triangleright$ indicates that $s : \langle g, h, x, y \rangle = \langle 0, 5, 2, 1 \rangle \in R_{q_1}^{q_3}$.

The rules in Definition 12 are interpreted as follows. The state space V is partitioned into $V_{①}$ (where $\mathcal{M}$ actions are allowed) and $V_{②}$ (where $\mathcal{A}$ actions are allowed), resembling a turn-based 2-player game. [R1] ensures that, if q is active in s, then only the transitions with the optimal action $\sigma_{\langle q, s_0 \rangle}(s)$ are allowed. [R2] ensures that, if $s \in R_q^q$, the active objective remains unchanged. If $s \in R_q^{q'}$, however, [R3] enforces switching the active objective to q'. The action τ is a stutter since $\forall v \xrightarrow{\tau} v'$, $\bar{L}(v) = \bar{L}(v')$.

Lemma 3 (Induced DTMC). $\mathcal{M}_{\mathcal{A}}^{\sigma}$ *constructed using Definition 12 is a DTMC.*

Lemma 3 dictates that the probability measure $\Pr_{\mathcal{M}_{\mathcal{A}}^{\sigma}}$ is well-defined. We will now use the notion of *stutter equivalence* [2] to prove that $\mathcal{M}_{\mathcal{A}}^{\sigma}$ is bisimilar to $\mathcal{M}^{\Pi}$. Basically, two paths π_1 and π_2 are stutter-equivalent, denoted by $\pi_1 \triangleq \pi_2$, if there exists a finite sequence $A_0 \dots A_n \in (\mathcal{P}(AP))^+$ such that $trace(\pi), trace(\hat{\pi}) \in A_0^+ A_1^+ \dots A_n^+$, where $A^+ = \{A, AA, \dots\}$ is the set of finite, non-empty repetitions.

Theorem 1 (Stutter-Equivalence). *Let $\mathcal{M}$, $\mathcal{A}$, and $\Pi \in \mathfrak{P}$ be such that $\mathcal{M}, \Pi \models \mathcal{A}$. For every $\pi \in FPath_{\mathcal{M}^{\Pi}}$ there exists $\hat{\pi} \in FPath_{\mathcal{M}_{\mathcal{A}}^{\sigma}}$ such that $\pi \triangleq \hat{\pi}$ and $\Pr_{\mathcal{M}^{\Pi}}(\pi) = \Pr_{\mathcal{M}_{\mathcal{A}}^{\sigma}}(\hat{\pi})$. For every $\hat{\pi} \in FPath_{\mathcal{M}_{\mathcal{A}}^{\sigma}}$, where $last(\hat{\pi}) \in V_{②}$, there exists $\hat{\pi} \in FPath_{\mathcal{M}^{\Pi}}$ such that $\hat{\pi} \triangleq \pi$ and $\Pr_{\mathcal{M}_{\mathcal{A}}^{\sigma}}(\hat{\pi}) = \Pr_{\mathcal{M}^{\Pi}}(\pi)$.*

Proof Sketch. We show that for every execution fragment $\varrho_1 = \langle s, q \rangle \xrightarrow{a,p} \langle s, q' \rangle$ there exists $\hat{\varrho}_1 = \langle s, q, ② \rangle \xrightarrow{\tau} \langle s, q, ① \rangle \xrightarrow{a,p} \langle s', q, ② \rangle$ Moreover, for every $\varrho_2 = \langle s, q \rangle \xrightarrow{w} \langle s', q \rangle$ there exists $\hat{\varrho}_2 = \langle s, q, ② \rangle \xrightarrow{w} \langle s, q', ② \rangle$. Using induction, we show that for every arbitrary execution ϱ there exists $\hat{\varrho}$ such that $\varrho \triangleq \hat{\varrho}$, where

$$trace(\varrho) = (A_0 + A_0 A_0)(A_1 + A_1 A_1) \dots (A_n + A_n A_n) \in (\mathcal{P}(AP))^+$$
$$trace(\hat{\varrho}) = (A_0 A_0) \qquad (A_1 A_1) \qquad \dots (A_n A_n) \qquad \in (\mathcal{P}(AP))^+$$

and $\Pr(\varrho) = \Pr(\hat{\varrho})$. Similarly, the other direction can be shown for every $last(\hat{\varrho})$ that ends with $last(\hat{\varrho}) \in V_{②}$. $\qquad \square$

We use Theorem 1 to devise the protocol synthesis procedure summarized in Algorithm 2. In the first part (lines 1–8), the procedure starts by synthesizing a local strategy $\sigma_{\langle q_0, s_0 \rangle}$ and obtaining the associated LFP vector $\mathbf{x}_{q_0} \in [0, 1]^R$. Next, R is partitioned using $\mathbf{x}_{q_0}$ to obtain $(R_{q_0}^q)_{q \in Q}$. If $R_{q_0}^q \neq \varnothing$ for some $q \neq q_0$, the same procedure is repeated for q to obtain $\langle q, s_0 \rangle$, $\mathbf{x}_q$ and $(R_q^{q'})_{q' \in Q}$. In the second part (lines 9–16), three modules are constructed based on Definition 12. The resulting parallel composition constitutes $\mathcal{M}_{\mathcal{A}}^{\sigma}$, which mimics a stochastic 2-player game between $\hat{\mathcal{M}}$ (player ①) and $\hat{\mathcal{A}}$ (player ②), where the players' choices are already resolved by $\hat{\sigma}$. Finally, Π is populated by a query that checks for the CAPTL satisfaction condition (line 17), i.e., a state $\langle s, q_i, \gamma \rangle$ is reached where $q_i = \mathbb{P}_{\max}[\lozenge \square B_i]$ is active, and $\square B_i$ holds. Notice that, based on the results from Lemma 1, Algorithm 2 synthesizes a local strategy at most once for every $q \in Q$, compared to Algorithm 1 where synthesis is performed at every reachable state.

Theorem 2. *Algorithm 2 terminates; and returns Π, c iff $\mathcal{M}, \Pi \models_c \mathcal{A}$.*

Example 4. (Protocol Synthesis). For the CAPTL requirement in Example 2 (see Fig. 3), Fig. 5 shows a visual representation of the protocol synthesized using Algorithm 2, where blue markers indicate actions in Act, and red markers indicate actions in W. While pursuing q_0, the robot can achieve the task by moving N(▲), N(▲), E(▶) if no obstacles are encountered, or if obstacles are encountered only once while moving E(▶). Switching from q_0 to q_1 via $w_{01}(\triangle)$ occurs in one state $(0, 7, 1, 2)$; while switching from q_0 to q_2 via $w_{02}(\triangledown)$ occurs in four states $(0, 8, 1, 1)$, $(0, 4, 3, 1)$, $(2, 7, 2, 3)$ and $(0, 4, 1, 3)$.

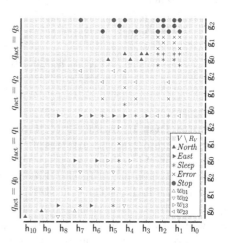

Fig. 5. The protocol synthesized based on the CAPTL requirement in Fig. 3, where $R_V = Reach(\mathcal{M}_{\mathcal{A}}^{\sigma}, v_0)$.

5   Experimental Evaluation

We demonstrate the use of CAPTL for protocol synthesis and analysis on two case studies. The first extends the robot task planning problem introduced in Sect. 2. The second considers the problem of synthesizing an error-resilient scheduler for digital microfluidic biochips. To this end, we implemented Algorithm 2 in MATLAB on top of a modified version of PRISM-games [19] (v4.4), where REACHP functionality was added. The experiments presented in this section were run on an Intel Core i7 2.6 GHz CPU with 16 GB RAM.

Algorithm 2: Synthesis Procedure for P-CAPTL

Input: $\mathcal{M} = (S, Act, \mathbf{P}, s_0, AP, L)$, $\mathcal{A} = (Q, W, \varXi, \hookrightarrow, q_0)$
Result: $\varPi, c$ such that $\mathcal{M}, \varPi \models_c \mathcal{A}$

1 **foreach** $(q, q') \in Q \times Q$ **do** $R_q^{q'} \leftarrow \varnothing$ // Initialize

2 $\varPi \leftarrow \varnothing$, $\hat{Q} \leftarrow \{q_0\}$, $\bar{Q} \leftarrow \varnothing$, $R \leftarrow \text{REACH}(\mathcal{M}, s_0)$

3 **while** $\hat{Q} \neq \varnothing$ **do**   // Partition R

4   Let $q \in \hat{Q}$, $\hat{Q} \leftarrow \hat{Q} \setminus \{q\}$, $\bar{Q} \leftarrow \bar{Q} \cup \{q\}$, $R_q^q \leftarrow R$

5     $\sigma_{\langle q, s_0 \rangle} \leftarrow \text{SYNTH}(\mathcal{M}; s_0, q)$, $\mathbf{x}_q \leftarrow \text{REACHP}(\mathcal{M}, s_0, \sigma_{\langle q, s_0 \rangle})$

6   **foreach** $w \in W(q)$ where $q' = Q(q, w)$ **do**

7        $R_q^{q'} \leftarrow \{s \mid \mathbf{x}_q[s] \in J_w\}$, $R_q^q \leftarrow R_q^q \setminus R_q^{q'}$

8   **if** $R_q^{q'} \neq \varnothing \wedge q' \notin \bar{Q}$ **then** $\hat{Q} \leftarrow \hat{Q} \cup \{q'\}$

9 **construct** $\hat{\mathcal{M}}$ module such that   // Construct $\mathcal{M}_{\mathcal{A}}^{\sigma}$

10   **foreach** $[a]\, s \to p_i : (s_i')$ **do** add $[a]\, s \wedge ① \to p_i : (s_i') \wedge ②$

11 **construct** $\hat{\mathcal{A}}$ module such that

12   **foreach** $q \in \bar{Q}$ **do** add $[\tau]\, q_{\text{act}} = q \wedge ② \wedge L(R_q^q; s) \to (q_{\text{act}} = q) \wedge ①$

13   **foreach** $q \xrightarrow{w} q'$ **do** add $[w]\, q_{\text{act}} = q \wedge ② \wedge L(R_q^{q'}; s) \to (q_{\text{act}} = q') \wedge ②$

14 **construct** $\hat{\sigma}$ module such that

15   **foreach** $\sigma_{\langle q, s_0 \rangle} \neq \varnothing$ and $s \in R$ **do** add $[\sigma_{\langle q, s_0 \rangle}(s)]\, q_{\text{act}} = q \wedge s \to \top$

16 $\mathcal{M}_{\mathcal{A}}^{\sigma} \leftarrow \hat{\mathcal{M}} \parallel \hat{\mathcal{A}} \parallel \hat{\sigma}$

17 $(\varPi, c) \leftarrow \text{SYNTH}\left(\mathcal{M}_{\mathcal{A}}^{\sigma}, \langle q_0, s_0, ② \rangle, \mathbb{P}[\bigvee_{q_i \in Q} \Diamond \square (q_{\text{act}} = q_i) \wedge B_i]\right)$

Robotic Task Planner. Table 1 summarizes the performance results for running Algorithm 2 on various sizes of the running example. Notice that the number of choices in $\mathcal{M}_{\mathcal{A}}^{\sigma}$ always matches the number of states, which agrees with the results from Lemma 3. In the three models, q_0 is always active in s_0, and thus is always verified. As the grid size grows larger, the probability of reaching the goal—and hence satisfying q_0—becomes lower, dropping below 0.85 at the initial state in both (6×6) and (9×9). As a result, q_1 is never active (and hence is never verified) in the second and third models. We also notice that the total time required to run Algorithm 2 does not necessarily grow as the size of the problem grows. In fact, the total time required for (6×6) and (9×9) is lower than the one for (3×3). This is primarily due to the fact that q_1 is never reached or verified in the second and third models as we described. When comparing the model size for $\mathcal{M}$ and $\mathcal{M}_{\mathcal{A}}^{\sigma}$, we notice that $|\mathcal{M}_{\mathcal{A}}^{\sigma}| < |\mathcal{M}|$, with the difference being in orders of magnitude for larger models. However, the time required to construct $\mathcal{M}_{\mathcal{A}}^{\sigma}$ is longer than the time required to construct $\mathcal{M}$.

MEDA-Biochip Scheduler. We now consider synthesizing error-resilient scheduler for micro-electrode-dot-array (MEDA) digital microfluidic biochips, where we borrow examples from [10,21]. A biochip segment consists of a $W \times H$ matrix of on-chip actuators and sensors to manipulate microfluidic droplets, and is further partitioned into 3×3 blocks. Two reservoirs are used to dispense droplets A and B. Various activation patterns can be applied to manipulate

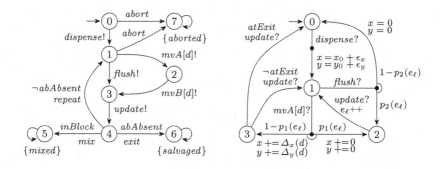

Fig. 6. The MEDA biochip scheduler model (left) and the droplet model (right).

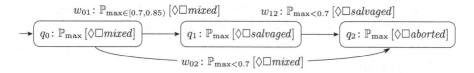

Fig. 7. P-CAPTL requirement for a MEDA-biochip segment scheduler.

the droplets, including moving (moving droplets individually), flushing (moving both droplets at the same time in the same direction) and mixing (merging two droplets occupying the same block). As the biochip degrades, the actuators become less reliable, and an actuation command may not result in the droplet moving as expected. The probability of an error occurring is proportional to the total number of errors occurred in the same block.

Figure 6 shows part of the segment scheduler (left) and the droplet (right) models. Initially, the scheduler can dispense both droplets through the *dispense* action, where the droplet location (x, y) can probabilistically deviate from the dispenser location (x_0, y_0) with error ϵ. Subsequently, droplets can be individually manipulated via $mvA[d]$ and $mvB[d]$ actions where d is the direction, or together via *flush*. The probability of successful manipulation $(1 - p(e_\ell))$ depends on both the number of errors within the same block (e_ℓ) and the activation pattern used. The scheduler executes *update* to sense droplet locations and register errors.

The primary task of the scheduler is to perform a mixing operation within the given segment (q_0). However, if the droplets are dispensed and (due to faulty blocks) the probability of a successful mixing operation is below 0.85 (w_{01}), salvaging the dispensed droplets by moving them to an adjacent segment is prioritized (q_1). If the mixing probability drops below 0.7 (w_{02}), or if the salvaging probability drops below 0.7 (w_{12}), the scheduler is to abort the operation (q_2). The aforementioned requirements are formalized using CAPTL as shown in Fig. 7. The set of objectives is $Q = \{q_0, q_1, q_2\}$, and the set of contexts is

Table 1. Protocol synthesis performance results for the robotic task planner (C1) and the MEDA-biochip scheduler (C2). (St.: states, Tr.: transitions, Ch.: choices).

Model Size	$\mathcal{M}$ Size			$\mathcal{M}_\mathcal{A}^\sigma$ Size			Construction/Synthesis Time (sec)							
Size	St.	Tr.	Ch.	St.	Tr.	Ch.	$\mathcal{M}$	q_0	q_1	q_2	q_3	$\mathcal{M}_\mathcal{A}^\sigma$	$q_\mathcal{A}$	Total
C1 3×3	233	1,117	745	142	163	142	0.438	0.031	0.029	0.033	0.106	0.557	0.052	25.5
6×6	595	2,692	1,874	159	190	159	0.495	0.041	–	0.083	0.260	0.662	0.112	24.2
9×9	733	3,242	2,278	96	116	96	0.508	0.037	–	0.059	0.313	0.691	0.083	21.9
C2 8×5	2,851	8,269	5,678	2,576	2,929	2,576	1.308	2.348	0.433	3.122	–	17.95	3.585	60.53
11×5	8,498	25,502	17,214	4,167	4,673	4,167	2.013	7.212	1.577	9.928	–	79.77	5.84	149.6
11×8	15,290	47,602	31,316	3,223	3,653	3,223	2.065	12.36	2.536	18.61	–	109.2	4.498	218.5
14×8	61,489	201,469	130,718	1,016	1,339	1,016	4.545	48.07	10.67	68.40	–	289.9	1.289	450.4

defined as $W = \{w_{01}, w_{02}, w_{12}\}$. The performance results for running Algorithm 2 on three different segment sizes is reported in Table 1.

6   Conclusion

In this paper we have introduced context-aware probabilistic temporal logic (CAPTL). The logic provides intuitive means to formalize requirements that comprises a number of objectives with an underlying priority structure. CAPTL allows for defining context (i.e., probabilistic conditions) as the basis for switching between two different objectives. We have presented CAPTL syntax and semantics for MDPs. We have also investigated the CAPTL synthesis problem, both from PCTL and CAPTL-based approaches, where we have shown that the latter provides significant performance improvements. To demonstrate our work, we have presented two case studies. As this work has primarily considered CAPTL semantics for MDPs, further investigation is required to generalize the results for stochastic multi-player games. Another research direction involves expanding the results to include PCTL fragments beyond persistence objectives, such as safety, bounded reachability and reward-based objectives.

Acknowledgments. This work was supported in part by the NSF CNS-1652544 and ECCS-1914796, ONR N00014-20-1-2745 and N00014-17-1-2504, as well as AFOSR FA9550-19-1-0169 awards.

References

1. Baier, C., Dubslaff, C., Korenčiak, L., Kučera, A., Řehák, V.: Synthesis of optimal resilient control strategies. In: D'Souza, D., Narayan Kumar, K. (eds.) ATVA 2017. LNCS, vol. 10482, pp. 417–434. Springer, Cham (2017). https://doi.org/10.1007/978-3-319-68167-2_27
2. Baier, C., Katoen, J.P., Larsen, K.G.: Principles of Model Checking. MIT Press, Cambridge (2008)

3. Barthe, G., Espitau, T., Ferrer Fioriti, L.M., Hsu, J.: Synthesizing probabilistic invariants via Doob's decomposition. In: Chaudhuri, S., Farzan, A. (eds.) CAV 2016. LNCS, vol. 9779, pp. 43–61. Springer, Cham (2016). https://doi.org/10.1007/978-3-319-41528-4_3
4. Blanchini, F.: Set invariance in control. Automatica **35**(11), 1747–1767 (1999)
5. Boutilier, C., Brafman, R.I., Geib, C.: Prioritized goal decomposition of Markov decision processes: toward a synthesis of classical and decision theoretic planning. In: IJCAI, pp. 1156–1162 (1997)
6. Bozkurt, A.K., Wang, Y., Zavlanos, M.M., Pajic, M.: Control synthesis from linear temporal logic specifications using model-free reinforcement learning. In: Proceedings of 2020 IEEE International Conference on Robotics and Automation (ICRA) (2020)
7. Brázdil, T., Kučera, A., Novotný, P.: Optimizing the expected mean payoff in energy Markov decision processes. In: Artho, C., Legay, A., Peled, D. (eds.) ATVA 2016. LNCS, vol. 9938, pp. 32–49. Springer, Cham (2016). https://doi.org/10.1007/978-3-319-46520-3_3
8. David, A., Jensen, P.G., Larsen, K.G., Mikučionis, M., Taankvist, J.H.: UPPAAL STRATEGO. In: Baier, C., Tinelli, C. (eds.) TACAS 2015. LNCS, vol. 9035, pp. 206–211. Springer, Heidelberg (2015). https://doi.org/10.1007/978-3-662-46681-0_16
9. Elfar, M., Wang, Y., Pajic, M.: Context-aware temporal logic for probabilistic systems. arXiv e-prints arXiv:2007.05793 (2020)
10. Elfar, M., Zhong, Z., Li, Z., Chakrabarty, K., Pajic, M.: Synthesis of error-recovery protocols for micro-electrode-dot-array digital microfluidic biochips. ACM Trans. Embed. Comput. Syst. (TECS) **16**(5s), 1–22 (2017)
11. Etessami, K., Kwiatkowska, M., Vardi, M.Y., Yannakakis, M.: Multi-objective model checking of Markov decision processes. In: Grumberg, O., Huth, M. (eds.) TACAS 2007. LNCS, vol. 4424, pp. 50–65. Springer, Heidelberg (2007). https://doi.org/10.1007/978-3-540-71209-1_6
12. Forejt, V., Kwiatkowska, M., Norman, G., Parker, D.: Automated verification techniques for probabilistic systems. In: Bernardo, M., Issarny, V. (eds.) SFM 2011. LNCS, vol. 6659, pp. 53–113. Springer, Heidelberg (2011). https://doi.org/10.1007/978-3-642-21455-4_3
13. Forejt, V., Kwiatkowska, M., Norman, G., Parker, D., Qu, H.: Quantitative multi-objective verification for probabilistic systems. In: Abdulla, P.A., Leino, K.R.M. (eds.) TACAS 2011. LNCS, vol. 6605, pp. 112–127. Springer, Heidelberg (2011). https://doi.org/10.1007/978-3-642-19835-9_11
14. Forejt, V., Kwiatkowska, M., Parker, D.: Pareto curves for probabilistic model checking. In: Chakraborty, S., Mukund, M. (eds.) ATVA 2012. LNCS, pp. 317–332. Springer, Heidelberg (2012). https://doi.org/10.1007/978-3-642-33386-6_25
15. Jiang, Z., Pajic, M., Moarref, S., Alur, R., Mangharam, R.: Modeling and verification of a dual chamber implantable pacemaker. In: Flanagan, C., König, B. (eds.) TACAS 2012. LNCS, vol. 7214, pp. 188–203. Springer, Heidelberg (2012). https://doi.org/10.1007/978-3-642-28756-5_14
16. Kattenbelt, M., Kwiatkowska, M., Norman, G., Parker, D.: A game-based abstraction-refinement framework for Markov decision processes. Form. Methods Syst. Des. **36**(3), 246–280 (2010)
17. Kofman, E., De Doná, J.A., Seron, M.M.: Probabilistic set invariance and ultimate boundedness. Automatica **48**(10), 2670–2676 (2012)

18. Kress-Gazit, H., Lahijanian, M., Raman, V.: Synthesis for robots: guarantees and feedback for robot behavior. Ann. Rev. Control Robot. Auton. Syst. **1**, 211–236 (2018)
19. Kwiatkowska, M., Parker, D., Wiltsche, C.: Prism-games: verification and strategy synthesis for stochastic multi-player games with multiple objectives. Int. J. Softw. Tools Technol. Transf. **20**(2), 195–210 (2018)
20. Lahijanian, M., Andersson, S., Belta, C.: Control of Markov decision processes from PCTL specifications. In: Proceedings of the 2011 American Control Conference, pp. 311–316. IEEE (2011)
21. Li, Z., et al.: Error recovery in a micro-electrode-dot-array digital microfluidic biochip. In: Proceedings of the 35th International Conference on Computer-Aided Design, pp. 1–8 (2016)
22. Neema, S., Sztipanovits, J., Karsai, G., Butts, K.: Constraint-based design-space exploration and model synthesis. In: Alur, R., Lee, I. (eds.) EMSOFT 2003. LNCS, vol. 2855, pp. 290–305. Springer, Heidelberg (2003). https://doi.org/10.1007/978-3-540-45212-6_19
23. Pajic, M., Mangharam, R., Sokolsky, O., Arney, D., Goldman, J., Lee, I.: Model-driven safety analysis of closed-loop medical systems. IEEE Trans. Ind. Inform. **10**(1), 3–16 (2012)
24. Puggelli, A., Sangiovanni-Vincentelli, A.L., Seshia, S.A.: Robust strategy synthesis for probabilistic systems applied to risk-limiting renewable-energy pricing. In: 2014 International Conference on Embedded Software (EMSOFT), pp. 1–10. IEEE (2014)
25. Seshia, S.A., Sadigh, D., Sastry, S.S.: Formal methods for semi-autonomous driving. In: 2015 52nd ACM/EDAC/IEEE Design Automation Conference (DAC), pp. 1–5 (2015)
26. Svoreňová, M., Kwiatkowska, M.: Quantitative verification and strategy synthesis for stochastic games. Eur. J. Control **30**, 15–30 (2016)
27. Wiltsche, C.: Assume-guarantee strategy synthesis for stochastic games. Ph.D. thesis, University of Oxford (2015)

Multi-head Monitoring of Metric Dynamic Logic

Martin Raszyk$^{(\boxtimes)}$ iD, David Basin iD, and Dmitriy Traytel iD

Institute of Information Security, Department of Computer Science,
ETH Zürich, Zurich, Switzerland
martin.raszyk@inf.ethz.ch

Abstract. We develop a monitoring algorithm for metric dynamic logic, an extension of metric temporal logic with regular expressions. The monitor computes whether a given formula is satisfied at every position in an input trace of time-stamped events. Our monitor follows the multi-head paradigm: it reads the input simultaneously at multiple positions and moves its reading heads asynchronously. This mode of operation results in unprecedented space complexity guarantees for metric dynamic logic: The monitor's memory consumption neither depends on the event-rate, i.e., the number of events within a fixed time-unit, nor on the numeric constants occurring in the quantitative temporal constraints in the given formula. We formally prove our algorithm correct in the Isabelle proof assistant, integrate it in the Hydra monitoring tool, and empirically demonstrate its strong performance.

1 Introduction

In runtime verification, monitoring is the task of detecting whether a system execution trace adheres to a given specification. One typically distinguishes online monitors that observe the trace event-wise as the system's execution proceeds from offline monitors that read the recorded trace from a log file, possibly after the system has finished its execution.

We have recently proposed third mode of operation for monitors: multi-head monitoring [20, 22]. Conceptually, a multi-head monitor has multiple pointers, called reading heads, into a single log file. The reading heads move over the file, independently of each other. In contrast to an offline monitor's random access to the log, a multi-head monitor's heads are restricted to move only in one direction, from left to right. Thus, an online monitor can be seen as the special case of a multi-head monitor that uses a single head.

In our previous work [20], we have demonstrated the benefits of multi-head monitoring for metric temporal logic (MTL) [17]. MTL is a widely used propositional specification language capable of expressing qualitative (e.g., happens before) and quantitative (e.g., within the last hour) temporal relationships. Our multi-head MTL monitor supports arbitrarily nested past and bounded future operators and produces a stream of Boolean verdicts denoting the formula's satisfaction (or violation) at each position in the trace. The monitor uses as many reading heads as there are leaves in the formula's

© Springer Nature Switzerland AG 2020
D. V. Hung and O. Sokolsky (Eds.): ATVA 2020, LNCS 12302, pp. 233–250, 2020.
https://doi.org/10.1007/978-3-030-59152-6_13

syntax tree. Its worst-case memory consumption is linear in the formula's *temporal size*, which is the sum of the formula's *size* (number of operators) and all *metric constants* occurring in the formula (the boundaries of intervals expressing quantitative temporal relationships). However, the monitor is *event-rate independent* [1], i.e., its space complexity does not depend on the trace length, the event rate, or other trace characteristics (assuming registers to store numbers as the underlying model of computation). The strong theoretical guarantees for our multi-head MTL monitor translate into practice: the monitor's implementation significantly outperforms its competitors with respect to both memory usage and the average time spent processing an event.

In this paper, we continue our investigation of the multi-head paradigm. We improve over our MTL monitor along three axis: (1) we consider a more expressive specification language than MTL, (2) we generalize the time domain to support both dense and discrete time, and (3) we achieve a space complexity that no longer depends on the metric constants occurring in the formula (again assuming the register model). As our specification language, we use metric dynamic logic (MDL) [1] (Sect. 2), an extension of MTL with regular expressions. The use of regular expressions instead of MTL's temporal operators increases the logic's expressiveness, which has prompted de Giacomo and Vardi to advocate linear dynamic logic (MDL's non-metric variant) over linear temporal logic [10].

Our main contribution is a space-efficient multi-head MDL monitor. On a high-level (Sect. 3), it resembles our multi-head MTL monitor [20]. In both logics, the main challenge for space-efficiency stems from the presence of both past and future operators, which may require the monitor to buffer the verdicts from the recursive subformula evaluation until a verdict for the overall formula can be produced. For MTL, the key insight is that a multi-head monitor can compress the information needed to evaluate MTL's temporal operators due to the simple fixed patterns of the direct subformulas' verdicts that the MTL semantics enforces. In contrast, MDL's regular expressions yield patterns that are neither simple nor fixed. We develop a data structure, called a *window*, that supports the space-efficient compression for this general case (Sect. 4). Consequently, our monitor is the first event-rate independent algorithm for MDL that outputs a stream of Boolean verdicts. Moreover, our new data structure's time and space complexity is independent of the formula's metric constants, a property we call *interval-obliviousness*, which the MTL monitor does not offer. Interval-obliviousness is relevant: large constants like 259 200 (three days expressed in seconds) often occur in realistic specifications [2,3].

The improvements over the multi-head MTL monitor come at a price: our MDL monitor's space consumption depends exponentially on the formula size. This follows alone from the fact that we will construct deterministic automata (on the fly) from the regular expressions occurring in the formula. Similarly, the number of required reading heads may be exponential in the formula size. In practice, however, specifications are small, while the traces are huge. It usually poses no problem for monitors to be exponential in the formula size, whereas a linear dependence on the trace or on the large numeric constants occurring in the formula is prohibitive. Our empirical evaluation of our multi-head MDL monitor confirms this "monitoring folk wisdom" (Sect. 5).

We used the Isabelle proof assistant to verify our monitor's functional correctness [21]. We proved its time and space complexity bounds on paper [23, Sect. 4.5].

Related Work. Event-rate independence is impossible to achieve for single-head monitors that support past and future temporal operators and output Boolean verdicts for every position in the trace (as we argue in Sect. 3.3). The multi-head paradigm overcomes this limitation for MTL [20]. Recently, we have used the multi-head model of computation to eliminate non-determinism from functional finite-state transducers [22]. This theoretical result provides a stepping stone towards our multi-head MDL monitor. Our core data structure resembles the multi-head transducer for the *all-suffix regular matching* problem studied in that work. However, significant extensions were necessary to handle quantitative temporal constraints, past operators, and the arbitrary nesting of formulas and regular expressions; these are all aspects not present in the transducer setting.

An alternative approach to achieving event-rate independence is to relax the requirement to output Boolean verdicts. Instead, an out-of-order mixture of Boolean and equivalence verdicts can be used to denote that the verdict is presently unknown, but will be equivalent to some other (also presently unknown) verdict [1]. This relaxation resulted in Aerial [7], the first event-rate independent MDL monitor. Our algorithm produces much more intelligible output, while also being event-rate independent. Moreover, Aerial's space and per-event-time complexity depend linearly on the sum of the formula's metric constants, whereas our monitor is interval-oblivious. This weakness of Aerial was also observed and improved upon empirically in the Reelay monitor for past-only MTL [25]. Reelay's space complexity, however, is still linear in the sum of the formula's constants.

Stream runtime verification (SRV) [24], pioneered by LOLA [9], generalizes logic-based specifications to recursive programs using stream expressions. Some specifications expressed in these languages can be efficiently monitored in constant space, but this fragment is rather restricted: specifications may refer to a bounded number of future events and the bound must be fixed statically. In contrast, MTL's and MDL's metric constraints, even if bounded, may require the monitor to wait for an unbounded number of future events before being able to output a verdict for an earlier position. (Metric constraints bound time, which is different from counting events.) Metric extensions of SRV languages were recently proposed [8, 11, 12]. They inherit the restricted efficiently monitorable fragment from non-metric SRV languages. A similar restriction applies to quantified regular expressions [18], which can be evaluated in constant space, but support neither metric constraints nor dependencies on future events.

Beyond propositional specification languages, first-order monitors [4, 13, 15], implemented in tools like MonPoly [6] and DejaVu [14], also produce streams of verdicts. Event-rate independence is however out of reach for these algorithms [4].

2   Metric Dynamic Logic

We recapitulate metric dynamic logic (MDL) [1]. While previous works on MDL focused on natural numbered time-stamps, we consider an abstract time domain $\mathbb{T}$. We assume that $\mathbb{T}$ forms an additive commutative monoid $(\mathbb{T}, +, 0)$, a partial order $(\mathbb{T}, <)$, and a join-semilattice $(\mathbb{T}, \sqcup)$. The partial order must be consistent with $\sqcup$ and $+$, i.e., $a \leq a \sqcup b, b \leq a \sqcup b, a \leq c \wedge b \leq c \implies a \sqcup b \leq c$, and $b < c \implies a + b < a + c$, for all $a, b, c \in \mathbb{T}$. Moreover, we assume the existence of an order-preserving embedding ι of natural numbers into $\mathbb{T}$ satisfying $\forall \tau \in \mathbb{T}. \exists n \in \mathbb{N}. \tau < \iota(n)$. For example, these assumptions are satisfied by both the discrete natural numbers $\mathbb{T} = \mathbb{N}$ and the dense real numbers $\mathbb{T} = \mathbb{R}$.

Further, let $\mathbb{I}$ be the set of non-empty intervals over $\mathbb{T}$. We write $\mathbb{I}$'s elements as $[l, r]$, where $l \in \mathbb{T}$, $r \in \mathbb{T} \cup \{\infty\}$, $l \leq r$, and $[l, r] = \{x \in \mathbb{T} \mid l \leq x \leq r\}$. We also define the operation of *shifting* an interval $[l, r] \in \mathbb{I}$ by a time-stamp $\tau \in \mathbb{T}$ as $\tau + [l, r] = [\tau + l, \tau + r]$. An event stream $\rho = \langle (\pi_i, \tau_i) \rangle_{i \in \mathbb{N}}$ is an infinite sequence of sets of atomic propositions $\pi_i \subseteq \Sigma$ along with their time-stamps $\tau_i \in \mathbb{T}$, which is monotone ($\forall i. \tau_i \leq \tau_{i+1}$) and progressing ($\forall \tau. \exists i. \tau < \tau_i$). The event stream's indices $i \in \mathbb{N}$ are called time-points. Consecutive time-points may carry the same time-stamp, and there might be time-stamps that no time-point carries. MDL's syntax is defined as follows, where $p \in \Sigma$ and $I \in \mathbb{I}$.

$$\varphi = p \mid \neg\varphi \mid \varphi \vee \varphi \mid |r\rangle_I \mid \langle r|_I \qquad\qquad r = \star \mid \varphi? \mid r + r \mid r \cdot r \mid r^*$$

Aside from Boolean operators, MDL contains the regular expression modalities. The future match operator $|r\rangle_I$ expresses that there exists some future time-point j whose time-stamp is in the interval $\tau + I$, where τ is the current time-point's time-stamp, and the regular expression r matches the portion of the event stream from the current point up to j. The past match operator $\langle r|_I$ expresses the dual property about a past time-point. Regular expressions themselves may nest arbitrary MDL formulas via the _? operator. We call the subformulas φ occurring as $\varphi?$ in a regular expression r the *direct tests* of r, thereby excluding any further _? operators that occur in φ itself. Regular expressions in MDL match portions of the event stream, i.e., words over 2^Σ. The expression $\star$ matches any character and $\varphi?$ matches the empty word starting at time-point i if the formula φ holds at i. Moreover, $+$, $\cdot$, and $*$ are the standard alternation, concatenation, and (Kleene) star operators.

We define the point-based semantics [5] of formulas and regular expressions by mutual recursion. A formula is evaluated over a fixed event stream $\rho = \langle (\pi_i, \tau_i) \rangle_{i \in \mathbb{N}}$ at a time-point $i \in \mathbb{N}$. We write $i \models \varphi$ if φ is true at i, whereby we omit the explicit reference to ρ. The regular expression r's semantics for a fixed ρ is a relation $\mathcal{R}(r) \subseteq \mathbb{N} \times \mathbb{N}$, where $(i, j) \in \mathcal{R}(r)$ are the starting and ending time-points of a match. Overloading notation, $\cdot$ and $\_^*$ denote relation composition and the reflexive transitive closure.

$i \models p$	iff $p \in \pi_i$	$\mathcal{R}(\star) = \{(i, i+1) \mid i \in \mathbb{N}\}$
$i \models \neg\varphi$	iff $i \not\models \varphi$	$\mathcal{R}(\varphi?) = \{(i, i) \mid i \models \varphi\}$
$i \models \varphi \vee \psi$	iff $i \models \varphi \vee i \models \psi$	$\mathcal{R}(r + s) = \mathcal{R}(r) \cup \mathcal{R}(s)$
$i \models |r\rangle_I$	iff $\exists j \geq i. \tau_j \in \tau_i + I \wedge (i, j) \in \mathcal{R}(r)$	$\mathcal{R}(r \cdot s) = \mathcal{R}(r) \cdot \mathcal{R}(s)$
$i \models \langle r|_I$	iff $\exists j \leq i. \tau_i \in \tau_j + I \wedge (j, i) \in \mathcal{R}(r)$	$\mathcal{R}(r^*) = \mathcal{R}(r)^*$

We assume that intervals $[l, r]$ of future match operators are bounded, i.e., $r \neq \infty$, and employ the usual syntactic sugar for additional constructs: *true* $= p \vee \neg p$, *false* $= \neg true$, and $\varphi \wedge \psi = \neg(\neg\varphi \vee \neg\psi)$. Given formulas φ and ψ, we define the MTL operators next

$\bigcirc_I \varphi$ as $|\star \cdot \varphi?\rangle_I$, previous $\bullet_I \varphi$ as $\langle\varphi? \cdot \star|_I$, until $\varphi \, U_I \, \psi$ as $|(\varphi? \cdot \star)^* \cdot \psi?\rangle_I$, and since $\varphi \, S_I \, \psi$ as $\langle\psi? \cdot (\star \cdot \varphi?)^*|_I$. These abbreviations faithfully implement MTL's point-based semantics.

Example 1. Many systems for user authentication follow a policy like: "A user should not be able to authenticate after entering a wrong password three times within the last hour without successfully authenticating in between." For a fixed user, we write ✗ for the event "User entered a wrong password" and ✓ for "User has successfully authenticated." Additionally, we abbreviate $\varphi? \cdot \star$ by φ. (This abbreviation is only used when φ appears in a regular expression position, e.g., as an argument of $\cdot$ or $\_^*$). Then the MDL formula $✓ \wedge \langle(✗ \cdot (\neg✓)^* \cdot ✗ \cdot (\neg✓)^* \cdot ✗ \cdot (\neg✓)^*)|_{[0,3600]}$ captures this policy's violations: it is satisfied at time-points at which the fixed user successfully authenticated after entering wrong credentials three times in the last $3\,600\,\mathrm{s}$, without intermediate successful authentications. We can express this property in MTL by nesting six temporal operators, namely one since and one previous operator for each of the ✗ subformulas. Yet, it is unclear which intervals to use as arguments to these operators beyond the fact that their upper bounds should sum up to $3\,600$. For $\mathbb{T} = \mathbb{N}$, a rather impractical solution exploits that there are finitely many ways to split the interval $[0, 3600]$ and constructs the disjunction of all possible splits, which yields $\binom{3605}{5} = 5\,059\,876\,272\,308\,221$ disjuncts in this case. For $\mathbb{T} = \mathbb{R}$, the previous solution no longer works and we conjecture that no equivalent MTL formula exists. MDL remediates these difficulties regardless of the time domain.

3   High-Level Overview

Our multi-head MDL monitor follows the monitored formula's recursive structure. We describe below the main ideas for propositions, Boolean, and temporal match operators.

3.1   Propositions and Boolean Operators

For an atomic proposition, a one-head monitor scans the trace and returns the corresponding Boolean verdicts. We view non-atomic formulas as being evaluated on streams of Boolean verdicts produced by submonitors for their subformulas. For $\varphi \vee \psi$, we evaluate $b_\varphi \vee b_\psi$ over the atomic propositions b_φ and b_ψ, which denote the satisfaction of φ and ψ at each time-point. The monitor for $\varphi \vee \psi$ uses a single head to combine its inputs b_φ and b_ψ at each time-point based on the semantics of $\vee$. Negation is evaluated similarly.

3.2   Temporal Match Operators

For a formula φ of the form $|r\rangle_I$ or $\langle r|_I$, we first convert r into an automaton over the alphabet $\mathbb{B}^k$, where k is the number of r's direct tests. For each time-point, the automaton's input symbol is constructed from k Boolean verdicts for r's direct tests at this time-point.

Key to our work is a data structure, called a *window*, that maintains a summary of the automaton runs on a finite subword of the automaton's input stream. The subword starts at a position i and ends at j. For a future match formula $\varphi = \langle r \rangle_I$, the position i is the time-point at which we need to produce φ's next Boolean verdict and j is a suitable lookahead time-point, determined by φ's interval I, which makes it possible to evaluate φ. Note that i and j can be arbitrarily far apart, but the window's size does not depend on this distance.

For a past match formula $\varphi = \langle r|_{[a,b]} \rangle$, the verdicts are computed at the window's end j. The window's start i is the earliest time-point with $\tau_j \notin \tau_i + [a, \infty]$ or it equals j if $a = 0$. The data structure uses two reading heads, a *start head* at i and an *end head* at j, to support operations that advance the window's start and end. Advancing the window's start requires a third auxiliary reading head that is obtained by cloning the start head. As with all reading heads, this additional head may move asynchronously after cloning.

Finally, the multi-head monitor M for the temporal match formula φ maintains the window data structure and uses it to compute the Boolean verdicts for φ. To assemble the next input symbol for the automaton, M runs k submonitors for r's direct tests. In particular, a reading head of the window data structure corresponds to the states of the k submonitors and thus cloning the reading head means cloning these submonitors.

3.3   Relation to Our Multi-head Monitor for MTL

Our multi-head MTL monitor [20] coincides with our MDL monitor except for the temporal operator cases. For MTL, we use a different data structure that only requires a single reading head per temporal operator. This is possible due to the special form of the regular expressions corresponding to MTL's operators. Although simpler, the MTL data structure is not interval-oblivious. Moreover, its time-stamps are fixed to the natural numbers.

In more detail, for since and until, the MTL monitor's state contains all time-stamp differences of relevant (for the interval) past or future matches. These time-stamp differences are stored compactly to avoid a linear dependence on the trace length. Yet, the number of stored time-stamp differences depends on the interval bounds.

For the until operator $\varphi \, U_I \, \psi$, producing a Boolean verdict at a time-point is delayed as long as all time-points satisfy φ and no time-point within the interval satisfies ψ. Nevertheless, all delayed time-points with the same time-stamp are guaranteed to be resolved to the same Boolean verdict. Hence, our MTL monitor stores only the number of delayed time-points for each time-stamp relevant for the interval. For MDL, it no longer holds that all delayed time-points with the same time-stamp must resolve to the same Boolean verdict. To see this, consider the formula $|\varphi? \cdot (\star)^* \cdot \psi?\rangle_{[0,0]}$, which holds at time-point i iff φ holds at i and ψ holds at some time-point $j \geq i$ with $\tau_i = \tau_j$. Producing a Boolean verdict at a time-point i for this formula must be delayed as long as no time-point j with the same time-stamp $\tau_j = \tau_i$ satisfies ψ. But if there exists such a time-point j, then all delayed time-points k, for $i \leq k \leq j$, are resolved to *true* iff φ is satisfied at k. Hence, the information to compute the Boolean verdicts for the delayed time-points cannot be compressed sublinearly with respect to the event rate. Our remedy is to use multiple reading heads, i.e., to run two monitors for φ and ψ, which process the time-points asynchronously.

4   Evaluating Temporal Match Operators

We now formally define the multi-head monitors for the past and future temporal match formulas $\langle r|_I$ and $|r\rangle_I$. First, we focus on a fixed regular expression r independently of both the interval I and whether r is used in a past or future match.

Let k be the number of direct tests of r and let ψ_j, for all $1 \leq j \leq k$, be the j-th direct test of r (according to some formula ordering). The i-th input symbol $b^i \in \mathbb{B}^k$ of the automaton, defined formally in Sect. 4.1, reflects the formula ψ_j's satisfaction at time-point i, i.e., b^i_j iff $i \models \psi_j$. To compute the input symbol b^i, a multi-head submonitor is run for each formula ψ_j, i.e., k synchronous multi-head monitors are run to compute b^i.

Our window data structure, defined formally in Sect. 4.2, reads the input symbols with multiple one-way reading heads. It has two heads positioned at the window's start and end. Advancing a head to the next time-point means advancing the corresponding k submonitors to the next time-point and assembling the next input symbol from their k Boolean verdicts. To update the window's state, a monitor may clone and advance the head at the window's start to read subsequent input symbols. Cloning does not affect the original reading head, i.e., there are always two heads at the window's start and end.

4.1   Translating Regular Expressions

We first convert MDL's regular expressions into nondeterministic automata with ε-transitions over an alphabet of vectors $b^i \in \mathbb{B}^k$. A slight peculiarity, due to MDL's semantics, requires our automata to consider the current input symbol even in ε-transitions. More precisely, a regular expression $\psi?$ always matches at most a *single* time-point, i.e., according to its semantics, only pairs of the form (i, i) are included in $\mathcal{R}(\psi?)$. In particular, even the regular expression $\psi? \cdot \varphi?$ matches at most a single time-point i, specifically $(i, i) \in \psi? \cdot \varphi?$ iff $i \models \psi$ and $i \models \varphi$. Matching such an expression therefore does not consume an input symbol. In contrast, matching the regular expression $\star$ is independent of the current input symbol b^i, but always consumes an input symbol.

A textbook ε-NFA's transitions are labeled by an input symbol or ε. In contrast, we distinguish three types of edges in the transition graph of our ε-NFA:

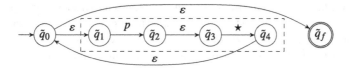

Fig. 1. The ε-NFA for $(p? \cdot \star)^*$, with the dashed rectangle showing the ε-NFA for $p? \cdot \star$

- *conditional ε-transition labeled by ψ_j*: observes the current input symbol b^i and can be taken if $b^i_j = true$; does not consume an input symbol;
- *unconditional ε-transition*: can always be taken; does not consume an input symbol;
- *$\star$-transition*: can always be taken; consumes the current input symbol.

To construct the transition graph, we use Thompson's standard construction mildly adapted to MDL regular expressions and the three types of edges in the transition graph. Because our window data structure described in the next section requires a deterministic automaton, we further determinize the obtained ε-NFA $\mathcal{A}_N$ using the subset construction. A difficulty arises from the conditional ε-transitions, which makes the ε-closure of a set of states S (i.e., the set of states reachable from a state in S using only ε-transitions) dependent on the input symbol. Thus, we compute the ε-closure of a set of states S *with respect to the input symbol* in both the transition function and while checking if the set of states S is accepting. To summarize, we convert an MDL regular expression r into a DFA $\mathcal{A}_D = (Q, \mathbb{B}^k, \delta, q_0, F)$ where

- Q is the set of states of $\mathcal{A}_D$ consisting of all subsets of the set of states of $\mathcal{A}_N$;
- $\delta : Q \times \mathbb{B}^k \to Q$ is the transition function for a state relative to an input symbol;
- q_0 is the initial state of $\mathcal{A}_D$, which is a singleton consisting of the initial state of $\mathcal{A}_N$;
- $F : Q \times \mathbb{B}^k \to \mathbb{B}$ is the accepting function for a state relative to an input symbol.

We label $\mathcal{A}_N$'s nondeterministic states by $\tilde{q}$ and $\mathcal{A}_D$'s deterministic states by q.

Example 2. Figure 1 shows the ε-NFA computed for the regular expression $(p? \cdot \star)^*$.

4.2 The Window Data Structure

Given a pair of time-points (i, j) with $i \le j$, we say that the DFA $\mathcal{A}_D$ *reaches a state q' from a state q on* (i, j), denoted $q \leadsto_{(i,j)} q'$, iff the state q' is reached by running $\mathcal{A}_D$ from the state q at time-point i until time-point j. In particular, we have $q \leadsto_{(i,i)} q$, for all q and i. Furthermore, we say that $\mathcal{A}_D$ *accepts from a state q on* (i, j), denoted $q \leadsto_{(i,j)} \checkmark$, iff the state q' reached by $\mathcal{A}_D$ from q on (i, j) is accepting with respect to the time-point j, i.e., $F(q', b^j)$ holds. We also use the following notation: $\text{dom}(f)$ of a partial function $f : X \to Y$ denotes f's domain, i.e., $\text{dom}(f) = \{x \in X \mid f(x) \ne \perp\}$. For a pair $tstp \in \mathbb{T} \times \mathbb{N}$ of a time-stamp and time-point, $ts(tstp)$ denotes the time-stamp and $tp(tstp)$ the time-point.

The window data structure consists of a pair of time-points (i, j) with $i \le j$ and two partial functions $s : Q \to Q \times ((\mathbb{T} \times \mathbb{N}) \cup \{\perp\})$ and $e : Q \to \mathbb{T}$. The function s represents the runs of $\mathcal{A}_D$ from a given state at the window's start to the state reached at the window's end and the last time-point (along with the corresponding time-stamp) within the window at which the run was in an accepting state (if such a time-point exits). The function e stores the time-stamp of the latest time-point before the window's start from which a given state at the window's end can be reached from the initial state.

Figure 2 visualizes the window data structure. Formally, the window is comprised of the table on the left. Figure 2 shows $\mathcal{A}_D$'s runs justifying the table's content. The individual runs are depicted by arrows from the initial state q_0. Whether a state is accepting depends on the current input symbol, which explains why a single state (e.g., p) may be both accepting and non-accepting at different time-points. We use standard notation for accepting states, including the smaller circles, which denote states whose name is irrelevant.

The domain of s are all the states reached by running $\mathcal{A}_D$ from the initial state at a time-point before the window's start i until i (including the initial state itself obtained by

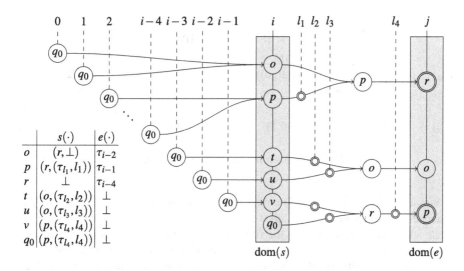

Fig. 2. The window data structure with start i and end j

running from i to i). The value of $s(q) = (q', tstp)$ for a state $q \in \mathrm{dom}(s)$ is obtained by running $\mathcal{A}_D$ further from the state q at the window's start i until the window's end j to a state q'. For example, the state r at the window's end j is reached from the states o and p at the window's start i in Fig. 2. Moreover, $tstp$ is the maximum time-point after i and strictly before j such that the current state in the run from q to q' is accepting. Hence, we have $s(o) = (r, \perp)$ in Fig. 2 because there is no such accepting state strictly before j in the run from the state o to r. In contrast, we have $s(p) = (r, (\tau_{l_1}, l_1))$ because the run from p to r contains an accepting state at time-point l_1 (which is the only accepting time-point in this run and thus also the maximum one). Similarly, we have $s(q_0) = (p, (\tau_{l_4}, l_4))$ because the time-point l_4 is the maximum of the two accepting time-points in the run from the initial state q_0 at time-point i to the state p at time-point j.

The domain of e are all the states reached by running $\mathcal{A}_D$ from the initial state at a time-point strictly before the window's start i until the window's end j. The value of $e(q) = \tau$ for a state $q \in \mathrm{dom}(e)$ is the time-stamp of the maximum time-point from which q was reached from the initial state q_0. For example, $e(p) = \tau_{i-1}$ in Fig. 2 because p is reached by running from q_0 at time-point $i-1$ until j. Note that p is also reached by running from i, but i is not strictly before the window's start and is thus not considered.

Formally, a window satisfies the invariant window(i, j, s, e) if the following holds:

- the window's start and end heads are at positions i and j;
- the domain of s, i.e., $\mathrm{dom}(s)$, are all states q such that $q_0 \rightsquigarrow_{(l,i)} q$, for some $l \leq i$;
- the domain of e, i.e., $\mathrm{dom}(e)$, are all states q such that $q_0 \rightsquigarrow_{(l,j)} q$, for some $l < i$;
- for any $q \in \mathrm{dom}(s)$: $s(q) = (q', tstp)$, where $q \rightsquigarrow_{(i,j)} q'$ and $tstp = (\tau_l, l)$ for the maximum time-point l with $i \leq l < j$ and $q \rightsquigarrow_{(i,l)} \checkmark$, or $tstp = \perp$ if no such l exists;
- for any $q \in \mathrm{dom}(e)$: $e(q) = \tau$, where $\tau = \tau_l$ is the time-stamp of the maximum time-point $l < i$ such that $q_0 \rightsquigarrow_{(l,j)} q$.

Trace:

τ_i	10	20	30	40
π_i	$\{p\}$	$\{\}$	$\{p\}$	$\{\}$

q	$s(\cdot)$	$e(\cdot)$		$s(\cdot)$	$e(\cdot)$		$s(\cdot)$	$e(\cdot)$		$s(\cdot)$	$e(\cdot)$
$\{\tilde{q}_0\}$	$(\{\tilde{q}_0\},\bot)$	$\bot$		$(\{\tilde{q}_4\},(10,0))$	$\bot$		$(\{\},(20,1))$	$\bot$		$(\{\},(20,1))$	$\bot$
$\{\tilde{q}_4\}$	$\bot$	$\bot$	adv_e	$\bot$	$\bot$	adv_e	$\bot$	$\bot$	adv_s	$(\{\},(20,1))$	$\bot$
$\{\}$	$\bot$	$\bot$	$\longrightarrow$	$\bot$	$\bot$	$\longrightarrow$	$\bot$	$\bot$	$\longrightarrow$	$\bot$	10
(i,j)	$(0,0)$			$(0,1)$			$(0,2)$			$(1,2)$	

Fig. 3. The trace and windows for Example 3

We now exemplify the window data structure by tracing its evolution through a sequence of window updates, which we manually selected. In the actual monitor, the update sequence is derived from the time-stamps in the event stream and the match operator's intervals. An update consists of advancing the window's start or end by one. We sketch the algorithms adv_s and adv_e that implement the window's start and end updates and their invariants in Sect. 4.3. The algorithms' pseudocode is given in our extended report [23, Sect. 4.3]. Their integration into the monitors for the match operators is described and the time and space complexity of the overall monitor is analyzed in Sect. 4.4.

Example 3. Consider again the MDL regular expression $r = (p? \cdot \star)^*$ from Example 2 with the corresponding ε-NFA in Fig. 1. We consider the trace given in Fig. 3 and the sequence of window updates, where the window's end is advanced twice followed by advancing the window's start. Figure 3 depicts the window's state after initialization ($i = 0$ and $j = 0$) and after each update. Recall that a deterministic state is a subset of the nondeterministic states in Fig. 1. For instance, the initial deterministic state is $q_0 = \{\tilde{q}_0\}$.

After advancing the window's end, e remains unchanged (its domain stays empty until the window's start advances). To update s, we perform a transition from $\{\tilde{q}_0\}$ at time-point 0 and arrive at the next state $\{\tilde{q}_4\}$. Because the state $\{\tilde{q}_0\}$ is accepting at time-point 0, we add time-point 0 (along with the corresponding time-stamp 10) to $s(\{\tilde{q}_0\})$.

To advance the window's end once more, no update of e is needed. To update s, we perform a transition from $\{\tilde{q}_4\}$ at time-point 1 and arrive at the state $\{\}$. Because $\{\tilde{q}_4\}$ is accepting at time-point 1, we update the time-stamp to 20 and time-point to 1 in $s(\{\tilde{q}_0\})$.

We now advance the window's start, i.e., update the window to $(1,2)$. To this end, we set $e(\{\}) = 10$ because from $s(\{\tilde{q}_0\}) = (\{\},(20,1))$ we derive that the state $\{\}$ is reached at the window's end 2 starting from the initial deterministic state $\{\tilde{q}_0\}$ at time-point 0. Next, we perform a transition (at time-point 0) from the state $\{\tilde{q}_0\}$ in $\mathrm{dom}(s)$, which yields the state $\{\tilde{q}_4\}$. Since the maximum accepting time-point 1 is within the new window $(1,2)$, we keep it and arrive at $s(\{\tilde{q}_4\}) = (\{\},(20,1))$. To compute $s(\{\tilde{q}_0\})$ for the initial deterministic state $\{\tilde{q}_0\}$, we perform two runs starting at time-point 1, one from $\{\tilde{q}_0\}$ and one from $\{\tilde{q}_4\}$, until the two states in the runs collapse or the window's end is reached. In this example, we carry out a single step and the two states collapse into $\{\}$ at time-point 2 (and the window's end is reached as well). Because time-point 1 in $s(\{\tilde{q}_4\})$ is strictly before the collapse at time-point 2, we cannot take it for $s(\{\tilde{q}_0\})$. However, since $\{\tilde{q}_0\}$ is accepting at time-point 1, we have $s(\{\tilde{q}_0\}) = (\{\}, (20, 1))$.

4.3 Initialization and Update of the Window Data Structure

The algorithms initializing and updating the window data structure are defined in our extended report [23, Sect. 4.3]. Here, we focus on their interfaces in terms of invariants. The window is initialized to time-points $(0,0)$ using $\mathsf{init_w}$, which also establishes the invariant.

Lemma 1. *The invariant* $\mathsf{window}(\mathsf{init_w})$ *holds for the initial window.*

The window (i, j, s, e) can be updated to time-points $(i, j+1)$ using the function $\mathsf{adv_e}$. This function updates s and e by performing transitions from states in the image of s and domain of e at the window's end. Overall, $\mathsf{adv_e}$ preserves the window invariant.

Lemma 2. *Assume that the invariant* $\mathsf{window}(i, j, s, e)$ *holds. Then the invariant holds after advancing the window's end, i.e.,* $\mathsf{window}(\mathsf{adv_e}(i, j, s, e))$.

To advance the window's start, we must advance the domain of s and then compute $s(q_0)$ at the new window's start. We first generalize the part of the window invariant characterizing s to take into account that $s(q_0)$ might not be computed yet. To this end, we define the generalized invariant $\mathsf{svalid}(i, i', j, s)$, which asserts that s is valid for the window (i', j), but its domain contains only states reached by running from a time-point before i. In particular, $\mathsf{window}(i, j, s, e)$ implies $\mathsf{svalid}(i, i, j, s)$. Formally, $\mathsf{svalid}(i, i', j, s)$ holds if:

- $\mathsf{dom}(s)$ consists of all states q such that $q_0 \leadsto_{(l,i')} q$, for some $l \le i$;
- for any $q \in \mathsf{dom}(s)$: $s(q) = (q', tstp)$, where $q \leadsto_{(i',j)} q'$ and $tstp = (\tau_l, l)$ for the maximum time-point l with $i' \le l < j$ and $q \leadsto_{(i',l)} \checkmark$, or $tstp = \bot$ if no such l exists.

The auxiliary function $\mathsf{adv_d}$ updates s by advancing time-point i' in the invariant $\mathsf{svalid}(i, i', j, s)$. This function is used when advancing the domain of s from i to $i+1$ and when computing $s(q_0)$. The invariant $\mathsf{svalid}(i, i', j, s)$ is preserved by $\mathsf{adv_d}$.

Lemma 3. *Assume that the invariant* $\mathsf{svalid}(i, i', j, s)$ *holds and that* $i' < j$. *Then the invariant holds for the updated function* s, *i.e.,* $\mathsf{svalid}(i, i' + 1, j, \mathsf{adv_d}(s, i', \tau_{i'}, b^{i'}))$.

The window (i, j, s, e) with $i < j$ can be updated to the time-points $(i+1, j)$ using the function $\mathsf{adv_s}$. This function first updates e to account for the run $q_0 \leadsto_{(i,j)} q'$. Next $\mathsf{adv_s}$ updates s. First, the domain of s is advanced by $\mathsf{adv_d}$. This way, the invariant on s becomes $\mathsf{svalid}(i, i+1, j, s)$. To establish $\mathsf{window}(i+1, j, s, e)$, however, $\mathsf{svalid}(i+1, i+1, j, s)$ is required. Thus, it remains to compute the value of $s(q_0)$ and update s accordingly. To this end, $\mathsf{adv_s}$ performs runs from q_0 as well as from all states in $\mathsf{dom}(s)$ until the current state q_{cur} in the run from q_0 collapses with the current state of the run from a state $q \in \mathsf{dom}(s)$ or the window's end is reached. Overall, $\mathsf{adv_s}$ preserves the window invariant.

Lemma 4. *Assume that the invariant* $\mathsf{window}(i, j, s, e)$ *holds and that* $i < j$. *Then the invariant holds after advancing the window's start, i.e.,* $\mathsf{window}(\mathsf{adv_s}(i, j, s, e))$.

4.4 Multi-head Monitors for Temporal Match Operators

The algorithms implementing a step of our multi-head monitor for a past or future temporal match operator are defined using pseudocode in Fig. 4.

To determine the Boolean verdict at a time-point j for a past match formula $\langle r|_{[a,b]}$, we must check if there exists a match from a time-point $l \leq j$ such that $\tau_j \in \tau_l + [a,b]$, i.e., $\tau_l + a \leq \tau_j \leq \tau_l + b$. Our multi-head monitor maintains a window (i,j,s,e) such that the invariant window(i,j,s,e) holds and $\tau_l + a \leq \tau_j$, for all $l < i$.

```
1  function evalP((a,b),(i,j,s,e)):
2      τi,_ := read start head
3      τj,bʲ := read end head
4      while i < j ∧ τi + a ≤ τj do
5          (i,j,s,e) := advs(i,j,s,e)
6          τi,_ := read start head
7      β := (∃q ∈ dom(e). τj ≤ e(q) + b ∧
           F(q,bʲ)) ∨ (a = 0 ∧ F(q0,bʲ))
8      return (β, adve(i,j,s,e))
```

Algorithm 1: Multi-head monitor's step on a formula $\langle r|_{[a\,b]}$

```
1  function evalF((a,b),(i,j,s,e)):
2      τi,_ := read start head
3      τj,_ := read end head
4      while τj ≤ τi + b do
5          (i,j,s,e) := adve(i,j,s,e)
6          τj,_ := read end head
7      let (q',tstp) = s(q0)
8      β := (tstp ≠ ⊥ ∧ τi + a ≤ ts(tstp))
9      return (β, advs(i,j,s,e))
```

Algorithm 2: Multi-head monitor's step on a formula $|r\rangle_{[a,b]}$

Fig. 4. Multi-head monitor's evaluation step on a past or future match operators

The algorithm evalP first adjusts the window so that the time-points $l < i$ strictly before the window's start are exactly those with $l < j$ and $\tau_l + a \leq \tau_j$. Using window(i,j,s,e), the first disjunct on line 7 then checks if there exists a match in the interval from a time-point $l < j$. The second disjunct checks a potential match in the interval of the form (j,j). Finally, we show that given a valid monitor's state, evalP computes a sound Boolean verdict at time-point j and returns a valid monitor's state at the next time-point $j+1$.

Lemma 5. *Assume that the invariant* window(i,j,s,e) *holds and* $\tau_l + a \leq \tau_j$, *for all* $l < i$. *Let* $(\beta,(i',j',s',e')) = $ evalP$((a,b),(i,j,s,e))$. *Then, (i)* β *iff* $j \models \langle r|_{[a,b]}$, *(ii)* $j' = j + 1$, *(iii)* window(i',j',s',e'), *and (iv)* $\tau_l + a \leq \tau_{j'}$, *for all* $l < i'$.

To determine the Boolean verdict at a time-point i for a future match formula $|r\rangle_{[a,b]}$, we need to check if there exists a match until a time-point $l \geq i$ such that $\tau_l \in \tau_i + [a,b]$, i.e., $\tau_i + a \leq \tau_l \leq \tau_i + b$. Our multi-head monitor maintains a window (i,j,s,e) such that the invariant window(i,j,s,e) holds and $\tau_l \leq \tau_i + b$, for all $i \leq l < j$.

The algorithm evalF first adjusts the window so that the time-points $i \leq l < j$ are exactly those with $\tau_l \leq \tau_i + b$. Using window(i,j,s,e), the function evalF then checks if there exists a match within the interval (lines 7–8). Finally, we show that given a valid monitor's state, evalF computes a sound Boolean verdict at time-point i and returns a valid monitor's state at the next time-point $i + 1$.

Lemma 6. *Assume that the invariant* window(i, j, s, e) *holds and* $\tau_l \leq \tau_i + b$ *for all* $i \leq l < j$. *Let* $(\beta, (i', j', s', e')) = \mathsf{eval}_\mathsf{F}((a, b), (i, j, s, e))$. *Then, (i)* β *iff* $i \vDash |r\rangle_{[a,b]}$, *(ii)* $i' = i + 1$, *(iii)* window(i', j', s', e'), *and (iv)* $\tau_l \leq \tau_{i'} + b$ *for all* $i' \leq l < j'$.

The soundness and completeness of the overall multi-head monitor follows by induction on the structure of MDL formulas using Lemmas 5 and 6 for the cases of temporal match formulas. We denote by init(φ) the initial multi-head monitor's state for an MDL formula φ and by eval(v) the evaluation function of the multi-head monitor's state v (both omitted). Then, soundness and completeness amount to the following theorem.

Theorem 1. *Let* φ *be a bounded-future MDL formula,* $n \in \mathbb{N}$, *and* v *the multi-head monitor's state after applying* n *times the evaluation function* eval *starting from* init(φ). *Let* $\mathsf{eval}(v) = (v', (t, \beta))$. *Then, (i)* $t = \tau_n$ *and (ii)* β *iff* $n \vDash \varphi$.

We state complexity bounds and prove them in our extended report [23, Sect. 4.5].

Theorem 2. *The amortized time complexity of evaluating an MDL formula* φ *is at most* $2^{O(|\varphi|)}$ *basic steps of computation. The space complexity of storing the multi-head monitor's state for evaluating the formula* φ *is at most* $2^{O(|\varphi|)}$ *registers representing deterministic automata states, time-stamps, and indices into the trace.*

5   Implementation and Evaluation

We have implemented our multi-head MDL monitor in a tool called HYDRA(MDL), consisting of roughly 3500 lines of C++ code [21]. Our implementation mirrors the structure of the multi-head monitor presented here and consists of C++ classes for monitoring atomic predicates, Boolean operators, and temporal match operators. In fact, the implementation extends HYDRA(MTL) [20] with classes for the temporal match operators.

In addition, we have exported OCaml code from our Isabelle formalization and augmented this verified core with unverified OCaml and C code for parsing the formula and log file. We call the resulting tool VYDRA(MDL). We have used it to successfully test the correctness of HYDRA(MDL) on thousands of pseudo-random formulas and traces.

To evaluate our tools' performance, we conduct a set of experiments comparing HYDRA(MDL) and VYDRA(MDL) with HYDRA(MTL) [20], AERIAL [7], REELAY [26], R2U2 [19] and PCRE [16], a library used in many regular expression engines, e.g., grep. We distinguish AERIAL(MDL) that supports MDL as defined in this paper and AERIAL(MTL) that is optimized for MTL formulas. Similarly, REELAY supports past-only MTL and untimed past-only regular expressions. Moreover, time-stamps for past-only MTL are (implicitly) equal to the time-points for REELAY (in particular, they are not explicitly part of the log). R2U2 restricts the time-stamps in the same way. In addition to past-only MTL, it supports future-only MTL, but not formulas mixing past and future operators. Because we focus on MDL and interval-obliviousness, we only include REELAY and R2U2 in an experiment that demonstrates that both tools are not interval-oblivious even in the restricted setting of past-only MTL with time-stamps coinciding to time-points. Finally, PCRE supports tests similar to MDL, but restricts them to be star-free.

The time-stamps and time-points used in our algorithm are represented as 32-bit integers in HYDRA(MDL) and as arbitrary precision integers in VYDRA(MDL). The other tools used in our experiments use bounded-precision machine integers as their representation. In our complexity analysis, we use an abstract model of computation, treating such values as being stored in registers that can be manipulated in a basic computation step.

We run our experiments on an Intel Core i7-8550U computer with 32 GB RAM. We measure the tools' total execution time and maximal writeable memory usage using a custom tool. Each experiment is repeated three times to minimize the impact of the execution environment. Each unfilled data point in our plots shows the average for the tool invocations with the same input parameters. We omit the negligible standard deviations. Each filled data point shows the average over a collection of a tool's data points with the same x-coordinate. We include trend lines over the filled data points in all plots. Note that the y-axis is always plotted in the logarithmic scale. Consequently, an exponential growth of a quantity looks linear and a polynomial growth looks logarithmic in the plots.

Experiment	Formula size	Number of formulas	Trace length	Scaling factor
IO	25	10	20 000	1–10
SZ	2–50	10	20 000	1

Fig. 5. The setup of the first two experiments

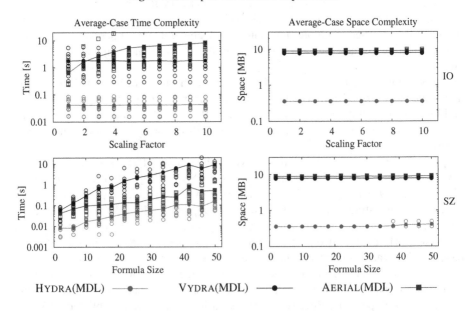

Fig. 6. Evaluation results for the randomized experiments IO and SZ

We now describe the experiments. In the first two experiments, HYDRA(MDL), VYDRA(MDL), and AERIAL are benchmarked on pseudo-random formulas and traces. In the first experiment (IO), the formulas are of a fixed size, with the time-stamp intervals of match operators scaled by a given scaling factor. In the second experiment (SZ), the formulas grow in size with small bounds in the intervals of match operators. In both experiments, the traces are of a fixed size. The parameters of the first two experiments are summarized in Fig. 5. The pseudo-random formulas are produced by mutually recursive generators for formula and regular expressions for a predefined size and maximum interval bounds. The pseudo-random traces are produced by a generator for a predefined event rate er [1]. Each trace contains events with 2000 different time-stamps.

Figure 6 summarizes the results for the experiments IO and SZ. The experiment IO shows that neither the time nor space complexity of HYDRA(MDL) and VYDRA(MDL) depends on the numerical values in the intervals, i.e., both tools are interval-oblivious. AERIAL(MDL)'s time complexity grows with increasing interval bounds because the algorithm works with formulas whose intervals are shifted by offsets up to the numerical bounds in the intervals [1]. Similarly, AERIAL(MDL)'s space complexity grows with increasing interval bounds, but it is dominated by the constant overhead of the runtime environment before AERIAL(MDL) times out. The experiment SZ shows that HYDRA(MDL) outperforms AERIAL(MDL) also when increasing the formulas' size.

The worst-case experiment (WC) reported in our previous work [20] results in space complexity of online monitoring that is exponential in the formula size. Here, all traces are of a fixed size, but their patterns depend on the parameter $n \in \mathbb{N}$. Our previous work [20] describes the traces and formulas.

Figure 7 summarizes the evaluation results. We observe that HYDRA(MDL)'s and VYDRA(MDL)'s time complexity is polynomial, whereas AERIAL(MDL)'s is exponential. (Recall that all y-axes are in logarithmic scale.) HYDRA(MTL) is the fastest here, as it is optimized for the more restricted logic.

The REELAY comparison experiment (RL) is conducted on formulas and traces described by Ulus [25]. The formulas are of the form: $\text{DELAY}(n) = p \, \mathsf{S}_{[n,n]} \, q$. A trace, parameterized by $n \in \mathbb{N}$, is constructed with p being always true and q being true at every other time-point (with time-stamps being equal to time-points). Figure 7 summarizes the results for this experiment. It confirms that the time complexity of both AERIAL(MTL) and REELAY grows when increasing n, i.e., neither of these tools is interval-oblivious. For AERIAL(MTL), the reason is again that the algorithm considers all interval-shifted formulas. The algorithm implemented in REELAY combines interval-shifted formulas with consecutive offsets. Nevertheless, the event pattern in the log files used in the experiment prevents this optimization and shows that REELAY's time and space complexity still depends on the interval bounds in the worst-case. Also, R2U2's space complexity depends on the interval bounds. Its time complexity is comparable to HYDRA(MDL)'s on this simple formula. In contrast, the time complexity of HYDRA(MTL), HYDRA(MDL), and VYDRA(MDL) is confirmed to be independent of the parameter n. Finally, the experiment shows that HYDRA(MTL)'s space complexity is not interval-oblivious.

The PCRE comparison experiment (RE) is conducted on formulas of the form: $\Psi_n = \langle (a? \cdot \star \cdot b? \cdot \star)^* \rangle_{[2n,2n]}$, which correspond to $r_n = \text{(?<=(ab)\{n\})}$. using the syntax

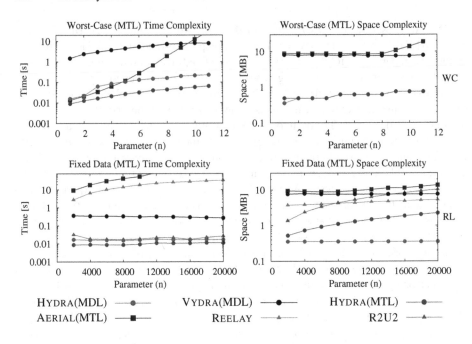

Fig. 7. Evaluation results for the experiment WC and RL

of Perl compatible regular expressions. We point out that *lookbehinds* do not consume matched symbols and thus produce overlapping matches (just like in MDL). The text in which the regular expressions r_n are searched consists of 10^5 occurrences of the pattern ab, i.e., a total of $2 \cdot 10^5$ symbols. For HYDRA(MDL) and VYDRA(MDL), this text is encoded into a log whose events correspond to the text's symbols.

The log's time-stamps are consecutive integers denoting the number of symbols up to the respective position. The evaluation results are summarized in Fig. 8. Because PCRE starts a new search for matching $(ab)\{n\}$ at each position in the text, its time complexity grows linearly in the parameter n. In contrast, HYDRA(MDL)'s and

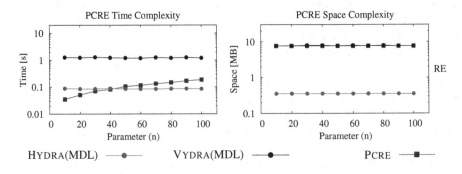

Fig. 8. Evaluation results for the experiment RE

VYDRA(MDL)'s time complexity does not depend on n, as the parameter n only occurs in the interval bounds of Ψ_n.

6   Conclusion

We presented a new monitoring algorithm for metric dynamic logic (MDL) that follows the multi-head paradigm. Our monitor is the first event-rate independent (assuming registers) monitor for MDL that produces a stream of Boolean verdicts. This is a significant improvement over the event-rate independent monitor AERIAL in terms of the monitor's interface: Boolean verdicts are much easier for humans to understand than AERIAL's non-standard equivalence verdicts. Additionally, our monitor is interval-oblivious: The constants occurring in the formula's metric constraints have no impact on the monitor's time- and memory consumption. To our knowledge, this property is unprecedented for monitors for metric specification languages in the point-based setting.

Our algorithm may, however, require exponentially many heads in the monitored formula's size. This exponential dependence seems daunting in theory, but it seems to be unproblematic in practice. We have validated this claim by implementing our algorithm in the HYDRA(MDL) tool and evaluating its performance in a series of case studies. For example, HYDRA(MDL) can process randomly generated MDL formulas with 50 operators on traces with 20000 events in about 100 ms on average.

Acknowledgment. This research is supported by the Swiss National Science Foundation grant "Big Data Monitoring" (167162). We thank the anonymous reviewers for detailed comments.

References

1. Basin, D., Bhatt, B.N., Krstić, S., Traytel, D.: Almost event-rate independent monitoring. Form. Methods Syst. Des. **54**(3), 449–478 (2019). https://doi.org/10.1007/s10703-018-00328-3
2. Basin, D., Caronni, G., Ereth, S., Harvan, M., Klaedtke, F., Mantel, H.: Scalable offline monitoring of temporal specifications. Form. Methods Syst. Des. **49**(1–2), 75–108 (2016)
3. Basin, D., Harvan, M., Klaedtke, F., Zalinescu, E.: Monitoring data usage in distributed systems. IEEE Trans. Softw. Eng. **39**(10), 1403–1426 (2013)
4. Basin, D., Klaedtke, F., Müller, S., Zalinescu, E.: Monitoring metric first-order temporal properties. J. ACM **62**(2), 15 (2015)
5. Basin, D., Klaedtke, F., Zălinescu, E.: Algorithms for monitoring real-time properties. In: Khurshid, S., Sen, K. (eds.) RV 2011. LNCS, vol. 7186, pp. 260–275. Springer, Heidelberg (2012). https://doi.org/10.1007/978-3-642-29860-8_20
6. Basin, D., Klaedtke, F., Zalinescu, E.: The MonPoly monitoring tool. In: RV-CuBES 2017. Kalpa Publications in Computing, vol. 3, pp. 19–28. EasyChair (2017)
7. Basin, D., Krstic, S., Traytel, D.: AERIAL: almost event-rate independent algorithms for monitoring metric regular properties. In: RV-CuBES 2017. Kalpa Publications in Computing, vol. 3, pp. 29–36. EasyChair (2017)
8. Convent, L., Hungerecker, S., Leucker, M., Scheffel, T., Schmitz, M., Thoma, D.: TeSSLa: temporal stream-based specification language. In: Massoni, T., Mousavi, M.R. (eds.) SBMF 2018. LNCS, vol. 11254, pp. 144–162. Springer, Cham (2018). https://doi.org/10.1007/978-3-030-03044-5_10

9. D'Angelo, B., et al.: LOLA: runtime monitoring of synchronous systems. In: TIME 2005, pp. 166–174. IEEE Computer Society (2005)
10. De Giacomo, G., Vardi, M.Y.: Linear temporal logic and linear dynamic logic on finite traces. In: IJCAI 2013, pp. 854–860. IJCAI/AAAI (2013)
11. Faymonville, P., et al.: StreamLAB: stream-based monitoring of cyber-physical systems. In: Dillig, I., Tasiran, S. (eds.) CAV 2019. LNCS, vol. 11561, pp. 421–431. Springer, Cham (2019). https://doi.org/10.1007/978-3-030-25540-4_24
12. Gorostiaga, F., Sánchez, C.: Striver: stream runtime verification for real-time event-streams. In: Colombo, C., Leucker, M. (eds.) RV 2018. LNCS, vol. 11237, pp. 282–298. Springer, Cham (2018). https://doi.org/10.1007/978-3-030-03769-7_16
13. Havelund, K., Peled, D., Ulus, D.: First order temporal logic monitoring with BDDs. In: FMCAD 2017, pp. 116–123. IEEE (2017)
14. Havelund, K., Peled, D., Ulus, D.: DejaVu: a monitoring tool for first-order temporal logic. In: MT@CPSWeek 2018, pp. 12–13. IEEE (2018)
15. Havelund, K., Reger, G., Thoma, D., Zălinescu, E.: Monitoring events that carry data. In: Bartocci, E., Falcone, Y. (eds.) Lectures on Runtime Verification. LNCS, vol. 10457, pp. 61–102. Springer, Cham (2018). https://doi.org/10.1007/978-3-319-75632-5_3
16. Hazel, P.: PCRE - Perl compatible regular expressions. https://www.pcre.org/ (2018)
17. Koymans, R.: Specifying real-time properties with metric temporal logic. Real-Time Syst. **2**(4), 255–299 (1990)
18. Mamouras, K., Raghothaman, M., Alur, R., Ives, Z.G., Khanna, S.: StreamQRE: modular specification and efficient evaluation of quantitative queries over streaming data. In: PLDI 2017, pp. 693–708. ACM (2017)
19. Moosbrugger, P., Rozier, K.Y., Schumann, J.: R2U2: monitoring and diagnosis of security threats for unmanned aerial systems. Form. Methods Syst. Des. **51**(1), 31–61 (2017). https://doi.org/10.1007/s10703-017-0275-x
20. Raszyk, M., Basin, D., Krstić, S., Traytel, D.: Multi-head monitoring of metric temporal logic. In: Chen, Y.-F., Cheng, C.-H., Esparza, J. (eds.) ATVA 2019. LNCS, vol. 11781, pp. 151–170. Springer, Cham (2019). https://doi.org/10.1007/978-3-030-31784-3_9
21. Raszyk, M., Basin, D., Traytel, D.: Formalization, implementation, and evaluation associated with this paper. https://bitbucket.org/krle/hydra/downloads/hydra-mdl.zip
22. Raszyk, M., Basin, D., Traytel, D.: From nondeterministic to multi-head deterministic finite-state transducers. In: ICALP 2019, LIPIcs, vol. 132, pp. 127:1–127:14. Schloss Dagstuhl–Leibniz-Zentrum für Informatik (2019)
23. Raszyk, M., Basin, D., Traytel, D.: Multi-head monitoring of metric dynamic logic (extended report). https://bitbucket.org/krle/hydra/src/master/HYDRA_MDL.pdf (2020)
24. Sánchez, C.: Online and offline stream runtime verification of synchronous systems. In: Colombo, C., Leucker, M. (eds.) RV 2018. LNCS, vol. 11237, pp. 138–163. Springer, Cham (2018). https://doi.org/10.1007/978-3-030-03769-7_9
25. Ulus, D.: Online monitoring of metric temporal logic using sequential networks. CoRR abs/1901.00175. http://arxiv.org/abs/1901.00175 (2019)
26. Ulus, D.: REELAY. https://github.com/doganulus/reelay-codegen (2019)

Techniques for Verification, Analysis and Testing

Faster Algorithms for Quantitative Analysis of MCs and MDPs with Small Treewidth

Ali Asadi[1], Krishnendu Chatterjee[2], Amir Kafshdar Goharshady[2(✉)],
Kiarash Mohammadi[3], and Andreas Pavlogiannis[4]

[1] Sharif University of Technology, Tehran, Iran
aasadi@ce.sharif.edu
[2] IST Austria, Klosterneuburg, Austria
{kchatterjee,goharshady}@ist.ac.at
[3] Ferdowsi University of Mashhad, Mashhad, Iran
kiarash.km@gmail.com
[4] Aarhus University, Aarhus, Denmark
pavlogiannis@cs.au.dk

Abstract. Discrete-time Markov Chains (MCs) and Markov Decision Processes (MDPs) are two standard formalisms in system analysis. Their main associated *quantitative* objectives are hitting probabilities, discounted sum, and mean payoff. Although there are many techniques for computing these objectives in general MCs/MDPs, they have not been thoroughly studied in terms of parameterized algorithms, particularly when treewidth is used as the parameter. This is in sharp contrast to *qualitative* objectives for MCs, MDPs and graph games, for which treewidth-based algorithms yield significant complexity improvements. In this work, we show that treewidth can also be used to obtain faster algorithms for the quantitative problems. For an MC with n states and m transitions, we show that each of the classical quantitative objectives can be computed in $O((n + m) \cdot t^2)$ time, given a tree decomposition of the MC with width t. Our results also imply a bound of $O(\kappa \cdot (n+m) \cdot t^2)$ for each objective on MDPs, where κ is the number of strategy-iteration refinements required for the given input and objective. Finally, we make an experimental evaluation of our new algorithms on low-treewidth MCs and MDPs obtained from the DaCapo benchmark suite. Our experiments show that on low-treewidth MCs and MDPs, our algorithms outperform existing well-established methods by one or more orders of magnitude.

Keywords: Markov Chains · Markov Decision Processes · Treewidth

A longer version is available at [1]. The research was partly supported by Austrian Science Fund (FWF) Grant No. NFN S11407-N23 (RiSE/SHiNE), Vienna Science and Technology Fund (WWTF) Project ICT15-003, the Facebook PhD Fellowship Program, and DOC Fellowship No. 24956 of the Austrian Academy of Sciences (ÖAW).

D. V. Hung and O. Sokolsky (Eds.): ATVA 2020, LNCS 12302, pp. 253–270, 2020.
https://doi.org/10.1007/978-3-030-59152-6_14

1   Introduction

MCs. Perhaps the most standard formalism for modeling randomness in discrete-time systems is that of discrete-time Markov Chains (MCs). MCs have immense applications in verification, and are used to express randomness both in the system and in the environment [11]. Besides the theoretical appeal, the analysis of MCs is also a core component in several model checkers [19,30].

MDPs. When the system exhibits both stochastic and non-deterministic behavior, the standard model of MCs is lifted to Markov Decision Processes (MDPs). For example, MDPs are used to model stochastic controllers, where the non-determinism models freedom of the controller and randomness models the behavior of the system. MDPs are also a topic of active study in verification [14].

Quantitative Analysis. Three of the most standard analysis objectives for MCs are the following: The *hitting probabilities* objective takes as input a set of target vertices $\mathfrak{T}$ of the MC, and asks to compute for each vertex u, the probability that a random walk from u eventually hits $\mathfrak{T}$. The *discounted sum* objective takes as input a discount factor $\lambda \in (0,1)$ and a reward function R that assigns a reward to each edge. The task is to compute for each vertex u the expected reward of a random walk starting from u, where the value of the walk is the sum of the rewards along its edges, discounted by the factor λ at each step[1]. Finally, the *mean payoff* objective is similar to discounted sum, except that the value of a walk is the long-run average of the rewards along its edges. In MDPs, the analyses ask for a strategy that maximizes the respective quantity.

Analysis Algorithms. Given the importance of quantitative objectives for MCs and MDPs, there have been various techniques for solving them efficiently. For MCs, the hitting probabilities and discounted sum objectives reduce to solving a system of linear equations [32]. For MDPs, all three objectives reduce to solving a linear program [32]. Besides the LP formulation, two popular approaches for solving quantitative objectives on MDPs are value iteration [3] and strategy iteration [28]. Value iteration is the most commonly used method in verification and operates by computing optimal policies for successive finite horizons. However, this process leads only to approximations of the optimal values, and for some objectives no stopping criterion for the optimal strategy is known [2]. In cases where such criteria are known (e.g. [35]), the number of iterations necessary before the numbers can be rounded to provide an optimal solution can be extremely high [10]. Nevertheless, value iteration has proved to be very successful in practice and is included in many probabilistic model checkers, such as [19,30]. On the other hand, strategy iteration lies on the observation that given a fixed strategy, the MDP reduces to an MC, and hence one can compute the value of each vertex using existing techniques on MCs. Then, the strategy can be refined to a new strategy that improves the value of each vertex. The running time of strategy iteration can be written as $O(\kappa \cdot f)$, where κ is the number of strategy

---

[1] The undiscounted sum objective is obtained by letting $\lambda = 1$ and our algorithms for discounted sum can be slightly modified to handle this case, too.

refinements and f is the time for evaluating the strategy. Although κ can be exponentially large [20], it behaves as a small constant in practice, which makes strategy iteration work well in practice [29].

Treewidth. *Treewidth* is a well-studied graph parameter. Many classes of graphs which arise in practice have constant treewidth. An example is that Control Flow Graphs (CFGs) of goto-free programs in many programming languages have constant treewidth [17,26,37]. Treewidth has important algorithmic implications, as many graph problems admit (more) efficient solutions on graphs of low treewidth [15,23,24,37]. In program analysis, treewidth has been exploited to develop improvements for register allocation [37], algebraic-path analysis [13], data-flow analysis [8,16], data-dependence analysis [7], and model checking [22,33].

Our Contributions. The contributions of this work are as follows:

1. *Theoretical Contributions.* Our general theoretical result is a linear-time algorithm for solving systems of linear equations whose primal graph has low treewidth. Given a linear system S of m equations over n unknowns, and a tree decomposition of the primal graph of S that has width t, our algorithm solves S in time $O((n+m) \cdot t^2)$. Given an MC M of treewidth t and a corresponding tree decomposition, our algorithm directly implies similar running times for the hitting probabilities and discounted sum objectives for M. In addition, we develop an algorithm that solves the mean-payoff objective for M in time $O((n+m) \cdot t^2)$. Our results on MCs also imply upper-bounds for the running time of strategy iteration on low-treewidth MDPs. Given an MDP P with treewidth t and a quantitative objective, our results imply that P can be solved in time $O(\kappa \cdot (n+m) \cdot t^2)$, where κ is the number of iterations until strategy iteration stabilizes for the respective input and objective.
2. *Practical Contributions.* We develop two practical algorithms for solving the hitting probabilities and discounted sum objectives on low-treewidth MCs. Although these algorithms have the same worst-case complexity of $O((n+m) \cdot t^2)$ as our general solution, they avoid its most practically time-consuming step, i.e. applying the Gram-Schmidt process, and replace it with simple changes to the MC. We report on an implementation of these algorithms and their performance in solving MCs and MDPs with low treewidth.

The existing works closest to this paper are [12,23]. The work of [12] considers the maximal end-component decomposition and the almost-sure reachability set computation in low-treewidth MDPs. These are both *qualitative* objectives, and thus very different from the *quantitative* objectives we consider here, which cannot be solved by [12]. Specifically, the main problem solved by [12] is almost-sure reachability, i.e. reachability with probability 1, which is a very special qualitative case of computing hitting probabilities. The work of [23] develops an algorithm for solving linear systems of low treewidth. Considering the computational complexity when applied to MCs/MDPs of treewidth t, the algorithms we develop in this work are a factor t faster compared to [23]. On the practical side, the algorithms in [23] have more complicated intermediate steps, which we expect will lead to large constant factors in the runtime of their implementations.

2 Preliminaries

Discrete Probability Distributions. Given a finite set X, a probability distribution over X is a function $d : X \rightarrow [0,1]$ such that $\sum_{x \in X} d(x) = 1$. We denote the set of all probability distributions over X by $\mathcal{D}(X)$.

Markov Chains (MCs). A *Markov chain* $C = (V, E, \delta)$ consists of a finite directed graph (V, E) and a probabilistic transition function $\delta : V \rightarrow \mathcal{D}(V)$, such that for any pair u, v of vertices, we have $\delta(u)(v) > 0$ only if $(u, v) \in E$. In an MC C, we start a random walk from a vertex $v_0 \in V$ and at each step, being in a vertex v, we probabilistically choose one of the successors of v and go there. The probability with which a successor w is chosen is given by $\delta(v)(w)$. Let $O \subseteq V^\omega$ be a measurable set of infinite paths on V, we use the notation $Pr_{v_0}(O)$ to denote the probability that our infinite random walk starting from v_0 is a member of O.

Markov Decision Processes (MDPs). A *Markov decision process* is a tuple $P = (V, E, V_1, V_P, \delta)$ which consists of a finite directed graph (V, E), a partitioning of V into two sets V_1 and V_P, and a probabilistic transition function $\delta : V_P \rightarrow \mathcal{D}(V)$, such that for any $(u, v) \in V_P \times V$, we have $\delta(u)(v) > 0$ only if $(u, v) \in E$. We assume that all vertices of an MDP have at least one outgoing edge. Intuitively, an MDP is a one-player game with two types of vertices: those controlled by Player 1, i.e. V_1, and those that behave probabilistically, i.e. V_P.

Strategies. In an MDP P, a *strategy* is a function $\sigma : V_1 \rightarrow V$, such that for every $v \in V_1$ we have $(v, \sigma(v)) \in E$. Informally, a strategy is a recipe for Player 1 that tells her which successor to choose based on the current state[2]. Given an MDP P with a strategy σ, we start a random walk from a vertex $v_0 \in V$ and at each step, being in a vertex v, choose the successor as follows: (i) if $v \in V_1$, then we go to $\sigma(v)$, and (ii) if $v \in V_P$ we act as in the case of MCs, i.e. we go to each successor w with probability $\delta(v)(w)$. As before, given a measurable set $O \subseteq V^\omega$ of infinite paths on V, we define $Pr_{v_0}^\sigma(O)$ as the probability that our infinite random walk becomes a member of O. Note that an MDP with a fixed strategy σ is basically an MC, in which for every $v \in V_1$ we have $\delta(v)(\sigma(v)) = 1$.

Hitting Probabilities [32]. Let $C = (V, E, \delta)$ be an MC and $\mathfrak{T} \subseteq V$ a designated set of *target* vertices. We define $Hit(\mathfrak{T}) \subseteq V^\omega$ as the set of all infinite sequences of vertices that intersect $\mathfrak{T}$. The *Hitting probability* $HitPr(u, \mathfrak{T})$ is defined as $Pr_u(Hit(\mathfrak{T}))$. In other words, $HitPr(u, \mathfrak{T})$ is the probability of eventually reaching $\mathfrak{T}$, assuming that we start our random walk at u. In case of MDPs, we assume that the player aims to maximize the hitting probability by choosing the best possible strategy. Therefore, we define $HitPr(u, \mathfrak{T})$ as $\max_\sigma Pr_u^\sigma(Hit(\mathfrak{T}))$.

---

[2] We only consider pure memoryless strategies because they are sufficient for our use-cases, i.e. there always exists an optimal strategy that is pure and memoryless [29].

Discounted Sums of Rewards [34]. Let $C = (V, E, \delta)$ be an MC and $R : E \to \mathbb{R}$ a *reward function* that assigns a real value to each edge. Also, let $\lambda \in (0, 1)$ be a *discount factor*. Given an infinite path $\pi = v_0, v_1, \ldots$ over (V, E), we define the total reward $R(\pi)$ of π as

$$\sum_{i=0}^{\infty} \lambda^i \cdot R(v_i, v_{i+1}) = R(v_0, v_1) + \lambda \cdot R(v_1, v_2) + \lambda^2 \cdot R(v_2, v_3) + \ldots.$$

For $u \in V$ we define *ExpDisSum(u)* as the expected value of the reward of our random walk if we begin it at u, i.e. $ExpDisSum(u) := \mathbb{E}_u[R(\pi)]$. As in the previous case, when considering MDPs, we assume that the player aims to maximize the discounted sum, hence given an MDP $P = (V, E, V_1, V_P, \delta)$, a reward function R and a discount factor λ, we define $ExpDisSum(u) := \max_\sigma \mathbb{E}_u^\sigma[R(\pi)]$.

Mean Payoff [29,34]. Let C be an MC and R a reward function. Given an infinite path $\pi = v_0, v_1, \ldots$ over C, we define the n-step average reward of π as

$$R(\pi[0..n]) := \tfrac{1}{n} \sum_{i=1}^{n} R(v_{i-1}, v_i).$$

Given a start vertex $u \in V$, the expected *long-time average* or *mean payoff* value from u is defined as $ExpMP(u) := \lim_{n\to\infty} \mathbb{E}_u[R(\pi[0..n])]$. In other words, $ExpMP(u)$ captures the expected reward per step in a random walk starting at u. For an MDP P, we define $ExpMP(u) := \max_\sigma \lim_{n\to\infty} \mathbb{E}_u^\sigma[R(\pi[0..n])]$. The limits in the former definitions are guaranteed to exist [29,34].

Problems. We consider the following problems for both MCs and MDPs:

- Given a target set $\mathfrak{T}$ compute $HitPr(u, \mathfrak{T})$ for every vertex u.
- Given a reward function R and a discount factor λ compute $ExpDisSum(u)$ for every vertex u.
- Given a reward function R, compute $ExpMP(u)$ for every vertex u.

Solving MCs [32]. A classical approach to the above problems for MCs is to reduce them to solving systems of linear equations. In case of hitting probabilities, we define one variable x_u for each vertex u, whose value in the solution to the system would be equal to $HitPr(u, \mathfrak{T})$. The system is constructed as follows:

- We add the equation $x_t = 1$ for every $t \in \mathfrak{T}$, and
- For every vertex $u \notin \mathfrak{T}$ with successors $u_1, \ldots, u_k$, we add the equation $x_u = \sum_{i=1}^{k} \delta(u)(u_i) \cdot x_{u_i}$.

If every vertex can reach a target, then it is well-known that the resulting system has a unique solution in which the value assigned to each x_u is equal to $HitPr(u, \mathfrak{T})$. A similar approach can be used in the case of discounted sums. We define one variable y_u per vertex u and if the successors of u are $u_1, \ldots, u_k$, then we add the equation $y_u = \sum_{i=1}^{k} \delta(u)(u_i) \cdot (R(u, u_i) + \lambda \cdot y_{u_i})$.

Primal Graphs. Let S be a system of linear equations with m equations and n unknowns (variables). The primal graph $G(S)$ of S is an undirected graph with n vertices, each corresponding to one unknown in S, in which there is an edge

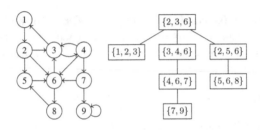

Fig. 1. A graph G (left) and a tree decomposition of G with width 2 (right).

between two unknowns x and y iff there exists an equation in S that contains both x and y with non-zero coefficients.

Solving MDPs. There are two classical approaches to solving the above problems for MDPs. One is to reduce the problem to Linear Programming (LP) in a manner similar to the reduction from MC to linear systems [21]. The other approach is to use dynamic programming [3]. We consider a widely-used variety of dynamic programming, called *strategy iteration* or *policy iteration* [28].

Strategy Iteration (SI) [3]. In SI we start with an arbitrary initial strategy σ_0 and attempt to find a better strategy in each step. Formally, assume that our strategy after i iterations is σ_i. Then, we compute $val_i(u) = HitPr^{\sigma_i}(u, \mathfrak{T})$ for every vertex u. This is equivalent to computing hitting probabilities in the MC that is obtained by considering our MDP together with the strategy σ_i. We use the values $val_i(u)$ to obtain a better strategy σ_{i+1} as follows: for every vertex $v \in V_1$ with successors $v_1, v_2, \ldots, v_k$, we set $\sigma_{i+1}(v) = \arg\max_{v_j} val_i(v_j)$. In case of discounted sum, we let $val_i(u) = ExpDisSum^{\sigma_i}(u)$ and $\sigma_{i+1}(v) = \arg\max_{v_j} R(v, v_j) + \lambda \cdot val_i(v_j)$. We repeat these steps until we reach a point where our strategy converges. It is well-known that strategy iteration always converges to the optimal strategy σ_κ, and at that point the values val_κ will be the desired hitting probabilities/discounted sums [21,28]. Given that SI solves the classic problems above on MDPs by several calls to a procedure for solving the same problems on MCs, our runtime improvements for MCs are naturally extended to MDPs. So, in the sequel we focus on MCs.

Tree Decompositions [36]. Given a directed or undirected graph $G = (V, E)$, a *tree decomposition* of G is a tree (T, E_T) such that:

- Each vertex $b \in T$ of the tree is associated with a subset $V_b \subseteq V$ of vertices of the graph. For clarity, we reserve the word "vertex" for vertices of G and use the word "bag" to refer to vertices of T. Also, we define $E_b := \{(u, v) \in E \mid u, v \in V_b\}$.
- Each vertex appears in at least one bag, i.e. $\bigcup_{b \in T} V_b = V$.
- Each edge appears in at least one bag, i.e. $\bigcup_{b \in T} E_b = E$.
- Each vertex appears in a connected subtree of T. In other words, for all $b, b', b'' \in T$, if b'' is in the unique path between b and b', then $V_b \cap V_{b'} \subseteq V_{b''}$.

Treewidth [36]. The *width* of a tree decomposition is the size of its largest bag minus one, i.e. $w(T) = \max_{b \in T} |V_b| - 1$. A tree decomposition of G is called *optimal* if it has the smallest possible width. The *treewidth* $tw(G)$ of G is defined as the width of its optimal tree decomposition(s).

Computing Treewidth and Tree Decompositions. The problem of computing the treewidth of a graph is solvable in linear time when parameterized by the treewidth itself [6]. The algorithm in [6] also finds an optimal tree decomposition in linear time. Moreover, [37] proves control-flow graphs of structured programs have constant treewidth and provides a linear-time algorithm for producing the tree decomposition by a single parse of the program.

3   Algorithms for MCs with Constant Treewidth

We now consider quantitative problems on MCs. As mentioned before, our improvements carry over to MDPs using SI. We build on classical state-elimination algorithms such as those used in [18,27]. The main novelty of our approach is that we use the tree decompositions to obtain a suitable *order* for eliminating vertices. This specific ordering significantly reduces the runtime complexity of classical state-elimination algorithms from cubic to linear.

3.1   A Simple Algorithm for Computing Hitting Probabilities

We begin by looking into the problem of computing hitting probabilities for general MCs without exploiting the treewidth. Without loss of generality, we can assume that our target set contains a single vertex. Otherwise, we add a new vertex t and add edges with probability 1 from every target vertex to t. This will keep the hitting probabilities intact. Consider our MC $C = (V, E, \delta)$ and our target vertex $t \in V$. If there is only one vertex in the MC then there is not much to solve. We just return that $HitPr(t, t) = 1$. Otherwise, we take an arbitrary vertex $u \neq t$ and try to remove it from the MC to obtain a smaller MC that can in turn be solved using the same method. We should do this in a manner that does not change $HitPr(v, t)$ for any vertex $v \neq u$. Figure 2 shows how to remove a vertex u from C in order to obtain a smaller MC $\overline{C} = (V \setminus \{u\}, \overline{E}, \overline{\delta})^3$. Basically, we remove u and all of its edges, and instead add new edges from every predecessor u' to every successor u''. We also update the transition function δ by setting $\overline{\delta}(u')(u'') = \delta(u')(u'') + \delta(u')(u) \cdot \delta(u)(u'')$. It is easy to verify that for every $v \neq u$, we have $\overline{HitPr}(v, t) = HitPr(v, t)$. Hence, we can compute hitting probabilities for every vertex $v \neq u$ in $\overline{C}$ instead of C. Finally, if $u_1, u_2, \ldots, u_k$ are the successors of u in C, we know that $HitPr(u, t) = \sum_{i=1}^{k} \delta(u)(u_i) \cdot HitPr(u_i, t) = \sum_{i=1}^{k} \delta(u)(u_i) \cdot \overline{HitPr}(u_i, t)$. Hence, we can easily compute the hitting probability for u using this formula. A pseudocode of is available in [1].

---

[3] We always use $\overline{C}$ to denote an MC that is obtained from C by removing one vertex. We apply this rule across our notation, e.g. $\overline{\delta}$ is the respective transition function.

Fig. 2. Removing a vertex u. The vertex u' is a predecessor of u and u'' is one of its successors. The left side shows the changes when there is no edge from u' to u'' and the right side shows the other case, where $(u', u'') \in E$. Edge labels are δ values.

A special case arises when there is a self-loop transition from u to u. If $\delta(u)(u) = 1$, i.e. u is an absorbing trap, then we can simply remove u, noting that $HitPr(u, t) = 0$. On the other hand if $0 < \delta(u)(u) < 1$, then we should distribute $\delta(u)(u)$ proportionately among the other successors of u because staying for a finite number of steps in the same vertex u does not change the hitting property of a path, and the probability of staying at u forever is 0.

Removing each vertex can take at most $O(n^2)$ time, given that it has $O(n)$ predecessors and successors. We should remove $n - 1$ vertices, leading to a total runtime of $O(n^3)$, which is worse than the reduction to system of linear equations and then applying Gaussian elimination. However, the runtime can be significantly improved if we remove vertices in an order that guarantees every vertex has a low degree upon removal.

3.2   Computing Hitting Probabilities in Constant Treewidth

The main idea behind our algorithm is simple: we take the algorithm from the previous section and use tree decompositions to obtain an ordering for the removal of vertices. Given that we can choose any bag in T as the root, without loss of generality, we assume that the target vertex t is in the root bag[4]. We base our approach on the following lemmas:

Lemma 1. *Let $l \in T$ be a leaf bag of the tree decomposition (T, E_T) of our MC C, and let $\bar{l}$ be the parent of l. If $V_l \subseteq V_{\bar{l}}$, then $(T \setminus \{l\}, E_T \setminus \{(\bar{l}, l)\})$ is also a valid tree decomposition for C.*

Proof. We just need to check that all the required properties of a tree decomposition hold after removal of l. Given that $V_l \subseteq V_{\bar{l}}$, any vertex that appears in l is also in $\bar{l}$ and hence removal of l does not cause any vertex to be unrepresented in the tree decomposition. The same applies to edges. Moreover, removing a *leaf* bag cannot disconnect the previously-connected set of bags containing a vertex.

Lemma 2. *Let $l \in T$ be a bag of the tree decomposition (T, E_T) and assume that the vertex $u \in V$ only appears in V_l, i.e. it does not appear in the vertex set of any other bag. Then, u has at most $|V_l|$ predecessors/successors in C.*

---

[4] If $|\mathfrak{T}| \geq 2$, we use the same technique as in the previous section to have only one target t. To keep the tree decomposition valid, we add t to every bag.

Proof. If u' is a predecessor/successor of u, then there is an edge between them. By definition, a tree decomposition should cover every edge. Hence, there should be a bag b such that $u, u' \in V_b$. By assumption, u only appears in V_l. Hence, every predecessor/successor u' must also appear in V_l.

The Algorithm. The above lemmas provide a convenient order for removing vertices. At each step, we choose an arbitrary *leaf* bag l. If there is a vertex u that appears *only* in V_l, then we eliminate u as in Fig. 2. In this case, Lemma 2 guarantees that u has $O(t)$ predecessors and successors. Otherwise, $V_l \subseteq V_{\bar{l}}$ (recall that each vertex appears in a connected subtree) and we can remove l from our tree decomposition according to Lemma 1. See [1] for a pseudocode.

Example. Consider the graph and tree decomposition in Fig. 1 with an arbitrary transition probability function δ and target vertex $\mathsf{t} = 6$. On this example, our algorithm would first choose an arbitrary leaf bag, say $\{7, 9\}$ and then realize that 9 has only appeared in this bag. Hence it removes vertex 9 from the MC using the same procedure as in the previous section. In the next iteration, it chooses the bag $\{7\}$ and realizes that the set of vertices in this bag is a subset of vertices that appear in its parent. Hence, it removes this unnecessary bag. The algorithm continues similarly, until only the target vertex 6 remains, at which point the problem is trivial. Figure 3 shows all the steps of our algorithm. Note that because the width of our tree decomposition is 2, at each step when we are removing a vertex u, it has at most 3 neighbors (counting itself).

Note that throughout this algorithm the tree decomposition remains valid, because we are only adding edges between vertices that are already in the same leaf bag l. Given that we remove at most $O(n)$ bags and $n - 1$ vertices and that removing each vertex takes only $O(t^2)$, the total runtime is $O(n \cdot t^2)$.

Theorem 1. *Given an MC with n vertices and treewidth t and an optimal tree decomposition of the MC, our algorithm computes hitting probabilities from every vertex to a designated target set in $O(n \cdot t^2)$.*

3.3 Computing Expected Discounted Sums in Constant Treewidth

We use a similar approach for handling the discounted sum problem. The only difference is in how a vertex is removed. Given an MC $C = (V, E, \delta)$, a tree decomposition (T, E_T) of C, a reward function $R : E \to \mathbb{R}$ and a discount factor $\lambda \in (0, 1)$, we first add a new vertex called $\hat{1}$ to the MC. The vertex $\hat{1}$ is disjoint from all other vertices and only has a single self-loop with probability 1 and reward $1 - \lambda$. In other words, we define $\delta(\hat{1})(\hat{1}) = 1$ and $R(\hat{1}, \hat{1}) = 1 - \lambda$. We also add $\hat{1}$ to the vertex set of every bag. The reason behind this gadget is that we have $ExpDisSum(\hat{1}) = (1 - \lambda) \cdot (1 + \lambda + \lambda^2 + \ldots) = 1$.

In our algorithm, the requirement that for all u, v we should have $0 \leq \delta(u)(v) \leq 1$ is unnecessary and becomes untenable, too. Therefore, we allow $\delta(u)(v)$ to have any real value, and use the linear system interpretation of C as in Sect. 2, i.e. instead of considering C as an MC, we consider it to be a representation of the linear system S_C defined as follows:

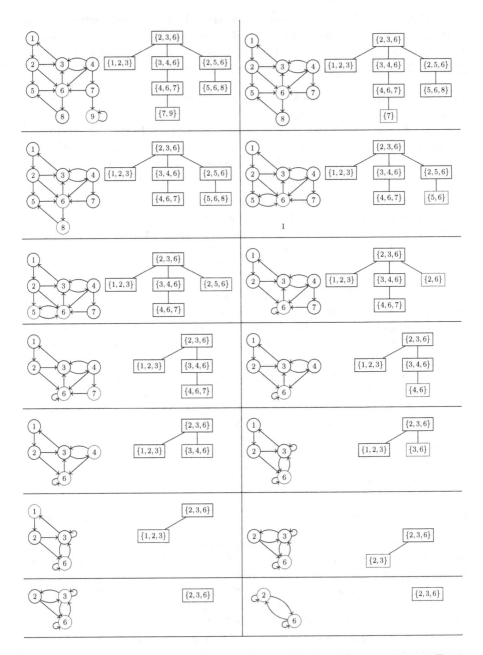

Fig. 3. The steps taken by our algorithm on the graph and tree decomposition in Fig. 1. The target vertex t = 6 is shown in green. At each step the vertex/bag that is being removed is shown in red. An active bag whose vertices, but not itself, are considered for removal is shown in blue. After removing vertex 2, the graph has only one vertex and the base case of the algorithm is run. (Color figure online)

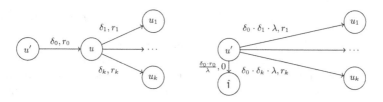

Fig. 4. Removing u from C (left) to obtain $\overline{C}$ (right). The vertex u' is a predecessor of u and $u_1, \ldots, u_k$ are its successors. Each edge is labelled with its δ and R values.

- For every vertex $u \in V$, the system S_C contains one unknown y_u, and
- For every vertex $u \in V$, whose successors are $u_1, u_2, \ldots, u_k$, the system S_C contains an equation $e_u := y_u = \sum_{i=1}^{k} \delta(u)(u_i) \cdot (R(u, u_i) + \lambda \cdot y_{u_i})$.

As mentioned in Sect. 2, in the solution to S_C, the value assigned to the unknown y_u is equal to $ExpDisSum(u)$ in the MC C. However, the definition above does not depend on the fact that C is an MC and can also be applied if δ has arbitrary real values.

Now suppose that we want to remove a vertex $u \neq \hat{1}$ with successors $u_1, \ldots, u_k$ from C. This is equivalent to removing y_u from S_C without changing the values of other unknowns in the solution. Given that we have $y_u = \sum_{i=1}^{k} \delta(u)(u_i) \cdot (R(u, u_i) + \lambda \cdot y_{u_i})$, we can simply replace every occurrence of y_u in other equations with the right-hand-side expression of this equation. If $u' \neq u$ is a predecessor of u, then we have $y_{u'} = A + \delta(u')(u) \cdot (R(u', u) + \lambda \cdot y_u)$, where A is an expression that depends on other successors of u'. We can rewrite this equation as $y_{u'} = A + \delta(u')(u) \cdot R(u', u) + \sum_{i=1}^{k} \delta(u')(u) \cdot \delta(u)(u_i) \cdot \lambda \cdot (R(u, u_i) + \lambda \cdot y_{u_i})$. This is equivalent to obtaining a new $\overline{C}$ from C by removing the vertex u and adding the following edges from every predecessor u' of u:

- An edge $(u', \hat{1})$, such that $R(u', \hat{1}) = 0$ and $\delta(u')(\hat{1}) = \frac{1}{\lambda} \cdot (\delta(u')(u) \cdot R(u', u))$,
- An edge (u', u_i) to every successor u_i of u, such that $R(u', u_i) = R(u, u_i)$ and $\delta(u')(u_i) = \delta(u')(u) \cdot \delta(u)(u_i) \cdot \lambda$.

This construction is shown in Fig. 4. Using this construction, the value of y_v remains the same in solutions of S_C and $S_{\overline{C}}$. There are a few special cases, e.g. when the graph has parallel edges or self-loops. See [1] for details.

As in the previous section, we can solve the problem on the smaller $\overline{C}$ and then use the equation e_u to compute the value of y_u in the solution to S_C. This algorithm's runtime can be analyzed exactly as before. We have to remove n vertices and each removal takes $O(n^2)$ for a total runtime of $O(n^3)$. To obtain a better algorithm that exploits tree decompositions, we can use the exact same removal order as in the previous section, leading to the same runtime, i.e. $O(n \cdot t^2)$. Note that we have added $\hat{1}$ to the associated vertex set of every bag, so the tree decomposition always remains valid throughout our algorithm.

Theorem 2. *Given an MC with n vertices and treewidth t and an optimal tree decomposition of the MC, the algorithm described in this section computes expected discounted sums from every vertex of the MC in $O(n \cdot t^2)$.*

3.4   Systems of Equations with Constant-Treewidth Primal Graphs

The ideas used in the previous section can be extended to obtain faster algorithms for solving any linear system whose primal graph has a small treewidth. However, new subtleties arise, given that general linear systems might have no solution or infinitely many solutions. In contrast, the systems S_C discussed in the previous section were guaranteed to have a unique solution. We consider a system S of m linear equations over n real unknowns as input, and assume that its primal graph $G(S)$ has treewidth t. Our algorithm for solving S is similar to our previous algorithms, and is actually what most students are taught in junior high school. We take an arbitrary unknown x and choose an arbitrary equation $\mathfrak{e}$ in which x appears with a non-zero coefficient. We then rewrite $\mathfrak{e}$ as $x = R_x$, where R_x is a linear expression based on other unknowns. Finally, we replace every occurrence of x in other equations with R_x and solve the resulting smaller system $\overline{S}$. If $\overline{S}$ has no solutions or infinitely many solutions, then so does S. Otherwise, we evaluate R_x in the solution of $\overline{S}$ to get the solution value for x. Using this algorithm, we have to remove $O(n)$ unknowns. When removing x, we might have to replace an expression of size $O(n)$, i.e. R_x, in $O(m)$ potential other equations where x has appeared. Hence, the overall runtime is $O(n^2 \cdot m)$.

Given a tree decomposition (T, E_T) of the primal graph $G(S)$, we choose the unknowns in the usual order, i.e. we always choose an unknown x that appears only in a leaf bag. If x does not appear in any equations, then we can simply remove it and then S is satisfiable iff $\overline{S}$ is satisfiable. Moreover, if S is satisfiable, then it has infinitely many solutions, given that x is not restricted. Otherwise, there is an equation $\mathfrak{e}$ in which x appears with non-zero coefficient, and hence we can rewrite this equation as $x = R_x$. Note that x has $O(t)$ neighbors in $G(S)$, given that it only appears in a leaf bag and all of its neighbors should also appear in the same bag, hence the length of R_x is $O(t)$, too. The problem is that x might have appeared in any of the other $O(m)$ equations. Hence, replacing it with R_x in every equation will lead to a runtime of $O(m \cdot t)$. We repeat this for every unknown, so our total runtime is $O(n \cdot m \cdot t)$, which is not linear.

The crucial observation is that while x might have appeared in as many as m equations, not all of them are linearly independent. Let $\mathfrak{E}_x$ be the set of equations containing x and l be the leaf bag in which x appears and assume that $V_l = \{x, y_1, \ldots, y_{k-1}\}$. Then the only unknowns that can appear together with x in an equation are $y_1, \ldots, y_{k-1}$. In other words, all equations in $\mathfrak{E}_x$ are over V_l. Hence, we can apply the Gram-Schmidt process on $\mathfrak{E}_x$ to remove the unnecessary equations and only keep at most k equations that form an orthogonal basis (or alternatively realize that the system is unsatisfiable). Given that we are operating in dimension $k = O(t)$, this will take $O(t^2 \cdot |\mathfrak{E}_x|)$ time. See [1] for a pseudocode. As in previous algorithms, our approach always keeps the tree decomposition valid. Moreover, as argued above, its runtime is $O((n + m) \cdot t^2)$.

Theorem 3. *Given a system of m linear equations over n unknowns, its primal graph, and a tree decomposition of the primal graph with width t, our algorithm solves the system in time $O((n + m) \cdot t^2)$.*

The algorithm can easily be extended to find a basis for the solution set. Moreover, it can also be combined with the algorithms in the previous sections to solve the mean-payoff objective, hence we have:

Theorem 4 (Proof and Details in [1]). *Given an MC with n vertices and treewidth t and an optimal tree decomposition, expected mean payoffs from every vertex can be computed in $O(n \cdot t^2)$.*

4   Experimental Results

We now report on a C/C++ implementation of our algorithms and provide a performance comparison with previous approaches. See [1] for details.

Compared Approaches. We consider the hitting probability and discounted sum problems for MCs and MDPs. In the case of MCs, we directly use our algorithms from Sect. 3.2 and Sect. 3.3. For MDPs, we use strategy iteration, where we use the above algorithms for the strategy evaluation step in each iteration. We compare our approach with the following alternatives:

- *Classical Approaches.* In case of MCs, we compare against an implementation of Gaussian elimination (Gauss). For MDPs, we consider our own implementation of value iteration (VI) and strategy iteration (SI).
- *Numerical and Industrial Optimizers.* We use Matlab [31] and Gurobi [25] to solve systems of linear equalities corresponding to MCs. For MDPs, we use Matlab [31], Gurobi [25] and lpsolve [4] to handle the corresponding LPs.
- *Probabilistic Model Checkers.* The model checkers Storm [19] and Prism [30] have standard procedures for computing hitting probabilities, but not for discounted sums. Hence, we compare with them on hitting probabilities only.

Benchmarks. We used CFGs of the 40 Java programs from the DaCapo suite [5] as our benchmarks. They have between 33 and 103918 vertices and transitions. To obtain MDPs, we randomly (with probability 1/2) turned each vertex into a Player 1 or a probabilistic one. We assigned random probabilities to each outgoing edge of a probabilistic vertex. To obtain MCs, we did the same, except that all vertices are probabilistic. For the hitting probabilities problem, we chose one random vertex from each connected component of the control flow graphs as a target. In case of discounted sum, we uniformly chose a discount factor

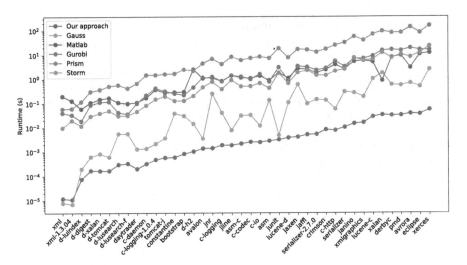

Fig. 5. Experimental results for computing hitting probabilities in MCs.

between 0 and 1 for each instance, and also assigned random integral rewards between -1000 to 1000 to each edge. Finally, we used JTDec [9] to compute tree decompositions. In each case the width of the obtained decomposition was no more than 9. The time and memory used for computing a tree decomposition are negligible, given that it is obtained by a single pass over the program. See [1] for details of the benchmarks and the motivation for using them.

Results. The runtimes for computing the values of hitting probabilities and discounted sums are shown in Figs. 5, 6, 7 and 8. The benchmarks are on the x-axes and ordered by their size. Note that the y-axes are in *logarithmic scale*. For example, Fig. 5 shows results for computing hitting probabilities in MCs, where Prism is the slowest tool by far, while our approach comfortably beats every other method. The gap is more apparent in MDPs (Figs. 7–8). Overall, we see that our new algorithms consistently outperform both classical approaches like VI and SI, and highly optimized solvers and model checkers like Gurobi, Prism and Storm, by one or more orders of magnitude. Hence, the theoretical improvements are also realized in practice. See [1] for raw numbers. It is also noteworthy that the outputs of the different approaches agreed with each other within an error range of 10^{-5}. Finally, note that our approach is only applicable to instances with small treewidth, such as CFGs of structured programs. For MCs/MDPs with arbitrary treewidth, the problem of computing an optimal tree decomposition is NP-hard [6].

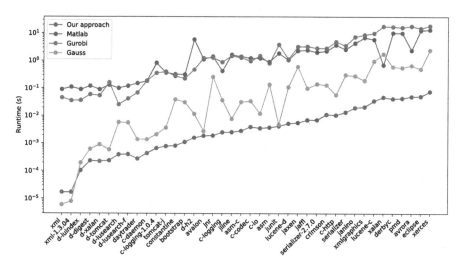

Fig. 6. Experimental results for computing expected discounted sums in MCs.

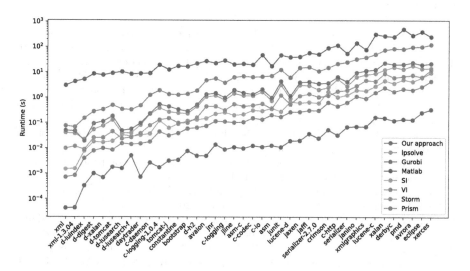

Fig. 7. Experimental results for computing hitting probabilities in MDPs.

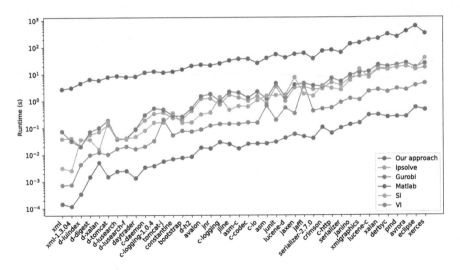

Fig. 8. Experimental results for computing expected discounted sums in MDPs.

References

1. Asadi, A., et al.: Faster algorithms for quantitative analysis of Markov chains and Markov decision processes with small treewidth. arXiv preprint:2004.08828 (2020)
2. Ashok, P., Chatterjee, K., Daca, P., Křetínský, J., Meggendorfer, T.: Value iteration for long-run average reward in Markov decision processes. In: CAV (2017)
3. Bellman, R.: A Markovian decision process. J. Math. Mech. **6**, 679–684 (1957)
4. Berkelaar, M., Eikland, K., Notebaert, P.: lpsolve linear programming system (2004)
5. Blackburn, S.M., et al.: The DaCapo benchmarks: Java benchmarking development and analysis. In: OOPSLA (2006)
6. Bodlaender, H.L.: A linear-time algorithm for finding tree-decompositions of small treewidth. SIAM J. Comput. **25**(6), 1305–1317 (1996)
7. Chatterjee, K., Choudhary, B., Pavlogiannis, A.: Optimal Dyck reachability for data-dependence and alias analysis. In: POPL (2017)
8. Chatterjee, K., Goharshady, A.K., Ibsen-Jensen, R., Pavlogiannis, A.: Optimal and perfectly parallel algorithms for on-demand data-flow analysis. In: ESOP (2020)
9. Chatterjee, K., Goharshady, A.K., Pavlogiannis, A.: JTDec: a tool for tree decompositions in soot. In: D'Souza, D., Narayan Kumar, K. (eds.) ATVA 2017. LNCS, vol. 10482, pp. 59–66. Springer, Cham (2017). https://doi.org/10.1007/978-3-319-68167-2_4
10. Chatterjee, K., Henzinger, T.A.: Value iteration. In: Grumberg, O., Veith, H. (eds.) 25 Years of Model Checking. LNCS, vol. 5000, pp. 107–138. Springer, Heidelberg (2008). https://doi.org/10.1007/978-3-540-69850-0_7
11. Chatterjee, K., Henzinger, T.A., Jobstmann, B., Singh, R.: Measuring and synthesizing systems in probabilistic environments. In: CAV (2010)
12. Chatterjee, K., Łącki, J.: Faster algorithms for Markov decision processes with low treewidth. In: Sharygina, N., Veith, H. (eds.) CAV 2013. LNCS, vol. 8044, pp. 543–558. Springer, Heidelberg (2013). https://doi.org/10.1007/978-3-642-39799-8_36

13. Chatterjee, K., et al.: Algorithms for algebraic path properties in concurrent systems of constant treewidth components. TOPLAS **40**(3), 1–43 (2018)
14. Chatterjee, K., Henzinger, M., Loitzenbauer, V., Oraee, S., Toman, V.: Symbolic algorithms for graphs and Markov decision processes with fairness objectives. In: Chockler, H., Weissenbacher, G. (eds.) CAV 2018. LNCS, vol. 10982, pp. 178–197. Springer, Cham (2018). https://doi.org/10.1007/978-3-319-96142-2_13
15. Chatterjee, K., et al.: Efficient parameterized algorithms for data packing. In: POPL (2019)
16. Chatterjee, K., et al.: Faster algorithms for dynamic algebraic queries in basic RSMs with constant treewidth. TOPLAS **41**(4), p. 23 (2019)
17. Chatterjee, K., et al.: The treewidth of smart contracts. In: SAC (2019)
18. Daws, C.: Symbolic and parametric model checking of discrete-time Markov chains. In: Liu, Z., Araki, K. (eds.) ICTAC 2004. LNCS, vol. 3407, pp. 280–294. Springer, Heidelberg (2005). https://doi.org/10.1007/978-3-540-31862-0_21
19. Dehnert, C., Junges, S., Katoen, J.-P., Volk, M.: A storm is coming: a modern probabilistic model checker. In: Majumdar, R., Kunčak, V. (eds.) CAV 2017. LNCS, vol. 10427, pp. 592–600. Springer, Cham (2017). https://doi.org/10.1007/978-3-319-63390-9_31
20. Fearnley, J.: Exponential lower bounds for policy iteration. In: Abramsky, S., Gavoille, C., Kirchner, C., Meyer auf der Heide, F., Spirakis, P.G. (eds.) ICALP 2010. LNCS, vol. 6199, pp. 551–562. Springer, Heidelberg (2010). https://doi.org/10.1007/978-3-642-14162-1_46
21. Feinberg, E.A.: Handbook of Markov Decision Processes. Springer, New York (2012)
22. Ferrara, A., Pan, G., Vardi, M.Y.: Treewidth in verification: local vs. global. In: Sutcliffe, G., Voronkov, A. (eds.) LPAR 2005. LNCS (LNAI), vol. 3835, pp. 489–503. Springer, Heidelberg (2005). https://doi.org/10.1007/11591191_34
23. Fomin, F.V., et al.: Fully polynomial-time parameterized computations for graphs and matrices of low treewidth. TALG **14**(3), 1–45 (2018)
24. Goharshady, A.K., Mohammadi, F.: An efficient algorithm for computing network reliability in small treewidth. Reliab. Eng. Syst. Saf. **193**, 106665 (2020)
25. Gurobi Optimization, L.: Gurobi optimizer (2019). http://www.gurobi.com
26. Gustedt, J., et al.: The treewidth of Java programs. In: ALENEX (2002)
27. Hahn, E.M., Hermanns, H., Wachter, B., Zhang, L.: PARAM: a model checker for parametric markov models. In: Touili, T., Cook, B., Jackson, P. (eds.) CAV 2010. LNCS, vol. 6174, pp. 660–664. Springer, Heidelberg (2010). https://doi.org/10.1007/978-3-642-14295-6_56
28. Howard, R.A.: Dynamic programming and Markov processes (1960)
29. Křetínský, J., Meggendorfer, T.: Efficient strategy iteration for mean payoff in Markov decision processes. In: D'Souza, D., Narayan Kumar, K. (eds.) ATVA 2017. LNCS, vol. 10482, pp. 380–399. Springer, Cham (2017). https://doi.org/10.1007/978-3-319-68167-2_25
30. Kwiatkowska, M., Norman, G., Parker, D.: PRISM 4.0: verification of probabilistic real-time systems. In: Gopalakrishnan, G., Qadeer, S. (eds.) CAV 2011. LNCS, vol. 6806, pp. 585–591. Springer, Heidelberg (2011). https://doi.org/10.1007/978-3-642-22110-1_47
31. MATLAB: The MathWorks Inc. (2018)
32. Norris, J.R.: Markov Chains. Cambridge University Press, Cambridge (1998)
33. Obdržálek, J.: Fast Mu-Calculus model checking when tree-width is bounded. In: Hunt, W.A., Somenzi, F. (eds.) CAV 2003. LNCS, vol. 2725, pp. 80–92. Springer, Heidelberg (2003). https://doi.org/10.1007/978-3-540-45069-6_7

34. Puterman, M.L.: Markov Decision Processes. Wiley, Hoboken (2014)
35. Quatmann, T., Katoen, J.-P.: Sound Value Iteration. In: Chockler, H., Weissenbacher, G. (eds.) CAV 2018. LNCS, vol. 10981, pp. 643–661. Springer, Cham (2018). https://doi.org/10.1007/978-3-319-96145-3_37
36. Robertson, N., Seymour, P.D.: Graph minors. iii. planar tree-width. J. Comb. Theor. Series B **36**(1), 49–64 (1984)
37. Thorup, M.: All structured programs have small tree width and good register allocation. Inf. Comput. **142**(2), 159–181 (1998)

Robustness Verification for Classifier Ensembles

Dennis Gross[1], Nils Jansen[1], Guillermo A. Pérez[2(✉)],
and Stephan Raaijmakers[3]

[1] Radboud University Nijmegen, Nijmegen, The Netherlands
[2] University of Antwerp, Antwerp, Belgium
guillermoalberto.perez@uantwerpen.be
[3] TNO and Leiden University, Leiden, The Netherlands

Abstract. We give a formal verification procedure that decides whether a classifier ensemble is robust against arbitrary randomized attacks. Such attacks consist of a set of deterministic attacks and a distribution over this set. The robustness-checking problem consists of assessing, given a set of classifiers and a labelled data set, whether there exists a randomized attack that induces a certain expected loss against all classifiers. We show the NP-hardness of the problem and provide an upper bound on the number of attacks that is sufficient to form an optimal randomized attack. These results provide an effective way to reason about the robustness of a classifier ensemble. We provide SMT and MILP encodings to compute optimal randomized attacks or prove that there is no attack inducing a certain expected loss. In the latter case, the classifier ensemble is provably robust. Our prototype implementation verifies multiple neural-network ensembles trained for image-classification tasks. The experimental results using the MILP encoding are promising both in terms of scalability and the general applicability of our verification procedure.

Keywords: Adversarial attacks · Ensemble classifiers · Robustness

1 Introduction

Recent years have seen a rapid progress in *machine learning* (ML) with a strong impact to fields like autonomous systems, computer vision, or robotics. As a consequence, many systems employing ML show an increasing interaction with aspects of our everyday life, consider autonomous cars operating amongst pedestrians and bicycles. While studies indicate that self-driving cars, inherently relying on ML techniques, make around 80% fewer traffic mistakes than human drivers [19], verifiable *safety* remains a major open challenge [5,13,23,26].

Research funded by the project NWA.BIGDATA.2019.002: "EXoDuS - EXplainable Data Science" and the FWO G030020N project "SAILor".

© Springer Nature Switzerland AG 2020
D. V. Hung and O. Sokolsky (Eds.): ATVA 2020, LNCS 12302, pp. 271–287, 2020.
https://doi.org/10.1007/978-3-030-59152-6_15

In the context of self-driving cars, for instance, certain camera data may contain noise that can be introduced randomly or actively via so-called adversarial attacks. We focus on the particular problem of such attacks in image classification. A successful attack perturbs the original image in a way such that a human does not recognize any difference while ML *misclassifies* the image. A measure of difference between the ground truth classification, for instance by a human, and a potentially perturbed ML classifier is referred as the *loss*.

A standard way to render image classification more robust against adversarial attacks is to employ a set of classifiers, also referred to as *classifier ensembles* [2, 3, 20, 21]. The underlying idea is to obscure the actual classifier from the attacker. One possible formalization of the competition between an adversarial attacker and the ensemble is that of a zero-sum game [20]: The attacker chooses first, the ensemble tries to react to the attack with minimal loss — that is, choosing a classifier that induces maximal classification accuracy.

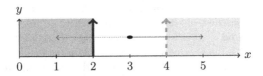

Fig. 1. We depict a single data point in $\mathbb{R}^2$ with label 1. The region to the left of the solid vertical line corresponds to points labelled with 2 by one classifier; the region to the right of the dashed line, those labelled with 2 by another classifier. Both (linear) classifiers label all other points in $\mathbb{R}^2$ with 1. (Hence, they correctly label the data point with 1.) The dotted attack, moving the data point left, induces a misclassification of the point by one of the classifiers. The solid attack, moving the data point right, induces a misclassification of the point by one of the classifiers. Note that every attack has a classifier which is "robust" to it, i.e. it does not misclassify the perturbed point. However, if the attacker chooses an attack uniformly at random, both of them misclassify the point with probability 1/2.

In this setting, the attacker may need to use randomization to behave optimally (see Fig. 1, cf. [6]). Such an attack is called optimal if the *expected loss* is maximized regardless of the choice of classifier.

Inspired by previous approaches for single classifiers [12, 15], we develop a formal verification procedure that decides if a classifier ensemble is *robust* against any randomized attack. In particular, the formal problem is the following. Given a set of classifiers and a labelled data set, we want to find a probability distribution and a set of attacks that induce an optimal randomized attack. Akin to the setting in [20], one can provide thresholds on potential perturbations of data points and the minimum shift in classification values. Thereby, it may happen that no optimal attack exists, in which case we call the classifier ensemble *robust*. Our aim is the development of a principled and effective method that is able to either find the optimal attack or prove that the ensemble is robust with respect to the predefined thresholds.

To that end, we first establish a number of theoretical results. First, we show that the underlying formal problem is **NP**-hard. Towards computational tractability, we also show that for an optimal attack there exists an upper bound on the number of attacks that are needed. Using these results, we provide an SMT encoding that computes suitable randomized attacks for a set of convolutional neural networks with ReLU activation functions and a labelled data set. In case there is no solution to that problem, the set of neural networks forms a robust classifier ensemble, see Fig. 2. Together with the state-of-the-art SMT solver Z3 [9], this encoding provides a complete method to solve the problem at hand. Yet, our experiments reveal that it scales only for small examples. We outline the necessary steps to formulate the problem as a mixed-integer linear programming (MILP), enabling the use of efficient optimization solvers like Gurobi [14].

Fig. 2. The verifier takes as input a set of classifiers, a set of labelled data points, the number of attacks, and the attack properties. If the verifier does not find a solution, we can be sure is robust against any attack with the specific properties. Otherwise, it returns the optimal attack.

In our experiments, we show the applicability of our approach by means of a benchmark set of binary classifiers, which were trained on the MNIST and German traffic sign datasets [10, 25].

Related Work

It is noteworthy that there is some recent work on robustness checking of decision-tree ensembles [22]. However, their approach is based on abstract interpretation and is thus not complete. Other approaches for robustness checking of machine learning classifiers focus on single classifiers (see, e.g., [7,12,15,18,24]). Akin to our approach, some of these works employ SMT solving. In [4], MILP-solving is used for verification tasks on (single) recurrent neural networks. In contrast, our framework allows to compute attacks for classifier ensembles.

In [11], Dreossi et al. propose a robustness framework which unifies the optimization and verification views on the robustness-checking problem and encompasses several existing approaches. They explicitly mention that their framework applies to *local robustness* and argue most of the existing work on finding adversarial examples and verifying robustness fits their framework. Our work, when we have a single classifier and a singleton data set, fits precisely into their framework. However, we generalize in those two dimensions by averaging over the *robustness target value* (in their jargon) for all points in a data set, and by considering ensemble classifiers. This means that our point of view of the *adversarial environment* is neither that of a white-box attacker nor is it a black-box attacker. Indeed, we know the set of classifiers but we do not know what strategy is used to choose which (convex combination of) classifiers to apply. Our environment is thus a gray-box attacker.

2   Preliminaries

Let $\mathbf{x}$ be a vector $(x_1, \ldots, x_d) \in \mathbb{R}^d$. We write $\|\mathbf{x}\|_1$ for the "Manhattan norm" of $\mathbf{x}$, that is $\sum_{i=1}^{d} |\mathbf{x}_i|$.

We will make use of a partial inverse of the max function. Consider a totally ordered set Y and a function $f: X \to Y$. Throughout this work we define the $\arg\max$ (arguments of the maxima) partial function as follows. For all $S \subseteq X$ we set $\arg\max_{s \in S} f(s) := m$ if m is the *unique* element of S such that $f(m) = \max_{s \in S} f(s)$. If more than one element of S witnesses the maximum then $\arg\max_{s \in S} f(s)$ is *undefined*.

A *probability distribution* over a finite set D is a function $\mu: D \to [0, 1] \subseteq \mathbb{R}$ with $\sum_{x \in D} \mu(x) = 1$. The set of all distributions on D is $Distr(D)$.

2.1   Neural Networks

We loosely follow the neural-network notation from [12,15]. A *feed-forward neural network* (NN for short) with d inputs and ℓ outputs encodes a function $f: \mathbb{R}^d \to \mathbb{R}^\ell$. We focus on NNs with *ReLU* activation functions. Formally, the function f is given in the form of

- a sequence $\mathbf{W}^{(1)}, \ldots, \mathbf{W}^{(k)}$ of *weight matrices* with $\mathbf{W}^{(i)} \in \mathbb{R}^{d_i \times d_{i-1}}$, for all $i = 1, \ldots, k$, and
- a sequence $\mathbf{B}^{(1)}, \ldots, \mathbf{B}^{(k)}$ of *bias vectors* with $\mathbf{B}^{(i)} \in \mathbb{R}^{d_i}$, for all $i = 1, \ldots, k$.

Additionally, we have that $d_0, \ldots, d_k \in \mathbb{N}$ with $d_0 = d$ and $d_k = \ell$. We then set $f = g^{(k)}(\mathbf{x})$ for all $\mathbf{x} \in \mathbb{R}^d$ where for all $i = 1, \ldots, k$ we define

$$g^{(i)}(\mathbf{x}) := \text{ReLU}(\mathbf{W}^{(i)} g^{(i-1)}(\mathbf{x}) + \mathbf{B}^{(i)}),$$

and $g^{(0)}(\mathbf{x}) := \mathbf{x}$. The ReLU function on vectors $\mathbf{u}$ is the element-wise maximum between 0 and the vector entries, that is, if $\mathbf{v} = \text{ReLU}(\mathbf{u})$ then $\mathbf{v}_i = \max(0, \mathbf{u}_i)$.

We sometimes refer to each $g^{(i)}$ as a *layer*. Note that each layer is fully determined by its corresponding weight and bias matrices.

2.2 Neural-Network Classifiers

A *data set* $X \subseteq \mathbb{R}^d$ is a finite set of (real-valued) data points $\mathbf{x} \in \mathbb{R}^d$ of dimension $d \in \mathbb{N}_{>0}$. A *classifier* $c \colon X \to [\ell]$ is a partial function that attaches to each data point a label from $[\ell] = \{1, \ldots, \ell\}$, the *set of labels*. We denote the set of all classifiers over X by $\mathbb{C}$. An NN-encoded classifier is simply a partial function $f \colon \mathbb{R}^d \to \mathbb{R}^k$ given as an NN that assigns to each data point $\mathbf{x} \in \mathbb{R}^d$ the label $\arg\max_{i \in [\ell]} h(i)$ where $h(i) = f(\mathbf{x})_i$. Intuitively, the label is the index of the largest entry in the vector resulting from applying f to $\mathbf{x}$. Note that if the image of x according to f has several maximal entries then the $\arg\max$ and the output label are undefined.

Definition 1 (Labelled data set). *A labelled data set* $\mathcal{X} = (X, c_t)$ *consists of a data set X and a total classifier c_t for X, i.e. c_t is a total function.*

In particular, $c_t(\mathbf{x})$ is defined for all $\mathbf{x} \in X$ and considered to be the "ground truth" classification for the whole data set X.

3 Problem Statement

We state the formal problem and provide the required notation. Recall that in our setting we assume to have an ensemble of classifiers $C \subseteq \mathbb{C}$. Such an ensemble is attacked by a set of attacks that are selected randomly.

Definition 2 (Deterministic attack). *A* deterministic attack *for a labelled data set (X, c_t) and a classifier $c \colon X \to [\ell]$ is a function $\delta \colon X \to \mathbb{R}^d$. An attack δ induces a* misclassification *for $\mathbf{x} \in X$ and c if $c(\mathbf{x} + \delta(\mathbf{x})) \neq c_t(\mathbf{x})$ or if $c(\mathbf{x} + \delta(\mathbf{x}))$ is undefined. The set of all deterministic attacks is Δ. An attack is ε-bounded if $\|\delta(\mathbf{x})\|_1 \leq \varepsilon$ holds for all $\mathbf{x} \in X$.*

We sometimes call the value $\mathbf{x} + \delta(\mathbf{x})$ the *attack point*. Note that the classifier c is not perfect, that is, $c(\mathbf{x}) \neq c_t(\mathbf{x})$ for some $\mathbf{x} \in X$, already a zero-attack $\delta(\mathbf{x}) = 0$ leads to a misclassification.

We extend deterministic attacks by means of probabilities.

Definition 3 (Randomized attack). *A* finite set $A \subseteq \Delta$ *of deterministic attacks together with a probability distribution $\mathbb{P} \in Distr(A)$ is a* randomized attack $(A, \mathbb{P})$. *A randomized attack is ε-bounded if for all attacks $\delta \in A$ with $\mathbb{P}(\delta) > 0$ it holds that $\|\delta(\mathbf{x})\|_1 \leq \varepsilon$ for all $\mathbf{x} \in X$.*

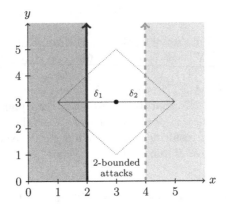

Fig. 3. The dotted diamond contains the set of all 2-bounded attacks in the setting described in Fig. 1. Both δ_1 and δ_2 are therefore 2-bounded (deterministic) attacks. Hence, any randomized attack with $A = \{\delta_1, \delta_2\}$ is also 2-bounded.

In general, a *loss function* $\ell \colon \mathbb{C} \times \mathbb{R}^d \times \mathbb{R}^d \to \mathbb{R}$ describes the *penalty* incurred by a classifier with respect to a labelled data point and an attack. In this work, we will focus on the widely used zero-one loss.

Definition 4 (Zero-one loss function). *The* $(0\text{--}1)$-loss function $\ell_{0-1} \colon \mathbb{C} \times \mathbb{R}^d \times \mathbb{R}^d \to \{0, 1\}$ *for a labelled data set* (X, c_t), *a classifier* $c \colon X \to [\ell]$, *and a deterministic attack* $\delta \in A$ *is given by the following for all* $\mathbf{x} \in X$

$$\ell_{0-1}(c, \mathbf{x}, \delta(\mathbf{x})) = \begin{cases} 0 & \text{if } c(\mathbf{x} + \delta(\mathbf{x})) = c_t(\mathbf{x}) \\ 1 & \text{otherwise.} \end{cases}$$

In particular, the loss function yields one if the image of the classifier c is undefined for the attack point $\mathbf{x} + \delta(\mathbf{x})$. Note furthermore that the loss is measured with respect to the ground truth classifier c_t. Thereby, the classifier c and the zero function as deterministic attack do not necessarily induce a loss of zero with respect to c_t. This assumption is realistic as, while we expect classifiers to perform well with regard to the ground truth, we cannot assume perfect classification in realistic settings.

We now connect a randomized attack to an ensemble, that is, a finite set $C \subseteq \mathbb{C}$ of classifiers. In particular, we quantify the overall value a randomized attack induces with respect to the loss function and the ensemble.

Definition 5 (Misclassification value). *The* misclassification value *of a randomized attack* $(A, \mathbb{P})$ *with respect to a labelled data set* $\mathcal{X} = (X, c_t)$ *and a finite set of classifiers* $C \subseteq \mathbb{C}$ *is given by*

$$\mathbf{Val}(A, \mathbb{P}) := \min_{c \in C} \frac{1}{|X|} \sum_{\mathbf{x} \in X} \mathop{\mathbb{E}}_{\delta \sim \mathbb{P}} [\ell_{0-1}(c, \mathbf{x}, \delta(\mathbf{x}))]. \tag{1}$$

This value is the minimum (over all classifiers) mean expected loss with respect to the randomized attack and the classifiers from C. An *optimal adversarial attack* against $C \subseteq \mathbb{C}$ with respect to a labelled data set (X, c_t) is a randomized attack which maximizes the value $\mathbf{Val}(A, \mathbb{P})$ in Eq. (1).

We are now ready to formalize a notion of robustness in terms of ε-bounded attacks and a *robustness bound* $\alpha \in \mathbb{R}$, as proposed in [20] for a set of classifiers.

Definition 6 (Bounded robustness). *A set of classifiers $C \in \mathbb{C}$ for a labelled data set (X, c_t) is called* robust bounded by ε and α *(ε, α-robust) if it holds that*

$$\forall (A, \mathbb{P}) \in 2^{\Delta} \times Distr(A). \mathbf{Val}(A, \mathbb{P}) < \alpha, \tag{2}$$

where the $(A, \mathbb{P})$ range over all ε-bounded randomized attacks.

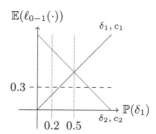

Fig. 4. Continuing with the example from Figs. 1 and 3, we now plot the expected loss per attack and the corresponding classifier. (That is, the classifier which misclassifies the perturbed point.) On the horizontal axis we have the probability x assigned to δ_1 and we assume $\mathbb{P}(\delta_2) = 1 - x$. Note that $x = 0.2$ is such that the minimal expected loss, i.e. the misclassification value, is strictly less than 0.3. Indeed, one classifier manages to correctly classifier the perturbed point with probability 0.8 in this case. With $x = 0.5$ we see that the misclassification value is 0.5. Hence, the ensemble is not $(2, 0.5)$-robust.

In other words, an (ε, α)-robust ensemble is such that for all possible ε-bounded random attacks $(A, \mathbb{P})$, there is at least one classifier $c \in C$ from the ensemble such that $\sum_{\mathbf{x} \in X} \mathbb{E}_{\delta \sim \mathbb{P}}[\ell_{0-1}(c, \mathbf{x}, \delta(\mathbf{x}))] < \alpha |X|$. Conversely, an ensemble is not (ε, α)-robust if there is an ε-bounded randomized attack with a misclassification value of at least α.

4 Theoretical Results

In this section we establish two key results that carry essential practical implication for our setting. First, we show that in order to obtain an optimal randomized attack, only a bounded number of deterministic attacks is needed.[1] Thereby, we

---

[1] An analogue of this property had already been observed by Perdomo and Singer in [20, Section 3] in the case when classifiers are chosen randomly.

only need to take a bounded number of potential attacks into account in order to prove the α-robustness of a set of classifiers and a given labelled data set. Second, we establish that our problem is in fact **NP**-hard, justifying the use of SMT and MILP solvers to (1) compute any optimal randomized attack and, more importantly, to (2) prove robustness against any such attack.

4.1   Bounding the Number of Attacks

In the following, we assume a fixed labelled data set (X, c_t). For every classifier $c \in C$ and every deterministic attack $\delta \in \Delta$, let us write $M_c(\delta)$ to denote the value $\sum_{x \in X} \ell_{0-1}(c, \mathbf{x}, \delta(\mathbf{x}))$. Observe that $0 \leq M_c(\delta) \leq |X|$ for all $c \in C$ and $\delta \in \Delta$. Furthermore, for all $c \in C$ and randomized attacks $(A, \mathbb{P})$ it holds that:

$$\sum_{\mathbf{x} \in X} \mathop{\mathbb{E}}_{\delta \sim \mathbb{P}} [\ell_{0-1}(c, \mathbf{x}, \delta(\mathbf{x}))] = \sum_{\mathbf{x} \in X} \sum_{\delta \in A} \mathbb{P}(\delta) \cdot \ell_{0-1}(c, \mathbf{x}, \delta(\mathbf{x}))$$

$$= \sum_{\delta \in A} \mathbb{P}(\delta) \underbrace{\left(\sum_{\mathbf{x} \in X} \ell_{0-1}(c, \mathbf{x}, \delta(\mathbf{x})) \right)}_{=M_c(\delta)} = \sum_{\delta \in A} \mathbb{P}(\delta) \cdot M_c(\delta)$$

We get that Eq. (2) from Definition 5 is false if and only if the following holds.

$$\exists (A, \mathbb{P}) \in 2^\Delta \times Distr(A). \forall c \in C. \sum_{\delta \in A} \mathbb{P}(\delta) \cdot M_c(\delta) \geq \alpha |X| \tag{3}$$

Proposition 1 (Bounded number of attacks). *Let $\alpha \in \mathbb{R}$ and consider the labelled data set (X, c_t) together with a finite set of classifiers $C \subseteq \mathbb{C}$. For all randomized attacks $(A, \mathbb{P})$, there exists a randomized attack $(A', \mathbb{P}')$ such that*

- $|A'| \leq (|X| + 1)^{|C|}$,
- **Val**$(A', \mathbb{P}')$ = **Val**$(A, \mathbb{P})$*, and*
- $(A', \mathbb{P}')$ *is ε-bounded if $(A, \mathbb{P})$ is ε-bounded.*

Proof. We proceed by contradiction. Let $(A, \mathbb{P})$ be an ε-bounded randomized attack with a misclassification value of α such that $|A| > (|X| + 1)^{|C|}$. Further suppose that $(A, \mathbb{P})$ is minimal (with respect to the size of A) amongst all such randomized attacks. It follows that there are attacks $\delta, \delta' \in A$ such that $M_c(\delta) = M_c(\delta')$ for all $c \in C$. We thus have that

$$\mathbb{P}(\delta) \cdot M_c(\delta) + \mathbb{P}(\delta') \cdot M_c(\delta') = (\mathbb{P}(\delta) + \mathbb{P}(\delta')) \cdot M_c(\delta).$$

Consider now the randomized attack $(A', \mathbb{P}')$ obtained by modifying $(A, \mathbb{P})$ so that $\mathbb{P}(\delta) = \mathbb{P}(\delta) + \mathbb{P}(\delta')$ and δ' is removed from A. From the above discussion and Eq. (3) it follows that $(A', \mathbb{P}')$, just like $(A, \mathbb{P})$, has a misclassification value of α. Furthermore, since $A' \subseteq A$, we have that $(A', \mathbb{P}')$ is ε-bounded and that $|A'| < |A|$. This contradicts our assumption regarding the minimality of $(A, \mathbb{P})$ amongst ε-bounded randomized attacks with the same value α. $\square$

4.2 NP Hardness of Non-robustness Checking

It is known that checking whether linear properties hold for a given NN with ReLU activation functions is **NP**-hard [15]. We restate this using our notation.

Proposition 2 (From)[15], Appendix I). *The following problem is* **NP***-hard: Given an NN-encoded function $f \colon \mathbb{R}^n \to \mathbb{R}^m$ and closed nonnegative intervals $(I_k)_1^n, (O_\ell)_1^m$, decide whether there exists $\mathbf{x} \in \prod_{k=1}^{n} I_k$ such that $f(\mathbf{x}) \in \prod_{\ell=1}^{m} O_\ell$.*

Intuitively, determining whether there exists a point in a given *box* — that is, a hypercube defined by a Cartesian product of intervals — from $\mathbb{R}^n$ whose image according to f is in a given box from $\mathbb{R}^m$ is **NP**-hard. We will now reduce this to the problem of determining if there is a randomized attack such that its misclassification value takes at least a given threshold.

Theorem 1. *The following problem is* **NP***-hard: For a labelled data set $\mathcal{X} = (X, c_t)$, a set C of classifiers, and a value $\alpha \in \mathbb{Q}$, decide if there exists an ε-bounded randomized attack $(A, \mathbb{P})$ w.r.t. $\mathcal{X}$ and C such that $\mathbf{Val}(A, \mathbb{P}) \geq \alpha$.*

Proof. We use Proposition 2 and show how to construct, for any NN-encoded function $g \colon \mathbb{R}^n \to \mathbb{R}$ and any constraint $\ell \leq g(\mathbf{x}) \leq u$, two classifiers c_ℓ, c_u such that a single deterministic attack δ causes $\mathbf{0}$, the single data point, to be misclassified by both c_ℓ and c_u if and only if the constraint holds. Note that the ε bound can be chosen to be large enough so that it contains the box $\prod_{k=1}^{n} I_k$ and that the identity function over nonnegative numbers is NN-encodable, that is, using the identity matrix as weight matrix $\mathbf{W}$ and a zero bias vector $\mathbf{B}$. For every instance of the problem from Proposition 2 we can therefore construct $2(n + m)$ NNs that encodes all input and output constraints: $2n$ of them based on the identity function to encode input constraints and $2m$ based on the input NN from the given instance. It follows that determining if there exists an ε-bounded deterministic attack δ that causes $\mathbf{0}$ to be *simultaneously misclassified* by a given classifier ensemble is **NP**-hard. Hence, to conclude, it suffices to argue that the latter problem reduces to our robustness-value threshold problem. The result follows from Lemmas 1 and 2. □

Enforcing Interval Constraints. Let $g \colon \mathbb{R}^n \to \mathbb{R}$ be an NN-encoded function and $\ell, u \in \mathbb{R}$ with $\ell \leq u$. Consider now the constraint $\ell \leq g(\mathbf{x}) \leq u$. Henceforth we will focus on the labelled data set (X, c_t) with $X = \{\mathbf{0}\}$ and $c_t(\mathbf{x}) = 1$.

Lower-Bound Constraint. We obtain c_ℓ by adding to the NN encoding of g a new final layer with weight and bias vectors

$$\mathbf{W} = \begin{pmatrix} 0 \\ 1 \end{pmatrix}, \mathbf{B} = \begin{pmatrix} \ell \\ 0 \end{pmatrix}$$

to obtain the NN-encoded function $\underline{g} \colon \mathbb{R}^n \to \mathbb{R}^2$. Note that $\underline{g}(\mathbf{v}) = (\ell, g(\mathbf{v}))^\mathsf{T}$ for all $\mathbf{v} \in \mathbb{R}^n$. It follows that $c_\ell(\mathbf{v}) = 2$ if $g(\mathbf{v}) > \ell$ and $c_\ell(\mathbf{v})$ is undefined if $g(\mathbf{v}) = \ell$. In all other cases the classifier yields 1.

Upper-Bound Constraint. To obtain c_u we add to the NN encoding of g two new layers. The corresponding weight matrices and bias vectors are as follows.

$$\mathbf{W}^{(1)} = (1), \ \mathbf{B}^{(1)} = (-u), \ \mathbf{W}^{(2)} = \begin{pmatrix} 0 \\ -1 \end{pmatrix}, \ \mathbf{B}^{(2)} = \begin{pmatrix} 1 \\ 1 \end{pmatrix}$$

Let us denote by $\bar{g} \colon \mathbb{R}^n \to \mathbb{R}^2$ the resulting function. Observe that $\bar{g}(\mathbf{v}) = (1, \max(0, 1 - \max(0, g(\mathbf{v}) - u)))^{\mathsf{T}}$ for all $\mathbf{v} \in \mathbb{R}^n$. Hence, we have that $c_u(\mathbf{v})$ is undefined if and only if $g(\mathbf{v}) \leq u$ and yields 1 otherwise.

Lemma 1. *Let $g \colon \mathbb{R}^n \to \mathbb{R}$ be an NN-encoded function and consider the constraint $\ell \leq g(\mathbf{x}) \leq u$. One can construct NN-encoded classifiers c_ℓ and c_u, of size linear with respect to g, for the labelled data set $(\{\mathbf{0}\}, \{\mathbf{0} \mapsto 1\})$ such that the deterministic attack $\delta \colon \mathbf{0} \mapsto \mathbf{v}$*

- *induces a misclassification of $\mathbf{0}$ with respect to c_ℓ if and only if $\ell \leq g(\mathbf{v})$ and*
- *it induces a misclassification of $\mathbf{0}$ with respect to c_u if and only if $g(\mathbf{v}) \leq u$.*

We now show how to modify the NN to obtain classifiers c_ℓ, c_u such that $\mathbf{x}$ is misclassified by both c_ℓ and c_u if and only if the constraint holds.

Enforcing Universal Misclassification. A randomized attack with misclassification value 1 can be assumed to be deterministic. Indeed, from Eq. (3) it follows that for any such randomized attack we must have $M_c(\delta) = |X|$ for all $\delta \in A$ and all $c \in C$. Hence, we can choose any such $\delta \in A$ and consider the randomized attack $(\{\delta\}, \{\delta \mapsto 1\})$ which also has misclassification value 1.

Lemma 2. *Consider the labelled data set $\mathcal{X} = (X, c_t)$ with the finite set of classifiers $C \subseteq \mathbb{C}$. There exists an ε-bounded randomized attack $(A, \mathbb{P})$ with $\mathrm{Val}(A, \mathbb{P}) = 1$ if and only if there exists a deterministic attack δ such that*

- $\|\delta(\mathbf{x})\|_1 \leq \varepsilon$ *for all $\mathbf{x} \in X$ and*
- *for all $\mathbf{x} \in X$ and all $c \in C$ we have that either $c(\mathbf{x} + \delta(\mathbf{x}))$ is undefined or it is not equal to $c_t(\mathbf{x})$.*

With Lemmas 1 and 2 established, the proof of Theorem 1 is now complete.

5   SMT and MILP Encodings

In this section, we describe the main elements of our SMT and MILP encodings to compute (optimal) randomized attacks or prove the robustness of classifier ensembles. We start with a base encoding and will afterwards explain how to explicitly encode the classifiers and the loss function.

5.1 Base Problem Encoding

First, we assume a labelled data set $\mathcal{X} = (X, c_t)$, the attack bound ε, and the robustness bound α are input to the problem. In particular, the data set $X = \{\mathbf{x}^1, \ldots, \mathbf{x}^{|X|}\} \subseteq \mathbb{R}^d$ has data points $\mathbf{x}^j = (x_1^j, \ldots, x_d^j) \in \mathbb{R}^d$ for $1 \leq j \leq |X|$. Furthermore, we assume the number $|A|$ of attacks that shall be computed is fixed. Recall that, to show that the set of classifiers is robust, we can compute a sufficient bound on the number of attacks — see Sec. 4.1.

For readability, we assume the classifiers C and the loss function ℓ_{0-1} are given as functions that can directly be used in the encodings, and we will use the absolute value $|x|$ for $x \in \mathbb{R}$. Afterwards, we discuss how to actually encode classifiers and the loss function. We use the following variables:

- For the attacks from A, we introduce $\delta_1, \ldots, \delta_{|A|}$ with $\delta_i \in \mathbb{R}^{|X| \times d}$ for $1 \leq i \leq |A|$. Specifically, δ_i shall be assigned all attack values for the i-th attack from A. That is, δ_i^j is the attack for the data point $\mathbf{x}^j = (x_1^j, \ldots, x_d^j) \in \mathbb{R}^d$ with $\delta_i^j = (\delta_i^{j,1}, \ldots, \delta_i^{j,d})$ for $1 \leq j \leq |X|$.
- We introduce $p_1, \ldots, p_{|A|}$ to form a probability distribution over deterministic attacks; p_i is assigned the probability to execute attack δ_i.

The classifier ensemble C is not ε, α-robust as in Definition 6 if and only if the following constraints are satisfiable.

$$\forall c \in C. \quad \sum_{j=1}^{|X|} \sum_{i=1}^{|A|} \left(p_i \cdot \ell_{0-1}(c, \mathbf{x}^j, \delta_i^j) \right) \geq \alpha \cdot |X| \quad (4)$$

$$\forall i \in \{1, \ldots, |A|\}, j \in \{1, \ldots, |X|\}. \quad \sum_{k=1}^{d} |\delta_i^{j,k}| \leq \varepsilon \quad (5)$$

$$\sum_{i=1}^{|A|} p_i = 1 \quad (6)$$

$$\forall i \in \{1, \ldots, |A|\}. \quad p_i \geq 0 \quad (7)$$

Indeed, (4) enforces the misclassification value to be at least α; (5) ensures an ε-bounded randomized attack; finally, by (6) and (7) the probability variables induce a valid probability distribution.

Specific Encodings. For the SMT encoding, we can make use of the $\max(\cdot)$ native to implement the absolute value. In particular for the MILP, however, we employ so-called "big-M" tricks to encode max functions and a (restricted) product operation (cf. [7]). Specifically, the product is required to obtain the value resulting from the multiplication of the loss function and probability variables.

As an example of "big-M" trick, suppose we have variables $a \in \mathbb{Q} \cap [0, 1], b \in \{0, 1\}$, and a constant $M \in \mathbb{Q}$ such that $M > a + b$. We introduce a variable $c \in \mathbb{Q} \cap [0, 1]$ and add the following constraints which clearly enforce that $c = ab$.

$$c \geq a - M(1 - b), \quad c \leq a + M(1 - b), \quad c \leq 0 + Mb .$$

Note that M can be chosen to be the constant 2 in this case.

Encoding the Loss Function. We encode the zero-one loss function from Definition 4 as an if-then-else expression making use of the ground truth classifier c_t. We introduce one variable $\ell_{i,j}^c$ per classifier $c \in C$ for all attacks $\delta_i \in A$ and all datapoints $\mathbf{x}^j \in X$. In the SMT encoding, we can then define

$$\ell_{i,j}^c = ITE((c(\mathbf{x}^j + \delta_i^j) = c_t(\mathbf{x}^j)), 0, 1) \qquad (8)$$

so that $\ell_{i,j}^c = \ell_{0-1}(c, \mathbf{x}^j, \delta_i^j)$. In our MILP encoding we have to simulate the *ITE* primitive using constraints similar to the ones mentioned above.

5.2 Classifier Encoding

As mentioned in the preliminaries, neural networks implement functions by way of layer composition. Intuitively, the input of a layer is by a previous layer. When fed forward, input values are multiplied by a weight, and a bias value will be added to it. Matrix operations realized by a neural network can thus be encoded as linear functions. For max-pooling operations and the ReLU activation function, one can use the native $\max(\cdot)$ operation or implement a maximum using a "big-M trick". For this, a suitable constant M has to be obtained beforehand (cf. [7]). We also use a (discrete) convolution operation, as a linear function.

6 Experiments

In the previous section, we showed that our problem of neural network robustness verification is **NP**-hard. Meaningful comparison between approaches, therefore, needs to be experimental. To that end, we use classifiers trained on multiple image data sets and report on the comparison between the SMT and MILP encodings. In what follows, we analyze the running time behavior of the different verifiers, the generated attacks and the misclassification value for the given data points, and whether a set of classifiers is robust against predefined thresholds.

6.1 Experimental Setup

For each experiment, we define a set of classifiers C, our data points $\mathcal{X}$, the number of attacks $|A|$, and both the ε- and α-values. Then, we generate the attacks A and the probability distribution $\mathbb{P}$ using SMT and MILP solvers. If no randomized attack $(A, \mathbb{P})$ is found (UNSAT), we have shown that our set of classifiers is ε, α-robust with respect to the predefined thresholds.

Toolchain. Our NN robustness verifier[2], is implemented as part of a Python 3.x toolchain. We use the SMT solver Z3 [9] and the MILP solver Gurobi [14] with their standard settings. To support arbitrary classifiers, we created a generic pipeline using the TensorFlow API, and support Max-Pooling layers, convolutional layers, and dense layers with ReLU activation functions [1]. We focus on binary classifiers by defining certain classification boundaries. We train the classifiers using the Adam optimizer [17] as well as stochastic gradient descent.

---

[2] Available at https://tinyurl.com/ensemble-robustness.

Table 1. SMT versus MILP

Benchmark Information								SMT		MILP	
ID	Name	$|C|$	$|A|$	$|\mathcal{X}|$	dim	α	ε	Time	**Val**$(A, \mathbb{P})$	Time	**Val**$(A, \mathbb{P})$
2	mnist_0_1	3	2	4	7×7	0.2	100	-TO-	–	12.43	0.25
4	mnist_0_1_2convs	3	2	4	8×8	0.4	100	-TO-	–	53.92	0.4
7	mnist_0_1	3	2	4	8×8	0.4	1000	-TO-	–	0.34	0.4
8	mnist_0_1	3	2	4	8×8	0.9	1000	-TO-	–	50.09	0.9
9	mnist_0_1	3	3	4	8×8	0.9	60	-TO-	–	34.02	1
13	mnist_4_5	3	4	4	10×10	0.9	50	-TO-	–	144.32	1
14	mnist_7_8	3	4	4	6×6	0.1	60	-TO-	–	18.94	0.25
16	mnist_4_5	3	2	4	10×10	0.1	1000	155.73	0.38	101.16	0.1
17	mnist_4_5	3	3	4	10×10	0.1	80	403.25	0.25	101.47	0.25
18	mnist_4_5	3	2	4	10×10	0.15	80	216.65	0.38	44.26	0.15
19	mnist_4_5	3	2	4	10×10	0.2	100	156.63	0.38	54.36	0.25
22	mnist_7_8	3	2	4	6×6	0.9	0.1	-TO-	–	4	robust
26	traffic_signs	3	2	4	10×10	1	0.01	-TO-	–	17	robust
27	traffic_signs	3	2	4	10×10	1	0.1	-TO-	–	-TO-	–

Table 2. MILP versus MaxMILP

Benchmark Information								MILP		MaxMILP	
ID	Name	$|C|$	$|A|$	$|l\mathcal{X}|$	dim	α	ε	Time	**Val**$(A, \mathbb{P})$	Time	**Val**$(A, \mathbb{P})$
1	mnist_0_1	3	2	4	7×7	0.1	1000	57.79	0.25	46.23	1*
3	mnist_0_1_2convs	3	2	4	8×8	0.2	1000	738.76	0.5	93.54	1*
7	mnist_0_1	3	2	4	8×8	0.4	1000	0.34	0.4	0.34	1*
10	mnist_0_1	3	4	4	8×8	0.9	60	51.39	1	51.39	1*
14	mnist_7_8	3	4	4	6×6	0.1	60	18.94	0.25	21.20	1
17	mnist_4_5	3	3	4	10×10	0.1	80	101.47	0.25	88.39	1
20	mnist_3_6	2	9	2	8×8	1	0.005	7	robust	7	robust
21	mnist_7_8	3	2	4	6×6	1	0.1	4	robust	4	robust
24	mnist_0_2	3	27	4	9×9	1	0.01	108	robust	108	robust
25	mnist_0_2	3	30	4	9×9	1	0.01	120	robust	120	robust
28	traffic_signs	3	3	4	10×10	1	0.01	45	robust	45	robust
29	traffic_signs	3	3	4	10×10	1	0.01	–TO–	-	–TO–	–

Data Sets. MNIST consists of 70 000 images of handwritten digits) [10] and is widely used for benchmarking in the field of machine learning [8, 16]. We trained classifiers to have a test accuracy of at least 90%.

German traffic sign is a multi-class and single-image classification data set, containing more than 50 000 images and more than 40 classes [25]. Traffic sign recognition and potential attacks are of utmost importance for self-driving cars [27]. We extracted the images for "Give way" and "priority" traffic signs from the data set and trained classifiers on this subset to have an accuracy of at least 80%.

Optimal Attacks. As MILP inherently solves optimization problems, we augment the base encoding from Eqs (4)–(7) with the following objective function:

$$\max \quad \sum_{k=1}^{|C|} \sum_{j=1}^{|\mathcal{X}|} \sum_{i=1}^{|A|} \left(p_i \cdot \ell_{0-1}(c_k, \mathbf{x}^j, \delta_i^j) \right).$$

An optimal solution with respect to the objective **may** yield a randomized attack inducing the maximal misclassification value among all ε-bounded attacks.[3]

Alternative Attacks. Our method generates attacks taking the whole ensemble of classifiers into account, which is computationally harder than just considering single classifiers [12,15] due to an increased number of constraints and variables in the underlying encodings. To showcase the need for our approach, we implemented two other ways to generate attacks that are based on individual classifiers and subsequently lifted to the whole ensemble. Recall that we assume the attacker does not know which classifier from the ensemble will be chosen.

First, for the classifier ensemble C we compute — using a simplified version of our MILP encoding — an optimal attack δ_c for each classifier $c \in C$. Each such δ_c maximizes the misclassification value, that is, the loss, for the classifier c. The attack set $A_C = \{\delta_c \mid c \in C\}$ together with a uniform distribution $Distr_A$ over A_C form the so-called *uniform attacker* $(A_C, Distr_A)$.

Second, to compare with deterministic attacks, we calculate for each attack from A_C the misclassification value over all classifiers. The *best deterministic attack* is any attack from A_C inducing a maximal misclassification value.

6.2 Evaluation

We report on our experimental results using the aforementioned data sets and attacks. For all experiments we used a timeout of 7200 s (TO). Each benchmark has an ID, a name, the number $|C|$ of classifiers, the number $|A|$ of attacks, the size $|\mathcal{X}|$ of the data set, the dimension of the image (dim), the robustness bound α, and the attack bound ε. The names of the MNIST benchmarks are of the form "mnist_x_y", where x and y are the labels; the additional suffix "_$n$convs" indicates that the classifier has n convolutional layers. We provide an excerpt of our experiments, full tables are available in the appendix.

SMT versus MILP. In Table 1, we report on the comparison between SMT and MILP. Note that for these benchmarks, the MILP solver just checks the feasibility of the constraints without an objective function. We list for both solvers the time in seconds and the misclassification value **Val**$(A, \mathbb{P})$, rounded to 2 decimal places, for the generated randomized attack $(A, \mathbb{P})$, if it can be computed before the timeout. If there is no solution, the classifier ensemble C is ε, α-robust, and instead of a misclassification value we list "robust".

---

[3] Note that we sum over classifiers instead of minimizing, as required in **Val**$(A, \mathbb{P})$.

We observe that SMT is only able to find solutions within the timeout for small α and large ε values. Moreover, if the ensemble is robust, that is, the problem is not satisfiable, the solver does not terminate for any benchmark. Nevertheless, for some benchmarks (see Table 1, entries 16–19) the SMT solver yields a higher misclassification value than the MILP solver — that is, it finds a better attack. The MILP solver, on the other hand, solves most of our benchmarks mostly within less than a minute, including the robust ones. Despite the reasonably low timeout of 7200 s, we are thus able to verify the robustness of NNs with around 6 layers. Running times visibly differ for other factors such as layer types.

MILP versus MaxMILP. Table 2 compares some of the MILP results to those where we optimize the mentioned objective function, denoted by MaxMILP. The MILP solver Gurobi offers the possibility of so-called *callbacks*, that is, while an intermediate solution is not proven to be optimal, it may already be feasible. In case optimality cannot be shown within the timeout, we list the current (feasible) solution, and mark optimal solutions with ∗. The misclassification value for the MaxMILP solver is always 1. For robust ensembles, it is interesting to see that the MaxMILP encoding sometimes needs less time.

Table 3. Attacker comparison

Benchmark Information							UA	BDA	MaxMILP
ID	Name	$|C|$	$|A|$	$|\mathcal{X}|$	dim	Epsilon	Alpha	$\mathbf{Val}(A,\mathbb{P})$	$\mathbf{Val}(A,\mathbb{P})$	$\mathbf{Val}(A,\mathbb{P})$
3	mnist_0_1_2convs	3	2	4	8×8	0.2	1000	0.33	0.25	1*
7	mnist_0_1	3	2	4	8×8	0.4	1000	0.33	0.5	1*
8	mnist_0_1	3	2	4	8×8	0.9	1000	0.33	0.5	1*
9	mnist_0_1	3	3	4	8×8	0.9	60	0.33	0.5	1*
10	mnist_0_1	3	4	4	8×8	0.9	60	0.33	0.5	1*
11	mnist_4_5	3	2	4	10×10	0.2	100	0.33	0.25	1*
14	mnist_7_8	3	4	4	6×6	0.1	60	0.33	0.5	1
15	mnist_7_8	3	10	4	6×6	0.1	60	0.33	0.5	1
16	mnist_4_5	3	2	4	10×10	0.1	1000	0.33	0.75	1*
17	mnist_4_5	3	3	4	10×10	0.1	80	0.33	0.5	1
18	mnist_4_5	3	2	4	10×10	0.15	80	0.33	0.5	1*

In Table 3, we compare the MaxMILP method to the *uniform attacker* (UA) and the *best deterministic attacker* (BDA). What we can see is that the best deterministic attacker usually achieves higher misclassification values than the uniform attacker, but none of them are able to reach the actual optimum of 1.

Discussion of the Results. Within the timeout, our method is able to generate optimal results for medium-sized neural networks. The running time is mainly influenced by the number and type of the used layers, in particular, it is governed by convolutional and max-pooling layers: these involve more matrix operations than dense layers. As expected, larger values of the robustness bound α and smaller values of the attack bound ε typically increase the running times.

7   Conclusion and Future Work

We presented a new method to formally verify the robustness or, vice versa, compute optimal attacks for an ensemble of classifiers. Despite the theoretical hardness, we were able to, in particular by using MILP-solving, provide results for meaningful benchmarks. In future work, we will render our method more scalable towards a standalone verification tool for neural network ensembles. Moreover, we will explore settings where we do not have white-box access to the classifiers and employ state-of-the-art classifier stealing methods.

References

1. Abadi, M.: Tensorflow: learning functions at scale. In: Garrigue, J., Keller, G., Sumii, E. (eds.) ICFP, p. 1. ACM (2016)
2. Abbasi, M., Gagné, C.: Robustness to adversarial examples through an ensemble of specialists. In: ICLR (Workshop), OpenReview.net (2017)
3. Abbasi, M., Rajabi, A., Gagné, C., Bobba, R.B.: Toward adversarial robustness by diversity in an ensemble of specialized deep neural networks. In: Goutte, C., Zhu, X. (eds.) Canadian AI 2020. LNCS (LNAI), vol. 12109, pp. 1–14. Springer, Cham (2020). https://doi.org/10.1007/978-3-030-47358-7_1
4. Akintunde, M.E., Kevorchian, A., Lomuscio, A., Pirovano, E.: Verification of RNN-based neural agent-environment systems. In: AAAI, pp. 6006–6013. AAAI Press (2019)
5. Amodei, D., Olah, C., Steinhardt, J., Christiano, P., Schulman, J., Mané, D.: Concrete problems in ai safety. CoRR abs/1606.06565 (2016)
6. Apt, K.R., Grädel, E.: Lectures in Game Theory for Computer Scientists. Cambridge University Press, Cambridge (2011)
7. Bunel, R., Turkaslan, I., Torr, P.H.S., Kohli, P., Mudigonda, P.K.: A unified view of piecewise linear neural network verification. In: NeurIPS, pp. 4795–4804 (2018)
8. Cohen, G., Afshar, S., Tapson, J., van Schaik, A.: EMNIST: extending MNIST to handwritten letters. In: IJCNN, pp. 2921–2926. IEEE (2017)
9. de Moura, L., Bjørner, N.: Z3: an efficient SMT solver. In: Ramakrishnan, C.R., Rehof, J. (eds.) TACAS 2008. LNCS, vol. 4963, pp. 337–340. Springer, Heidelberg (2008). https://doi.org/10.1007/978-3-540-78800-3_24
10. Deng, L.: The MNIST database of handwritten digit images for machine learning research [best of the web]. IEEE Signal Process. Mag. **29**(6), 141–142 (2012)
11. Dreossi, T., Ghosh, S., Sangiovanni-Vincentelli, A.L., Seshia, S.A.: A formalization of robustness for deep neural networks. CoRR abs/1903.10033 (2019)
12. Ehlers, R.: Formal verification of piece-wise linear feed-forward neural networks. In: D'Souza, D., Narayan Kumar, K. (eds.) ATVA 2017. LNCS, vol. 10482, pp. 269–286. Springer, Cham (2017). https://doi.org/10.1007/978-3-319-68167-2_19
13. Freedman, R.G., Zilberstein, S.: Safety in AI-HRI: challenges complementing user experience quality. In: AAAI Fall Symposium Series (2016)
14. Gurobi Optimization Inc: Gurobi optimizer reference manual. http://www.gurobi.com (2013)
15. Katz, G., Barrett, C., Dill, D.L., Julian, K., Kochenderfer, M.J.: Reluplex: an efficient SMT solver for verifying deep neural networks. In: Majumdar, R., Kunčak, V. (eds.) CAV 2017. LNCS, vol. 10426, pp. 97–117. Springer, Cham (2017). https://doi.org/10.1007/978-3-319-63387-9_5

16. Keysers, D.: Comparison and combination of state-of-the-art techniques for hand-written character recognition: topping the mnist benchmark. arXiv preprint arXiv:0710.2231 (2007)
17. Kingma, D.P., Ba, J.: Adam: a method for stochastic optimization. In: Bengio, Y., LeCun, Y. (eds.) ICLR (2015). http://arxiv.org/abs/1412.6980
18. Kwiatkowska, M.Z.: Safety verification for deep neural networks with provable guarantees (invited paper). In: CONCUR, LIPIcs, vol. 140, pp. 1–5. Schloss Dagstuhl - Leibniz-Zentrum für Informatik (2019)
19. Nyholm, S.: The ethics of crashes with self-driving cars: a roadmap, ii. Philos. Compass **13**(7), e12506 (2018)
20. Perdomo, J.C., Singer, Y.: Robust attacks against multiple classifiers. CoRR abs/1906.02816 (2019)
21. Pinot, R., Ettedgui, R., Rizk, G., Chevaleyre, Y., Atif, J.: Randomization matters. how to defend against strong adversarial attacks. CoRR abs/2002.11565 (2020)
22. Ranzato, F., Zanella, M.: Robustness verification of decision tree ensembles. OVERLAY@AI*IA, **2509**, pp. 59–64 (2019). CEUR-WS.org
23. Science, N.: National Science Technology and Council: Preparing for the Future of Artificial Intelligence, T.C. (2016)
24. Singh, G., Gehr, T., Püschel, M., Vechev, M.T.: An abstract domain for certifying neural networks. Proc. ACM Program. Lang. **3**(POPL), 1–30 (2019). https://doi.org/10.1145/3290354
25. Stallkamp, J., Schlipsing, M., Salmen, J., Igel, C.: The German traffic sign recognition benchmark: a multi-class classification competition. In: IJCNN, pp. 1453–1460. IEEE (2011)
26. Stoica, I., et al.: A Berkeley view of systems challenges for AI. CoRR abs/1712.05855 (2017)
27. Yan, C., Xu, W., Liu, J.: Can you trust autonomous vehicles: contactless attacks against sensors of self-driving vehicle. DEF CON **24**(8), 109 (2016)

Verification of Indefinite-Horizon POMDPs

Alexander Bork[1], Sebastian Junges[2(✉)], Joost-Pieter Katoen[1], and Tim Quatmann[1]

[1] RWTH Aachen University, Aachen, Germany
[2] University of California, Berkeley, USA
sjunges@berkeley.edu

Abstract. The verification problem in MDPs asks whether, for any policy resolving the nondeterminism, the probability that something bad happens is bounded by some given threshold. This verification problem is often overly pessimistic, as the policies it considers may depend on the complete system state. This paper considers the verification problem for partially observable MDPs, in which the policies make their decisions based on (the history of) the observations emitted by the system. We present an abstraction-refinement framework extending previous instantiations of the Lovejoy-approach. Our experiments show that this framework significantly improves the scalability of the approach.

1 Introduction

Markov decision processes are *the* model to reason about systems involving nondeterministic choice and probabilistic branching. They have widespread usage in planning and scheduling, robotics, and formal methods. In the latter, the key *verification question* is whether for any policy, i.e., for any resolution of the nondeterminism, the probability to reach the bad states is below a threshold [3]. The verification question may be efficiently analysed using a variety of techniques such as linear programming, value iteration, or policy iteration, readily available in mature tools such as STORM [16], PRISM [23] and MODEST [14].

However, those verification results are often overly *pessimistic*. They assume that the adversarial policy may depend on the specific state. Consider a game like mastermind, where the adversary has a trivial strategy if it knows the secret they have to guess. Intuitively, to analyse an adversary that has to find a secret, we must assume it cannot observe this secret. For a range of privacy, security, and robotic domains, we may instead assume that the adversary must decide based on system observations. Consider, e.g., surveillance problems, where the

---

This work has been supported by the ERC Advanced Grant 787914 (FRAPPANT) the DFG RTG 2236 'UnRAVeL', NSF grants 1545126 (VeHICaL) and 1646208, the DARPA Assured Autonomy program, Berkeley Deep Drive, and by Toyota under the iCyPhy center.

D. V. Hung and O. Sokolsky (Eds.): ATVA 2020, LNCS 12302, pp. 288–304, 2020.
https://doi.org/10.1007/978-3-030-59152-6_16

aim is to compute the probability that an intruder accesses a (physical or cyber) location with critical information or infrastructure.

Partially observable MDPs [20,30] cater to this need. They extend MDPs with observation labels, and restrict policies to be *observation-based*: paths with the same observation traces are indistinguishable and yield the same decisions. The verification problem for POMDPs with *indefinite horizon specifications* such as unbounded undiscounted reachability is whether all observation-based policies satisfy this specification, e.g., whether for each policy, a bad state is reached with a probability less than 0.1. This problem is undecidable [25]. Intuitively, undecidability follows from the fact that optimal policies require the full history.

Nevertheless, the analysis of POMDPs is a vibrant research area. Traditionally, the focus has been on finding some "good" policy, in planning, control, and robotics [21,32,36] and in software verification [10]. Many works have been devoted to finding a policy that behaves "almost optimal" for *discounted* or *bounded* reachability, most prominently (variants of) point-based solvers [4,22,29,31,34]. These methods can be exploited to find policies for temporal specifications [7]. *Error bounds provided by those methods do require a discounting factor (or a finite horizon).* A notable exception is the recent Goal-HSVI [17], which explores the computation tree and cuts off exploration using sound bounds. Another popular approach to overcome the hardness of the problem is to limit the policies, i.e., by putting a (small) a-priori bound on the memory of the policy [1,9,13,19,26,28,35]. We remark that it is often undesirable to assume small memory bounds on adversarial policies.

Orthogonally, we focus on the *undiscounted and unbounded* (aka the *indefinitive horizon*) case. Reachability in this case is *the* key question to soundly support temporal logic properties [3]. Discounting is optimistic about events in the future, i.e., it under-approximates the probability that a bad state is reached after many steps, and is therefore inadequate in some safety analyses. Furthermore, we do *not* make assumptions on the amount of memory the policies may use. This means that we give absolute guarantees about the performance of an optimal policy. *While techniques for discounting, finite horizons, or finite memory policies may yield policies that are almost optimal in the unbounded case, they are inadequate to prove the absence of better policies.*

Like [27], we use a result from Lovejoy [24]. Whereas [27] focuses on supporting a wider range of properties and *partially-observable* probabilistic timed automata, we focus on the performance of the basic approach. In this paper, we discuss a method constructing a finite MDP such that the optimal policy in this MDP over-approximates the optimal observation-based policy in the POMDP. Thus, model checking this MDP may be used to prove the absence of POMDP policies. We use ideas similar to Goal-HSVI [17] in providing cut-offs: instead of the computation tree, we do these cut-offs on top of the MDP.

Contributions. We provide a concise method for the verification problem that builds upon the Lovejoy construction [24]. Contrary to [24,27], we describe a flexible variant of the approach in terms of the underlying MDP. Among other benefits, this enables an on-the-fly construction of this MDP, enables further

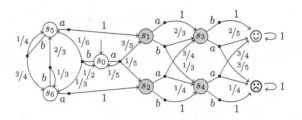

Fig. 1. POMDP $\mathcal{M}$ as running example with 9 states, and 5 observations, partitioning the states by the observation function yields: $\{s_0, s_5, s_6\}, \{s_1, s_2\}, \{s_3, s_4\}, \{\smiley\}, \{\frownie\}$.

(tailored) abstractions on this MDP, and clarifies how to analyse this MDP using standard methods. The approach is embedded in an automated abstraction-refinement loop. Our implementation is part of the next release of the open-source model checker STORM. Experiments show superior scalability over [27].

2   Preliminaries and Problem Statement

Models We introduce partially observable MDPs by first considering MDPs.

Definition 1 (MDP). *A Markov decision process (MDP) is a tuple $M = \langle S, Act, \mathbf{P}, s_I \rangle$ with a countable set S of states, an initial state $s_I \in S$, a finite set Act of actions, and a transition function $\mathbf{P}: S \times Act \times S \to [0, 1]$ with $\sum_{s' \in S} \mathbf{P}(s, \alpha, s') \in \{0, 1\}$ for all $s \in S$ and $\alpha \in Act$.*

Definition 2 (POMDP). *A partially observable MDP (POMDP) is a tuple $\mathcal{M} = \langle M, Z, O \rangle$ where $M = \langle S, Act, \mathbf{P}, s_I \rangle$ is the underlying MDP with finite S, Z is a finite set of observations, and $O: S \to Z$ is an observation function[1].*

We fix a POMDP $\mathcal{M} := \langle M, Z, O \rangle$ with underlying MDP $M := \langle S, Act, \mathbf{P}, s_I \rangle$. For $s \in S$ and $\alpha \in Act$, let $post^M(s, \alpha) = \{s' \in S \mid \mathbf{P}(s, \alpha, s') > 0\}$. The set of enabled actions for s is given by $Act(s) = \{\alpha \in Act \mid post^M(s, \alpha) \neq \emptyset\}$. W.l.o.g., we assume that states with the same observation have the same set of enabled actions, i.e. $\forall s, s' \in S: O(s) = O(s') \implies Act(s) = Act(s')$. Therefore, we can also write $Act(z) = Act(s)$ for observation z and state s with $O(s) = z$.

Policies. We want to make a statement about each possible resolution of the nondeterminism. Nondeterminism is resolved using policies that map paths to distributions over actions. A (finite) path is a sequence of states and actions, i.e., $\hat{\pi} = s_0 \xrightarrow{\alpha_0} s_1 \xrightarrow{\alpha_1} \dots \xrightarrow{\alpha_{n-1}} s_n$, such that $\alpha_i \in Act(s_i)$ and $s_{i+1} \in post^M(s_i, \alpha_i)$ for all $0 \le i < n$. Let $last(\hat{\pi})$ denote the last state of $\hat{\pi}$, and $Paths^M_{\text{fin}}$ denote the set of all paths in an MDP. We may (by slight misuse of notation) lift the observation function to paths: $O(\hat{\pi}) = O(s_0) \xrightarrow{\alpha_0} O(s_1) \xrightarrow{\alpha_1} \dots \xrightarrow{\alpha_{n-1}} O(s_n)$. Two paths $\hat{\pi}_1, \hat{\pi}_2$ with $O(\hat{\pi}_1) = O(\hat{\pi}_2)$ are *observation-equivalent*.

---

[1] More general observation functions can be efficiently encoded in this formalism [11].

Example 1. We depict a POMDP in Fig. 1. The following two paths are observation-equivalent:

$$s_0 \xrightarrow{a} s_1 \xrightarrow{b} s_4 \xrightarrow{a} \otimes \quad \text{and} \quad s_0 \xrightarrow{a} s_2 \xrightarrow{b} s_4 \xrightarrow{a} \otimes$$

For finite set A let $Dist(A) = \{\mu \colon A \to [0,1] \mid \sum_{a \in A} \mu(a) = 1\}$ be the set of distributions over A and for $\mu \in Dist(A)$ let $supp(\mu) = \{a \in A \mid \mu(a) > 0\}$.

Definition 3 (Policies). *A policy is a mapping* $\sigma \colon Paths_{fin}^M \to Dist(Act)$ *that for path* π *yields a distribution over actions with* $supp(\sigma(\pi)) \subseteq Act(last(\pi))$. *A policy* σ *is* observation-based, *if for paths* $\hat{\pi}$, $\hat{\pi}'$

$$O(\hat{\pi}) = O(\hat{\pi}') \text{ implies } \sigma(\hat{\pi}) = \sigma(\hat{\pi}').$$

A policy σ *is* memoryless, *if for paths* $\hat{\pi}$, $\hat{\pi}'$

$$last(\hat{\pi}) = last(\hat{\pi}') \text{ implies } \sigma(\hat{\pi}) = \sigma(\hat{\pi}').$$

Let Σ_{obs}^M denote the set of observation-based policies for a POMDP $\mathcal{M}$, and Σ^M all policies for an MDP M.

Reachability Probability. The reachability probability $\mathsf{Pr}_\mathcal{M}^\sigma(s \models \Diamond \mathsf{Bad})$ to reach a set of states Bad from s using a policy σ is defined as standard, by considering the probability in the induced Markov chain (with state space $Paths_{fin}^M$). For details, consider e.g. [3]. We write $\mathsf{Pr}_\mathcal{M}^\sigma(\Diamond \mathsf{Bad})$ to denote $\mathsf{Pr}_\mathcal{M}^\sigma(s_I \models \Diamond \mathsf{Bad})$.

> **Problem 1.** For a given POMDP $\mathcal{M}$, a set $\mathsf{Bad} \subseteq S$ of bad states, and a rational threshold $\lambda \in (0,1)$, decide whether $\sup_{\sigma \in \Sigma_{obs}^M} \mathsf{Pr}_\mathcal{M}^\sigma(\Diamond \mathsf{Bad}) \leq \lambda$.

We emphasise that the techniques in this paper are applicable to upper and lower bounds, and to expected rewards properties[2]. LTL properties can be supported by the standard encoding of the corresponding automaton into the MDP state space. The technique also applies (but is inefficient) for $\lambda \in \{0,1\}$.

Example 2. Consider the POMDP in Fig. 1. Using the (memoryless) policy $\sigma = \{s_3, s_6 \mapsto a, \; s_i \mapsto b(i \neq 3,6)\}$, state $\otimes$ is reached with probability one, but this policy is not observation-based: e.g. $\sigma(s_5) \neq \sigma(s_6)$. Now consider the policy $\{s_i \mapsto a\}$, which is memoryless and observation-based. Indeed, this policy is optimal among the memoryless observation policies (the probability to reach $\otimes$ is $37/64 \approx 0.57$). A policy taking b in the first step and then resorting to the memoryless policy $\{s_0, s_5, s_6 \mapsto a, \; s_1, s_2, s_3, s_4 \mapsto b\}$ is better: the induced probability to reach $\otimes$ is $23/26 \approx 0.639$. The questions we aim to answer is whether there exists a strategy that achieves probability $65/100$ (yes), or even $7/10$ (no).

---

[2] The implementation discussed in Sect. 5 supports all these combinations.

3   Belief MDPs and Their Approximation

A central notion in the analysis of POMDPs is *belief*: A distribution over the states that describes the likelihood of being in a particular state given the observation-based history $O(\hat{\pi})$. We reformulate our problem in terms of the *belief MDP*, a standard way of defining operational semantics of POMDPs, discuss some essential properties, and discuss abstractions of this infinite belief MDP.

3.1   Infinite MDP Semantics

We first give an example and then formalise the belief MDP. The states B of the belief MDP are the beliefs, i.e., $B := \{\boldsymbol{b} \in \mathit{Dist}(S) \mid \forall\, s, s' \in \mathit{supp}(\boldsymbol{b})\colon O(s) = O(s')\}$. We write $O(\boldsymbol{b})$ to denote the unique $O(s)$ with $s \in \mathit{supp}(\boldsymbol{b})$.

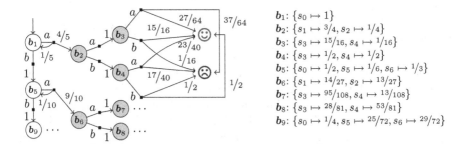

$b_1\colon \{s_0 \mapsto 1\}$
$b_2\colon \{s_1 \mapsto {}^3/_4, s_2 \mapsto {}^1/_4\}$
$b_3\colon \{s_3 \mapsto {}^{15}/_{16}, s_4 \mapsto {}^1/_{16}\}$
$b_4\colon \{s_3 \mapsto {}^1/_2, s_4 \mapsto {}^1/_2\}$
$b_5\colon \{s_0 \mapsto {}^1/_2, s_5 \mapsto {}^1/_6, s_6 \mapsto {}^1/_3\}$
$b_6\colon \{s_1 \mapsto {}^{14}/_{27}, s_2 \mapsto {}^{13}/_{27}\}$
$b_7\colon \{s_3 \mapsto {}^{95}/_{108}, s_4 \mapsto {}^{13}/_{108}\}$
$b_8\colon \{s_3 \mapsto {}^{28}/_{81}, s_4 \mapsto {}^{53}/_{81}\}$
$b_9\colon \{s_0 \mapsto {}^1/_4, s_5 \mapsto {}^{25}/_{72}, s_6 \mapsto {}^{29}/_{72}\}$

Fig. 2. (Fraction of) the belief MDP of the running example. Beliefs are given in the table on the right. Colours indicate $O(b_i)$. We omitted self-loops at the sink states. (Color figure online)

Example 3. Figure 2 shows part of the belief MDP for the POMDP from Fig. 1. We start with the belief that POMDP $\mathcal{M}$ is in the initial state s_0. Upon executing action a, we observe with probability $^1/_5$ that $\mathcal{M}$ is in state s_0, and with $^4/_5$ that $\mathcal{M}$ is in either state s_1 or s_2. In the first case, based on the observations, we surely are in state s_0. In the latter case, the belief is computed by normalising the transition probabilities on the observation: The belief $\boldsymbol{b}_1$ indicates that $\mathcal{M}$ is in s_2 with probability $\frac{1/5}{4/5}$, and in s_1 with probability $\frac{3/5}{4/5}$. Upon executing action a again after observing that $\mathcal{M}$ is in s_1 or s_2, we reach state s_3 with probability

$$\boldsymbol{b}_1(s_1) \cdot \mathbf{P}(s_1, a, s_3) + \boldsymbol{b}_1(s_2) \cdot \mathbf{P}(s_2, a, s_3) = {}^3/_4 \cdot 1 + {}^1/_4 \cdot {}^3/_4 = {}^{15}/_{16}.$$

In the following, let $\mathbf{P}(s, \alpha, z) := \sum_{s' \in S}[O(s') {=} z] \cdot \mathbf{P}(s, \alpha, s')$ denote the probability[3] to move to (a state with) observation z from state s using action α. Then, $\mathbf{P}(\boldsymbol{b}, \alpha, z) := \sum_{s \in S} \boldsymbol{b}(s) \cdot \mathbf{P}(s, \alpha, z)$ is the probability to observe z after

---

[3] In the formula, we use Iverson brackets: $[x] = 1$ if x is true and 0 otherwise.

taking α in $\mathbf{b}$. We define the *belief obtained by taking α from $\mathbf{b}$, conditioned on observing z*:

$$[\![\mathbf{b}|\alpha, z]\!](s') := \frac{[O(s') = z] \cdot \sum_{s \in S} \mathbf{b}(s) \cdot \mathbf{P}(s, \alpha, s')}{\mathbf{P}(\mathbf{b}, \alpha, z)}.$$

Definition 4 (Belief MDP). *The belief MDP of POMDP $\mathcal{M} = \langle M, Z, O \rangle$ is the MDP $bel(\mathcal{M}) := \langle B, Act, \mathbf{P}^B, \mathbf{b}_I \rangle$ with B as above, initial belief state $\mathbf{b}_I := \{s_I \mapsto 1\}$, and transition function $\mathbf{P}^B$ given by*

$$\mathbf{P}^B(\mathbf{b}, \alpha, \mathbf{b}') := \begin{cases} \mathbf{P}^B(\mathbf{b}, \alpha, O(\mathbf{b}')) & \text{if } \mathbf{b}' = [\![\mathbf{b}|\alpha, O(\mathbf{b}')]\!], \\ 0 & \text{otherwise.} \end{cases}$$

To ease further notation, we denote $\overline{\mathsf{Bad}} := \{\mathbf{b} \mid \sum_{s \in \mathsf{Bad}} \mathbf{b}(s) = 1\}$, and we define the (standard notion of the) *value of a belief $\mathbf{b}$*,

$$V(\mathbf{b}) := \sup_{\sigma \in \Sigma^{bel(\mathcal{M})}} \mathsf{Pr}^{\sigma}_{bel(\mathcal{M})}(\mathbf{b} \models \Diamond\overline{\mathsf{Bad}}) \quad \text{and for action } \alpha:$$

$$V_{\alpha}(\mathbf{b}) := \sup_{\sigma \in \Sigma^{bel(\mathcal{M})}, \sigma(\mathbf{b}) = \alpha} \mathsf{Pr}^{\sigma}_{bel(\mathcal{M})}(\mathbf{b} \models \Diamond\overline{\mathsf{Bad}}).$$

Theorem 1. *For any POMDP $\mathcal{M}$ and $\mathbf{b}_I$, the initial state of $bel(\mathcal{M})$:*

$$V(\mathbf{b}_I) \quad = \quad \sup_{\sigma \in \Sigma^{\mathcal{M}}_{\mathrm{obs}}} \mathsf{Pr}^{\sigma}_{\mathcal{M}}(\Diamond\mathsf{Bad}).$$

We can now restrict ourselves to memoryless deterministic schedulers, but face a potentially infinite MDP[4]. Instead of solving Problem 1, we consider:

Problem 2. Given a belief MDP $bel(\mathcal{M})$, a set $\overline{\mathsf{Bad}}$ of bad beliefs, and a threshold $\lambda \in (0, 1)$, decide whether $V(\mathbf{b}_I) \leq \lambda$.

In the remainder of this section, we discuss two types of approximations, but not before reviewing an essential property of the value in belief MDPs. We discuss how we combine these abstractions in Sect. 4.

Value Function. Assuming a fixed total order on the POMDP states $s_1 < \cdots < s_n$, we interpret belief states as vectors $\mathbf{b} \in [0, 1]^n$ where the ith entry corresponds to $\mathbf{b}(s_i)$. In particular, we can encode a belief by a tuple $\langle z, [0, 1]^{n_z} \rangle$, where n_z denotes the number of states with observation z. This encoding also justifies the representation of beliefs in Fig. 3 and 4.

Figure 3(a) contains a typical belief-to-value plot for $z = O(s_3) = O(s_4)$. On the x-axis, we depict the belief to be in state s_3 (from 1 to 0), and thus, the

---

[4] In general, the set of states of the belief MDP is uncountable. However, a given belief state $\mathbf{b}$ only has a finite number of successors for each action α, i.e. $post^{bel(M)}(\mathbf{b}, \alpha)$ is finite, and thus the belief MDP is countably infinite. Acyclic POMDPs always give rise to finite belief MDPs (but may be exponentially large).

belief to be in state s_4 (from 0 to 1). On the y-axis, we denote the value of the belief. This value is constructed as follows: A policy takes action a or action b (or randomise, more about that later). We have plotted the corresponding V_a and V_b. In Fig. 3(b), we depict the same functions for observing that we are in either s_1 or s_2. This plot can be constructed as the maximum of four policy applications. Formally, the following relations hold (from the Bellman equations):

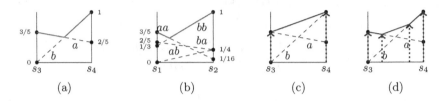

(a)   (b)   (c)   (d)

Fig. 3. Illustrating the discretised belief approximation ideas. (Color figure online)

Lemma 1. Let $\overline{\mathsf{Zero}} := \{b \mid \mathrm{Pr}^{\max}_{\mathcal{M}}(b \models \Diamond\overline{\mathsf{Bad}}) = 0\}$. For each $b \notin (\overline{\mathsf{Bad}} \cup \overline{\mathsf{Zero}})$:

$$V_\alpha(b) = \sum_{b'} \mathbf{P}^B(b, \alpha, b') \cdot V(b'), \quad with \quad V(b) = \max_{\alpha \in Act(O(b))} V_\alpha(b).$$

Furthermore: $V(b) = 0$ for $b \in \overline{\mathsf{Zero}}$, and $V(b) = 1$ for $b \in \overline{\mathsf{Bad}}$.

Remark 1. As we are over-approximating V, we do not need to precompute $\overline{\mathsf{Zero}}$.

Note that the function V is *convex* iff for each $b_1, b_2 \in B$ and for each $\alpha \in [0, 1]$, it holds that $V(\alpha \cdot b_1 + (1-\alpha) \cdot b_2) \leq \alpha \cdot V(b_1) + (1-\alpha) \cdot V(b_2)$.

For $b \in (\overline{\mathsf{Bad}} \cup \overline{\mathsf{Zero}})$, the value function is constant and thus convex. The n-step reachability for a particular action is a linear combination over the $(n-1)$-step reachabilities, and we take the maximum over these values to get the n-step reachability. The value $V(b)$ is the limit for n towards infinity. As convex functions are closed under linear combinations with non-negative coefficients, under taking the maximum, and under taking the limit, we obtain:

Theorem 2. *For any POMDP, the value-function V is convex.*

3.2   Finite Exploration Approximation

One way to circumvent building the complete state space is to *cut-off* its exploration after some steps, much like we depicted part of the belief POMDP in Fig. 2. To ensure that the obtained finite MDP over-approximates the probability to reach a bad state, we simply assume that all transitions we cut go to a bad state immediately. Elaborate techniques for this approach (on general MDPs) have been discussed in the context of verification [8], and have been successfully adapted to other models [2,18,33]. It shares many ideas with the SARSOP and GOAL-HSVI approaches for POMDPs [17,22]. This approach may be applied directly to belief MDPs, and we may use the POMDP $\mathcal{M}$ to guide the cut-off process. In particular, using Theorem 2 and that the maximising policy over *all* policies is necessarily overapproximating the maximum over all *observation-based* policies, we obtain the following inequality:

$$V(\boldsymbol{b}) \quad \leq \quad \sum_{s \in S} \boldsymbol{b}(s) \cdot V(\{s \mapsto 1\}) \quad \leq \quad \sum_{s \in S} \boldsymbol{b}(s) \cdot \sup_{\sigma \in \Sigma^{\mathcal{M}}} \mathrm{Pr}^{\sigma}_{\mathcal{M}}(s \models \Diamond \mathsf{Bad}) \quad (1)$$

We may use this inequality to cut-off with a less pessimistic value than assuming that we reach the bad states with probability one.

Nevertheless, this approach has limited applicability on its own. It may well get stuck in regions of the belief space that are not near the goal. From state s_5, s_6 in Fig. 1 the maximal reachability according to the underlying MDP is 1, which is too pessimistic to provide a good cut-off. Another issue is that the belief converges slowly along $\boldsymbol{b}_1, \boldsymbol{b}_5, \boldsymbol{b}_9$ in Fig. 2, and that cut-offs do not immediately allow to reason that the belief converged.

3.3 Discretised Belief Approximation

The idea of this approach is to select a finite set $\mathcal{F} \subseteq B$ of beliefs, and construct an approximation of the belief MDP using only $\mathcal{F}$ as states. We refer to $\mathcal{F}$ as the *foundation*. (Reachable) beliefs $\boldsymbol{b}$ not in $\mathcal{F}$ are approximated using beliefs in $\mathcal{N}_{\mathcal{F}}(\boldsymbol{b})$, where $\mathcal{N}_{\mathcal{F}}(\boldsymbol{b}) \subseteq \mathcal{F}$ is the *neighbourhood* of $\boldsymbol{b}$. We clarify the selection of these neighbourhoods later, and we omit the subscript $\mathcal{F}$ whenever possible.

Definition 5. *A neighbourhood $\mathcal{N}(\boldsymbol{b})$ of belief $\boldsymbol{b}$ is* convex-containing, *if there exists $\delta_b \in Dist(\mathcal{N}(\boldsymbol{b}))$ such that $\boldsymbol{b} = \sum_{\boldsymbol{b}' \in \mathcal{N}(\boldsymbol{b})} \delta_b(\boldsymbol{b}') \cdot \boldsymbol{b}'$.*

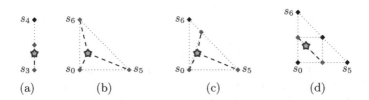

    (a)   (b)   (c)   (d)

Fig. 4. Belief-spaces with foundation (diamonds), a belief state (blue star), a fixed neighbourhood (red diamonds), and vertex-weights. (Color figure online)

Example 4. In Fig. 4, we depict various neighbourhoods. In Fig. 4(a), the belief $\{s_3 \mapsto 2/3, s_4 \mapsto 1/3\}$ lies in the neighbourhood $\{\{s_3 \mapsto 1,\}\{s_3, s_4 \mapsto 1/2\}\}$. All other subfigures depict belief-spaces for observations where three states have this observation (the third dimension implicitly follows). For the belief state $\boldsymbol{b}_5 = \{s_0 \mapsto 1/2, s_5 \mapsto 1/6, s_6 \mapsto 1/3\}$ from Fig. 2 and a neighbourhood as in Fig. 4(b), the vertex-weights δ_b follow straightforwardly from the belief. Observe

that a small distance to a vertex induces a large weight. In Fig. 4(c), we adapt
the neighbourhood to $x = \{s_5 \mapsto 1\}, y = \{s_0 \mapsto 1\}, z = \{s_5 \mapsto 1/4, s_6 \mapsto 3/4\}$.
Then, the vertex weights follow from the following linear equations:

$$\delta_{b_5}(x) = 1/2, \quad \delta_{b_5}(y) + 1/4 \cdot \delta_{b_5}(z) = 1/6, \quad \text{and } 3/4 \cdot \delta_{b_5}(z) = 1/3.$$

From the convexity of the value function V (Theorem 2), it follows that:

Lemma 2. *Given b, $\mathcal{N}(b)$ and δ_b as in Definition 5, it holds:*

$$V(b) \quad \leq \quad \sum_{b' \in \mathcal{N}(b)} \delta_b(b') \cdot V(b').$$

We emphasise that this inequality also holds if one over-approximates the values
of the beliefs in the neighbourhood.

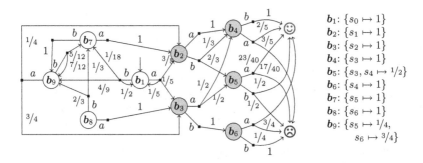

Fig. 5. Reachable fragment of the discretised belief MDP (fully observable). Actual
beliefs are given in the table on the right. Colours indicate $O(b_i)$ in the POMDP.
(Color figure online)

Example 5. Figure 3(c) depicts the belief-to-value from Fig. 3(a) and (in blue)
depicts the over-approximation based on Lemma 2. As neighbourhood, we use
$\{s_3 \mapsto 1\}$ and $\{s_4 \mapsto 1\}$. In Fig. 3(d), we depict the over-approximation using
a partitioning into three neighbourhoods, using the foundation $\{s_3 \mapsto 1\}$,
$\{s_3 \mapsto 1/4, s_4 \mapsto 3/4\}$, $\{s_3 \mapsto 3/4, s_4 \mapsto 1/4\}$ and $\{s_4 \mapsto 1\}$. We see that
the outer neighbourhoods now yield a tight over-approximation, and the inner
neighbourhood yields a much better approximation compared to Fig. 3(c).

We select some finite foundation $\mathcal{F}$ such that for each reachable b in $bel(\mathcal{M})$,
there exists a convex containing neighbourhood $\mathcal{N}(b)$. We call such a foundation
adequate. One small adequate $\mathcal{F}$ is $\{\{s \mapsto 1\} \in B \mid s \in \mathcal{M}\}$.

Definition 6 (Discretised Belief MDP). *Let $\mathcal{F} \subseteq B$ be an adequate foundation. Let $\mathcal{N}$ be arbitrarily fixed such that $\mathcal{N}(b) \subseteq \mathcal{F}$ is convex-containing for
any b. The discretised belief MDP of POMDP $\mathcal{M} = \langle M, Z, O \rangle$ is the MDP*

$db_{\mathcal{F}}(\mathcal{M}) := \langle \mathcal{F}, Act, \mathbf{P}^{\mathcal{F}}, \mathbf{b}_I \rangle$ with initial belief state $\mathbf{b}_I = \{s_I \mapsto 1\}$, and—using the auxiliary notation from before Definition 4—transition function $\mathbf{P}^{\mathcal{F}}$ given by

$$\mathbf{P}^{\mathcal{F}}(\mathbf{b}, \alpha, \mathbf{b}') := \begin{cases} \delta_{[\![b|\alpha,z]\!]}(\mathbf{b}') \cdot \mathbf{P}^B(\mathbf{b}, \alpha, z) & \text{if } \mathbf{b}' \in \mathcal{N}([\![b|\alpha, z]\!]), \\ 0 & \text{otherwise.} \end{cases}$$

Example 6. Consider Fig. 5. We fixed $\mathcal{F} = \{s \mapsto 1 \mid s \in S\} \cup \{s_3, s_4 \mapsto 1/2\} \cup \{s_5 \mapsto 1/4,\ s_6 \mapsto 3/4\}$. The weights for $post(\mathbf{b}_2, b)$ and $post(\mathbf{b}_1, b)$ follow from the computations in Example 4. Observe that $\mathbf{b}_8$ is not reachable. The optimal policy in this MDP induces probability $3/4$, which is an upper bound on $V(\mathbf{b}_1)$.

Theorem 3. *For POMDP $\mathcal{M}$ with discretised belief MDP $db_{\mathcal{F}}(\mathcal{M})$ and $\mathbf{b} \in \mathcal{F}$*

$$V(\mathbf{b}) \quad \leq \quad \sup_{\sigma \in \Sigma^{db_{\mathcal{F}}(\mathcal{M})}} \Pr^{\sigma}_{db_{\mathcal{F}}(\mathcal{M})}(\mathbf{b} \models \Diamond \overline{\mathsf{Bad}}).$$

As the MDP is finite and fully observable, the supremum is achieved by a memoryless policy, and we use MDP model checking to compute these values.

4   Abstraction-Refinement

In this section, we discuss a framework that combines the two types of abstraction discussed before. Roughly, the approach is a typical abstraction-refinement loop. We start with an abstraction of the belief MDP; model checking this abstraction yields an upper bound on the values $V(\mathbf{b})$. In every iteration, we update the MDP and then obtain more and more accurate bounds. The abstraction applies cut-offs on a discretised belief MDP with some foundation $\mathcal{F}$. For the refinement, we either explore beliefs that were previously cut off, we extend the foundation $\mathcal{F}$, or we rewire the successors $\mathbf{b}' \in post^{bel(\mathcal{M})}(\mathbf{b}, \alpha)$ of some belief $\mathbf{b}$ and action α to a new $\mathcal{N}_{\mathcal{F}}(\mathbf{b}')$. Thus, rewiring updates neighbourhoods, typically after refining the foundation. We give an example and then clarify the precise procedure.

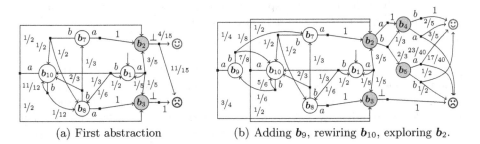

(a) First abstraction   (b) Adding $\mathbf{b}_9$, rewiring $\mathbf{b}_{10}$, exploring $\mathbf{b}_2$.

Fig. 6. Beliefs as in Fig. 5, with $\mathbf{b}_{10} = \{s_5 \mapsto 1/2, s_6 \mapsto 1/2\}$.

Example 7. In Fig. 6(a), we used a foundation as in Fig. 5, but with b_{10} replacing b_9. Furthermore, we used cut-offs in b_2 and b_3 with the overapproximation from Eq. (1). In Fig. 6(b) we refined as follows: We *extended the foundation* with $b_9 = \{s_5 \mapsto 1/4, s_6 \mapsto 3/4\}$, we *explored* from b_2, b_9, and we rewired *only* $\langle b_{10}, b \rangle$.

Algorithm 1 sketches the abstraction-refinement loop. The algorithm iteratively constructs an abstraction MDP $\mathcal{A}$ via a breath-first-search on the state space of the discretised belief MDP $db_{\mathcal{F}}(\mathcal{M})$ (Lines 3 to 21). In Line 7, a heuristic `explore` decides for each visited belief to either *explore* or *cut-off*. If we explore, we may encounter a state that was previously explored. Heuristic `rewire` decides in Line 9 whether we *rewire*, i.e., whether we explore the successors again (to account for potentially updated neighbourhoods) or whether we keep the existing successor states. When cutting off, we use Eq. (1) to obtain an upper bound $U(b)$ for $V(b)$ and add a transition to some bad state with probability $U(b)$ and a transition to a sink state with probability $1 - U(b)$.[5] The foundation is extended in Line 20. This only has an effect in the next refinement step.

After building the MDP $\mathcal{A}$, it is analysed in Line 19 using model checking. This analysis yields a new upper bound $U(b_I) \geq V(b_I)$. The loop can be stopped at any time, e.g., when threshold λ is shown as upper bound. Next, we describe how the foundation $\mathcal{F}$ is initialised, extended, and iteratively explored.

Picking Foundations. *The initial foundation.* We discretise the beliefs using the foundation $\mathcal{F}$. The choice of this foundation is driven by the need to easily determine the neighbourhood and the vertex-weights. Furthermore, the cardinality of the neighbourhood affects the branching factor of the approximation MDP. As [24], we use a triangulation scheme based on *Freudenthal Triangulation* [12], illustrated by Fig. 4(d). Given fixed resolutions $\eta_z \in \mathbb{N}_{>0}$, $z \in Z$, the triangulation scheme yields discretised beliefs b with $\forall s \colon b(s) \in \{i/\eta_z \mid z = O(b), 0 \leq i \leq \eta_z\}$.

In the refinement loop shown in Algorithm 1, we initialise $\mathcal{F}$ (Line 1) by setting the observation-dependent resolutions η_z to a fixed value η_{init}. Notice that it suffices to determine the neighbourhoods on-the-fly during the belief exploration. To compute the neighbourhood, we find $n_z + 1$ neighbours as intuitively depicted in Fig. 4(d). The intricate computation of these neighbours [12] involves changing the basis for the vector space, ordering the coefficients and adequately manipulating single entries, before finally inverting the basis change, see [24] for an example.

Extension of Foundation. The set Z_{extend} of observations for which the foundation will be extended is determined by assigning a *score*: $Z \to [0,1]$. Low scoring observations are refined first. Intuitively, the score is assigned such that a score close to 0 indicates that one of the approximated beliefs with observation z is far away from all points in its neighbourhood, and a high score (close to 1) then means that all approximated beliefs are close to one of their neighbours.

---

[5] The implementation actually still connects b with already explored successors and only redirects the 'missing' probabilities w.r.t. $U(b')$, $b' \in post^{db_{\mathcal{F}}(\mathcal{M})}(s, \alpha) \setminus S_{expl}$.

We set $Z_{\text{extend}} = \{z \in Z \mid score(z) \leq \rho_Z\}$ for some threshold $\rho_Z \in [0,1]$. When the value of ρ_Z is iteratively increased towards 1, each observation is eventually considered for refinement. Details are given in [6].

Input   : POMDP $\mathcal{M} = \langle M, Z, O \rangle$ with $M = \langle S, Act, \mathbf{P}, s_I \rangle$, bad beliefs $\overline{\text{Bad}}$, threshold λ
Output   : An upper bound $\lambda \geq U(\boldsymbol{b}_I) \geq V(\boldsymbol{b}_I)$

1 $\mathcal{F} \leftarrow$ initial adequate foundation
2 $\mathcal{A} \leftarrow$ MDP $\left\langle S^{\mathcal{A}}, Act, \mathbf{P}^{\mathcal{A}}, \boldsymbol{b}_I \right\rangle$ with $\boldsymbol{b}_I = \{s_I \mapsto 1\}$ and $S^{\mathcal{A}} = \{\boldsymbol{b}_I\}$
3 **repeat**
4 $\quad$ $S_{expl} \leftarrow \{\boldsymbol{b}_I\};\; Q \leftarrow$ FIFO Queue initially containing $\boldsymbol{b}_I$
5 $\quad$ **while** Q not empty **do**
6 $\quad\quad$ take $\boldsymbol{b}$ from Q
7 $\quad\quad$ **if** $\boldsymbol{b} \in S^{\mathcal{A}}$ or explore($\boldsymbol{b}$) **then**   // decide to explore $\boldsymbol{b}$ or not
8 $\quad\quad\quad$ **foreach** $\alpha \in Act(\boldsymbol{b})$ **do**
9 $\quad\quad\quad\quad$ **if** $\boldsymbol{b} \notin S^{\mathcal{A}}$ or rewire($\boldsymbol{b}, \alpha$) **then**   // decide to rewire $\langle \boldsymbol{b}, \alpha \rangle$ or not
10 $\quad\quad\quad\quad\quad$ clear $\mathbf{P}^{\mathcal{A}}(\boldsymbol{b}, \alpha, \boldsymbol{b}')$ for all $\boldsymbol{b}' \in S^{\mathcal{A}}$ // delete old transitions
11 $\quad\quad\quad\quad\quad$ **foreach** $\boldsymbol{b}' \in post^{db_{\mathcal{F}}(\mathcal{M})}(\boldsymbol{b}, \alpha)$ **do**   // cf. Definition 6
12 $\quad\quad\quad\quad\quad\quad$ $\mathbf{P}^{\mathcal{A}}(\boldsymbol{b}, \alpha, \boldsymbol{b}') \leftarrow \mathbf{P}^{\mathcal{F}}(\boldsymbol{b}, \alpha, \boldsymbol{b}')$
13 $\quad\quad\quad\quad\quad\quad$ **if** $\boldsymbol{b}' \notin S_{expl}$ **then**
14 $\quad\quad\quad\quad\quad\quad\quad$ insert $\boldsymbol{b}'$ into $S^{\mathcal{A}}$, Q, and S_{expl}

15 $\quad\quad\quad\quad$ **else**   // keep the current successors
16 $\quad\quad\quad\quad\quad$ insert all $\boldsymbol{b}' \in post^{\mathcal{A}}(\boldsymbol{b}, \alpha) \setminus S_{expl}$ into Q and S_{expl}

17 $\quad\quad$ **else**   // do not explore $\boldsymbol{b}$
18 $\quad\quad\quad$ cutoff($\boldsymbol{b}, \mathcal{A}$)   // redirect outgoing transitions to $\overline{\text{Bad}}$

19 $\quad$ $U(\boldsymbol{b}_I) \leftarrow \sup_{\sigma \in \Sigma^{\mathcal{A}}} \mathrm{Pr}^{\sigma}_{\mathcal{A}}(\boldsymbol{b}_I \models \Diamond\overline{\text{Bad}})$ // MDP model checking
20 $\quad$ $\mathcal{F} \leftarrow$ extend($\mathcal{F}$)   // consider refined neighbourhoods in next iteration
21 **until** $U(\boldsymbol{b}_I) \leq \lambda$

Algorithm 1: Abstraction-refinement loop.

Iterative Exploration. The iterative exploration is guided using an estimate of how coarse the approximation is for the current belief state $\boldsymbol{b}$, and by an estimate of how likely we reach $\boldsymbol{b}$ under the optimal policy (which is unknown). If either of these values is small, then the influence of a potential cut-off at $\boldsymbol{b}$ is limited.

Bounds on Reaching the Bad State. We use a lower bound $L(\boldsymbol{b})$ and an upper bound $U(\boldsymbol{b})$ for the value $V(\boldsymbol{b})$. Equation (1) yields an easy-to-compute initial over-approximation $U(\boldsymbol{b})$. Running the refinement-loop improves this bound. For the lower bound, we exploit that any policy on the POMDP under-approximates the performance of the best policy. Thus, we guess some set of observation-based policies[6] on the POMDP and evaluate them. If these policies are memoryless, the induced Markov chain is in the size of the POMDP and is typically easy to evaluate. Using a better under-approximation (e.g., by picking better policies, possibly exploiting the related work) is a promising direction for future research.

Estimating Reachability Likelihoods. As a naive proxy for this likelihood, we consider almost optimal policies from the previous refinement step as well as the

---

[6] We guess policies in $\Sigma^{\mathcal{M}}_{\text{obs}}$ by distributing over actions of optimal policies for MDP M.

distance of b to the initial belief b_I. Since the algorithm performs a breadth-first exploration, the distance from b_I to b is reflected by the number of beliefs explored before b.

State Exploration. In Line 7 of Algorithm 1, explore decides whether the successors of the current belief b are explored or cut off. We only explore the successors of b if: (1) *the approximation is coarse*, i.e., if the relative gap between $U(b)$ and $L(b)$ is above (a decreasing) ρ_{gap}[7]. (2) *the state is likely relevant for the optimal scheduler*, i.e., if (i) at most ρ_{step} [8] beliefs were explored (or rewired) before and (ii) b is reachable under a ρ_Σ-optimal policy[9] from the previous refinement step.

Rewiring. We apply the same criteria for rewire in Line 9. In addition, we only rewire the successors for action α if (i) α is selected by some ρ_Σ-optimal policy and (ii) the rewiring actually has an effect, i.e. , for at least one successor the foundation has been extended since the last exploration of b and α.

5   Experiments

Implementation. We integrated the abstraction-refinement framework in the model checker STORM [16]. The implementation constructs the abstraction MDP as detailed in Algorithm 1 using sparse matrices. The computation in Line 19 is performed using STORM's implementation of *optimistic value iteration* [15], yielding sound precision guarantees up to relative precision $\varepsilon = 10^{-6}$. Our implementation supports arbitrary combinations of minimisation and maximisation of reachability and reach-avoid specifications, and indefinite-horizon expected rewards. For minimisation, lower and upper bounds are swapped. Additionally, our implementation may compute lower bounds by iteratively exploring (a fragment of) the belief MDP, *without* discretisation. The state-space exploration is cut off after exploring an increasing number of states[10].

Models. We use *all* sets of POMDPs from [27]. Small versions of these benchmarks are omitted. We additionally introduced some variants, e.g., added uncertainty to the movement in the grid examples. Finally, we consider three scalable variants of typical grid-world planning domains in artificial intelligence, cf. [6].

Set-Up. We evaluate our implementation with and without the refinement loop. In the former case, the refinement loop runs a given amount of time and we report the results obtained so far. In the latter case, a single iteration of Algorithm 1 is performed with a fixed triangulation resolution η—a set-up as in [27]. We compare with the implementation [27] in PRISM. We used a simple SCC analysis to find POMDPs where the reachable belief MDP is finite. All POMDPs

---

[7] ρ_{gap} is set to 0.1 initially and after each iteration we update it to $\rho_{gap}/4$.

[8] ρ_{step} is set to ∞ initially and after each iteration we update it to $4 \cdot |S^{\mathcal{A}}|$.

[9] A policy σ is ρ_Σ-optimal if $\forall b \colon V_{\sigma(b)}(b) + \rho_\Sigma \geq V(b)$. We set $\rho_\Sigma = 0.001$.

[10] In refinement step i, we explore $2^{i-1} \cdot |S| \cdot \max_{z \in Z} |O^{-1}(z)|$ states.

Table 1. Results for POMDPs with infinite belief MDP.

Benchmark		Data		MDP	bel($\mathcal{M}$)	$\eta = 4$		$\eta = 12$			refine	
Model	ϕ	S/Act	Z	STORM	PRISM	STORM	PRISM	STORM	PRISM	STORM	$t=60$	$t=1800$
					$t=60$	$\rho_{gap}=0$		$\rho_{gap}=0$		$\rho_{gap}=0.2$		
Drone 4-1	P_{max}	1226 / 3026	384	0.98	≥ 0.84 (6)	TO	≤ 0.96 (6.67)	MO	MO	MO	**≤ 0.97** (2)	**≤ 0.97†** (3)
Drone 4-2	P_{max}	1226 / 3026	761	0.98	≥ 0.96 (7)	TO	≤ 0.98 (<1)	MO	≤ 0.97 (194)	**≤ 0.97** (173)	**≤ 0.97** (3)	**≤ 0.97†** (4)
Grid-av 4-0.1	P_{max}	17 / 59	4	1	≥ 0.93 (13)	[0.21, 1.0] (2.03)	≤ 1 (<1)	MO	≤ 0.94 (164)	**≤ 0.94** (168)	**≤ 0.94** (3)	**≤ 0.94†** (3)
Grid 4-0.1	R_{min}	17 / 62	3	3.56	≤ 4.7 (13)	[4.06, 4.7] (2.02)	≥ 4.06 (<1)	MO	≥ 4.59 (264)	**≥ 4.59** (268)	**≥ 4.56** (3)	**≥ 4.61†** (4)
Grid 4-0.3	R_{min}	17 / 62	3	4.57	≤ 6.37 (13)	[5.4, 6.31] (3.05)	≥ 5.4 (<1)	MO	≥ 6.18 (217)	**≥ 6.18** (214)	**≥ 5.92** (3)	**≥ 5.92†** (3)
Maze2 0.1	R_{min}	15 / 54	8	5.64	≤ 6.32 (14)	[6.29, 6.32] (1.35)	≥ 6.29 (<1)	**[6.32, 6.32]** (4.91)	≥ 6.32 (<1)	**≥ 6.32** (<1)	**≥ 6.32** (7)	**≥ 6.32†** (8)
Refuel 06	P_{max}	208 / 574	50	0.98	≥ 0.67 (10)	TO	≤ 0.71 (<1)	MO	≤ 0.68 (2.08)	**≤ 0.68** (2.08)	**=0.67*** (59)	**=0.67*** (59)
Refuel 08	P_{max}	470 / 1446	66	0.99	≥ 0.45 (7)	MO	≤ 0.76 (7.3)	MO	MO	MO	**≤ 0.75** (2)	**≤ 0.58†** (3)
Rocks 12	R_{min}	6553 / $3 \cdot 10^4$	1645	16.5	≤ 35.4 (6)	TO	≥ 19.9 (1.26)	MO	≥ 20 (18.9)	**≥ 20** (19.1)	**=20*** (9)	**=20*** (9)
Rocks 16	R_{min}	$1 \cdot 10^4$ / $5 \cdot 10^4$	2761	22	≤ 44 (5)	MO	≥ 25.6 (2.55)	MO	≥ 26 (37.2)	**≥ 26** (35.9)	**≥ 25.9** (8)	**≥ 25.9** (9)

from [27] are in this category. We refer to the remaining POMDPs as infinite belief POMDPs.

All experiments were run on 4 cores[11] of an Intel® Xeon® Platinum 8160 CPU with a time limit of 1 h (unless indicated otherwise) and 32 GB RAM.

Results. We consider the infinite belief POMDPs in Table 1. The first columns indicate the POMDP model instance, the type of the checked property (probabilities (P) or rewards (R), minimising or maximising policies), as well as the number of states, state-action pairs, and observations of the POMDP. The column 'MDP' shows the model checking result on the underlying, fully-observable MDP. The column '$bel(\mathcal{M})$' considers the refinement loop for the non-discretised belief MDP as discussed above and lists the best result obtained within 60 s, and the number of iterations. The subsequent columns show our result for a single approximation step with fixed resolution η and cut-off threshold ρ_{gap}, as well as the results of PRISM when invoked with resolution η. 'TO' and 'MO' indicate a time-out (>1 h) and a memory-out (>32 GB), respectively. Each cell contains the obtained bounds on the result and the analysis time in seconds. Finally, the last two columns report on running the refinement loop for at most t (60 and 1800) s. The cells contain the best bound on the result and the number of loop iterations of Algorithm 1. In addition, ∗ indicates that no further refinement was possible (in this case the model-checking result corresponds to the precise value) and † indicates that an MO occurred before t seconds.

---

[11] STORM uses one core, PRISM uses four cores in garbage collection only.

Table 2. Results for POMDPs with finite belief MDP.

Benchmark		Data		MDP	bel($\mathcal{M}$)	$\eta=4$		$\eta=12$			refine	
Model	ϕ	S/Act	Z	STORM	STORM	PRISM	STORM	PRISM	STORM			
							$\rho_{gap}=0$		$\rho_{gap}=0$	$\rho_{gap}=0.2$	t = 60	t = 1800
Crypt	$P_{\max}$	1972	510	1	=0.33	[0.33, 0.79]	≤0.79	MO	≤0.33	≤0.33	=0.33*	=0.33*
4		4612			3.51	20.3	< 1		1.36	6.12	6	6
Crypt	$P_{\max}$	$7 \cdot 10^4$	6678	1	=0.2	MO	≤1	MO	≤0.84	≤0.84	≤0.97	≤0.94
6		$2 \cdot 10^5$			8.47	17.8	< 1		155	159	2	4
Grid-av	$P_{\max}$	17	4	1	=0.93	[0.21, 1.0]	≤1	MO	≤0.94	≤0.94	=0.93	≤0.93†
4-0		59			< 1	1.51	< 1		< 1	< 1	9	26
Maze2	$R_{\min}$	15	8	5.08	=5.69	[5.69, 5.69]	≥5.69	[5.69, 5.69]	≥5.69	≥5.69	=5.69*	=5.69*
0		54			< 1	1.43	< 1	3.17	< 1	< 1	4	4
Netw-p	$R_{\max}$	$2 \cdot 10^4$	4909	566	=557	[557, 559]	≤560	TO	≤557	≤566	≤557	≤557
2-8-20		$3 \cdot 10^4$			612	503	2.17		4.25	< 1	10	18
Netw-p	$R_{\max}$	$2 \cdot 10^5$	$2 \cdot 10^4$	849	TO	TO	≤832	MO	TO	≤849	≤849	≤825
3-8-20		$3 \cdot 10^5$					514			8.2	0	2
Netw	$R_{\min}$	4589	1173	2.56	=3.2	[3.03, 3.2]	≥2.97	[3.17, 3.2]	≥3.17	≥3.16	≥3.2	≥3.2
2-8-20		6973			38.4	42.1	< 1	521	< 1	< 1	10	23
Netw	$R_{\min}$	$2 \cdot 10^4$	2205	3.88	MO	[5.54, 6.77]	≥5.11	MO	≥6.35	≥6.33	≥6.26	≥6.72†
3-8-20		$3 \cdot 10^4$				1777	4.82		34.5	34.3	3	5
Nrp	$P_{\max}$	125	41	1	=0.12	[0.13, 0.38]	≤0.38	[0.13, 0.22]	≤0.22	≤0.22	=0.12*	=0.12*
8		161				1.57	< 1	22.9	< 1	< 1	70	70

Table 2 provides the experimental results for benchmark models with finite belief MDP. The columns are similar as in Table 1 except that column '$bel(\mathcal{M})$' indicates the model checking result and analysis time in seconds for the complete finite belief MDP. The technical report [6] contains further experiments.

Discussion. Consider Table 1. First, our implementation outperforms the implementation of [27] by several orders of magnitude, most likely due to the on-the-fly state-space construction, and by an engineering effort. This difference cannot be explained by the currently implemented cut-offs; indeed, when choosing a static foundation, cut-offs do not noticeably improve performance. Second, our refinement loop avoids the need for a user-picked resolution, but a hand-picked resolution is sometimes faster (e.g. Maze) or yields better results (e.g. Grid). On the other hand, the refinement loop might find finite abstractions that concisely represent the belief MDP reachable under the optimal policy (e.g. Rocks). Here, cut-offs are essential. Third, often, the refinement loop finds the crucial part of the abstraction within a minute, however, Refuel profits from extra time.

We want to share three further observations: First, it seems interesting to investigate finite-belief POMDPs as these occur quite frequently (see Table 2) and can be analysed straightforwardly. Second, the current bottleneck is the bookkeeping of the belief states and the computation of neighbourhoods, not the model checking. Finally, even more than for MDPs, the size of the POMDP (or the number of observations) is not at all a proxy for the difficulty of verification.

Data Availability. The implementation, models, and log files are available at [5].

6 Conclusion and Future Work

We presented an abstraction-refinement for solving the verification problem for indefinite-horizon properties in POMDPs, e.g., for proving that all policies reach a bad state with at most probability λ. As the original problem is undecidable, we compute a sequence of over-approximations by iteratively refining an abstraction of the belief MDP. Our prototype shows superior performance over [27] in PRISM. The next step is to integrate better under-approximations.

References

1. Amato, C., Bernstein, D.S., Zilberstein, S.: Optimizing fixed-size stochastic controllers for POMDPs and decentralized POMDPs. Auton. Agent. Multi-Agent Syst. **21**(3), 293–320 (2010)
2. Ashok, P., Butkova, Y., Hermanns, H., Křetínský, J.: Continuous-time Markov decisions based on partial exploration. In: Lahiri, S.K., Wang, C. (eds.) ATVA 2018. LNCS, vol. 11138, pp. 317–334. Springer, Cham (2018). https://doi.org/10.1007/978-3-030-01090-4_19
3. Baier, C., Katoen, J.P.: Principles of Model Checking. The MIT Press, Cambridge (2008)
4. Bonet, B., Geffner, H.: Solving POMDPs: RTDP-Bel vs. point-based algorithms. In: IJCAI, pp. 1641–1646 (2009)
5. Bork, A., Junges, S., Katoen, J.P., Quatmann, T.: Experiments for 'Verification of indefinite- horizon POMDPs'. https://doi.org/10.5281/zenodo.3924577
6. Bork, A., Junges, S., Katoen, J.P., Quatmann, T.: Verification of indefinite-horizon POMDPs. CoRR abs/2007.00102 (2020)
7. Bouton, M., Tumova, J., Kochenderfer, M.J.: Point-based methods for model checking in partially observable Markov decision processes. In: AAAI, pp. 10061–10068. AAAI Press (2020)
8. Brázdil, T., et al.: Verification of Markov decision processes using learning algorithms. In: Cassez, F., Raskin, J.-F. (eds.) ATVA 2014. LNCS, vol. 8837, pp. 98–114. Springer, Cham (2014). https://doi.org/10.1007/978-3-319-11936-6_8
9. Braziunas, D., Boutilier, C.: Stochastic local search for POMDP controllers. In: AAAI. pp. 690–696. AAAI Press / The MIT Press (2004)
10. Černý, P., Chatterjee, K., Henzinger, T.A., Radhakrishna, A., Singh, R.: Quantitative synthesis for concurrent programs. In: Gopalakrishnan, G., Qadeer, S. (eds.) CAV 2011. LNCS, vol. 6806, pp. 243–259. Springer, Heidelberg (2011). https://doi.org/10.1007/978-3-642-22110-1_20
11. Chatterjee, K., Chmelik, M., Gupta, R., Kanodia, A.: Qualitative analysis of POMDPs with temporal logic specifications for robotics applications. In: ICRA. pp. 325–330. IEEE (2015)
12. Freudenthal, H.: Simplizialzerlegungen von beschrankter Flachheit. Ann. Math. **43**(3), 580–582 (1942)
13. Hansen, E.A.: Solving POMDPs by searching in policy space. In: UAI, pp. 211–219. Morgan Kaufmann (1998)
14. Hartmanns, A., Hermanns, H.: The Modest Toolset: an integrated environment for quantitative modelling and verification. In: Ábrahám, E., Havelund, K. (eds.) TACAS 2014. LNCS, vol. 8413, pp. 593–598. Springer, Heidelberg (2014). https://doi.org/10.1007/978-3-642-54862-8_51

15. Hartmanns, A., Kaminski, B.L.: Optimistic value iteration. In: Lahiri, S., Wang, C. (eds.) Computer Aided Verification. CAV 2020. LNCS, vol. 12225. Springer, Cham (2020). https://doi.org/10.1007/978-3-030-53291-8_26

16. Hensel, C., Junges, S., Katoen, J.P., Quatmann, T., Volk, M.: The probabilistic model checker Storm. CoRR abs/2002.07080 (2020)

17. Horák, K., Bosanský, B., Chatterjee, K.: Goal-HSVI: heuristic search value iteration for goal POMDPs. In: IJCAI, pp. 4764–4770. ijcai.org (2018)

18. Jansen, N., Dehnert, C., Kaminski, B.L., Katoen, J.-P., Westhofen, L.: Bounded model checking for probabilistic programs. In: Artho, C., Legay, A., Peled, D. (eds.) ATVA 2016. LNCS, vol. 9938, pp. 68–85. Springer, Cham (2016). https://doi.org/10.1007/978-3-319-46520-3_5

19. Junges, S., et al.: Finite-state controllers of POMDPs using parameter synthesis. In: UAI, pp. 519–529. AUAI Press (2018)

20. Kaelbling, L.P., Littman, M.L., Cassandra, A.R.: Planning and acting in partially observable stochastic domains. Artif. Intell. **101**(1–2), 99–134 (1998)

21. Kochenderfer, M.J.: Decision Making Under Uncertainty. The MIT Press, Cambridge (2015)

22. Kurniawati, H., Hsu, D., Lee, W.S.: SARSOP: efficient point-based POMDP planning by approximating optimally reachable belief spaces. In: Robotics: Science and Systems. The MIT Press (2008)

23. Kwiatkowska, M., Norman, G., Parker, D.: PRISM 4.0: verification of probabilistic real-time systems. In: Gopalakrishnan, G., Qadeer, S. (eds.) CAV 2011. LNCS, vol. 6806, pp. 585–591. Springer, Heidelberg (2011). https://doi.org/10.1007/978-3-642-22110-1_47

24. Lovejoy, W.S.: Computationally feasible bounds for partially observed Markov decision processes. Oper. Res. **39**(1), 162–175 (1991)

25. Madani, O., Hanks, S., Condon, A.: On the undecidability of probabilistic planning and related stochastic optimization problems. Artif. Intell. **147**(1–2), 5–34 (2003)

26. Meuleau, N., Kim, K., Kaelbling, L.P., Cassandra, A.R.: Solving POMDPs by searching the space of finite policies. In: UAI, pp. 417–426. Morgan Kaufmann (1999)

27. Norman, G., Parker, D., Zou, X.: Verification and control of partially observable probabilistic systems. Real-Time Syst. **53**(3), 354–402 (2017)

28. Pajarinen, J., Peltonen, J.: Periodic finite state controllers for efficient POMDP and DEC-POMDP planning. In: NIPS, pp. 2636–2644 (2011)

29. Pineau, J., Gordon, G.J., Thrun, S.: Point-based value iteration: an anytime algorithm for POMDPs. In: IJCAI, pp. 1025–1032. Morgan Kaufmann (2003)

30. Russell, S.J., Norvig, P.: Artificial Intelligence - A Modern Approach. Pearson Education (2010)

31. Shani, G., Pineau, J., Kaplow, R.: A survey of point-based POMDP solvers. Auton. Agents Multi Agent Syst. **27**(1), 1–51 (2013)

32. Thrun, S., Burgard, W., Fox, D.: Probabilistic Robotics. The MIT Press, Cambridge (2005)

33. Volk, M., Junges, S., Katoen, J.P.: Fast dynamic fault tree analysis by model checking techniques. IEEE Trans. Ind. Inform. **14**(1), 370–379 (2018)

34. Walraven, E., Spaan, M.T.J.: Point-based value iteration for finite-horizon POMDPs. J. Artif. Intell. Res. **65**, 307–341 (2019)

35. Winterer, L., et al.: Motion planning under partial observability using game-based abstraction. In: CDC, pp. 2201–2208. IEEE (2017)

36. Wongpiromsarn, T., Frazzoli, E.: Control of probabilistic systems under dynamic, partially known environments with temporal logic specifications. In: CDC, pp. 7644–7651. IEEE (2012)

Verification of a Generative Separation Kernel

Inzemamul Haque[1(✉)], D. D'Souza[1], P. Habeeb[1], A. Kundu[2],
and Ganesh Babu[2]

[1] Indian Institute of Science, Bangalore, India
inzemamul@iisc.ac.in
[2] CAIR, Defence Research and Development Organization, Bangalore, India

Abstract. We present a formal verification of the functional correctness of the Muen Separation Kernel. Muen is representative of the class of modern separation kernels that leverage hardware virtualization support, and are *generative* in nature in that they generate a specialized kernel for each system configuration. We propose a verification framework called conditional parametric refinement which allows us to formally reason about generative systems. We use this framework to prove the correctness of Muen. Our analysis of several system configurations shows that our technique is effective in producing mechanized proofs of correctness, and also in identifying issues that may compromise the separation property.

1 Introduction

A separation kernel (SK) is a small specialized operating system or microkernel, that provides a sand-boxed or "separate" execution environment for a given set of processes (or "subjects"). The subjects may communicate only via declared memory channels, and are otherwise isolated from each other. Unlike a general operating system these kernels have a fixed set of subjects to run according to a specific schedule on the different CPUs of a processor-based system. Such kernels are often employed in security and safety-critical applications in military and aerospace domains, and the correct functioning of the kernel is of critical importance in guaranteeing the secure and timely execution of the subjects.

One way of obtaining a high level of assurance in the correct functioning of a system is to carry out a refinement-based proof of functional correctness [17,18], as has been done in the context of OS verification [22,31]. Here one specifies an abstract model of the system's behaviour, and then shows that the system implementation conforms to the abstract specification. Such a proof subsumes standard security properties related to separation, like no-exfiltration/infiltration and temporal and spatial separation of subjects considered for instance in [16].

Our aim here is to carry out a similar refinement-based proof of functional correctness for the Muen separation kernel [6], which is an open-source representative of a class of modern separation kernels (including commercial products [13,25,27,34,36]) that use hardware virtualization support and are *generative*

© Springer Nature Switzerland AG 2020
D. V. Hung and O. Sokolsky (Eds.): ATVA 2020, LNCS 12302, pp. 305–322, 2020.
https://doi.org/10.1007/978-3-030-59152-6_17

in nature. By the latter we mean that these tools take an input specification describing the subjects and the schedule of execution, and generate a tailor-made processor-based system that includes subject binaries, page tables, and a kernel that acts like a Virtual Machine Monitor (VMM).

There are several challenges in carrying out such an exercise. Each generated system employs a mix of Ada, Assembly, hardware virtualization features, and complex 4-level paging structures, and is challenging to reason about as a stand-alone system. However, the main challenge lies in reasoning about the generative aspect of such a system: we need to show that for *every* possible input specification, the kernel generator produces a correct system. A possible approach to handle this challenge could be to verify the generator code, along the lines of the CompCert project [24]. However with the generator code running close to 41K LOC, with little compositional structure, this would be a formidable task. Translation validation [30] is another possibility but would require manual effort from scratch each time.

We overcame the challenge of virtualization by simply choosing to model the virtualization layer (in this case Intel's VT-x layer) along with the rest of the hardware components like registers and memory, programmatically in software. Thus we modeled VT-x components like the per-CPU VMX-Timer and EPTP as 64-bit variables in Ada, and implicit structures like the VMCS as a record with appropriate fields as specified by Intel [19]. Instructions like VMLAUNCH were then implemented as methods that accessed these variables. In many ways, virtualization turned out to be more of a boon than a bane. We solved the problem of generativeness (and the problem of handling page tables too), by leveraging a key feature of such systems: the kernel is essentially a *template* which is largely fixed, independent of the input specification. The kernel accesses variables which represent input-specific details like subject details and the schedule, and these structures are generated by Muen based on the given input specification. The kernel can thus be viewed as a *parametric* program, much like a method that computes using its formal parameter variables. In fact, taking a step back, the whole processor system generated by Muen can be viewed as a parametric program with parameter values like the schedule, subject details, page tables, and memory elements being filled in by the generator based on the input specification. This view of Muen as a parametric program turned out to be the key enabler for us.

Such a view suggests a novel two-step technique for verifying generative systems that can be represented as parametric programs. We call this approach *conditional parametric refinement*. We first perform a general verification step (independent of the input spec) to verify that the parametric program refines a parametric abstract specification, *assuming* certain natural conditions on the parameter values (for example *injectivity* of the page tables) that are to be filled in. This first step essentially tells us that for *any* input specification P, if the parameter values generated by the system generator satisfy the assumed conditions, then the generated system is correct vis-a-vis the abstract specification. In the second step, which is *input-specific*, we check that for a given input specification, the generated parameter values actually satisfy the assumed conditions. This gives us an effective verification technique for verifying generative systems that lies somewhere between verifying the generator and translation validation.

We carried out the first step of this proof technique for Muen, using the Spark Ada [2] verification environment. The effort involved about 20K lines of source code and annotation. No major issues were found, modulo some subjective assumptions we discuss in Sect. 4.3. We have also implemented a tool that automatically and efficiently performs the Step 2 check for a given SK configuration. The tool is effective in proving the assumptions, leading to machine-checked proofs of correctness for 16 different input configurations, as well as in detecting issues like undeclared sharing of memory components in some seeded faulty configurations.

In the sequel we sketch the main components of our theory and its application to the verification of Muen. For further details we refer the reader to the longer version [15].

2 Conditional Parametric Refinement

2.1 Machines and Refinement

A convenient way to reason about systems such as Muen is to view them as an *Abstract Data Type* or *machine* [1]. A machine $\mathcal{A}$ is essentially a set of states along with a set of operations, each of which takes an argument, transforms the current state, and returns an output value. We have a designated intialization operation called *init*. The machine $\mathcal{A}$ induces a transition system $\mathcal{T}_{\mathcal{A}}$ in a natural way, whose states are the states of $\mathcal{A}$, and transitions from one state to another are labelled by triples of the form (n, a, b), representing that operation n with input a was invoked and the return value was b. We denote the language of *initialized* sequences of operation calls produced by this transition system, by $L_{init}(\mathcal{A})$.

We will consider machines represented as a program in an imperative programming language. Valuations for the variables of the program make up the state of the machine, while each operation n is given by a method definition of the same name. We call such a program a *machine program*. Figure 1(a) shows a program in a C-like language, that represents a "set" machine with operations *init*, *add* and *elem*. The set stores a subset of the numbers 0–3, in a Boolean array of size 4. However, for certain extraneous reasons, it uses an array T to permute the positions where information for an element x is stored. Thus to indicate that x is present in the set the bit $S[T[x]]$ is set to true.

Refinement [1,17,18] is a way of saying that a "concrete" machine conforms to an "abstract" one, behaviourally. In our setting of total and deterministic machines, we say that machine $\mathcal{B}$ *refines* machine $\mathcal{A}$ if $L_{init}(\mathcal{B}) \subseteq L_{init}(\mathcal{A})$. Refinement is typically exhibited using a "gluing" relation ρ which relates the states of $\mathcal{B}$ to those of $\mathcal{A}$. We say ρ is *adequate* to show that $\mathcal{B}$ refines $\mathcal{A}$ if it satisfies the conditions: (init) the states of $\mathcal{B}$ and $\mathcal{A}$ after initialization are related by ρ, and (sim) if states p and q are related by ρ then after doing any operation n

```
typedef univ          // Abstract spec      const unsigned        // Abstract param spec
  0..3;               typedef univ            Usize;              const unsigned absUsize;
bool S[4];              0..3;                typedef univ          typedef absUniv
univ T[4] :=          bool absS[4];            0..Usize-1;           0..absUsize-1
  {1,2,3,0};          void add(univ x){     bool S[Usize];        bool absS[absUsize];
                        absS[x] :=          univ T[Usize];
void init(){            true;                                     void add(absUniv x){
  for (int i:=0;      }                     void init(){            absS[x] := true;
   i < 4; i++)                                 for (int i:=0;     }
  S[i] := false;        ...                      i < Usize; i++)
}                                                S[i] := false;      ...
                      // Gluing             }
void add(univ x){     // relation
  S[T[x]] := true;    \forall univ x:       void add(univ x){     // Assumption R:
}                       S[T[x]] =             S[T[x]] := true;       Usize = absUsize
                        absS[x]             }                        && T injective
bool elem(univ x){
  return S[T[x]];                           bool elem(univ x){     // Param gluing relation
}                                             return S[T[x]];     \forall univ x:
                                            }                        S[T[x]] = absS[x]

        (a)                 (b)                   (c)                     (d)
```

Fig. 1. (a) A machine program P implementing a set machine, (b) an abstract specification A and gluing relation, (c) a parametric machine program $Q[Usize, T]$ representing a parametric set machine, and (d) abstract parametric specification $B[absUsize]$ and parametric gluing predicate.

with input a in these states, the output values agree and the resulting states are again ρ-related. To check the adequacy of a gluing relation, we can use Floyd-Hoare logic based code-level verification tools (like VCC [7] for C, or GNAT Pro [2] for Ada Spark), to phrase the refinement conditions (init) and (sim) as pre/post annotations and carry out a machine-checked proof of refinement [12]. Figure 1(b) shows an abstract specification and a gluing relation, for the set machine program of part (a).

2.2 Generative Systems and Parametric Refinement

A *generative system* is a program G that given an input specification I (in some space of valid inputs), generates a machine program P_I. As an example, one can think of a set machine generator *SetGen*, that given a number k of type unsigned int (representing the universe size), generates a program P_k similar to the one in Fig. 1(a), which uses the constant k in place of the set size 4, and an array T_k of size k, which maps each x in $[0..k-1]$ to $(x+1) \bmod k$. For every I, let us say we have an abstract machine (again similar to the one in Fig. 1(b)) say A_I, describing the intended behaviour of the machine P_I. Then the verification problem of interest to us, for the generative system G, is to show that for *each* input specification I, P_I refines A_I. This is illustrated in Fig. 2(a). We propose a way to address this problem using refinement of *parametric* programs, which we describe next.

Parametric Refinement. A *parametric* program is like a standard program, except that it has certain read-only variables which are left *uninitialized*. These uninitialized variables act like "parameters" to the program. We denote by $P[\bar{V}]$ a parametric program P with a list of uninitialized variables $\bar{V}$. As such a parametric program has no useful meaning, but if we initialize the variables $\bar{V}$ with the values $\bar{v}$ passed to the program, we get a standard program which we denote by $P[\bar{v}]$. Let N be a set of operation names. A *parametric machine program* of type N is a parametric program $Q[\bar{V}]$ containing a method f_n for each operation $n \in N$. The input/output types of f_n may be dependent on and derived from the parameter values. Given a parameter value $\bar{v}$ for $\bar{V}$, we obtain the machine program $Q[\bar{v}]$. Each method f_n now has a concrete input/output type which we denote by $I_n^{\bar{v}}$ and $O_n^{\bar{v}}$ respectively. Figure 1(c) shows an example parametric machine program $Q[Usize, T]$, representing a parametric version of the set program in Fig. 1(a). Given a value 4 for $Usize$ and a list $[1, 2, 3, 0]$ for T, we get the machine program $Q[4, [1, 2, 3, 0]]$, which behaves similar to the one of Fig. 1(a). We note that the input type of the methods *add* and *elem* depend on the value of the parameter $Usize$.

Given two parametric machine programs $Q[\bar{V}]$ and $B[\bar{U}]$ of type N, we are interested in exhibiting a refinement relation between instances of $Q[\bar{V}]$ and $B[\bar{U}]$. Let R be a relation on parameter values $\bar{u}$ for $\bar{U}$ and $\bar{v}$ for $\bar{V}$, given by a predicate on the variables in $\bar{U}$ and $\bar{V}$. We say that $Q[\bar{V}]$ *parametrically refines* $B[\bar{U}]$ w.r.t. the condition R, if whenever two parameter values $\bar{u}$ for $\bar{U}$ and $\bar{v}$ for $\bar{V}$ are such that $R(\bar{u}, \bar{v})$ holds, then $Q[\bar{v}]$ refines $B[\bar{u}]$. We propose a way to exhibit such a conditional refinement using a *single* "universal" gluing relation. A *parametric gluing relation* on $Q[\bar{V}]$ and $B[\bar{U}]$ is a relation π on the state spaces S^Q of $Q[\bar{V}]$ and S^B of $B[\bar{U}]$, given by a predicate on the variables of $Q[\bar{V}]$ and $B[\bar{U}]$. We say π is *adequate*, with respect to the condition R, if the following conditions are satisfied. In the conditions below, we use the standard Hoare triple notation for total correctness $\{G\} \boxed{P} \{H\}$, to mean that a program P, when started in a state satisfying predicate G, always terminates in a state satisfying H. We use the superscript Q or B to differentiate the components pertaining to the programs $Q[\bar{V}]$ and $B[\bar{U}]$ respectively, and assume that the programs have disjoint state spaces.

1. (type) For each $n \in N$: $R(\bar{u}, \bar{v}) \implies (I_n^{Q,\bar{v}} = I_n^{B,\bar{u}} \wedge O_n^{Q,\bar{v}} = O_n^{B,\bar{u}})$.
2. (init) $\{R\} \boxed{init^B(); init^Q()} \{\pi\}$.
3. (sim) For each $n \in N$: $\{R \wedge \pi\} \boxed{r_B := f_n^B(a); r_Q := f_n^Q(a)} \{\pi \wedge r_B = r_Q\}$.

We can now state the following theorem:

Theorem 1. *Let $Q[\bar{V}]$ and $B[\bar{U}]$ be parametric machine programs of type N. Let R be a predicate on $\bar{U}$ and $\bar{V}$, and let π be an adequate parametric gluing relation for $Q[\bar{V}]$ and $B[\bar{U}]$ w.r.t. R. Then $Q[\bar{V}]$ parametrically refines $B[\bar{U}]$ w.r.t. the condition R.* $\qquad\square$

Consider the parametric machine program $Q[Usize, T]$ in Fig. 1(c), and the abstract parametric program in Fig. 1(d), which we call $B[absUsize]$. Consider the condition R which requires that $absUsize = Usize$ and T to be injective. Let

π be the parametric gluing predicate $\forall x$: unsigned, $(x < Usize) \implies S[T[x]] = absS[x])$. Then π can be seen to be adequate w.r.t. the condition R, and thus $Q[Usize, T]$ parametrically refines $B[absUsize]$ w.r.t. R.

Verifying Generative Systems using Parametric Refinement. Consider a generative system G that given a specification I, generates a machine program P_I by filling a template with values derived from I, and let A_I be the abstract specification for input I. Recall that our aim is to show that for each I, P_I refines A_I. We achieve this by applying the following steps:

1. Associate a parametric program $Q[V]$ with G, such that for each I, G can be viewed as generating the value v_I for the parameter V, so that $Q[v_I]$ is behaviourally equivalent to P_I. $Q[V]$ can be constructed from the template which is filled by G.
2. Construct a parametric abstract specification $B[U]$, and concrete value u_I for each I, such that A_I is equivalent to $B[u_I]$.
3. Construct a condition R on the parameters U and V, and show that $Q[V]$ parametrically refines $B[U]$ w.r.t. R, using an adequate gluing predicate.
4. For a given I, check if u_I and v_I satisfy R. If so, conclude that P_I refines A_I.

We note that the Steps 1–3 are done only once for G, while the last step needs to be done for each I of interest. Figure 2 illustrates this approach.

As a final illustration in our running example, to verify the correctness of the set machine generator *SetGen*, we use the parametric programs $Q[Usize, T]$ and $B[absUsize]$ to capture the concrete program generated and the abstract specification respectively. We then show that $Q[Usize, T]$ parametrically refines $B[absUsize]$ w.r.t. the condition R, using the gluing predicate π, as described above. We note that the actual values generated for the parameters in this case (recall that these are values for the parameters $Usize$, $absUsize$ and T) do indeed satisfy the conditions required by R, namely that $Usize$ and $absUsize$ be equal, and T be injective. Thus we can conclude that for each input universe size k, the machine program P_k refines A_k, and we are done.

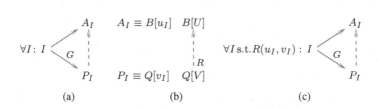

(a)   (b)   (c)

Fig. 2. Proving correctness of a generative system using parametric refinement. (a) The goal, (b) proof artifacts and obligation, and (c) the guarantee. Dashed arrows represent refinement, dashed arrow with R at tail represents conditional refinement w.r.t. R.

3   The Muen Kernel Generator

3.1   Intel X86/64 Processor

The kernel that Muen generates runs on an x86/64 processor with VMX support. We briefly describe this platform (see [19] for more details) and how to view a processor-based system as a machine. Figure 3 depicts the processor system and its components. The CPU components like the 64-bit general purpose registers, model-specific registers like the Time Stamp Counter (TSC), and physical memory components are standard. The layer above shows components like the VMCS pointer (VMPTR), the VMX-timer, and extended page table pointer (EPTP), which are part of the VT-x layer of the VMX mode that supports virtualization. The VMPTR on each CPU points to a VMCS structure, which is used by the VMM (here the kernel) to control launch/exit of subjects. The CR3 register and the EPTP component (set by the active VMCS) control the virtual-to-physical address translation. The top-most layer shows the kernel code that runs on each CPU, with an "Init" component that runs on system initialization, and a "Handler" component that handles VM-exits due to interrupts. The Muen kernel essentially runs as a VMM, and subjects as VMs provided by the VMM. To launch a subject in a VM, the kernel sets the VMPTR to point to one of the VMCSs using the VMPTRLD instruction, and then calls VMLAUNCH which sets the timer, CR3, and EPTP components from the VMCS fields. A subject is caused to exit its VM and return control to the kernel by events like VMX-timer expiry, page table exceptions, and interrupts.

We would like to view such a processor system as a machine of Sect. 2.1. The state of the machine is the contents of all its components. The operations are (a) *Init*, where the init code of the kernel is executed on each of the processors starting with the BSP (CPU0); (b) *Execute*, which takes a CPU id and executes the next instruction pointed to by the IP on that CPU. The instruction could be one that does not access memory (like *add*), or one that accesses memory (like *mov*) in which case the given address is translated via the page tables pointed to by the CR3 and EPTP components; or (c) *Event*, which could be timer tick event on a CPU causing the TSC to increment and the VMX-timer of the active

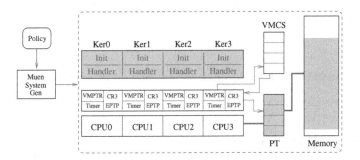

Fig. 3. An x86/64bit VMX processor. Shaded components are generated by Muen.

VM to decrement. If the VMX-timer becomes 0, a VM exit is caused and the corresponding handler invoked. Another kind of event is generated by external interrupts. External interrupts cause a VM exit. The cause of all VM exits is stored in the subject's VMCS, which the handler checks and takes appropriate action for.

3.2 Policy Specification

The input specification to Muen is an XML file called a *policy*. It specifies details of the host processor, subjects to be run, and a precise schedule of execution on each CPU of the host processor system. For each subject the policy specifies the size and starting addresses of the components in its virtual memory which could include shared memory components called *channels*.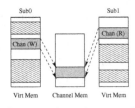

The policy specifies the size and location of each channel in a subject's virtual address space, and read/write permissions, as depicted alongside.

The schedule is a sequence of *major frames* to be performed repeatedly. A major frame specifies for each CPU a sequence of *minor frames*, which specifies a subject and the number of ticks to run it. The beginning of each major frame is a synchronization point for the CPUs. An example scheduling policy in XML is shown in Fig. 4(a), while Fig. 4(b) shows the same schedule viewed as a clock. The shaded portion depicts the passage of time (the tick count) on each CPU.

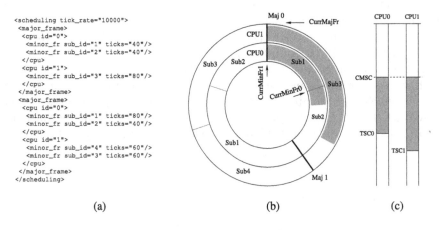

Fig. 4. (a) Example schedule, (b) its clock view, and (c) its implementation in Muen.

3.3 Muen Kernel Generator

Given a policy C, Muen generates the components of a processor system S_C, which is meant to run according to the specified schedule. This is depicted in Fig. 3, where the Muen toolchain generates the shaded components of the processor system, like the initial memory contents, page tables, and kernel code. The toolchain generates a kernel for each CPU, to orchestrate the execution of the subjects according to the specified schedule on that CPU. The kernel is actually a *template* of code written in Spark Ada, and the toolchain generates the constants for this template based on the given policy. The kernel uses data structures like *subject-specs* to store details like page table and VMCS address for each subject. To implement scheduling, the kernel uses a multidimensional array called *scheduling-plans* representing the schedule for each CPU. The kernel knows the number of ticks elapsed on each CPU from the TSC register. It uses a shared variable called CMSC, which is updated by the BSP, to keep track of the start of the current major frame, as shown in Fig. 4(c). The structure *vector-routing* is also generated by the toolchain to represent the table which maps an interrupt vector to the corresponding destination subject and the destination vector to be sent to the destination subject. The

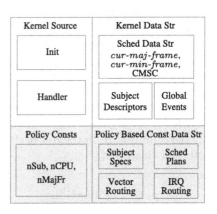

Fig. 5. Components of the generated kernel. Shaded components are generated by the toolchain.

kernel also uses a data structure called *global-events* for each subject to save pending interrupts when the destination subject is not active. The components of the kernel are shown in Fig. 5.

At system startup the Init part of the kernel performs the initialization tasks like setting up the VMCS for each subject, making use of the *subject-specs* structure generated by Muen. The handler part of the kernel is invoked whenever there is a VM exit. For instance if the exit is due to a VMX-timer expiry, it uses *scheduling-plans* to decide whether to schedule the subject in the next minor frame, or to wait for synchronization at the end of a major frame. If the exit is due to an external interrupt, it uses *vector-routing* to decide the subject which will handle the interrupt, and the destination vector which should be sent to the handler subject. The structure *global-events* is used to store the pending interrupt. When the handler subject becomes active, the pending interrupt is *injected* via the VMCS and the pending interrupt is removed from *global-events*.

We have focussed on Ver. 0.7 of Muen. The toolchain implemented in Ada and C, comprises about 41K LoC, while the kernel template is about 3K LoC in Ada.

4   Proof Overview

Given a policy C, let S_C denote the processor system generated by Muen. Let T_C denote an abstract machine spec for the system S_C (we describe T_C next). Our aim is to show that for each valid policy C, S_C refines T_C. We use the parametric refinement technique of Sect. 2 to do this. We first define a parametric program $Q[\bar{V}]$ that models the generic system generated by Muen, so that for a given policy C, if $\bar{v}_C$ corresponds to the parameter values generated by Muen, then S_C and $Q[\bar{v}_C]$ are behaviourally equivalent. In a similar way we define the abstract parametric program $B[\bar{U}]$, so that with appropriate parameters $\bar{u}_C$, $B[\bar{u}_C]$ captures the abstract spec T_C. Next we show that $Q[\bar{V}]$ parametrically refines $B[\bar{U}]$ w.r.t. a condition R. The figure alongside shows the proof artifacts and obligations. Finally, for a given policy C, we check that the parameter values $\bar{u}_C$ and $\bar{v}_C$ satisfy the condition R. In the rest of this section we elaborate on the components and steps of this proof.

$$T_C \equiv B[\bar{u}_C] \qquad B[\bar{U}]$$
$$C \qquad\qquad\qquad\qquad\uparrow R$$
$$Muen \qquad S_C \equiv Q[\bar{v}_C] \qquad Q[\bar{V}]$$

4.1   Abstract Specification

The abstract specification T_C implements a simple system that realizes the behaviour specified by a policy C. In T_C each subject s is run on a *separate*, dedicated, single-CPU processor system M_s. The system M_s has its own CPU with registers, and 2^{64} bytes of physical memory *VMem* with permissions as specified in the policy. The policy maps each subject to a CPU of the concrete machine on which it is meant to run. To model this we use a set of *logical* CPUs (corresponding to the number of CPUs specified in the policy), and we associate with each logical CPU, the (disjoint) group of subjects mapped to that CPU. Figure 6 shows a schematic representation of T_C. To model channels, we use a separate memory array *chmem*, as depicted in Sect. 3.2. Memory contents for a subject s are fetched from $VMem_s$ or from *chmem* accordingly. There is no kernel in this system, but a *supervisor* whose job is to process events directed to a logical CPU or subject, and to enable and disable subjects based on the scheduling policy and the current "time". Towards this end it maintains a flag *enabled*$_s$ for each subject s, which is set whenever the subject is enabled to run based on the current time. To implement the specified schedule it keeps track of time using the clock-like abstraction depicted in Fig. 4(b).

In the *init* operation the supervisor initializes the processor systems M_s, permissions array *perms*, the channel memory *chmem*, and also the schedule-related variables, based on the policy. The *execute* operation, given a logical CPU id, executes the next instruction on the subject machine currently active for that logical CPU id. An *execute* operation does not affect the state of other subject processors, except possibly via the shared memory *chmem*. If the instruction accesses an invalid memory address, the system is assumed to shut down in an error state. Finally, for the *event* operation, which is a tick/interrupt event

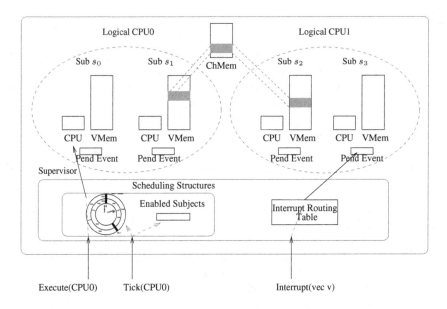

Fig. 6. Schematic diagram of the abstract specification T_C

directed to a logical CPU or subject, the supervisor updates the scheduling state, or pending event array, appropriately.

To represent the system T_C concretely, we use an Ada program which we call A_C. A_C is a programmatic realization of T_C, with processor registers represented as 64-bit numeric variables, and memory as byte arrays of size 2^{64}. The operations *init*, *execute*, and *event* are implemented as methods that implement the operations as described above. Finally, we obtain a parametric program $B[\bar{U}]$ from A_C, by parameterizing it as illustrated in Sect. 2. We call the list of parameters $\bar{U}$. By construction, it is evident that if we generate appropriate values $\bar{u}_C$ for the parameters in $\bar{U}$, we will get a machine program $B[\bar{u}_C]$ which is equivalent in behaviour to A_C.

4.2 Parametric Refinement Proof

We begin by describing how we view Muen as a parametric program. Let C be a given policy. We first define a machine program P_C that represents the processor system S_C generated by Muen. This is done similar to A_C, except that we now have a *single* physical memory array which we call *PMem*. Further, since the processor system S_C makes use of the VT-x components, we need to model these components in P_C as well. For example we represent each page table *ptab*, as a 2^{64} size array PT_{ptab} of 64-bit numbers, with the translation *ptab*(a) of an address a being modelled as $PT_{ptab}[a]$. The operations *init*, *execute*, and *event* are implemented as method calls. The *init* code comes from the Init component of the kernel. In the *execute* method, memory accesses are translated via the active page table to access the physical memory *PMem*. The implementation of the *event* operation comes from the Handler part of the kernel code. We then move from P_C to a parametric program $Q[\bar{V}]$, by using parameters such as *NSubs*, *scheduling-plans*, *subject-specs*, *PMem*, and *PT*. Once again, for an appropriate list of values $\bar{v}_C$ generated by Muen from a given policy C, $Q[\bar{v}_C]$ is equivalent to P_C, which in turn is equivalent to S_C.

Next we show that the parametric version of the Muen system $Q[\bar{V}]$ conditionally refines the parametric abstract spec $B[\bar{U}]$. From Sect. 2.2, this requires us to identify the condition R, and find a gluing relation π on the state of parametric programs Q and B such that the refinement conditions (type), (init), and (sim) are satisfied. The key conjuncts of our condition R are:

- R_1: The page tables $ptab_s$ associated with a subject s must be *injective* in that no two virtual addresses, within a subject or across subjects, may be mapped to the same physical address, *unless* specified to be part of a channel;
- R_2: For each subject s, the permissions (rd/wr/ex/present) associated with an address a should match with the permissions for a in $ptab_s$;
- R_3: For each subject s, no invalid virtual address is mapped to a physical address by page table $ptab_s$.
- R_4: The values of the parameters (like *NSubs*, *subject-specs*, *scheduling-plans* and *IOBitmap*) in the concrete should match with those in the abstract.

The gluing relation π has the following key conjuncts: The CPU register contents of each subject in the abstract match with the register contents of the CPU on which the subject is active, if the subject is enabled, and with the subject descriptor, otherwise; For each subject s and valid address a in its virtual address space, the contents of $VMem_s(a)$ and $PMem(ptab_s(a))$ should match; The value $(TSC - CMSC)$ on each CPU in the concrete, should match with how much the ideal clock for the subject's logical CPU is ahead of the beginning of the current major frame in the abstract.

We carry out the adequacy check for π, described in Sect. 2.2, by constructing a "combined" version of Q and B that has the disjoint union of their state variables, as well as a joint version of their operations, and phrase

$B[U]$		$Q[V]$		Combined	
LoC	LoA	LoC	LoA	LoC	LoA
793	0	1,914	0	13,970	6,214

the adequacy conditions as pre/post conditions on the joint operations. We carry out these checks using the Spark Ada tool [2] which uses provers Z3 [28], CVC4 [3], and Alt-Ergo [8] in the backend. We faced several challenges in carrying out this proof to completion. For instance, to prove the kernel's handling of the tick event correct, we used 8 subcases to break up the reasoning into manageable subgoals for both the engineer and the prover. The table alongside shows details of our proof effort in terms of lines of code (LoC) and lines of annotations (LoA) in the combined proof artifact. In the combined artifact the LoC count includes comments and repetition of code due to case-splits. All the proof artifacts used in this project are available at shorturl.at/ilqMU.

4.3   Checking Condition R

We now describe how to efficiently check that for a given policy C, the parameters generated by Muen and those of the abstract specification, satisfy the condition R. A naive way to check R would be to iterate over the virtual addresses for each subject and check the conditions. This runs in time $\mathcal{O}(N_v)$ where N_v is the size of the virtual address space (typically 2^{48}), and would take days to run. Instead we exploit the fact that the actual size of the memory components is relatively small. We make use of Muen's B-policy which defines the physical address and size of physical memory segments, and the mapping of virtual components to it, so that checking R_1 reduces to checking overlap of physical components. To check R_3, we exploit the fact that translation of a valid virtual address uses certain entries of paging structures which have their "present" bit set to 1. We check that the present bit is set only in the entries which are used for translation of valid virtual addresses. These checks run in time $\mathcal{O}(N_u)$ where N_u is the actual used virtual address space of a subject.

We implemented our algorithms above in C and Ada, using the Libxml2 library to process policy files, and a Linux utility xxd to convert the Muen image and individual files from raw format to hexadecimal format. We ran our tool on 16 system configs, 9 of which (D7-*,D9-*) were available as demo configurations from Muen. The remaining configs (DL-*) were configured by us to mimic a Multi-Level Security (MLS) system from [32]. Details of representative configs are shown alongside. We used

System	Sub	CPU	PMem (MB)	Image (MB)	Time (s)	Check Passed
D7_Bochs	8	4	527.4	13.8	3.7	✓
DL_conf1	8	4	506.5	12.9	3.7	✓
DL_conf2	9	4	1552.7	15.1	6.8	✓
DL_conf3	12	4	1050.1	23.3	6.7	✓
DL_conf4	16	4	1571.4	15.1	9.2	✓
D9_Bochs	10	2	532.9	16.2	4.9	✗
D9_vtd	16	4	1057.8	18.4	5.9	✗
D9_IntelNuc	10	2	567.0	16.2	5.5	✗

the 3 configs D9-* (from Ver. 0.9 of Muen) as seeded faults to test our tool. Ver. 0.9 of Muen generates *implicit* shared memory components, and this undeclared sharing was correctly flagged by our tool. The average running time on a configuration was 5.6s. The experiments were carried out on an Intel Core i5 machine with 4GB RAM running Ubuntu 16.04.

Discussion. We believe that the property we have proved for Muen (namely conformance to an abstract specification via a refinement proof) is the canonical security property needed of a separation kernel. However security standards often require specific basic security properties to be satisfied. In [15] we discuss how some of these properties mentioned in [11,16] follow from our proof.

The validity of the verification proof carried out in this work depends on several assumptions we have made. Apart from implicit assumptions like page table translation and VMX instructions behave the way we have modelled them, we made explicit assumptions like the 64-bit TSC counter does not overflow (it would take *years* to happen), and a minor frame length is never more than 2^{32}

ticks. If any of these assumptions are violated, the proof will not go through, and we would have counter-examples to conformance with the abstract specification.

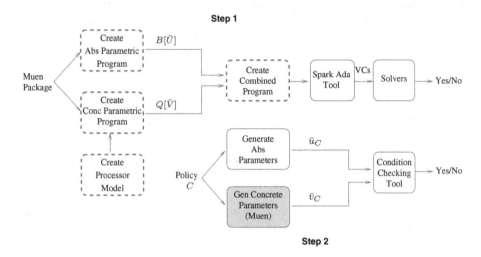

Fig. 7. Components in Muen verification. Untrusted components are shown shaded while non-automated (manual) steps are shown with dashed boxes.

Finally, we show the various components used in our verification in Fig. 7. Each box represents a automated tool (full boxes) or manual transformation carried out (dashed boxes). Components that we trust in the proof are unshaded, while untrusted components are shown shaded.

We would like to mention that the developers of Muen were interested in adding our condition checking tool to the Muen distribution, as they felt it would strengthen the checks they carry out during the kernel generation. We have updated our tool to work on the latest version (v0.9) of Muen, and handed it over to the developers.

5   Related Work

We classify related work based on general OS verification, verification of separation kernels, and translation validation based techniques.

Operating System Verification. There has been a great deal of work in formal verification of operating system kernels in the last few decades. Klein [20] gives an excellent survey of the work till around 2000. In recent years the most comprehensive work on OS verification has been the work on seL4 [21], which gave a refinement-based proof of the functional correctness of a microkernel using the Isabelle/HOL theorem prover. They also carry out an impressive verification of page table translation [35]. The CertiKOS project [14] provides a technique for proving contextual functional correctness across the implementation stack of a kernel, and also handles concurrency. Other recent efforts include verification of a type-safe OS [37], security invariants in ExpressOS [26], and the Hyperkernel project [29].

While verification of a general purpose OS is a more complex task than ours— in particular a general kernel has to deal with dynamic creation of processes while in our setting we have a *fixed* set of processes and a fixed schedule—the techniques used there cannot readily reason about generative kernels like Muen. We would also like to note here that while it is true in such verification one often needs to reason about parametric components (like a method that computes based on its parameters), the whole programs themselves are *not* parametric. In particular, a standard operating system is *not* parametric: it begins with a concrete initial state, unlike a parametric program in which the initial state has unitialized parameters. Thus the techniques developed in this paper are needed to reason about such programs. Finally, we point out that none of these works address the use of VT-x virtualization support.

Verification of Separation Kernels. There has been substantial work in formal verification of separation kernels/hypervisors. seL4 [21] can also be configured as a separation kernel, and the underlying proof of functional correctness was used to prove information flow enforcement. Heitmeyer et al. [16] proved data separation properties using a refinement-based approach for a special-purpose SK called ED, in an embedded setting. As far as we can make out these systems are not generative in nature, and either do not use or do not verify hardware virtualization support. Additionally, unlike our work, none of these works (including OS verification works) are *post-facto*: they are developed *along* with verification.

Dam et al. [10] verify a prototype SK called PROSPER, proving information flow security on the specification and showing a bisimulation between the specification and the implementation. PROSPER works for a minimal configuration with exactly two subjects, and is not a generative system. The Verisoft XT project [4] attempted to prove the correctness of Microsoft's Hyper-V hypervisor [23] and Sysgo's PikeOS, using VCC [7]. While the Hyper-V project was not completed, the PikeOS memory manager was proved correct in [5]. Sanan et al. [33] propose an approach towards verification of the XtratuM kernel [9] in Isabelle/HOL, but the verification was not completed.

Translation Validation Techniques. Our verification problem can also be viewed as translation validation problem, where the Muen generator translates the input policy specification to an SK system. The two kinds of approaches here aim to verify the generator code itself (for example the CompCert project [24]) which can be a challenging task in our much less structured, *post-facto* setting; or aim to verify the generated output for each specific instance [30]. Our work can be viewed as a via-media between these two approaches: we leverage the template-based nature of the generated system to verify the generator conditionally, and then check whether the generated parameter values satisfy our assumed conditions.

6   Conclusion

In this work we have proposed a technique to reason about *template*-based generative systems, and used it to carry out effective *post-facto* verification of the separation property of a complex, generative, virtualization-based separation kernel. In future work we plan to extend the scope of verification to address concurrency issues that we presently ignore in this work.

Acknowledgement. We thank the developers of Muen, Reto Buerki and Adrian-Ken Rueegsegger, for their painstaking efforts in helping us understand the Muen separation kernel. We also thank Arka Ghosh for his help in the proof of interrupt handling.

References

1. Abrial, J.R.: Modeling in Event-B - System and Software Engineering. Cambridge University Press, Cambridge (2010)
2. AdaCore: GNAT Pro Ada toolsuite (2018). https://www.adacore.com/gnatpro
3. Barrett, C., et al.: CVC4. In: Gopalakrishnan, G., Qadeer, S. (eds.) CAV 2011. LNCS, vol. 6806, pp. 171–177. Springer, Heidelberg (2011). https://doi.org/10.1007/978-3-642-22110-1_14
4. Baumann, C., Bormer, T.: Verifying the PikeOS microkernel: first results in the Verisoft XT avionics project. In: Doctoral Symposium on Systems Software Verification. p. 20 (2009)
5. Baumann, C., Bormer, T., Blasum, H., Tverdyshev, S.: Proving memory separation in a microkernel by code level verification. In: Proceedings of the 14th Object/Component/Service-Oriented Real-Time Distributed Computing Workshops, pp. 25–32. IEEE (2011)
6. Buerki, R., Rueegsegger, A.K.: Muen - An x86/64 separation kernel for high assurance. Technical report, Univ. Applied Sc. Rapperswils (HSR) (2013). https://muen.codelabs.ch/
7. Cohen, E., et al.: VCC: a practical system for verifying concurrent C. In: Berghofer, S., Nipkow, T., Urban, C., Wenzel, M. (eds.) TPHOLs 2009. LNCS, vol. 5674, pp. 23–42. Springer, Heidelberg (2009). https://doi.org/10.1007/978-3-642-03359-9_2
8. Conchon, S.: SMT techniques and their applications: from Alt-Ergo to Cubicle. Thèse d'habilitation, Université Paris-Sud (Dec 2012)
9. Crespo, A., Ripoll, I., Masmano, M.: Partitioned Embedded Architecture Based on Hypervisor: The XtratuM approach. In: European Dependable Computing Conference (EDCC), Spain. pp. 67–72. IEEE (2010)
10. Dam, M., Guanciale, R., Khakpour, N., Nemati, H., Schwarz, O.: Formal verification of information flow security for a simple ARM-based separation kernel. In: Proeedings. ACM Conference on Computer and Communications Security, CCS 2013. pp. 223–234. ACM (2013)
11. Directorate, I.A.: U.S. Government Protection Profile for Separation Kernels in Environments Requiring High Robustness, Version 1.03 29 June 2007 (2007). https://www.niap-ccevs.org/Profile/Info.cfm?id=65
12. Divakaran, S., D'Souza, D., Sridhar, N.: Efficient refinement checking in VCC. In: Giannakopoulou, D., Kroening, D. (eds.) VSTTE 2014. LNCS, vol. 8471, pp. 21–36. Springer, Cham (2014). https://doi.org/10.1007/978-3-319-12154-3_2

13. Green Hills Software: INTEGRITY Multivisor (2019). https://www.ghs.com
14. Gu, R., et a: CertiKOS: an extensible architecture for building certified concurrent OS kernels. In: USENIX Symposium Operating Systems Design and Implementation (OSDI), pp. 653–669 (2016)
15. Haque, I., D'Souza, D., P, H., Kundu, A., Babu, G.: Verification of a generative separation kernel (2020). https://arxiv.org/abs/2001.10328v2
16. Heitmeyer, C.L., Archer, M., Leonard, E.I., McLean, J.D.: Formal specification and verification of data separation in a separation kernel for an embedded system. In: Proceedings of the Conference on Computer and Communications Security (CCS), pp. 346–355. ACM (2006)
17. Hoare, C.A.R.: Proof of correctness of data representations. In: Bauer, F.L., et al. (eds.) Language Hierarchies and Interfaces. LNCS, vol. 46, pp. 183–193. Springer, Heidelberg (1976). https://doi.org/10.1007/3-540-07994-7_54
18. Hoare, C.A.R., et al.: Data Refinement Refined (Draft). Technical report, Oxford University (1985)
19. Intel Corp.: Intel 64 and IA-32 architectures software developer's manual, vol 3C (May 2018)
20. Klein, G.: Operating system verification: an overview. Sadhana $34(1)$, 27–69 (2009)
21. Klein, G., et al.: Comprehensive formal verification of an OS microkernel. ACM Trans. Comput. Syst. 32, 1–70 (2014). Article 2
22. Klein, G., et al.: seL4: formal verification of an OS kernel. In: Proceedings of the 22nd ACM Symposium on Operating Systems Principles 2009, Big Sky. pp. 207–220. ACM (2009)
23. Leinenbach, D., Santen, T.: Verifying the Microsoft hyper-v hypervisor with VCC. In: Cavalcanti, A., Dams, D.R. (eds.) FM 2009. LNCS, vol. 5850, pp. 806–809. Springer, Heidelberg (2009). https://doi.org/10.1007/978-3-642-05089-3_51
24. Leroy, X.: Formal certification of a compiler back-end or: programming a compiler with a proof assistant. In: Proceedings of the Principles of Program Languages (POPL), pp. 42–54. ACM (2006)
25. LynxSecure: LynxSecure Sep. Kernel Hypervisor (2019). http://www.lynx.com/
26. Mai, H., Pek, E., Xue, H., King, S.T., Madhusudan, P.: Verifying security invariants in ExpressOS. In: Proceedings of the Architectural Support for Programming Languages and Operating Systems (ASPLOS), pp. 293–304. ACM (2013)
27. Masmano, M., Ripoll, I., Crespo, A., Jean-Jacques, M.: XtratuM: A Hypervisor for Safety Critical Embedded Systems. In: Real Time Linux Workshop (2009)
28. de Moura, L., Bjørner, N.: Z3: an efficient SMT solver. In: Ramakrishnan, C.R., Rehof, J. (eds.) TACAS 2008. LNCS, vol. 4963, pp. 337–340. Springer, Heidelberg (2008). https://doi.org/10.1007/978-3-540-78800-3_24
29. Nelson, L., et al.: Hyperkernel: push-button verification of an OS kernel. In: Proceedings of the Symposium Operating Systems Principles (SOSP), pp. 252–269. ACM (2017)
30. Pnueli, A., Siegel, M., Singerman, E.: Translation validation. In: Steffen, B. (ed.) TACAS 1998. LNCS, vol. 1384, pp. 151–166. Springer, Heidelberg (1998). https://doi.org/10.1007/BFb0054170
31. Rushby, J.M.: Design and verification of secure systems. In: Proceedings of the Symposium Operating System Principles (SOSP), pp. 12–21. ACM (1981)
32. Rushby, J.M.: Proof of separability a verification technique for a class of security kernels. In: Dezani-Ciancaglini, M., Montanari, U. (eds.) Programming 1982. LNCS, vol. 137, pp. 352–367. Springer, Heidelberg (1982). https://doi.org/10.1007/3-540-11494-7_23

33. Sanan, D., Butterfield, A., Hinchey, M.: Separation kernel verification: the xtratum case study. In: Proceedings of the Verified Software: Theories, Tools and Exp. (VSTTE), pp. 133–149 (2014)
34. Sysgo AG: PikeOS 4.2 hypervisor (2018). https://www.sysgo.com/
35. Tuch, H., Klein, G.: Verifying the L4 virtual memory subsystem. In: Proceedings of the NICTA Formal Methods Workshop on Operating Systems Verification, pp. 73–97 (2004)
36. Wind River: VxWorks MILS Platform (2019). https://www.windriver.com
37. Yang, J., Hawblitzel, C.: Safe to the last instruction: automated verification of a type-safe operating system. In: Proceedings of the Programming Language Design and Implementation (PLDI), pp. 99–110. ACM (2010)

Model Checking and Decision Procedures

A Decision Procedure for Path Feasibility of String Manipulating Programs with Integer Data Type

Taolue Chen[1], Matthew Hague[2], Jinlong He[3,6], Denghang Hu[3,6], Anthony Widjaja Lin[4], Philipp Rümmer[5], and Zhilin Wu[3,7,8(✉)]

[1] University of Surrey, Guildford, UK
[2] Royal Holloway, University of London, Egham, UK
[3] State Key Laboratory of Computer Science, Institute of Software, Chinese Academy of Sciences, Beijing, China
wuzl@ios.ac.cn
[4] Technical University of Kaiserslautern, Kaiserslautern, Germany
[5] Uppsala University, Uppsala, Sweden
[6] University of Chinese Academy of Sciences, Beijing, China
[7] Shanghai Key Laboratory of Trustworthy Computing, East China Normal University, Shanghai, China
[8] Institute of Intelligent Software, Guangzhou, China

Abstract. In this paper, we propose a decision procedure for a class of string-manipulating programs which includes not only a wide range of string operations such as concatenation, replaceAll, reverse, and finite transducers, but also those involving the integer data-type such as length, indexof, and substring. To the best of our knowledge, this represents one of the most expressive string constraint languages that is currently known to be decidable. Our decision procedure is based on a variant of cost register automata. We implement the decision procedure, giving rise to a new solver OSTRICH+. We evaluate the performance of OSTRICH+ on a wide range of existing and new benchmarks. The experimental results show that OSTRICH+ is the first string decision procedure capable of tackling finite transducers and integer constraints, whilst its overall performance is comparable with the state-of-the-art string constraint solvers.

1 Introduction

String-manipulating programs are notoriously subtle, and their potential bugs may bring severe security consequences. A typical example is cross-site scripting (XSS), which is among the OWASP Top 10 Application Security Risks [29]. Integer data type occurs naturally and extensively in string-manipulating programs. An effective and increasingly popular method for identifying bugs, including XSS, is symbolic execution [11]. In a nutshell, this technique analyses static paths through the program being considered. Each of these paths can be viewed as a constraint φ over appropriate data domains, and symbolic execution tools demand fast constraint solvers to check the satisfiability of φ. Such constraint solvers need to support all data-type operations occurring in a program.

© Springer Nature Switzerland AG 2020
D. V. Hung and O. Sokolsky (Eds.): ATVA 2020, LNCS 12302, pp. 325–342, 2020.
https://doi.org/10.1007/978-3-030-59152-6_18

Typically, mainstream programming languages provide standard string functions such as concatenation, replace, and replaceAll. Moreover, Web programming languages usually provide complex string operations (e.g. htmlEscape and trim), which are conveniently modelled as finite transducers, to sanitise malicious user inputs [19]. Nevertheless, apart from these operations involving only the string data type, functions such as length, indexOf, and substring, which can convert strings to integers and vice versa, are also heavily used in practice; for instance, it was reported [26] that length, indexOf, substring, and variants thereof, comprise over 80% of string function occurrences in 18 popular JavaScript applications, notably outnumbering concatenation. The introduction of integers exacerbates the intricacy of string-manipulating programs, and poses new theoretical and practical challenges in solver development.

When combining strings and integers, decidability can easily be lost; for instance, the string theory with concatenation and letter counting functions is undecidable [8,15]. Remarkably, it is still a major open problem whether the string theory with concatenation (arguably the simplest string operation) and length function (arguably the most common string-number function) is decidable [17,22]. One promising approach to retain decidability is to enforce a syntactic restriction to the constraints. In the literature, these restriction include solved forms [17], acyclicity [2,3,5], and straight-line fragment (aka programs in single static assignment form) [12,14,18,21]. On the one hand, such a restriction has led to decidability of string constraint solving with complex string operations (not only concatenation, but also finite transducers) and integer operations (letter-counting, length, indexOf, etc.); see, e.g., [21]. On the other hand, there is a lot of evidence (e.g. from benchmark) that many practical string constraints do satisfy such syntactic restrictions.

Approaches to building practical string solvers could essentially be classified into two categories. Firstly, one could support as many constraints as possible, but primarily resort to heuristics, offering no completeness/termination guarantee. This is a realistic approach since, as mentioned above, the problem involving both string and integer data types is in general undecidable. Many solvers belong to this category, e.g., CVC4 [20], Z3 [7,16], Z3-str3 [6], S3(P) [27,28], Trau [1] (or its variants Trau+ [3] and Z3-Trau [9]), ABC [10], and Slent [32]. Completeness guarantees are, however, valuable since the performance of heuristics can be difficult to predict. The second approach is to develop solvers for decidable fragments supporting both strings and integers (e.g. [2,3,5,12,14,17,18,21]). Solvers in this category include Norn [2], SLOTH [18], and OSTRICH [14]. The fragment *without* complex string operations (e.g. replaceAll and finite transducers, but length) can be handled quite well by Norn. The fragment *without* length constraints (but replaceAll and finite transducers) can be handled effectively by OSTRICH and SLOTH. Moreover, most existing solvers that belong to the first category do not support complex string operations like replaceAll and finite transducers as well. This motivates the following problem: *provide a decision procedure that supports both string and integer data type, with completeness guarantee and meanwhile admitting efficient implementation.*

We argue that this problem is highly challenging. A deeper examination of the algorithms used by OSTRICH and SLOTH reveals that, unlike the case for Norn, it would *not* be straightforward to extend OSTRICH and SLOTH with integer constraints. First and foremost, the complexity of the fragment used by Norn (i.e. without transducers and replaceAll) is solvable in exponential time, even in the presence of integer constraints. This is not the case for the straight-line fragments with transducers/replaceAll, which require at least double exponential time (regardless of the integer constraints). This unfortunately manifests itself in the size of symbolic representations of the solutions. SLOTH [18] computes a representation of all solutions "eagerly" as (alternating) finite transducers. Dealing with integer data type requires to compute the Parikh images of these transducers [21], which would result in a quantifier-free linear integer arithmetic formula (LIA for short) of double exponential size, thus giving us a triple exponential time algorithm, since LIA formulas are solved in exponential time (see e.g. [30]). Lin and Barcelo [21] provided a double exponential upper bound in the length of the strings in the solution, and showed that the double exponential time theoretical complexity could be retained. This, however, does not result in a practical algorithm since it requires all strings of double exponential size to be enumerated. OSTRICH [14] adopted a "lazy" approach and computed the pre-images of regular languages step by step, which is more scalable than the "eager" approach adopted by SLOTH and results in a highly competitive solver. It uses *recognisable relations* (a finite union of products of regular languages) as symbolic representations. Nevertheless, extending this approach to integer constraints is not obvious since integer constraints break the independence between different string variables in the recognisable relations.

Contribution. We provide a decision procedure for an expressive class of string constraints involving the integer data type, which includes not only concatenation, replace/replaceAll, reverse, finite transducers, and regular constraints, but also length, indexOf and substring. The decision procedure utilizes a variant of cost-register automata introduced by Alur et al. [4], which are called *cost-enriched finite automata* (CEFA) for convenience. Intuitively, each CEFA records the connection between a string variable and its associated integer variables. With CEFAs, the concept of recognisable relations is then naturally extended to accommodate integers. The integer constraints, however, are detached from CEFAs rather than being part of CEFAs. This allows to preserve the independence of string variables in the recognisable relation. The crux of the decision procedure is to compute the backward images of CEFAs under string functions, where each cost register (integer variable) might be split into several ones, thus extending but still in the same flavour as OSTRICH for string constraints *without* the integer data type [14]. Such an approach is able to treat a wide range of string functions in a generic, and yet simple, way. To the best of our knowledge, the class of string constraints considered in this paper is currently one of the most expressive string theories involving the integer data type known to enjoy a decision procedure.

We implement the decision procedure based on the recent OSTRICH solver [14], resulting in OSTRICH+. We perform experiments on a wide range of benchmark suites, including those where both replace/replaceAll/finite transducers and length/indexOf/substring occur, as well as the well-known benchmarks KALUZA and PYEX. The results show that 1) OSTRICH+ so far is the only string constraint solver capable of dealing with finite transducers and integer constraints, and 2) its overall performance is comparable with the best state-of-the-art string constraint solvers (e.g. CVC4 and Z3-Trau) which are short of completeness guarantees.

The rest of the paper is structured as follows: Sect. 2 introduces the preliminaries. Section 3 defines the class of string-manipulating programs with integer data type. Section 4 presents the decision procedure. Section 5 presents the benchmarks and experiments for the evaluation. The paper is concluded in Sect. 6. Missing proofs, implementation details and further examples can be found in the full version [13].

2   Preliminaries

We write $\mathbb{N}$ and $\mathbb{Z}$ for the sets of natural and integer numbers, respectively. For $n \in \mathbb{N}$ with $n \geq 1$, $[n]$ denotes $\{1, \ldots, n\}$; for $m, n \in \mathbb{N}$ with $m \leq n$, $[m, n]$ denotes $\{i \in \mathbb{N} \mid m \leq i \leq n\}$. Throughout the paper, Σ is a finite alphabet, ranged over by $a, b, \ldots$.

Strings, Languages, and Transductions. A string over Σ is a (possibly empty) sequence of elements from Σ, denoted by $u, v, w, \ldots$. An empty string is denoted by ε. We write Σ^* (resp., Σ^+) for the set of all (resp. nonempty) strings over Σ. For a string u, we use $|u|$ to denote the number of letters in u. In particular, $|\varepsilon| = 0$. Moreover, for $a \in \Sigma$, let $|u|_a$ denote the number of occurrences of a in u. Assume $u = a_0 \cdots a_{n-1}$ is nonempty and $i < j \in [0, n-1]$. We let $u[i]$ denote a_i and $u[i, j]$ for the substring $a_i \cdots a_j$.

Let u, v be two strings. We use $u \cdot v$ to denote the *concatenation* of u and v. The string u is said to be a *prefix* of v if $v = u \cdot v'$ for some string v'. In addition, if $u \neq v$, then u is said to be a *strict* prefix of v. If $v = u \cdot v'$ for some string v', then we use $u^{-1}v$ to denote v'. In particular, $\varepsilon^{-1}v = v$. If $u = a_0 \cdots a_{n-1}$ is nonempty, then we use $u^{(r)}$ to denote the *reverse* of u, that is, $u^{(r)} = a_{n-1} \cdots a_0$.

A *transduction* over Σ is a binary relation over Σ^*, namely, a subset of $\Sigma^* \times \Sigma^*$. We will use $T_1, T_2, \ldots$ to denote transductions. For two transductions T_1 and T_2, we will use $T_1 \cdot T_2$ to denote the *composition* of T_1 and T_2, namely, $T_1 \cdot T_2 = \{(u, w) \in \Sigma^* \times \Sigma^* \mid there\ exists\ v \in \Sigma^*\ \text{s.t.}\ (u, v) \in T_1\ and\ (v, w) \in T_2\}$.

Recognisable Relations. We assume familiarity with standard regular language. Recall that a regular language L can be represented by a regular expression $e \in \mathsf{RegExp}$ whereby we usually write $L = \mathcal{L}(e)$.

Intuitively, a *recognisable relation* is simply a finite union of Cartesian products of regular languages. Formally, an r-ary relation $R \subseteq \Sigma^* \times \cdots \times \Sigma^*$ is *recognisable* if $R = \bigcup_{i=1}^n L_1^{(i)} \times \cdots \times L_r^{(i)}$ where $L_j^{(i)}$ is regular for each

$j \in [r]$. A *representation* of a recognisable relation $R = \bigcup_{i=1}^{n} L_1^{(i)} \times \cdots \times L_r^{(i)}$ is $(\mathcal{A}_1^{(i)}, \ldots, \mathcal{A}_r^{(i)})_{1 \leq i \leq n}$ such that each $\mathcal{A}_j^{(i)}$ is an NFA with $\mathscr{L}(\mathcal{A}_j^{(i)}) = L_j^{(i)}$. The tuples $(\mathcal{A}_1^{(i)}, \ldots, \mathcal{A}_r^{(i)})$ are called the *disjuncts* of the representation and the NFAs $\mathcal{A}_j^{(i)}$ are called the *atoms* of the representation.

Automata Models. A *(nondeterministic) finite automaton* (NFA) is a tuple $\mathcal{A} = (Q, \Sigma, \delta, I, F)$, where Q is a finite set of states, Σ is a finite alphabet, $\delta \subseteq Q \times \Sigma \times Q$ is the transition relation, $I, F \subseteq Q$ are the set of initial and final states respectively. For readability, we write a transition $(q, a, q') \in \delta$ as $q \xrightarrow[\delta]{a} q'$ (or simply $q \xrightarrow{a} q'$). The *size* of an NFA $\mathcal{A}$, denoted by $|\mathcal{A}|$, is defined as the number of transitions of $\mathcal{A}$. A *run* of $\mathcal{A}$ on a string $w = a_1 \cdots a_n$ is a sequence of transitions $q_0 \xrightarrow{a_1} q_1 \cdots q_{n-1} \xrightarrow{a_n} q_n$ with $q_0 \in I$. The run is *accepting* if $q_n \in F$. A string w is accepted by an NFA $\mathcal{A}$ if there is an accepting run of $\mathcal{A}$ on w. In particular, the empty string ε is accepted by $\mathcal{A}$ if $I \cap F \neq \emptyset$. The language of $\mathcal{A}$, denoted by $\mathscr{L}(\mathcal{A})$, is the set of strings accepted by $\mathcal{A}$. An NFA $\mathcal{A}$ is said to be *deterministic* if I is a singleton and, for every $q \in Q$ and $a \in \Sigma$, there is at most one state $q' \in Q$ such that $(q, a, q') \in \delta$. It is well-known that finite automata capture regular languages precisely.

A *nondeterministic finite transducer* (NFT) $\mathcal{T}$ is an extension of NFA with outputs. Formally, an NFT $\mathcal{T}$ is a tuple $(Q, \Sigma, \delta, I, F)$, where Q, Σ, I, F are as in NFA and the transition relation δ is a finite subset of $Q \times \Sigma \times Q \times \Sigma^*$. Similarly to NFA, for readability, we write a transition $(q, a, q', u) \in \delta$ as $q \xrightarrow[\delta]{a,u} q'$ or $q \xrightarrow{a,u} q'$. The *size* of an NFT $\mathcal{T}$, denoted by $|\mathcal{T}|$, is defined as the sum of the sizes of the transitions of $\mathcal{T}$, where the size of a transition $q \xrightarrow{a,u} q'$ is defined as $|u| + 3$. A run of $\mathcal{T}$ over a string $w = a_1 \cdots a_n$ is a sequence of transitions $q_0 \xrightarrow{a_1,u_1} q_1 \cdots q_{n-1} \xrightarrow{a_n,u_n} q_n$ with $q_0 \in I$. The run is accepting if $q_n \in F$. The string $u_1 \cdots u_n$ is called the output of the run. The transduction defined by $\mathcal{T}$, denoted by $\mathscr{T}(\mathcal{T})$, is the set of string pairs (w, u) such that there is an accepting run of T on w, with the output u. An NFT $\mathcal{T}$ is said to be *deterministic* if I is a singleton, and, for every $q \in Q$ and $a \in \Sigma$ there is at most one pair $(q', u) \in Q \times \Sigma^*$ such that $(q, a, q', u) \in \delta$. In this paper, we are primarily interested in *functional* finite transducers (FFT), i.e., finite transducers that define functions instead of relations. (For instance, deterministic finite transducers are always functional.)

We will also use standard quantifier-free/existential *linear integer arithmetic* (LIA) formulae, which are typically ranged over by ϕ, φ, etc.

3   String-Manipulating Programs with Integer Data Type

In this paper, we consider logics involving two data-types, i.e., the string data-type and the integer data-type. As a convention, $u, v, \ldots$ denote string constants, $c, d, \ldots$ denote integer constants, $x, y, \ldots$ denote string variables, and $i, j, \ldots$ denote integer variables.

We consider symbolic execution of string-manipulating programs with numeric conditions (abbreviated as SL$_{\text{int}}$), defined by the following rules,

$$S ::= x := y \cdot z \mid x := \text{replaceAll}_{e,u}(y) \mid x := \text{reverse}(y) \mid x := \mathcal{T}(y) \mid$$
$$x := \text{substring}(y, t_1, t_2) \mid \text{assert}\,(\varphi) \mid S; S,$$
$$\varphi ::= x \in \mathcal{A} \mid t_1 \, o \, t_2 \mid \varphi \vee \varphi \mid \varphi \wedge \varphi,$$

where e is a regular expression over Σ, $u \in \Sigma^*$, $\mathcal{T}$ is an FFT, $\mathcal{A}$ is an NFA, $o \in \{=, \neq, \geq, \leq, >, <\}$, and t_1, t_2 are integer terms defined by the following rules,

$$t ::= i \mid c \mid \text{length}(x) \mid \text{indexOf}_v(x, i) \mid ct \mid t + t, \text{ where } c \in \mathbb{Z}, v \in \Sigma^+.$$

We require that the string-manipulating programs are in **single static assignment (SSA) form**. Note that SSA form imposes restrictions only on the assignment statements, but not on the assertions. A string variable x in an SL$_{\text{int}}$ program S is called an *input string variable* of S if it does not appear on the left-hand side of the assignment statements of S. A variable in S is called an *input variable* if it is either an input string variable or an integer variable.

Semantics. The semantics of SL$_{\text{int}}$ is explained as follows.

- The assignment $x := y \cdot z$ denotes that x is the concatenation of two strings y and z.
- The assignment $x := \text{replaceAll}_{e,u}(y)$ denotes that x is the string obtained by replacing all occurrences of e in y with u, where the *leftmost and longest* matching of e is used. For instance, $\text{replaceAll}_{(ab)^+,c}(aababaab) = ac \cdot \text{replaceAll}_{(ab)^+,c}(aab) = acac$, since the leftmost and longest matching of $(ab)^+$ in $aababaab$ is $abab$. Here we require that the language defined by e does *not* contain the empty string, in order to avoid the troublesome definition of the semantics of the matching of the empty string. The formal semantics of the replaceAll function can be found in [12].
- The assignment $x := \text{reverse}(y)$ denotes that x is the reverse of y.
- The assignment $x := \mathcal{T}(y)$ denotes that $(y, x) \in \mathscr{T}(\mathcal{T})$.
- The assignment $x := \text{substring}(y, t_1, t_2)$ denotes that x is equal to the return value of $\text{substring}(y, t_1, t_2)$, where

$$\text{substring}(y, t_1, t_2) = \begin{cases} \epsilon & \text{if } t_1 < 0 \vee t_1 \geq |y| \vee t_2 = 0 \\ y[t_1, \min\{t_1 + t_2 - 1, |y| - 1\}] & o/w \end{cases}$$

For instance, $\text{substring}(abaab, -1, 1) = \varepsilon$, $\text{substring}(abaab, 3, 0) = \varepsilon$, $\text{substring}(abaab, 3, 2) = ab$, and $\text{substring}(abaab, 3, 3) = ab$.

- The conditional statement $\text{assert}\,(x \in \mathcal{A})$ denotes that x belongs to $\mathscr{L}(\mathcal{A})$.
- The conditional statement $\text{assert}\,(t_1 \, o \, t_2)$ denotes that the value of t_1 is equal to (not equal to, ...) that of t_2, if $o \in \{=, \neq, \geq, >, \leq, <\}$.
- The integer term $\text{length}(x)$ denotes the length of x.
- The function $\text{indexOf}_v(x, i)$ returns the starting position of the first occurrence of v in x after the position i, if such an occurrence exists, and -1 otherwise. Note that if $i < 0$, then $\text{indexOf}_v(x, i)$ returns $\text{indexOf}_v(x, 0)$,

and if $i \geq$ length(x), then indexOf$_v(x, i)$ returns -1. For instance, indexOf$_{Ab}(aaba, -1) = 1$, indexOf$_{Ab}(aaba, 1) = 1$, indexOf$_{Ab}(aaba, 2) = -1$, and indexOf$_{Ab}(aaba, 4) = -1$.

Path Feasibility Problem. Given an SL$_{\text{int}}$ program S, decide whether there are valuations of the input variables so that S can execute to the end.

4 Decision Procedures for Path Feasibility

In this section, we present a decision procedure for the path feasibility problem of SL$_{\text{int}}$. A distinguished feature of the decision procedure is that it conducts backward computation which is lazy and can be done in a modular way. To support this, we extend a regular language with quantitative information of the strings in the language, giving rise to cost-enriched regular languages and corresponding finite automata (Sect. 4.1). The crux of the decision procedure is thus to show that the pre-images of cost-enriched regular languages under the string operations in SL$_{\text{int}}$ (i.e., concatenation $\cdot$, replaceAll$_{e,u}$, reverse, FFTs $\mathcal{T}$, and substring) are representable by so called cost-enriched recognisable relations (Sect. 4.2). The overall decision procedure is presented in Sect. 4.3, supplied by additional complexity analysis.

4.1 Cost-Enriched Regular Languages and Recognisable Relations

Let $k \in \mathbb{N}$ with $k > 0$. A k-cost-enriched string is $(w, (n_1, \cdots, n_k))$ where w is a string and $n_i \in \mathbb{Z}$ for all $i \in [k]$. A k-cost-enriched language L is a subset of $\Sigma^* \times \mathbb{Z}^k$. For our purpose, we identify a "regular" fragment of cost-enriched languages as follows.

Definition 1 (Cost-enriched regular languages). *Let $k \in \mathbb{N}$ with $k > 0$. A k-cost-enriched language is regular (abbreviated as CERL) if it can be accepted by a cost-enriched finite automaton.*

A cost-enriched finite automaton (CEFA) $\mathcal{A}$ is a tuple $(Q, \Sigma, R, \delta, I, F)$ where

- *Q, Σ, I, F are defined as in NFAs,*
- *$R = (r_1, \cdots, r_k)$ is a vector of (mutually distinct) cost registers,*
- *δ is the transition relation which is a finite set of tuples (q, a, q', η) where $q, q' \in Q$, $a \in \Sigma$, and $\eta : R \to \mathbb{Z}$ is a cost register update function. For convenience, we usually write $(q, a, q', \eta) \in \Delta$ as $q \xrightarrow{a, \eta} q'$.*

A run of $\mathcal{A}$ on a k-cost-enriched string $(a_1 \cdots a_m, (n_1, \cdots, n_k))$ is a transition sequence $q_0 \xrightarrow{a_1, \eta_1} q_1 \cdots q_{m-1} \xrightarrow{a_m, \eta_m} q_m$ such that $q_0 \in I$ and $n_i = \sum\limits_{1 \leq j \leq m} \eta_j(r_i)$ for each $i \in [k]$ (Note that the initial values of cost registers are zero). The run is accepting if $q_m \in F$. A k-cost-enriched string $(w, (n_1, \cdots, n_k))$ is accepted by $\mathcal{A}$ if there is an accepting run of $\mathcal{A}$ on $(w, (n_1, \cdots, n_k))$. In particular, (ε, n) is accepted by $\mathcal{A}$ if $n = 0$ and $I \cap F \neq \emptyset$. The k-cost-enriched language defined by $\mathcal{A}$, denoted by $\mathscr{L}(\mathcal{A})$, is the set of k-cost-enriched strings accepted by $\mathcal{A}$.

The *size* of a CEFA $\mathcal{A} = (Q, \Sigma, R, \delta, I, F)$, denoted by $|\mathcal{A}|$, is defined as the sum of the sizes of its transitions, where the size of each transition (q, a, q', η) is $\sum_{r \in R} \lceil \log_2(|\eta(r)|) \rceil + 3$. Note here the integer constants in $\mathcal{A}$ are encoded in binary.

Remark 1. CEFAs can be seen as a variant of Cost Register Automata [4], by admitting nondeterminism and discarding partial final cost functions. CEFAs are also closely related to monotonic counter machines [21]. The main difference is that CEFAs discard guards in transitions and allow binary-encoded integers in cost updates, while monotonic counter machines allow guards in transitions but restrict the cost updates to being monotonic and unary, i.e. $0, 1$ only. Moreover, we explicitly define CEFAs as language acceptors for cost-enriched languages.

Example 1 (CEFA for length*).* The string function length can be captured by CEFAs. For any NFA $\mathcal{A} = (Q, \Sigma, \delta, I, F)$, it is not difficult to see that the cost-enriched language $\{(w, \mathsf{length}(w)) \mid w \in \mathscr{L}(\mathcal{A})\}$ is accepted by a CEFA, i.e., $(Q, \Sigma, (r_1), \delta', I, F)$ such that for each $(q, a, q') \in \delta$, we let $(q, a, q', \eta) \in \delta'$, where $\eta(r_1) = 1$.

For later use, we identify a special $\mathcal{A}_{\mathsf{len}} = (\{q_0\}, \Sigma, (r_1), \{(q_0, a, q_0, \eta) \mid \eta(r_1) = 1\}, \{q_0\}, \{q_0\})$. In other words, $\mathcal{A}_{\mathsf{len}}$ accepts $\{(w, \mathsf{length}(w)) \mid w \in \Sigma^*\}$.

We can show that the function $\mathsf{indexOf}_v(\cdot, \cdot)$ can be captured by a CEFA as well, in the sense that, for any NFA $\mathcal{A}$ and constant string v, we can construct a CEFA $\mathcal{A}_{\mathsf{indexOf}_v}$ accepting $\{(w, (n, \mathsf{indexOf}_v(w, n))) \mid w \in \mathscr{L}(\mathcal{A}),\ n \le \mathsf{indexOf}_v(w, n) < |w|\}$. The construction is slightly technical and can be found in the full version [13].

Note that $\mathcal{A}_{\mathsf{indexOf}_v}$ does not model the corner cases in the semantics of $\mathsf{indexOf}_v$, for instance, $\mathsf{indexOf}_v(w, n) = -1$ if v does not occur after the position n in w.

Given two CEFAs $\mathcal{A}_1 = (Q_1, \Sigma, R_1, \delta_1, I_1, F_1)$ and $\mathcal{A}_2 = (Q_2, \Sigma, \delta_2, R_2, I_2, F_2)$ with $R_1 \cap R_2 = \emptyset$, the product of $\mathcal{A}_1$ and $\mathcal{A}_2$, denoted by $\mathcal{A}_1 \times \mathcal{A}_2$, is defined as $(Q_1 \times Q_2, \Sigma, R_1 \cup R_2, \delta, I_1 \times I_2, F_1 \times F_2)$, where δ comprises the tuples $((q_1, q_2), \sigma, (q'_1, q'_2), \eta)$ such that $(q_1, \sigma, q'_1, \eta_1) \in \delta_1$, $(q_2, \sigma, q'_2, \eta_2) \in \delta_2$, and $\eta = \eta_1 \cup \eta_2$.

For a CEFA $\mathcal{A}$, we use $R(\mathcal{A})$ to denote the vector of cost registers occurring in $\mathcal{A}$. Suppose $\mathcal{A}$ is CEFA with $R(\mathcal{A}) = (r_1, \cdots, r_k)$ and $\boldsymbol{i} = (i_1, \cdots, i_k)$ is a vector of mutually distinct integer variables such that $R(\mathcal{A}) \cap \boldsymbol{i} = \emptyset$. We use $\mathcal{A}[\boldsymbol{i}/R(\mathcal{A})]$ to denote the CEFA obtained from $\mathcal{A}$ by simultaneously replacing r_j with i_j for $j \in [k]$.

Definition 2 (Cost-enriched recognisable relations). *Let* $(k_1, \cdots, k_l) \in \mathbb{N}^l$ *with* $k_j > 0$ *for every* $j \in [l]$*. A cost-enriched recognisable relation (CERR)* $\mathcal{R} \subseteq (\Sigma^* \times \mathbb{Z}^{k_1}) \times \cdots \times (\Sigma^* \times \mathbb{Z}^{k_l})$ *is a finite union of products of CERLs. Formally,*
$$\mathcal{R} = \bigcup_{i=1}^{n} L_{i,1} \times \cdots \times L_{i,l},$$
where for every $j \in [l]$*,* $L_{i,j} \subseteq \Sigma^* \times \mathbb{Z}^{k_j}$ *is a CERL.*
A CEFA representation of $\mathcal{R}$ *is a collection of CEFA tuples* $(\mathcal{A}_{i,1}, \cdots, \mathcal{A}_{i,l})_{i \in [n]}$ *such that* $\mathscr{L}(\mathcal{A}_{i,j}) = L_{i,j}$ *for every* $i \in [n]$ *and* $j \in [l]$*.*

4.2   Pre-images of CERLs Under String Operations

To unify the presentation, we consider string functions $f : (\Sigma^* \times \mathbb{Z}^{k_1}) \times \cdots \times (\Sigma^* \times \mathbb{Z}^{k_l}) \to \Sigma^*$. (If there is no integer input parameter, then $k_1, \cdots, k_l$ are zero.)

Definition 3 (Cost-enriched pre-images of CERLs). *Suppose that $f : (\Sigma^* \times \mathbb{Z}^{k_1}) \times \cdots \times (\Sigma^* \times \mathbb{Z}^{k_l}) \to \Sigma^*$ is a string function, $L \subseteq \Sigma^* \times \mathbb{Z}^{k_0}$ is a CERL defined by a CEFA $\mathcal{A} = (Q, \Sigma, R, \delta, I, F)$ with $R = (r_1, \cdots, r_{k_0})$. Then the R-cost-enriched pre-image of L under f, denoted by $f_R^{-1}(L)$, is a pair $(\mathcal{R}, t)$ such that*

- $\mathcal{R} \subseteq (\Sigma^* \times \mathbb{Z}^{k_1+k_0}) \times \cdots \times (\Sigma^* \times \mathbb{Z}^{k_l+k_0})$;
- $t = (t_1, \cdots, t_{k_0})$ *is a vector of linear integer terms where for each $i \in [k_0]$, t_i is a term whose variables are from $\left\{ r_i^{(1)}, \cdots, r_i^{(l)} \right\}$ which are fresh cost registers and are disjoint from R in $\mathcal{A}$;*
- L *is equal to the language comprising the k_0-cost-enriched strings*

$$\left(w_0, t_1 \left[d_1^{(1)}/r_1^{(1)}, \cdots, d_1^{(l)}/r_1^{(l)} \right], \cdots, t_{k_0} \left[d_{k_0}^{(1)}/r_{k_0}^{(1)}, \cdots, d_{k_0}^{(l)}/r_{k_0}^{(l)} \right] \right),$$

such that

$$w_0 = f((w_1, c_1), \cdots, (w_l, c_l)) \text{ for some } ((w_1, (c_1, d_1)), \cdots, (w_l, (c_l, d_l))) \in \mathcal{R},$$

where $c_j \in \mathbb{Z}^{k_j}$, $d_j = (d_1^{(j)}, \cdots, d_{k_0}^{(j)}) \in \mathbb{Z}^{k_0}$ for $j \in [l]$.

The R-cost-enriched pre-image of L under f, say $f_R^{-1}(L) = (\mathcal{R}, t)$, is said to be CERR-definable if $\mathcal{R}$ is a CERR.

Definition 3 is essentially a semantic definition of the pre-images. For the decision procedure, one desires an effective representation of a CERR-definable $f_R^{-1}(L) = (\mathcal{R}, t)$ in terms of CEFAs. Namely, a CEFA representation of $(\mathcal{R}, t)$ (where t_j is over $\left\{ r_j^{(1)}, \cdots, r_j^{(l)} \right\}$ for $j \in [k_0]$) is a tuple $((\mathcal{A}_{i,1}, \cdots, \mathcal{A}_{i,l})_{i \in [n]}, t)$ such that $(\mathcal{A}_{i,1}, \cdots, \mathcal{A}_{i,l})_{i \in [n]}$ is a CEFA representation of $\mathcal{R}$, where $R(\mathcal{A}_{i,j}) = \left(r'_{j,1}, \cdots, r'_{j,k_j}, r_1^{(j)}, \cdots, r_{k_0}^{(j)} \right)$ for each $i \in [n]$ and $j \in [l]$. (The cost registers $r'_{1,1}, \cdots, r'_{1,k_1}, \cdots, r'_{l,1}, \cdots, r'_{l,k_l}$ are mutually distinct and freshly introduced.)

Example 2 (substring$_R^{-1}(L)$). Let $\Sigma = \{a\}$ and $L = \{(w, |w|) \mid w \in \mathscr{L}((aa)^*)\}$. Evidently L is a CERL defined by a CEFA $\mathcal{A} = (Q, \Sigma, R, \delta, \{q_0\}, \{q_0\})$ with $Q = \{q_0, q_1\}$, $R = (r_1)$ and $\delta = \{(q_0, a, q_1), (q_1, a, q_0)\}$. Since substring is from $\Sigma^* \times \mathbb{Z}^2$ to Σ^*, substring$_R^{-1}(L)$, the R-cost-enriched pre-image of L under substring, is the pair $(\mathcal{R}, t)$, where $t = r_1^{(1)}$ (note that in this case $l = 1$, $k_0 = 1$, and $k_1 = 2$) and

$$\mathcal{R} = \{(w, n_1, n_2, n_2) \mid w \in \mathscr{L}(a^*), n_1 \geq 0, n_2 \geq 0, n_1 + n_2 \leq |w|, n_2 \text{ is even}\},$$

which is represented by $(\mathcal{A}', t)$ such that $\mathcal{A}' = (Q', \Sigma, R', \delta', I', F')$, where

– $Q' = Q \times \{p_0, p_1, p_2\}$, (Intuitively, p_0, p_1, and p_2 denote that the current position is before the starting position, between the starting position and ending position, and after the ending position of the substring respectively.)

– $R' = \left(r'_{1,1}, r'_{1,2}, r_1^{(1)}\right)$,

– $I' = \{(q_0, p_0)\}$, $F' = \{(q_0, p_2), (q_0, p_0)\}$ (where (q_0, p_0) is used to accept the 3-cost-enriched strings $(w, n_1, 0, 0)$ with $0 \leq n_1 \leq |w|$), and

– δ' is

$$\left\{ \begin{array}{l} (q_0, p_0) \xrightarrow{a, \eta_1} (q_0, p_0), (q_0, p_0) \xrightarrow{a, \eta_2} (q_1, p_1), (q_1, p_1) \xrightarrow{a, \eta_2} (q_0, p_1), \\ (q_0, p_1) \xrightarrow{a, \eta_2} (q_1, p_1), (q_1, p_1) \xrightarrow{a, \eta_2} (q_0, p_2), (q_0, p_2) \xrightarrow{a, \eta_3} (q_0, p_2) \end{array} \right\},$$

where $\eta_1(r'_{1,1}) = 1$, $\eta_1(r'_{1,2}) = 0$, $\eta_1(r_1^{(1)}) = 0$, $\eta_2(r'_{1,1}) = 0$, $\eta_2(r'_{1,2}) = 1$, and $\eta_2(r_1^{(1)}) = 1$, $\eta_3(r'_{1,1}) = 0$, $\eta_3(r'_{1,2}) = 0$, and $\eta_3(r_1^{(1)}) = 0$.

Therefore, $\mathsf{substring}_R^{-1}(L)$ is CERR-definable.

It turns out that for each string function f in the assignment statements of $\mathrm{SL}_{\mathrm{int}}$, the cost-enriched pre-images of CERLs under f are CERR-definable.

Proposition 1. *Let L be a CERL defined by a CEFA $\mathcal{A} = (Q, \Sigma, R, \delta, I, F)$. Then for each string function f ranging over $\cdot$, $\mathsf{replaceAll}_{e,u}$, $\mathsf{reverse}$, FFTs $\mathcal{T}$, and $\mathsf{substring}$, $f_R^{-1}(L)$ is CERR-definable. In addition,*

– *a CEFA representation of $\cdot_R^{-1}(L)$ can be computed in time $O(|\mathcal{A}|^2)$,*
– *a CEFA representation of $\mathsf{reverse}_R^{-1}(L)$ (resp. $\mathsf{substring}_R^{-1}(L)$) can be computed in time $O(|\mathcal{A}|)$,*
– *a CEFA representation of $(\mathcal{T}(\mathcal{T}))_R^{-1}(L)$ can be computed in time polynomial in $|\mathcal{A}|$ and exponential in $|\mathcal{T}|$,*
– *a CEFA representation of $(\mathsf{replaceAll}_{e,u})_R^{-1}(L)$ can be computed in time polynomial in $|\mathcal{A}|$ and exponential in $|e|$ and $|u|$.*

The proof of Proposition 1 is given in the full version [13].

4.3   The Decision Procedure

Let S be an $\mathrm{SL}_{\mathrm{int}}$ program. Without loss of generality, we assume that for every occurrence of assignments of the form $y := \mathsf{substring}(x, t_1, t_2)$, it holds that t_1 and t_2 are integer variables. This is not really a restriction, since, for instance, if in $y := \mathsf{substring}(x, t_1, t_2)$, neither t_1 nor t_2 is an integer variable, then we introduce fresh integer variables i and j, replace t_1, t_2 by i, j respectively, and add $\mathsf{assert}\,(i = t_1)\,; \mathsf{assert}\,(j = t_2)$ in S. We present a decision procedure for the path feasibility problem of S which is divided into five steps.

Step I: Reducing to atomic assertions.
Note first that in our language, each assertion is a positive Boolean combination of atomic formulas of the form $x \in \mathcal{A}$ or $t_1 \, o \, t_2$ (cf. Sect. 3). Nondeterministically choose, for each assertion $\mathsf{assert}\,(\varphi)$ of S, a set of atomic formulas $\Phi_\varphi = \{\alpha_1, \cdots, \alpha_n\}$ such that φ holds when atomic formulas in Φ_φ are true.

Then each assertion $\mathsf{assert}\,(\varphi)$ in S with $\Phi_\varphi = \{\alpha_1, \cdots, \alpha_n\}$ is replaced by $\mathsf{assert}\,(\alpha_1)\,;\cdots\,;\mathsf{assert}\,(\alpha_n)$, and thus S constrains atomic assertions only.

Step II: Dealing with the case splits in the semantics of $\mathsf{indexOf}_v$ and substring.
For each integer term of the form $\mathsf{indexOf}_v(x, i)$ in S, nondeterministically choose one of the following five options (which correspond to the semantics of $\mathsf{indexOf}_v$ in Sect. 3).

(1) Add $\mathsf{assert}\,(i < 0)$ to S, and replace $\mathsf{indexOf}_v(x, i)$ with $\mathsf{indexOf}_v(x, 0)$ in S.
(2) Add $\mathsf{assert}\,(i < 0)\,;\mathsf{assert}\,(x \in \mathscr{A}_{\overline{\Sigma^* v \Sigma^*}})$ to S; replace $\mathsf{indexOf}_v(x, i)$ with -1 in S.
(3) Add $\mathsf{assert}\,(i \geq \mathsf{length}(x))$ to S, and replace $\mathsf{indexOf}_v(x, i)$ with -1 in S.
(4) Add $\mathsf{assert}\,(i \geq 0)\,;\mathsf{assert}\,(i < \mathsf{length}(x))$ to S.
(5) Add

$$\mathsf{assert}\,(i \geq 0)\,;\mathsf{assert}\,(i < \mathsf{length}(x))\,;\mathsf{assert}\,(j = \mathsf{length}(x) - i)\,;$$
$$y := \mathsf{substring}(x, i, j);\mathsf{assert}\,(y \in \mathscr{A}_{\overline{\Sigma^* v \Sigma^*}})$$

to S, where y is a fresh string variable, j is a fresh integer variable, and $\mathscr{A}_{\overline{\Sigma^* v \Sigma^*}}$ is an NFA defining the language $\{w \in \Sigma^* \mid v$ does not occur as a substring in $w\}$. Replace $\mathsf{indexOf}_v(x, i)$ with -1 in S.

For each assignment $y := \mathsf{substring}(x, i, j)$, nondeterministically choose one of the following three options (which correspond to the semantics of substring in Sect. 3).

(1) Add the statements $\mathsf{assert}\,(i \geq 0)\,;\mathsf{assert}\,(i + j \leq \mathsf{length}(x))$ to S.
(2) Add the statements $\mathsf{assert}\,(i \geq 0)\,;\mathsf{assert}\,(i \leq \mathsf{length}(x))\,;\mathsf{assert}\,(i + j > \mathsf{length}(x));\mathsf{assert}\,(i' = \mathsf{length}(x) - i)$ to S, and replace $y := \mathsf{substring}(x, i, j)$ with $y := \mathsf{substring}(x, i, i')$, where i' is a fresh integer variable.
(3) Add the statement $\mathsf{assert}\,(i < 0)\,;\mathsf{assert}\,(y \in \mathscr{A}_\varepsilon)$ to S, and remove $y := \mathsf{substring}(x, i, j)$ from S, where $\mathscr{A}_\varepsilon$ is the NFA defining the language $\{\varepsilon\}$.

Step III: Removing length and indexOf.
For each term $\mathsf{length}(x)$ in S, we introduce a *fresh* integer variable i, replace every occurrence of $\mathsf{length}(x)$ by i, and add the statement $\mathsf{assert}\,(x \in \mathscr{A}_{\mathsf{len}}[i/r_1])$ to S. (See Example 1 for the definition of $\mathscr{A}_{\mathsf{len}}$.)

For each term $\mathsf{indexOf}_v(x, i)$ occurring in S, introduce two fresh integer variables i_1 and i_2, replace every occurrence of $\mathsf{indexOf}_v(x, i)$ by i_2, and add the statements $\mathsf{assert}\,(I = i_1)\,;\mathsf{assert}\,(x \in \mathscr{A}_{\mathsf{indexOf}_v}[i_1/r_1, i_2/r_2])$ to S.

Step IV: Removing the assignment statements backwards.
Repeat the following procedure until S contains no assignment statements.

Suppose $y := f(x_1, \boldsymbol{i_1}, \cdots, x_l, \boldsymbol{i_l})$ is the *last* assignment of S, where $f : (\Sigma^* \times \mathbb{Z}^{k_1}) \times \cdots \times (\Sigma^* \times \mathbb{Z}^{k_l}) \to \Sigma^*$ is a string function and $\boldsymbol{i_j} = (i_{j,1}, \cdots, i_{j,k_j})$ for each $j \in [l]$.

Let $\{\mathcal{A}_1, \cdots, \mathcal{A}_s\}$ be the set of all CEFAs such that $\mathsf{assert}\,(y \in \mathcal{A}_j)$ occurs in S for every $j \in [s]$. Let $j \in [s]$ and $R(\mathcal{A}_j) = (r_{j,1}, \cdots, r_{j,\ell_j})$. Then from Proposition 1, a CEFA representation of $f_{R(\mathcal{A}_j)}^{-1}(\mathscr{L}(\mathcal{A}_j))$, say

$$\left(\left(\mathcal{B}_{j,j'}^{(1)}, \cdots, \mathcal{B}_{j,j'}^{(l)} \right)_{j' \in [m_j]}, t \right), \text{ can be effectively computed from } \mathcal{A} \text{ and } f,$$

where we write

$$R\left(\mathcal{B}_{j,j'}^{(j'')} \right) = \left((r')_j^{(j'',1)}, \cdots, (r')_j^{(j'',k_{j''})}, r_{j,1}^{(j'')}, \cdots, r_{j,\ell_j}^{(j'')} \right)$$

for each $j' \in [m_j]$ and $j'' \in [l]$, and $t = (t_1, \cdots, t_{\ell_j})$. Note that the cost registers $(r')_j^{(1,1)}, \cdots, (r')_j^{(1,k_1)}, \cdots, (r')_j^{(l,1)}, \cdots, (r')_j^{(l,k_l)}, r_{j,1}^{(1)}, \cdots, r_{j,\ell_j}^{(1)}, \cdots,$ $r_{j,1}^{(l)}, \cdots, r_{j,\ell_j}^{(l)}$ are mutually distinct and freshly introduced, moreover, $R\left(\mathcal{B}_{j,j_1'}^{(j'')} \right) = R\left(\mathcal{B}_{j,j_2'}^{(j'')} \right)$ for distinct $j_1', j_2' \in [m_j]$.

Remove $y := f(x_1, i_1, \cdots, x_l, i_l)$, as well as all the statements $\mathsf{assert}\,(y \in \mathcal{A}_1), \cdots, \mathsf{assert}\,(y \in \mathcal{A}_s)$ from S. For every $j \in [s]$, nondeterministically choose $j' \in [m_j]$, and add the following statements to S,

$$\mathsf{assert}\left(x_1 \in \mathcal{B}_{j,j'}^{(1)} \right); \cdots ; \mathsf{assert}\left(x_l \in \mathcal{B}_{j,j'}^{(l)} \right); S_{j,j',i_1,\cdots,i_l}; S_{j,t}$$

where

$$S_{j,j',i_1,\cdots,i_l} \equiv \mathsf{assert}\left(i_{1,1} = (r')_{j,j'}^{(1,1)} \right); \cdots ; \mathsf{assert}\left(i_{1,k_1} = (r')_{j,j'}^{(1,k_1)} \right);$$

$$\cdots$$

$$\mathsf{assert}\left(i_{l,1} = (r')_{j,j'}^{(l,1)} \right); \cdots ; \mathsf{assert}\left(i_{l,k_l} = (r')_{j,j'}^{(l,k_l)} \right)$$

and

$$S_{j,t} \equiv \mathsf{assert}\,(r_{j,1} = t_1); \cdots, \mathsf{assert}\left(r_{j,\ell_j} = t_{\ell_j} \right).$$

Step V: Final satisfiability checking.

In this step, S contains no assignment statements and only assertions of the form $\mathsf{assert}\,(x \in \mathcal{A})$ and $\mathsf{assert}\,(t_1 \circ t_2)$ where $\mathcal{A}$ are CEFAs and t_1, t_2 are linear integer terms. Let X denote the set of string variables occurring in S. For each $x \in X$, let $\Lambda_x = \{\mathcal{A}_x^1, \cdots, \mathcal{A}_x^{s_x}\}$ denote the set of CEFAs $\mathcal{A}$ such that $\mathsf{assert}\,(x \in \mathcal{A})$ appears in S. Moreover, let ϕ denote the conjunction of all the LIA formulas $t_1 \circ t_2$ occurring in S. It is straightforward to observe that ϕ is over $R' = \bigcup_{x \in X, j \in [s_x]} R(\mathcal{A}_x^j)$. Then the path feasibility of S is reduced to *the satisfiability problem of LIA formulas w.r.t. CEFAs (abbreviated as* $\mathrm{SAT}_{\mathrm{CEFA}}[\mathrm{LIA}]$ *problem)* which is defined as

deciding whether ϕ is satisfiable w.r.t. $(\Lambda_x)_{x \in X}$, namely, whether there are an assignment function $\theta : R' \to \mathbb{Z}$ and strings $(w_x)_{x \in X}$ such that $\phi[\theta(R')/R']$ holds and $(w_x, \theta(R(\mathcal{A}_x^j))) \in \mathscr{L}(\mathcal{A}_x^j)$ for every $x \in X$ and $j \in [s_x]$.

This $\mathrm{SAT}_{\mathrm{CEFA}}[\mathrm{LIA}]$ problem is decidable and PSPACE-complete; The proof can be found in the full version [13].

Proposition 2. $\mathrm{SAT_{CEFA}}[\mathrm{LIA}]$ *is* PSPACE-*complete.*

An example to illustrate the decision procedure can be found in the full version [13].

Complexity Analysis of the Decision Procedure. Step I and Step II can be done in nondeterministic linear time. Step III can be done in linear time. In Step IV, for each input string variable x in S, at most exponentially many CEFAs can be generated for x, each of which is of at most exponential size. Therefore, Step IV can be done in nondeterministic exponential space. By Proposition 2, Step V can be done in exponential space. Therefore, we conclude that the path feasibility problem of $\mathrm{SL_{int}}$ programs is in NEXPSPACE, thus in EXPSPACE by Savitch's theorem [23].

Remark 2. In this paper, we focus on functional finite transducers (cf. Sect. 2). Our decision procedure is applicable to general finite transducers as well with minor adaptation. However, the EXPSPACE complexity upper-bound does not hold any more, because the distributive property $f^{-1}(L_1 \cap L_2) = f^{-1}(L_1) \cap f^{-1}(L_2)$ for regular languages L_1, L_2 only holds for functional finite transducers f.

5 Evaluations

We have implemented the decision procedure presented in the preceding section based on the recent string constraint solver OSTRICH [14], resulting in a new solver OSTRICH+. OSTRICH is written in Scala and based on the SMT solver Princess [25]. OSTRICH+ reuses the parser of Princess, but replaces the NFAs from OSTRICH with CEFAs. Correspondingly, in OSTRICH+, the pre-image computation for concatenation, replaceAll, reverse, and finite transducers is reimplemented, and a new pre-image operator for substring is added. OSTRICH+ also implements CEFA constructions for length and indexOf. More details can be found in the full version [13].

We have compared OSTRICH+ with some of the state-of-the-art solvers on a wide range of benchmarks. We discuss the benchmarks in Sect. 5.1 and present the experimental results in Sect. 5.2.

5.1 Benchmarks

Our evaluation focuses on problems that combine string with integer constraints. To this end, we consider the following four sets of benchmarks, all in SMT-LIB 2 format.

TRANSDUCER+ is derived from the TRANSDUCER benchmark suite of OSTRICH [14]. The TRANSDUCER suite involves seven transducers: toUpper (replacing all lowercase letters with their uppercase ones) and its dual toLower, htmlEscape and its dual htmlUnescape, escapeString, addslashes, and trim. These transducers are collected from Stranger [33] and SLOTH [18]. Initially none of the benchmarks involved integers. In TRANSDUCER+, we encode four security-relevant properties of transducers [19], with the help of the functions charAt and length:

- idempotence: given $\mathcal{T}$, whether $\forall x.\ \mathcal{T}(\mathcal{T}(x)) = \mathcal{T}(x)$;
- duality: given $\mathcal{T}_1$ and $\mathcal{T}_2$, whether $\forall x.\ \mathcal{T}_2(\mathcal{T}_1(x)) = x$;
- commutativity: given $\mathcal{T}_1$ and $\mathcal{T}_2$, whether $\forall x.\ \mathcal{T}_2(\mathcal{T}_1(x)) = \mathcal{T}_1(\mathcal{T}_2(x))$;
- equivalence: given $\mathcal{T}_1$ and $\mathcal{T}_2$, whether $\forall x.\ \mathcal{T}_1(x) = \mathcal{T}_2(x)$.

Table 1. Experimental results on different benchmark suites. '–' means that the tool is not applicable to the benchmark suite, and 'inconclusive' means that a tool gave up, timed out, or crashed.

Benchmark	Output	CVC4	Z3-str3	Z3-Trau	OSTRICH[1]	OSTRICH[2]	OSTRICH+
TRANSDUCER+ Total: 94	sat	–	–	–	0	0	84
	unsat	–	–	–	1	1	4
	inconcl.	–	–	–	93	93	6
SLOG+(REPLACEALL) Total: 120	sat	104	–	–	0	0	98
	unsat	11	–	–	7	5	12
	inconcl.	5	–	–	113	115	10
SLOG+(REPLACE) Total: 3,391	sat	1,309	878	–	0	169	584
	unsat	2,082	2,066	–	2,079	2,075	2,082
	inconcl.	0	447	–	1,312	1,147	725
PYEX-td Total: 5,569	sat	4,224	4,068	4,266	68	96	4,141
	unsat	1,284	1,289	1,295	95	93	1,203
	inconcl.	61	212	8	5,406	5,380	225
PYEX-z3 Total: 8,414	sat	6,346	6,040	7,003	76	100	5,489
	unsat	1,358	1,370	1,394	61	53	1,239
	inconcl.	710	1,004	17	8,277	8,261	1,686
PYEX-zz Total: 11,438	sat	10,078	8,804	10,129	71	98	9,033
	unsat	1,204	1,207	1,222	91	61	868
	inconcl.	156	1,427	87	11,276	11,279	1,537
KALUZA Total: 47,284	sat	35,264	33,438	34,769	23,397	28,522	27,962
	unsat	12,014	11,799	12,014	10,445	10,445	9,058
	inconcl.	6	2,047	501	13,442	8,317	10,264
Total: 76,310	solved	75,278	70,959	72,092	36,391	41,718	61,857
	unsolved	1,032	5,351	4,218	39,919	34,592	14,453

For instance, we encode the non-idempotence of $\mathcal{T}$ into the path feasibility of the $\mathrm{SL}_{\mathrm{int}}$ program $y := \mathcal{T}(x); z := \mathcal{T}(y); S_{y \neq z}$, where y and z are two fresh string variables, and $S_{y \neq z}$ is the $\mathrm{SL}_{\mathrm{int}}$ program encoding $y \neq z$ (see the full version [13] for the details). We also include in TRANSDUCER+ three instances generated from a program to sanitize URLs against XSS attacks (see the full version [13] for the details), where $\mathcal{T}_{\mathrm{trim}}$ is used. In total, we obtain 94 instances for the TRANSDUCER+ suite.

SLOG+ is adapted from the SLOG benchmark suite [31], containing 3,511 instances about strings only. We obtain SLOG+ by choosing a string variable x for each instance, and adding the statement $\mathsf{assert}\,(\mathsf{length}(x) < 2\mathsf{indexOf}_A (x, 0))$ for some $a \in \Sigma$. As in [14], we split SLOG+ into SLOG+(REPLACE) and SLOG+(REPLACEALL), comprising 3,391 and 120 instances respectively.

In addition to the indexOf and length functions, the benchmarks use regular constraints and concatenation; SLOG+(REPLACE) also contains the replace function (replacing the first occurrence), while SLOG+(REPLACEALL) uses the replaceAll function (replacing all occurrences).

PYEX [24] contains 25,421 instances derived by the PyEx tool, a symbolic execution engine for Python programs. The PYEX suite was generated by the CVC4 group from four popular Python packages: httplib2, pip, pymongo, and requests. These instances use regular constraints, concatenation, length, substring, and indexOf functions. Following [24], the PYEX suite is further divided into three parts: PYEX-td, PYEX-z3 and PYEX-zz, comprising 5,569, 8,414 and 11,438 instances, respectively.

KALUZA [26] is the most well-known benchmark suite in literature, containing 47,284 instances with regular constraints, concatenation, and the length function. The 47,284 benchmarks include 28,032 satisfiable and 9,058 unsatisfiable problems in SSA form.

5.2 Experiments

We compare OSTRICH+ to CVC4 [20], Z3-str3 [34], and Z3-Trau [9], as well as two configurations of OSTRICH [14] with standard NFAs. The configuration OSTRICH$^{(1)}$ is a direct implementation of the algorithm in [14], and does not support integer functions. In OSTRICH$^{(2)}$, we integrated support for the length function as in Norn [2], based on the computation of length abstractions of regular languages, and handle indexOf, substring, and charAt via an encoding to word equations. The experiments are executed on a computer with an Intel Xeon Silver 4210 2.20 GHz and 2.19 GHz CPU (2-core) and 8 GB main memory, running 64bit Ubuntu 18.04 LTS OS and Java 1.8. We use a timeout of 30 s (wall-clock time), and report the number of satisfiable and unsatisfiable problems solved by each of the systems. Table 1 summarises the experimental results. We did not observe incorrect answers by any tool.

There are two additional state-of-the-art solvers Slent and Trau+ which were not included in the evaluation. We exclude Slent [32] because it uses its own input format laut, which is different from the SMT-LIB 2 format used for our benchmarks; also, TRANSDUCER+ is beyond the scope of Slent. Trau+ [3] integrates Trau with Sloth to deal with both finite transducers and integer constraints. We were unfortunately unable to obtain a working version of Trau+, possibly because Trau requires two separate versions of Z3 to run. In addition, the algorithm in [3] focuses on length-preserving transducers, which means that TRANSDUCER+ is beyond the scope of Trau+.

OSTRICH+ and OSTRICH are the only tools applicable to the problems in TRANSDUCER+. With a timeout of 30 s, OSTRICH+ can solve 88 of the benchmarks, but this number rises to 94 when using a longer timeout of 600 s. Given the complexity of those benchmarks, this is an encouraging result. OSTRICH can only solve one of the benchmarks, because the encoding of charAt in the benchmarks using equations almost always leads to problems that are not in SSA form.

On SLOG+(REPLACEALL), OSTRICH+ and CVC4 are very close: OSTRICH+ solves 98 satisfiable instances, slightly less than the 104 instances solved by CVC4, while OSTRICH+ solves one more unsatisfiable instance than CVC4 (12 versus 11). The suite is beyond the scope of Z3-str3 and Z3-Trau, which do not support replaceAll.

On SLOG+(REPLACE), OSTRICH+, CVC4, and Z3-str3 solve a similar number of unsatisfiable problems, while CVC4 solves the largest number of satisfiable instances (1,309). The suite is beyond the scope of Z3-Trau which does not support replace.

On the three PYEX suites, Z3-Trau consistently solves the largest number of instances by some margin. OSTRICH+ solves a similar number of instances as Z3-str3. Interpreting the results, however, it has to be taken into account that PYEX includes 1,334 instances that are *not* in SSA form, which are beyond the scope of OSTRICH+.

The KALUZA problems can be solved most effectively by CVC4. OSTRICH+ can solve almost all of the around 80% of the benchmarks that are in SSA form, however.

OSTRICH+ consistently outperforms OSTRICH[1] and OSTRICH[2] in the evaluation, except for the KALUZA benchmarks. For OSTRICH[1], this is expected because most benchmarks considered here contain integer functions. For OSTRICH[2], it turns out that the encoding of indexOf, substring, and charAt as word equations usually leads to problems that are not in SSA form, and therefore are beyond the scope of OSTRICH.

In summary, we observe that OSTRICH+ is competitive with other solvers, while is able to handle benchmarks that are beyond the scope of the other tools due to the combination of string functions (in particular transducers) and integer constraints. Interestingly, the experiments show that OSTRICH+, at least in its current state, is better at solving unsatisfiable problems than satisfiable problems; this might be an artefact of the use of nuXmv for analysing products of CEFAs. We expect that further optimisation of our algorithm will lead to additional performance improvements. For instance, a natural optimisation that is to be included in our implementation is to use standard finite automata, as opposed to CEFAs, for simpler problems such as the KALUZA benchmarks. Such a combination of automata representations is mostly an engineering effort.

6   Conclusion

In this paper, we have proposed an expressive string constraint language which can specify constraints on both strings and integers. We provided an automata-theoretic decision procedure for the path feasibility problem of this language. The decision procedure is simple, generic, and amenable to implementation, giving rise to a new solver OSTRICH+. We have evaluated OSTRICH+ on a wide range of existing and newly created benchmarks, and have obtained very encouraging results. OSTRICH+ is shown to be the first solver which is capable of tackling finite transducers and integer constraints with completeness guarantees. Meanwhile, it demonstrates competitive performance against some of the best state-of-the-art string constraint solvers.

Acknowledgements. T. Chen and Z. Wu are supported by Guangdong Science and Technology Department grant (No. 2018B010107004); T. Chen is also supported by Overseas Grant (KFKT2018A16) from the State Key Laboratory of Novel Software Technology, Nanjing University, China and Natural Science Foundation of Guangdong Province, China (No. 2019A1515011689). M. Hague is supported by EPSRC [EP/T00021X/1];. A. Lin is supported by the European Research Council (ERC) under the European Union's Horizon 2020 research and innovation programme (grant agreement no 759969). P. Rümmer is supported by the Swedish Research Council (VR) under grant 2018-04727, and by the Swedish Foundation for Strategic Research (SSF) under the project WebSec (Ref. RIT17-0011). Z. Wu is supported by the Open Project of Shanghai Key Laboratory of Trustworthy Computing (No. 07dz22304201601), the NSFC grants (No. 61872340), and the INRIA-CAS joint research project VIP.

References

1. Abdulla, P.A., et al.: Flatten and conquer: a framework for efficient analysis of string constraints. In: PLDI, pp. 602–617 (2017)
2. Abdulla, P.A., et al.: String constraints for verification. In: CAV, pp. 150–166 (2014)
3. Abdulla, P.A., Atig, M.F., Diep, B.P., Holík, L., Janku, P.: Chain-free string constraints. In: ATVA, pp. 277–293 (2019)
4. Alur, R., D'Antoni, L., Deshmukh, J., Raghothaman, M., Yuan, Y.: Regular functions and cost register automata. In: LICS, pp. 13–22. IEEE Computer Society (2013)
5. Barceló, P., Figueira, D., Libkin, L.: Graph logics with rational relations. Logical Meth. Comput. Sci. **9**(3) (2013)
6. Berzish, M., Ganesh, V., Zheng, Y.: Z3str3: a string solver with theory-aware heuristics. In: FMCAD, pp. 55–59 (2017)
7. Bjørner, N., Tillmann, N., Voronkov, A.: Path feasibility analysis for string-manipulating programs. In: TACAS, pp. 307–321 (2009)
8. Büchi, J.R., Senger, S.: Definability in the existential theory of concatenation and undecidable extensions of this theory. In: Collected Works of J. R. Büchi, pp. 671–683 (1990)
9. Bui, D. and contributors. Z3-trau (2019)
10. Bultan, T. and contributors. Abc string solver (2015)
11. Cadar, C., Sen, K.: Symbolic execution for software testing: three decades later. Commun. ACM **56**(2), 82–90 (2013)
12. Chen, T., Chen, Y., Hague, M., Lin, A.W., Wu, Z.: What is decidable about string constraints with the replaceall function. PACMPL **2**(POPL), 3:1–3:29 (2018)
13. Chen, T., et al.: A decision procedure for path feasibility of string manipulating programs with integer data type (full version) (2020). http://arxiv.org/abs/2007.06913
14. Chen, T., Hague, M., Lin, A.W., Rümmer, P., Wu., Z.: Decision procedures for path feasibility of string-manipulating programs with complex operations. PACMPL, **3**(POPL) (2019)
15. Day, J.D., Ganesh, V., He, P. , Manea, F., Nowotka, D.: RP, pp. 15–29 (2018)

16. de Moura, L., Bjørner, N.: Z3: an efficient SMT solver. In: TACAS, pp. 337–340 (2008)
17. Ganesh, V., Minnes, M., Solar-Lezama, A., Rinard, M.C.: Word equations with length constraints: what's decidable? HVC **2012**, 209–226 (2012)
18. Holík, L., Janku, P., Lin, A.W., Rümmer, P., Vojna, T.: String constraints with concatenation and transducers solved efficiently. PACMPL **2**(POPL), 4:1–4:32 (2018)
19. Hooimeijer, P., Livshits, B., Molnar, D., Saxena, P., Veanes, M.: Fast and precise sanitizer analysis with BEK. In: USENIX Security Symposium (2011)
20. Liang, T., Reynolds, A., Tinelli, C., Barrett, C., Deters, M.: DPLL(T) theory solver for a theory of strings and regular expressions. In: CAV, pp. 646–662 (2014)
21. Lin, A.W., Barceló, P.: String solving with word equations and transducers: towards a logic for analysing mutation XSS. In: POPL, pp. 123–136. ACM (2016)
22. Lin, A.W., Majumdar, R.: Quadratic word equations with length constraints, counter systems, and presburger arithmetic with divisibility. In: ATVA, pp. 352–369 (2018)
23. Papadimitriou, C.H.: Computational Complexity. Addison-Wesley, Reading (1994)
24. Reynolds, A., Woo, M., Barrett, C., Brumley, D., Liang, T., Tinelli, C.: Scaling Up DPLL(T) string solvers using context-dependent simplification. In: Majumdar, R., Kunčak, V. (eds.) CAV 2017. LNCS, vol. 10427, pp. 453–474. Springer, Cham (2017). https://doi.org/10.1007/978-3-319-63390-9_24
25. Rümmer, P.: A constraint sequent calculus for first-order logic with linear integer arithmetic. In: LPAR, pp. 274–289 (2008)
26. Saxena, P., Akhawe, D., Hanna, S., Mao, F., McCamant, S., Song, D.: A symbolic execution framework for Javascript. In: S&P, pp. 513–528 (2010)
27. Trinh, M., Chu, D., Jaffar, J.: S3: a symbolic string solver for vulnerability detection in web applications. In: CCS, pp. 1232–1243 (2014)
28. Trinh, M.-T., Chu, D.-H., Jaffar, J.: Progressive reasoning over recursively-defined strings. In: Chaudhuri, S., Farzan, A. (eds.) CAV 2016. LNCS, vol. 9779, pp. 218–240. Springer, Cham (2016). https://doi.org/10.1007/978-3-319-41528-4_12
29. van der Stock, A., Glas, B., Smithline, N., Gigler, T.: OWASP Top 10–2017 (2017)
30. Verma, K.N., Seidl, H., Schwentick, T.: On the complexity of equational horn clauses. In: CADE, pp. 337–352 (2005)
31. Wang, H.-E., Tsai, T.-L., Lin, C.-H., Yu, F., Jiang, J.-H.R.: String analysis via automata manipulation with logic circuit representation. In: Chaudhuri, S., Farzan, A. (eds.) CAV 2016. LNCS, vol. 9779, pp. 241–260. Springer, Cham (2016). https://doi.org/10.1007/978-3-319-41528-4_13
32. Wang, H.-E., Chen, S.-Y., Yu, F., Jiang, J.-H.R.: A symbolic model checking approach to the analysis of string and length constraints. In: ASE, pp. 623–633. ACM (2018)
33. Yu, F., Alkhalaf, M., Bultan, T., Ibarra, O.H.: Automata-based symbolic string analysis for vulnerability detection. Formal Methods Syst. Des. **44**(1), 44–70 (2013). https://doi.org/10.1007/s10703-013-0189-1
34. Zheng, Y., Zhang, X., Ganesh, V.: Z3-str: a Z3-based string solver for web application analysis. In: ESEC/SIGSOFT FSE, pp. 114–124 (2013)

From Checking to Inference: Actual Causality Computations as Optimization Problems

Amjad Ibrahim[(⊠)] and Alexander Pretschner

Department of Informatics, Technical University of Munich, Munich, Germany
{ibrahim,pretschn}@in.tum.de

Abstract. Actual causality is increasingly well understood. Recent formal approaches, proposed by Halpern and Pearl, have made this concept mature enough to be amenable to automated reasoning. Actual causality is especially vital for building accountable, explainable systems. Among other reasons, causality reasoning is computationally hard due to the requirements of counterfactuality and the minimality of causes. Previous approaches presented either inefficient or restricted, and domain-specific, solutions to the problem of automating causality reasoning. In this paper, we present a novel approach to formulate different notions of causal reasoning, over binary acyclic models, as optimization problems, based on quantifiable notions within counterfactual computations. We contribute and compare *two* compact, non-trivial, and sound integer linear programming (ILP) and Maximum Satisfiability (MaxSAT) encodings to *check* causality. Given a candidate cause, both approaches identify what a minimal cause is. Also, we present an ILP encoding to *infer* causality without requiring a candidate cause. We show that both notions are efficiently automated. Using models with more than 8000 variables, checking is computed in a matter of seconds, with MaxSAT outperforming ILP in many cases. In contrast, inference is computed in a matter of minutes.

1 Introduction

Actual causality is the retrospective linking of *effects* to *causes* [13,30]. As part of their cognition, humans reason about actual causality to explain particular past events, to control future events, or to attribute moral responsibility and legal liability [14]. Similar to humans, it is useful for systems in investigating security protocols [21], safety accidents [22], software or hardware models [5,9,23], and database queries [28]. More importantly, actual causality is central for enabling social constructs such as accountability in Cyber-Physical systems [16,17,19], in information systems [10], and explainability in artificial intelligence systems [29].

Work supported by the Deutsche Forschungsgemeinschaft (DFG, German Research Foundation) under grant no. PR1266/4-1, Conflict resolution and causal inference with integrated socio-technical models.

© Springer Nature Switzerland AG 2020
D. V. Hung and O. Sokolsky (Eds.): ATVA 2020, LNCS 12302, pp. 343–359, 2020.
https://doi.org/10.1007/978-3-030-59152-6_19

Attempts to formalize a precise definition of an *actual cause* go back to the eighteenth century when Hume [15] introduced *counterfactual reasoning*. Simply put, counterfactual reasoning concludes that event A is a cause of event B if B does not occur if A does not occur. However, this simple reasoning cannot be used with interdependent, multi-factorial, and complex causes [24]. Recently, Halpern and Pearl formalized HP–a seminal model-based definition of actual causality that addresses many of the challenges facing naive counterfactual reasoning [13].

Because of its formal foundation, HP enables automated causality reasoning. We distinguish two notions of reasoning: *checking* and *inference*. *Checking* refers to verifying if a candidate cause is an actual cause of an effect, i.e., answering the question "is $\vec{X}$ a cause of φ?" *Inference* involves finding a cause without any candidates, i.e., answering the question "why φ?" Using HP, causality checking is, in general, D_1^P-complete and *NP*-complete for singleton (one-event) causes [12]; the difference is due to a minimality requirement in the definition (details in Sect. 2). Intuitively, *inference* is at least as hard. The complexity led to restricted (e.g., singleton causes, single-equation models [28]) utilizations of HP (Sect. 5). All these utilizations exploit domain-specificities (e.g., database repairs [28,33] [6]), which hinders taking advantage of the available approximations for general queries. In prior work, we proposed an approach to *check* causality in acyclic models *with binary variables* based on the satisfiability problem (SAT) [18]. The approach required enumerating all the satisfying assignments of a formula (ALL-SAT), which obviously is impacted by the solver's performance [35]. Thus, previous approaches fail to automate answering queries for larger models.

Large models of causal factors are likely to occur especially when generated automatically from other sources for purposes of accountability and explainability [16,17,29]. Further, models of real-world accidents are sufficiently large to require efficient approaches. For instance, a model of the 2002 mid-air collision in Germany consists of 95 factors [34] (discussed in [17]). Thus, in this paper, we present a novel approach to formulate actual causality computations in binary models as optimization problems. We show how to construct quantifiable notions within counterfactual computations, and use them for checking and inference.

We encode our checking approach as integer linear programs (ILP), or weighted MaxSAT formulae [25]. Both are well-suited alternatives for Boolean optimization problems. However, MaxSAT has an inherent advantage with binary propositional constraints [25]. On the other hand, ILP has an expressive objective language that allows us to tackle the problem of causality inference as a multi-objective program. Accordingly, we contribute an approach with *three* encodings. The first two cover causality *checking*, and better they can determine a *minimal* HP cause from a potentially non-minimal candidate cause; we refer to this ability as *semi-inference*. The third encoding tackles causality *inference*. All these encodings benefit from the rapid development in solving complex and large (tens of thousands of variables and constraints) optimization problems [2,20].

We consider our work to be the first to provide an efficient solution to the problem of checking and inferring HP causality, for a large class of models (binary models) without any dependency on domain-specific technologies. We contribute:

1.) A sound formulation of causality computations for acyclic binary models as optimization problems, **2.)** A Java library[1] that implements the approaches. **3.)** An empirical evaluation, using models from multiple domains, of the efficiency and scalability of the approaches in comparison with previous work.

2 Halpern-Pearl Definition of Actual Causality

HP uses variables to describe the world, and *structural equations* to define its mechanics [30]. The variables are split into *exogenous* and *endogenous*. The values of the former, called a *context* $\vec{u}$, are governed by factors that are not part of the modeled world (they represent the environment). The endogenous variables, in contrast, are determined by equations of exogenous and endogenous variables. In this formulation, we look at causes within a specified universe of discourse represented by the endogenous variables, while exogenous variables are not considered to be part of a cause but rather as given information. An equation represents the semantics of the dependency of the endogenous variable on other variables. Similar to Halpern, we limit ourselves to acyclic models in which we can compute a unique solution for the equations given a context $\vec{u}$, which we refer to as *actual evaluation* of the model. A binary model (Boolean variables only) is formalized in Definition 1.

Definition 1. *[30]* **Binary Causal Model**
A causal model is a tuple $M = (\mathcal{U}, \mathcal{V}, \mathcal{R}, \mathcal{F})$, where

- $\mathcal{U}$, $\mathcal{V}$ *are sets of exogenous variables and endogenous variables respectively,*
- $\mathcal{R}$ *associates with $Y \in \mathcal{U} \cup \mathcal{V}$ a set of possible values $\mathcal{R}(Y)$, i.e., $\{0,1\}$,*
- $\mathcal{F}$ *maps $X \in \mathcal{V}$ to a function $F_X : (\times_{U \in \mathcal{U}} \mathcal{R}(U)) \times (\times_{Y \in \mathcal{V} \setminus \{X\}} \mathcal{R}(Y)) \rightarrow \{0,1\}$*

Definition 1 makes precise the fact that F_X determines the value of X, given the values of all the other variables. We summarize the causality notations before defining the cause in Definition 2. A *primitive event* is a formula of the form $X = x$, for $X \in \mathcal{V}$ and x is a value $\in \{0,1\}$. A sequence of variables $X_1, ..., X_n$ is abbreviated as $\vec{X}$. Analogously, $X_1 = x_1, ..., X_n = x_n$ is abbreviated $\vec{X} = \vec{x}$. φ is a Boolean combination of such events. $(M, \vec{u}) \models X = x$ if the variable X has value x in the unique solution to the equations in M given context $\vec{u}$. The value of variable Y can be overwritten by a value y (known as an intervention) writing $Y \leftarrow y$ (analogously $\vec{Y} \leftarrow \vec{y}$ for vectors). Then, a causal formula is of the form $[Y_1 \leftarrow y_1, ..., Y_k \leftarrow y_k]\varphi$, where $Y_1, ..., Y_k$ are variables in $\mathcal{V}$ that make φ hold when they are set to $y_1, .., y_k$. We write $(M, \vec{u}) \models \varphi$ if the causal formula φ is true in M given $\vec{u}$. Lastly, $(M, \vec{u}) \models [\vec{Y} \leftarrow \vec{y}]\varphi$ holds if we replace variable equations' in $\vec{Y}$ by equations of the form $Y = y$ denoted by $(M_{\vec{Y}=\vec{y}}, \vec{u}) \models \varphi$ [13].

Definition 2. **Actual Cause** *[12]*
$\vec{X} = \vec{x}$ *is an actual cause of φ in $(M, \vec{u})$ if the following three conditions hold:*

---

[1] https://github.com/amjadKhalifah/HP2SAT1.0/tree/hp-optimization-library.

AC1. $(M, \vec{u}) \models (\vec{X} = \vec{x})$ and $(M, \vec{u}) \models \varphi$.

AC2. There is a set $\vec{W}$ of variables in $\mathcal{V}$ and a setting $\vec{x}'$ of the variables in $\vec{X}$ such that if $(M, \vec{u}) \models \vec{W} = \vec{w}$, then $(M, \vec{u}) \models [\vec{X} \leftarrow \vec{x}', \vec{W} \leftarrow \vec{w}]\neg\varphi$.

AC3. $\vec{X}$ is minimal: no non-empty subset of $\vec{X}$ satisfies AC1 and AC2.

AC1 checks that the cause $\vec{X} = \vec{x}$ and the effect φ occurred within the actual evaluation of M given context $\vec{u}$, i.e., the cause is sufficient for the occurrence of the effect. AC2 checks the counterfactual (necessary) relation between the cause and effect. It holds if there exists a setting $\vec{x}'$ for the cause variables $\vec{X}$ different from the actual evaluation $\vec{x}$ (in binary models such a setting is the negation of the actual setting [18]), and another set of variables $\vec{W}$, referred to as a contingency set, that we use to *fix* variables at their actual values, such that φ does not occur. The contingency set $\vec{W}$ is meant to deal with issues such as preemption and redundancy. Preemption is a problematic situation where multiple possible causes coincide (illustrated by an example below) [24]; thus a naive counterfactual check cannot determine the cause [23]. AC3 checks that $\vec{X}$ is minimal in fulfilling the previous conditions. To check a cause, we need to think of two worlds (variable assignments): the *actual* world with all the values known to us, and the counterfactual one in which the *cause* and *effect* take on different values. Two factors further complicate the search for this counterfactual world. First, finding an arbitrary $\vec{W}$, such that AC2 holds which is exponential in the worst case. Second, no (non-empty) subset of $\vec{X}$ is sufficient for constructing such a counterfactual world. Halpern shows that checking causality is in general D_1^P-complete [1,12], i.e., checking *AC1* is P, checking *AC2* is NP-complete, and checking *AC3* is $co-NP$-complete. Complexity considerations for binary models suggest a reduction to SAT or ILP [12]; in this paper, we show concrete ILP and MaxSAT formulations to check, and an ILP formulation to infer a cause.

Example: *Throwing rocks* [24] is a problematic example from philosophy: Suzy and Billy both throw a rock at a bottle that shatters if one of them hits. We know Suzy's rock hits the bottle slightly earlier than Billy's and both are accurate throwers. Halpern models this story using the endogenous variables ST, BT for "Suzy/Billy throws", with values 0 (the person does not throw) and 1 (s/he does), SH, BH for "Suzy/Billy hits", and BS for "bottle shatters." Two exogenous variables ST_{exo}, BT_{exo} are used to set the values. The equations:

$$- ST = ST_{exo} \qquad - BT = BT_{exo} \qquad - SH = ST$$
$$- BH = BT \wedge \neg SH \qquad - BS = SH \vee BH$$

Assuming a context (exogenous variables' values) $\vec{U} = \vec{u}$: $ST_{exo} = 1, BT_{exo} = 1$ (both actually threw), the actual evaluation of the model is: $ST = 1$, $BT = 1$, $BH = 0$, $SH = 1$, and $BS = 1$. Assume we want to *check* whether $ST = 1$ is a cause of $BS = 1$, i.e., is Suzy's throw a cause for the bottle shattering? Obviously, AC1 is fulfilled as both appear in the actual evaluation. As a candidate cause, we set $ST = 0$ (for binary models a candidate cause is negated to check counterfactuality; see Lemma 1 in [18]). A first attempt with $\vec{W} = \emptyset$ shows that AC2 does *not* hold. However, if we randomly let $\vec{W} = \{BH\}$, i.e., we replace the equation of BH with $BH = 0$, then AC2 holds because $(M, \vec{u}) \models [ST \leftarrow 0, BH \leftarrow 0]BS = 0$, and AC3 automatically holds since the cause is a singleton. Thus, $ST = 1$ is a cause of $BS = 1$. Let us check if $ST = 1 \wedge BT = 1$ is a cause for $BS = 1$. AC1 and AC2 hold (obviously if they both did not throw, the bottle would not shatter with a $\vec{W} = \emptyset$) but AC3 does not. As we saw earlier, $ST = 1$ alone satisfies AC2. Hence $ST = 1 \wedge BT = 1$ are not a cause.

As opposed to the all-or-nothing treatment of causality, Chockler and Halpern added ([8], modified in [13]) a notion of *responsibility* to a cause. They introduced a metric, degree of responsibility (dr), that "measures the minimal number of changes needed to make φ counterfactually depend on X."[2] Definition 3 shows a shortened version of dr [8,13], which we use for causality inference in our work.

Definition 3. *The degree of responsibility of $X = x$ w.r.t. a cause $\vec{X} = \vec{x}$ for φ, denoted $dr((\vec{X} = \vec{x}), (X = x), \varphi)$, is 0 if $X = x$ is not in $\vec{X} = \vec{x}$; otherwise is $1/(|\vec{W}| + |\vec{X}|)$ given that $|\vec{W}|$ is the smallest set of variables that satisfies AC2.*

3   Approach

Given the triviality of AC1, we presented in prior work, a SAT-based approach to check causality, focusing on AC2 [18]. The contribution was in how AC2 is encoded into a formula F, so that an efficient conclusion of $\vec{W}$ without iterating over the power-set of all variables, is possible. Briefly, F described a counterfactual world that incorporated (1) $\neg\varphi$, (2) a context $\vec{u}$ (size n), (3) a setting $\vec{x}'$ for a candidate cause, $\vec{X}$, and (4) a method to infer $\vec{W}$, while maintaining the semantics of M. Because checking is done in hindsight, we have the actual evaluation of the variables. Thus, the first three requirements are represented using literals. The semantics of M, given by each function F_{V_i} corresponding to V_i (according to Definition 1), is expressed using an equivalence operator between a variable and its function, i.e., $V_i \leftrightarrow F_{V_i}$. This is not done for the cause variables because they are represented by a negation. To account for $\vec{W}$, we add a disjunction to the equivalence sub-formula with the positive or negative literal of V_i, according to its actual evaluation (1 or 0). With this representation of each variable, we check if such a counterfactual world is satisfiable, and hence AC2 holds.

By generalizing F, we can also check minimality (AC3). Assume we remove the restriction on the cause variables $\vec{X}$, of only be negated literals (allowing them to take on their original values also), and call the new formula G. Then G might be satisfiable for the negated cause $\vec{X} = \vec{x}'$ as well as all the other combinations of the cause set. Analyzing all the satisfying assignments of G (All-SAT), allows us to check minimality. Specifically, if we find an assignment such that at least one conjunct of $\vec{X} = \vec{x}$ takes on a value that equals the one

---

[2] Their idea is often motivated with an example of 11 voters that can vote for Suzy or Billy. If Suzy wins 6–5, we can show that each Suzy voter is a cause of her winning. If Suzy wins 11–0, then each subset of size six of the voters is a cause. The authors argue that in 11–0 scenario, "a voter feels less responsible" compared to 6–5 situation.

computed from its equation, it means that it is not a required part of the cause, and hence, the cause is not minimal. In many situations, All-SAT is problematic and decreases the performance, especially if G is satisfiable for a large number of assignments [35]. Equation 1 shows the construction of G. Because Y_i is the variable form, and y_i is the value, we use $f(Y_i = y_i)$ to convert the variable to a positive or a negative literal, i.e., Y or $\neg Y$.

$$G := \neg\varphi \wedge \bigwedge_{i=1...n} f(U_i = u_i) \wedge \bigwedge_{i=1...m, \nexists j \bullet X_j = V_i} (V_i \leftrightarrow F_{V_i} \vee f(V_i = v_i)) \quad (1)$$

F and G aid us in *checking* if a candidate cause $\vec{X}$ is a *minimal, counterfactual* cause of φ. If it is not, we cannot use them to *find* a minimal cause from within $\vec{X}$, i.e., *semi-inference*. We, also, cannot use them to find a cause without requiring a candidate cause, i.e., *inference*. To efficiently achieve such abilities, we present a novel formulation of causal queries as optimization problems.

3.1   Checking and Semi-inference Queries as Optimization Problems

In this section, we focus on the computation of the minimality requirement in causality checking. For that, we conceptualize a technique to check AC2 and AC3 as one problem (AC1 is explicitly checked solely). The result of solving this problem can then be interpreted to conclude AC2, $\vec{W}$, AC3, and, better, what is a minimal subset of the cause if AC3 is violated (semi-inference). To compare the efficiency, we formulate the problem as an integer program and a MaxSAT formula. Both techniques solve the problem based on an *objective* function— a function whose value is minimized or maximized among feasible alternatives.

To quantify an *objective* for a causal check, we introduce an *integer* variable that we call the *distance*. Similar to the Hamming distance, it measures the difference between the cause values when φ holds true, i.e., actual world, and when it holds false, i.e., the counterfactual world. As shown in Eq. 2, it is computed by counting the cause variables whose values assigned by a solver (x_i') is different from their value under the given context (x_i). As we shall see, the *distance* is equivalent to the size of the (minimal) cause within our check of a possibly non-minimal cause. As such, the *distance* must be greater than 0, since a cause is non-empty, and less or equal to the size of $\vec{X}$ (ℓ), i.e., $1 \leq distance \leq \ell$.

$$distance = \sum_{i=1}^{\ell} d(i) \quad s.t \quad d(i) = \begin{cases} 1 - x_i', & x_i = 1 \\ x_i', & x_i = 0 \end{cases} \quad (2)$$

According to AC3, our *objective function* is then to minimize the distance; we encode a causality check as an optimization problem that *minimizes* the number of cause variables while satisfying the constraints for AC2 (counterfactuality and $\vec{W}$). In the following, we present how to derive these constraints for the ILP formulation and the MaxSAT encoding. Then, we discuss how to interpret the results to (semi-)infer a minimal cause from a possibly non-minimal cause.

ILP is an optimization program with integer variables and linear constraints and objectives. To formulate such a program, we need three elements: *decision* *variables, constraints, and objective(s).* Our *decision variables* are, in addition to the *distance*, the set of exogenous and endogenous variables from the model, i.e., $\vec{U} \cup \vec{V}$. Since we only consider binary variables, their values are bound to be 0 or 1. Since ILP and SAT solvers can be used as complementary tools, the translation from SAT to ILP is standard [26]. Therefore, we reuse formula G (Eq. 1) to create the *constraints*. Constraints from G contain the **a.)** effect not holding true, **b.)** the context, **c.)** each endogenous variable either follows the model equation or the actual value, i.e., part of the set $\vec{W}$, **d.)** each element in the cause set $\vec{X} = \vec{x}$ is not constrained, i.e., its equation is removed. Transforming these constraints (on the Conjunctive Normal Form (CNF) level) into linear inequalities is straightforward; we have clauses that can be reduced to ILP directly, e.g., express $y = x_1 \vee x_2$ as $1 \geq 2*y - x_1 - x_2 \geq 0$ [26]. In addition, we add a constraint to calculate the distance according to Eq. 2.

MaxSAT. The maximum satisfiability problem (MaxSAT) is an optimization variant of SAT [25]. In contrast to SAT, which aims to find a satisfying assignment of all the clauses in a formula, MaxSAT aims to find an assignment that maximizes the number of satisfied clauses. Thus, MaxSAT allows the potential that some clauses are unsatisfied. In this paper, we use *partial* MaxSAT solving, which allows specific clauses to be unsatisfied, referred to as *soft clauses*; contrary to the *hard* clauses that must be satisfied [25]. A soft clause can be assigned a *weight* to represent the cost of not satisfying it. In essence, a weighted partial MaxSAT problem is a minimization problem that minimizes the cost over all solutions. Unlike ILP, the objective in MaxSAT is immutable. Thus, we need to construct our formula in a way that mimics the concept of the distance.

As shown in Eq. 3, the MaxSAT encoding also uses G (shown in Eq. 1) as a base. G embeds all the mandatory parts of any solution. Thus, we use the CNF clauses of G as *hard* clauses. On the other hand, we need to append the cause variables $(\vec{X})$ as *soft* clauses (underlined in Eq. 3). Since the solver would minimize the cost of unsatisfying the $(\vec{X})$ clauses, we represent each cause variable as a literal according to its original value (when φ holds). Because this is already in CNF, it is easier to assign weights. We assign 1 as a cost for unsatisfying each cause variable's clause, i.e., when X_i is negated in the (solved) counterfactual world. Then, the overall cost of unsatisfying the underlined parts of the formula is the count of the negated causes, i.e., the size of the minimal cause. Essentially, this concept maps directly to the *distance*, which the MaxSAT solver will minimize. In contrast to ILP, we cannot specify a lower bound on the MaxSAT objective. Thus, we need to express the non-emptiness of a cause, as *hard* clauses. A *non-empty* cause means that at least one cause variable X_j does not take its original value, *and* does not follow its equation due to an intervention. The first conjunction (after G) in Eq. 3 ensures the first requirement, while the second corresponds to the second case.

$$G_{max} := G \wedge \neg(\bigwedge_{i=1...\ell} f(X_i = x_i)) \wedge \neg(\bigwedge_{i=1...\ell} X_i \leftrightarrow F_{X_i}) \wedge \underline{\bigwedge_{i=1...\ell} f(X_i = x_i)} \qquad (3)$$

Results. With the above, we illustrated the formulation of a causal checking problem. We now discuss how to translate their results to a causal answer once

Algorithm 1. Interpreting the Optimization Problem's Results

Input: causal model M, context $\langle U_1, \ldots, U_n \rangle = \langle u_1, \ldots, u_n \rangle$, effect φ, candidate cause
$\langle X_1, \ldots, X_\ell \rangle = \langle x_1, \ldots, x_\ell \rangle$, evaluation $\langle V_1, \ldots, V_m \rangle = \langle v_1, \ldots, v_m \rangle$
1: **function** CHECKCAUSE($M, \vec{U} = \vec{u}, \varphi, \vec{X} = \vec{x}, \vec{V} = \vec{v}$)
2:     **if** $\langle U_1 = u_1 \ldots U_n = u_n, V_1 = v_1' \ldots V_m = v_m' \rangle = solve(\vec{C}, objective)$ **then**
3:         $\vec{X}_{min} := \langle X_1' \ldots X_d' \rangle$ s.t. $\forall i \forall j \bullet (i \neq j \Rightarrow X_i' \neq X_j') \wedge (X_i' = V_j \Leftrightarrow v_j' \neq v_j)$
4:         $\vec{W} := \langle W_1 \ldots W_s \rangle$ s.t. $\forall i \forall j \bullet (i \neq j \Rightarrow W_i \neq W_j) \wedge (W_i = V_j \Leftrightarrow v_j' = v_j)$
5:         **return** $\vec{X}_{min}, \vec{W}$
6:     **else return** *infeasible (unsatisfiable)*
7:     **end if**
8: **end function**

---

they are solved; Algorithm 1 formalizes this. The evaluation, in the input, is a list of the variables in M and their values under $\vec{u}$. Assuming $\vec{C}$ is a representation of the optimization problem (a set of linear constraints (without the objective), or hard/soft clauses), then in Line 2, we solve this problem and process the results in Lines 3–4. The feasibility (satisfiability) of the problem implies that either $\vec{X}$ or a non-empty subset of it is a minimal cause (fulfills AC2 and AC3). If *distance* (cost returned by the MaxSAT solver) equals the size of $\vec{X}$, then the whole candidate cause is minimal. Otherwise, to find a minimal cause $\vec{X}_{min}$ (semi-inference), we choose the parts of $\vec{X}$ that have different values between the actual and the solved values (Line 3). To determine $\vec{W}$, in Line 4, we take the variables whose solved values are the same as the actual evaluation (potentially including $\vec{X}$ variables). Obviously, this is not a minimal $\vec{W}$, which is not a requirement for *checking* HP [18]. If the model is *infeasible or unsatisfiable*, then HP for the given $\vec{X}$ (checking) and its subsets (semi-inference) does not hold.

Throwing Rocks Example: To illustrate our approach, we show the ILP and MaxSAT encodings to answer the query is $ST = 1, BT = 1$ a cause of $BS = 1$?

$$min\ d \text{ s.t. } \{BS = 0,\ ST_{exo} = 1,\ BT_{exo} = 1,\ -SH + BS \geq 0,\ -BH + BS \geq 0,$$
$$-ST + SH \geq 0,\ BT - BH \geq 0,\ -SH - BH \geq -1,\ ST + BT + d = 2\}$$
$$G_{max} = \neg BS \wedge ST_{exo} \wedge BT_{exo} \wedge (BS \leftrightarrow SH \vee BH) \wedge ((SH \leftrightarrow ST) \vee SH) \wedge$$
$$((BH \leftrightarrow BT \wedge \neg SH) \vee \neg BH) \wedge \neg(ST \wedge BT) \wedge \underline{(ST \wedge BT)}$$

Both encodings are solved with a *distance(d)* (cost) value of 1, which indicates that ST, BT is not minimal, and a cause of size 1 is (semi)-inferred, namely ST. The optimal assignment $(\neg BS, ST_{exo}, BT_{exo}, \neg SH, \neg BH, \neg ST, BT)$ showed that the constraints can be guaranteed without changing the value of BT, which violates AC3. This shows the enhancement of finding a minimal cause rather than only checking AC3. Theorem 1 states the soundness of our approach (for proofs see Appendix of https://arxiv.org/abs/2006.03363).

Theorem 1. *The generated optimization problem (ILP program or G_{max}) is feasible iff AC3 holds for $\vec{X}$ or a non-empty subset of $\vec{X}$.*

3.2   Causality Inference with ILP

The previous approaches utilized the candidate cause $\vec{X}$ to help describe a counterfactual world that proves $\vec{X}$ is a cause of φ. In this section, we present a method, ILP_{why}, to *infer* causality (answer *why φ?* questions) without requiring $\vec{X}$. Unlike checking, in inference, we cannot aid the solver in a description of the counterfactual world (e.g., negating values of $\vec{X}$). Instead, we describe characteristics of the actual cause that have caused an effect φ.

In addition to requirements of counterfactuality and minimality imposed by the conditions in Definition 2, we utilize the *degree of responsibility* (dr) as a mean to compare actual causes [8]. While the conditions are suitable for determining if $\vec{X}$ is a cause, dr judges the "quality" of the cause based on an aggregation of its characteristics. Because we may find multiple causes for which the conditions hold, dr is reasonable for comparison. We require our answer to an inference question to be an actual cause with the maximum dr. We come back to this after we construct a formula G^* that is the base of ILP_{why}.

Both negating the effect formula $(\neg\varphi)$ and setting the context $f(U_i = u_i)$ remain as in Eq. 1. Because the variables that appear in the effect formula cannot be part of the cause, we represent each with the simple *equivalence* relation, i.e., $V_i \leftrightarrow F_{V_i}$. The complicated part is representing the other variables because any variable can be: **a.** a cause, **b.** a contingency-set, or **c.** a normal variable. Recall, in a counterfactual computation, a cause does not follow its equation, *and* differs from its original value; a contingency-set variable does not follow its equation while keeping its original value; a normal variable follows its equation, regardless of whether it equals the original value or not. Thus, we need to allow variables to be classified in any category in the "best" possible way.

To that end, we represent each (non-effect) variable V_i with a disjunction between the equivalence holding and not holding, *and* a disjunction between its original value and its negation: $((V_i \leftrightarrow F_{V_i}) \vee \neg(V_i \leftrightarrow F_{V_i})) \wedge (V_{i_{orig}} \vee \neg V_{i_{orig}})$. Clearly, each disjunction is a tautology. However, this redundancy facilitates the classification into the categories; more importantly, we can incentivize the solver to classify those variables according to specific criteria.

To be able to guide the solver, we add auxiliary boolean variables (indicators) to each clause (left and right parts of a disjunction). They serve two functions. The first is to *indicate* which clauses hold. Since the two parts of the conjunction are not mutually exclusive, i.e., a variable can follow its equation, yet have its original value, we need *two* indicators $C^1 C^2$. Secondly, similar to the concept of *distance* from Subsect. 3.1, we use the indicators to describe the criteria of the solution. For each variable V_i, C_i^1 is appended to the first two clauses: $((V_i \leftrightarrow F_{V_i}) \wedge C_i^1) \vee (\neg(V_i \leftrightarrow F_{V_i}) \wedge \neg C_i^1)$. Similarly C^2 is appended to the other clauses. As such, the category of each endogenous variable is determined based on the values of C^1 and C^2. A cause variable would have a $C^1 C^2 : 00$ (not following the formula nor its original value); a contingency-set variable has a $C^1 C^2 : 01$; and a normal variable has a $C^1 C^2 : 10$, or 11. Formula G^* follows (equivalence relations of effect variables are omitted for space).

$$G^* := \neg\varphi \wedge \bigwedge_{i=1...n} f(U_i = u_i) \wedge \bigwedge_{i=1...m} \left(\left((V_i \leftrightarrow F_{V_i}) \wedge C_i^1 \right) \vee \left(\neg (V_i \leftrightarrow F_{V_i}) \wedge \neg C_i^1 \right) \right)$$
$$\wedge \left((V_{orig} \wedge C_i^2) \vee (\neg V_{orig} \wedge \neg C_i^2) \right)$$

Theorem 2. *Formula G^* is satisfiable iff $\exists\ \vec{X} = \vec{x}$ such that AC2 holds for $\vec{X}$*

We now discuss the *objectives* of this formulation. We aim to find an assignment to the constraints in G^* that corresponds to a cause with a maximum dr. Recall that dr is $1/(|\vec{X}| + |\vec{W}|)$. *Maximizing dr entails minimizing $|X| + |W|$.* Since the three sets (cause, contingency, and normal) form the overall model size (excluding effect and exogenous variables), then minimizing $|X| + |W|$ is equivalent to maximizing the number of normal variables, which concludes our *first objective*. The sum of C^1 variables resembles the number of normal variables; thus, *objective$_1$* is to *maximize* the sum of C^1 variables.

The above formulation minimizes $\vec{X}$, and $\vec{W}$ as a whole, following dr. For our purpose, we think it is valid to look for causes with higher responsibility first (fewer variables to negate or fix) and favor them over smaller causes. For example, if an effect has two actual causes: one with 2 variables in $\vec{X}$, 3 in $\vec{W}$, and the second with 1 variable in $\vec{X}$, 5 in $\vec{W}$, we pick the first. That said, we still want to distinguish between $\vec{X}$ and $\vec{W}$ in causes with the same dr. Assume we have two causes: the first with 2 variables in $\vec{X}$, 3 in $\vec{W}$, and the second with 3 in $\vec{X}$, 2 in $\vec{W}$. Although both are optimal solutions to *objective$_1$*, we would like to pick the one with fewer causes. Thus, we add *objective$_2$* to *minimize* causes, i.e., the number of variables with C^1 and C^2 equal to 0. We use hierarchical objectives in ILP, for which the solver finds the optimal solution(s) based on the first objective, and then use the second objective to optimize the solution(s).

We wrap-up with Algorithm 2, which omits the construction of G^*. We start by turning G^* into linear constraints in Line 2. The first objective obj_1, which maximizes dr by maximizing the sum of C_i^1 is added in Line 3. The second objective, obj_2, handles minimizing the size of the cause set. We process the results after solving the program in Lines 5–7. The feasibility of the program means we found a cause (size obj_2) with the maximum dr for the effect. For the details, we check the indicators of each variable. The cause is composed of variables that have C^1 and C^2 equal 0; variables in $\vec{W}$, have $C^1 = 0$ and $C^2 = 1$.

Throwing Rocks Example. Assume we want to answer *why did the bottle shatter $BS = 1$? (given both threw)*. The generated program is not shown, but it was solved with ($obj_1 = 2$), i.e., *two* normal variables, and $obj_2 = 1$, one cause variable. Based on the indicators, $SH = 1$ is the actual cause of $BS = 1$, given that $BH = 0$. This is the result of having $C_{SH}^1 = 0 \wedge C_{SH}^2 = 0$ as opposed to $C_{BH}^1 = 0 \wedge C_{BH}^2 = 1$. The result is correct; SH is a cause of BS, with the maximum dr. Previous references of this example concluded ST as a cause; however, since SH is an identity function, this does not compromise our result.[3]

---

[3] Arguably, the (geodesic) distance between the cause and effect nodes in the graph, can be taken into consideration. In this paper, we do not consider this issue.

Algorithm 2. Causality Inference using ILP_{why}

Input: causal model M, context $\langle U_1, \ldots, U_n \rangle = \langle u_1, \ldots, u_n \rangle$, effect φ, evaluation
$\langle V_1, \ldots, V_m \rangle = \langle v_1, \ldots, v_m \rangle$

1: **function** FINDCAUSE($M, \vec{U} = \vec{u}, \varphi, \vec{V} = \vec{v}$)
2:   $\langle Con_1, \ldots Con_n \rangle = convertToILP(CNF(G^*))$
3:   $obj_1 = Maximize \sum_{i=1}^{m} C_i^1 \ s.t. \ obj_1 \leq |\vec{V}|$
4:   $obj_2 = Minimize \sum_{i=1}^{m} (1 - C_i^1) * (1 - C_i^2) \ s.t. \ |\vec{V}| \geq obj_2 \geq 1$
5:   **if** $\langle V_1 = v_1' \ldots V_m = v_m', C_1^1 = c_1^1 \ldots C_m^1 = c_m^1, C_1^2 = c_1^2 \ldots C_m^2 = c_m^2 \rangle$
        $\hookrightarrow \ = solve(\vec{Con}, obj_1, obj_2)$ **then**
6:     $\vec{X'} := \langle X_1' \ldots X_{obj_2}' \rangle \ s.t. \ \forall i \forall j \bullet (i \neq j \Rightarrow X_i' \neq X_j') \wedge (X_i' = V_j \Leftrightarrow \neg c_j^1 \wedge \neg c_j^2)$
7:     $\vec{W} := \langle W_1 \ldots W_s \rangle \ s.t. \ \forall i \forall j \bullet (i \neq j \Rightarrow W_i \neq W_j) \wedge (W_i = V_j \Leftrightarrow (\neg c_j^1 \wedge c_j^2))$
8:     **return** $\vec{X'}, \vec{W}$
9:   **else return** *infeasible*
10: **end if**
11: **end function**

---

4 Evaluation

To evaluate their efficiency, we implemented our strategies as an open-source library. We used state of the art solvers: *Gurobi* [11] for ILP, and Open-WBO for MaxSAT [27]. In this section, we evaluate the performance, in terms of *execution time* and *memory allocation*, of the strategies in comparison with previous work.

Experiment Setup. Unfortunately, there are no standard data-sets to benchmark causality computations. Thus, we gathered a dataset of 37 models, which included 21 *small* models ($\leq$400 endogenous variables)–from domains of causality, security, safety, and accident investigation– and 16 larger security models from an industrial partner, in addition to artificially generated models. The smaller models contained 9 illustrative examples from literature (number of endogenous variables in brackets) such as $Throwing - Rocks(5)$, $Railroad(4)$ [12], 2 variants of a safety model that describes a leakage in a subsea production system $LSP(41)$ and $LSP2(41)$ [7], and an aircraft accident model (Ueberlingen, 2002) $Ueb(95)$ [34], 7 generated binary trees, and a security model obtained from an industrial partner which depicts how insiders within a company steal a master encryption key SMK. Because it can be parameterized by the number of employees in a company, we have 14 variants of SMK, 2 small ones $SMK1(36)$ and $SMK8(91)$, and 12 large models of sizes (550–7150). In addition, we artificially generated 4 models: 2 binary trees with different heights, denoted as $BT(2047 - 4095)$, and 2 trees combined with non-tree random models, denoted as $ABT(4103)$, and $ABT2(8207)$. We have evidence that such large models are likely to occur when built automatically from architectures or inferred from other sources [16,17]. Details on the models and the results can be found online.[4]

---

[4] Machine-readable models and their description available at https://git.io/Jf8iH.

We formulated a total of **484** *checking* queries that vary in the context, cause, effect, and consequently differ in the result of AC1-AC3, the size of $\vec{W}$, and the size of the minimal cause. For the smaller models, we specified the queries manually according to their sources in literature and verified that our results match the sources. The approaches, including previous ALL-SAT approach, answered these queries in under a second; hence, we exclude them from our discussion. For the larger models, we constructed a total of **224** checking queries. We specified some effects (e.g., root of *BT*, or *steal passphrase* in *SMK*) and used different contexts, and randomly selected causes (sizes 1, 2, 3, 4, 10, 15, and 50) from the models. Since we can reuse the checking queries for inference by omitting the cause, we created **180** inference queries including **67** queries of large models.

We collected the results for: SAT - the original SAT-based approach [18], and the presented three approaches: ILP, MaxSAT, and ILP$_{why}$- the inference approach. We ran each query for 30 warm-ups (dry-runs before collecting results to avoid accounting for factors like JVM warm-up), and 30 measurement iterations on an i7 Ubuntu machine with 16 GB RAM. We set the cut-off threshold to 2 h.

Discussion. Generally, we use cactus plots to compare the performance of the approaches. The x-axis shows the number of queries an approach answered ordered by the execution time, which is shown on the y-axis; a point (x, y) on the plot reads as x queries can be answered in y or less. Next, we discuss the overall trends of the results; however, since we are interested in notions of checking, and inference, we also mention specific queries in which AC3 does not hold.

As expected, the experiments confirmed the problems with the SAT encoding— significant solver slow-down and memory exhaustion—[35]. Thus, as shown in Fig. 1a, SAT only answered **187** of the **224** checking queries; for the remaining either it ran out of memory or took more than 2 h. For instance, queries on *SMK(6600)* checking causes of sizes 2, 3, 4 were not answered because the program ran out of memory. With almost all answered queries, SAT took al least two to four times as much as ILP, and up to twenty times as much as MaxSAT. In extreme cases, SAT took around 113 mins to finish, whereas others stayed under 5 s for the same cases. Memory allocation, shown in Fig. 1b, was similar to the execution time. However, it showed less difference with ILP and sometimes better allocation. Although it is not surprising that an ALL-SAT encoding performs poorly in some situations, the key result is that both ILP and MaxSAT provide more informative answers to a query while performing better.

According to our dataset, both ILP and MaxSAT, answered all queries in less than 70–100 s. Especially for semi-inference, cases of *non-minimal* causes and a minimal cause can be found, they are effective. For instance, with queries using *ABT(4103)*, we found causes of size 2, 5, and 11 out of candidate causes of sizes 5, 10, 15, and 50. All these queries were answered in around 5 s using ILP, and 2 s using MaxSAT. For larger and more complex models e.g., *SMK(7150)*, answering similar queries jumped to 98 s with ILP and 71 s MaxSAT.

As shown in Fig. 1a and Fig. 1b, MaxSAT outperformed ILP in execution time and memory; a scatter plot to compare them is shown in Fig. 1c. The propositional nature of the problem gives an advantage to MaxSAT. Especially for easier queries, as shown in Fig. 1c bottom left, MaxSAT is much faster because no linear transformation is needed, which explains why the gap between the two decreases among the larger queries. Further, we used Open-WBO —a solver that uses cores to initiate (UN)SAT instances [27]— which performs better, especially when the number of hard clauses is high [3]. That said, in addition to the comparison, we used ILP for binary computations to incorporate quantifiable notions to infer causality using multi-objective ILP in ILP$_{why}$.

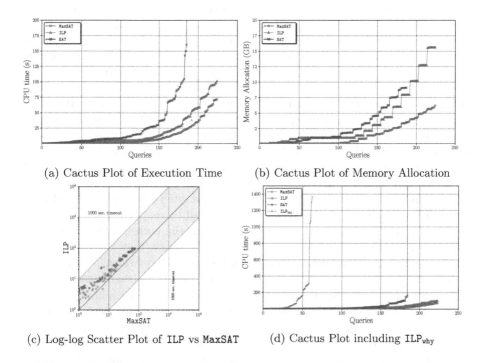

(a) Cactus Plot of Execution Time   (b) Cactus Plot of Memory Allocation

(c) Log-log Scatter Plot of ILP vs MaxSAT   (d) Cactus Plot including ILP$_{why}$

Fig. 1. Execution Time and Memory Results on the Larger Models

Although we have fewer inference queries (67), for comparison, we plot the checking approaches with ILP$_{why}$ in Fig. 1d. ILP$_{why}$ answered **63** out of **67** queries. In comparison, it was slower than the checking approaches. Still, it scaled to large and complex queries. For instance, with basic tree models of 4000 variables (BT_{11}, ABT), it took 8 s, and scaled to 8000 variable $ABT2$ within 63 s. However, it slowed down with larger models with complex semantics, i.e., SMK different variants. For instance, $SMK(5500)$ took 280 s, while $SMK(6600)$ jumped to 1400 s. The slow down is related to the memory allocation because the program, finally, ran out of memory with queries on $SMK(7150)$. Given sufficient memory, we think ILP$_{why}$ computes *inference* for even larger models.

In summary, we argue that the three approaches efficiently automates actual causality reasoning over binary models. Our MaxSAT encoding performs well for purposes of causality checking and semi-inference. Although slower, ILP$_{why}$ is also efficient and scalable for purposes of inference.

5   Related Work

There are three versions of HP (*original* 2001, *updated* 2005, *modified* 2015) [13]. We use the latest because it solves issues with the previous versions, and reduces the complexity [12]. To the best of our knowledge, no previous work tackled the implementation of the (*modified*) HP. Still, we discuss the implementations of previous versions. Previous work has proposed simplified adaptations of the definition for various applications. First, in the domain of databases [6,28,33], (updated) HP was utilized to explain conjunctive query results. The approaches heavily depend on the correspondence between causes and domain-specific concepts such as lineage, database repairs, and denial constraints. The simplification in that line of work is the limitation to a single-equation causal model based on the lineage of the query in [28], or no-equation model in [6,33], in addition to the elimination of preemption treatment. Similar simplification has been made for Boolean circuits in [9]. Second, in the context of software and hardware verification, (updated) HP is used to explain counterexamples returned by a model checker [5]. The authors also restricted the definition to singleton causes and no-equation models. Third, in [4,23], the authors adapted HP to debug models of safety-critical systems. Similar to our approach, all the papers above use acyclic binary models. However, they depend heavily on the correspondence between causes and domain-specific concepts. Also, for efficiency, they relax the definition by restricting the model, i.e., one equation [28], no-equations [5,6,33], or by restricting the cause, i.e., singleton [5,33]; the complexity is then relaxed, because AC2 is straightforward (no $\vec{W}$) or AC3 is not needed. While such limitations are sufficient for the particular use-case, we argue that they cannot be used outside their respective domains, e.g., for accountability. In contrast, our approach is a general method to automate HP. We focus on the minimality, which, to the best of our knowledge, no previous work has tackled. We employ optimization solving, which was not utilized before in this context. Alternatively, previous work used SAT directly [18], indirectly [4], or answer set programming [6]. Sharing our generality, Hopkins proposed methods to check (original) HP using search-based algorithms [14]. Our approach scales to thousands of variables, while the results presented in the search-based approaches showed a limit of 30 variables.

Fault tree analysis (FTA) is an established design-time method to analyze safety risks of a system [32]. FTA's primary analysis is the computation of minimal cut sets MCSs of a fault tee; a CS is a set of events that, together, cause the top-level event. Approaches to determine MCS use Boolean manipulation, or Binary decision diagrams [32]. These methods are similar to our computations; however, the conceptual difference is the definition of a cause. While a cause covers two notions: sufficiency and necessity, a CS presents a sufficient cause only. The occurrence of the events in the cut leads to the occurrence of the top-level event. This roughly corresponds to AC1, while the minimality of the cut set corresponds to AC3. The difference lies in the necessity of the cause (AC2). An MCS computation does not include this step, which is the core of actual causality computation. Cut sets are all the enumerations that make the effect true. Similarly, model-based diagnosis (MBD) aims to detect faulty components to explain anomalies in system behavior [31]. The model is a set of logical expressions over a set of components. MBD requires a set of observations that correspond to the context $\vec{U}$; using logical inference, MBD outputs a set of hypotheses for how the system differs from its model, i.e., diagnoses. While MBD can be considered as an approach to infer causality, it does not require counterfactuality of the cause. Although MBD uses a notion of intervention (setting some components to abnormal), this is not counterfactual reasoning. Instead, it is a sufficiency check since MBD uses a behavioral model, i.e., a representation of the correct behavior. Like FTA, diagnoses are sufficient causes, but not actual causes.

6   Conclusions and Future Work

According to HP, a set of events $(\vec{X})$ causes an effect (φ) if (1) both actually happen; (2) changing some values of $\vec{X}$ while fixing a set $\vec{W}$ of the remaining variables at their original value leads to φ not happening; and (3) $\vec{X}$ is minimal. The complexity of the general problem has been established elsewhere. We show that when restricting to binary models, the problem of checking or inferring causality can effectively and efficiently be solved as an optimization problem. The problem is not trivial because intuitively, we need to enumerate all sets $\vec{W}$ from condition (2) and need to check minimality for condition (3). We show how to formulate both properties as an optimization problem instead which immediately gives rise to using a solver to determine if a cause satisfies all conditions, or find one that does. For that, we define an objective function that encodes the distance between cause values in the actual and counterfactual worlds. If we now manage to optimize the problem with a smaller cause, then we know that it satisfies condition (2) but is not minimal. With an additional objective to quantify responsibility, we also formulate inference as an optimization problem. Using models with 8000 variables, which we deem realistic and necessary for automatically inferred causal models, we show that our approaches answer checking queries in seconds, and inference queries in minutes. In the future, we plan to explore the extension of the approach to support non-binary models.

References

1. Aleksandrowicz, G., Chockler, H., Halpern, J.Y., Ivrii, A.: The computational complexity of structure-based causality. In: Proceedings of the Twenty-Eighth AAAI Conference on Artificial Intelligence (2014)
2. Bacchus, F., Järvisalo, M., Martins, R., et al.: MaxSAT evaluation 2018 (2018)
3. Bacchus, F., Narodytska, N.: Cores in core based MaxSAT algorithms: an analysis. In: International Conference on Theory and Applications of Satisfiability Testing (2014)

4. Beer, A., Heidinger, S., Kühne, U., Leitner-Fischer, F., Leue, S.: Symbolic causality checking using bounded model checking. In: Model Checking Software - 22nd International Symposium, SPIN (2015)

5. Beer, I., Ben-David, S., Chockler, H., Orni, A., Trefler, R.J.: Explaining counter examples using causality. Formal Methods Syst. Des. **40**(1), 20–40 (2012)

6. Bertossi, L.: Characterizing and computing causes for query answers in databases from database repairs and repair programs. In: Ferrarotti, F., Woltran, S. (eds.) Foundations of Information and Knowledge Systems, pp. 55–76. Springer, Cham (2018). https://doi.org/10.1007/978-3-319-90050-6_4

7. Cheliyan, A.S., Bhattacharyya, S.K.: Fuzzy fault tree analysis of oil and gas leakage in subsea production systems. J. Ocean Eng. Sci. **3**, 38–48 (2018)

8. Chockler, H., Halpern, J.Y.: Responsibility and blame: a structural-model approach. J. Artif. Intell. Res. **22**, 93–115 (2004). https://doi.org/10.1613/jair.1391

9. Chockler, H., Halpern, J.Y., Kupferman, O.: What causes a system to satisfy a specification? ACM Trans. Comput. Logic (TOCL) **9**(3), 20 (2008)

10. Feigenbaum, J., Hendler, J.A., Jaggard, A.D., Weitzner, D.J., Wright, R.N.: Accountability and deterrence in online life. In: Web Science (2011)

11. Gurobi, L.: Optimization: Gurobi optimizer reference manual (2018)

12. Halpern, J.Y.: A modification of the Halpern-Pearl definition of causality. In: Proceedings of the Twenty-Fourth International Joint Conference on Artificial Intelligence, IJCAI. pp. 3022–3033 (2015)

13. Halpern, J.Y.: Actual Causality. MIT Press, Cambridge (2016)

14. Hopkins, M.: Strategies for determining causes of events. In: AAAI/IAAI (2002)

15. Hume, D.: An Enquiry Concerning Human Understanding (1748)

16. Ibrahim, A., Kacianka, S., Pretschner, A., Hartsell, C., Karsai, G.: Practical causal models for cyber-physical systems. In: NASA Formal Methods, pp. 211–227 (2019)

17. Ibrahim, A., Klesel, T., Zibaei, E., Kacianka, S., Pretschner, A.: Actual causality canvas: A general framework for explanation-based socio-technical constructs. In: ECAI 2020, the 24th European Conference on Artificial Intelligence. Frontiers in Artificial Intelligence and Applications, IOS Press (2020)

18. Ibrahim, A., Rehwald, S., Pretschner, A.: Efficient checking of actual causality with sat solving. Eng. Secure Dependable Softw. Syst. **53**, 241 (2019)

19. Kacianka, S., Ibrahim, A., Pretschner, A., Trende, A., Lüdtke, A.: Extending causal models from machines into humans. Electron. Proc. Theor. Comput. Sci. **308**, 17–31 (2019). https://doi.org/10.4204/eptcs.308.2

20. Koch, T., Martin, A., Pfetsch, M.E.: Progress in academic computational integer programming. In: Facets of Combinatorial Optimization. Springer, Heidelberg (2013). https://doi.org/10.1007/978-3-642-38189-8

21. Künnemann, R., Esiyok, I., Backes, M.: Automated verification of accountability in security protocols. CoRR abs/1805.10891 (2018)

22. Ladkin, P., Loer, K.: Why-because analysis: Formal reasoning about incidents. Bielefeld, Germany, Document RVS-Bk-98-01, Technischen Fakultat der Universitat Bielefeld, Germany (1998)

23. Leitner-Fischer, F., Leue, S.: Causality checking for complex system models. In: Giacobbazzi, R., Berdine, J., Mastroeni, I. (eds.) VMCAI 2013. LNCS, vol. 7737, pp. 248–267. Springer, Heidelberg (2013). https://doi.org/10.1007/978-3-642-35873-9_16

24. Lewis, D.: Causation. J. Philosophy **70**(17), 556–567 (1973)

25. Li, C.M., Manyà, F.: MaxSAT, hard and soft constraints. In: Handbook of Satisfiability, pp. 613–631 (2009)

26. Li, R., Zhou, D., Du, D.: Satisfiability and integer programming as complementary tools. In: Proceedings of the 2004 Asia and South Pacific Design Automation Conference, pp. 879–882. IEEE Press (2004)
27. Martins, R., Manquinho, V., Lynce, I.: Open-WBO: A modular MaxSAT solver. In: International Conference on Theory and Applications of Satisfiability Testing. pp. 438–445. Springer (2014). https://doi.org/10.1007/978-3-319-09284-3_33
28. Meliou, A., Gatterbauer, W., Halpern, J.Y., Koch, C., Moore, K.F., Suciu, D.: Causality in databases. IEEE Data Eng. Bull. **33**(3), 59–67 (2010)
29. Miller, T.: Explanation in artificial intelligence: insights from the social sciences. Artif. Intell. **267**, 1–38 (2018)
30. Pearl, J.: Causation, action and counterfactuals. In: Proceedings of the Sixth Conference on Theoretical Aspects of Rationality and Knowledge, pp. 51–73 (1996)
31. Reiter, R.: A theory of diagnosis from first principles. Artif. Intell. **312**, 57–95 (1987)
32. Ruijters, E., Stoelinga, M.: Fault tree analysis: a survey of the state-of-the-art in modeling, analysis and tools. Comput. Sci. Rev. **15**, 29–62 (2015)
33. Salimi, B., Bertossi, L.: From causes for database queries to repairs and model-based diagnosis and back (2014)
34. Stuphor, J.: WBG of the 2002 Überlingen Mid-Air Collision. https://rvs-bi.de/Bieleschweig/5.5/Stuphorn_Ueberlingen_WBA.pdf
35. Zhao, W., Wu, W.: ASIG: an all-solution SAT solver for CNF formulas. In: 11th International Conference on Computer-Aided Design and Computer Graphics (2009)

Boosting Sequential Consistency Checking Using Saturation

Rachid Zennou[1,2(✉)], Mohamed Faouzi Atig[3], Ranadeep Biswas[1],
Ahmed Bouajjani[1], Constantin Enea[1], and Mohammed Erradi[2]

[1] Université de Paris, Paris, France
{ranadeep,abou,cenea}@irif.fr
[2] ENSIAS, Mohammed V University, Rabat, Morocco
rachid.zennou@gmail.com, mohamed.erradi@gmail.com
[3] Uppsala University, Uppsala, Sweden
mohamed_faouzi.atig@it.uu.se

Abstract. We address the problem of checking that an execution of a shared memory concurrent program is sequentially consistent (SC). This problem is NP-hard due to the necessity of finding a total order between the write operations that induces an acyclic happen-before relation. We propose an approach allowing to avoid falling systematically in the worst case, and to check SCness in polynomial-time in most cases in practice. The approach is based on a simple yet powerful saturation-based procedure for computing write constraints that must hold for SCness, allowing on one hand fast detection of SC violations, and on the other hand reducing drastically the search space for a total order witnessing SCness.

1 Introduction

Sequential Consistency (SC, for short) [19] is a fundamental model of shared memory, where write and read operations are atomic, and operations issued by different threads are interleaved arbitrarily while the order between operations issued by a same thread is preserved. SC offers the best programming abstraction, since each write operation is considered to be immediately visible to all threads. While adopting SC as a memory model is desirable by memory users as it simplifies their task, implementing sequential consistency is extremely complex and error prone due to various optimisations and complex caching mechanisms that must be adopted in order to achieve acceptable performances. Therefore, it is important to develop automated methods and tools for checking that the executions of an implementation of the memory are sequentially consistent (for every possible client, or for some given client). A crucial problem for developing SC conformance testing tools, is checking if a given single execution is SC. This problem has been shown to be hard. Intuitively, it amounts in finding a total order on write operations that explains the execution, in the sense that the happen-before relation induced by this order (that includes causality and conflict constraints between writes and reads) is acyclic. It has been shown that the

D. V. Hung and O. Sokolsky (Eds.): ATVA 2020, LNCS 12302, pp. 360–376, 2020.
https://doi.org/10.1007/978-3-030-59152-6_20

problem is NP-complete [15,17], which means that in the worst case, it is necessary to enumerate the exponentially many possible store orderings in order to solve the problem. Therefore, it is important to investigate methods that avoid falling systematically in the worst case, and that are able to solve the problem in polynomial time (in the size of the execution) as often as possible in practice.

In [25], we introduced *gradual consistency checking* (GCC, for short) to address this issue. The approach consists in using weaker consistency models (than SC) that are known to be polynomially checkable, such as causal consistency, in two ways. First, finding violations for these "cheaper" models allows to detect efficiently many of the SC violations. Second, and this is the important point, GCC uses weak consistency models for which checking conformance is based on computing, by a polynomial time fixpoint calculation, a set of order constraints on writes that are *included in every store order witnessing SC conformance*, if any. So, computing these constraints reduces the number of pairs of writes for which an order must be found non-deterministically. In [25], we proposed for that a model called Convergence Causal Memory (CCM, for short) that is stronger than all known variants of causal consistency, constructed by combining the constraints imposed by CCv [8] and CM [3,20].

Then, a natural question is how far the GCC approach can be pushed (i.e., is CCM the strongest model that can be used in this approach)? This paper tackles this question. Our main contribution is the definition of a new consistency criterion called *weak sequential consistency* (wSC, for short) that can be used for this purpose. wSC is defined using a simple *saturation rule* for introducing *store order* constraints. Compared to the definition of CCM, the one of wSC is much more natural and simpler. Interestingly, we prove that wSC is strictly stronger than CCM. This is due to the fact that wSC saturation computes a larger set of constraints on pairs of writes than CCM. Then, the question is still whether it is possible to do better using a saturation-based approach. This question leads to the following more general one: Given an execution that is SC, let us call the SC-kernel of this execution the intersection of all store order relations allowing to establish that the execution is SC (i.e., for which the induced happen-before relation is acyclic). Then, is the store order imposed by wSC always equal to the SC-kernel when the execution is SC? More generally, is it possible to compute the SC-kernel of any execution using saturation when the execution is SC?[1]

First, we show that the wSC saturation rule does not compute the whole SC-kernel in general. We analyze the reason of this by providing several families of counterexamples. We show that there are order constraints that must be imposed on pairs of writes to avoid happen-before cycles including not only one conflict (as wSC saturation does), but several (actually any number) of conflicts involving an arbitrary number of writes. Moreover, we show that in order to impose an order constraint on pairs of writes, in some cases it is necessary to enumerate the

---

[1] The facts that checking SC conformance is NP-hard and that saturation-based computations are polynomial-time do not imply P = NP: given an arbitrary execution, the saturation-based computation would lead to a set of store order constraints, but whether they can be extended to a total order witnessing SC-ness must be checked.

possible order of several other pairs of writes, and the number of these pairs can be arbitrarily high. This shows that the design of a saturation-based schema for computing the SC-kernel would require the addition of an unbounded number of saturation rules. This provides and interesting insight on the hard instances of the SC checking problem. (Though, this leaves open the theoretical question of the complexity of computing the SC-kernel of an SC execution).

Nevertheless, an interesting question is how far is wSC saturation from computing the SC-kernel in practice? We show experimentally that, interestingly, in practice[2], wSC allows to compute the full SC-kernel in most of the cases (more than 74% of the considered executions), and in general it computes almost the whole SC-kernel (around 99.9% of it). The experiments also show that CCM computes 100% of the SC-kernel for only 0.7% of the executions of the considered benchmark. This shows that the wSC saturation rule is very powerful and efficient in practice, despite its simplicity (and that it is theoretically not complete). In fact, as discussed above, we could have considered other saturation rules to define stronger and stronger consistency models approximating SC. But our experiments show that the benefit would not be important w.r.t. what is already achieved with wSC.

Furthermore, we compare the performances of GCC using CCM versus GCC using wSC. In each case we apply the corresponding saturation procedure to compute a partial order on writes (or partial store order), and then the completion of this order to a *total* order is done using a SAT solver. The two algorithms obtained this way are called CCM+ENUM and wSC+ENUM. Our experiments show that wSC+ENUM is significantly more efficient and more scalable than CCM+ENUM.

Finally, we compare our methods with the approach implemented in DBCOP [7] based on a polynomial search algorithm for checking SC-ness assuming that the number of threads is fixed [1,7]. While DBCOP is efficient for a small number of threads, its performances degrade quite fast when this number grows, whereas WSC+ENUM is efficient and scales very well in this case. Then, we consider combining saturation with DBCOP. We use wSC saturation to compute a large set of store order constraints that are given to DBCOP in order to reduce the number of interleavings to be explored for SC conformance checking. We obtain this way an efficient algorithm, called wSC+DBCOP, that has better performances than both DBCOP and wSC+ENUM.

Related Work. The problem of checking whether a history is SC has been proved to be NP-hard by Gibbons and Korach [17]. In [1,7], this problem is shown to be polynomial in the size of the history when the number of threads is fixed. The problem of verifying that a finite-state shared-memory implementations (over a bounded number of threads, variables, and values) has been shown to be undecidable by Alur et al. [5].

Several static techniques have been developed to prove that a shared-memory implementation (or cache coherence protocol) satisfies SC [2,5,9–12,14,16,18,21, 22], however only few have addressed dynamic techniques such as testing and runtime verification (which scale to more realistic implementations).

---

[2] We consider executions of 4 cache coherence protocols within the Gem5 platform.

The idea of using weaker approximations of a memory consistency model (TSO) in order to detect violations has been used, e.g., in [23]. In that paper the authors use a form of saturation that corresponds to a variant of causal consistency (similar to convergence consistency [8]). However, their method is not complete. This idea of saturation is generalized in the framework of gradual consistency checking introduced in [25] where SC is approximated using several variants of causal consistency (including a new one called CCM).

The McVerSi framework [13] addresses test generation (i.e., finding clients that increase the probability of uncovering bugs in shared memory implementations). Their methodology for checking SC lies within the context of white-box testing, i.e., the user is required to annotate the shared memory implementation with events that define the store order in an execution. In the approach we follow, the implementation is treated as a black-box requiring less user intervention.

2 Preliminaries

We introduce in this section basic notions that will be used throughout the paper. We use similar notations and definitions as in [4, 25].

Binary Relations. For a binary relation $r \subseteq A \times A$ over a given set A, we use r^+ (resp. r^*) to denote the transitive (resp. reflexive transitive) closure of r. We use r^{-1} to denote the inverse relation of r (i.e., $(a, b) \in r^{-1}$ iff $(b, a) \in r$). We say that r is a partial order if it is irreflexive (i.e., $(a, a) \notin r$ for all $a \in A$). We say that r is total if, for every $a, b \in A$, we have either $(a, b) \in r$ or $(b, a) \in r$. For two binary relations r_1 and r_2, we use $r_1 \circ r_2$ (resp. $r_1 \cup r_2$) to denote the composition (resp. union) of r_1 and r_2, i.e., $(a, b) \in r_1 \circ r_2$ iff there is an $c \in A$ such that $(a, c) \in r_1$ and $(c, b) \in r_2$ (resp. $(a, b) \in r_1 \cup r_2$ iff $(a, b) \in r_1$ or $(a, b) \in r_2$).

Programs. We consider multi-threaded programs over a set of shared variables $\mathsf{Var} = \{x, y, \ldots\}$. Let Val be an unspecified set of values and $\mathsf{Old} \subseteq \mathbb{N}$ be a set of operation identifiers. We assume that the set of (visible) operations issued by the threads of the program are read and write operations. Formally, the set Op of operations reading or writing a value v to a variable x is defined as $\mathsf{Op} = \{\mathsf{read}_i(x, v), \mathsf{write}_i(x, v) : i \in \mathsf{Old}, x \in \mathsf{Var}, v \in \mathsf{Val}\}$. We omit operation identifiers when it is clear from the context. We use $\mathcal{R}$, (resp. $\mathcal{W}$) to denote the set of read (resp. write) operations. Given an operation $o \in \mathsf{Op}$, we use $\mathsf{var}(o)$ to denote the variable accessed by o. Let O be a subset of Op. We use $\mathcal{R}(O)$ (resp. $\mathcal{W}(O)$) to denote the set of read (resp. write) operations in O.

Histories. A *history* is an abstraction of a program execution. It consists of a set of write or read operations ordered according to two relations: (1) a *partial program order* po that totally orders operations issued by the same thread, and (2) a *write-read* relation wr that identifies the write operation from which each read operation gets it value. Formally, a *history* $\langle O, \mathsf{po}, \mathsf{wr} \rangle$ is a set of operations O along with a strict partial *program order* po and a *write-read* relation $\mathsf{wr} \subseteq \mathcal{W}(O) \times \mathcal{R}(O)$, such that the inverse of wr is a total function and if $(\mathsf{write}(x, v), \mathsf{read}(x', v')) \in \mathsf{wr}$, then $x = x'$ and $v = v'$. We assume that every *history* includes a write operation writing the initial value for each variable x. These write operations precede all other operations in po. Mentioning these initial write operations is omitted when it is clear from the context.

In the following, we assume also that each value is written at most once. This is not a restriction since shared-memory implementations (or cache coherence protocols) are data-independent [24] in practice, i.e., their behavior doesn't depend on the concrete values read or written in the program, and therefore any potential buggy behavior can be exposed by executions where each value is written at most once. Observe that in this case, the *write-read* relation can be easily extracted by just looking to the value fetched by each read operation.

t_0: t_1:
write$(x, 1)$ write$(y, 1)$
read$(y, 0)$ read$(x, 1)$

(a) CCM, wSC and SC

t_0: t_1:
write$(x, 1)$ write$(x, 2)$
read$(y, 0)$ read$(y, 0)$
write$(y, 1)$ write$(y, 2)$
read$(x, 1)$ read$(x, 2)$

(b) CCM but not wSC nor SC

t_0:	t_1:	t_2:	t_3:	t_4:	t_5:
read$(z, 2)$	write$(x, 1)$	write$(t, 1)$	read$(z, 2)$	read$(z, 1)$	read$(z, 1)$
write$(y, 2)$	write$(y, 1)$	write$(s, 1)$	write$(x, 2)$	write$(t, 2)$	write$(s, 2)$
read$(x, 1)$	write$(z, 1)$	write$(z, 2)$	read$(y, 1)$	read$(s, 1)$	read$(t, 1)$

(c) wSC but not SC

Fig. 1. Comparison of different consistency models.

Sequential Consistency. In the following, we recall the formal definition of the Sequential Consistency (SC) memory model [4]. A *history* $\langle O, \text{po}, \text{wr} \rangle$ is *sequentially consistent* if there exists a total relation (called *store order*) ww $\subseteq \mathcal{W}(O) \times \mathcal{W}(O)$ such that the relation po $\cup$ wr $\cup$ ww $\cup$ rw is acyclic, where rw is the *read-write* relation defined by rw = wr$^{-1} \circ$ ww. Intuitively, rw expresses the fact that when a read operation read(x, v) reads a value v from a write operation write(x, v), and some other write operation write(x, v') comes after write(x, v) in the store order, then there is a conflict between read(x, v) and write(x, v'), and read(x, v) must happen before write(x, v').

Figure 1a shows a *history* that is SC. Since read$(y, 0)$ should precede write$(y, 1)$, this *history* admits a total order where the operations of thread t_0 are executed before thread t_1 operations. Figure 1b presents a *history* that does not satisfy SC. The reason is that a total order cannot be found. Since read$(x, 1)$ reads the value from write$(x, 1)$ and read$(x, 2)$ reads the value from write$(x, 2)$, all operations of t_0 should be executed before the operations of t_1, or vice versa. This does not allow either t_0 or t_1 to read the value 0 on variable y.

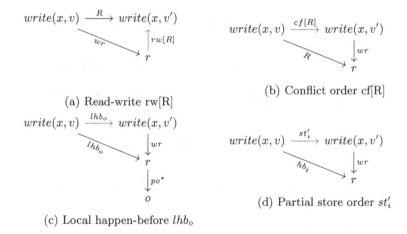

(a) Read-write rw[R]

(b) Conflict order cf[R]

(c) Local happen-before lhb_o

(d) Partial store order st'_i

Fig. 2. Definitions of relations used to define consistency models.

Convergent Causal Memory. The gradual consistency checking approach for checking SC in [25] relies on the use of a weak consistency model called Convergent Causal Memory (CCM) as a polynomially checkable SC approximation. CCM is defined as a strengthening of existing variants of causal consistency. We omit here the definition of these variants and give directly the formal definition of CCM as presented in [25] . For that, some preliminary notions must be introduced. Given a binary relation R on the set of operations, let R_{WW} (resp. R_{WR}) denotes the projection of R on pairs of writes (resp. pairs of writes and reads) on the same variable. We define also the parametric read-write relation rw[R] as follows: $rw[R] = wr^{-1} \circ R_{WW}$ (see Fig. 2a), i.e.,

$$(\text{read}(x, v), \text{write}(x, v')) \in rw[R] \text{ iff } (\text{write}(x, v), \text{write}(x, v')) \in R \text{ and}$$
$$(\text{write}(x, v), \text{read}(x, v)) \in wr$$

Let co be the *causality relation* defined as the transitive closure of the union of the program order and the write-read relation (i.e., $co = (po \cup wr)^+$). Then, we consider a *local happen-before relation* defined with respect to each operation. Given a *history* $h = \langle O, po, wr \rangle$, for every operation o in h, lhb_o[3] is the smallest transitive relation such that:

- if two operations are causally related, and each one is causally related to o, then they are related by the *local happen-before* relation lhb_o, i.e., $(o_1, o_2) \in lhb_o$ if $(o_1, o_2) \in co$, $(o_1, o) \in co$, and $(o_2, o) \in co^*$, and
- two writes w_1 and w_2 are related by the *local happen-before* relation lhb_o (Fig. 2c) if w_1 is lhb_o-related to a read taking its value from w_2, and that read is issued before o by the same thread executing o, i.e.,

---

[3] This relation was denoted hb_o in [25]. We denote it lhb_o to avoid confusion with other happen-before relations considered in the paper.

$$(\text{write}(x, v), \text{write}(x, v')) \in \text{lhb}_o \text{ if } (\text{write}(x, v), \text{read}(x, v')) \in \text{lhb}_o,$$
$$(\text{write}(x, v'), \text{read}(x, v')) \in \text{wr}, \text{ and}$$
$$(\text{read}(x, v'), o) \in \text{po}^*, \text{ for some } \text{read}(x, v').$$

Finally, a *history* $\langle O, \text{po}, \text{wr} \rangle$ is conform to CCM if $\text{po} \cup \text{wr} \cup \text{pww} \cup \text{rw}[\text{pww}]$ is acyclic, where the *partial store order* pww is defined by

$$\text{pww} = (\text{lhb}_{\text{WW}} \cup \text{cf}[\text{lhb}])^+ \text{ with } \text{lhb} = \left(\bigcup_{o \in O} \text{lhb}_o \right)^+$$

where the conflict relation $\text{cf}[R]$ induced by a relation R is defined as $\text{cf}[R] = R_{\text{WR}} \circ \text{wr}^{-1}$ (Fig. 2b), i.e.,

$$(\text{write}(x, v), \text{write}(x, v')) \in \text{cf}[R] \text{ iff } (\text{write}(x, v), \text{read}(x, v')) \in R \text{ and}$$
$$(\text{write}(x, v'), \text{read}(x, v')) \in \text{wr}, \text{ for some } \text{read}(x, v')$$

Notice that the relation rw used in the definition of SC corresponds to rw[ww] according to this parametric definition.

3 Weak Sequential Consistency

We propose in this section a new consistency model (called Weak Sequential Consistent) obtained by computing a partial store order using a simple *saturation rule*. This partial store order is inductively defined unlike the SC case where the total store order is existentially quantified. Formally, let st and hb be the smallest relations such that:

$$\text{st} = ((\text{hb}_{\text{WR}} \circ \text{wr}^{-1}) \cup \text{hb}_{\text{WW}})^+$$
$$\text{hb} = (\text{po} \cup \text{wr} \cup \text{st} \cup \text{rw}[\text{st}])^+$$
$$\text{rw}[\text{st}] = \text{wr}^{-1} \circ \text{st}$$

Recall that hb_{WR} (resp. hb_{WW}) denote the projection of the relation hb on pairs of writes and reads (resp. pairs of writes on the same variable). Intuitively, the store order st contains the composition of the projection of happen-before relation on pairs of writes and reads and write-read relation, union the projection of happen-before on pairs of writes.

The happen-before relation is similar to the SC one (which corresponds to $\text{po} \cup \text{wr} \cup \text{ww} \cup \text{rw}$), it is just that, the store order is deterministically computed using the above saturation rule. Then, a *history* $\langle O, \text{po}, \text{wr} \rangle$ is weakly sequentially consistent (wSC) if hb is acyclic.

Our first contribution consists in showing that wSC is stronger than CCM (which is already stronger than all known variants of causal consistency) [25].

Lemma 1. *If a* history *satisfies* wSC, *then it satisfies* CCM.

Proof. Let $h = \langle O, \mathsf{po}, \mathsf{wr} \rangle$ be a *history* satisfying wSC i.e., $\mathsf{po} \cup \mathsf{wr} \cup \mathsf{st} \cup \mathsf{rw[st]}$ is acyclic. We prove that $(\mathsf{po} \cup \mathsf{wr} \cup \mathsf{pww} \cup \mathsf{rw[pww]})^+ \subseteq \mathsf{hb}$ (hence the history satisfies also CCM). We will first show that for every operation o in h, $\mathsf{lhb}_o \subseteq \mathsf{hb}$. For that we will prove that hb satisfies the two properties of lhb_o:

- If $(o_1, o_2) \in \mathsf{co}$, $(o_1, o) \in \mathsf{co}$, and $(o_2, o) \in \mathsf{co}^*$ then $(o_1, o_2) \in \mathsf{hb}$ trivially holds (since $\mathsf{co} \subseteq \mathsf{hb}$), and
- if $(\mathsf{write}(x, v), \mathsf{read}(x, v')) \in \mathsf{hb}$ and $(\mathsf{write}(x, v'), \mathsf{read}(x, v')) \in \mathsf{wr}$ then $(\mathsf{write}(x, v), \mathsf{write}(x, v')) \in (\mathsf{hb} \circ \mathsf{wr}^{-1})$ and hence $(\mathsf{write}(x, v), \mathsf{write}(x, v')) \in \mathsf{st}$ and $(\mathsf{write}(x, v), \mathsf{write}(x, v')) \in \mathsf{hb}$.

Thus, we have that $\mathsf{lhb}_o \subseteq \mathsf{hb}$ and hence $\mathsf{lhb} \subseteq \mathsf{hb}$.

Let us now show that $\mathsf{pww} = (\mathsf{lhb}_{\mathsf{WW}} \cup \mathsf{cf}[\mathsf{lhb}])^+ \subseteq \mathsf{st}$. It is easy to see that $\mathsf{lhb}_{\mathsf{WW}} \subseteq \mathsf{hb}_{\mathsf{WW}}$ (since $\mathsf{lhb} \subseteq \mathsf{hb}$). By definition, we have also that $\mathsf{cf}[\mathsf{lhb}] = (\mathsf{lhb}_{\mathsf{WR}} \circ \mathsf{wr}^{-1})$ and hence $\mathsf{cf}[\mathsf{lhb}] \subseteq (\mathsf{hb}_{\mathsf{WR}} \circ \mathsf{wr}^{-1})$. This implies that $\mathsf{pww} = (\mathsf{lhb}_{\mathsf{WW}} \cup \mathsf{cf}[\mathsf{lhb}])^+ \subseteq \mathsf{st} = ((\mathsf{hb}_{\mathsf{WR}} \circ \mathsf{wr}^{-1}) \cup \mathsf{hb}_{\mathsf{WW}})^+$. Finally, it is easy to deduce that $(\mathsf{po} \cup \mathsf{wr} \cup \mathsf{pww} \cup \mathsf{rw[pww]})^+ \subseteq \mathsf{hb} = (\mathsf{po} \cup \mathsf{wr} \cup \mathsf{st} \cup \mathsf{rw[st]})^+$. □

The reverse of this lemma does not hold. Figure 1b presents a *history* that satisfies CCM but not wSC. A possible partial store order for CCM is to consider that the writes of each thread are not visible to the other thread. The *history* does not satisfy wSC. Since $\mathsf{rw[st]}$ is included in hb, $\mathsf{read}(y, 0)$ is visible to $\mathsf{write}(y, 2)$ then $\mathsf{write}(x, 1)$ precedes $\mathsf{read}(x, 2)$ in hb. Thus, $\mathsf{write}(x, 2)$ should be executed before $\mathsf{write}(x, 1)$. Similarly $\mathsf{write}(x, 2)$ precedes $\mathsf{read}(x, 1)$ in hb as well and $\mathsf{write}(x, 1)$ should be executed before $\mathsf{write}(x, 2)$.

We prove now that wSC is indeed weaker than SC. For that, we need to consider the subrelations of st and hb obtained by iterative least fixpoint calculation. Let $\mathsf{st} = \bigcup_i st_i$ and $\mathsf{hb} = \bigcup_i hb_i$ where $st_i = (hb_{i\mathsf{WW}} \cup st_i')^+$ and st_i' (Fig. 2d) is defined by:

$$(\mathsf{write}(x, v), \mathsf{write}(x, v')) \in st_i' \text{ iff } (\mathsf{write}(x, v), \mathsf{read}(x, v')) \in hb_i \text{ and}$$
$$(\mathsf{write}(x, v'), \mathsf{read}(x, v')) \in \mathsf{wr}$$

where, for every $i \geq 0$, hb_i is defined by:

$$hb_0 = (\mathsf{po} \cup \mathsf{wr})^+$$
$$hb_{i+1} = (hb_i \cup st_i \cup \mathsf{rw}[st_i])^+$$

We now show that the partial store order st_i is included in any store order ww witnessing for SC satisfaction.

Lemma 2. *Let $h = \langle O, \mathsf{po}, \mathsf{wr} \rangle$ be a history and ww be a total store order such that $\mathsf{po} \cup \mathsf{wr} \cup \mathsf{ww} \cup \mathsf{rw}$ is acyclic. Then, $st_i \subseteq \mathsf{ww}$ and $hb_i \subseteq (\mathsf{po} \cup \mathsf{wr} \cup \mathsf{ww} \cup \mathsf{rw})^+$.*

Proof. The proof is by induction on the index i of hb_i and st_i.

Base Case (i=0). We have $hb_0 = (\mathsf{po} \cup \mathsf{wr})^+$ is included in $(\mathsf{po} \cup \mathsf{wr} \cup \mathsf{ww} \cup \mathsf{rw})^+$. Since $hb_0 \subseteq (\mathsf{po} \cup \mathsf{wr} \cup \mathsf{ww} \cup \mathsf{rw})^+$, if $(\mathsf{write}(x, v), \mathsf{read}(x, v')) \in hb_0$

and there exists a $\mathsf{read}(x, v')$ such that $(\mathsf{write}(x, v'), \mathsf{read}(x, v')) \in \mathsf{wr}$, then $(\mathsf{write}(x, v), \mathsf{write}(x, v')) \in \mathsf{ww}$. Otherwise, assuming by contradiction that $(\mathsf{write}(x, v'), \mathsf{write}(x, v)) \in \mathsf{ww}$, we get $(\mathsf{read}(x, v'), \mathsf{write}(x, v)) \in \mathsf{rw}$. Since $\mathsf{write}(x, v), \mathsf{read}(x, v')) \in hb_0 \subseteq (\mathsf{po} \cup \mathsf{wr} \cup \mathsf{ww} \cup \mathsf{rw})^+$, this implies that there is a cycle in $(\mathsf{po} \cup \mathsf{wr} \cup \mathsf{ww} \cup \mathsf{rw})^+$ which is a contradiction. So, $(\mathsf{write}(x, v), \mathsf{write}(x, v')) \in \mathsf{ww}$. Thus, st_0' is included in ww and hence $st_0 = (hb_{0\mathsf{ww}} \cup st_0')^+$ is also in ww since $hb_{0\mathsf{ww}} \subseteq \mathsf{ww}$ (otherwise it leads to a contradiction since $hb_0 \subseteq (\mathsf{po} \cup \mathsf{wr} \cup \mathsf{ww} \cup \mathsf{rw})^+$ and $(\mathsf{po} \cup \mathsf{wr} \cup \mathsf{ww} \cup \mathsf{rw})^+$ is acyclic).

Induction Step. Assume that $hb_i \subseteq (\mathsf{po} \cup \mathsf{wr} \cup \mathsf{ww} \cup \mathsf{rw})^+$ and $st_i \subseteq \mathsf{ww}$. Now, let's show that this holds for $i + 1$ as well. By induction hypothesis, $st_i \subseteq \mathsf{ww}$, so using the definition of $\mathsf{rw}[st_i]$ we have $\mathsf{rw}[st_i] \subseteq \mathsf{rw}$. Then, $hb_{i+1} = (hb_i \cup st_i \cup \mathsf{rw}[st_i])^+ \subseteq (\mathsf{po} \cup \mathsf{wr} \cup \mathsf{ww} \cup \mathsf{rw})^+$. Now, we show that $st_{i+1}' \subseteq \mathsf{ww}$. If $(\mathsf{write}(x, v), \mathsf{read}(x, v')) \in hb_i$ and $(\mathsf{write}(x, v'), \mathsf{read}(x, v')) \in \mathsf{wr}$, then $(\mathsf{write}(x, v), \mathsf{write}(x, v')) \in \mathsf{ww}$. Otherwise, using the same argument as in the base case, we get that $(\mathsf{read}(x, v'), \mathsf{write}(x, v)) \in \mathsf{rw}$ and a contradiction of the fact that $(\mathsf{po} \cup \mathsf{wr} \cup \mathsf{ww} \cup \mathsf{rw})^+$ is acyclic. Hence, if $(\mathsf{write}(x, v), \mathsf{write}(x, v')) \in st_{i+1}'$ then $(\mathsf{write}(x, v), \mathsf{write}(x, v')) \in \mathsf{ww}$ and so $st_{i+1}' \subseteq \mathsf{ww}$. Furthermore, we have $hb_{i+1\mathsf{ww}} \subseteq \mathsf{ww}$ since $hb_{i+1} \subseteq (\mathsf{po} \cup \mathsf{wr} \cup \mathsf{ww} \cup \mathsf{rw})^+$ (otherwise it leads to a contradiction of the fact that $(\mathsf{po} \cup \mathsf{wr} \cup \mathsf{ww} \cup \mathsf{rw})^+$ is acyclic). Since $st_{i+1} = (hb_{i+1\mathsf{ww}} \cup st_{i+1}')^+$, $st_{i+1}' \subseteq \mathsf{ww}$ and $hb_{i+1\mathsf{ww}} \subseteq \mathsf{ww}$, we get that $st_{i+1} \subseteq \mathsf{ww}$ (since ww is a total store order). □

As an immediate corollary of Lemma 2, we get:

Lemma 3. *If a history satisfies SC, then it satisfies wSC.*

Proof. The proof is by contradiction. Assume that a history $h = \langle O, \mathsf{po}, \mathsf{wr} \rangle$ satisfies SC and it does not satisfy wSC. Since h satisfies SC, then there exists a total store order ww such that $\mathsf{po} \cup \mathsf{wr} \cup \mathsf{ww} \cup \mathsf{rw}$ is acyclic. Since h does not satisfy wSC, this means that hb is cyclic. Since $hb = \bigcup_i hb_i$ and $hb_i \subseteq (\mathsf{po} \cup \mathsf{wr} \cup \mathsf{ww} \cup \mathsf{rw})^+$ (from Lemma 2), we can deduce that $(\mathsf{po} \cup \mathsf{wr} \cup \mathsf{ww} \cup \mathsf{rw})^+$ is also cyclic which constitutes a contradiction. □

The reverse of the above lemma doesn't hold. Figure 1c shows a *history* which satisfies wSC but it is not SC. To show that it satisfies wSC, one can consider a partial store order st where the writes $\mathsf{write}(z, 1)$ and $\mathsf{write}(z, 2)$ are not ordered. In the other hand, since there is no valid store order for the writes $\mathsf{write}(z, 1)$ and $\mathsf{write}(z, 2)$, this *history* does not satisfy SC.

Notice that, at each step of the calculation of hb and st, at least one pair of operations is added to one of these two relations and that number of such pairs is polynomially bounded (in the size of the computation). Thus, the acyclicity of hb can be decided in polynomial time.

Theorem 1. *Checking whether a history h satisfies wSC can be done in polynomial time in the size of the history.*

4   The Sequential Consistency Kernel

Given a history $h = \langle O, \mathsf{po}, \mathsf{wr} \rangle$ that satisfies SC, we define the SC-Kernel of h as the intersection of all store order orders allowing to establish the SCness of h. We know already, from the previous section (Lemma 2), that the store order st, computed by the wSC saturation

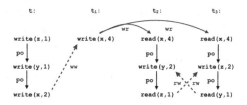

Fig. 3. SC-Kernel counter example

procedure, is included in any total store order ww such that $\mathsf{po} \cup \mathsf{wr} \cup \mathsf{ww} \cup \mathsf{rw}$ is acyclic. This means that the computed st is always a subset of SC-Kernel. Then, the question is whether the computed store order st is equal to SC-Kernel or not.

In the following, we show that the saturation procedure of wSC may in some cases not be able to compute the SC-Kernel (but rather a strict subset of it). To see why, consider the history given in Fig. 3. The wSC rules do not generate any st relation and therefore the saturation procedure of wSC returns that the store order st is empty while the happens-before relation hb is equal to $(\mathsf{po} \cup \mathsf{wr})^+$. However, any total store order ww that allows to show the SCness of this history should order $\mathsf{write}(x, 4)$ before $\mathsf{write}(x, 2)$ (and hence the pair $(\mathsf{write}(x, 4), \mathsf{write}(x, 2))$ is in the SC-Kernel). We prove that $(\mathsf{write}(x, 4), \mathsf{write}(x, 2))$ belongs to the SC-Kernel by contradiction. Assume that $(\mathsf{write}(x, 4), \mathsf{write}(x, 2))$ is not in SC-Kernel. Then, there is a total store order ww such that (1) $(\mathsf{write}(x, 2), \mathsf{write}(x, 4))$ is in ww (represented in Fig. 3 by a dashed arrow) and (2) $(\mathsf{po} \cup \mathsf{wr} \cup \mathsf{ww} \cup \mathsf{rw})^+$ is acyclic (since the history h is SC). However, if $(\mathsf{write}(x, 2), \mathsf{write}(x, 4))$ is in ww then $(\mathsf{po} \cup \mathsf{wr} \cup \mathsf{ww} \cup \mathsf{rw})^+$ is not acyclic (as shown in Fig. 3 by the dashed arrows) and which is a contradiction.

One way to overcome this problem is to include such a pattern in the definition of st'_i used in the saturation procedure. Thus, the definition of st'_i is updated as follows: $(\mathsf{write}(x, v'), \mathsf{write}(x, v)) \in st'_i$ iff one of the following cases holds:

- $(\mathsf{write}(x, v'), \mathsf{read}(x, v)) \in hb_i$ and $(\mathsf{write}(x, v), \mathsf{read}(x, v)) \in \mathsf{wr}$, or
- $(\mathsf{write}(z, v_z), \mathsf{write}(x, v))$, $(\mathsf{write}(y, v_y), \mathsf{write}(x, v))$, $(\mathsf{write}(x, v'), \mathsf{write}(y, v'_y))$, $(\mathsf{write}(y, v'_y), \mathsf{read}(z, v_z))$, $(\mathsf{write}(x, v'), \mathsf{write}(z, v'_z))$, $(\mathsf{write}(z, v'_z), \mathsf{read}(y, v_y))$ are in hb_i and $(\mathsf{write}(z, v_z), \mathsf{read}(z, v_z))$, $(\mathsf{write}(y, v_y), \mathsf{read}(y, v_y))$ are in wr.

Observe that the pattern added to st'_i contains six write operations. Unfortunately, this pattern is not enough to allow us to capture the SC-Kernel. In fact, we can construct a family of counter-examples (see Fig. 4) such that in order to capture all of them, we need to add to the relation st'_i patterns involving a strictly increasing number of writes (which is not feasible in practice).

One way to address the problem raised by the family of counter-examples given in Fig. 4 is to guess for a given pair of writes $\mathsf{write}(x, v)$ and $\mathsf{write}(x, v')$ that are not related by the computed store relation st (i.e., $(\mathsf{write}(x, v), \mathsf{write}(x, v'))$

and $(\mathsf{write}(x,v'), \mathsf{write}(x,v))$ are not in st) one possible order and check if it can make the history h infeasible under SC and if it is the case we add the other order to st. For instance, in the history given in Fig. 3, one would guess that the $(\mathsf{write}(x,2), \mathsf{write}(x,4))$ is in st. This guess makes the history infeasible under SC due to the existence of a cycle in $(\mathsf{po} \cup \mathsf{wr} \cup \mathsf{ww} \cup \mathsf{rw})^+$ and hence $(\mathsf{write}(x,4), \mathsf{write}(x,2))$ is added to st. Observe that this still results in a saturation procedure which works in polynomial time since we are only allowed to guess the order of at most two unrelated writes.

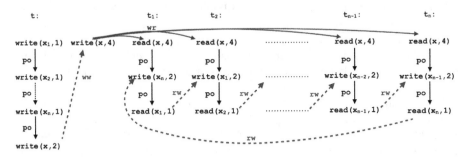

Fig. 4. SC-Kernel counter-examples with cycles involving an arbitrary number of writes

So the question is whether this extended saturation procedure calculates the SC-Kernel. Alas, this is not true. Consider the history given in Fig. 5. The previous saturation procedure of wSC (augmented with the guessing of the order of one pair of writes) results in an empty store order st. However, this history satisfies SC and $(\mathsf{write}(x,1), \mathsf{write}(x,2))$ and $(\mathsf{write}(t,2), \mathsf{write}(t,1))$ are in SC-Kernel. In fact, ordering $\mathsf{write}(x,2)$ before $\mathsf{write}(x,1)$ and $\mathsf{write}(t,2)$ before $\mathsf{write}(t,1)$ creates a happens-before cycle in the top-left block of Fig. 5 (in similar manner to the example given in Fig. 3). While ordering $\mathsf{write}(x,2)$ before $\mathsf{write}(x,1)$ and $\mathsf{write}(t,1)$ before $\mathsf{write}(t,2)$ creates a happens-before cycle in the top-right block of Fig. 5. Finally, ordering $\mathsf{write}(x,1)$ before $\mathsf{write}(x,2)$ and $\mathsf{write}(t,1)$ before $\mathsf{write}(t,2)$ creates a happens-before cycle in the top-middle block of Fig. 5. This shows the necessity of augmenting the saturation procedure with the enumeration of the order between two pairs of writes in order to compute the SC-Kernel. Even worst, we can easily extend the history given in Fig. 5 in order to force the enumeration of the order between several pairs of writes in order to be able to compute the SC-Kernel. The main idea is to add a number of blocks (in similar manner to the examples given in Figure 3 and Figure 4) to forbid all order combinations between certain pairs of write except one.

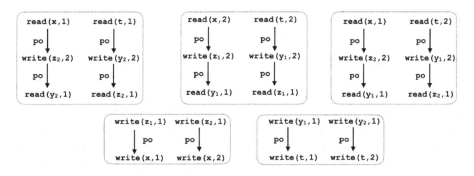

Fig. 5. SC-Kernel counter-example requiring the enumeration of the possible order between two pairs of writes

5 Algorithms for Checking SC Conformance

We define in this section algorithms for SC checking that exploit the partial store order st computed by the wSC saturation. Following the approach of gradual consistency checking [25], we start by checking that the given history is wSC. If not, then we conclude that it is not SC neither (by Lemma 3). If yes, we exploit st in order to enhance the SC verification of the history. This verification amounts in finding a total store order extending st. To solve this problem we adopt two approaches, one is based on reducing the SC verification problem to SAT i.e., a direct encoding of the axioms defining SC into a propositional formula, and the second one is based on using the bounded-thread approach of [1,7] implemented in the tool DBCOP. Both of these approaches are enhanced by the fact that they will use the st constraints in order to reduce their search space. The two obtained algorithms are called wSC+ENUM and wSC+DBCOP, respectively.

The algorithm wSC+ENUM uses an encoding of SC conformance of a given history (defined with its po and wr constraints) as the satisfaction of a Boolean formula. The latter expresses the constraints on the relations involved in the definition of SC, including the fact that the *store oder* ww is a total order relation (so every pair of writes must be order in one direction or the other), and that the happen-before relation (i.e., $(\text{po} \cup \text{wr} \cup \text{ww} \cup \text{rw})^+$) is transitive and acyclic. Moreover, the order constraints corresponding to the relation st computed for wSC are added to the formula since st $\subseteq$ ww.

The algorithm wSC+DBCOP is based on the algorithm implemented in DBCOP [7]. Given a history (again defined by its po and wr relations), DBCOP searches for an interleaving of all the operations of the history that respects the constraints imposed by SC. Then, wSC+DBCOP is an adaptation of DBCOP that exploits st in addition to po and wr as fixed constraints during its search.

For our experiments in next section, we will compare wSC+ENUM and wSC+DBCOP to each other, to DBCOP, and also to CCM+ENUM which is the analogous of wSC+ENUM using CCM saturation instead of wSC saturation. CCM+ENUM is the algorithm proposed in [25].

6 Experimental Results

We evaluate in this section the efficiency of our approach and its scalability. We first report on the efficiency of the wSC saturation in computing the SC-kernel. Then, we present an evaluation of the approach in checking SC conformance by taking into account two parameters: the number of operations and the number of threads. The experimental results consider three kinds of benchmarks: The first one consists of only valid histories (i.e., satisfying SC). The second one consists of invalid histories (i.e., violating SC). The third benchmark consists of mixture of valid and invalid histories. These benchmarks are generated by running random clients on realistic cache coherence protocols within the Gem5 simulator [6] in system emulation mode. We use 4 cache coherence protocols that are available in Gem5: MI, MEOSI HAMMER, MESI TWO LEVEL, and MEOSI AMD Base.

Approximating the SC-Kernel. We know already that the store orders computed by the saturation procedures of CCM and wSC are part of the SC-kernel (Lemma 2). The questions are then what is the computed proportion of the SC-kernel, and what is the proportion of the set of pairs of writes in the execution that are not ordered by the saturation procedures. Our experimental results show that wSC computes the SC-kernel in 74.24% of all the 1742 tested histories, and that for the rest of the histories, it computes in average 99.97% of their kernel. For CCM, we found that it computes the SC-kernel only in 0.7% of the same set of executions. We also found that the wSC saturation procedure orders 98.51% of the pairs of writes of a history in average, and that CCM orders in average 97,89% of the pairs of writes. This is interesting since in terms of coverage of the sets of pairs of write, CCM is not far from wSC, however, only for very few histories it can fully cover its SC-kernel.

SC Conformance Checking for Valid Histories. We consider in this section the case of histories that satisfy SC. The experiments are made by varying the number of operations and the number of threads. For each number of operations (threads), we have tested 200 histories and computed the running time average.

Figure 6 reports the running time (in seconds) of the 4 algorithms wSC+ENUM, CCM+ENUM, DPCOP, and wSC+DBCOP while increasing the number of operations from 200 to 800 (by an increase of 100) with a fixed number of 6 threads. It shows that for a relatively small number of threads, DBCOP has the best performances, while wSC+ENUM has good performances and is clearly superior than CCM+ENUM. This can be partly explained by the difference in the coverage of store order constraints between the two algorithms, but most

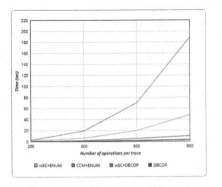

Fig. 6. Checking SCness for valid histories while varying the number of operations.

importantly by their time complexity.
In fact, the difference in the coverage
in average between the two algorithms is small (98.51% vs 97,89%). Thus, the
time complexity of the two algorithms plays also an important role: for CCM,
the saturation schema requires computing local happen-before relation for each
operation, which is very expensive compared with the much simpler saturation
schema in wSC.

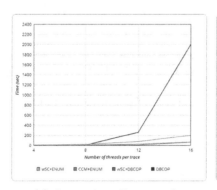
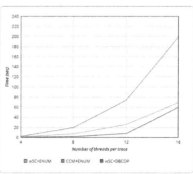

(a) Comparing all approaches.   (b) Comparison of wSC+ENUM,
                                           CCM+ENUM and wSC+DBCOP.

Fig. 7. Checking SC for valid histories while varying the number of threads.

Figure 7 reports the running time while increasing the number of threads
from 4 to 16, by steps of 4. We have considered 50 operations per thread. Notice
that increasing the number of threads increases also the total number of operations. Figure 7(a) shows that the performances of DBCOP degrade beyond
8 threads, while the other algorithms exploiting saturation are more scalable.
wSC+DBCOP achieves the best performances while wSC+ENUM performs better than CCM+ENUM. Figure 7(b) is a zoom of Figure 7(a) for a smaller time
scale in order to examine more closely the separation between CCM+ENUM,
wSC+ENUM, and wSC+DBCOP. It can be seen that the combination of wSC
saturation with DBCOP leads to an efficient procedure that takes advantage
from the DBCOP strategy for small number of threads, and exploits wSC saturation to stay scalable when both the number of threads and operations increase.

SC Conformance Checking for (in)valid Histories. We now consider a
set of histories containing 50% of violations. The violations are generated by
randomly changing the write-read relation: for some reads, chosen randomly, we
modify the writes from which they get their values. The new writes are chosen
randomly within a bounded distance from their corresponding reads. As in the
previous paragraph, we consider histories with 4 to 16 threads and we test 200
histories for each number of threads. The experimental results are presented in
Fig. 8 and they are very similarly to the case with only valid histories.

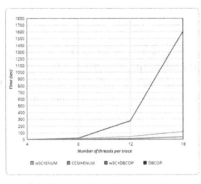
(a) Comparing all approaches.

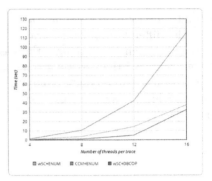
(b) Comparison of wSC+ENUM,
CCM+ENUM and wSC+DBCOP.

Fig. 8. Checking SC for a set of 50% of valid and 50% of invalid histories.

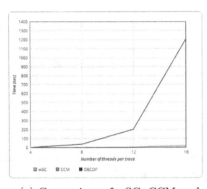
(a) Comparison of wSC, CCM and
DBCOP.

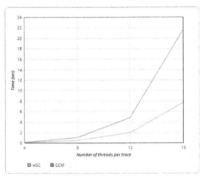
(b) Comparison of wSC and CCM.

Fig. 9. Checking SC for Invalid Histories.

SC Conformance Checking for Invalid Histories. In the following, we consider invalide histories with 4 to 16 threads and 50 operations per thread. For each number of threads, we consider 100 histories and compute the average running time. Since all found violations are already wSC violations, we only compare the saturation steps of wSC, CCM, and DBCOP. Figure 9b shows that wSC is more efficient than CCM. In addition, wSC captures more SC violations: 1,25% of the violations are not captured by CCM. Figure 9 shows that wSC has better performance, by factors of 70 times (in the 8 threads case) and higher, compared to DBCOP. In fact, wSC terminates in less than 8 s for all the tested histories. This shows the efficiency of wSC in detecting consistency violations. Furthermore, wSC scales very well when increasing the number of threads (and therefore the total number of operations).

7   Conclusion

We have proposed an efficient approach for verifying the conformance of an execution to SC (known to be NP-hard). The approach is based on using a powerful saturation rule for computing in polynomial time a large subset of the SC-kernel of the given execution. Our experimental results show that in practice (1) this allows to catch very quickly almost all SC-violations, and (2) our method allows to compute almost always the whole SC-kernel, and leaves only a very small number of store order constraints to be found in order to check SC-ness. We considered two ways for finding the remaining constraints: either using SAT-solving, or using the search procedure of DBCOP. The latter option, exploiting saturation to enhance DBCOP, is the best one experimentally, leading to a performant and scalable algorithm. An interesting problem for future work is the development of similar approaches for other consistency models for which the conformance verification problem is NP-hard, such as for instance the Total Store Order (TSO) model.

References

1. Abdulla, P.A., Atig, M.F., Jonsson, B., Lång, M., Ngo, T.P., Sagonas, K.: Optimal stateless model checking for reads-from equivalence under sequential consistency. Proc. ACM Program. Lang. 3(OOPSLA) (2019)
2. Abdulla, P.A., Haziza, F., Holík, L.: Parameterized verification through view abstraction. STTT 18(5), 495–516 (2016)
3. Ahamad, M., Neiger, G., Burns, J.E., Kohli, P., Hutto, P.W.: Causal memory: definitions, implementation, and programming. Distributed Comput. 9(1), 37–49 (1995)
4. Alglave, J., Maranget, L., Tautschnig, M.: Herding cats: modelling, simulation, testing, and data mining for weak memory. ACM Trans. Program. Lang. Syst. 36(2), 7:1–7:74 (2014)
5. Alur, R., McMillan, K.L., Peled, D.A.: Model-checking of correctness conditions for concurrent objects. Inf. Comput. 160(1–2), 167–188 (2000)
6. Binkert, N., et al.: The Gem5 Simulator. SIGARCH Comput. Archit. News 39(2), 1–7 (2011)
7. Biswas, R., Enea, C.: On the complexity of checking transactional consistency. Proc. ACM Program. Lang. 3(OOPSLA) (2019)
8. Burckhardt, S.: Principles of Eventual Consistency. Now Publishers (2014)
9. Clarke, E.M., et al.: Verification of the futurebus+ cache coherence protocol. In: Agnew, D., Claesen, L.J.M., Camposano, R. (eds.) CHDL. IFIP Transactions, vol. A-32, pp. 15–30. North-Holland (1993)
10. Delzanno, G.: Automatic verification of parameterized cache coherence protocols. In: Emerson, E.A., Sistla, A.P. (eds.) CAV 2000. LNCS, vol. 1855, pp. 53–68. Springer, Heidelberg (2000). https://doi.org/10.1007/10722167_8
11. Delzanno, G.: Constraint-based verification of parameterized cache coherence protocols. Formal Methods Syst. Des. 23(3), 257–301 (2003)
12. Eiríksson, Á.T., McMillan, K.L.: Using formal verification/analysis methods on the critical path in system design: a case study. In: Wolper, P. (ed.) CAV 1995. LNCS, vol. 939, pp. 367–380. Springer, Heidelberg (1995). https://doi.org/10.1007/3-540-60045-0_63

13. Elver, M., Nagarajan, V.: Mcversi: a test generation framework for fast memory consistency verification in simulation. In: HPCA, pp. 618–630. IEEE Computer Society (2016)
14. Esparza, J., Finkel, A., Mayr, R.: On the verification of broadcast protocols. In: LICS, pp. 352–359. IEEE Computer Society (1999)
15. Furbach, F., Meyer, R., Schneider, K., Senftleben, M.: Memory-model-aware testing: a unified complexity analysis. ACM Trans. Embedded Comput. Syst. **14**(4), 63:1–63:25 (2015)
16. German, S.M., Sistla, A.P.: Reasoning about systems with many processes. J. ACM **39**(3), 675–735 (1992)
17. Gibbons, P.B., Korach, E.: Testing shared memories. SIAM J. Comput. **26**(4), 1208–1244 (1997)
18. Ip, C.N., Dill, D.L.: Better verification through symmetry. Formal Methods Syst. Des. **9**(1/2), 41–75 (1996)
19. Lamport, L.: How to make a multiprocessor computer that correctly executes multiprocess programs. IEEE Trans. Comput. **28**(9), 690–691 (1979)
20. Perrin, M., Mostefaoui, A., Jard, C.: Causal consistency: beyond memory. In: PPoPP, pp. 26:1–26:12. ACM (2016)
21. Pong, F., Dubois, M.: A new approach for the verification of cache coherence protocols. IEEE Trans. Parallel Distrib. Syst. **6**(8), 773–787 (1995)
22. Qadeer, S.: Verifying sequential consistency on shared-memory multiprocessors by model checking. IEEE Trans. Parallel Distrib. Syst. **14**(8), 730–741 (2003)
23. Roy, A., Zeisset, S., Fleckenstein, C.J., Huang, J.C.: Fast and generalized polynomial time memory consistency verification. In: Ball, T., Jones, R.B. (eds.) CAV 2006. LNCS, vol. 4144, pp. 503–516. Springer, Heidelberg (2006). https://doi.org/10.1007/11817963_46
24. Wolper, P.: Expressing interesting properties of programs in propositional temporal logic. In: POPL, pp. 184–193. ACM Press (1986)
25. Zennou, R., Bouajjani, A., Enea, C., Erradi, M.: Gradual consistency checking. In: Dillig, I., Tasiran, S. (eds.) CAV 2019. LNCS, vol. 11562, pp. 267–285. Springer, Cham (2019). https://doi.org/10.1007/978-3-030-25543-5_16

Parallel Graph-Based Stateless Model Checking

Magnus Lång$^{(\boxtimes)}$ and Konstantinos Sagonas

Department of Information Technology, Uppsala University, Uppsala, Sweden
{Magnus.Lang,Konstantinos.Sagonas}@it.uu.se

Abstract. Stateless model checking (SMC) is an automatic technique with low memory requirements for finding errors in concurrent programs or for checking for their absence. To be effective, SMC tools require algorithms that combat the combinatorial explosion in the number of process/thread interactions that need to be explored. In recent years, a plethora of such algorithms have emerged, which can be classified broadly in those that explore *interleavings* (i.e., complete serializations of events) and those that explore *traces* (i.e., graphs of events). In either case, an SMC algorithm is *optimal* if it explores exactly one representative from each class of equivalent executions. In this paper, we examine the parallelization of a state-of-the-art graph-based algorithm for SMC under sequential consistency, based on the reads-from relation. The algorithm is provably optimal, and in practice spends only polynomial time per equivalence class. We present the modifications to the algorithm that its parallelization requires and implementation aspects that allow us to make it scalable. We report on the performance and scalability that we were able to achieve on C/pthread programs, and how this performance compares to that of other SMC tools. Finally, we argue for the inherent advantages that graph-based algorithms have over interleaving-based ones for achieving scalability when parallelism enters the picture.

1 Introduction

Stateless model checking (SMC) [12] is a fully automatic technique to systematically, and often *exhaustively*, test concurrent programs written in general-purpose programming languages for bugs and other concurrency issues. The programs, which must be data-deterministic and terminating, are executed many times under the control of a stateless model checker, each time controlled to exhibit a different interleaving. One approach to combating the combinatorial explosion in the number of executions that need to be explored in SMC is called *Dynamic Partial-Order Reduction* [2,11], which drives the scheduling of the program, and systematically explores the different orderings of *dependent events*, for example conflicting accesses to the same shared variable. Recently, a new kind of SMC reduction algorithms [3,16,17] has emerged, which views program executions not as schedules but as *traces*, i.e., labelled *graphs* of program events. These new graph-based SMC algorithms are conceptually easier to understand and often

© Springer Nature Switzerland AG 2020
D. V. Hung and O. Sokolsky (Eds.): ATVA 2020, LNCS 12302, pp. 377–393, 2020.
https://doi.org/10.1007/978-3-030-59152-6_21

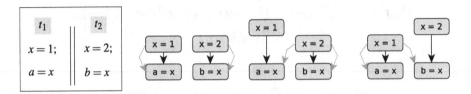

Fig. 1. Simple program (left) and its three READSFROM-SMC traces. (Color figure online)

simpler to implement in an efficient way. More importantly, as we will show in this paper, they are more amenable to effective parallelization.

In either type of SMC algorithms, the partial order relation and the traces, respectively, divide the interleavings of the program into equivalence classes. If an algorithm explores exactly one representative from each equivalence class, we say that it is *optimal*. Non-optimal algorithms may spend exponentially more time than optimal ones exploring multiple different elements of each equivalence class.

SMC algorithms have low memory requirements in practice, but run in time at least linear in the number of different concurrency behaviours of the program. In order to apply SMC to challenging programs, users are often required to carefully constrain the programs to minimize the number of concurrency behaviours that are independent of the part of the program they want to test. Having the ability to scale SMC algorithms using, for example, the nowadays abundant availability of multicore machines could allow users to apply stateless model checking more frequently, or to even more challenging programs. Last but not least, we hold that it is particularly desirable to parallelize optimal SMC algorithms, as the slowdown of non-optimality could easily trump the speedup gained by parallelization, no matter how powerful a platform one uses.

One example of an optimal graph-based SMC algorithm is the recently proposed READSFROM-SMC algorithm of Abdulla et al. [3], hereafter abbreviated RF-SMC, which runs programs under the *sequential consistency* (SC) memory model. In RF-SMC, traces consist of two types of edges: 1) "Program order", which contains the sequencing of operations from the program source code, but also orderings like a thread-spawn event before the thread-start, and 2) "Reads-from", which associates read events with the corresponding write event from which they got their value.

As an illustration, consider the program in Fig. 1. Two threads, t_1 and t_2, access a shared variable x. Each thread writes to the variable and reads from it into a local register, a resp. b. The three traces that RF-SMC will examine are also shown in the figure. Program order is drawn with black arrows, and Reads-from with green. We can see that either both threads read their own writes, or both threads read the same write (from t_1 resp. t_2). When RF-SMC explores the example program, it starts by running an arbitrary interleaving of the program events and constructs the corresponding trace. Let us assume that it is the first trace in Fig. 1. By analyzing the reads in this trace, the algorithm discovers that the source writes can be changed, leading to the two other traces, which it then proceeds to run, one at a time. They too will be analyzed, but will only lead back to the initial trace. Here, there is an opportunity to parallelize the algorithm by running and analyzing the second and third trace concurrently.

In this paper, we present PAR-RF-SMC (Sect. 4), a parallel version of the RF-SMC algorithm (Sect. 3), as well as an implementation on top of NIDHUGG and the changes that were needed to make the implementation parallel (Sect. 5). We experimentally evaluate its performance and scalability in Sect. 6. The paper ends by reviewing related work (Sect. 7) and some concluding remarks.

2   READSFROM-SMC by Example

Let us explore in depth how RF-SMC operates, using the program in Fig. 1 as an example. The algorithm represents an execution as a sequence of *events*. Each event records a side-effect of a program statement, such as a read or a write of a shared variable. There are two write events here $x = 1$ and $x = 2$, denoted e_1 and e_2. Read events record from which write event they read (the rf relation). The initialization of shared variables (x in the example) is also represented as write events, but we will omit them for brevity.

The goal of the algorithm is to explore all the execution graphs of the program, which we call *traces*. We represent a trace by a linearization of its events. For example, we may represent the first trace in Fig. 1 by $x = 1 \ a = x^{e_1} \ x = 2 \ b = x^{e_2}$, where $a = x^{e_1}$ denotes the event where $a = x$ reads from e_1. Note that these linearizations are not necessarily executions; i.e. read events do not necessarily read from the most recent write event.

To structure the exploration, RF-SMC maintains traces in an *exploration tree*. Branches of this tree are gradually pruned, achieving low memory consumption in practice, but in this section, for simplicity, we will show complete exploration trees.

The algorithm starts by running an arbitrary execution, and acquires its corresponding trace. Let's assume it is $x = 1 \ a = x^{e_1} \ x = 2 \ b = x^{e_2}$. The exploration tree is initialized with the first trace. In Fig. 2, it is shown as the leftmost trace, τ_1. The algorithm then explores if any if the reads in this trace can have their source writes changed. First, it considers if $b = x$ could have read from e_1 instead, and generates a trace prefix $x = 1 \ a = x^{e_1} \ x = 2 \ b = x^{e_1}$. In general, it may not always be possible to have read from this new source. In order to test it, RF-SMC employs a procedure called GETWITNESS (Sect. 3.1). This procedure will either report that the change would violate SC-consistency, or produces a *witness*, an execution in which that source is realized. In this case, the witness shown in the lower box in Fig. 2 is returned, and RF-SMC inserts the prefix in the exploration tree to create a new $b = x^{e_1}$ node, and associates it with the witness. Next, it considers if $a = x$ could read from e_2. For this, the prefix $x = 1 \ a = x^{e_2}$ would not be self-contained, since $e_2 : x = 2$ is not included, so the missing event(s) are appended to create the prefix $x = 1 \ a = x^{e_2} \ x = 2$.

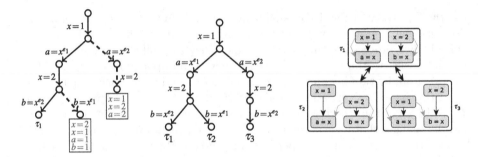

Fig. 2. Exploring the program of Fig. 1: (left) the first trace and two witnesses from it, shown in green. (middle) the tree of traces after the full exploration. (right) the "discoverability" relation of the three traces: there is an edge from trace τ to trace τ' if τ' is discoverable from τ. This affects available concurrency. (Color figure online)

Again, note that the ordering of a linearization of a trace only needs to preserve program order. This prefix will also be found to be consistent, so this prefix, and its witness are inserted into the exploration tree, whose state at this point is as in the left of Fig. 2.

The sequential algorithm could in principle continue with either of these two witnesses, but will pick the leftmost one for space reduction reasons. Starting from the $b = x^{e_1}$ node, the algorithm takes the witness out of the tree, extends it to a complete execution, and adds any newly found nodes under $b = x^{e_1}$. In this case, the witness was already a complete execution. The algorithm then again looks for new sources for the read events in the trace. However, this time it finds that both the $b = x^{e_2}$ and $a = x^{e_2}$ nodes already exist in the exploration tree, and so does nothing. Last, it backtracks to the witness for $a = x^{e_2}$. This time, the execution is not complete and a final $b = x^{e_2}$ event is added to the end of the tree, to create the tree shown in the middle of Fig. 2. Once more, the algorithm will consider if any reads-from sources can be changed. For a, $a = x^{e_1}$ is still in the tree, but for b, the algorithm will generate the trace prefix $x = 1\ a = x^{e_2}\ x = 2\ b = x^{e_1}$. (Note that this does not correspond to the $b = x^{e_1}$ node already in the tree.) However, this trace is not consistent, as, under SC, there is no way to interleave the program statements so that both a reads 2 and b reads 1. Thus, no more nodes are inserted into the exploration tree, and the algorithm terminates at this point.

As we can see, most of the algorithm is agnostic to the order that the newly found traces are explored. The only point where the logic differs is when the exploration tree is checked to see if a certain node already exists. We may further note that the only purpose of this check is to avoid redundant work, as the witness or lack thereof would be identical to that found the last time that trace prefix was checked. Simplifying slightly, the exploration of traces can be compared to exploration of a strongly connected digraph, where the set of all nodes is found by computing the neighbour sets of known nodes. Then, it should be clear why an algorithm on this form is parallelizable. Any time several new traces are discovered, these could in principle be explored in parallel.

The rightmost part of Fig. 2 shows this digraph of traces as induced by this example. If trace τ_1 is explored first, traces τ_2 and τ_3 may be explored in parallel. However, if exploration starts with trace τ_2 or τ_3, the remaining two traces can only be explored sequentially. Thus, the scheduling decisions made during arbitrary exploration can affect the available concurrency.

3   Sequential READSFROM-SMC

In this section, we review RF-SMC [3], a sequential SMC algorithm which optimally explores the complete consistent traces of a given concurrent program. The exploration algorithm is centered around a test GETWITNESS for checking whether a given trace is consistent under SC, described in Sect. 3.1.

For a read event e_R, let $e_R.src$ be the write event that it reads from, and for any read or write event e, let $e.var$ be the variable, or memory address, that is accessed. Recall that traces are labelled graphs represented by some linearization. We say that two traces τ and τ' are *equivalent*, denoted $\tau \equiv \tau'$, if they are linearizations of the same graph. For a trace τ, let $\leq_\tau$ be the relation containing all of the edges labelled "program order", and $\mathtt{rf}$ be the relation containing all edges labelled "reads-from". Define a *cut* of τ to be a subsequence τ' of τ such that whenever e and e' are events in τ, such that τ' contains e and $e' [\leq_\tau \cup \mathtt{rf}]^* e$, then τ' also contains e'. That is, a cut is closed under causal dependencies (in the sense of $\leq_\tau \cup \mathtt{rf}$). Note that a cut is also a trace.

For a trace τ and an event $e \in \tau$ let

$pre(\tau, e)$ denote the prefix of τ up to, but not including, e;

$post(\tau, e)$ denote the suffix of τ after, but not including, e;

$predecs(\tau, e)$ denote the minimal cut of τ which contains e, i.e., the set of events (including e) on which e is causally dependent.

As an example, if τ is the trace τ_3 in Fig. 2, i.e., $\tau := x=1\ a=x^{e_2}\ x=1\ b=x^{e_2}$, then $predecs(\tau, b=x^{e_1})$ is $x=1\ x=2\ b=x^{e_2}$.

Algorithm 1 gives the pseudocode of RF-SMC(τ, E), where τ is an SC-consistent trace and E is an execution and a witness for τ. Exploration begins with a call RF-SMC($\langle\rangle, \langle\rangle$).

An important element in RF-SMC is to analyze an explored trace to see whether another trace can be formed by changing the source of one of its read events. In order to explore every consistent combination of sources for all the reads in the program exactly once, the reads are organized in the exploration tree, as shown in Sect. 2. For this to be sound, the order of read events in the traces must be preserved throughout the exploration. However, sometimes read events must be "lifted" because they are injected in the causal history of a prior read event when its source is changed. The algorithm must not explore alternative sources for lifted read events, or the algorithm might explore redundant traces, and even be unsound. To avoid this, we extend the representation of events

Algorithm 1: RF-SMC.

```
1  RF-SMC(τ, E)
2  |  extend E to a complete execution E · Ê where each event of Ê is unmarked
3  |  τ' := τ · Ê
4  |  for each read event e_R ∈ Ê do schedules(pre(τ', e_R)) := ∅
5  |  for each e_R, e_W ∈ τ' :  e_W.var = e_R.var and e_W ≠ e_R.src and
6  |                  (e_R ∈ Ê or e_W ∈ Ê) and unmarked(e_R) and
7  |                  MayRead(τ', e_R, e_W) do
8  |  |  τ'' := pre(τ', e_R)
9  |  |  π := predecs(τ', e_W) ∩ post(τ', e_R)
10 |  |  σ := e_R[src := e_W] · mark(π)
11 |  |  E'' := GetWitness(τ'' · σ, E · Ê)
12 |  |  if E'' ≠ ⟨⟩ and ¬∃ ⟨σ', −⟩ ∈ schedules(τ'') : σ' ≡ σ then
13 |  |  |  add ⟨σ, E''⟩ to schedules(τ'')
14 |  for each read event e_R ∈ Ê starting from the end do
15 |  |  τ'' := pre(τ', e_R)
16 |  |  for each ⟨σ, E''⟩ ∈ schedules(τ'') do RF-SMC(τ'' · σ, E'')
17 |  |  erase schedules(τ'')
```

with a field whose value is either ⊤ or ⊥. When ⊤, we say that the event is *marked*; when ⊥, that it is *unmarked*. For a sequence π of events, let $mark(\pi)$ be π but with each element marked. By marking any events that are "lifted" in the exploration tree, RF-SMC will not analyse any such event for alternate sources.

For some trace prefix τ in the exploration tree, RF-SMC represents the set of children of that node by a set $schedules(\tau)$. Each element is a tuple $\langle \tau', E' \rangle$ of the child trace τ' and a witness E' of its consistency. As we saw in Sect. 2, the exploration tree serves two purposes. First, for any read event e_R in a trace τ, the set $schedules(pre(\tau, e_R))$ keeps track of all read sources for e_R that have been found so far. Secondly, $schedules$ also keeps track of what trace prefixes, with associated executions, to explore in the future.

The algorithm is structured in three phases: i) exploration (lines 2–3); ii) new-source-detection (lines 4–13); and iii) recursive-exploration (lines 14–17).

In the exploration phase, RF-SMC(τ, E) extends E to an arbitrary complete execution $E \cdot \hat{E}$, and its complete trace τ' is computed. Correctness properties are checked on $E \cdot \hat{E}$.

In the new-source-detection phase, for every read event e_R, any possibly consistent source e_W from the same trace are considered. The MayRead(τ', e_R, e_W) predicate checks whether e_R reading from e_W would cause a causal loop, or whether there is another write event e'_W causally after e_W and before e_R. This is an efficient necessary but not sufficient check for whether e_R can read from e_W. If the check passes, the algorithm will construct the trace prefix $\tau'' \cdot \sigma$ containing e_R with the new source, as well as a sequence π of any new causal dependencies of e_R. On line 9, as an abuse of notation we take the intersection ∪ of two sequences, and mean the subsequence of both that contain the elements common to both sequences. Note that this is well-defined because both sequences agree on the ordering of common elements. The trace prefix $\tau'' \cdot \sigma$ is fed to the GETWITNESS decision procedure, along with the current execution $E \cdot \hat{E}$ as a hint. If it is found to be consistent, and there is no equivalent node already in the tree, it is inserted into the exploration tree along with the witness found by GETWITNESS.

In the recursive-exploration phase, the algorithm calls itself recursively on any consistent trace prefixes that were found by the new-source-detection phase, starting from the bottom of the tree. Note that the recursive calls to RF-SMC may add elements to $schedules(\tau'')$. When all sources of e_R have been recursively explored, the set $schedules(\tau'')$ may safely be erased to keep memory use low.

The algorithm satisfies the following three properties [3]: *Soundness*, *Completeness*, and *Optimality* (cf. Sect. 4).

3.1 Checking Consistency: The GETWITNESS Procedure

Let us briefly overview the GETWITNESS(τ, E) procedure. (For more details, refer to our previous paper [3].) The procedure checks the consistency of τ, returning either a witness or $\langle \rangle$. It takes an execution E as a hint for the ordering of write events to the same variable when it cannot infer the ordering, or when any ordering is valid.

The core of the procedure is a sound but incomplete heuristic which runs in polynomial time, but falls back on a sound and complete decision procedure which is polynomial time when the number of threads is fixed [3]. The heuristic is based on the concept of *saturation*. When a trace τ is saturated, the rf and $\leq_\tau$ relations are extended to a *saturated-happens-before* relation shb, which extends $\leq_\tau \cup$ rf by orderings that must be respected by any witness of τ. If shb is cyclic, then τ is inconsistent.

3.2 Implementation

An implementation of RF-SMC is available in the tool NIDHUGG [1]. In this section, we describe that implementation.

NIDHUGG takes C or C++ programs as input, but does its analysis on the level of LLVM IR, produced by the Clang compiler. Executions are checked for assertion violations and crashes, such as segmentation faults. For programs that do not terminate in bounded time, and hence have an infinite trace space, automatic loop bounding, sometimes called loop unrolling, can be requested by the user. As with any bounding technique, this makes the exploration exhaustive only up to the given bound, which means that bugs may be missed if they do not manifest in any trace within the bound.

In order to do efficient trace equivalence comparison, as needed on line 12 of Algorithm 1, NIDHUGG maintains a directed graph which is the union of all $(\leq_\tau \cup$ rf$)$ graphs for all the traces in *schedules*. Each node is duplicated for every possible reads-from assignment and program-order predecessor node. Insertions are *interned*, which means that if, when inserting a node for some event with some predecessor set, there is already a node for that program event with the same predecessor set, that node is reused. Thus, to compare two traces identified by the nodes of their last events, it suffices to compare the nodes for reference equality, which is an $O(1)$ operation. In the source code of NIDHUGG, this graph is called the *unfolding tree*.

As an optimization, in addition to the *schedules* sets, NIDHUGG maintains a cache of traces that GETWITNESS has found to be inconsistent. Before querying GETWITNESS, it checks both *schedules*(τ'') and the cache of inconsistent traces, so that consistency is never queried for the same trace twice.

As an additional optimization, for every read event e_R in τ tried in the new-source-detection phase, NIDHUGG caches the shb graph for $pre(\tau', e_R)$. Then, when shb is needed for a new trace τ'', the longest prefix of τ'' for which there is an shb cached is found and reused, adding only the missing suffix of events and re-saturating. In order to efficiently support this use, NIDHUGG represents shb graphs using persistent immutable data structures that provide $O(1)$ copying and $O(\log n)$ updates.

4   Parallelization of READSFROM-SMC

In this section, we present PAR-RF-SMC, a parallel version of RF-SMC. While the sequential version is expressed in a recursive form, PAR-RF-SMC is expressed in a task-based form, where each task explores one trace and spawns zero or more new tasks. Algorithm 2 shows its code. The algorithm consists of creating an initial task PAR-RF-SMC($\langle\rangle, \langle\rangle$), and terminates when all tasks have finished.

Recall from Sect. 3 that in RF-SMC, the global data structure *schedules* serves two purposes. It keeps track of both all read sources that have been found so far for any read event, as well as of what trace prefixes, with associated executions, to explore in the future. In PAR-RF-SMC, the trace prefixes to explore in the future are kept as tasks and do not need to be stored as global variables, but the set of all sources found for some read event e_R in some trace τ is still required to avoid redundant (duplicate) exploration. Therefore, PAR-RF-SMC uses a variable *attempted*($pre(\tau, e_R)$), shared by all tasks, to keep track of this set. This is the only shared data structure.

The algorithm of PAR-RF-SMC is structured in three phases: i) exploration (lines 2–3); ii) new-source-detection (lines 4–13); and iii) cleanup (lines 14–17). As can be seen, there is no recursive-exploration phase. Instead, new tasks are spawned for all new sources found in the new-source-detection phase, and then the cleanup phase deletes all the *attempted* sets that are no longer needed after all sub-tasks have finished.

The exploration phase is identical to that of RF-SMC. A trace prefix τ and execution E is extended to an arbitrary complete execution $E \cdot \hat{E}$ and corresponding trace τ', and correctness properties are checked.

Algorithm 2: PAR-RF-SMC.

1 PAR-RF-SMC(τ, E)
2   **extend** E to a complete execution $E \cdot \hat{E}$ where each event of $\hat{E}$ is unmarked
3      $\tau' := \tau \cdot \hat{E}$
4   **for each** read event $e_R \in \hat{E}$ **do**
5 | $attempted(pre(\tau', e_R)) := \{pre(\tau', e_R) \cdot e_R\}$
6   **for each** $e_R, e_W \in \tau' : \ e_W.var = e_R.var$ and $e_W \neq e_R.src$ and
7                      $(e_R \in \hat{E}$ or $e_W \in \hat{E})$ and $unmarked(e_R)$ and
8   MAYREAD(τ', e_R, e_W) **do**
9        $\tau'' := pre(\tau', e_R)$
10       $\pi := predecs(\tau', e_W) \cap post(\tau', e_R)$
11       $\sigma := e_R[src := e_W] \cdot mark(\pi)$
12   **if** $\neg \exists \sigma' \in attempted(\tau'') : \sigma' \equiv \sigma$ **then**
13   **add** σ to $attempted(\tau'')$ // atomically with the test above
14         $E'' := $ GETWITNESS($\tau'' \cdot \sigma, E \cdot \hat{E}$)
15   **if** $E'' \neq \langle\rangle$ **then** **spawn** PAR-RF-SMC(σ, E'')
16   **join** all sub-tasks
17   **for each** read event $e_R \in \hat{E}$ **do** **erase** $attempted(pre(\tau', e_R))$

The new-source-detection phase is very similar to that of RF-SMC. The differences lie in the changes to the global data structure *attempted*. The set *attempted* of possible sources for a read event is initialized on line 5, just like *schedules* in RF-SMC. Possible alternative sources for reads are looped over on line 6, however on line 12 we see the first difference. Before we invoke the potentially expensive consistency check GETWITNESS, we first check that the source e_W for e_R has not been previously attempted, by this or any other thread. This ensures that the algorithm never queries consistency for the same trace prefix twice. Thus lines 12 and 13 need to be executed atomically, for example with a mutex guarding $attempted(\tau'')$. Finally, if we did not find this source in $attempted(\tau'')$ and GETWITNESS found it to be consistent, we add the new trace to the work-queue on line 15.

Just like RF-SMC, PAR-RF-SMC satisfies the following three properties:

(i) *Soundness*: each complete trace explored by the algorithm is a consistent trace of the program.
(ii) *Completeness*: the algorithm explores all consistent traces of the program.
(iii) *Optimality*: each trace is explored exactly once.

Proof. We can establish these properties by observing that any run of PAR-RF-SMC can be rearranged to produce an equivalent run of RF-SMC. Every time the sequential algorithm adds an element to *schedules* for future exploration, the parallel algorithm spawns a task with the same parameters, and vice versa. Every time the parallel algorithm runs a new task, the sequential algorithm makes a recursive call to itself. In order to be allowed to rearrange the execution of the parallel algorithm like this, we must show that it does not affect the set of traces explored. To do that, it suffices to look at the only source of scheduling non-determinism in the algorithm; the access to the *attempted* set. When two tasks both try to insert equivalent σ's into *attempted*, whichever of them "wins" and gets to insert into *attempted* is exactly the one that will run GETWITNESS and, if σ is consistent, the one that will spawn a task to explore it. After that, the system is in the same state, no matter which task "won".   □

The order in which tasks are scheduled is not specified. The algorithm keeps its correctness and optimality properties with any scheduling, but depth-first and left-to-right policies minimize memory use. Work-stealing scheduling policies [7], where each thread has its own depth-first queue but when empty "steals" a shallowest task from another thread's queue, may also be employed to maximize locality while bounding the increase in memory use.

As was described at the end of Sect. 2, the scheduling of the arbitrary execution during the exploration phase on line 2 affects the amount of concurrency exposed to this algorithm. It is possible to devise a program where under one scheduling, PAR-RF-SMC would explore it entirely sequentially, and under another scheduling, would find all other traces by examining the first one it explores. However, we have neither encountered nor we expect realistic programs with large numbers of traces to behave this way.

5 Implementation

PAR-RF-SMC has been implemented in NIDHUGG. The language NIDHUGG is written in, C++, does not have a task-based scheduler in its runtime system. There are libraries that provide such functionality, but we chose to write our own work-stealing task scheduler. The scheduler detects when there are no more tasks in the queue or running, and terminates at that point. Figure 3 shows a diagram of the components of the implementation.

In the sequential implementation, the *schedules* sets are stored as a stack, one entry per read event. However, in our parallel version, the *attempted* sets cannot be stored in a stack. Instead, they are organized in a tree. This tree is effectively the exploration tree, as described in Sect. 2. Unlike the pseudocode of Algorithm 2, our implementation does not do explicit deletions of *attempted* sets, as on lines 16–17. Rather, nodes in this *attempted* tree are reference counted, and each task holds references to the attempted sets of all read events in their input traces. Every node in the tree has an associated mutex which is held during the atomic check-and-insert operation on lines 12–13. The *attempted* tree is shown in the middle of Fig. 3.

We preserve the unfolding tree data structure from sequential RF-SMC, but we extend it with mutexes that guard the child lists used for interning. For the special list of root nodes for each thread, we employ a readers-writer mutex due to high contention and high hit-rate (i.e., most queries for a root node return an interned node, and thus need not modify the list). The unfolding tree is shown in the bottom of Fig. 3.

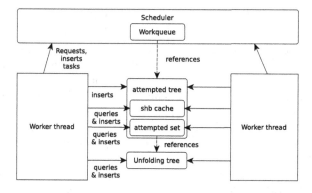

Fig. 3. Components of PAR-RF-SMC's implementation in NIDHUGG.

In sequential RF-SMC, the cache of shb graphs was represented using persistent immutable data structures [21], which had structural sharing that was memory managed through reference counting. These were stored along the sets on the *schedules* stack. For PAR-RF-SMC, we could simply move the cache into the nodes of the *attempted* tree, and ensure that write-accesses were properly synchronized. Luckily, the library that was used to provide these data structures was designed with threading in mind [21], and offered thread-safe atomic reference counting. However, as we were benchmarking our implementation, we found that the reference counting on these data structures became a scalability bottleneck. We were able to lift this bottleneck by redesigning these data structures to be more tailored to the needs of PAR-RF-SMC. In particular, because nodes in the *attempted* tree are always erased *after* all of their children, and because an shb graph is never updated after being installed into the cache, the memory management can be designed so that each piece of memory has exactly one owner, and thus does not require reference counting.

NIDHUGG supports early termination when it finds an error in the program, so naturally we wanted to support this in PAR-RF-SMC. We achieve this by telling the task scheduler to stop scheduling new tasks when an error is found. Thus, once all tasks that were running at that point terminate, so does the algorithm.

6   Performance and Scalability Evaluation

In this section, we report on the performance and scalability of NIDHUGG/rfsc. To put the numbers in perspective, we first compare its performance to three other SMC tools that implement state-of-the-art algorithms. Subsequently, we evaluate NIDHUGG/rfsc's scalability on a large multicore machine.

Tools. Let us briefly present the SMC tools we compare against and the algorithms they employ. By VC-DPOR we refer to a prototype tool, based on

NIDHUGG, that implements the recently proposed *Value-Centric Dynamic Partial Order Reduction* algorithm [9]. This algorithm, which is sensitive to the *values* used by the events during an execution rather than the read events themselves, in principle provides a coarser partitioning than reads-from. However, neither the VC-DPOR algorithm nor its implementation provide any optimality guarantees and often explore—partially—considerably more executions than NIDHUGG/rfsc, as we will soon see. The second tool, CDSCHECKER [20], is a high-performance stateless model checker for C/C++11 programs. It employs a variant of the interleaving-based DPOR algorithm of Flanagan and Godefroid [11]. Although CDSCHECKER's implementation is well-engineered, the tool often explores a significant number of executions that are redundant, as this DPOR algorithm is not optimal. The last tool, GENMC [17], is a high-performance generic stateless model checker for concurrent C programs. As its algorithm is also graph-based, GENMC is the tool which is more similar to NIDHUGG/rfsc. However, rather than focusing on SC, GENMC provides a framework into which consistency checks for different (weak) memory models and program semantics can be plugged and even combined. GENMC offers a mode for SMC under rf-equivalence, which is the default, as well as a mode that tracks the modification order. We compare against the default mode of GENMC. In this mode, GENMC is optimal when consistency checks are not needed for SMC under SC. It is also faster than NIDHUGG/rfsc, both due to not checking consistency and due to being well-engineered.

Platform and Benchmarks. Our benchmarking platform is a machine with two Intel(R) Xeon(R) Platinum 8168 CPUs (2.70 GHz each with 24 cores and hyperthreading, giving a total of 48 physical/96 logical cores), has 192 GB of RAM and ran Debian 10.3. All tools used Clang version 7.0.1 to translate the C source to LLVM IR. For benchmarks, we use the subset of programs from our previous paper [3] that can be handled by most tools and, more importantly for this paper, whose execution time is more than a few seconds, and hence their parallel execution makes sense. Refer to that paper for the programs' origin and characteristics, and to the artifact [4] of that paper for their sources.

Performance. Table 1 shows the results: number of executions that the various tools explore and the time (in seconds) that this requires.[1] Since all these programs have a scaling parameter, often the number of threads involved, we show

---

[1] In Table 1, entries n/a signify that the tool cannot handle that program; a ⊙ symbol that the benchmark does not complete after running for more than ten hours. The circular-buffer program contains a concurrency error which only manifests itself for parameter values ≥ 10. The CDSCHECKER tool finds this error immediately (within the first few executions), hence the † symbols for its circular-buffer(10) entries. The remaining three tools are not so lucky in their search, and catch the error after exploring many executions. The parallel version of NIDHUGG/rfsc detects this error at a point that is influenced by the distribution of tasks to threads, which also explains the slight variation in the curve of circular-buffer(10) in Fig. 4.

Table 1. Performance comparison of four SMC tools in terms of the number of executions that explore and the time (in secs) it takes to do so using one thread. The last column shows the time performance of parallel NIDHUGG/rfsc using 48 threads.

Benchmark	CDSCHECKER		VC-DPOR		GENMC		NIDHUGG/rfsc		rfsc-48
	Execs	Time	Execs	Time	Execs	Time	Execs	Time	Time
fib-bench(4)	n/a	n/a	70937	6.93	34205	0.88	19605	1.66	0.15
fib-bench(5)	n/a	n/a	788940	87.69	525630	33.48	218243	21.28	0.76
fib-bench(6)	n/a	n/a	8543518	1182.25	8149694	3718.86	2364418	255.03	8.31
parker(12)	n/a	n/a	6601	0.92	69658	11.61	9407	2.24	0.13
parker(16)	n/a	n/a	11425	1.76	203754	43.60	21195	5.85	0.23
parker(20)	n/a	n/a	17561	3.09	475210	132.08	40087	12.73	0.41
circular-buffer(8)	12870	0.72	303149	50.44	12870	3.21	12870	2.51	0.15
circular-buffer(9)	48620	2.91	1147421	226.36	48620	13.58	48620	10.32	0.39
circular-buffer(10)	†	†	2964067	635.99	59279	19.13	59280	13.90	0.52
casrot(9)	372735	27.24	n/a	n/a	8597	0.08	8597	0.89	0.14
casrot(10)	3456845	284.27	n/a	n/a	38486	0.30	38486	4.28	0.23
casrot(11)	35407921	3230.99	n/a	n/a	182905	1.40	182905	22.39	0.89
lastzero(11)	184331	21.15	170515	33.09	7168	0.28	7168	1.13	0.13
lastzero(13)	1888624	255.84	1192108	317.12	32768	1.25	32768	5.89	0.26
lastzero(15)	19478080	3057.60	8264353	3061.91	147456	6.25	147456	30.76	1.00
readers(13)	13311	1.75	67108864	21224.93	8192	0.59	8192	1.25	0.14
readers(15)	53247	8.10	☉	☉	32768	2.46	32768	5.81	0.26
readers(17)	212991	37.24	☉	☉	131072	10.94	131072	25.23	0.89
sigma(7)	509861	48.08	46232	4.97	5040	0.23	5040	0.52	0.11
sigma(8)	9057756	977.89	409112	56.27	40320	1.67	40320	4.40	0.28
sigma(9)	180337837	22286.21	4037912	668.64	362880	15.94	362880	44.17	2.17
race-parametric(5)	34904	12.41	14967	3.92	8953	1.04	8953	3.60	0.21
race-parametric(6)	372436	134.75	88432	26.38	73789	8.24	73789	30.35	0.96
race-parametric(7)	4027216	1479.37	591352	209.40	616227	69.59	616227	255.43	7.69
approxds-append(5)	390728	25.69	121883	11.36	9945	0.60	9945	1.72	0.15
approxds-append(6)	30603290	2425.28	5353219	622.40	198936	12.83	198936	41.45	1.21
approxds-append(7)	☉	☉	☉	☉	4645207	342.52	4645207	1143.28	34.86

three rows for each. This allows to see the complexity of the different SMC algorithms and their scalability in terms of the number of executions explored as the state space increases. We notice the following:

- In terms of sequential performance, no tool is fastest overall. GENMC is fastest in the last six benchmarks where it is optimal and explores the same number of executions as NIDHUGG/rfsc. However, when it is not optimal and on circular-buffer, it is slower roughly by an order of magnitude compared to other tools (NIDHUGG/rfsc on fib-bench, VC-DPOR and NIDHUGG/rfsc on parker, and CDSCHECKER and NIDHUGG/rfsc on circular-buffer).
- VC-DPOR explores significantly less executions only on one program (parker) and only a few less on race-parametric(7). It is faster than the other tools only on parker. In the remaining seven programs, it examines a big number of partially explored executions —on readers even exponentially more!— and its numbers explode.

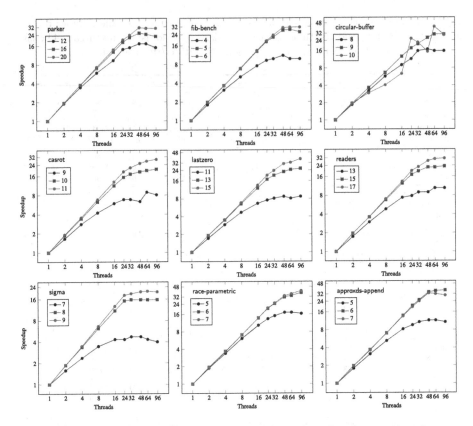

Fig. 4. Speedups (y-axes) obtained by running the benchmarks when varying the number of threads (x-axes) on a machine with 48 physical/96 logical cores.

- The performance of the sequential NIDHUGG/rfsc is quite decent, but GENMC is 2.4 to five times faster than NIDHUGG/rfsc in the last four benchmarks where both tools explore the same number of executions. Also, in the casrot benchmark, GENMC is an order of magnitude faster. However, both tools scale similarly and better than the other two.
- When parallelism enters the picture, NIDHUGG/rfsc becomes the fastest tool across the board. (The last column of Table 1 shows times when executing with 48 threads, which is the number of physical cores in our machine.) Note that this would not have been possible if NIDHUGG/rfsc were examining a significant number of redundant executions (e.g., similar to those that CDSCHECKER or VC-DPOR often explore).

Scalability. Let us now examine the scalability of PAR-RF-SMC compared to its sequential counterpart as implemented in NIDHUGG/rfsc. Figure 4 shows speedups obtained for executions of all benchmark/parameter combinations. All graphs show a very similar picture. The speedup is almost linear up to 24 threads, which is the number of physical cores per chip on this machine, and becomes on average 32× when using all 48 physical cores (which are located on two different NUMA nodes). In most programs, there is a moderate speedup increase above 32× when hyperthreading is also used.

Two more points worth noting are that i) the speedups are in general highest for the benchmark configuration with the largest parameter value (brown lines in the plots), and ii) the speedup obtained for the configuration with the smallest parameter value (blue lines) often drops when using more threads than physical cores. This is due to threads not having much work to do after some point in time during the execution of the benchmark and/or trying to steal from other threads, causing memory traffic.

7 Related Work

To address the inherent complexity of testing concurrent software, researchers have developed a variety of methods for finding and reproducing concurrency errors. In the area of stateless model checking [12] numerous tools and research prototypes [1,10,16,17,19,20] have been developed in the last decade, and SMC has been successfully applied to important concurrent programs (e.g., [13,18]).

In recent years, a wide variety of SMC algorithms has been put forward (e.g., [2,3,5,6,8,9,11,16,22,26]) with the aim to effectively combat the combinatorial explosion in the number of executions that must be explored. However, only a selected few of them [2,3,6,17] come with optimality guarantees, and none of them has been parallelized. To the best of our knowledge READSFROM-SMC is the first *optimal* algorithm for SMC with a parallel implementation.

Still, non-optimal Dynamic Partial-Order Reduction (DPOR) algorithms have been parallelized in the past (e.g., by Yang et al. [25] and by Simsa et al. [23]), although the focus of those works has been on obtaining *distributed* versions of these algorithms rather than algorithms suitable for running on multicores. Also, their focus has been on techniques and heuristics on how to avoid situations where different workers end up exploring identical (N.B. not just from the same equivalence class!) parts of the search space, due to the non-local nature in which interleaving-based DPOR algorithms update their exploration frontier and the need, for scalability, to avoid a central coordinator.

Of course, distributed execution and parallelization of explicit state model checkers has also been investigated (e.g., [14,15,24]). Stateful exploration is less common for software model checking and often suffers from memory explosion.

8 Concluding Remarks

We have presented PAR-RF-SMC, the parallel version of a state-of-the-art graph-based SMC algorithm for SC. The algorithm retains its main properties (soundness, completeness and, most importantly, optimality), can be implemented with moderate additional effort on top of its sequential counterpart, and achieves very good scalability; on average 32 times speedup on a 48 core machine.

Our performance evaluation shows that parallel NIDHUGG/rfsc currently outperforms all tools in its area, and offers the possibility for SMC to be applied to programs which are currently very challenging.

Acknowledgments. We would like to acknowledge the work of Nodari Kankava and Alexis Remmers for an initial prototype implementation of the algorithm which formed the basis for PAR-RF-SMC's implementation in NIDHUGG. This work has been partially supported by the Swedish Research Council through grant #621-2017-04812, and by the Swedish Foundation for Strategic Research through the aSSIsT project.

References

1. Abdulla, P.A., Aronis, S., Atig, M.F., Jonsson, B., Leonardsson, C., Sagonas, K.: Stateless model checking for TSO and PSO. In: Baier, C., Tinelli, C. (eds.) TACAS 2015. LNCS, vol. 9035, pp. 353–367. Springer, Heidelberg (2015). https://doi.org/10.1007/978-3-662-46681-0_28
2. Abdulla, P.A., Aronis, S., Jonsson, B., Sagonas, K.: Source sets: a foundation for optimal dynamic partial order reduction. J. ACM **64**(4), 25:1–25:49 (2017). http://doi.acm.org/10.1145/3073408
3. Abdulla, P.A., Atig, M.F., Jonsson, B., Lång, M., Ngo, T.P., Sagonas, K.: Optimal stateless model checking for reads-from equivalence under sequential consistency. Proc. ACM Program. Lang. **3**(OOPSLA), 150:1–150:29 (2019). https://doi.org/10.1145/3360576
4. Abdulla, P.A., Atig, M.F., Jonsson, B., Lång, M., Ngo, T.P., Sagonas, K.: Optimal Stateless Model Checking for Reads-From Equivalence under Sequential Consistency (2019). https://doi.org/10.5281/zenodo.3401442, artifact for the OOPSLA 2019 paper with the same title
5. Albert, E., Arenas, P., de la Banda, M.G., Gómez-Zamalloa, M., Stuckey, P.J.: Context-sensitive dynamic partial order reduction. In: Majumdar, R., Kunčak, V. (eds.) CAV 2017. LNCS, vol. 10426, pp. 526–543. Springer, Cham (2017). https://doi.org/10.1007/978-3-319-63387-9_26
6. Aronis, S., Jonsson, B., Lång, M., Sagonas, K.: Optimal dynamic partial order reduction with observers. In: Beyer, D., Huisman, M. (eds.) TACAS 2018. LNCS, vol. 10806, pp. 229–248. Springer, Cham (2018). https://doi.org/10.1007/978-3-319-89963-3_14
7. Blumofe, R.D., Leiserson, C.E.: Scheduling multithreaded computations by work stealing. J. ACM **46**(5), 720–748 (1999). https://doi.org/10.1145/324133.324234
8. Chalupa, M., Chatterjee, K., Pavlogiannis, A., Sinha, N., Vaidya, K.: Data-centric dynamic partial order reduction. Proc. ACM Program. Lang. **2**(POPL), 31:1–31:30 (2018). http://doi.acm.org/10.1145/3158119
9. Chatterjee, K., Pavlogiannis, A., Toman, V.: Value-centric dynamic partial order reduction. Proc. ACM Program. Lang. **3**(OOPSLA), 124:1–124:29 (2019). https://doi.org/10.1145/3360550
10. Christakis, M., Gotovos, A., Sagonas, K.: Systematic testing for detecting concurrency errors in Erlang programs. In: Sixth IEEE International Conference on Software Testing, Verification and Validation, pp. 154–163. ICST 2013, IEEE, Los Alamitos, CA, USA, March 2013. https://doi.org/10.1109/ICST.2013.50
11. Flanagan, C., Godefroid, P.: Dynamic partial-order reduction for model checking software. In: Principles of Programming Languages, (POPL). pp. 110–121. ACM, New York, NY, USA, January 2005. http://doi.acm.org/10.1145/1040305.1040315

12. Godefroid, P.: Model checking for programming languages using VeriSoft. In: Principles of Programming Languages, (POPL), pp. 174–186. ACM Press, New York, NY, USA, January 1997. http://doi.acm.org/10.1145/263699.263717
13. Godefroid, P., Hanmer, R.S., Jagadeesan, L.: Model checking without a model: an analysis of the heart-beat monitor of a telephone switch using VeriSoft. In: Proceedings of the ACM SIGSOFT International Symposium on Software Testing and Analysis, pp. 124–133. ISSTA, ACM, New York, NY, USA, March 1998. https://doi.org/10.1145/271771.271800
14. Holzmann, G.J., Bosnacki, D.: The design of a multicore extension of the SPIN model checker. IEEE Trans. Softw. Eng. **33**(10), 659–674 (2007). https://doi.org/10.1109/TSE.2007.70724
15. Holzmann, G.J., Joshi, R., Groce, A.: Swarm verification techniques. IEEE Trans. Softw. Eng. **37**(6), 845–857 (2011). https://doi.org/10.1109/TSE.2010.110
16. Kokologiannakis, M., Lahav, O., Sagonas, K., Vafeiadis, V.: Effective stateless model checking for C/C++ concurrency. Proc. ACM on Program. Lang. **2**(POPL), 17:1–17:32 (2018). https://doi.org/10.1145/3158105
17. Kokologiannakis, M., Raad, A., Vafeiadis, V.: Model checking for weakly consistent libraries. In: Proceedings of the 40th ACM SIGPLAN Conference on Programming Language Design and Implementation, pp. 96–110. PLDI 2019, ACM, New York, NY, USA, June 2019. https://doi.org/10.1145/3314221.3314609
18. Kokologiannakis, M., Sagonas, K.: Stateless model checking of the Linux kernel's read-copy update (RCU). Int. J. Softw. Tools Technol. Transfer **21**(3), 287–306 (2019). https://doi.org/10.1007/s10009-019-00514-6
19. Musuvathi, M., Qadeer, S., Ball, T., Basler, G., Nainar, P.A., Neamtiu, I.: Finding and reproducing heisenbugs in concurrent programs. In: Proceedings of the 8th USENIX Symposium on Operating Systems Design and Implementation, pp. 267–280. OSDI 2008, USENIX Association, Berkeley, CA, USA, December 2008. http://dl.acm.org/citation.cfm?id=1855741.1855760
20. Norris, B., Demsky, B.: A practical approach for model checking C/C++11 code. ACM Trans. Program. Lang. Syst. **38**(3), 10:1–10:51 (2016). http://doi.acm.org/10.1145/2806886
21. Puente, J.P.B.: Persistence for the masses: RRB-vectors in a systems language. Proc. ACM Program. Lang. **1**(ICFP) (2017). https://doi.org/10.1145/3110260
22. Rodríguez, C., Sousa, M., Sharma, S., Kroening, D.: Unfolding-based partial order reduction. In: 26th International Conference on Concurrency Theory (CONCUR 2015). LIPIcs, vol. 42, pp. 456–469. Schloss Dagstuhl-Leibniz-Zentrum fuer Informatik, August 2015. http://dx.doi.org/10.4230/LIPIcs.CONCUR.2015.456
23. Simsa, J., Bryant, R., Gibson, G., Hickey, J.: Scalable dynamic partial order reduction. In: Qadeer, S., Tasiran, S. (eds.) RV 2012. LNCS, vol. 7687, pp. 19–34. Springer, Heidelberg (2013). https://doi.org/10.1007/978-3-642-35632-2_4
24. Stern, U., Dill, D.L.: Parallelizing the murφ verifier. Formal Methods Syst. Des. **18**, 117–129 (2001). https://doi.org/10.1023/A:1008771324652
25. Yang, Y., Chen, X., Gopalakrishnan, G., Kirby, R.M.: Distributed dynamic partial order reduction based verification of threaded software. In: Bošnački, D., Edelkamp, S. (eds.) SPIN 2007. LNCS, vol. 4595, pp. 58–75. Springer, Heidelberg (2007). https://doi.org/10.1007/978-3-540-73370-6_6
26. Zhang, N., Kusano, M., Wang, C.: Dynamic partial order reduction for relaxed memory models. In: Programming Language Design and Implementation (PLDI), pp. 250–259. ACM, New York, NY, USA, June 2015. http://doi.acm.org/10.1145/2737924.2737956

Model Checking Branching Properties
on Petri Nets with Transits

Bernd Finkbeiner[1], Manuel Gieseking[2(✉)], Jesko Hecking-Harbusch[1],
and Ernst-Rüdiger Olderog[2]

[1] CISPA Helmholtz Center for Information Security, Saarbrücken, Germany
{finkbeiner,jesko.hecking-harbusch}@cispa.saarland
[2] University of Oldenburg, Oldenburg, Germany
{gieseking,olderog}@informatik.uni-oldenburg.de

Abstract. To model check concurrent systems, it is convenient to distinguish between the data flow and the control. Correctness is specified on the level of data flow whereas the system is configured on the level of control. Petri nets with transits and Flow-LTL are a corresponding formalism. In Flow-LTL, both the correctness of the data flow and assumptions on fairness and maximality for the control are expressed in linear time. So far, branching behavior cannot be specified for Petri nets with transits. In this paper, we introduce Flow-CTL* to express the intended branching behavior of the data flow while maintaining LTL for fairness and maximality assumptions on the control. We encode physical access control with policy updates as Petri nets with transits and give standard requirements in Flow-CTL*. For model checking, we reduce the model checking problem of Petri nets with transits against Flow-CTL* via automata constructions to the model checking problem of Petri nets against LTL. Thereby, physical access control with policy updates under fairness assumptions for an unbounded number of people can be verified.

1 Introduction

Petri nets with transits [8] superimpose a transit relation onto the flow relation of Petri nets. The flow relation models the *control* in the form of tokens moving through the net. The transit relation models the *data flow* in the form of flow chains. The configuration of the system takes place on the level of the control whereas correctness is specified on the level of the data flow. Thus, Petri nets with transits allow for an elegant separation of the data flow and the control without the complexity of unbounded colored Petri nets [14]. We use *physical access control* [11–13] as an application throughout the paper. It defines and enforces access policies in physical spaces. People are represented as the data

This work has been supported by the German Research Foundation (DFG) through Grant Petri Games (392735815) and through the Collaborative Research Center "Foundations of Perspicuous Software Systems" (TRR 248, 389792660), and by the European Research Council (ERC) through Grant OSARES (683300).

D. V. Hung and O. Sokolsky (Eds.): ATVA 2020, LNCS 12302, pp. 394–410, 2020.
https://doi.org/10.1007/978-3-030-59152-6_22

flow in the building. The control defines which policy enforcement points like doors are open to which people identified by their RFID cards [19]. Changing access policies is error-prone as closing one door for certain people could be circumvented by an alternative path. Therefore, we need to verify such updates.

Flow-LTL [8] is a logic for Petri nets with transits. It specifies linear time requirements on both the control and the data flow. Fairness and maximality assumptions on the movement of tokens are expressed in the control part. The logic lacks branching requirements for the data flow. In physical access control, branching requirements can specify that a person has the *possibility* to reach a room but not necessarily has to visit it. In this paper, we introduce *Flow-CTL** which maintains LTL to specify the control and adds CTL* to specify the data flow. Fairness and maximality assumptions in the control part dictate which executions, represented by runs, are checked against the data flow part.

This leads to an interesting encoding for physical access control in Petri nets with transits. Places represent rooms to collect the data flow. Transitions represent doors between rooms to continue the data flow. The selection of runs by fairness and maximality assumptions on the control restricts the branching behavior to transitions. Hence, the data flow is split at transitions: Every room has exactly one outgoing transition enabled unless all outgoing doors are closed. This transition splits the data flow into all successor rooms and thereby represents the maximal branching behavior.

We present a reduction of the model checking problem of safe Petri nets with transits against Flow-CTL* to the model checking problem of safe Petri nets against LTL. This enables for the first time the automatic verification of physical access control with *policy updates* under fairness and maximality assumptions for an unbounded number of people. Policy updates occur for example in the evening when every employee is expected to eventually leave the building and therefore access is more restricted. Such a policy update should prevent people from entering the building but should not trap anybody in the building.

Our reduction consists of three steps: First, each data flow subformula of the given Flow-CTL* formula is represented, via an alternating tree automaton, an alternating word automaton, and a nondeterministic Büchi automaton, by a finite Petri net to guess and then to verify a counterexample tree. Second, the original net for the control subformula of the Flow-CTL* formula and the nets for the data flow subformulas are connected in sequence. Third, an LTL formula encodes the control subformula, the acceptance conditions of the nets for the data flow subformulas, and the correct skipping of subnets in the sequential order. This results in a model checking problem of safe Petri nets against LTL.

The remainder of this paper is structured as follows: In Sect. 2, we motivate our approach with an example. In Sect. 3, we recall Petri nets and their extension to Petri nets with transits. In Sect. 4, we introduce Flow-CTL*. In Sect. 5, we express fairness, maximality, and standard properties for physical access control in Flow-CTL*. In Sect. 6, we reduce the model checking problem of Petri nets with transits against Flow-CTL* to the model checking problem of Petri nets

Fig. 1. The layout of a simple building is shown. There are three rooms indicated by gray boxes which are connected by doors indicated by small black boxes.

against LTL. Section 7 presents related work and Sect. 8 concludes the paper. Further details can be found in the full version of the paper [10].

2   Motivating Example

We motivate our approach with a typical example for physical access control. Consider the very simple building layout in Fig. 1. There are three rooms connected by two doors. An additional door is used to enter the building from the outside. Only employees have access to the building. A typical specification requires that employees can access the *lab* around the clock while allowing access to the *kitchen* only during daytime to discourage too long working hours. Meanwhile, certain safety requirements have to be fulfilled like not trapping anybody in the building. During the day, a correct access policy allows access to all rooms whereas, during the night, it only allows access to the *hall* and to the *lab*.

Figure 2 shows a Petri nets with transits modeling the building layout from Fig. 1. There are corresponding places (represented by circles) with tokens (represented by dots) for the three rooms: *hall*, *lab*, and *kitchen*. These places are connected by transitions (represented by squares) of the form *from→to* for *from* and *to* being rooms. The doors from the *kitchen* and *lab* to the *hall* cannot be closed as this could trap people. For all other doors, places of the form $o_{from→to}$ and $c_{from→to}$ exist to represent whether the door is open or closed.

In (safe) Petri nets, transitions define the movement of tokens: Firing a transition removes one token from each place with a black arrow leaving to the transition and adds one token to each place with a black arrow coming from the transition. Firing transition *evening* moves one token from place $o_{h→k}$ to place $c_{h→k}$ as indicated by the single-headed, black arrows and one token from and to each of the places *hall*, *lab*, and *kitchen* as indicated by the double-headed, black arrows. Firing transitions modeling doors returns all tokens to the same places while the transit relation as indicated by the green, blue, and orange arrows represents employees moving through the building. Dashed and dotted arrows only distinguish them from black arrows in case colors are unavailable.

Firing transition *enterHall* starts a flow chain modeling an employee entering the building as indicated by the single-headed, green (dashed) arrow. Meanwhile, the double-headed, blue (dotted) arrow maintains all flow chains previously in *hall*. All flow chains collectively represent the data flow in the modeled system incorporating all possible control changes. Firing transitions *from→to*, which correspond to doors, continues all flow chains from place *from* to place *to* as indicated by the single-headed, green (dashed) arrows and merges them with all flow chains in the place *to* as indicated by the double-headed, blue (dotted) arrows. For example, firing transition *hall→lab* lets all employees in the *hall* enter the *lab*. When employees *leave* the *hall*, their flow chain ends because it is not continued as indicated by the lack of colored arrows at transition *leaveHall*.

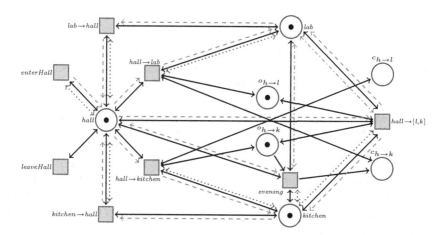

Fig. 2. The Petri net with transits encoding the building from Fig. 1 is depicted. Rooms are modeled by corresponding places, doors by transitions. Tokens in places starting with *o* configure the most permissive access policy during the day. In the *evening*, access to the *kitchen* is restricted. Employees in the building are modeled by the transit relation depicted by green, blue, and orange arrows. (Color figure online)

Flow-CTL* allows the splitting of flow chains in transitions. Splitting flow chains corresponds to branching behavior. Thus, when the doors to the *lab* and *kitchen* are open, we represent this situation by *one* transition which splits the flow chains. Transition *hall→[l,k]* realizes this by the single-headed, green (dashed) arrows from the *hall* to the *lab* and *kitchen*. Branching results in a *flow tree* for the possible behavior of an employee whereas a flow chain represents one explicit path from this flow tree, i.e., each employee has one flow tree with possibly many flow chains. Notice that transition *hall→[l,k]* can only be fired during the day, because, when firing transition *evening*, access to the *kitchen* is revoked. Then, only transition *hall→lab* can be fired for moving flow chains from the *hall*. For simplicity, we restrict the example to only one time change which implies that the transition *hall→kitchen* can never be fired. Firing transition *evening* continues all flow chains in the three places *hall*, *lab*, and *kitchen*, respectively, as indicated by the distinctly colored, double-headed arrows. Thus, we can specify requirements for the flow chains after the time change.

We specify the correctness of access policies with formulas of the logic *Flow-CTL**. The formula $\mathbb{A}\,\mathbf{AGEF}\,lab$ expresses *persistent permission* requiring that all flow chains ($\mathbb{A}$) on all paths globally (**AG**) have the possibility (**EF**) to reach the *lab*. The formula $\mathbb{A}\,\mathbf{A}((\mathbf{EF}\,kitchen)\mathbf{U}\,evening)$ expresses *dependent permission* requiring that all flow chains on all paths (**A**) have the possibility to reach the *kitchen* until (**U**) *evening*. Both properties require weak or strong fairness for all transitions modeling doors to be satisfied. The second property additionally requires weak or strong fairness for transition *evening* to be satisfied. Flow-CTL* and specifying properties with it are discussed further in Sect. 4 and Sect. 5.

3   Petri Nets with Transits

We recall the formal definition of Petri nets with transits [8] as extension of Petri nets [17]. We refer the reader to the full paper for more details [10]. A safe *Petri net* is a structure $\mathcal{N} = (\mathcal{P}, \mathcal{T}, \mathcal{F}, In)$ with the set of *places* $\mathcal{P}$, the set of *transitions* $\mathcal{T}$, the *(control) flow relation* $\mathcal{F} \subseteq (\mathcal{P} \times \mathcal{T}) \cup (\mathcal{T} \times \mathcal{P})$, and the *initial marking* $In \subseteq \mathcal{P}$. In *safe* Petri nets, each reachable marking contains at most one token per place. The elements of the disjoint union $\mathcal{P} \cup \mathcal{T}$ are considered as *nodes*. We define the *preset* (and *postset*) of a node x from Petri net $\mathcal{N}$ as $pre^{\mathcal{N}}(x) = \{y \in \mathcal{P} \cup \mathcal{T} \mid (y,x) \in \mathcal{F}\}$ (and $post^{\mathcal{N}}(x) = \{y \in \mathcal{P} \cup \mathcal{T} \mid (x,y) \in \mathcal{F}\}$). A safe *Petri net with transits* is a structure $\mathcal{N} = (\mathcal{P}, \mathcal{T}, \mathcal{F}, In, \Upsilon)$ which additionally contains a *transit relation* Υ refining the flow relation of the net to define the data flow. For each transition $t \in \mathcal{T}$, $\Upsilon(t)$ is a relation of type $\Upsilon(t) \subseteq (pre^{\mathcal{N}}(t) \cup \{\triangleright\}) \times post^{\mathcal{N}}(t)$, where the symbol $\triangleright$ denotes a *start*. With $\triangleright \Upsilon(t)\, q$, we define the start of a new data flow in place q via transition t and with $p\, \Upsilon(t)\, q$ that all data in place p *transits* via transition t to place q. The *postset regarding* Υ of a place $p \in \mathcal{P}$ and a transition $t \in post^{\mathcal{N}}(p)$ is defined by $post^{\Upsilon}(p,t) = \{p' \in \mathcal{P} \mid (p,p') \in \Upsilon(t)\}$.

The graphic representation of $\Upsilon(t)$ in Petri nets with transits uses a *color coding* as can be seen in Fig. 2. Black arrows represent the usual *control flow*. Other matching colors per transition are used to represent the transits of the *data flow*. Transits allow us to specify where the data flow is moved forward, split, and merged, where it ends, and where data is newly created. The data flow can be of infinite length and at any point in time (possibly restricted by the control) new data can enter the system at different locations.

As the data flow is a local property of each distributed component (possibly shared via joint transitions) it is convenient that Petri nets with transits use a true concurrency semantics to define the data flow. Therefore, we recall the notions of unfoldings and runs [5,6] and their application to Petri nets with transits. In the unfolding of a Petri net $\mathcal{N}$, every transition stands for the unique occurrence (instance) of a transition of $\mathcal{N}$ during an execution. To this end, every loop in $\mathcal{N}$ is unrolled and every backward branching place is expanded by multiplying the place. Forward branching, however, is preserved. Formally, an *unfolding* is a branching process $\beta^U = (\mathcal{N}^U, \lambda^U)$ consisting of an occurrence net $\mathcal{N}^U$ and a homomorphism λ^U that labels the places and transitions in $\mathcal{N}^U$ with the corresponding elements of $\mathcal{N}$. The unfolding exhibits concurrency, causality, and nondeterminism (forward branching) of the unique occurrences of the transitions in $\mathcal{N}$ during all possible executions. A *run* of $\mathcal{N}$ is a subprocess $\beta^R = (\mathcal{N}^R, \rho)$ of β^U, where $\forall p \in \mathcal{P}^R : |post^{\mathcal{N}^R}(p)| \leq 1$ holds, i.e., all nondeterminism has been resolved but concurrency is preserved. Thus, a run formalizes one concurrent execution of $\mathcal{N}$. We lift the transit relation of a Petri net with transits to any branching process and thereby obtain notions of runs and unfoldings for Petri nets with transits. Consider a run $\beta^R = (\mathcal{N}^R, \rho)$ of $\mathcal{N}$ and a finite or infinite firing sequence $\zeta = M_0[t_0\rangle M_1[t_1\rangle M_2 \cdots$ of $\mathcal{N}^R$ with $M_0 = In^R$. This sequence *covers* β^R if $(\forall p \in \mathcal{P}^R : \exists i \in \mathbb{N} : p \in M_i) \wedge (\forall t \in \mathcal{T}^R : \exists i \in \mathbb{N} : t = t_i)$, i.e., all places and transitions in $\mathcal{N}^R$ appear in ζ. Several firing sequences may cover β^R.

We define flow chains by following the transits of a given run. A (*data*) *flow chain* of a run $\beta^R = (\mathcal{N}^R, \rho)$ of a Petri net with transits $\mathcal{N}$ is a *maximal* sequence $\xi = t_0, p_0, t_1, p_1, t_2 \ldots$ of connected places and transitions of $\mathcal{N}^R$ with

(I) $(\triangleright, p_0) \in \Upsilon^R(t_0)$,
(con) $(p_{i-1}, p_i) \in \Upsilon^R(t_i)$ for all $i \in \mathbb{N} \setminus \{0\}$ if ξ is infinite and for all $i \in \{1, \ldots n\}$
     if $\xi = t_0, p_0, t_1, \ldots, t_n, p_n$ is finite,
(max) if $\xi = t_0, p_0, t_1, \ldots, t_n, p_n$ is finite there is no transition $t \in \mathcal{T}^R$ and place
     $q \in \mathcal{P}^R$ such that $(p_n, q) \in \Upsilon^R(t)$.

A *flow chain suffix* $\xi' = t_0, p_0, t_1, p_1, t_2 \ldots$ of a run β^R requires constraints (con), (max), and in addition to (I) allows that the chain has already started, i.e., $\exists p \in \mathcal{P}^R : (p, p_0) \in \Upsilon^R(t_0)$.

A Σ-labeled *tree* over a set of *directions* $\mathscr{D} \subset \mathbb{N}$ is a tuple (T, v), with a labeling function $v : T \to \Sigma$ and a tree $T \subseteq \mathscr{D}^*$ such that if $x \cdot c \in T$ for $x \in \mathscr{D}^*$ and $c \in \mathscr{D}$, then both $x \in T$ and for all $0 \leq c' < c$ also $x \cdot c' \in T$ holds. A (*data*) *flow tree* of a run $\beta^R = (\mathcal{N}^R, \rho)$ represents all branching behavior in the transitions of the run w.r.t. the transits. Formally, for each $t_0 \in \mathcal{T}^R$ and place $p_0 \in \mathcal{P}^R$ with $(\triangleright, p_0) \in \Upsilon^R(t_0)$, there is a $\mathcal{T}^R \times \mathcal{P}^R$-labeled tree $\tau = (T, v)$ over directions $\mathscr{D} \subseteq \{0, \ldots, \max\{|post^{\Upsilon^R}(p, t)| - 1 \mid p \in \mathcal{P}^R \wedge t \in post^{\mathcal{N}^R}(p)\}\}$ with

1. $v(\epsilon) = (t_0, p_0)$ for the root ϵ, and
2. if $n \in T$ with $v(n) = (t, p)$ then for the only transition $t' \in post^{\mathcal{N}^R}(p)$ (if existent) we have for all $0 \leq i < |post^{\Upsilon^R}(p, t')|$ that $n \cdot i \in T$ with $v(n \cdot i) = (t', q)$ for $q = \langle post^{\Upsilon^R}(p, t')\rangle_i$ where $\langle post^{\Upsilon^R}(p, t')\rangle_i$ is the i-th value of the ordered list $\langle post^{\Upsilon^R}(p, t')\rangle$.

Figure 3 shows a finite run of the example from Fig. 2 with two flow trees. The first tree starts with transition $enterHall_0$, i.e., $v(\epsilon) = (enterHall_0, hall_1)$ and is indicated by the gray shaded area. This tree represents an extract of the possibilities of a person entering the hall during the day ending with the control change to the evening policy. The second tree ($v(\epsilon) = (enterHall_1, hall_3), v(0) = (lab \to hall, hall_4), v(00) = (kitchen \to hall, hall_5), v(000) = (evening, hall_6)$) shows the possibilities of a person in this run who later enters the hall and can, because of the run, only stay there. Note that the trees only end due to the finiteness of the run. For maximal runs, trees can only end when transition *leaveHall* is fired.

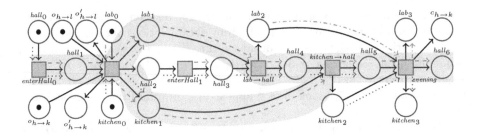

Fig. 3. A finite run of the Petri net with transits from Fig. 2 with two data flow trees is depicted. The first one is indicated by the gray shaded area.

4   Flow-CTL* for Petri Nets with Transits

We define the new logic *Flow*-CTL* to reason about the Petri net behavior and the data flow individually. Properties on the selection of runs and the general behavior of the net can be stated in LTL, requirements on the data flow in CTL*.

4.1   LTL on Petri Net Unfoldings

We recall LTL with *atomic propositions* $AP = \mathcal{P} \cup \mathcal{T}$ on a Petri net $\mathcal{N} = (\mathcal{P}, \mathcal{T}, \mathcal{F}, In)$ and define the semantics on runs and their firing sequences. We use the *ingoing* semantics, i.e., we consider the marking and the transition used to enter the marking, and *stutter* in the last marking for finite firing sequences.

Syntactically, the set of *linear temporal logic* (LTL) formulas LTL over AP is defined by $\psi ::= true \mid a \mid \neg \psi \mid \psi_1 \wedge \psi_2 \mid \bigcirc \psi \mid \psi_1 \, \mathcal{U} \, \psi_2$, with $a \in AP$ and $\bigcirc$ being the *next* and $\mathcal{U}$ the *until* operator. As usual, we use the propositional operators $\vee$, $\rightarrow$, and $\leftrightarrow$, the temporal operators $\Diamond \psi = true \, \mathcal{U} \, \psi$ (the *eventually* operator) and $\Box \psi = \neg \Diamond \neg \psi$ (the *always* operator) as abbreviations.

For a Petri net $\mathcal{N}$, we define a *trace* as a mapping $\sigma : \mathbb{N} \rightarrow 2^{AP}$. The i-th suffix $\sigma^i : \mathbb{N} \rightarrow 2^{AP}$ is a trace defined by $\sigma^i(j) = \sigma(j + i)$ for all $j \in \mathbb{N}$. To a (finite or infinite) covering firing sequence $\zeta = M_0[t_0\rangle M_1[t_1\rangle M_2 \cdots$ of a run $\beta^R = (\mathcal{N}^R, \rho)$ of $\mathcal{N}$, we associate a trace $\sigma(\zeta) : \mathbb{N} \rightarrow 2^{AP}$ with $\sigma(\zeta)(0) = \rho(M_0)$, $\sigma(\zeta)(i) = \{\rho(t_{i-1})\} \cup \rho(M_i)$ for all $i \in \mathbb{N} \setminus \{0\}$ if ζ is infinite and $\sigma(\zeta)(i) = \{\rho(t_{i-1})\} \cup \rho(M_i)$ for all $0 < i \leq n$, and $\sigma(\zeta)(j) = \rho(M_n)$ for all $j > n$ if $\zeta = M_0[t_0\rangle \cdots [t_{n-1}\rangle M_n$ is finite. Hence, a trace of a firing sequence covering a run is an infinite sequence of states collecting the corresponding marking and ingoing transition of $\mathcal{N}$, which stutters on the last marking for finite sequences.

The *semantics* of an LTL formula $\psi \in$ LTL on a Petri net $\mathcal{N}$ is defined over the traces of the covering firing sequences of its runs: $\mathcal{N} \models_{\text{LTL}} \psi$ iff for all runs β^R of $\mathcal{N}$: $\beta^R \models_{\text{LTL}} \psi$, $\beta^R \models_{\text{LTL}} \psi$ iff for all firing sequences ζ covering β^R : $\sigma(\zeta) \models_{\text{LTL}} \psi$, $\sigma \models_{\text{LTL}} true$, $\sigma \models_{\text{LTL}} a$ iff $a \in \sigma(0)$, $\sigma \models_{\text{LTL}} \neg \psi$ iff not $\sigma \models_{\text{LTL}} \psi$, $\sigma \models_{\text{LTL}} \psi_1 \wedge \psi_2$ iff $\sigma \models_{\text{LTL}} \psi_1$ and $\sigma \models_{\text{LTL}} \psi_2$, $\sigma \models_{\text{LTL}} \bigcirc \psi$ iff $\sigma^1 \models_{\text{LTL}} \psi$, and $\sigma \models_{\text{LTL}} \psi_1 \, \mathcal{U} \, \psi_2$ iff there exists a $j \geq 0$ with $\sigma^j \models_{\text{LTL}} \psi_2$ and $\sigma^i \models_{\text{LTL}} \psi_1$ holds for all $0 \leq i < j$.

4.2   CTL* on Flow Chains

To specify the data flow of a Petri net with transits $\mathcal{N} = (\mathcal{P}, \mathcal{T}, \mathcal{F}, In, \Upsilon)$, we use the complete *computation tree logic* (CTL*). The set of CTL* formulas CTL* over $AP = \mathcal{P} \cup \mathcal{T}$ is given by the following *syntax* of *state formulas*: $\Phi ::= a \mid \neg\Phi \mid \Phi_1 \wedge \Phi_2 \mid \mathbf{E}\phi$ where $a \in AP$, Φ, Φ_1, Φ_2 are state formulas, and ϕ is a *path formula* with the following *syntax*: $\phi ::= \Phi \mid \neg\phi \mid \phi_1 \wedge \phi_2 \mid \mathbf{X}\phi \mid \phi_1\mathbf{U}\phi_2$ where Φ is a state formula and ϕ, ϕ_1, ϕ_2 are path formulas. We use the propositional operators $\vee$, $\rightarrow$, $\leftrightarrow$, the path quantifier $\mathbf{A}\phi = \neg\mathbf{E}\neg\phi$, and the temporal operators $\mathbf{F}\phi = true\ \mathbf{U}\ \phi$, $\mathbf{G}\phi = \neg\mathbf{F}\neg\phi$, $\phi_1\mathbf{R}\phi_2 = \neg(\neg\phi_1\mathbf{U}\neg\phi_2)$ as abbreviations.

To a (finite or infinite) flow chain suffix $\xi = t_0, p_0, t_1, p_1, t_2, \ldots$ of a run $\beta^R = (\mathcal{N}^R, \rho)$ of $\mathcal{N}$, we associate a trace $\sigma(\xi) : \mathbb{N} \to \mathcal{S} = \{\{t, p\}, \{p\} \mid p \in \mathcal{P}^R \wedge t \in \mathcal{T}^R\}$ with $\sigma(\xi)(i) = \{t_i, p_i\}$ for all $i \in \mathbb{N}$ if ξ is infinite and $\sigma(\xi)(i) = \{t_i, p_i\}$ for all $i \leq n$, and $\sigma(\xi)(j) = \{p_n\}$ for all $j > n$ if $\xi = t_0, p_0, t_1, p_1, \ldots, t_n, p_n$ is finite. Hence, a trace of a flow chain suffix is an infinite sequence of states collecting the current place and ingoing transition of the flow chain, which stutters on the last place p of a finite flow chain suffix. We define $\sigma_s(\{p\})(i) = \{p\}$ for all $i \in \mathbb{N}$ to stutter on the last place of a finite flow chain suffix.

The *semantics* of a computation tree logic formula $\varphi \in$ CTL* is evaluated on a given run $\beta^R = (\mathcal{N}^R, \rho)$ of the Petri net with transits $\mathcal{N}$ and a state $s \in \mathcal{S}$ of a trace $\sigma(\xi)$ of a flow chain suffix ξ or the trace itself:

$\beta^R, s \models_{\text{CTL}^*} a$ iff $a \in \rho(s)$

$\beta^R, s \models_{\text{CTL}^*} \neg\Phi$ iff not $\beta^R, s \models_{\text{CTL}^*} \Phi$

$\beta^R, s \models_{\text{CTL}^*} \Phi_1 \wedge \Phi_2$ iff $\beta^R, s \models_{\text{CTL}^*} \Phi_1$ and $\beta^R, s \models_{\text{CTL}^*} \Phi_2$

$\beta^R, s \models_{\text{CTL}^*} \mathbf{E}\phi$ iff there *exists* some flow chain suffix $\xi = t_0, p_0, \ldots$ of β^R with $p_0 \in s$ such that $\beta^R, \sigma(\xi) \models_{\text{CTL}^*} \phi$ holds for $s \not\subseteq \mathcal{P}$ and $\beta^R, \sigma_s(s) \models_{\text{CTL}^*} \phi$ holds for $s \subseteq \mathcal{P}$

$\beta^R, \sigma \models_{\text{CTL}^*} \Phi$ iff $\beta^R, \sigma(0) \models_{\text{CTL}^*} \Phi$

$\beta^R, \sigma \models_{\text{CTL}^*} \neg\phi$ iff not $\beta^R, \sigma \models_{\text{CTL}^*} \phi$

$\beta^R, \sigma \models_{\text{CTL}^*} \phi_1 \wedge \phi_2$ iff $\beta^R, \sigma \models_{\text{CTL}^*} \phi_1$ and $\beta^R, \sigma \models_{\text{CTL}^*} \phi_2$

$\beta^R, \sigma \models_{\text{CTL}^*} \mathbf{X}\phi$ iff $\beta^R, \sigma^1 \models_{\text{CTL}^*} \phi$

$\beta^R, \sigma \models_{\text{CTL}^*} \phi_1\mathbf{U}\phi_2$ iff there exists some $j \geq 0$ with $\beta^R, \sigma^j \models_{\text{CTL}^*} \phi_2$ and for all $0 \leq i < j$ the following holds: $\beta^R, \sigma^i \models_{\text{CTL}^*} \phi_1$

with atomic propositions $a \in AP$, state formulas Φ, Φ_1, and Φ_2, and path formulas ϕ, ϕ_1, and ϕ_2. Note that since the formulas are evaluated on the runs of $\mathcal{N}$, the branching is in the transitions and not in the places of $\mathcal{N}$.

4.3   Flow-CTL*

Like in [8], we use Petri nets with transits to enable reasoning about two separate timelines. Properties defined on the run of the system concern the *global* timeline and allow to reason about the global behavior of the system like its general control or fairness. Additionally, we can express requirements about the individual data flow like the access possibilities of people in buildings. These requirements concern the *local* timeline of the specific data flow. In Flow-CTL*, we can reason about these two parts with LTL in the *run* and with CTL* in the *flow* part of the formula. This is reflected in the following *syntax*:

$$\Psi ::= \psi \mid \Psi_1 \wedge \Psi_2 \mid \Psi_1 \vee \Psi_2 \mid \psi \rightarrow \Psi \mid \mathbb{A}\,\varphi$$

where Ψ, Ψ_1, Ψ_2 are Flow-CTL* formulas, ψ is an LTL formula, and φ is a CTL* formula. We call $\varphi_{\mathbb{A}} = \mathbb{A}\,\varphi$ *flow formulas* and all other subformulas *run formulas*.

The *semantics* of a Petri net with transits $\mathcal{N} = (\mathcal{P}, \mathcal{T}, \mathcal{F}, In, \Upsilon)$ satisfying a Flow-CTL* formula Ψ is defined over the covering firing sequences of its runs:

$$
\begin{array}{ll}
\mathcal{N} \models \Psi & \text{iff for all runs } \beta^R \text{ of } \mathcal{N} : \beta^R \models \Psi \\
\beta^R \models \Psi & \text{iff for all firing sequences } \zeta \text{ covering } \beta^R : \beta^R, \sigma(\zeta) \models \Psi \\
\beta^R, \sigma \models \psi & \text{iff } \sigma \models_{\text{LTL}} \psi \\
\beta^R, \sigma \models \Psi_1 \wedge \Psi_2 & \text{iff } \beta^R, \sigma \models \Psi_1 \text{ and } \beta^R, \sigma \models \Psi_2 \\
\beta^R, \sigma \models \Psi_1 \vee \Psi_2 & \text{iff } \beta^R, \sigma \models \Psi_1 \text{ or } \beta^R, \sigma \models \Psi_2 \\
\beta^R, \sigma \models \psi \rightarrow \Psi & \text{iff } \beta^R, \sigma \models \psi \text{ implies } \beta^R, \sigma \models \Psi \\
\beta^R, \sigma \models \mathbb{A}\,\varphi & \text{iff for all flow chains } \xi \text{ of } \beta^R : \beta^R, \sigma(\xi) \models_{\text{CTL}^*} \varphi
\end{array}
$$

Due to the covering of the firing sequences and the maximality constraint of the flow chain suffixes, every behavior of the run is incorporated. The operator $\mathbb{A}$ chooses flow chains rather than flow trees as our definition is based on the common semantics of CTL* over paths. Though it suffices to find one of the possibly infinitely many flow trees for each flow formula to invalidate the subformula, checking the data flow while the control changes the system complicates the direct expression of the model checking problem within a finite model. In Sect. 6, we introduce a general reduction method for a model with a finite state space.

5   Example Specifications

We illustrate Flow-CTL* with examples from the literature on physical access control [13,18]. Branching properties like permission and way-pointing are given as flow formulas, linear properties like fairness and maximality as run formulas.

5.1   Flow Formulas

Figure 4 illustrates six typical specifications for physical access control [13,18].

Permission. Permission (cf. Fig. 4a) requires that a subformula φ can be reached on one path ($\mathbb{A}\mathbf{EF}\varphi$). In our running example, permission can be required for the *hall* and the *lab*. Permission can be extended as it requires

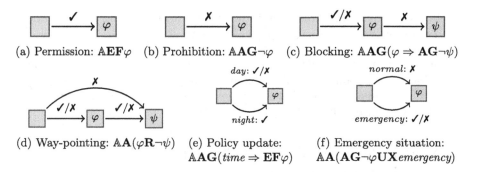

Fig. 4. Illustrations for standard properties of physical access control are depicted. Gray boxes represent rooms and arrows represent directions of doors that can be opened (✓), closed (✗), or are not affected by the property (✓/✗).

reaching the subformula once. Persistent permission then requires that, on all paths, the subformula φ can be repeatedly reached on a path ($\mathbb{A}\mathbf{AGEF}\varphi$).

Prohibition. Prohibition (cf. Fig. 4b) requires that a subformula φ, for example representing a room, can never be reached on any path ($\mathbb{A}\mathbf{AG}\neg\varphi$). In our running example, closing the door to the *kitchen* would satisfy prohibition for the *kitchen*.

Blocking. Blocking (cf. Fig. 4c) requires for all paths globally that, after reaching subformula φ, the subformula ψ cannot be reached ($\mathbb{A}\mathbf{AG}(\varphi \Rightarrow \mathbf{AG}\neg\psi)$). This can be used to allow a new employee to only enter one of many labs.

Way-Pointing. Way-pointing (cf. Fig. 4d) ensures for all paths that subformula ψ can only be reached if φ was reached before ($\mathbb{A}\mathbf{A}(\varphi\mathbf{R}\neg\psi)$). This can be used to enforce a mandatory security check when entering a building.

Policy Update. A policy update (cf. Fig. 4e) allows access to subformula φ according to a time schedule ($\mathbb{A}\mathbf{AG}(time \Rightarrow \mathbf{EF}\varphi)$) with *time* being a transition. This can be used to restrict access during the night.

Emergency. An emergency situation (cf. Fig. 4f) can revoke the prohibition of subformula φ at an arbitrary time ($\mathbb{A}\mathbf{A}(\mathbf{AG}\neg\varphi\mathbf{UX}emergency)$) with *emergency* being a transition. An otherwise closed door could be opened to evacuate people. The next operator $\mathbf{X}$ is necessary because of the ingoing semantics of Flow-CTL*.

5.2 Run Formulas

Flow formulas require behavior on the maximal flow of people in the building. Doors are assumed to allow passthrough in a fair manner. Both types of assumptions are expressed in Flow-CTL* as run formulas.

Maximality. A run β^R is *interleaving-maximal* if, whenever some transition is enabled, some transition will be taken: $\beta^R \models \Box(\bigvee_{t\in\mathcal{T}} pre(t) \to \bigvee_{t\in\mathcal{T}} \bigcirc t)$. A run β^R is *concurrency-maximal* if, when a transition t is from a moment on always enabled, infinitely often a transition t' (including t itself) sharing a precondition with t is taken: $\beta^R \models \bigwedge_{t \in \mathcal{T}} (\Diamond\square \, pre(t) \rightarrow \square\Diamond \bigvee_{p \in pre(t), t' \in post(p)} t')$.

Fairness. A run β^R is *weakly fair* w.r.t. a transition t if, whenever t is always enabled after some point, t is taken infinitely often: $\beta^R \models \Diamond\square \, pre(t) \rightarrow \square\Diamond t$. A run β^R is *strongly fair* w.r.t. t if, whenever t is enabled infinitely often, t is taken infinitely often: $\beta^R \models \square\Diamond \, pre(t) \rightarrow \square\Diamond t$.

6   Model Checking Flow-CTL* on Petri Nets with Transits

We solve the model checking problem for a given Flow-CTL* formula Ψ and a safe Petri net with transits $\mathcal{N}$ in four steps:

1. For each flow subformula $\mathbb{A}\,\varphi_i$ of Ψ, a subnet $\mathcal{N}_i^>$ is created via a sequence of automata constructions which allows to guess a counterexample, i.e., a flow tree not satisfying φ_i, and to check for its correctness.
2. The Petri net $\mathcal{N}^>$ is created by composing the subnets $\mathcal{N}_i^>$ to a copy of $\mathcal{N}$ such that every firing of a transition subsequently triggers each subnet.

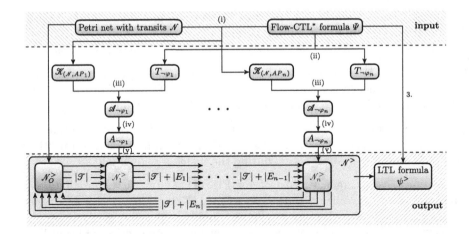

Fig. 5. Overview of the model checking procedure: For a given safe Petri net with transits $\mathcal{N}$ and a Flow-CTL* formula Ψ, a standard Petri net $\mathcal{N}^>$ and an LTL formula $\psi^>$ are created: For each flow subformula $\mathbb{A}\,\varphi_i$, create (i) a labeled Kripke structure $\mathcal{K}_{(\mathcal{N}, AP_i)}$ and (ii) the alternating tree automaton $T_{\neg\varphi_i}$, construct (iii) the alternating word automaton $\mathcal{A}_{\neg\varphi_i} = T_{\neg\varphi_i} \times \mathcal{K}_{(\mathcal{N}, AP_i)}$, and from that (iv) the Büchi automaton $A_{\neg\varphi_i}$ with edges E_i, which then (v) is transformed into a Petri net $\mathcal{N}_i^>$. These subnets are composed to a Petri net $\mathcal{N}^>$ such that they get subsequently triggered for every transition fired by the original net. The constructed formula $\psi^>$ skips for the run part of Ψ these subsequent steps and checks the acceptance of the guessed tree for each automaton. The problem is then solved by checking $\mathcal{N}^> \models_{\text{LTL}} \psi^>$.

3. The formula $\Psi^>$ is created such that the subnets $\mathcal{N}_i^>$ are adequately skipped for the run part of Ψ, and the flow parts are replaced by LTL formulas checking the acceptance of a run of the corresponding automaton.
4. $\mathcal{N}^> \models_{\text{LTL}} \Psi^>$ is checked to answer $\mathcal{N} \models \Psi$.

The construction from a given safe Petri net with transits $\mathcal{N} = (\mathcal{P}, \mathcal{T}, \mathcal{F}, In, \Upsilon)$ and a Flow-CTL* formula Ψ with $n \in \mathbb{N}$ flow subformulas $\varphi_{\mathbb{A}i} = \mathbb{A}\varphi_i$ with atomic propositions AP_i to a Petri net $\mathcal{N}^> = (\mathcal{P}^>, \mathcal{T}^>, \mathcal{F}^>, \mathcal{F}_I^>, In^>)$ with inhibitor arcs (denoted by $\mathcal{F}_I^>$) and an LTL formula $\Psi^>$ is defined in the following sections. More details and proofs can be found in the full paper [10]. An *inhibitor arc* connects a place p and a transition t of a Petri net such that t is only enabled when p is empty. Figure 5 gives a schematic overview of the procedure.

6.1   Automaton Construction for Flow Formulas

In Step 1, we create for each flow subformula $\mathbb{A}\varphi_i$ of Ψ with atomic propositions AP_i a nondeterministic Büchi automaton $A_{\neg\varphi_i}$ which accepts a sequence of transitions of a given run if the corresponding flow tree satisfies $\neg\varphi_i$. This construction has four steps:

(i) Create the labeled Kripke structure $\mathcal{K}_{(\mathcal{N}, AP_i)}$ which, triggered by transitions $t \in \mathcal{T}$, tracks every flow chain of $\mathcal{N}$. Each path corresponds to a flow chain.
(ii) Create the alternating tree automaton $T_{\neg\varphi_i}$ for the negation of the CTL* formula φ_i and the set of directions $\mathcal{D} \subseteq \{0, \ldots, \max\{|post^{\Upsilon}(p,t)| - 1 \mid p \in \mathcal{P} \wedge t \in post^{\mathcal{N}}(p)\}\}$ which accepts all 2^{AP_i}-labeled trees with nodes of degree in $\mathcal{D}$ satisfying $\neg\varphi_i$ [15].
(iii) Create the alternating word automaton $\mathcal{A}_{\neg\varphi_i} = T_{\neg\varphi_i} \times \mathcal{K}_{(\mathcal{N}, AP_i)}$ like in [15].
(iv) Alternation elimination for $\mathcal{A}_{\neg\varphi_i}$ yields the nondeterministic Büchi automaton $A_{\neg\varphi_i}$ [4,16].

Step (ii) and Step (iv) are well-established constructions. For Step (iii), we modify the construction of [15] by applying the algorithm for the groups of equally labeled edges. By this, we obtain an alternating word automaton with the alphabet $A = \mathcal{T} \cup \{\mathfrak{s}\}$ of the labeled Kripke structure rather than an alternating word automaton over a 1-letter alphabet. This allows us to check whether the, by the input transition dynamically created, system satisfies the CTL* subformula φ_i.

Step (i) of the construction creates the labeled Kripke structure $\mathcal{K}_{(\mathcal{N}, AP_i)} = (AP, S, S_0, L, A, R)$ with a set of *atomic propositions* $AP = AP_i$, a finite set of *states* $S = ((\mathcal{T} \cap AP) \times \mathcal{P}) \cup \mathcal{P}$, the *initial states* $S_0 \subseteq S$, the *labeling function* $L : S \rightarrow 2^{AP}$, the *alphabet* $A = \mathcal{T} \cup \{\mathfrak{s}\}$, and the *labeled transition relation* $R \subseteq S \times A \times S$. The Kripke structure serves (in combination with the tree automaton) for checking the satisfaction of a flow tree of a given run. Hence, the states track the current place of the considered chain of the tree and additionally, when the transition extending the chain into the place occurs in the formula, also this ingoing transition. The initial states S_0 are either the tuples of transitions t_j and places p_j which start a flow chain, i.e., all $(t_j, p_j) \in \mathcal{T} \times \mathcal{P}$ with $(\triangleright, p_j) \in \Upsilon(t_j)$

when $t_j \in AP$ or only the place p_j otherwise. The labeling function L labels the states with its components. The transition relation R connects the states with respect to the transits, connects each state $(t, p) \in S$ with $\mathfrak{s}$-labeled edges to the state $p \in S$, and loops with $\mathfrak{s}$-labeled edges in states $s \in \mathscr{P}$ to allow for the stuttering of finite chains.

Lemma 1 (Size of the Kripke Structure). *The constructed Kripke structure $\mathscr{K}_{(\mathcal{N}, AP_i)}$ has $\mathcal{O}(|AP_i \cap \mathcal{T}| \cdot |\mathcal{N}| + |\mathcal{N}|)$ states and $\mathcal{O}(|\mathcal{N}^3|)$ edges.*

Note that the number of edges stems from the number of transits $(p, t, q) \in \mathscr{P} \times \mathcal{T} \times \mathscr{P}$ used in the Petri net with transits $\mathcal{N}$.

The size of the Büchi automaton is dominated by the tree automaton construction and the removal of the alternation. Each construction adds one exponent for CTL*.

Lemma 2 (Size of the Büchi Automaton). *The size of the Büchi automaton $A_{\neg\varphi_i}$ is in $\mathcal{O}(2^{2^{|\varphi| \cdot |\mathcal{N}|^3}})$ for specifications φ_i in CTL* and in $\mathcal{O}(2^{|\varphi| \cdot |\mathcal{N}|^3})$ for specifications in CTL.*

6.2   From Petri Nets with Transits to Petri Nets

In Step 2, we construct for the Petri net with transits $\mathcal{N}$ and the Büchi automata $A_{\neg\varphi_i}$ for each flow subformula $\varphi_{\mathbb{A}i} = \mathbb{A} \varphi_i$ of Ψ, a Petri net $\mathcal{N}^>$ by composing a copy of $\mathcal{N}$ (without transits), denoted by $\mathcal{N}_O^>$, to subnets $\mathcal{N}_i^>$ corresponding to $A_{\neg\varphi_i}$ such that each copy is sequentially triggered when a transition of $\mathcal{N}_O^>$ fires. The subnet $\mathcal{N}_i^>$, when triggered by transitions $t \in \mathcal{T}$, guesses nondeterministically the violating flow tree of the operator $\mathbb{A}$ and simulates $A_{\neg\varphi_i}$. Thus, a token from the initially marked place $[\iota]_i$ is moved via a transition for each transition $t \in \mathcal{T}$ starting a flow chain to the place corresponding to the initial state of $A_{\neg\varphi_i}$. For each state s of $A_{\neg\varphi_i}$, we have a place $[s]_i$, and, for each edge (s, l, s'), a transition labeled by l which moves the token from $[s]_i$ to $[s']_i$.

There are two kinds of stutterings: *global* stuttering for finite runs and *local* stuttering for finite flow chains. To guess the starting time of both stutterings, there is an initially marked place $\mathbf{N}$, a place $\mathbf{S}$, and a transition which can switch from *normal* to *stuttering* mode for the global stuttering in $\mathcal{N}_O^>$ and for the local stutterings in each subnet $\mathcal{N}_i^>$ (denoted by $[\mathbf{N}], [\mathbf{S}]$). The original transitions of $\mathcal{N}_O^>$ and the transitions of a subnet $\mathcal{N}_i^>$ corresponding to a transition $t \in \mathcal{T}$ depend on the normal mode. The $\mathfrak{s}$-labeled transitions (used for global stuttering) of the subnet depend on the stuttering mode. To enable local stuttering, we add, for each edge $e = (s, \mathfrak{s}, s')$ of $A_{\neg\varphi_i}$, a transition $t^>$ for each transition $t \in \mathcal{T}$ for which no edge (s, t, s'') exists in $A_{\neg\varphi_i}$. These transitions depend on the stuttering mode and move the token according to their corresponding edge e.

The original part $\mathcal{N}_O^>$ and the subnets $\mathcal{N}_i^>$ are connected in a sequential manner. The net $\mathcal{N}_O^>$ has an initially marked activation place $\rightarrow_o$ in the preset of each transition, the subnets have one activation place $[\rightarrow_t]$ in the preset of every transition $t^>$ corresponding to a transition $t \in \mathcal{T}$ (normal as well as stuttering).

The transitions move the activation token to the corresponding places of the next subnet (or back to $\mathcal{N}_O^>$). To ensure the continuation even though the triggering transition does not extend the current flow tree (e.g., because it is a concurrent transition of the run), there is a skipping transition for each transition $t \in \mathcal{T}$ which moves the activation token when none of the states having a successor edge labeled with t are active. For the global stuttering, each subnet has an activation place $[\rightarrow_\mathfrak{s}]_i$, in which an additional transition $t_\mathfrak{s}$ in $\mathcal{N}_O^>$ puts the active token if the stuttering mode of $\mathcal{N}_O^>$ is active. Each $\mathfrak{s}$-labeled transition of the subnets moves this token to the next subnet (or back to $\mathcal{N}_O^>$).

By that, we can check the acceptance of each $A_{\neg\varphi_i}$ by checking if the subnet infinitely often reaches any places corresponding to a Büchi state of $A_{\neg\varphi_i}$. This and only allowing to correctly guess the time point of the stutterings is achieved with the formula described in Sect. 6.3. A formal definition is given in in the full paper [10]. The size of the constructed Petri net is dominated by the respective single- or double-exponential size of the nondeterministic Büchi automata.

Lemma 3 (Size of the Constructed Net). *The constructed Petri net with inhibitor arcs $\mathcal{N}^>$ for a Petri net with transits $\mathcal{N}$ and n nondeterministic Büchi automata $A_{\neg\varphi_i} = (\mathcal{T} \cup \{\mathfrak{s}\}, Q_i, I_i, E_i, F_i)$ has $\mathcal{O}(|\mathcal{N}| \cdot n + |\mathcal{N}| + \sum_{i=1}^n |Q_i|)$ places and $\mathcal{O}(|\mathcal{N}|^2 \cdot n + |\mathcal{N}| + \sum_{i=1}^n |E_i| + |\mathcal{N}| \cdot \sum_{i=1}^n |Q_i|)$ transitions.*

6.3   From Flow-CTL* Formulas to LTL Formulas

The formula transformation from a given Flow-CTL* formula Ψ and a Petri net with transits $\mathcal{N}$ into an LTL formula (Step 3) consists of three parts:

First, we substitute the flow formulas $\varphi_{\mathbb{A}i} = \mathbb{A}\,\varphi_i$ with the acceptance check of the corresponding automaton $A_{\neg\varphi_i}$, i.e., we substitute $\varphi_{\mathbb{A}i}$ with $\neg\Box\Diamond\bigvee_{b\in F_i}[b]_i$ for the Büchi states F_i of $A_{\neg\varphi_i}$.

Second, the sequential manner of the constructed net $\mathcal{N}^>$ requires an adaptation of the run part of Ψ. For a subformula $\psi_1\,\mathcal{U}\,\psi_2$ with transitions $t \in \mathcal{T}$ as atomic propositions or a subformula $\bigcirc \psi$ in the run part of Ψ, the sequential steps of the subnets have to be skipped. Let $\mathcal{T}_O^>$ be the transition of the original copy $\mathcal{N}_O^>$, $\mathcal{T}_i^>$ the transitions of the subnet $\mathcal{N}_i^>$, $\mathcal{T}_{\Rightarrow_i}$ the transitions of the subnet $\mathcal{N}_i^>$ which skip the triggering of the automaton in the normal mode, and $t_{\mathcal{N}\rightarrow\mathcal{S}}$ the transition switching $\mathcal{N}_O^>$ from normal to stuttering mode. Then, because of the ingoing semantics, we can select all states corresponding to the run part with $\mathtt{M} = \bigvee_{t\in\mathcal{T}_O^>\setminus\{t_{\mathcal{N}\rightarrow\mathcal{S}}\}} t$ together with the initial state $\mathtt{i} = \neg\bigvee_{t\in\mathcal{T}^>} t$. Hence, we replace each subformula $\psi_1\,\mathcal{U}\,\psi_2$ containing transitions $t \in \mathcal{T}$ as atomic propositions with $((\mathtt{M}\vee\mathtt{i}) \rightarrow \psi_1)\,\mathcal{U}\,((\mathtt{M}\vee\mathtt{i}) \rightarrow \psi_2)$ from the inner- to the outermost occurrence. For the next operator, the second state is already the correct next state of the initial state also in the sense of the global timeline of $\psi^>$. For all other states belonging to the run part (selected by the until construction above), we have to get the next state and then skip all transitions of the subnet. Thus, we replace each subformula $\bigcirc \psi$ with $\mathtt{i} \rightarrow \bigcirc \psi \wedge \neg\mathtt{i} \rightarrow \bigcirc(\bigvee_{t\in\mathcal{T}^>\setminus\mathcal{T}_O^>} t\,\mathcal{U}\,\bigvee_{t'\in\mathcal{T}_O^>} t'\wedge\psi)$ from the inner- to the outermost occurrence.

Third, we have to ensure the correct switching into the stuttering mode. By $\text{skip}_i = \neg \Diamond \Box ((\bigvee_{t \in \mathcal{T}_i^>} t) \to (\bigvee_{t' \in \mathcal{T}_{\Rightarrow_i}} t'))$ a subnet is enforced to switch into its stuttering mode if necessary. If it wrongly selects the time point of the global stuttering, the run stops. Hence, we obtain the formula $\psi^> = ((\Box \Diamond \to_o) \wedge \bigwedge_{i \in \{1,\dots,n\}} \text{skip}_i) \to \psi$ by only selecting the runs where the original part is infinitely often activated and each subnet chooses its stuttering mode correctly.

Since the size of the formula depends on the size of the constructed Petri net $\mathcal{N}^>$, it is also dominated by the Büchi automaton construction.

Lemma 4 (Size of the Constructed Formula). *The size of the constructed formula $\psi^>$ is double-exponential for specifications given in CTL* and single-exponential for specifications in CTL.*

We can show that the construction of the net and the formula adequately fit together such that the additional sequential steps of the subnets are skipped in the formula and the triggering of the subnets simulating the Büchi automata as well as the stuttering is handled properly.

Lemma 5 (Correctness of the Transformation). *For a Petri net with transits $\mathcal{N}$ and a Flow-CTL* formula Ψ, there exists a safe Petri net $\mathcal{N}^>$ with inhibitor arcs and an LTL formula $\Psi^>$ such that $\mathcal{N} \models \Psi$ iff $\mathcal{N}^> \models_{\text{LTL}} \Psi^>$.*

The complexity of the model checking problem of Flow-CTL* is dominated by the automata constructions for the CTL* subformulas. The need of the alternation removal (Step (iv) of the construction) is due to the checking of branching properties on structures chosen by linear properties. In contrast to standard CTL* model checking on a static Kripke structure, we check on Kripke structures dynamically created for specific runs.

Theorem 1. *A safe Petri net with transits $\mathcal{N}$ can be checked against a Flow-CTL* formula Ψ in triple-exponential time in the size of $\mathcal{N}$ and Ψ. For a Flow-CTL formula Ψ', the model checking algorithm runs in double-exponential time in the size of $\mathcal{N}$ and Ψ'.*

Note that a single-exponential time algorithm for Flow-LTL is presented in [8].

7   Related Work

There is a large body of work on physical access control: Closest to our work are *access nets* [12] which extend Petri nets with mandatory transitions to make people leave a room at a policy update. Branching properties can be model checked for a fixed number of people in the building. Fixing the number of people enables explicit interaction between people. In logic-based access-control frameworks, credentials are collected from distributed components to open policy enforcement points according to the current policy [2,3]. Techniques from networking can be applied to physical access control to detect redundancy, shadowing, and spuriousness in policies [11]. Our model prevents such situations by definition as a door can be either open or closed for people with the same access rights.

A user study has been carried out to identify the limitations of physical access control for real-life professionals [1]. Here, it was identified that policies are made by multiple people which is a problem our approach of global control solves. Types of access patterns are also studied [7,13,18]: Access policies according to time schedules and emergencies, access policies for people without RFID cards, and dependent access are of great importance. The first and the third problem are solvable by our approach and the second one seems like an intrinsic problem to physical access control. Policies for physical access control can be synthesized if no policy updates are necessary [18]. It is an interesting open question whether policy updates can be included in the synthesis of access policies.

8 Conclusion

We present the first model checking approach for the verification of physical access control with policy updates under fairness assumptions and with an unbounded number of people. Our approach builds on Petri nets with transits which superimpose a transit relation onto the flow relation of Petri nets to differentiate between data flow and control. We introduce Flow-CTL* to specify branching properties on the data flow and linear properties on the control in Petri nets with transits. We outline how Petri nets with transits can model physical access control with policy updates and how Flow-CTL* can specify properties on the behavior before, during, and after updates including fairness and maximality. To solve the model checking problem, we reduce the model checking problem of Petri nets with transits against Flow-CTL* via automata constructions to the model checking problem of Petri nets against LTL. In the future, we plan to evaluate our approach in a tool implementation and a corresponding case study. We can build on our tool ADAMMC [9] for Petri nets with transits and Flow-LTL.

References

1. Bauer, L., Cranor, L.F., Reeder, R.W., Reiter, M.K., Vaniea, K.: Real life challenges in access-control management. In: Proceedings of the CHI (2009)
2. Bauer, L., Garriss, S., Reiter, M.K.: Distributed proving in access-control systems. In: Proceedings of S&P (2005)
3. Bauer, L., Garriss, S., Reiter, M.K.: Efficient proving for practical distributed access-control systems. In: Biskup, J., López, J. (eds.) ESORICS 2007. LNCS, vol. 4734, pp. 19–37. Springer, Heidelberg (2007). https://doi.org/10.1007/978-3-540-74835-9_3
4. Dax, C., Klaedtke, F.: Alternation elimination by complementation (extended abstract). In: Cervesato, I., Veith, H., Voronkov, A. (eds.) LPAR 2008. LNCS, vol. 5330, pp. 214–229. Springer, Heidelberg (2008). https://doi.org/10.1007/978-3-540-89439-1_16
5. Engelfriet, J.: Branching processes of Petri nets. Acta Inf. **28**(6), 575–591 (1991). https://doi.org/10.1007/BF01463946

6. Esparza, J., Heljanko, K.: Unfoldings - A Partial-Order Approach to Model Checking. Springer, Heidelberg (2008). https://doi.org/10.1007/978-3-540-77426-6
7. Fernandez, E.B., Ballesteros, J., Desouza-Doucet, A.C., Larrondo-Petrie, M.M.: Security patterns for physical access control systems. In: Barker, S., Ahn, G.J. (eds.) DBSec 2007. LNCS, vol. 4602, pp. 259–274. Springer, Heidelberg (2007). https://doi.org/10.1007/978-3-540-73538-0_19
8. Finkbeiner, B., Gieseking, M., Hecking-Harbusch, J., Olderog, E.-R.: Model checking data flows in concurrent network updates. In: Chen, Y.-F., Cheng, C.-H., Esparza, J. (eds.) ATVA 2019. LNCS, vol. 11781, pp. 515–533. Springer, Cham (2019). https://doi.org/10.1007/978-3-030-31784-3_30
9. Finkbeiner, B., Gieseking, M., Hecking-Harbusch, J., Olderog, E.-R.: ADAMMC: a model checker for petri nets with transits against flow-LTL. In: Lahiri, S.K., Wang, C. (eds.) CAV 2020. LNCS, vol. 12225, pp. 64–76. Springer, Cham (2020). https://doi.org/10.1007/978-3-030-53291-8_5
10. Finkbeiner, B., Gieseking, M., Hecking-Harbusch, J., Olderog, E.: Model checking branching properties on Petri nets with transits (full version). arXiv preprint arXiv:2007.07235 (2020)
11. Fitzgerald, W.M., Turkmen, F., Foley, S.N., O'Sullivan, B.: Anomaly analysis for physical access control security configuration. In: Proceedings of CRiSIS (2012)
12. Frohardt, R., Chang, B.-Y.E., Sankaranarayanan, S.: Access nets: modeling access to physical spaces. In: Jhala, R., Schmidt, D. (eds.) VMCAI 2011. LNCS, vol. 6538, pp. 184–198. Springer, Heidelberg (2011). https://doi.org/10.1007/978-3-642-18275-4_14
13. Geepalla, E., Bordbar, B., Du, X.: Spatio-temporal role based access control for physical access control systems. In: Proceedings of EST (2013)
14. Jensen, K.: Coloured Petri Nets: Basic Concepts, Analysis Methods and Practical Use, vol. 1. Springer, Heidelberg (1992). https://doi.org/10.1007/978-3-642-60794-3
15. Kupferman, O., Vardi, M.Y., Wolper, P.: An automata-theoretic approach to branching-time model checking. J. ACM **47**(2), 312–360 (2000)
16. Miyano, S., Hayashi, T.: Alternating finite automata on omega-words. Theor. Comput. Sci. **32**, 321–330 (1984)
17. Reisig, W.: Petri Nets: An Introduction. Springer, Heidelberg (1985). https://doi.org/10.1007/978-3-642-69968-9
18. Tsankov, P., Dashti, M.T., Basin, D.A.: Access control synthesis for physical spaces. In: Proceedings of CSF (2016)
19. Welbourne, E., et al.: Building the internet of things using RFID: the RFID ecosystem experience. IEEE Internet Comput. **13**(3), 48–55 (2009)

Synthesis

Explainable Reactive Synthesis

Tom Baumeister[1(✉)], Bernd Finkbeiner[2], and Hazem Torfah[3]

[1] Saarland University, Saarland Informatics Campus, Saarbrücken, Germany
s8tobaum@stud.uni-saarland.de
[2] CISPA Helmholtz Center for Information Security, Saarbrücken, Germany
finkbeiner@cispa.saarland
[3] University of California, Berkeley, USA
torfah@berkeley.edu

Abstract. Reactive synthesis transforms a specification of a reactive system, given in a temporal logic, into an implementation. The main advantage of synthesis is that it is automatic. The main disadvantage is that the implementation is usually very difficult to understand. In this paper, we present a new synthesis process that explains the synthesized implementation to the user. The process starts with a simple version of the specification and a corresponding simple implementation. Then, desired properties are added one by one, and the corresponding transformations, repairing the implementation, are explained in terms of counterexample traces. We present SAT-based algorithms for the synthesis of repairs and explanations. The algorithms are evaluated on a range of examples including benchmarks taken from the SYNTCOMP competition.

Keywords: Reactive synthesis · Temporal logic · SAT-based synthesis

1 Introduction

In reactive synthesis, an implementation of a reactive system is automatically constructed from its formal specification. Synthesis allows developers to define the behavior of a system in terms of a list of its desired high-level properties, delegating the detailed implementation decisions to an automatic procedure. However, the great advantage of synthesis, that it is *automatic*, can also be an obstacle, because it makes it difficult for the user to *understand* why the system reacts in a particular way. This is particularly troublesome in case the user has written an incorrect specification or forgotten to include an important property. The declarative nature of formal specifications gives the synthesis process the liberty to resolve unspecified behavior in an arbitrary way. This may result in

This work was partially supported by the Collaborative Research Center "Foundations of Perspicuous Software Systems" (TRR: 248, 389792660), the European Research Council (ERC) Grant OSARES (No. 683300), the DARPA Assured Autonomy program, the iCyPhy center, and by Berkeley Deep drive.

D. V. Hung and O. Sokolsky (Eds.): ATVA 2020, LNCS 12302, pp. 413–428, 2020.
https://doi.org/10.1007/978-3-030-59152-6_23

implementations that satisfy the specification, yet still behave very differently from the developer's expectations.

In this paper, we propose a new synthesis process that, while still fully automatic, provides the user with an explanation for the decisions made by the synthesis algorithm. The *explainable synthesis* process builds the implementation incrementally, starting with a small subset of the desired properties and then adding more properties, one at a time. In each step, the algorithm presents an implementation that satisfies the currently considered specification and explains the changes that were required from the previous implementation in order to accomodate the additional property. Such an explanation consists of a counterexample trace, which demonstrates that the previous implementation violated the property, and a transformation that minimally repairs the problem.

As an example, consider the specification of a two-client arbiter in linear-time temporal logic (LTL) shown in Fig. 1a. The specification consists of three properties: $\varphi_{mutex}, \varphi_{fairness}$ and $\varphi_{non\text{-}spurious}$, requiring *mutual exclusion*, i.e., there is at most one grant at a time, *fairness*, i.e., every request is eventually granted, and *non-spuriousness*, i.e., a grant is only given upon receiving a request[1]. Let us suppose that our synthesis algorithm has already produced the transition system shown in Fig. 1b for the partial specification $\varphi_{mutex} \wedge \varphi_{fairness}$. This solution does not satisfy $\varphi_{non\text{-}spurious}$. To repair the transition system, the synthesis algorithm carries out the transformations depicted in Figs. 1c to 1g. The transformations include a label change in the initial state and the redirection of five transitions. The last four redirections require the expansion of the transition system to two new states t_2 and t_3. The synthesis algorithm justifies the transformations with counterexamples, depicted in red in Figs. 1c to 1f.

The algorithm justifies the first two transformations, (1) changing the label in the initial state to $\emptyset$ as depicted in Fig. 1c and (2) redirecting the transition $(t_0, \emptyset, t_1)$ to $(t_0, \emptyset, t_0)$, as shown in Fig. 1d, by a path in the transition system that violates $\varphi_{non\text{-}spurious}$, namely the path that starts with transition $(t_0, \emptyset, t_1)$. Changing the label of the initial state causes, however, a violation of $\varphi_{fairness}$, because no grant is given to client 0. This justifies giving access to a new state t_2, as shown in Fig. 1e and redirecting the transition with $\{r_0\}$ from t_0 to t_2. The third transformation, leading to Fig. 1f, is justified by the counterexample that, when both clients send a request at the same time, then only client 1 would be given access. Finally, the last two transformations, redirecting $(t_1, \{r_0\}, t_0)$ to $(t_1, \{r_0\}, t_3)$ and $(t_1, \{r_0, r_1\}, t_0)$ to $(t_1, \{r_0, r_1\}, t_3)$, are justified by the counterexample that if both clients alternate between sending a request then client 0 will not get a grant. This final transformation results in the transition system shown in Fig. 1g, which satisfies all three properties from Fig. 1a.

We implement the explainable synthesis approach in the setting of *bounded synthesis* [4,9]. Bounded synthesis finds a solution that is minimal in the number

---

[1] The sub-formula $r_i \mathcal{R} \neg g_i$ states that initially no grant is given to client i as long as no request is received from this client. After that, the formula $\Box(g_i \rightarrow r_i \vee (\bigcirc(r_i \mathcal{R} \neg g_i)))$ ensures that a grant is active only if the current request is still active, otherwise, and from this point on, no grants are given as long as no new request is received.

$$\varphi_{mutex} := \quad \Box(\neg g_0 \lor \neg g_1)$$

$$\varphi_{fairness} := \bigwedge_{i \in \{0,1\}} \Box(r_i \to \Diamond g_i)$$

$$\varphi_{non\text{-}spurious} := \bigwedge_{i \in \{0,1\}} ((r_i \mathcal{R} \neg g_i) \land \Box(g_i \to r_i \lor (\bigcirc(r_i \mathcal{R} \neg g_i))))$$

(a) Specification of a two-client arbiter

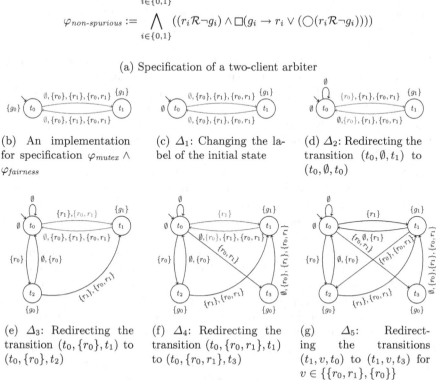

(b) An implementation for specification $\varphi_{mutex} \land \varphi_{fairness}$

(c) Δ_1: Changing the label of the initial state

(d) Δ_2: Redirecting the transition $(t_0, \emptyset, t_1)$ to $(t_0, \emptyset, t_0)$

(e) Δ_3: Redirecting the transition $(t_0, \{r_0\}, t_1)$ to $(t_0, \{r_0\}, t_2)$

(f) Δ_4: Redirecting the transition $(t_0, \{r_0, r_1\}, t_1)$ to $(t_0, \{r_0, r_1\}, t_3)$

(g) Δ_5: Redirecting the transitions (t_1, v, t_0) to (t_1, v, t_3) for $v \in \{\{r_0, r_1\}, \{r_0\}\}$

Fig. 1. Using explainable reactive synthesis to synthesize an implementation for a two-client arbiter. Clients request access to the shared resource via the signals r_0 and r_1. Requests are granted by the arbiter via the signals g_0 and g_1. (Color figure online)

of states; this generalizes here to a solution that is obtained from the previous solution with a minimal number of transformations. Like bounded synthesis, we use a SAT encoding to find the transition system, with additional constraints on the type and number of transformations. As explained above, the transformations involve a change of a state label or a redirection of a transition. Within the given budget of states, new states are accessed by redirecting transitions to these states. In the example in Fig. 1, a budget of four states is fixed and initially unreachable states, such as t_2 and t_3, are accessed by redirecting transitions to them as done in Fig. 1e and Fig. 1f. For the construction of explanations, we use bounded model checking [9]. In this way, both the repair and the explanation can be ensured to be minimal. We evaluate our approach on a series of examples, including benchmarks from the SYNTCOMP competition [12].

Related Work

The importance of incremental algorithms for solving the reactive synthesis problem has quickly manifested itself in the research community after the introduction of the problem. By decomposing a synthesis problem into smaller instances and combining the results of these instances to a solution for the full problem, the hope is to provide scalable algorithms for solving the in general difficult problem [6,15–17,20,21]. For example, for a set of system specifications, one can construct implementations for the individual specifications and construct an implementation for the full specification by composing the results for the smaller specifications [15]. To check the realizability of a specification, one can check the realizability of gradually larger parts of the specification [21]. Refinement-based synthesis algorithms incrementally construct implementations starting with an abstraction that is gradually refined with respect to a given partial order that guarantees correctness [6,16,17,20]. The key difference between our approach and the incremental approaches mentioned above is the underlying repair process. The advantage of program repair is that it constructs an implementation that is close to the original erroneous implementation. In our approach, this makes it possible to derive explanations that justify the repairs applied to the previous implementation. Other repair problems for temporal logics have previously been considered in [3,13]. In [13], an expression or a left-hand side of an assignment is assumed to be erroneous and replaced by one that satisfies the specification. In [3], the repair removes edges from the transition system. By contrast, our repair algorithm changes labels of states and redirects transitions.

A completely different approach to make synthesized implementation more understandable is by posing conditions on the structure of synthesized implementations [8,14]. Bounded synthesis [9] allows us to bound the size of the constructed implementation. Bounded cycle synthesis [7] additionally bounds the number of cycles in the implementation. Skeleton synthesis [10] establishes the relations between the specification and the synthesized implementation to clarify which parts of the implementation are determined by the specification and which ones where chosen by the synthesis process.

2   Preliminaries

Linear-Time Temporal Logic: As specification language, we use Linear-Time Temporal Logic (LTL) [19], with the usual temporal operators Next $\bigcirc$, Until $\mathcal{U}$ and the derived operators Release $\mathcal{R}$, which is the dual operator of $\mathcal{U}$, Eventually $\lozenge$ and Globally $\square$. Informally, the Release operator $\varphi_1 \mathcal{R} \varphi_2$ says that φ_2 holds in every step until φ_1 *releases* this condition. LTL formulas defining specifications for reactive systems are defined over a set of atomic propositions $AP = I \cup O$, which is partitioned into a set I of input propositions and a set O of output propositions. We denote the satisfaction of an LTL formula φ by an infinite sequence $\sigma \colon \mathbb{N} \to 2^{AP}$ of valuations of the atomic propositions by $\sigma \vDash \varphi$. For an LTL formula φ we define the language $\mathcal{L}(\varphi)$ by the set $\{\sigma \in (\mathbb{N} \to 2^{AP}) \mid \sigma \vDash \varphi\}$.

Implementations: We represent implementations as *labeled transition systems.*
For a given finite set Υ of directions and a finite set Σ of labels, a Σ-labeled
Υ-transition system is a tuple $\mathcal{T} = (T, t_0, \tau, o)$, consisting of a finite set of states
T, an initial state $t_0 \in T$, a transition function $\tau \colon T \times \Upsilon \to T$, and a labeling
function $o \colon T \to \Sigma$. For a set I of input propositions and a set O of output
propositions, we represent reactive systems as 2^O-labeled 2^I-transition systems.
For reactive systems, a *path* in $\mathcal{T}$ is a sequence $\pi \in \mathbb{N} \to T \times 2^I$ of states and
directions that follows the transition function, i.e., for all $i \in \mathbb{N}$, if $\pi(i) = (t_i, e_i)$
and $\pi(i+1) = (t_{i+1}, e_{i+1})$, then $t_{i+1} = \tau(t_i, e_i)$. We call a path initial if it starts
with the initial state: $\pi(0) = (t_0, e)$ for some $e \in 2^I$. We denote the set of initial
paths of $\mathcal{T}$ by $Paths(\mathcal{T})$. For a path $\pi \in Paths(\mathcal{T})$, we denote the sequence
$\sigma_\pi \colon i \mapsto o(\pi(i))$, where $o(t, e) = (o(t) \cup e)$ by the *trace* of π. We call the set of
traces of the paths of a transition system $\mathcal{T}$ the language of $\mathcal{T}$, denoted by $\mathcal{L}(\mathcal{T})$.

For a given finite sequence $v^* \in (2^I)^*$, we denote the transitions sequence
where we reach a state t' from state t after applying the transition function τ for
every letter in v^* starting in t by $\tau^*(t, v^*) = t'$. The size of a transition system
is the size of its set of states, which we denote by $|\mathcal{T}|$.

For a set of atomic propositions $AP = I \cup O$, we say that a 2^O-labeled 2^I-
transition system $\mathcal{T}$ satisfies an LTL formula φ, if and only if $\mathcal{L}(\mathcal{T}) \subseteq \mathcal{L}(\varphi)$, i.e.,
every trace of $\mathcal{T}$ satisfies φ. In this case, we call $\mathcal{T}$ a model of φ.

3   Minimal Repairs and Explanations

In this section, we lay the foundation for explainable reactive synthesis. We
formally define the transformations that are performed by our repair algorithm
and determine the complexity of finding a minimal repair, i.e., a repair with the
fewest number of transformations, with respect to a given transition system and
an LTL specification and show how repairs can be explained by counterexamples
that justify the repair.

3.1   Generating Minimal Repairs

For a 2^O-labeled 2^I-transition system $\mathcal{T} = (T, t_0, \tau, o)$, an *operation* Δ is either
a *change of a state labeling* or a *redirection of a transition* in $\mathcal{T}$. We denote the
transition system $\mathcal{T}'$ that results from applying an operation Δ to the transition
system $\mathcal{T}$ by $\mathcal{T}' = apply(\mathcal{T}, \Delta)$.

A state labeling change is denoted by a tuple $\Delta_{\text{label}} = (t, v)$, where $t \in T$
and $v \in 2^O$ defines the new output v of state t. The transition system $\mathcal{T}' =
apply(\mathcal{T}, \Delta_{\text{label}})$ is defined by $\mathcal{T}' = (T, t_0, \tau, o')$, where $o'(t) = v$ and $o'(t') = o(t')$
for all $t' \in T$ with $t' \neq t$.

A transition redirection is denoted by a tuple $\Delta_{\text{transition}} = (t, t', V)$, where
$t, t' \in T$ and $V \subseteq 2^I$. For a transition redirection operation $\Delta_{\text{transition}} = (t, t', V)$,
the transition system $\mathcal{T}' = apply(\mathcal{T}, \Delta_{\text{transition}})$ is defined by $\mathcal{T}' = (T, t_0, \tau', o)$,
with $\tau'(t, v) = t'$ for $v \in V$ and $\tau'(t, v) = \tau(t, v)$ for $v \notin V$. For $t'' \neq t$ and
$v \in 2^I$, $\tau'(t'', v) = \tau(t'', v)$.

A finite set of operations ξ is called a *transformation*. A transformation ξ is *consistent* if there is no transition system T and $\Delta_1, \Delta_2 \in \xi$ such that $apply(apply(T, \Delta_1), \Delta_2) \neq apply(apply(T, \Delta_2), \Delta_1)$, i.e. the resulting transition system does not differ depending on the order in which operations are applied. For a consistent transformation ξ, we denote the 2^O-labeled 2^I-transition system T' that we reach after applying every operation in ξ starting with a 2^O-labeled 2^I-transition system T by $T' = apply^*(T, \xi)$.

Note that there is no operation which explicitly adds a new state. In the example in Fig. 1, we assume a fixed number of available states (some that might be unreachable in the initial transition system). We reach new states by using a transition redirection operation to these states.

Definition 1 (Minimal Repair). *For an LTL-formula φ over $AP = I \cup O$ and a 2^O-labeled 2^I-transition system T, a consistent transformation ξ is a repair for T and φ if $apply^*(T, \xi) \vDash \varphi$. A repair ξ is minimal if there is no repair ξ' with $|\xi'| < |\xi|$.*

Example 1. The arbiter Arb_1 in Fig. 1c can be obtained from the round-robin arbiter Arb_0, shown in Fig. 1b, by applying $\Delta_{\text{label}} = (t_0, \emptyset)$, i.e. $Arb_1 = apply(Arb_0, \Delta_{\text{label}})$. Arbiter Arb_3, depicted in Fig. 1e is obtained from Arb_1 with the transformation $\xi_1 = \{\Delta_{\text{transition1}}, \Delta_{\text{transition2}}\}$ where $\Delta_{\text{transition1}} = (t_0, t_0, \{\emptyset\})$ and $\Delta_{\text{transition2}} = (t_0, t_2, \{\{r_0\}\})$ such that $apply^*(Arb_1, \xi_1) = Arb_3$. A minimal repair for Arb_0 and $\varphi_{mutex} \wedge \varphi_{fairness} \wedge \varphi_{non\text{-}spurious}$, defined in Sect. 1, is $\xi_2 = \{\Delta_{\text{label}}, \Delta_{\text{transition1}}, \Delta_{\text{transition2}}, \Delta_{\text{transition3}}, \Delta_{\text{transition4}}\}$ with $\Delta_{\text{transition3}} = (t_0, t_3, \{\{r_0, r_1\}\})$ and $\Delta_{\text{transition}} = (t_1, t_2, \{\{r_0\}, \{r_0, r_1\}\})$. The resulting full arbiter Arb_5 is depicted in Fig. 1g, i.e. $apply^*(Arb_0, \xi_2) = Arb_5$.

We are interested in finding minimal repairs. The *minimal repair synthesis problem* is defined as follows.

Problem 1 (Minimal Repair Synthesis). *Let φ be an LTL-formula over a set of atomic propositions $AP = I \cup O$ and T be a 2^O-labeled 2^I-transition system. Find a minimal repair for φ and T?*

In the next lemma, we show that for a fixed number of operations, the problem of checking if there is a repair is polynomial in the size of the transition system and exponential in the number of operations. For a small number of operations, finding a repair is cheaper than synthesizing a new system, which is 2EXPTIME-complete in the size of the specification [18].

Lemma 1. *For an LTL-formula φ, a 2^O-labeled 2^I-transition system T, and a bound k, deciding whether there exists a repair ξ for T and φ with $|\xi| = k$ can be done in time polynomial in the size of T, exponential in k, and space polynomial in the length of φ.*

Proof. Checking for a transformation ξ if $apply^*(T, \xi) \vDash \varphi$ is PSPACE-complete [22]. There are $|T| \cdot 2^{|O|}$ different state labeling operations and $|T|^2 \cdot 2^{|I|}$ transition redirections. Thus, the number of transformations ξ with $|\xi| = k$ is bounded by $\mathcal{O}((|T|^2)^k)$. Hence, deciding the existence of such a repair is polynomial in $|T|$ and exponential in k. $\qquad\square$

The size of a minimal repair is bounded by a polynomial in the size of the transition system under scrutiny. Thus, the minimal repair synthesis problem can be solved in time at most exponential in $|\mathcal{T}|$. In most cases, we are interested in small repairs resulting in complexities that are polynomial in $|\mathcal{T}|$.

Theorem 1. *For an LTL-formula φ, a 2^O-labeled 2^I-transition system $\mathcal{T}$, finding a minimal repair for $\mathcal{T}$ and φ can be done in time exponential in the size of $\mathcal{T}$, and space polynomial in the length of φ.*

3.2   Generating Explanations

For an LTL-formula φ over $AP = I \cup O$, a transformation ξ for a 2^O-labeled 2^I-system $\mathcal{T}$ is *justified* by a counterexample σ if $\sigma \nvDash \varphi$, $\sigma \in \mathcal{L}(\mathcal{T})$ and $\sigma \notin \mathcal{L}(apply^*(\mathcal{T},\xi))$. We call σ a *justification* for ξ. A transformation ξ is called *justifiable* if there exists a justification σ for ξ.

A transformation ξ for $\mathcal{T}$ and φ is *minimally* justified by σ if ξ is justified by σ and there is no $\xi' \subset \xi$ where σ is a justification for ξ'. If a transformation ξ is minimally justified by a counterexample σ, we call σ a *minimal* justification.

Definition 2 (Explanation). *For an LTL-formula φ over $AP = I \cup O$, an initial 2^O-labeled 2^I-transition system $\mathcal{T}$, and a minimal repair ξ, an explanation ex is defined as a sequence of pairs of transformations and counterexamples. For an explanation $ex = (\xi_1, \sigma_1), \ldots, (\xi_n, \sigma_n)$, it holds that all transformations $\xi_1, \ldots, \xi_n$ are disjoint, $\xi = \bigcup_{1 \leq i \leq n} \xi_i$, and each transformation ξ_i with $1 \leq i \leq n$ is minimally justified by σ_i for $apply^*(\mathcal{T}, \bigcup_{1 \leq j < i} \xi_j)$ and φ.*

Example 2. Let $\varphi_1 = g \wedge \bigcirc \neg g$ over $I = \{r\}$ and $O = \{g\}$ and consider the 2^O-labeled 2^I-transition system $\mathcal{T}$ with states $\{t_0, t_1\}$, depicted in Fig. 2.

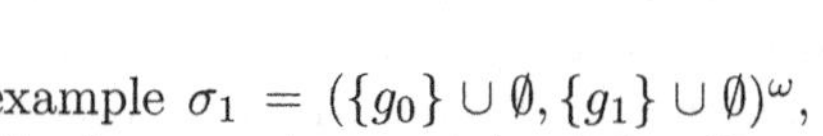

For $\mathcal{T}$ and φ_1, the transformation ξ with $\xi = \{\Delta_{\text{transition}}\}$ where $\Delta_{\text{transition}} = (t_0, t_1, \{\{g\}, \emptyset\})$, is not justifiable because $\mathcal{L}(\mathcal{T}) = \mathcal{L}(apply^*(\mathcal{T}, \xi))$. For our running example, introduced in Sect. 1, the transformation $\xi_1 = \{\Delta_{\text{label}}\}$ that is defined in Example 1, is justifiable for the round-robin arbiter Arb_0 and $\varphi_{\text{mutex}} \wedge \varphi_{\text{fairness}} \wedge$

$\{g\}\ (t_0)\ \circlearrowright\ \emptyset, \{r\}$ $\{g\}\ (t_1)\ \circlearrowright\ \emptyset, \{r\}$

Fig. 2. A transition system over $I = \{r\}$ and $O = \{g\}$ that is not a model of φ_1.

$\varphi_{\text{non-spurious}}$. It is justified by the counterexample $\sigma_1 = (\{g_0\} \cup \emptyset, \{g_1\} \cup \emptyset)^\omega$, indicated by the red arrows in Fig. 1b. Further, σ_1 is a minimal justification. The transformation $\xi_2 = \{\Delta_{\text{label}}, \Delta_{\text{transition1}}\}$ for Arb_0 is not minimally justified by σ_1 as σ_1 is a justification for ξ_1 and $\xi_1 \subset \xi_2$. An explanation ex for Arb_0, the LTL-formula $\varphi_{\text{mutex}} \wedge \varphi_{\text{fairness}} \wedge \varphi_{\text{non-spurious}}$ and the minimal repair $\xi_3 = \{\Delta_{\text{label}}, \Delta_{\text{transition1}}, \Delta_{\text{transition2}}, \Delta_{\text{transition3}}, \Delta_{\text{transition4}}\}$ is $ex = (\Delta_{\text{label}}, \sigma_1), (\Delta_{\text{transition1}}, \sigma_2), (\Delta_{\text{transition2}}, \sigma_3), (\Delta_{\text{transition3}}, \sigma_4), (\Delta_{\text{transition4}}, \sigma_5)$ with $\sigma_2 = (\emptyset \cup \emptyset, \{g_1\} \cup \emptyset)^\omega$, $\sigma_3 = (\emptyset \cup \{r_0\}, \{g_1\} \cup \{r_0\})^\omega$, $\sigma_4 = (\emptyset \cup \{r_0, r_1\}, \{g_1\} \cup \emptyset)^\omega$ and $\sigma_5 = (\emptyset \cup \{r_1\}, \{g_1\} \cup \{r_0\})^\omega$. The different justifications are indicated in the subfigures of Fig. 1.

In the next theorem, we show that there exists an explanation for every minimal repair.

Theorem 2. *For every minimal repair ξ for an* LTL-*formula φ over $AP = I \cup O$ and a 2^O-labeled 2^I-transition system $\mathcal{T}$, there exists an explanation.*

Proof. Let $\xi = \{\Delta_1, \ldots, \Delta_n\}$ be a minimal repair for the LTL-formula φ and the transition system $\mathcal{T}$. An explanation ex can be constructed as follows. Let $\sigma \in \mathcal{L}(\mathcal{T})$ with $\sigma \nvDash \varphi$. Since ξ is a minimal repair, $\sigma \notin \mathcal{L}(apply^*(\mathcal{T}, \xi))$. The smallest subset $\xi' \subseteq \xi$ with $\sigma \notin \mathcal{L}(apply^*(\mathcal{T}, \xi'))$ is minimally justified by σ. Thus (ξ', σ) is the first element of the explanation ex. For the remaining operations in $\xi \backslash \xi'$, we proceed analogously. The counterexample σ is now determined for $apply^*(\mathcal{T}, \xi')$. The construction is finished if either every transformation is minimally justified by a counterexample and there is no operation left or there is no justification for a transformation which clearly contradicts that ξ is a minimal repair. Hence, ex is an explanation for ξ.   □

From the last theorem we know that we can find an explanation for every minimal repair. It is however important to notice that it is not necessarily the case that we can find justifications for each singleton transformation in the repair as shown by the following example. Let $\varphi_2 = \neg g \wedge \bigcirc \neg g \wedge ((\square \neg r) \rightarrow \bigcirc \bigcirc g)$ over $I = \{r\}$, $O = \{g\}$ and consider the 2^O-labeled 2^I-transition system $\mathcal{T}$ with the set of states $\{t_0, t_1, t_2\}$, depicted in Fig. 3.

For φ_2 and $\mathcal{T}$, the transformation ξ with $\xi = \{\Delta_{\text{transition1}}, \Delta_{\text{transition2}}\}$ where $\Delta_{\text{transition1}} = (t_0, t_1, \{\emptyset\})$, and $\Delta_{\text{transition2}} = (t_1, t_2, \{\emptyset\})$, is a minimal repair. The counterexample $\sigma = \emptyset^\omega$ is the only one with $\sigma \in \mathcal{L}(\mathcal{T})$. For an explanation $ex = (\xi_1, \sigma_1), (\xi_2, \sigma_2)$ where ξ_i is a singleton, for all $1 \leq i \leq 2$, either $\xi_1 = \{\Delta_{\text{transition1}}\}$ or $\xi_1 = \{\Delta_{\text{transition2}}\}$. However, in both

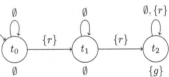

Fig. 3. A transition system over $I = \{r\}$ and $O = \{g\}$ that is not a model of φ_2.

cases, $\sigma \in \mathcal{L}(apply^*(\mathcal{T}, \xi_1))$. Thus, there are minimal repairs where not every operation can be justified on its own. Furthermore, it should be noted that explanations are not unique as there can exist different justifications for the same transformation, i.e. there can exist multiple different explanations for the same minimal repair. For the round-robin arbiter in Fig. 1b and the specification $\varphi_{mutex} \wedge \varphi_{fairness} \wedge \varphi_{non\text{-}spurious}$, the transformation $\xi_1 = \{\Delta_{\text{label}}\}$ can be minimally justified by $(\{g_0\} \cup \emptyset, \{g_1\} \cup \emptyset)^\omega$ and by $(\{g_0\} \cup \{r_1\}, \{g_1\} \cup \emptyset)^\omega$.

We refer to the problem of finding an explanation for a minimal repair as the *explanation synthesis problem*.

Problem 2 (Explanation Synthesis). *Let φ be an LTL-formula over $AP = I \cup O$, $\mathcal{T}$ be a 2^O-labeled 2^I-transition system and ξ be a minimal repair. Find an explanation ex for φ, $\mathcal{T}$ and ξ.*

Algorithm 1. MINIMALREPAIR$(\mathcal{T}, \varphi)$

1: $left \leftarrow 0$
2: $right \leftarrow |\mathcal{T}| + |\mathcal{T}| \cdot |\mathcal{T}|$
3: $exist \leftarrow false$
4: **while** $left < right$ **do**
5:     $k \leftarrow \lfloor \frac{left + right}{2} \rfloor$
6:     $(found, \xi) \leftarrow$ REPAIR$(\mathcal{T}, \varphi, k)$
7:     **if** $found$ **then**
8:         $right \leftarrow k - 1$
9:         $\xi_{min} \leftarrow \xi$
10:        $exists \leftarrow true$
11:    **else**
12:       $left \leftarrow k + 1$

13: $(found', \xi') \leftarrow$ REPAIR$(\mathcal{T}, \varphi, left)$
14: **if** $!exists$ **then**
15:    **return** no minimal repair exists
16: **if** $found'$ **then**
17:    **return** ξ'
18: **else**
19:    **return** ξ_{min}

4   SAT-Based Algorithms for Minimal Repair and Explanation Synthesis

In this section, we present SAT-based algorithms to solve the minimal repair synthesis problem and the explanation synthesis problem.

4.1   Generating Minimal Repairs

The procedure MINIMALREPAIR$(\mathcal{T}, \varphi)$, shown in Algorithm 1, solves the minimal repair synthesis problem. For a given LTL-formula φ over $AP = I \cup O$ and 2^O-labeled 2^I-transition system $\mathcal{T}$, Algorithm 1 constructs a minimal repair ξ if one exists. We use binary search to find the minimal number k of required operations. The possible number of operations can be bounded by $|\mathcal{T}| + |\mathcal{T}| \cdot |\mathcal{T}|$ as there are only $|\mathcal{T}|$ state labelings and $|\mathcal{T}| \cdot |\mathcal{T}|$ transition redirects. Checking whether there is a transformation ξ with $|\xi| \leq k$ such that $apply^*(\mathcal{T}, \xi) \vDash \varphi$ is done by using the procedure REPAIR$(\mathcal{T}, \varphi, k)$ which is explained next.

REPAIR$(\mathcal{T}, \varphi, k)$: To check whether there is a repair ξ for a 2^O-labeled 2^I-transition system $\mathcal{T}$ with k operations, we need to ensure that the resulting transition system is a model for φ, i.e. $apply^*(\mathcal{T}, \xi) \vDash \varphi$. To check the existence of a transition system $\mathcal{T}'$ with bound $n = |\mathcal{T}'|$ that implements φ, we use the SAT-based encoding of bounded synthesis [4]. Bounded synthesis is a synthesis procedure for LTL-formulas that produces size-optimal transition systems [9]. For a given LTL formula φ, a universal co-Büchi automaton $\mathcal{A}$ that accepts $\mathcal{L}(\varphi)$ is constructed. A transition system $\mathcal{T}$ satisfies φ if every path of the run graph, i.e. the product of $\mathcal{T}$ and $\mathcal{A}$, visits a rejecting state only finitely often. An annotation function λ confirms that this is the case. The bounded synthesis approach constructs a transition system with bound n by solving a constraint system that checks the existence of a transition system $\mathcal{T}$ and a valid annotation

$$\phi_{cost} = \bigwedge_{0 \le t,n < |T|, c \le k} rdTrans_{t,n,c} \wedge notRdTrans_{t,n,c} \wedge \neg cost_{t,n,k+1}$$

$$\bigwedge_{0 \le t < |T|, c \le k} changeLabel_{t,c} \wedge notChangeLabel_{t,c} \wedge \neg cost_{t,|T|,k+1}$$

$$rdTrans_{t,n,c} = \begin{cases} trans_{0,0} \rightarrow cost_{0,0,1} & \text{if } t = 0 \wedge n = 0 \\ cost_{t-1,|T|,c} \wedge trans_{t,n} \rightarrow cost_{t,n,c+1} & \text{if } t > 0 \wedge n = 0 \\ cost_{t,n-1,c} \wedge trans_{t,n} \rightarrow cost_{t,n,c+1} & \text{if } n > 0 \end{cases}$$

$$notRdTrans_{t,n,c} = \begin{cases} \neg trans_{0,0} \rightarrow cost_{0,0,0} & \text{if } t = 0 \wedge n = 0 \\ cost_{t-1,|T|,c} \wedge \neg trans_{t,n} \rightarrow cost_{t,n,c} & \text{if } t > 0 \wedge n = 0 \\ cost_{t,n-1,c} \wedge \neg trans_{t,n} \rightarrow cost_{t,n,c} & \text{if } n > 0 \end{cases}$$

$$changeLabel_{t,c} = cost_{t,|T|-1,c} \wedge label_t \rightarrow cost_{t,|T|,c+1}$$
$$notChangeLabel_{t,c} = cost_{t,|T|-1,c} \wedge \neg label_t \rightarrow cost_{t,|T|,c}$$

$$label_t = \bigvee_{o \in O} \begin{cases} o'_t & \text{if } o \notin o(t) \\ \neg o'_t & \text{if } o \in o(t) \end{cases}$$

$$trans_{t,t'} = \bigvee_{i \in 2^I} \begin{cases} \tau'_{t,i,t'} & \text{if } \tau(t,i) \ne t' \\ \bot & \text{if } \tau(t,i) = t' \end{cases}$$

Fig. 4. The constraint ϕ_{cost} ensures that at most k operations are applied.

function λ. In the bounded synthesis constraint system for the 2^O-labeled 2^I-transition system $T' = (T, t_0, \tau', o')$, the transition function τ' is represented by a variable $\tau'_{t,i,t'}$ for every $t, t' \in T$ and $i \in 2^I$. The variable $\tau'_{t,i,t'}$ is true if and only if $\tau'(t,i) = t'$. The labeling function o' is represented by a variable o'_t for every $o \in O$ and $t \in T$ and it holds that o'_t is true if and only if $o \in o'(t)$. For simplicity, states are represented by natural numbers.

To ensure that the transition system T' can be obtained with at most k operations from a given transition system $T = (T, t_0, \tau, o)$, the bounded synthesis encoding is extended with the additional constraint ϕ_{cost} shown in Fig. 4. For states t, t', the constraint $trans_{t,t'}$ holds iff there is a redirected transition from t to t', i.e. there exists an $i \in 2^I$ with $\tau'(t,i) = t'$ and $\tau(t,i) \ne t'$. The constraint $label_t$ holds iff the state labeling of state t is changed, i.e. $o(t) \ne o'(t)$. To count the number of applied operations, we use an implicit ordering over all the possible operations: starting from state 0, we first consider all potential transition redirects to states $0, 1, \dots, |T| - 1$, then the potential state label change of state 0, then the transition redirects from state 1, and so on. For state t and operation n, where n ranges from 0 to $|T|$ (where $n < |T|$ refers to the transition redirect operation to state n and $n = |T|$ refers to the state label change operation), the

Algorithm 2. EXPLANATION$(\mathcal{T}, \varphi, \xi)$

```
1: Told ← T
2: ex ← ()
3: while ξ ≠ ∅ do
4:     σ ← BMC(Told, φ)
5:     minimal ← false
6:     ξ' ← ξ
7:     while !minimal do
8:         minimal ← true
9:         for Δ ∈ ξ' do
10:            Tnew ← apply*(Told, ξ'\{Δ})
11:            if σ ∉ L(Tnew) then
12:                minimal ← false
13:                ξ' ← ξ'\{Δ}
14:     Told ← apply*(Told, ξ')
15:     ex ← ex.APPEND(ξ', σ)
16:     ξ ← ξ\ξ'
17: return ex
```

variable $cost_{t,n,c}$ is true if the number of applied operations so far is c. This book-keeping is done by constraints $rdTrans_{t,n,c}$, $notRdTrans_{t,n,c}$, $changeLabel_{t,c}$ and $notChangeLabel_{t,c}$. Constraints $rdTrans$ and $notRdTrans$ account for the presence and absence, respectively, of transition redirects, constraints $changeLabel_{t,c}$ and $notChangeLabel_{t,c}$ for the presence and absence of state label changes. In order to bound the total number of operations by k, ϕ_{cost} requires that $cost_{t,n,k+1}$ is false for all states t and operations n.

In the next theorem, we state the size of the resulting constraint system, based on the size of the bounded synthesis constraint system given in [4].

Theorem 3. *The size of the constraint system is in* $\mathcal{O}(nm^2 \cdot 2^{|I|} \cdot (|\delta_{q,q'}| + n\log(nm)) + kn^2)$ *and the number of variables is in* $\mathcal{O}(n(m\log(nm) + 2^{|I|} \cdot (|O| + n)) + kn^2)$, *where* $n = |\mathcal{T}'|$, $m = |Q|$ *and* k *the number of allowed operations.*

4.2 Generating Explanations

We describe now how we can solve the explanation synthesis problem for a given LTL-formula φ over $AP = I \cup O$, a 2^O-labeled 2^I-transition system $\mathcal{T}$ and a minimal repair ξ. The minimal repair ξ can be obtained from Algorithm 1. The construction of the explanation follows the idea from the proof of Theorem 2 and is shown in Algorithm 2. An explanation ex is a sequence of transformations ξ_i and counterexamples σ_i such that every transformation ξ_i can be minimally justified by σ_i. A counterexample σ for the current transition system $\mathcal{T}_{old}$ is obtained by Bounded Model Checking (BMC) [2] and is a justification for ξ as ξ is a minimal repair. BMC checks if there is a counterexample of a given bound n that satisfies the negated formula $\neg\varphi$ and is contained in $\mathcal{L}(\mathcal{T})$. The constraint system $\phi_{\mathcal{T}} \wedge \phi_{loop} \wedge [\![\neg\varphi]\!]$ is composed of three components. $\phi_{\mathcal{T}}$ encodes the transition system $\mathcal{T}$, where each state $t \in T$ is represented as a boolean vector. ϕ_{loop} ensures the existence of exactly one loop of the counterexample, and the fixpoint formula $[\![\neg\varphi]\!]$ ensures that the counterexample satisfies the LTL formula. To obtain a minimal justification, we need to ensure that there is no transformation $\xi' \subset \xi$ such that σ justifies ξ'. As long as there is an operation Δ such that $\sigma \notin \mathcal{L}(apply^*(\mathcal{T}_{old}, \xi'\backslash\{\Delta\}))$, σ is not a minimal justification for ξ'. Otherwise σ minimally justifies ξ' and (ξ', σ) can be appended to the explanation. The algorithm terminates and returns an explanation if ξ is empty, i.e. every operation is justified. The presented algorithm solves the BMC-problem at most $|\xi|$-times and the number of checks if a counterexample is contained in the language of a transition system is bounded by $|\xi|^2$. The correctness of Algorithm 2 is shown in Theorem 2.

5   Experimental Results

We compare our explainable synthesis approach with **BoSy** [5], a traditional synthesis tool, on several benchmarks. After describing the different benchmark families and technical details, we explain the observable results.

5.1   Benchmark Families

The benchmarks families for arbiter, AMBA and load balancer specifications are standard specifications of SYNTCOMP [11]. For the scaling benchmarks only a constant number of operations is needed. The remaining benchmarks synthesize support for different layers of the OSI communication network.

- **Arbiter:** An *arbiter* is a control unit that manages a shared resource. Arb_n specifies a system to eventually grant every request for each of the n clients and includes mutual exclusion, i.e. at most one grant is given at any time. $ArbFull_n$ additionally does not allow spurious grants, i.e. there is only given a grant for client i if there is an open request of client i.
- **AMBA:** The *ARM Advanced Microcontroller Bus Architecture* (AMBA) is an arbiter allowing additional features like locking the bus for several steps. The specification $AMBAEnc_n$ is used to synthesize the encode component of the decomposed AMBA arbiter with n clients that need to be controlled. $AMBAArb_n$ specifies the arbiter component of a decomposed AMBA arbiter with an n-ary bus, and $AMBALock_n$ specifies the lock component.
- **Load Balancer:** A *load balancer* distributes a number of jobs to a fixed number of server. $LoadFull_n$ specifies a load balancer with n clients.
- **Bit Stuffer:** *Bit stuffing* is a part of the physical layer of the OSI communication network which is responsible for the transmission of bits. Bit stuffing inserts non-information bits into a bit data stream whenever a defined pattern is recognized. $BitStuffer_n$ specifies a system to signal every recurrence of a pattern with length n.

Table 1. Benchmarking results of BoSy and our explainable synthesis tool

Initial		Extended		Size Aut.	Operations chL/rdT	Number Just.	Time in sec. BoSy	Time in sec. Explainable
Ben.	Size	Ben.	Size					
Arb_2	2	Arb_4	4	5	0/3	3	0.348	1.356
Arb_4	4	Arb_5	5	6	0/2	2	2.748	12.208
Arb_4	4	Arb_6	6	7	0/3	3	33.64	139.088
Arb_4	4	Arb_8	–	9	–	–	Timeout	Timeout
Arb_2	2	$ArbFull_2$	4	6	3/7	10	0.108	0.352
$ArbFull_2$	4	$ArbFull_3$	8	8	1/18	19	26.14	288.168
$AMBAEnc_2$	2	$AMBAEnc_4$	4	6	1/11	12	0.26	7.16
$AMBAEnc_4$	4	$AMBAEnc_6$	6	10	1/21	22	5.76	973.17
$AMBAArb_2$	–	$AMBAArb_4$	–	17	–	–	Timeout	Timeout
$AMBAArb_4$	–	$AMBAArb_6$	–	23	–	–	Timeout	Timeout
$AMBALock_2$	–	$AMBALock_4$	–	5	–	–	Timeout	Timeout
$AMBALock_4$	–	$AMBALock_6$	–	5	–	–	Timeout	Timeout
$LoadFull_2$	3	$LoadFull_3$	6	21	1/10	10	6.50	49.67
$Loadfull_3$	6	$LoadFull_4$	–	25	–	–	Timeout	Timeout
$BitStuffer_2$	5	$BitStuffer_3$	7	7	2/7	9	0.08	1.02
$BitStuffer_3$	7	$BitStuffer_4$	9	9	1/6	7	0.21	3.97
$ABPRec_1$	2	$ABPRec_2$	4	9	2/5	7	0.11	1.52
$ABPRec_2$	4	$ABPRec_3$	8	17	4/9	13	2.87	326.98
$ABPTran_1$	2	$ABPTran_2$	4	31	1/5	5	0.76	76.93
$ABPTran_2$	4	$ABPTran_3$	–	91	–	–	Timeout	Timeout
TCP_1	2	TCP_2	4	6	1/4	5	0.05	0.19
TCP_2	4	TCP_3	8	8	3/14	17	0.58	14.47
$Scaling_4$	4	$Scaling'_4$	4	4	4/0	4	0.02	0.10
$Scaling_5$	5	$Scaling'_5$	5	5	4/0	4	0.03	0.22
$Scaling_6$	6	$Scaling'_6$	6	6	4/0	4	0.04	0.51
$Scaling_8$	8	$Scaling'_8$	8	8	4/0	4	0.12	2.54
$Scaling_{12}$	12	$Scaling'_{12}$	12	12	4/0	4	34.02	167.03

- **ABP:** The *alternating bit protocol* (ABP) is a standard protocol of the data link layer of the OSI communication network which transmits packets. Basically, in the ABP, the current bits signals which packet has to be transmitted or received. $ABPRec_n$ specifies the ABP with n bits for the receiver and $ABPTran_n$ for the transmitter.
- **TCP-Handshake:** A *transmission control protcol* (TCP) supports the transport layer of the OSI communication network which is responsible for the end-to-end delivery of messages. A TCP-handshake starts a secure connection between a client and a server. TCP_n implements a TCP-handshake where n clients can continuously connect with the server.
- **Scaling:** The $Scaling_n$ benchmarks specify a system of size n. To satisfy the specification $Scaling'_n$ a constant number of operations is sufficient.

5.2   Technical Details

We instantiate BoSy with an explicit encoding, a linear search strategy, an input-symbolic backend and moore semantics to match our implementation. Both tools only synthesize winning strategies for system players. We use **ltl3ba** [1] as the converter from an LTL-specification to an automaton for both tools. As both constraint systems only contain existential quantifiers, **CryptoMiniSat** [23] is used as the SAT-solver. The solution bound is the minimal bound that is given as input and the initial transition system is synthesized using BoSy, at first. The benchmarks results were obtained on a single quad-core Intel Xeon processor (E3-1271 v3, 3.6 GHz) with 32 GB RAM, running a GNU/Linux system. A timeout of 2 h is used.

5.3   Observations

The benchmark results are shown in Table 1. For each benchmark, the table contains two specifications, an initial and an extended one. For example, the initial specification for the first benchmark Arb_2 specifies a two-client arbiter and the extended one Arb_4 specifies a four-client arbiter. Additionally, the table records the minimal solution bound for each of the specifications. Our explainable synthesis protoype starts by synthesizing a system for the initial specification and then synthesizes a minimal repair and an explanation for the extended one. If the minimal repair has to access additional states, that are initially unreachable, our prototype initializes them with a self loop for all input assignments where no output holds. The traditional synthesis tool BoSy only synthesizes a solution for the extended specification. The size of the universal co-Büchi automaton, representing the extended specification is reported. For the explainable synthesis, the applied operations of the minimal repair and the number of justifications is given. For both tools, the runtime is reported in seconds.

The benchmark results reveal that our explainable synthesis approach is able to solve the same benchmarks like BoSy. In all cases, except two, we are able to synthesize explanations where every operation can be single justified. The applied operations show that there are only a small number of changed state labelings, primarily for reaching additional states. Since only minimal initial systems are synthesized, the outputs in the given structure are already fixed. Redirecting transitions repairs the system more efficient. In general, the evaluation reveals that the runtime for the explainable synthesis process takes a multiple of BoSy with respect to the number of applied operations. Thus, the constraint-based synthesis for minimal repairs is not optimal if a small number of operations is sufficient since the repair synthesis problem is polynomial in the size of the system as proven in Lemma 1. To improve the runtime and to solve more instances, many optimizations, used in existing synthesis tools, can be implemented. These extensions include different encodings such as QBF or DQBF or synthesizing strategies for the environment or a mealy semantics.

6   Conclusion

In this paper, we have developed an explainable synthesis process for reactive systems. For a set of specification, expressed in LTL, the algorithm incrementally builds an implementation by repairing intermediate implementations to satisfy the currently considered specification. In each step, an explanation is derived to justify the taken changes to repair an implementation. We have shown that the decision problem of finding a repair for a fixed number of transformations is polynomial in the size of the system and exponential in the number of operations. By extending the constraint system of bounded synthesis, we can synthesize minimal repairs where the resulting system is size-optimal. We have presented an algorithm that constructs explanations by using Bounded Model Checking to obtain counterexample traces. The evaluation of our prototype showed that explainable synthesis, while more expensive, can still solve the same benchmarks as a standard synthesis tool. In future work, we plan to develop this approach into a comprehensive tool that provides rich visual feedback to the user. Additionally, we plan to investigate further types of explanations, including quantitative and symbolic explanations.

References

1. Babiak, T., Křetínský, M., Řehák, V., Strejček, J.: LTL to Büchi automata translation: fast and more deterministic. In: Flanagan, C., König, B. (eds.) TACAS 2012. LNCS, vol. 7214, pp. 95–109. Springer, Heidelberg (2012). https://doi.org/10.1007/978-3-642-28756-5_8

2. Biere, A., Cimatti, A., Clarke, E.M., Strichman, O., Zhu, Y., et al.: Bounded model checking. Adv. Comput. 58(11), 117–148 (2003)

3. Bonakdarpour, B., Finkbeiner, B.: Program repair for hyperproperties. In: Chen, Y.-F., Cheng, C.-H., Esparza, J. (eds.) ATVA 2019. LNCS, vol. 11781, pp. 423–441. Springer, Cham (2019). https://doi.org/10.1007/978-3-030-31784-3_25

4. Faymonville, P., Finkbeiner, B., Rabe, M.N., Tentrup, L.: Encodings of bounded synthesis. In: Legay, A., Margaria, T. (eds.) TACAS 2017. LNCS, vol. 10205, pp. 354–370. Springer, Heidelberg (2017). https://doi.org/10.1007/978-3-662-54577-5_20

5. Faymonville, P., Finkbeiner, B., Tentrup, L.: BoSy: an experimentation framework for bounded synthesis. In: Majumdar, R., Kunčak, V. (eds.) CAV 2017. LNCS, vol. 10427, pp. 325–332. Springer, Cham (2017). https://doi.org/10.1007/978-3-319-63390-9_17

6. Finkbeiner, B., Jacobs, S.: Lazy synthesis. In: Kuncak, V., Rybalchenko, A. (eds.) VMCAI 2012. LNCS, vol. 7148, pp. 219–234. Springer, Heidelberg (2012). https://doi.org/10.1007/978-3-642-27940-9_15

7. Finkbeiner, B., Klein, F.: Bounded cycle synthesis. In: Chaudhuri, S., Farzan, A. (eds.) CAV 2016. LNCS, vol. 9779, pp. 118–135. Springer, Cham (2016). https://doi.org/10.1007/978-3-319-41528-4_7

8. Finkbeiner, B., Klein, F.: Reactive synthesis: towards output-sensitive algorithms. In: Pretschner, A., Peled, D., Hutzelmann, T. (eds.) Dependable Software Systems Engineering, Volume 50 of NATO Science for Peace and Security Series, D: Information and Communication Security, pp. 25–43. IOS Press (2017)

9. Finkbeiner, B., Schewe, S.: Bounded synthesis. Int. J. Softw. Tools Technol. Transf. 15(5–6), 519–539 (2013). https://doi.org/10.1007/s10009-012-0228-z

10. Finkbeiner, B., Torfah, H.: Synthesizing skeletons for reactive systems. In: Artho, C., Legay, A., Peled, D. (eds.) ATVA 2016. LNCS, vol. 9938, pp. 271–286. Springer, Cham (2016). https://doi.org/10.1007/978-3-319-46520-3_18

11. Jacobs, S., et al.: The 4th reactive synthesis competition (SYNTCOMP 2017): benchmarks, participants and results. In: SYNT 2017, Volume 260 of EPTCS, pp. 116–143 (2017)

12. Jacobs, S., et al.: The 5th reactive synthesis competition (SYNTCOMP 2018): benchmarks, participants & results. CoRR, abs/1904.07736 (2019)

13. Jobstmann, B., Griesmayer, A., Bloem, R.: Program repair as a game. In: Etessami, K., Rajamani, S.K. (eds.) CAV 2005. LNCS, vol. 3576, pp. 226–238. Springer, Heidelberg (2005). https://doi.org/10.1007/11513988_23

14. Kress-Gazit, H., Torfah, H.: The challenges in specifying and explaining synthesized implementations of reactive systems. In: Proceedings CREST@ETAPS, EPTCS, pp. 50–64 (2018)

15. Kupferman, O., Piterman, N., Vardi, M.Y.: Safraless compositional synthesis. In: Ball, T., Jones, R.B. (eds.) CAV 2006. LNCS, vol. 4144, pp. 31–44. Springer, Heidelberg (2006). https://doi.org/10.1007/11817963_6

16. Nilsson, P., Ozay, N.: Incremental synthesis of switching protocols via abstraction refinement. In: 53rd IEEE Conference on Decision and Control, pp. 6246–6253 (2014)

17. Peter, H.J., Mattmüller, R.: Component-based abstraction refinement for timed controller synthesis. In: Baker, T. (ed.) Proceedings of the 30th IEEE Real-Time Systems Symposium, RTSS 2009, Washington, D.C., USA, 1–4 December 2009, pp. 364–374, Los Alamitos, CA, USA, December 2009. IEEE Computer Society (2009)

18. Pnueli, A., Rosner, R.: On the synthesis of a reactive module. Automata Lang. Program. **372**, 179–190 (1989)

19. Pnueli, A.: The temporal logic of programs. In: Proceedings of the 18th Annual Symposium on Foundations of Computer Science, SFCS 1977, USA, pp. 46–57. IEEE Computer Society (1977)

20. Reissig, G., Weber, A., Rungger, M.: Feedback refinement relations for the synthesis of symbolic controllers. IEEE Trans. Autom. Control **62**(4), 1781–1796 (2017)

21. Ryzhyk, L., Walker, A.: Developing a practical reactive synthesis tool: experience and lessons learned. In: Piskac, R., Dimitrova, R. (eds.) Proceedings Fifth Workshop on Synthesis, SYNT@CAV 2016, Toronto, Canada, 17–18 July 2016, Volume 229 of EPTCS, pp. 84–99 (2016)

22. Sistla, A., Clarke, E.: The complexity of propositional linear temporal logics. J. ACM **32**, 733–749 (1985)

23. Soos, M., Nohl, K., Castelluccia, C.: Extending SAT solvers to cryptographic problems. In: Kullmann, O. (ed.) SAT 2009. LNCS, vol. 5584, pp. 244–257. Springer, Heidelberg (2009). https://doi.org/10.1007/978-3-642-02777-2_24

Robust Controller Synthesis
for Duration Calculus

Kalyani Dole$^{(\boxtimes)}$, Ashutosh Gupta, and Shankara Narayanan Krishna

Department of Computer Science and Engineering, IIT Bombay, Mumbai, India
dole.kalyani@gmail.com

Abstract. In automatic control synthesis, we may need to handle specifications with timing constraints and control such that the system meets the specification as much as possible, which is called robust control. In this paper, we present a method for open loop robust controller synthesis from duration calculus (DC) specifications. For robust synthesis, we propose an approach to evaluate the robustness of DC specifications on a given run of a system. We leverage a CEGIS like method for synthesizing robust control signals. In our method, the DC specifications and the system under control are encoded into mixed integer linear problems, and the optimization problem is solved to yield a control signal. We have implemented a tool (ControlDC) based on the method and applied it on a set of benchmarks.

Keywords: Controller synthesis · Robustness · Duration calculus

1 Introduction

Temporal logics have played a significant role in compactly specifying desired behaviours of a system, and in synthesizing controllers. There has been a rich body of work on the verification and synthesis of systems that abide by some specification given by temporal logics. The synthesis of controllers for a hybrid system satisfying a temporal logic specification in the presence of an uncontrollable environment is practically relevant in many domains like robotics, modern medical devices, space vehicles, and so on. The automated development of controllers, called *controller synthesis*, is an active area of research. Controller synthesis addresses the question of how to control the behavior of a given system to meet its specification, regardless of the behavior enforced by the environment. To respond to environmental factors, a cyber-physical system (CPS) may include controllers, i.e., a component that takes environmental signals as input and steers the system, to meet the goals. A simple example is that of a traffic controller which decides on the fly, the duration of red, green and orange depending on the traffic at any point of time. Synthesizing an optimal controller is non-trivial [1], especially when software based systems are considered, since environmental factors can cause disturbances. In CPS, we express the goals of the system in terms of logical formulae, that are formally called specifications. For reactive

© Springer Nature Switzerland AG 2020
D. V. Hung and O. Sokolsky (Eds.): ATVA 2020, LNCS 12302, pp. 429–446, 2020.
https://doi.org/10.1007/978-3-030-59152-6_24

systems, the behaviour changes over time, and temporal logic is a widely used formalism to express such specifications.

Linear temporal logic (LTL), Computation tree logic (CTL) [2], Metric temporal logic (MTL) [3], Signal temporal logic (STL) [4] are some of the well-known temporal logics. There have been attempts to synthesize controllers from these temporal logics, as we explain below. [5] investigates the synthesis of controllers enforcing linear temporal logic specifications on discrete-time linear systems. [6] studies an optimization variant of synthesis from LTL formulas, and designs controllers which satisfy a set of hard specifications and minimally violates a set of soft specifications. In [7], controller synthesis has been studied for systems allowing probability and non-determinism with respect to probabilistic CTL. In the case of timed logics like MTL, a robust interpretation of formulas over signals has been adopted in [8] thereby proposing multi-valued semantics for MTL formulas, capturing not the usual Boolean satisfiability, but information regarding the distance from unsatisfiability. Using this, they propose an algorithm for under-approximate analysis of robustness satisfaction of the MTL specification with respect to a given finite timed state sequence. This notion of robust satisfaction has been investigated in [9] for STL formulas and used in controller synthesis for discrete-time continuous systems in the presence of an adverse environment.

In this paper, we work on the robust controller synthesis problem with respect to systems specified as hybrid automata, in the presence of an adversarial environment, with a specification given in Duration Calculus(DC, [10]). DC is one of the oldest interval temporal logics known. The syntax of DC allows modalities like the duration ($\int_I \varphi$) operator, and chop (†) operator[1] which makes it very expressive. The duration modality $\int_I \varphi$ measures the real time over which a formula φ is true in an interval I, while the chop operator allows us to write specifications modularly. The duration modality makes DC more expressive than LTL, CTL, STL and MTL in capturing specifications where the time durations are critical. The chop operator, as the name suggests, allows us to specify properties φ_1, φ_2 over smaller time intervals I_1, I_2 and "stitch them" together, to obtain a property $\varphi_1 † \varphi_2$ over the larger time interval I obtained by concatenating intervals I_1, I_2. The chop modality helps in making DC very succinct, as opposed to logics like LTL for expressing many specifications.

There has been a renewed interest in synthesizing controllers for DC very recently [11,12]. [12] considers specifications in quantified discrete duration calculus (QDDC), the discrete counterpart of DC, known to be equivalent to regular languages [13]. [12] considers controller specifications, given as a pair of QDDC formulae (D_A, D_C) called assumption and commitment, and looks at the notions of hard and soft robustness. In hard robustness, the requirement is that, in all behaviours of the controller, the commitment formula D_C must hold if the assumption formula D_A holds, while in soft robustness, D_C should be met as much as possible irrespective of D_A. This approach has been implemented in a tool DCSynth [11].

---

[1] Traditionally denoted as ⌒.

Contributions. In this paper, we synthesize controllers that robustly satisfy the given DC specification. As a first contribution, we propose a notion of robust satisfaction for DC formulae. The robust satisfaction associates real values or weights with each formula, as opposed to a Boolean value. As our second contribution, we consider systems given as hybrid automata, and synthesize control behaviours under which, the system robustly satisfies the specification, in the presence of adversarial environmental inputs. To the best of our knowledge, robust synthesis with respect to hybrid automata has not been considered in the literature. The inputs to our synthesis algorithm consist of the hybrid automaton as the system, the initial state of the system, a disturbance vector, and the DC constraints that need to be satisfied. Our approach for controller synthesis is based on encoding DC constraints, which are either environmental or system constraints into optimization of mixed integer linear programs (MILP) [9,14]. We follow a counter example guided approach (CEGIS) to find the optimal control sequence, and synthesize controllers using the open-loop synthesis technique [15]. At each step, we minimize the robustness and find the worst adversarial input that leads to the violation of the specification. If an adversary is found, we add it to the list of adversaries to consider it for future iterations, and if no such adversary is found, then we return the satisfying control sequence. This way, we create an optimisation problem that can be solved using MILP solvers like Gurobi [16] to yield a satisfying control sequence. As the third contribution, we have implemented our algorithm in a tool ControlDC. ControlDC automatically synthesizes robust controllers from DC specifications. We have tested ControlDC on some benchmark examples, and find the results encouraging.

The rest of the paper is organized as follows. Section 2 gives the necessary definitions related to hybrid automata and DC needed for later sections. The robust satisfaction of DC is described in Sect. 3. The open-loop synthesis algorithm is presented in Sect. 4. Our experimental results, along with some ideas for future work, can be found in Sect. 5.

2   Preliminaries

Let $\mathbb{R}_{\geq 0}$ be the set of non-negative real-numbers with the usual order. A hybrid system is a dynamical system with both discrete and continuous components. Hybrid automata [17] is a well accepted formal model for hybrid systems. Given a finite set of variables Var, let $|Var|$ denote the cardinality of the set Var and $\dot{Var} = \{\dot{x} \mid x \in Var\}$, $Var' = \{x' \mid x \in Var\}$ respectively denote the first derivatives of variables in Var during continuous change, and the values of variables after a discrete change. For a set of variables Var, $\mathsf{Pred}(Var)$ denotes a predicate over Var, and $\mathsf{Exp}(Var)$ denotes an expression over Var. For example, $2x - 3y = 5$ is a predicate over variables x, y, while $2x + 3y$ is an expression over x, y. Given a predicate π over a set of variables Var, $[\![\pi]\!]$ denotes the set of valuations over $\mathbb{R}^{|Var|}$ which satisfy π. For example, $(\frac{5}{2}, 0) \in [\![2x - 3y = 5]\!]$.

Hybrid Automata. A hybrid automaton [17] $H = (Q, I, Var, \delta, \mathsf{Inv}, \mathsf{flow})$ is a finite state automaton equipped with a finite set of locations Q called *control* *modes*, a subset $I \subseteq Q$ of *initial* locations, a finite set $Var = \{x_1, \ldots, x_n\}$ of variables. *Var* consists of variables of 4 kinds: (1) Input variables (U) (2) Output variables (Y) (3) State variables (X) and (4) Environment variables (W). Let $X_1 = U \cup X$ be the disjoint union of input and state variables, s.t. *Var* is a disjoint union of X_1, W, Y. Input variables represent the control inputs, state variables represent the logical system states, environment variables represent the adversarial external disturbances, and output variables are a function of all the variables.

Discrete transitions or control switches have the form $\delta \subseteq Q \times Pred(X_1 \cup W) \times Q \times \mu(Z')$ where $Z \subseteq Var$. A discrete transition from a location q to a location q' is labeled by predicates over $X_1 \cup W$, and $\mu : Z' \mapsto Exp(Var)$ is a function which assigns to variables $Z \subseteq Var$ values obtained by evaluating some expressions over *Var*. Inv, flow called *invariants* and *flows* respectively, are functions labeling locations with predicates over X_1 and $X_1 \cup \dot{X}_1$. A state of the hybrid automaton is a member of $Q \times \mathbb{R}^{|Var|}$ consisting of a location, along with the values of all the variables. An initial state of the automaton is $(q_0, \overline{0})$ where $q_0 \in I$, and $\overline{0} = 0^{|Var|}$.

Transitions in H are either *discrete* transitions or *continuous* transitions. For states (q, v) and (q', v'), a continuous transition denoted $(q, v) \overset{t}{\to} (q', v')$ is enabled for $t \in \mathbb{R}_{\geq 0}$ iff (1) $q = q'$, (2) there is a differentiable function $f : [0, t] \mapsto \mathbb{R}^{|Var|}$ with the first derivative $\dot{f} : (0, t) \mapsto \mathbb{R}^{|Var|}$ s.t. $f(0) = v, f(t) = v'$, and for all $\epsilon \in (0, t)$, both $Inv(q)[Var := f(\epsilon)]$ and $flow(q)[Var, \dot{Var} := f(\epsilon), \dot{f}(\epsilon)]$ are true.

For example, if we have $Inv(q) = (x = 2)$ and $Inv(q') = (x = 4, y \leq 2)$, $flow(q) = (\dot{x} = 2, \dot{y} = 0)$, then we have $(q, (2, 2)) \overset{1}{\to} (q', (4, 2))$, since in one unit of time, y remains the same and x doubles.

A discrete transition from (q, v) to (q', v') on predicate $\pi(Var)$ and assignment $\mu(Z')$ denoted $(q, v) \xrightarrow[\mu(Z')]{\pi(Var)} (q', v')$ is enabled iff (1) $(q, \pi, q', \mu) \in \delta$, (2) $v \in [\![Inv(q)]\!], [\![\pi]\!]$, and (3) $v' \in [\![Inv(q')]\!]$, where $v' = v[Z' := \mu(Z')]$ is obtained by assigning to all variables in $Z \subseteq Var$ the values given by the function μ.

For example, if we have the control switch $cs = (q, x \geq 2y, q', (x' = 3))$ in δ with $Inv(q) = (x = 5)$ and $Inv(q') = (y > 1)$, $flow(q) = (\dot{x} = 2)$ then we have the discrete transition from state $(q, (5, 2))$ to state $(q', (3, 2))$ denoted $(q, (5, 2)) \overset{cs}{\to} (q', (3, 2))$.

A *run* in the hybrid automaton H is a finite or infinite sequence of alternating continuous and discrete transitions starting from an initial state $s_0 = (q_0, \overline{0})$. The sequence of states $s_0 s_1 s_2 \ldots$ in a run is called a *signal*. For an initial state $s_0 = (q_0, \alpha_0)$, $N \in \mathbb{N}$, a N-horizon run of the system has the form

$$(q_0, \alpha_0) \overset{t_0}{\to} (q_0, \alpha_0') \xrightarrow[\mu_1]{pred_1} (q_1, \alpha_1) \ldots (q_{N-1}, \alpha_{N-1}) \overset{t_{N-1}}{\to} (q_{N-1}, \alpha_{N-1}') \xrightarrow[\mu_N]{pred_N} (q_1, \alpha_N)$$

If $T = \sum_{i=0}^{N-1} t_i \in \mathbb{R}_{\geq 0}$ is the sum of all time elapses along the run, then the run defines a signal in the time interval $[0, T]$ and uniquely gives the sequence of values $u_0 u_1 \ldots u_N$ of input variables, $w_0 w_1 \ldots w_N$ of environment variables,

$x_0 x_1 \ldots x_N$ of state variables and $y_0 y_1 \ldots y_N$ of output variables seen along the run in the time interval $[0, T]$. The ith value u_i (respectively x_i, y_i, w_i) can be written as $u(t_{i-1})$ (respectively $x(t_{i-1}), y(t_{i-1}), w(t_{i-1})$) to denote the value at time point t_{i-1}.

In the following, let $I = [b, e]$ where $b \leq e$ are non-negative reals be an interval. A signal (or behaviour) over a set of variables Var with respect to interval I is a sequence, which specifies for each $p \in Var$, a real value $p(t)$, $t \in I$. The terms signal and behaviour may be used interchangeably in the following.

Duration Calculus. Duration calculus (DC) [10,18] is a highly expressive real time logic, with duration and length modalities.

The syntax of a DC formula over variables Var is defined as follows. Let $x \in Var$, $c \in \mathbb{R}$, and $op \in \{\leq, <, =, >, \geq, >\}$. First we define propositions P as $P ::= \bot \mid \top \mid x \; op \; c \mid P \wedge P \mid \neg P$, where $\top, \bot$ respectively represent true and false. Using the propositions P, we define a set of formulae D for DC as follows.

$$D ::= P \mid D \wedge D \mid \neg D \mid \lceil P \rceil_I \mid \lceil\rceil \mid \dagger_I(D, ..., D) \mid c \, op \int_I P \mid c \, op \, \ell$$

where $I = [b, e]$ is an interval. Note that the DC modalities $\lceil \; \rceil_I, \dagger_I, \int_I$ are parameterized with an interval I. We will explain the interval I used in these DC modalities in the semantics below.

For a given behaviour θ, an interval $[x, y]$, and a DC formula ψ, the satisfaction relation denoted $\theta, [x, y] \models \psi$ is defined inductively as follows.

1. $\theta, [x, y] \models P$ for a proposition P if $\theta(P(x))$ is true. Recall that P in its simplest form (other than $\top, \bot$) looks like $\alpha \; op \; c$, where $\alpha \in Var$. For propositions, the value at the beginning of the interval is compared with c, obtaining a Boolean value.
2. $\theta, [x, y] \models \neg P$ for a proposition P if $\theta(P(x))$ is False.
3. $\theta, [x, y] \models \lceil P \rceil_{[b,e]}$. The behaviour θ is over the interval $[x, y]$ while the formula $\lceil P \rceil$ to be evaluated has the interval $[b, e]$ tagged to it. The evaluation of $\lceil P \rceil$ happens at relative distance $[b, e]$ wrt the interval $[x, y]$, and it must be that $[b + x, e + x] \subseteq [x, y]$ since the behaviour is defined till the time point y. $\theta, [x, y] \models \lceil P \rceil_{[b,e]}$ iff for all $b + x \leq t \leq e + x \leq y$, $\theta, [t, t] \models P$.
4. $\theta, [x, y] \models D_1 \wedge D_2$ if $\theta, [x, y] \models D_1$ and $\theta, [x, y] \models D_2$.
5. $\theta, [x, y] \models \ell \, op \, c$ if $Eval(\ell)([x, y]) \; op \; c$ is true. $Eval(\ell)([x, y])$ is defined as $y - x$, the length of the interval.
6. $\theta, [x, y] \models \int_I P \, op \, c$ if $Eval(\int_{I+x} P)(\theta, [x, y]) \; op \; c$ evaluates to true, and $e + x \leq y$. $Eval(\int_{I+x} P)(\theta, [x, y])$ is defined as $\int_{b+x}^{e+x} \theta(P(t)) dt$ for $I = [b, e]$. That is, for each $t \in [b + x, e + x]$, check if $\theta(P(t))$ evaluates to true or false. The accumulated duration where $\theta(P(t))$ is true in $[b + x, e + x] \subseteq [x, y]$ is what $(\int_{I+x} P)(\theta, [x, y])$ evaluates to. This is compared against c using op obtaining a Boolean answer.
7. $\theta, [x, y] \models \dagger_{[b,e]}(D_1, ..., D_n)$ if there exist points $z_1, z_2, \ldots, z_{n-1}$ s.t. $b + x \leq z_1 \leq z_2 \leq \cdots \leq z_{n-1} \leq e + x \leq y$, and $\theta, [b + x, z_1] \models D_1, \theta, [z_1, z_2] \models D_2, \ldots, \theta, [z_{n-1}, e + x] \models D_n$.

The measurement operators length and duration are collectively represented as $mt\,op\,c$, where $mt \in \{\ell, \int_r, P\}$.

Derived Operators. Using †, we define the following derived operators. $\Diamond_I D = {\dagger}_I(\top, D, \top)$ holds provided D holds for some sub interval in I. $\Box_I D = \neg\Diamond_I\neg D$ holds provided D holds for all admissible sub intervals in I.

- The formula $\Box[(\ell = 50) \rightarrow (30 \leq \int_{[0,50]} (h_b = 1) \leq 45)]$ says that within any sub interval of length 50, the accumulated duration for which the variable h_b is 1 should lie between 30 and 45.
- The formula $\Box_{[0,n]}((p > 100) \Rightarrow [(\ell < 40) \dagger (p < 50)])$ says that in any subinterval of length n, whenever the value of variable p exceeds 100, it must come below 50 within an interval of length < 40.

3   Robust Satisfaction of DC

Robust or quantitative satisfaction associates a real number instead of a Boolean value to formulae. As we will see below, this number indicates "how far" the formula is, from being satisfiable in the usual Boolean sense. A robustness value of ∞ indicates perfect satisfaction of the formula, while $-\infty$ is the worst possible robustness indicating maximal distance from satisfaction. Thus, robust satisfaction defines a real-valued function $\rho(\theta, [x, y], D)$ of DC formula D, behaviour θ and interval $[x, y]$ s.t. $\theta, [x, y] \models D \equiv \rho(\theta, [x, y], D) > 0$.

The robust semantics for other operators is computed recursively from the DC semantics in a straightforward manner, by propagating the values of the functions associated with each operand using min and max corresponding to the various DC modalities. The complete robust satisfaction is defined inductively below.

1. $\rho(\theta, [x, y], \top) = +\infty$, $\rho(\theta, [x, y], \bot) = -\infty$

2. $\rho(\theta, [x, y], P\,op\,c) = \begin{cases} \theta(P(x)) - c & \text{if } op \text{ is } > \\ c - \theta(P(x)) & \text{if } op \text{ is } < \\ -|c - \theta(P(x))| & \text{if } op \text{ is } = \end{cases}$

3. $\rho(\theta, [x, y], P \wedge Q) = \min\{\rho(\theta, [x, y], P), \rho(\theta, [x, y], Q)\}$. is one of the oldest interval temporal logics known. The syntax of DC allows modalities like the duration $(\int_I \varphi)$ operator, and chop (†) operator[2] which makes it very expressive. The duration modality $\int_I \varphi$ measures the real time over which a formula φ has been true in an interval I, while

4. $\rho(\theta, [x, y], \neg P) = -\rho(\theta, [x, y], P)$.

5. $\rho(\theta, [x, y], \lceil P \rceil_{[b,e]}) = \inf_{z \in ([b+x, e+x])} \rho(\theta, [z, z], P)$, and $e + x \leq y$. The robustness of P is evaluated at all points in the interval $[b + x, e + x] \subseteq [x, y]$. The infimum of all possible values is taken as the robustness of $\lceil P \rceil$. Indeed, if

---

[2] Traditionally denoted as ⌢.

we obtain a negative value, we know that there is at least one point in the interval $[b + x, e + x]$ where the Boolean satisfaction is violated.

If the interval is not a point interval, the robustness is $-K$, where $K > 0$ is the size of the interval. This measures how much bigger the interval is, from what it should be. When we have a point interval, the robustness is 0, indicating that we are exactly where we should have been.

6. $\rho(\theta, [x, y], \int_I P \ op \ c) = \begin{cases} \alpha - c & \text{if } op \text{ is } > \\ c - \alpha, & \text{if } op \text{ is } < \\ -|\alpha - c| & \text{if } op \text{ is } = \end{cases}$

where $\alpha = Eval(\int_{I+x} P)(\theta, [x, y])$ is obtained as explained in the DC semantics (it should be that $e + x \leq y$). The difference between α and c is the robustness and the sign depends on the operator used. The explanation here is analogous to $mt \ op \ c$.

7. $\rho(\theta, [x, y], \ell \ op \ c) = \begin{cases} \beta - c & \text{if } op \text{ is } > \\ c - \beta & \text{if } op \text{ is } < \\ -|\beta - c| & \text{if } op \text{ is } = \end{cases}$

where $\beta = Eval(\ell)([x, y])$ and $e + x \leq y$. Here again, we compute the difference between $y - x$ and c, and depending op, obtain the result.

8. $\rho(\theta, [x, y], \neg D_{[b,e]}) = -\{\rho(\theta, [x, y], D)\}$, and $e + x \leq y$. The robustness of $\neg D$ is obtained by flipping the sign of the robustness of D.

9. $\rho(\theta, [x, y], D_1 \wedge D_2) = \min\{\rho(\theta, [x, y], D_1, \rho(\theta, [x, y], D_2)\}, e + x \leq y$. The minimum of the robustness values of D_1, D_2 is the robustness of $D_1 \wedge D_2$.

10. $\rho(\theta, [x, y], \dagger_{[b,e]}(D_1 \ldots D_n))$ is defined as

$$\sup_{z_1,\ldots,z_{n-1}\in[b+x,e+x]} \{\min\{\rho(\theta, [b + x, z_1], D_1) \ldots \rho(\theta, [z_{n-1}, e + x], D_n)\}\}$$

and $e + x \leq y$.

For a choice of $b + x \leq z_1 \leq z_2 \leq \cdots \leq z_{n-1} \leq e + x$, find the minimum robustness value from $\rho(\theta, [z_{i-1}, z_i], D_i)$. However, the robustness of chop is the supremum across all possible ways of chopping (all possible ways of finding $z_1, \ldots, z_{n-1}$).

- As an example to illustrate robustness, consider the formula $[(\ell = 50) \rightarrow (30 \leq \int_{[0,50]} (h_b = 1) \leq 45)]$. If we have a signal such that the duration for which $h_b = 1$ is 25 or 50 in the interval $[0,50]$, then the robustness value will be -5, since the accumulated duration is 5 away from the required range.

- As yet another example, consider the formula $\dagger([p > 2], \ell = 2)$. The formula can be evaluated on any interval of length at least 2. If we have a signal over an interval $[x, y]$ where the values of p range in the interval $[-100, 10]$ in the sub interval $[x, y - 2]$, then the robustness is -102, the distance from the ideal value 2 at some point in the signal.

4   Synthesis Algorithm

In this Section, we present our algorithm for synthesizing controllers satisfying a DC specification for a system. The inputs to our synthesis algorithm are a system given as a hybrid automaton H, adversarial external environmental disturbances, a time horizon N, time granularity dt, and a DC specification. The goal is to synthesize a sequence of control variables (or an input signal) resulting in behaviours of the system H which have maximum robustness in satisfying the DC specification. The output of the algorithm is hence this sequence of input variables such that the robustness value of the behaviour of the system is maximized.

We assume that the signals (input, state, output and environment) we deal with in the algorithm are finitely piecewise linear and continuous. A signal y over an interval $[t_0, t_n]$ is said to be finitely piecewise linear, continuous (f.p.l.c.) if there exists a finite sequence of time points $(t_i)_{0 \le i \le n}$ such that for all $0 \le i < n$, y is continuous at t_i and is affine on the interval $[t_i, t_{i+1})$.

4.1   The Algorithm

In Algorithm 1, we present an algorithm for synthesizing control for finite trajectories maximizing robustness of bounded specifications. The algorithm generates a sequence of control inputs for a bounded DC specification $\phi_e \implies \phi_s$, which must be bounded by horizon length N. The specification $\phi_e \implies \phi_s$ has two parts, the DC specification on the system ϕ_s and the DC specification on the environment ϕ_e. The algorithm also takes a hybrid system H as input. The quality of learned controls is judged based on its effect on the robust satisfaction of the specification. Higher the positive robustness value, the more desirable the control input. The approach is iterative and collects the adversarial environment inputs. In each iteration, we synthesize a control signal that satisfies the specification for the environment inputs (ϕ_e) seen so far and check if there is an environmental input such that the learned control signal may cause violation of the specifications. If such an environment input is found, we go for the next iteration. Otherwise, our method terminates with the learned control signal.

Let us present our algorithm in detail. We expect the input system H has variable vectors X, Y, U, and W representing internal state, outputs, inputs, and environment inputs respectively. At first, we translate the system H into a formula F^H using the $EncodeBMC$ method that implements the bounded model-checking encoding of H using the method presented in [19, 20]. The encoding produces formula $F_H(\mathbf{x}, \mathbf{y}, \mathbf{u}, \mathbf{w})$ over symbolic vector of signals for internal states $\mathbf{x}$, outputs $\mathbf{y}$, inputs $\mathbf{u}$, and environment $\mathbf{w}$. To keep the exposition clear, we have differentiated between the program variables and the symbolic signals by changing fonts. Afterwards, we encode the DC property ϕ_s over signals of H using function $EncodeProp$ (see Sect. 4.2 for details of the encoding from DC to mixed integer linear programming). The function returns two values. The first is a symbolic expression $r^s_{[0,N]}(\mathbf{x}, \mathbf{y}, \mathbf{u})$ that encodes the robustness of ϕ_s over signals $\mathbf{x}$, $\mathbf{y}$, and $\mathbf{u}$. The second is the condition F_s under which the robustness

```
1  Function Synthesis(H(X,Y,U,W), N, dt, φ_e ⟹ φ_s):
       Result: u*
2      F_H(x,y,u,w) = EncodeBMC(H(X,Y,U,W), dt);
3      r^s_{[0,N]}(x,y,u), F_s(x,y,u) = EncodeProp(φ_s(X,Y,W), dt, [x,y,u], N);
4      F(x,y,u,w) = F_H(x,y,u,w) ∧ F_s(x,y,u);
5      u* = random control input;
6      maxr := −∞;
7      maxu := u*;
8      W_worst = ∅;
9      while runtime < TIMEOUT do
10         w*,r* ← arg min_w r^s_{[0,N]}(x,y,u*) s.t. w ⊨ φ_e ∧ F(x,y,u*,w) ;
11         if r* > 0 then
12             Return u*,r* ;
13         end
14         W_worst ← W_worst ∪ {w*} ;
15         if r* > maxr then
16             maxr = r*;
17             maxu = u*;
18         end
19         u*,r' ← arg min_u max_{w^0∈W_worst} − r^s_{[0,N]}(x,y,u) s.t. F(x,y,u,w^0) ;
20         if r' == ∞ then
21             Return INFEASIBLE;
22         end
23     end
24     Return maxu,maxr
25 end
```

Algorithm 1: Synthesis algorithm

expression is correct. We conjunct the formulas F_s and F_H to obtain the overall condition to be true in our analysis. At line 5, we initialize the control sequence input u^* at random. We also initialize maxu and $maxr$ that records the best input seen so far and the value of robustness at the input. We will present the encoding for DC formulas to constraint system in the next subsection.

The iterative loop at line 9 finds inputs that perform better on already seen adverse environments. In each iteration, we start by finding an environment w^* that forces worst behavior under input u^*. In line 10 we solve an optimization problem that minimizes the robustness of ϕ_s by varying the environmental input. In the problem, we minimize expression $r^s_{[0,N]}(x,y,u^*)$ for all values of w such that w satisfies ϕ_e and the side conditions $F(x,y,u^*,w)$ is satisfied. The minimization returns a pair of the worst environment w^* for input u^* and the minimum robustness value r^*. If the robustness is positive, then no environment can falsify ϕ_s given the control input u^*. Therefore, we return the control input u^*. Otherwise, we update the W_{worst} set adding one more adversarial input to the list in line 14 in the algorithm.

In line 19 of the algorithm, we try to find a control input such that it maximizes the robustness, given the adversarial environment signals of the system. The condition at line 19 ensures that we only search for the control signals that satisfy ϕ_s and all the variables respect the behavior of the system and the property. We again use the encoding to translate this into an optimization query. Note that we are minimizing the negation of the robustness. Therefore, we compute a new u^* which performs best against all environments in W_{worst}. If no such satisfying control input exists, then we return infeasible.

During every cycle, we either find a satisfying control input or some adversarial input that leads to the violation of the specification. We expand W_{worst} every time we find such an adversarial input. The algorithm may run indefinitely. Therefore, we stop the loop after some timeout.

The proof of the following theorem is straightforward from the algorithm.

Theorem 1. *If our algorithm returns a control input u^* and robustness r then under any execution $[x, y, u^*, w]$ of H under environment $w \models \psi_e$ the following holds.*

$$\rho([x, y, u], [0, N], \psi_s) \geq r$$

To avoid any impact of discrete time, we compute a range of possible outcomes in our encoding [20] to approximate the non-linear behaviors of the differential equations. Therefore, we ignore the impact of dt in the above theorem. The algorithm may not terminate; however, we stop the algorithm after a finite number of steps to report the best control input found.

The satisfaction conditions in line 10 and 19 are converted to constraints encoding satisfaction of a mixed integer linear problem (MILP). In the above discussion, we have not illustrated how we translate the DC specification to MILP encoding. Therefore, in the next subsection, we describe the encoding of the DC operators to MILP.

4.2   Encoding DC Formulas in MILP

We encode the DC specification as a Mixed-Integer Linear Programming(MILP) problem. We are using the robustness semantics of DC to encode into MILP such that the robustness value ≥ 0 indicates the satisfaction of the specification. In the call to $EncodeProp(\psi(X), X, N)$, we expect formula ψ over variables X, corresponding symbolic signals X, and a time horizon N as parameters. For each sub-formula ϕ of ψ and a time interval $[t, t'] \subseteq [0, N]$, we introduce a real valued variable $r^{\phi}_{[t,t']}$ to represent robustness of ϕ in the interval $[t, t']$. The variable $r^{\psi}_{[0,N]}$ represents the robustness of the full formula in the interval $[0, N]$, and this is returned. We also return constraints F that encodes correctness conditions which check that the variable indeed represents the robustness. Our encoding also uses some Boolean variables $p^{\phi}_{[t,t']}$ as well as a predefined large positive number M to represent choices to be made in the case of some formulae. In Table 1, we present the encoding for DC formulas. Using the robustness variables $r_{[t,t']}$ and Boolean variables $p_{[t,t']}$ (omitting here, the superscript denoting which formulae), we obtain the MILP encoding for each DC formulae.

Table 1. Encoding for DC formulas. $\mathbf{x}$ is the symbolic signal in the encoding for $x \in X$.

ψ	Contribution to F for encoding $\psi_{[t,t']}$
$x \geq c$	$r^{\psi}_{[t,t']} = \mathbf{x}_t - c$
$x \leq c$	$r^{\psi}_{[t,t']} = c - \mathbf{x}_t$
$x = c$	$r^{\psi}_{[t,t']} = -\lvert \mathbf{x}_t - c \rvert$
$\neg \phi$	$r^{\psi}_t = -r^{\phi}_t$
$\phi_1 \wedge \phi_2$	$p^{\phi_1}_{[t,t']} + p^{\phi_2}_{[t,t']} = 1 \wedge r^{\psi}_{[t,t']} \leq r^{\phi_1}_{[t,t']}, i = 1,2$ $r^{\phi_i}_{[t,t']} - (1 - p^{\phi_i}_{[t,t']})M \leq r^{\psi}_{[t,t']} \leq r^{\phi_i}_{[t,t']} + M(1 - p^{\phi_i}_{[t,t']})$
$\phi_1 \vee \phi_2$	$r^{\psi}_{[t,t']} = max(r^{\phi_1}_{[t,t']}, r^{\phi_2}_{[t,t']})$
$\square_{[a,b]} \phi$	$r^{\psi}_{[t,t']} = min(\{r^{\phi}_{[s,t']} \mid s \in [t+a, t+b]\})$ if $t + b \leq t'$
$\lozenge_{[a,b]} \phi$	$r^{\psi}_{[t,t']} = max(\{r^{\phi}_{[s,t']} \mid s \in [t+a, t+b]\})$ if $t + b \leq t'$
$\phi_1 \dagger_{[a,b]} \phi_2$	Use $\psi \Leftrightarrow \wedge^b_{i=a}(\square_{[a,i]}\phi_1 \wedge \square_{[i,b]}\phi_2)$ to define $r^{\psi}_{[t,t']}$
$\int_{[a,b]} \phi > c$	$\wedge^b_{i=a}[p^{\phi}_{[t+i,t']}M \geq r^{\phi}_{[t+i,t']} \geq M(p^{\phi}_{[t+i,t']} - 1)] \wedge$ $r^{\psi}_{[t,t']} = dt \sum\limits^b_{i=a} p^{\phi}_{[t+i,t']} - c$
$\int_{[a,b]} \phi < c$	$\wedge^b_{i=a}[p^{\phi}_{[t+i,t']}M \geq r^{\phi}_{[t+i,t']} \geq M(p^{\phi}_{[t+i,t']} - 1)] \wedge$ $r^{\psi}_{[t,t']} = c - dt \sum\limits^b_{i=a} p^{\phi}_{[t+i,t']}$
$\int_{[a,b]} \phi = c$	$\wedge^b_{i=a}[p^{\phi}_{[t+i,t']}M \geq r^{\phi}_{[t+i,t']} \geq M(p^{\phi}_{[t+i,t']} - 1)] \wedge$ $r^{\psi}_{[t,t']} = -\lvert c - dt \sum\limits^b_{i=a} p^{\phi}_{[t+i,t']} \rvert$
$\ell > c$	$r^{\psi}_{[t,t']} = (t' - t) - c$
$\ell < c$	$r^{\psi}_{[t,t']} = c - (t' - t)$
$\ell = c$	$r^{\psi}_{[t,t']} = -\lvert c - (t' - t) \rvert$

Let $\mathbf{x}_t$ denote the variable corresponding to $x \in X$ in the MILP encoding, at time t in the signal $\mathbf{x}$. Following the semantics of DC formulas, we encode $x \geq c$ at $[t, t']$ by checking the difference of the value of x at time t from c. To encode a conjunction $\psi = \phi_1 \wedge \phi_2$, we need to compute the minimum of the two robustness values with respect to ϕ_1 and ϕ_2. We use Boolean variables p^{ϕ_1}, p^{ϕ_2} to encode which of the subformulas ϕ_1, ϕ_2 has the minimum robustness. The formula $p^{\phi_1}_{[t,t']} + p^{\phi_2}_{[t,t']} = 1$ says that we choose one of the two, the formula $r^{\psi}_{[t,t']} \leq r^{\phi_i}_{[t,t']}, i = 1, 2$ says that the robustness of ψ is the minimum robustness value between those of ϕ_1, ϕ_2. Further, using a large positive number M, we encode the relation between the robustness values of ψ and ϕ_1, ϕ_2 as follows: $r^{\phi_i}_{[t,t']} - (1 - p^{\phi_i}_{[t,t']})M \leq r^{\psi}_{[t,t']} \leq r^{\phi_i}_{[t,t']} + M(1 - p^{\phi_i}_{[t,t']})$. Thus, we encode min using the Boolean variables and M. Similarly, we encode max for disjunction, which we have not explicitly illustrated in the Table. We use similar ideas to encode minimum or maximum in the semantics of $\square$, $\lozenge$, and $\dagger$ (for brevity, in the Table, we have used min, max notations for $\vee, \square, \lozenge$ and provide an equivalent characterization using $\square$ for $\dagger$. In the actual MILP encoding, the min, max are handled as explained above).

We need to be careful about the time ranges. If $[t, t']$ does not provide enough space, i.e. $t' - t < b$, to interpret temporal formulas $\psi_{[a,b]}$ then our encoding is not applicable. In our implementation, we throw exceptions. In measurement operators, we compare the evaluated output of the measurement operators with a constant. So, for each of the comparison operators $>, <$ and $=$ we have a different encoding. The value of the state duration operator, is the time for which the specification ϕ is true. We again use Boolean variables p to count the number of times for which the robustness of ϕ is greater than 0. We multiply the count by time steps dt to compute the real time value of the duration operator. Then, depending on the comparison operator we take the difference of the evaluation with the constant. The encoding of the length operator is simple. We take the difference from the available time interval depending on the comparison operator used.

5 Experimental Evaluation

We have implemented the above algorithm in a tool called ControlDC. In this Section, we will present the results of our tool on case studies on four examples. ControlDC is implemented in about 2000 lines of Python code and takes hybrid automata and DC formulas as input, which are declared using a Python like syntax. We allow non-linear dynamics in the hybrid automata we take as input. Our implementation uses an SMT solver Z3 [21] as an optimization tool. We choose the solver, since it can optimize with non-linearity and disjunctions. All our queries to Z3 remain quantifier-free. ControlDC returns an input signal that satisfies the property as best as possible given the timing constraints. We run our experiments on a standard PC with 100 min timeout and limit on five rounds of the algorithm.

Pacemaker System

We consider the problem of controlling the behaviour of the heart. We use the random heart model from [22] as the system to control. We present the model in Fig. 1. Our objective is to maintain the heart beat in a given range. The function of the pacemaker or the controller is to balance the atrial and ventricular events. The heart and the pacemaker communicate with each other using events. The heart generates the intrinsic heart events $Aget$ and $Vget$, representing atrial and ventricular events that the pacemaker takes as inputs. The pacemaker generates events AP and VP to the corresponding components in the heart. The model non deterministically generates an intrinsic heart event $Xget$ within the time interval $[Xminwait, Xmaxwait]$, after each intrinsic heart event $Xget$ or pacing XP where, X is either atrial (A) or ventricular (V).

Our goal is to satisfy a given specification which is expressed in DC to simulate proper working of the heart. The property states that there are between 60 and 100 heart beats (ventricular events $Vevent \in \{Vget, VP\}$) in an interval of one

minute. We write the specification using the duration and always operator as fol-
lows: $\square_{[0,n]}[(\ell=60) \rightarrow (60 \leq \int_{[0,60]} (Vevent=1) \leq 100)]$. We can choose a behaviour
σ with horizon n to check this property. Therefore in 5 s, the number of heartbeats
should $\in [5,9]$ (rounding 8 upward to 9). So, we test the following property on our
system on n horizon runs $\square_{[0,n]}[(\ell = 5) \rightarrow (4 < \int_{[0,5]} (Vevent = 1) < 10)]$

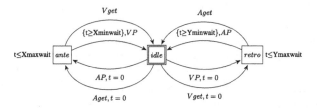

Fig. 1. The heart model. The flow dynamics has been omitted for brevity.

In the Table below, we present the robustness values for different choices
of the timing variables. ControlDC synthesizes the control input for which the
robustness is found to be positive. If it does not find a control with positive
robustness in given time and rounds, then we report the best robustness so far.
If the *minwait* values are greater than 2, and we are unable to find a satisfying
control, then we report a control with known maximum possible robustness.

Xminwait	Xmaxwait	Yminwait	Ymaxwait	Robustness	Time (mins)
0.2	0.6	0.2	1	0.6	0.28
0.4	0.6	0.4	1	0.8	4.14
1	2	1	2	0.2	3.06
2.4	4	2.2	4	−0.2	2.39

Metro System

Let us consider the problem of a metro train transporting passengers across two
stations in an optimal way. We present the hybrid model of the metro system in
the Fig. 2. The location *sn1o* in the model is the starting location of the system
indicating that the metro is in Station 1, the door of the metro is open, and
passengers can enter the train. Passengers enter the train at a rate depending
on the number of people inside the train and on the platform. The passenger
dynamics is illustrated in the Figure. The system transitions to the location
sn1c where the door of the metro is closed. When the metro starts running, it
enters the location *run*. In the end, when the metro reaches the Station 2 and
the door opens, it enters the *sn2o* location. In case of unwanted events such
as overcrowding, negative speed etc. occurring in the system, it transitions to

the *error* state. The state variables in the system are *pin, pout, poutst2*, which represent the number of passengers inside the metro, the number of passengers standing outside the metro at a station, and the number of passengers who have got out of the metro at Station 2. Additionally, the variable *sp* is the speed of the train and *dct* is the distance covered by the train depending on *sp*. The parameter *cap* represents the number of passengers that can be accommodated by the train. The controller controls the acceleration of the train. This controls the dynamics of the train in the location *run* in the usual way. The number of passengers who have arrived at the station outside the metro is the adversarial environment input to our system.

The goal of the system is to transport as many passengers as possible in the least amount of time. We will write a specification which allows us to fulfill this condition. In an interval $[a, b]$, the train should pick up more than x number of passengers from Station 1 and within c time units it should reach Station 2, where at least d passengers must be transported. We write the property using the chop operator as follows: $\dagger_{a,b}(pin > x, len < c, poutst2 > d)$.

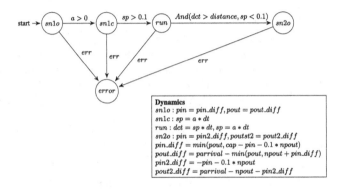

Fig. 2. The metro model. The flow dynamics is shown in the figure.

In the following Table, we consider the specification with different values of the state variables, the interval length under consideration, and compare the robustness of the synthesized control. We fix the acceleration range between $[-1,1]$.

Sr. no.	Initial pin	Initial poutst2	distance	interval	Robustness	Time (mins)
1	5	4	1	2	−4	23.47
2	5	4	1	2.6	2.6	3.21
3	10	10	1	3	3	6.28
4	9	7	2	1	−7	0.68
5	20	20	2	3.2	−10.8	61.75

In the first row of the Table, the robustness of the control is negative, the executions under the control are stuck in the run state and do not reach the Station 2. The reason is that the distance 1 unit in the specification was not covered in the interval of length 2 units successfully. In the second and third row, the robustness is positive, the train always reaches the Station 2, and enough number of people are transported to Station 2. As we change the distance in our specification, the train may take more time to reach Station 2, and the robustness for smaller length interval properties is negative since the distance between the two stations could not be covered in that interval. Another reason for negative robustness is, that the number of people transported to Station 2 was below the required number. The last two rows have negative robustness due to these reasons.

Gas Burner System

In Fig. 3, we present the model of a gas burner. The flow of gas is determined by the degree of opening of the valve. The variable *flame* indicates the presence of flame and variable *leak* is a function of *gas* and *flame* as follows: $leak = gas \wedge \neg(flame)$. The system has three locations. Initially, the system is in location $gsoff$ where the gas is off, and the timer is set to 0. As soon as the presence of gas and flame is detected, or the timer rises above 0.1, the transition to the location $gfon$ (indicating flame is on) is triggered. In the case of the absence of flame when the gas is on, it goes to location $glon$ (indicating leak). The environment variable e governs the transitions between the $glon$ and $gfon$ locations.

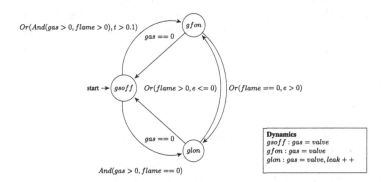

Fig. 3. Gas burner. The flow dynamics is shown in the figure.

Our goal is to try to minimize the leak as much as possible. We want to control the functioning of the valve in the system. Our specification is $\square_{[0,n]}(\int_{[0,int]}(leak > 0) < b)$, i.e., in any interval of int seconds, the duration of leak should not exceed b seconds. In the table below, we change int (interval length) and b (duration) used in the specification and run ControlDC to synthesize input control.

Interval (int)	Duration (b)	Robustness	Time (mins)
1	0.2	−0.2	1.17
1	0.6	0	0.81
2	0.4	−0.4	3.20
2	1.2	0.6	0.66
3	1	−0.2	4.51
3	1.4	0.4	0.81

Car System

We consider an example from [9] of an autonomous car driving in the presence of another adversary vehicles. The system involves two kinds of vehicles. The vehicle which we control, is the *self* vehicle whereas, the other is the *adv* vehicle. Both the vehicles need to cross an intersection at some time. The model has a single location without transitions. The position of vehicles, their speed, and their accelerations are the state variables. The environment variables control the speed of *adv* and input variables control the speed of *self*.

The goal is to avoid collision of the *self* and *adv*. The prospect of making our vehicle to come to an abrupt stop when the other vehicle is approaching is not practical. We want to avoid over speeding when both the vehicles are close enough, so as to avoid a crash. The solution is to ensure that our vehicle will not cross some threshold speed more than a fixed amount of time when the two vehicles come in a zone of some distance apart. Formally, we require that whenever the *self* and *adv* are less than 2 m apart, the time for which the speed of the self vehicle is greater than 2 should be less than 4 units. $\phi_s = \Box_{[0,\infty]}[|x_t^{self} - x_t^{adv}| < 2] \implies [\int(|v_t^{self}| > 2) < 4]$. ControlDC finds the robust control of the system in 30.41 s.

References

1. Pinzon, L.E., Hanisch, H.-M., Jafari, M.A., Boucher, T.: A comparative study of synthesis methods for discrete event controllers. Formal Methods Syst. Des. **15**(2), 123–167 (1999). https://doi.org/10.1023/A:1008740917111
2. Baier, C., Katoen, J.-P.: Principles of Model Checking. MIT Press, Cambridge (2008)
3. Koymans, R.: Specifying real-time properties with metric temporal logic. Real-Time Syst. **2**(4), 255–299 (1990). https://doi.org/10.1007/BF01995674
4. Maler, O., Nickovic, D.: Monitoring temporal properties of continuous signals. In: Lakhnech, Y., Yovine, S. (eds.) FORMATS/FTRTFT -2004. LNCS, vol. 3253, pp. 152–166. Springer, Heidelberg (2004). https://doi.org/10.1007/978-3-540-30206-3_12
5. Rungger, M., Mazo Jr, M., Tabuada, P.: Specification-guided controller synthesis for linear systems and safe linear-time temporal logic. In: Proceedings of the 16th International Conference on Hybrid Systems: Computation and Control, pp. 333–342. ACM (2013)

6. Dimitrova, R., Ghasemi, M., Topcu, U.: Reactive synthesis with maximum realizability of linear temporal logic specifications. Acta Inf. **57**(1), 107–135 (2020). https://doi.org/10.1007/s00236-019-00348-4

7. Baier, C., Größer, M., Leucker, M., Bollig, B., Ciesinski, F.: Controller synthesis for probabilistic systems (extended abstract). In: Levy, J.-J., Mayr, E.W., Mitchell, J.C. (eds.) TCS 2004. IIFIP, vol. 155, pp. 493–506. Springer, Boston, MA (2004). https://doi.org/10.1007/1-4020-8141-3_38

8. Fainekos, G.E., Pappas, G.J.: Robustness of temporal logic specifications for continuous-time signals. Theor. Comput. Sci. **410**(42), 4262–4291 (2009)

9. Raman, V., Donzé, A., Sadigh, D., Murray, R.M., Seshia, S.A.: Reactive synthesis from signal temporal logic specifications. In: Proceedings of the 18th International Conference on Hybrid Systems: Computation and Control, pp. 239–248. ACM (2015)

10. Chaochen, Z., Hansen, M.R.: Duration Calculus - A Formal Approach to Real-Time Systems. Monographs in Theoretical Computer Science. An EATCS Series. Springer, Heidelberg (2004). https://doi.org/10.1007/978-3-662-06784-0

11. Wakankar, A., Pandya, P.K., Matteplackel, R.M.: DCSYNTH: guided reactive synthesis with soft requirements. In: Verified Software. Theories, Tools, and Experiments - 11th International Conference, VSTTE 2019, New York City, NY, USA, 13–14 July 2019, Revised Selected Papers, pp. 124–142 (2019)

12. Pandya, P.K., Wakankar, A.: Logical specification and uniform synthesis of robust controllers. In: Proceedings of the 17th ACM-IEEE International Conference on Formal Methods and Models for System Design, MEMOCODE 2019, La Jolla, CA, USA, 9–11 October 2019, pp. 15:1–15:11 (2019)

13. Pandya, P.K.: Specifying and deciding quantified discrete-time duration calculus formulae using DCVALIDS. In: Proceedings of RTTOOLS 2001 (Affiliated with CONCUR 2001) (2001)

14. Wolff, E.M., Topcu, U., Murray, R.M.: Optimization-based trajectory generation with linear temporal logic specifications. In: 2014 IEEE International Conference on Robotics and Automation, ICRA 2014, Hong Kong, China, 31 May–7 June 2014, pp. 5319–5325 (2014)

15. Raman, V., Donzé, A., Maasoumy, M., Murray, R.M., Sangiovanni-Vincentelli, A.L., Seshia, S.A.: Model predictive control with signal temporal logic specifications. In: 53rd IEEE Conference on Decision and Control, CDC 2014, Los Angeles, CA, USA, 15–17 December 2014, pp. 81–87 (2014)

16. Gurobi Optimization. Inc.: Gurobi optimizer reference manual (2014) (2015). http://www.gurobi.com

17. Henzinger, T.A.: The theory of hybrid automata. In: Proceedings, 11th Annual IEEE Symposium on Logic in Computer Science, New Brunswick, New Jersey, USA, 27–30 July 1996, pp. 278–292 (1996)

18. Pandya, P.K., Krishna, S.N., Loya, K.: On sampling abstraction of continuous time logic with durations. In: Grumberg, O., Huth, M. (eds.) TACAS 2007. LNCS, vol. 4424, pp. 246–260. Springer, Heidelberg (2007). https://doi.org/10.1007/978-3-540-71209-1_20

19. Biere, A., Cimatti, A., Clarke, E.M., Strichman, O., Zhu, Y.: Bounded model checking. Adv. Comput. **58**, 117–148 (2003)

20. Kong, S., Gao, S., Chen, W., Clarke, E.: dReach: δ-reachability analysis for hybrid systems. In: Baier, C., Tinelli, C. (eds.) TACAS 2015. LNCS, vol. 9035, pp. 200–205. Springer, Heidelberg (2015). https://doi.org/10.1007/978-3-662-46681-0_15

21. de Moura, L., Bjørner, N.: Z3: an efficient SMT solver. In: Ramakrishnan, C.R., Rehof, J. (eds.) TACAS 2008. LNCS, vol. 4963, pp. 337–340. Springer, Heidelberg (2008). https://doi.org/10.1007/978-3-540-78800-3_24

22. Jiang, Z., Pajic, M., Moarref, S., Alur, R., Mangharam, R.: Modeling and verification of a dual chamber implantable pacemaker. In: Flanagan, C., König, B. (eds.) TACAS 2012. LNCS, vol. 7214, pp. 188–203. Springer, Heidelberg (2012). https://doi.org/10.1007/978-3-642-28756-5_14

Dependency-Based Compositional Synthesis

Bernd Finkbeiner[iD] and Noemi Passing[(✉)][iD]

CISPA Helmholtz Center for Information Security, Saarbrücken, Germany
{finkbeiner,noemi.passing}@cispa.saarland

Abstract. Despite many recent advances, reactive synthesis is still not really a practical technique. The grand challenge is to scale from small transition systems, where synthesis performs well, to complex multi-component designs. Compositional methods, such as the construction of dominant strategies for individual components, reduce the complexity significantly, but are usually not applicable without extensively rewriting the specification. In this paper, we present a refinement of compositional synthesis that does not require such an intervention. Our algorithm decomposes the system into a sequence of components, such that every component has a strategy that is dominant, i.e., performs at least as good as any possible alternative, provided that the preceding components follow their (already synthesized) strategies. The decomposition of the system is based on a dependency analysis, for which we provide semantic and syntactic techniques. We establish the soundness and completeness of the approach and report on encouraging experimental results.

1 Introduction

Compositionality breaks the analysis of a complex system into several smaller tasks over individual components. It has long been recognized as the key technique that makes a "significant difference" [16] for the scalability of verification algorithms. In synthesis, it has proven much harder to develop successful compositional techniques. In a nutshell, synthesis corresponds to finding a winning strategy for the system in a game against its environment. In compositional synthesis, the system player controls an individual component, the environment player all remaining components [9]. In practice, however, a winning strategy rarely exists for an individual component, because the specification can usually only be satisfied if several components collaborate.

Remorsefree dominance [3], a weaker notion than winning, accounts for such situations. Intuitively, a dominant strategy is allowed to violate the specification as long as no other strategy would have satisfied it in the same situation.

This work was partially supported by the German Research Foundation (DFG) as part of the Collaborative Research Center "Foundations of Perspicuous Software Systems" (TRR 248, 389792660), and by the European Research Council (ERC) Grant OSARES (No. 683300).

D. V. Hung and O. Sokolsky (Eds.): ATVA 2020, LNCS 12302, pp. 447–463, 2020.
https://doi.org/10.1007/978-3-030-59152-6_25

In other words, if the violation is the fault of the environment, we do not blame the component. Looking for strategies that are dominant, rather than winning, allows us to find strategies that do not necessarily satisfy the specification for all input sequences, but satisfy the specification for sequences that are *realistic* in the sense that they might actually occur in a system that is built from components that all do their best to satisfy the specification.

For safety specifications, it was shown that dominance is a compositional notion: the composition of two dominant strategies is again dominant. Furthermore, if a winning strategy exists, then all dominant strategies are winning. This directly leads to a compositional synthesis approach that synthesizes individual dominant strategies [4]. In general, however, there is no guarantee that a dominant strategy exists. Often, a component A depends on the well-behavior of another component B in the sense that A needs to anticipate some future action of B. In such situations, there is no dominant strategy for A alone since the decision which strategy is best for A depends on the specific strategy for B.

In this paper, we address this problem with an *incremental* synthesis approach. Like in standard compositional synthesis, we split the system into components. However, we do not try to find dominant strategies for each component individually. Rather, we proceed in an incremental fashion such that each component can already assume a particular strategy for the previously synthesized components. We call the order, in which the components are constructed, the *synthesis order*. Instead of requiring the existence of dominant strategies for all components, we only require the existence of a dominant strategy *under the assumption* of the previous strategies. Similar to standard compositional synthesis, this approach reduces the complexity of synthesis by decomposing the system; additionally, it overcomes the problem that dominant strategies generally do not exist for all components without relying on other strategies.

The key question now is how to find the synthesis order. We propose two methods that offer different trade-offs between precision and computational cost. The first method is based on a semantic dependency analysis of the output variables of the system. We build equivalence classes of variables based on cyclic dependencies, which then form the components of the system. The synthesis order is defined on the dependencies between the components, resolving dependencies that prevent the existence of dominant strategies. The second method is based on a syntactic analysis of the specification, which conservatively overapproximates the semantic dependencies.

We have implemented a prototype of the incremental synthesis algorithm and compare it to the state-of-the-art synthesis tool BoSy [6] on scalable benchmarks. The results are very encouraging: our algorithm clearly outperforms classical synthesis for larger systems.

Proofs and the benchmark specifications are provided in the full version [8].

Related Work. Kupferman et al. introduce a safraless compositional synthesis algorithm transforming the synthesis problem into an emptiness check on Büchi tree automata [13]. Kugler and Sittal introduce two compositional algorithms for synthesis from Live Sequence Charts specifications [12]. Yet, neither of them is sound and complete. While they briefly describe a sound and complete extension of their algorithms, they did not implement it. Filiot et al. introduce a compositional synthesis algorithm for LTL specifications [7] based on the composition of safety games. Moreover, they introduce a non-complete heuristic for dropping conjuncts of the specification. All of the above approaches search for winning strategies and thus fail if cooperation between the components is needed.

The notion of remorsefree dominance was first introduced in the setting of reactive synthesis by Damm and Finkbeiner [3]. They introduce a compositional synthesis algorithm for safety properties based on dominant strategies [4].

In the setting of controller synthesis, Baier et al. present an algorithm that incrementally synthesizes so-called most general controllers and builds their parallel composition in order to synthesize the next one [1]. In contrast to our approach, they do not decompose the system in separate components. Incremental synthesis is only used to handle cascades of objectives in an online fashion.

2   Motivating Example

In safety-critical systems such as self-driving cars, correctness of the implementation with respect to a given specification is crucial. Hence, they are an obvious target for synthesis. However, a self-driving car consists of several components that interact with each other, leading to enormous state spaces when synthesized together. While a compositional approach may reduce the complexity, in most scenarios there are neither winning nor dominant strategies for the separate components. Consider a specification for a gearing unit and an acceleration unit of a self-driving car. The latter one is required to decelerate before curves and to not accelerate in curves. To prevent traffic jams, the car is required to accelerate eventually if no curve is ahead. In order to safe fuel, it should not always accelerate or decelerate. This can be specified in LTL as follows:

$$\varphi_{acc} = \Box(curve\_ahead \rightarrow \bigcirc dec) \wedge \Box(in\_curve \rightarrow \bigcirc \neg acc) \wedge \Box \Diamond keep$$
$$\wedge \Box((\neg in\_curve \wedge \neg curve\_ahead) \rightarrow \Diamond acc) \wedge \Box \neg(acc \wedge dec)$$
$$\wedge \Box \neg(acc \wedge keep) \wedge \Box \neg(dec \wedge keep) \wedge \Box(acc \vee dec \vee keep),$$

where $curve\_ahead$ and in_curve are input variables denoting whether a curve is ahead or whether the car is in a curve, respectively. The output variables are acc and dec, denoting acceleration and deceleration, and $keep$, denoting that the current speed is kept. Note that φ_{acc} is only realizable if we assume that a curve is not followed by another one with only one step in between infinitely often.

The gearing unit can choose between two gears. It is required to use the smaller gear when the car is accelerating and the higher gear if the car reaches a steady speed after accelerating. This can be specified in LTL as follows, where $gear_i$ are output variables denoting whether the first or the second gear is used:

$$\varphi_{gear} = \Box((acc \wedge \bigcirc acc) \rightarrow \bigcirc \bigcirc gear_1) \wedge \Box((acc \wedge \bigcirc keep) \rightarrow \bigcirc \bigcirc gear_2)$$
$$\wedge \Box \neg(gear_1 \wedge gear_2) \wedge \Box(gear_1 \vee gear_2).$$

When synthesizing a strategy s for the acceleration unit, it does not suffice to consider only φ_{acc} since s affects the gearing unit. Yet, there is clearly no winning strategy for $\varphi_{car} := \varphi_{acc} \wedge \varphi_{gear}$ when considering the acceleration unit separately. There is no dominant strategy either: As long as the car accelerates after a curve, the conjunct $\Box((\neg in\_curve \wedge \neg curve\_ahead) \rightarrow \Diamond acc)$ is satisfied. If the gearing unit does not react correctly, φ_{car} is violated. Yet, an alternative strategy for the acceleration unit that accelerates at a different point in time at which the gearing unit reacts correctly, satisfies φ_{car}. Thus, neither a compositional approach using winning strategies, nor one using dominant strategies, is able to synthesize strategies for the components of the self-driving car.

However, the lack of a dominant strategy for the acceleration unit is only due to the uncertainty whether the gearing unit will comply with the acceleration strategy. The only dominant strategy for the gearing unit is to react correctly to the change of speed. Hence, providing this knowledge to the acceleration unit by synthesizing the strategy for the gearing unit beforehand and making it available, yields a dominant and even winning strategy for the acceleration unit. Thus, synthesizing the components *incrementally* instead of *compositionally* allows for separate strategies even if there is a dependency between the components.

3 Preliminaries

LTL. Linear-time temporal logic (LTL) is a specification language for linear-time properties. Let Σ be a finite set of atomic propositions and let $a \in \Sigma$. The syntax of LTL is given by $\varphi, \psi :: = a \mid \neg\varphi \mid \varphi \vee \psi \mid \varphi \wedge \psi \mid \bigcirc\varphi \mid \varphi\, \mathcal{U}\, \psi \mid \varphi\, \mathcal{W}\, \psi$. We define the abbreviations $true := a \vee \neg a$, $false := \neg true$, $\Diamond\varphi = true\, \mathcal{U}\, \varphi$, and $\Box\varphi = \neg\Diamond\neg\varphi$ as usual and use the standard semantics. The language $\mathcal{L}(\varphi)$ of a formula φ is the set of infinite words that satisfy φ.

Automata. Given a finite alphabet Σ, a universal co-Büchi automaton is a tuple $\mathcal{A} = (Q, q_0, \delta, F)$, where Q is a finite set of states, $q_0 \in Q$ is the initial state, $\delta : Q \times 2^{\Sigma} \times Q$ is a transition relation, and $F \subseteq Q$ is a set of rejecting states. Given an infinite word $\sigma = \sigma_0\sigma_1 \cdots \in (2^{\Sigma})^{\omega}$, a run of σ on $\mathcal{A}$ is an infinite sequence $q_0 q_1 \cdots \in Q^{\omega}$ of states where $(q_i, \sigma_i, q_{i+1}) \in \delta$ holds for all $i \geq 0$. A run is called accepting if it contains only finitely many rejecting states. $\mathcal{A}$ accepts a word σ if all runs of σ on $\mathcal{A}$ are accepting. The language $\mathcal{L}(\mathcal{A})$ of $\mathcal{A}$ is the set of all accepted words. An LTL specification φ can be translated into an equivalent universal co-Büchi automaton $\mathcal{A}_{\varphi}$ with a single exponential blow up [14].

Decomposition. A decomposition is a partitioning of the system into components. A component p is defined by its input variables $inp(p) \subseteq (inp \cup out)$ and output variables $out(p) \subseteq out$ with $inp(p) \cap out(p) = \emptyset$, where inp and out are the input and output variables of the system and $V = inp \cup out$. The output variables of components are pairwise disjoint and their union is equivalent to out. The *implementation order* defines the communication interface between the components. It assigns a rank $rank_{impl}(p)$ to every component p. If $rank_{impl}(p) <$

$rank_{impl}(p')$, then p' sees the valuations of the variables in $inp(p') \cap out(p)$ one step in advance, i.e., it is able to directly react to them, modeling knowledge about these variables in the whole system. The implementation order is not necessarily total.

Strategies. A strategy is a function $s : (2^{inp(p)})^* \to 2^{out(p)}$ that maps a history of inputs of a component p to outputs. We model strategies as Moore machines $\mathcal{T} = (T, t_0, \tau, o)$ with a finite set of states T, an initial state t_0, a transition function $\tau : T \times 2^{inp(p)} \to T$, and an output function $o : T \to 2^{out(p)}$ that is is independent of the input. Given an input sequence $\gamma = \gamma_0 \gamma_1 \ldots \in (2^{V \setminus out(p)})^\omega$, $\mathcal{T}$ produces a path $\pi = (t_0, \gamma_0 \cup o(t_0, \gamma_0))(t_1, \gamma_1 \cup o(t_1, \gamma_1)) \ldots \in (T \times 2^V)^\omega$, where $\tau(t_j, i_j) = t_{j+1}$. The projection of a path to the variables is called trace. The trace produced by $\mathcal{T}$ on γ is called the computation of strategy s represented by $\mathcal{T}$ on γ, denoted $comp(s, \gamma)$. A strategy s is *winning* for φ if $comp(s, \gamma) \models \varphi$ for all $\gamma \in (2^{inp})^\omega$. A strategy s is *dominated* by a strategy t for φ if for all $\gamma \in (2^{V \setminus out(p)})^\omega$ with $comp(s, \gamma) \models \varphi$, $comp(t, \gamma) \models \varphi$ holds as well. A strategy is *dominant* if it dominates every other strategy. A specification φ is called *admissible* if there exists a dominant strategy for φ.

Bounded Synthesis. Given a specification, synthesis derives an implementation that is correct by construction. Bounded synthesis [10] additionally requires a bound $b \in \mathbb{N}$ on the size of the implementation as input. It produces size-optimal strategies. The search for a strategy satisfying the specification is encoded into a constraint system. If it is unsatisfiable, then the specification is unrealizable for the given size bound. Otherwise, the solution defines a winning strategy. There exist SMT [10] as well as SAT, QBF, and DQBF [5] encodings.

4   Synthesis of Dominant Strategies

In our incremental synthesis approach, we seek for dominant strategies, rather than for winning ones. To synthesize dominant strategies, we construct a universal co-Büchi automaton $\mathcal{A}_\varphi^{dom}$ for a specification φ that accepts exactly the computations of dominant strategies following the ideas in [3,4]. As for the universal co-Büchi automaton $\mathcal{A}_\varphi$ with $\mathcal{L}(\mathcal{A}_\varphi) = \mathcal{L}(\varphi)$, the size of $\mathcal{A}_\varphi^{dom}$ is exponential in the length of φ [4]. In bounded synthesis, the automaton $\mathcal{A}_\varphi^{dom}$ is then used instead of $\mathcal{A}_\varphi$ to derive dominant strategies.

Since we synthesize independent components compositionally, dominance of the parallel composition of dominant strategies is crucial for both soundness and completeness. Yet, in contrast to winning strategies, the parallel composition of dominant strategies is not guaranteed to be dominant in general. Consider a system with components p_1 and p_2 that send each other messages m_1 and m_2, and the specification $\varphi = \Diamond m_1 \wedge \Diamond m_2$. For p_1, it is dominant to wait for m_2 before sending m_1 since this strategy only violates $\Diamond m_1$ if $\Diamond m_2$ is violated as well. Analogously, it is dominant for p_2 to wait for m_1 before sending m_2. The parallel composition of these strategies, however, never sends any message.

It violates φ in every situation while there are strategies that are winning for φ. Nevertheless, dominant s strategies are compositional for safety specifications:

Theorem 1 ([4]). *Let φ be a safety property and let s_1 and s_2 be strategies for components p_1 and p_2. If s_1 is dominant for φ and p_1 and s_2 is dominant for φ and p_2, then the parallel composition $s_1 \| s_2$ is dominant for φ and $p_1 \| p_2$.*

We extend this result to specifications where only a single component affects the liveness part. Intuitively, then a violation of the liveness part can always be lead back to the single component affecting it, contradicting the assumption that its strategy is dominant.

Theorem 2. *Let φ be a property where only output variables of component p_1 affect the liveness part of φ, and let s_1 and s_2 be two strategies for components p_1 and p_2, respectively. If s_1 is dominant for φ and p_1 and s_2 is dominant for φ and p_2, then the parallel composition $s_1 \| s_2$ is dominant for φ and $p_1 \| p_2$.*

To lift compositional synthesis to real-world settings where strategies have to rely on the fact that other components will not maliciously violate the specification, we circumvent the need for the existence dominant strategies for every component in the following sections: We model the assumption that other components behave in a dominant fashion by synthesizing strategies incrementally.

5   Incremental Synthesis

In this section, we introduce a synthesis algorithm based on dominant strategies, where, in contrast to compositional synthesis, the components are not necessarily synthesized independently but one after another. The strategies that are already synthesized provide further information to the one under consideration.

For the self-driving car from Sect. 2, for instance, there is no dominant strategy for the acceleration unit. However, when provided with a dominant gearing strategy, there is even a winning strategy for the acceleration unit. Therefore, synthesizing strategies for the components incrementally, rather than compositionally, allows us to synthesize a strategy for the self-driving car.

The incremental synthesis algorithm is described in Algorithm 1. Besides a specification φ, it expects an array of arrays of components that are ordered by the *synthesis order* $<_{syn}$ as input. The synthesis order assigns a rank $rank_{syn}(p_i)$ to every component p_i. Strategies for components with lower ranks are synthesized before strategies for components with higher ranks. Strategies for components with the same rank are synthesized compositionally. Thus, to guarantee soundness, the synthesis order has to ensure that either φ is a safety property, or that at most one of these components affects the liveness part of φ.

First, we synthesize dominant strategies $s_1, \ldots, s_i$ for the components with the lowest rank in the synthesis order. Then, we synthesize dominant strategies $s_{i+1}, \ldots, s_j$ for the components with the next rank *under the assumption* of the parallel composition of $s_1, \ldots, s_i$, denoted $s_1 \| \ldots \| s_i$. Particularly, we seek for

---

Algorithm 1: Incremental Synthesis

Input: specification φ, array C of arrays of k components ordered by $<_{syn}$
Output: strategies $s_1, \ldots, s_k$ such that $s_1 \,||\, \ldots \,||\, s_k$ is dominant for φ
array[k] strategies
strategy assumedStrategies
for $i = 1$ **to** $C.length()$ **by** 1 **do**
    strategy addForLayer
    for $j = 1$ **to** $C[i].length()$ **by** 1 **do**
        synthesize strategy s for $C[i][j]$ such that (assumedStrategies $||$ s) is
        dominant for φ
        int component $= C[i][j].getLabel()$
        strategies[component] $= s$
        addForLayer $=$ addForLayer $||$ s
    assumedStrategies $=$ assumedStrategies $||$ addForLayer

---

strategies such that $s_1 \,||\, \ldots \,||\, s_i \,||\, s_{i+\ell}$ is dominant for φ and $p_1 \,||\, \ldots \,||\, p_i \,||\, p_{i+\ell}$, where $1 \leq \ell \leq j - i$. We continue until strategies for all components have been synthesized. The soundness follows directly from the construction of the algorithm as well as Theorems 1 to 2.

Theorem 3 (Soundness). *Let φ be a specification and let $s_1, \ldots, s_k$ be the strategies produced by the incremental synthesis algorithm. Then $s_1 \,||\, \ldots \,||\, s_k$ is dominant for φ. If φ is realizable, then $s_1 \,||\, \ldots \,||\, s_k$ is winning.*

The success of incremental synthesis relies heavily on the choice of components. Clearly, it succeeds if compositional synthesis does. Otherwise, the synthesis order has to guarantee admissibility of every component when provided with the strategies of components with a lower rank. In this regard, it is crucial that the parallel composition of the components with the same rank is dominant. Thus, we introduce techniques for component selection inducing a synthesis order that ensure completeness of incremental synthesis in the following sections.

6   Semantic Component Selection

The component selection algorithm introduced in this section is based on dependencies between the output variables of the system. It directly induces a synthesis order ensuring completeness of incremental synthesis.

We require specifications to be of the form $(\varphi_1^A \wedge \cdots \wedge \varphi_n^A) \rightarrow (\varphi_1^G \wedge \cdots \wedge \varphi_m^G)$, where the conjuncts are conjunction-free in negation normal form. When seeking for dominant strategies, assumptions can be treated as conjuncts as long as the system is not able to satisfy the specification by violating the assumptions. Since it is a modeling flaw if the assumptions can be violated by the system, we assume specifications to be of the form $(\varphi_1^A \wedge \cdots \wedge \varphi_n^A) \wedge (\varphi_1^G \wedge \cdots \wedge \varphi_m^G)$ in the following.

First, we introduce an algorithm for component selection that ensures completeness of incremental synthesis in the absence of input variables. Afterwards, we extend it to achieve completeness in general. The algorithm identifies equivalence classes of variables based on dependencies between them. These equivalence classes then build the components. Intuitively, a variable u depends on the current or future valuation of a variable v if changing the valuation of u yields a violation of the specification φ that can be fixed by changing the valuation of v at the same point in time or at a strictly later point in time, respectively. The change of the valuation of v needs to be necessary for the satisfaction of φ in the sense that not changing it would not yield a satisfaction of φ.

Definition 1 (Minimal Satisfying Changeset). *Let φ be a specification, let $\gamma \in (2^{inp})^\omega$, $\pi \in (2^{out})^\omega$ be sequences such that $\gamma \cup \pi \not\models \varphi$, let $u \in out$ and let i be a position. For sets $P \subseteq out \setminus \{u\}$, $F \subseteq out$, let $\Pi^{P,F}$ be the set of output sequences $\pi^{P,F} \in (2^{out})^\omega$ such that $\pi_j^{P,F} = \pi_j$ for all $j < i$ and*

$$- \ \forall v \in P. \ v \in \pi_i^{P,F} \leftrightarrow v \notin \pi_i \ and \ \forall v \in V \setminus P. \ v \in \pi_i^{P,F} \leftrightarrow v \in \pi_i, \ and$$
$$- \ \forall v \in F. \ \exists j > i. \ v \in \pi_j^{P,F} \leftrightarrow v \notin \pi_j \ and \ \forall v \in V \setminus F. \ \forall j > i. \ v \in \pi_j^{P,F} \leftrightarrow v \in \pi_j.$$

If there is a sequence $\pi^{P,F} \in \Pi^{P,F}$, such that $\gamma \cup \pi^{P,F} \models \varphi$ and for all $P' \subset P$, $F' \subset F$, we have $\gamma \cup \pi^{P',F'} \not\models \varphi$ for all $\pi^{P',F'} \in \Pi^{P',F'}$, then (P,F) is called minimal satisfying changeset *with respect to φ, γ, π, i.*

Definition 2 (Semantic Dependencies). *Let φ be a specification and $u \in out$. Let $\eta, \eta' \in (2^V)^*$ be sequences of length $i + 1$ such that $u \in \eta_i' \leftrightarrow u \notin \eta_i$, $\forall v \in V \setminus \{u\}. v \in \eta_i' \leftrightarrow v \in \eta_i$, and $\forall j < i. \eta_j' = \eta_j$. If there are $\gamma \in (2^{inp})^\omega$, $_\gamma\pi \in (2^{out})^\omega$ with $\gamma_0 \ldots \gamma_i = \eta \cap inp$, $_\gamma\pi_0 \ldots _\gamma\pi_i = \eta \cap out$, and $\gamma \cup _\gamma\pi \models \varphi$, then*

- *u depends on (P,F) for $P \subseteq out \setminus \{u\}$, $F \subseteq out$ if there is $_\gamma\pi' \in (2^{out})^\omega$ with $_\gamma\pi_0' \ldots _\gamma\pi_i' = \eta' \cap out$ and $_\gamma\pi_j = _\gamma\pi_j'$ for all $j > i$ such that $\gamma \cup _\gamma\pi' \not\models \varphi$ and (P,F) is a minimal satisfying changeset w.r.t. φ, γ, $_\gamma\pi'$, i. We say that u depends semantically on the current or future valuation of v, if there are P, F such that u depends on (P,F) and $v \in P$ or $v \in F$, respectively.*
- *u depends on the input, if for all $_\gamma\pi'' \in (2^{out})^\omega$ with $_\gamma\pi_0'' \ldots _\gamma\pi_i'' = \eta' \cap out$, we have $\gamma \cup _\gamma\pi'' \not\models \varphi$, while there are $\gamma' \in (2^{inp})^\omega$, $_{\gamma'}\pi'' \in (2^{out})^\omega$ with $\gamma_0' \ldots \gamma_i' = \eta \cap inp$ and $_{\gamma'}\pi_0'' \ldots _{\gamma'}\pi_i'' = \eta' \cap out$ such that $\gamma' \cup _{\gamma'}\pi'' \models \varphi$.*

The specification of the self-driving car induces, for instance, a present dependency from acc to dec: Let $\gamma = \emptyset^\omega$, $\eta = \{gear_1, dec\}$, $\eta' = \{gear_1, dec, acc\}$. For $_\gamma\pi = \{gear_1, dec\}\{gear_2\}^\omega$, $\gamma \cup _\gamma\pi$ clearly satisfies φ_{car}. In contrast, for $_\gamma\pi' = \{gear_1, dec, acc\}\{gear_2\}^\omega$, $\gamma \cup _\gamma\pi' \not\models \varphi_{car}$ since mutual exclusion of acc and dec is violated. For $P = \{dec\}$, $F = \emptyset$, (P,F) is a minimal satisfying changeset w.r.t. φ, γ, $_\gamma\pi'$, i. Thus, acc depends on the current valuation of dec.

If a variable u depends on the future valuation of some variable v, a strategy for u most likely has to predict the future, preventing the existence of a dominant strategy for u. In our setting, strategies cannot react directly to an input. Thus, present dependencies may prevent admissibility as well. Yet, the implementation order resolves a present dependency from u to v if $rank_{impl}(v) < rank_{impl}(u)$: Then, the valuation of v is known to u one step in advance and thus a strategy for u does not have to predict the future. Hence, if u neither depends on the input, nor on the future valuation of some $v \in out$, nor on its current valuation if $rank_{impl}(u) \leq rank_{impl}(v)$, then the specification is admissible for u.

To show this formally, we construct a dominant strategy for u. It maximizes the set of input sequences for which there is an output sequence that satisfies the specification. In general, this strategy is not dominant since these output sequences may not be computable by a strategy. Yet, this can only be the case if a strategy needs to predict the valuations of variables outside its control and this need is exactly what is captured by semantic present and future dependencies.

Theorem 4. *Let φ be a specification and let $O \subseteq out$. If for all $u \in O$, u neither depends semantically on the future valuation of v, nor on the current valuation of v if $rank_{impl}(u) \leq rank_{impl}(v)$ for all $v \in V \setminus O$, nor on the input, then φ is admissible for the component p with $out(p) = O$.*

We build a dependency graph in order to identify the components of the system. The vertices represent the variables and edges denote semantic dependencies between them. Formally, the *Semantic Dependency Graph* $\mathcal{D}_{\varphi}^{sem} = (V_{\varphi}, E_{\varphi}^{sem})$ of φ is given by $V_{\varphi} = V$ and $E_{\varphi}^{sem} = E_{\varphi,p}^{sem} \cup E_{\varphi,f}^{sem} \cup E_{\varphi,i}^{sem}$, where $(u, v) \in E_{\varphi,p}^{sem}$ if u depends on the current valuation of $v \in out$, $(u, v) \in E_{\varphi,f}^{sem}$ if u depends on the future valuation of $v \in out$, and $(u, v) \in E_{\varphi,i}^{sem}$ if u depends on $v \in inp$.

To identify the components, we proceed in three steps. First, we eliminate vertices representing input variables since they are not part of the components. Second, we resolve present dependencies. Since future dependencies subsume present ones, we remove (u, v) from $E_{\varphi,p}^{sem}$ if $(u, v) \in E_{\varphi,f}^{sem}$. Then, we resolve present dependencies by refining the implementation order: If $(u, v) \in E_{\varphi,p}^{sem}$, we add $rank_{impl}(v) < rank_{impl}(u)$ and remove (u, v) from $E_{\varphi,p}^{sem}$. This is only possible if the implementation order does not become contradictory. In particular, at most one present dependency between u and v can be resolved in this way. Third, we identify the strongly connected components $\mathcal{C} := \{C_1, \ldots, C_k\}$ of $\mathcal{D}_{\varphi}^{sem}$. They define the decomposition of the system: We obtain k components $p_1, \ldots, p_k$ with $out(p_i) = C_i$ for $1 \leq i \leq k$. Thus, the number of strongly connected components should be maximized when resolving present dependencies in step two.

The dependency graph induces the *synthesis order*: Let $\mathcal{C}^i \subseteq \mathcal{C}$ be the set of strongly connected components that do not have any direct predecessor when removing $\mathcal{C}^0 \cup \cdots \cup \mathcal{C}^{i-1}$ from $\mathcal{D}_{\varphi}^{sem}$. For all $C_n \in \mathcal{C}^0$, $rank_{syn}(p_n) = 1$. For $C_n \in \mathcal{C}^i$, $C_m \in \mathcal{C}^j$, $rank_{syn}(p_n) < rank_{syn}(p_m)$ if $i > j$ and $rank_{syn}(p_n) > rank_{syn}(p_m)$ if $i < j$. If $i = j$, $rank_{syn}(p_n) = rank_{syn}(p_m)$ if φ is a safety property or only one of the components affects the liveness part of φ. Otherwise, choose an ordering, i.e., either $rank_{syn}(p_n) < rank_{syn}(p_m)$ or $rank_{syn}(p_m) < rank_{syn}(p_n)$.

For the specification of the self-driving car, we obtain the semantic dependency graph shown in Fig. 1a. It induces three components p_1, p_2, p_3 with $out(p_1) = \{gear_1\}$, $out(p_2) = \{gear_2\}$, and $out(p_3) = \{acc, dec, keep\}$. When adding $rank_{impl}(gear_2) < rank_{impl}(gear_1)$ to the implementation order, we obtain $rank_{syn}(p_1) < rank_{syn}(p_2) < rank_{syn}(p_3)$ and thus $p_1 <_{syn} p_2 <_{syn} p_3$.

Incremental synthesis with the semantic component selection algorithm is complete for specifications that do not contain dependencies to input variables:

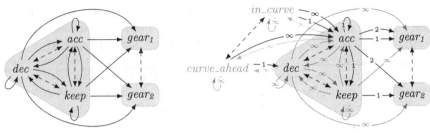

(a) Semantic Dependency Graph   (b) Syntactic Dependency Graph

Fig. 1. Semantic and Syntactic Dependency Graphs for the self-driving car. Dashed edges denote present dependencies, solid ones future dependencies. Gray boxes denote induced components. In (b), blue edges are obtained by transitivity, orange ones by derivation, and green ones by transitivity after derivation. For the sake of readability, not all transitive and derived edges are displayed. (Color figure online)

By construction, a component $p \in \mathcal{C}^0$ has no unresolved semantic dependencies to variables outside of p. Thus, by Theorem 4, φ is admissible. Moreover, by the incremental synthesis algorithm as well as Theorems 1 to 2, for every component $p \in \mathcal{C}^i$, the parallel composition of the strategies of components p' with $rank_{syn}(p') < rank_{syn}(p)$ is dominant. Thus, by construction, there is a dominant strategy for $\mathcal{C}^0 \cup \cdots \cup \mathcal{C}^i$ as well.

Lemma 1. *Let φ be a specification. If for all $u \in out$, u does not depend semantically on the input, then incremental synthesis yields strategies for all components and the synthesis order induced by the component selection algorithm.*

Since semantic dependencies to input variables cannot be resolved, admissibility is not guaranteed in general. Yet, if the specification is realizable, admissibility of completely independent components follows: If p does not depend on the input, admissibility of φ follows directly with Lemma 1. Otherwise, φ can only be non-admissible for p if a strategy has to predict the valuation of an input variable. Since p is completely independent of other components, a different valuation of an output variable outside of p cannot affect the need to predict input variables. But then a strategy for the whole system has to predict inputs as well, yielding a contradiction.

Theorem 5. *Let φ be a specification, let p be a component such that for all p', $rank_{syn}(p') \leq rank_{syn}(p)$, and for all $u \in out(p)$, u neither depends semantically on the future valuation of $v \in out \setminus out(p)$, nor on its current valuation if $rank_{impl}(u) \leq rank_{impl}(v)$. If φ is realizable, then φ is admissible for p.*

Thus, when encountering a component for which φ is not admissible in incremental synthesis, we can directly deduce non-realizability of φ if there is no component with a higher rank in the synthesis order. Yet, this does not hold in general. Consider $\varphi = a \vee ((\bigcirc b) \leftrightarrow (\bigcirc \bigcirc i))$, where i is an input variable and both a and b are output variables. Since a depends on b while b does not depend on a, a strategy for b has to be synthesized first. Yet, there is no dominant strategy for b since it has to predict the future valuation of i, while there is a dominant strategy for the whole system, namely the one that sets a in the first step.

Thus, we combine a component for which φ is not admissible with a direct successor in the synthesis order until either φ is admissible or only a single component is left. With this extension, the completeness of incremental synthesis follows directly from Lemma 1 and Theorem 5.

Theorem 6 (Completeness). *Let φ be a specification. If φ is realizable, incremental synthesis yields strategies for all components and the synthesis order induced by the extended semantic component selection algorithm.*

7 Syntactic Analysis

While analyzing semantic dependencies for component selection ensures completeness of incremental synthesis, computing the dependencies is hard. In particular, the semantic definition of dependencies is a hyperproperty [2], i.e., a property relating multiple execution traces, with quantifier alternation. To determine the present and future dependencies between variables more efficiently, we introduce a dependency definition based on the syntax of the LTL formula.

Definition 3 (Syntactic Dependencies). *Let φ be an LTL formula in negation normal form. Let $\mathcal{T}(\varphi)$ be the syntax tree of φ, where $\Box\Diamond$ is considered to be a separate operator. Let q be a node of $\mathcal{T}(\varphi)$ with child q', if q is a unary operator, and left child q' and right child q'', if q is a binary operator. We assign a set $D_q \in 2^{2^{V \times \mathbb{N} \times \mathbb{B}}}$ to each node q of $\mathcal{T}(\varphi)$ as follows:*

- *if q is a leaf, then $q = u \in V$ and $D_q = \{\{(u, 0, \mathit{false})\}\}$,*
- *if $q = \neg$, then $D_q = D_{q'}$,*
- *if $q = \wedge$, then $D_q = D_{q'} \cup D_{q''}$,*
- *if $q = \vee$, then $D_q = \bigcup_{M \in D_{q'}} \bigcup_{M' \in D_{q''}} \{M \cup M'\}$,*
- *if $q = \bigcirc$, then $D_q = \bigcup_{M \in D_{q'}} \{\{(u, x+1, y) \mid (u, x, y) \in M\}\}$,*
- *if $q = \Box$, then $D_q = D_{q'} \cup \bigcup_{M \in D_{q'}} \{\{(u, x, \mathit{true})\} \mid (u, x, y) \in M\}$,*
- *if $q = \Diamond$, then $D_q = D_{q'} \cup \left\{\bigcup_{M \in D_{q'}} \{(u, x, \mathit{true}), (u, x, \mathit{false}) \mid (u, x, y) \in M\}\right\}$*
- *if $q = \Box\Diamond$, then $D_q = \bigcup_{M \in D_{q'}} \{\{(u, x, \mathit{true})\} \mid (u, x, y) \in M\}$,*
- *if $q = \mathcal{U}$ or $q = \mathcal{W}$, then*

$$D_q = \bigcup_{M \in D_{q'}} \bigcup_{M' \in D_{q''}} \{M \cup M'\}$$
$$\cup \bigcup_{M \in D_{q'}} \bigcup_{M' \in D_{q''}} \bigcup_{(u,x,y) \in M} \{\{(u, x, \mathit{true})\} \cup M'\}$$
$$\cup \left\{\bigcup_{M' \in D_{q''}} \{(u, x, \mathit{true}), (u, x, \mathit{false}) \mid (u, x, y) \in M'\}\right\}$$

Let q be the root node of $T(\varphi)$ and let $(u, x, y), (v, x', y') \in M$ for some $M \in D_q$, $u, v \in V$, $x, x' \in \mathbb{N}$, and $y, y' \in \mathbb{B}$ with $(u, x, y) \neq (v, x', y')$. Then u depends syntactically on the current valuation of v, if $u \neq v$ and either $y = y' = false$ and $x = x'$, or $y = true$ and $y' = false$ and $x \leq x'$, or $y = false$ and $y' = true$ and $x \geq x'$, or $y = y' = true$. Furthermore, u depends syntactically on the future valuation of v, if either $y' = true$, or $y' = false$ and $x < x'$. The offset of the future dependency is ∞ in the former case and $x' - x$ in the latter case.

For (u, x, y), x denotes the number of $\bigcirc$-operators under which u occurs and y denotes whether u occurs under an unbounded temporal operator. Since the specification is in negation normal form, negation only occurs in front of variables and thus does not influence the dependencies. Disjunction introduces dependencies between the disjuncts ψ and ψ' since the satisfaction of ψ affects the need of satisfaction of ψ' and vice versa. A conjunct, however, has to be satisfied irrespective of other conjuncts and thus conjunction does not introduce dependencies. Analogously, $\Diamond \psi$ introduces future dependencies between the variables in ψ, while $\Box \psi$ does not. Adding triples with both *true* and *false* is necessary for the $\Diamond$-operator in order to obtain future dependencies from a variable to itself also if ψ contains only a single variable, e.g., for $\Diamond u$. For $\psi \mathcal{U} \psi'$ and $\psi \mathcal{W} \psi'$, there are dependencies between ψ and ψ' as well as future dependencies between the variables in ψ' analogously to disjunction and the $\Diamond$-operator. Furthermore, there are future dependencies from ψ' to ψ since whether or not ψ is satisfied in the future affects the need of satisfaction of ψ' in the current step. The $\Box\Diamond$-operator takes a special position. Although including $\Diamond$, changing the valuation of a variable at a single position does not yield a violation of $\Box\Diamond \psi$ and thus there is no semantic dependency. Hence, $\Box\Diamond \psi$ does not introduce syntactic dependencies between the variables in ψ either.

For the specification of the self-driving car from Sect. 2, we annotate, for instance, node q representing the $\Box$-operator of the conjunct $\Box \neg(acc \wedge dec)$ with $D_q = \{\{(acc, 0, false), (dec, 0, false)\}, \{(acc, 0, true)\}, \{(dec, 0, true)\}\}$, yielding a syntactic present dependency from acc to dec and vice versa. For the node q representing the $\Box$-operator of $\Box((acc \wedge \bigcirc acc) \rightarrow \bigcirc\bigcirc gear_1)$, we obtain amongst others $\{(acc, 0, false), (acc, 1, false), (gear_1, 2, false)\} \in D_q$, yielding future dependencies from acc to acc with offset 1 and to $gear_1$ with offsets 1 and 2.

As long as semantic dependencies do not range over several conjuncts, every semantic dependency is captured by a syntactic one as well: If there is a semantic dependency from u to v and if φ does not contain any conjunction, u and v occur in the same set $M \in D_q$, where q is the root node of $T(\varphi)$, by construction. With structural induction on φ, it thus follows that every semantic dependency has a syntactic counterpart.

Lemma 2. *Let φ be an LTL formula in negation normal form that does not contain any conjunction. Let $u, v \in V$ be variables. If u depends semantically on* *the current or future valuation of v, then u depends syntactically on the current or future valuation of v, respectively, as well.*

Yet, the above definition of syntactic dependencies does not capture all semantic dependencies in general. Particularly, semantic dependencies ranging over several conjuncts cannot be detected. To capture all dependencies, we build the *syntactic dependency graph* analogously to the semantic one, additionally annotating future dependency edges with their offsets. We build the *transitive closure* over output variables: Let $u, v \in out$ and let there be $u_1, \ldots, u_j \in out$ for some $j \geq 1$ with $(u, u_1) \in E_{\varphi}^{syn}$, $(u_j, v) \in E_{\varphi}^{syn}$, and $(u_i, u_{i+1}) \in E_{\varphi}^{syn}$ for all $1 \leq i < j$. If all these edges are present dependency edges, then $(u, v) \in E_{\varphi,p}^{syn}$. Otherwise, $(u, v) \in E_{\varphi,f}^{syn}$. If there are connecting edges for u and v containing a future dependency cycle, the offset of the transitive edge is ∞. Otherwise, it is the sum of the offsets of the connecting edges. To capture the synergy of dependencies, let $u, v, w \in V$ be variables with $u, w \in out$ and $u \neq v$ or $u \neq w$. Let $(u, w) \in E_{\varphi,f}^{syn}$ with offset x and $(v, w) \in E_{\varphi,f}^{syn}$ with offset y. If $x \neq \infty$ and $y \neq \infty$, then, if $x = y$, add (u, v) and (v, u) to $E_{\varphi,p}^{syn}$, and if $x < y$ or $x > y$, add (v, u) or (u, v) to $E_{\varphi,f}^{syn}$ with offset $y - x$ or $x - y$, respectively. If $x = \infty$, add both $(u, v), (v, u)$ to $E_{\varphi,p}^{syn}$ and $E_{\varphi,f}^{syn}$ with offset ∞. Build the transitive closure again.

The resulting syntactic dependency graph for the self-driving car is shown in Fig. 1b. Unlike the semantic one, it contains outgoing dependencies from input variables. While such dependencies are not relevant for component selection and thus are not defined in the semantic algorithm, they are needed to derive dependencies *to* input variables with the syntactic technique.

After the derivation of further dependencies in the dependency graph, every semantic dependency has a syntactic counterpart, even if it ranges over several conjuncts. Intuitively, the derivation of a minimal satisfying changeset for a semantic dependency induces several separate semantic present and future dependencies that only affect single conjuncts of the specification. With Lemma 2, the claim follows by induction on the number of these separate dependencies.

Theorem 7. *Let φ be an LTL formula and let $u, v \in out$. If $(u, v) \in E_{\varphi,p}^{sem}$, then $(u, v) \in E_{\varphi,p}^{syn}$. If $(u, v) \in E_{\varphi,f}^{sem}$, then $(u, v) \in E_{\varphi,f}^{syn}$. If u depends semantically on the input, then there are variables $w \in out$, $w' \in inp$ such that $(w, w') \in E_{\varphi}^{syn}$.*

Thus, since semantic dependencies have a syntactic counterpart, completeness of incremental synthesis using syntactic dependency analysis for selecting components follows directly with Theorem 6. However, the syntactic analysis is a conservative overapproximation of the semantic dependencies. This can be easily seen when comparing the semantic and syntactic dependency graphs for the self-driving car shown in Fig. 1. For instance, there is a syntactic future dependency from *acc* to *in_curve* while there is no such semantic dependency. In particular, the derivation rules are blamable for the overapproximation.

8   Specification Simplification

In this section, we identify conjuncts that are not relevant for the component p under consideration to reduce the size of the specification. In general, leaving out conjuncts is not sound since the missing conjuncts may invalidate admissibility of the specification [4]. However, non-admissible components cannot become admissible by leaving out conjuncts that do not refer to output variables of p:

Theorem 8 ([4])**.** *Let φ be an LTL formula over $V \setminus out(p)$ and let ψ be an LTL formula over V. If ψ is admissible, then $\varphi \wedge \psi$ is admissible as well.*

Yet, an admissible component may become non-admissible. For instance, consider the specification $\varphi = \Box(a \leftrightarrow \bigcirc i) \wedge \Box i$, where i is an input variable and a is an output variable. While always outputting a is a dominant strategy for φ, leaving out $\Box i$ yields non-admissibility of φ since a dominant strategy for a needs to predict i. A conjunct that does not contain variables on which the component under consideration depends, however, can be eliminated since its satisfaction does not influence the admissibility of the specification for p:

Theorem 9. *Let φ be an LTL formula such that $\varphi = \psi \wedge \psi'$, where ψ is an LTL formula over $V' \subseteq V \setminus out(p)$ not containing assumption conjuncts and ψ' is an LTL formula over V. If for all $u \in out(p)$ and $v \in out \setminus out(p)$, u neither depends on the future valuation of v, nor on the present valuation of v if $rank_{impl}(u) \leq rank_{impl}(v)$, and if φ is realizable for the whole system, then ψ' is admissible for p if, and only if, φ is admissible for p.*

If ψ' is admissible, admissibility of φ follows since the truth value of ψ is solely determined by the input of p. Otherwise, a strategy for p has to predict the input. Since p is independent of all other components, φ can only be realizable if ψ restricts the input behavior, contradicting the assumption that it does not contain assumption conjuncts. This directly leads to the following observation:

Corollary 1. *Let $\varphi = \psi \wedge \psi'$ be an LTL formula inducing two components p, p' with $rank_{syn}(p) = rank_{syn}(p')$ for either the semantic or the syntactic technique, where ψ and ψ' range over $V \setminus out(p')$ and $V \setminus out(p)$, respectively. If φ is realizable, then there are winning strategies for p and p' for ψ and ψ', respectively.*

Moreover, in incremental synthesis the strategies of components with a lower rank in the synthesis order are provided to the component p under consideration. Hence, if these strategies are winning for a conjunct, it may be eliminated from the specification for p since its satisfaction is already guaranteed.

Theorem 10. *Let φ, ψ be LTL formulas over V. Let s' be the parallel composition of the strategies for the components p_i with $rank_{syn}(p_i) < rank_{syn}(p)$. If s' is winning for φ, then there is a strategy s such that $s' \parallel s$ is dominant for ψ if, and only if, there is a strategy s such that $s' \parallel s$ is dominant for $\varphi \wedge \psi$.*

Table 1. Experimental results on scalable benchmarks. Reported is the parameter and the time in seconds. We used a machine with a 3.1 GHz Dual-Core Intel Core i5 processor and 16 GB of RAM, and a timeout of 60 min.

Benchmark	Parameter	BoSy	Incremental Synthesis
n-ary Latch	2	**2.61**	4.76
	3	**3.66**	6.58
	4	11.55	**8.74**
	5	TO	**10.98**
	...	...	...
	1104	TO	**3599.04**
Generalized Buffer	1	37.04	**5.08**
	2	TO	**6.21**
	3	TO	**66.03**
Sensors	2	**1.99**	6.08
	3	**2.31**	8.79
	4	**6.99**	11.73
	5	92.79	**16.99**
	6	TO	**43.50**
	7	TO	**2293.85**
Robot Fleet	2	**2.49**	6.25
	3	TO	**10.51**
	4	TO	**269.09**

9   Experimental Results

We implemented a prototype of the incremental synthesis algorithm. It expects an LTL specification as well as a decomposition of the system and a synthesis order as input. Our prototype extends the state-of-the-art synthesis tool BoSy [6] to the synthesis of dominant strategies. Furthermore, it converts the synthesized strategy from the AIGER-circuit produced by our extension of BoSy to an equivalent LTL formula that is added to the specification of the next component.

We compare our prototype to BoSy on four scalable benchmarks. The results are presented in Table 1. The first two benchmarks stem from the reactive synthesis competition (SYNTCOMP 2018) [11]. The latch is parameterized in the number of bits and the Generalized Buffer in the number of receivers. For the n-ary latch, both the semantic and the syntactic component selection algorithms identify n separate components, one for each bit of the latch. For the Generalized Buffer, both techniques identify two components, one for the communication with the senders and one for the communication with the receivers. After simplifying the specification using Theorem 9, we are able to synthesize separate winning strategies for the components for both benchmarks, making use of Corollary 1. The incremental synthesis approach clearly outperforms BoSy's classical bounded synthesis approach for the Generalized Buffer in all cases. For the n-ary latch, the advantage becomes clear from $n = 4$ on.

Furthermore, we consider a benchmark describing n sensors and a managing unit that requests and collects sensor data. The semantic component selection technique identifies n separate components for the sensors as well as a component for the managing unit that depends on the other components. For this decomposition, the incremental synthesis approach outperforms BoSy for $n \geq 5$. The syntactic technique, however, does not identify the separability of the sensors from the managing unit due to the overapproximation in the derivation rules.

Lastly, we consider a benchmark describing a fleet of n robots that must not collide with a further robot crossing their way. Both the semantic and the syntactic technique identify n separate components for the robots in the fleet as well as a component for the further robot depending on the former components. Our prototype outperforms BoSy from $n \geq 3$ on. It still terminates in less than 5 min when BoSy is not able to synthesize a strategy within 60 min.

10   Conclusions

We have presented an incremental synthesis algorithm that reduces the complexity of synthesis by decomposing large systems. Furthermore, it is, unlike compositional approaches, applicable if the components depend on the strategies of other components. We have introduced two techniques to select the components, one based on a semantic dependency analysis of the output variables and one based on a syntactic analysis of the specification. Both induce a synthesis order that guarantees soundness and completeness of incremental synthesis. Moreover, we have presented rules for reducing the size of the specification for the components. We have implemented a prototype of the algorithm and compared it to a state-of-the-art synthesis tool. Our experiments clearly demonstrates the advantage of incremental synthesis over classical synthesis for large systems. The prototype uses a bounded synthesis approach. However, the incremental synthesis algorithm applies to other synthesis approaches, e.g., explicit approaches as implemented in the state-of-the-art tool Strix [15], as well if they are extended with the possibility of synthesizing dominant strategies.

References

1. Baier, C., Klein, J., Klüppelholz, S.: A compositional framework for controller synthesis. In: Katoen, J.-P., König, B. (eds.) CONCUR 2011. LNCS, vol. 6901, pp. 512–527. Springer, Heidelberg (2011). https://doi.org/10.1007/978-3-642-23217-6_34

2. Clarkson, M.R., Schneider, F.B.: Hyperproperties. J. Comput. Secur. 18(6), 1157–1210 (2010). https://doi.org/10.3233/JCS-2009-0393

3. Damm, W., Finkbeiner, B.: Does it pay to extend the perimeter of a world model? In: Butler, M., Schulte, W. (eds.) FM 2011. LNCS, vol. 6664, pp. 12–26. Springer, Heidelberg (2011). https://doi.org/10.1007/978-3-642-21437-0_4

4. Damm, W., Finkbeiner, B.: Automatic compositional synthesis of distributed systems. In: Jones, C., Pihlajasaari, P., Sun, J. (eds.) FM 2014. LNCS, vol. 8442, pp. 179–193. Springer, Cham (2014). https://doi.org/10.1007/978-3-319-06410-9_13

5. Faymonville, P., Finkbeiner, B., Rabe, M.N., Tentrup, L.: Encodings of bounded synthesis. In: Legay, A., Margaria, T. (eds.) TACAS 2017. LNCS, vol. 10205, pp. 354–370. Springer, Heidelberg (2017). https://doi.org/10.1007/978-3-662-54577-5_20

6. Faymonville, P., Finkbeiner, B., Tentrup, L.: BoSy: an experimentation framework for bounded synthesis. In: Majumdar, R., Kunčak, V. (eds.) CAV 2017. LNCS, vol. 10427, pp. 325–332. Springer, Cham (2017). https://doi.org/10.1007/978-3-319-63390-9_17

7. Filiot, E., Jin, N., Raskin, J.-F.: Compositional algorithms for LTL synthesis. In: Bouajjani, A., Chin, W.-N. (eds.) ATVA 2010. LNCS, vol. 6252, pp. 112–127. Springer, Heidelberg (2010). https://doi.org/10.1007/978-3-642-15643-4_10

8. Finkbeiner, B., Passing, N.: Dependency-based compositional synthesis (Full Version). CoRR abs/2007.06941 (2020)

9. Finkbeiner, B., Schewe, S.: Semi-automatic distributed synthesis. In: Peled, D.A., Tsay, Y.-K. (eds.) ATVA 2005. LNCS, vol. 3707, pp. 263–277. Springer, Heidelberg (2005). https://doi.org/10.1007/11562948_21

10. Finkbeiner, B., Schewe, S.: Bounded synthesis. STTT (2013). https://doi.org/10.1007/s10009-012-0228-z

11. Jacobs, S., et al.: The 5th reactive synthesis competition (SYNTCOMP 2018): benchmarks, participants & results. CoRR abs/1904.07736 (2019)

12. Kugler, H., Segall, I.: Compositional synthesis of reactive systems from live sequence chart specifications. In: Kowalewski, S., Philippou, A. (eds.) TACAS 2009. LNCS, vol. 5505, pp. 77–91. Springer, Heidelberg (2009). https://doi.org/10.1007/978-3-642-00768-2_9

13. Kupferman, O., Piterman, N., Vardi, M.Y.: Safraless compositional synthesis. In: Ball, T., Jones, R.B. (eds.) CAV 2006. LNCS, vol. 4144, pp. 31–44. Springer, Heidelberg (2006). https://doi.org/10.1007/11817963_6

14. Kupferman, O., Vardi, M.Y.: Safraless Decision Procedures. In: Proceedings of FOCS (2005). https://doi.org/10.1109/SFCS.2005.66

15. Meyer, P.J., Sickert, S., Luttenberger, M.: Strix: explicit reactive synthesis strikes back!. In: Chockler, H., Weissenbacher, G. (eds.) CAV 2018. LNCS, vol. 10981, pp. 578–586. Springer, Cham (2018). https://doi.org/10.1007/978-3-319-96145-3_31

16. de Roever, W.-P., Langmaack, H., Pnueli, A. (eds.): COMPOS 1997. LNCS, vol. 1536. Springer, Heidelberg (1998). https://doi.org/10.1007/3-540-49213-5

Randomization and Probabilistic Systems

Proving Non-inclusion of Büchi Automata Based on Monte Carlo Sampling

Yong Li[1], Andrea Turrini[1,3], Xuechao Sun[1,2], and Lijun Zhang[1,2,3(✉)]

[1] State Key Laboratory of Computer Science,
Institute of Software, Chinese Academy of Sciences, Beijing, China
zhanglj@ios.ac.cn
[2] University of Chinese Academy of Sciences, Beijing, China
[3] Institute of Intelligent Software, Guangzhou, China

Abstract. The search for a proof of correctness and the search for counterexamples (bugs) are complementary aspects of verification. In order to maximize the practical use of verification tools it is better to pursue them at the same time. While this is well-understood in the termination analysis of programs, this is not the case for the language inclusion analysis of Büchi automata, where research mainly focused on improving algorithms for proving language inclusion, with the search for counterexamples left to the expensive complementation operation.

In this paper, we present IMC^2, a specific algorithm for proving Büchi automata non-inclusion $\mathcal{L}(\mathcal{A}) \not\subseteq \mathcal{L}(\mathcal{B})$, based on Grosu and Smolka's algorithm MC^2 developed for Monte Carlo model checking against LTL formulas. The algorithm we propose takes $M = \lceil \ln \delta / \ln(1 - \varepsilon) \rceil$ random lasso-shaped samples from $\mathcal{A}$ to decide whether to reject the hypothesis $\mathcal{L}(\mathcal{A}) \not\subseteq \mathcal{L}(\mathcal{B})$, for given error probability ε and confidence level $1 - \delta$. With such a number of samples, IMC^2 ensures that the probability of witnessing $\mathcal{L}(\mathcal{A}) \not\subseteq \mathcal{L}(\mathcal{B})$ via further sampling is less than δ, under the assumption that the probability of finding a lasso counterexample is larger than ε. Extensive experimental evaluation shows that IMC^2 is a fast and reliable way to find counterexamples to Büchi automata inclusion.

1 Introduction

The language inclusion checking of Büchi automata is a fundamental problem in the field of automated verification. Specially, in the automata-based model checking [25] framework, when both system and specification are given as Büchi automata, the model checking problem of verifying whether some system's behavior violates the specification reduces to a language inclusion problem between the corresponding Büchi automata.

This work has been supported by the Guangdong Science and Technology Department (grant no. 2018B010107004) and by the National Natural Science Foundation of China (grant nos. 61761136011, 61532019, and 61836005).

© Springer Nature Switzerland AG 2020
D. V. Hung and O. Sokolsky (Eds.): ATVA 2020, LNCS 12302, pp. 467–483, 2020.
https://doi.org/10.1007/978-3-030-59152-6_26

In this paper, we target at the language inclusion checking problem of Büchi automata. Since this problem has already been proved to be PSPACE-complete [18], researchers have been focusing on devising algorithms to reduce its practical cost. A naïve approach to checking the inclusion between Büchi automata $\mathcal{A}$ and $\mathcal{B}$ is to first construct a complement automaton $\mathcal{B}^c$ such that $\mathcal{L}(\mathcal{B}^c) = \Sigma^\omega \setminus \mathcal{L}(\mathcal{B})$ and then to check the language emptiness of $\mathcal{L}(\mathcal{A}) \cap \mathcal{L}(\mathcal{B}^c)$, which is the algorithm implemented in SPOT [11], a highly optimized symbolic tool for manipulating LTL formulas and ω-automata.

The bottleneck of this approach is computing the automaton $\mathcal{B}^c$, which can be exponentially larger than $\mathcal{B}$ [26]. As a result, various optimizations—such as *subsumption* and *simulation*—have been proposed to avoid exploring the whole state-space of $\mathcal{B}^c$, see, e.g., [1,2,9,10,13,14]. For instance, RABIT is currently the state-of-the-art tool for checking language inclusion between Büchi automata, which has integrated the simulation and subsumption techniques proposed in [1,2,9]. All these techniques improving the language inclusion checking, however, focus on *proving* inclusion. In particular, the simulation techniques in [9,13] are specialized algorithms mainly proposed to obtain such proof, which ensures that for every initial state q_a of $\mathcal{A}$, there is an initial state q_b of $\mathcal{B}$ that simulates every possible behavior from q_a.

From a practical point of view, it is widely believed that the witness of a counterexample (or bug) found by a verification tool is equally valuable as a proof for the correctness of a program; we would argue that showing why a program violates the specification is also intuitive for a programmer, since it gives a clear way to identify and correct the error. Thus, the search for a proof and the search for counterexamples (bugs) are complementary activities that need to be pursued at the same time in order to maximize the practical use of verification tools. This is well-understood in the termination analysis of programs, as the techniques for searching the proof of the termination [6,7,20] and the counterexamples [12,16,21] are evolving concurrently. Counterexamples to Büchi automata language inclusion, instead, are the byproducts of a failure while proving language inclusion. Such a failure may be recognized after a considerable amount of efforts has been spent on proving inclusion, in particular when the proposed improvements are not effective. In this work, instead, we focus directly on the problem of finding a counterexample to language inclusion.

The main contribution is a novel algorithm called IMC^2 for showing language non-inclusion based on sampling and statistical hypothesis testing. Our algorithm is inspired by the Monte Carlo approach proposed in [15] for model checking systems against LTL specifications. The algorithm proposed in [15] takes as input a Büchi automaton $\mathcal{A}$ as system and an LTL formula φ as specification and then checks whether $\mathcal{A} \not\models \varphi$ by equivalently checking $\mathcal{L}(\mathcal{A}) \not\subseteq \mathcal{L}(\mathcal{B}_\varphi)$, where $\mathcal{B}_\varphi$ is the Büchi automaton constructed for φ. The main idea of the algorithm for showing $\mathcal{L}(\mathcal{A}) \not\subseteq \mathcal{L}(\mathcal{B}_\varphi)$ is to sample lasso words from the product automaton $\mathcal{A} \times \mathcal{B}_\varphi^c$ for $\mathcal{L}(\mathcal{A}) \cap \mathcal{L}(\mathcal{B}_\varphi^c)$; lasso words are of the form uv^ω and are obtained as soon as a state is visited twice. If one of such lasso words is accepted by $\mathcal{A} \times \mathcal{B}_\varphi^c$, then it is surely a witness to $\mathcal{L}(\mathcal{A}) \not\subseteq \mathcal{L}(\mathcal{B}_\varphi)$, i.e., a counterexample to $\mathcal{A} \models \varphi$.

Since in [15] the algorithm gets an LTL formula φ as input, the construction of $\mathcal{B}_{\varphi}^{c}$ reduces to the construction of $\mathcal{B}_{\neg\varphi}$ and it is widely assumed that the translation into a Büchi automaton is equally efficient for a formula and its negation. In this paper, we consider the general case, namely the specification is given as a generic Büchi automaton $\mathcal{B}$, where the construction of $\mathcal{B}^{c}$ from $\mathcal{B}$ can be very expensive [26].

To avoid the heavy generation of $\mathcal{B}^{c}$, the algorithm IMC^{2} we propose directly sampling lasso words in $\mathcal{A}$, without making the product $\mathcal{A} \times \mathcal{B}^{c}$. We show that usual lasso words, like the ones used in [15], do not suffice in our case, and propose a rather intriguing sampling procedure. We allow the lasso word uv^{ω} to visit each state of $\mathcal{A}$ multiple times, i.e., the run σ of $\mathcal{A}$ on the finite word uv can present small cycles on both the u and the v part of the lasso word. We achieve this by setting a bound K on the number of times a state can be visited: each state in σ is visited at most $K - 1$ times, except for the last state of σ that is visited at most K times. We show that IMC^{2} gives a probabilistic guarantee in terms of finding a counterexample to inclusion when K is sufficiently large, as described in Theorem 4. This notion of generalized lasso allows our approach to find counterexamples that are not valid lassos in the usual sense. The extensive experimental evaluation shows that our approach is generally very fast and reliable in finding counterexamples to language inclusion. In particular, the prototype tool we developed is able to manage easily Büchi automata with very large state space and alphabet on which the state-of-the-art tools such as RABIT and SPOT fail. This makes our approach fit very well among tools that make use of Büchi automata language inclusion tests, since it can quickly provide counterexamples before having to rely on the possibly time and resource consuming structural methods, in case an absolute guarantee about the result of the inclusion test is desired.

Organization of the Paper. In the remainder of this paper, we briefly recall some known results about Büchi automata in Sect. 2. We then present the algorithm IMC^{2} in Sect. 3 and give the experimental results in Sect. 4 before concluding the paper with some remark in Sect. 5.

All missing proofs can be found in the report [23].

2   Preliminaries

Büchi Automata. Let Σ be a finite set of *letters* called *alphabet*. A finite sequence of letters is called a *word*. An infinite sequence of letters is called an ω-*word*. We use $|\alpha|$ to denote the length of the finite word α and we use λ to represent the empty word, i.e., the word of length 0. The set of all finite words on Σ is denoted by Σ^{*}, and the set of all ω-words is denoted by Σ^{ω}. Moreover, we also denote by Σ^{+} the set $\Sigma^{*} \setminus \{\lambda\}$.

A *nondeterministic Büchi automaton* (NBA) is a tuple $\mathcal{B} = (\Sigma, Q, Q_{I}, \mathrm{T}, Q_{F})$, consisting of a finite *alphabet* Σ of input letters, a finite set Q of *states* with a non-empty set $Q_{I} \subseteq Q$ of *initial states*, a set $\mathrm{T} \subseteq Q \times \Sigma \times Q$ of *transitions*, and a set $Q_{F} \subseteq Q$ of *accepting states*.

A *run* of an NBA $\mathcal{B}$ over an ω-word $\alpha = a_0a_1a_2\cdots \in \Sigma^\omega$ is an infinite alternation of states and letters $\rho = q_0a_0q_1a_1q_2\cdots \in (Q\times\Sigma)^\omega$ such that $q_0\in Q_I$ and, for each $i\geq 0$, $\big(\rho(i),a_i,\rho(i+1)\big)\in \mathrm{T}$ where $\rho(i) = q_i$. A run ρ is *accepting* if it contains infinitely many accepting states, i.e., $\mathrm{Inf}(\rho)\cap Q_F\neq\emptyset$, where $\mathrm{Inf}(\rho) = \{q\in Q\mid \forall i\in\mathbb{N}.\exists j > i : \rho(j) = q\}$. An ω-word α is *accepted* by $\mathcal{B}$ if $\mathcal{B}$ has an accepting run on α, and the set of words $\mathcal{L}(\mathcal{B}) = \{\alpha\in\Sigma^\omega\mid \alpha \text{ is accepted by } \mathcal{B}\}$ accepted by $\mathcal{B}$ is called its *language*.

We call a subset of Σ^ω an ω-*language* and the language of an NBA an ω-*regular language*. Words of the form uv^ω are called *ultimately periodic* words. We use a pair of finite words (u,v) to denote the ultimately periodic word $w = uv^\omega$. We also call (u,v) a *decomposition* of w. For an ω-language L, let $\mathrm{UP}(L) = \{uv^\omega\in L\mid u\in\Sigma^*, v\in\Sigma^+\}$ be the set of all ultimately periodic words in L. The set of ultimately periodic words can be seen as the fingerprint of L:

Theorem 1 (Ultimately Periodic Words [8]). *Let L, L' be two ω-regular languages. Then $L = L'$ if, and only if, $\mathrm{UP}(L) = \mathrm{UP}(L')$.*

An immediate consequence of Theorem 1 is that, for any two ω-regular languages L_1 and L_2, if $L_1\neq L_2$ then there is an ultimately periodic word $xy^\omega\in\big(\mathrm{UP}(L_1)\setminus\mathrm{UP}(L_2)\big)\cup\big(\mathrm{UP}(L_2)\setminus\mathrm{UP}(L_1)\big)$. It follows that $xy^\omega\in L_1\setminus L_2$ or $xy^\omega\in L_2\setminus L_1$. Let $\mathcal{A}, \mathcal{B}$ be two NBAs and assume that $\mathcal{L}(\mathcal{A})\setminus\mathcal{L}(\mathcal{B})\neq\emptyset$. One can find an ultimately periodic word $xy^\omega\in\mathcal{L}(\mathcal{A})\setminus\mathcal{L}(\mathcal{B})$ as a counterexample to $\mathcal{L}(\mathcal{A})\subseteq\mathcal{L}(\mathcal{B})$.

Language inclusion between NBAs can be reduced to *complementation*, *intersection*, and *emptiness* problems on NBAs. The complementation operation of an NBA $\mathcal{B}$ is to construct an NBA $\mathcal{B}^c$ accepting the complement language of $\mathcal{L}(\mathcal{B})$, i.e., $\mathcal{L}(\mathcal{B}^c) = \Sigma^\omega\setminus\mathcal{L}(\mathcal{B})$.

Lemma 1 (cf. [17,19]). *Let $\mathcal{A}, \mathcal{B}$ be NBAs with n_a and n_b states, respectively.*

1. *It is possible to construct an NBA $\mathcal{B}^c$ such that $\mathcal{L}(\mathcal{B}^c) = \Sigma^\omega\setminus\mathcal{L}(\mathcal{B})$ whose number of states is at most $(2n_b+2)^{n_b}\times 2^{n_b}$, by means of the complement construction.*
2. *It is possible to construct an NBA $\mathcal{C}$ such that $\mathcal{L}(\mathcal{C}) = \mathcal{L}(\mathcal{A})\cap\mathcal{L}(\mathcal{B}^c)$ whose number of states is at most $2\times n_a\times(2n_b+2)^{n_b}\times 2^{n_b}$, by means of the product construction. Note that $\mathcal{L}(\mathcal{A})\subseteq\mathcal{L}(\mathcal{B})$ holds if and only if $\mathcal{L}(\mathcal{C}) = \emptyset$ holds.*
3. *$\mathcal{L}(\mathcal{C}) = \emptyset$ is decidable in time linear in the number of states of $\mathcal{C}$.*

Further, testing whether an ω-word w is accepted by a Büchi automaton $\mathcal{B}$ can be done in time polynomial in the size of the decomposition (u,v) of $w = uv^\omega$.

Lemma 2 (cf. [17]). *Let $\mathcal{B}$ be an NBA with n states and an ultimately periodic word (u,v) with $|u| + |v| = m$. Then checking whether uv^ω is accepted by $\mathcal{B}$ is decidable in time and space linear in $n\times m$.*

Random Sampling and Hypothesis Testing. Statistical hypothesis testing is a statistical method to assign a confidence level to the correctness of the interpretation given to a small set of data sampled from a population, when this interpretation is extended to the whole population.

Let Z be a Bernoulli random variable and X the random variable with parameter p_Z whose value is the number of independent trials required until we see that $Z = 1$. Let δ be the *significance level* that $Z = 1$ will not appear within N trials. Then $N = \lceil \ln \delta / \ln(1 - p_Z) \rceil$ is the number of attempts needed to get a counterexample with probability at most $1 - \delta$.

If the exact value of p_Z is unknown, given an *error probability* ε such that $p_Z \geq \varepsilon$, we have that $M = \lceil \ln \delta / \ln(1 - \varepsilon) \rceil \geq N = \lceil \ln \delta / \ln(1 - p_Z) \rceil$ ensures that $p_Z \geq \varepsilon \implies \Pr[X \leq M] \geq 1 - \delta$. In other words, M is the minimal number of attempts required to find a counterexample with probability $1 - \delta$, under the assumption that $p_Z \geq \varepsilon$. See, e.g., [15,27] for more details about statistical hypothesis testing in the context of formal verification.

3 Monte Carlo Sampling for Non-inclusion Testing

In this section we present our Monte Carlo sampling algorithm IMC^2 for testing non-inclusion between Büchi automata.

3.1 MC^2: Monte Carlo Sampling for LTL Model Checking

In [15], the authors proposed a Monte Carlo sampling algorithm MC^2 for verifying whether a given system A satisfies a Linear Temporal Logic (LTL) specification φ. MC^2 works directly on the product Büchi automaton $\mathcal{P}$ that accepts the language $\mathcal{L}(A) \cap \mathcal{L}(\mathcal{B}_{\neg \varphi})$. It essentially checks whether $\mathcal{L}(\mathcal{P})$ is empty.

First, MC^2 takes two statistical parameters ε and σ as input and computes the number of samples M for this experiment. Since every ultimately periodic word $xy^\omega \in \mathcal{L}(\mathcal{P})$ corresponds to some cycle run (or "lasso") in $\mathcal{P}$, MC^2 can just find *an accepting lasso* whose corresponding ultimately periodic word xy^ω is such that $xy^\omega \in \mathcal{L}(\mathcal{P})$. In each sampling procedure, MC^2 starts from a randomly chosen initial state and performs a random walk on $\mathcal{P}$'s transition graph until a state has been visited twice, which consequently gives a lasso in $\mathcal{P}$. MC^2 then checks whether there exists an accepting state in the repeated part of the sampled lasso. If so, MC^2 reports it as a counterexample to the verification, otherwise it continues with another sampling process if necessary. The correctness of MC^2 is straightforward, as the product automaton $\mathcal{P}$ is non-empty if and only if there is an accepting lasso.

3.2 The Lasso Construction Fails for Language Inclusion

The Monte Carlo Sampling algorithm in [15] operates directly on the product. For language inclusion, as discussed in the introduction, this is the bottleneck of the construction. Thus, we aim at a sampling algorithm operating on the automata A and B, separately. With this in mind, we show first that, directly applying MC^2 can be incomplete for language inclusion checking.

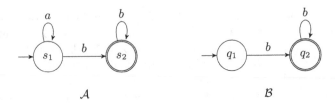

Fig. 1. Two NBAs $\mathcal{A}$ and $\mathcal{B}$.

Example 1. Consider checking the language inclusion of the Büchi automata $\mathcal{A}$ and $\mathcal{B}$ in Fig. 1. As we want to exploit MC^2 to find a counterexample to the inclusion, we need to sample a word from $\mathcal{A}$ that is accepted by $\mathcal{A}$ but not accepted by $\mathcal{B}$. In [15], the sampling procedure is terminated as soon as a state is visited twice. Thus, the set of lassos that can be sampled by MC^2 is $\{s_1as_1, s_1bs_2bs_2\}$, which yields the set of words $\{a^\omega, b^\omega\}$. It is easy to see that neither of these two words is a counterexample to the inclusion. The inclusion, however, does not hold: the word $ab^\omega \in \mathcal{L}(\mathcal{A}) \setminus \mathcal{L}(\mathcal{B})$ is a counterexample.   ◊

According to Theorem 1, if $\mathcal{L}(\mathcal{A}) \setminus \mathcal{L}(\mathcal{B}) \neq \emptyset$, then there must be an ultimately periodic word $xy^\omega \in \mathcal{L}(\mathcal{A}) \setminus \mathcal{L}(\mathcal{B})$ as a counterexample to the inclusion. It follows that there exists some lasso in $\mathcal{A}$ whose corresponding ultimately periodic word is a counterexample to the inclusion. The *limit of* MC^2 *in checking the inclusion* is that MC^2 only samples simple lasso runs, which may miss non-trivial lassos in $\mathcal{A}$ that correspond to counterexamples to the inclusion. The reason that it is sufficient for checking non-emptiness in the product automaton is due to the fact that the product automaton already synchronizes behaviors of $\mathcal{A}$ and $\mathcal{B}_{\neg\varphi}$.

In the remainder of this section, we shall propose a new definition of lassos by allowing multiple occurrences of states, which is the key point of our extension.

3.3   IMC^2: Monte Carlo Sampling for Inclusion Checking

We now present our Monte Carlo sampling algorithm called IMC^2 specialized for testing the language inclusion between two given NBAs $\mathcal{A}$ and $\mathcal{B}$.

We first define the lassos of $\mathcal{A}$ in Definition 1 and show how to compute the probability of a sample lasso in Definition 2. Then we prove that with our definition of the lasso probability space in $\mathcal{A}$, the probability of a sample lasso whose corresponding ultimately periodic word xy^ω is a counterexample to the inclusion is greater than 0 under the hypothesis $\mathcal{L}(\mathcal{A}) \not\subseteq \mathcal{L}(\mathcal{B})$. Thus we eventually get for sure a sample from $\mathcal{A}$ that is a counterexample to the inclusion, if inclusion does not hold. In other words, we are able to obtain a counterexample to the inclusion with high probability from a large amount of samples.

In practice, a lasso of $\mathcal{A}$ is sampled via a random walk on $\mathcal{A}$'s transition graph, starting from a randomly chosen initial state and picking uniformly one outgoing transition. In the following, we fix a natural number $K \geq 2$ unless explicitly stated otherwise and two NBAs $\mathcal{A} = (\Sigma, Q, Q_I, T, Q_F)$ and $\mathcal{B}$. We assume that each state in $\mathcal{A}$ can reach an accepting state and has at least one outgoing transition. Note that each NBA $\mathcal{A}$ with $\mathcal{L}(\mathcal{A}) \neq \emptyset$ can be pruned to satisfy such assumption; only NBAs $\mathcal{A}'$ with $\mathcal{L}(\mathcal{A}') = \emptyset$ do not satisfy the assumption, but for these automata the problem $\mathcal{L}(\mathcal{A}') \subseteq \mathcal{L}(\mathcal{B})$ is trivial.

Definition 1 (Lasso). *Given two NBAs $\mathcal{A}$, $\mathcal{B}$ and a natural $K \geq 2$, a finite run $\sigma = q_0 a_0 q_1 \cdots a_{n-1} q_n a_n q_{n+1}$ of $\mathcal{A}$ is called a K-lasso if (1) each state in $\{q_0, \ldots, q_n\}$ occurs at most $K - 1$ times in $q_0 a_0 q_1 \cdots a_{n-1} q_n$ and (2) $q_{n+1} = q_i$ for some $0 \leq i \leq n$ (thus, q_{n+1} occurs at most K times in σ). We write $\sigma \perp$ for the terminating K-lasso σ, where $\perp$ is a fresh symbol denoting termination. We denote by $S_{\mathcal{A}}^K$ the set of all terminating K-lassos for $\mathcal{A}$.*

We call $\sigma \perp \in S_{\mathcal{A}}^K$ a witness for $\mathcal{L}(\mathcal{A}) \setminus \mathcal{L}(\mathcal{B}) \neq \emptyset$ if the associated ω-word $(a_0 \cdots a_{i-1}, a_i \cdots a_n)$ is accepted by $\mathcal{A}$ but not accepted by $\mathcal{B}$.

It is worth noting that not every finite cyclic run of $\mathcal{A}$ is a valid K-lasso. Consider the NBA $\mathcal{A}$ shown in Fig. 1 for instance: the run $s_1 a s_1 b s_2 b s_2$ is not a lasso when $K = 2$ since by Definition 1 every state except the last one is allowed to occur at most $K - 1 = 1$ times; s_1 clearly violates this requirement since it occurs twice and it is not the last state of the run. The run $s_1 b s_2 b s_2$ instead is obviously a valid lasso when $K = 2$.

Remark 1. A K-lasso σ is also a K'-lasso for any $K' > K$. Moreover, a terminating K-lasso can be a witness without being an accepting run: according to Definition 1, a terminating K-lasso $\sigma \perp$ is a witness if its corresponding word uv^ω is accepted by $\mathcal{A}$ but not accepted by $\mathcal{B}$. This does not imply that σ is an accepting run, since there may be another run σ' on the same word uv^ω that is accepting.

In order to define a probability space over $S_{\mathcal{A}}^K$, we first define the probability of a terminating K-lasso of $\mathcal{A}$. We denote by $\#(\sigma, q)$ the number of occurrences of the state q in the K-lasso σ.

Definition 2 (Lasso Probability). *Given an NBA $\mathcal{A}$, a natural number $K \geq 2$, and a stopping probability $p_\perp \in (0, 1)$, the probability $\mathbf{Pr}_{p_\perp}[\sigma \perp]$ of a terminating K-lasso $\sigma \perp = q_0 a_0 \cdots q_n a_n q_{n+1} \perp \in S_{\mathcal{A}}^K$ is defined as follows:*

$$\mathbf{Pr}_{p_\perp}[\sigma \perp] = \begin{cases} \mathbf{Pr}'_{p_\perp}[\sigma] & \text{if } \#(\sigma, q_{n+1}) = K, \\ p_\perp \cdot \mathbf{Pr}'_{p_\perp}[\sigma] & \text{if } \#(\sigma, q_{n+1}) < K; \end{cases}$$

$$\mathbf{Pr}'_{p_\perp}[\sigma] = \begin{cases} \frac{1}{|Q_I|} & \text{if } \sigma = q_0; \\ \mathbf{Pr}'_{p_\perp}[\sigma'] \cdot \pi[q_l a_l q_{l+1}] & \text{if } \sigma = \sigma' a_l q_{l+1} \text{ and } \#(\sigma', q_l) = 1; \\ (1 - p_\perp) \cdot \mathbf{Pr}'_{p_\perp}[\sigma'] \cdot \pi[q_l a_l q_{l+1}] & \text{if } \sigma = \sigma' a_l q_{l+1} \text{ and } \#(\sigma', q_l) > 1, \end{cases}$$

where $\pi[qaq'] = \frac{1}{m}$ if $(q, a, q') \in \mathrm{T}$ and $|\mathrm{T}(q)| = m$, 0 otherwise.

We extend $\mathbf{Pr}_{p_\perp}$ to sets of terminating K-lassos in the natural way, i.e., for $S \subseteq S_{\mathcal{A}}^K$, $\mathbf{Pr}_{p_\perp}[S] = \sum_{\sigma \perp \in S} \mathbf{Pr}_{p_\perp}[\sigma \perp]$.

Assume that the current state of run σ is q. Intuitively, if the last state s of the run σ has been already visited at least twice but less than K times, the run σ can either terminate at s with probability $p_\perp$ or continue with probability $1 - p_\perp$ by taking uniformly one of the outgoing transitions from the state q. However, as soon as the state q has been visited K times, the run σ has to terminate.

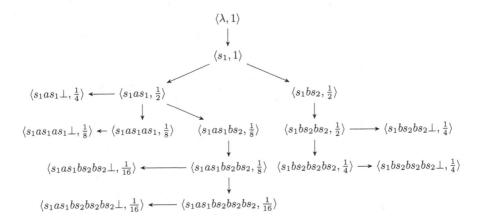

Fig. 2. An instance $\mathcal{T}$ of the trees used in the proof of Theorem 2. Each leaf node is labeled with a terminating 3-lasso $\sigma\perp \in S_{\mathcal{A},\mathcal{B}}^3$ for the NBAs $\mathcal{A}$ and $\mathcal{B}$ shown in Fig. 1, and its corresponding probability value $\mathbf{Pr}_{\frac{1}{2}}[\sigma\perp]$.

Theorem 2 (Lasso Probability Space). *Let $\mathcal{A}$ be an NBA, $K \geq 2$, and a stopping probability $p_\perp \in (0,1)$. The σ-field $(S_{\mathcal{A}}^K, 2^{S_{\mathcal{A}}^K})$ together with $\mathbf{Pr}_{p_\perp}$ defines a discrete probability space.*

Proof (sketch). The facts that $\mathbf{Pr}_{p_\perp}[\sigma]$ is a non-negative real value for each $\sigma \in S$ and that $\mathbf{Pr}_{p_\perp}[S_1 \cup S_2] = \mathbf{Pr}_{p_\perp}[S_1] + \mathbf{Pr}_{p_\perp}[S_2]$ for each $S_1, S_2 \subseteq S_{\mathcal{A}}^K$ such that $S_1 \cap S_2 = \emptyset$ are both immediate consequences of the definition of $\mathbf{Pr}_{p_\perp}$.

The interesting part of the proof is about showing that $\mathbf{Pr}_{p_\perp}[S_{\mathcal{A}}^K] = 1$. To prove this, we make use of a tree $\mathcal{T} = (N, \langle \lambda, 1 \rangle, E)$, like the one shown in Fig. 2, whose nodes are labelled with finite runs and probability values. In particular, we label the leaf nodes of $\mathcal{T}$ with the terminating K-lassos in $S_{\mathcal{A}}^K$ while we use their finite run prefixes to label the internal nodes. Formally, the tree $\mathcal{T}$ is constructed as follows. Let $P = \{\sigma' \in Q \times (\Sigma \times Q)^* \mid \sigma'$ is a prefix of some $\sigma\perp \in S_{\mathcal{A}}^K\}$ be the set of prefixes of the K-lassos in $S_{\mathcal{A}}^K$. $\mathcal{T}$'s components are defined as follows.

- $N = (P \times (0,1]) \cup (S_{\mathcal{A}}^K \times (0,1]) \cup \{\langle \lambda, 1 \rangle\}$ is the set of nodes,
- $\langle \lambda, 1 \rangle$ is the root of the tree, and

$$- \ E \subseteq \Big(\{ \langle \lambda, 1 \rangle \} \times \big(P \times (0,1] \big) \Big) \cup \Big(P \times (0,1] \Big)^2 \cup \Big(\big(P \times (0,1] \big) \times \big(S_{\mathcal{A}}^K \times (0,1] \big) \Big)$$

is the set of edges defined as

$$
\begin{aligned}
E = \ & \{ \, (\langle \lambda, 1 \rangle, \langle q, \tfrac{1}{|Q_I|} \rangle) \mid q \in Q_I \, \} \\
& \cup \{ \, (\langle \sigma, p \rangle, \langle \sigma a q, \tfrac{p}{|T(\sigma_l)|} \rangle) \mid \sigma a q \in P \wedge \#(\sigma, \sigma_l) = 1 \, \} \\
& \cup \{ \, (\langle \sigma, p \rangle, \langle \sigma a q, \tfrac{p \cdot (1 - p_\perp)}{|T(\sigma_l)|} \rangle) \mid \sigma a q \in P \wedge \#(\sigma, \sigma_l) > 1 \, \} \\
& \cup \{ \, (\langle \sigma, p \rangle, \langle \sigma \perp, p \rangle) \mid \sigma \perp \in S_{\mathcal{A}}^K \wedge \#(\sigma, \sigma_l) = K \, \} \\
& \cup \{ \, (\langle \sigma, p \rangle, \langle \sigma \perp, p \cdot p_\perp \rangle) \mid \sigma \perp \in S_{\mathcal{A}}^K \wedge \#(\sigma, \sigma_l) < K \, \}
\end{aligned}
$$

where σ_l denotes the last state s_n of the finite run $\sigma = s_0 a_0 s_1 \ldots a_{n-1} s_n$.

Then we show a correspondence between the reachable leaf nodes and the terminating K-lassos with their $\mathbf{Pr}_{p_\perp}$ probability values, and that the probability value in each internal node equals the sum of the probabilities of its children. By the finiteness of the reachable part of the tree we then derive $\mathbf{Pr}_{p_\perp}[S_{\mathcal{A}}^K] = 1$. □

Example 2 (Probability of lassos). Consider the Büchi automaton $\mathcal{A}$ of Fig. 1 and $p_\perp = \frac{1}{2}$. For $K = 2$, there are only two terminating 2-lassos, namely $s_1 a s_1 \perp$ and $s_1 b s_2 b s_2 \perp$. According to Definition 2, we know that each lasso occurs with probability $\frac{1}{2}$ and they are not witnesses since the corresponding ultimately periodic words a^ω and bb^ω do not belong to the language $\mathcal{L}(\mathcal{A}) \setminus \mathcal{L}(\mathcal{B})$. If we set $K = 2$ to check whether $\mathcal{L}(\mathcal{A}) \subseteq \mathcal{L}(\mathcal{B})$, we end up concluding that the inclusion holds with probability 1 since the probability to find some lasso of $\mathcal{A}$ related to the ω-word $ab^\omega \in \mathcal{L}(\mathcal{A}) \setminus \mathcal{L}(\mathcal{B})$ is 0. If we want to find a witness K-lasso, we need to set $K = 3$ at least, since now the terminating 3-lasso $s_1 a s_1 b s_2 b s_2 \perp$ with corresponding ω-word $abb^\omega \in \mathcal{L}(\mathcal{A}) \setminus \mathcal{L}(\mathcal{B})$ can be found with probability $\frac{1}{16} > 0$.

We remark that the Monte Carlo method proposed in [15] uses lassos that are a special instance of Definition 2 when we let $K = 2$ and $p_\perp = 1$, thus their method is not complete for NBA language inclusion checking. ◇

According to Theorem 2, the probability space of the sample terminating K-lassos in $\mathcal{A}$ can be organized in the tree, like the one shown in Fig. 2. Therefore, it is easy to see that the probability to find the witness 3-lasso $s_1 a s_1 b s_2 b s_2 \perp$ of $\mathcal{A}$ is $\frac{1}{16}$, as indicated by the leaf node $\langle s_1 a s_1 b s_2 b s_2 \perp, \frac{1}{16} \rangle$.

Definition 3 (Lasso Bernoulli Variable). *Let $K \geq 2$ be a natural number and $p_\perp$ a stopping probability. The random variable associated with the probability space $(S_{\mathcal{A}}^K, 2^{S_{\mathcal{A}}^K}, \mathbf{Pr}_{p_\perp})$ of the NBAs $\mathcal{A}$ and $\mathcal{B}$ is defined as follows: $p_Z = \mathbf{Pr}_{p_\perp}[Z = 1] = \sum_{\sigma \perp \in S_w} \mathbf{Pr}_{p_\perp}[\sigma \perp]$ and $q_Z = \mathbf{Pr}_{p_\perp}[Z = 0] = \sum_{\sigma \perp \in S_n} \mathbf{Pr}_{p_\perp}[\sigma \perp]$, where $S_w, S_n \subseteq S_{\mathcal{A}}^K$ are the set of witness and non-witness lassos, respectively.*

476   Y. Li et al.

Under the assumption $\mathcal{L}(A) \setminus \mathcal{L}(B) \neq \emptyset$, there exists some witness K-lasso $\sigma\bot \in S_w$ that can be sampled with positive probability if $\mathbf{Pr}_{p_\bot}[Z = 1] > 0$, as explained by Example 3.

Example 3. For the NBAs $\mathcal{A}$ and $\mathcal{B}$ shown in Fig. 1, $K = 3$, and $p_\bot = \frac{1}{2}$, the lasso probability space is organized as in Fig. 2. The lasso Bernoulli variable has associated probabilities $p_Z = \frac{1}{8}$ and $q_Z = \frac{7}{8}$ since the only witness lassos are $s_1 a s_1 b s_2 b s_2 \bot$ and $s_1 a s_1 b s_2 b s_2 b s_2 \bot$, both occurring with probability $\frac{1}{16}$.   ◇

Therefore, if we set $K = 3$ and $p_\bot = \frac{1}{2}$ to check the inclusion between $\mathcal{A}$ and $\mathcal{B}$ from Fig. 1, we are able to find with probability $\frac{1}{8}$ the ω-word ab^ω as a counterexample to the inclusion $\mathcal{L}(\mathcal{A}) \subseteq \mathcal{L}(\mathcal{B})$. It follows that the probability we do not find any witness 3-lasso after 50 trials would be less than 0.002, which can be made even smaller with a larger number of trials.

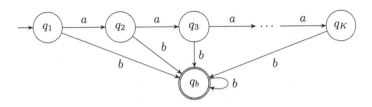

Fig. 3. NBA $\mathcal{K}_K$ making $p_Z = 0$ when checking $\mathcal{L}(\mathcal{A}) \subseteq \mathcal{L}(\mathcal{K}_K)$ by means of sampling terminating K-lassos from $\mathcal{A}$ shown in Fig. 1.

As we have seen in Example 2, the counterexample may not be sampled with positive probability if K is not sufficiently large, that is the main problem with MC^2 algorithm from [15] for checking language inclusion. The natural question is then: how large should K be for checking the inclusion? First, let us discuss about K without taking the automaton $\mathcal{B}$ into account. Consider the NBA $\mathcal{A}$ of Fig. 1: it seems that no matter how large K is, one can always construct an NBA $\mathcal{K}$ with $K+1$ states to make the probability $p_Z = 0$, as the counterexample $a^l b^\omega \in \mathcal{L}(\mathcal{A}) \setminus \mathcal{L}(\mathcal{B})$ can not be sampled for any $l \geq K$. Figure 3 depicts such NBA $\mathcal{K}$, for which we have $\mathcal{L}(K) = \{b^\omega, ab^\omega, aab^\omega, \ldots, a^{K-1}b^\omega\}$. One can easily verify that the counterexample $a^l b^\omega$ can not be sampled from $\mathcal{A}$ when $l \geq K$, as sampling this word requires the state s_1 to occur $l+1$ times in the run, that is not a valid K-lasso. This means that K is a value that depends on the size of $\mathcal{B}$. To get a K sufficiently large for every $\mathcal{A}$ and $\mathcal{B}$, one can just take the product of $\mathcal{A}$ with the complement of $\mathcal{B}$ and check how many times in the worst case a state of $\mathcal{A}$ occurs in the shortest accepting run of the product.

Lemma 3 (Sufficiently Large K). *Let $\mathcal{A}, \mathcal{B}$ be NBAs with n_a and n_b states, respectively, and Z be the random variable defined in Definition 3. Assume that $\mathcal{L}(\mathcal{A}) \setminus \mathcal{L}(\mathcal{B}) \neq \emptyset$. If $K \geq 2 \times (2n_b + 2)^{n_b} \times 2^{n_b} + 1$, then $\mathbf{Pr}_{p_\bot}[Z = 1] > 0$.*

Algorithm 1. IMC^2 Algorithm

1: **procedure** IMC^2($\mathcal{A}, \mathcal{B}, K, p_\perp, \varepsilon, \delta$)
2:     $M := \lceil \ln \delta / \ln(1 - \varepsilon) \rceil$;
3:     **for** ($i := 1; i \leq M; i++$) **do**
4:         $(u, v) := \mathsf{sample}(\mathcal{A}, K, p_\perp)$;
5:         **if** $\mathsf{membership}(\mathcal{A}, (u, v))$ **then**
6:             **if not** $\mathsf{membership}(\mathcal{B}, (u, v))$ **then**
7:                 **return** (*false*, (u, v));
8:     **return** *true*;

Remark 2. We want to stress that choosing K as given in Lemma 3 is a sufficient condition for sampling a counterexample with positive probability; choosing this value, however, is not a necessary condition. In practice, we can find counterexamples with positive probability with K being set to a value much smaller than $2 \times (2n_b + 2)^{n_b} \times 2^{n_b} + 1$, as experiments reported in Sect. 4 indicate.

Now we are ready to present our IMC^2 algorithm, given in Algorithm 1. On input the two NBAs $\mathcal{A}$ and $\mathcal{B}$, the bound K, the stopping probability $p_\perp$, and the statistical parameters ε and δ, the algorithm at line 2 first computes the number M of samples according to ε and δ. Then, for each ω-word $(u, v) = uv^\omega$ associated with a terminating lasso sampled at line 4 according to Definitions 1 and 2, it checks whether the lasso is a witness by first (line 5) verifying whether $uv^\omega \in \mathcal{L}(\mathcal{A})$, and then (line 6) whether $uv^\omega \notin \mathcal{L}(\mathcal{B})$. If the sampled lasso is indeed a witness, a counterexample to $\mathcal{L}(\mathcal{A}) \subseteq \mathcal{L}(\mathcal{B})$ has been found, so the algorithm can terminate at line 7 with the correct answer *false* and the counterexample (u, v). If none of the M sampled lassos is a witness, then the algorithm returns *true* at line 8, which indicates that hypothesis $\mathcal{L}(\mathcal{A}) \not\subseteq \mathcal{L}(\mathcal{B})$ has been rejected and $\mathcal{L}(\mathcal{A}) \subseteq \mathcal{L}(\mathcal{B})$ is assumed to hold. It follows that IMC^2 gives a probabilistic guarantee in terms of finding a counterexample to inclusion when K is sufficient large, as formalized by the following proposition.

Proposition 1. *Let $\mathcal{A}, \mathcal{B}$ be two NBAs and K be a sufficiently large number. If $\mathcal{L}(\mathcal{A}) \backslash \mathcal{L}(\mathcal{B}) \neq \emptyset$, then IMC^2 finds a counterexample to the inclusion $\mathcal{L}(\mathcal{A}) \subseteq \mathcal{L}(\mathcal{B})$ with positive probability.*

In general, the exact value of p_Z, the probability of finding a word accepted by $\mathcal{A}$ but not accepted by $\mathcal{B}$, is unknown or at least very hard to compute. Thus, we summarize our results about IMC^2 in Theorems 3 and 4 with respect to the choice of the statistical parameters ε and δ.

Theorem 3 (Correctness). *Let $\mathcal{A}, \mathcal{B}$ be two NBAs, K be a sufficiently large number, and ε and δ be statistical parameters. If IMC^2 returns false, then $\mathcal{L}(\mathcal{A}) \not\subseteq \mathcal{L}(\mathcal{B})$ is certain. Otherwise, if IMC^2 returns true, then the probability that we would continue and with probability $p_Z \geq \varepsilon$ find a counterexample is less than δ.*

Theorem 4 (Complexity). *Given two NBAs $\mathcal{A}, \mathcal{B}$ with n_a and n_b states, respectively, and statistical parameters ε and δ, let $M = \lceil \ln \delta / \ln(1 - \varepsilon) \rceil$ and $n = \max(n_a, n_b)$. Then IMC^2 runs in time $\mathcal{O}(M \cdot K \cdot n^2)$ and space $\mathcal{O}(K \cdot n^2)$.*

4   Experimental Evaluation

We have implemented the Monte Carlo sampling algorithm proposed in Sect. 3 in ROLL [22] to evaluate it. We performed our experiments on a desktop PC equipped with a 3.6 GHz Intel i7-4790 processor with 16 GB of RAM, of which 4 GB were assigned to the tool. We imposed a timeout of 300 s (5 min) for each inclusion test. In the experiments, we compare our sampling inclusion test algorithm with RABIT 2.4.5 [1,2,9] and SPOT 2.8.4 [11]. ROLL and RABIT are written in Java while SPOT is written in C/C++. This gives SPOT some advantage in the running time, since it avoids the overhead caused by the Java Virtual Machine. For RABIT we used the option -fastc while for ROLL we set parameters $\varepsilon = 0.1\%$ and $\delta = 2\%$, resulting in sampling roughly 4 000 words for testing inclusion, $p_\perp = \frac{1}{2}$, and K to the maximum of the number of states of the two automata. The automata we used in the experiment are represented in two formats: the BA format used by GOAL[1] [24] and the HOA format [4]. RABIT supports only the former, SPOT only the latter, while ROLL supports both. We used ROLL to translate between the two formats and then we compared ROLL (denoted $ROLL_H$) with SPOT on the HOA format and ROLL (denoted $ROLL_B$) with RABIT on the BA format. When we present the outcome of the experiments, we distinguish them depending on the used automata format. This allows us to take into account the possible effects of the automata representation, on both the language they represent and the running time of the tools.

Table 1. Experiment results on random automata with fixed state space and alphabet.

Tool	Included	Not included	Timeout	Memory out	Other failures
SPOT	1 803	10 177 + 53	1 780	670	1 517
$ROLL_H$	2 497(5)	10 177 + 3194	119	0	13
$ROLL_B$	2 501(45)	12 436 + 1054	0	0	9
RABIT	2 205	12 436 + 45	306	1 008	0

4.1   Experiments on Randomly Generated Büchi Automata

To run the different tools on randomly generated automata, we used SPOT to generate 50 random HOA automata for each combination of state space size $|Q| \in \{10, 20, \ldots, 90, 100, 125, \ldots, 225, 250\}$ and alphabet size $|\Sigma| \in \{2, 4, \ldots, 18, 20\}$, for a total of 8 000 automata, that we have then translated to the BA format. We then considered 100 different pairs of automata for each combination of state space size and alphabet size (say, for instance, 100 pairs of automata with 50

---

[1] GOAL is omitted in our experiments as it is shown in [9] that RABIT performs much better than GOAL.

states and 10 letters or 100 pairs with 175 states and 4 letters). The resulting 16 000 experiments are summarized in Table 1.

For each tool, we report the number of inclusion test instances that resulted in an answer for language inclusion and not inclusion, as well as the number of cases where a tool went timeout, ran out of memory, or failed for any other reason. For the "included" case, we indicate in parenthesis how many times ROLL has failed to reject the hypothesis $\mathcal{L}(\mathcal{A}) \subseteq \mathcal{L}(\mathcal{B})$, that is, ROLL returned "included" instead of the expected "not included". For the "non included" case, instead, we split the number of experiments on which multiple tools returned "not included" and the number of times only this tool returned "not included"; for instance, we have that both SPOT and $ROLL_H$ returned "not included" on 10 177 cases, that only SPOT returned so in 53 more experiments (for a total of 10 230 "not included" results), and that only $ROLL_H$ identified non inclusion in 3 194 additional experiments (for a total of 13 371 "not included" results).

We can see in Table 1 that both $ROLL_H$ and $ROLL_B$ were able to solve many more cases than their counterparts SPOT and RABIT, respectively, on both "included" and "not included" outcomes. In particular, we can see that both $ROLL_H$ and $ROLL_B$ have been able to find a counterexample to the inclusion for many cases (3 194 and 1 052, respectively) where SPOT on the HOA format and RABIT on the BA format failed, respectively.

On the other hand, there are only few cases where SPOT or RABIT proved non inclusion while ROLL failed to do so. In particular, since ROLL implements a statistical hypothesis testing algorithm for deciding language inclusion, we can expect few experiments where ROLL fails to reject the alternative hypothesis $\mathcal{L}(\mathcal{A}) \subseteq \mathcal{L}(\mathcal{B})$. In the experiments this happened 5 ($ROLL_H$) and 45 ($ROLL_B$) times; this corresponds to a failure rate of less than 0.6%, well below the choice of the statistical parameter $\delta = 2\%$.

Regarding the 13 failures of $ROLL_H$ and the 9 ones of $ROLL_B$, they are all caused by a stack overflow in the strongly connected components (SCC) decomposition procedure for checking membership $uv^\omega \in \mathcal{L}(\mathcal{A})$ or $uv^\omega \in \mathcal{L}(\mathcal{B})$ (i.e., $\mathcal{L}(\mathcal{A}) \cap \{uv^\omega\} = \emptyset$ or $\mathcal{L}(\mathcal{B}) \cap \{uv^\omega\} = \emptyset$, cf. [17]) at lines 5 and 6 of Algorithm 1, since checking whether the sampled lasso is an accepting run of $\mathcal{A}$ does not suffice (cf. Remark 1). The 119 timeouts of $ROLL_H$ occurred for 3 pairs of automata with 200 states and 20 letters, 12/21 pairs of automata with 225 states and 18/20 letters, respectively, and 40/43 pairs of automata with 250 states and 18/20 letters, respectively. We plan to investigate why $ROLL_H$ suffered of these timeouts while $ROLL_B$ avoided them, to improve ROLL's performance.

About the execution running time of the tools, they are usually rather fast in giving an answer, as we can see from the plot in Fig. 4. In this plot, we show on the y axis the total number of experiments, each one completed within the time marked on the x axis; the vertical gray line marks the timeout limit. The plot is relative to the number of "included" and "not included" outcomes combined together; the shape of the plots for the two outcomes kept separated is similar to the combined one we present in Fig. 4; the only difference is that in the "not included" case, the plots for $ROLL_B$ and $ROLL_H$ would terminate earlier,

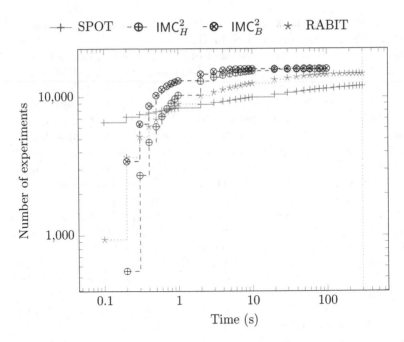

Fig. 4. Experiment running time on the random automata with fixed state space and alphabet.

since all experiments returning "not included" are completed within a smaller time than for the "included" case. As we can see, we have that ROLL rather quickly overcame the other tools in giving an answer. This is likely motivated by the fact that by using randomly generated automata, the structure-based tools such as RABIT and SPOT are not able to take advantage of the symmetries or other structural properties one can find in automata obtained from, e.g., logical formulas. From the result of the experiments presented in Table 1 and Fig. 4, we have that the use of a sampling-based algorithm is a very fast, effective, and reliable way to rule out that $\mathcal{L}(\mathcal{A}) \subseteq \mathcal{L}(\mathcal{B})$ holds. Moreover, we also conclude that IMC^2 complements existing approaches rather well, as it finds counterexamples to the language inclusion for a lot of instances that other approaches fail to manage.

4.2 Effect of the Statistical Parameters ε and δ

To analyze the effect of the choice of ε and δ on the execution of the sampling algorithm we proposed, we have randomly taken 100 pairs of automata where, for each pair $(\mathcal{A}, \mathcal{B})$, the automata $\mathcal{A}$ and $\mathcal{B}$ have the same alphabet but possibly different state space. On these 100 pairs of automata, we repeatedly ran $ROLL_H$ 10 times with different values of ε in the set $\{0.00001, 0.00051, \ldots, 0.00501\}$ and of δ in the set $\{0.0001, 0.0051, \ldots, 0.0501\}$, for a total of 121 000 inclusion tests.

The choice of ε and δ plays essentially no role in the running time for the cases where a counterexample to the language inclusion is found: the average running time is between 1.67 and 1.77 s. This can be expected, since ROLL stops its sampling procedure as soon as a counterexample is found (cf. Algorithm 1). If we consider the number of experiments, again there is almost no difference, since for all combinations of the parameters it ranges between 868 and 870.

On the other hand, ε and δ indeed affect the running time for the "included" cases, since they determine the number M of sampled words and all such words have to be sampled and tested before rejecting the "non included" hypothesis. The average running time is 1 s or less for all choices of $\varepsilon \neq 0.00001$ and δ, while for $\varepsilon = 0.00001$, the average running time ranges between 12 and 36 s when δ moves from 0.0501 to 0.0001, which corresponds to testing roughly 300 000 to 1 000 000 sample words, respectively.

4.3 Effect of the Lasso Parameters K and $p_\perp$

At last, we also experimented with different values of K and $p_\perp$ while keeping the statistical parameters unchanged: we have generated other 100 pairs of automata as in Sect. 4.2 and then checked inclusion 10 times for each pair and each combination of $K \in \{2, 3, 4, 5, 6, 8, 11, 51, 101, 301\}$ and $p_\perp \in \{0.05, 0.1, \ldots, 0.95\}$.

As one can expect, low values for $p_\perp$ and large values of K allow IMC^2 to find more counterexamples, at the cost of a higher running time. It is worth noting that $K = 2$ is still rather effective in finding counterexamples: out of the 1 000 executions on the pairs, IMC^2 returned "non included" between 906 and 910 times; for $K = 3$ it ranged between 914 and 919 for $p_\perp \leq 0.5$ and between 909 and 912 for $p_\perp > 0.5$. Larger values of K showed similar behavior. Regarding the running time, except for $K = 2$ the running time of IMC^2 is loosely dependent on the choice of K, for a given $p_\perp$; this is likely motivated by the fact that imposing e.g. $K = 51$ still allows IMC^2 to sample lassos that are for instance 4-lassos. Instead, the running time is affected by the choice of $p_\perp$ for a given $K \geq 3$: as one can expect, the smaller $p_\perp$ is, the longer IMC^2 takes to give an answer; a small $p_\perp$ makes the sampled words $uv^\omega \in \mathcal{L}(\mathcal{B}_1)$ to be longer, which in turn makes the check $uv^\omega \in \mathcal{L}(\mathcal{B}_2)$ more expensive.

Experiments suggest that taking $0.25 \leq p_\perp \leq 0.5$ and $3 \leq K \leq 11$ gives a good tradeoff between running time and number of "non included" outcomes. Very large values of K, such as $K > 50$, are usually not needed, also given the fact that usually lassos with several repetitions occur with rather low probability.

5   Conclusion and Discussion

We presented IMC^2, a sample-based algorithm for proving language non-inclusion between Büchi automata. Experimental evaluation showed that IMC^2 is very fast and reliable in finding such witnesses, by sampling them in many cases where traditional structure-based algorithms fail or take too long to complete the analysis. We believe that IMC^2 is a very good technique to disprove $\mathcal{L}(\mathcal{A}) \subseteq$

$\mathcal{L}(\mathcal{B})$ and complements well the existing techniques for checking Büchi automata language inclusion. As future work, our algorithm can be applied to scenarios like black-box testing and PAC learning [3], in which inclusion provers are either not applicable in practice or not strictly needed. A uniform word sampling algorithm was proposed in [5] for concurrent systems with multiple components. We believe that extending our sampling algorithms to concurrent systems with multiple components is worthy of study.

References

1. Abdulla, P.A., et al.: Simulation subsumption in Ramsey-based Büchi automata universality and inclusion testing. In: Touili, T., Cook, B., Jackson, P. (eds.) CAV 2010. LNCS, vol. 6174, pp. 132–147. Springer, Heidelberg (2010). https://doi.org/10.1007/978-3-642-14295-6_14
2. Abdulla, P.A., et al.: Advanced Ramsey-based Büchi automata inclusion testing. In: Katoen, J.-P., König, B. (eds.) CONCUR 2011. LNCS, vol. 6901, pp. 187–202. Springer, Heidelberg (2011). https://doi.org/10.1007/978-3-642-23217-6_13
3. Angluin, D.: Queries and concept learning. Mach. Learn. 2(4), 319–342 (1987). https://doi.org/10.1023/A:1022821128753
4. Babiak, T., et al.: The Hanoi omega-automata format. In: Kroening, D., Păsăreanu, C.S. (eds.) CAV 2015. LNCS, vol. 9206, pp. 479–486. Springer, Cham (2015). https://doi.org/10.1007/978-3-319-21690-4_31
5. Basset, N., Mairesse, J., Soria, M.: Uniform sampling for networks of automata. In: CONCUR, pp. 36:1–36:16 (2017)
6. Ben-Amram, A.M., Genaim, S.: On multiphase-linear ranking functions. In: Majumdar, R., Kunčak, V. (eds.) CAV 2017. LNCS, vol. 10427, pp. 601–620. Springer, Cham (2017). https://doi.org/10.1007/978-3-319-63390-9_32
7. Bradley, A.R., Manna, Z., Sipma, H.B.: The polyranking principle. In: Caires, L., Italiano, G.F., Monteiro, L., Palamidessi, C., Yung, M. (eds.) ICALP 2005. LNCS, vol. 3580, pp. 1349–1361. Springer, Heidelberg (2005). https://doi.org/10.1007/11523468_109
8. Büchi, J.R.: On a decision method in restricted second order arithmetic. In: Mac, L.S., Siefkes, D. (eds.) The Collected Works of J. Richard Büchi, pp. 425–435. Springer, New York (1990). https://doi.org/10.1007/978-1-4613-8928-6_23
9. Clemente, L., Mayr, R.: Efficient reduction of nondeterministic automata with application to language inclusion testing. LMCS 15(1), 12:1–12:73 (2019)
10. Doyen, L., Raskin, J.: Antichains for the automata-based approach to model-checking. LMCS 5(1) (2009)
11. Duret-Lutz, A., Lewkowicz, A., Fauchille, A., Michaud, T., Renault, É., Xu, L.: Spot 2.0—A framework for LTL and ω-automata manipulation. In: Artho, C., Legay, A., Peled, D. (eds.) ATVA 2016. LNCS, vol. 9938, pp. 122–129. Springer, Cham (2016). https://doi.org/10.1007/978-3-319-46520-3_8
12. Emmes, F., Enger, T., Giesl, J.: Proving non-looping non-termination automatically. In: Gramlich, B., Miller, D., Sattler, U. (eds.) IJCAR 2012. LNCS (LNAI), vol. 7364, pp. 225–240. Springer, Heidelberg (2012). https://doi.org/10.1007/978-3-642-31365-3_19
13. Etessami, K., Wilke, T., Schuller, R.A.: Fair simulation relations, parity games, and state space reduction for Büchi automata. SIAM J. Comput. 34(5), 1159–1175 (2005)

14. Fogarty, S., Vardi, M.Y.: Efficient Büchi universality checking. In: Esparza, J., Majumdar, R. (eds.) TACAS 2010. LNCS, vol. 6015, pp. 205–220. Springer, Heidelberg (2010). https://doi.org/10.1007/978-3-642-12002-2_17
15. Grosu, R., Smolka, S.A.: Monte Carlo model checking. In: Halbwachs, N., Zuck, L.D. (eds.) TACAS 2005. LNCS, vol. 3440, pp. 271–286. Springer, Heidelberg (2005). https://doi.org/10.1007/978-3-540-31980-1_18
16. Gupta, A., Henzinger, T.A., Majumdar, R., Rybalchenko, A., Xu, R.: Proving non-termination. In: POPL, pp. 147–158 (2008)
17. Kupferman, O.: Automata theory and model checking. Handbook of Model Checking, pp. 107–151. Springer, Cham (2018). https://doi.org/10.1007/978-3-319-10575-8_4
18. Kupferman, O., Vardi, M.Y.: Verification of fair transition systems. In: Alur, R., Henzinger, T.A. (eds.) CAV 1996. LNCS, vol. 1102, pp. 372–382. Springer, Heidelberg (1996). https://doi.org/10.1007/3-540-61474-5_84
19. Kupferman, O., Vardi, M.Y.: Weak alternating automata are not that weak. TOCL **2**(3), 408–429 (2001)
20. Leike, J., Heizmann, M.: Ranking templates for linear loops. LMCS **11**(1), 1–27 (2015)
21. Leike, J., Heizmann, M.: Geometric nontermination arguments. In: Beyer, D., Huisman, M. (eds.) TACAS 2018. LNCS, vol. 10806, pp. 266–283. Springer, Cham (2018). https://doi.org/10.1007/978-3-319-89963-3_16
22. Li, Y., Sun, X., Turrini, A., Chen, Y.-F., Xu, J.: ROLL 1.0: ω-regular language learning library. In: Vojnar, T., Zhang, L. (eds.) TACAS 2019. LNCS, vol. 11427, pp. 365–371. Springer, Cham (2019). https://doi.org/10.1007/978-3-030-17462-0_23
23. Li, Y., Turrini, A., Sun, X., Zhang, L.: Proving non-inclusion of Büchi automata based on Monte Carlo sampling. CoRR abs/2007.02282 (2020)
24. Tsai, M.-H., Tsay, Y.-K., Hwang, Y.-S.: GOAL for games, omega-automata, and logics. In: Sharygina, N., Veith, H. (eds.) CAV 2013. LNCS, vol. 8044, pp. 883–889. Springer, Heidelberg (2013). https://doi.org/10.1007/978-3-642-39799-8_62
25. Vardi, M.Y., Wolper, P.: An automata-theoretic approach to automatic program verification (preliminary report). In: LICS, pp. 332–344 (1986)
26. Yan, Q.: Lower bounds for complementation of omega-automata via the full automata technique. LMCS **4**(1) (2008)
27. Younes, H.L.S.: Planning and verification for stochastic processes with asynchronous events. Ph.D. thesis. Carnegie Mellon University (2005)

Probabilistic Hyperproperties of Markov Decision Processes

Rayna Dimitrova[1(✉)], Bernd Finkbeiner[1], and Hazem Torfah[2]

[1] CISPA Helmholtz Center for Information Security, Saarbrücken, Germany
dimitrova@cispa.de
[2] University of California at Berkeley, Berkeley, USA

Abstract. Hyperproperties are properties that describe the correctness of a system as a relation between multiple executions. Hyperproperties generalize trace properties and include information-flow security requirements, like noninterference, as well as requirements like symmetry, partial observation, robustness, and fault tolerance. We initiate the study of the specification and verification of hyperproperties of Markov decision processes (MDPs). We introduce the temporal logic *PHL (Probabilistic Hyper Logic)*, which extends classic probabilistic logics with quantification over schedulers and traces. PHL can express a wide range of hyperproperties for probabilistic systems, including both classical applications, such as probabilistic noninterference, and novel applications in areas such as robotics and planning. While the model checking problem for PHL is in general undecidable, we provide methods both for proving and for refuting formulas from a fragment of the logic. The fragment includes many probabilistic hyperproperties of interest.

1 Introduction

Ten years ago, Clarkson and Schneider coined the term *hyperproperties* [10] for the class of properties that describe the correctness of a system as a relation between multiple executions. Hyperproperties include information-flow security requirements, like noninterference [17], as well as many other types of system requirements that cannot be expressed as trace properties, including symmetry, partial observation, robustness, and fault tolerance. Over the past decade, a rich set of tools for the specification and verification of hyperproperties have been developed. HYPERLTL and HYPERCTL* [9] are extensions to LTL and CTL* that can express a wide range of hyperproperties. There are a number of algorithms and tools for hardware model checking [11,16], satisfiability checking [15], and reactive synthesis [14] for hyperproperties.

This work was partially supported by the Collaborative Research Center "Foundations of Perspicuous Software Systems" (TRR 248, 389792660), the European Research Council (ERC) Grant OSARES (No. 683300), the DARPA Assured Autonomy program, the iCyPhy center, and by Berkeley Deep Drive.

D. V. Hung and O. Sokolsky (Eds.): ATVA 2020, LNCS 12302, pp. 484–500, 2020.
https://doi.org/10.1007/978-3-030-59152-6_27

The natural next step is to consider probabilistic systems. Randomization plays a key role in the design of security-critical and distributed systems. In fact, randomization is often added specifically to implement a certain hyperproperty. For example, randomized mutual exclusion protocols use a coin flip to decide which process gets access to the critical resource in order to avoid breaking the symmetry based on the process id [4]. Databases employ privacy mechanisms based on randomizaton in order to guarantee (differential) privacy [13].

Previous work on probabilistic hyperproperties [2] has focussed on the specification and verification of probabilistic hyperproperties for Markov chains. The logic HyperPCTL [2] extends the standard probabilistic logic PCTL with quantification over states. For example, the HyperPCTL formula

$$\forall s.\forall s'. \, (init_s \wedge init_{s'}) \rightarrow \mathbb{P}(\Diamond \, terminate_s) = \mathbb{P}(\Diamond \, terminate_{s'})$$

specifies that the probability that the system terminates is the same from all initial states. If the initial state encodes some secret, then the property guarantees that this secret is not revealed through the probability of termination.

Because Markov chains lack nondeterministic choice, they are a limited modeling tool. In an open system, the secret would likely be provided by an external environment, whose decisions would need to be represented by nondeterminism. In every step of the computation, such an environment would typically set the values of some low-security and some high-security input variables. In such a case, we would like to specify that the publicly observable behavior of our system does not depend on the infinite sequence of the values of the high-security input variables. Similarly, nondeterminism is needed to model the possible strategic decisions in autonomous systems, such as robots, or the content of the database in a privacy-critical system.

In this paper, we initiate the study of hyperproperties for *Markov decision processes* (MDPs). To formalize hyperproperties in this setting, we introduce PHL, a general temporal logic for probabilistic hyperproperties. The nondeterministic choices of an MDP are resolved by a *scheduler*[1]; correspondingly, our logic quantifies over schedulers. For example, in the PHL formula

$$\forall \sigma.\forall \sigma'. \, \mathbb{P}(\Diamond \, terminate_\sigma) = \mathbb{P}(\Diamond \, terminate_{\sigma'})$$

the variables σ and σ' refer to schedulers. The formula specifies that the probability of termination is the same for all of the possible (infinite) combinations of the nondeterministic choices. If we wish to distinguish different types of inputs, for example those that are provided through a high-security variable h vs. those provided through a low-security variable l, then the quantification can be restricted to those schedulers that make the same low-security choices:

$$\forall \sigma.\forall \sigma'. \, (\forall \pi : \sigma.\forall \pi' : \sigma'. \, \Box(l_\pi \leftrightarrow l_{\pi'})) \rightarrow \mathbb{P}(\Diamond \, terminate_\sigma) = \mathbb{P}(\Diamond \, terminate_{\sigma'})$$

The path quantifier $\forall \pi : \sigma$ works analogously to the quantifiers in HYPERCTL*, here restricted to the paths of the Markov chain induced by the scheduler

---

[1] In the literature, schedulers are also known as strategies or policies.

assigned to variable σ. The formula thus states that all schedulers that agree on the low-security inputs induce the same probability of termination.

As we show in the paper, PHL is a very expressive logic, thanks to the combination of scheduler quantifiers, path quantifiers and a probabilistic operator. PHL has both classical applications, such as differential privacy, as well as novel applications in areas such as robotics and planning. For example, we can quantify the interference of the plans of different agents in a multi-agent system, such as the robots in a warehouse, or we can specify the existence of an approximately optimal policy that meets given constraints. A consequence of the generality of the logic is that it is impossible to simply reduce the model checking problem to that of a simpler temporal logic in the style of the reduction of HyperPCTL to PCTL [2]. In fact, we show that the emptiness problem for probabilistic Büchi automata (PBA) can be encoded in PHL, which implies that the model checking problem for PHL is, in general, undecidable.

We present two verification procedures that approximate the model checking problem from two sides. The first algorithm *overapproximates* the model checking problem by quantifying over a combined monolithic scheduler rather than a tuple of independent schedulers. Combined schedulers have access to more information than individual ones, meaning that the set of allowed schedulers is overapproximated. This means that if a universal formula is true for all combined schedulers it is also true for all tuples of independent schedulers. The second procedure is a bounded model checking algorithm that *underapproximates* the model checking problem by bounding the number of states of the schedulers. This algorithm is obtained as a combination of a bounded synthesis algorithm for hyperproperties, which generates the schedulers, and a model checking algorithm for Markov chains, which computes the probabilities on the Markov chains induced by the schedulers. Together, the two algorithms thus provide methods both for proving and for refuting a class of probabilistic hyperproperties for MDPs.

Related Work. Probabilistic noninterference originated in information-flow security [18,21] and is a security policy that requires that the probability of every low trace should be the same for every low equivalent initial state. Volpano and Smith [24] presented a type system for checking probabilistic noninterference of concurrent programs with probabilistic schedulers. Sabelfeld and Sands [23] defined a secure type system for multi-threaded programs with dynamic thread creation which improves on that of Volpano and Smith. None of these works is concerned with models combining probabilistic choice with nondeterminism, nor with general temporal logics for probabilistic hyperproperties.

The specification and verification of probabilistic hyperproperties have recently attracted significant attention. Abraham and Bonakdarpour [2] are the first to study a temporal logic for probabilistic hyperproperties, called Hyper-PCTL. The logic allows for explicit quantification over the states of a Markov chain, and is capable of expressing information-flow properties like probabilistic noninterference. The authors present a model checking algorithm for verifying HyperPCTL on finite-state Markov chains. HyperPCTL was extended to a logic called HyperPCTL* [25] that allows nesting of temporal and probabilistic operators, and a statistical model checking method for HyperPCTL* was proposed. Our present work, on the other hand is concerned with the specification and model checking of probabilistic hyperproperties for system models featuring both probabilistic choice and nondeterminism, which are beyond the scope of all previous temporal logics for probabilistic hyperproperties. Probabilistic logics with quantification over schedulers have been studied in [6] and [3]. However, these logics do not include quantifiers over paths.

Independently and concurrently to our work, probabilistic hyperproperties for MDPs were also studied in [1] (also presented at ATVA'20). The authors extend HYPERPCTL with quantifiers over schedulers, while our new logic PHL extends HYPERCTL* with the probabilistic operator and quantifiers over schedulers. Thus, HYPERPCTL quantifies over states (i.e., the computation trees that start from the states), while PHL quantifies over paths. Both papers show that the model checking problem is undecidable for the respective logics. The difference is in how the approaches deal with the undecidability result. For both logics, the problem is decidable when quantifiers are restricted to non-probabilistic memoryless schedulers. [1] provides an SMT-based verification procedure for HYPERPCTL for this class of schedulers. We consider general memoryful schedulers and present two methods for proving and for refuting formulas from a fragment of PHL.

Due to lack of space we have omitted the proofs of our results and details of the presented model checking procedures, which can be found in [12].

2   Preliminaries

Definition 1 (Markov Decision Process (MDP)). *A* Markov Decision Process (MDP) *is a tuple* $M = (S, Act, \mathbf{P}, \iota, \mathsf{AP}, L)$ *where* S *is a finite set of states,* Act *is a finite set of actions,* $\mathbf{P} : S \times Act \times S \to [0,1]$ *is the transition probability function such that* $\sum_{s' \in S} \mathbf{P}(s, a, s') \in \{0, 1\}$ *for every* $s \in S$ *and* $a \in Act$, $\iota : S \to [0,1]$ *is the initial distribution such that* $\sum_{s \in S} \iota(s) = 1$, AP *is a finite set of atomic propositions and* $L : S \to 2^{\mathsf{AP}}$ *is a labelling function.*

A finite path in an MDP $M = (S, Act, \mathbf{P}, \iota, \mathsf{AP}, L)$ is a sequence $s_0 s_1 \ldots s_n$ where for every $0 \leq i < n$ there exists $a_i \in Act$ such that $\mathbf{P}(s_i, a_i, s_{i+1}) > 0$. Infinite paths in M are defined analogously. We denote with $Paths_{fin}(M)$ and $Paths_{inf}(M)$ the sets of finite and infinite paths in M. For an infinite path $\rho = s_0 s_1 \ldots$ and $i \in \mathbb{N}$ we denote with $\rho[i, \infty)$ the infinite suffix $s_i s_{i+1} \ldots$. Given $s \in S$, define $Paths_{fin}(M, s) = \{s_0 s_1 \ldots s_n \in Paths_{fin}(M) \mid s_0 = s\}$, and similarly $Paths_{inf}(M, s)$. We denote with $M_s = (S, Act, \mathbf{P}, \iota_s, \mathsf{AP}, L)$ the MDP obtained from M by making s the single initial state, i.e., $\iota_s(s) = 1$ and $\iota_s(t) = 0$ for $t \neq s$.

For a set A we denote with $\mathcal{D}(A)$ the set of probability distributions on A.

Definition 2 (Scheduler). *A* scheduler *for an MDP* $M = (S, Act, \mathbf{P}, \iota, \mathsf{AP}, L)$ *is a function* $\mathfrak{S} : (S \cdot Act)^* S \to \mathcal{D}(Act)$ *such that for all sequences* $s_0 a_0 \ldots a_{n-1} s_n \in (S \cdot Act)^* S$ *it holds that if* $\mathfrak{S}(s_0 a_0 \ldots a_{n-1} s_n)(a) > 0$ *then*

$\sum_{t \in S} \mathbf{P}(s_n, a, t) > 0$, that is, each action in the support of $\mathfrak{S}(s_0 a_0 \ldots a_{n-1} s_n)$ is enabled in s_n. We define $Sched(M)$ to be the set consisting of all schedulers for an MDP M.

Given an MDP $M = (S, Act, \mathbf{P}, \iota, \mathsf{AP}, L)$ and a scheduler $\mathfrak{S}$ for M, we denote with $M_{\mathfrak{S}}$ the *Markov chain of M induced by* $\mathfrak{S}$, which is defined as the tuple $M_{\mathfrak{S}} = ((S \cdot Act)^* S, \mathbf{P}_{\mathfrak{S}}, \iota, \mathsf{AP}, L_{\mathfrak{S}})$ where for every sequence $h = s_0 a_0 \ldots a_{n-1} s_n \in (S \cdot Act)^* S$ it holds that $\mathbf{P}_{\mathfrak{S}}(h, h \cdot s_{n+1}) = \sum_{a \in Act} \mathfrak{S}(h)(a) \cdot \mathbf{P}(s_n, a, s_{n+1})$ and $L_{\mathfrak{S}}(h) = L(s_n)$. Note that $M_{\mathfrak{S}}$ is infinite even when M is finite. The different types of paths in a Markov chain are defined as for MDPs.

Of specific interest are *finite-memory* schedulers, which are schedulers that can be represented as finite-state machines. Formally, a finite-memory scheduler for M is represented as a tuple $\mathcal{T}_{\mathfrak{S}} = (Q, \delta, q_0, act)$, where Q is a finite set of states, representing the memory of the scheduler, $\delta : Q \times S \times Act \to Q$ is a memory update function, q_0 is the initial state of the memory, and $act : Q \times S \to \mathcal{D}(Act)$ is a function that based on the current memory state and the state of the MDP returns a distribution over actions. Such a representation defines a function $\mathfrak{S} : (S \cdot Act)^* S \to \mathcal{D}(Act)$ as follows. First, let us define the function $\delta^* : Q \times (S \cdot Act)^* \to Q$ as follows: $\delta^*(q, \epsilon) = q$ for all $q \in Q$, and $\delta^*(q, s_0 a_0 \ldots s_n a_n s_{n+1} a_{n+1}) = \delta(\delta^*(q, s_0 a_0 \ldots s_n a_n), s_{n+1}, a_{n+1})$ for all $q \in Q$ and all $s_0 a_0 \ldots s_n a_n s_{n+1} a_{n+1} \in (S \cdot Act)^*$. Now, we define the scheduler function represented by $\mathcal{T}_{\mathfrak{S}}$ by $\mathfrak{S}(s_0 a_0 \ldots s_n a_n s_{n+1}) = act(\delta^*(s_0 a_0 \ldots s_n a_n), s_{n+1})$.

Finite-memory schedulers induce finite Markov chains with simpler representation. A finite memory scheduler $\mathfrak{S}$ represented by $\mathcal{T}_{\mathfrak{S}} = (Q, \delta, q_0, act)$ induces the Markov chain $M_{\mathfrak{S}} = (S \times Q, \mathbf{P}_{\mathfrak{S}}, \iota_{\mathfrak{S}}, \mathsf{AP}, L_{\mathfrak{S}})$ where $\mathbf{P}_{\mathfrak{S}}((s, q), (s', q')) = \sum_{a \in Act} act(q, s)(a) \cdot \mathbf{P}(s, a, s')$ if $q' = \delta(q, s)$, otherwise $\mathbf{P}_{\mathfrak{S}}((s, q), (s', q')) = 0$, and $\iota_{\mathfrak{S}}(s, q) = \iota(s)$ if $q = q_0$ and $\iota_{\mathfrak{S}}(s, q) = 0$ otherwise.

A scheduler $\mathfrak{S}$ is *deterministic* if for every $h \in (S \cdot Act)^* S$ it holds that $\mathfrak{S}(h)(a) = 1$ for exactly one $a \in Act$. By abuse of notation, a deterministic scheduler can be represented as a function $\mathfrak{S} : S^+ \to Act$, that maps a finite sequence of states to the single action in the support of the corresponding distribution. Note that for deterministic schedulers we omit the actions from the history as they are uniquely determined by the sequence of states. We write $DetSched(M)$ for the set of deterministic schedulers for the MDP M.

A *probability space* is a triple $(\Omega, \mathcal{F}, Prob)$, where Ω is a sample space, $\mathcal{F} \subseteq 2^{\Omega}$ is a σ-algebra and $Prob : \mathcal{F} \to [0, 1]$ is a probability measure.

Given a Markov chain $C = (S, \mathbf{P}, \iota, \mathsf{AP}, L)$, it is well known how to associate a probability space $(\Omega^C, \mathcal{F}^C, Prob^C)$ with C. The sample space $\Omega^C = Paths_{inf}(C)$ is the set of infinite paths in C, where the sets of finite and infinite paths for a Markov chain are defined in the same way as for MDP. The σ-algebra $\mathcal{F}^C$ is the smallest σ-algebra that for each $\pi \in Paths_{fin}(C)$ contains the set $Cyl_C(\pi) = \{\rho \in Paths_{inf}(C) \mid \exists \rho' \in Paths_{inf}(C) : \rho = \pi \cdot \rho'\}$ called the cylinder set of the finite path π. $Prob^C$ is the unique probability measure such that for each $\pi = s_0 \ldots s_n \in Paths_{fin}(C)$ it holds that $Prob^C(Cyl(\pi)) = \iota(s_0) \cdot \prod_{i=0}^{n-1} \mathbf{P}(s_i, s_{i+1})$.

Analogously, given any state $s \in S$ we denote with $(\Omega^C, \mathcal{F}^C, Prob_s^C)$ the probability space for paths in C originating in the state s, i.e., the probability space associated with the Markov chain C_s (where C_s is defined as for MDPs).

When considering a Markov chain $M_{\mathfrak{S}}$ induced by an MDP M and a scheduler $\mathfrak{S}$, we write $Prob_{M,\mathfrak{S}}$ and $Prob_{M,\mathfrak{S},s}$ for the sake of readability.

3   The Logic PHL

In this section we define the syntax and semantics of PHL, the logic which we introduce and study in this work. PHL allows for quantification over schedulers and integrates features of temporal logics for hyper properties, such as HYPER-LTL and HYPERCTL* [9], and probabilistic temporal logics such as PCTL*.

3.1   Examples of PHL Specifications

We illustrate the expressiveness of PHL with two applications beyond information-flow security, from the domains of robotics and planning.

Example 1 (Action Cause). Consider the question whether a car on a highway that enters the opposite lane (action b) when there is a car approaching from the opposite direction (condition p) increases the probability of an accident (effect e). This can be formalized as the property stating that there exist two deterministic schedulers σ_1 and σ_2 such that (i) in σ_1 the action b is never taken when p is satisfied, (ii) the only differences between σ_1 and σ_2 can happen when σ_2 takes action b when p is satisfied, and (iii) the probability of e being true eventually is higher in the Markov chain induced by σ_2 than in the one for σ_1. To express this property in our logic, we will use *scheduler quantifiers* quantifying over the schedulers for the MDP. To capture the condition on the way the schedulers differ, we will use *path quantifiers* quantifying over the paths in the Markov chain induced by each scheduler. The atomic propositions in a PHL formula are indexed with path variables when they are interpreted on a given path, and with scheduler variables when they are interpreted in the Markov chain induced by that scheduler. Formally, we can express the property with the PHL formula

$$\exists \sigma_1 \exists \sigma_2. \, (\forall \pi_1 : \sigma_1 \forall \pi_2 : \sigma_2. \, (\Box \neg (p_{\pi_1} \wedge \bigcirc b_{\pi_1})) \wedge \psi) \wedge \mathbb{P}(\Diamond e_{\sigma_1}) < \mathbb{P}(\Diamond e_{\sigma_2}),$$

where $\psi = \left(\left(\bigwedge_{a \in Act} (\bigcirc a_{\pi_1} \leftrightarrow \bigcirc a_{\pi_2}) \right) \vee (p_{\pi_2} \wedge \bigcirc b_{\pi_2}) \right) \mathcal{W} (\bigvee_{q \in \mathsf{AP} \setminus Act} (q_{\pi_1} \not\leftrightarrow q_{\pi_2}))$.

The two conjuncts of $\forall \pi_1 : \sigma_1 \forall \pi_2 : \sigma_2. \, (\Box \neg (p_{\pi_1} \wedge \bigcirc b_{\pi_1})) \wedge \psi$ capture conditions (i) and (ii) above respectively, and $\mathbb{P}(\Diamond e_{\sigma_1}) < \mathbb{P}(\Diamond e_{\sigma_2})$ formalizes (iii). Here we assume that actions are represented in AP, i.e., $Act \subseteq \mathsf{AP}$ □

Example 2 (Plan Non-interference). Consider two robots in a warehouse, possibly attempting to reach the same location. Our goal is to determine whether all plans for the first robot to move towards the goal are robust against interferences from arbitrary plans of the other robot. That is, we want to check whether for every plan of robot 1 the probability that it reaches the goal under an arbitrary plan of robot 2 is close to that of the same plan for robot 1 executed under any other plan for robot 2. We can express this property in PHL by using *quantifiers over schedulers* to quantify over the joint deterministic plans of the robots, and using *path quantifiers* to express the condition that in both joint plans robot 1 behaves the same. Formally, we can express the property with the PHL formula

$$\forall\sigma_1\forall\sigma_2.\ (\forall\pi_1:\sigma_1\forall\pi_2:\sigma_2.\ \Box(move1_{\pi_1} \leftrightarrow move1_{\pi_2})) \rightarrow$$
$$\mathbb{P}(\Diamond(goal1_{\sigma_1} \wedge \neg goal2_{\sigma_1})) - \mathbb{P}(\Diamond(goal1_{\sigma_2} \wedge \neg goal2_{\sigma_2})) \leq \varepsilon,$$

where σ_1 and σ_2 are scheduler variables, π_1 is a path variable associated with the scheduler for σ_1, and π_2 is a path variable associated with the scheduler for σ_2. The condition $\forall\pi_1:\sigma_1\forall\pi_2:\sigma_2.\ \Box(move1_{\pi_1} \leftrightarrow move1_{\pi_2})$ states that in both joint plans robot 1 executes the same moves, where the proposition *move1* corresponds to robot 1 making a move towards the goal. The formula $\mathbb{P}(\Diamond(goal1_{\sigma_1} \wedge \neg goal2_{\sigma_1})) - \mathbb{P}(\Diamond(goal1_{\sigma_2} \wedge \neg goal2_{\sigma_2})) \leq \varepsilon$ states that the difference in the probability of robot 1 reaching the goal under scheduler σ_1 and the probability of it reaching the goal under scheduler σ_2 does not exceed ε. □

3.2 Syntax

As we are concerned with hyperproperties interpreted over MDPs, our logic allows for quantification over schedulers and quantification over paths.

To this end, let $\mathcal{V}_{sched}$ be a countably infinite set of *scheduler variables* and let $\mathcal{V}_{path}$ be a countably infinite set of *path variables*. According to the semantics of our logic, quantification over path variables ranges over the paths in a Markov chain associated with the scheduler represented by a given scheduler variable. To express this dependency we will associate path variables with the corresponding scheduler variable, writing $\pi : \sigma$ for a path variable π associated with a scheduler variable σ. The precise use and meaning of this notation will become clear below, once we define the syntax and semantics of the logic.

Given a set AP of atomic propositions, PHL formulas over AP will use atomic propositions indexed with scheduler variables or with path variables. We define the sets of propositions indexed with scheduler variables as $\mathsf{AP}_{\mathcal{V}_{sched}} = \{a_\sigma \mid a \in \mathsf{AP}, \sigma \in \mathcal{V}_{sched}\}$ and with path variables as $\mathsf{AP}_{\mathcal{V}_{path}} = \{a_\pi \mid a \in \mathsf{AP}, \pi \in \mathcal{V}_{path}\}$. *PHL (Probabilistic Hyper Logic) formulas* are defined by the grammar

$$\Phi ::= \ \forall\sigma.\ \Phi \ \mid \ \Phi \wedge \Phi \ \mid \ \neg\Phi \ \mid \ \chi \ \mid \ P \bowtie c$$

where $\sigma \in \mathcal{V}_{sched}$ is a scheduler variable, χ is a HYPERCTL* formula, P is a *probabilistic expression* defined below, $\bowtie \in \{<, \leq, \geq, >\}$, and $c \in \mathbb{Q}$.

Formulas in HYPERCTL*, introduced in [9], are constructed by the grammar

$$\chi ::= a_\pi \ \mid \ \chi \wedge \chi \ \mid \ \neg\chi \ \mid \ \bigcirc\chi \ \mid \ \chi \mathcal{U} \chi \ \mid \ \forall\pi : \sigma.\ \chi$$

where π is a path variable associated with a scheduler variable σ, and $a \in \mathsf{AP}$.

Probability expressions are defined by the grammar

$$P ::= \mathbb{P}(\varphi) \mid P + P \mid c \cdot P$$

where $\mathbb{P}$ is the *probabilistic operator*, $c \in \mathbb{Q}$, and φ is an LTL formula [22] defined by the grammar below, where $a \in \mathsf{AP}$ and σ is a scheduler variable.

$$\varphi ::= a_\sigma \mid \varphi \wedge \varphi \mid \neg\varphi \mid \bigcirc\varphi \mid \varphi \mathcal{U} \varphi.$$

We call formulas of the form $P \bowtie c$ *probabilistic predicates*.

A PHL formula Φ is *well-formed* if each path quantifier for $\pi : \sigma$ that appears in Φ is in the scope of a scheduler quantifier with the scheduler variable σ.

A PHL formula is *closed* if all occurrences of scheduler and path variables are bound by scheduler and path quantifiers respectively.

In the following we consider only closed and well-formed PHL formulas.

Discussion. Intuitively, a PHL formula is a Boolean combination of formulas consisting of a scheduler quantifier prefix followed by a formula without scheduler quantifiers constructed from probabilistic predicates and HYPERCTL* formulas via propositional operators. Thus, interleaving path quantifiers and probabilistic predicates is not allowed in PHL. This design decision is in line with the fact that probabilistic temporal logics like PCTL* replace the path quantifiers with the probabilistic operator that can be seen as their quantitative counterpart. We further chose to not allow nesting of probabilistic predicates and temporal operators, as in all the examples that we considered we never encountered the need for nested $\mathbb{P}$ operators. Moreover, allowing arbitrary nesting of probabilistic and temporal operators would immediately make the model checking problem for the resulting logic undecidable, following from the results in [8].

3.3   Self-composition for MDPs

In order to define the semantics of PHL we first introduce the self-composition operation for MDPs, which lifts to MDPs the well-known self-composition of transition systems that is often used in the model checking of hyperproperties.

Let us fix, for the reminder of the section, an MDP $M = (S, Act, \mathbf{P}, \iota, \mathsf{AP}, L)$.

Definition 3 (*n*-Self-composition of MDP). *Let* $M = (S, Act, \mathbf{P}, \iota, \mathsf{AP}, L)$ *be an MDP and* $n \in \mathbb{N}_{>0}$ *be a constant. The n-self-composition of M is the MDP* $M^n = (S^n, Act^n, \widehat{\mathbf{P}}, \widehat{\iota}, \mathsf{AP}, \widehat{L})$ *with the following components.* $S^n = \{(s_1, \ldots, s_n) \mid s_i \in S \text{ for all } 1 \leq i \leq n\}$ *is the set of states.* $Act^n = \{(a_1, \ldots, a_n) \mid a_i \in Act \text{ for all } 1 \leq i \leq n\}$ *is the set of actions. The transition probability function* $\widehat{\mathbf{P}}$ *is such that for every* $(s_1, \ldots, s_n), (s'_1, \ldots, s'_n) \in S^n$ *and* $(a_1, \ldots, a_n) \in Act^n$ *we have* $\widehat{\mathbf{P}}((s_1, \ldots, s_n), (a_1, \ldots, a_n), (s'_1, \ldots, s'_n)) = \prod_{i=1}^{n} \mathbf{P}(s_i, a_i, s'_i)$. *The initial distribution such that* $\widehat{\iota}((s_1, \ldots, s_n)) = \iota(s_1)$ *if* $s_1 = \ldots = s_n = s$ *and* $\widehat{\iota}((s_1, \ldots, s_n)) = 0$ *otherwise. The labelling function* $\widehat{L} : S^n \to (2^{\mathsf{AP}})^n$ *maps states to n-tuples of subsets of* AP *(in contrast to Definition 1 where states are mapped to subsets of* AP) *and is given by* $\widehat{L}((s_1, \ldots, s_n)) = (L(s_1), \ldots, L(s_n))$.

Naturally, a scheduler $\widehat{\mathfrak{S}} \in Sched(M^n)$ induces a Markov chain $M^n_{\widehat{\mathfrak{S}}}$.

Given schedulers $\mathfrak{S}_1, \ldots, \mathfrak{S}_n \in Sched(M)$, their *composition*, a scheduler $\overline{\mathfrak{S}} : (S^n \cdot Act^n)^* S^n \rightarrow \mathcal{D}(Act^n)$ for M^n, is denoted $\overline{\mathfrak{S}} = \mathfrak{S}_1 \| \cdots \| \mathfrak{S}_n$ and such that for every $\overline{h} = (s_{1,1}, \ldots, s_{1,n})(a_{1,1}, \ldots, a_{1,n}) \cdots (s_{k,1}, \ldots, s_{k,n}) \in (S^n \cdot Act^n)^* S^n$ and $\overline{a} = (a_{k+1,1}, \ldots, a_{k+1,n}) \in Act^n$, $\overline{\mathfrak{S}}(\overline{h})(\overline{a}) = \prod_{i=1}^n \mathfrak{S}_i(s_{1,i}a_{1,i} \cdots s_{k,i})(a_{k+1,i})$.

3.4 Scheduler and Path Assignments

Let $\mathcal{V}_{sched}$ and $\mathcal{V}_{path}$ be the sets of scheduler and path variables respectively.

A *scheduler assignment* is a vector of pairs $\Sigma \in \bigcup_{n \in \mathbb{N}} (\mathcal{V}_{sched} \times Sched(M))^n$ that assigns schedulers to some of the scheduler variables. Given a scheduler assignment $\Sigma = ((\sigma_1, \mathfrak{S}_1), \ldots, (\sigma_n, \mathfrak{S}_n))$, we denote by $|\Sigma|$ the length (number of pairs) of the vector. For a scheduler variable $\sigma \in \mathcal{V}_{sched}$ we define $\Sigma(\sigma) = \mathfrak{S}_i$ where i is the maximal index such that $\sigma_i = \sigma$. If such an index i does not exits, $\Sigma(\sigma)$ is undefined. For a scheduler assignment $\Sigma = ((\sigma_1, \mathfrak{S}_1), \ldots, (\sigma_n, \mathfrak{S}_n))$, a scheduler variable $\sigma \in \mathcal{V}_{sched}$, and a scheduler $\mathfrak{S} \in Sched(M)$ we define the scheduler assignment $\Sigma[\sigma \mapsto \mathfrak{S}] = ((\sigma_1, \mathfrak{S}_1), \ldots, (\sigma_n, \mathfrak{S}_n), (\sigma, \mathfrak{S}))$ obtained by adding the pair $(\sigma, \mathfrak{S})$ to the end of the vector Σ.

Given the MDP M, let $\Sigma = ((\sigma_1, \mathfrak{S}_1), \ldots, (\sigma_n, \mathfrak{S}_n))$ be a scheduler assignment, and consider $M^{|\Sigma|}$, the $|\Sigma|$-self composition of M. Σ defines a scheduler for $M^{|\Sigma|}$, which is the product of the schedulers in Σ, i.e., $\overline{\mathfrak{S}} = \mathfrak{S}_1 \| \cdots \| \mathfrak{S}_n$. Let M_Σ be the Markov chain induced by $\overline{\mathfrak{S}}$. If $\widehat{s}$ is a state in M_Σ, we denote by $M_{\Sigma, \widehat{s}}$ the Markov chain obtained from M_Σ by making $\widehat{s}$ the single initial state.

Note that the labeling function $\widehat{L}$ in $M^{|\Sigma|}$ maps the states in $S^{|\Sigma|}$ to $|\Sigma|$-tuples of sets of atomic predicates, that is $\widehat{L}(\widehat{s}) = (L_1, \ldots, L_{|\Sigma|})$. Given a scheduler variable σ for which $\Sigma(\sigma)$ is defined, we write $\widehat{L}(\widehat{s})(\sigma)$ for the set of atomic predicates L_i, where i is the maximal position in Σ in which σ appears.

We define path assignments similarly to scheduler assignments. A *path assignment* is a vector of pairs of path variables and paths in $Paths_{inf}(M)$. More precisely, a path assignment Π is an element of $\bigcup_{m \in \mathbb{N}} (\mathcal{V}_{path} \times Paths_{inf}(M))^m$. Analogously to scheduler assignments, for a path variable π and a path $\rho \in Paths_{inf}(M)$, we define $\Pi(\pi)$ and $\Pi[\pi \mapsto \rho]$. For $\Pi = ((\pi_1, \rho_1), \ldots, (\pi_n, \rho_n))$ and $j \in \mathbb{N}$, we define $\Pi[j, \infty] = ((\pi_1, \rho_1[j, \infty]), \ldots, (\pi_n, \rho_n[j, \infty]))$ to be the path assignment that assigns to each π_i the suffix $\rho_i[j, \infty]$ of the path ρ_i.

3.5 Semantics of PHL

We are now ready to define the semantics of PHL formulas. Recall that we consider only closed and well-formed PHL formulas. PHL formulas are interpreted over an MDP and a scheduler assignment. The interpretation of HYPERCTL* formulas requires additionally a path assignment. Probabilistic expressions and LTL formulas are evaluated in the Markov chain for an MDP induced by a scheduler assignment. As usual, the satisfaction relations are denoted by $\models$.

For an MDP M and a scheduler assignment Σ we define

$$
\begin{aligned}
&M, \Sigma \models \forall \sigma.\Phi && \text{iff} && \text{for all } \mathfrak{S} \in Sched(M): M, \Sigma[\sigma \mapsto \mathfrak{S}] \models \Phi; \\
&M, \Sigma \models \Phi_1 \wedge \Phi_2 && \text{iff} && M, \Sigma \models \Phi_1 \text{ and } M, \Sigma \models \Phi_2; \\
&M, \Sigma \models \neg\Phi && \text{iff} && M, \Sigma \not\models \Phi; \\
&M, \Sigma \models \chi && \text{iff} && M, \Sigma, \Pi_\emptyset \models \chi, \text{where } \Pi_\emptyset \text{ is the empty path assignment;} \\
&M, \Sigma \models P \bowtie c && \text{iff} && [\![P]\!]_{M_\Sigma} \bowtie c.
\end{aligned}
$$

For an MDP M, scheduler assignment Σ, and path assignment Π we define

$$
\begin{aligned}
&M, \Sigma, \Pi \models a_\pi && \text{iff} && a \in L(\Pi(\pi)[0]); \\
&M, \Sigma, \Pi \models \chi_1 \wedge \chi_2 && \text{iff} && M, \Sigma, \Pi \models \chi_1 \text{ and } M, \Sigma, \Pi \models \chi_2; \\
&M, \Sigma, \Pi \models \neg\chi && \text{iff} && M, \Sigma, \Pi \not\models \chi; \\
&M, \Sigma, \Pi \models \bigcirc\chi && \text{iff} && M, \Sigma, \Pi[1, \infty] \models \chi; \\
&M, \Sigma, \Pi \models \chi_1 \mathcal{U} \chi_2 && \text{iff} && \text{there exists } i \geq 0: M, \Sigma, \Pi[i, \infty] \models \chi_2 \text{ and} \\
&&&&& \quad \text{for all } j < i: M, \Sigma, \Pi[j, \infty] \models \chi_1; \\
&M, \Sigma, \Pi \models \forall \pi : \sigma.\, \chi && \text{iff} && \text{for all } \rho \in Paths_{inf}(C): M, \Sigma, \Pi[\pi \mapsto \rho] \models \chi,
\end{aligned}
$$

where in the last item C is the Markov chain $M_{\Sigma(\sigma)}$ when Π is the empty path assignment, and otherwise the Markov chain $M_{\Sigma(\sigma), \Pi(\pi')[0]}$ where π' is the path variable associated with scheduler variable σ that was most recently added to Π.

For Markov chain C of the form M_Σ or $M_{\Sigma, \hat{s}}$, where Σ is a scheduler assignment and $\hat{s}$ is a state in M_Σ the semantics $[\![\cdot]\!]_C$ of probabilistic expressions is:

$$
\begin{aligned}
[\![\mathbb{P}(\varphi)]\!]_C &= Prob^C(\{\rho \in Paths_{inf}(C) \mid C, \rho \models \varphi\}); \\
[\![P_1 + P_2]\!]_C &= [\![P_1]\!]_C + [\![P_2]\!]_C; \quad [\![c \cdot P]\!]_C = c \cdot [\![P]\!]_C,
\end{aligned}
$$

where the semantics of path formulas (i.e., LTL formulas) is defined by

$$
\begin{aligned}
&C, \rho \models a_\sigma && \text{iff} && a \in \widehat{L}(\rho[0])(\sigma); \\
&C, \rho \models \varphi_1 \wedge \varphi_2 && \text{iff} && C, \rho \models \varphi_1 \text{ and } C, \rho \models \varphi_2; \\
&C, \rho \models \neg\varphi && \text{iff} && C, \rho \not\models \varphi; \\
&C, \rho \models \bigcirc\varphi && \text{iff} && C, \rho[1, \infty] \models \varphi; \\
&C, \rho \models \varphi_1 \mathcal{U} \varphi_2 && \text{iff} && \text{there exists } i \geq 0: C, \rho[i, \infty] \models \varphi_2 \text{ and} \\
&&&&& \quad \text{for all } j < i: C, \rho[j, \infty] \models \varphi_1.
\end{aligned}
$$

Note that $Prob^C(\{\rho \in Paths_{inf}(C) \mid C, \rho \models \varphi\})$ is well-defined as it is a known fact [7] that the set $\{\rho \in Paths_{inf}(C) \mid C, \rho \models \varphi\}$ is measurable.

We say that an MDP M *satisfies* a closed well-formed PHL formula Φ, denoted $M \models \Phi$ iff $M, \Sigma_\emptyset \models \Phi$, where $\Sigma_\emptyset$ is the empty scheduler assignment.

Since PHL includes both scheduler and path quantification, the sets of deterministic and randomized schedulers are not interchangeable with respect to the PHL semantics. That is, there exists an MDP M and formula Φ such that if quantifiers are interpreted over $Sched(M)$, then $M \models \Phi$, and if quantifiers are interpreted over $DetSched(M)$ then $M \not\models \Phi$. See [12] for an example.

3.6   Undecidability of PHL Model Checking

Due to the fact that PHL allows quantification over both schedulers and paths, the model checking problem for PHL is undecidable. The proof is based on a reduction from the emptiness problem for probabilistic Büchi automata (PBA), which is known to be undecidable [5].

Theorem 1. *The model checking problem for PHL is undecidable.*

We saw in the previous section an example of a probabilistic hyperproperty expressed as a PHL formulas of the form $\forall \sigma_1 \ldots \forall \sigma_n.\ \big((\forall \pi_1 : \sigma_1 \ldots \forall \pi_n : \sigma_n.\ \psi) \to P \bowtie c\big)$. Analogously to Theorem 1, we can show that the model checking problem for PHL formulas of the form $\exists \sigma_1 \ldots \exists \sigma_n.\ (\forall \pi_1 : \sigma_1 \ldots \forall \pi_n : \sigma_n.\ \psi \wedge P \bowtie c)$ is undecidable. The undecidability for formulas of the form $\forall \sigma_1 \ldots \forall \sigma_n.\ \big((\forall \pi_1 : \sigma_1 \ldots \forall \pi_n : \sigma_n.\ \psi) \to P \bowtie c\big)$ then follows by duality. In the next two sections, we present an approximate model checking procedure and a bounded model checking procedure for PHL formulas in these two classes.

However, since there are finitely many deterministic schedulers with a given fixed number of states, the result stated in the next theorem is easily established.

Theorem 2. *For any constant $b \in \mathbb{N}$, the model checking problem for PHL restricted to deterministic finite-memory schedulers with b states is decidable.*

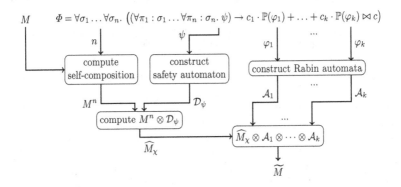

Fig. 1. Approximate model checking of PHL formulas of the form (1).

4   Approximate Model Checking

In this section we provide a sound but incomplete procedure for model checking a fragment of PHL. The fragment we consider consists of those PHL formulas that are positive Boolean combinations of formulas of the form

$$\Phi = \forall \sigma_1 \ldots \forall \sigma_n.\ \big(\chi \to c_1 \cdot \mathbb{P}(\varphi_1) + \ldots + c_k \cdot \mathbb{P}(\varphi_k) \bowtie c\big) \qquad (1)$$

where $\chi = \forall \pi_1 : \sigma_1 \ldots \forall \pi_n : \sigma_n$. ψ and the formula ψ does not contain path quantifiers and describes an n-safety property (i.e., a safety property on M^n [10]). The PHL formula in Example 2 falls into this class.

The formula ψ contains at most one path variable associated with each scheduler variable in $\{\sigma_1, \ldots \sigma_n\}$. This allows us to use the classical self-composition approach to obtain an automaton for χ. Requiring that ψ describes an n-safety property enables us to consider a deterministic safety automaton for χ which, intuitively, represents the most general scheduler in M^n, such that every scheduler that refines it results in a Markov chain in which all paths satisfy ψ.

Since for every Markov chain C we have $Prob^C(\{\pi \in Paths_{inf}(C) \mid \pi \models \varphi\}) = 1 - Prob^C(\{\pi \in Paths_{inf}(C) \mid \pi \models \neg\varphi\})$, it suffices to consider the case when $\bowtie$ is $\leq$ (or $<$) and $c_i \geq 0$ for each $i = 1, \ldots, k$.

We now describe a procedure for checking whether a given MDP $M = (S, Act, \mathbf{P}, \iota, AP, L)$ satisfies a PHL formula Φ of the form (1). If the answer is positive, then we are guaranteed that $M \models \Phi$, but otherwise the result is inconclusive. The method, outlined in Fig. 1, proceeds as follows.

We first compute a deterministic safety automaton $\mathcal{D}_\psi$ for the n-hypersafety property ψ. The language of $\mathcal{D}_\psi$ is defined over words in $(S^n)^\omega$. It holds that $w \in \mathcal{L}(\mathcal{D}_\psi)$ if and only if for an arbitrary scheduler assignment Σ it holds that $M, \Sigma, \Pi_w \models \psi$, where Π_w is the path assignment corresponding to the word w. As a second step we construct the n-self-composition MDP M^n, and then build the product of M^n with the deterministic safety automaton $\mathcal{D}_\psi$. The language of the resulting automaton $\widehat{M_\chi}$ consists of the n-tuples of infinite paths in M such that each such tuple satisfies the n-hypersafety property ψ.

After constructing the MDP $\widehat{M_\chi}$, our goal is to check that for every scheduler assignment $\Sigma = ((\sigma_1, \mathfrak{S}_1), \ldots, (\sigma_n, \mathfrak{S}_n))$ for M such that $\overline{\mathfrak{S}} = \mathfrak{S}_1 \parallel \ldots \parallel \mathfrak{S}_n \in Sched(\widehat{M_\chi})$ the inequality $\sum_{i=1}^{k}(c_i \cdot Prob_{\widehat{M_\chi}, \overline{\mathfrak{S}}}(\varphi_i)) \leq c$ is satisfied. That would mean, intuitively, that every scheduler assignment that satisfies χ also satisfies the above inequality, which is the property stated by Φ. Note that, if we establish that $\max_{\overline{\mathfrak{S}} = \mathfrak{S}_1 \parallel \ldots \parallel \mathfrak{S}_n} \sum_{i=1}^{k}(c_i \cdot Prob_{\widehat{M_\chi}, \overline{\mathfrak{S}}}(\varphi_i)) \leq c$, then we have established the above property. Computing exactly the value $\max_{\overline{\mathfrak{S}} = \mathfrak{S}_1 \parallel \ldots \parallel \mathfrak{S}_n} \sum_{i=1}^{k}(c_i \cdot Prob_{\widehat{M_\chi}, \overline{\mathfrak{S}}}(\varphi_i))$, however, is not algorithmically possible in light of the undecidability results in the previous section. Therefore, we will overapproximate this value by computing a value $c^* \geq \max_{\overline{\mathfrak{S}} = \mathfrak{S}_1 \parallel \ldots \parallel \mathfrak{S}_n} \sum_{i=1}^{k}(c_i \cdot Prob_{\widehat{M_\chi}, \overline{\mathfrak{S}}}(\varphi_i))$ and if $c^* \leq c$, then we can conclude that the property holds. The value c^* is computed as $c^* = \max_{\widehat{\mathfrak{S}} \in Sched(\widehat{M_\chi})} \sum_{i=1}^{k}(c_i \cdot Prob_{\widehat{M_\chi}, \widehat{\mathfrak{S}}}(\varphi_i))$. For the schedulers $\widehat{\mathfrak{S}}$ considered in this maximization, it is not in general possible to decompose $\widehat{\mathfrak{S}}$ into schedulers $\mathfrak{S}_1, \ldots, \mathfrak{S}_n \in Sched(M)$. Therefore we have that

$$\max_{\widehat{\mathfrak{S}} \in Sched(\widehat{M_\chi})} \sum_{i=1}^{k}(c_i \cdot Prob_{\widehat{M_\chi}, \widehat{\mathfrak{S}}}(\varphi_i)) \geq \max_{\overline{\mathfrak{S}} = \mathfrak{S}_1 \parallel \ldots \parallel \mathfrak{S}_n} \sum_{i=1}^{k}(c_i \cdot Prob_{\widehat{M_\chi}, \overline{\mathfrak{S}}}(\varphi_i)),$$

which implies that c^* has the desired property. We compute c^* as follows.

We construct deterministic Rabin automata $\mathcal{A}_1, \ldots, \mathcal{A}_k$ for the formulas $\varphi_1, \ldots, \varphi_k$. We compute the product $\widetilde{M}$ of the MDP $\widetilde{M}_\chi$ constructed earlier and $\mathcal{A}_1, \ldots, \mathcal{A}_k$. Let $\widetilde{S}$ be the set of states of $\widetilde{M}$. We consider each combination of formulas in $\{\varphi_1, \ldots, \varphi_k\}$, i.e., each subset $I \subseteq \{1, \ldots, k\}$ such that $I \neq \emptyset$. For each I, we take the conjunction of the accepting conditions of the deterministic Rabin automata $\mathcal{A}_i$ for $i \in I$ and apply the methods in [7] to compute the so called *success set* $U_I \subseteq \widetilde{S}$ for this conjunction. Intuitively, in the states in U_I there exists a scheduler that can enforce the conjunction of the properties in I.

Finally, we solve the linear program that asks to minimize $\sum_{\widetilde{s} \in \widetilde{S}} x_{\widetilde{s}}$ subject to (i) $x_{\widetilde{s}} \geq 0$ for all $\widetilde{s} \in \widetilde{S}$, (ii) $x_{\widetilde{s}} \geq \sum_{i \in I} c_i$ for all $I \subseteq \{1, \ldots, k\}$ and $\widetilde{s} \in U_I$ and (iii) $x_{\widetilde{s}} \geq \sum_{\widetilde{t} \in \widetilde{S}} \mathbf{P}(\widetilde{s}, a, \widetilde{t}) \cdot x_{\widetilde{t}}$ for all $\widetilde{s} \in \widetilde{S}$ and $a \in Act^n$. If $(x_{\widetilde{s}}^*)_{s \in \widetilde{S}}$ is the optimal solution of the linear program, let $c^* = \sum_{\widetilde{s} \in \widetilde{S}} \widetilde{\iota}(\widetilde{s}) \cdot x_{\widetilde{s}}^*$.

If $c^* \leq c$, then for all tuples of schedulers $\mathfrak{S}_1, \ldots, \mathfrak{S}_n$ we have that if $M_{\mathfrak{S}_1 \| \ldots \| \mathfrak{S}_n} \models \chi$, then for their product $\overline{\mathfrak{S}} = \mathfrak{S}_1 \| \ldots \| \mathfrak{S}_n$ it holds that $\sum_{i=1}^{k} (c_i \cdot Prob_{M^n, \overline{\mathfrak{S}}}(\varphi_i)) \leq c$, and we conclude that $M \models \Phi$. If, on the other hand, we have $c^* > c$, then the result is inconclusive. When this is the case, we can use bounded model checking to search for counterexamples to formulas of the form (1). For the procedure above, we establish the following result.

Theorem 3 (Complexity). *Given an MDP* $M = (S, Act, \mathbf{P}, \iota, \mathsf{AP}, L)$ *and a PHL formula* Φ *of the form (1) the model checking procedure above runs in time polynomial in the size of* M *and doubly exponential in the size of* Φ.

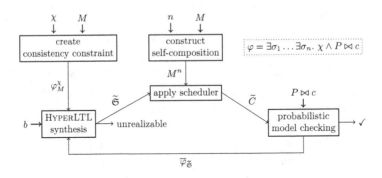

Fig. 2. Bounded model checking of MDPs against PHL formulas for the form (2).

5   Bounded Model Checking

We present a bounded model-checking procedure for PHL formulas of the form

$$\Phi = \exists \sigma_1 \ldots \exists \sigma_n. \left(\chi \wedge c_1 \cdot \mathbb{P}(\varphi_1) + \ldots + c_k \cdot \mathbb{P}(\varphi_k) \bowtie c \right) \qquad (2)$$

where $\chi = \forall \pi_1 : \sigma_1 \ldots \forall \pi_n : \sigma_n. \psi$ is in the $\forall^*$ fragment of HYPERLTL [14]. An example of a formula in this fragment is the formula in Example 1. By finding a scheduler assignment that is a witness for a PHL formula of the form (2) we can find counterexamples to PHL formulas of the form (1).

Given an MDP $M = (S, Act, \mathbf{P}, \iota, \mathsf{AP}, L)$, a bound $b \in \mathbb{N}$, and a PHL formula $\Phi = \exists \sigma_1 \ldots \exists \sigma_n. \left(\chi \wedge c_1 \cdot \mathbb{P}(\varphi_1) + \ldots + c_k \cdot \mathbb{P}(\varphi_k) \bowtie c \right)$, the *bounded model checking problem for M, b and Φ* is to determine whether there exists a *deterministic finite-memory scheduler* $\widetilde{\mathfrak{S}} = \mathfrak{S}_1 || \ldots || \mathfrak{S}_n$ for M^n composed of deterministic finite-memory schedulers $\mathfrak{S}_i = (Q^i, \delta^i, q_0^i, act_i)$ for M for $i \in \{1, \ldots, n\}$, with $|\widetilde{\mathfrak{S}}| = b$ such that $M_{\widetilde{\mathfrak{S}}}^n \models \chi \wedge \sum_{i=1}^k (c_i \cdot \mathbb{P}(\varphi_i)) \bowtie c$.

Our bounded model checking procedure employs bounded synthesis for the logic HYPERLTL [14] and model checking of Markov chains [19]. The flow of our procedure is depicted in Fig. 2. The procedure starts by checking whether there is a scheduler $\widetilde{\mathfrak{S}}$ for M^n composed of schedulers $\mathfrak{S}_1, \ldots, \mathfrak{S}_n$ for M that satisfies the constraint given by the hyperproperty χ. This is done by synthesizing a scheduler of size b for the HYPERLTL formula φ_M^χ composed of the formula χ, an encoding of M, which ensures that the schedulers $\mathfrak{S}_1, \ldots, \mathfrak{S}_n$ defining $\widetilde{\mathfrak{S}}$ follow the structure of M, and an additional consistency constraint that requires $\widetilde{\mathfrak{S}}$ to be a composition of n schedulers $\mathfrak{S}_1, \ldots, \mathfrak{S}_n$ for M.

If φ_M^χ is realizable, then the procedure proceeds by applying the synthesized scheduler $\widetilde{\mathfrak{S}}$ to the n-self-composition of the MDP M, which results in a Markov chain $\widetilde{C} = M_{\widetilde{\mathfrak{S}}}^n$. To check whether the synthesized scheduler also satisfies the probabilistic constraint $P \bowtie c$, we apply a probabilistic model checker to the Markov chain $\widetilde{C}$ to compute for each φ_i the probability $Prob_{\widetilde{C}}(\varphi_i)$, and then we evaluate the probabilistic predicate $P \bowtie c$. If $\widetilde{C}$ satisfies $P \bowtie c$, then $M_{\widetilde{\mathfrak{S}}}^n \models \chi \wedge \sum_{i=1}^k (c_i \cdot \mathbb{P}(\varphi_i)) \bowtie c$, implying that $M \models \Phi$. If not, we return back to the synthesizer to construct a new scheduler. In order to exclude the scheduler $\widetilde{\mathfrak{S}}$ from the subsequent search, a new constraint $\overline{\varphi}_{\widetilde{\mathfrak{S}}}$ is added to φ_M^χ. The formula $\varphi_{\widetilde{\mathfrak{S}}}$ imposes the requirement that the synthesized scheduler should be different from $\widetilde{\mathfrak{S}}$. This process is iterated until a scheduler that is a witness for Φ is found, or all schedulers within the given bound b have been checked. The complexity of the procedure is given in the next theorem and follows from complexity of probabilistic model checking [19] and that of synthesis for HYPERLTL [14].

Theorem 4 (Complexity). *Given an MDP $M = (S, Act, \mathbf{P}, \iota, \mathsf{AP}, L)$, a bound $b \in \mathbb{N}$, and a PHL formula $\Phi = \exists \sigma_1 \ldots \exists \sigma_n. \chi \wedge c_1 \cdot \mathbb{P}(\varphi_1) + \ldots + c_k \cdot \mathbb{P}(\varphi_k) \bowtie c$, the bounded model checking problem for M, b and Φ can be solved in time polynomial in the size of M, exponential in b, and exponential in the size of Φ.*

5.1   Evaluation

We developed a proof-of-concept implementation of the approach in Fig. 2. We used the tool BoSyHyper [14] for the scheduler synthesis and the tool PRISM [20] to model check the Markov chains resulting from applying the synthesized

Table 1. Experimental results from model checking plan non-interference.

Benchmark	MDP size	# Iterations	Synthesis time (s)	Model checking time (s)
Arena 3	16	6	12.04	2.68
Arena 4	36	5	17.23	2.19
Arena 5	81	5	18.49	2.76
Arena 7	256	5	19.46	3.01
Arena 9	625	7	168.27	4.72
3-Robots Arena 4	36	9	556.02	4.5

scheduler to the self-composition of the input MDP. For our experiments, we used a machine with 3.3 GHz dual-core Intel Core i5 and 16 GB of memory.

Table 1 shows the results of model checking the "plan non-interference" specification introduced in Sect. 3.1 against MDP's representing two robots that try to reach a designated cell on grid arenas of different sizes ranging from 3-grid to a 9-grid arena. In the last instance, we increased the number of robots to three to raise the number of possible schedulers. The specification thus checks whether the probability for a robot to reach the designated area changes with the movements the other robots in the arena. In the initial state, every robot is positioned on a different end of the grid, i.e., the farthest point from the designated cell.

In all instances in Table 1, the specification with $\varepsilon = 0.25$ is violated. We give the number of iterations, i.e., the number of schedulers synthesized, until a counterexample was found. The synthesis and model checking time represent the total time for synthesizing and model checking all schedulers. Table 1 shows the feasibility of approach, however, it also demonstrates the inherent difficulty of the synthesis problem for hyperproperties.

Table 2. Detailed experimental results for the 3-Robots Arena 4 benchmark.

Iteration	Synthesis (s)	Model checking (s)
1	3.723	0.504
2	3.621	0.478
3	3.589	0.469
4	3.690	0.495
5	3.934	0.514
6	4.898	0.528
7	11.429	0.535
8	60.830	0.466
9	460.310	0.611

Table 2 shows that the time needed for the overall model checking approach is dominated by the time needed for synthesis: The time for synthesizing a scheduler quickly increases in the last iterations, while the time for model checking the resulting Markov chains remains stable for each scheduler. Despite recent advances on the synthesis from hyperproperties [14], synthesis tools for hyperproperties are still in their infancy. PHL model checking will directly profit from future progress on this problem.

6   Conclusion

We presented a new logic, called PHL, for the specification of probabilistic temporal hyperproperties. The novel and distinguishing feature of our logic is the combination of quantification over both schedulers and paths, and a probabilistic operator. This makes PHL uniquely capable of specifying hyperproperties of MDPs. PHL is capable of expressing interesting properties both from the realm of security and from the planning and synthesis domains. While, unfortunately, the expressiveness of PHL comes at a price as the model checking problem for PHL is undecidable, we show how to approximate the model checking problem from two sides by providing sound but incomplete procedures for proving and for refuting universally quantified PHL formulas. We developed a proof-of-concept implementation of the refutation procedure and demonstrated its principle feasibility on an example from planning.

We believe that this work opens up a line of research on the verification of MDPs against probabilistic hyperproperties. One direction of future work is identifying fragments of the logic or classes of models that are practically amenable to verification. Furthermore, investigating the connections between PHL and simulation notions for MDPs, as well studying the different synthesis questions expressible in PHL are both interesting avenues for future work.

References

1. Abraham, E., Bartocci, E., Bonakdarpour, B., Dobe, O.: Probabilistic hyperproperties with nondeterminism. In: Proceedings of Automated Technology for Verification and Analysis, ATVA 2020 (2020)
2. Ábrahám, E., Bonakdarpour, B.: HyperPCTL: a temporal logic for probabilistic hyperproperties. In: McIver, A., Horvath, A. (eds.) QEST 2018. LNCS, vol. 11024, pp. 20–35. Springer, Cham (2018). https://doi.org/10.1007/978-3-319-99154-2_2
3. Aminof, B., Kwiatkowska, M., Maubert, B., Murano, A., Rubin, S.: Probabilistic strategy logic. In: Proceedings of the Twenty-Eighth International Joint Conference on Artificial Intelligence, IJCAI 2019, pp. 32–38 (2019)
4. Baier, C.: On model checking techniques for randomized distributed systems. In: Méry, D., Merz, S. (eds.) IFM 2010. LNCS, vol. 6396, pp. 1–11. Springer, Heidelberg (2010). https://doi.org/10.1007/978-3-642-16265-7_1
5. Baier, C., Bertrand, N., Größer, M.: On decision problems for probabilistic Büchi automata. In: Amadio, R. (ed.) FoSSaCS 2008. LNCS, vol. 4962, pp. 287–301. Springer, Heidelberg (2008). https://doi.org/10.1007/978-3-540-78499-9_21
6. Baier, C., Brázdil, T., Größer, M., Kucera, A.: Stochastic game logic. Acta Inform. **49**(4), 203–224 (2012). https://doi.org/10.1007/s00236-012-0156-0
7. Baier, C., Katoen, J.: Principles of Model Checking. MIT Press, Cambridge (2008)
8. Brázdil, T., Brozek, V., Forejt, V., Kucera, A.: Stochastic games with branching-time winning objectives. In: Proceedings of 21th IEEE Symposium on Logic in Computer Science (LICS 2006), pp. 349–358. IEEE Computer Society (2006)
9. Clarkson, M.R., Finkbeiner, B., Koleini, M., Micinski, K.K., Rabe, M.N., Sánchez, C.: Temporal logics for hyperproperties. In: Abadi, M., Kremer, S. (eds.) POST 2014. LNCS, vol. 8414, pp. 265–284. Springer, Heidelberg (2014). https://doi.org/10.1007/978-3-642-54792-8_15
10. Clarkson, M.R., Schneider, F.B.: Hyperproperties. J. Comput. Secur. **18**(6), 1157–1210 (2010)
11. Coenen, N., Finkbeiner, B., Sánchez, C., Tentrup, L.: Verifying hyperliveness. In: Dillig, I., Tasiran, S. (eds.) CAV 2019. LNCS, vol. 11561, pp. 121–139. Springer, Cham (2019). https://doi.org/10.1007/978-3-030-25540-4_7

12. Dimitrova, R., Finkbeiner, B., Torfah, H.: Probabilistic hyperproperties of Markov decision processes. CoRR arxiv:2005.03362 (2020)
13. Dwork, C.: Differential privacy. In: van Tilborg, H.C.A., Jajodia, S. (eds.) Encyclopedia of Cryptography and Security, 2nd edn., pp. 338–340. Springer, Boston (2011). https://doi.org/10.1007/978-1-4419-5906-5_752
14. Finkbeiner, B., Hahn, C., Lukert, P., Stenger, M., Tentrup, L.: Synthesizing reactive systems from hyperproperties. In: Chockler, H., Weissenbacher, G. (eds.) CAV 2018. LNCS, vol. 10981, pp. 289–306. Springer, Cham (2018). https://doi.org/10.1007/978-3-319-96145-3_16
15. Finkbeiner, B., Hahn, C., Stenger, M.: EAHyper: satisfiability, implication, and equivalence checking of hyperproperties. In: Majumdar, R., Kunčak, V. (eds.) CAV 2017. LNCS, vol. 10427, pp. 564–570. Springer, Cham (2017). https://doi.org/10.1007/978-3-319-63390-9_29
16. Finkbeiner, B., Rabe, M.N., Sánchez, C.: Algorithms for model checking HyperLTL and HyperCTL*. In: Kroening, D., Păsăreanu, C.S. (eds.) CAV 2015. LNCS, vol. 9206, pp. 30–48. Springer, Cham (2015). https://doi.org/10.1007/978-3-319-21690-4_3
17. Goguen, J.A., Meseguer, J.: Security policies and security models. In: 1982 IEEE Symposium on Security and Privacy. IEEE Computer Society (1982)
18. Gray, J.W.: Toward a mathematical foundation for information flow security. J. Comput. Secur. 1(3–4), 255–294 (1992)
19. Kwiatkowska, M., Norman, G., Parker, D.: Probabilistic model checking: advances and applications. In: Drechsler, R. (ed.) Formal System Verification, pp. 73–121. Springer, Cham (2018). https://doi.org/10.1007/978-3-319-57685-5_3
20. Kwiatkowska, M., Norman, G., Parker, D.: PRISM 4.0: verification of probabilistic real-time systems. In: Gopalakrishnan, G., Qadeer, S. (eds.) CAV 2011. LNCS, vol. 6806, pp. 585–591. Springer, Heidelberg (2011). https://doi.org/10.1007/978-3-642-22110-1_47
21. O'Neill, K.R., Clarkson, M.R., Chong, S.: Information-flow security for interactive programs. In: 19th IEEE Computer Security Foundations Workshop, (CSFW-19 2006), pp. 190–201. IEEE Computer Society (2006)
22. Pnueli, A.: The temporal logic of programs. In: 18th Annual Symposium on Foundations of Computer Science, pp. 46–57. IEEE Computer Society (1977)
23. Sabelfeld, A., Sands, D.: Probabilistic noninterference for multi-threaded programs. In: Proceedings of the 13th IEEE Computer Security Foundations Workshop, CSFW 2000, pp. 200–214. IEEE Computer Society (2000)
24. Volpano, D.M., Smith, G.: Probabilistic noninterference in a concurrent language. J. Comput. Secur. 7(1), 231–253 (1999)
25. Wang, Y., Zarei, M., Bonakdarpour, B., Pajic, M.: Statistical verification of hyperproperties for cyber-physical systems. ACM Trans. Embed. Comput. Syst. 18(5s), 1–23 (2019)

Minimal Witnesses for Probabilistic Timed Automata

Simon Jantsch[✉], Florian Funke[✉], and Christel Baier

Technische Universität Dresden, Dresden, Germany
{simon.jantsch,florian.funke,christel.baier}@tu-dresden.de

Abstract. Witnessing subsystems have proven to be a useful concept in the analysis of probabilistic systems, for example as diagnostic information on why a given property holds or as input to refinement algorithms. This paper introduces witnessing subsystems for reachability problems in probabilistic timed automata (PTA). Using a new operation on difference bounds matrices, it is shown how Farkas certificates of finite-state bisimulation quotients of a PTA can be translated into witnessing subsystems. We present algorithms for the computation of minimal witnessing subsystems under three notions of minimality, which capture the timed behavior from different perspectives, and discuss their complexity.

1 Introduction

A *witnessing subsystem* is a part of a probabilistic system that by itself carries enough probability to satisfy a given constraint. Hence, it provides insight into which components of the system are sufficient for the desired behavior, and on the other hand, which can be disabled without interfering with it. The concept of witnessing subsystems (sometimes, dually, referred to as *critical subsystems*) for discrete-time Markov chains (DTMC) and Markov decision processes (MDP) has received considerable attention [14,17,18,34]. Apart from providing diagnostic information on why a property holds, witnessing subsystems have been used for automated refinement and synthesis algorithms [10,16].

In this paper we introduce witnessing subsystems for reachability constraints in probabilistic timed automata (PTA) [6,23]. PTAs combine real-time, non-deterministic, and probabilistic behavior and are a widely used formalism for the modeling and verification of reactive systems such as communication protocols and scheduler optimization tasks [24,28]. However, as the state space of PTAs is inherently uncountable, the theory of witnessing subsystems in finite-state probabilistic systems is not applicable. Our generalization applies to both maximal and minimal reachability probabilities, where particularly the latter needs to be treated with special care in the timed setting.

This work was funded by DFG grant 389792660 as part of TRR 248, the Cluster of Excellence EXC 2050/1 (CeTI, project ID 390696704, as part of Germany's Excellence Strategy), DFG-projects BA-1679/11-1 and BA-1679/12-1, and the Research Training Group QuantLA (GRK 1763).

D. V. Hung and O. Sokolsky (Eds.): ATVA 2020, LNCS 12302, pp. 501–517, 2020.
https://doi.org/10.1007/978-3-030-59152-6_28

A continuous algebraic counterpart to witnessing subsystems in MDPs are *Farkas certificates*, which are vectors certifying threshold properties of the form $\mathbf{Pr}_{\mathcal{M}}^{\min}(\Diamond\text{goal}) \geq \lambda$ or $\mathbf{Pr}_{\mathcal{M}}^{\max}(\Diamond\text{goal}) \geq \lambda$ [14]. We pave a two-way street between witnessing subsystems in a PTA and Farkas certificates of finite-state bisimulation quotients by giving explicit procedures how one can be obtained from the other. It is noteworthy that this translation makes finite-state methods available for the certification of threshold properties in infinite-state models.

Relevant information from a subsystem can only be expected after optimization along suitable minimality criteria, the most prevalent of which for MDPs is state-minimality. In the timed setting, however, the usefulness of a minimality criterion is more volatile under changing the specific practical problem. For this reason, we introduce three notions of minimality aimed at finding witnessing subsystems with few locations, strong invariants, or small invariant volume.

In all three cases, we present single-exponential algorithms for the computation of minimal witnessing subsystems. They heavily rely on the connection between PTA subsystems and Farkas certificates of bisimulation quotients and can also be adapted to faster heuristic approaches. Furthermore, we observe that while comparing two subsystems according to their location number or invariance strength is not difficult, it is inherently harder (**PP**-hard) to compare their invariance volume. All omitted proofs can be found in the technical report [19].

Contributions. The notion of (strong) subsystem for PTAs is introduced (Definition 3.1) and justified by proving that reachability probabilities do not increase under passage to a subsystem (Corollary 3.4). It is shown that subsystems of a PTA induce Farkas certificates in time-abstracting bisimulation quotients (Theorem 3.3). Vice versa, a conceptual construction of PTA subsystems from Farkas certificates of such quotients is given (Definition 3.9 and Proposition 3.11), which relies on a new operation on difference bounds matrices (DBMs), see Definition 3.5. Three notions of minimality for PTA subsystems are introduced and compared. We present mixed integer linear programs for computing location- and invariance-minimal subsystems. Volume-minimal subsystems can be computed with the aid of a *multi-objective* mixed integer linear program (Sect. 4). Regarding volume-minimality, we establish **PP**-hardness of comparing two witnessing subsystems according to their volume (Theorem 4.11).

Related Work. Exact and heuristic approaches for computing minimal and small witnessing subsystems in DTMCs have been proposed in [17,18], and generalizations to MDPs have been considered in [3,14,34]. The approach in [33] is most closely related to our work as it finds counterexamples for a high-level description (a guarded command language for MDPs). Model checking PTAs against PTCTL specifications has first been described in [23]. Subsequent approaches use digital clocks [25], symbolic model checking techniques [26], or the boundary region graph [20]. The work [9] presents an algorithm for price-bounded reachability in PTAs. The complexity of model checking PTAs was studied in [21,27]. The notion of bisimulation that we use was introduced in [11] and used for verification techniques in [31]. The computation and analysis of counterexamples in (non-probabilistic) timed automata was studied in [12,22]. Certification of unreachability was recently examined for timed automata [35]. DBMs are a widely used data structure for timed systems (see [26,32]) that were first analyzed in [13] and most notably used in the model checker UPPAAL[7].

2   Preliminaries

For any set S we denote by $\mathrm{Dist}(S)$ the set of probability distributions on S (seen as a discrete measurable space). Given $s \in S$, we let $\delta_s \in \mathrm{Dist}(S)$ denote the Dirac distribution on s, i.e. $\delta_s(t) = 0$ for all $t \neq s$ and $\delta_s(s) = 1$.

Markov Decision Processes. A *Markov decision process* (MDP) is a tuple $\mathcal{M} = (S, \mathrm{Act}, T, s_0)$, where S is a set of *states*, Act is a finite set of *actions*, $T: S \to 2^{\mathrm{Act} \times \mathrm{Dist}(S)}$ is a *transition function*, and $s_0 \in S$ is the *initial state*. We assume that $T(s)$ is non-empty and finite for all $s \in S$. A finite path is a sequence $\pi = s_0(\alpha_0, \mu_0)s_1(\alpha_1, \mu_1)...s_n$ such that for all $0 \leq i \leq n - 1$ we have $(\alpha_i, \mu_i) \in T(s_i)$ and $\mu_i(s_{i+1}) > 0$. A *scheduler* $\mathfrak{S}$ selects for each such finite path π in $\mathcal{M}$ an element of $T(s_n)$. Infinite paths are defined accordingly. For $s \in S$ and $G \subseteq S$ the supremum $\mathbf{Pr}^{\max}_{\mathcal{M},s}(\Diamond G) := \sup_{\mathfrak{S}} \mathrm{Pr}^{\mathfrak{S}}_{\mathcal{M},s}(\Diamond G)$ and infimum $\mathbf{Pr}^{\min}_{\mathcal{M},s}(\Diamond G) := \inf_{\mathfrak{S}} \mathrm{Pr}^{\mathfrak{S}}_{\mathcal{M},s}(\Diamond G)$, ranging for all schedulers $\mathfrak{S}$ over the probability of those $\mathfrak{S}$-paths starting in s and eventually reaching G, are attained (see, for example, [5, Lemmata 10.102 and 10.113]). We define $\mathbf{Pr}^*_{\mathcal{M}}(\Diamond G) = \mathbf{Pr}^*_{\mathcal{M},s_0}(\Diamond G)$ for $* \in \{\min, \max\}$. Let $\mathcal{M} = (S_{\mathrm{all}}, \mathrm{Act}, T, s_0)$ be an MDP with two distinguished absorbing states goal and fail. A *(weak) subsystem* $\mathcal{M}'$ of $\mathcal{M}$, denoted $\mathcal{M}' \subseteq \mathcal{M}$, is an MDP $\mathcal{M}' = (S'_{\mathrm{all}}, \mathrm{Act}, T', s_0)$ with goal, fail $\in S'_{\mathrm{all}} \subseteq S_{\mathrm{all}}$, and for each $(\alpha, \mu') \in T'(s)$ there exists $(\alpha, \mu) \in T(s)$ such that for $v \neq$ fail we have $\mu'(v) \in \{0, \mu(v)\}$. Intuitively, in a subsystem some states and actions of $\mathcal{M}$ are deleted and some edges are redirected to fail. A subsystem is *strong* if, vice versa, for each $(\alpha, \mu) \in T(s)$ there exists $(\alpha, \mu') \in T'(s)$ with $\mu'(v) \in \{0, \mu(v)\}$.[1]

Farkas Certificates. Let us assume that for all $s \in S := S_{\mathrm{all}} \backslash \{\mathrm{goal}, \mathrm{fail}\}$ we have $\mathbf{Pr}^{\min}_s(\Diamond(\mathrm{goal} \vee \mathrm{fail})) > 0$. In the following we write $\mathbb{R}^{\mathcal{M}}$ for the real vector space indexed by $\bigcup_{s \in S}\{s\} \times T(s)$. To each of the threshold properties $\mathbf{Pr}^*_{s_0}(\Diamond \mathrm{goal}) \sim \lambda$ for $* \in \{\min, \max\}$ and $\sim \in \{\leq, <, \geq, >\}$, one can associate a polytope (possibly with non-closed faces) sitting either in $\mathbb{R}^S$ or $\mathbb{R}^{\mathcal{M}}$ that is non-empty if and only if the threshold is satisfied. Elements in this polytope are called *Farkas certificates* for the respective threshold property. The polytope of Farkas certificates for lower-bound thresholds $\mathbf{Pr}^*_{s_0}(\Diamond \mathrm{goal}) \geq \lambda$ are of the form

---

[1] This is a slight deviation from [14], where only strong subsystems were considered. Here we distinguish between weak and strong subsystems since it will reflect the corresponding notions for PTAs established in Sect. 3.

$$\mathcal{P}_{\mathcal{M}}^{\min}(\lambda) = \{\mathbf{z} \in \mathbb{R}_{\geq 0}^{S} \mid \mathbf{A}\mathbf{z} \leq \mathbf{b} \wedge \mathbf{z}(s_0) \geq \lambda\}, \quad \text{for } * = \min$$

$$\mathcal{P}_{\mathcal{M}}^{\max}(\lambda) = \{\mathbf{y} \in \mathbb{R}_{\geq 0}^{\mathcal{M}} \mid \mathbf{y}\mathbf{A} \leq \delta_{s_0} \wedge \mathbf{y}\mathbf{b} \geq \lambda\}, \quad \text{for } * = \max,$$

where $\mathbf{A} \in \mathbb{R}^{\mathcal{M} \times S}$ and $\mathbf{b} \in \mathbb{R}^{S}$ can be taken as a black box in this paper. The main result of [14] states that to any Farkas certificate $\mathbf{z} \in \mathcal{P}_{\mathcal{M}}^{\min}(\lambda)$ one can associate a strong subsystem $\mathcal{M}' \subseteq \mathcal{M}$ whose states are contained in $\mathrm{supp}(\mathbf{z}) = \{s \in S \mid \mathbf{z}(s) > 0\}$ and which satisfies $\mathbf{Pr}_{\mathcal{M}',s_0}^{\min}(\Diamond\mathrm{goal}) \geq \lambda$. The corresponding statement holds for $\mathbf{y} \in \mathcal{P}_{\mathcal{M}}^{\max}(\lambda)$ and subsystems with states contained in $\mathrm{supp}_S(\mathbf{y}) = \{s \in S \mid \exists \alpha \in T(s). \, \mathbf{y}(s, \alpha) > 0\}$.

Clock Constraints and Difference Bounds Matrices. We fix a finite number of *clocks* $\mathcal{C} = \{c_0, c_1, ..., c_n\}$, where by convention c_0 is a designated clock always representing 0 so that absolute and relative time bounds can be written in a uniform manner. A *valuation* on $\mathcal{C}$ is a map $v \colon \mathcal{C} \to \mathbb{R}_{\geq 0}$ such that $v(c_0) = 0$. The set of all valuations on $\mathcal{C}$ is denoted by $\mathrm{Val}(\mathcal{C})$. For a valuation v and $t \in \mathbb{R}_{\geq 0}$ we denote by $v+t$ the valuation with $(v+t)(c) = v(c)+t$ for all $c \in \mathcal{C}\backslash\{c_0\}$. Given $C \subseteq \mathcal{C}$ we let $v[C := 0]$ be the *reset* valuation with $v[C := 0](c) = 0$ for $c \in C$ and $v[C := 0](c) = v(c)$ for $c \notin C$. The set of *clock constraints* $\mathrm{CC}(\mathcal{C})$ is formed according to the following grammar: $g :: = \mathrm{true} \mid \mathrm{false} \mid c - c' \sim x \mid g \wedge g$, where $c, c' \in \mathcal{C}$, $x \in \mathbb{Z} \cup \{\infty, -\infty\}$, and $\sim \in \{\leq, <, \geq, >\}$. A valuation v satisfies a clock constraint g, written as $v \models g$, if replacing every clock variable c in g with the value $v(c)$ leads to a true formula. We set $\mathrm{Val}(g) = \{v \in \mathrm{Val}(\mathcal{C}) \mid v \models g\}$ and define $g_1 \Vdash g_2$ if $\mathrm{Val}(g_1) \subseteq \mathrm{Val}(g_2)$. A subset $Z \subseteq \mathrm{Val}(\mathcal{C})$ is a *zone* if $Z = \mathrm{Val}(g)$ for some clock constraint g. We commonly represent a clock constraint by a *difference bounds matrix* (DBM), which is a $\mathcal{C} \times \mathcal{C}$-matrix M over $(\mathbb{Z} \cup \{\infty, -\infty\}) \times \{<, \leq\}$. The intended meaning of an entry $M_{ij} = (a, \lhd)$ is the constraint $c_i - c_j \lhd a$. To each DBM M one can associate a DBM M^* containing constraints that are as tight as possible while still satisfying $\mathrm{Val}(M^*) = \mathrm{Val}(M)$ (see [13, Theorem 2]). We make use of the operations $\sqcap$ from [13] (corresponding to logical conjunction of the associated clock constraints) and the *time closure* operation $\uparrow$ of [8] (there called **up**), which removes all absolute time bounds from the DBM, see also the technical report [19, Lemma A.2].

Probabilistic Timed Automata. A *probabilistic timed automaton* (PTA) is a tuple $\mathcal{T} = (\mathrm{Loc}, \mathcal{C}, \mathrm{Act}, \mathrm{inv}, T, l_0)$, where Loc is a finite set of *locations*, $\mathcal{C}$ is a finite set of *clocks*, Act is a finite set of *actions*, $\mathrm{inv} \colon \mathrm{Loc} \to \mathrm{CC}(\mathcal{C})$ is the *invariance condition*, $T \colon \mathrm{Loc} \to 2^{\mathrm{CC}(\mathcal{C}) \times \mathrm{Act} \times \mathrm{Dist}(2^{\mathcal{C}} \times \mathrm{Loc})}$ is the transition function with $T(l)$ non-empty and finite for every $l \in \mathrm{Loc}$, and $l_0 \in \mathrm{Loc}$ is the *initial location*, for which we assume that $0 \models \mathrm{inv}(l_0)$. A transition $(g, \alpha, \mu) \in T(l)$ is written as $l \xrightarrow{g:\alpha} \mu$ and the element g is called the *guard*. The intended meaning of $T(l)$ is that from location l one first chooses non-deterministically a transition $l \xrightarrow{g:\alpha} \mu$, provided that the guard g is satisfied by the current clock valuation. Then an element $(C, l') \in 2^{\mathcal{C}} \times \mathrm{Loc}$ is picked according to the distribution μ, the clocks in C are reset and the next location is set to l'.

A *timed probabilistic system* (TPS) is a tuple $\mathcal{S} = (S, \text{Act}', T, s_0)$, where S is a set of states, $\text{Act}' = \text{Act} \uplus \mathbb{R}_+$ is a set of actions (Act is assumed to be finite), $T : S \to 2^{\text{Act}' \times \text{Dist}(S)}$ is the transition function, and s_0 the *initial state*. For a pair $(\alpha, \mu) \in T(s)$ (or $s \xrightarrow{\alpha} \mu$) we assume that μ has finite support. Transitions indexed by $\mathbb{R}_+$ are called *time delays* and transitions indexed by Act are *discrete actions*. Schedulers are defined as for MDPs, and a scheduler $\mathfrak{S}$ is *time-divergent* if for almost every path compatible with $\mathfrak{S}$ the series of time delays is divergent. Reachability probabilities $\mathbf{Pr}^*_{\mathcal{S},s}(\lozenge T)$ for $* \in \{\min, \max\}$ are defined as for MDPs, but only taking time-divergent schedulers into account.

A *pointed* PTA $(\mathcal{T}, \text{goal}, \text{fail})$ consists of a PTA $\mathcal{T} = (\text{Loc}, \mathcal{C}, \text{Act}, \text{inv}, T, l_0)$ and two distinguished absorbing locations goal, fail $\in$ Loc. The *semantics* of a pointed PTA is the TPS $\mathcal{S}(\mathcal{T}) = (S, \text{Act}', T_{\text{sem}}, s_0)$ with $S = \{(l, v) \in \text{Loc} \times \text{Val}(\mathcal{C}) \mid v \models \text{inv}(l)\}$, $\text{Act}' = \text{Act} \uplus \mathbb{R}_+$, $s_0 = (l_0, 0)$, and T_{sem} is the smallest function satisfying the inference rules

$$\frac{t \in \mathbb{R}_+, \forall t' \leq t. \ v + t' \models \text{inv}(l)}{(l, v) \xrightarrow{t} \delta_{(l,v+t)} \in T_{\text{sem}}} \quad \text{and} \quad \frac{l \xrightarrow{g:\alpha} \mu \in T, \ v \models g}{(l, v) \xrightarrow{\alpha} \mu_{\text{sem}} \in T_{\text{sem}}}, \text{ where}$$

$$\mu_{\text{sem}}(l', v') = \sum_{\substack{(C, l') \\ v' = v[C := 0]}} \mu(C, l') \quad \text{for } l' \neq \text{fail and } v' \models \text{inv}(l') \tag{2.1}$$

$$\mu_{\text{sem}}(\text{fail}, v') = \sum_{\substack{(C, \text{fail}) \\ v' = v[C := 0]}} \mu(C, \text{fail}) + \sum_{\substack{(C, l'), \ l' \neq \text{fail} \\ v' = v[C := 0] \not\models \text{inv}(l')}} \mu(C, l') \tag{2.2}$$

We define the goal set of $\mathcal{S}(\mathcal{T})$ to be $\text{goal}_{\mathcal{S}(\mathcal{T})} = \{(l, v) \in S \mid l = \text{goal}\}$. For $* \in \{\min, \max\}$ the probability to reach goal in $\mathcal{T}$ is defined as

$$\mathbf{Pr}^*_{\mathcal{T}, l_0}(\lozenge\text{goal}) := \mathbf{Pr}^*_{\mathcal{S}(\mathcal{T}), s_0}(\lozenge\text{goal}_{\mathcal{S}(\mathcal{T})})$$

Remark 2.1. Typically, the semantics is only defined if the PTA is *well-formed*. This means that no transition leads to a violation of the invariance condition of the target. We relax this condition and, in the case that $v' = v[C := 0] \not\models \text{inv}(l')$, add the probability of (C, l') to the edge $(l, v) \xrightarrow{\alpha} (\text{fail}, v')$ (this is the second sum in Eq. (2.2)). This generalization will facilitate our translation from Farkas certificates of quotients of $\mathcal{S}(\mathcal{T})$ to PTA subsystems.

Probabilistic Time-Abstracting Bisimulation. As in [11], we define a *probabilistic time-abstracting bisimulation* (PTAB) on a TPS $\mathcal{S} = (S, \text{Act} \uplus \mathbb{R}_+, T, s_0)$ to be an equivalence relation $\sim$ on S such that if $s \sim s'$ we have:

(1) for any time delay $s \xrightarrow{t} u$ there exists a time delay $s' \xrightarrow{t'} u'$ such that $u \sim u'$;

(2) for any discrete action $s \xrightarrow{\alpha} \mu$, there exists a discrete action $s' \xrightarrow{\alpha} \mu'$ such that for all $E \in S/\sim$ we have $\sum_{s \in E} \mu(s) = \sum_{s \in E} \mu'(s)$.

If $\mathcal{S}$ has distinguished sets goal, fail $\subseteq S$, we say that a PTAB $\sim$ *respects* goal and fail if whenever $(l, v) \sim (\text{goal}, v')$, then $l = \text{goal}$, and likewise for fail. The *quotient* of $\mathcal{S}$ by $\sim$ is the MDP $\mathcal{M}(\mathcal{S}/\sim) = (S/\sim, \text{Act} \cup \{\tau\}, T', [s_0])$ with

$$T'([s]) = \{(\tau, \delta_{[s']}) \mid \exists(t, \delta_{s'}) \in T(s)\} \cup \{(\alpha, \mu/\sim) \mid \exists(\alpha, \mu) \in T(s)\}$$

with $\mu/\sim(E') = \sum_{s' \in E'} \mu(s')$. As we could not find a formal proof for the following lemma in the literature, we included one in the technical report [19].

Lemma 2.2. *Let $\mathcal{S}$ be a TPS and $\sim$ a PTAB on $\mathcal{S}$ that respects* goal *and* fail. *Then for all $s \in S$ and $* \in \{\min, \max\}$ we have*

$$\mathbf{Pr}^*_{\mathcal{S},s}(\lozenge \text{goal}) = \mathbf{Pr}^*_{\mathcal{M}(\mathcal{S}/\sim),[s]}(\lozenge \text{goal}).$$

3   Witnessing Subsystems for Reachability in PTAs

In this chapter we generalize the notion of subsystems formalized first for Markov chains in [17] and MDPs in [34] to PTAs. From now on we assume for all pointed PTAs $(\mathcal{T}, \text{goal}, \text{fail})$ that the probability to eventually reach goal or fail is 1 for each time-divergent scheduler over the semantics $\mathcal{S}(\mathcal{T})$. This is necessary to apply the results of [14]. An important application that justifies this assumption is *time-bounded* reachability, where goal needs to be reached before an absolute time-bound K. This can be encoded in our setting by adding a clock c^* that is never reset, and adding $c^* \leq K$ to the invariance of every location.

3.1   Subsystems for PTAs

Definition 3.1 (Subsystem). *Let $(\mathcal{T}, \text{goal}, \text{fail})$ be a pointed PTA with $\mathcal{T} = (\text{Loc}, \mathcal{C}, \text{Act}, \text{inv}, T, l_0)$. A PTA $\mathcal{T}' = (\text{Loc}', \mathcal{C}, \text{Act}, \text{inv}', T', l_0)$ is a (weak) subsystem of $\mathcal{T}$ if the following three conditions hold:*

(1) goal, fail $\in \text{Loc}' \subseteq \text{Loc}$;
(2) for all locations $l \in \text{Loc}'$ we have $\text{inv}'(l) \Vdash \text{inv}(l)$;
(3) for all $l \in \text{Loc}'$ there is an injective map $\Phi: T'(l) \to T(l)$ such that for
$$\Phi(l \xrightarrow{g':\alpha'} \mu') = l \xrightarrow{g:\alpha} \mu \text{ we have (3a) } g' \Vdash g, \text{ (3b) } \alpha' = \alpha, \text{ and (3c) for all}$$
$(C, l') \in 2^{\mathcal{C}} \times \text{Loc}'$ with $l' \neq \text{fail}$ we have $\mu'(C, l') \in \{0, \mu(C, l')\}$.

We call $\mathcal{T}'$ a strong *subsystem if, additionally, the following two conditions hold for all $l \in \text{Loc}'$:*

(3*) there is a left-inverse $\Psi: T(l) \to T'(l)$ of Φ such that for $\Psi(l \xrightarrow{g:\alpha} \mu) = l \xrightarrow{g':\alpha'} \mu'$ we have (3a*) $g' \equiv g \wedge \text{inv}'(l)$, and (3b) and (3c) as above;
(4) if $v \in \text{Val}(\mathcal{C})$ and $t \in \mathbb{R}_+$ satisfy $v \models \text{inv}'(l)$ and $v + t \models \text{inv}(l)$, then also $v + t \models \text{inv}'(l)$.

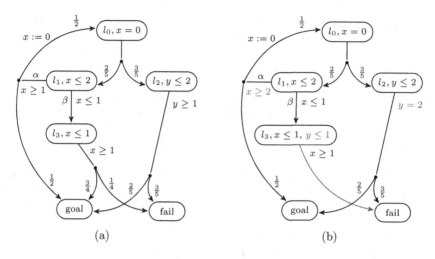

Fig. 1. A pointed PTA (left) and a weak subsystem therein (right).

In other words, in the passage from $\mathcal{T}$ to a subsystem, it is allowed to discard locations and elements in $T(l)$, redirect individual transitions to fail, and shrink invariants and guards. This will be sufficient for witnessing lower bounds on $\mathbf{Pr}^{\max}$ (see Corollary 3.4 below). For witnessing lower bounds on $\mathbf{Pr}^{\min}$ we need the extra assumptions that elements in $T(l)$ must not be deleted, guards can only shrink as much as the invariance and that $\mathrm{inv}'(l)$ is closed under time successors. On the level of quotients of the semantics of $\mathcal{T}$, this reflects the difference between weak and strong subsystems for MDPs (see Sect. 2). We demand Ψ to be a left-inverse of Φ instead of requiring that both are bijections since two different elements of $T(l)$ might coincidentally be shrunk to the same element of $T'(l)$.

Example 3.2. Consider the PTA $\mathcal{T}$ displayed in Fig. 1a. A scheduler $\mathfrak{S}$ in $\mathcal{T}$ principally has to choose between α and β whenever in l_1 (and letting time pass accordingly). Action α in state $(l_1, (x,y)) \in \mathcal{S}(\mathcal{T})$ leads to a higher probability to reach goal exactly when $y \leq 2$, the reason being that then the right-hand branch of $\mathcal{T}$ contributes towards $\mathrm{Pr}^{\mathfrak{S}}(\Diamond \text{goal})$ upon leaving l_0 the next time. Thus choosing β upon leaving l_1 for the first time leads to a scheduler attaining $\mathbf{Pr}_{\mathcal{T}}^{\min}(\Diamond \text{goal})$ (cf. Example B.1 in the technical report [19]). An example of a weak subsystem $\mathcal{T}' \subseteq \mathcal{T}$ is portrayed in Fig. 1b, with differences to $\mathcal{T}$ indicated in red. Even though $\mathcal{T}'$ fails to be a strong subsystem (e.g. the guard of α is shrunk more than allowed), we have $\mathbf{Pr}_{\mathcal{T}}^{\min}(\Diamond \text{goal}) \geq \mathbf{Pr}_{\mathcal{T}'}^{\min}(\Diamond \text{goal})$. However, this is not true for all weak subsystems: Take $\mathcal{T}''$ obtained from $\mathcal{T}$ by changing only the guard of the action β at l_1 from $x \leq 1$ to $x \leq 1 \wedge y \geq 2$. Then any scheduler is forced to take α at least once, resulting in $\mathbf{Pr}_{\mathcal{T}}^{\min}(\Diamond \text{goal}) < \mathbf{Pr}_{\mathcal{T}''}^{\min}(\Diamond \text{goal})$. Removing action β and location l_3 altogether has the same effect. This example illustrates that strong subsystems are indeed needed in order to deal with $\mathbf{Pr}^{\min}$ (cf. Corollary 3.4). More details can be found in the technical report [19].

We show that subsystems of a PTA $\mathcal{T}$ induce Farkas certificates in finite-state quotients of $\mathcal{S}(\mathcal{T})$, which are supported on the states induced by the subsystem. In other words, subsystems are reflected *purely algebraically* on the level of Farkas certificates. This is a generalization of the forward direction of [14, Theorem 5.4].

Theorem 3.3 (PTA Subsystems Induce Farkas Certificates). *Let* $(\mathcal{T}, \text{goal}, \text{fail})$ *be a pointed PTA, and let* $\sim$ *be a PTAB on* $\mathcal{S}(\mathcal{T})$ *that respects* goal *and* fail *and has finite index. Let* $\mathcal{M} = \mathcal{M}(\mathcal{S}(\mathcal{T})/_\sim)$ *be the associated quotient MDP with states* $S \cup \{\text{goal}, \text{fail}\}$. *Given a subsystem* $\mathcal{T}' \subseteq \mathcal{T}$, *let* $S' = \{[s] \in S \mid s \text{ is a state of } \mathcal{S}(\mathcal{T}')\}$.

Then there is a Farkas certificate $\mathbf{y} \in \mathbb{R}^{\mathcal{M}}$ *for* $\mathbf{Pr}_{\mathcal{M}}^{\max}(\lozenge\text{goal}) \geq \mathbf{Pr}_{\mathcal{T}'}^{\max}(\lozenge\text{goal})$ *with* $\text{supp}_S(\mathbf{y}) \subseteq S'$. *If* $\mathcal{T}'$ *is a strong subsystem, then there also exists a Farkas certificate* $\mathbf{z} \in \mathbb{R}^S$ *for* $\mathbf{Pr}_{\mathcal{M}}^{\min}(\lozenge\text{goal}) \geq \mathbf{Pr}_{\mathcal{T}'}^{\min}(\lozenge\text{goal})$ *such that* $\text{supp}(\mathbf{z}) \subseteq S'$.

Corollary 3.4. *Let* $(\mathcal{T}, \text{goal}, \text{fail})$ *be a pointed PTA.*

(1) If $\mathcal{T}' \subseteq \mathcal{T}$ *is a subsystem, then* $\mathbf{Pr}_{\mathcal{T}}^{\max}(\lozenge\text{goal}) \geq \mathbf{Pr}_{\mathcal{T}'}^{\max}(\lozenge\text{goal})$.
(2) If $\mathcal{T}' \subseteq \mathcal{T}$ *is a strong subsystem, then* $\mathbf{Pr}_{\mathcal{T}}^{\min}(\lozenge\text{goal}) \geq \mathbf{Pr}_{\mathcal{T}'}^{\min}(\lozenge\text{goal})$.

3.2 Zone Closure for DBMs

Our next aim is to show how Farkas certificates of the quotient $\mathcal{M}(\mathcal{S}/_\sim)$ can be translated back into PTA subsystems. As location invariants are described by zones, this requires to pass from states of the quotient (which represent equivalence classes of clock valuations) to zones that include these valuations and are as small as possible. We do this using the following operation, which relies on the lexicographic order on DBMs (see also the technical report [19, Section A.1]).

Definition 3.5 (Zone Closure). *Let* M *and* N *be DBMs over* $\mathcal{C}$. *The* zone closure $M \sqcup N$ *is the DBM defined by*

$$(M \sqcup N)_{ij} = \max\{M_{ij}, N_{ij}\} \text{ for all } i, j \in \mathcal{C}.$$

The zone closure satisfies the following properties:

Lemma 3.6. *Let* M, N *be DBMs such that* $M = M^*$ *and* $N = N^*$. *Then*

(1) $\text{Val}(M \sqcup N)$ *is the smallest zone in* $\text{Val}(\mathcal{C})$ *containing* $\text{Val}(M) \cup \text{Val}(N)$.
(2) We have $(M \sqcup N)^* = (M \sqcup N)$.

Given an arbitrary subset $R \subseteq \text{Val}(\mathcal{C})$ the *canonical DBM* M_R associated to R is defined as $(M_R)_{ij} = (\sup\{v(i) - v(j) \mid v \in R\}, \lhd)$ for $i, j \in \mathcal{C}$, where $\lhd = \leq$ exactly if the supremum is attained, and otherwise $<$. Then $M_R = M_R^*$ and $\text{Val}(M_R)$ is the smallest zone of $\text{Val}(\mathcal{C})$ that contains R (see the technical report [19, Lemma A.1]). Applying Lemma 3.6 to the canonical DBM associated to sets of clock valuations gives:

Proposition 3.7. *Let* $R_1, ..., R_n \subseteq \text{Val}(\mathcal{C})$ *be sets of clock valuations. For every* i *let* M_{R_i} *be the canonical DBM of* R_i *and set* $M = \bigsqcup_{i=1}^n M_{R_i}$. *Then,* $\text{Val}(M)$ *is the smallest zone in* $\text{Val}(\mathcal{C})$ *that contains all sets* R_i.

3.3   From Farkas Certificates to Witnessing Subsystems

We are now in a position to outline a construction which reverses Theorem 3.3, i.e., which passes from Farkas certificates for threshold properties in finite-state quotients of the PTA semantics to PTA subsystems. Of course, the constructed subsystems should *witness* the same threshold on the level of the PTA, as follows:

Definition 3.8 (Witness). *Let* $(\mathcal{T}, \text{goal}, \text{fail})$ *be a pointed PTA and let* $\lambda \in [0,1]$. *A witnessing subsystem or simply a witness for* $\mathbf{Pr}_{\mathcal{T}}^{\max}(\Diamond\text{goal}) \geq \lambda$ *is a subsystem* $\mathcal{T}' \subseteq \mathcal{T}$ *such that* $\mathbf{Pr}_{\mathcal{T}'}^{\max}(\Diamond\text{goal}) \geq \lambda$. *A witnessing subsystem or witness for* $\mathbf{Pr}_{\mathcal{T}}^{\min}(\Diamond\text{goal}) \geq \lambda$ *is a* strong *subsystem* $\mathcal{T}' \subseteq \mathcal{T}$ *such that* $\mathbf{Pr}_{\mathcal{T}'}^{\min}(\Diamond\text{goal}) \geq \lambda$.

By Corollary 3.4 a witnessing subsystem is indeed a witness for the given threshold property. The next definition shows how to construct a witness from Farkas certificates of finite-state quotients of the PTA semantics. Here and for the rest of this section we use the notation $S = S_{\text{all}} \setminus \{\text{goal}, \text{fail}\}$, where S_{all} are the states of a PTAB quotient of $\mathcal{S}(\mathcal{T})$.

Definition 3.9 (Induced Subsystems). *Let* $(\mathcal{T}, \text{goal}, \text{fail})$ *be a pointed PTA, and let* $\mathcal{M} = (S_{\text{all}}, \text{Act}, T, s_0)$ *the quotient of* $\mathcal{S}(\mathcal{T})$ *by a PTAB* $\sim$ *that respects* goal *and* fail *and has finite index. Given* $s \in S$ *and* $l \in \text{Loc}$ *we put*

$$s_{|l} = \{v \in \text{Val}(\mathcal{C}) \mid (l, v) \in s\}.$$

For a fixed $R \subseteq S$ *we define subsystems* $\mathcal{T}_R^w = (\text{Loc}', \mathcal{C}, \text{Act}, \text{inv}^w, T^w, l_0)$ *and* $\mathcal{T}_R^s = (\text{Loc}', \mathcal{C}, \text{Act}, \text{inv}^s, T^s, l_0)$ *induced by* R *as follows:*

- *Both have locations:* $\text{Loc}' = \{l \in \text{Loc} \mid \exists s \in R.\ s_{|l} \neq \emptyset\} \cup \{\text{goal}, \text{fail}\}$
- *For each location* $l \in \text{Loc}'$ *we consider the DBMs*

$$M_l^w = \bigsqcup_{s \in R} M_{s_{|l}} \quad and \quad M_l^s = (\uparrow M_l^w) \sqcap M_{\text{inv}(l)}$$

and let $\text{inv}^w(l) = M_l^w$ *and* $\text{inv}^s(l) = M_l^s$.
- *For every* $l \xrightarrow{g:\alpha} \mu$ *in* $T(l)$ *with* $l \in \text{Loc}'$ *let*

$$g^w = g \sqcap \bigsqcup_{\substack{s \in R \\ \exists(l,v) \in s.\ v \models g}} M_{s_{|l}} \quad and \quad g^s = g \sqcap \text{inv}^s(l)$$

For $C \subseteq \mathcal{C}$ *and* $l' \in \text{Loc}' \setminus \{\text{fail}\}$ *let*

$$\mu'(C, l') = \begin{cases} \mu(C, l') & \text{if } \exists s, s' \in R, (l, v) \in s.\ (l', v[C := 0]) \in s' \\ 0 & \text{otherwise} \end{cases}$$

and assign the remaining probability to $\mu'(\text{fail}, \emptyset)$. *Now add a transition* $l \xrightarrow{g^w:\alpha} \mu'$ *to* $T^w(l)$ *and* $l \xrightarrow{g^s:\alpha} \mu'$ *to* $T^s(l)$.

The intuition behind this construction is that one completes all states of T whose equivalence class is in R to a smallest (weak or strong) subsystem of T whose state space contains this set. In each location, the set of clock valuations which induce states in R is turned into a viable invariance condition using the operation $\sqcup$. Guards of transitions in T are shrunk accordingly, and their support is restricted to those pairs (C, l') which – on the level of the quotient $\mathcal{M}$ – induce at least one transition between two elements of R.

Lemma 3.10. *Let $(T, \text{goal}, \text{fail})$ be a pointed PTA and $\mathcal{M} = (S_{\text{all}}, \text{Act}, T, s_0)$ the quotient of $\mathcal{S}(T)$ by a PTAB that respects* goal *and* fail. *Then for any $R \subseteq S$, T_R^w is a subsystem and T_R^s is a strong subsystem of T.*

The following proposition states that Farkas certificates for any PTAB quotient of the PTA can be used to find witnesses for probabilistic reachability constraints. It is a generalization of the backward direction of [14, Theorem 5.4] and provides a converse of Theorem 3.3.

Proposition 3.11 (Farkas Certificates to Witnesses). *Let $(T, \text{goal}, \text{fail})$ be a pointed PTA and $\mathcal{M} = (S_{\text{all}}, \text{Act}, T, s_0)$ the quotient of $\mathcal{S}(T)$ by a PTAB $\sim$ that respects* goal *and* fail. *Fix $\lambda \in [0, 1]$ and $R \subseteq S$.*

If there exists a Farkas certificate $\mathbf{z} \in \mathcal{P}_{\mathcal{M}}^{\min}(\lambda)$ with $\text{supp}(\mathbf{z}) \subseteq R$, then T_R^s is a witness for $\mathbf{Pr}_T^{\min}(\Diamond\text{goal}) \geq \lambda$. Likewise, if there exists a Farkas certificate $\mathbf{y} \in \mathcal{P}_{\mathcal{M}}^{\max}(\lambda)$ with $\text{supp}_S(\mathbf{y}) \subseteq R$, then T_R^w is a witness for $\mathbf{Pr}_T^{\max}(\Diamond\text{goal}) \geq \lambda$.

4   Computing Minimal Witnessing Subsystems

We now introduce three notions of minimality for subsystems of PTAs and show how minimal (or small) subsystems can be computed. Henceforth let $\mathcal{M}$ be the quotient (with states S_{all}) of the semantics of a pointed PTA $(T, \text{goal}, \text{fail})$ by a PTAB $\sim$ that has finite index and let $S = S_{\text{all}} \backslash \{\text{goal}, \text{fail}\}$.

As the threshold problem for min and max-reachability constraints of PTAs is directly reducible to the *existence* of a witness for the same property, computing (minimal) witnessing subsystems is at least as hard as this problem. Deciding $\mathbf{Pr}_T^{\max}(\Diamond\text{goal}) \geq 1$ is EXPTIME-hard [27, Theorem 3.1] for PTAs, which holds already for time-bounded reachability. PSPACE-hardness of $\mathbf{Pr}_T^{\min}(\Diamond\text{goal}) \geq 1$ (which is equivalent to $\mathbf{Pr}_T^{\max}(\Diamond\text{goal}) > 0$ in the time-bounded setting) follows from PSPACE-hardness of non-probabilistic reachability [2, Theorem 4.17].

4.1   Notions of Minimality for PTA Subsystems

For a set of valuations $R \subseteq \text{Val}(\mathcal{C})$ we denote by $\text{vol}(R)$ the Lebesgue volume of R considered as a subset of $\mathbb{R}^{\mathcal{C}\backslash\{c_0\}}$. The *volume* of a PTA T is defined as

$$\text{vol}(T) = \sum_{l \in \text{Loc}(T)} \text{vol}\big(\text{Val}(\text{inv}(l))\big) \in \mathbb{R}_{\geq 0} \cup \{\infty\}.$$

Definition 4.1 (Notions of Minimality). *We define three partial orders on subsystems T_1, T_2 of a PTA T as follows:*

(1) $T_1 \leq_{\mathrm{loc}} T_2$ if $|\mathrm{Loc}(T_1)| \leq |\mathrm{Loc}(T_2)|$;
(2) $T_1 \leq_{\mathrm{inv}} T_2$ if $\mathrm{Loc}(T_1) \subseteq \mathrm{Loc}(T_2)$ and for all $l \in \mathrm{Loc}(T_1) : \mathrm{inv}_{T_1}(l) \Vdash \mathrm{inv}_{T_2}(l)$;
(3) $T_1 \leq_{\mathrm{vol}} T_2$ if $\mathrm{vol}(T_1) \leq \mathrm{vol}(T_2)$.

We say that a witness $T' \subseteq T$ for some threshold property as defined in Definition 3.8 is loc-minimal *(respectively,* inv-minimal *or* vol-minimal*) if T' is a $\leq_{\mathrm{loc}}$-minimal element (respectively, $\leq_{\mathrm{inv}}$-minimal or $\leq_{\mathrm{vol}}$-minimal element) among all witnesses of T for the same threshold property.*

When considering inv- and vol-minimality, we will assume that $\mathrm{Val}(\mathrm{inv}(l))$ is bounded for every location $l \in \mathrm{Loc}$, or, equivalently, that a finite upper bound on all clocks exists. This will guarantee that the set of witnesses that we have to consider is finite, and, for vol-minimality, that their volume is finite.

The rationale for considering vol-minimal witnesses is that they have – in a precise measure-theoretic sense – a minimal number of states. Note that in contrast to $\leq_{\mathrm{loc}}$ and $\leq_{\mathrm{vol}}$, the partial order $\leq_{\mathrm{inv}}$ is not a total order and thus results in general in many incomparable inv-minimal witnesses.

Example 4.2. Consider the PTA of Example 3.2. Table 1 lists minimal witnesses for $\lambda = 6/25$ for all three notions of minimality. The inv-minimal witnesses for $\mathbf{Pr}^{\max}$ also encode corresponding schedulers with probability of at least $6/25$ (e.g. the first one encodes waiting in l_1 for one time unit, choosing α, and on the branch going through l_0 repeating this once more). For $\mathbf{Pr}^{\min}$, the inv-minimal witnesses ensure that whatever choice the scheduler makes the induced probability will be at least $6/25$. See Example C.1 in the technical report [19] for more details.

Lemma 4.3. *We have $\leq_{\mathrm{inv}} \subseteq \leq_{\mathrm{loc}} \cap \leq_{\mathrm{vol}}$. Moreover, $\leq_{\mathrm{vol}}$ and $\leq_{\mathrm{loc}}$ are incomparable in general.*

Note that Lemma 4.3 does not imply that inv-minimal witness are loc-minimal or vol-minimal. This is because an inv-minimal witness might be $\leq_{\mathrm{inv}}$-incomparable to witnesses with smaller volume (see also Example 4.2).

4.2   Computing Loc-Minimal Witnesses

In this section we will assume that whenever $(l_1, v_1) \sim (l_2, v_2)$, then $l_1 = l_2$. To compute a loc-minimal strong subsystem of T we use a mixed integer linear program (MILP) over the inequalities defining $\mathcal{P}_{\mathcal{M}}^{\min}(\lambda)$ (see Sect. 2). We first define the linear inequalities:

$$\mathbf{z} \in \mathcal{P}_{\mathcal{M}}^{\min}(\lambda) \text{ and } \mathbf{z}_{[(l,v)]} \leq \zeta_l \text{ for all } [(l,v)] \in S \qquad \text{(LOC-CONSTR)}$$

This adds exactly $|S|$ inequalities to the ones defining $\mathcal{P}_{\mathcal{M}}^{\min}(\lambda)$. The idea is that as the variable $\mathbf{z}_{[(l,v)]}$ measures whether $[(l, v)]$ should be contained in the MDP subsystem associated with a Farkas certificate, the new variable ζ_l measures whether location l is needed *at all* in the corresponding PTA subsystem.

Table 1. Every indent describes a minimal witness for the PTA $\mathcal{T}$ in Fig. 1a. For inv-minimal ones, invariants are highlighted in blue after colons of the corresponding location, where the clock x is drawn on the horizontal axis, y on the vertical axis, and gridlines have unit 1.

	$\mathbf{Pr}_{\mathcal{T}}^{\max}(\Diamond \text{goal}) \geq 6/25$	$\mathbf{Pr}_{\mathcal{T}}^{\min}(\Diamond \text{goal}) \geq 6/25$
loc	– keeping l_0 and l_1; – keeping l_0 and l_2;	– keeping l_0 and l_2;
inv	– l_0: ▢ , l_1: ▨ – l_0: ▢ , l_2: ▨ – l_0: ▢ , l_1: ▢ , l_3: ▨ – l_0: ▢ , l_1: ▨ , l_3: ▢	– l_0: ▢ , l_2: ▨ – l_0: ▢ , l_1: ▨ , l_3: ▨
vol	– the bottom three inv-minimal witnesses from above (vol = 0)	– the top inv-minimal witness from above (vol = 0)

Proposition 4.4. *There exists a witnessing subsystem for* $\mathbf{Pr}_{\mathcal{T}}^{\min}(\Diamond \text{goal}) \geq \lambda$ *with at most k locations (excluding* goal *and* fail*) if and only if there exists a pair* $(\mathbf{z}, \zeta)$ *that satisfies* (LOC-CONSTR)*, where ζ has at most k non-zero entries.*

Restricting ζ_l to the domain $\{0, 1\}$ leads to the following MILP:

$$\min \sum_{l \in \text{Loc}} \zeta_l \quad \text{s.t.} \quad (\mathbf{z}, \zeta) \text{ satisfies (LOC-CONSTR)} \qquad \text{(LOC-MILP)}$$

By Proposition 4.4, solutions of (LOC-MILP) correspond to loc-minimal witnesses for $\mathbf{Pr}_{\mathcal{T}}^{\min}(\Diamond \text{goal}) \geq \lambda$. Although the size of (LOC-MILP) is exponential in the size of $\mathcal{T}$, it has only $|\text{Loc}|$ many binary variables. Hence, if the size of $\mathcal{M}$ is single-exponential (as is already the case for the *region graph*, see [1,23]), a loc-minimal witness can be computed in single-exponential time:

Proposition 4.5. *A loc-minimal witness for* $\mathbf{Pr}_{\mathcal{T}}^{\min}(\Diamond \text{goal}) \geq \lambda$ *can be computed in time* $\mathcal{O}(2^{|\text{Loc}|} \cdot \text{poly}(|\mathcal{M}|))$*, if one exists.*

One can deal with $\mathbf{Pr}_{\mathcal{T}}^{\max}(\Diamond \text{goal}) \geq \lambda$ similarly. In [14] the *quotient sum heuristic* was introduced as an approach for finding vectors with many zeros in a given polytope by iteratively solving LPs whose objective function is the inverse of the last optimal solution. This approach can be adapted to maximize zeros in only part of the dimensions by assigning the objective value 0 to the rest. In the case of loc-minimal witnesses one discards all variables $\mathbf{z}_{[(l,v)]}$ and optimizes only over the new variables ζ_l (which are non-binary in the LP-based QS heuristic).

4.3 Computing Inv-Minimal Witnesses

We now assume that $\mathrm{Val}(\mathrm{inv}(l))$ is bounded in every location l, and take K to be an upper bound on all clocks that must then exist. While for loc-minimality we assumed that $\sim$ distinguishes locations, now we additionally assume that if $(l_1, v_1) \sim (l_2, v_2)$, then there is no clock constraint γ such that $v_1 \models \gamma$ and $v_2 \not\models \gamma$. So, equivalent valuations must be indistinguishable by clock constraints. The coarsest PTAB that achieves this is the region equivalence (see [1,23]).

To encode invariance strength, we will use $n = 4K + 1$ binary variables $\xi_{ij}^l(k)$ with $k \in \{-2K, \ldots, 2K\}$ for every location l and ordered pair of clocks c_i, c_j. The intended meaning of $\xi_{ij}^l(k) = 1$ is that $\lceil k/2 \rceil$ is an upper bound for $v(i) - v(j)$ for all $v \in \mathrm{Val}(\mathrm{inv}(l))$. We have introduced the granularity $1/2$ in order to distinguish between strict and non-strict inequalities. For even k, which will represent $\leq$, the upper bound will always be met. Formally, we consider the following constraints, ranging over $l \in \mathrm{Loc}$ and $c_i, c_j \in \mathcal{C}$ with $j \neq 0$:

$$\mathbf{z} \in \mathcal{P}_{\mathcal{M}}^{\min}(\lambda)$$

$$\mathbf{z}_{[(l,v)]} \leq \begin{cases} \xi_{ij}^l(2a - 1) & \text{if } (M_{[(l,v)]})_{ij} = (a, <) \\ \xi_{ij}^l(2a) & \text{if } (M_{[(l,v)]})_{ij} = (a, \leq) \end{cases} \qquad (\text{INV-CONSTR})$$

$$\xi_{ij}^l(k) \leq \xi_{ij}^l(k - 1) \quad \text{for all } k \in \{-2K + 1, \ldots, 2K\}$$

In the above, $M_{[(l,v)]}$ is the canonical DBM for the set of valuations $\{v' \in \mathrm{Val}(\mathcal{C}) \mid (l, v') \in [(l, v)]\}$ as defined in Sect. 3.2. The reason for excluding the constraints where c_j is the zero clock is that for strong subsystems a stronger invariant cannot be achieved by strengthening the upper bound of a clock, cf. Definition 3.1, (4). On top of these constraints we now define the MILP:

$$\min \sum_{l,i,j,k} \xi_{ij}^l(k) \quad \text{s.t } (\mathbf{z}, \xi) \text{ satisfies } (\text{INV-CONSTR}). \qquad (\text{INV-MILP})$$

Proposition 4.6. *If $(\mathbf{z}, \xi)$ is a solution of (INV-MILP), then $\mathcal{T}_{\mathrm{supp}(\mathbf{z})}^s$ is an inv-minimal witness for $\mathbf{Pr}_{\mathcal{T}}^{\min}(\Diamond\mathrm{goal}) \geq \lambda$.*

The number of binary variables in (INV-MILP) is $n \cdot |\mathrm{Loc}| \cdot (|\mathcal{C}|^2 - |\mathcal{C}|)$. However, due to the constraints $\xi_{ij}^l(k) \leq \xi_{ij}^l(k - 1)$, there are only n possible configurations of the binary variables $\xi_{ij}^l(k)$ for every location l and pair of clocks c_i, c_j. Hence, the number of satisfying configurations of ξ is bounded by $n^{|\mathrm{Loc}| \cdot (|\mathcal{C}|^2 - |\mathcal{C}|)}$. In a similar way as for Proposition 4.5 we get:

Proposition 4.7. *An inv-minimal witness for $\mathbf{Pr}_{\mathcal{T}}^{\min}(\Diamond\mathrm{goal}) \geq \lambda$ can be computed in time $\mathcal{O}(2^{\log(n) \cdot |\mathrm{Loc}| \cdot |\mathcal{C}|^2} \cdot \mathrm{poly}(|\mathcal{M}|))$, if one exists.*

Again, $\mathbf{Pr}_{\mathcal{T}}^{\max}$ can be treated similarly and the same idea of deriving heuristics that was outlined to loc-minimal witnesses can be used here.

4.4 Computing Vol-Minimal Witnesses

As for inv-minimality, we will assume that $\sim$ distinguishes states that are distinguishable by clock constraints and that K is an upper bound on all clocks. To get a candidate set of possible vol-minimal witnesses, we use the following lemma:

Lemma 4.8. *For* $* \in \{\min, \max\}$, *there is at least one witness for* $\mathbf{Pr}_{\mathcal{T}}^{*}(\Diamond \mathrm{goal})$ $\geq \lambda$ *that is both inv- and vol-minimal.*

Hence, to find a vol-minimal witness it suffices to compute (1) *all* inv-minimal witnesses and (2) compare their volumes. Using the results of the previous section, for (1) it is enough to solve the *multi-objective* mixed integer linear program

$$\text{for all } \begin{smallmatrix} l \in \mathrm{Loc} \\ c_i, c_j \in \mathcal{C} \\ j \neq 0 \end{smallmatrix} : \ \min \sum_k \xi_{ij}^l(k) \ \text{ s.t. } \ (\mathbf{z}, \xi) \text{ satisfies } (\texttt{INV-CONSTR}) \qquad (\texttt{INV-MO})$$

A solution of this program is a vector that satisfies ($\texttt{INV-CONSTR}$) and such that all other vectors satisfying ($\texttt{INV-CONSTR}$) evaluate worse on at least one objective function. This implies that the set of solutions of ($\texttt{INV-MO}$) encodes precisely the set of inv-minimal witnesses for $\mathbf{Pr}_{\mathcal{T}}^{\min}(\Diamond \mathrm{goal}) \geq \lambda$. Techniques for solving such programs efficiently are presented in [29, 30].

Let $\mathrm{VOL}(|\mathcal{C}|^2, \log(K))$ be the time complexity of computing the volume of a DBM over clocks $\mathcal{C}$ with entries bounded from above by K. This factor is exponential in general, but polynomial if the number of clocks is fixed [15]. Then we get the following time complexity for computing vol-minimal witnesses:

Proposition 4.9. *A vol-minimal witness for* $\mathbf{Pr}_{\mathcal{T}}^{\min}(\Diamond \mathrm{goal}) \geq \lambda$ *can be computed in time* $\mathcal{O}(2^{\log(n) \cdot |\mathrm{Loc}| \cdot |\mathcal{C}|^2} \cdot \mathrm{VOL}(|\mathcal{C}|^2, \log(K)) \cdot \mathrm{poly}(|\mathcal{M}|))$, *if one exists.*

4.5 Hardness of Deciding $\leq_{\mathrm{vol}}$

Computing the volume of a polytope generally requires exponential time in the number of dimensions. However, as the invariants of PTA have a restricted form involving only linear inequalities with at most two clocks, one might hope that computing their volume is easier. We now show that this is not the case (under the standard complexity theoretic assumptions).

We recall that #P is the counting complexity class that includes the functions that can be expressed as the number of accepting runs of a polynomial time, non-deterministic Turing machine (NTM) for a given input. Hardness for #P is typically defined using polynomial-time Turing reductions. The analogous decision class is PP, where $L \in$ PP if there is a polynomial time NTM such that $x \in L$ if and only if the majority of runs of the NTM on x is accepting (see [4, Chapter 9] for an introduction). Via a reduction from #P-hardness results on polytope volume computation, we obtain:

Proposition 4.10. *Computing* vol(Val(M)) *for a DBM M is* #P-*hard.*

Using this proposition we can show that deciding the $\leq_{\mathrm{vol}}$ relation for two PTA subsystems is substantially harder than for $\leq_{\mathrm{loc}}$ and $\leq_{\mathrm{inv}}$.

Theorem 4.11. *Given two subsystems T_1, T_2 in a PTA T, deciding whether $T_1 \leq_{\mathrm{vol}} T_2$ holds is* PP-*hard under polynomial-time Turing reductions.*

Hence, in particular, there is no polynomial time algorithm to decide $T_1 \leq_{\mathrm{vol}} T_2$, unless P = NP. This should be contrasted with the relations $\leq_{\mathrm{loc}}$ and $\leq_{\mathrm{inv}}$. To decide $T_1 \leq_{\mathrm{loc}} T_2$ one just counts the locations, and for $T_1 \leq_{\mathrm{inv}} T_2$ one checks the inclusion of locations and inspects the entries of the canonical DBMs associated to the invariants. In fact, these observations for $\leq_{\mathrm{loc}}$ and $\leq_{\mathrm{inv}}$ are the main ingredients for the MILP formulations (LOC-MILP) and (INV-MILP).

5 Conclusion

This paper introduces witnessing subsystems for PTAs. These subsystems give insight into which (hopefully small) part of the system is sufficient for a certain property to hold. We have studied three notions of minimality for witnessing subsystems: location number, invariant strength, and invariant volume. For all three we derive single-exponential algorithms to compute a minimal witness. Our approaches are based on Farkas certificates for quotient MDPs under probabilistic time-abstracting bisimulations. The time complexities are relative to the sizes of these quotients, so coarse bisimulations can substantially benefit the approach. While comparing two subsystems with respect to their location number or invariance strength is relatively easy, comparing the volume is shown to be PP-hard. This result notably extends also to non-probabilistic timed automata.

An open question is how to extend the scope of witnessing subsystems to probabilistic hybrid automata (PHA). It is conceivable that our approach extends naturally to *rectangular* PHAs, as they admit finite bisimulation quotients [31]. Exploring how PTA subsystems can be used in timed versions of refinement and synthesis algorithms [10, 16] is another interesting line of future work.

References

1. Alur, R., Courcoubetis, C., Dill, D.: Model-checking in dense real-time. Inf. Comput. **104**(1), 2–34 (1993). https://doi.org/10.1006/inco.1993.1024
2. Alur, R., Dill, D.L.: A theory of timed automata. Theor. Comput. Sci. **126**(2), 183–235 (1994). https://doi.org/10.1016/0304-3975(94)90010-8
3. Andrés, M.E., D'Argenio, P., van Rossum, P.: Significant diagnostic counterexamples in probabilistic model checking. In: Chockler, H., Hu, A.J. (eds.) HVC 2008. LNCS, vol. 5394, pp. 129–148. Springer, Heidelberg (2009). https://doi.org/10.1007/978-3-642-01702-5_15
4. Arora, S., Barak, B.: Computational Complexity - A Modern Approach. Cambridge University Press, Cambridge (2009)

5. Baier, C., Katoen, J.P.: Principles of Model Checking (Representation and Mind Series). MIT Press, Cambridge (2008)
6. Beauquier, D.: On probabilistic timed automata. Theor. Comput. Sci. **292**(1), 65–84 (2003). https://doi.org/10.1016/S0304-3975(01)00215-8
7. Behrmann, G., et al.: Uppaal 4.0. In: Quantitative Evaluation of Systems, QEST (2006). https://doi.org/10.1109/QEST.2006.59
8. Bengtsson, J., Yi, W.: Timed automata: semantics, algorithms and tools. In: Desel, J., Reisig, W., Rozenberg, G. (eds.) ACPN 2003. LNCS, vol. 3098, pp. 87–124. Springer, Heidelberg (2004). https://doi.org/10.1007/978-3-540-27755-2_3
9. Berendsen, J., Jansen, D.N., Katoen, J.: Probably on time and within budget: on reachability in priced probabilistic timed automata. In: Quantitative Evaluation of Systems QEST (2006). https://doi.org/10.1109/QEST.2006.43
10. Češka, M., Hensel, C., Junges, S., Katoen, J.-P.: Counterexample-driven synthesis for probabilistic program sketches. In: ter Beek, M.H., McIver, A., Oliveira, J.N. (eds.) FM 2019. LNCS, vol. 11800, pp. 101–120. Springer, Cham (2019). https://doi.org/10.1007/978-3-030-30942-8_8
11. Chen, T., Han, T., Katoen, J.: Time-abstracting bisimulation for probabilistic timed automata. In: International Symposium on Theoretical Aspects of Software Engineering, pp. 177–184 (2008). https://doi.org/10.1109/TASE.2008.29
12. Dierks, H., Kupferschmid, S., Larsen, K.G.: Automatic abstraction refinement for timed automata. In: Raskin, J.-F., Thiagarajan, P.S. (eds.) FORMATS 2007. LNCS, vol. 4763, pp. 114–129. Springer, Heidelberg (2007). https://doi.org/10.1007/978-3-540-75454-1_10
13. Dill, D.L.: Timing assumptions and verification of finite-state concurrent systems. In: Sifakis, J. (ed.) CAV 1989. LNCS, vol. 407, pp. 197–212. Springer, Heidelberg (1990). https://doi.org/10.1007/3-540-52148-8_17
14. Funke, F., Jantsch, S., Baier, C.: Farkas certificates and minimal witnesses for probabilistic reachability constraints. TACAS 2020. LNCS, vol. 12078, pp. 324–345. Springer, Cham (2020). https://doi.org/10.1007/978-3-030-45190-5_18
15. Gritzmann, P., Klee, V.: On the complexity of some basic problems in computational convexity. In: Bisztriczky, T., McMullen, P., Schneider, R., Weiss, A.I. (eds.) Polytopes: Abstract Convex and Computational. Springer, Dordrecht (1994). https://doi.org/10.1007/978-94-011-0924-6_17
16. Hermanns, H., Wachter, B., Zhang, L.: Probabilistic CEGAR. In: Gupta, A., Malik, S. (eds.) CAV 2008. LNCS, vol. 5123, pp. 162–175. Springer, Heidelberg (2008). https://doi.org/10.1007/978-3-540-70545-1_16
17. Jansen, N., Ábrahám, E., Katelaan, J., Wimmer, R., Katoen, J.-P., Becker, B.: Hierarchical counterexamples for discrete-time Markov chains. In: Bultan, T., Hsiung, P.-A. (eds.) ATVA 2011. LNCS, vol. 6996, pp. 443–452. Springer, Heidelberg (2011). https://doi.org/10.1007/978-3-642-24372-1_33
18. Jansen, N., et al.: Symbolic counterexample generation for large discrete-time Markov chains. Sci. Comput. Program. **91**, 90–114 (2014). https://doi.org/10.1016/j.scico.2014.02.001
19. Jantsch, S., Funke, F., Baier, C.: Minimal witnesses for probabilistic timed automata. arXiv:2007.00637 (2020)
20. Jurdziński, M., Kwiatkowska, M., Norman, G., Trivedi, A.: Concavely-priced probabilistic timed automata. In: Bravetti, M., Zavattaro, G. (eds.) CONCUR 2009. LNCS, vol. 5710, pp. 415–430. Springer, Heidelberg (2009). https://doi.org/10.1007/978-3-642-04081-8_28

21. Jurdziński, M., Laroussinie, F., Sproston, J.: Model checking probabilistic timed automata with one or two clocks. In: Grumberg, O., Huth, M. (eds.) TACAS 2007. LNCS, vol. 4424, pp. 170–184. Springer, Heidelberg (2007). https://doi.org/10.1007/978-3-540-71209-1_15
22. Kölbl, M., Leue, S., Wies, T.: Clock bound repair for timed systems. In: Dillig, I., Tasiran, S. (eds.) CAV 2019. LNCS, vol. 11561, pp. 79–96. Springer, Cham (2019). https://doi.org/10.1007/978-3-030-25540-4_5
23. Kwiatkowska, M., Norman, G., Segala, R., Sproston, J.: Automatic verification of real-time systems with discrete probability distributions. Theor. Comput. Sci. **282**(1), 101–150 (2002). https://doi.org/10.1016/S0304-3975(01)00046-9
24. Kwiatkowska, M., Norman, G., Sproston, J.: Probabilistic model checking of deadline properties in the IEEE 1394 FireWire root contention protocol. Form. Asp. Comput. **14**(3), 295–318 (2003). https://doi.org/10.1007/s001650300007
25. Kwiatkowska, M.Z., Norman, G., Parker, D., Sproston, J.: Performance analysis of probabilistic timed automata using digital clocks. Form. Method Syst. Des. **29**, 33–78 (2006). https://doi.org/10.1007/s10703-006-0005-2
26. Kwiatkowska, M.Z., Norman, G., Sproston, J., Wang, F.: Symbolic model checking for probabilistic timed automata. Inf. Comput. **205**(7), 1027–1077 (2007). https://doi.org/10.1016/j.ic.2007.01.004
27. Laroussinie, F., Sproston, J.: State explosion in almost-sure probabilistic reachability. Inf. Process. Lett. **102**(6), 236–241 (2007). https://doi.org/10.1016/j.ipl.2007.01.003
28. Norman, G., Parker, D., Sproston, J.: Model checking for probabilistic timed automata. Form. Methods Syst. Des. **43**, 164–190 (2013). https://doi.org/10.1007/s10703-012-0177-x
29. Özpeynirci, Ö., Köksalan, M.: An exact algorithm for finding extreme supported nondominated points of multiobjective mixed integer programs. Manag. Sci. **56**(12), 2302–2315 (2010). https://doi.org/10.1287/mnsc.1100.1248
30. Pettersson, W., Ozlen, M.: Multi-objective mixed integer programming: an objective space algorithm. AIP Conf. Proc. **2070**(1), 020039 (2019). https://doi.org/10.1063/1.5090006
31. Sproston, J.: Discrete-time verification and control for probabilistic rectangular hybrid automata. In: Eight International Conference on Quantitative Evaluation of Systems, QEST 2011, pp. 79–88 (2011). https://doi.org/10.1109/QEST.2011.18
32. Tripakis, S.: L'analyse formelle des systèmes temporisés en pratique. Ph.D. thesis, Université Joseph Fourier (1998)
33. Wimmer, R., Jansen, N., Ábrahám, E., Katoen, J.P.: High-level counterexamples for probabilistic automata. Log. Methods Comput. Sci. **11**(1) (2015). https://doi.org/10.2168/LMCS-11(1:15)2015
34. Wimmer, R., Jansen, N., Ábrahám, E., Katoen, J., Becker, B.: Minimal counterexamples for linear-time probabilistic verification. Theor. Comput. Sci. **549**, 61–100 (2014). https://doi.org/10.1016/j.tcs.2014.06.020
35. Wimmer, S., Mutius, J.: Verified certification of reachability checking for timed automata. TACAS 2020. LNCS, vol. 12078, pp. 425–443. Springer, Cham (2020). https://doi.org/10.1007/978-3-030-45190-5_24

Probabilistic Hyperproperties with Nondeterminism

Erika Ábrahám[1], Ezio Bartocci[2], Borzoo Bonakdarpour[3(✉)], and Oyendrila Dobe[3]

[1] RWTH-Aachen, Aachen, Germany
abraham@informatik.rwth-aachen.de
[2] Technische Universität Wien, Vienna, Austria
ezio.bartocci@tuwien.ac.at
[3] Michigan State University, East Lansing, USA
{borzoo,dobeoyen}@msu.edu

Abstract. We study the problem of formalizing and checking probabilistic hyperproperties for models that allow nondeterminism in actions. We extend the temporal logic HyperPCTL, which has been previously introduced for discrete-time Markov chains, to enable the specification of hyperproperties also for Markov decision processes. We generalize HyperPCTL by allowing explicit and simultaneous quantification over schedulers and probabilistic computation trees and show that it can express important quantitative requirements in security and privacy. We show that HyperPCTL model checking over MDPs is in general undecidable for quantification over probabilistic schedulers with memory, but restricting the domain to memoryless non-probabilistic schedulers turns the model checking problem decidable. Subsequently, we propose an SMT-based encoding for model checking this language and evaluate its performance.

1 Introduction

Hyperproperties [1] extend the conventional notion of *trace properties* [2] from a set of traces to a set of sets of traces. In other words, a hyperproperty stipulates a *system* property and not the property of just individual traces. It has been shown that many interesting requirements in computing systems are hyperproperties and cannot be expressed by trace properties. Examples include (1) a wide range of information-flow security policies such as *noninterference* [3] and *observational determinism* [4], (2) sensitivity and robustness requirements in cyber-physical systems [5], and consistency conditions such as *linearizability* in concurrent data structures [6].

Hyperproperties can describe the requirements of probabilistic systems as well. They generally express probabilistic relations between multiple executions

This research has been partially supported by the United States NSF SaTC Award 181338, by the Vienna Science and Technology Fund ProbInG Grant ICT19-018 and by the DFG Research and Training Group UnRAVeL. The order of authors is alphabetical and all authors made equal contribution.

© Springer Nature Switzerland AG 2020
D. V. Hung and O. Sokolsky (Eds.): ATVA 2020, LNCS 12302, pp. 518–534, 2020.
https://doi.org/10.1007/978-3-030-59152-6_29

of a system. For example, in information-flow security, adding probabilities is motivated by establishing a connection between information theory and information flow across multiple traces. A prominent example is probabilistic schedulers that open up an opportunity for an attacker to set up a probabilistic covert channel. Or, *probabilistic causation* compares the probability of occurrence of an effect between scenarios where the cause is or is not present.

The state of the art on probabilistic hyperproperties has exclusively been studied in the context of discrete-time Markov chains (DTMCs). In [7], we proposed the temporal logic HyperPCTL, which extends PCTL by allowing explicit and simultaneous quantification over computation trees. For example, the DTMC in Fig. 1 satisfies the following HyperPCTL formula:

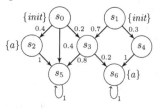

Fig. 1. Example DTMC.

$$\psi = \forall \hat{s}.\forall \hat{s}'.\Big(init_{\hat{s}} \wedge init_{\hat{s}'} \Big) \Rightarrow \Big(\mathbb{P}(\lozenge a_{\hat{s}}) = \mathbb{P}(\lozenge a_{\hat{s}'}) \Big) \tag{1}$$

which means that the probability of reaching proposition a from any pair of states $\hat{s}$ and $\hat{s}'$ labeled by *init* should be equal. Other works on probabilistic hyperproperties for DTMCs include parameter synthesis [8] and statistical model checking [5,9].

An important gap in the spectrum is verification of probabilistic hyperproperties with regard to models that allow *nondeterminism*, in particular, *Markov decision processes* (MDP). Nondeterminism plays a crucial role in many probabilistic systems. For instance, nondeterministic queries can be exploited in order to make targeted attacks to databases with private information [10]. To motivate the idea, consider the MDP in Fig. 2, where h

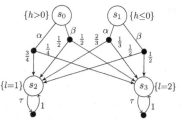

Fig. 2. Example MDP.

is a high secret and l is a low publicly observable variable. To protect the secret, there should be no probabilistic dependencies between observations on the low variable l and the value of h. However, an attacker that chooses a scheduler that always takes action α from states s_0 and s_1 can learn whether or not $h \leq 0$ by observing the probability of obtaining $l = 1$ (or $l = 2$). On the other hand, a scheduler that always chooses action β, does not leak any information about the value of h. Thus, a natural question to ask is whether a certain property holds for all or some schedulers.

With the above motivation, in this paper, we focus on probabilistic hyperproperties in the context of MDPs. Such hyperproperties inherently need to consider different nondeterministic choices in different executions, and naturally call for quantification over schedulers. There are several challenges to achieve this. In general, there are schedulers whose reachability probabilities cannot be achieved

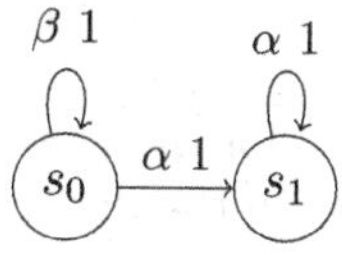

Fig. 3. Example MDP.

by any memoryless non-probabilistic scheduler, and, hence finding a scheduler is not reducible to checking non-probabilistic memoryless schedulers, as it is done in PCTL mode checking for MDPs. Consider for example the MDP in Fig. 3, for which we want to know whether there is a scheduler such that the probability to reach s_1 from s_0 equals 0.5. There are two non-probabilistic memoryless schedulers, one choosing action α and the other, action β in s_0. The first one is the maximal scheduler for which s_1 is reached with probability 1, and the second one is the minimal scheduler leading to probability 0. However, the probability 0.5 cannot be achieved by any non-probabilistic scheduler. *Memoryless* probabilistic schedulers can neither achieve probability 0.5: if a memoryless scheduler would take action α with any positive probability, then the probability to reach s_1 is always 1. The only way to achieve the reachability probability 0.5 (or any value strictly between 0 and 1) is by a probabilistic scheduler with memory, e.g., taking α and β in s_0 with probabilities 0.5 each when this is the first step on a path, and β with probability 1 otherwise.

Our contributions in this paper are as follows. We first extend the temporal logic HyperPCTL [7] to the context of MDPs. To this end, we augment the syntax and semantics of HyperPCTL to quantify over schedulers and relate probabilistic computation trees for different schedulers. For example, the following formula generalizes (1) by requiring that the respective property should hold for all computation trees starting in any states $\hat{s}$ and $\hat{s}'$ of the DMTC induced by any scheduler $\hat{\sigma}$:

$$\forall \hat{\sigma}. \forall \hat{s}(\hat{\sigma}). \forall \hat{s}'(\hat{\sigma}). \Big(init_{\hat{s}} \wedge init_{\hat{s}'} \Big) \Rightarrow \Big(\mathbb{P}(\Diamond a_{\hat{s}}) = \mathbb{P}(\Diamond a_{\hat{s}'}) \Big)$$

On the negative side, we show that the problem to check HyperPCTL properties for MDPs is in general undecidable. On the positive side, we show that the problem becomes decidable when we restrict the scheduler quantification domain to memoryless non-probabilistic schedulers. We also show that this restricted problem is already NP-complete (respectively, coNP-complete) in the size of the given MDP for HyperPCTL formulas with a single existential (respectively, universal) scheduler quantifier. Subsequently, we propose an SMT-based encoding to solve the restricted model checking problem. We have implemented our method and analyze it experimentally on three case studies: probabilistic scheduling attacks, side-channel timing attacks, and probabilistic conformance (available at https://github.com/oreohere/HyperOnMDP).

It is important to note that the work in [11] (also published in ATVA'20) independently addresses the problem under investigation in this paper. The authors propose the temporal logic PHL. Similar to HyperPCTL, PHL also allows quantification over schedulers, but path quantification of the induced DTMC is achieved by using HyperCTL*. Both papers show that the model checking problem is undecidable for the respective logics. The difference, however, is in our approaches to deal with the undecidability result, which leads two complementary and orthogonal techniques. For both logics the problem is decidable for non-probabilistic memoryless schedulers. We provide an SMT-based verification procedure for HyperPCTL for this class of schedulers. The work in [11] presents two methods for proving and for refuting formulas from a fragment of PHL for general memoryful schedulers. The two papers offer disjoint case studies for evaluation.

Organization. Preliminary concepts are discussed in Sect. 2. We present the syntax and semantics of HyperPCTL for MDPs and discuss its expressive power in Sect. 3. Section 4 is dedicated to the applications of HyperPCTL. Sections 5 and 6 present our results on memoryless non-probabilistic schedulers and their evaluation before concluding in Sect. 7. More technical details and all proofs appear in [12].

2   Preliminaries

2.1   Discrete-Time Markov Models

Definition 1. *A* discrete-time Markov chain (DTMC) *is a tuple* $\mathcal{D} = (S, \mathbf{P}, \mathsf{AP}, L)$ *with the following components:*

- *S is a nonempty finite set of* states;
- *$\mathbf{P} : S \times S \to [0, 1]$ is a* transition probability function *with* $\sum_{s' \in S} \mathbf{P}(s, s') = 1$, *for all $s \in S$;*
- *AP is a finite set of* atomic propositions, *and*
- *$L : S \to 2^{\mathsf{AP}}$ is a* labeling function. ∎

Figure 1 shows a simple DTMC. An (*infinite*) *path of* $\mathcal{D}$ is an infinite sequence $\pi = s_0 s_1 s_2 \ldots \in S^{\omega}$ of states with $\mathbf{P}(s_i, s_{i+1}) > 0$, for all $i \geq 0$; we write $\pi[i]$ for s_i. Let $Paths_s^{\mathcal{D}}$ denote the set of all (infinite) paths of $\mathcal{D}$ starting in s, and $fPaths_s^{\mathcal{D}}$ denote the set of all non-empty finite prefixes of paths from $Paths_s^{\mathcal{D}}$, which we call *finite paths*. For a finite path $\pi = s_0 \ldots s_k \in fPaths_{s_0}^{\mathcal{D}}$, $k \geq 0$, we define $|\pi| = k$. We will also use the notations $Paths^{\mathcal{D}} = \cup_{s \in S} Paths_s^{\mathcal{D}}$ and $fPaths^{\mathcal{D}} = \cup_{s \in S} fPaths_s^{\mathcal{D}}$. A state $t \in S$ is *reachable* from a state $s \in S$ in $\mathcal{D}$ if there exists a finite path in $fPaths_s^{\mathcal{D}}$ with last state t; we use $fPaths_{s,T}^{\mathcal{D}}$ to denote the set of all finite paths from $fPaths_s^{\mathcal{D}}$ with last state in $T \subseteq S$. A state $s \in S$ is *absorbing* if $\mathbf{P}(s, s) = 1$.

The *cylinder set* $Cyl^{\mathcal{D}}(\pi)$ of a finite path $\pi \in fPaths_s^{\mathcal{D}}$ is the set of all infinite paths of $\mathcal{D}$ with prefix π. The *probability space for $\mathcal{D}$ and state* $s \in S$ is $(Paths_s^{\mathcal{D}}, \{\cup_{\pi \in R} Cyl^{\mathcal{D}}(\pi) \mid R \subseteq fPaths_s^{\mathcal{D}}\}, \mathrm{Pr}_s^{\mathcal{D}})$, where the *probability* of the cylinderset of $\pi \in fPaths_s^{\mathcal{D}}$ is $\mathrm{Pr}_s^{\mathcal{D}}(Cyl^{\mathcal{D}}(\pi)) = \Pi_{i=1}^{|\pi|} \mathbf{P}(\pi[i-1], \pi[i])$.

Note that the cylinder sets of two finite paths starting in the same state are either disjoint or one is contained in the other. According to the definition of the probability spaces, the total probability for a set of cylinder sets defined by the finite paths $R \subseteq fPaths_s^{\mathcal{D}}$ is $\mathrm{Pr}^{\mathcal{D}}(R) = \sum_{\pi \in R'} \mathrm{Pr}_s^{\mathcal{D}}(\pi)$ with $R' = \{\pi \in R \mid$ no $\pi' \in R \setminus \{\pi\}$ *is a prefix of* $\pi\}$. To improve readability, we sometimes omit the DTMC index $\mathcal{D}$ in the notations when it is clear from the context.

Definition 2. *The* parallel composition *of two DTMCs $\mathcal{D}_i = (S_i, \mathbf{P}_i, \mathsf{AP}_i, L_i)$, $i = 1, 2$, is the DTMC $\mathcal{D}_1 \times \mathcal{D}_2 = (S, \mathbf{P}, \mathsf{AP}, L)$ with the following components:*

- $S = S_1 \times S_2$;
- $\mathbf{P} : S \times S \to [0,1]$ *with* $\mathbf{P}((s_1, s_2), (s_1', s_2')) = \mathbf{P}_1(s_1, s_1') \cdot \mathbf{P}_2(s_2, s_2')$, *for all states* $(s_1, s_2), (s_1', s_2') \in S$;
- $AP = AP_1 \cup AP_2$, *and*
- $L : S \to 2^{AP}$ *with* $L((s_1, s_2)) = L_1(s_1) \cup L_2(s_2)$. ∎

Definition 3. *A Markov decision process (MDP) is a tuple* $\mathcal{M} = (S, Act, \mathbf{P}, AP, L)$ *with the following components:*

- S *is a nonempty finite set of* states;
- Act *is a nonempty finite set of* actions;
- $\mathbf{P} : S \times Act \times S \to [0,1]$ *is a* transition probability function *such that for all* $s \in S$ *the set of enabled actions in* s $Act(s) = \{\alpha \in Act \mid \sum_{s' \in S} \mathbf{P}(s, \alpha, s') = 1\}$ *is not empty and* $\sum_{s' \in S} \mathbf{P}(s, \alpha, s') = 0$ *for all* $\alpha \in Act \setminus Act(s)$;
- AP *is a finite set of* atomic propositions, *and*
- $L : S \to 2^{AP}$ *is a* labeling function. ∎

Figure 2 shows a simple MDP. Schedulers can be used to eliminate the non-determinism in MDPs, inducing DTMCs with well-defined probability spaces.

Definition 4. *A scheduler for an MDP* $\mathcal{M} = (S, Act, \mathbf{P}, AP, L)$ *is a tuple* $\sigma = (Q, act, mode, init)$, *where*

- Q *is a countable set of* modes;
- $act : Q \times S \times Act \to [0,1]$ *is a function for which* $\sum_{\alpha \in Act(s)} act(q, s, \alpha) = 1$ *and* $\sum_{\alpha \in Act \setminus Act(s)} act(q, s, \alpha) = 0$ *for all* $s \in S$ *and* $q \in Q$;
- $mode : Q \times S \to Q$ *is a mode transition* function, *and*
- $init : S \to Q$ *is a function selecting a starting mode for each state of* $\mathcal{M}$. ∎

Let $\Sigma^{\mathcal{M}}$ denote the set of all schedulers for the MDP $\mathcal{M}$. A scheduler is *finite-memory* if Q is finite, *memoryless* if $|Q| = 1$, and *non-probabilistic* if $act(q, s, \alpha) \in \{0,1\}$ for all $q \in Q$, $s \in S$ and $\alpha \in Act$.

Definition 5. *Assume an MDP* $\mathcal{M} = (S, Act, \mathbf{P}, AP, L)$ *and a scheduler* $\sigma = (Q, act, mode, init) \in \Sigma^{\mathcal{M}}$ *for* $\mathcal{M}$. *The DTMC induced by* $\mathcal{M}$ *and* σ *is defined as* $\mathcal{M}^{\sigma} = (S^{\sigma}, \mathbf{P}^{\sigma}, AP, L^{\sigma})$ *with* $S^{\sigma} = Q \times S$,

$$\mathbf{P}^{\sigma}((q, s), (q', s')) = \begin{cases} \sum_{\alpha \in Act(s)} act(q, s, \alpha) \cdot \mathbf{P}(s, \alpha, s') & \text{if } q' = mode(q, s) \\ 0 & \text{otherwise} \end{cases}$$

and $L^{\sigma}(q, s) = L(s)$ *for all* $s, s' \in S$ *and all* $q, q' \in Q$. ∎

A state s' is *reachable* from $s \in S$ in MDP $\mathcal{M}$ is there exists a scheduler σ for $\mathcal{M}$ such that s' is reachable from s in $\mathcal{M}^{\sigma}$. A state $s \in S$ is *absorbing* in $\mathcal{M}$ if s is absorbing in $\mathcal{M}^{\sigma}$ for all schedulers σ for $\mathcal{M}$. We sometimes omit the MDP index $\mathcal{M}$ in the notations when it is clear from the context.

3   HyperPCTL for MDPs

3.1   HyperPCTL Syntax

HyperPCTL (quantified) state formulas φ^q are inductively defined as follows:

$$
\begin{array}{lll}
\textit{quantified formula} & \varphi^q & ::= \forall\hat{\sigma}.\varphi^q \mid \exists\hat{\sigma}.\varphi^q \mid \forall\hat{s}(\hat{\sigma}).\varphi^q \mid \exists\hat{s}(\hat{\sigma}).\varphi^q \mid \varphi^{nq} \\
\textit{non-quantified formula} & \varphi^{nq} & ::= \texttt{true} \mid a_{\hat{s}} \mid \varphi^{nq} \wedge \varphi^{nq} \mid \neg\varphi^{nq} \mid \varphi^{pr} < \varphi^{pr} \\
\textit{probability expression} & \varphi^{pr} & ::= \mathbb{P}(\varphi^{path}) \mid f(\varphi_1^{pr},\ldots,\varphi_k^{pr}) \\
\textit{path formula} & \varphi^{path} & ::= \bigcirc\varphi^{nq} \mid \varphi^{nq}\,\mathcal{U}\,\varphi^{nq} \mid \varphi^{nq}\,\mathcal{U}^{[k_1,k_2]}\,\varphi^{nq}
\end{array}
$$

where $\hat{\sigma}$ is a *scheduler variable*[1] from an infinite set $\hat{\Sigma}$, $\hat{s}$ is a *state variable* from an infinite set $\hat{S}$, φ^{nq} is a quantifier-free state formula, $a \in \mathsf{AP}$ is an atomic proposition, φ^{pr} is a *probability expression*, $f : [0,1]^k \to \mathbb{R}$ are k-ary arithmetic operators (binary addition, unary/binary subtraction, binary multiplication) over probabilities, where constants are viewed as 0-ary functions, and φ^{path} is a *path formula*, such that $k_1 \le k_2 \in \mathbb{N}_{\ge 0}$. The probability operator $\mathbb{P}$ allows the usage of probabilities in arithmetic constraints and relations.

A HyperPCTL construct φ (probability expression φ^{pr}, state formula φ^q, φ^{nq} or path formula φ^{path}) is *well-formed* if each occurrence of any $a_{\hat{s}}$ with $a \in \mathsf{AP}$ and $\hat{s} \in \hat{S}$ is in the scope of a *state quantifier* for $\hat{s}(\hat{\sigma})$ for some $\hat{\sigma} \in \hat{\Sigma}$, and any quantifier for $\hat{s}(\hat{\sigma})$ is in the scope of a *scheduler quantifier* for $\hat{\sigma}$. We restrict ourselves to quantifying first the schedulers then the states, i.e., different state variables can share the same scheduler. One can consider also *local* schedulers when different players cannot explicitly share the same scheduler, or in other words, each scheduler quantifier belongs to exactly one of the quantified states.

HyperPCTL formulas are well-formed HyperPCTL state formulas, where we additionally allow standard syntactic sugar like $\texttt{false} = \neg\texttt{true}$, $\varphi_1 \vee \varphi_2 = \neg(\neg\varphi_1 \wedge \neg\varphi_2)$, $\Diamond\varphi = \texttt{true}\,\mathcal{U}\,\varphi$, and $\mathbb{P}(\Box\varphi) = 1 - \mathbb{P}(\Diamond\neg\varphi)$. For example, the HyperPCTL state formula $\forall\hat{\sigma}.\exists\hat{s}(\hat{\sigma}).\mathbb{P}(\bigcirc a_{\hat{s}}) < 0.5$ is a HyperPCTL formula. The HyperPCTL state formula $\mathbb{P}(\bigcirc a_{\hat{s}}) < 0.5$ is not a HyperPCTL formula, but can be extended to such. The HyperPCTL state formula $\forall\hat{s}(\hat{\sigma}).\exists\hat{\sigma}.\mathbb{P}(\bigcirc a_{\hat{s}}) < 0.5$ is not a HyperPCTL formula, and it even cannot can be extended to such.

3.2   HyperPCTL Semantics

Definition 6. *The n-ary self-composition of an MDP $\mathcal{M} = (S, Act, \mathbf{P}, \mathsf{AP}, L)$ for a sequence $\boldsymbol{\sigma} = (\sigma_1,\ldots,\sigma_n) \in (\Sigma^{\mathcal{M}})^n$ of schedulers for $\mathcal{M}$ is the DTMC parallel composition $\mathcal{M}^{\boldsymbol{\sigma}} = \mathcal{M}_1^{\sigma_1} \times \ldots \times \mathcal{M}_n^{\sigma_n}$, where $\mathcal{M}_i^{\sigma_i}$ is the DTMC induced by $\mathcal{M}_i$ and σ_i, and where $\mathcal{M}_i = (S, Act, \mathbf{P}, \mathsf{AP}_i, L_i)$ with $\mathsf{AP}_i = \{a_i \mid a \in \mathsf{AP}\}$ and $L_i(s) = \{a_i \mid a \in L(s)\}$, for all $s \in S$.* ∎

HyperPCTL state formulas are evaluated in the context of an MDP $\mathcal{M} = (S, Act, \mathbf{P}, \mathsf{AP}, L)$, a sequence $\boldsymbol{\sigma} = (\sigma_1,\ldots,\sigma_n) \in (\Sigma^{\mathcal{M}})^n$ of schedulers, and a

---

[1] We use the notation $\hat{\sigma}$ for scheduler variables and σ for schedulers, and analogously $\hat{s}$ for state variables and s for states.

sequence $r = ((q_1, s_1), \ldots, (q_n, s_n))$ of $\mathcal{M}^\sigma$ states; we use $()$ to denote the empty sequence (of any type) and $\circ$ for concatenation. Intuitively, these sequences store instantiations for scheduler and state variables. The satisfaction of a HyperPCTL quantified formula by $\mathcal{M}$ is defined by

$$\mathcal{M} \models \varphi \quad \textit{iff} \quad \mathcal{M}, (), () \models \varphi .$$

The semantics evaluates HyperPCTL formulas by structural recursion. Let in the following $\mathbb{Q}, \mathbb{Q}', \ldots$ denote quantifiers from $\{\forall, \exists\}$. When instantiating $\mathbb{Q}\hat{\sigma}.\varphi$ by a scheduler $\sigma \in \Sigma^\mathcal{M}$, we replace in φ each subformula $\mathbb{Q}'\hat{s}(\hat{\sigma}).\varphi'$, that is not in the scope of a quantifier for $\hat{\sigma}$ by $\mathbb{Q}'\hat{s}(\sigma).\varphi'$, and denote the result by $\varphi[\hat{\sigma} \rightsquigarrow \sigma]$. For instantiating a state quantifier $\mathbb{Q}\hat{s}(\sigma).\varphi$ by a state s, we append $\sigma = (Q, act, mode, init)$ and $(init(s), s)$ at the end of the respective sequences, and replace each $a_{\hat{s}}$ in the scope of the given quantifier by a_s, resulting in a formula that we denote by $\varphi[\hat{s} \rightsquigarrow s]$. To evaluate probability expressions, we use the n-ary self-composition of the MDP.

Formally, the semantics judgment rules are as follows:

$$
\begin{array}{lll}
\mathcal{M}, \sigma, r \models \mathbf{true} & & \\
\mathcal{M}, \sigma, r \models a_i & \textit{iff} & a_i \in L^\sigma(r) \\
\mathcal{M}, \sigma, r \models \varphi_1 \wedge \varphi_2 & \textit{iff} & \mathcal{M}, \sigma, r \models \varphi_1 \text{ and } \mathcal{M}, \sigma, r \models \varphi_2 \\
\mathcal{M}, \sigma, r \models \neg\varphi & \textit{iff} & \mathcal{M}, \sigma, r \not\models \varphi \\
\mathcal{M}, \sigma, r \models \forall\hat{\sigma}.\varphi & \textit{iff} & \forall \sigma \in \Sigma^\mathcal{M}.\ \mathcal{M}, \sigma, r \models \varphi[\hat{\sigma} \rightsquigarrow \sigma] \\
\mathcal{M}, \sigma, r \models \exists\hat{\sigma}.\varphi & \textit{iff} & \exists \sigma \in \Sigma^\mathcal{M}.\ \mathcal{M}, \sigma, r \models \varphi[\hat{\sigma} \rightsquigarrow \sigma] \\
\mathcal{M}, \sigma, r \models \forall\hat{s}(\sigma).\varphi & \textit{iff} & \forall s_{n+1} \in S.\ \mathcal{M}, \sigma \circ \sigma, r \circ (init(s_{n+1}), s_{n+1}) \models \varphi[\hat{s} \rightsquigarrow s_{n+1}] \\
\mathcal{M}, \sigma, r \models \exists\hat{s}(\sigma).\varphi & \textit{iff} & \exists s_{n+1} \in S.\ \mathcal{M}, \sigma \circ \sigma, r \circ (init(s_{n+1}), s_{n+1}) \models \varphi[\hat{s} \rightsquigarrow s_{n+1}] \\
\mathcal{M}, \sigma, r \models \varphi_1^{pr} < \varphi_2^{pr} & \textit{iff} & [\![\varphi_1^{pr}]\!]_{\mathcal{M},\sigma,r} < [\![\varphi_2^{pr}]\!]_{\mathcal{M},\sigma,r} \\
[\![\mathbb{P}(\varphi_{path})]\!]_{\mathcal{M},\sigma,r} & = & \mathrm{Pr}^{\mathcal{M}^\sigma}\left(\{\pi \in Paths_r^{\mathcal{M}^\sigma} \mid \mathcal{M}, \sigma, \pi \models \varphi_{path}\}\right) \\
[\![f(\varphi_1^{pr}, \ldots \varphi_k^{pr})]\!]_{\mathcal{M},\sigma,r} & = & f\left([\![\varphi_1^{pr}]\!]_{\mathcal{M},\sigma,r} \cdots, [\![\varphi_k^{pr}]\!]_{\mathcal{M},\sigma,r}\right)
\end{array}
$$

where $\mathcal{M}$ is an MDP; $n \in \mathbb{N}_{\geq 0}$ is non-negative integer; $\sigma \in (\Sigma^\mathcal{M})^n$; r is a state of $\mathcal{M}^\sigma$; $a \in \mathsf{AP}$ is an atomic proposition and $i \in \{1, \ldots, n\}$; $\varphi, \varphi_1, \varphi_2$ are HyperPCTL state formulas; $\sigma = (Q, act, mode, init) \in \Sigma^\mathcal{M}$ is a scheduler for $\mathcal{M}$; $\varphi_1^{pr} \cdots \varphi_k^{pr}$ are probability expressions, and φ_{path} is a HyperPCTL path formula whose satisfaction relation is as follows:

$$
\begin{array}{lll}
\mathcal{M}, \sigma, \pi \models \bigcirc\varphi & \textit{iff} & \mathcal{M}, \sigma, r_1 \models \varphi \\
\mathcal{M}, \sigma, \pi \models \varphi_1 \mathcal{U} \varphi_2 & \textit{iff} & \exists j \geq 0.\left(\mathcal{M}, \sigma, r_j \models \varphi_2 \wedge \forall i \in [0, j).\ \mathcal{M}, \sigma, r_i \models \varphi_1\right) \\
\mathcal{M}, \sigma, \pi \models \varphi_1 \mathcal{U}^{[k_1, k_2]} \varphi_2 & \textit{iff} & \exists j \in [k_1, k_2].\left(\mathcal{M}, \sigma, r_j \models \varphi_2 \wedge \forall i \in [0, j).\mathcal{M}, \sigma, r_i \models \varphi_1\right)
\end{array}
$$

where $\pi = r_0 r_1 \cdots$ with $r_i = ((q_{i,1}, s_{i,1}), \ldots, (q_{i,n}, s_{i,n}))$ is a path of $\mathcal{M}^\sigma$; formulas $\varphi, \varphi_1,$ and φ_2 are HyperPCTL state formulas, and $k_1 \leq k_2 \in \mathbb{N}_{\geq 0}$.

For MDPs with $|Act(s)| = 1$ for each of its states s, the HyperPCTL semantics reduces to the one proposed in [7] for DTMCs.

For MDPs with non-determinism, the standard PCTL semantics defines that in order to satisfy a PCTL formula $\mathbb{P}_{\sim c}(\psi)$ in a given MDP state s, all schedulers should induce a DTMC that satisfies $\mathbb{P}_{\sim c}(\psi)$ in s. Though it should hold for all schedulers, it is known that there exist minimal and maximal schedulers that are non-probabilistic and memoryless, therefore it is sufficient to restrict the reasoning to such schedulers. Since for MDPs with finite state and action spaces, the number of such schedulers is finite, PCTL model checking for MDPs is decidable. Given this analogy, one would expect that HyperPCTL model checking should be decidable, but it is not.

Theorem 1. *HyperPCTL model checking for MDPs is in general undecidable.*

4   Applications of HyperPCTL on MDPs

Side-channel timing leaks open a channel to an attacker to infer the value of a secret by observing the execution time of a function. For example, the heart of the RSA public-key encryption algorithm is the modular exponentiation algorithm that computes $(a^b \bmod n)$, where a is an integer representing the plaintext and b is the integer encryption key. A careless implementation can leak b through a probabilistic scheduling channel (see Fig. 4). This program is not secure since the two branches of the *if* have different timing behaviors. Under a fair execution sched-

```
1 void mexp(){
2    c = 0; d = 1; i = k;
3    while (i >= 0){
4       i = i-1; c = c*2;
5       d = (d*d) % n;
6       if (b(i) = 1)
7          c = c+1;
8          d = (d*a) % n;
9       }
10 }
11 /************/
12 t = new Thread(mexp());
13 j = 0; m = 2 * k;
14 while (j < m & !t.stop) j++;
15 /************/
```

Fig. 4. Modular exponentiation.

uler for parallel threads, an attacker thread can infer the value of b by running in parallel to a modular exponentiation thread and iteratively incrementing a counter variable until the other thread terminates (lines 12–14). To model this program by an MDP, we can use two nondeterministic actions for the two branches of the *if* statement, such that the choice of different schedulers corresponds to the choice of different bit configurations b(i) for the key b. This algorithm should satisfy the following property: the probability of observing a concrete value in the counter j should be independent of the bit configuration of the secret key b:

$$\forall \hat{\sigma}_1.\forall \hat{\sigma}_2.\forall \hat{s}(\hat{\sigma}_1).\forall \hat{s}'(\hat{\sigma}_2).\Big(init_{\hat{s}} \wedge init_{\hat{s}'}\Big) \;\Rightarrow\; \bigwedge_{l=0}^{m} \Big(\mathbb{P}(\lozenge(j=l)_{\hat{s}}) = \mathbb{P}(\lozenge(j=l)_{\hat{s}'})\Big)$$

Another example of timing attacks that can be implemented through a probabilistic scheduling side channel is password verification which is typically implemented by comparing an input string with another confidential string (see Fig. 5). Also here, an attacker thread can measure the time necessary to break the loop, and use this information to infer the prefix of the input string matching the secret string.

```
1 int str_cmp(char * r){
2    char * s = 'Bg\$4\0';
3    i = 0;
4    while (s[i] != '\0'){
5       i++;
6       if (s[i]!=r[i]) return 0;
7    }
8    return 1;
9 }
```

Fig. 5. String comparison.

Scheduler-specific observational determinism policy (SSODP) [13] is a confidentiality policy in multi-threaded programs that defends against an attacker that chooses an appropriate scheduler to control the set of possible traces. In particular, given any scheduler and two initial states that are indistinguishable with respect to a secret input (i.e., low-equivalent), any two executions from these two states should terminate in low-equivalent states with equal probability. Formally, given a proposition h representing a secret:

$$\forall \hat{\sigma}. \forall \hat{s}(\hat{\sigma}). \forall \hat{s}'(\hat{\sigma}). \left(h_{\hat{s}} \oplus h_{\hat{s}'} \right) \Rightarrow \bigwedge_{l \in L} \left(\mathbb{P}(\Diamond l_{\hat{s}}) = \mathbb{P}(\Diamond l_{\hat{s}'}) \right)$$

where $l \in L$ are atomic propositions that classify low-equivalent states and $\oplus$ is the exclusive-or operator. A stronger variation of this policy is that the executions are stepwise low-equivalent:

$$\forall \hat{\sigma}. \forall \hat{s}(\hat{\sigma}). \forall \hat{s}'(\hat{\sigma}). \left(h_{\hat{s}} \oplus h_{\hat{s}'} \right) \Rightarrow \mathbb{P}\square \left(\bigwedge_{l \in L} \left((\mathbb{P} \bigcirc l_{\hat{s}}) = (\mathbb{P} \bigcirc l_{\hat{s}'}) \right) \right) = 1.$$

Probabilistic conformance describes how well a model and an implementation conform with each other with respect to a specification. As an example, consider a 6-sided die. The probability to obtain one possible side of the die is $1/6$. We would like to synthesize a protocol that simulates the 6-sided die behavior only by repeatedly tossing a fair coin. We know that such an implementation exists [14], but our aim is to find such a solution automatically by modeling the die as a DTMC and by using an MDP to model all the possible coin-implementations with a given maximum number of states, including 6 absorbing final states to model the outcomes. In the MDP, we associate to each state a set of possible nondeterministic actions, each of them choosing two states as successors with equal probability $1/2$. Then, each scheduler corresponds to a particular implementation. Our goal is to check whether there exists a scheduler that induces a DTMC over the MDP, such that repeatedly tossing a coin simulates die-rolling with equal probabilities for the different outcomes:

$$\exists \hat{\sigma}. \forall \hat{s}(\hat{\sigma}). \exists \hat{s}'(\hat{\sigma}). \left(init_{\hat{s}} \wedge init_{\hat{s}'} \right) \Rightarrow \bigwedge_{l=1}^{6} \left(\mathbb{P}(\Diamond (die = l)_{\hat{s}}) = \mathbb{P}(\Diamond (die = l)_{\hat{s}'}) \right)$$

5   HyperPCTL Model Checking for Non-probabilistic Memoryless Schedulers

Due to the undecidability of model checking HyperPCTL formulas for MDPs, we noe restrict ourselves the semantics, where scheduler quantification ranges over non-probabilistic memoryless schedulers only. It is easy to see that this restriction makes the model checking problem decidable, as there are only finitely many such schedulers that can be enumerated. Regarding complexity, we have the following property.

Theorem 2. *The problem to decide for MDPs the truth of HyperPCTL formulas with a single existential (respectively, universal) scheduler quantifier over non-probabilistic memoryless schedulers is NP-complete (respectively, coNP-complete) in the state set size of the given MDP.*

Next we propose an SMT-based technique for solving the model checking problem for non-probabilistic memoryless scheduler domains, and for the simplified case of having a single scheduler quantifier; the general case for an arbitrary number of scheduler quantifiers is similar, but a bit more involved, so the simplified setting might be more suitable for understanding the basic ideas.

The main method listed in Algorithm 1 constructs a formula E that is satisfiable if and only if the input MDP $\mathcal{M}$ satisfies the input HyperPCTL formula with a single scheduler quantifier over the non-probabilistic memoryless scheduler domain. Let us first deal with the case that the scheduler quantifier is *existential*. In line 2 we encode possible instantiations σ for the scheduler variable $\hat{\sigma}$, for which we use a variable σ_s for each MDP

Algorithm 1: Main SMT encoding algorithm

Input : $\mathcal{M} = (S, Act, \mathbf{P}, AP, L)$: MDP; $Q\hat{\sigma}.Q_1\hat{s}_1(\hat{\sigma}).\ldots.Q_n\hat{s}_n(\hat{\sigma}).\varphi^{nq}$: HyperPCTL formula.
Output : Whether $\mathcal{M}$ satisfies the input formula.
1 Function $Main(\mathcal{M},\ Q\hat{\sigma}.\ Q_1\hat{s}_1(\hat{\sigma}).\ldots.Q_n\hat{s}_n(\hat{\sigma}).\ \varphi^{nq})$
2 $\quad E := \bigwedge_{s \in S}(\bigvee_{\alpha \in Act(s)} \sigma_s = \alpha)$ // scheduler choice
3 $\quad$ **if** Q *is existential* **then**
4 $\qquad E := E\wedge$ Semantics$(\mathcal{M},\ \varphi^{nq},\ n)$;
5 $\qquad E := E\wedge$ Truth$(\mathcal{M},\ \exists\hat{\sigma}.\ Q_1\hat{s}_1(\hat{\sigma}).\ldots.Q_n\hat{s}_n(\hat{\sigma}).\ \varphi^{nq})$;
6 $\qquad$ **if** $check(E) = SAT$ **then return** $TRUE$;
7 $\qquad$ **else return** $FALSE$;
8 $\quad$ **else if** Q *is universal* **then**
9 $\qquad$ // $\overline{Q}_i$ is $\forall$ if $Q_i = \exists$ and $\exists$ else
10 $\qquad E := E\wedge$ Semantics$(\mathcal{M},\ \neg\varphi^{nq},\ n)$;
11 $\qquad E := E\wedge$ Truth$(\mathcal{M},\ \exists\hat{\sigma}.\overline{Q}_1\hat{s}_1(\hat{\sigma}).\ldots.\overline{Q}_n\hat{s}_n(\hat{\sigma}).\neg\varphi^{nq})$;
12 $\qquad$ **if** $check(E) = SAT$ **then return** $FALSE$;
$\qquad$ **else return** $TRUE$;

---

state $s \in S$ to encode which action is chosen in that state. In line 4 we encode the meaning of the quantifier-free inner part φ^{nq} of the input formula, whereas line 5 encodes the meaning of the state quantifiers, i.e. for which sets of composed states φ^{nq} needs to hold in order to satisfy the input formula. In lines 6–7 we check the satisfiability of the encoding and return the corresponding answer. Formulas with a *universal* scheduler quantifier $\forall\hat{\sigma}.\varphi$ are semantically equivalent to $\neg\exists\hat{\sigma}.\neg\varphi$. We make use of this fact in lines 8–12 to check first the satisfaction of an encoding for $\exists\hat{\sigma}.\neg\varphi$ and return the inverted answer.

Algorithm 2: SMT encoding for the meaning of the input formula

Input	: $\mathcal{M} = (S, Act, \mathbf{P}, AP, L)$: MDP;
	φ: quantifier-free HyperPCTL formula or expression;
	n: number of state variables in φ.
Output	: SMT encoding of the meaning of φ in the n-ary self-composition of $\mathcal{M}$.

1 **Function** $Semantics(\mathcal{M}, \varphi, n)$
2   **if** φ is true **then** $E := \bigwedge_{s \in S^n} holds_{s,\varphi}$;
3   **else if** φ is $a_{\hat{s}_i}$ **then**
4        $E := (\bigwedge_{s \in S^n,\ a \in L(s_i)} (holds_{s,\varphi})) \wedge (\bigwedge_{s \in S^n,\ a \notin L(s_i)} (\neg holds_{s,\varphi}))$;
5   **else if** φ is $\varphi_1 \wedge \varphi_2$ **then**
6        $E := Semantics(\mathcal{M}, \varphi_1, n) \wedge Semantics(\mathcal{M}, \varphi_2, n) \wedge$
7        $\bigwedge_{s \in S^n} ((holds_{s,\varphi} \wedge holds_{s,\varphi_1} \wedge holds_{s,\varphi_2}) \vee (\neg holds_{s,\varphi} \wedge (\neg holds_{s,\varphi_1} \vee \neg holds_{s,\varphi_2})))$;
8   **else if** φ is $\neg\varphi'$ **then**
9        $E := Semantics(\mathcal{M}, \varphi', n) \wedge \bigwedge_{s \in S^n} (holds_{s,\varphi} \oplus holds_{s,\varphi'})$;
10   **else if** φ is $\varphi_1 < \varphi_2$ **then**
11        $E := Semantics(\mathcal{M}, \varphi_1, n) \wedge Semantics(\mathcal{M}, \varphi_2, n) \wedge$
12        $\bigwedge_{s \in S^n} ((holds_{s,\varphi} \wedge prob_{s,\varphi_1} < prob_{s,\varphi_2}) \vee (\neg holds_{s,\varphi} \wedge prob_{s,\varphi_1} \geq prob_{s,\varphi_2}))$;
13   **else if** φ is $\mathbb{P}(\bigcirc\varphi')$ **then**
14        $E := Semantics(\mathcal{M}, \varphi', n) \wedge$
15        $\bigwedge_{s \in S^n} ((holdsToInt_{s,\varphi'} = 1 \wedge holds_{s,\varphi'}) \vee (holdsToInt_{s,\varphi'} = 0 \wedge \neg holds_{s,\varphi'}))$;
16   **foreach** $s = (s_1, \ldots, s_n) \in S^n$ **do**
17   **foreach** $\alpha = (\alpha_1, \ldots, \alpha_n) \in Act(s_1) \times \ldots \times Act(s_n)$ **do**
18              $E := E \wedge ([\bigwedge_{i=1}^{n} \sigma_{s_i} = \alpha_i] \rightarrow [prob_{s,\varphi} =$
19              $\sum_{s' \in supp(\alpha_1) \times \ldots \times supp(\alpha_n)} ((\Pi_{i=1}^{n} \mathbf{P}(s_i, \alpha_i, s_i')) \cdot holdsToInt_{s',\varphi'})])$;
20   **else if** φ is $\mathbb{P}(\varphi_1 \mathcal{U} \varphi_2)$ **then** $E := SemanticsUnboundedUntil(\mathcal{M}, \varphi, n)$;
21   **else if** φ is $\mathbb{P}(\varphi_1 \mathcal{U}^{[k_1,k_2]} \varphi_2)$ **then** $E := SemanticsBoundedUntil(\mathcal{M}, \varphi, n)$;
22   **else if** φ is c **then** $E := \bigwedge_{s \in S^n} (prob_{s,\varphi} = c)$;
23   **else if** φ is φ_1 op φ_2 /* $op \in \{+, -, *\}$ */   **then**
24        $E := Semantics(\mathcal{M}, \varphi_1, n) \wedge Semantics(\mathcal{M}, \varphi_2, n) \wedge$
          $\bigwedge_{s \in S^n} (prob_{s,\varphi} = (prob_{s,\varphi_1}\ op\ prob_{s,\varphi_2}))$;
25   **return** E;

The Semantics method, shown in Algorithm 2, applies structural recursion to encode the meaning of its quantifier-free input formula. As variables, the encoding uses (1) propositions $holds_{s,\varphi^{nq}} \in \{\texttt{true}, \texttt{false}\}$ to encode the truth of each Boolean sub-formula φ^{nq} of the input formula in each state $s \in S^n$ of the n-ary self-composition of $\mathcal{M}$, (2) numeric variables $prob_{s,\varphi^{pr}} \in [0,1] \subseteq \mathbb{R}$ to encode the value of each probability expression φ^{pr} in the input formula in the context of each composed state $s \in S^n$, (3) variables $holdsToInt_{s,\varphi^{pr}} \in \{0,1\}$ to encode truth values in a pseudo-Boolean form, i.e. we set $holdsToInt_{s,\varphi^{pr}} = 1$ for $holds_{s,\varphi^{nq}} = \texttt{true}$ and $prob_{s,\varphi^{pr}} = 0$ else and (4) variables $d_{s,\varphi}$ to encode the existence of a loop-free path from state s to a state satisfying φ.

There are two base cases: the Boolean constant $\texttt{true}$ holds in all states (line 2), whereas atomic propositions hold in exactly those states that are labelled by them (line 3). For conjunction (line 5) we recursively encode the truth values of the operands and state that the conjunction is true iff both operands are true. For negation (line 8) we again encode the meaning of the operand recursively and flip its truth value. For the comparison of two probability expressions (line 10), we recursively encode the probability values of the operands and state the respective relation between them for the satisfaction of the comparison.

Algorithm 3: SMT encoding for the meaning of unbounded until formulas

---

Input : $\mathcal{M} = (S, Act, \mathbf{P}, AP, L)$: MDP; φ: HyperPCTL unbounded until formula of the form $\mathbb{P}(\varphi_1 \, \mathcal{U} \, \varphi_2)$; n: number of state variables in φ.

Output : SMT encoding of φ's meaning in the n-ary self-composition of $\mathcal{M}$.

1 **Function** $SemanticsUnboundedUntil(\mathcal{M}, \, \varphi = \mathbb{P}(\varphi_1 \, \mathcal{U} \, \varphi_2), \, n)$

2    $E := \mathrm{Semantics}(\mathcal{M}, \varphi_1, n) \wedge \mathrm{Semantics}(\mathcal{M}, \varphi_2, n)$;

3   **foreach** $s = (s_1, \ldots, s_n) \in S^n$ **do**

4      $E :=$
$$E \wedge (holds_{s,\varphi_2} \rightarrow prob_{s,\varphi}{=}1) \wedge ((\neg holds_{s,\varphi_1} \wedge \neg holds_{s,\varphi_2}) \rightarrow prob_{s,\varphi}{=}0);$$

5   **foreach** $\alpha = (\alpha_1, \ldots, \alpha_n) \in Act(s_1) \times \ldots \times Act(s_n)$ **do**

6        $E := E \wedge \Big(\big[holds_{s,\varphi_1} \wedge \neg holds_{s,\varphi_2} \wedge \bigwedge_{i=1}^{n} \sigma_{s_i} = \alpha_i \big] \rightarrow$

7        $\big[prob_{s,\varphi} = \sum_{s' \in supp(\alpha_1) \times \ldots \times supp(\alpha_n)} ((\Pi_{i=1}^{n} \mathbf{P}(s_i, \alpha_i, s_i')) \cdot prob_{s',\varphi}) \wedge$

8        $(prob_{s,\varphi}{>}0 \rightarrow (\bigvee_{s' \in supp(\alpha_1) \times \ldots \times supp(\alpha_n)} (holds_{s',\varphi_2} \vee d_{s,\varphi_2}{>}d_{s',\varphi_2}))) \big] \Big)$;

9   **return** E;

The remaining cases encode the semantics of probability expressions. The cases for constants (line 22) and arithmetic operations (line 23) are straightforward. For the probability $\mathbb{P}(\bigcirc \varphi')$ (line 13), we encode the Boolean value of φ' in the variables $holds_{s,\varphi'}$ (line 14), turn them into pseudo-Boolean values $holdsToInt_{s,\varphi'}$ (1 for true and 0 for false, line 15), and state that for each composed state, the probability value of $\mathbb{P}(\bigcirc \varphi')$ is the sum of the probabilities to get to a successor state where the operand φ' holds; since the successors and their probabilities are scheduler-dependent, we need to iterate over all scheduler choices and use $supp(\alpha_i)$ to denote the support $\{s \in S \mid \alpha_i(s) > 0\}$ of the distribution α_i (line 17). The encodings for the probabilities of unbounded until formulas (line 20) and bounded until formulas (line 21) are listed in Algorithm 3 and 4, respectively.

For the probabilities $\mathbb{P}(\varphi_1 \, \mathcal{U} \, \varphi_2)$ to satisfy an unbounded until formula, the method SemanticsUnboundedUntil shown in Algorithm 3 first encodes the meaning of the until operands (line 2). For each composed state $s \in S^n$, the probability of satisfying the until formula in s is encoded in the variable $prob_{s,\mathbb{P}(\varphi_1 \, \mathcal{U} \, \varphi_2)}$. If the second until-operand φ_2 holds in s then this probability is 1 and if none of the operands are true in s then it is 0 (line 4). Otherwise, depending on the scheduler σ of $\mathcal{M}$ (line 5), the value of $prob_{s,\mathbb{P}(\varphi_1 \, \mathcal{U} \, \varphi_2)}$ is a sum, adding up for each successor state s' of s the probability to get from s to s' in one step times the probability to satisfy the until-formula on paths starting in s' (line 7). However, these encodings work only when at least one state satisfying φ_2 is reachable from s with a positive probability: for any bottom SCC whose states all violate φ_2, the probability $\mathbb{P}(\varphi_1 \, \mathcal{U} \, \varphi_2)$ is obviously 0, however, assigning any fixed value from $[0,1]$ to all states of this bottom SCC would yield a fixed-point for the underlying equation system. To assure correctness, in line 8 we enforce smallest fixed-points by requiring that if $prob_{s,\mathbb{P}(\varphi_1 \, \mathcal{U} \, \varphi_2)}$ is positive then there exists a loop-free path from s to any state satisfying φ_2. In the encoding of this

---

Algorithm 4: SMT encoding for the meaning of bounded until formulas

---

Input : $\mathcal{M} = (S, Act, \mathbf{P}, AP, L)$: MDP; φ: HyperPCTL bounded until formula
of the form $\mathbb{P}(\varphi_1 \mathcal{U}^{[k_1,k_2]}\varphi_2)$; n: number of state variables in φ.

Output : SMT encoding of φ's meaning in the n-ary self-composition of $\mathcal{M}$.

1 **Function** *SemanticsBoundedUntil*$(\mathcal{M}, \varphi = \mathbb{P}(\varphi_1 \mathcal{U}^{[k_1,k_2]}\varphi_2), n)$

2   **if** $k_2 = 0$ **then**

3      $E := \text{Semantics}(\mathcal{M}, \varphi_1, n) \wedge \text{Semantics}(\mathcal{M}, \varphi_2, n)$;

4   **foreach** $s = (s_1, \ldots, s_n) \in S^n$ **do**

5        $E := E \wedge (holds_{s,\varphi_2} \rightarrow prob_{s,\varphi} = 1) \wedge (\neg holds_{s,\varphi_2} \rightarrow prob_{s,\varphi} = 0)$;

6   **else if** $k_1 = 0$ **then**

7      $E := \text{SemanticsBoundedUntil}(\mathcal{M}, \mathbb{P}(\varphi_1 \mathcal{U}^{[0,k_2-1]}\varphi_2), n)$;

8   **foreach** $s = (s_1, \ldots, s_n) \in S^n$ **do**

9        $E :=$
$E \wedge (holds_{s,\varphi_2} \rightarrow prob_{s,\varphi} = 1) \wedge ((\neg holds_{s,\varphi_1} \wedge \neg holds_{s,\varphi_2}) \rightarrow prob_{s,\varphi} = 0)$;

10   **foreach** $\alpha = (\alpha_1, \ldots, \alpha_n) \in Act(s_1) \times \ldots \times Act(s_n)$ **do**

11          $E :=$

           $E \wedge \Big(\big[\ holds_{s,\varphi_1} \wedge \neg holds_{s,\varphi_2} \wedge \bigwedge_{i=1}^{n} \sigma_{s_i} = \alpha_i\ \big] \rightarrow \big[prob_{s,\varphi} =$

12            $\sum_{s' \in supp(\alpha_1) \times \ldots \times supp(\alpha_n)}((\Pi_{i=1}^{n}\mathbf{P}(s_i, \alpha_i, s'_i)) \cdot$

           $prob_{s',\mathbb{P}(\varphi_1 \mathcal{U}^{[0,k_2-1]}\varphi_2)})\ \big]\ \Big)$;

13   **else if** $k_1 > 0$ **then**

14      $E := \text{SemanticsBoundedUntil}(\mathcal{M}, \mathbb{P}(\varphi_1 \mathcal{U}^{[k_1-1,k_2-1]}\varphi_2), n)$;

15   **foreach** $s = (s_1, \ldots, s_n) \in S^n$ **do**

16        $E := E \wedge (\neg holds_{s,\varphi_1} \rightarrow prob_{s,\varphi} = 0)$;

17   **foreach** $\alpha = (\alpha_1, \ldots, \alpha_n) \in Act(s_1) \times \ldots \times Act(s_n)$ **do**

18          $E := E \wedge \Big(\big[\ holds_{s,\varphi_1} \wedge \bigwedge_{i=1}^{n} \sigma_{s_i} = \alpha_i\ \big] \rightarrow \big[\ prob_{s,\varphi} =$

19          $\sum_{s' \in supp(\alpha_1) \times \ldots \times supp(\alpha_n)}((\Pi_{i=1}^{n}\mathbf{P}(s_i, \alpha_i, s'_i)) \cdot$

         $prob_{s',\mathbb{P}(\varphi_1 \mathcal{U}^{[k_1-1,k_2-1]}\varphi_2)})\ \big]\ \Big)$;

20   **return** E;

---

property we use fresh variables d_{s,φ_2} and require a path over states with strong monotonically decreasing d_{s,φ_2}-values to a φ_2-state (where the decreasing property serves to exclude loops). The domain of the distance-variables d_{s,φ_2} can be e.g. integers, rationals or reals; the only restriction is that is should contain at least $|S|^n$ ordered values. Especially, it does not need to be lower bounded (note that each solution assigns to each d_{s,φ_2} a fixed value, leading a finite number of distance values).

The SemanticsBoundedUntil method, listed in Algorithm 4, encodes the probability $\mathbb{P}(\varphi_1 \, \mathcal{U}^{[k_1,k_2]} \varphi_2)$ of a bounded until formula in the numeric variables $prob_{s,\mathbb{P}(\varphi_1 \mathcal{U}^{[k_1,k_2]}\varphi_2)}$ for all (composed) states $s \in S^n$ and recursively reduced time bounds. There are three main cases: (i) the satisfaction of $\varphi_1 \, \mathcal{U}^{[0,k_2-1]} \varphi_2$

Algorithm 5: SMT encoding of the truth of the input formula

Input	: $\mathcal{M} = (S, Act, \mathbf{P}, AP, L)$: MDP; $\exists \hat{\sigma}.Q_1\hat{s}_1(\hat{\sigma}).\ldots.Q_n\hat{s}_n(\hat{\sigma}).\varphi^{nq}$: HyperPCTL formula.
Output	: Encoding of the truth of the input formula in $\mathcal{M}$.

1 **Function** $Truth(\mathcal{M}, \exists \hat{\sigma}. \, Q_1\hat{s}_1(\hat{\sigma}). \, \ldots \, Q_n\hat{s}_n(\hat{\sigma}). \, \varphi^{nq})$
2   **foreach** $i = 1,\ldots,n$ **do**
3   **if** $Q_i = \forall$ **then** $B_i :=$ "$\bigwedge_{s_i \in S}$";
4   **else** $B_i :=$ "$\bigvee_{s_i \in S}$";
5   **return** $B_1 \, \ldots \, B_n \, holds_{(s_1,\ldots,s_n),\varphi^{nq}}$;

---

requires to satisfy φ_2 immediately (lines 2–5); (ii) $\varphi_1 \, \mathcal{U}^{[0,k_2-1]} \varphi_2$ can be satisfied by either satisfying φ_2 immediately or satisfying it later, but in the latter case φ_1 needs to hold currently (lines 6–12); (iii) φ_1 has to hold and φ_2 needs to be satisfied some time later (lines 13–19). To avoid the repeated encoding of the semantics of the operands, we do it only when we reach case (i) where recursion stops (line 3). For the other cases, we recursively encode the probability to reach a φ_2-state over φ_1 states where the deadlines are reduced with one step (lines 7 resp. 14) and use these to fix the values of the variables $prob_{s,\mathbb{P}(\varphi_1 \mathcal{U}^{[k_1,k_2]}\varphi_2)}$, similarly to the unbounded case but under additional consideration of time bounds.

Finally, the Truth method listed in Algorithm 5 encodes the meaning of the state quantification: it states for each universal quantifier that instantiating it with any MDP state should satisfy the formula (conjunction over all states in line 9), and for each existential state quantification that at least one state should lead to satisfaction (disjunction in line 4).

Theorem 3. *Algorithm 1 returns a formula that is true iff its input HyperPCTL formula is satisfied by the input MDP.*

We note that the satisfiability of the generated SMT encoding for a formula with an existential scheduler quantifier does not only prove the truth of the formula but provides also a scheduler as witness, encoded in the solution of the SMT encoding. Conversely, unsatisfiability of the SMT encoding for a formula with a universal scheduler quantifier provides a counterexample scheduler.

6 Evaluation

We developed a prototypical implementation of our algorithm in python, with the help of several libraries. There is an extensive use of STORMPY [15,16], which provides efficient solution to parsing, building, and storage of MDPs. We used the SMT-solver Z3 [17] to solve the logical encoding generated by Algorithm 1. All of our experiments were run on a MacBook Pro laptop with a 2.3 GHz i7 processor with 32 GB of RAM. The results are presented in Table 1.

As the first case study, we model and analyze information leakage in the modular exponentiation algorithm (function modexp in Fig. 4); the corresponding results in Table 1 are marked by **TA**. We experimented with 1, 2, and 3 bits for the encryption key (hence, $m \in \{2, 4, 6\}$). The specification checks whether there is a timing channel for all possible schedulers, which is the case for the implementation in `modexp`.

Our second case study is verification of password leakage thorough the string comparison algorithm (function `str_cmp` in Fig. 5). Here, we also experimented with $m \in \{2, 4, 6\}$; results in Table 1 are denoted by **PW**.

In our third case study, we assume two concurrent processes. The first process decrements the value of a secret h by 1 as long as the value is still positive, and after this it sets a low variable l to 1. A second process just sets the value of the same low variable l to 2. The two threads run in parallel; as long as none of them terminated, a fair scheduler chooses for each CPU cycle the next executing thread. As discussed in Sect. 1, this MDP opens a probabilistic thread scheduling channel and leaks the value of h. We denote this case study by **TS** in Table 1, and compare observations for executions with different secret values h_1 and h_2 (denoted as $h = (h_1, h_2)$ in the table). There is an interesting relation between the execution times for **TA** and **TS**. For example, although the MDP for **TA** with $m = 4$ has 60 reachable states and the MDP for **TS** comparing executions for $h = (0, 15)$ has 35 reachable states, verification of **TS** takes 20 times more than **TA**. We believe this is because the MDP of **TS** is twice deeper than the MDP of **TA**, making the SMT constraints more complex.

Our last case study is on probabilistic conformance, denoted **PC**. The input is a DTMC that encodes the behavior of a 6-sided die as well as a structure of actions having probability distributions with two successor states each; these transitions can be pruned using a scheduler to obtain a DTMC which simulates the die outcomes using a fair coin. Given a fixed state space, we experiment with different numbers of transitions. In particular, we started from the implementation in [14] and then we added all the possible nondeterministic transitions from the first state to all the other states ($s = 0$), from the first and second states to all the others ($s = 0, 1$), and from the first, second, and third states to all the others ($s = 0, 1, 2$). Each time we were able not only to satisfy the formula, but also to obtain the witness corresponding to the scheduler satisfying the property.

Regarding the running times listed in Table 1, we note that our implementation is only prototypical and there are possibilities for numerous optimizations. Most importantly, for purely existentially or purely universally quantified formulas, we could define a more efficient encoding with much less variables. However, it is clear that the running times for even relatively small MPDs are large. This is simply because of the high complexity of the verification of hyperproperties. In addition, the HyperPCTL formulas in our case studies have multiple scheduler and/or state quantifiers, making the problem significantly more difficult.

Table 1. Experimental results. **TA:** Timing attack. **PW:** Password leakage. **TS:** Thread scheduling. **PC:** Probabilistic conformance.

Case study		Running time (s)			#SMT variables	#subformulas	#states	#transitions
		SMT encoding	SMT solving	Total				
TA	$m = 2$	5.43	0.31	5.74	8088	50654	24	46
	$m = 4$	114	20	134	50460	368062	60	136
	$m = 6$	1721	865	2586	175728	1381118	112	274
PW	$m = 2$	5.14	0.3	8.14	8088	43432	24	46
	$m = 4$	207	40	247	68670	397852	70	146
	$m = 6$	3980	1099	5079	274540	1641200	140	302
TS	$h = (0, 1)$	0.83	0.07	0.9	1379	7913	7	13
	$h = (0, 15)$	60	1607	1667	34335	251737	35	83
	$h = (4, 8)$	11.86	17.02	28.88	12369	87097	21	48
	$h = (8, 15)$	60	1606	1666	34335	251737	35	83
PC	s=(0)	277	1996	2273	21220	1859004	20	158
	s=(0,1)	822	5808	6630	21220	5349205	20	280
	s=(0,1,2)	1690	58095	59785	21220	11006581	20	404

7   Conclusion and Future Work

We investigated the problem of specifying and model checking probabilistic hyperproperties of Markov decision processes (MDPs). Our study is motivated by the fact that many systems have probabilistic nature and are influenced by nondeterministic actions of their environment. We extended the temporal logic HyperPCTL for DTMCs [7] to the context of MDPs by allowing formulas to quantify over schedulers. This additional expressive power leads to undecidability of the HyperPCTL model checking problem on MDPs, but we also showed that the undecidable fragment becomes decidable for non-probabilistic memoryless schedulers. Indeed, all applications discussed in this paper only require this type of schedulers.

Due to the high complexity of the problem, more efficient model checking algorithms are greatly needed. An orthogonal solution is to design less accurate and/or approximate algorithms such as statistical model checking that scale better and provide certain probabilistic guarantees about the correctness of verification. Another interesting direction is using counterexample-guided techniques to manage the size of the state space.

References

1. Clarkson, M.R., Schneider, F.B.: Hyperproperties. J. Comput. Secur. **18**(6), 1157–1210 (2010)
2. Alpern, B., Schneider, F.B.: Defining liveness. Inf. Process. Lett. **21**, 181–185 (1985)

3. Goguen, J.A., Meseguer, J.: Security policies and security models. In: IEEE Symposium on Security and Privacy, pp. 11–20 (1982)
4. Zdancewic, S., Myers, A.C.: Observational determinism for concurrent program security. In: Proceedings of CSFW 2003, p. 29 (2003)
5. Wang, Y., Zarei, M., Bonakdarpour, B., Pajic, M.: Statistical verification of hyperproperties for cyber-physical systems. ACM Trans. Embedded Comput. Syst. (TECS) 18(5s), 1–23 (2019)
6. Bonakdarpour, B., Sanchez, C., Schneider, G.: Monitoring hyperproperties by combining static analysis and runtime verification. In: Margaria, T., Steffen, B. (eds.) ISoLA 2018. LNCS, vol. 11245, pp. 8–27. Springer, Cham (2018). https://doi.org/10.1007/978-3-030-03421-4_2
7. Ábrahám, E., Bonakdarpour, B.: HyperPCTL: a temporal logic for probabilistic hyperproperties. In: McIver, A., Horvath, A. (eds.) QEST 2018. LNCS, vol. 11024, pp. 20–35. Springer, Cham (2018). https://doi.org/10.1007/978-3-319-99154-2_2
8. Ábrahám, E., Bartocci, E., Bonakdarpour, B., Dobe, O.: Parameter synthesis for probabilistic hyperproperties. In: Proceedings of 23rd International Conference on Logic for Programming, Artificial Intelligence and Reasoning, LPAR 23, EPiC Series in Computing. EasyChair, vol. 73, pp. 12–31 (2020)
9. Wang, Y., Nalluri, S., Bonakdarpour, B., Pajic, M.: Statistical model checking for hyperproperties. In: Proceedings of the IEEE 34th Computer Security Foundations (CSF), (2021, to appear)
10. Guarnieri, M., Marinovic, S., Basin, D.: Securing databases from probabilistic inference. In: Proceedings of CSF 2017, pp. 343–359 (2017)
11. Dimitrova, R., Finkbeiner, B., Torfah, H.: Probabilistic hyperproperties of Markov decision processes. In: Proceedings of the 18th Symposium on Automated Technology for Verification and Analysis (ATVA) (2020, to appear)
12. Ábrahám, E., Bartocci, E., Bonakdarpour, B., Dobe, O.: Probabilistic hyperproperties with nondeterminism. CoRR abs/2005.06115 (2020)
13. Minh Ngo, T., Stoelinga, M., Huisman, M.: Confidentiality for probabilistic multithreaded programs and its verification. In: Jürjens, J., Livshits, B., Scandariato, R. (eds.) ESSoS 2013. LNCS, vol. 7781, pp. 107–122. Springer, Heidelberg (2013). https://doi.org/10.1007/978-3-642-36563-8_8
14. Knuth, D., Yao, A.: The complexity of nonuniform random number generation. In: Algorithms and Complexity: New Directions and Recent Results. Academic Press (1976)
15. STORMPY. https://moves-rwth.github.io/stormpy/
16. Dehnert, C., Junges, S., Katoen, J.-P., Volk, M.: A storm is coming: a modern probabilistic model checker. In: Majumdar, R., Kunčak, V. (eds.) CAV 2017. LNCS, vol. 10427, pp. 592–600. Springer, Cham (2017). https://doi.org/10.1007/978-3-319-63390-9_31
17. de Moura, L., Bjørner, N.: Z3: an efficient SMT solver. In: Ramakrishnan, C.R., Rehof, J. (eds.) TACAS 2008. LNCS, vol. 4963, pp. 337–340. Springer, Heidelberg (2008). https://doi.org/10.1007/978-3-540-78800-3_24

Tool Papers

ReachNN*: A Tool for Reachability Analysis of Neural-Network Controlled Systems

Jiameng Fan[1($\boxtimes$)], Chao Huang[2], Xin Chen[3], Wenchao Li[1], and Qi Zhu[2]

[1] Boston University, Massachusetts, USA
{jmfan,wenchao}@bu.edu
[2] Northwestern University, Illinois, USA
{chao.huang,qzhu}@northwestern.edu
[3] University of Dayton, Ohio, USA
xchen4@udayton.edu

Abstract. We introduce ReachNN*, a tool for reachability analysis of neural-network controlled systems (NNCSs). The theoretical foundation of ReachNN* is the use of Bernstein polynomials to approximate any Lipschitz-continuous neural-network controller with different types of activation functions, with provable approximation error bounds. In addition, the sampling-based error bound estimation in ReachNN* is amenable to GPU-based parallel computing. For further improvement in runtime and error bound estimation, ReachNN* also features optional controller re-synthesis via a technique called *verification-aware knowledge distillation* (KD) to reduce the Lipschitz constant of the neural-network controller. Experiment results across a set of benchmarks show 7× to 422× efficiency improvement over the previous prototype. Moreover, KD enables proof of reachability of NNCSs whose verification results were previously unknown due to large overapproximation errors. An open-source implementation of ReachNN* is available at https://github.com/JmfanBU/ReachNNStar.git.

Keywords: Neural-network controlled systems · Reachability · Bernstein polynomials · GPU acceleration · Knowledge distillation.

1 Introduction

There has been a growing interest in using neural networks as controllers in areas of control and robotics, e.g., deep reinforcement learning [13], imitation learning [7,14], and model predictive control (MPC) approximating [3,9]. We consider

---

J. Fan and C. Huang contributed equally.

We acknowledge the support from NSF grants 1646497, 1834701, 1834324, 1839511, 1724341, ONR grant N00014-19-1-2496, and the US Air Force Research Laboratory (AFRL) under contract number FA8650-16-C-2642.

D. V. Hung and O. Sokolsky (Eds.): ATVA 2020, LNCS 12302, pp. 537–542, 2020.
https://doi.org/10.1007/978-3-030-59152-6_30

neural-network controlled systems (NNCSs) that are closed-loop sampled-data systems where a neural-network controller controls a continuous physical plant in a periodic manner. Given a sampling period $\delta > 0$, the neural-network (NN) controller reads the state x of the plant at the time $t = i\delta$ for $i = 0, 1, 2, \ldots$, feeds it to a neural network to obtain the output u, and updates the control input in the plant's dynamics to u. Our tool ReachNN* aims to solve the following reachability problem of NNCSs.

Problem 1. The *reach-avoid problem* of a NNCS is to decide whether from any state in an initial set X_0, the system can reach a target set X_f, while avoiding an unsafe set X_u within the time interval $[0, T]$.

A major challenge facing reachability analysis for NNCSs is the presence of non-linearity in the NN controllers. Existing reachability analysis tools for NNCSs typically target specific classes of NN controllers [2,5,12,15]. Sherlock [5] and NNV [15] for instance only consider neural networks with RELU activation functions, while Verisig [12] requires the neural networks to have differentiable activation functions such as tanh/Sigmoid.

In this paper, we present our tool ReachNN*, which is a significantly extended implementation of our previous prototype ReachNN [11]. ReachNN* provides two main features. First, it can verify an NNCS with any activation functions by Bernstein polynomial approximation [11]. Second, based on the proportionality relationship between approximation error estimation Lipschitz constant of the NN controller, ReachNN* can use knowledge distillation (KD) [10] to retrain a verification-friendly NN controller that preserves the performance of the original network but has a smaller Lipschitz constant, as proposed in [6].

Another significant improvement in ReachNN* is the acceleration of the sampling-based error analysis in ReachNN by using GPU-based parallel computing. The sampling-based approach uniformly samples the input space for a given sample density and evaluates the neural network controller and the polynomial approximation at those sample points. We use the Lipschitz constant of the neural network and the samples to establish an upper bound on the true error (details in [11]). For networks with many inputs, this approach may require many sample points to avoid a blowup in the overapproximation. Here, we make the observation that the sampling-evaluation step is a single instruction, multiple data (SIMD) computation which is amenable to GPU-based acceleration. Experimental results across a set of benchmarks show 7× to 422× efficiency improvement over the previous prototype.

2   Tool Design

The architecture of ReachNN* is shown in Fig. 1. The input consists of three parts: (1) a file containing the plant dynamics and the (bounded) reach-avoid specification, (2) a file describing the NN controller, and (3) an optional target Lipschitz constant for controller retraining. The tool then works as follows. For every sampling step $[i\delta, (i + 1)\delta]$ for $i = 0, 1, 2 \ldots$, a polynomial approximation

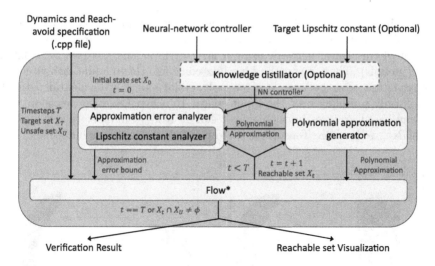

Fig. 1. Structure of ReachNN*.

along with a guaranteed error bound for the NN controller output is computed and then used to update the plant's continuous dynamics. The evolution of the plant is approximated by flowpipes using Flow*. During the flowpipe construction, it checks every computed flowpipe whether it lies entirely inside the target set X_f and outside the avoid set X_u. The tool terminates when (1) the reachable set at some time $t \leq T$ lies inside the target set and all computed flowpipes do not intersect with the avoid set, i.e. the reach-avoid specification is satisfied; or (2) an unsafe flowpipe is detected, i.e. it enters the avoid set X_u; or (3) the reachable set at some time t intersects with but is not entirely contained in X_f, in which case the verification result is unknown. The tool also terminates if Flow* fails due to a blowup in the size of the flowpipes. Along with the verification result (Yes, No or Unknown), the tool generates a Gnuplot script for producing the visualization of the computed flowpipes relative to X_0, X_f and X_u.

When the tool returns Unknown, it is often caused by a large overapproximation of the reachable set. As noted before, the overapproximation error is directly tied to the Lipschitz constant of the network in our tool. In such cases, the user can enable the knowledge distillation option to retrain a new neural network. The retrained network has similar performance compared to the original network but a smaller Lipschitz constant. The tool will then perform reachability analysis on the retrained network. We describe the function of each model in ReachNN* in more detail below.

[**Polynomial Approximation Generator**]. We implement this module in Python. It generates the approximation function of a given neural network over a general hyper-rectangle, with respect to a given order bound for the Bernstein polynomials. The generated polynomial is represented as a list of monomials' orders and the associated coefficients.

[**Approximation Error Analyzer**]. This module is implemented in Python. It first invokes a sub-module – Lipschitz constant analyzer, to compute a Lipschitz constant of the neural network using a layer-by-layer analysis (see Sect. 3.2 of [11] for details). Then, given the Lipschitz constant, this module estimates the approximation error between a given polynomial and a given neural network by uniformly sampling over the input space. To achieve a given precision, this sampling-based error estimation may result in a large number of samples. In ReachNN*, we leverage Tensorflow [1] to parallelize this step using GPUs.

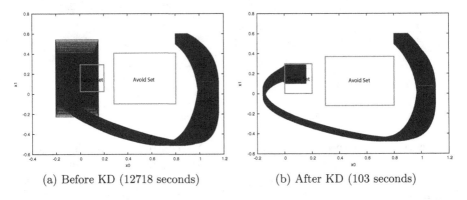

(a) Before KD (12718 seconds)   (b) After KD (103 seconds)

Fig. 2. Reachability analysis results: Red lines represent boundaries of the obstacles and form the avoid set. Green rectangle represents the target region. Blue rectangle represents the computed flowpipes. (Color figure online)

[**Flow***]. We use the C++ APIs in Flow* [4] to carry out the following tasks: (a) flowpipe construction under continuous dynamics using symbolic remainders, (b) checking whether a flowpipe intersects the given avoid set, (c) checking whether a flowpipe lies entirely in the given target set, and (d) generating a visualization file for the flowpipes.

[**Knowledge Distillator**]. This module is implemented in Python with GPU support for retraining. The inputs for this module are the original NN, a target Lipschitz constant number, and a user-specified tolerance of the training error between the new network and the original network. The output is a retrained network. Details of the distillation procedure can be found in [6]. We note that this module also supports distilling the original network into a new network with a different architecture, which can be specified as an additional input.

Example 1. Consider the following nonlinear control system [8]: $\dot{x}_0 = x_1, \dot{x}_1 = ux_1^2 - x_0$, where u is computed from a NN controller κ that has two hidden layers, twenty neurons in each layer, and ReLU and tanh as activation functions. Given a control stepsize $\delta_c = 0.2$, we want to check if the system will reach $[0, 0.2] \times [0.05, 0.3]$ from the initial set $[0.8, 0.9] \times [0.5, 0.6]$ while avoiding $[0.3, 0.8] \times [-0.1, 0.4]$ over the time interval $[0, 7]$.

Table 1. Comparison with ReachNN. We use l to represent the number of layers in the neural network controller, n to represent the number of neurons in the hidden layers, and $\bar{\varepsilon}$ for the error bound in sampling-based analysis. We use the same benchmarks from [11]. The dimensions of states are from 2 to 4 for these benchmarks. Time shows the runtime of the reachability analysis module. The *After KD* results do not include the runtime for knowledge distillation. The average runtime for knowledge distillation is 245 s (The runtime of the knowledge distillation module does not vary much across different benchmarks.). *Acc* (short for acceleration) denotes the ratio between the runtime of ReachNN and that of ReachNN* on the same NNCS without applying knowledge distillation.

#	NN Controller			Setting	Verification Result		Time (Seconds)			Acc
	Act	l	n	$\bar{\varepsilon}$	Before KD	After KD	ReachNN [11]	ReachNN*	After KD	
1	ReLU	3	20	0.001	Yes(35)	–	3184	26	–	112×
	sigmoid	3	20	0.005	Yes(35)	–	779	76	–	10×
	tanh	3	20	0.005	Unknown(35)	Yes(35)	543	76	70	7×
	ReLU + tanh	3	20	0.005	Yes(35)	–	589	76	–	7×
2	ReLU	3	20	0.01	Yes(9)	–	128	5	–	25×
	sigmoid	3	20	0.001	Yes(9)	–	280	13	–	21×
	tanh	3	20	0.01	Unknown(7)	Yes(7)	642	71	69	9×
	ReLU + tanh	3	20	0.01	Yes(7)	–	543	25	–	21×
6	ReLU	4	20	0.01	Yes(10)	Yes(10)	7842	1126	12	7×
	sigmoid	4	20	0.01	No(7)	–	32499	77	–	422×
	tanh	4	20	0.01	No(7)	–	3683	11	–	334×
	ReLU + tanh	4	20	0.01	Yes(10)	Yes(10)	10032	1410	674	7×

The verification finished in 12718 s and the result is Unknown, which indicates the computed flowpipes intersect with (and are not contained entirely in) the avoid set or the target set. The flowpipes are shown in Fig. 2a. With KD enabled, we retrain a new NN controller with the same architecture, a target Lipschitz constant as 0 (0 means the knowledge distillator will try to minimize the Lipschitz constant) and a regression error tolerance of 0.4. The resulting flowpipes are shown in Fig. 2b. We can see that the new NN controller can be verified to satisfy the reach-avoid specification. In addition, the verification for the new NN controller is 123× faster compared to verifying the original NNCS.

3 Experiments

We provide a full comparison between ReachNN* and the prototype ReachNN on all the examples in [11]. If the verification result is Unknown, we apply our verification-aware knowledge distillation framework to synthesize a new NN controller and check the resulting system with ReachNN*. All experiments are performed on a desktop with 12-core 3.60 GHz Intel Core i7 and NVIDIA GeForce RTX 2060 (ReachNN does not make use of GPU).

We highlight part of the results for Benchmark #1, #2 and #6 in Table 1 due to space constraint (results on all benchmarks can be found in

https://github.com/JmfanBU/ReachNNStar.git). ReachNN* achieves from 7×
to 422× efficiency improvement on the same NNCSs (across all benchmarks
also). In Benchmark #1 and #2 with Unknown results, we applied our knowledge distillation procedure to obtain new NN controllers and performed reachability analysis again on the resulting systems. Observe that ReachNN* produces
a Yes answer for these systems. In addition, it took a shorter amount of time
to compute the verification results compared to ReachNN. In Benchmark #6,
ReachNN* took more than 1000 s to obtain a Yes result in two cases. We run
knowledge distillation for these two cases to evaluate whether KD can be beneficial solely from an efficiency perspective. In both cases, ReachNN* with KD
significantly improves runtime compared to ReachNN* without KD.

References

1. Abadi, M., et al.: Tensorflow: a system for large-scale machine learning. In: OSDI, pp. 265–283 (2016)
2. Bogomolov, S., Forets, M., Frehse, G., Potomkin, K., Schilling, C.: Juliareach: a toolbox for set-based reachability. In: HSCC, pp. 39–44 (2019)
3. Chen, S., et al.: Approximating explicit model predictive control using constrained neural networks. In: ACC, pp. 1520–1527. IEEE (2018)
4. Chen, X., Ábrahám, E., Sankaranarayanan, S.: Flow*: an analyzer for non-linear hybrid systems. In: Sharygina, N., Veith, H. (eds.) CAV 2013. LNCS, vol. 8044, pp. 258–263. Springer, Heidelberg (2013). https://doi.org/10.1007/978-3-642-39799-8_18
5. Dutta, S., Chen, X., Sankaranarayanan, S.: Reachability analysis for neural feed-back systems using regressive polynomial rule inference. In: HSCC, pp. 157–168 (2019)
6. Fan, J., Huang, C., Li, W., Chen, X., Zhu, Q.: Towards verification-aware knowl-edge distillation for neural-network controlled systems. In: ICCAD. IEEE (2019)
7. Finn, C., Yu, T., Zhang, T., Abbeel, P., Levine, S.: One-shot visual imitation learning via meta-learning. In: Conference on Robot Learning, pp. 357–368 (2017)
8. Gallestey, E., Hokayem, P.: Lecture notes in nonlinear systems and control (2019)
9. Hertneck, M., Köhler, J., Trimpe, S., Allgöwer, F.: Learning an approximate model predictive controller with guarantees. IEEE Control Syst. Lett. **2**(3), 543–548 (2018)
10. Hinton, G.E., Vinyals, O., Dean, J.: Distilling the knowledge in a neural network. CoRR abs/1503.02531 (2015)
11. Huang, C., Fan, J., Li, W., Chen, X., Zhu, Q.: REACHNN: reachability analysis of neural-network controlled systems. TECS **18**(5s), 1–22 (2019)
12. Ivanov, R., Weimer, J., Alur, R., Pappas, G.J., Lee, I.: Verisig: verifying safety properties of hybrid systems with neural network controllers. In: HSCC, pp. 169–178 (2019)
13. Lillicrap, T.P., et al.: Continuous control with deep reinforcement learning. In: International Conference on Learning Representation (2016)
14. Pan, Y., et al.: Agile autonomous driving using end-to-end deep imitation learning. In: RSS (2018)
15. Tran, H.D., Cai, F., Diego, M.L., Musau, P., Johnson, T.T., Koutsoukos, X.: Safety verification of cyber-physical systems with reinforcement learning control. TECS **18**(5s), 1–22 (2019)

RVX - A Tool for Concolic Testing of Embedded Binaries Targeting RISC-V Platforms

Vladimir Herdt[1]([✉])[iD], Daniel Große[1,2][iD], and Rolf Drechsler[1,3][iD]

[1] Cyber-Physical Systems, DFKI GmbH, 28359 Bremen, Germany
{vherdt,grosse,drechsle}@informatik.uni-bremen.de
[2] Chair of Complex Systems, Johannes Kepler University Linz, Linz, Austria
[3] Institute of Computer Science, University of Bremen, 28359 Bremen, Germany

Abstract. We present RVX, a tool for concolic testing of embedded binaries targeting RISC-V platforms with peripherals. RVX integrates the *Concolic Testing Engine* (CTE) with an *Instruction Set Simulator* (ISS) supporting the RISC-V RV32IMC *Instruction Set Architecture* (ISA). Further, RVX provides a designated CTE-interface for additional extensions. It is an extensible command layer that provides support for verification functions and enables integration of peripherals into the concolic simulation. The experiments demonstrate the applicability and efficiency of RVX in analyzing real-world embedded applications. In addition, we found a new serious bug in the RISC-V port of the *newlib* C library.

Keywords: RISC-V · Concolic testing · Verification · Embedded binaries

1 Introduction

Performing application *Software* (SW) verification on the binary level is very important to achieve accurate verification results. However, at the same time it is very challenging due to the detailed low level semantics. Concolic testing has been shown to be very effective for binary analysis [2,3,5,9]. Recently, we proposed a methodology for concolic testing of embedded binaries targeting platforms with peripherals, using the RISC-V *Instruction Set Architecture* (ISA)[1]

This work was supported in part by the German Federal Ministry of Education and Research (BMBF) within the project Scale4Edge under contract no. 16ME0127 and within the project VerSys under contract no. 01IW19001 and within the project SATiSFy under contract no. 16KIS0821K, and by the German Research Foundation (DFG) as part of the Collaborative Research Center (Sonderforschungsbereich) 1320 EASE – Everyday Activity Science and Engineering, University of Bremen (http://www.ease-crc.org/) in subproject P04.

[1] Find the RISC-V ISA specification documents at https://riscv.org/specifications/.

© Springer Nature Switzerland AG 2020
D. V. Hung and O. Sokolsky (Eds.): ATVA 2020, LNCS 12302, pp. 543–559, 2020.
https://doi.org/10.1007/978-3-030-59152-6_31

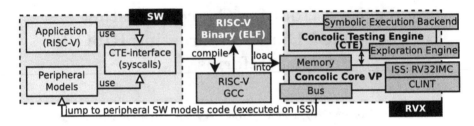

Fig. 1. RVX architecture overview. The Core VP is based on our RISC-V VP from [6].

as a case-study [7]. This initial prototype implementation has been extended, resulting in the tool RVX. To the best of our knowledge, RVX is the first available concolic testing tool targeting the RISC-V ISA[2]. In particular, RVX supports the RISC-V RV32IMC ISA, i.e. a 32 bit architecture with the mandatory base Integer instruction set together with the Multiplication extension and support for Compressed instructions, in combination with the RISC-V machine mode *Control and Status Registers* (CSRs) and interrupt handling instruction. In addition RVX provides a designated *Concolic Testing Engine* (CTE) interface to access verification functions from the SW and integrate additional peripherals into the concolic simulation by means of SW models. The CTE-interface peripheral integration is tailored for SystemC-based peripherals with TLM 2.0 communication [8]. Our experiments demonstrate the efficiency of RVX in analyzing real-world embedded binaries.

Compared to our initial paper [7], this tool paper focuses on additional implementation details and adds the following extensions and **contributions: 1)** several architectural improvements, including a search heuristic to speed-up bug hunting and an optimized memory system for more efficiency (lazy initialization and instruction fetch optimization); **2)** extended support for the RISC-V privileged ISA which enables to use the Zephyr *Operating System* (OS); and **3)** new set of experiments based on the Zephyr OS and we found a new serious bug in the RISC-V port of the *newlib* C library.

2   RVX Overview and Implementation

2.1   Architecture Overview

RVX is implemented in C++. Figure 1 shows an overview of the architecture. RVX operates on the binary level. Starting point of the analysis is a RISC-V binary (ELF). The RISC-V binary is obtained by compiling and linking the SW application together with our CTE-interface and an optional set of peripheral SW models. We expect that calls to the verification functions (functions provided

---

[2] Visit http://systemc-verification.org/risc-v for the most recent updates on our RISC-V related approaches.

through our CTE-interface SW stub), to mark symbolic input variables and encode (safety) properties (i.e. *make_symbolic*, *assume* and *assert* with their usual semantic), have been embedded in the ELF already.

RVX performs concolic testing of the RISC-V ELF. Essentially, RVX consists of two parts: The concolic core *Virtual Prototype* (VP) and the CTE, as shown on the right side of Fig. 1. The CTE successively generates new inputs to explore new paths through the ELF. Based on the inputs the VP, and in particular the *Instruction Set Simulator* (ISS) component, performs the actual execution one after another and tracks symbolic constraints in order to generate new inputs. Therefore, the VP is operating with concolic data types in place of concrete values. Essentially, a concolic data type is a pair of a concrete value and a (optional) symbolic expression.

We implemented symbolic expressions as lightweight wrapper classes that provide a thin layer around KLEE [1] symbolic expressions. Beside, enabling to change the symbolic backend more easily, the wrapper provides expression simplification rules, based on term rewriting. We leverage KLEE constraint sets and use the solver API of KLEE (combining the counterexample and caching solvers) for constraint solving.

2.2 Exploration Engine and Memory Model

The **exploration engine** collects inputs in a priority queue to enable easy integration of different search algorithms. We prioritize inputs that lead to new program counter values (i.e. essentially increase branch coverage by selecting a branch direction that has not yet been executed). In case of multiple/none available candidates, we randomize the decision. By using the search depth as criteria a *Depth First Search* (DFS) or *Breadth First Search* (BFS) can be selected instead.

Memory is modeled as mapping from address to concolic byte. The mapping is constructed on-demand in a lazy fashion. A lazy implementation enables a significantly faster startup of the VP and reduces memory consumption, since the VP can have a large amount of memory and construction of symbolic data is resource intensive. The memory is initialized by loading the ELF file[3]. All other memory locations are uninitialized and will return a symbolic value on access. A memory access (read or write) with symbolic address will be concretized to a concrete address. Symbolic constraints are collected to enable generation of different concrete addresses. To speed-up instruction fetching we provide an option to load the *text* section of the ELF file into a native array and perform instruction fetching from that array.

---

[3] Essentially, this will copy code and data from the text and data sections, respectively, as well as zero initialize memory according to the *bss* section, as specified in the ELF program headers.

2.3   CTE-Interface and Peripheral Integration

Verification Interface. We provide the *make_symbolic, assume* and *assert* verification functions with their usual semantic, i.e. to make variables (memory locations in general) symbolic as well as constrain and check their values. Besides that, we provide two functions to set/unset memory regions to be access protected. These functions enable to e.g. implement heap buffer overflow protection by allocating a larger buffer and marking the beginning and end of the allocated buffer to be access protected. RVX reports an error in case an access to such a memory region is detected at runtime.

Peripheral Integration. Both the actual application SW as well as the SW peripheral models are executed on the core VP. In case a memory access is routed to a SW peripheral the ISS performs a context switch to the peripheral handler. Therefore, the ISS sets the program counter to the handler address. Arguments between the ISS and the SW peripherals are passed through registers. Arguments are the access address, length, type (read or write) and a pointer to the data that is written or to be read (therefore a designated array is reserved). At the end of the handler, the CTE *return* function is called. It restores the previous execution context in the ISS.

Besides the *return* function that transfers control back to the caller of a peripheral function, RVX provides four additional CTE-interface functions for peripheral integration: *notify, cancel, delay* and *trigger_irq*. Notify registers a callback function to be called after a specified delay by the core VP (based on the core VP timing model, i.e. execution cycles per instructions). Cancel removes a pending notification callback. Notify and cancel enable to implement a simple event-based synchronization targeting simple SystemC-based process (i.e. SC_THREAD and SC_METHOD) functionality. The *delay* function allows to annotate a processing delay that is added to the VPs internal timing model. The *trigger_irq* function triggers the given interrupt number. Please note, we provide an SW model of the RISC-V PLIC (*Platform Level Interrupt Controller*) that receives interrupts from other peripherals and prioritizes them. Finally, the PLIC is using the *trigger_irq* interface function to signal to the core VP that some interrupt is pending and requires processing.

Virtual Instructions. Load instructions are split in the ISS into smaller virtual instructions. The reason is that they need to store the result of the memory access into a destination register (encoded in the instruction format). However, the result of a peripheral memory access is only available after context switching between the peripheral, which involves execution of several additional instructions (code from the peripheral) in-between. Splitting load instructions into two virtual instructions, where the first performs the memory access and the second stores the result in the destination register, enables the ISS to resume execution of the load instruction correctly.

2.4 ISS Main Loop

The ISS is the main component of the core VP. Algorithm 1 shows the instruction processing loop of the ISS. It executes instructions until the simulation terminates (19, by issuing a special system call from the SW).

The ISS either executes application code (the default mode) or peripheral code (*in-peripheral* is *True*). In both cases the ISS might be executing virtual instructions (*in-virtual-mode* is True) to process load instruction correctly. Please note, *in-virtual-mode* is set to *False* when entering peripheral code and restored to its previous state on leaving (i.e. by storing *in-virtual-mode* on the context stack).

Pending notifications from peripherals (2–7) as well as external system calls (not CTE-interface, e.g. Zephyr OS context switches) and interrupts (8–10) are only processed if the ISS is currently executing normal application code. The *switch-to-trap-handler* function jumps to the trap/interrupt handler in SW, following the RISC-V trap/interrupt handling convention.

In each step either a virtual (12) or normal (13–18) instruction is executed. In case of a normal instruction the ISS timing model is updated and the delay of the registered pending peripheral notifications is updated accordingly.

Algorithm 1: Main instruction processing loop inside the ISS

```
 1 do
 2 |   if ¬ in-virtual-mode ∧ ¬ in-peripheral then
 3 |   |   foreach e ← pending-notifications do
 4 |   |   |   if delay(e) ≤ 0 then              /* notification time elapsed */
   |   |   |   |   /* context switch to peripheral code                   */
 5 |   |   |   |   context-switch-to-event-handler(function(e))
 6 |   |   |   |   pending-notifications.remove(e)
 7 |   |   |   |   break
   |
 8 |   |   if ¬ in-peripheral then
 9 |   |   |   if has-pending-system-call ∨ has-pending-enabled-interrupts then
10 |   |   |   |   switch-to-trap-handler()   /* follow RISC-V convention */
   |
11 |   if in-virtual-mode then
12 |   |   exec-virtual-step()               /* continue with instruction part */
13 |   else
   |   |   /* exec-normal-step() might enter virtual mode and context
   |   |      switch to peripheral or set status to Terminated            */
14 |   |   if in-peripheral then
15 |   |   |   exec-normal-step()     /* peripherals have separate timing */
16 |   |   else
   |   |   |   /* execute SW instruction and update core timing          */
17 |   |   |   Instruction op ← exec-normal-step()
18 |   |   |   timing-and-pending-notifications-update(op)
   |
19 while status != Terminated
```

The updates only happen for application code (18), since the peripheral models emulate hardware devices and hence require a different timing model (we provide the *delay* system call to annotate the execution delay). The ISS uses a simple timing model that assigns each instruction a fixed (though configurable) execution time.

3   Experiments and Conclusion

All experiments have been performed on an Ubuntu 16.04 Linux system with an Intel Core i5-7200U processor. As symbolic backend we use KLEE [1] v1.4.0 with STP [4] solver v2.3.1. Table 1 shows the results. The columns show: the application SW name, the number of executed instruction (*#instr*), lines of code in C and assembly, overall execution time (*time*), solver time (*stime*), number of concolic execution paths (*#paths*), and number of solver queries (*#queries*).

First, we consider two applications (each with and without a bug as indicated by the name) based on the Zephyr OS. Both applications use a consumer and producer thread and a sensor peripheral attached to an *Interrupt Service Routine* (ISR). The sensor generates symbolic data that is passed through the ISR to the producer (which applies post-processing) and finally the consumer (contains assertions) thread using message queues. The first application (*zephyr-filter-**) generates ten values, applies a filter and asserts that the sum and maximum value stays within a valid range. The second application (*zephyr-sort-**) generates six values, sorts the data (using the BSD *qsort* implementation) and then asserts that it is sorted. These applications demonstrate RVX's ability in analyzing complex embedded binaries.

Table 1. Experiment results (all times reported in seconds) - using RVX to analyze embedded SW targeting the RISC-V ISA and use the i) Zephyr OS, and ii) the RISC-V port of the *newlib* C library. In case of a bug (*-bug) RVX stops the analysis and reports a counterexample. Otherwise (*-ok), RVX performs an exhaustive concolic execution based on the symbolic inputs.

Application SW	#instr	C	ASM	time (S)	stime (S)	#paths	#queries
zephyr-filter-ok	421,206,516	265	4293	196.17	141.73	1024	2048
zephyr-filter-bug	24,628,768	265	4293	7.66	4.79	72	127
zephyr-sort-ok	180,274,083	408	4650	249.25	223.05	724	5043
zephyr-sort-bug	996,518	408	4648	1.43	1.27	4	34
memcpy-opt-bug	182,943	207	566	12.80	11.87	18	473

In addition, we found a new bug in the RISC-V port of the *newlib* C library. In particular, the bug is in the (speed) optimized *memcpy* function[4] and causes

---

[4] https://github.com/riscv/riscv-newlib/blob/master/newlib/libc/machine/riscv/memcpy.c.

overwriting of nearly the entire address space due to an integer overflow in a length calculation. It is triggered by copying a small block to a destination (*dst*) address that is close to zero. We found the bug (last row in Table 1) by making the source (*src*) and *dst* address as well as the copy size symbolic. We added constraints that *src* and *dst* are not overlapping, and placed before the code segment. To catch buffer overflows we added a protected memory region (access is monitored by the ISS) around the buffer memory. Finally, we placed assertions after the memcpy to ensure it copies the data correctly from *src* to *dst*.

In summary, the experiments demonstrate the applicability and efficiency of RVX in analyzing real-world embedded binaries and finding bugs.

References

1. Cadar, C., Dunbar, D., Engler, D.R.: KLEE: unassisted and automatic generation of high-coverage tests for complex systems programs. In: OSDI, pp. 209–224 (2008)
2. Cha, S.K., Avgerinos, T., Rebert, A., Brumley, D.: Unleashing mayhem on binary code. In: IEEE S & P, pp. 380–394 (2012)
3. Chipounov, V., Kuznetsov, V., Candea, G.: S2E: a platform for in-vivo multi-path analysis of software systems. In: ASPLOS, pp. 265–278 (2011)
4. Ganesh, V., Dill, D.L.: A decision procedure for bit-vectors and arrays. In: CAV, pp. 519–531 (2007)
5. Godefroid, P., Levin, M.Y., Molnar, D.A.: Automated whitebox fuzz testing. In: NDSS (2008)
6. Herdt, V., Große, D., Le, H.M., Drechsler, R.: Extensible and configurable RISC-V based virtual prototype. In: Forum on Specification and Design Languages, pp. 5–16 (2018)
7. Herdt, V., Große, D., Le, H.M., Drechsler, R.: Early concolic testing of embedded binaries with virtual prototypes: a RISC-V case study. In: DAC, pp. 188:1–188:6 (2019)
8. IEEE Std. 1666: IEEE Standard SystemC Language Reference Manual (2011)
9. Shoshitaishvili, Y., et al.: SOK: (state of) the art of war: offensive techniques in binary analysis. In: IEEE S & P, pp. 138–157 (2016)

Peregrine 2.0: Explaining Correctness of Population Protocols Through Stage Graphs

Javier Esparza[ID], Martin Helfrich[ID], Stefan Jaax[ID], and Philipp J. Meyer[(✉)][ID]

Technical University of Munich, Munich, Germany
{esparza,helfrich,jaax,meyerphi}@in.tum.de

Abstract. We present a new version of Peregrine, the tool for the analysis and parameterized verification of population protocols introduced in [Blondin et al., CAV'2018]. Population protocols are a model of computation, intensely studied by the distributed computing community, in which mobile anonymous agents interact stochastically to perform a task. Peregrine 2.0 features a novel verification engine based on the construction of stage graphs. Stage graphs are proof certificates, introduced in [Blondin et al., CAV'2020], that are typically succinct and can be independently checked. Moreover, unlike the techniques of Peregrine 1.0, the stage graph methodology can verify protocols whose executions never terminate, a class including recent fast majority protocols. Peregrine 2.0 also features a novel proof visualization component that allows the user to interactively explore the stage graph generated for a given protocol.

Keywords: Population protocols · Distributed computing · Parameterized verification · Stage graphs.

1 Introduction

We present Peregrine 2.0[1], a tool for analysis and parameterized verification of population protocols. Population protocols are a model of computation, intensely studied by the distributed computing community, in which an arbitrary number of indistinguishable agents interact stochastically in order to decide a given property of their initial configuration. For example, agents could initially be in one of two possible states, "yes" and "no", and their task could consist of deciding whether the initial configuration has a majority of "yes" agents or not.

Verifying correctness and/or efficiency of a protocol is a very hard problem, because the semantics of a protocol is an infinite collection of finite-state Markov

This project has received funding from the European Research Council (ERC) under the European Union's Horizon 2020 research and innovation programme under grant agreement No. 787367 (PaVeS). We thank Michael Blondin for contributions to the frontend and Philip Offtermatt for improvements of the simulation backend.

[1] Peregrine 2.0 is available at https://peregrine.model.in.tum.de/.

D. V. Hung and O. Sokolsky (Eds.): ATVA 2020, LNCS 12302, pp. 550–556, 2020.
https://doi.org/10.1007/978-3-030-59152-6_32

chains, one for each possible initial configuration. Peregrine 1.0 [5] was the first tool for the automatic verification of population protocols. It relies on theory developed in [6], and is implemented on top of the Z3 SMT-solver.

Peregrine 1.0 could only verify protocols whose agents eventually never change their state (and not only their answer). This constraint has become increasingly restrictive, because it is not satisfied by many efficient and succinct protocols recently developed for different tasks [1, 2, 4]. Further, Peregrine 1.0 was unable to provide correctness certificates and the user had to trust the tool. Finally, Peregrine 1.0 did not provide any support for computing parameterized bounds on the expected number of interactions needed to reach a stable consensus, i.e., bounds like "$\mathcal{O}(n^2 \log n)$ interactions, where n is the number of agents".

Peregrine 2.0 addresses these three issues. It features a novel verification engine based on theory developed in [3, 7], which, given a protocol and a task description, attempts to construct a stage graph. Stage graphs are proof certificates that can be checked by independent means, and not only prove the protocol correct, but also provide a bound on its expected time-to-consensus. Stages represent milestones reached by the protocol on the way to consensus. Stage graphs are usually small, and help designers to understand why a protocol works. The second main novel feature of Peregrine 2.0 is a visualization component that offers a graphical and explorable representation of the stage graph.

The paper is organized as follows. Section 2 introduces population protocols and sketches the correctness proof of a running example. Section 3 describes the stage graph generated for the example by Peregrine 2.0, and shows that it closely matches the human proof. Section 4 describes the visualization component.

2   Population Protocols

A *population protocol* consists of a set Q of *states* with a subset $I \subseteq Q$ of *initial states*, a set $T \subseteq Q^2 \times Q^2$ of *transitions*, and an *output function* $O : Q \to \{0, 1\}$ assigning to each state a boolean output. Intuitively, a transition $q_1, q_2 \mapsto q_3, q_4$ means that two agents in states q_1, q_2 can interact and simultaneously move to states q_3, q_4. A *configuration* is a mapping $C : Q \to \mathbb{N}$, where $C(q)$ represents the number of agents in a state q. An *initial configuration* is a mapping $C : I \to \mathbb{N}$. A configuration has *consensus* $b \in \{0, 1\}$ if all agents are in states with output b. We write configurations using a set-like notation, e.g. $C = \langle y, n, n \rangle$ or $C = \langle y, 2 \cdot n \rangle$ is the configuration where $C(y) = 1$, $C(n) = 2$ and $C(q) = 0$ for $q \notin \{y, n\}$.

Running Example: Majority Voting. The goal of this protocol is to conduct a vote by majority in a distributed way. The states are $\{Y, N, y, n\}$. Initially, all agents are in state Y or N, according to how they vote. The goal of the protocol is that the agents determine whether at least 50% of them vote "yes".

The output function is $O(Y) = O(y) = 1$ and $O(N) = O(n) = 0$. When two agents interact, they change their state according to the following transitions:

$$a : \text{YN} \mapsto \text{yn} \qquad b : \text{Yn} \mapsto \text{Yy} \qquad c : \text{Ny} \mapsto \text{Nn} \qquad d : \text{yn} \mapsto \text{yy}$$

Intuitively, agents are either active (Y, N) or passive (y, n). By transition a, when active agents with opposite opinions meet, they become passive. Transitions b and c let active agents change the opinion of passive agents. Transition d handles the case of a tie.

Computations in Population Protocols. Computations use a stochastic model: starting from an initial configuration C_0, two agents are repeatedly picked, uniformly at random, and the corresponding transition is applied. This gives rise to an infinite sequence $C_0 \xrightarrow{t_1} C_1 \xrightarrow{t_2} \dots$ of configurations, called a *run*. A run *stabilizes* to consensus $b \in \{0, 1\}$ if from some point on all configurations have consensus b. Intuitively, in a run that stabilizes to b the agents eventually agree on the answer b. Given a population protocol $\mathcal{P}$ and a *predicate* φ that maps every configuration C to a value in $\{0, 1\}$, we say that $\mathcal{P}$ *computes* φ if for every initial configuration C, a run starting at C stabilizes to consensus $\varphi(C)$ with probability 1. The *correctness problem* consists of deciding, given $\mathcal{P}$ and φ, whether $\mathcal{P}$ computes φ. Intuitively, a correct protocol almost surely converges to the consensus specified by the predicate. Majority Voting is correct and computes the predicate that assigns 1 to the configurations where initially at least 50% of the agents are in state Y, i.e. we have $\varphi(C) = (C(\text{Y}) \geq C(\text{N}))$.

Majority Voting is Correct. To intuitively understand why the protocol is correct, it is useful to split a run into *phases*. The first phase starts in the initial configuration, and ends when two agents interact using transition a for the last time. Observe that this moment arrives with probability 1 because passive agents can never become active again. Further, at the end of the first phase either all active agents are in state Y, or they are all in state N. The second phase ends when the agents reach a consensus for the first time, that is, the first time that either all agents are in states Y, y, or all are in states N, n. To see that the second phase ends with probability 1, consider three cases. If initially there is a majority of "yes", then at the end of the first phase no agent is in state N, and at least one is in state Y. This agent eventually moves all passive agents in state n to state y using transition b, reaching a "yes" consensus. The case with an initial majority of "no" is symmetric. If initially there is a tie, then at the end of the first phase all agents are passive, and transition d eventually moves all agents in state n to y, again resulting in a "yes" consensus. The third phase is the rest of the run. We observe that once the agents reach a consensus no transition is enabled, and so the agents remain in this consensus, proving that the protocol is correct.

3   Protocol Verification with Peregrine 2.0

Peregrine 2.0 allows the user to specify and edit population protocols. (Our running example is listed in the distribution as *Majority Voting*.) After choosing a protocol, the user can simulate it and gather statistics, as in Peregrine 1.0 [5]. The main feature of Peregrine 2.0 is its new verification engine based on stage graphs, which closely matches the "phase-reasoning" of the previous section.

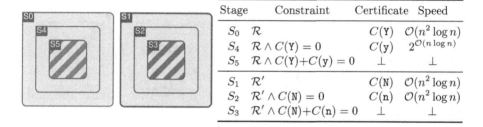

Stage	Constraint	Certificate	Speed
S_0	$\mathcal{R}$	$C(\text{Y})$	$\mathcal{O}(n^2 \log n)$
S_4	$\mathcal{R} \wedge C(\text{Y}) = 0$	$C(\text{y})$	$2^{\mathcal{O}(n \log n)}$
S_5	$\mathcal{R} \wedge C(\text{Y}){+}C(\text{y}) = 0$	$\bot$	$\bot$
S_1	$\mathcal{R}'$	$C(\text{N})$	$\mathcal{O}(n^2 \log n)$
S_2	$\mathcal{R}' \wedge C(\text{N}) = 0$	$C(\text{n})$	$\mathcal{O}(n^2 \log n)$
S_3	$\mathcal{R}' \wedge C(\text{N}){+}C(\text{n}) = 0$	$\bot$	$\bot$

Fig. 1. Stage graphs for Majority Voting protocol with constraints, certificates and speeds. The expression $\mathcal{R}$ and $\mathcal{R}'$ denote abstractions of the reachability relation, which are a bit long and therefore omitted for clarity.

Stage Graphs. A *stage graph* is a directed acyclic graph whose nodes, called *stages*, are possibly infinite sets of configurations, finitely described by a Presburger formula. Stages are *inductive*, i.e. closed under reachability. There is an edge $S \rightarrow S'$ to a *child* stage S' if $S' \subset S$, and no other stage S'' satisfies $S' \subset S'' \subset S$. Peregrine 2.0 represents stage graphs as Venn diagrams like the ones on the left of Fig. 1. Stages containing no other stages are called *terminal*, and otherwise *non-terminal*. Intuitively, a phase starts when a run enters a stage, and ends when it reaches one of its children.

Each non-terminal stage S comes equipped with a *certificate*. Intuitively, a certificate proves that runs starting at any configuration of S will almost surely reach one of its children and, since S is inductive, get trapped there forever. Loosely speaking, certificates take the form of ranking functions bounding the distance of a configuration to the children of S, and are also finitely represented by Presburger formulas. Given a configuration C and a certificate f, runs starting at C reach a configuration C' satisfying $f(C') < f(C)$ with probability 1.

To verify that a protocol computes a predicate φ we need two stage graphs, one for each output. The roots of the first stage graph contain all initial configurations C with $\varphi(C) = 0$ and the terminal stages contain only configurations with consensus 0. The second handles the case when $\varphi(C) = 1$.

Stage Graphs for Majority Voting. For the Majority Voting protocol Peregrine 2.0 generates the two stage graphs of Fig. 1 in a completely automatic way. By clicking on a stage, say S_4, the information shown in Fig. 2 is displayed. The constraint describes the set of configurations of the stage (Fig. 1 shows the constraints for all stages). In particular, all the configurations of S_4 satisfy $C(\text{Y}) = 0$, that is, all agents initially in state Y have already become passive. The certificate indicates that a run starting at a configuration $C \in S_4 \setminus S_5$ eventually reaches S_5 or a configuration $C' \in S_4 \setminus S_5$ such that $C'(\text{y}) < C(\text{y})$. Peregrine 2.0 also displays a list of *dead transitions* that can never occur again from any configuration of S_4, and a list of *eventually dead transitions*, which will become dead whenever a child stage, in this case S_5, is reached.

Stage S4

Speed: $2^{\mathcal{O}(n \log n)}$
Certificate: C[y]
Certificate Value: 2
Constraint: PotReach(¬(C[Y] ≥ C[N])) ∧ C[Y]=0

Eventually dead transitions (2):

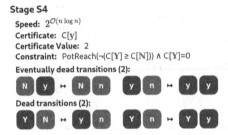

Dead transitions (2):

Fig. 2. Details of stage S_4 in Fig. 1 at configuration $\langle N, 4 \cdot n, 2 \cdot y \rangle$. The terms C[q] are the number of agents $C(q)$ in state q.

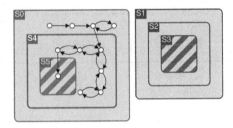

Fig. 3. Partially constructed Markov chain after a simulation of the Majority Voting protocol inside the protocol's stage graphs, with $O = \langle N, 4 \cdot n, 2 \cdot y \rangle$ selected. (Color figure online)

While they are automatically generated, these stage graphs closely map the intuition above. The three stages of each graph naturally correspond to the three phases of the protocol: S_0 and S_1 correspond to the first phase (we reduce $C(Y)$ or $C(N)$), S_2 and S_4 to the second phase ($C(Y)$ or $C(N)$ is zero, and we reduce $C(y)$ or $C(n)$), and S_3 and S_5 to the third phase (all agents are in consensus).

Speed. Because agents interact randomly, the length of the phase associated to a stage is a random variable (more precisely, a variable for each number of agents). The expected value of this variable is called the *speed* of the stage. A stage has speed $\mathcal{O}(f(n))$ if for every n the expected length of the phase for configurations with n agents is at most $c \cdot f(n)$ for some constant c. Peregrine 2.0 computes an upper bound for the speed of a stage using the techniques of [7]. The last column of Fig. 1 gives the upper bounds on the speed of all stages. Currently, Peregrine 2.0 can prove one of the bounds $\mathcal{O}(n^2 \log n)$, $\mathcal{O}(n^3)$, $\mathcal{O}(n^k)$ for some k and $2^{\mathcal{O}(n \log n)}$. Observe that for stage S_4 of Majority Voting the tool returns $2^{\mathcal{O}(n \log n)}$. Majority Voting is indeed very inefficient, much faster protocols exist.

4   Visualizing Runs in the Stage Graph

To further understand the protocol, Peregrine 2.0 allows the user to simulate a run and monitor its progress through the stage graph. The simulation is started at a chosen initial configuration or a precomputed example configuration of a stage. The current configuration is explicitly shown and also highlighted as a yellow circle in the stage graph. To choose the next pair of interacting agents, the user can click on them. The resulting interaction is visualized, and the successor configuration is automatically placed in the correct stage, connected to the previous configuration. After multiple steps, this partially constructs the underlying Markov chain of the system as shown in Fig. 3. One can also navigate the current run by clicking on displayed configurations or using the PREV and NEXT buttons.

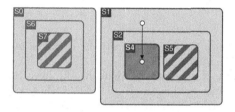

Fig. 4. Counterexample automatically found by Peregrine when verifying Majority Voting (broken), shown in the stage graphs as a run from $O = \langle Y, N \rangle$ to $O = \langle y, n \rangle$. The graph with root S_1 is only a partial stage graph, because stage S_4 contains configurations that do not have the correct consensus.

Beyond choosing pairs of agents one by one, the user can simulate a full run of the protocol by clicking on PLAY. The acceleration slider allows to speed up this simulation. However, if the overall speed of the protocol is very slow, a random run might not make progress in a reasonable time frame. An example for this is the Majority Voting protocol for populations with a small majority for N, where the expected number of interactions to go from S_4 to S_5 is $2^{\mathcal{O}(n \log n)}$. Thus, even for relatively small configurations like $\langle 4 \cdot Y, 5 \cdot N \rangle$ a random run is infeasible. To make progress in these cases, one can click on PROGRESS. This automatically chooses a transition that reduces the value of the certificate. Intuitively, reducing the certificate's value guides the run towards a child stage and thus, the run from S_4 to S_5 needs at most n steps. To visualize the progress, the value of the stage's certificate for the current configuration is displayed in the stage details as in Fig. 2 and next to the PROGRESS button.

Finding Counterexamples. The speed of stage S_4 with certificate $C(y)$ is so low because of transition $d : y \, n \mapsto y \, y$ that increases the value of the certificate and may be chosen with high probability. Removing the transition d makes the protocol faster (this variant is listed in the distribution as "Majority Voting (broken)"). However, then Peregrine cannot verify the protocol anymore, and it even finds a counterexample: a run that does not stabilize to the correct consensus. Figure 4 shows the counterexample ending in the configuration $\langle y, n \rangle$ from the initial configuration $\langle Y, N \rangle$, i.e. a configuration with a tie. In this case, the configuration should stabilize to 1, but no transition is applicable at $\langle y, n \rangle$, which does not have consensus 1. This clearly shows why we need the transition d. Note however that the left part with root stage S_0 in Fig. 4 is a valid stage graph, so the modified protocol works correctly in the ‚negative case. This helps locate the cause of the problem.

References

1. Alistarh, D., Gelashvili, R.: Recent algorithmic advances in population protocols. SIGACT News **49**(3), 63–73 (2018)
2. Blondin, M., Esparza, J., Genest, B., Helfrich, M., Jaax, S.: Succinct population protocols for Presburger arithmetic. In: STACS. LIPIcs, vol. 154, pp. 40:1–40:15 (2020). https://doi.org/10.4230/LIPIcs.STACS.2020.40
3. Blondin, M., Esparza, J., Helfrich, M., Kučera, A., Meyer, P.J.: Checking qualitative liveness properties of replicated systems with stochastic scheduling. In: Lahiri, S.K., Wang, C. (eds.) CAV 2020. LNCS, vol. 12225, pp. 372–397. Springer, Cham (2020). https://doi.org/10.1007/978-3-030-53291-8_20
4. Blondin, M., Esparza, J., Jaax, S.: Large flocks of small birds: on the minimal size of population protocols. In: STACS. LIPIcs, vol. 96, pp. 16:1–16:14 (2018)
5. Blondin, M., Esparza, J., Jaax, S.: PEREGRINE: a tool for the analysis of population protocols. In: Chockler, H., Weissenbacher, G. (eds.) CAV 2018. LNCS, vol. 10981, pp. 604–611. Springer, Cham (2018). https://doi.org/10.1007/978-3-319-96145-3_34
6. Blondin, M., Esparza, J., Jaax, S., Meyer, P.J.: Towards efficient verification of population protocols. In: PODC, pp. 423–430. ACM (2017)
7. Blondin, M., Esparza, J., Kučera, A.: Automatic analysis of expected termination time for population protocols. In: CONCUR. LIPIcs, pp. 33:1–33:16 (2018)

DG: Analysis and Slicing of LLVM Bitcode

Marek Chalupa[✉]

Masaryk University, Brno, Czech Republic
chalupa@fi.muni.cz

Abstract. DG is a library written in C++ that provides several types of program analysis for LLVM bitcode. The main parts of DG are a parametric points-to analysis, a call graph construction, a data dependence analysis, and a control dependence analysis. The project includes several tools built around the analyses, the main one being a static slicer for LLVM bitcode. This paper describes what analyses are implemented in DG and its use cases with the focus on program slicing.

1 Introduction

DG is a library providing data structures and algorithms for program analysis. The library was created during the re-implementation of the static slicer in the tool SYMBIOTIC [8] and its original purpose was the construction of *dependence graphs* [12] for LLVM bitcode [14]. During the development, we re-designed DG from a single-purpose library for the construction of dependence graphs to a library providing data structures and basic algorithms for program analysis.

The main parts of DG are a parametric *points-to analysis* and a *call graph construction*, a *data dependence analysis* based on the transformation of writes to memory into static single assignment (SSA) form [18], and a *control dependence analysis* providing two different algorithms with different characteristics. The results of these analyses can be used to construct a *dependence graph* [12] of the program that supports forward and backward slicing, among others.

Most of the implemented algorithms are designed to be independent of the programming language. Currently, DG has an LLVM backend that allows using the algorithms with LLVM infrastructure.

Analyses in DG have a public API that is used also in communication between analyses inside DG. As a result, a particular implementation of analysis can be easily replaced by an external analysis. The benefit of being able to integrate an external analysis is that one can use features of DG (e.g., program slicing) along with features of the external analysis (e.g., better speed or precision). At this moment, DG integrates a points-to analysis from the SVF library [19].

The work is supported by The Czech Science Foundation grant GA18-02177S.

D. V. Hung and O. Sokolsky (Eds.): ATVA 2020, LNCS 12302, pp. 557–563, 2020.
https://doi.org/10.1007/978-3-030-59152-6_33

```
entry:
  %y = alloca i32
  %x = alloca i32
  %p = alloca i32*
  store 0 to %y
  store %y to %p
  %c = call @nondet()
  store %c to %x
  br label %while.cond

while.cond:
  %0 = load %x
  %cmp = icmp sgt %0, 0
  br %cmp, label %while.body,
          label %while.end

while.body:
  %dec = add %0, -1
  store %dec to %x
  br label %while.cond

while.end:
  %1 = load %p
  %2 = load %1
  %cmp1 = icmp eq %2, 0
  call @assert(i1 %cmp1)
```

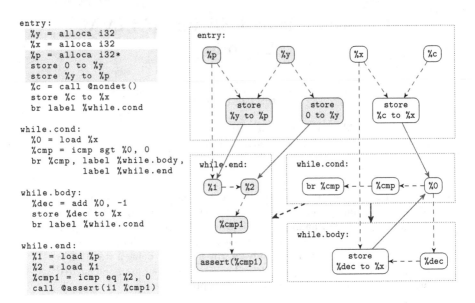

Fig. 1. A simplified LLVM bitcode and its dependence graph. For clarity, we left out nodes with no dependencies. Black dashed edges are use dependencies, red edges are data dependencies, and blue edges are control dependencies. The dashed control dependence is present in the graph only when NTSCD algorithm is used. Highlighted are the nodes that are in the slice with respect to the call of **assert** (using SCD). (Color figure online)

LLVM. DG works with LLVM [14], which is a strongly typed assembly-like intermediate language for compilers. Instructions in LLVM are arranged into labeled basic blocks to which we can jump using the **br** instruction. Variables on the stack are created by the **alloca** instruction and can be later accessed via the **load** and **store** instructions. The meaning of the rest of the instructions used in this paper should be clear from the text. An example of LLVM bitcode can be found in Fig. 1.

In the rest of the paper, we describe the main analyses in DG and its use cases.

2   Points-To Analysis

Points-to analysis is a cornerstone of many other program analyses. It answers the queries: "What is the memory referenced by the pointer?". For each points-to analysis, we can identify the following basic traits. Points-to analysis is *flow-sensitive* (FS) if it takes into account the flow of control in the program and thus computes information specifically for each program location. Otherwise, it is *flow-insensitive* (FI). It is *field-sensitive* if it differentiates between individual elements of aggregate objects, e.g., arrays or structures.

In DG, we have implemented a parametric points-to analysis framework [6] that supports FS and FI analysis and has dynamically configurable field-sensitivity. Moreover, the analysis can construct a call graph of the program. The FS analysis has also an option to track what memory has been freed [9].

3   Data Dependence Analysis

Data dependence analysis is a crucial part of program slicing. Informally, we say that instruction r is data dependent on instruction w if r reads values from memory that may have been written by w. In Fig. 1, for example, instruction %0 = load %x is data dependent on instructions store %c to %x and store %dec to %x as it may read values written by both of these instructions.

In DG, the data dependence analysis constructs SSA representation of writes to memory, the so-called memory SSA form [16]. The input to the data dependence analysis in DG is a program whose instructions are annotated with information about what memory *may/must* be written, and what memory *may* be read by the instructions. These annotations are derived from the results of the points-to analysis.

Our analysis algorithm is based on the algorithm of Braun [5]. We extended the Braun's algorithm, which works only with scalar variables, to handle aggregated data structures, heap-allocated objects and accesses to memory via pointers, and also accesses to unknown memory objects (occurring due to a lack of information about the accessed memory). Also, the algorithm has been modified to handle procedure calls, therefore it yields interprocedural results.

4   Control Dependence Analysis

Informally, control dependence arises between two program instructions if whether one is executed depends on a jump performed at the other. There are several formal notions of control dependence. In DG, we implement analyses that compute two of them. The first one is *standard control dependence* (SCD) as defined by Ferrante et al. [12] and the other is *non-termination sensitive control dependence* (NTSCD) introduced by Ranganath et al. [17]. The difference between these two is that NTSCD takes into account also the possibility that an instruction is not executed because of a non-terminating loop.

For example, in Fig. 1, instructions in while.body basic block are (standard and non-termination sensitive) control dependent on the br %cmp instruction from while.cond block as the jump performed by the br %cmp instruction may avoid their execution. If the loop in the program does not terminate, we will never get to while.end basic block, and therefore NTSCD marks also instructions from this block to be dependent on the br %cmp instruction.

The classical algorithms compute control dependencies per instruction. For efficiency, our implementation allows also control dependencies between basic blocks, where if basic block A depends on basic block B than it represents that all instructions from the basic block A depend on the jump instruction at the end of the basic block B. See, for example, the control dependence edge between `while.cond` and `while.body` basic blocks in Fig. 1.

We have also an implementation of the computation of interprocedural control dependencies that arise e.g., when calling `abort()` inside procedures. This analysis runs independently of SCD and NTSCD analysis.

5   Dependence Graphs and Program Slicing

The results of hitherto mentioned analyses can be used to construct a dependence graph of the program. A dependence graph is a directed graph that has instructions of the program as nodes and there is an edge from node n_1 to node n_2 if n_2 depends on n_1.

In DG, we distinguish three types of dependencies. The first two types are control and data dependencies as computed by control and data dependence analysis. The last dependence is *use* dependence that is the syntactic relation between instruction and its operands. For instance, in Fig. 1, there is use dependence from instruction `%y = alloca i32` to `%0 = load %y` as the later uses `%y`.

Program Slicing. *Static backward program slicing* [21] is a method that removes parts of a program that cannot affect a given set of instructions (called *slicing criteria*). Dependence graphs are a suitable representation for program slicing [12] as they capture dependencies between instructions. The set of instructions that comprise a slice is obtained by traversing the graph in the backward direction from nodes corresponding to slicing criteria. In our example in Fig. 1, the slice with respect to the call to function **assert** contains all instructions that are backward reachable from the call node in the dependence graph. Depending on whether we use SCD or NTSCD, the slice contains either the highlighted instructions (SCD) or all instructions (NTSCD).

One of the prominent features of our slicer is that we produce executable slices. That is, unlike tools that just output the set of instructions in the slice, we produce a valid sliced bitcode that can be run or further analyzed.

6   Evaluation and Use Cases

We evaluated the effectiveness of our analyses by running our slicer on a set of 8107 reachability benchmarks from Software Verification Competition[1]. These benchmarks range from small artificial programs (tens of instructions) to complex code generated from Linux kernel modules (up to 130000 of instructions). The average size of a benchmark is approximately 5320 instructions. Each benchmark contains calls to an error function which we used as slicing criteria (all together if there were multiple calls). The experiments ran on a machine with *Intel i7-8700 CPU @ 3.2* GHz. Each benchmark run was constrained to 6 GB of memory and 120 s of CPU time.

---

[1] https://github.com/sosy-lab/sv-benchmarks, rev. `6c4d8bc`.

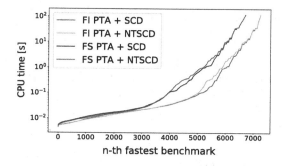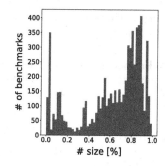

Fig. 2. The plot on the left shows CPU time of slicing using FS or FI points-to analysis (PTA) and NTSCD or SCD control dependence analysis. On the right is depicted the ratio of the number of instructions after and before slicing for FI PTA + SCD setup.

Figure 2 on the left shows a quantile plot of the CPU time of slicing with different setups of pointer and control dependence analyses. Slicing is mostly very fast – more than 75 % of benchmarks is sliced in 1 s (more than 80 % for FI setups). However, in each setup are benchmarks on which slicing either timeouts (around 380 benchmarks for FI setups and 280 for FS setups) or crashed e.g., due to hitting the memory limit (around 860 for FI setups and 1400 for FS setups).

In Fig. 2 on the right is depicted the distribution of the ratio of the number of instructions after and before slicing for *FI PTA + SCD* setup (the slicer's default). On average, for this setup, the size of the sliced bitcode was reduced to 67 % of the size before slicing, but there are also numerous cases of reduction to less than 30 %. FS points-to analysis has no big influence on these numbers.

Use Cases. Since its creation, DG has proved to be useful in many cases, e.g., software verification and bug finding [7–9,15,20] cyber-security [3,13] cyber-physical systems analysis [10], and network software analysis [11].

Availability. DG library and documentation is available under the MIT license at https://github.com/mchalupa/dg.

7 Related Work

Many analyses, including memory SSA construction and various alias analyses, are contained directly in the LLVM project. However, these analyses are usually only intraprocedural and thus too imprecise for sensible program slicing.

Now we survey the projects providing backward program slicing for LLVM. *ParaSlicer* [2] and *llvm-slicing* [22] are projects written in Haskell that make use of procedure summaries to generate more precise slices than the classical slicing algorithms. These slicers only output a list of instructions that should be in the slice. *SemSlice* [4] is a slicer for semantic slicing of LLVM bitcode. The bottle-neck of semantic slicing is the use of SMT solving, which can be inefficient.

Finally, there is the obsolete slicer from Symbiotic called *LLVMSlicer* [1] which is no longer maintained.

Acknowledgements. The author would like to thank Jan Strejček for his valuable comments on the paper. Further, many thanks go to other contributors to the DG library, mainly Tomáš Jašek, Lukáš Tomovič, and Martina Vitovská.

References

1. LLVMSlicer. https://github.com/jslay/LLVMSlicer
2. ParaSlicer. https://archive.codeplex.com/?p=paraslicer
3. Ahmadvand, M., Hayrapetyan, A., Banescu, S., Pretschner, A.: Practical integrity protection with oblivious hashing. In: ACSAC 2018, pp. 40–52. ACM (2018)
4. Beckert, B., Bormer, T., Gocht, S., Herda, M., Lentzsch, D., Ulbrich, M.: SEMSLICE: exploiting relational verification for automatic program slicing. In: Polikarpova, N., Schneider, S. (eds.) IFM 2017. LNCS, vol. 10510, pp. 312–319. Springer, Cham (2017). https://doi.org/10.1007/978-3-319-66845-1_20
5. Braun, M., Buchwald, S., Hack, S., Leißa, R., Mallon, C., Zwinkau, A.: Simple and efficient construction of static single assignment form. In: CC2013, LNCS 7791, pp. 102–122. Springer, Heidelberg (2013). https://doi.org/10.1007/978-3-642-37051-9_6
6. Chalupa, M.: Slicing of LLVM Bitcode. Master's thesis, Masaryk University, Faculty of Informatics, Brno (2016). https://is.muni.cz/th/vik1f/
7. Chalupa, M., Strejček, J.: Evaluation of program slicing in software verification. In: Ahrendt, W., Tapia Tarifa, S.L. (eds.) IFM 2019. LNCS, vol. 11918, pp. 101–119. Springer, Cham (2019). https://doi.org/10.1007/978-3-030-34968-4_6
8. Chalupa, M., et al.: Symbiotic 7: Integration of Predator and More. TACAS 2020. LNCS, vol. 12079, pp. 413–417. Springer, Cham (2020). https://doi.org/10.1007/978-3-030-45237-7_31
9. Chalupa, M., Strejček, J., Vitovská, M.: Joint forces for memory safety checking revisited. Int. J. Softw. Tools Technol. Transf. **22**(2), 115–133 (2020)
10. Cheng, L., Tian, K., Yao, D., Sha, L., Beyah, R.A.: Checking is believing: event-aware program anomaly detection in cyber-physical systems. CoRR, abs/1805.00074 (2018)
11. Deng, B., Wu, W., Song, L.: Redundant logic elimination in network functions. In: SOSR 2020, pp. 34–40. ACM (2020)
12. Ferrante, J., Ottenstein, K.J., Warren, J.D.: The program dependence graph and its use in optimization. ACM Trans. Program. Lang. Syst. **9**(3), 319–349 (1987)
13. Hamadeh, H., Almomani, A., Tyagi, A.: Probabilistic verification of outsourced computation based on novel reversible PUFs. In: Brogi, A., Zimmermann, W., Kritikos, K. (eds.) ESOCC 2020. LNCS, vol. 12054, pp. 30–37. Springer, Cham (2020). https://doi.org/10.1007/978-3-030-44769-4_3
14. Lattner, C., Adve, V.S.: LLVM: a compilation framework for lifelong program analysis & transformation. In: CGO 2004, pp. 75–88. IEEE Computer Society (2004)
15. Li, Z., Zou, D., Xu, S., Chen, Z., Zhu, Y., Jin, H.: VulDeeLocator: a deep learning-based fine-grained vulnerability detector. CoRR, abs/2001.02350 (2020). http://arxiv.org/abs/2001.02350

16. Novillo, D.: Memory SSA - A Unified Approach for Sparsely Representing Memory Operations (2006)
17. Ranganath, V.P., Amtoft, T., Banerjee, A., Dwyer, M.B., Hatcliff, J.: A new foundation for control-dependence and slicing for modern program structures. In: Sagiv, M. (ed.) ESOP 2005. LNCS, vol. 3444, pp. 77–93. Springer, Heidelberg (2005). https://doi.org/10.1007/978-3-540-31987-0_7
18. Rosen, B.K., Wegman, M.N., Zadeck, F.K.: Global value numbers and redundant computations. In POPL 1888, pp. 12–27. ACM Press (1988)
19. Sui, Y., Xue, J.: SVF: interprocedural static value-flow analysis in LLVM. In CC 2016, pp. 265–266. ACM (2016)
20. Trabish, D., Mattavelli, A., Rinetzky, N., Cadar, C.: Chopped symbolic execution. In: ICSE 2018, pp. 350–360. ACM (2018)
21. Weiser, M.: Program slicing. IEEE Trans. Software Eng. 10(4), 352–357 (1984)
22. Zhang, Y.: Sympas: Symbolic program slicing. CoRR, abs/1903.05333 (2019). http://arxiv.org/abs/1903.05333

RTAMT: Online Robustness Monitors
from STL

Dejan Ničković[1(✉)] and Tomoya Yamaguchi[2]

[1] AIT Austrian Institute of Technology, Vienna, Austria
dejan.nickovic@ait.ac.at
[2] Toyota Research Institute - North America, Ann Arbor, Michigan, USA

Abstract. We present rtamt, an online monitoring library for Signal Temporal Logic (STL) and its interface-aware variant (IA-STL), providing both discrete- and dense-time interpretation of the logic. We also introduce rtamt4ros, a tool that integrates rtamt with Robotic Operating System (ROS), a common environment for developing robotic applications. We evaluate rtamt and rtamt4ros on two robotic case studies.

1 Introduction

Robotic applications are complex autonomous cyber-physical systems (CPS). Robotic Operating System (ROS) [1] provides a meta-operating system that helps development of robotic applications. Verification remains a bottleneck, as existing techniques do not scale to this level of complexity, thus making static safety assurance a very costly, if not impossible, activity. Run-time assurance (RTA) is an alternative approach for ensuring the safe operation of robotic CPS that cannot be statically verified. RTA allows the use of untrusted components in a system that implements a safe fallback mechanism for (1) detecting anomalies during real-time system operations and (2) invoking a recovery mechanism that brings the system back to its safe operation. Runtime verification (RV) provides a reliable and rigorous way for finding violations in system executions and consequently represents a viable solution for the monitoring RTA component.

Formal specifications play an important role in RV and enable formulating system properties. Signal Temporal Logic (STL) [2] is a formal specification language used to describe CPS properties. It admits *robustness* semantics that measure how far is an observed behavior from satisfying/violating a specification.

We introduce rtamt[1], an online STL monitoring library. rtamt supports standard STL and its *interface-aware* extension (IA-STL) [3] as specification languages. It provides automated generation of *online robustness* monitors from specifications under both *discrete* and *continuous* interpretation of time. We also present rtamt4ros[2], an extension that integrates rtamt to ROS, thus enabling the use of specification-based RV methods in robotic applications. We assess the library on two robotic applications.

---

[1] https://github.com/nickovic/rtamt.
[2] https://github.com/nickovic/rtamt4ros.

© Springer Nature Switzerland AG 2020
D. V. Hung and O. Sokolsky (Eds.): ATVA 2020, LNCS 12302, pp. 564–571, 2020.
https://doi.org/10.1007/978-3-030-59152-6_34

Related Work. Several tools support *offline* monitoring of STL with qualitative (AMT2.0 [4]) and quantitative semantics (S-TaLiRo [5] and Breach [6]). Reelay [7] implements past Metric Temporal Logic (MTL) monitors over discrete and continuous time and with qualitative and quantitative semantics. PyMTL [8] is a library for quantitative offline evaluation of MTL specifications. R2U2 tool [9] combines runtime observers for the discrete *mission-time linear temporal logic* (mtLTL), with Bayesian networks, sensor filters and Boolean testers. MONTRE [10] implements monitoring algorithms for *timed regular expressions* (TRE). MONAA [11] implements an automata-based matching algorithms for TREs. StreamLAB [12] and TeSSLa [13] are tools for evaluating real-time CPS streams. The problem of online robustness monitoring was studied in [14], where the authors propose an interval-based approach of online evaluation that allows estimating the minimum and the maximum robustness with respect to both the observed prefix and unobserved trace suffix. RVROS [15] is a specification-agnostic monitoring framework for improving safety and security of robots using ROS. To the best of our knowledge, rtamt/rtamt4ros is the only tool that implements online robustness STL monitors with both future and past operators and ROS support.

2   RTAMT Design and Functionality

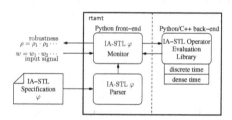

Fig. 1. RTAMT architecture.

The main functionality of rtamt is the automatic generation of online robustness monitors from declarative specifications. Given an input signal in the form of a sequence of (time, value) pairs and a specification, rtamt computes at different points in time how robust is the observed signal to the specification, i.e. how far is it from satisfying or violating it. The library consists of 3 major parts: (1) *specifications* expressed in a declarative specification language, (2) a *front-end* with an Application Programming Interface (API) to parse specifications and generate the monitor, and (3) a *back-end* that implements the actual evaluation algorithm used by the monitor. The rtamt library uses a modular architecture depicted in Fig. 1. It uses ANTLR4 parser generator to translate textual (IA-)STL specifications into an abstract parse tree (APT) data structure used to build the actual monitor. The front-end implements the Application Programming Interface (API) and the pre-processing steps such as the translation of bounded-future (IA-)STL to past (IA-)STL in Python. The back-end implements the monitoring algorithms in Python (for discrete-time and dense-time interpretation) and C++ (for discrete-time interpretation). The library is compatible with both Python 2.7 and 3.7.

Specification language in rtamt is STL with infinity-norm quantitative semantics [16]. The library supports four variants of the specification language – standard STL and interface-aware STL [3] interpreted over discrete and dense time.

IA-STL extends STL with an input/output signature of the variables and provides two additional semantic interpretations: (1) output robustness and (2) input vacuity. Output robustness measures robustness of output signals with respect to some fixed input. Input vacuity measures how vacuously is a specification satisfied with input signals only. rtamt accepts as input *bounded-future* STL (bfSTL) that restricts the use of the future temporal operators (eventually, always and until) to bounded intervals.

Parsing and preprocessing follows a two-step procedure. The first step consists in translating the specification given in a textual form to an abstract parse tree (APT). The translation uses ANTLR4 to generate a Python parser for the (IA-)STL grammar. This translation is still not suitable for online monitors – the specification may have future temporal operator that would require clair-voyant monitoring capability. Hence, we implement the *pastification* procedure [17] that translates the bfSTL formula ϕ into an *equi-satisfiable* past STL formula ψ, which uses only past temporal operators and postpones the formula evaluation from time index t, to the end of the (bounded) horizon $t + h$ where all the inputs necessary for computing the robustness degree are available.

Monitoring consists of evaluating in online fashion the past STL specification according to its quantitative semantics, interpreted in discrete or dense time [3].

Discrete-time monitors follow a time-triggered approach in which sensing of inputs and output generation are done at a periodic rate. This choice is motivated by [18], which shows that by weakening/strengthening real-time specifications, discrete-time evaluation of properties preserves important properties of dense-time interpretation. This approach admits an upper bound on the use of computation resources. rtamt implements two back-ends for STL monitors – one in Python (for rapid prototyping) and one in C++ (for efficiency). rtamt uses Boost.Python library to integrate the Python front-end with the C++ backend. *Dense-time monitors* follow an event-driven approach. Their implementation combines the incremental evaluation approach from [19] with the optimal streaming algorithm to compute the min and max of a numeric sequence over a sliding window from [20]. Unlike their discrete-time counterparts, continuous-time monitors do not have bounds on memory requirements.

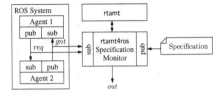

Fig. 2. Integration of RTAMT to ROS.

Integration of RTAMT to ROS ROS supports several messaging approaches, including the *subscriber* and *publisher* pattern. A *publisher* categorizes a message into a class (called *topic* in ROS) and sends it without knowing who will read the message. A *subscriber* subscribes to a topic and receives its associated messages, without knowing who sent the message[4]. The

---

[3] Due to pastification, rtamt only needs to evaluate past temporal operators.

[4] Unless the publisher encodes its identity into the message itself.

messages are received and processed in callback() functions. Common ROS applications associate a callback() function per subscribed variable.

rtamt4ros, illustrated in Fig. 2, integrates rtamt into ROS using *rospy*. The integration is non-intrusive and provides the user with a generic and transparent monitoring solution for (IA-)STL specifications. The ROS system under observation is implemented with ROS nodes, which interact by publishing and receiving ROS messages on dedicated topics. To publish values of a variable x of type T on a topic t, ROS node associates x and T to t. Similarly, we declare in the STL specification variables that we want to monitor, declare their types and associate them to ROS subscription/publication topics using annotations. Variable names, their types and associated topics are specification-dependent. rtamt4ros implements a *dynamic* subscription/publication mechanism that uses the concepts of *introspection* and *reflection* (the ability to passively infer the type of an object and actively change its properties at runtime). Given a (IA-)STL specification, rtamt4ros infers all the specification variables and dynamically creates their associated subscribers and publishers. The use of reflection allows us to associate a single callback() function to all specification variables, by passing the variable object as an argument to the function. We use the callback() function only to collect input data and the main ROS loop to make robustness monitor updates.

3   Experiments and Use Scenario

We now present experiments performed using rtamt and rtamt4ros. We apply rtamt and rtamt4ros on two ROS case studies: Simple Two Dimensional Simulator (STDR) and Toyota's Human Support Robot (HSR) platform [21]. We use the STDR example to show step-by-step usage of the rtamt and rtamt4ros for online monitoring of robotic applications. We note that rtamt is versatile and could be used for instance for offline monitoring and non-robotic applications. We then evaluate the computation time requirements of the library. The experiments were performed on a Dell Latitude 7490 with an i7-8650U processor and 16 GB of RAM, running Ubuntu 16.04 on a virtual machine.

Online Monitoring of Robotic Applications: STDR is a ROS-compliant environment for easy multi-robot 2D simulation (see Fig. 3). We use a simple robot controller with commands encoded as ROS Twist messages that expresses velocity in free space consisting of its linear and angular parts. The robot state is encoded as a ROS Odometry message that represents an estimate of the position (pose) and velocity (twist) in free space. We then use the rtamt4ros and rtamt to monitor its low-level requirement stating that every step in the command must be followed by the observed response. The specification spec.stl requires that at all times the distance between the linear velocity on the x dimension of the command and the robot is smaller than 0.5. The user first needs to import data types used in the specification (lines 1–3). Then, it declares variables used in specification, with their data type and (optionally) their input/output signature (lines 4, 6 and 8). Special comments in lines 5 and 7 are annotations that provide additional information about variables - in this case they associate variables to ROS topics. Finally, line 9 defines the IA-STL property.

```
1  from geometry_msgs.msg import Twist
2  from nav_msgs.msg import Odometry
3  from rtamt_msgs.msg import FloatMessage
4  input Twist cmd
5  @ topic(cmd, robot0/cmd_vel)
6  output Odometry robot
7  @ topic(res, robot0/odom)
8  output FloatMessage out
9  out.value = always(abs(cmd.linear.x - robot.twist.twist.
       linear.x) <= 0.5)
```

To monitor the IA-STL specification spec.stl with rtamt/rtamt4ros , it suffices to run the following command in the ROS environment.

```
1  roscore rtamt4ros ros_stl_monitor.py --stl spec.stl --
       period 100 --unit ms
```

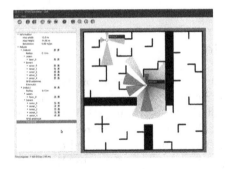

Fig. 3. STDR simulator.

Fig. 4. HSR service robotics application.

HSR is a robot with 8 degrees of freedom (DoF), combining 3 DoF of its mobile base, 4 DoF of the arm and 1 DoF of the torso lift (see Fig. 4). The robot is equipped with ROS modules for localization, path planning and obstacle avoidance. We used this example to experiment with *system-level properties* in a multi-agent environment. We were interested in particular in monitoring the following requirements: (1) *no-collision* requirement stating that two robots are never closer than some d_{min} distance from each other, and (2) when robot 2 is closer than d distance from robot 1, then robot 2 two goes in at most T seconds within d' distance of some location L. For this industrial application, we present an abstracted formalization of the above requirements.

```
1  out1 = always (abs(rob1.pos - rob2.pos) < d)
2  out2 = abs(rob1.pos - rob2.pos) < d implies
3          eventually[0:T](rob1.pos - L) < d'
```

This experiment demonstrates the use of the library in a sophisticated ROS/Gazebo environment in an industrial case study. The addition of monitors is orthogonal to the development of the application and the monitors are non-intrusive.

Table 1. Timing requirement per single monitor update.

k bound	C++ (s)	Python (s)
100	0.00014	0.00023
1k	0.0002	0.00085
10k	0.0008	0.029
100k	0.0047	0.31
1M	0.046	72

Timing Figures: For online monitors, the most important quantitative measure is the computation time of a single monitoring update step. We compared the difference in timing requirements between the C++ and the Python implementation of the discrete-time monitoring algorithm. We used for the experiment the STL specification out = always[0:k] (a + b > -2) where k is the upper bound on the timing modality of the always operator that we varied between 100 and 1 million. Table 1 summarized the results of the experiment. The outcomes clearly demonstrate the efficiency of the C++ back-end, especially for large upper bounds in temporal modalities.

4 Conclusions

In this paper, we presented rtamt a library for generating online monitors from declarative specifications and rtamt4ros, its ROS extension, demonstrating their usability and versatility two robotic case studies.

Acknowledgements. This work was partially supported by iDev40 project, which has received funding from the ECSEL Joint Undertaking (JU) under grant agreement No 783163. The JU receives support from the European Union's Horizon 2020 research and innovation programme. It is co-funded by the consortium members, grants from Austria, Germany, Belgium, Italy, Spain and Romania.

References

1. Quigley, M., et al.: ROS: an open-source robot operating system. In: ICRA workshop on open source software, vol. 3, p. 5. Kobe, Japan (2009)
2. Maler, O., Nickovic, D.: Monitoring temporal properties of continuous signals. In: Lakhnech, Y., Yovine, S. (eds.) FORMATS/FTRTFT -2004. LNCS, vol. 3253, pp. 152–166. Springer, Heidelberg (2004). https://doi.org/10.1007/978-3-540-30206-3_12
3. Ferrère, T., Nickovic, D., Donzé, A., Ito, H., Kapinski, J.: Interface-aware signal temporal logic. In: HSCC, pp. 57–66 (2019)
4. Nickovic, D., Lebeltel, O., Maler, O., Ferrère, T., Ulus, D.: AMT 2.0: Qualitative and quantitative trace analysis with extended signal temporal logic. In: TACAS 2018, pp. 303–319 (2018)

5. Annpureddy, Y., Liu, C., Fainekos, G., Sankaranarayanan, S.: S-TALIRo: a tool for temporal logic falsification for hybrid systems. In: Abdulla, P.A., Leino, K.R.M. (eds.) TACAS 2011. LNCS, vol. 6605, pp. 254–257. Springer, Heidelberg (2011). https://doi.org/10.1007/978-3-642-19835-9_21

6. Donzé, A.: Breach, a toolbox for verification and parameter synthesis of hybrid systems. In: Touili, T., Cook, B., Jackson, P. (eds.) CAV 2010. LNCS, vol. 6174, pp. 167–170. Springer, Heidelberg (2010). https://doi.org/10.1007/978-3-642-14295-6_17

7. Ulus, D.: Online monitoring of metric temporal logic using sequential networks. CoRR, abs/1901.00175 (2019)

8. Vazquez-Chanlatte, M.: mvcisback/py-metric-temporal-logic: v0.1.1 (2019)

9. Schumann, J., Moosbrugger, P., Rozier, K.Y.: Runtime analysis with R2U2: a tool exhibition report. In: Falcone, Y., Sánchez, C. (eds.) RV 2016. LNCS, vol. 10012, pp. 504–509. Springer, Cham (2016). https://doi.org/10.1007/978-3-319-46982-9_35

10. Ulus, D.: MONTRE: a tool for monitoring timed regular expressions. In: Majumdar, R., Kunčak, V. (eds.) CAV 2017. LNCS, vol. 10426, pp. 329–335. Springer, Cham (2017). https://doi.org/10.1007/978-3-319-63387-9_16

11. Waga, M., Hasuo, I., Suenaga, K.: MONAA: A tool for timed pattern matching with automata-based acceleration. In: 3rd Workshop on Monitoring and Testing of Cyber-Physical Systems, MT-CPSWeek 2018, 10 April 2018, Porto, Portugal, pp. 14–15 (2018)

12. Faymonville, P.: StreamLAB: stream-based monitoring of cyber-physical systems. In: Dillig, I., Tasiran, S. (eds.) CAV 2019. LNCS, vol. 11561, pp. 421–431. Springer, Cham (2019). https://doi.org/10.1007/978-3-030-25540-4_24

13. Leucker, M., Sánchez, C., Scheffel, T., Schmitz, M., Schramm, A.: Tessla: runtime verification of non-synchronized real-time streams. In: Proceedings of the 33rd Annual ACM Symposium on Applied Computing, SAC 2018, Pau, France, 09–13 April 2018, pp. 1925–1933 (2018)

14. Deshmukh, J.V., Donzé, A., Ghosh, S., Jin, X., Juniwal, G., Seshia, S.A.: Robust online monitoring of signal temporal logic. Form. Methods Syst. Des. 51(1), 5–30 (2017). https://doi.org/10.1007/s10703-017-0286-7

15. Huang, J.: ROSRV: runtime verification for robots. In: Bonakdarpour, B., Smolka, S.A. (eds.) RV 2014. LNCS, vol. 8734, pp. 247–254. Springer, Cham (2014). https://doi.org/10.1007/978-3-319-11164-3_20

16. Donzé, A., Maler, O.: Robust satisfaction of temporal logic over real-valued signals. In: Chatterjee, K., Henzinger, T.A. (eds.) FORMATS 2010. LNCS, vol. 6246, pp. 92–106. Springer, Heidelberg (2010). https://doi.org/10.1007/978-3-642-15297-9_9

17. Maler, O., Nickovic, D., Pnueli, A.: On synthesizing controllers from bounded-response properties. In: Damm, W., Hermanns, H. (eds.) CAV 2007. LNCS, vol. 4590, pp. 95–107. Springer, Heidelberg (2007). https://doi.org/10.1007/978-3-540-73368-3_12

18. Henzinger, T.A., Manna, Z., Pnueli, A.: What good are digital clocks? In: Kuich, W. (ed.) ICALP 1992. LNCS, vol. 623, pp. 545–558. Springer, Heidelberg (1992). https://doi.org/10.1007/3-540-55719-9_103

19. Nickovic, D., Maler, O.: AMT: a property-based monitoring tool for analog systems. In: Raskin, J.-F., Thiagarajan, P.S. (eds.) FORMATS 2007. LNCS, vol. 4763, pp. 304–319. Springer, Heidelberg (2007). https://doi.org/10.1007/978-3-540-75454-1_22

20. Donzé, A., Ferrère, T., Maler, O.: Efficient robust monitoring for STL. In: Sharygina, N., Veith, H. (eds.) CAV 2013. LNCS, vol. 8044, pp. 264–279. Springer, Heidelberg (2013). https://doi.org/10.1007/978-3-642-39799-8_19

21. Yamamoto, T., Terada, K., Ochiai, A., Saito, F., Asahara, Y., Murase, K.: Development of human support robot as the research platform of a domestic mobile manipulator. ROBOMECH J. 6(1), 1–15 (2019). https://doi.org/10.1186/s40648-019-0132-3

Author Index

Printed in the United States
By Bookmasters